Victorian Poet

baic 2006

Formalism

Chartism

John
Singer
Sargeant

BLACKWELL ANNOTATED ANTHOLOGIES

Advisory Editors

Robert Cummings, University of Glasgow; David Fairer, University of Leeds; Christine Gerrard, University of Oxford; Andrew Hadfield, University of Wales, Aberystwyth; Angela Leighton, University of Hull; Michael O'Neill, University of Durham; Duncan Wu, University of Glasgow.

This series of mid-length anthologies is devoted to poetry and the provision of key texts, canonical and post-canonical, with detailed annotation, sufficient to facilitate close reading, for use on specialist and appropriate survey courses. Headnotes and foot-of-page notes are designed to provide contexts for poets and poems alike, elucidating references and pointing to allusions. Selected variants may be given, where these provide vitally illuminating clues to a work's evolution and editorial history, and there are cross-references between poems.

Seventeenth-century Poetry: An Annotated Anthology
Edited by Robert Cummings

Eighteenth-century Poetry: An Annotated Anthology, Second Edition
Edited by David Fairer and Christine Gerrard

Victorian Poetry: An Annotated Anthology
Edited by Francis O'Gorman

Forthcoming
Sixteenth-century Poetry: An Annotated Anthology
Edited by Gordon Braden

Victorian Poetry

An Annotated Anthology

Edited by

Francis O'Gorman

Blackwell
Publishing

Editorial material and organization © 2004 by Blackwell Publishing Ltd

BLACKWELL PUBLISHING
350 Main Street, Malden, MA 02148-5020, USA
9600 Garsington Road, Oxford OX4 2DQ, UK
550 Swanston Street, Carlton, Victoria 3053, Australia

First published 2004 by Blackwell Publishing Ltd

10   2012

Library of Congress Cataloging-in-Publication Data

Victorian poetry: an annotated anthology / edited by Francis O'Gorman.
p. cm. – (Blackwell annotated anthologies)
Includes bibliographical references (p.) and index.
ISBN 978-0-631-23435-7 (alk. paper) – ISBN 978-0-631-23436-4 (pbk.: alk. paper)
1. English poetry – 19th century.   I. O'Gorman, Francis.   II. Series.
PR1223.V535 2004
821'.808 – dc22
2003020732

A catalogue record for this title is available from the British Library.

Set in 9.5 on 11 pt Ehrhardt
by SNP Best-set Typesetter Ltd., Hong Kong
Printed and bound in Singapore by C.O.S. Printers Pte Ltd

The publisher's policy is to use permanent paper from mills that operate a sustainable forestry policy, and which has been manufactured from pulp processed using acid-free and elementary chlorine-free practices. Furthermore, the publisher ensures that the text paper and cover board used have met acceptable environmental accreditation standards.

For further information on
Blackwell Publishing, visit our website:
www.blackwellpublishing.com

For Dinah Birch

Contents

Suggested Contents by Theme and Genre   xii
Alphabetical List of Authors   xxvi
List of Plates   xxvii
Abbreviations   xxviii
Chronology   xxix
Acknowledgements   xxxvi
Introduction   xxxvii

Thomas Babington (First Baron) Macaulay (1800–1859)   1
    'Horatius: A Lay made about the Year of the City CCCLX'   1

Elizabeth Barrett Browning (1806–1861)   18
    'Bertha in the Lane'   18
    'The Cry of the Children'   25
    'Rime of the Duchess May'   29
    'The Runaway Slave at Pilgrim's Point'   44
    'Hiram Powers' *Greek Slave*'   51
    Sonnets from the Portuguese (selection):
        'I thought once how Theocritus had sung'   53
        'I never gave a lock of hair away'   53
        'If I leave all for thee'   54
        'How do I love thee? Let me count the ways' 54
        'Belovèd, thou has brought me many flowers' 54
    'Lord Walter's Wife'   55
    'A Musical Instrument'   57
    'Amy's Cruelty'   59

Alfred Tennyson (Lord Tennyson) (1809–1892)   62
    'The Dying Swan'   62
    'Mariana'   64
    'The Lotos-Eaters'   66
    'The Lady of Shalott'   71
    'The Epic/Morte d'Arthur'   76
    'Ulysses'   85
    'Now sleeps the crimson petal'   87
    In Memoriam A.H.H. OBIIT MDCCCXXXIII   88
    'The Charge of the Light Brigade'   165
    'To the Marquis of Dufferin and Ava'   167
    'Crossing the Bar'   169

Robert Browning (1812–1889)   171
    'Porphyria's Lover'   171
    'My Last Duchess'   173
    'The Bishop Orders his Tomb at Saint Praxed's Church' 175
    'Fra Lippo Lippi'   179
    'Andrea del Sarto'   189

'"Childe Roland to the Dark Tower Came"'   195
'A Toccata of Galuppi's'   202
'Two in the Campagna'   204
'Caliban upon Setebos'   207
'Eurydice to Orpheus: A Picture by Leighton'   214
'Inapprehensiveness'   215

Emily (Jane) Brontë (1818–1848)   217
   'High waving heather'   217
   'The Night-Wind'   218
   'Shall Earth no more inspire thee[?]'   219
   'To Imagination'   220
   'Remembrance'   222
   'The Prisoner: A Fragment'   223
   'No coward soul is mine'   225

Arthur Hugh Clough (1819–1861)   227
   'Say not the struggle nought availeth'   227
   Amours de Voyage   228
   'The Latest Decalogue'   262

Matthew Arnold (1822–1888)   264
   'A Summer Night'   264
   'To Marguerite – Continued'   267
   'Empedocles on Etna'   268
   'The Buried Life'   296
   'The Scholar-Gipsy'   298
   'Stanzas from the Grande Chartreuse'   305
   'Dover Beach'   312

Adelaide Anne Procter (1825–1864)   314
   'Philip and Mildred'   314
   'A Legend of Provence'   320

George Meredith (1828–1909)   328
   Modern Love   328

Dante Gabriel Rossetti (1828–1882)   350
   'The Burden of Nineveh'   350
   'Sestina. Of the Lady Pietra degli Scrovigni' 356
   'Jenny'   358
   'Nuptial Sleep'   367
   'Song 8: The Woodspurge'   368

Christina G. Rossetti (1830–1894)   370
   'In an Artist's Studio'   370
   'An Apple-Gathering'   371
   'A Birthday'   372
   'Goblin Market'   373
   'Song: When I am dead, my dearest'   385

'Winter: My Secret'   386
'The Lambs of Grasmere, 1860'   387
'Shut Out'   388
'The World'   389
'A Christmas Carol: In the bleak mid-winter'   390
'In life our absent friend'   391
'Resurgam'   392
'Babylon the Great'   393

James Thomson, 'B. V.' (1834–1882)   394
The City of Dreadful Night   394

William Morris (1834–1896)   423
'The Haystack in the Floods'   423
'The Defence of Guenevere'   428
'Concerning Geffray Teste Noire'   438
'Iceland First Seen'   445

Alfred Austin (1835–1913)   448
'Henry Bartle Edward Frere'   448

(Julia) Augusta Webster (1837–1894)   450
'Circe'   450
'A Castaway'   456
'Faded'   471

Algernon Charles Swinburne (1837–1909)   476
'Hymn to Proserpine'   476
'Anactoria'   480
'Laus Veneris'   487
'*Ave Atque Vale*: In Memory of Charles Baudelaire'   500
'A Forsaken Garden'   506

Thomas Hardy (1840–1928)   510
'Hap'   510
'Drummer Hodge'   511
'The Darkling Thrush'   512
'In the Old Theatre, Fiesole'   513
'The Ruined Maid'   514
'The Self Unseeing'   516
'In Tenebris I'   516
'Shelley's Skylark'   517
'Lausanne: In Gibbon's Old Garden'   519
'The Revisitation'   520

Gerard M[anley] Hopkins (1844–1889)   525
'The Wreck of the *Deutschland*'   525
'Spring and Fall'   534
'As kingfishers catch fire'   535
'God's Grandeur'   536

'Pied Beauty'   537
'The Windhover'   538
'Inversnaid'   539
'That Nature is a Heraclitean Fire and of the Comfort of the Resurrection'   540
'Harry Ploughman'   541
'Binsey Poplars'   542
'No worst, there is none'   543
'My own heart let me more have pity on'   544

Eugene (Jacob) Lee-Hamilton (1845–1907)   545
'The New Medusa'   545
Imaginary Sonnets: 'Laura to Petrarch'   553
'Carmagnola to the Republic of Venice'   554
'Fallopius to his Dissecting Knife'   555
'Charles Edward to his Last Friend'   556

**Michael Field (Katherine Harris Bradley [1846–1914] and Edith Emma
Cooper [1862–1913])**   557
'Maids, not to you my mind doth change'   557
'La Gioconda'   558
'A Portrait: Bartolommeo Veneto'   560
'A Girl'   562
'Cyclamens'   563
'Sometimes I do despatch my heart'   563
'It was deep April'   564
'Nests in Elms'   565

Four Victorian Hymns   566
'The day thou gavest' (Ellerton)   566
'Take my life, and let it be' (Havergal)   567
'Onward, Christian soldiers' (Baring-Gould)   567
'My God, how wonderful Thou art' (Faber)   569

W[illiam] E[rnest] Henley (1849–1903)   571
In Hospital   571

Oscar (Fingal O'Flahertie Wills) Wilde (1854–1900)   587
'Fantaisies Décoratives: II. Les Ballons'   587
'Symphony in Yellow'   588
The Ballad of Reading Gaol   588

John Davidson (1857–1909)   606
'Thirty Bob a Week'   606
'A Woman and her Son'   609
'Snow'   616
'The Crystal Palace'   618

May Kendall (1861–?1943)   627
'Lay of the Trilobite'   627

Amy Levy (1861–1889)   630
   'Xantippe: A Fragment'   630
   'A Minor Poet'   636
   'A Ballad of Religion and Marriage'   642

Rudyard Kipling (1865–1936)   644
   'Fuzzy-Wuzzy'   644
   'Gunga Din'   646
   'Tommy'   649
   'Recessional, A Victorian Ode'   650
   'The White Man's Burden'   652
   'If –'   654
   'The Way through the Woods'   655

Arthur (William) Symons (1865–1945)   657
   'From Théophile Gautier: Posthumous Coquetry'   657
   'The Absinthe Drinker'   658
   'Javanese Dancers'   659
   'Prologue'   660
   'Paris'   662
   'Hands'   663
   'White Heliotrope'   663
   'Stella Maris'   664

Ernest (Christopher) Dowson (1867–1900)   667
   'Nuns of the Perpetual Adoration'   667
   'Extreme Unction'   668
   '*Non sum qualis eram bonae sub regno Cynarae*'   670
   '*Vitae summa brevis spem nos vetat incohare longam*'   671

Lionel (Pigot) Johnson (1867–1902)   672
   'Oxford'   672
   'By the Statue of King Charles at Charing Cross'   674
   'The Dark Angel'   677

Charlotte Mew (1869–1928)   680
   'The Forest Road'   680
   'Madeleine in Church'   682
   'The Trees are Down'   687

Select Bibliography   690
Index of Titles   694
Index of First Lines   696

Suggested Contents by Theme and Genre

History/Historiography: General

Thomas Macaulay, 'Horatius: A Lay made about the Year of the City CCCLX'   1
Robert Browning, 'The Bishop Orders his Tomb at Saint Praxed's Church'   175
    'Fra Lippo Lippi'   179
    'Andrea del Sarto'   189
    'A Toccata of Galuppi's'   202
Matthew Arnold, 'Empedocles on Etna'   268
Dante Gabriel Rossetti, 'The Burden of Nineveh'   350
Christina G. Rossetti, 'Babylon the Great'   393
William Morris, 'The Haystack in the Floods'   423
    'The Defence of Guenevere'   428
    'Concerning Geffray Teste Noire'   438
    'Iceland First Seen'   445
Algernon Charles Swinburne, 'Hymn to Proserpine'   476
Thomas Hardy, 'Lausanne: In Gibbon's Old Garden'   519
    'The Darkling Thrush'   512
    'The Revisitation'   520
    'In the Old Theatre, Fiesole'   513
Eugene Lee-Hamilton, 'Laura to Petrarch'   553
    'Carmagnola to the Republic of Venice'   554
    'Fallopius to his Dissecting Knife'   555
    'Charles Edward to his Last Friend'   556
May Kendall, 'Lay of the Trilobite'   627
Amy Levy, 'Xantippe: A Fragment'   630
Lionel Johnson, 'By the Statue of King Charles at Charing Cross'   674

History: Classical

Thomas Macaulay, 'Horatius: A Lay made about the Year of the City CCCLX'   1
Matthew Arnold, 'Empedocles on Etna'   268
Algernon Charles Swinburne, 'Hymn to Proserpine'   476
Thomas Hardy, 'In the Old Theatre, Fiesole'   513
Amy Levy, 'Xantippe: A Fragment'   630

History: Renaissance

Robert Browning, 'The Bishop Orders his Tomb at Saint Praxed's Church'   175
    'Fra Lippo Lippi'   179
    'Andrea del Sarto'   189
Eugene Lee-Hamilton, 'Laura to Petrarch'   553
    'Carmagnola to the Republic of Venice'   554

Myth and Legend: Classical

Thomas Macaulay, 'Horatius: A Lay made about the Year of the City CCCLX'   1
Elizabeth Barrett Browning, 'A Musical Instrument'   57
Alfred Tennyson, 'Ulysses'   85
    'The Lotos-Eaters'   66
Robert Browning, 'Eurydice to Orpheus: A Picture by Leighton'   214
Augusta Webster, 'Circe'   450
Eugene Lee-Hamilton, 'The New Medusa'   545

Myth and Legend: Middle Ages

Elizabeth Barrett Browning, 'Rime of the Duchess May'   29
Alfred Tennyson, 'The Lady of Shalott'   71
    'Morte d'Arthur'   76
Robert Browning, '"Childe Roland to the Dark Tower Came"'   195
Adelaide Anne Procter, 'A Legend of Provence'   314
William Morris, 'The Defence of Guenevere'   428
Algernon Charles Swinburne, 'Laus Veneris'   487

Death

Elizabeth Barrett Browning, 'Rime of the Duchess May'   29
Alfred Tennyson, 'The Dying Swan'   62
    'Charge of the Light Brigade'   165
    'To the Marquis of Dufferin and Ava'   167
    'The Lady of Shalott'   71
    'Morte d'Arthur'   76
    'Crossing the Bar'   169
    In Memoriam A.H.H.   88
Robert Browning, 'Porphyria's Lover'   171
    'The Bishop Orders his Tomb at Saint Praxed's Church'   175
    'Eurydice to Orpheus: A Picture by Leighton'   214
Emily Brontë, 'No coward soul is mine'   225
Christina G. Rossetti, 'Song: When I am dead, my dearest'   385
    'Resurgam'   392
Alfred Austin, 'Henry Bartle Edward Frere'   448
Algernon Charles Swinburne, '*Ave Atque Vale*: In Memory of Charles Baudelaire'   500
    'A Forsaken Garden'   506
Thomas Hardy, 'Shelley's Skylark'   517
    'The Darkling Thrush'   512
    'Drummer Hodge'   511
Gerard M. Hopkins, 'The Wreck of the *Deutschland*'   525
    'That Nature is a Heraclitean Fire and of the Comfort of the Resurrection'   540
Eugene Lee-Hamilton, 'Carmagnola to the Republic of Venice'   554
    'Fallopius to his Dissecting Knife'   555
Michael Field, 'A Portrait: Bartolommeo Veneto'   560
    'Sometimes I do despatch my heart'   563
    'Nests in Elms'   565

W. E. Henley, *In Hospital*   571
Oscar Wilde, *The Ballad of Reading Gaol*   588
John Davidson, 'A Woman and her Son'   609
Amy Levy, 'A Minor Poet'   636
Ernest Dowson, 'Extreme Unction'   668

Fallen Women

Adelaide Anne Procter, 'A Legend of Provence'   320
Dante Gabriel Rossetti, 'Jenny'   358
Christina G. Rossetti, 'Goblin Market'   373
                        'An Apple-Gathering'   371
William Morris, 'The Defence of Guenevere'   428
Augusta Webster, 'A Castaway'   450
Thomas Hardy, 'The Ruined Maid'   514
Charlotte Mew, 'Madeleine in Church'   682

Homoeroticism

Alfred Tennyson, *In Memoriam A.H.H.*   88
Christina G. Rossetti, 'Goblin Market'   373
Algernon Charles Swinburne, 'Anactoria'   480
Gerard M. Hopkins, 'Pied Beauty'   537
                    'The Windhover'   538
                    'Inversnaid'   539
                    'Harry Ploughman'   541
Michael Field, 'A Girl'   562
               'Maids, not to you my mind doth change'   557
               'Sometimes I do despatch my heart'   563
               'It was deep April'   564
Lionel Johnson, 'The Dark Angel'   677
                'By the Statue of King Charles at Charing Cross'   674
Charlotte Mew, 'The Forest Road'   680

Science/Technology/Medicine

Alfred Tennyson, *In Memoriam A.H.H.*   88
Eugene Lee-Hamilton, 'The New Medusa'   545
                     'Fallopius to his Dissecting Knife'   555
W. E. Henley, *In Hospital*   571
John Davidson, 'Snow'   616
               'The Crystal Palace'   618

'Modern Love'

Elizabeth Barrett Browning, 'I thought once how Theocritus had sung'   52
                            'I never gave a lock of hair away'   52
                            'If I leave all for thee'   54

'How do I love thee? Let me count the ways'   54
'Beloved, thou has brought me many flowers'   54
'Amy's Cruelty'   59
Arthur Hugh Clough, *Amours de Voyage*   228
Matthew Arnold, 'The Buried Life'   296
'To Marguerite – Continued'   267
Adelaide Anne Procter, 'Philip and Mildred'   314
George Meredith, *Modern Love*   328
Dante Gabriel Rossetti, 'Nuptial Sleep'   367
Charlotte Mew, 'The Forest Road'   680
'Madeleine in Church'   682

Art/Painting/The Image/Representation/Visuality

Elizabeth Barrett Browning, 'Hiram Powers' *Greek Slave*'   51
Alfred Tennyson, 'The Lady of Shalott'   71
Robert Browning, 'My Last Duchess'   173
'The Bishop Orders his Tomb at Saint Praxed's Church'   175
'Fra Lippo Lippi'   179
'Andrea del Sarto'   189
'Eurydice to Orpheus: A Picture by Leighton'   214
Christina G. Rossetti, 'In an Artist's Studio'   370
Augusta Webster, 'Faded'   450
Michael Field, 'La Gioconda'   558
'A Portrait: Bartolommeo Veneto'   560
Oscar Wilde, 'Fantaisies Décoratives: II. Les Ballons'   587
'Symphony in Yellow'   588

Empire

Thomas Macaulay, 'Horatius: A Lay made about the Year of the City CCCLX'   1
Alfred Tennyson, 'To the Marquis of Dufferin and Ava'   167
Robert Browning, 'Caliban upon Setebos'   207
Alfred Austin, 'Henry Bartle Edward Frere'   448
Thomas Hardy, 'In the Old Theatre, Fiesole'   513
Four Victorian Hymns, 'The day thou gavest' (Ellerton)   566
'Onward, Christian Soldiers' (Baring-Gloud)   567
Rudyard Kipling, 'Fuzzy-Wuzzy'   644
'Gunga Din'   646
'Tommy'   649
'Recessional, a Victorian Ode'   650
'The White Man's Burden'   652
'If –'   654
'The Way through the Woods'   655

Female Sexuality/Desire/Love

Elizabeth Barrett Browning, 'Bertha in the Lane'   18
'Rime of the Duchess May'   29

'The Runaway Slave at Pilgrim's Point'   44
'I thought once how Theocritus had sung'   52
'I never gave a lock of hair away'   52
'If I leave all for thee'   54
'How do I love thee? Let me count the ways'   54
'Beloved, thou has brought me many flowers'   54
'Lord Walter's Wife'   55
'Amy's Cruelty'   59
Robert Browning, 'Eurydice to Orpheus: A Picture by Leighton'   214
Adelaide Anne Procter, 'A Legend of Provence'   320
George Meredith, *Modern Love*   328
Dante Gabriel Rossetti, 'Jenny'   358
                  'Nuptial Sleep'   367
Christina G. Rossetti, 'Goblin Market'   373
William Morris, 'The Defence of Guenevere'   428
Augusta Webster, 'Circe'   450
                  'A Castaway'   456
                  'Faded'   471
Algernon Charles Swinburne, 'Anactoria'   480
Eugene Lee-Hamilton, 'The New Medusa'   545
                  'Laura to Petrarch'   553
Michael Field, 'Maids, not to you my mind doth change'   557
Amy Levy, 'A Ballad of Religion and Marriage'   642
Charlotte Mew, 'The Forest Road'   680
                  'Madeleine in Church'   682

Marriage

Elizabeth Barrett Browning, 'Bertha in the Lane'   18
                  'Rime of the Duchess May'   29
                  'The Runaway Slave at Pilgrim's Point'   44
                  'I thought once how Theocritus had sung'   52
                  'I never gave a lock of hair away'   52
                  'If I leave all for thee'   54
                  'How do I love thee? Let me count the ways'   54
                  'Beloved, thou has brought me many flowers'   54
                  'Lord Walter's Wife'   55
                  'Amy's Cruelty'   59
Robert Browning, 'My Last Duchess'   173
                  'Andrea del Sarto'   189
                  'Two in the Campagna'   204
                  'Eurydice to Orpheus: A Picture by Leighton' 214
Adelaide Anne Procter, 'Philip and Mildred'   314
George Meredith, *Modern Love*   328
Dante Gabriel Rossetti, 'Nuptial Sleep'   367
Christina G. Rossetti, 'Goblin Market'   373
Eugene Lee-Hamilton, 'Laura to Petrarch'   553
Amy Levy, 'A Ballad of Religion and Marriage'   642

Epic

Thomas Macaulay, 'Horatius: A Lay made about the Year of the City CCCLX'   1
Alfred Tennyson, 'The Epic/Morte d'Arthur'   62
      'The Lotos-Eaters'   66
Augusta Webster, 'Circe'   450

Domestic Poetry

Elizabeth Barrett Browning, 'Bertha in the Lane'   18
      'Lord Walter's Wife'   55
      'Amy's Cruelty'   59
Adelaide Anne Procter, 'Philip and Mildred'   314

Dramatic Poetry/Dramatic Monologue

Elizabeth Barrett Browning, 'Bertha in the Lane'   18
      'The Cry of the Children'   25
      'The Runaway Slave at Pilgrim's Point'   44
      'Lord Walter's Wife'   57
      'Amy's Cruelty'   59
Alfred Tennyson, 'The Lotos-Eaters'   66
      'Ulysses'   85
Robert Browning, 'My Last Duchess'   173
      'Porphyria's Lover'   171
      'The Bishop Orders his Tomb at Saint Praxed's Church'   175
      'Fra Lippo Lippi'   179
      'Andrea del Sarto'   189
      'A Toccata of Galuppi's'   202
      'Two in the Campagna'   204
      '"Childe Roland to the Dark Tower Came"'   195
      'Caliban upon Setebos'   207
      'Eurydice to Orpheus: A Picture by Leighton'   214
      'Inapprehensiveness'   215
Matthew Arnold, 'Empedocles on Etna'   268
Dante Gabriel Rossetti, 'Jenny'   358
William Morris, 'The Defence of Guenevere'   428
Augusta Webster, 'Circe'   450
      'A Castaway'   456
      'Faded'   471
Algernon Charles Swinburne, 'Hymn to Proserpine'   476
      'Anactoria'   476
      'Laus Veneris'   487
Thomas Hardy, 'The Ruined Maid'   514
      'The Revisitation'   520
Eugene Lee-Hamilton, 'The New Medusa'   545
      'Laura to Petrarch'   553
      'Carmagnola to the Republic of Venice'   554
      'Fallopius to his Dissecting Knife'   555
      'Charles Edward to his Last Friend'   556

John Davidson, 'Thirty Bob a Week'   606
            'A Woman and her Son'   606
            'The Crystal Palace'   618
May Kendall, 'Lay of the Trilobite'   627
Amy Levy, 'Xantippe: A Fragment'   630
            'A Minor Poet'   636
Rudyard Kipling, 'Fuzzy-Wuzzy'   644
            'Gunga Din'   646
            'Tommy'   649
            'If –'   654
Charlotte Mew, 'The Forest Road'   680
            'Madeleine in Church'   680

Sonnet/Sonnet Sequence/Curtal Sonnet

Elizabeth Barrett Browning, 'Hiram Powers' *Greek Slave*'   51
            'I thought once how Theocritus had sung'   52
            'I never gave a lock of hair away'   52
            'If I leave all for thee'   54
            'How do I love thee? Let me count the ways'   54
            'Beloved, thou has brought me many flowers'   54
Dante Gabriel Rossetti, 'Nuptial Sleep'   367
Christina G. Rossetti, 'In an Artist's Studio'   370
            'A Birthday'   372
            'The World'   389
            'In life our absent friend'   391
            'Resurgam'   392
            'Babylon the Great'   393
Thomas Hardy, 'In the Old Theatre, Fiesole'   513
            'Lausanne: In Gibbon's Old Garden'   519
Gerard M. Hopkins, 'God's Grandeur'   536
            'Pied Beauty'   537
            'The Windhover'   538
            'As kingfishers catch fire'   535
Eugene Lee-Hamilton, 'Laura to Petrarch'   553
            'Carmagnola to the Republic of Venice'   554
            'Fallopius to his Dissecting Knife'   555
            'Charles Edward to his Last Friend'   556
W. E. Henley, *In Hospital*   571
Michael Field, 'A Girl'   562
            'Sometimes I do despatch my heart'   563
Arthur Symons, 'The Absinthe Drinker'   658

Elegy

Alfred Tennyson, 'Morte d'Arthur'   76
            In Memoriam A.H.H.   88
            'To the Marquis of Dufferin and Ava'   167

Robert Browning, 'A Toccata of Galuppi's'   202
Alfred Austin, 'Henry Bartle Edward Frere'   448
Algernon Charles Swinburne, '*Ave Atque Vale*: In Memory of Charles Baudelaire'   500
Thomas Hardy, 'Drummer Hodge'   511
Gerard M. Hopkins, 'Binsey Poplars'   542
Michael Field, 'Sometimes I do despatch my heart'   563
Oscar Wilde, *The Ballad of Reading Gaol*   588
Charlotte Mew, 'The Trees are Down'   687

Hymn

Christina G. Rossetti, 'A Christmas Carol: In the bleak mid-winter'   390
Four Victorian Hymns, 'The day thou gavest' (Ellerton)   566
                      'Take my life, and let it be' (Havergal)   567
                      'Onward, Christian soldiers' (Baring-Gould)   567
                      'My God, how wonderful Thou art' (Faber)   569

Translation

Dante Gabriel Rossetti, 'Sestina. Of the Lady Pietra degli Scrovigni'   356
Arthur Symons, 'From Théophile Gautier: Posthumous Coquetry'   657

Pre-Raphaelitism/Pre-Raphaelite Poetry

Robert Browning, 'Fra Lippo Lippi'   179
Dante Gabriel Rossetti, 'The Burden of Nineveh'   350
                       'Sestina. Of the Lady Pietra degli Scrovigni'   356
                       'Jenny'   358
                       'Nuptial Sleep'   367
                       'Song 8: The Woodspurge'   368
Christina G. Rossetti, 'In an Artist's Studio'   370
William Morris, 'The Haystack in the Floods'   423
               'The Defence of Guenevere'   428
               'Concerning Geffray Teste Noire'   438
Gerard M. Hopkins, 'Spring and Fall'   534
                  'As kingfishers catch fire'   535
                  'God's Grandeur'   536
                  'Pied Beauty'   537
                  'The Windhover'   538
                  'Inversnaid'   539

Decadence/The 1890s/Anti-Decadence

Alfred Austin, 'Henry Bartle Edward Frere'   448
Oscar Wilde, 'Fantaisies Décoratives: II. Les Ballons'   587
            'Symphony in Yellow'   588
            The Ballad of Reading Gaol   588

Arthur Symons, 'From Théophile Gautier: Posthumous Coquetry'   657
               'The Absinthe Drinker'   657
               'Javanese Dancers'   658
               'Prologue'   659
               'Paris'   660
               'Hands'   663
               'White Heliotrope'   663
               'Stella Maris'   664
Ernest Dowson, 'Nuns of the Perpetual Adoration'   667
               'Extreme Unction'   668
               '*Non sum qualis eram bonae sub regno Cynarae*'   670
               '*Vitae summa brevis spem nos vetat incohare longam*'   671

The City

Elizabeth Barrett Browning, 'The Cry of the Children'   25
                            'Amy's Cruelty'   59
Arthur Hugh Clough, *Amours de Voyage*   228
Matthew Arnold, 'A Summer Night'   264
Adelaide Anne Procter, 'Philip and Mildred'   314
Dante Gabriel Rossetti, 'Jenny'   358
Christina G. Rossetti, 'Babylon the Great'   393
James Thomson, *The City of Dreadful Night*   394
Augusta Webster, 'A Castaway'   456
W. E. Henley, *In Hospital*   571
Oscar Wilde, 'Symphony in Yellow'   588
John Davidson, 'Thirty Bob a Week'   606
               'A Woman and her Son'   609
               'The Crystal Palace'   618
Amy Levy, 'A Minor Poet'   636
Arthur Symons, 'The Absinthe Drinker'   658
               'Javanese Dancers'   659
               'Prologue'   660
               'Paris'   662
               'Hands'   663
               'Stella Maris'   664
Lionel Johnson, 'Oxford'   672
               'By the Statue of King Charles at Charing Cross'   674
Charlotte Mew, 'Madeleine in Church'   682
               'The Trees are Down'   687

Britain and France

Matthew Arnold, 'Dover Beach'   312
Adelaide Anne Procter, 'A Legend of Provence'   320
George Meredith, *Modern Love*   328
William Morris, 'The Haystack in the Floods'   423
               'Concerning Geffray Teste Noire'   438
Algernon Charles Swinburne, '*Ave Atque Vale*: In Memory of Charles Baudelaire'   500

Oscar Wilde, 'Fantaisies Décoratives: II. Les Ballons'   587
       'Symphony in Yellow'   588
Arthur Symons, 'From Théophile Gautier: Posthumous Coquetry'   657
       'The Absinthe Drinker'   658
       'Javanese Dancers'   659
       'Prologue'   660
       'Paris'   662
       'Hands'   663
       'White Heliotrope'   663
       'Stella Maris'   664
Ernest Dowson, 'Nuns of the Perpetual Adoration'   667
       'Extreme Unction'   668
       'Non sum qualis eram bonae sub regno Cynarae'   670
       'Vitae summa brevis spem nos vetat incohare longam'   671

Britain and Italy

Thomas Macaulay, 'Horatius: A Lay made about the Year of the City CCCLX'   18
Robert Browning, 'My Last Duchess'   173
       'The Bishop Orders his Tomb at Saint Praxed's Church'   175
       'Fra Lippo Lippi'   179
       'Andrea del Sarto'   189
       'A Toccata of Galuppi's'   202
       'Two in the Campagna'   204
       'Inapprehensiveness'   215
Arthur Hugh Clough, *Amours de Voyage*   228
Dante Gabriel Rossetti, 'Sestina. Of the Lady Pietra degli Scrovigni'   356
Thomas Hardy, 'In the Old Theatre, Fiesole'   513
Eugene Lee-Hamilton, 'Laura to Petrarch'   553
       'Carmagnola to the Republic of Venice'   554
       'Charles Edward to his Last Friend'   556
Michael Field, 'La Gioconda'   558
       'A Portrait: Bartolommeo Veneto'   560

Britain and Greece

Elizabeth Barrett Browning, 'Hiram Powers' *Greek Slave*'   51
       'A Musical Instrument'   57
Robert Browning, 'Eurydice to Orpheus'   214
Matthew Arnold, 'Empedocles on Etna'   268
Augusta Webster, 'Circe'   450
Algernon Charles Swinburne, 'Hymn to Proserpine'   476
       'Anactoria'   480
       'Ave Atque Vale: In Memory of Charles Baudelaire'   500
Gerard M. Hopkins, 'That Nature is a Heraclitean Fire and of the Comfort
       of the Resurrection'   540
Eugene Lee-Hamilton, 'The New Medusa'   545
Michael Field, 'Maids, not to you my mind doth change'   557
       'It was deep April'   564
Amy Levy, 'Xantippe: A Fragment'   630

Victorian/Modern Transition

Thomas Hardy, 'The Darkling Thrush'   511
John Davidson, 'Thirty Bob a Week'   606
                    'A Woman and her Son'   609
                    'Snow'   616
                    'The Crystal Palace'   618
Amy Levy, 'A Ballad of Religion and Marriage'   642
Rudyard Kipling, 'The Way through the Woods'   655
Charlotte Mew, 'The Forest Road'   680
                    'Madeleine in Church'   682
                    'The Trees are Down'   687

Social Critique

Elizabeth Barrett Browning, 'The Cry of the Children'   25
                    'The Runaway Slave at Pilgrim's Point'   44
                    'Hiram Powers' *Greek Slave*'   51
Arthur Hugh Clough, 'The Latest Decalogue'   262
Dante Gabriel Rossetti, 'The Burden of Nineveh'   350
Christina G. Rossetti, 'Babylon the Great'   393
Alfred Austin, 'Henry Bartle Edward Frere'   448
W. E. Henley, *In Hospital*   571
Oscar Wilde, *The Ballad of Reading Gaol*   588
John Davidson, 'Thirty Bob a Week'   606
                    'The Crystal Palace'   618

Divided Self

Arthur Hugh Clough, *Amours de Voyage*   228
Matthew Arnold, 'A Summer Night'   264
                    'To Marguerite – Continued'   267
                    'Empedocles on Etna'   268
                    'The Buried Life'   296
                    'Stanzas from the Grande Chartreuse'   305
                    'Dover Beach'   312
Gerard M. Hopkins, 'No worst, there is none'   543
                    'My own heart let me more have pity on'   544
Michael Field, 'A Portrait: Bartolommeo Veneto'   560
                    'A Girl'   562
                    'Sometimes I do despatch my heart'   563
Lionel Johnson, 'The Dark Angel'   677
Charlotte Mew, 'The Forest Road'   680
                    'Madeleine in Church'   682

Religion/God

Elizabeth Barrett Browning, 'The Cry of the Children'   18
                    'The Runaway Slave at Pilgrim's Point'   44

Alfred Tennyson, 'The Epic/Morte d'Arthur'   76
         In Memoriam A.H.H.   88
         'Crossing the Bar'   169
Robert Browning, 'The Bishop Orders his Tomb at Saint Praxed's Church'   175
         'Caliban Upon Setebos'   207
Matthew Arnold, 'Empedocles on Etna'   268
         'Stanzas from the Grande Chartreuse'   305
         'Dover Beach'   312
Adelaide Anne Procter, 'A Legend of Provence'   320
Dante Gabriel Rossetti, 'The Burden of Nineveh'   350
Christina G. Rossetti, 'Goblin Market'   373
         'The World'   389
         'A Christmas Carol: In the bleak mid-winter'   390
         'Resurgam'   392
         'Babylon the Great'   393
James Thomson, *The City of Dreadful Night*   394
Algernon Charles Swinburne, 'Hymn to Proserpine'   476
         'A Forsaken Garden'   506
Thomas Hardy, 'Hap'   510
Gerard M. Hopkins, 'Spring and Fall'   534
         'The Wreck of the *Deutschland*'   534
         'As kingfishers catch fire'   535
         'God's Grandeur'   536
         'Pied Beauty'   537
         'The Windhover'   538
         'Inversnaid'   539
         'That Nature is a Heraclitean Fire and of the Comfort of the
         Resurrection'   540
         'Harry Ploughman'   541
         'No worst, there is none'   543
         'My own heart let me more have pity on'   544
Four Victorian Hymns, 'The day thou gavest' (Ellerton)   566
         'Take my life, and let it be' (Havergal)   567
         'Onward, Christian soldiers' (Baring-Gould)   567
         'My God, how wonderful Thou art' (Faber)   569
Oscar Wilde, *The Ballad of Reading Gaol*   588
John Davidson, 'A Woman and her Son'   609
Amy Levy, 'A Ballad of Religion and Marriage'   642
Ernest Dowson, 'Nuns of the Perpetual Adoration'   667
         'Extreme Unction'   668
Lionel Johnson, 'By the Statue of King Charles at Charing Cross'   674
Charlotte Mew, 'Madeleine in Church'   680

Religious Doubt/Critique of Religion

Alfred Tennyson, 'The Epic/Morte d'Arthur'   76
         In Memoriam A.H.H.   88
Matthew Arnold, 'Empedocles on Etna'   268
         'Stanzas from the Grande Chartreuse'   305
         'Dover Beach'   312

Dante Gabriel Rossetti, 'The Burden of Nineveh'   350
James Thomson, *The City of Dreadful Night*   394
Algernon Charles Swinburne, 'Hymn to Proserpine'   476
                            'A Forsaken Garden'   506
Thomas Hardy, 'Hap'   510
John Davidson, 'A Woman and her Son'   609
Amy Levy, 'A Ballad of Religion and Marriage'   642
Charlotte Mew, 'Madeleine in Church'   682

The Poet/Authorship

Elizabeth Barrett Browning, 'Hiram Powers' *Greek Slave*'   51
Alfred Tennyson, 'The Dying Swan'   62
                 'The Lady of Shalott'   71
Algernon Charles Swinburne, '*Ave Atque Vale*: In Memory of Charles Baudelaire'   500
Thomas Hardy, 'The Darkling Thrush'   512
Amy Levy, 'A Minor Poet'   636

Sappho

Algernon Charles Swinburne, '*Ave Atque Vale*: In Memory of Charles Baudelaire'   500
                            'Anactoria'   480
Michael Field, 'Maids, not to you my mind doth change'   557
               'A Girl'   562
               'It was deep April'   564

Crime

Robert Browning, 'Porphyria's Lover'   171
                 'My Last Duchess'   173
                 'Fra Lippo Lippi'   179
                 'Andrea del Sarto'   189
                 '"Childe Roland to the Dark Tower Came"'   195
                 'Caliban upon Setebos'   207
Emily Brontë, 'The Prisoner: A Fragment'   223
William Morris, 'The Haystack in the Floods'   423
                'The Defence of Guenevere'   428
                'Concerning Geffray Teste Noire'   438
Eugene Lee-Hamilton, 'The New Medusa'   545
                     'Carmagnola to the Republic of Venice'   554
Oscar Wilde, *The Ballad of Reading Gaol*   588

Suicide

Elizabeth Barrett Browning, 'Rime of the Duchess May'   29
Matthew Arnold, 'Empedocles on Etna'   268
George Meredith, *Modern Love*   328
William Ernest Henley, *In Hospital*   571
Amy Levy, 'Xantippe: A Fragment'   630
          'A Minor Poet'   363

Late Victorian Demotic Voices

William Ernest Henley, *In Hospital* 571
Oscar Wilde, *The Ballad of Reading Gaol* 588
John Davidson, 'Thirty Bob a Week' 606
    'A Woman and her Son' 609
    'The Crystal Palace' 618
Amy Levy, 'A Minor Poet' 636
Rudyard Kipling, 'Fuzzy-Wuzzy' 644
    'Gunga Din' 646
    'Tommy' 649

Post-Romantic Negotiations

Alfred Tennyson, 'The Dying Swan' 62
Robert Browning, 'My Last Duchess' 173
Emily Brontë, 'Shall Earth no more inspire thee[?]' 219
    'The Night-Wind' 218
    'To Imagination' 220
Matthew Arnold, 'Empedocles on Etna' 268
    'Stanzas from the Grande Chartreuse' 305
Dante Gabriel Rossetti, 'Song 8: The Woodspurge' 368
Christina G. Rossetti, 'Lambs of Grasmere, 1860' 387
Thomas Hardy, 'The Darkling Thrush' 512
    'Shelley's Skylark' 517
Gerard M. Hopkins, 'The Windhover' 538
    'Binsey Poplars' 542
Michael Field, 'Cyclamens' 563
Amy Levy, 'A Minor Poet' 636
Arthur Symons, 'White Heliotrope' 663

Natural Theology/Contesting Natural Theology

Robert Browning, 'Two in the Campagna' 204
    'Caliban upon Setebos' 207
Emily Brontë, 'High waving heather' 217
    'The Night-Wind' 218
    'Shall Earth no more inspire thee[?]' 219
Matthew Arnold, 'Dover Beach' 312
Dante Gabriel Rossetti, 'Song 8: The Woodspurge' 368
Algernon Charles Swinburne, 'A Forsaken Garden' 506
Thomas Hardy, 'The Darkling Thrush' 512
Gerard M. Hopkins, 'As kingfishers catch fire' 535
    'God's Grandeur' 536
    'Pied Beauty' 537
    'The Windhover' 538
    'Inversnaid' 539
    'That Nature is a Heraclitean Fire and of the Comfort of the
    Resurrection' 540
    'Binsey Poplars' 542
Michael Field, 'Cyclamens' 563

Alphabetical List of Authors

Matthew Arnold (1822–1888)   264
Alfred Austin (1835–1913)   448
Sabine Baring-Gould (1834–1924)   567
Emily Brontë (1818–1848)   217
Elizabeth Barrett Browning
(1806–1861)   18
Robert Browning (1812–1889)   171
Arthur Hugh Clough (1819–1861)   227
John Davidson (1857–1909)   606
Ernest Dowson (1867–1900)   667
John Ellerton (1826–1893)   566
Frederick William Faber (1814–1863)   569
Michael Field (Katherine Bradley
[1846–1914] and Edith Cooper
[1862–1913])   557
Thomas Hardy (1840–1928)   510
Frances Ridley Havergal (1836–1879)   567
William Ernest Henley (1849–1903)   571
Gerard M. Hopkins (1844–1889)   525

Lionel Johnson (1867–1902)   672
May Kendall (1861–?1943)   627
Rudyard Kipling (1865–1936)   644
Eugene Lee-Hamilton (1845–1907)   545
Amy Levy (1861–1889)   630
Thomas Macaulay (1800–1859)   1
George Meredith (1828–1909)   328
Charlotte Mew (1869–1928)   680
William Morris (1834–1896)   394
Adelaide Anne Procter (1825–1864)   314
Christina G. Rossetti (1830–1894)   370
Dante Gabriel Rossetti (1828–1882)   350
Algernon Charles Swinburne
(1837–1909)   476
Arthur Symons (1865–1945)   657
Alfred Tennyson (1809–1892)   62
James Thomson, 'B. V.' (1834–1882)   394
Augusta Webster (1837–1894)   450
Oscar Wilde (1854–1900)   587

Plates

1   B. R. Haydon, *Marcus Curtius* (1843), The National Gallery of Victoria,
    Melbourne, Australia   30
2   Hiram Powers, *Greek Slave* (1846), Corcoran Gallery of Art, Washington DC   52
3   Filippo Lippi, *Coronation of the Virgin* (1441–7), Uffizi, Florence   188
4   Sir Frederick Leighton, *Orpheus and Eurydice* (*c.*1864), Leighton House, London   214
5   Raphael, *St Michael trampling Satan* (1518), Louvre   342
6   Albrecht Dürer, *Melencolia* I (1514), engraving   421
7   Leonardo da Vinci, *La Gioconda*, Louvre   559
8   Bartolomeo Veneto, *Portrait of a Woman*, Städelsches Kunstinstitut, Frankfurt   560
9   Edgar Degas, *The Absinthe Drinkers* (1876), Musée d'Orsay, Paris   659
10 Edgar Degas, *L'étoile* [*La danseuse sur la scène*] (*The Star* [*Dancer on Stage*])
    (1878), Musée d'Orsay, Paris   661

Abbreviations

cf.	*compare* (from Latin, *confer*)
colloq.	*colloquialism*
derog.	*derogatory*
OED	*Oxford English Dictionary*, 2nd edition
pron.	*pronounced*

Chronology

Date of first publication (excluding Emily Brontë, whose poems are listed by date of writing as it is exactly known; other exceptions noted).

1830 Tennyson, 'The Dying Swan', 'Mariana'

1832 Tennyson, 'The Lotos-Eaters' (first version), 'The Lady of Shalott' (first version)

1836 R. Browning, 'Porphyria's Lover', Brontë, 'High waving heather'

1830 Death of **George IV**; accession of **William IV**; Wellington's Tories oppose electoral **reform**; Tory government falls; **Whig administration** commences, sympathetic to reform though not united; opening of **Liverpool and Manchester railway**; **Charles X** of France refuses to accept election results that have returned a majority liberal opposition, precipitating riots and eventually his **abdication**; replaced by Louis Philippe, the 'citizen king'; various European **revolutions** follow (Belgium, Italy, Poland).

1831 **Reform crisis** continues.

1832 Grey's Whigs succeed in passing the **Great Reform Act**, increasing the electorate to around 700,000 men, abolishing rotten boroughs and increasing the representation of cities.

1833 John Keble preaches the 'Assize Sermon' in St Mary's, the University Church at Oxford, inaugurating the **Oxford Movement**; **Factory Act** prohibits children under 9 from working in textile mills and restricts those between 9 and 13 from working more than 8 hours a day; end of the institution of **slavery** in British colonies.

1834 **Poor Law Amendment Act** ('New Poor Law') shifts responsibility for poor relief to unions of parishes administered by boards of guardians; it insists that all able-bodied poor could receive relief only in workhouses; **Tolpuddle Martyrs**: six agricultural labourers from Tolpuddle, Dorset, are sentenced to 7 years' transportation for unlawfully joining a trade union; the national outcry leads to the men being pardoned 2 years later.

1835 Henry Fox Talbot begins to experiment with paper repeatedly coated with salt and silver nitrate to improve the earliest **photographic techniques**.

1836 **First train in London** – between London Bridge and Greenwich.

1837 Death of William IV; accession of **Victoria** (–1901).

1838 **Anti Corn-Law League** founded. The Corn Laws – which fixed the price of corn and impeded free trade – have become symbolic of aristocratic privilege and maladministration. Brunel's *Great Western* crosses the Atlantic, the largest wooden ship then afloat; **'The People's Charter'** issued (foundational document of Chartism), which calls for universal adult male suffrage; secret ballot; abolition of property qualifications for MPs; payment of MPs; equal electoral districts; annual parliaments.

1839   Abortive **Chartist riots**; Fox Talbot and Daguerre announce rival processes for taking **photographs**.

1840   Brontë, 'The Night-Wind'

1840   **Penny post** introduced by Roland Hill, the first pre-paid postal service in the modern world; **marriage** of Victoria and Albert; international **Anti-Slavery Convention** held in London; difficulties for women delegates attending lead Lucretia Mott and Elizabeth Cady Stanton to formulate the idea for a women's rights convention in the USA, a major initial step in the **women's rights movement**.

1841   Brontë, 'Shall Earth no more inspire thee[?]'

1841   First **paperbacks** published by Tauchnitz Verlag, Germany.

1842   Tennyson, 'The Lotos-Eaters' (revised version), 'The Lady of Shalott' (revised version), 'The Epic/Morte d'Arthur', 'Ulysses'; R. Browning, 'My Last Duchess'

1842   **Chartist riots** after the rejection of the Chartist petition, containing some 3 million signatures (not all authentic); Chartism proving immensely important in forming members of the working class into a **political organization**; **Mudie's Lending Library** opened, the self-appointed guardian of bourgeois family values.

1843   Wordsworth becomes **Poet Laureate** on the death of Southey.

1844   E. Barrett Browning, 'Bertha in the Lane', 'The Cry of the Children', 'Rime of the Duchess May'; Brontë, 'To Imagination'

1844   **Factory Act** further shortens the working day for children and increases the amount of mandatory schooling; makes women textile workers into protected persons, giving them additional rights in law; the **electrical telegraph** is used to announce the birth of Victoria's second son, Alfred Ernest.

1845   R. Browning, 'The Bishop Orders his Tomb at Saint Praxed's Church'; Brontë, 'Remembrance'

1845   **John Henry Newman** converts to Roman Catholicism, a blow to the Oxford Movement; **Irish 'Great Famine'** (1845–51) caused by potato blight and inept government attempts at relief; 1 million people die.

1846   Brontë, 'No coward soul is mine'

1846   **Ragged School Union** founded to provide education to the extremely poor and potentially criminal children; a later ragged school teacher was Dr Barnardo; **repeal of the Corn Laws**, a major advance for the free traders; **railway boom** underway.

1847   E. Barrett Browning, 'The Runaway Slave at Pilgrim's Point'; Tennyson, *The Princess* ('Now sleeps the crimson petal')

1847   There are now 4,000 miles of **telegraph lines** in Britain, owned by the Electrical Telegraph Co.; **10 Hours Factory Act** establishes the much-desired $10\frac{1}{2}$-hour day; James Young Simpson announces the success of **chloroform** as an anaesthetic.

1848   **European revolutions** in favour of liberal reform; election in France of **Louis**

Napoleon Bonaparte as president of the republic; failure of the second **Chartist Petition**; serious **cholera** outbreak; formation of the **Pre-Raphaelite Brotherhood**.

1849   **Siege of Rome** and the subsequent restoration of Pius IX; **Disraeli** becomes Conservative leader.

1850   E. Barrett Browning, 'Hiram Powers' *Greek Slave*', *Sonnets from the Portuguese*; Tennyson, *In Memoriam A.H.H.*

1850   Tennyson becomes **Poet Laureate** on the death of Wordsworth; **North London Collegiate School** (for girls) founded by educational pioneer Frances Mary Buss; Pius IX restores Roman Catholic **ecclesiastical hierarchy** in England; **Public Libraries Act** permits cities and towns to provide a library service funded by local taxes if they wish.

1851   **Great Exhibition** opens in London; Louis Napoleon's *coup d'état* restores the **Empire**; ratified by a plebiscite the following year (he becomes Napoleon III); **invasion anxieties** in England.

1852   Matthew Arnold, 'A Summer Night', 'To Marguerite – Continued', 'Empedocles on Etna', 'The Buried Life'

1853   Arnold, 'The Scholar-Gipsy'

1853   Turkey declares war on Russia to commence the **Crimean War** (–1856); Britain, anxious to avoid a Russian presence in the Mediterranean, joins forces in due course with France, the Ottoman empire and Sardinia to attack Russia.

1854   Tennyson, 'The Charge of the Light Brigade'

1854   *The Times* (established 1785) now selling 50,000 copies a day; **Working Men's College** London founded; disastrous **charge of the Light Brigade** at Balaclava; Queen and Prince Albert open the **Crystal Palace** containing material from the Great Exhibition; it is later moved to Sydenham.

1855   Arnold, 'Stanzas from the Grande Chartreuse'; R. Browning, 'Fra Lippo Lippi', 'Andrea del Sarto', '"Childe Roland to the Dark Tower Came"', 'A Toccata of Galuppi's', 'Two in the Campagna'; Clough, 'Say not the struggle naught availeth'

1856   C. G. Rossetti, 'In an Artist's Studio' (written); D. G. Rossetti, 'The Burden of Nineveh'

1855   Abolition of the remaining **newspaper duty**, which has impeded growth; papers such as the *Liverpool Daily Post*, *Manchester Guardian* and the *Daily Telegraph* are able to come into existence; Scottish missionary and explorer **David Livingstone** discovers **Victoria Falls** as part of the extensive exploration of **Africa**, then largely unknown in Britain; formation of the **Langham Place Group** of feminists urging change in marriage law.

1857   **Indian Uprising** ('Indian Mutiny'), the most serious threat to date to British rule in India. The Uprising (1857–8) leads to the replacement of the rule of the English East India Company by the British government direct, and reform of military and civil services. **Matrimonial Causes Act** allows women limited access to divorce; right of access to children extended and women are able under certain circumstances to repossess their property after separation or following the husband's desertion.

1858 Clough, *Amours de Voyage*; Morris, 'The Haystack in the Floods', 'The Defence of Guenevere', 'Concerning Geffray Teste Noire'; Procter, 'Philip and Mildred', 'A Legend of Provence'

1858 Darwin and Wallace present joint paper on evolution; **Jewish Disabilities Act** allows Jews to take their seats in both Houses of Parliament without having to swear a Christian oath; abolition of the **property qualification** for MPs allows working-class candidates for Parliament.

1859 J. S. Mill, *On Liberty*; Charles Darwin, *The Origin of Species*; Mrs Beeton's *Book of Household Management*.

1860 T. H. Huxley v. Bishop Wilberforce debate in the Oxford Museum widely viewed as a victory for **evolutionary science**; Garibaldi takes Naples leading to **unification of Italy**; Bradlaugh founds the secularist/atheist *National Reformer*.

1861 C. G. Rossetti, 'An Apple-Gathering', 'A Birthday'; D. G. Rossetti, 'Sestina. Of the Lady Pietra degli Scrovigni'

1861 Beginning of the **American Civil War** (to 1865); **death of Prince Albert** and Victoria's withdrawal into mourning; William Morris and others form **interior design company** (Morris, Marshall, Faulkner & Co.), a key moment in the Arts and Crafts Movement; **Criminal Law Consolidation Act** reduces the large number of capital crimes to four: murder, high treason, arson in a royal dockyard, piracy.

1862 E. Barrett Browning, 'Lord Walter's Wife', 'A Musical Instrument', 'Amy's Cruelty'; Clough, 'The Latest Decalogue'; Meredith, *Modern Love*; C. G. Rossetti, 'Goblin Market', 'Song: When I am dead, my dearest', 'Winter: My Secret', 'Shut Out', 'The World'

1862 **London Exposition**, showcasing many international developments in science and technology.

1864 R. Browning, 'Eurydice to Orpheus', 'Caliban upon Setebos'

1864 First of the **Contagious Diseases Acts**, controversial efforts to control prostitution more effectively; Louis Pasteur invents **'pasteurization'**, a breakthrough in food safety; Geneva Convention establishes **Red Cross**.

1865 Abolition of **slavery** in the USA at the end of the Civil War; Governor Edward **Eyre** viciously suppresses a slave revolt led by Paul Bogle prompting both outcry in England and support from leading intellectuals (Carlyle, Dickens, Kingsley, Ruskin, Tennyson).

1866 Swinburne, 'Hymn to Proserpine', 'Laus Veneris', 'Anactoria'

1866 Second **Contagious Diseases Act**; first petition to Parliament for **female suffrage**; first functional underwater **telegraph** cable laid between North America and Europe.

1867 Arnold, 'Dover Beach' (probably written early 1850s)

1867 **Second Reform Act** raises electorate to around 2 million; Marx, *Das Kapital* (vol. 1); Nobel invents **dynamite**.

1868 **Trades Union Congress** formed in Manchester; Society of Missionaries for Africa founded; W. E. Gladstone begins first term of office as Liberal prime minister (1868–74, 1880–5, 1886, 1892–4).

1869 **Girton College Cambridge** for women founded; **Suez Canal** opened; Third

Contagious Diseases Act; margarine invented; Arnold, *Culture and Anarchy*; J. S. Mill, *Subjection of Women*.

1870 D. G. Rossetti, 'Jenny', 'Song 8: The Woodspurge', 'Nuptial Sleep'; Webster, 'Circe', 'A Castaway', 'Faded' (intended for publication in 1870)

1870 William Forster's **Education Act** creates school boards to examine the provision of elementary education across the newly created school districts (*c.*2,500); **women** are allowed to serve on the school boards, an important step in recognizing women's ability in public administration; **Married Women's Property Act** allows women to keep earnings, property acquired after marriage and open a separate savings account.

1871 **Religious tests** abolished at Durham, Cambridge and Oxford; **FA Cup** established (Wanderers beat Royal Engineers 1–0 in the first final [1872]).

1872 C. G. Rossetti, 'A Christmas Carol: In the bleak mid-winter'

1872 **Girls' Public Day School Trust** established for independent girls' schools.

1873 Population of the UK at **26 million**.

1874 Thomson, *The City of Dreadful Night* (first version)

1874 **Women's Trade Union League** formed; first **Impressionist Exhibition** in Paris.

1875 Henley, *In Hospital* (first version); Gerard M. Hopkins, 'The Wreck of the *Deutschland*' (written)

1875 **Public Health Act** requires a Medical Officer and a sanitary inspector for each district and gives councils powers to build sewers, drains and public toilets; **Third Republic** proclaimed in France.

1876 Alexander Graham Bell patents the **telephone**; **Cruelty to Animals Act** provides for protection for all vertebrate animals, requiring licensing of vivisection and inspection of facilities.

1877 Queen Victoria crowned **Empress of India**; Edison perfects the **phonograph** (early sound recording device); **Grosvenor Gallery** opened in London (centre of Aesthetic Movement art); William Morris helps found the **Society for the Protection of Ancient Buildings**; first **public telephone**; frozen meat first shipped across the Atlantic; first All-England Lawn Tennis championship at **Wimbledon**.

1878 Swinburne, '*Ave Atque Vale*: In Memory of Charles Baudelaire', 'A Forsaken Garden'

1878 Paris Exhibition (**Exposition Universelle**) of arts, science and technology; *English Men of Letters* series begun by John Morley; **Second Afghan War** (1878–9); **Lady Margaret Hall** founded as a college for women in Oxford.

1879 **Somerville Hall** founded as a college for women in Oxford; defeat of the British Army at **Battle of Isandhlwana** (South Africa); **Rorke's Drift** (some 150 British soldiers defend remote outpost against 4,000 Zulu warriors, a celebrated incident of British Army history); **Battle of Ulundi** (Zulu army defeated by Britain to bring an end to the war widely seen as caused by Sir Bartle Frere).

1880 Levy, 'Xantippe: A Fragment'; Thomson, *The City of Dreadful Night* (second version)

1880 First **Anglo-Boer** War (1880–1); Owens College Manchester granted a Royal Charter as the **Victoria University** (later Manchester University); **Elementary Education Act** (Mundella's Act) extends the provisions of 1876 Act about compulsory school attendance for children aged 5 to 10 years; **Greenwich Mean Time** adopted officially by British Parliament; now 30,000 telephones in use around the world.

1881 C. G. Rossetti, 'In life our absent friend'

1881 Pretoria convention recognizes independence of **Transvaal** and **Orange Free State**.

1882 Lee-Hamilton, 'The New Medusa'; C. G. Rossetti, 'Resurgam'

1882 Recognition of British protectorate over **Egypt**; commercial **domestic lighting** used for the first time (Central Station, New York); Leslie Stephen begins to edit the *Dictionary of National Biography*; **Phoenix Park Murders** (Lord Frederick Cavendish, British secretary for Ireland, and Thomas Henry Burke, his undersecretary, are stabbed to death by Fenian splinter group in Dublin); Society for Psychical Research founded by group of Cambridge scholars to examine 'allegedly paranormal phenomena in a scientific and unbiased way'.

1883 **Women's Cooperative Guild** founded.

1884 Levy, 'A Minor Poet'; Austin, 'Henry Bartle Edward Frere' (written)

1884 **Third Reform Act**, extending franchise to most adult males; Murray begins *Oxford English Dictionary* (to 1928); **Fabian Society** formed (socialist society committed to gradual rather than revolutionary social reform, named after Roman general Quintus Fabius from his strategy of delaying battle until the right moment); **machine gun** invented; **petrol engine** invented.

1885 **Motor car** invented; first **electric tramway** at Blackpool; death of General Gordon at Khartoum.

1886 Repeal of **Contagious Diseases Acts**; Gladstone's first Irish Home Rule Bill (fails).

1887 Kendall, 'Lay of the Trilobite'; Wilde, 'Fantaisies Décoratives: II. Les Ballons'

1887 Queen Victoria's **golden jubilee**.

1888 Henley, *In Hospital* (second version); Lee-Hamilton, *Imaginary Sonnets*

1888 Kodak **box camera** invented; Dunlop patents pneumatic **tyre**; County Councils Act establishes **County Councils** (system of voting **enfranchises unmarried women**); **match girls' strike** at Bryant & May's match factory against use of fatal red phosphorus, long hours and poor pay (prominent early instance of organized industrial action).

1889 R. Browning, 'Inapprehensiveness'; Field, 'Maids, not to you my mind doth change'; Tennyson, 'Crossing the Bar', 'To the Marquis of Dufferin and Ava'; Wilde, 'Symphony in Yellow'; Johnson, 'By the Statue of King Charles at Charing Cross' (written)

1889 **London Dock Strike** (part of a wave of strikes following the match girls involving new role for unions); **Board of Education** established; 35,000 unique **telegraphic addresses** are now registered with British Post Office.

1890 Johnson, 'Oxford' (written)

1890 Tennyson makes **wax cylinder recordings**; Frazer's *The Golden Bough* (–1915) begins.

1891 Morris, 'Iceland First Seen' (written early in the 1870s)

1891 The great **Trans-Siberian Railway** begins; **International Copyright law**.

1892   Kipling, 'Fuzzy-Wuzzy', 'Gunga Din', 'Tommy'; Field, 'La Gioconda', 'A Portrait: Bartolommeo Veneto'; Symons, 'The Absinthe Drinker', 'Javanese Dancers'

1893   Field, 'A Girl', 'Cyclamens', 'Sometimes I do despatch my heart', 'It was deep April'; C. G. Rossetti, 'Babylon the Great'; Johnson, 'The Dark Angel' (written)

1894   Davidson, 'Thirty Bob a Week'

1895   Symons, 'Prologue', 'Paris', 'Hands'

1896   Dowson, 'Nuns of the Perpetual Adoration', 'Extreme Unction', '*Non sum qualis eram bonae sub regno Cynarae*', '*Vitae summa brevis spem nos vetat incohare longam*'

1897   Davidson, 'A Woman and her Son'; Kipling, 'Recessional, A Victorian Ode'; Symons, 'White Heliotrope', 'Stella Maris'

1898   Hardy, 'Hap'; Wilde, *The Ballad of Reading Gaol*

1899   Hardy, 'Drummer Hodge'; Kipling, 'The White Man's Burden'

1900   Hardy, 'The Darkling Thrush'

1901   Hardy, 'In the Old Theatre, Fiesole'

1902   Hardy, 'The Ruined Maid', 'The Self-Unseeing', 'In Tenebris I', 'Shelley's Skylark', 'Lausanne: In Gibbon's Old Garden'
1904   Hardy, 'The Revisitation'
1908   Davidson, 'The Crystal Palace' [1908–9]
1909   Davidson, 'Snow'
1910   Kipling, 'If –', 'The Way through the Woods'
1916   Mew, 'The Forest Road', 'Madeleine in Church'
1918   Gerard M. Hopkins, *Poems . . . now first published*, edited with notes by Robert Bridges
1929   Mew, 'The Trees are Down'

1892   Coal miner, unionist and journalist Kier Hardie becomes first **Independent Labour MP**; last major outbreak of **cholera** in Europe (Hamburg); first automatic **telephone exchange**.

1893   **Ford** builds his first car; **diesel engine** patented; second Irish Home Rule Bill (fails).

1894   **Armenian massacres,** a great liberal cause in the UK.

1895   Marconi sucessfully transmits a 'dot-dot-dot' radio signal (Morse code for 'S') – the beginning of **radio communication**; the Cinématographe, based on Edison's experimental Kinetograph, is used by Louis and Auguste Lumière in Paris (the beginning of **moving images**); Oscar Wilde imprisoned for **homosexual offences**.

1896   First modern **Olympic Games** (Athens); Wilhelm Conrad Röntgen (1845–1923), experimenting on cathode rays in December 1895, is amazed to see the bones in his own hand; in January 1896, he announces publicly the discovery of **X-rays**; Lord Northcliffe founds *Daily Mail* (founds *Daily Mirror* in 1903); **Alfred Austin** is, to the disappointment of many, appointed Poet Laureate.

1897   Queen Victoria's **diamond jubilee**; **Workmen's Compensation Act** insists employers compensate injured workmen and dependants if killed; gold discovered in the **Klondike** (Seattle, USA).

1898   M. and Mme Curie discover **radium**; Zeppelin builds **airship**.

1899   **Second Anglo-Boer War** (–1902); **International Women's Congress**, London; **aspirin** invented; first **international radio transmission**.

1900   Formation of **Labour Representation Committee** (predecessor of the Labour Party); 'black body' radiation explained by Max Planck (a step towards **quantum theory**).

1901   Death of **Queen Victoria**, accession of Edward VII; population of Great Britain **32 million**.

Acknowledgements

In the first place, a long-standing debt: I must thank Dr Nicholas Shrimpton, a great critic of Victorian poetry, for inspiring teaching. Thanks to a significant number of people who have helped me with queries both small and large during the editing of this book. For advice about individual poems or poets, thanks to Dr Catherine Batt, Professor Elleke Boehmer, Professor Shirley Chew, Dr Dominique Collon, Dr Máire ní Fhlathúin, Professor Paul Hammond, Professor David Lindley, Dr Gail Marshall, Dr Catherine Maxwell, Dr Rory McTurk, Dr Nicholas Shrimpton (again), Alistair Stead, Dr Marion Thain, Professor Andrew Wawn and Professor Peter Widdowson. I'm especially grateful to Professor David Fairer. Emma Bennett from Blackwell Publishing has provided encouragement and practical advice at important stages while I have been writing. Brigitte Lee saw the book through its final stages. My mother, Joyce O'Gorman, patiently answered a large number of questions about translations from French, Latin and Italian. Many thanks also to Stella Pilling for replying to other translation questions. Thanks to my brother Chris O'Gorman for suggestions, and for information about the British Army and, separately, the Catholic Church. I'm grateful to Dr John Whale for guidance about natural history. To Jane Wright for advice on Tennyson and support for this book, especially in its early stages, thank you. Editors of individual poets or of other anthologies have also provided me with information from their work, and I am grateful to them as any reader will plainly see. I am very happy to thank the two people who read this edition in manuscript, Dr Matthew Campbell and Dr Alison Chapman: they made valuable suggestions and strengthened it. Thanks to the University of Leeds Faculty of Arts for an extra semester's research leave 2002–3, and to friends and colleagues, especially Dr Tracy Hargreaves, Dr Juliet John, Dr Anthony Mellors, Dr Clare Palmer, Dr Clare Pettitt, Dr Cristiano Ristuccia, Dr Fiona Robertson, Dr Helen Small and Dr Katherine Turner, for helping keep me on course. Professor Dinah Birch's wisdom, good humour and friendship have been invaluable. This book is for her, with love and thanks.

There are no doubt errors still here, and unpolished sentences. They are my responsibility.

Francis O'Gorman
Campo Santa Maria Gloriosa dei Frari,
Venezia

The editor and publishers also wish to thank the following for permission to use copyright material: A. P. Watt Ltd on behalf of the National Trust for Places of Historical Interest or Natural Beauty for permission to include the poetry of Rudyard Kipling.

Introduction

The Victorian period now seems, suddenly, further away. Of course, the change has not really been sudden, but the arrival of the new millennium has thrown a peculiarly clear light on the gradual shift that has taken place in our relationship with the nineteenth century over the last few years. It is now not 'the previous century'; it is impossible to meet anyone who remembers it first hand. Alfred Tennyson's voice can be heard, chanting slowly the words of 'The Charge of the Light Brigade' from the Internet. Technology has preserved estranged voices, but the nineteenth century is no longer the age of our grandparents, of living memories we can still access. The beginning of the twenty-first century is an opportune moment to think again about what constitutes the Victorian. For literary scholars, new readers, it is to be hoped, will begin to come to the period's literature without some of the presuppositions that have distorted it in the past.

This collection is specifically aimed at those new readers to the period, particularly its students who want and need accessible but appropriate information about the texts they are considering. Its aim is to provide a well-annotated selection of diversity, a collection of writing that reveals something of the period's enormous poetic range, but which is also, in the broadest of terms, coherent, and in which links and relationships are suggested explicitly and implicitly. The canon of Victorian poetry has expanded significantly in the last few years. Women poets have been the most obvious beneficiaries, and recent editions of nineteenth-century female poets by Angela Leighton and Margaret Reynolds (Blackwell), Isobel Armstrong, Joseph Bristow and Cath Sharrock (Oxford) and Virginia Blain (Longman) have made available texts beyond the reach of those outside a copyright library for the first time in over a century. The present edition continues the representation of a wide range of female poets from Emily Brontë to Augusta Webster to Charlotte Mew.

'Victorian poetry' is, for the most part here, understood to be that published between 1830 and 1900. But it would be a falsification to be absolutely strict. The dating of Thomas Hardy's poems is difficult: many poems published in the twentieth century were written much earlier. My selection includes work published in the first decade of the twentieth century. Gerard M. Hopkins's poems were, of course, written in the nineteenth century, but only published in 1918; Charlotte Mew's poetry volumes were both published in the twentieth century, the second posthumously in 1929. But Mew is one of the last of the Victorian poets in mood and theme, so she is included as a terminal figure. Her last poem reproduced here, 'The Trees are Down', is a lament for the passing of time. John Davidson's poetry reflects on the relation between an idea of the Victorian and an idea of the modern, so I have added a number of his early twentieth-century pieces because they reveal ways in which the Victorian was constructed at the beginning of the new century. Kipling spills over the edge too, but readers would not want to miss the two twentieth-century poems, one of which is a reflection on the Victorian past.

Like David Fairer's and Christine Gerrard's collection of eighteenth-century verse in the same series (2nd edn, 2003), this volume does not claim to offer the 'best' poems of the Victorian era, even were such a category decidable. But this anthology does give an introduction to the glories of the period, nevertheless – a glimpse of its peculiarly introspective energies and uncertainties, its bravura explorations of human character, its engagement with modern questions of politics, industry, war, science and love, its changing relationship with the natural world, its restless exploration of religious belief, its seductive and destructive *fin de siècle* pleasures, its stark realism, its fragile beauties and its yearning sexuality.

As a general rule, this volume has reproduced poems in their entirety, eschewing selection and abridgement. The Victorians diversely experimented with long poems – the idyll, the sonnet sequence, the collection of lyrics, the epistolary poem, the Dantesque journey into hell, the detective novel in verse – and substantial poems by Matthew Arnold, Arthur Hugh Clough, W. E. Henley, George Meredith, Alfred Tennyson, James Thomson and Oscar Wilde are represented in full, together with many other poems of considerable length such as Elizabeth Barrett Browning's 'Rime of the Duchess May', John Davidson's 'The Crystal Palace', Gerard M. Hopkins's 'The Wreck of the *Deutschland*', Adelaide Anne Procter's 'A Legend of Provence', Christina G. Rossetti's 'Goblin Market' and Augusta Webster's 'A Castaway'. The reluctantly made exceptions to my selection rule are mostly extracts from sonnet sequences (Elizabeth Barrett Browning, Christina Rossetti, Dante Gabriel Rossetti) and from Tennyson's *The Princess*, all for the same reason of space and balance.

Biographical notes are provided, and each poem is preceded by a headnote that includes details of first publication and context and sources where appropriate. This volume justifies itself among various other important collections of Victorian poetry available – such as those edited by Thomas Collins and Vivienne Rundle (Broadview), Valentine Cunningham (Blackwell), Christopher Ricks (Oxford) and J. R. Watson (Everyman) – on the basis of its annotation and its effort to assist its readers in making sense of the texts before them. My interpretative steers are there to give readers a start. They may not agree with my views – it would be wrong if they whole-heartedly did – but in an edition of this kind, it seems to me most helpful to give readers new to the field a point of departure for their own thinking. This is not, however, a *textual* edition. I have barely ever included textual variants and I have not sought to adjudicate between different revisions where disagreements exist. I have used the most widely published texts, the ones now most frequently quoted and most frequently discussed in critical prose, as plainly the appropriate choice for a volume of this kind. On the few occasions where language or punctuation have been modernized (e.g., Emily Brontë's spelling), I have said so. I have throughout, however, changed Roman numerals into Arabic (except in titles) on the grounds that few students now read them confidently. Victorian poetry is saturated in Classical and Biblical reference. I have given Classical translations in modern English but have throughout used the King James version for the Bible, a text that one can be sure all Victorians could have seen if they had wanted. Shakespeare is also given in modern English as the Victorians knew him (though for convenience I use an edition standard for us, namely Stanley Wells's and Gary Taylor's *The Complete Works* [Oxford, 1986]). The poets are arranged in chronological order, based on year of birth; their poems are also ordered chronologically by date of publication. Where a date of writing can be confidently established and is of relevance because it is significantly different from the date of publication, I have used that instead. The list of suggested thematic groups is obviously not exhaustive but might serve as another starting point for readers' own investigations (readers will find a significant number of the headings relate to essay titles in Alison Chapman, Richard Cronin and Antony H. Harrison, eds, *A Companion to Victorian Poetry* [Blackwell, 2002]). Readers might finally want to know that I have sometimes glossed the singular version of a word that appears as a plural in the poem, or vice versa, for reasons of clarity.

No anthologist can satisfy all his or her readers, and I certainly have no illusions that my sins of omission will be overlooked. But it is to be hoped that readers fresh to the subject will be truly excited – with an excitement that will grow through reading and rereading – by the many varied examples of Victorian poetry that now lie in front of them.

Thomas Babington (First Baron) Macaulay
(1800–1859)

Macaulay was the son of Zachary Macaulay (1768–1838), a prominent Scottish anti-slavery campaigner and reformer. A child prodigy, he was encouraged to write from an early age and possessed a remarkable memory. Macaulay graduated from Trinity College Cambridge, was called to the bar and extended his involvement with the Anti-Slavery Society, but an essay in August 1825 on Milton in the *Edinburgh Review* – the pro-reform, Whig periodical – brought him fame and tempted him into a career as an essayist. He entered Parliament as a Whig in 1830 and took a lively part in the passing of the Great Reform Bill in 1832. In 1834, he left for India as a new member of the East India Company's ruling council. His important 'Minute on Indian Education' announced that the best way of using education to spread civilization through overseas territories in which Britain had an interest was through the propagation of the English language and its literature. The 'Minute' helped define colonial educational policy throughout the century. Macaulay returned from India in 1838 and continued his career as an essayist, served as Secretary for War in the Cabinet, and began to write his most famous prose work, *The History of England*. This heroic achievement of partial but compelling narration covered the events of the Glorious Revolution of 1688 and its immediate aftermath; it remained unfinished at his death. Gifted with a novelist's command of narrative, his *Lays of Ancient Rome* (1842) – from where 'Horatius' comes – was an extraordinary success too, selling 100,000 copies by 1875. Macaulay, raised to the peerage in 1857, had created with *The History of England* a new form of popular history, but some viewed this as disastrous, making it more or less impossible to write serious history without dressing it up as heroic, glamorized narrative thereafter. He died in 1859 after several years of ill health.

Horatius: A Lay made about the Year of the City CCCLX [360]

A high point of early Victorian heroic narrative, Macaulay's poem – taken from his *Lays of Ancient Rome* (1842) – turned to the early years of the Roman Republic for a balladic tale of bravery and selfless loyalty to a city. Its literary debts are firstly to Sir Walter Scott and the Romantic ballad tradition. The political context of the story is as follows: the Tarquinii (semi-legendary Etruscan rulers in the 6th and 5th centuries BC) sought refuge with Lars Porse(n)na, Etruscan prince of Clusium, at the end of the 6th century BC. He, believing it an honourable thing for there to be an Etruscan king of Rome, launched an attack on the city to impose one. The faithful defence of the city by three men, led by Horatius, followed.

The major historical source is Livy's *History of Ancient Rome*, Book 2.10. Macaulay's version stresses the collective integrity of the Roman citizens over Livy's less impressively heroic men. In Livy, Horatius is a guardsman on the bridge who is deserted by his companions when they perceive the advance of the enemy. Only two remain with him, spurred by a sense of shame for the cowardliness of the others. They defend the bridge until it collapses, and Horatius is left to swim across the river. Where Macaulay notes the enemy conquer their feelings of adversity and cheer him as he makes for the opposite bank of the Tiber, in Livy, they throw spears at him. Macaulay's Horatius defends a nobler city than Livy's, and assails a nobler enemy.

Macaulay's poem constructs a golden age of Roman history, and emphasizes the values of continuity, historical inheritance, legitimacy and what we might call a notion of ethnic purity. Two of the defenders of the city belong to the ancient tribes from whom the first Roman people were formed. They attack, moreover, an army including the 'false Sixtus', whose 'deed of shame' (the rape of Lucrece) had led to the end of a dynasty of rulers dating back to Romulus and Remus, the legendary founders of Rome.

But the speaker of the poem is not simply Macaulay. Indeed, Macaulay proclaimed himself doubtful of its politics of nostalgia, and made clear a separation between the narrator's values and his own. 'The author', he said in the Preface to the 'Lay' (lay = song), 'seems to have been an honest citizen, proud of the military glory of his country, sick of the disputes of factions, and much given to pining after good old times which had never really existed.' 'Horatius' celebrates and commemorates the hero, whose central role in the unfolding of history Thomas Carlyle had articulated in his lectures *On Heroes, Hero-Worship, and the Heroic in History* (pub. 1841). It also offers a way of crossing the gap between the high culture of Classical learning and a popular readership by transforming an event from ancient Roman history into an arresting balladic tale of heroic action. For poems that explore the possibilities of *female* heroic endeavour, see Elizabeth Barrett Browning, 'Rime of the Duchess May', 29–44, and Christina G. Rossetti, 'Goblin Market', 373–85. For a contrasting treatment of the faithful hero – the 'broken heart' of fidelity – see Macaulay's 'Epitaph on a Jacobite' (1845).

'Horatius' was enormously successful and later writers had only to catch the Macaulay rhythm to suggest the heroism of a great action. The defence of Rome certainly struck Bertram Mitford as a natural comparison with the events of Rorke's Drift, 22–3 January 1879; here, a tiny band of British officers and men defended a remote mission station against overwhelming numbers of Zulu warriors following the British invasion of KwaZulu in South Africa at the beginning of the year. Mitford's 'The Defence of Rorke's Drift' (1882) begins:

> Come listen for a moment
> All ye whose peaceful life
> In even flow is ne'er disturbed
> By scenes of blood and strife –
> Who sit around your hearth-fires
> Secure from war's alarms;
> This humble lay sets forth to-day
> A British deed of arms.
>
> Left on the wild lone border,
> A small but fearless band,
> Guarding the river entrance
> To savage Zululand;
> On the warm mid-day breezes,
> Like thunder's distant sound,
> Came the long roll of cannon
> From far o'er the hostile ground . . .

Cf. Alfred Austin, 'Henry Bartle Edward Frere', 448–9.

Text: *The Works of Lord Macaulay* (1898).

> Lars Porsena of Clusium
> By the Nine Gods[1] he swore
> That the great house of Tarquin
> Should suffer wrong no more.
> By the Nine Gods he swore it,   5
> And named a trysting[2] day,
> And bade his messengers ride forth,
> East and west and south and north,
> To summon his array.

> 2
> East and west and south and north   10
> The messengers ride fast,
> And tower and town and cottage
> Have heard the trumpet's blast.
> Shame on the false Etruscan[3]
> Who lingers in his home,   15
> When Porsena of Clusium
> Is on the march for Rome.

> 3
> The horsemen and the footmen
> Are pouring in amain[4]
> From many a stately market-place;   20
> From many a fruitful plain;

---

[1] *Nine Gods* Juno, Minerva and Tin'ia (the three chief); Vulcan, Mars, Saturn, Hercules, Summanus and Vedius.
[2] *trysting* meeting (usually with an association of love, here ironic).
[3] *Etruscan* area of ancient Italy (Tuscany).
[4] *amain* with full force.

From many a lonely hamlet,
Which, hid by beech and pine,
Like an eagle's nest, hangs on the crest
Of purple Apennine;[5]   25

4

From lordly Volaterræ,[6]
Where scowls the far-famed hold
Piled by the hands of giants
For godlike kings of old;
From seagirt Populonia,[7]   30
Whose sentinels descry
Sardinia's[8] snowy mountain-tops
Fringing the southern sky;

5

From the proud mart of Pisæ,[9]
Queen of the western waves,   35
Where ride Massilia's triremes[10]
Heavy with fair-haired slaves;
From where sweet Clanis[11] wanders
Through corn and vines and flowers;
From where Cortona[12] lifts to heaven   40
Her diadem of towers.

6

Tall are the oaks whose acorns
Drop in dark Auser's rill;[13]
Fat are the stags that champ the boughs
Of the Ciminian[14] hill;   45
Beyond all streams Clitumnus[15]
Is to the herdsman dear;
Best of all pools the fowler loves
The great Volsinian[16] mere.[17]

7

But now no stroke of woodman   50
Is heard by Auser's rill;
No hunter tracks the stag's green path
Up the Ciminian hill;
Unwatched along Clitumnus
Grazes the milk-white steer;   55
Unharmed the water fowl may dip
In the Volsinian mere.

---

[5] *Apennine* mountain range running down the centre of Italy.
[6] *Volaterræ* ancient Etruscan town.
[7] *Populonia* ancient Etruscan coastal town.
[8] *Sardinia* large island to the west of the Tyrrhenian Sea.
[9] *Pisæ* ancient Italian city (Pisa).
[10] *triremes* ancient galleys – ships – with three ranks of oars one above another.
[11] *Clanis* Etruscan river.
[12] *Cortona* ancient hill town between Perugia and Arezzo.
[13] *Auser's rill* tributary stream of the River Arno.
[14] *Ciminian* the area around Lake Ciminus.
[15] *Clitumnus* small river in Umbria.
[16] *Volsinian* the Volsci were a tribe of central Italy.
[17] *mere* lake.

8

The harvests of Arretium,[18]
This year, old men shall reap;
This year, young boys in Umbro[19]
Shall plunge the struggling sheep;   60
And in the vats of Luna,[20]
This year, the must[21] shall foam
Round the white feet of laughing girls[22]
Whose sires have marched to Rome.   65

9

There be thirty chosen prophets,
The wisest of the land,
Who alway by Lars Porsena
Both morn and evening stand:
Evening and morn the Thirty   70
Have turned the verses o'er,
Traced from the right on linen white
By mighty seers of yore.

10

And with one voice the Thirty
Have their glad answer given: 75
'Go forth, go forth, Lars Porsena;
Go forth, beloved of Heaven;
Go, and return in glory
To Clusium's royal dome;
And hang round Nurscia's[23] altars   80
The golden shields of Rome.'

11

And now hath every city
Sent up her tale of men;
The foot are fourscore thousand,
The horse are thousands ten.   85
Before the gates of Sutrium[24]
Is met the great array.
A proud man was Lars Porsena
Upon the trysting day.

12

For all the Etruscan armies   90
Were ranged beneath his eye,
And many a banished Roman,
And many a stout ally;
And with a mighty following
To join the muster came   95

[18] *Arretium* large town in Etruria (Arezzo).
[19] *Umbro* Umbria.
[20] *Luna* ancient Etruscan town.
[21] *must* juice of grapes for wine making.
[22] *white feet . . . girls* the grapes are being crushed in the traditional manner: by foot.
[23] *Nurscia* ancient Umbrian town.
[24] *Sutrium* ancient Etruscan town.

The Tusculan[25] Mamilius,
Prince of the Latian[26] name.

13
But by the yellow Tiber[27]
Was tumult and affright:
From all the spacious champaign[28]   100
To Rome men took their flight.
A mile around the city,
The throng stopped up the ways;
A fearful sight it was to see
Through two long nights and days.   105

14
For aged folks on crutches,
And women great with child,
And mothers sobbing over babes
That clung to them and smiled,
And sick men borne in litters[29]   110
High on the necks of slaves,
And troops of sun-burned husbandmen[30]
With reaping-hooks and staves,

15
And droves of mules and asses
Laden with skins of wine,   115
And endless flocks of goats and sheep,
And endless herds of kine,[31]
And endless trains of waggons
That creaked beneath the weight
Of corn-sacks and of household goods,   120
Choked every roaring gate.

16
Now, from the rock Tarpeian,[32]
Could the wan burghers[33] spy
The line of blazing villages
Red in the midnight sky.   125
The Fathers of the City,
They sat all night and day,
For every hour some horseman came
With tidings of dismay.

17
To eastward and to westward   130
Have spread the Tuscan bands;
Nor house, nor fence, nor dovecote

---

[25] *Tusculan* Etruscan.
[26] *Latian* small region to the south-east of Rome.
[27] *Tiber* river of Rome.
[28] *champaign* countryside outside Rome, the Campagna di Roma (cf. Browning's 'Two in the Campagna', 204–6).
[29] *litter* frame supporting a bed or couch for moving the sick or wealthy.

[30] *husbandmen* farmers.
[31] *kine* cows.
[32] *Tarpeian* rock-face on the Capitoline Hill at Rome over which those convicted of treason to the state were thrown.
[33] *wan burghers* pale citizens.

In Crustumerium[34] stands.
Verbenna down to Ostia[35]
Hath wasted all the plain;
Astur hath stormed Janiculum,[36]   135
And the stout guards are slain.

18

I wis,[37] in all the Senate,
There was no heart so bold,
But sore it ached, and fast it beat,   140
When that ill news was told.
Forthwith up rose the Consul,[38]
Up rose the Fathers all;
In haste they girded up their gowns,
And hied[39] them to the wall.   145

19

They held a council standing,
Before the River-Gate;
Short time was there, ye well may guess,
For musing or debate.
Out spake the Consul roundly: 150
'The bridge must straight go down;
For, since Janiculum is lost,
Nought else can save the town.'

20

Just then a scout came flying,
All wild with haste and fear: 155
'To arms! to arms! Sir Consul:
Lars Porsena is here.'
On the low hills to westward
The Consul fixed his eye,
And saw the swarthy[40] storm of dust   160
Rise fast along the sky.

21

And nearer fast and nearer
Doth the red whirlwind come;
And louder still and still more loud,
From underneath that rolling cloud,   165
Is heard the trumpet's war-note proud,
The trampling, and the hum.
And plainly and more plainly
Now through the gloom appears,
Far to left and far to right,   170

[34] *Crustumerium* ancient Sabine town.
[35] *Ostia* important Roman port at the mouth of the River Tiber.
[36] *Janiculum* hill on the west bank of the Tiber, opposite Rome (not one of the seven hills). Cf. the end of Clough's *Amours de Voyage*, 228–62, for a later occasion when the seizure of the Janiculum heights signified the defeat of Rome.

[37] *wis* know.
[38] *Consul* one of two elected magistrates who formed the supreme authority of the Roman Republic.
[39] *hied* hastened.
[40] *swarthy* dark or black.

In broken gleams of dark-blue light,
The long array of helmets bright,
The long array of spears.

22

And plainly and more plainly,
Above that glimmering line,   175
Now might ye see the banners
Of twelve fair cities shine;
But the banner of proud Clusium
Was highest of them all,
The terror of the Umbrian,   180
The terror of the Gaul.[41]

23

And plainly and more plainly
Now might the burghers know,
By port and vest,[42] by horse and crest,
Each warlike Lucumo.[43]   185
There Cilnius of Arretium
On his fleet roan[44] was seen;
And Astur of the four-fold shield,
Girt with the brand none else may wield,
Tolumnius with the belt of gold,   190
And dark Verbenna from the hold
By reedy Thrasymene.[45]

24

Fast by the royal standard,
O'erlooking all the war,
Lars Porsena of Clusium   195
Sat in his ivory car.[46]
By the right wheel rode Mamilius,
Prince of the Latian name;
And by the left false Sextus,
That wrought the deed of shame.[47]   200

25

But when the face of Sextus
Was seen among the foes,
A yell that rent the firmament
From all the town arose.
On the house-tops was no woman   205
But spat towards him and hissed,
No child but screamed out curses,
And shook its little fist.

---

[41] *Gaul* French.

[42] *vest* i.e., garment.

[43] *Lucumo* Etruscan nobles, who combined the functions of priest and prince.

[44] *roan* horse.

[45] *Thrasymene* Etruscan lake.

[46] *car* chariot.

[47] *Sextus* 'the ill-famed Sextus Tarquinius, son of Lucius Tarquinius (called Superbus for his strength and pride). His "deed of shame" was the ravishment of Lucrece, the wife of Collatinus, a Roman noble and one of Sextus' officers. As a result of the rape and a general disgust at the tyranny of Superbus, the Tarquins were banished from Rome, ending the line of Kings going back to Romulus. Thereafter, Rome was administered by Consuls elected yearly' (Macaulay's note).

26

But the Consul's brow was sad,
And the Consul's speech was low,
And darkly looked he at the wall,
And darkly at the foe.
'Their van[48] will be upon us
Before the bridge goes down;
And if they once may win the bridge,
What hope to save the town?'

210

215

27

Then out spake brave Horatius,
The Captain of the Gate:
'To every man upon this earth
Death cometh soon or late.
And how can man die better
Than facing fearful odds,
For the ashes of his fathers,
And the temples of his Gods,

220

28

'And for the tender mother
Who dandled him to rest,
And for the wife who nurses
His baby at her breast,
And for the holy maidens
Who feed the eternal flame,[49]
To save them from false Sextus
That wrought the deed of shame?

225

230

29

'Hew down the bridge, Sir Consul,
With all the speed ye may;
I, with two more to help me,
Will hold the foe in play.
In yon strait path a thousand
May well be stopped by three.
Now who will stand on either hand,
And keep the bridge with me?'

235

240

30

Then out spake Spurius Lartius;
A Ramnian[50] proud was he:
'Lo, I will stand at thy right hand,
And keep the bridge with thee.'
And out spake strong Herminius;
Of Titian[51] blood was he:
'I will abide on thy left side,
And keep the bridge with thee.'

245

---

[48] *van* foremost division.
[49] *holy maidens . . . flame* in ancient Rome, the temple of Vesta, goddess of the hearth, was superintended by priestesses known as Vestal Virgins; they guarded a perpetual fire at her altar.

[50] *Ramnian* the Ramnes formed one of the three tribes from which the first Roman people were formed.
[51] *Titian* the Tities comprised another of the original three Roman tribes (see note 50).

31

'Horatius,' quoth the Consul,
'As thou sayest, so let it be.'   250
And straight against that great array
Forth went the dauntless Three.
For Romans in Rome's quarrel
Spared neither land nor gold,
Nor son nor wife, nor limb nor life,   255
In the brave days of old.

32

Then none was for a party;
Then all were for the state;
Then the great man helped the poor,
And the poor man loved the great: 260
Then lands were fairly portioned;
Then spoils were fairly sold:
The Romans were like brothers
In the brave days of old.

33

Now Roman is to Roman   265
More hateful than a foe,
And the Tribunes beard the high,
And the Fathers grind the low.
As we wax hot in faction,
In battle we wax cold: 270
Wherefore men fight not as they fought
In the brave days of old.

34

Now while the Three were tightening
Their harness on their backs,
The Consul was the foremost man   275
To take in hand an axe:
And Fathers mixed with Commons
Seized hatchet, bar, and crow,
And smote upon the planks above,
And loosed the props below.   280

35

Meanwhile the Tuscan army,
Right glorious to behold,
Come flashing back the noonday light,
Rank behind rank, like surges bright
Of a broad sea of gold.   285
Four hundred trumpets sounded
A peal of warlike glee,
As that great host, with measured tread,
And spears advanced, and ensigns[52] spread,
Rolled slowly towards the bridge's head,   290
Where stood the dauntless Three.

[52] *ensigns* military flags.

36
The Three stood calm and silent,
And looked upon the foes,
And a great shout of laughter
From all the vanguard rose: 295
And forth three chiefs came spurring
Before that deep array;
To earth they sprang, their swords they drew,
And lifted high their shields, and flew
To win the narrow way;   300

37
Aunus from green Tifernum,[53]
Lord of the Hill of Vines;
And Seius, whose eight hundred slaves
Sicken in Ilva's[54] mines;
And Picus, long to Clusium   305
Vassal[55] in peace and war,
Who led to fight his Umbrian powers
From that grey crag where, girt with towers,
The fortress of Nequinum[56] lowers
O'er the pale waves of Nar.[57]   310

38
Stout Lartius hurled down Aunus
Into the stream beneath;
Herminius struck at Seius,
And clove him to the teeth;
At Picus brave Horatius   315
Darted one fiery thrust;
And the proud Umbrian's gilded arms
Clashed in the bloody dust.

39
Then Ocnus of Falerii[58]
Rushed on the Roman Three;   320
And Lausulus of Urgo,
The rover of the sea;
And Aruns of Volsinium,
Who slew the great wild boar,
The great wild boar that had his den   325
Amidst the reeds of Cosa's[59] fen,
And wasted fields, and slaughtered men,
Along Albinia's shore.

40
Herminius smote down Aruns:
Lartius laid Ocnus low: 330
Right to the heart of Lausulus

[53] *Tifernum* ancient Umbrian town.
[54] *Ilva* now the Island of Elba.
[55] *Vassal* feudal tenant.
[56] *Nequinum* ancient Umbrian town.

[57] *Nar* tributary river of the Tiber.
[58] *Falerii* capital of the ancient Falisci people.
[59] *Cosa* ancient Etruscan colony.

Horatius sent a blow.
'Lie there,' he cried, 'fell pirate!
No more, aghast and pale,
From Ostia's walls the crowd shall mark   335
The track of thy destroying bark.
No more Campania's[60] hinds shall fly
To woods and caverns when they spy
Thy thrice accursed sail.'

41

But now no sound of laughter   340
Was heard among the foes.
A wild and wrathful clamour
From all the vanguard rose.
Six spears' lengths from the entrance
Halted that deep array,   345
And for a space no man came forth
To win the narrow way.

42

But hark! the cry is Astur:
And lo! the ranks divide;
And the great Lord of Luna   350
Comes with his stately stride.
Upon his ample shoulders
Clangs loud the four-fold shield,
And in his hand he shakes the brand
Which none but he can wield.   355

43

He smiled on those bold Romans
A smile serene and high;
He eyed the flinching Tuscans,
And scorn was in his eye.
Quoth he, 'The she-wolf's litter[61]   360
Stand savagely at bay:
But will ye dare to follow,
If Astur clears the way?'

44

Then, whirling up his broadsword
With both hands to the height,   365
He rushed against Horatius,
And smote with all his might.
With shield and blade Horatius
Right deftly turned the blow.
The blow, though turned, came yet too nigh;   370
It missed his helm, but gashed his thigh:
The Tuscans raised a joyful cry
To see the red blood flow.

[60] *Campania* region of central Italy.
[61] *she-wolf's litter* the twins Romulus and Remus, the legendary founders of Rome, were suckled by a she-wolf after they had been thrown into then recovered from the Tiber.

45

He reeled, and on Herminius
He leaned one breathing-space;   375
Then, like a wild cat mad with wounds,
Sprang right at Astur's face.
Through teeth, and skull, and helmet
So fierce a thrust he sped,
The good sword stood a hand-breadth out   380
Behind the Tuscan's head.

46

And the great Lord of Luna
Fell at that deadly stroke,
As falls on Mount Alvernus[62]
A thunder smitten oak.   385
Far o'er the crashing forest
The giant arms lie spread;
And the pale augurs, muttering low,
Gaze on the blasted head.

47

On Astur's throat Horatius   390
Right firmly pressed his heel,
And thrice and four times tugged amain,
Ere he wrenched out the steel.
'And see,' he cried, 'the welcome,
Fair guests, that waits you here!   395
What noble Lucumo comes next
To taste our Roman cheer?'

48

But at his haughty challenge
A sullen murmur ran,
Mingled of wrath, and shame, and dread,   400
Along that glittering van.
There lacked not men of prowess,
Nor men of lordly race;
For all Etruria's noblest
Were round the fatal place.   405

49

But all Etruria's noblest
Felt their hearts sink to see
On the earth the bloody corpses,
In the path the dauntless Three:
And, from the ghastly entrance   410
Where those bold Romans stood,
All shrank, like boys who unaware,
Ranging the woods to start a hare,
Come to the mouth of the dark lair
Where, growling low, a fierce old bear   415
Lies amidst bones and blood.

---

[62] *Alvernus* Mount Alverno, in the Apennines.

50

Was none who would be foremost
    To lead such dire attack:
But those behind cried 'Forward!'
    And those before cried 'Back!'   420
And backward now and forward
    Wavers the deep array;
And on the tossing sea of steel,
    To and fro the standards reel;
And the victorious trumpet-peal   425
    Dies fitfully away.

51

Yet one man for one moment
    Strode out before the crowd;
Well known was he to all the Three,
    And they gave him greeting loud.   430
'Now welcome, welcome, Sextus!
    Now welcome to thy home!
Why dost thou stay, and turn away?
    Here lies the road to Rome.'

52

Thrice looked he at the city;   435
    Thrice looked he at the dead;
And thrice came on in fury,
    And thrice turned back in dread:
And, white with fear and hatred,
    Scowled at the narrow way   440
Where, wallowing in a pool of blood,
    The bravest Tuscans lay.

53

But meanwhile axe and lever
    Have manfully been plied;
And now the bridge hangs tottering   445
    Above the boiling tide.
'Come back, come back, Horatius!'
    Loud cried the Fathers all.
'Back, Lartius! back, Herminius!
    Back, ere the ruin fall!'   450

54

Back darted Spurius Lartius;
    Herminius darted back:
And, as they passed, beneath their feet
    They felt the timbers crack.
But when they turned their faces,   455
    And on the farther shore
Saw brave Horatius stand alone,
    They would have crossed once more.

55

But with a crash like thunder
    Fell every loosened beam,   460

And, like a dam, the mighty wreck
Lay right athwart the stream:
And a long shout of triumph
Rose from the walls of Rome,
As to the highest turret-tops   465
Was splashed the yellow foam.

56
And, like a horse unbroken
When first he feels the rein,
The furious river struggled hard,
And tossed his tawny mane,   470
And burst the curb and bounded,
Rejoicing to be free,
And whirling down, in fierce career,
Battlement, and plank, and pier,
Rushed headlong to the sea.   475

57
Alone stood brave Horatius,
But constant still in mind;
Thrice thirty thousand foes before,
And the broad flood behind.
'Down with him!' cried false Sextus.   480
With a smile on his pale face.
'Now yield thee,' cried Lars Porsena,
'Now yield thee to our grace.'

58
Round turned he, as not deigning
Those craven[63] ranks to see;   485
Nought spake he to Lars Porsena,
To Sextus nought spake he;
But he saw on Palatinus[64]
The white porch of his home;
And he spake to the noble river   490
That rolls by the towers of Rome.

59
'Oh, Tiber! father Tiber!
To whom the Romans pray,
A Roman's life, a Roman's arms,
Take thou in charge this day!'   495
So he spake, and speaking sheathed
The good sword by his side,
And with his harness on his back,
Plunged headlong in the tide.

60
No sound of joy or sorrow   500
Was heard from either bank;
But friends and foes in dumb surprise,

---

[63] *craven* cowardly.   [64] *Palatinus* one of the seven hills of Rome.

With parted lips and straining eyes,
   Stood gazing where he sank;
And when above the surges   505
   They saw his crest appear,
All Rome sent forth a rapturous cry,
   And even the ranks of Tuscany
Could scarce forbear to cheer.

61

But fiercely ran the current,   510
   Swollen high by months of rain:
And fast his blood was flowing;
   And he was sore in pain,
And heavy with his armour,
   And spent with changing blows: 515
And oft they thought him sinking,
   But still again he rose.

62

Never, I ween,[65] did swimmer,
   In such an evil case,
Struggle through such a raging flood   520
   Safe to the landing place:
But his limbs were borne up bravely
   By the brave heart within,
And our good father Tiber
   Bare bravely up his chin.   525

63

'Curse on him!' quoth false Sextus;
   'Will not the villain drown?
But for this stay, ere close of day
   We should have sacked the town!'
'Heaven help him!' quoth Lars Porsena,   530
   'And bring him safe to shore;
For such a gallant feat of arms
   Was never seen before.'

64

And now he feels the bottom;
   Now on dry earth he stands;   535
Now round him throng the Fathers;
   To press his gory hands;
And now, with shouts and clapping,
   And noise of weeping loud,
He enters through the River-Gate,   540
   Borne by the joyous crowd.

65

They gave him of the corn-land,
   That was of public right,
As much as two strong oxen

[65] *ween* think.

Could plough from morn till night;   545
And they made a molten image,
And set it up on high,
And there it stands unto this day
To witness if I lie.

66

It stands in the Comitium,[66]   550
Plain for all folk to see;
Horatius in his harness,
Halting upon one knee:
And underneath is written,
In letters all of gold,   555
How valiantly he kept the bridge
In the brave days of old.

67

And still his name sounds stirring
Unto the men of Rome,
As the trumpet-blast that cries to them   560
To charge the Volscian home;
And wives still pray to Juno[67]
For boys with hearts as bold
As his who kept the bridge so well
In the brave days of old.   565

68

And in the nights of winter,
When the cold north winds blow,
And the long howling of the wolves
Is heard amidst the snow;
When round the lonely cottage   570
Roars loud the tempest's din,
And the good logs of Algidus[68]
Roar louder yet within;

69

When the oldest cask is opened,
And the largest lamp is lit;   575
When the chestnuts glow in the embers,
And the kid turns on the spit;
When young and old in circle
Around the firebrands close;
When the girls are weaving baskets,   580
And the lads are shaping bows;

70

When the goodman mends his armour,
And trims his helmet's plume;

---

[66] *Comitium* main place of political assembly in Rome.   [68] *Algidus* mountain near Rome.
[67] *Juno* goddess of marriage and childbirth, wife of
Jupiter.

When the goodwife's shuttle merrily
  Goes flashing through the loom;   585
With weeping and with laughter
  Still is the story told,
How well Horatius kept the bridge
  In the brave days of old.

Elizabeth Barrett Browning (1806–1861)

Born into a family of wealthy Jamaican sugar-planters (with slave-owning interests), Elizabeth Barrett Moulton-Barrett was a child of remarkable intellectual energy and ability. Although not formally trained – probably a good thing, given the limited nature of much early nineteenth-century girls' education – she learned ancient Greek with her brother, and her father printed privately her long Popean poem *The Battle of Marathon* in 1820. Other pieces followed, including the *Essay on Mind* in 1826 and a translation of *Prometheus Unbound* in 1833. But her early life was soon to be afflicted with grief. Elizabeth Barrett began to suffer during her teenage years from some kind of lingering condition – consumption? – and a spinal injury that kept her bedridden or, at best, confined indoors. Her mother died in 1828 and her beloved brother Edward – 'Bro' – drowned at Torquay in 1840 after – to make things worse – they had fallen out. In 1845, following the publication of her *Poems* (1844), she began a correspondence with Robert Browning, then a struggling young poet, who much admired her work and, increasingly, her. Forbidden by her exceptionally possessive father to marry, she and Browning eventually eloped after wedding in secret to live in Italy, chiefly Florence. Her love for Browning was poured into the *Sonnets from the Portuguese* (1850), and into what outsiders saw as a happy marriage (though they certainly fell out about politics and spiritualism). Confident in the powers of art to intervene in political questions – slavery, child labour, Italian unification, sexual corruption – Elizabeth Barrett Browning's poetry seemed predicated on the belief in *Aurora Leigh*, her novel-in-verse of 1857, that poets were 'the only truth-tellers now left to God,/The only speakers of essential truth,/Opposed to relative, comparative,/And temporal truths'. James Thomson, the author of *The City of Dreadful Night*, 394–422, wrote after her death (in 'E.B.B. 1861') that she was a writer whose 'spirit pure and brave' had fought for her land 'With . . . grand impassioned thought'. Elizabeth Barrett Browning (I use this name throughout the anthology to avoid confusion even when it is proleptic) published *Casa Guidi Windows* in 1851 – a long poem on the struggle for Italian unification – and *Poems Before Congress* in 1860; *Last Poems* (1862) was posthumous. Throughout the period, her stature was recognized (during her life, she was more celebrated than her husband). Amy Sharp, Fellow of Newnham College Cambridge, expressed the prevailing view when she remarked in a University Extension lecture in 1891 that 'No other poetess has reached Mrs. Browning's level of achievement, or anything like it'. Elizabeth Barrett Browning died in Casa Guidi – the Brownings' residence in Florence – in 1861, survived by her husband and their only son, Robert Wiedemann 'Pen' Browning

Bertha in the Lane

'Bertha in the Lane' (1844) presents a dramatic speaker whose life offers, it appears, a stark drama of female choice. The speaker addresses her younger sister, Bertha, and reveals that Bertha took the speaker's fiancé, Robert, to be her own husband. The unnamed monologist has made a wedding gown for Bertha, but a shroud for herself. In doing so, she has seemingly expressed – through sewing, a medium peculiarly associated with the duties of Victorian domestic femininity – the limited options available in her life: marriage or self-sacrifice for another's happiness.

But, the poem indicates, rhetoric is a powerful tool of protest and self-expression. The speaker ostensibly maintains her affection for Bertha but her often-repeated 'Dear' is suspiciously over-repeated. Deftly, the speaker shapes her narrative and tone to bruise her sister beneath the seemingly loving words, exacting a subtle form of verbal revenge. The more generous she appears, the more pain she can inflict. The speaker's sensitivity to rhetoric, the crafting of language for specific effect, is most obvious in the final line.

The poem, notable for its eroticized landscape, offers an extreme response to lost love and is one of a number of poems in which Barrett Browning investigates – and here ironizes – the occasions and politics of female self-sacrifice; cf. 'Rime of the Duchess May', 29–44. Its consideration of how a sister deprives another sister of life and love makes for a stark contrast with Christina G. Rossetti's celebration of sisterly love in 'Goblin Market', 373–85. Barrett Browning's 'Bianca Among the Nightingales' (1862) can be compared as a text representing with plainer bitterness a further scene of a man lost to another lover. In terms of form, the workings of sympathy and the reader's relation to the speaker in 'Bertha in the Lane' can be contrasted with Robert Browning's handling of the monologue form (e.g., 'My Last Duchess', 173–5, 'Andrea del Sarto', 189–95).

Text: *Poems* (1844).

Put the broidery-frame[1] away,
For my sewing is all done:
The last thread[2] is used to-day,
And I need not join it on.[3]
Though the clock stands at the noon   5
I am weary. I have sewn,
Sweet, for thee, a wedding-gown.

2

Sister, help me to the bed,
And stand near me, Dearest-sweet.
Do not shrink nor be afraid,   10
Blushing with a sudden heat!
No one standeth in the street? –
By God's love I go to meet,
Love I thee with love complete.

3

Lean thy face down; drop it in   15
These two hands, that I may hold
'Twixt their palms thy cheek and chin,
Stroking back the curls of gold:
'Tis a fair, fair face, in sooth[4] –
Larger eyes and redder mouth   20
Than mine were in my first youth.

4

Thou art younger by seven years –
Ah! – so bashful at my gaze,
That the lashes, hung with tears,
Grow too heavy to upraise?   25
I would wound thee by no touch
Which thy shyness feels as such.
Dost thou mind me, Dear, so much?

5

Have I not been nigh[5] a mother
To thy sweetness – tell me, Dear?   30
Have we not loved one another
Tenderly, from year to year,
Since our dying mother mild
Said with accents undefiled,
'Child, be mother to this child'!   35

6

Mother, mother, up in heaven,
Stand up on the jasper[6] sea,
And be witness I have given

---

[1] *broidery-frame* wooden frame with material to be embroidered stretched across it; a familiar nineteenth-century female occupation.
[2] *last thread* with a pun on the notion of the thread of life.
[3] *join it on* each finished thread was spliced onto the next, creating a smooth surface.
[4] *sooth* truth.
[5] *nigh* nearly.
[6] *jasper* green precious stone.

All the gifts required of me, –
Hope that blessed me, bliss that crowned,   40
Love that left me with a wound,
Life itself that turneth round!

7

Mother, mother, thou art kind,
Thou art standing in the room,
In a molten glory shrined   45
That rays off into the gloom!
But thy smile is bright and bleak
Like cold waves – I cannot speak,
I sob in it, and grow weak.

8

Ghostly mother, keep aloof   50
One hour longer from my soul,
For I still am thinking of
Earth's warm-beating joy and dole![7]
On my finger is a ring
Which I still see glittering   55
When the night hides everything.

9

Little sister, thou art pale!
Ah, I have a wandering brain –
But I lose that fever-bale,[8]
And my thoughts grow calm again.   60
Lean down closer – closer still!
I have words thine ear to fill,
And would kiss thee at my will.

10

Dear, I heard thee in the spring,
Thee and Robert – through the trees, –   65
When we all went gathering
Boughs of May-bloom[9] for the bees.
Do not start so! think instead
How the sunshine overhead
Seemed to trickle through the shade.   70

11

What a day it was, that day!
Hills and vales did openly
Seem to heave and throb away
At the sight of the great sky:
And the silence, as it stood   75
In the glory's golden flood,
Audibly did bud, and bud.

---

[7] *dole* sadness.
[8] *bale* evil, injury.
[9] *May-bloom* blossom of may (hawthorn).

12

Through the winding hedgerows green,
How we wandered, I and you,
With the bowery tops shut in,   80
And the gates that showed the view!
How we talked there; thrushes soft
Sang our praises out, or oft
Bleatings took them from the croft:[10]

13

Till the pleasure grown too strong   85
Left me muter evermore,
And, the winding road being long,
I walked out of sight, before,
And so, wrapt in musings fond,
Issued (past the wayside pond)   90
On the meadow-lands beyond.

14

I sate down beneath the beech
Which leans over to the lane,
And the far sound of your speech
Did not promise any pain;   95
And I blessed you full and free,
With a smile stooped tenderly
O'er the May-flowers on my knee.

15

But the sound grew into word
As the speakers drew more near –   100
Sweet, forgive me that I heard
What you wished me not to hear.
Do not weep so, do not shake,
Oh, – I heard thee, Bertha, make
Good true answers for my sake.   105

16

Yes, and he too! let him stand
In thy thoughts, untouched by blame.
Could he help it, if my hand[11]
He had claimed with hasty claim?
That was wrong perhaps – but then   110
Such things be – and will, again.
Women cannot judge for men.

17

Had he seen thee when he swore
He would love but me alone?
Thou wast absent, sent before   115
To our kin[12] in Sidmouth[13] town.

---

[10] *croft* piece of enclosed, cultivated land.
[11] *hand* in marriage.
[12] *kin* family.
[13] *Sidmouth* Devon coastal resort.

When he saw thee who art best
Past compare, and loveliest,
He but judged thee as the rest.

18

Could we blame him with grave words,   120
Thou and I, Dear, if we might?
Thy brown eyes have looks like birds
Flying straightway to the light:
Mine are older. – Hush! – look out –
Up the street! Is none without?   125
How the poplar swings about!

19

And that hour – beneath the beech,
When I listened in a dream,
And he said in his deep speech
That he owed me all esteem,[14] –   130
Each word swam in on my brain
With a dim, dilating pain,
Till it burst with that last strain.

20

I fell flooded with a dark,
In the silence of a swoon.[15]   135
When I rose, still cold and stark,
There was night; I saw the moon
And the stars, each in its place,
And the May-blooms on the grass,
Seemed to wonder what I was.   140

21

And I walked as if apart
From myself, when I could stand,
And I pitied my own heart,
As if I held it in my hand –
Somewhat coldly, with a sense   145
Of fulfilled benevolence,
And a 'Poor thing' negligence.

22

And I answered coldly too,
When you met me at the door;
And I only heard the dew   150
Dripping from me to the floor:
And the flowers, I bade you see,
Were too withered for the bee, –
As my life, henceforth, for me.

23

Do not weep so – Dear, – heart-warm!   155
All was best as it befell.

---

[14] *esteem* that is, not love: he breaks off the engagement.   [15] *swoon* faint.

If I say he did me harm,
I speak wild, – I am not well.
All his words were kind and good –
He esteemed me. Only, blood   160
Runs so faint in womanhood!

24
Then I always was too grave, –
Like the saddest ballad sung, –
With that look, besides, we have
In our faces, who die young.   165
I had died, Dear, all the same;
Life's long, joyous, jostling game
Is too loud for my meek shame.

25
We are so unlike each other,
Thou and I, that none could guess   170
We were children of one mother,
But for mutual tenderness.
Thou art rose-lined from the cold,
And meant verily[16] to hold
Life's pure pleasures manifold.   175

26
I am pale as crocus grows
Close beside a rose-tree's root;
Whosoe'er would reach the rose,
Treads the crocus underfoot.
I, like May-bloom on thorn-tree,   180
Thou, like merry summer-bee, –
Fit that I be plucked[17] for thee!

27
Yet who plucks me? – no one mourns,
I have lived my season out,
And now die of my own thorns   185
Which I could not live without.
Sweet, be merry! How the light
Comes and goes! If it be night,
Keep the candles in my sight.

28
Are there footsteps at the door?   190
Look out quickly. Yea, or nay?
Some one might be waiting for
Some last word that I might say.
Nay? So best! – so angels would
Stand off clear from deathly road,   195
Not to cross the sight of God.

[16] *verily* truly.

[17] *plucked* with a pun on its Victorian sense of 'failed', as in an examination.

29

Colder grow my hands and feet.
When I wear the shroud I made,
Let the folds lie straight and neat,
And the rosemary[18] be spread,   200
That if any friend should come,
(To see thee, Sweet!) all the room
May be lifted out of gloom.

30

And, dear Bertha, let me keep
On my hand this little ring,   205
Which at nights, when others sleep,
I can still see glittering!
Let me wear it out of sight,
In the grave, – where it will light
All the dark up, day and night.   210

31

On that grave drop not a tear!
Else, though fathom[19]-deep the place,
Through the woollen shroud I wear
I shall feel it on my face.
Rather smile there, blessèd one,   215
Thinking of me in the sun,
Or forget me – smiling on!

32

Art thou near me? nearer! so –
Kiss me close upon the eyes,
That the earthly light may go   220
Sweetly, as it used to rise
When I watched the morning-grey
Strike, betwixt the hills, the way
He was sure to come that day.

33

So, – no more vain words be said!   225
The hosannas[20] nearer roll.
Mother, smile now on thy Dead,
I am death-strong in my soul.
Mystic Dove[21] alit on cross,
Guide the poor bird of the snows   230
Through the snow-wind above loss!

34

Jesus, Victim, comprehending
Love's divine self-abnegation,[22]

---

[18] *rosemary* fragrant shrub that signifies remembrance and, at funerals, the soul's immortality.
[19] *fathom* measurement of six feet.
[20] *hosannas* hosanna is an exclamation that means 'save now'; it has been used from early times in the Christian Church as praise to God.

[21] *Mystic Dove* symbol of the Holy Spirit.
[22] *Love's divine self-abnegation* Jesus, the embodiment of love, gave his life, according to Christian theology, for humankind on the cross.

Cleanse my love in its self-spending,
And absorb the poor libation![23]
Wind my thread of life up higher,
Up, through angels' hands of fire!
I aspire while I expire.

235

[23]*libation* drink offering (to God).

Helen Jane Eare
sent. tropes

The Cry of the Children

Elizabeth Barrett Browning had been reading William Blake's *Songs of Innocence* in 1842, and the portrayal of innocent, cruelly inhibited lives in 'The Cry of the Children' (1844) testifies to its influence (her taste was unusual: Blake was barely known through much of the nineteenth century). Like her Romantic period predecessor, Barrett Browning shares disgust for the way in which child labour supports modern society; the natural world is imagined in Blakean terms; and the final lines mimic a Blakean aphorism.

'The Cry of the Children' also draws on the cluster of women's writing on factory conditions in the decade of Queen Victoria's accession, including Caroline Norton's *A Voice from the Factories* (1836). A stanza gives a flavour:

Ever a toiling *child* doth make us sad:
'Tis an unnatural and mournful sight,
Because we feel their smiles should be so glad
Because we know their eyes should be so bright.
What is it, then, when, tasked beyond their might,
They labour all day long for others' gain, –
Nay, trespass on the still and pleasant night,
While uncompleted hours of toil remain?
Poor little *Factory Slaves* – for *You* these
lines complain!

Barrett Browning's tone was to be harder edged, more ironic, her meaning more layered. R. H. Horne's work (he was a friend of Barrett Browning) for a Royal Commission investigating the employment of children in factories and mines lay behind the poem too.

Like 'The Runaway Slave at Pilgrim's Point', 44–51, 'The Cry of the Children' is centrally engaged with questions of human cruelty and oppression, and preoccupied with how a wretched environment inflicts suffering not only on the body but also on the mind. The children's conceptions of God here are corrupted by their factory conditions, and stanza 11 adds that Christianity has been cynically co-opted into the oppressive discourses of industrial capitalism. Part of the protest of the poem – whose rhythms capture something of the new experience of the factory's ceaseless operation – is to remind its Christian readers that souls are being endangered as well as bodies in modern labour.

Barrett Browning transforms the traditional association between femininity and children to produce a political statement that gives voice to the voiceless (cf. 'Hiram Powers' *Greek Slave*', 51–2) and suggests the ignorance of the modern adult by counterpointing a naive grown-up speaker with the views of labouring children. As a poem on the nature of labour in the contemporary world, 'The Cry of the Children' can be compared with Tennyson's 'The Lady of Shalott', 71–6, and 'The Lotos-Eaters', 66–71, Gerard M. Hopkins's 'Harry Ploughman', 541–2, and John Davidson's 'Thirty Bob a Week', 606–9. The Factory Act of 1844 reduced the hours children aged between 8 and 13 could work in the textile industry to six and a half a day.

Text: *Poems* (1844).

Not iambic
stark contrast, rhythm?
to sentimental

'Φεῦ, φεῦ, τί προσδέρκεσθε μ' 'ὄμμασιυ, τέκνα;' – Medea.[1]

Do ye hear the children weeping, O my brothers,   *adheres to brotherhood*
Ere the sorrow comes with years?
They are leaning their young heads against their mothers,
And that cannot stop their tears.

[1] 'Φεῦ, φεῦ, τί προσδέρκεσθε μ' 'ὄμμασιυ, τέκνα;'
'Alas, alas, why do you work upon me with your eyes, my children', Euripides, *Medea*, first produced in 431 BC. The play concerns Medea, an enchantress and niece of Circe; in Euripides's text, she slays her own children as she knows they will die at the hands of her enemies.

The young lambs are bleating in the meadows,   5
    The young birds are chirping in the nest,
The young fawns are playing with the shadows,
    The young flowers are blowing toward the west –
But the young, young children, O my brothers,
    They are weeping bitterly!   10
They are weeping in the playtime of the others,
    In the country of the free.[2]

                        2
Do you question the young children in the sorrow
    Why their tears are falling so?
The old man may weep for his to-morrow   15
    Which is lost in Long Ago;
The old tree is leafless in the forest,
The old year is ending in the frost,
The old wound, if stricken, is the sorest,
    The old hope is hardest to be lost: 20
But the young, young children, O my brothers,
    Do you ask them why they stand
Weeping sore before the bosoms of their mothers,
    In our happy Fatherland?

                        3
They look up with their pale and sunken faces,   25
    And their looks are sad to see,
For the man's hoary[3] anguish draws and presses
    Down the cheeks of infancy;
'Your old earth,' they say, 'is very dreary,
Our young feet,' they say, 'are very weak;   30
Few paces have we taken, yet are weary –
    Our grave-rest is very far to seek:
Ask the aged why they weep, and not the children,
    For the outside earth is cold,
And we young ones stand without, in our bewildering,   35
    And the graves are for the old.

                        4
'True,' say the children, 'it may happen
    That we die before our time:
Little Alice died last year, her grave is shapen
    Like a snowball, in the rime.[4]   40
We looked into the pit prepared to take her:
    Was no room for any work in the close clay!
From the sleep wherein she lieth none will wake her,
    Crying, "Get up, little Alice! it is day."'
If you listen by that grave, in sun and shower,   45
    With your ear down, little Alice never cries;
Could we see her face, be sure we should not know her,
    For the smile has time for growing in her eyes:
And merry go her moments, lulled and stilled in

---

[2] *free* ironically emphasizes the official absence of slavery in   [3] *hoary* grey with age.
Great Britain and her colonies since the Abolition of   [4] *rime* freezing mist.
Slavery Act, 1833.

The shroud by the kirk-chime.[5]   50
'It is good when it happens,' say the children,
    'That we die before our time.'

                    5
Alas, alas, the children! they are seeking
    Death in life, as best to have:
They are binding up their hearts away from breaking,   55
    With a cerement[6] from the grave.
Go out, children, from the mine and from the city,
    Sing out, children, as the little thrushes do;
Pluck your handfuls of the meadow-cowslips pretty,
    Laugh aloud, to feel your fingers let them through! 60
But they answer, 'Are your cowslips of the meadows
    Like our weeds anear the mine?
Leave us quiet in the dark of the coal-shadows,
    From your pleasures fair and fine!

                    6
'For oh,' say the children, 'we are weary,   65
    And we cannot run or leap;
If we cared for any meadows, it were merely
    To drop down in them and sleep.
Our knees tremble sorely in the stooping,
    We fall upon our faces, trying to go;   70
And, underneath our heavy eyelids drooping
    The reddest flower would look as pale as snow.
For, all day, we drag our burden tiring
    Through the coal-dark, underground;
Or, all day, we drive the wheels of iron   75
    In the factories, round and round.

                    7
'For all day the wheels are droning, turning;
    Their wind comes in our faces,
Till our hearts turn, our heads with pulses burning,
    And the walls turn in their places: 80
Turns the sky in the high window, blank and reeling,
    Turns the long light that drops adown the wall,
Turn the black flies that crawl along the ceiling:
    All are turning, all the day, and we with all.
And all day the iron wheels are droning,   85
    And sometimes we could pray,
"O ye wheels" (breaking out in a mad moaning),
    "Stop! be silent for to-day!"'

                    8
Ay, be silent! Let them hear each other breathing
    For a moment, mouth to mouth!   90
Let them touch each other's hands, in a fresh wreathing
    Of their tender human youth!
Let them feel that this cold metallic motion

---

[5] *kirk-chime* church clock.   [6] *cerement* garment for the grave.

Is not all the life God fashions or reveals:
Let them prove their living souls against the notion   95
That they live in you, or under you, O wheels!
Still, all day, the iron wheels go onward,
Grinding life down from its mark;
And the children's souls, which God is calling sunward,
Spin on blindly in the dark.   100

9

Now tell the poor young children, O my brothers,
To look up to Him and pray;
So the blessed One who blesseth all the others,
Will bless them another day.
They answer, 'Who is God that He should hear us,[7]   105
While the rushing of the iron wheels is stirred?
When we sob aloud, the human creatures near us
Pass by, hearing not, or answer not a word.
And we hear not (for the wheels in their resounding)
Strangers speaking at the door: 110
Is it likely God, with angels singing round Him,
Hears our weeping any more?

10

'Two words, indeed, of praying we remember,
And at midnight's hour of harm,
"Our Father,"[8] looking upward in the chamber,   115
We say softly for a charm.
We know no other words except "Our Father,"
And we think that, in some pause of angels' song,
God may pluck them with the silence sweet to gather,
And hold both within His right hand which is strong.[9]   120
"Our Father!" If He heard us, He would surely
(For they call Him good and mild)
Answer, smiling down the steep world very purely,
'Come and rest with me, my child.'[10]

11

'But, no!' say the children, weeping faster,   125
'He is speechless as a stone:
And they tell us, of His image is the master
Who commands us to work on.
'Go to!'[11] say the children, – 'up in Heaven,
Dark, wheel-like, turning clouds are all we find.   130
Do not mock us; grief has made us unbelieving:
We look up for God, but tears have made us blind.'
Do you hear the children weeping and disproving,
O my brothers, what ye preach?

---

[7] *who is God . . . hear us* ironic allusion to Psalm 8.4: 'What is man, that thou art mindfull of him? and the sonne of man, that thou visitest him?'
[8] *Our Father* first words of the Lord's Prayer: Matthew 6.9–13.
[9] *right hand . . . strong* cf. 'Shewe thy marueilous louing kindnesse, O thou that sauest by thy right hand, them which put their trust in thee', Psalm. 17.7.
[10] *'Come rest . . . child'* cf. Jesus's words: 'Come vnto me all yee that labour, and are heauy laden, and I will giue you rest', Matthew 11.28.
[11] *Go to!* exclamation of disbelief.

For God's possible is taught by His world's loving,   135
And the children doubt of each.

12

And well may the children weep before you!
They are weary ere they run;
They have never seen the sunshine, nor the glory
Which is brighter than the sun.[12]   140
They know the grief of man, without its wisdom;
They sink in man's despair, without its calm;
Are slaves, without the liberty in Christdom,[13]
Are martyrs, by the pang without the palm:[14]
Are worn as if with age, yet unretrievingly   145
The harvest of its memories cannot reap, –
Are orphans of the earthly love and heavenly.
Let them weep! let them weep!

13

They look up with their pale and sunken faces,
And their look is dread to see,   150
For they mind[15] you of their angels in high places,
With eyes turned on Deity.
'How long,' they say, 'how long,[16] O cruel nation,
Will you stand, to move the world, on a child's heart, –[17]
Stifle down with a mailed[18] heel its palpitation,   155
And tread onward to your throne amid the mart?[19]
Our blood splashes upward, O gold-heaper,
And your purple[20] shows your path!
But the child's sob in the silence curses deeper
Than the strong man in his wrath.'   160

[12] *glory . . . sun* God.
[13] *without the liberty in Christdom* ignorant of Christianity's faith that true freedom comes through Jesus.
[14] *palm* symbolizing the victory of the Christian martyr.
[15] *mind* remind.
[16] *How long . . . how long* cf. 'And when hee had opened the fift seale, I saw vnder the altar, the soules of them that were slaine for the word of God, and for the testimony which they held. And they cried with a lowd voice, saying, How long, O Lord, holy and true, doest thou not iudge and auenge our blood on them that dwell on the earth?' Revelation 6.9–10.
[17] *Will you stand . . . heart* cf. Archimedes's statement about the powers of levers and pulleys: 'Give me a place to stand and I will move the earth'. Browning would have found this line as one of the epigraphs of Shelley's *Queen Mab* (1813).
[18] *mailed* armoured.
[19] *mart* market.
[20] *purple* suggestive of riches.

Rime of the Duchess May

Romantic-period poets found in ballad form a vehicle for serious poetry, but it is more associated in the Victorian era with ephemeral popular literature or with culturally marginalized women's writing. Indeed, at the very end of the century, the poet A. Mary F. Robinson (1857–1944) made a virtue of this, claiming women's peculiar authority over popular forms as a source of strength in the 1901 'Preface' to her *Collected Poems*: 'Some persons of culture have refused me the right to express myself in those simple forms of popular song which I have loved since childhood as sincerely as any peasant . . . [But we] women have a privilege in these matters . . . We have always been the prime makers of ballads and love songs, of anonymous snatches and screeds of popular song.' Elizabeth Barrett Browning, however, approached the matter differently. She had much earlier sought to make the ballad into a genre for serious reflective verse, using the traditional form – with its concentration on action, repetitions, archaisms and stock characterization – to explore contemporary questions of sexual politics. In 'Rime of the Duchess May' (1844), Barrett Browning transforms the culturally familiar idea of female self-sacrifice – treated from a very different modern angle in her 'Bertha in the Lane', 18–25 – into a statement of heroism and a declaration of the integrity of a woman's sexual desire (cf. *Aurora Leigh* [1857]).

A significant source was the old ballad 'Edom O' Gordon' which Barrett Browning would have found in Thomas Percy's *Reliques of Ancient English Poetry* (1765). This commemorates Margaret Campbell's defence of her Aberdeenshire castle, in the absence of her husband, against Adam Gordon in 1571. It concludes in atrocity as the castle is fired and 'Baith lady and babes were brent [burned]'. Margaret's daughter, wanting to escape, moreover, is lowered down the castle wall but killed 'on the point o' Gordon's spear'. Barrett Browning's poem rejects such ideas of female death. Instead, the 'Rime' presents a woman who resists her husband's efforts to determine her actions; she demands the right to control her own future and insists that her love for him is to be taken seriously (cf. 'Lord Walter's Wife', 55–7). The tense moral drama of the 'Rime' is counterpointed by the words of the narrator, whose limited intellectual and emotional outlook means that he or she is not able to comprehend the full significance of the story.

Benjamin Robert Haydon's picture *Marcus Curtius* (1836–42) (plate 1) also survives in the intertext of the 'Rime'. It shows Curtius in 362 BC, a Roman officer, leaping on horseback into a chasm in the Roman Forum. The void was created by an earthquake that soothsayers declared could only be closed by throwing in the most valuable treasure of the city. When Barrett Browning wrote about this painting in letters (she was a friend of Haydon's), she concentrated on

Plate 1   B. R. Haydon, *Marcus Curtius* (1843), The National Gallery of Victoria, Melbourne, Australia.

the appearance of the horse. In the poem, at the moment of climax, it is also on the horse that her imagination is fixed. The reactions of the married lovers themselves at the moment before their heroic death – a radical rewriting of the tradition of Sappho's final plunge in despair over unrequited love – remain powerfully beyond the representational limits of the poem. The link with Curtius also reminds the reader that Barrett Browning was aiming to create a literary *heroine*, the depiction of a woman rather than a man

acting valiantly (cf. Macaulay's male heroic poem, 'Horatius: A Lay made about the Year of the City CCCLX', 1–17). Christina G. Rossetti's 'Goblin Market, 373–85, similarly ponders on the representation of female heroism in poetry. It is often said that the 'Rime' is parodied as 'The Rhyme of Sir Launcelot Bogle' in the 'Bon Gaultier' *Book of Ballads* (1859 edition), but it is not a close relationship.

Text: *Poems* (1844).

To the belfry, one by one, went the ringers from the sun,
Toll slowly.
And the oldest ringer said, 'Ours is music for the dead
When the rebecks[1] are all done.'

2

Six abeles[2] i' the churchyard grow on the north side in a row,   5
Toll slowly.
And the shadows of their tops rock across the little slopes
Of the grassy graves below.

3

On the south side and the west a small river runs in haste,
Toll slowly.   10
And, between the river flowing and the fair green trees a-growing,
Do the dead lie at their rest.

4

On the east I sate[3] that day, up against a willow grey:
Toll slowly.
Through the rain of willow-branches I could see the low hill-ranges   15
And the river on its way.

5

There I sate beneath the tree, and the bell tolled solemnly,
Toll slowly.
While the trees' and river's voices flowed between the solemn noises, –
Yet death seemed – more loud to me.   20

6

There I read this ancient rhyme while the bell did all the time
Toll slowly.
And the solemn knell fell in with the tale of life and sin,
Like a rhythmic fate sublime.

THE RHYME

Broad the forests stood (I read) on the hills of Linteged,[4]   25
Toll slowly.
And three hundred years had stood mute adown each hoary wood,
Like a full heart having prayed.

---

[1] *rebeck* (rebec) medieval precursor to the violin.
[2] *abeles* white poplar trees.
[3] *sate* sat.
[4] *Linteged* imaginary location, with a Welsh resonance.

2

And the little birds sang east, and the little birds sang west,
 Toll slowly.   30
And but little thought was theirs of the silent antique years,
 In the building of their nest.

3

Down the sun dropt large and red on the towers of Linteged, –
 Toll slowly.
Lance and spear upon the height, bristling strange in fiery light, 35
 While the castle stood in shade.

4

There the castle stood up black with the red sun at its back –
 Toll slowly –
Like a sullen smouldering pyre⁵ with a top that flickers fire
 When the wind is on its track.   40

5

And five hundred archers tall did besiege the castle wall –
 Toll slowly.
And the castle, seethed⁶ in blood, fourteen days and nights had stood
 And to-night was near its fall.

6

Yet thereunto, blind to doom, three months since, a bride did come – 45
 Toll slowly.
One who proudly trod the floors and softly whispered in the doors,
 'May good angels bless our home.'

7

Oh, a bride of queenly eyes, with a front of constancies:
 Toll slowly.   50
Oh, a bride of cordial mouth⁷ where the untired smile of youth
 Did light outward its own sighs!

8

'Twas a Duke's fair orphan-girl, and her uncle's ward – the Earl –
 Toll slowly.
Who betrothed her twelve years old,⁸ for the sake of dowry gold, 55
 To his son Lord Leigh the churl.⁹

9

But what time she had made good all her years of womanhood –
 Toll slowly.
Unto both these lords of Leigh spake she out right sovranly,¹⁰
 'My will runneth as my blood.   60

10

'And while this same blood makes red this same right hand's veins,' she said –
 Toll slowly –

---

⁵ *pyre* heap of combustible material, often associated with funeral cremations.
⁶ *seethed* boiled.
⁷ *cordial mouth* speaking warmly, sincerely.

⁸ *twelve years old* the poem's medieval setting means such an age is acceptable for betrothal.
⁹ *churl* man of low rank.
¹⁰ *sovranly* royally.

"'Tis my will, as lady free, not to wed a lord of Leigh,
But Sir Guy of Linteged.'

11

The old Earl he smilèd smooth, then he sighed for wilful youth –   65
Toll slowly.
'Good my niece, that hand withal looketh somewhat soft and small
For so large a will, in sooth.'

12

She too smiled by that same sign, but her smile was cold and fine –
Toll slowly.   70
'Little hand clasps muckle[11] gold, or it were not worth the hold
Of thy son, good uncle mine!'

13

Then the young lord jerked his breath, and sware thickly in his teeth –
Toll slowly –
'He would wed his own betrothed, an she loved him an she loathed,   75
Let the life come or the death.'

14

Up she rose with scornful eyes, as her father's child might rise –
Toll slowly.
'Thy hound's blood, my lord of Leigh, stains thy knightly heel,' quoth she,
'And he moans not where he lies: 80

15

'But a woman's will dies hard, in the hall or on the sward'[12] –
Toll slowly.
'By that grave, my lords, which made me orphaned girl and dowered lady,
I deny you wife and ward!'

16

Unto each she bowed her head and swept past with lofty tread.   85
Toll slowly.
Ere the midnight-bell had ceased, in the chapel had the priest
Blessed her, bride of Linteged.

17

Fast and fain[13] the bridal train along the night-storm rode amain[14] –
Toll slowly.   90
Hard the steeds of lord and serf[15] struck their hoofs out on the turf,
In the pauses of the rain.

18

Fast and fain the kinsmen's train along the storm pursued amain –
Toll slowly.
Steed on steed-track, dashing off, – thickening, doubling, hoof on hoof,   95
In the pauses of the rain.

---

[11] *muckle* great quantity of.
[12] *sward* surface of soil covered with grass.
[13] *fain* glad.

[14] *amain* vehemently.
[15] *serf* slave, bondman.

19

And the bridegroom led the flight on his red-roan[16] steed of might –
                    Toll slowly.
And the bride lay on his arm, still, as if she feared no harm,
                    Smiling out into the night.   100

20

'Dost thou fear?' he said at last. 'Nay,' she answered him in haste, –
                    Toll slowly.
'Not such death as we could find – only life with one behind.
                    Ride on fast as fear, ride fast!'

21

Up the mountain wheeled the steed – girth to ground, and fetlocks[17] spread –   105
                    Toll slowly.
Headlong bounds, and rocking flanks, – down he staggered, down the banks,
                    To the towers of Linteged.

22

High and low the serfs looked out, red the flambeaus[18] tossed about –
                    Toll slowly.   110
In the courtyard rose the cry, 'Live the Duchess and Sir Guy!'
                    But she never heard them shout.

23

On the steed she dropped her cheek, kissed his mane and kissed his neck –
                    Toll slowly.
'I had happier died by thee than lived on, a Lady Leigh,'   115
                    Were the first words she did speak.

24

But a three months' joyaunce[19] lay 'twixt that moment and to-day –
                    Toll slowly.
When five hundred archers tall stand beside the castle wall
                    To recapture Duchess May.   120

25

And the castle standeth black with the red sun at its back –
                    Toll slowly.
And a fortnight's siege is done, and, except the duchess, none
                    Can misdoubt the coming wrack.[20]

26

Then the captain, young Lord Leigh, with his eyes so grey of blee[21] –   125
                    Toll slowly.
And thin lips that scarcely sheathe the cold white gnashing of his teeth,
                    Gnashed in smiling, absently, –

27

Cried aloud, 'So goes the day, bridegroom fair of Duchess May!'
                    Toll slowly.   130

---

[16] *red-roan* of a horse: red, thickly interspersed with another colour.
[17] *fetlock* part of a horse's leg.
[18] *flambeaus* fire torches.

[19] *joyaunce* happiness.
[20] *wrack* revenge, hostile action.
[21] *blee* colour.

'Look thy last upon that sun! if thou seest to-morrow's one
'Twill be through a foot of clay.

28
'Ha, fair bride! dost hear no sound save that moaning of the hound?'
Toll slowly.
'Thou and I have parted troth, yet I keep my vengeance-oath,   135
And the other may come round.

29
'Ha! thy will is brave to dare, and thy new love past compare' –
Toll slowly.
'Yet thine old love's falchion[22] brave is as strong a thing to have,
As the will of lady fair.   140

30
'Peck on blindly, netted dove! If a wife's name thee behove'[23] –
Toll slowly –
'Thou shalt wear the same to-morrow, ere the grave has hid the sorrow
Of thy last ill-mated love.

31
'O'er his fixed and silent mouth, thou and I will call back troth':   145
Toll slowly.
'He shall altar be and priest, – and he will not cry at least
'I forbid you, I am loth!'[24]

32
'I will wring thy fingers pale in the gauntlet[25] of my mail':
Toll slowly.   150
'"Little hand and muckle gold" close shall lie within my hold,
As the sword did, to prevail.'

33
Oh, the little birds sang east, and the little birds sang west –
Toll slowly.
Oh, and laughed the Duchess May, and her soul did put away   155
All his boasting, for a jest.

34
In her chamber did she sit, laughing low to think of it, –
Toll slowly.
'Tower is strong and will is free: thou canst boast, my lord of Leigh,
But thou boastest little wit.'   160

35
In her tire-glass[26] gazèd she, and she blushed right womanly –
Toll slowly.
She blushed half from her disdain, half her beauty was so plain,
– 'Oath for oath, my lord of Leigh!'

---

[22] *falchion* curved broad sword.
[23] *behove* be in want of.
[24] *loth* averse.

[25] *gauntlet* armoured glove.
[26] *tire-glass* dressing-glass.

36
Straight she called her maidens in – 'Since ye gave me blame herein' –   165
Toll slowly –
'That a bridal such as mine should lack gauds[27] to make it fine,
Come and shrive[28] me from that sin.

37
'It is three months gone to-day since I gave mine hand away':
Toll slowly.   170
'Bring the gold and bring the gem, we will keep bride-state in them,
While we keep the foe at bay.

38
'On your arms I loose mine hair; comb it smooth and crown it fair'
Toll slowly.
'I would look in purple pall[29] from this lattice down the wall,   175
And throw scorn to one that's there!'

39
Oh, the little birds sang east, and the little birds sang west –
Toll slowly.
On the tower the castle's lord leant in silence on his sword,
With an anguish in his breast.   180

40
With a spirit-laden weight did he lean down passionate:
Toll slowly.
They have almost sapped[30] the wall, – they will enter therewithal
With no knocking at the gate.

41
Then the sword he leant upon, shivered, snapped upon the stone –   185
Toll slowly.
'Sword,' he thought, with inward laugh, 'ill thou servest for a staff
When thy nobler use is done!

42
'Sword, thy nobler use is done! tower is lost, and shame begun!' –
Toll slowly.   190
'If we met them in the breach, hilt to hilt or speech to speech,
We should die there, each for one.

43
'If we met them at the wall, we should singly, vainly fall' –
Toll slowly.
'But if I die here alone, – then I die who am but one,   195
And die nobly for them all.

44
'Five true friends lie for my sake in the moat and in the brake[31] –
Toll slowly.

[27] *gauds* pieces of finery.
[28] *shrive* minister forgiveness to.
[29] *pall* fine, rich cloth.
[30] *sapped* undermined.
[31] *brake* bracken, undergrowth.

'Thirteen warriors lie at rest with a black wound in the breast,
           And not one of these will wake.   200

45
'So, no more of this shall be! heart-blood[32] weighs too heavily' –
                    Toll slowly.
'And I could not sleep in grave, with the faithful and the brave
           Heaped around and over me.

46
'Since young Clare a mother hath, and young Ralph a plighted faith'[33] –   205
                    Toll slowly.
'Since my pale young sister's cheeks blush like rose when Ronald speaks,
           Albeit never a word she saith –

47
'These shall never die for me: life-blood falls too heavily':
                    Toll slowly.   210
'And if I die here apart, o'er my dead and silent heart
           They shall pass out safe and free.

48
'When the foe hath heard it said – "Death holds Guy of Linteged"' –
                    Toll slowly.
'That new corse[34] new peace shall bring, and a blessèd, blessèd thing   215
           Shall the stone be at its head.

49
'Then my friends shall pass out free, and shall bear my memory' –
                    Toll slowly.
'Then my foes shall sleek[35] their pride, soothing fair my widowed bride
           Whose sole sin was love of me: 220

50
'With their words all smooth and sweet, they will front her and entreat' –
                    Toll slowly.
'And their purple pall will spread underneath her fainting head
           While her tears drop over it.

51
'She will weep her woman's tears, she will pray her woman's prayers' –   225
                    Toll slowly.
'But her heart is young in pain, and her hopes will spring again
           By the suntime of her years.

52
'Ah, sweet May! ah, sweetest grief! – once I vowed thee my belief' –
                    Toll slowly –   230
'That thy name expressed thy sweetness, – May of poets, in completeness!
           Now my May-day seemeth brief.'

---

[32] *heart-blood* affection, conscience.
[33] *plighted faith* solemnly promised engagement (to a woman
or knighthood).

[34] *corse* dead body.
[35] *sleek* lay back.

53

All these silent thoughts did swim o'er his eyes grown strange and dim –
Toll slowly.
Till his true men, in the place, wished they stood there face to face   235
With the foe instead of him.

54

'One last oath, my friends that wear faithful hearts to do and dare!'
Toll slowly.
'Tower must fall and bride be lost – swear me service worth the cost!'
Bold they stood around to swear.   240

55

'Each man clasp my hand and swear by the deed we failed in there' –
Toll slowly.
'Not for vengeance, not for right, will ye strike one blow to-night!'
Pale they stood around to swear.

56

'One last boon, young Ralph and Clare! faithful hearts to do and dare!'   245
Toll slowly.
'Bring that steed up from his stall, which she kissed before you all:
Guide him up the turret-stair.

57

'Ye shall harness him aright, and lead upward to this height:'
Toll slowly.   250
'Once in love and twice in war hath he borne me strong and far:
He shall bear me far to-night.'

58

Then his men looked to and fro, when they heard him speaking so –
Toll slowly.
''Las![36] the noble heart,' they thought, 'he in sooth[37] is grief-distraught: 255
Would we stood here with the foe!'

59

But a fire flashed from his eye, 'twixt their thought and their reply –
Toll slowly.
'Have ye so much time to waste? We who ride here, must ride fast
As we wish our foes to fly.'   260

60

They have fetched the steed with care, in the harness he did wear –
Toll slowly.
Past the court and through the doors, across the rushes of the floors,
But they goad him up the stair.

61

Then from out her bower chambère[38] did the Duchess May repair: 265
Toll slowly.
'Tell me now what is your need,' said the lady, 'of this steed,
That ye goad him up the stair?'

---

[36] '*Las* Alas.
[37] *sooth* truth.
[38] *bower chambère* bedroom.

62

Calm she stood; unbodkined[39] through, fell her dark hair to her shoe:
Toll slowly.   270
And the smile upon her face, ere she left the tiring-glass,
Had not time enough to go.

63

'Get thee back, sweet Duchess May! hope is gone like yesterday'
Toll slowly.
'One half-hour completes the breach; and thy lord grows wild of speech –   275
Get thee in, sweet lady, and pray!

64

'In the east tower, high'st of all, loud he cries for steed from stall':
Toll slowly.
' 'He would ride as far,' quoth he, 'as for love and victory,
Though he rides the castle-wall!'   280

65

'And we fetch the steed from stall, up where never a hoof did fall' –
Toll slowly.
'Wifely prayer meets deathly need: may the sweet Heavens hear thee plead
If he rides the castle-wall!'

66

Low she dropt her head, and lower, till her hair coiled on the floor –   285
Toll slowly.
And tear after tear you heard fall distinct as any word
Which you might be listening for.

67

'Get thee in, thou soft ladye![40] here is never a place for thee!'
Toll slowly.   290
'Braid thine hair and clasp thy gown, that thy beauty in its moan[41]
May find grace with Leigh of Leigh.'

68

She stood up in bitter case, with a pale yet steady face:
Toll slowly.
Like a statue thunderstruck, which, though quivering, seems to look   295
Right against the thunder-place.

69

And her foot trod in, with pride, her own tears i' the stone beside –
Toll slowly.
'Go to, faithful friends, go to! judge no more what ladies do,
No, nor how their lords may ride!'   300

70

Then the good steed's rein she took, and his neck did kiss and stroke:
Toll slowly.

[39] *unbodkined* without a bodkin, a hair pin.
[40] *ladye* archaic bisyllabic version of 'lady' with accent on second syllable.
[41] *moan* state of lamentation.

Soft he neighed to answer her, and then followed up the stair
For the love of her sweet look:

71

Oh, and steeply, steeply wound up the narrow stair around –   305
Toll slowly.
Oh, and closely, closely speeding, step by step beside her treading
Did he follow, meek as hound.

72

On the east tower, high'st of all, – there, where never a hoof did fall –
Toll slowly.   310
Out they swept, a vision steady, noble steed and lovely lady,
Calm as if in bower or stall.

73

Down she knelt at her lord's knee, and she looked up silently –
Toll slowly.
And he kissed her twice and thrice, for that look within her eyes   315
Which he could not bear to see.

74

Quoth he, 'Get thee from this strife, and the sweet saints bless thy life!'
Toll slowly.
'In this hour I stand in need of my noble red-roan steed,
But no more of my noble wife.'   320

75

Quoth she, 'Meekly have I done all thy biddings under sun':
Toll slowly.
'But by all my womanhood, which is proved so, true and good,
I will never do this one.

76

'Now by womanhood's degree[42] and by wifehood's verity' –   325
Toll slowly.
'In this hour if thou hast need of thy noble red-roan steed,
Thou hast also need of me.

77

'By this golden ring ye see on this lifted hand pardiè'[43] –
Toll slowly.   330
'If, this hour, on castle-wall can be room for steed from stall,
Shall be also room for me.

78

'So the sweet saints with me be,' (did she utter solemnly) –
Toll slowly.
'If a man, this eventide, on this castle-wall will ride,   335
He shall ride the same with me.'

---

[42] *womanhood's degree* status as a woman.   [43] *pardiè* form of oath ('By God!'), hence certainly,
assuredly; trisyllabic, accent on second syllable.

79
Oh, he sprang up in the selle[44] and he laughed out bitter-well –
Toll slowly.
'Wouldst thou ride among the leaves, as we used on other eves,
To hear chime a vesper-bell?'[45]   340

80
She clung closer to his knee – 'Ay, beneath the cypress-tree!'[46]
Toll slowly.
'Mock me not, for otherwhere than along the greenwood fair
Have I ridden fast with thee.

81
'Fast I rode with new-made vows from my angry kinsman's house':   345
Toll slowly.
'What, and would you men should reck[47] that I dared more for love's sake
As a bride than as a spouse?

82
'What, and would you it should fall, as a proverb, before all' –
Toll slowly.   350
'That a bride may keep your side while through castle-gate you ride,
Yet eschew the castle-wall?'

83
Ho! the breach yawns into ruin and roars up against her suing[48] –
Toll slowly.
With the inarticulate din and the dreadful falling in –   355
Shrieks of doing and undoing!

84
Twice he wrung her hands in twain, but the small hands closed again.
Toll slowly.
Back he reined the steed – back, back! but she trailed along his track
With a frantic clasp and strain.   360

85
Evermore the foemen pour through the crash of window and door –
Toll slowly.
And the shouts of Leigh and Leigh, and the shrieks of 'kill!' and 'flee!'
Strike up clear amid the roar.

86
Thrice he wrung her hands in twain, but they closed and clung again –   365
Toll slowly.
While she clung, as one, withstood, clasps a Christ upon the rood,[49]
In a spasm of deathly pain.

87
She clung wild and she clung mute with her shuddering lips half-shut:
Toll slowly.   370

---

[44] *selle* (French) saddle.
[45] *vesper-bell* bell for the evening service.
[46] *cypress-tree* tree associated with mourning.

[47] *reck* care.
[48] *against her suing* as a result of the action against her.
[49] *rood* cross.

Her head fallen as half in swound,[50] hair and knee swept on the ground,
    She clung wild to stirrup and foot.

88

Back he reined his steed back-thrown on the slippery coping-stone:[51]
    Toll slowly.
Back the iron hoofs did grind on the battlement behind   375
    Whence a hundred feet went down:

89

And his heel did press and goad on the quivering flank bestrode –
    Toll slowly.
'Friends and brothers, save my wife! Pardon, sweet, in change for life, –
    But I ride alone to God.'   380

90

Straight as if the Holy name had upbreathed her like a flame –
    Toll slowly.
She upsprang, she rose upright, in his selle she sate in sight,
    By her love she overcame.

91

And her head was on his breast where she smiled as one at rest –   385
    Toll slowly.
'Ring,' she cried, 'O vesper-bell in the beechwood's old chapelle[52] –
    But the passing-bell[53] rings best!'

92

They have caught out at the rein which Sir Guy threw loose – in vain –
    Toll slowly.   390
For the horse in stark despair, with his front hoofs poised in air,
    On the last verge rears amain.

93

Now he hangs, he rocks between, and his nostrils curdle in –
    Toll slowly.
Now he shivers head and hoof and the flakes of foam fall off,   395
    And his face grows fierce and thin:

94

And a look of human woe from his staring eyes did go:
    Toll slowly.
And a sharp cry uttered he, in a foretold agony
    Of the headlong death below, –   400

95

And, 'Ring, ring, thou passing-bell,' still she cried, 'i' the old chapelle!'
    Toll slowly.
Then, back-toppling, crashing back – a dead weight flung out to wrack,[54]
    Horse and riders overfell.

---

[50] *swound* faint (rhymes with ground).
[51] *coping* uppermost course of masonry in a wall.
[52] *chapelle* chapel (accent on second syllable).
[53] *passing-bell* bell tolled to announce a death.
[54] *wrack* disaster.

1

Oh, the little birds sang east, and the little birds sang west –   405
Toll slowly.
And I read this ancient Rhyme, in the churchyard, while the chime
Slowly tolled for one at rest.

2

The abeles moved in the sun, and the river smooth did run –
Toll slowly.   410
And the ancient Rhyme rang strange, with its passion and its change,
Here, where all done lay undone.

3

And beneath a willow tree I a little grave did see –
Toll slowly –
Where was graved – Here, undefiled, lieth Maud, a three-year child,   415
Eighteen hundred forty-three.

4

Then, O spirits, did I say, ye who rode so fast that day –
Toll slowly.
Did star-wheels and angel wings with their holy winnowings[55]
Keep beside you all the way?   420

5

Though in passion ye would dash, with a blind and heavy crash –
Toll slowly –
Up against the thick-bossed shield[56] of God's judgment in the field, –
Though your heart and brain were rash, –

6

Now, your will is all unwilled; now, your pulses are all stilled: 425
Toll slowly.
Now, ye lie as meek and mild (whereso laid) as Maud the child
Whose small grave was lately filled.

7

Beating heart and burning brow, ye are very patient now –
Toll slowly.   430
And the children might be bold to pluck the kingcups[57] from your mould
Ere a month had let them grow.

8

And you let the goldfinch[58] sing in the alder[59] near in spring –
Toll slowly.
Let her build her nest and sit all the three weeks out on it,   435
Murmuring not at anything.

9

In your patience ye are strong, cold and heat ye take not wrong –
Toll slowly.

[55] *winnowings* beating (of wings).
[56] *thick-bossed shield* cf. Haydon's *Curtius*, plate 1, discussed in headnote, 30.
[57] *kingcups* bright yellow marsh flowers.
[58] *goldfinch* bird associated in Christian iconography with Jesus's suffering and death.
[59] *alder* tree related to the birch.

When the trumpet of the angel blows eternity's evangel,[60]
Time will seem to you not long.   440

10

Oh, the little birds sang east, and the little birds sang west –
Toll slowly.
And I said in underbreath, – All our life is mixed with death,
And who knoweth which is best?

11

Oh, the little birds sang east, and the little birds sang west –   445
Toll slowly.
And I smiled to think God's greatness flowed around our incompleteness, –
Round our restlessness, His rest.

[60] *eternity's evangel* herald of eternity.

The Runaway Slave at Pilgrim's Point

In 1845, Elizabeth Barrett Browning was asked to write a poem for a Boston anti-slavery organization. This, her response, was published in an anti-slavery annual, *The Liberty Bell*, in 1847 for 1848. By this stage, the British Abolition of Slavery Bill (1833) had come into effect in British colonies, but the slavery issue in the United States was emerging as central in arguments that would lead to the Civil War (1861–5). Congress eventually abolished slavery throughout the United States by the thirteenth constitutional amendment in 1865.

Barrett Browning, from a family with earlier slave-owning interests, was committed to the anti-slavery position. She exploited to the full the irony of the Pilgrim settlers – who left England seeking freedom from religious persecution – founding a nation that deprived many black men, women and children of liberty. In 'The Cry of the Children', 25–9, Barrett Browning considered the consequences of oppression – on both body and mind – of the factory workers. She is similarly interested in 'The Runaway Slave' in the mental as well as corporeal consequences of slavery, indicating how a barbaric system leads a despairing slave to a barbaric act. In detailing the social conditions that result in infanticide, Barrett Browning was at once offering an instance of the obscene consequences of slavery on human beings, and making a wider, provocative statement about a society's responsibility for the crimes that are committed within it (cf. Wilde's *The Ballad of Reading Gaol*, 588–605).

Oppression of many forms angered Barrett Browning and she invested hope in poetry as a moral agent. 'The Runaway Slave' can be compared, in its confidence about the liberal principles of art, to 'Hiram Powers' *Greek Slave*', 51–2). Like that sonnet, it is also confident in women as agents for social change. 'The Runaway Slave' relates suggestively to

'Lord Walter's Wife', 55–7, a poem that celebrates married love as a basis for moral action. It is a feature of the corrupt slave society of 'The Runaway Slave' that the speaker's love for her fellow slave is renounced by her white masters. Legitimate love, with its morally enabling consequences, is outlawed.

'The Runaway Slave' draws on and reconfigures two poems by the popular early nineteenth-century poet Felicia Hemans (1793–1835), whose death Barrett Browning commemorated in the elegy 'Felicia Hemans'. Firstly, 'The Runaway Slave' ironizes Hemans's 'The Landing of the Pilgrim Fathers', with its hymn to liberty in North America:

. . . What sought they thus afar?
Bright jewels of the mine?
The wealth of seas, the spoils of war? –
They sought a faith's pure shrine!

Ay, call it holy ground,
The soil where first they trod!
They have left unstain'd what there they found –
Freedom to worship God!

It also politicizes Hemans's 'Indian Woman's Death Song', a sorrowful monologue spoken by an Indian woman about to drown herself and her child in response to her husband's desertion. Like Hemans's poem, Barrett Browning's is a rhyming monologue, sharply different in its treatment of sympathy from Robert Browning's (non-rhyming) approach to the form. It powerfully captures the apostrophizing voice of a woman in crisis and exemplifies the speaker's declaration in Barrett Browning's 'A Curse of a Nation' (1860) that 'A curse from the depths of womanhood / Is very salt, and bitter, and good.'

Text: *Poems* (1850).

I stand on the mark beside the shore
Of the first white pilgrim's bended knee,
Where exile turned to ancestor,[1]
And God was thanked for liberty.
I have run through the night, my skin is as dark,   5
I bend my knee down on this mark:
I look on the sky and the sea.

2

O pilgrim-souls, I speak to you!
I see you come proud and slow
From the land of the spirits pale as dew   10
And round me and round me ye go.
O pilgrims, I have gasped and run
All night long from the whips of one
Who in your names works sin and woe!

3

And thus I thought that I would come   15
And kneel here where ye knelt before,
And feel your souls around me hum
In undertone to the ocean's roar;
And lift my black face, my black hand,
Here, in your names, to curse this land   20
Ye blessed in freedom's, evermore.

4

I am black, I am black,
And yet God made me, they say:
But if He did so, smiling back
He must have cast His work away   25
Under the feet of His white creatures,[2]
With a look of scorn, that the dusky[3] features
Might be trodden again to clay.

5

And yet He has made dark things
To be glad and merry as light: 30
There's a little dark bird sits and sings,
There's a dark stream ripples out of sight,
And the dark frogs chant in the safe morass,[4]
And the sweetest stars are made to pass
O'er the face of the darkest night.   35

6

But we who are dark, we are dark!
Ah God, we have no stars!
About our souls in care and cark[5]

---

[1] *I stand . . . ancestor* the Pilgrim settlers, chiefly English *émigrés*, arrived at Plymouth, Massachusetts, in 1620, fleeing to the New World to escape religious restraint. Although the poem begins in Massachusetts, slavery in the 1840s was chiefly a southern state practice.

[2] *He must . . . creatures* cf. 'And the LORD God said vnto the Serpent, Because thou hast done this, thou art cursed aboue all cattel, and aboue euery beast of the field: vpon thy belly shalt thou goe, and dust shalt thou eate, all the dayes of thy life', Genesis 3.14.

[3] *dusky* dark.

[4] *morass* swampy tract, bog.

[5] *cark* troubled state of mind, distress.

Our blackness shuts like prison-bars:
The poor souls crouch so far behind   40
That never a comfort can they find
By reaching through the prison-bars.

7

Indeed we live beneath the sky,
That great smooth Hand of God stretched out
On all His children fatherly,   45
To save them from the dread and doubt
Which would be if, from this low place,
All opened straight up to His face
Into the grand eternity.

8

And still God's sunshine and His frost,   50
They make us hot, they make us cold,
As if we were not black and lost;
And the beasts and birds, in wood and fold,
Do fear and take us for very men:
Could the whip-poor-will[6] or the cat of the glen[7]   55
Look into my eyes and be bold?

9

I am black, I am black!
But, once, I laughed in girlish glee,
For one of my colour stood in the track
Where the drivers drove, and looked at me,   60
And tender and full was the look he gave –
Could a slave look so at another slave? –
I look at the sky and the sea.

10

And from that hour our spirits grew
As free as if unsold, unbought: 65
Oh, strong enough, since we were two,
To conquer the world, we thought.
The drivers drove us day by day;
We did not mind, we went one way,
And no better a freedom sought.   70

11

In the sunny ground between the canes,
He said 'I love you' as he passed;
When the shingle[8]-roof rang sharp with the rains,
I heard how he vowed it fast:
While others shook he smiled in the hut,   75
As he carved me a bowl of the cocoa-nut
Through the roar of the hurricanes.

---

[6] *whip-poor-will* kind of American goatsucker, a bird
believed to suck the udders of goats.

[7] *cat of the glen* unspecified wild cat.
[8] *shingle* thin piece of wood used as a house-tile.

12

I sang his name instead of a song,
Over and over I sang his name,
Upward and downward I drew it along   80
My various notes, – the same, the same!
I sang it low, that the slave-girls near
Might never guess, from aught they could hear,
It was only a name – a name.

13

I look on the sky and the sea.   85
We were two to love, and two to pray:
Yes, two, O God, who cried to Thee,
Though nothing didst Thou say!
Coldly Thou sat'st behind the sun:
And now I cry who am but one,   90
Thou wilt not speak to-day.

14

We were black, we were black,
We had no claim to love and bliss,
What marvel if each went to wrack?[9]
They wrung my cold hands out of his,   95
They dragged him – where? I crawled to touch
His blood's mark in the dust . . . not much,
Ye pilgrim-souls, though plain as this!

15

Wrong, followed by a deeper wrong!
Mere grief's too good for such as I: 100
So the white men brought the shame[10] ere long
To strangle the sob of my agony.
They would not leave me for my dull
Wet eyes! – it was too merciful
To let me weep pure tears and die.   105

16

I am black, I am black!
I wore a child upon my breast,
An amulet[11] that hung too slack,
And, in my unrest, could not rest:
Thus we went moaning, child and mother,   110
One to another, one to another,
Until all ended for the best.

17

For hark! I will tell you low, low,
I am black, you see, –
And the babe who lay on my bosom so,   115
Was far too white, too white for me;
As white as the ladies who scorned to pray

---

[9] *wrack* violence, punishment.
[10] *brought the shame* in modern terms, she is gang raped.

[11] *amulet* anything worn about the person as a charm against evil.

Beside me at church but yesterday,
Though my tears had washed a place for my knee.

18

My own, own child! I could not bear   120
To look in his face, it was so white;
I covered him up with a kerchief[12] there,
I covered his face in close and tight:
And he moaned and struggled, as well might be,
For the white child wanted his liberty –   125
Ha, ha! he wanted the master-right.[13]

19

He moaned and beat with his head and feet,
His little feet that never grew;
He struck them out, as it was meet,
Against my heart to break it through: 130
I might have sung and made him mild,
But I dared not sing to the white-faced child
The only song I knew.

20

I pulled the kerchief very close:
He could not see the sun, I swear,   135
More, then, alive, than now he does
From between the roots of the mango . . . where?
I know where. Close! A child and mother
Do wrong to look at one another
When one is black and one is fair.   140

21

Why, in that single glance I had
Of my child's face, . . . I tell you all,
I saw a look that made me mad!
The master's look, that used to fall
On my soul like his lash . . . or worse!   145
And so, to save it from my curse,
I twisted it round in my shawl.

22

And he moaned and trembled from foot to head,
He shivered from head to foot;
Till after a time, he lay instead   150
Too suddenly still and mute.
I felt, beside, a stiffening cold:
I dared to lift up just a fold,
As in lifting a leaf of the mango-fruit.

23

But my fruit . . . ha, ha! – there, had been   155
(I laugh to think on't at this hour!)

---

[12] *kerchief* cloth used to cover the head.

[13] *master-right* both the general human right to liberty, and the right of the white man to liberty (over the oppressed blacks).

Your fine white angels (who have seen
Nearest the secret of God's power)
And plucked my fruit to make them wine,
And sucked the soul of that child of mine   160
As the humming-bird sucks the soul of the flower.

24

Ha, ha, the trick of the angels white!
They freed the white child's spirit so.
I said not a word, but day and night
I carried the body to and fro,   165
And it lay on my heart like a stone, as chill.
– The sun may shine out as much as he will:
I am cold, though it happened a month ago.

25

From the white man's house, and the black man's hut,
I carried the little body on;   170
The forest's arms did round us shut,
And silence through the trees did run:
They asked no question as I went,
They stood too high for astonishment,
They could see God sit on His throne.   175

26

My little body, kerchiefed fast,
I bore it on through the forest, on;
And when I felt it was tired at last,
I scooped a hole beneath the moon:
Through the forest-tops the angels far,   180
With a white sharp finger from every star,
Did point and mock at what was done.

27

Yet when it was all done aright, –
Earth, 'twixt me and my baby, strewed, –
All, changed to black earth, – nothing white, –   185
A dark child in the dark! – ensued
Some comfort, and my heart grew young;
I sate[14] down smiling there and sung
The song I learnt in my maidenhood.

28

And thus we two were reconciled,   190
The white child and black mother, thus;
For as I sang it soft and wild,
The same song, more melodious,
Rose from the grave whereon I sate:
It was the dead child singing that,   195
To join the souls of both of us.

[14] *sate* sat.

29

I look on the sea and the sky.
Where the pilgrims' ships first anchored lay
The free sun rideth gloriously,
But the pilgrim-ghosts have slid away   200
Through the earliest streaks of the morn:
My face is black, but it glares with a scorn
Which they dare not meet by day.

30

Ha! – in their stead, their hunter sons!
Ha, ha! they are on me – they hunt in a ring!   205
Keep off! I brave you all at once,
I throw off your eyes like snakes that sting!
You have killed the black eagle at nest, I think:
Did you ever stand still in your triumph, and shrink
From the stroke of her wounded wing?   210

31

(Man, drop that stone you dared to lift! –)
I wish you who stand there five abreast,
Each, for his own wife's joy and gift,
A little corpse as safely at rest
As mine in the mangoes! Yes, but she   215
May keep live babies on her knee,
And sing the song she likes the best.

32

I am not mad: I am black.
I see you staring in my face –
I know you staring, shrinking back,   220
Ye are born of the Washington-race,[15]
And this land is the free America,
And this mark on my wrist – (I prove what I say)
Ropes tied me up here to the flogging-place.

33

You think I shrieked then? Not a sound!   225
I hung, as a gourd[16] hangs in the sun;
I only cursed them all around
As softly as I might have done
My very own child: from these sands
Up to the mountains, lift your hands,   230
O slaves, and end what I begun!

34

Whips, curses; these must answer those!
For in this Union[17] you have set
Two kinds of men in adverse rows,
Each loathing each; and all forget   235

---

[15] *Ye are . . . Washington-race* symbolically descended from
George Washington, first president of the United States of
America (himself a slave owner).

[16] *gourd* large fleshy fruit often dried and used ornamentally.
[17] *Union* of American states.

The seven wounds in Christ's body fair,[18]
While He sees gaping everywhere
Our countless wounds that pay no debt.[19]

35

Our wounds are different. Your white men
Are, after all, not gods indeed,   240
Nor able to make Christs again
Do good with bleeding. We who bleed
(Stand off!) we help not in our loss!
We are too heavy for our cross,
And fall and crush you and your seed.[20]   245

36

I fall, I swoon![21] I look at the sky.
The clouds are breaking on my brain;
I am floated along, as if I should die
Of liberty's exquisite pain.
In the name of the white child waiting for me   250
In the death-dark where we may kiss and agree,
White men, I leave you all curse-free
In my broken heart's disdain!

---

[18] *seven wounds . . . fair* Christian tradition usually refers to Jesus's five wounds from the crucifixion.
[19] *pay no debt* cf. Jesus's death that, in Christian theology, paid the price for human sin.

[20] *seed* descendants.
[21] *swoon* faint.

Hiram Powers' *Greek Slave*

Robert and Elizabeth Barrett Browning knew the North American sculptor Hiram Powers (1805–73), who lived for much of his life in Florence (where the Brownings also lived after their marriage). Powers's well-known and controversial statue 'The Greek Slave' was completed in 1843 and depicts supposedly a Greek woman about to be sold into slavery by the Turks during the struggle for Greek independence, which finally concluded in 1832 (see plate 2). To what extent the political association was Powers's shrewd device to legitimate the depiction of a full nude is not of interest to Barrett Browning; neither is the question of the troubling eroticism of the statue. Barrett Browning may have seen it, or one of its various replicas, either in Florence or in London, where it was first exhibited in 1845. Her sonnet, characterized, as her sonnets mostly are, by fluid language that sounds as if spoken, by syntax that is not confined to the line length for its unit of sense, is buoyant about the power of art to effect political and social change, and confident in its identification of that power with a woman (cf. 'A Runaway Slave at Pilgrim's Point', 44–51). Like 'The Cry of the Children', 25–9, 'Hiram Powers' *Greek Slave*' (1850) explores the expressive powers of the silent or silenced. Barrett Browning's own family's involvement with slavery adds further energy to its poised outrage.

Text: *Poems* (1850).

They say Ideal beauty cannot enter
The house of anguish. On the threshold stands
An alien Image with enshackled hands,
Called the Greek Slave! as if the artist meant her
(That passionless perfection which he lent her,   5

Shadowed not darkened where the sill expands)
To so confront man's crimes in different lands
With man's ideal sense. Pierce to the centre,
Art's fiery finger, and break up ere long
The serfdom[1] of this world. Appeal, fair stone,   10
From God's pure heights of beauty against man's wrong!
Catch up in thy divine face, not alone
East griefs but west,[2] and strike and shame the strong,
By thunders of white silence, overthrown.

[1] *serfdom* bondage, slavery.
[2] *East griefs but west* the statue should expose oppression not only in the east (Greece and Turkey) but everywhere, including the slavery practised by the United States (the west).

VENERABLE : Accorded A great Deal of Respect, esp. b/c of age, wisdom or character. distinguished

Sonnets from the Portuguese (selection)

The sonnet sequence as a form of poetry that records a male lover's feelings for a woman has a venerable history. Drawing on Petrarch and an established European tradition, Sir Philip Sidney's *Astophil and Stella* (1591) inaugurated its popularity in Renaissance England, clinching its association with formal tributes from a man to his (silent) beloved. Elizabeth Barrett Browning's sequence about her love for Robert Browning – only nominally disguised by the fictitious title – challenges the traditional associations of the

Plate 2   Hiram Powers, *Greek Slave* (1846), Corcoran Gallery of Art, Washington DC.

form. She investigates the enabling doubleness that follows from being – in terms of the sonnet sequence's history – both lover and beloved. She is, throughout the 44-poem sequence, the lover of the man and, in turn, the object of his love (yet she controls the representation of that love). Elizabeth Barrett and Robert Browning were married in secret in September 1846, after a correspondence begun in 1845 that had led to their meeting and engagement. The title, the claim that the sonnets were translations of a Portuguese poet's work, was an easily penetrated device to disguise the autobiographical origin.

In *Sonnets from the Portuguese* (1850), Barrett Browning makes a space for the expression of female desire, its patterns and integrity, and the sequence can be compared with her narrative poem that pivots on the recognition of female love *in extremis*, 'Rime of the Duchess May', 29–44. As fluid, conversational sonnets, these poems compare with the handling of the form in 'Hiram Powers' *Greek Slave*', 51–2. At a more general thematic level, *Sonnets from the Portuguese* require comparison with other mid-century poems on the nature of modern love such as George Meredith's *Modern Love*, 328–49, A. H. Clough's

Amours de Voyage, 228–62, and Coventry Patmore's *The Angel in the House* (1854–63).

Although more explicitly about life than art (in contrast to her long novel in verse *Aurora Leigh* [1857], which continually debates the relationship between private life and public writing), the tropes than run through the sequence amount to a set of probing comments on the Petrarchan and sentimental traditions of the sonnet and continue Elizabeth Barrett Browning's self-figuring as a poet. The poems are open about the griefs of her life, griefs that help constitute her identity and maintain a sense of individual selfhood in the midst of love. By keeping this grave personal discourse in the foreground of the sonnets, Barrett Browning sustains herself as a more fully realized individual, as a woman with her own history who is not simply to be absorbed into the beloved's identity. The question of the lover's absorption of the beloved is treated ironically in 'Bertha in the Lane', 18–25, and Barrett Browning's poems on this subject contrast with her husband's 'Two in the Campagna', 204–6.

Text: *Poems* (1850).

I thought once how Theocritus[1] had sung
Of the sweet years, the dear and wished-for years,
Who each one in a gracious hand appears
To bear a gift for mortals, old or young:
And, as I mused it in his antique tongue,[2]   5
I saw, in gradual vision through my tears,
The sweet, sad years, the melancholy years,
Those of my own life, who by turns had flung
A shadow across me. Straightway I was 'ware,[3]
So weeping, how a mystic Shape did move   10
Behind me, and drew me backward by the hair;   *Roughly? Smooth?*
And a voice said in mastery, while I strove, –
'Guess now who holds thee?' – 'Death,' I said. But, there,
The silver answer rang, – 'Not Death, but Love.' –   *Love produces same effect of death – "Lock upon"*

18

I never gave a lock of hair away   15
To a man, Dearest, except this to thee,
Which now upon my fingers thoughtfully,
I ring out to the full brown length and say
'Take it.' My day of youth went yesterday;[4]
My hair no longer bounds to my foot's glee,   20

[1] *I thought . . . Theocritus* see the 'Hymn to Adonis' in the ancient Greek poet Theocritus's *Fifteenth Idyll*: 'Tardiest of the Immortals are the beloved Hours, / But dear and desired they come, / For always, to all mortals, / They bring some gift with them.'

[2] *antique tongue* ancient language.
[3] *'ware* aware.
[4] *My day . . . yesterday* Elizabeth Barrett was 40 when she married Robert Browning on 12 September 1846.

Nor plant I it from rose or myrtle-tree,[5]
  As girls do, any more: it only may
Now shade on two pale cheeks the mark of tears,
Taught drooping from the head that hangs aside
Through sorrow's trick. I thought the funeral-shears   25
  Would take this first, but Love is justified, –
Take it thou, – finding pure, from all those years,
  The kiss my mother left here when she died.[6]

thought death would take her hair/ youth before love

25

If I leave all for thee, wilt thou exchange
  And be all to me? Shall I never miss   30
Home-talk and blessing and the common kiss
That comes to each in turn, nor count it strange,
  When I look up, to drop on a new range
Of walls and floors, another home than this?
Nay, wilt thou fill that place by me which is   35
Filled by dead eyes[7] too tender to know change?
That's hardest. If to conquer love, has tried,
To conquer grief, tries more, as all things prove;
  For grief indeed is love and grief beside.
Alas, I have grieved so I am hard to love.[8]   40
Yet love me – wilt thou? Open thine heart wide,   *Love last 2 lines*
  And fold within the wet wings of thy dove.

43   *RB Love*

How do I love thee? Let me count the ways.
I love thee to the depth and breadth and height
My soul can reach, when feeling out of sight   45
  For the ends of Being and ideal Grace.
I love thee to the level of everyday's
  Most quiet need, by sun and candle-light.
I love thee freely, as men strive for Right;
I love thee purely, as they turn from Praise.   50
  I love thee with the passion put to use
In my old griefs,[9] and with my childhood's faith.
I love thee with a love I seemed to lose
With my lost saints,[10] – I love thee with the breath,
Smiles, tears, of all my life! – and, if God choose,   55
  I shall but love thee better after death.

44   *P12*

Belovèd, thou hast brought me many flowers
Plucked in the garden, all the summer through
And winter, and it seemed as if they grew

---

[5] *myrtle* shrub growing abundantly in Southern Europe; it
was sacred to Venus, Roman goddess of love and beauty.
[6] *The kiss . . . died* Mary Moulton-Barrett died on 7 October
1828. Barrett Browning was 22.
[7] *dead eyes* Barrett Browning lost her mother in 1828 and,
in 1840, her brother Edward ('Bro') drowned off Torquay.

[8] *Alas . . . love* British Library MS has 'Alas, I have grieved
so, I am hard to love'.
[9] *old griefs* her extended illness from 1821 and
bereavements.
[10] *lost saints* chiefly Bro: see note 7.

In this close room, nor missed the sun and showers.   60
   So, in the like name of that love of ours,
   Take back these thoughts which here unfolded too,
   And which on warm and cold days I withdrew
From my heart's ground. Indeed, those beds and bowers
   Be overgrown with bitter weeds and rue,[11]   65
   And wait thy weeding; yet here's eglantine,[12]
   Here's ivy! – take them, as I used to do
Thy flowers, and keep them where they shall not pine.
   Instruct thine eyes to keep their colours true,
   And tell thy soul their roots are left in mine.   70

[11] *rue* Shakespeare's Queen calls this the 'sour herb-of-grace' in *Richard II* 3.4.106.

[12] *eglantine* sweet briar; like ivy, a trailing plant.

Lord Walter's Wife

Elizabeth Barrett Browning sent 'Lord Walter's Wife' in 1861 to William Makepeace Thackeray's *Cornhill Magazine*, a successful middle-class family journal. But he turned it down: it is, he said, 'an account of an unlawful passion felt by a man for a woman . . . so I have not published the poem'. Barrett Browning replied sharply with a manifesto for poetry: 'I don't like coarse subjects, or the coarse treatment of any subject. But I am deeply convinced that the corruption of our society requires not shut doors and windows, but light and air: and that it is exactly because pure and prosperous women choose to *ignore* vice, that miserable women suffer wrong by it everywhere.'

The poem, published in *Last Poems* (1862), takes a commonplace idea of a moral debate about a man's sexual interest in a woman but reworks it to present a strong-minded figure exposing the shabbiness of her husband's friend's assumptions about women. The Lady, the opposite of a *femme fatale*, believes wholly in her wedding vows and appropriately has her husband's name only: the poem proposes the role of faithful marriage in preserving a morally decent society and in giving a woman the basis for authoritative repudiation of slack male sexual standards (cf. 'Rime of the Duchess May', 29–44, and 'The Runaway Slave at Pilgrim's Point', 44–51). Barrett Browning's monologue deftly catches the verbal characteristics of the two antagonistic speakers with a lightness of touch far remote from any coarseness.

Text: *Last Poems* (1862).

'But why do you go?' said the lady, while both sat under the yew,
And her eyes were alive in their depth, as the kraken[1] beneath the sea-blue.

2
'Because I fear you,' he answered; – 'because you are far too fair,
And able to strangle my soul in a mesh of your gold-coloured hair.'[2]

3
'Oh, that,' she said, 'is no reason! Such knots are quickly undone,   5
And too much beauty, I reckon, is nothing but too much sun.'

4
'Yet farewell so,' he answered; – 'the sun-stroke's fatal at times.
I value your husband, Lord Walter, whose gallop rings still from the limes.'[3]

[1] *kraken* mythical sea-monster of enormous size.
[2] *strangle . . . hair* conventional trope of the dangerous female.

[3] *from the limes* the drive up to the mansion which is lined with lime trees.

5
'Oh, that,' she said, 'is no reason. You smell a rose through a fence:
If two should smell it, what matter? who grumbles, and where's the pretence?'   10

6
'But I,' he replied, 'have promised another, when love was free,
To love her alone, alone, who alone and afar loves me.'

7
'Why, that,' she said, 'is no reason. Love's always free, I am told.
Will you vow to be safe from the headache on Tuesday, and think it will hold?'

8
'But you,' he replied, 'have a daughter, a young little child, who was laid   15
In your lap to be pure; so I leave you: the angels would make me afraid.'

9
'Oh, that,' she said, 'is no reason. The angels keep out of the way;
And Dora, the child, observes nothing, although you should please me and stay.'

10
At which he rose up in his anger, – 'Why, now, you no longer are fair!
Why, now, you no longer are fatal,[4] but ugly and hateful, I swear.'   20

11
At which she laughed out in her scorn: 'These men! Oh, these men overnice,[5]
Who are shocked if a colour not virtuous is frankly put on by a vice.'

12
Her eyes blazed upon him – 'And you! You bring us your vices so near
That we smell them! You think in our presence a thought 'twould defame us to hear!

13
'What reason had you, and what right, – I appeal to your soul from my life, –   25
To find me too fair as a woman? Why, sir, I am pure, and a wife.

14
'Is the day-star too fair up above you? It burns you not. Dare you imply
I brushed you more close than the star does, when Walter had set me as high?

15
'If a man finds a woman too fair, he means simply adapted too much
To uses unlawful and fatal. The praise! – shall I thank you for such?   30

16
'Too fair? – not unless you misuse us! and surely if, once in a while,
You attain to it, straightway you call us no longer too fair, but too vile.

17
'A moment, – I pray your attention! – I have a poor word in my head
I must utter, though womanly custom would set it down better unsaid.

---

[4] *fatal* as in *femme fatale*, dangerously attractive woman.   [5] *overnice* too fastidious, over-particular.

18

'You grew, sir, pale to impertinence, once when I showed you a ring.   35
You kissed my fan when I dropped it. No matter! – I've broken the thing.

19

'You did me the honour, perhaps, to be moved at my side now and then
In the senses – a vice, I have heard, which is common to beasts and some men.

20

'Love's a virtue for heroes! – as white as the snow on high hills,
And immortal as every great soul is that struggles, endures, and fulfils.   40

21

'I love my Walter profoundly, – you, Maude, though you faltered a week,
For the sake of . . . what was it – an eyebrow? or, less still, a mole on a cheek?[6]

22

'And since, when all's said, you're too noble to stoop to the frivolous cant[7]
About crimes irresistible, virtues that swindle, betray and supplant,

23

'I determined to prove to yourself that, whate'er you might dream or avow   45
By illusion, you wanted precisely no more of me than you have now.

24

'There! Look me full in the face! – in the face. Understand, if you can,
That the eyes of such women as I am are clean as the palm of a man.

25

'Drop his hand, you insult him. Avoid us for fear we should cost you a scar –
You take us for harlots, I tell you, and not for the women we are.   50

26

'You wronged me: but then I considered . . . there's Walter! And so at the end
I vowed that he should not be mulcted,[8] by me, in the hand of a friend.

27

'Have I hurt you indeed? We are quits then. Nay, friend of my Walter, be mine!
Come, Dora, my darling, my angel, and help me to ask him to dine.'

[6] *For the sake . . . cheek* Maude has been tempted to infidelity before.

[7] *cant* empty, bombastic language.
[8] *mulcted* punished.

A Musical Instrument

'A Musical Instrument' presents itself as a charming fragment of a mythic narrative, almost a child's story. But it disguises a violent truth. The poem refers to a Greek myth of sexual violation. The god of fields and woodland, Pan, who was half man, half goat, fell in love with the Arcadian nymph, Syrinx. Syrinx disdained him and fled from his pursuit. In her flight, she reached a tributary of the River Ladon, and, being trapped, asked the river nymphs for assistance. They did what they could, and turned her into marsh reeds. When Pan arrived, he found nothing but the sound of the reeds in the wind. Hearing this, he declared, as Ovid puts it (in Dryden's translation), 'Thou, he sed, / Who can'st not be the Partner of my Bed, / At least shall be the Consort of my Mind'. Pulling out the reeds and binding them together, he invented the musical instrument with which he was thereafter associated: the *syrinx* or pan-pipes.

In 1844, Barrett Browning had published 'The Dead Pan' in which she rejected Classical myth in favour of Christian poetry of the real. But 'A Musical Instrument', published in *Last Poems* (1862), shows that she continued to be drawn to the signifying possibilities of ancient Greek narratives. The poem poses an uncomfortable question about the relation of artistic production to sexual exploitation, of male artistic success to female destruction. Some have seen Pan representing the kind of poet with whom Barrett Browning was never content, one for whom the imag-

ination was privileged over the real with its harsh pains. Certainly, she might be understood as defining herself on the outside of dominant forms of poetic production in 'A Musical Instrument', associating herself with the marginalized and oppressed whose modes of self-representation have been outlawed or silenced. The poem's apparent innocence of tone creates friction with the underlying narrative – cf. the disjunction in 'Bertha in the Lane', 18–25 – and the repetition of 'the great god Pan' grows increasingly, brutally ironic.

Text: *Last Poems* (1862).

What was he doing, the great god Pan,
   Down in the reeds by the river?
Spreading ruin and scattering ban,[1]
Splashing and paddling with hoofs of a goat,[2]
And breaking the golden lilies afloat   5
   With the dragon-fly on the river.

2

He tore out a reed, the great god Pan,
   From the deep cool bed of the river:
The limpid water turbidly ran,
   And the broken lilies a-dying lay,   10
And the dragon-fly had fled away,
   Ere he brought it out of the river.

3

High on the shore sat the great god Pan
   While turbidly flowed the river;
And hacked and hewed as a great god can,   15
With his hard bleak steel at the patient reed,
Till there was not a sign of the leaf indeed
   To prove it fresh from the river.

4

He cut it short, did the great god Pan,
   (How tall it stood in the river!)   20
Then drew the pith, like the heart of a man,
   Steadily from the outside ring,
And notched the poor dry empty thing
   In holes, as he sat by the river.

5

'This is the way,' laughed the great god Pan   25
   (Laughed while he sat by the river),
'The only way, since gods began
   To make sweet music, they could succeed.'

[1] *ban* ill, malevolence.   [2] *hoofs of a goat* the lower part of Pan's body was a goat's.

Then, dropping his mouth to a hole in the reed,
He blew in power by the river.   30

6

Sweet, sweet, sweet, O Pan!
Piercing sweet by the river!
Blinding sweet, O great god Pan!
The sun on the hill forgot to die,
And the lilies revived, and the dragon-fly   35
Came back to dream on the river.[3]

7

Yet half a beast is the great god Pan,
To laugh as he sits by the river,
Making a poet out of a man:
The true gods sigh for the cost and pain, –   40
For the reed which grows nevermore again
As a reed with the reeds in the river.

[3] *Sweet, sweet . . . river* cf. the story of Orpheus who played
the lyre to such perfection that fellow mortals, animals,
trees and rocks were entranced.

Amy's Cruelty

The late poem 'Amy's Cruelty' (*Last Poems*, 1862), evidence of Elizabeth Barrett Browning's persistent originality, is provocatively unclassifiable. It treats a question of sexual politics with a mixture of playfulness and seriousness, tonally distinct from the graver manner of 'Lord Walter's Wife', 55–7, or 'Rime of the Duchess May', 29–44. Its subject is possessiveness and obsessiveness in love. The poem's ironization of the problems of giving all, of the absorption of the lover by the beloved and vice versa, offers a comparison with *Sonnets from the Portuguese*, 52–5, where distance and self-preservation are cherished. 'Amy's Cruelty' is set in the modern location of the 'terraced house', a rapidly growing phenomenon in mid-nineteenth-century England. The poem wittily ironizes the sexual politics of a member of the lower middle class, a dweller in the new environment of suburbia. For alternative, later poems on the suburban, see James Thomson, *The City of Dreadful Night*, 394–422, and John Davidson, 'Thirty Bob a Week', 606–9, and 'A Woman and her Son', 609–15.

Robert Browning said that he organized the contents of *Last Poems* from a list drawn up by his wife shortly before her death. Accordingly, 'Amy's Cruelty' was paired with 'May's Love', adding further to its curious and lively ironies:

You love all, you say,
Round, beneath, above me:
Find me then some way
Better than to love me,
Me, too, dearest May!

O world-kissing eyes
Which the blue heavens melt to;
I, sad, overwise,
Loathe the sweet looks dealt to
All things – men and flies.

You love all, you say:
Therefore, Dear, abate me
Just your love, I pray!
Shut your eyes and hate me –
Only me – fair May!

Text: *Last Poems* (1862).

Fair Amy of the terraced house,
Assist me to discover
Why you who would not hurt a mouse
Can torture so your lover.

2
You give your coffee to the cat,   5
You stroke the dog for coming,[1]
And all your face grows kinder at
The little brown bee's humming.

3
But when *he* haunts your door . . . the town
Marks coming and marks going[2] . . .   10
You seem to have stitched your eyelids down
To that long piece of sewing!

4
You never give a look, not you,
Nor drop him a 'Good morning,'
To keep his long day warm and blue,   15
So fretted by your scorning.

5
She shook her head – 'The mouse and bee
For crumb or flower will linger:
The dog is happy at my knee,
The cat purrs at my finger.   20

6
'But *he* . . . to *him*, the least thing given
Means great things at a distance;
He wants my world, my sun, my heaven,
Soul, body, whole existence.

7
'They say love gives as well as takes;   25
But I'm a simple maiden, –
My mother's first smile when she wakes
I still have smiled and prayed in.

8
'I only know my mother's love
Which gives all and asks nothing;   30
And this new loving sets the groove[3]
Too much the way of loathing.

9
'Unless he gives me all in change,[4]
I forfeit all things by him:

---

[1] *You give . . . coming* 'you give your cat treats and reward
your dog for doing as it is told'.
[2] *the town . . . going* 'other people see what happens'.

[3] *groove* direction.
[4] *change* exchange.

The risk is terrible and strange –   35
    I tremble, doubt, . . . deny him.

10
'He's sweetest friend or hardest foe,
    Best angel or worst devil;
I either hate or . . . love him so,
    I can't be merely civil!   40

11
'You trust a woman who puts forth
    Her blossoms thick as summer's?
You think she dreams what love is worth,
    Who casts it to new-comers?

12
'Such love's a cowslip-ball⁵ to fling,   45
    A moment's pretty pastime;
I give . . . all me, if anything,
    The first time and the last time.

13
'Dear neighbour of the trellised house,
    A man should murmur never,   50
Though treated worse than dog and mouse,
    Till doted on for ever!'

⁵ *cowslip-ball* ball of cowslip-blossoms, often made by
children.

Alfred Tennyson (Lord Tennyson) (1809–1892)

Alfred Tennyson was born in the remote village of Somersby in Lincolnshire where his father was rector of a group of parishes. A family possessed of striking good looks and bearing, it was also plagued by melancholy and, at worst, insanity. The rector was an intelligent and, in some ways, enabling man, but he drank heavily and was consumed by anger against his own father, who had passed over a rightful inheritance to his younger son, Charles Tennyson d'Eyncourt. The bitterness at this injustice remained with Alfred too (it is perhaps a shadowy subtext even of 'Mariana'). Alfred read widely in his father's ample library and endured some time in Louth Grammar School before going up to Trinity College Cambridge – he left without a degree – where he became briefly a member of the elite debating society, the Apostles Club, and, crucially, met Arthur Henry Hallam, who became his most important friend and early critic. Tennyson's *Poems, Chiefly Lyrical* was published in 1830 – he already had a part in *Poems by Two Brothers* (1827) – and it was famously supported by Hallam's essay in *The Englishman's Magazine* in August 1831. Celebrating Tennyson as a poet of 'sensation', the article drew attention to the focus of much of Tennyson's early writing on human feeling, the experience of consciousness, but accidentally it made it difficult for readers to think of the *intellectual* achievement of Tennyson's verse thereafter. Hallam's unexpected death in Vienna in 1833 devastated Tennyson and the lyrics he composed over the next 17 years documenting his grief and the changing intellectual uncertainties to which the bereavement gave rise were eventually published in 1850 as *In Memoriam A.H.H.* Tennyson felt sufficiently recovered to marry Emily Sellwood later in 1850 and he succeeded Wordsworth in November that year as Poet Laureate (Tennyson did not attempt to make a living by any kind of labour other than poetry and, less successfully, drama; he was a professional writer).

In 1847 Tennyson's long poem on female education, *The Princess*, had appeared, and in 1855 another long work, the 'monodrama' *Maud*, was issued, a provocative reflection on the Crimean War, class, madness, the relationship between poetry and insanity, and sexuality; the first four of the *Idylls of the King* followed in 1859, the beginning of Tennyson's substantial Arthurian poem on heroism, nationhood and sexual responsibility. He worked at these over the next decades and the complete *Idylls* was published in the form in which it is now known only in 1891. Other volumes include *Enoch Arden and other Poems* (1864), *Tiresias and other Poems* (1885) and *Demeter and other Poems* (1889). Tennyson, the supreme Victorian lyricist and poet of the elegiac, died in 1892 and was buried in Westminster Abbey, the highest funerary honour the state can confer.

The Dying Swan

Published in 1830, 'The Dying Swan' explores what would be named in 1856 the 'pathetic fallacy': the saturation of landscape with human feeling (cf. 'Mariana', 64–6). If Romantic period poets such as Wordsworth and Coleridge found the divine in nature, here it is expressive only of human emotion in a poem of melancholy secularism. The grey of the sky is not, of course, really doleful; the adjective describes the human perception superimposed on the susceptible scene. 'The Dying Swan' is more generally part of Tennyson's first anxious negotiations with his Romantic inheritance. Writing of bird song in order to discuss poetry is a familiar practice from Classical antiquity, but Tennyson's most immediate predecessors are Coleridge, Keats, Shelley and Charlotte Smith. Romantic poems on the nightingale and skylark typically argue about the nature of poetry, the imagination and the writer's relationship with the earth. Tennyson's text is equally concerned with poetry, but more uncertainly. The poet-swan here sings only when it is dying (the ancient legend of the swan song), and, despite the epic simile of the last section that evokes great crowds, no human beings are listening. Doubts both about the future and the audience of poetry seem obliquely present. Certainly, the poem registers perceptions elsewhere discussed by contemporary commentators on poetry. Lecturing to the Royal Institution in 1830 and 1831, James Montgomery declared that Romanticism – or what we now know as Romanticism – had been a great high tide mark of English poetry but that the enthusiasm for verse had 'much fallen within these last ten years'. A new generation was struggling to find its audience.

The voice of poetry is female in 'The Dying Swan', a characteristic Tennysonian cross-gender movement that may be compared to 'The Lady of Shalott', 71–6, and the androgynous voice of 'Now sleeps the crimson petal', 87–8. Like 'Ulysses', 85–7, 'The Dying Swan' fixes on a moment in time *before* a significant event, in this case the swan's death. Poetry suspends action, focusing instead on the distinctively realized details of a material landscape and the paradoxes of the swan's music. Cf. Thomas Hardy's 'The Darkling Thrush', 512–13, for a later Victorian bird poem that negotiates with a Romantic legacy and ideals about the poet's role.

Text: *Poems, Chiefly Lyrical* (1830).

d bare,
e air,
here
gray.   5
r ran,
wan,

lay.
on,
went.   10
ce rose,
ite sky,
ows.
ept,
did sigh;   15
allow,
l will,
and still
slept,
and yellow.   20

k the soul
oy
he ear
d clear;
-sky,   25
ach[3] stole
Sometimes afar, and sometimes anear;
But anon her awful[4] jubilant voice,
With a music strange and manifold,
Flow'd forth on a carol[5] free and bold;   30
As when a mighty people rejoice
With shawms,[6] and with cymbals, and harps of gold,
And the tumult of their acclaim is roll'd
Thro' the open gates of the city afar,
To the shepherd who watcheth the evening star.   35

[1] *marish* marsh.
[2] *water-courses* streams or brooks.
[3] *coronach* Celtic funeral song.
[4] *awful* in the sense of awe-ful.
[5] *carol* song.
[6] *shawm* medieval musical instrument, close to a modern oboe.

And the creeping mosses and clambering weeds,
And the willow-branches hoar[7] and dank,
And the wavy swell of the soughing[8] reeds,
And the wave-worn horns of the echoing bank,
And the silvery marish-flowers that throng   40
The desolate creeks and pools among,
Were flooded over with eddying song.

[7] *hoar* grey and bare.   [8] *soughing* murmuring.

Mariana

Tennyson took his inspiration for this early poem, published in 1830, from Duke Vicentio's words in Shakespeare's *Measure for Measure* 3.1.215–67: 'She [Mariana] should this Angelo have married; was affianced to her by oath, and the nuptial appointed; between which time of the contract and limit of the solemnity, her brother Frederick was wrecked at sea, having in that perished vessel the dowry of his sister. But mark how heavily this befell to the poor gentlewoman. There she lost a noble and renowned brother, in his love toward her ever most kind and natural; with him, the portion and sinew of her fortune, her marriage dowry; with both, her combinate husband, this well-seeming Angelo . . . [He left] her in her tears, and dried not one of them with his comfort; swallowed his vows whole, pretending in her discoveries of dishonour: in few, bestowed her on her own lamentation, which she yet wears for his sake; and he, a marble to her tears, is washed with them, but relents not. . . . [T]here at the moated grange resides this dejected Mariana.' At the root of Mariana's suffering in Shakespeare's version, then, lies the financial consideration of the lost dowry: economics, and the idea of woman as commodity, are the unspokens of her plight. Tennyson – acutely conscious of the fragility of his own family's finances and the history of its lost fortune – may have this dowry loss, and its resulting misery, in mind.

Arthur Hallam, Tennyson's friend and early critic (and the subject of *In Memoriam A.H.H.*, 88–165), noted in an essay in 1831 that one of the distinguishing features of Tennyson's early art was his 'vivid, pic-

turesque delineation of objects, and the peculiar skill with which he holds all of them *fused* . . . in a medium of strong emotion'. 'Mariana' is certainly an essay in the *fusion* of landscape with human feeling, a defining example of what Hallam meant by Tennyson as a poet of *sensation*. Unlike nature for Wordsworth, Tennyson's landscape gives back nothing but the human mind. The poem's meditation on the stagnant life of a confined woman has been read as a reflection on early nineteenth-century gender politics – cf. Augusta Webster's 'Circe', 450–5 – but it is also one of Tennyson's early considerations of a self-dramatizing speaker who is securely in control of her own rhetoric. Contemporary critics recognized immediately Tennyson's ability to enter the minds of others – an ability most strikingly displayed in the dramatic monologues such as 'Ulysses', 85–7, and 'St Simeon Stylites'. William Johnson Fox remarked in 1831 that 'Our author has the secret of the transmigration of the soul. He can cast his own spirit into any living thing, real or imaginary.' The melancholy lament of 'Mariana' helped define the Tennysonian voice early on as expressive of regret, loss, sorrow: *In Memoriam A.H.H.* was its natural climax. The well-defined particularities of place here have, proleptically, a Pre-Raphaelite feel, and indeed John Everett Millais (1829–96) painted a much-discussed 'Mariana' in 1851. For a comparison, see Tennyson's 'Mariana in the South'.

Text: *Poems, Chiefly Lyrical* (1830).

'Mariana in the Moated Grange' (Shakespeare, *Measure for Measure*)[1]

With blackest moss the flower-plots
Were thickly crusted, one and all:
The rusted nails fell from the knots
That held the pear to the gable-wall.
The broken sheds look'd sad and strange: 5

[1] *'Mariana . . . Measure for Measure'* see headnote, above.

Unlifted was the clinking latch;
Weeded and worn the ancient thatch
Upon the lonely moated grange.[2]
She only said, 'My life is dreary,
    He cometh not,' she said;   10
She said, 'I am aweary, aweary,
    I would that I were dead!'

                        2
Her tears fell with the dews at even;
Her tears fell ere the dews were dried;
She could not look on the sweet heaven,   15
    Either at morn or eventide.
    After the flitting of the bats,
When thickest dark did trance the sky,
She drew her casement[3]-curtain by,
And glanced athwart[4] the glooming[5] flats.   20
She only said, 'The night is dreary,
    He cometh not,' she said;
She said, 'I am aweary, aweary,
    I would that I were dead!'

                        3
    Upon the middle of the night,   25
Waking she heard the night-fowl crow:
The cock sung out an hour ere light:
    From the dark fen[6] the oxen's low
Came to her: without hope of change,
    In sleep she seem'd to walk forlorn,   30
Till cold winds woke the gray-eyed morn
    About the lonely moated grange.
She only said, 'The day is dreary,
    He cometh not,' she said;
She said, 'I am aweary, aweary,   35
    I would that I were dead!'

                        4
    About a stone-cast from the wall
A sluice[7] with blacken'd waters slept,
And o'er it many, round and small,
    The cluster'd marish[8]-mosses crept.   40
    Hard by a poplar shook alway,
All silver-green with gnarled bark:
For leagues no other tree did mark
    The level waste, the rounding gray.
She only said, 'My life is dreary,   45
    He cometh not,' she said;
She said 'I am aweary, aweary
    I would that I were dead!'

[2] *grange* country house with farm buildings attached.
[3] *casement* frame or sash that is part of a window.
[4] *athwart* from side to side.
[5] *glooming* twilight.
[6] *fen* area of lowland covered partly by shallow water.
[7] *sluice* small stream carrying off surplus water.
[8] *marish* marsh.

5

And ever when the moon was low,
And the shrill winds were up and away,   50
In the white curtain, to and fro,
She saw the gusty shadow sway.
But when the moon was very low
And wild winds bound within their cell,[9]
The shadow of the poplar fell   55
Upon her bed, across her brow.
She only said, 'The night is dreary,
He cometh not,' she said;
She said 'I am aweary, aweary,
I would that I were dead!'   60

6

All day within the dreamy house,
The doors upon their hinges creak'd;
The blue fly sung in the pane; the mouse
Behind the mouldering wainscot[10] shriek'd,
Or from the crevice peer'd about.   65
Old faces glimmer'd thro' the doors
Old footsteps trod the upper floors,
Old voices called her from without.
She only said, 'My life is dreary,
He cometh not,' she said;   70
She said, 'I am aweary, aweary,
I would that I were dead!'

7

The sparrow's chirrup on the roof,
The slow clock ticking, and the sound
Which to the wooing wind aloof   75
The poplar made, did all confound
Her sense; but most she loathed the hour
When the thick-moted[11] sunbeam lay
Athwart the chambers, and the day
Was sloping toward his western bower.   80
Then said she, 'I am very dreary,
He will not come,' she said;
She wept, 'I am aweary, aweary,
Oh God, that I were dead!'

[9] *wild winds . . . cell* allusion to the Greek myth of Aeolus who kept the winds in an island cave.

[10] *wainscot* wooden panel-work lining the walls of a room.
[11] *moted* with motes, specks of dust.

The Lotos-Eaters

Tennyson's chief source for this poem, published in its first version in 1832 and significantly revised in 1842, was Book 9 of Homer's *Odyssey*: 'for nine days I was driven by ravening winds across the sea. On the tenth day we made the land of the Lotos-eaters, men who browse on a food of flowers. We landed there to fill our water-butts, while my crews snatched a meal on the shore, beside their likely vessels. As soon as the first hunger for food and drink had passed, I chose out two fellows and added to them a third, as runner, that they might go inland to spy out and enquire what were the human beings there existing. Off they went at once and met a party of these Lotos-eaters, who had no notion of slaying my emissaries: instead they gave them a dish of their Lotos-flower. And so it was that as each tasted of this honey-seed plant, the wish to bring news or return grew faint in him: rather he preferred to dwell for ever with the Lotos-eating men, feeding upon Lotos and letting fade from his mind all memory of home. I had to seek them and drag them back on board. They wept: yet into the ships we brought them perforce and chained them beneath the thwarts, deep in the well, while I constrained the rest of my adherents to hurry abroad, lest perhaps more of them might eat Lotos and lose their longing for home'.

The nineteenth-century Italian opera composer Giuseppe Verdi (1813–1901) gave some of his most seductive arias to his villainous characters, expressing a creative anxiety about the moral power of beautiful music. Tennyson explores a similar anxiety about the seductive power of poetic language to beguile; here, to entice the reader into a fantasy of escape. The mariners' desire to detach themselves from the world of work and marriage in preference for drugged idleness, a state where they have almost become plants, may be read not only in terms of concerns about the power of poetic language, but also as a displaced debate about the role of poetry more generally. The question is one of a poet's involvement in the external world of politics and labour, or his retreat into an isolated aesthetic that pretends to itself that it has no relation to the world beyond. In the 1842 version of the poem, reproduced here, Tennyson made the

ethical question of the mariners' decision clearer by including a new section (ll. 114–32), in which they recall the 'wedded lives' they are readily prepared to leave behind.

'The Dying Swan', 62–4, and 'The Lady of Shalott', 71–6, may be compared as other poems meditating obliquely on the place of art in relation to the public world (cf. also 'The Palace of Art'). Like 'The Lady of Shalott', 'The Lotos-Eaters' is political at another subtle level, musing on what Karl Marx would call alienated labour. The scene it describes could also be shaped in general terms by Tennyson's knowledge of Parliament during the Reform Bill crisis. The poem was begun in 1830 as debates about electoral reform were dominating discussions in the Commons and Lords, and the first version published in the year the Reform Act was passed (1832). Tennyson broadly supported reform and the idle mariners of 'The Lotos-Eaters' perhaps obliquely image a Parliament seemingly indifferent to its responsibilities – as it may have appeared to outsiders – in the build-up to the Act. The mariners are not *simply* depictions of Tory MPs, who were far from passive in trying to obstruct the Bill, but more broadly the poem's representation of stalled movement, impeded progress and carelessness of the world beyond a small homosocial gathering suggests a reflection on the political situation in England and the public reach of Tennyson's Homeric imagination even in a poem that contemplates withdrawal from the world. For another poem distantly engaging with these events, see 'Ulysses', 85–7.

Text: *Poems* (1842).

'Courage!' he said, and pointed toward the land,
'This mounting wave will roll us shoreward soon.'
In the afternoon they came unto a land
In which it seemed always afternoon.
All round the coast the languid air did swoon,   5
Breathing like one that hath a weary dream.
Full-faced above the valley stood the moon;
And like a downward smoke, the slender stream
Along the cliff to fall and pause and fall did seem.

2

A land of streams! some, like a downward smoke,   10
Slow-dropping veils of thinnest lawn,[1] did go;
And some thro' wavering lights and shadows broke,
Rolling a slumbrous[2] sheet of foam below.
They saw the gleaming river seaward flow
From the inner land: far off, three mountain-tops,   15

---

[1] *lawn* fine linen.   [2] *slumbrous* sleepy.

Three silent pinnacles of aged snow,
Stood sunset-flush'd: and, dew'd with showery drops,
Up-clomb[3] the shadowy pine above the woven copse.

3

The charmed sunset linger'd low adown
In the red West: thro' mountain clefts the dale   20
Was seen far inland, and the yellow down
Border'd with palm, and many a winding vale
And meadow, set with slender galingale;[4]
A land where all things always seem'd the same!
And round about the keel with faces pale,   25
Dark faces pale against that rosy flame,
The mild-eyed melancholy Lotos-eaters came.

4

Branches they bore of that enchanted stem,
Laden with flower and fruit, whereof they gave
To each, but whoso did receive of them,   30
And taste, to him the gushing of the wave
Far far away did seem to mourn and rave
On alien shores; and if his fellow spake,
His voice was thin, as voices from the grave;
And deep-asleep he seem'd, yet all awake,   35
And music in his ears his beating heart did make.

5

They sat them down upon the yellow sand,
Between the sun and moon upon the shore;
And sweet it was to dream of Fatherland,
Of child, and wife, and slave; but evermore   40
Most weary seem'd the sea, weary the oar,
Weary the wandering fields of barren foam.
Then some one said, 'We will return no more;'
And all at once they sang, 'Our island home
Is far beyond the wave; we will no longer roam.'   45

CHORIC SONG[5]

There is sweet music here that softer falls
Than petals from blown[6] roses on the grass,
Or night-dews on still waters between walls
Of shadowy granite, in a gleaming pass;
Music that gentlier on the spirit lies,   50
Than tir'd eyelids upon tir'd eyes;
Music that brings sweet sleep down from the blissful skies.
Here are cool mosses deep,
And thro' the moss the ivies creep,
And in the stream the long-leaved flowers weep,   55
And from the craggy ledge the poppy hangs in sleep.

---

[3] *clomb* climbed.
[4] *galingale* plant with an aromatic root used for cooking and medicine.

[5] *Choric Song* song sung by a chorus (an ancient Greek literary form).
[6] *blown* blossomed, in full bloom.

2

Why are we weigh'd upon with heaviness,
And utterly consumed with sharp distress,
While all things else have rest from weariness?
All things have rest: why should we toil alone,   60
We only toil, who are the first of things,[7]
    And make perpetual moan,
Still from one sorrow to another thrown:
    Nor ever fold our wings,
    And cease from wanderings,   65
Nor steep our brows in slumber's holy balm;
Nor harken what the inner spirit sings,
    'There is no joy but calm!'
Why should we only toil, the roof and crown of things?

3

    Lo! in the middle of the wood,   70
The folded leaf is woo'd from out the bud
With winds upon the branch, and there
Grows green and broad, and takes no care,
    Sun-steep'd at noon, and in the moon
    Nightly dew-fed; and turning yellow   75
    Falls, and floats adown the air.
    Lo! sweeten'd with the summer light,
The full-juiced apple, waxing over-mellow,
    Drops in a silent autumn night.
    All its allotted length of days,   80
    The flower ripens in its place,
Ripens and fades, and falls, and hath no toil,
    Fast-rooted in the fruitful soil.

4

    Hateful is the dark-blue sky,
    Vaulted o'er the dark-blue sea.   85
    Death is the end of life; ah, why
        Should life all labour be?
Let us alone. Time driveth onward fast,
And in a little while our lips are dumb.
Let us alone. What is it that will last?   90
All things are taken from us, and become
Portions and parcels of the dreadful Past.
Let us alone. What pleasure can we have
    To war with evil? Is there any peace
In ever climbing up the climbing wave?   95
All things have rest, and ripen toward the grave
    In silence; ripen, fall and cease:[8]
Give us long rest or death, dark death, or dreamful ease.

5

How sweet it were, hearing the downward stream,
    With half-shut eyes ever to seem   100

---

[7] *first of things* human beings as the supreme species (ironic).

[8] *fall and cease* appropriate allusion to *King Lear* (folio), 5.3.239.

Falling asleep in a half-dream!
To dream and dream, like yonder amber light,
Which will not leave the myrrh-bush[9] on the height;
To hear each other's whisper'd speech;
Eating the Lotos day by day,   105
To watch the crisping ripples on the beach,
And tender curving lines of creamy spray;
To lend our hearts and spirits wholly
To the influence of mild-minded melancholy;
To muse and brood and live again in memory,   110
With those old faces of our infancy
Heap'd over with a mound of grass,
Two handfuls of white dust, shut in an urn of brass!

6

Dear is the memory of our wedded lives,
And dear the last embraces of our wives   115
And their warm tears: but all hath suffer'd change:
For surely now our household hearths are cold:
Our sons inherit us: our looks are strange:
And we should come like ghosts to trouble joy.
Or else the island princes over-bold   120
Have eat our substance, and the minstrel sings
Before them of the ten years' war in Troy,[10]
And our great deeds, as half-forgotten things.
Is there confusion in the little isle?
Let what is broken so remain.   125
The Gods are hard to reconcile:
'Tis hard to settle order once again.
There is confusion worse than death,
Trouble on trouble, pain on pain,
Long labour unto aged breath,   130
Sore task to hearts worn out by many wars
And eyes grown dim with gazing on the pilot-stars.

7

But, propt on beds of amaranth[11] and moly,[12]
How sweet (while warm airs lull us, blowing lowly)
With half-dropt eyelid still,   135
Beneath a heaven dark and holy,
To watch the long bright river drawing slowly
His waters from the purple hill –
To hear the dewy echoes calling
From cave to cave thro' the thick-twined vine –   140
To watch the emerald-colour'd water falling
Thro' many a wov'n acanthus[13]-wreath divine!
Only to hear and see the far-off sparkling brine,
Only to hear were sweet, stretch'd out beneath the pine.

[9] *myrrh-bush* bush that yields a gum resin; associated with death.
[10] *Troy* the siege of the city of Troy by the Greeks is the subject of Homer's *Iliad*.
[11] *amaranth* legendary flower reputed never to fade.
[12] *moly* legendary herb given to Odysseus to protect him against the charms of Circe (cf. Augusta Webster, 'Circe', 450–5).
[13] *acanthus* plant celebrated by the Greeks and Romans for the elegance of its leaves.

8

The Lotos blooms below the barren peak: 145
The Lotos blows by every winding creek:
All day the wind breathes low with mellower tone:
Thro' every hollow cave and alley lone
Round and round the spicy downs the yellow Lotos-dust is blown.
We have had enough of action, and of motion we,   150
Roll'd to starboard,[14] roll'd to larboard,[15] when the surge was seething[16] free,
Where the wallowing monster spouted his foam-fountains in the sea.
Let us swear an oath, and keep it with an equal mind,
In the hollow Lotos-land to live and lie reclined
On the hills like Gods together, careless of mankind.   155
For they lie beside their nectar,[17] and the bolts[18] are hurl'd
Far below them in the valleys, and the clouds are lightly curl'd
Round their golden houses, girdled with the gleaming world:
Where they smile in secret, looking over wasted lands,
Blight and famine, plague and earthquake, roaring deeps and fiery sands,   160
Clanging fights, and flaming towns, and sinking ships, and praying hands.
But they smile, they find a music centred in a doleful song
Steaming up, a lamentation and an ancient tale of wrong,
Like a tale of little meaning tho' the words are strong;
Chanted from an ill-used race of men that cleave[19] the soil,   165
Sow the seed, and reap the harvest with enduring toil,
Storing yearly little dues of wheat, and wine and oil;
Till they perish and they suffer – some, 'tis whisper'd – down in hell
Suffer endless anguish, others in Elysian[20] valleys dwell,
Resting weary limbs at last on beds of asphodel.[21]   170
Surely, surely, slumber is more sweet than toil, the shore
Than labour in the deep mid-ocean, wind and wave and oar;
Oh rest ye, brother mariners, we will not wander more.

[14] *starboard* right-hand side in nautical terms.
[15] *larboard* left-hand side in nautical terms (now 'port').
[16] *seething* boiling.
[17] *nectar* drink of the gods on their mountain home of Olympus.
[18] *bolts* lightning bolts were the weapons of Zeus, king of the gods.

[19] *cleave* cut (in ploughing).
[20] *Elysian* to the Greeks, paradise (few of the dead went there).
[21] *asphodel* immortal flower that covers the fields of Elysium.

The Lady of Shalott

Tennyson's celebrated poem, published first in 1832 then revised in 1842, presents itself as an episode from an Arthuriad. Set near Camelot, the castle of King Arthur and the Knights of the Round Table, its ballad form shows the influence of both medieval literature and the popular heroic poetry of Sir Walter Scott (1771–1832). Like a ballad, the poem is not concerned with psychological credibility. Centred on the mysteriously cursed Lady of Shalott, its narrative hinges on the sexual power of the glimpse. Charged in its depiction of the erotic, sexuality is throughout associated with transgression.

'The Lady of Shalott', with its ruptured romance plot, has sustained a wide range of readings. It has been most usually understood in gender terms as a reflection on the consequences of the notion of separate spheres (male public world v. female domestic world). Certainly, 'The Lady of Shalott' is a poem that *constructs* a strong sense of separate spheres within which its drama is acted out, but to what extent it asks its reader to believe these true of early Victorian England is an open question. Other readers have seen it as a statement about the artist's troubled relation with the world beyond the self, and a poem anxious about what kind of knowledge art provides (the artist here is unable to regard the real world beyond her window without paying the penalty of death). Tennyson's employment of a woman to represent the creative artist suggests his association of poetry with the female, as did 'The Dying Swan', 62–4. Like 'The Dying Swan', 'The Lady of Shalott' seems fretful about the future and audience of verse, figured in the solitariness and fate of the Lady, and in Lancelot's final, formulaic words that reveal no understanding of her desires. Others have considered the text's hidden politics of work, seeing it as an intervention into debates about alienated labour, cf. 'The Lotos-Eaters', 66–71, or, more locally, as a poem shaped by the plight of English handloom weavers at the beginning of the Victorian period facing poverty and the destruction of

their way of life consequent on increasing levels of mechanization. The mythic power of Tennyson's Lady appealed to artists including William Holman Hunt (1827–1910) and J. W. Waterhouse (1849–1917); by the end of the century there were some 50 images of her in the public domain. This erotic, tragic medievalist poem can be compared with William Morris's even darker scrutiny of the violence of the Middle Ages in 'The Haystack in the Floods', 423–7, and 'Concerning Geffray Teste Noire', 438–45.

Text: *Poems* (1842).

On either side the river lie
Long fields of barley and of rye,
That clothe the wold[1] and meet the sky;
And thro' the field the road runs by
To many-tower'd Camelot;
And up and down the people go,
Gazing where the lilies blow
Round an island there below,
The island of Shalott.

2

Willows whiten, aspens[2] quiver,
Little breezes dusk[3] and shiver
Thro' the wave that runs for ever
By the island in the river
Flowing down to Camelot.
Four gray walls, and four gray towers,
Overlook a space of flowers,
And the silent isle imbowers
The Lady of Shalott.

3

By the margin, willow-veil'd,
Slide the heavy barges trail'd
By slow horses; and unhail'd
The shallop[4] flitteth silken-sail'd
Skimming down to Camelot:
But who hath seen her wave her hand?
Or at the casement[5] seen her stand?
Or is she known in all the land,
The Lady of Shalott?

4

Only reapers, reaping early
In among the bearded barley,
Hear a song that echoes cheerly
From the river winding clearly,

5

10

15

20

25

30

---

[1] *wold* downs.
[2] *aspens* trees of the poplar family, the leaves of which are especially liable to tremulous motion.
[3] *dusk* as a verb: to become dusk.
[4] *shallop* small dingy.
[5] *casement* frame or sash that is part of a window.

Down to tower'd Camelot:
And by the moon the reaper weary,
Piling sheaves in uplands airy,
Listening, whispers ''Tis the fairy   35
Lady of Shalott.'

PART 2

There she weaves by night and day
A magic web with colours gay.
She has heard a whisper say,
A curse is on her if she stay   40
To look down to Camelot.
She knows not what the curse may be,
And so she weaveth steadily,
And little other care hath she,
The Lady of Shalott.   45

2
And moving thro' a mirror[6] clear
That hangs before her all the year,
Shadows of the world appear.
There she sees the highway near
Winding down to Camelot: 50
There the river eddy whirls,
And there the surly village-churls,[7]
And the red cloaks of market girls,
Pass onward from Shalott.

3
Sometimes a troop of damsels glad,   55
An abbot on an ambling pad,[8]
Sometimes a curly shepherd-lad,
Or long-hair'd page in crimson clad,
Goes by to tower'd Camelot;
And sometimes thro' the mirror blue   60
The knights come riding two and two:
She hath no loyal knight and true,
The Lady of Shalott.

4
But in her web she still delights
To weave the mirror's magic sights,   65
For often thro' the silent nights
A funeral, with plumes and lights
And music, went to Camelot:
Or when the moon was overhead,
Came two young lovers lately wed;   70
'I am half sick of shadows,' said
The Lady of Shalott.

---

[6] *mirror* loom workers used a mirror as, working from the back of a tapestry, it enabled them to see the front.

[7] *village-churls* serfs or bondmen of the village.
[8] *pad* road-horse.

PART 3

A bow-shot[9] from her bower-eaves,
He rode between the barley-sheaves,
The sun came dazzling thro' the leaves,
And flamed upon the brazen[10] greaves[11]   75
    Of bold Sir Lancelot.[12]
A red-cross knight for ever kneel'd
    To a lady in his shield,
    That sparkled on the yellow field,   80
    Beside remote Shalott.

2

The gemmy[13] bridle glitter'd free,
Like to some branch of stars we see
    Hung in the golden Galaxy.
    The bridle bells rang merrily   85
As he rode down to Camelot:
And from his blazon'd[14] baldric[15] slung
    A mighty silver bugle hung,
    And as he rode his armour rung,
    Beside remote Shalott.   90

3

All in the blue unclouded weather
Thick-jewell'd shone the saddle-leather,
The helmet and the helmet-feather
Burn'd like one burning flame together,
    As he rode down to Camelot.   95
As often thro' the purple night,
    Below the starry clusters bright,
    Some bearded meteor, trailing light,
    Moves over still Shalott.

4

His broad clear brow in sunlight glow'd;   100
On burnish'd hooves his war-horse trode;
From underneath his helmet flow'd
His coal-black curls as on he rode,
    As he rode down to Camelot.
From the bank and from the river   105
    He flash'd into the crystal mirror,
    'Tirra lirra,'[16] by the river
    Sang Sir Lancelot.

---

[9] *bow-shot* distance an arrow travels.

[10] *brazen* brass.

[11] *greaves* armour for the leg below the knee.

[12] *Lancelot* peerless knight of Arthur's realm, whose adultery with Queen Guinevere helped bring about the end of the Round Table. Cf. William Morris's 'The Defence of Guenevere', 428–38.

[13] *gemmy* covered in gems.

[14] *blazon'd* covered in heraldic images.

[15] *baldric* strap or girdle.

[16] *Tirra lira* words taken from a bawdy context: Tennyson alludes to Autolycus's song in *The Winter's Tale* 4.3.9–12: 'The lark, that tirra-lyra chants, / With heigh, with heigh, the thrush and the jay, / Are summer songs for me and my aunts / While we lie tumbling in the hay.' 'Aunts' are whores.

5

She left the web, she left the loom,
She made three paces thro' the room,   110
She saw the water-lily bloom,
She saw the helmet and the plume,
She look'd down to Camelot.
Out flew the web and floated wide;
The mirror crack'd from side to side;   115
'The curse is come upon me,' cried
The Lady of Shalott.

PART 4

In the stormy east-wind straining,
The pale yellow woods were waning,
The broad stream in his banks complaining,   120
Heavily the low sky raining
Over tower'd Camelot;
Down she came and found a boat
Beneath a willow left afloat,
And round about the prow she wrote   125
The Lady of Shalott.

2

And down the river's dim expanse
Like some bold seër[17] in a trance,
Seeing all his own mischance[18] –
With a glassy countenance   130
Did she look to Camelot.
And at the closing of the day
She loosed the chain, and down she lay;
The broad stream bore her far away,
The Lady of Shalott.   135

3

Lying, robed in snowy white
That loosely flew to left and right –
The leaves upon her falling light –
Thro' the noises of the night
She floated down to Camelot: 140
And as the boat-head wound along
The willowy hills and fields among,
They heard her singing her last song,
The Lady of Shalott.

4

Heard a carol,[19] mournful, holy,   145
Chanted loudly, chanted lowly,
Till her blood was frozen slowly,
And her eyes were darken'd wholly,
Turn'd to tower'd Camelot.

[17] *seër* prophet, someone able to see into the future.   [19] *carol* song.
[18] *mischance* ill luck.

For ere she reach'd upon the tide   150
The first house by the water-side,
Singing in her song she died,
    The Lady of Shalott.

5

Under tower and balcony,
By garden-wall and gallery,   155
A gleaming shape she floated by,
Dead-pale between the houses high,
    Silent into Camelot.
Out upon the wharfs they came,
Knight and burgher,[20] lord and dame,   160
And round the prow they read her name,
    The Lady of Shalott.

6

Who is this? and what is here?
And in the lighted palace near
Died the sound of royal cheer;   165
And they cross'd themselves for fear,
    All the knights at Camelot:
But Lancelot mused a little space;
He said, 'She has a lovely face;
God in his mercy lend her grace,   170
    The Lady of Shalott.'

[20] *burgher* citizen.

The Epic/Morte d'Arthur

Tennyson's interest in writing an Arthuriad would eventually result in the long poem *The Idylls of the King* (Tennyson wanted the word pronounced 'idols'). In this, the 'Morte d'Arthur', originally published in 1842, would be reused as the core of the final Idyll, 'The Passing of Arthur' (1869). The framing 'Epic', not included in the 1842 trial edition, reveals Tennyson's nervousness about writing medievalist verse at this stage of his career, his aspirations for it none the less, and – in its conclusion – an effort to direct the reader to perceive the constructive possibilities of imagining the antique in the nineteenth century. W. B. Donne, one of Tennyson's Cambridge friends, reflected that 'We have long sold our birthright to oblivion and neglect. Our rich fountains of legendary tales and patriotic superstition are sealed up; their echoes have died away on the lips of a manufacturing people.' Tennyson's Arthuriad forms one response to such a lament. The title of 'Morte d'Arthur', which simply means 'The Death of Arthur', deliberately recalls the substantial late medieval text, Thomas Malory's *Morte Darthur*, an important source for all Tennyson's Arthurian poems.

Tennyson did not want to be thought merely escapist in his approach to the Middle Ages – 'The Lotos-Eaters', 66–71, muses on the ethics of escape more generally – and he invites his reader to imagine the poem's implications for the modern world. Partly, this has to do with the politics of nostalgia: the poem is a meditation on the end of a society with a firmer code of principle than – by implication – the modern (and a society in which the writing of epic, with its assumption of heroic men, was possible [cf. the Homeric allusion in the description of Arthur's final journey]). More plainly, Tennyson asks the reader to understand Arthur's death in terms of the decline of Christianity, the 'general decay of faith', announced by Holmes in the first part of the 'Epic'. The conclusion endeavours to efface the impression by grafting an overtly Christian ending onto the poem, linking, implicitly, the reading of medievalist poetry with the restoration of Christian belief.

'Morte d'Arthur' is, we are told by Hall, a fragment of a larger work, and the notion of traces, of the last remains, dominates the poem itself. Where 'The Lotos-Eaters' considered men keen to detach themselves from their past and to enter a state in which history had more or less ended, 'Morte d'Arthur' aims to recover a past that has left almost nothing behind except its own narratives and myths. The relation of this to a concern about the historical basis of Christianity is obvious. The poem's private theme is lament for the loss of another Arthur: Tennyson's friend, Arthur Hallam (1811–33), the subject of *In Memoriam A.H.H.*, 88–165, and the initial inspiration behind 'Ulysses', 85–7, written shortly after his death.

Medievalism would prove a particular attraction to many writers in the Victorian period, to say nothing of architects, interior designers, painters and utopists (for other examples in this anthology, see Robert Browning, '"Childe Roland to the Dark Tower Came"', 195–202, and William Morris, 'Haystack in the Floods', 423–7, 'The Defence of Guenevere', 428–38, and 'Concerning Geffray Teste Noire', 438–45).

Text: *Poems* (1842).

At Francis Allen's on the Christmas-eve, –
The game of forfeits[1] done – the girls all kiss'd
Beneath the sacred bush and past away –
The parson Holmes, the poet Everard Hall,
The host, and I sat round the wassail-bowl,[2]   5
Then half-way ebb'd: and there we held a talk,
How all the old honour had from Christmas gone,
Or gone, or dwindled down to some odd games
In some odd nooks like this; till I, tired out
With cutting eights[3] that day upon the pond,   10
Where, three times slipping from the outer edge,
I bump'd the ice into three several stars,
Fell in a doze; and half-awake I heard
The parson taking wide and wider sweeps,
Now harping on the church-commissioners,[4]   15
Now hawking at Geology[5] and schism;[6]
Until I woke, and found him settled down
Upon the general decay of faith
Right thro' the world, 'at home was little left,
And none abroad: there was no anchor, none,   20
To hold by.' Francis, laughing, clapt his hand
On Everard's shoulder, with 'I hold by him.'
'And I,' quoth Everard, 'by the wassail-bowl.'
'Why yes,' I said, 'we knew your gift that way
At college: but another which you had,   25
I mean of verse (for so we held it then),
What came of that?' 'You know,' said Frank, 'he burnt
His epic, his King Arthur, some twelve books' –
And then to me demanding why? 'Oh, sir,
He thought that nothing new was said, or else   30
Something so said 'twas nothing – that a truth
Looks freshest in the fashion of the day:
God knows: he has a mint of reasons: ask.
It pleased me well enough.' 'Nay, nay,' said Hall,
'Why take the style of those heroic times?   35

[1] *forfeits* party game in which a player gives up something by way of penalty for making some mistake, and afterwards redeems it by performing a ludicrous task.
[2] *wassail-bowl* receptacle for drinking festive toasts.
[3] *cutting eights* ice skating (in a figure of eight pattern).
[4] *church-commissioners* official investigators in the Church of England.
[5] *Geology* the New Geology of the first part of the nineteenth century – including the work of Sir Charles Lyell (1797–1875) – radically challenged the Biblical chronology of creation.
[6] *schism* division in the Church.

For nature brings not back the Mastodon,[7]
Nor we those times; and why should any man
Remodel models? these twelve books of mine
Were faint Homeric[8] echoes, nothing-worth,
Mere chaff and draff,[9] much better burnt.' 'But I,'   40
Said Francis, 'pick'd the eleventh from this hearth
And have it: keep a thing, its use will come.
I hoard it as a sugar-plum for Holmes.'
He laugh'd, and I, tho' sleepy, like a horse
That hears the corn-bin open, prick'd my ears;   45
For I remember'd Everard's college fame
When we were Freshmen:[10] then at my request
He brought it; and the poet little urged,
But with some prelude of disparagement,
Read, mouthing out his hollow oes and aes,   50
Deep-chested music, and to this result.

MORTE D'ARTHUR

So all day long the noise of battle roll'd
Among the mountains by the winter sea;
Until King Arthur's table, man by man,
Had fallen in Lyonnesse about their Lord,   55
King Arthur: then, because his wound was deep,
The bold Sir Bedivere uplifted him,
Sir Bedivere, the last of all his knights,
And bore him to a chapel nigh[11] the field,
A broken chancel[12] with a broken cross,   60
That stood on a dark strait of barren land.
On one side lay the Ocean, and on one
Lay a great water, and the moon was full.

Then spake King Arthur to Sir Bedivere:
'The sequel of to-day unsolders all   65
The goodliest fellowship of famous knights
Whereof this world holds record. Such a sleep
They sleep – the men I loved. I think that we
Shall never more, at any future time,
Delight our souls with talk of knightly deeds,   70
Walking about the gardens and the halls
Of Camelot, as in the days that were.
I perish by this people which I made, –
Tho' Merlin[13] sware that I should come again
To rule once more – but let what will be, be,   75
I am so deeply smitten[14] thro' the helm[15]
That without help I cannot last till morn.
Thou therefore take my brand Excalibur,[16]

---

[7] *Mastodon* large extinct mammal resembling the elephant.
[8] *Homeric* Homer (prob. 8th century BC), Greek epic poet regarded from antiquity as the author of the two great epics, the *Iliad* and *Odyssey*.
[9] *draff* refuse.
[10] *Freshmen* in the first year at University.
[11] *nigh* near.
[12] *chancel* eastern part of a church, of great sanctity.
[13] *Merlin* wizard of Arthur's court.
[14] *smitten* struck.
[15] *helm* helmet.
[16] *Excalibur* Arthur's sword, mysteriously fashioned.

Which was my pride: for thou rememberest how
In those old days, one summer noon, an arm   80
Rose up from out the bosom of the lake,
Clothed in white samite,[17] mystic, wonderful,
Holding the sword – and how I row'd across
And took it, and have worn it, like a king:
    And, wheresoever I am sung or told   85
In aftertime, this also shall be known:
But now delay not: take Excalibur,
And fling him far into the middle mere:[18]
Watch what thou seëst, and lightly bring me word.'

    To him replied the bold Sir Bedivere: 90
'It is not meet,[19] Sir King, to leave thee thus,
Aidless, alone, and smitten thro' the helm.
A little thing may harm a wounded man.
Yet I thy hest[20] will all perform at full,
Watch what I see, and lightly bring thee word.'   95
So saying, from the ruin'd shrine he stept
And in the moon athwart the place of tombs,
Where lay the mighty bones of ancient men,
Old knights, and over them the sea-wind sang
Shrill, chill, with flakes of foam. He, stepping down   100
    By zig-zag paths, and juts of pointed rock,
    Came on the shining levels of the lake.

    There drew he forth the brand Excalibur,
And o'er him, drawing it, the winter moon,
Brightening the skirts of a long cloud, ran forth   105
And sparkled keen with frost against the hilt:
For all the haft twinkled with diamond sparks,
Myriads[21] of topaz[22]-lights, and jacinth[23]-work
    Of subtlest jewellery. He gazed so long
That both his eyes were dazzled, as he stood,   110
This way and that dividing the swift mind,
    In act to throw: but at the last it seem'd
    Better to leave Excalibur conceal'd
There in the many-knotted waterflags,[24]
That whistled stiff and dry about the marge.   115
So strode he back slow to the wounded King.

    Then spake King Arthur to Sir Bedivere:
'Hast thou perform'd my mission which I gave?
What is it thou hast seen? or what hast heard?'
    And answer made the bold Sir Bedivere: 120
'I heard the ripple washing in the reeds,
And the wild water lapping on the crag.'

    To whom replied King Arthur, faint and pale:
'Thou hast betray'd thy nature and thy name,

---

[17] *samite* rich silk fabric, sometimes interwoven with gold.
[18] *mere* marsh, water, lake.
[19] *meet* proper, fitting.
[20] *hest* behest, request.

[21] *Myriads* countless numbers.
[22] *topaz* precious stone.
[23] *jacinth* reddish-orange gem.
[24] *waterflags* yellow flags (plants).

Not rendering true answer, as beseem'd   125
    Thy fëalty,[25] nor like a noble knight:
For surer sign had follow'd, either hand,
Or voice, or else a motion of the mere.
This is a shameful thing for men to lie.
Yet now, I charge thee, quickly go again   130
As thou art lief[26] and dear, and do the thing
I bad[27] thee, watch, and lightly bring me word.'

Then went Sir Bedivere the second time
Across the ridge, and paced beside the mere,
Counting the dewy pebbles, fix'd in thought;   135
But when he saw the wonder of the hilt,
How curiously and strangely chased,[28] he smote
His palms together, and he cried aloud,
    'And if indeed I cast the brand away,
Surely a precious thing, one worthy note,   140
Should thus be lost for ever from the earth,
Which might have pleased the eyes of many men.
What good should follow this, if this were done?
What harm, undone? deep harm to disobey,
Seeing obedience is the bond of rule.   145
Were it well to obey then, if a king demand
An act unprofitable, against himself?
The King is sick, and knows not what he does.
What record, or what relic of my lord
Should be to aftertime, but empty breath   150
And rumours of a doubt? but were this kept,
Stored in some treasure-house of mighty kings,
Some one might show it at a joust of arms,
Saying, 'King Arthur's sword, Excalibur,
Wrought by the lonely maiden of the Lake.   155
Nine years she wrought it, sitting in the deeps
Upon the hidden bases of the hills.'
So might some old man speak in the aftertime
To all the people, winning reverence.
But now much honour and much fame were lost.'   160

So spake he, clouded with his own conceit,[29]
    And hid Excalibur the second time,
And so strode back slow to the wounded King.
Then spoke King Arthur, breathing heavily:
'What is it thou hast seen? or what hast heard?   165

And answer made the bold Sir Bedivere:
'I heard the water lapping on the crag,
And the long ripple washing in the reeds.'
To whom replied King Arthur, much in wrath:
'Ah, miserable and unkind, untrue,   170
Unknightly, traitor-hearted! Woe is me!

---

[25] *fëalty* feudal obligation of fidelity.
[26] *lief* beloved, precious.
[27] *bad* bade, asked.

[28] *chased* adorned.
[29] *conceit* conception.

Authority forgets a dying king,
Laid widow'd of the power in his eye
That bow'd the will. I see thee what thou art,
For thou, the latest-left of all my knights,   175
In whom should meet the offices of all,
Thou wouldst betray me for the precious hilt;
Either from lust of gold, or like a girl
Valuing the giddy pleasure of the eyes.
Yet, for a man may fail in duty twice,   180
And the third time may prosper, get thee hence:
But, if thou spare to fling Excalibur,
I will arise and slay thee with my hands.'

Then quickly rose Sir Bedivere, and ran,
And, leaping down the ridges lightly, plunged   185
Among the bulrush-beds, and clutch'd the sword,
And strongly wheel'd and threw it. The great brand
Made lightnings in the splendour of the moon,
And flashing round and round, and whirl'd in an arch,
Shot like a streamer of the northern morn,   190
Seen where the moving isles of winter shock
By night, with noises of the northern sea.
So flash'd and fell the brand Excalibur:
But ere he dipt the surface, rose an arm
Clothed in white samite, mystic, wonderful,   195
And caught him by the hilt, and brandish'd him
Three times, and drew him under in the mere.
And lightly went the other to the King.

Then spoke King Arthur, drawing thicker breath:
'Now see I by thine eyes that this is done.   200
Speak out: what is it thou hast heard, or seen?'

And answer made the bold Sir Bedivere:
'Sir King, I closed mine eyelids, lest the gems
Should blind my purpose, for I never saw,
Nor shall see, here or elsewhere, till I die,   205
Not tho' I live three lives of mortal men,
So great a miracle as yonder hilt.
Then with both hands I flung him, wheeling him;
But when I look'd again, behold an arm,
Clothed in white samite, mystic, wonderful,   210
That caught him by the hilt, and brandish'd him
Three times, and drew him under in the mere.'

And answer made King Arthur, breathing hard:
'My end draws nigh; 'tis time that I were gone.
Make broad thy shoulders to receive my weight,   215
And bear me to the margin; yet I fear
My wound hath taken cold, and I shall die.'
So saying, from the pavement he half rose,
Slowly, with pain, reclining on his arm,
And looking wistfully with wide blue eyes   220
As in a picture. Him Sir Bedivere
Remorsefully regarded thro' his tears,

And would have spoken, but he found not words,
Then took with care, and kneeling on one knee,
O'er both his shoulders drew the languid hands,   225
And rising bore him thro' the place of tombs.

But, as he walk'd, King Arthur panted hard,
Like one that feels a nightmare on his bed
When all the house is mute. So sigh'd the King,
Muttering and murmuring at his ear, 'Quick, quick!   230
    I fear it is too late, and I shall die.'
But the other swiftly strode from ridge to ridge,
Clothed with his breath, and looking, as he walk'd,
    Larger than human on the frozen hills.
He heard the deep behind him, and a cry   235
Before. His own thought drove him, like a goad.
    Dry clash'd his harness in the icy caves
    And barren chasms, and all to left and right
The bare black cliff clang'd round him, as he based
    His feet on juts of slippery crag that rang   240
Sharp-smitten with the dint of armed heels –
    And on a sudden, lo! the level lake,
    And the long glories of the winter moon.

Then saw they how there hove[30] a dusky barge,
    Dark as a funeral scarf from stem to stern,   245
Beneath them; and descending they were ware
That all the decks were dense with stately forms
Black-stoled,[31] black-hooded, like a dream – by these
Three Queens with crowns of gold – and from them rose
    A cry that shiver'd to the tingling stars,   250
    And, as it were one voice, and agony
Of lamentation, like a wind, that shrills
All night in a waste land, where no one comes,
Or hath come, since the making of the world.

Then murmur'd Arthur, 'Place me in the barge,'   255
And to the barge they came. There those three Queens
Put forth their hands, and took the King, and wept.
    But she, that rose the tallest of them all
    And fairest, laid his head upon her lap,
And loosed the shatter'd casque,[32] and chafed his hands,   260
    And call'd him by his name, complaining loud,
    And dropping bitter tears against his brow
Striped with dark blood: for all his face was white
    And colourless, and like the wither'd moon
    Smote by the fresh beam of the springing east;   265
And all his greaves[33] and cuisses[34] dash'd with drops
    Of onset;[35] and the light and lustrous curls –
    That made his forehead like a rising sun

---

[30] *hove* moved into view.
[31] *stoled* a stole is a long robe or, in ecclesiastical use, a
vestment made from a narrow strip of silk or linen.
[32] *casque* helmet.

[33] *greaves* armour for lower part of the leg, beneath the
knee.
[34] *cuisses* armour for protecting the front part of the thighs.
[35] *onset* blood that signified the coming of death.

High from the daïs-throne[36] – were parch'd with dust;
Or, clotted into points and hanging loose,   270
Mix'd with the knightly growth that fringed his lips.
So like a shatter'd column lay the King;
Not like that Arthur who, with lance in rest,
From spur to plume a star of tournament,
Shot thro' the lists[37] at Camelot, and charged   275
Before the eyes of ladies and of kings.

Then loudly cried the bold Sir Bedivere,
'Ah! my Lord Arthur, whither shall I go?
Where shall I hide my forehead and my eyes?
For now I see the true old times are dead,   280
When every morning brought a noble chance,
And every chance brought out a noble knight.
Such times have been not since the light that led
The holy Elders with the gift of myrrh.[38]
But now the whole round table is dissolved   285
Which was an image of the mighty world;
And I, the last, go forth companionless,
And the days darken round me, and the years,
Among new men, strange faces, other minds.'

And slowly answered Arthur from the barge: 290
'The old order changeth, yielding place to new,
And God fulfils Himself in many ways,
Lest one good custom should corrupt the world.
Comfort thyself: what comfort is in me?
I have lived my life, and that which I have done   295
May He within Himself make pure! but thou,
If thou shouldst never see my face again,
Pray for my soul. More things are wrought by prayer
Than this world dreams of. Wherefore, let thy voice
Rise like a fountain for me night and day.   300
For what are men better than sheep or goats
That nourish a blind life within the brain,
If, knowing God, they lift not hands of prayer
Both for themselves and those who call them friend?
For so the whole round earth is every way   305
Bound by gold chains about the feet of God.
But now farewell. I am going a long way
With these thou seëst – if indeed I go –
(For all my mind is clouded with a doubt)
To the island-valley of Avilion;[39]   310
Where falls not hail, or rain, or any snow,
Nor ever wind blows loudly; but it lies
Deep-meadow'd, happy, fair with orchard-lawns

---

[36] *daïs-throne* throne on a dais, a raised platform.
[37] *lists* enclosed space in which tilting-matches and tournaments were held.
[38] *holy . . . myrrh* visit to the newborn Jesus by the wise men of the east who brought gold, frankincense and myrrh (Matthew 2.11).

[39] *Avilion* 'From which he will some day return – the Isle of the Blest,' Tennyson noted, with more confidence than Arthur.

And bowery hollows crown'd with summer sea,
Where I will heal me of my grievous wound.'[40]   315

So said he, and the barge with oar and sail
Moved from the brink, like some full-breasted swan
That, fluting a wild carol[41] ere her death,
Ruffles her pure cold plume, and takes the flood
With swarthy[42] webs. Long stood Sir Bedivere   320
Revolving many memories, till the hull
Look'd one black dot against the verge of dawn,
And on the mere the wailing died away.

[THE EPIC]

Here ended Hall, and our last light, that long
Had wink'd and threaten'd darkness, flared and fell: 325
At which the Parson, sent to sleep with sound,
And waked with silence, grunted 'Good!' but we
Sat rapt: it was the tone with which he read –
Perhaps some modern touches here and there
Redeem'd it from the charge of nothingness –   330
Or else we loved the man, and prized his work;
I know not: but we sitting, as I said,
The cock crew loud; as at that time of year
The lusty bird takes every hour for dawn:
Then Francis, muttering, like a man ill-used,   335
'There now – that's nothing!' drew a little back,
And drove his heel into the smoulder'd log,
That sent a blast of sparkles up the flue:
And so to bed; where yet in sleep I seem'd
To sail with Arthur under looming shores,   340
Point after point; till on to dawn, when dreams
Begin to feel the truth and stir of day,
To me, methought, who waited with a crowd,
There came a bark[43] that, blowing forward, bore
King Arthur, like a modern gentleman   345
Of stateliest port;[44] and all the people cried,
'Arthur is come again: he cannot die.'
Then those that stood upon the hills behind
Repeated – 'Come again, and thrice as fair;'
And, further inland, voices echo'd – 'Come   350
With all good things, and war shall be no more.'
At this a hundred bells began to peal,
That with the sound I woke, and heard indeed
The clear church-bells ring in the Christmas-morn.

[40] *I am going . . . grievous wound* cf. Homer's *Odyssey* (trans. A. T. Murray), 'But for thyself, Menelaus, fostered by Zeus, it is not ordained that thou shouldst die and meet thy fate in horse-pasturing Argos, but to the Elysian plain and the bounds of the earth will the immortals convey thee, where dwells fair-haired Rhadamanthus, and where life is easiest for men. No snow is there, nor heavy storm, nor ever rain, but ever does Ocean send up blasts of the shrill-blowing West Wind that they may give cooling to men.'
[41] *carol* song.
[42] *swarthy* black, blackish.
[43] *bark* small sailing boat.
[44] *port* manner of bearing or carrying oneself.

Ulysses

Tennyson began independently to explore the possibilities of what would eventually be known as the dramatic monologue at almost exactly the same time as Robert Browning (cf. Browning's 'Andrea del Sarto', 189–95, or 'Fra Lippo Lippi', 179–88). A curious moment in literary history and a defining point in the emergence of distinctively *Victorian* poetry. Like Browning, Tennyson exploited to the full the dramatic monologue's possibilities for subtle investigation of human action and thought through ventriloquization and the enabling space it opened up between poet and speaker. It was, for Tennyson, an ideal form for the expression of equivocation.

'Ulysses', published in 1842, certainly leaves the reader in two minds. It is a poem carefully balanced between the heroic and the morally questionable. Ulysses is at once a courageous figure who bravely resists the coming of age, and foolhardy, irresponsible. As an investigation of the ethics of withdrawal from the quotidian world, the poem can be compared with 'The Lotos-Eaters', 66–71. Tennyson's focus on Ulysses as a figure indifferent to his domestic political responsibilities, to the legal injustices of his kingdom, suggests more reflection on the events surrounding the 1832 Reform Act (cf. 'The Lotos-Eaters'). Ulysses, like Wellington's Tory administration, is unsympathetic to the abuses in his native land. Cf. Tennyson's 'Ode on the Death of the Duke of Wellington', which concentrates on Arthur Wellesley's military career and significantly omits comment on his role in the Reform crisis.

Tennyson said that the monologue 'was written soon after Arthur Hallam's death [1833], and it gives the feeling about the need of going forward and braving the struggle of life perhaps more simply than anything in *In Memoriam*'. Many readers have, however, discerned the tension in this celebrated text between heroic diction and enervated rhythm, the fissure between the substance of the language and its sound, particularly in the final line. The heroic sentiment of 'To strive, to seek, to find, and not to yield' conflicts sharply with the line's weary rhythm, as if the utterance of brave words consumes the energies of the brave.

At a literary level, the obvious source is Homer's *Odyssey*; the more important one is canto 26 of Dante's *Hell* from the *Divine Comedy*. In Henry Cary's translation (1805–14), which Tennyson admired, the relevant passage reads:

> [Ulysses]: 'When I escap'd
> From Circe, who beyond a circling year
> Had held me near Caieta, by her charms,
> Ere thus Aeneas yet had nam'd the shore,
> Nor fondness for my son, nor reverence
> Of my old father, nor return of love,
> That should have crown'd Penelope with joy,
> Could overcome in me the zeal I had
> T'explore the world, and search the ways of life,
> Man's evil and his virtue. Forth I sail'd
> Into the deep illimitable main,
> With but one bark, and the small faithful band
> That yet cleav'd to me. As Iberia far,
> Far as Morocco either shore I saw,
> And the Sardinian and each isle beside
> Which round that ocean bathes. Tardy with age
> Were I and my companions, when we came
> To the strait pass, where Hercules ordain'd
> The bound'ries not to be o'erstepp'd by man.
> The walls of Seville to my right I left,
> On the other hand already Ceuta past.
> "O brothers!" I began, "who to the west
> Through perils without number now have reach'd,
> To this the short remaining watch, that yet
> Our senses have to wake, refuse not proof
> Of the unpeopled world, following the track
> Of Phoebus. Call to mind from whence we sprang:
> Ye were not form'd to live the life of brutes
> But virtue to pursue and knowledge high.
> With these few words I sharpen'd for the voyage
> The mind of my associates, that I then
> Could scarcely have withheld them. To the dawn
> Our poop we turn'd, and for the witless flight
> Made our oars wings [. . .]"'

Text: *Poems* (1842).

It little profits that an idle king,
By this still hearth, among these barren crags,
Match'd with an aged wife,[1] I mete[2] and dole
Unequal laws[3] unto a savage race,
That hoard, and sleep, and feed, and know not me.   5

---

[1] *aged wife* Penelope.
[2] *mete* measure.
[3] *Unequal laws* inconsistent laws.

I cannot rest from travel: I will drink
Life to the lees:[4] all times I have enjoy'd
Greatly, have suffer'd greatly, both with those
That loved me, and alone; on shore, and when
    Thro' scudding drifts the rainy Hyades[5]   10
Vext the dim sea: I am become a name;
    For always roaming with a hungry heart
Much have I seen and known; cities of men
And manners, climates, councils, governments,
    Myself not least, but honour'd of them all;   15
And drunk delight of battle with my peers,
    Far on the ringing plains of windy Troy.[6]
    I am a part of all that I have met;
    Yet all experience is an arch wherethro'
Gleams that untravell'd world, whose margin fades   20
    For ever and for ever when I move.
    How dull it is to pause, to make an end,
To rust unburnish'd, not to shine in use!
As tho' to breathe were life. Life piled on life
    Were all too little, and of one to me   25
    Little remains: but every hour is saved
From that eternal silence, something more,
A bringer of new things; and vile it were
For some three suns to store and hoard myself,
    And this gray spirit yearning in desire   30
To follow knowledge like a sinking star,
Beyond the utmost bound of human thought.
    This is my son, mine own Telemachus,
To whom I leave the sceptre[7] and the isle –
    Well-loved of me, discerning to fulfil   35
This labour, by slow prudence to make mild
A rugged people, and thro' soft degrees
Subdue them to the useful and the good.
Most blameless is he, centred in the sphere
    Of common duties, decent not to fail   40
    In offices of tenderness, and pay
Meet[8] adoration to my household gods,
When I am gone. He works his work, I mine.

There lies the port; the vessel puffs her sail:
There gloom the dark broad seas. My mariners,   45
Souls that have toil'd, and wrought, and thought with me –
    That ever with a frolic welcome took
The thunder and the sunshine, and opposed
Free hearts, free foreheads – you and I are old;
    Old age hath yet his honour and his toil;   50
Death closes all: but something ere the end,
Some work of noble note, may yet be done,

---

[4] *lees* sediment at the bottom of a liquid.
[5] *Hyades* ('rainers') group of stars near the Pleiades, in the head of the constellation Taurus; their rising was thought to indicate rain.
[6] *Troy* Odysseus, himself once a suitor of Helen of Troy, fought with the Greek expedition to Troy to recover her.
[7] *sceptre* ceremonial rod, a symbol of rule.
[8] *Meet* proper.

Not unbecoming men that strove with Gods.[9]
The lights begin to twinkle from the rocks:
The long day wanes: the slow moon climbs: the deep   55
Moans round with many voices. Come, my friends,
'Tis not too late to seek a newer world.
Push off, and sitting well in order smite
The sounding furrows; for my purpose holds
To sail beyond the sunset, and the baths   60
Of all the western stars,[10] until I die.
It may be that the gulfs will wash us down:
It may be we shall touch the Happy Isles,[11]
And see the great Achilles,[12] whom we knew.
Tho' much is taken, much abides; and tho'   65
We are not now that strength which in old days
Moved earth and heaven; that which we are, we are;
One equal temper of heroic hearts,
Made weak by time and fate, but strong in will
To strive, to seek, to find, and not to yield.   70

[9] *strove with Gods* in the Trojan war.
[10] *baths . . . stars* i.e., beyond the horizon.
[11] *Happy Isles* Elysium, the Paradise of Greek myth where only a few mortals went.

[12] *Achilles* chief Greek hero in the Trojan war though also a figure associated with the abnegation of responsibility. For much of the *Iliad*, he remains sulking in his tent while Agamemnon, king of men, fights the enemy.

Now sleeps the crimson petal

An exquisite example of Tennyson's short lyrics, 'Now sleeps the crimson petal' is one of the songs from his long poem, *The Princess* (1847), a work in which Tennyson endeavoured to throw off his equivocations about the public role of poetry (cf. 'The Lady of Shalott', 71–6) and embrace a political theme – the education of women. None the less, the lyrical interludes provide moments of poetic language seemingly distant from the political concerns of the narrative. 'Now sleeps the crimson petal' owes much to the Persian form of the *ghazal*, and the vocabulary of cypresses, peacocks, stars and lilies are familiar ornaments of Persian love poetry (Persia is the modern Iran). The absorption of the landscape into the preoccupations of the speaker may be compared to the fashioning of place in 'Mariana', 64–6.

Tennyson's ability as a poet in technical terms was well regarded in his own century and the complex sound patterns of his verse were from the start recognized as an unparalleled accomplishment. He occupied the supreme place among nineteenth-century lyricists, casting a long shadow over his fellows, just as *In Memoriam*, 88–165, loomed large over later Victorian conceptions of the elegy (this anxiety of influence is something Swinburne wrestles with extensively in *Poems and Ballads second series* [1878]). The critic Amy

Sharp summed up in 1891 some of the admiration – and problems – readers had. 'Lord Tennyson', she said, 'has set a new standard of perfection in technical excellence; his own art is so perfect that we, simply as readers, rarely notice or think about it at all, – when every word seems just what it should be, we are led along in happy unconsciousness of effort, and are even apt to be a little blinded to the power of his work by his faultless execution. Yet Tennyson never for a moment sacrifices meaning to sensuous effect.'

The poem's curious uneasiness comes partly from the Classical reference to the rape of Danae: dreadful sexual violation is in the intertext of this seductively elegant poem. The recognition of the speaker's desire to exert power over the beloved to the point of total absorption is also a disturbing element of its sexual politics. And uncertainty is to be found in the shifting gender position of the speaker. Line 6 suggests the speaker is male, but ll. 9–10 female. Delicate lyrical eroticism is, perhaps, as Catherine Maxwell argues, being associated with androgyny (for different cross-gender movements in Tennyson's work, see 'The Dying Swan', 62–4, and 'The Lady of Shalott').

Text: *The Princess* (1847).

'Now sleeps the crimson petal, now the white;
Nor waves the cypress in the palace walk;
Nor winks the gold fin in the porphyry[1] font:
The fire-fly wakens: waken thou with me.

Now droops the milkwhite peacock like a ghost,   5
And like a ghost she glimmers on to me.

Now lies the Earth all Danaë[2] to the stars,
And all thy heart lies open unto me.

Now slides the silent meteor on, and leaves
A shining furrow, as thy thoughts in me.   10

Now folds the lily all her sweetness up,
And slips into the bosom of the lake:
So fold thyself, my dearest, thou, and slip
Into my bosom and be lost in me.'

[1] *porphyry* highly polished valuable stone.
[2] *Danaë* Danae was the daughter of the King of Argos, who had been warned by an oracle that her son would kill him, so he kept her in a bronze chamber or tower. But Zeus, king of the gods, made love to her as a shower of golden rain. Here, the earth lies open, like Danae, to the sexual power of the stars.

In Memoriam A.H.H. OBIIT MDCCCXXXIII

20p/day

Tennyson's *In Memoriam A.H.H.* – the full title means 'In memory of A.H.H., died 1833' – achieved public status almost from the day of its appearance in 1850. It created powerful expectations of what confessional poetry could be in the middle of the nineteenth century, and amply satisfied them. *In Memoriam* seemed to produce the audience that could admire it. Queen Victoria, after the death of her husband Prince Albert in 1861, found particular consolation in this great poem of bereavement, and her approval might be taken as symbolic of the way in which *In Memoriam* became public property, a text that helped define a particular quality of what it meant to be Victorian in the middle of the century. It has had both its admirers and detractors ever since – understandably, for no poem shows the difficulties and the achievements of Tennyson's art as a lyricist so clearly.

The poem commemorates Arthur Henry Hallam, Tennyson's closest friend from their time together as undergraduates at Trinity College Cambridge. Hallam's essay on Tennyson's poetry in the *Englishman's Magazine* for 1831 – 'On Some of the Characteristics of Modern Poetry, and on the Lyrical Poems of Alfred Tennyson' – provocatively defined modern poetry as either the poetry of ideas or the poetry of senses, of reflection or sensation. Tennyson, Hallam thought, in a judgement to have profound (and increasingly unwelcome) consequences for readers of Tennyson's thereafter, was 'decidedly' a poet of sensation.

Hallam, who was engaged to marry Emily, Tennyson's sister, died suddenly of a brain haemorrhage on 15 September 1833 while touring in Vienna. The poet heard the news some two weeks later. Both 'Morte d'Arthur', 76–84, and 'Ulysses', 85–7, were displaced responses to Arthur Hallam's shockingly unexpected death. *In Memoriam* is centrally about the bereavement. The poem was not, however, conceived initially either as a whole or as something intended for publication (Tennyson, when finally he agreed to publish it, wanted it to be anonymous). Its composition took place over 17 years – 1833–50 – and the final poem is persistently fragmentary. Readers should not expect to find each successive lyric tracing a unitary and coherently developing response, or consistently working out logical resolutions to the religious and personal uncertainties that confront the poet. *In Memoriam*'s relation with linearity follows, like George Meredith's *Modern Love*, 328–49, an emotional rather than a formal logic, its aesthetic is chiefly of the moment.

An underlying narrative of a very broad kind there is, none the less. At its most general level, the poem maps a pattern of progress from deep distress to an exultant celebration – though to what extent the poem is convinced of its own conclusion has long been debated – of Hallam as a forerunner of a higher race of men. The stages of that development are most clearly visible through comparison of the three Christmases, and an important turning point is the quasi-mystical experience of Hallam's 'living soul' in lyric 95. The 'Epilogue' is a wedding – a celebration of the real marriage between Tennyson's sister Cecilia and the Classical scholar Edmund Lushington, a replacement for the marriage that should have taken place between Emily Tennyson and Hallam. The 'Epilogue' marks most plainly the poem's movement from loss to union and continuation. None the less, *In Memoriam* gives its greatest weight and its most affective lyricism to grief, not to confidence and emotional restoration. Doubt and loss extrude from the poem as its dominant terms, and it secured the association between Tennyson's voice and elegy – a powerful strain in English writing and music altogether – which was widely influential for poetry and, to an extent, fiction, in the nineteenth century.

Hallam's death precipitates multiple anxieties, and *In Memoriam* is one of the most distinctive poems of male inner conflict from the period. Like Tennyson's *Maud: A Monodrama* (1855) and Clough's *Amours de Voyage* (1858), 228–62, it debates with and redefines conventional terms of masculine identity (part of Tennyson's redefinition here involves the occupation of different class and gender subject positions in a restless search for adequate tropes to articulate his grief). The intellectual anxieties Hallam's death prompts include the nature of life beyond the grave (cf. 'Crossing the Bar', 169–70), the purposes of human development, and the knowledge provided by natural

theology (cf. Browning's 'Caliban upon Setebos', 207–13). On this last point, Tennyson's concern about the science of geology – e.g., lyric 56 – provides an example of how *In Memoriam* moves between private grief and public themes, inviting the reader to see in Tennyson's loss a concentration of issues challenging the whole mid-century. Tennyson as poet mediates between poetry as 'overheard' and as addressed to the social. *In Memoriam*'s engagement with the New Geology also helped define the relationship between science and religion at the mid-century as conflictual, a definition that assisted in setting the terms for the reception of Darwin's *The Origin of Species* in 1859.

Tennyson's poem meditates on metamorphosed bodies, having a pre-Darwinian, quasi-Gothic interest in the transformation of corporeal forms. It returns compellingly to images of transitional spaces, and to hands, clasped and clasping, investing its emotional energies in recurrent, articulate motifs. *In Memoriam*'s affection for Hallam is intense, and some critics have discerned a strong homoerotic current in its grief. Uneven in its poetic accomplishment, the poem remains an indispensable text in understanding the lyrical achievement of the Victorians.

The four-line stanza form with its abba rhyme scheme swiftly became known as the '*In Memoriam* stanza' and Tennyson (and others) tellingly reused it for later elegies (cf. 'To the Marquis of Dufferin and Ava', 167–9). The rhyme scheme has seemed to many in harmony with the mood of the poem: the second two lines move away from the sound of the first, as if making some form of progress, a development away from an initial point, but the final line pulls backwards to the opening, as if memory and history continue to weigh on the present.

Text: *In Memoriam* (1850). (I follow A. C. Bradley and Christopher Ricks in using the titles 'Prologue' and 'Epilogue'; all Roman numerals have been changed to Arabic for convenience.)

[PROLOGUE]

Strong Son of God, immortal Love,
Whom we, that have not seen thy face,
By faith, and faith alone, embrace,
Believing where we cannot prove;

Directing the Poem to God

Thine are these orbs of light and shade;[1]   5
Thou madest Life in man and brute;
Thou madest Death; and lo, thy foot
Is on the skull which thou hast made. *A. H. H. ?*

[1] *orbs . . . shade* sun and moon.

Thou wilt not leave us in the dust:
Thou madest man, he knows not why,
He thinks he was not made to die;
And thou hast made him: thou art just.

Thou seemest human and divine,
The highest, holiest manhood,[2] thou:
Our wills are ours, we know not how,
Our wills are ours, to make them thine.

Our little systems[3] have their day;
They have their day and cease to be:
They are but broken lights of thee,
And thou, O Lord, art more than they.

We have but faith: we cannot know;
For knowledge is of things we see;
And yet we trust it comes from thee,
A beam in darkness: let it grow.

Let knowledge grow from more to more,
But more of reverence in us dwell;
That mind and soul, according well,
May make one music as before,

But vaster. We are fools and slight;
We mock thee when we do not fear:
But help thy foolish ones to bear;
Help thy vain worlds to bear thy light.

Forgive what seem'd my sin in me;
What seem'd my worth since I began;
For merit lives from man to man,
And not from man, O Lord, to thee.

Gives
A.H.H
to God

Forgive my grief for one removed,
Thy creature, whom I found so fair.
I trust he lives in thee, and there
I find him worthier to be loved.

Forgive these wild and wandering cries,
Confusions of a wasted youth;
Forgive them where they fail in truth,
And in thy wisdom make me wise.

1

I held it truth, with him who sings
To one clear harp in divers[4] tones,
That men may rise on stepping-stones
Of their dead selves to higher things.

10

15

20

25

30

35

40

45

---

[2] *highest . . . manhood* God in the human form of Jesus.   [4] *divers* diverse.
[3] *systems* of belief and thought.

But who shall so forecast the years
And find in loss a gain to match? 50
Or reach a hand thro' time to catch
The far-off interest of tears?

Let Love clasp Grief lest both be drown'd,
Let darkness keep her raven[5] gloss:
Ah, sweeter to be drunk with loss, 55
To dance with death, to beat the ground,

Than that the victor Hours should scorn
The long result of love, and boast,
'Behold the man that loved and lost,[6]
But all he was is overworn.' 60

2

Old Yew,[7] which graspest at the stones[8]
That name the under-lying dead,
Thy fibres net the dreamless head,
Thy roots are wrapt about the bones.

Physical union btwn trees & the dead underground

The seasons bring the flower again, 65
And bring the firstling to the flock;
And in the dusk of thee, the clock
Beats out the little lives of men.

O not for thee the glow, the bloom,
Who changest not in any gale,
Nor branding[9] summer suns avail 70
To touch thy thousand years[10] of gloom:

Tree lives longer

And gazing on thee, sullen tree,
Sick for thy stubborn hardihood,
I seem to fail from out my blood 75
And grow incorporate into thee.

3

O Sorrow, cruel fellowship,
O Priestess in the vaults of Death,
O sweet and bitter in a breath,
What whispers from thy lying lip? 80

'The stars,' she whispers, 'blindly run;
A web is wov'n across the sky;
From out waste places comes a cry,
And murmurs from the dying sun:

'And all the phantom, Nature, stands – 85
With all the music in her tone,

---

[5] *raven* black.
[6] *Behold . . . lost* cf. ll. 567–8.
[7] *Yew* evergreen tree of great longevity, often found in English country churchyards.

[8] *stones* gravestones.
[9] *branding* perhaps with the Old English sense of scorching, burning.
[10] *thousand years* yews can grow to a great age.

A hollow echo of my own, –
A hollow form with empty hands.'

And shall I take a thing so blind,
Embrace her as my natural good;   90
Or crush her, like a vice of blood,
Upon the threshold of the mind?

4

To Sleep I give my powers away;
My will is bondsman to the dark;
I sit within a helmless bark,[11]   95
And with my heart I muse and say:

O heart, how fares it with thee now,
That thou should'st fail from thy desire,
Who scarcely darest to inquire,
'What is it makes me beat so low?'   100

Something it is which thou hast lost,
Some pleasure from thine early years.
Break, thou deep vase of chilling tears,
That grief hath shaken into frost![12]

Such clouds of nameless trouble cross   105
All night below the darken'd eyes;
With morning wakes the will, and cries,
'Thou shalt not be the fool of loss.'

5

I sometimes hold it half a sin
To put in words the grief I feel;   110
For words, like Nature, half reveal
And half conceal the Soul within.

But, for the unquiet heart and brain,
A use in measured[13] language lies;
The sad mechanic exercise,   115
Like dull narcotics, numbing pain.

In words, like weeds,[14] I'll wrap me o'er,
Like coarsest clothes against the cold:
But that large grief which these enfold
Is given in outline and no more.   120

6

One writes, that 'Other friends remain,'
That 'Loss is common to the race' –

---

[11] *helmless bark* rudderless boat.
[12] *Break . . . frost* Tennyson noted, 'Water can be brought
below freezing-point and not turn into ice – if it be kept
still; but if it be moved suddenly it turns into ice and may
break the vase'.

[13] *measured* metred, rhythmical.
[14] *weeds* garments of mourning (esp. a widow's).

And common is the commonplace,
And vacant chaff well meant for grain.

That loss is common would not make   125
My own less bitter, rather more:
Too common! Never morning wore
To evening, but some heart did break.

O father, wheresoe'er thou be,
Who pledgest[15] now thy gallant son;   130
A shot, ere half thy draught[16] be done,
Hath still'd the life that beat from thee.

O mother, praying God will save
Thy sailor, – while thy head is bow'd,
His heavy-shotted[17] hammock-shroud   135
Drops in his vast and wandering grave

Ye know no more than I who wrought
At that last hour to please him well;[18]
Who mused on all I had to tell,
And something written, something thought;   140

Expecting still his advent[19] home;
And ever met him on his way
With wishes, thinking, 'here to-day,'
Or 'here to-morrow will he come.'

O somewhere, meek, unconscious dove,   145
That sittest ranging golden hair;
And glad to find thyself so fair,
Poor child, that waitest for thy love!

For now her father's chimney glows
In expectation of a guest;   150
And thinking 'this will please him best,'
She takes a riband[20] or a rose;

For he will see them on to-night;
And with the thought her colour burns;
And, having left the glass,[21] she turns   155
Once more to set a ringlet right;

And, even when she turn'd, the curse
Had fallen, and her future Lord
Was drown'd in passing thro' the ford,
Or kill'd in falling from his horse.   160

O what to her shall be the end?
And what to me remains of good?

---

[15] *pledgest* drinks a toast to.
[16] *draught* of the toast.
[17] *heavy-shotted* weighted with lead shot to make it sink.
[18] *last hour . . . well* Tennyson was writing to Arthur Hallam during the hour in which he died.
[19] *advent* coming.
[20] *riband* ribbon.
[21] *glass* mirror.

To her, perpetual maidenhood,
And unto me no second friend.

(7) *Really loved this man*

Dark house,[22] by which once more I stand   165
Here in the long unlovely street,
Doors, where my heart was used to beat
So quickly, waiting for a hand,

A hand that can be clasp'd no more –
Behold me, for I cannot sleep,   170
And like a guilty thing I creep
At earliest morning to the door.

He is not here; but far away[23]
The noise of life begins again,
And ghastly thro' the drizzling rain   175
On the bald street breaks the blank day.

8

A happy lover who has come
To look on her that loves him well,
Who 'lights[24] and rings the gateway bell,
And learns her gone and far from home;   180

He saddens, all the magic light
Dies off at once from bower and hall,
And all the place is dark, and all
The chambers emptied of delight:

Hmmm...   So find I every pleasant spot   185
In which we two were wont[25] to meet,
The field, the chamber and the street,
For all is dark where thou art not.

Yet as that other, wandering there
In those deserted walks, may find   190
A flower beat with rain and wind,
Which once she foster'd up with care;

So seems it in my deep regret,
O my forsaken heart, with thee
And this poor flower of poesy[26]   195
Which little cared for fades not yet.

But since it pleased a vanish'd eye,
I go to plant it on his tomb,
That if it can it there may bloom,
Or dying, there at least may die.   200

[22] *Dark house* 67 Wimpole Street, London, where Hallam had lived.
[23] *He . . . away* good example of the way in which enjambment teases the reader with a meaning that is then changed.
[24] *'lights* alights.
[25] *wont* accustomed.
[26] *poesy* archaic word for poetry (also referring to flowers [posy]).

9

Fair ship,[27] that from the Italian shore
 Sailest the placid ocean-plains
 With my lost Arthur's loved remains,
Spread thy full wings, and waft him o'er.

So draw him home to those that mourn   205
 In vain; a favourable speed
 Ruffle thy mirror'd mast,[28] and lead
Thro' prosperous floods his holy urn.

All night no ruder air perplex
 Thy sliding keel, till Phosphor,[29] bright   210
 As our pure love, thro' early light
Shall glimmer on the dewy decks.

Sphere all your lights around, above;
 Sleep, gentle heavens, before the prow;
 Sleep, gentle winds, as he sleeps now,   215
 My friend, the brother of my love;

My Arthur, whom I shall not see
 Till all my widow'd race be run;
 Dear as the mother to the son,
More than my brothers are to me.   220

10

I hear the noise about thy keel;
 I hear the bell struck in the night: *Ship bringing his body?*
 I see the cabin-window bright;
 I see the sailor at the wheel.

Thou bring'st the sailor to his wife,   225
 And travell'd men from foreign lands;
 And letters unto trembling hands;
And, thy dark freight, a vanish'd life.

So bring him: we have idle dreams:
 This look of quiet flatters thus   230
 Our home-bred fancies: O to us,
The fools of habit, sweeter seems

To rest beneath the clover sod,
 That takes the sunshine and the rains,
 Or where the kneeling hamlet drains   235
The chalice of the grapes of God;[30]

Than if with thee the roaring wells
 Should gulf him fathom[31] -deep in brine;

---

[27] *Fair ship* that brought Hallam's body home by sea from Trieste (Italian port on the east coast of the Adriatic).
[28] *mirror'd mast* one reflected in the sea.
[29] *Phosphor* morning star.

[30] *kneeling hamlet . . . God* country church where villagers take communion (chalice = cup in which consecrated wine is administered at the eucharist).
[31] *fathom* nautical measurement of six feet.

And hands so often clasp'd in mine,
Should toss with tangle[32] and with shells.   240

11

Calm is the morn without a sound,
Calm as to suit a calmer grief,
And only thro' the faded leaf
The chestnut pattering to the ground:

Calm and deep peace on this high wold,[33]   245
And on these dews that drench the furze,[34]
And all the silvery gossamers[35]
That twinkle into green and gold:

Calm and still light on yon great plain
That sweeps with all its autumn bowers,   250
And crowded farms and lessening towers,
To mingle with the bounding main:[36]

Calm and deep peace in this wide air,
These leaves that redden to the fall;
And in my heart, if calm at all,   255
If any calm, a calm despair:

Calm on the seas, and silver sleep,
And waves that sway themselves in rest,
And dead calm in that noble breast
Which heaves but with the heaving deep.   260

12   Enjoyed

Lo, as a dove when up she springs
To bear thro' Heaven a tale of woe,[37]
Some dolorous[38] message knit below
The wild pulsation of her wings;

Like her I go; I cannot stay;   265
I leave this mortal ark[39] behind,
A weight of nerves without a mind,
And leave the cliffs, and haste away

O'er ocean-mirrors rounded large,
And reach the glow of southern skies,   270
And see the sails at distance rise,
And linger weeping on the marge,[40]

---

[32] *tangle* species of seaweed with long leathery fronds.
[33] *wold* piece of open country (chiefly Lincolnshire wolds, where Tennyson grew up).
[34] *furze* spiny evergreen shrub with yellow flowers.
[35] *gossamers* fine threads of spiders' web.
[36] *main* sea.
[37] *Lo . . . woe* inversion of the Genesis story from Noah and the Ark: 'And [Noah] stayed yet other seuen dayes; and

againe hee sent foorth the doue out of the Arke. And the doue came in to him in the euening, and loe, in her mouth was an Oliue leafe pluckt off: So Noah knew that the waters were abated from off the earth', Genesis 8.10–11.
[38] *dolorous* sorrowful.
[39] *ark* cf. note 37.
[40] *marge* margin, edge.

And saying; 'Comes he thus, my friend?
　　Is this the end of all my care?'
　　And circle moaning in the air:
'Is this the end? Is this the end?'[41]　　　　　　　　275

And forward dart again, and play
　　About the prow, and back return
　　To where the body sits, and learn
That I have been <u>an hour away.</u> *?*　　　　　　　280

13 *Husband ?*

Tears of the widower, when he sees
　　A late-lost form that sleep reveals,
Comparing And moves his doubtful arms, and feels
himself — Her place is empty, fall like these;[42]
& A HH to ?
a couple　　　　Which weep a loss for ever new,　　　285
　　A void where heart on heart reposed;
And, where warm hands have prest and closed,
　　Silence, till I be silent too.

Which weep the <u>comrade of my choice,</u>
　　An awful thought, a life removed,　　　　　290
　　The <u>human-hearted man</u> I loved,
　　A Spirit, not a breathing voice.

Come Time, and teach me, many years,
　　I do not suffer in a dream;
For now so strange do these things seem,　　　295
　　Mine eyes have leisure for their tears;

　　My fancies time to rise on wing,
And glance about the approaching sails,
As tho' they brought but merchants' bales,
　　And not the burthen that they bring.　　　　300

14
If one should bring me this report,
　　That thou hadst touch'd the land to-day,
　　And I went down unto the quay,
　　And found thee lying[43] in the port;

And standing, muffled round with woe,　　　　305
　　Should see thy passengers in rank
Come stepping lightly down the plank,
　　And beckoning unto those they know;

And if along with these should come
　　The man I held as half-divine;　　　　　　310

[41] *Is this . . . end?* cf. *King Lear* (folio) 5.3.237–8, as Lear
enters with the dead Cordelia in his arms: '*Kent.* Is this the
promised end? *Edgar.* Or image of that horror.'
[42] *Tears . . . like these* cf. Milton's 'Methought I saw my late
espoused Saint' on his dead wife, which concludes 'But O

as to embrace me she enclin'd / I wak'd, she fled, and day
brought back my night'.
[43] *lying* staying.

Should strike a sudden hand in mine,
And ask a thousand things of home;

And I should tell him all my pain,
And how my life had droop'd of late,
And he should sorrow o'er my state   315
And marvel what possess'd my brain;

And I perceived no touch of change,
No hint of death in all his frame,
But found him all in all the same,
I should not feel it to be strange.   320

15

To-night the winds begin to rise
And roar from yonder dropping day:
The last red leaf is whirl'd away,
The rooks are blown about the skies;

The forest crack'd, the waters curl'd,   325
The cattle huddled on the lea;[44]
And wildly dash'd on tower and tree
The sunbeam strikes along the world:

And but for fancies, which aver
That all thy motions[45] gently pass   330
Athwart a plane of molten glass,[46]
I scarce could brook[47] the strain and stir

That makes the barren branches loud;
And but for fear it is not so,
The wild unrest that lives in woe   335
Would dote and pore on yonder cloud

That rises upward always higher,
And onward drags a labouring breast,
And topples round the dreary west,
A looming bastion fringed with fire.[48]   340

16

What words are these have fall'n from me?
Can calm despair and wild unrest
Be tenants of a single breast,
Or sorrow such a changeling be?

Or doth she only seem to take   345
The touch of change in calm or storm;
But knows no more of transient form
In her deep self, than some dead lake

---

[44] *lea* meadow.
[45] *thy motions* movement of Hallam's body on the ship.
[46] *plane of molten glass* the sea (an awkward Tennysonian circumlocution).
[47] *brook* endure.

[48] *And but for fear . . . fringed with fire* if he thought that Hallam's body was not being brought back, his 'wild unrest' would lead him to indulgent fixation with the correspondence between the natural world and his own plight.

That holds the shadow of a lark
Hung in the shadow of a heaven? 350
Or has the shock, so harshly given,
Confused me like the unhappy bark

That strikes by night a craggy shelf,
And staggers blindly ere she sink?
And stunn'd me from my power to think 355
And all my knowledge of myself;

And made me that delirious man
Whose fancy fuses old and new,
And flashes into false and true,
And mingles all without a plan? 360

17

Thou comest, much wept for: such a breeze
Compell'd thy canvas,[49] and my prayer
Was as the whisper of an air
To breathe thee over lonely seas.

For I in spirit saw thee move 365
Thro' circles of the bounding sky,
Week after week: the days go by:
Come quick, thou bringest all I love.

Henceforth, wherever thou may'st roam,
My blessing, like a line of light, 370
Is on the waters day and night,
And like a beacon guards thee home.

So may whatever tempest mars
Mid-ocean, spare thee, sacred bark;
And balmy drops in summer dark 375
Slide from the bosom of the stars.

So kind an office hath been done,
Such precious relics brought by thee;
The dust of him I shall not see
Till all my widow'd race be run. 380

18

'Tis well; 'tis something; we may stand
Where he in English earth is laid,[50]
And from his ashes may be made
The violet[51] of his native land.

'Tis little; but it looks in truth 385
As if the quiet bones were blest

---

[49] *canvas* sail.
[50] *English . . . laid* Hallam is buried at Clevedon, Somerset, a county in the south-west of England.
[51] *violet* small purple wild flower (long associated mythologically with resurrection).

> Among familiar names[52] to rest
> And in the places of his youth.
>
> Come then, pure hands, and bear the head
> That sleeps or wears the mask of sleep,   390
> And come, whatever loves to weep,
> And hear the ritual of the dead.[53]
>
> Ah yet, ev'n yet, if this might be,
> I, falling on his faithful heart,
> Would breathing thro' his lips impart   395
> The life that almost dies in me;
>
> That dies not, but endures with pain,
> And slowly forms the firmer mind,
> Treasuring the look it cannot find,
> The words that are not heard again.   400

19

Water

> The Danube[54] to the Severn[55] gave   *Interesting connection*
> The darken'd heart that beat no more;   *btwn bodies of water*
> They laid him by the pleasant shore,
> And in the hearing of the wave.
>
> There twice a day the Severn fills;   405
> The salt sea-water passes by,[56]
> And hushes half the babbling Wye,[57]
> And makes a silence in the hills.[58]
>
> The Wye is hush'd nor moved along,
> And hush'd my deepest grief of all,   410
> When fill'd with tears that cannot fall,
> I brim with sorrow drowning song.
>
> The tide flows down, the wave again
> Is vocal in its wooded walls;
> My deeper anguish also falls,   415
> And I can speak a little then.

20

Mourning servants

> The lesser griefs that may be said,
> That breathe a thousand tender vows,
> Are but as servants in a house
> Where lies the master newly dead;   420
>
> Who speak their feeling as it is,
> And weep the fulness from the mind:

---

[52] *familiar names* some of Hallam's family are also buried at Clevedon.
[53] *ritual . . . dead* funeral service.
[54] *Danube* river that flows through Vienna where Hallam died.
[55] *Severn* English river that flows into the Bristol Channel, overlooked by Clevedon.

[56] *twice . . . passes by* Tennyson refers to the tidal movement of the Severn estuary.
[57] *Wye* river that flows into the Severn estuary from the north.
[58] *silence . . . hills* Tennyson said that, from his own observation, the rising sea stilled the rapids of the Wye.

'It will be hard,' they say, 'to find
Another service such as this.'

My lighter moods are like to these, 425
That out of words a comfort win;
But there are other griefs within,
And tears that at their fountain freeze;

Cannot reveal certain grifs – tears must "freeze"

For by the hearth the children sit
Cold in that atmosphere of Death, 430
And scarce endure to draw the breath,
Or like to noiseless phantoms flit:

But open converse is there none,
So much the vital spirits sink
To see the vacant chair, and think, 435
'How good! how kind! and he is gone.'

(21 ?)

I sing to him that rests below,
And, since the grasses round me wave,
I take the grasses of the grave,
And make them pipes whereon to blow. 440

The traveller[59] hears me now and then,
And sometimes harshly will he speak:
'This fellow would make weakness weak,
And melt the waxen hearts of men.'

Another answers, 'Let him be, 445
He loves to make parade of pain
That with his piping he may gain
The praise that comes to constancy.'

A third is worth:[60] 'Is this an hour
For private sorrow's barren song, 450
When more and more the people throng[61]
The chairs and thrones of civil power?

'A time to sicken and to swoon,
When Science reaches forth her arms
To feel from world to world, and charms 455
Her secret from the latest moon?

Behold, ye speak an idle thing:
Ye never knew the sacred dust:
I do but sing because I must,
And pipe but as the linnets[62] sing: 460

---

[59] *traveller* one unsympathetic to Tennyson's grief.
[60] *is worth* i.e., has this to say.
[61] *more and more . . . throng* general reference to the

agitations of Chartism and to the European revolutions
from the French revolution of 1789 onwards.
[62] *linnet* English song bird.

And one is glad; her note is gay,
For now her little ones have ranged;
And one is sad; her note is changed,
Because her brood is stol'n away.

22   *Only knew eachother 4 years*

The path by which we twain did go,   465
Which led by tracts that pleased us well,
Thro' four sweet years[63] arose and fell,
From flower to flower, from snow to snow:

And we with singing cheer'd the way,
And, crown'd with all the season lent,   470
From April on to April went,
And glad at heart from May to May:

But where the path we walk'd began
To slant the fifth autumnal slope,[64]
As we descended following Hope,   475
There sat the Shadow fear'd of man;

Who broke our fair companionship,
And spread his mantle dark and cold,
And wrapt thee formless in the fold,
And dull'd the murmur on thy lip,   480

And bore thee where I could not see
Nor follow, tho' I walk in haste,
And think, that somewhere in the waste
The Shadow sits and waits for me.

23

Now, sometimes in my sorrow shut,   485
Or breaking into song by fits,
Alone, alone, to where he sits,
The Shadow cloak'd from head to foot,

Who keeps the keys of all the creeds,[65]
I wander, often falling lame,   490
And looking back to whence I came,
Or on to where the pathway leads;

And crying, How changed from where it ran
Thro' lands where not a leaf was dumb;
But all the lavish hills would hum   495
The murmur of a happy Pan:[66]

When each by turns was guide to each,
And Fancy light from Fancy caught,
And Thought leapt out to wed with Thought
Ere Thought could wed itself with Speech;   500

---

[63] *four sweet years* Tennyson first met Hallam late in 1828.
[64] *fifth . . . slope* Hallam died on 15 September 1833.
[65] *creeds* beliefs.

[66] *Pan* cheerful and mischievous Greek god of field and woodland.

And all we met was fair and good,
And all was good that Time could bring,
And all the secret of the Spring
Moved in the chambers of the blood;

And many an old philosophy   505
On Argive[67] heights divinely sang,
And round us all the thicket rang
To many a flute of Arcady.[68]

24
And was the day of my delight
As pure and perfect as I say?   510
The very source and fount of Day
Is dash'd with wandering isles of night.

If all was good and fair we met,
This earth had been the Paradise
It never look'd to human eyes   515
Since our first Sun arose and set.

And is it that the haze of grief
Makes former gladness loom so great?
The lowness of the present state,
That sets the past in this relief?   520

Or that the past will always win
A glory from its being far;
And orb into the perfect star
We saw not, when we moved therein?   *Interesting*
                                      glny stronger?

25
I know that this was Life, – the track   525
Whereon with equal feet we fared;
And then, as now, the day prepared
The daily burden for the back.

But this it was that made me move
As light as carrier-birds in air;   530
I loved the weight I had to bear,
Because it needed help of Love:

Nor could I weary, heart or limb,
When mighty Love would cleave in twain
The lading[69] of a single pain,   535
And part it, giving half to him.

26
Still onward winds the dreary way
I with it; for I long to prove

---

[67] *Argive* referring to the ancient city of Argos or, more generally, to Classical Greece.

[68] *Arcady* pastoral ideal of Classical Greece.

[69] *lading* loading.

No lapse of moons can canker[70] Love,
   Whatever fickle[71] tongues may say.   540

And if that eye which watches guilt
And goodness, and hath power to see
Within the green the moulder'd tree,
And towers fall'n as soon as built –

   Oh, if indeed that eye foresee   545
   Or see (in Him is no before)
   In more of life true life no more
   And Love the indifference to be,

Then might I find, ere yet the morn
   Breaks hither over Indian seas,   550
   That Shadow waiting with the keys,
To shroud me from my proper[72] scorn.

27

   I envy not in any moods
   The captive void of noble rage,
   The linnet born within the cage,   555
That never knew the summer woods:

   I envy not the beast that takes
   His license in the field of time,
   Unfetter'd by the sense of crime,
   To whom a conscience never wakes;   560

Nor, what may count itself as blest,
The heart that never plighted troth[73]
But stagnates in the weeds of sloth;
   Nor any want-begotten rest.

   I hold it true, whate'er befall;   565
   I feel it, when I sorrow most;
   'Tis better to have loved and lost
   Than never to have loved at all.

28

The time draws near the birth of Christ:
   The moon is hid; the night is still;   570
   The Christmas bells from hill to hill
   Answer each other in the mist.

Four voices of four hamlets round,
From far and near, on mead[74] and moor,
   Swell out and fail, as if a door   575
Were shut between me and the sound:

---

[70] *canker* corrupt, destroy.
[71] *fickle* unreliable, changeful.
[72] *proper* 'appropriate', also 'own'.

[73] *plighted troth* took a vow of faithfulness.
[74] *mead* meadow.

Each voice four changes on the wind,
That now dilate, and now decrease,
Peace and goodwill, goodwill and peace,
Peace and goodwill, to all mankind.[75]   580

This year I slept and woke with pain,
I almost wish'd no more to wake,
And that my hold on life would break
Before I heard those bells again:

But they my troubled spirit rule,   585
For they controll'd me when a boy;
They bring me sorrow touch'd with joy,
The merry merry bells of Yule.[76]

29

With such compelling cause to grieve
As daily vexes household peace,   590
And chains regret to his decease,
How dare we keep our Christmas-eve;

Which brings no more a welcome guest
To enrich the threshold of the night
With shower'd largess[77] of delight   595
In dance and song and game and jest?

Yet go, and while the holly boughs
Entwine the cold baptismal font,
Make one wreath more for Use and Wont,
That guard the portals[78] of the house;   600

Old sisters of a day gone by,
Gray nurses, loving nothing new;
Why should they miss their yearly due
Before their time? They too will die.

30 *why*

With trembling fingers did we weave   605
The holly round the Christmas hearth;
A rainy cloud possess'd the earth,
And sadly fell our Christmas-eve.

At our old pastimes in the hall
We gambol'd, making vain pretence   610
Of gladness, with an awful sense
Of one mute Shadow watching all.

We paused: the winds were in the beech:
We heard them sweep the winter land;

---

[75] *Peace and goodwill . . . mankind* cf. the announcement of Jesus's birth to the shepherds: 'And suddenly there was with the Angel a multitude of the heauenly hoste praising God, and saying, Glory to God in the highest, and on earth peace, good wil towards men', Luke 2.13–14.

[76] *Yule* Christmas.
[77] *largess* largesse, generosity, bounty.
[78] *portals* gates.

> And in a circle hand-in-hand   615
> Sat silent, looking each at each.

Then echo-like our voices rang;
We sung, tho' every eye was dim,
A merry song we sang with him
Last year: impetuously we sang: 620

We ceased: a gentler feeling crept
Upon us: surely rest is meet:
'They rest,' we said, 'their sleep is sweet,'
And silence follow'd, and we wept.

Our voices took a higher range;   625
Once more we sang: 'They do not die
Nor lose their mortal sympathy,
Nor change to us, although they change;

'Rapt from the fickle and the frail
With gather'd power, yet the same,   630
Pierces the keen seraphic[79] flame[80]
From orb to orb, from veil to veil.'

Rise, happy morn, rise, holy morn,
Draw forth the cheerful day from night:
O Father, touch the east, and light   635
The light that shone when Hope was born.[81]

31

When Lazarus[82] left his charnel-cave,[83]
And home to Mary's[84] house return'd,
Was this demanded – if he yearn'd
To hear her weeping by his grave?   640

'Where wert thou, brother, those four days?[85]
There lives no record of reply,
Which telling what it is to die
Had surely added praise to praise.

From every house the neighbours met,   645
The streets were fill'd with joyful sound,
A solemn gladness even crown'd
The purple brows of Olivet.[86]

Behold a man raised up by Christ!
The rest remaineth unreveal'd;   650

---

[79] *seraphic* of seraphim, an order of angels.
[80] *Pierces the keen seraphic flame* i.e., 'the keen seraphic flame pierces'.
[81] *light . . . born* cf. 'Now when Iesus was borne in Bethlehem of Iudea, in the dayes of Herod the king, behold, there came Wise men from the East to Hierusalem, Saying, Where is he that is borne King of the Iewes? for we haue seene his Starre in the East, and are come to worship him', Matthew 2.1–2.

[82] *Lazarus* friend of Jesus whom Jesus raised from the dead (see John 11.30–45).
[83] *charnel-cave* tomb in a cave.
[84] *Mary* Lazarus's sister.
[85] *those four days* Lazarus had lain dead for this period, John 11.39.
[86] *Olivet* Mount of Olives.

He told it not; or something seal'd
The lips of that Evangelist.[87]

32

Her[88] eyes are homes of silent prayer,
Nor other thought her mind admits
But, he was dead, and there he sits,   655
And he that brought him back is there.

Then one deep love doth supersede
All other, when her ardent gaze
Roves from the living brother's face,
And rests upon the Life[89] indeed.   660

All subtle thought, all curious fears,
Borne down by gladness so complete,
She bows, she bathes the Saviour's feet
With costly spikenard[90] and with tears.[91]

Thrice blest whose lives are faithful prayers,   665
Whose loves in higher love endure;
What souls possess themselves so pure,
Or is there blessedness like theirs?

33

O thou that after toil and storm
Mayst seem to have reach'd a purer air,   670
Whose faith has centre everywhere,
Nor cares to fix itself to form,

Leave thou[92] thy sister when she prays,
Her early Heaven, her happy views;
Nor thou with shadow'd hint confuse   675
A life that leads melodious days.

Her faith thro' form is pure as thine,
Her hands are quicker unto good:
Oh, sacred be the flesh and blood
To which she links a truth divine!   680

See thou, that countest reason ripe
In holding by the law within,

[87] *Evangelist* accepted title for the authors of the gospels; here, St John.

[88] *Her* Mary's.

[89] *Life* Jesus (cf. John 11.25, 'Iesus said vnto her, I am the resurrection, and the life: hee that beleeueth in me, though he were dead, yet shall he liue').

[90] *spikenard* aromatic substance (employed in ancient times in the preparation of a costly ointment or oil).

[91] *She bows . . . tears* cf. John 12.3 (after the raising of Lazarus): 'Then tooke Mary a pound of ointment, of Spikenard, very costly, and anointed the feet of Iesus, & wiped his feet with her haire: and the house was filled with the odour of the ointment.'

[92] *thou* cf. 'And shee [Martha] had a sister called Mary, which also sate at Iesus feet, and heard his word: But Martha was cumbred about much seruing, and came to him, and said, Lord, doest thou not care that my sister hath left mee to serue alone? Bid her therefore that she helpe me. And Iesus answered, and saide vnto her, Martha, Martha, thou art carefull, and troubled about many things: But one thing is needefull, and Mary hath chosen that good part, which shall not bee taken away from her', Luke 20.39–42. Tennyson does not refer to this with precision.

Thou fail not in a world of sin,
And ev'n for want of such a type.

(34) *RR*

My own dim life should teach me this,   685
   That life shall live for evermore,
   Else earth is darkness at the core,
    And dust and ashes all that is;

This round of green, this orb of flame,
   Fantastic beauty; such as lurks   690
   In some wild Poet, when he works
    Without a conscience or an aim.

What then were God to such as I?
'Twere hardly worth my while to choose
   Of things all mortal, or to use   695
    A little patience ere I die;

'Twere best at once to sink to peace,
Like birds the charming serpent draws,
   To drop head-foremost in the jaws
    Of vacant darkness and to cease.   700

35

Yet if some voice that man could trust
Should murmur from the narrow house,
   'The cheeks drop in; the body bows;
   Man dies: nor is there hope in dust:'

Might I not say? 'Yet even here,   705
   But for one hour, O Love, I strive
   To keep so sweet a thing alive:'
    But I should turn mine ears and hear

The moanings of the homeless sea,
The sound of streams that swift or slow   710
   Draw down Æonian[93] hills, and sow
    The dust of continents to be;

And Love would answer with a sigh,
   'The sound of that forgetful shore
Will change my sweetness more and more,   715
   Half-dead to know that I shall die.'

O me, what profits it to put
An idle case? If Death were seen
   At first as Death, Love had not been,
   Or been in narrowest working shut,   720

---

[93] *Æonian* everlasting.

> Mere fellowship of sluggish moods,
> Or in his coarsest Satyr-shape[94]
> Had bruised the herb and crush'd the grape,
> And bask'd and batten'd[95] in the woods.

36

Tho' truths in manhood darkly join,   725
Deep-seated in our mystic frame,
We yield all blessing to the name
Of Him[96] that made them current coin;

For Wisdom dealt with mortal powers,
Where truth in closest words shall fail,   730
When truth embodied in a tale
Shall enter in at lowly doors.[97]

And so the Word[98] had breath, and wrought
With human hands the creed of creeds
In loveliness of perfect deeds,   735
More strong than all poetic thought;

Which he may read that binds the sheaf,
Or builds the house, or digs the grave,
And those wild eyes[99] that watch the wave
In roarings round the coral reef.   740

37

Urania[100] speaks with darken'd brow:
'Thou pratest here where thou art least;
This faith has many a purer priest,
And many an abler voice than thou.

'Go down beside thy native rill,   745
On thy Parnassus[101] set thy feet,
And hear thy laurel whisper sweet
About the ledges of the hill.'

And my Melpomene[102] replies,
A touch of shame upon her cheek: 750
'I am not worthy ev'n to speak
Of thy prevailing mysteries;

'For I am but an earthly Muse,
And owning but a little art

---

[94] *Satyr-shape* in the form of a satyr, a largely human creature with some animal elements in Classical myth, given to excessive consumption of wine and sexual pleasure.
[95] *batten'd* glutted.
[96] *Him* Jesus.
[97] *For wisdom . . . doors* Tennyson said, 'For divine Wisdom had to deal with the limited powers of humanity, to which truth logically argued out could be ineffectual, whereas truth coming in the story of the Gospel can influence the poorest'.

[98] *Word* Jesus (cf. John 1.1, 'In the beginning was the Word, & the Word was with God, and the Word was God').
[99] *wild eyes* 'the Pacific Islanders', Tennyson said.
[100] *Urania* 'heavenly one', the Muse of astronomy (the Muses were Greek deities on whom mortals depended for inspiration).
[101] *Parnassus* Greek mountain believed to be the home of the Muses.
[102] *Melpomene* Muse of tragedy.

To lull with song an aching heart,   755
And render human love his dues;

'But brooding on the dear one dead,
And all he said of things divine,
(And dear to me as sacred wine
    To dying lips is all he said),   760

'I murmur'd, as I came along,
Of comfort clasp'd in truth reveal'd;
And loiter'd in the master's field,[103]
And darken'd sanctities with song.'

38

With weary steps I loiter on,   765
Tho' always under alter'd skies
The purple from the distance dies,
My prospect and horizon gone.

No joy the blowing season gives,
The herald melodies of spring,   770
But in the songs I love to sing
A doubtful gleam of solace lives.

If any care for what is here
Survive in spirits render'd free,
Then are these songs I sing of thee   775
Not all ungrateful to thine ear.

39

Old warder[104] of these buried bones,
And answering now my random stroke
With fruitful cloud and living smoke,[105]
Dark yew, that graspest at the stones   780

And dippest toward the dreamless head,
To thee too comes the golden hour
When flower is feeling after flower;[106]
But Sorrow – fixt upon the dead,

And darkening the dark graves of men, –   785
What whisper'd from her lying lips?
Thy gloom is kindled at the tips,
And passes into gloom again.

40

Could we forget the widow'd hour
And look on Spirits breathed away,   790

---

[103] *master's field* 'God's acre' (Tennyson).
[104] *warder* the poet addresses the yew.
[105] *living smoke* 'The yew, when flowering, in a wind or if struck send up its pollen like smoke' (Tennyson).

[106] *flower . . . flower* the yew has separate unisexual male and female flowers.

As on a maiden in the day
When first she wears her orange-flower![107]

When crown'd with blessing she doth rise
To take her latest[108] leave of home,
And hopes and light regrets that come   795
Make April of her tender eyes;

And doubtful joys the father move,
And tears are on the mother's face,
As parting with a long embrace
She enters other realms of love;   800

Her office there to rear, to teach,
Becoming as is meet and fit
A link among the days, to knit
The generations each with each;

And, doubtless, unto thee is given   805
A life that bears immortal fruit
In those great offices that suit
The full-grown energies of heaven.

Ay me, the difference I discern!
How often shall her old fireside   810
Be cheer'd with tidings of the bride,
How often she herself return,

And tell them all they would have told,
And bring her babe, and make her boast,
Till even those that miss'd her most   815
Shall count new things as dear as old:

But thou and I have shaken hands,
Till growing winters lay me low;
My paths are in the fields I know.
And thine in undiscover'd lands.   820

41
Thy spirit ere our fatal loss
Did ever rise from high to higher;
As mounts the heavenward altar-fire,[109]
As flies the lighter thro' the gross.[110]

But thou art turn'd to something strange,[111]   825
And I have lost the links that bound
Thy changes; here upon the ground,
No more partaker of thy change.

[107] *orange-flower* Queen Victoria revived a fashion for wearing orange blossom as a bride at her marriage on 10 February 1840 to Prince Albert.

[108] *latest* last.

[109] *As mounts . . . fire* cf. Judges 13.20, 'For it came to passe, when the flame went vp toward heauen from off the altar, that the Angel of the Lord ascended in the flame of the altar'.

[110] *gross* bodily.

[111] *But thou . . . strange* cf. *The Tempest* 1.2.401–4, 'Nothing of him that doth fade / But doth suffer a sea-change / Into something rich and strange'.

Deep folly! yet that this could be –
That I could wing my will with might   830
To leap the grades of life and light,
And flash at once, my friend, to thee.

For tho' my nature rarely yields
To that vague fear implied in death;
Nor shudders at the gulfs beneath,   835
The howlings from forgotten fields;[112]

Yet oft when sundown skirts the moor
An inner trouble I behold,
A spectral doubt which makes me cold,
That I shall be thy mate no more,   840

Tho' following with an upward mind
The wonders that have come to thee,
Thro' all the secular to-be,[113]
But evermore a life behind.

42

I vex my heart with fancies dim: 845
He still outstript me in the race;
It was but unity of place
That made me dream I rank'd with him.

And so may Place retain us still,
And he the much-beloved again,   850
A lord of large experience, train
To riper growth the mind and will:

And what delights can equal those
That stir the spirit's inner deeps,
When one that loves but knows not, reaps   855
A truth from one that loves and knows?

43

If Sleep and Death be truly one,
And every spirit's folded bloom
Thro' all its intervital[114] gloom
In some long trance should slumber on;   860

Unconscious of the sliding hour,
Bare of the body, might it last,
And silent traces of the past
Be all the colour of the flower:

So then were nothing lost to man;   865
So that still garden of the souls
In many a figured leaf enrolls
The total world since life began;

---

[112] *The howlings . . . fields* 'The eternal miseries of the Inferno' (Tennyson).
[113] *secular to-be* 'æons [ages] of the future' (Tennyson).
[114] *intervital* neologism, existing between two lives or stages of existence.

And love will last as pure and whole
As when he loved me here in Time,
  And at the spiritual prime[115]
Rewaken with the dawning soul.   870

44

How fares it with the happy dead?
For here the man is more and more;
  But he forgets the days before   875
God shut the doorways of his head.

The days have vanish'd, tone and tint,
And yet perhaps the hoarding sense
Gives out at times (he knows not whence)
  A little flash, a mystic hint;   880

And in the long harmonious years
(If Death so taste Lethean[116] springs),
May some dim touch of earthly things
  Surprise thee ranging with thy peers.

If such a dreamy touch should fall,   885
O turn thee round, resolve the doubt;
  My guardian angel will speak out
In that high place, and tell thee all.[117]

45

The baby new to earth and sky,
What time his tender palm is prest   890
  Against the circle of the breast,
Has never thought that 'this is I:'

But as he grows he gathers much,
And learns the use of 'I', and 'me,'
  And finds 'I am not what I see,   895
And other than the things I touch.'

So rounds he to a separate mind
From whence clear memory may begin,
  As thro' the frame that binds him in
His isolation grows defined.   900

This use may lie in blood and breath,
Which else were fruitless of their due,
  Had man to learn himself anew
Beyond the second birth of Death.

---

[115] *prime* morning, dawn.
[116] *Lethean* the Lethe is the river of forgetfulness in Classical mythology.
[117] *If such . . . all* Tennyson said, 'if you *have* forgot all earthly things – yet as a man has faint memories, even so in the new life a sort of vague memory of the past would come. This is fortified by considering that the use of flesh & blood were lost if they do not establish an identity.'

46

We ranging down this lower track,   905
  The path we came by, thorn and flower,
  Is shadow'd by the growing hour,
Lest life should fail in looking back.

So be it: there no shade can last
  In that deep dawn behind the tomb,   910
But clear from marge to marge shall bloom
  The eternal landscape of the past;

A lifelong tract of time reveal'd;
  The fruitful hours of still increase;
  Days order'd in a wealthy peace,   915
And those five years[118] its richest field.

O Love, thy province were not large,
  A bounded field, nor stretching far;
  Look also, Love, a brooding star,
A rosy warmth from marge to marge.   920

47

That each, who seems a separate whole,
  Should move his rounds, and fusing all
  The skirts of self again, should fall
Remerging in the general Soul,

Is faith as vague as all unsweet:[119]   925
  Eternal form shall still divide
  The eternal soul from all beside;
And I shall know him when we meet:

And we shall sit at endless feast,
  Enjoying each the other's good: 930
What vaster dream can hit the mood
  Of Love on earth? He seeks at least

Upon the last and sharpest height,
  Before the spirits fade away,[120]
Some landing-place, to clasp and say,   935
  'Farewell! We lose ourselves in light.'

48

If these brief lays,[121] of Sorrow born,
  Were taken to be such as closed
Grave doubts and answers here proposed,
Then these were such as men might scorn: 940

---

[118] *five years* duration of Tennyson's friendship with Hallam (1828–33).

[119] *That each . . . unsweet* Tennyson remarked, 'The individuality lasts after death, and we are not utterly absorbed into the Godhead. If we are to be finally merged in the Universal Soul, Love asks to have at least one more parting before we lose ourselves.'

[120] *Before . . . away* Tennyson said, 'into the Universal Spirit – but at least one last parting! and always would want it again – of course'.

[121] *lays* songs.

Her care is not to part and prove;
She takes, when harsher moods remit,
What slender shade of doubt may flit,
And makes it vassal[122] unto love:

And hence, indeed, she sports with words,   945
But better serves a wholesome law,
And holds it sin and shame to draw
The deepest measure from the chords:

Nor dare she trust a larger lay,
But rather loosens from the lip   950
Short swallow-flights of song, that dip
Their wings in tears, and skim away.

49

From art, from nature, from the schools,[123]
Let random influences glance,
Like light in many a shiver'd lance   955
That breaks about the dappled pools:

The lightest wave of thought shall lisp,
The fancy's tenderest eddy wreathe,
The slightest air of song shall breathe
To make the sullen surface crisp.   960

And look thy look, and go thy way,[124]
But blame not thou the winds that make
The seeming-wanton ripple break,
The tender-pencil'd shadow play.

Beneath all fancied hopes and fears   965
Ay me, the sorrow deepens down,
Whose muffled motions blindly drown
The bases of my life in tears.

50

Be near me when my light is low,
When the blood creeps, and the nerves prick   970
And tingle; and the heart is sick,
And all the wheels of Being slow.

Be near me when the sensuous frame
Is rack'd with pangs that conquer trust;
And Time, a maniac scattering dust,   975
And Life, a Fury slinging flame.

Be near me when my faith is dry,
And men the flies of latter spring,
That lay their eggs, and sting and sing
And weave their petty cells and die.   980

---

[122] *vassal* servant, subordinate.
[123] *schools* (medieval) divisions of knowledge, universities.

[124] *And look . . . way* Tennyson said this was addressed to the reader.

Be near me when I fade away,
To point the term of human strife,
And on the low dark verge of life
The twilight of eternal day.

51

Do we indeed desire the dead   985
Should still be near us at our side?
Is there no baseness we would hide?
No inner vileness that we dread?

Shall he for whose applause I strove,
I had such reverence for his blame,   990
See with clear eye some hidden shame
And I be lessen'd in his love?

I wrong the grave with fears untrue:
Shall love be blamed for want of faith?
There must be wisdom with great Death: 995
The dead shall look me thro' and thro'.

Be near us when we climb or fall:
Ye watch, like God, the rolling hours
With larger other eyes than ours,
To make allowance for us all.   1000

52

I cannot love thee as I ought,
For love reflects the thing beloved;
My words are only words, and moved
Upon the topmost froth of thought.

'Yet blame not thou thy plaintive song,'   1005
The Spirit of true love replied;
'Thou canst not move me from thy side,
Nor human frailty do me wrong.

'What keeps a spirit wholly true
To that ideal which he bears?   1010
What record? not the sinless years
That breathed beneath the Syrian[125] blue:

'So fret not, like an idle girl,
That life is dash'd with flecks of sin.
Abide: thy wealth is gather'd in,   1015
When Time hath sunder'd shell from pearl.'

53

How many a father have I seen,
A sober man, among his boys,
Whose youth was full of foolish noise,
Who wears his manhood hale[126] and green:[127]   1020

---

[125] *Syrian* of Syria, i.e., the blue of the sea and skies of a country at the far eastern point of the Mediterranean.

[126] *hale* healthy.

[127] *green* fresh, vigorous, young.

And dare we to this fancy give,
That had the wild oat not been sown,
The soil, left barren, scarce had grown
The grain by which a man may live?

Or, if we held the doctrine sound   1025
For life outliving heats of youth,
Yet who would preach it as a truth
To those that eddy round and round?

Hold thou the good: define it well:
For fear divine Philosophy   1030
Should push beyond her mark, and be
Procuress to the Lords of Hell.

54   *seems better here*

Oh yet we trust that somehow good
Will be the final goal of ill,
To pangs of nature, sins of will,   1035
Defects of doubt, and taints of blood;

That nothing walks with aimless feet;
That not one life shall be destroy'd,
Or cast as rubbish to the void,
When God hath made the pile complete;   1040

That not a worm is cloven in vain;
That not a moth with vain desire
Is shrivell'd in a fruitless fire,
Or but subserves[128] another's gain.

Behold, we know not anything;   1045
I can but trust that good shall fall
At last – far off – at last, to all,
And every winter change to spring.

So runs my dream: but what am I?
An infant crying in the night: 1050
An infant crying for the light:
And with no language but a cry.[129]

55

The wish, that of the living whole
No life may fail beyond the grave,
Derives it not from what we have   1055
The likest God within the soul?

Are God and Nature then at strife,
That Nature lends such evil dreams?
So careful of the type[130] she seems,
So careless of the single life;   1060

---

[128] *subserves* is subservient to.
[129] *no language . . . cry* 'infant' derives from the Latin 'infans', 'unable to speak'.
[130] *type* species.

That I, considering everywhere
Her secret meaning in her deeds,
And finding that of fifty seeds
She often brings but one to bear,

I falter where I firmly trod,   1065
And falling with my weight of cares
Upon the great world's altar-stairs
That slope thro' darkness up to God,

I stretch lame hands of faith, and grope,
And gather dust and chaff, and call   1070
To what I feel is Lord of all,
And faintly trust the larger hope.

(56) ? ₧₧

'So careful of the type?' but no.
From scarpèd[131] cliff and quarried stone
She cries, 'A thousand types are gone:[132]   1075
I care for nothing, all shall go.

'Thou makest thine appeal to me:
I bring to life, I bring to death:
The spirit does but mean the breath:
I know no more.' And he, shall he,   1080

Man, her last work, who seem'd so fair,
Such splendid purpose in his eyes,
Who roll'd the psalm to wintry skies,
Who built him fanes[133] of fruitless prayer,

Who trusted God was love[134] indeed   1085
And love Creation's final law –
Tho' Nature, red in tooth and claw
With ravine,[135] shriek'd against his creed –

Who loved, who suffer'd countless ills,
Who battled for the True, the Just,   1090
Be blown about the desert dust,
Or seal'd within the iron hills?

No more? A monster then, a dream,
A discord. Dragons of the prime,[136]
That tare each other in their slime,   1095
Were mellow music match'd with him.

O life as futile, then, as frail!
O for thy voice to soothe and bless!

[131] *scarpèd* with a steep face cut into it, reduced to a steep face.
[132] *thousand . . . gone* the quarries and cliffs reveal fossils of species lost in their entirety.
[133] *fanes* temples.

[134] *God was love* cf. John 4.16, 'God is loue, and hee that dwelleth in loue, dwelleth in God, and God in him'.
[135] *ravine* violence, force.
[136] *prime* morning of life on earth, primal.

What hope of answer, or redress?
Behind the veil, behind the veil.   1100

57

Peace; come away: the song of woe
Is after all an earthly song:
Peace; come away: we do him wrong
To sing so wildly: let us go.

Come; let us go: your cheeks are pale;   1105
But half my life I leave behind:
Methinks my friend is richly shrined;
But I shall pass; my work will fail.

Yet in these ears, till hearing dies,
One set slow bell will seem to toll   1110
The passing of the sweetest soul
That ever look'd with human eyes.

I hear it now, and o'er and o'er
Eternal greetings to the dead;
And 'Ave, Ave, Ave,'[137] said,   1115
'Adieu, adieu'[138] for evermore.

58

In those sad words I took farewell:
Like echoes in sepulchral[139] halls,
As drop by drop the water falls
In vaults and catacombs,[140] they fell;   1120

And, falling, idly broke the peace
Of hearts that beat from day to day,
Half-conscious of their dying clay,
And those cold crypts[141] where they shall cease

The high Muse answer'd: 'Wherefore grieve   1125
Thy brethren with a fruitless tear?
Abide a little longer here,
And thou shalt take a nobler leave.'

59

O Sorrow, wilt thou live with me
No casual mistress, but a wife,   1130
My bosom-friend and half of life;
As I confess it needs must be;

O Sorrow, wilt thou rule my blood,
Be sometimes lovely like a bride,

---

[137] *Ave, Ave, Ave* reference to Catullus, '*Accipe fraterno
multum manantia fletu, / atque in perpetuum, frater, ave atque
vale*' ('Take them, wet with many tears of a brother, and for
ever, O my brother, hail and farewell!'). Tennyson said of
these lines that no 'modern elegy, so long as men retain the
least hope in the after-life of those whom they loved, equal
in pathos the desolation of that everlasting farewell'. Cf.

Swinburne's '*Ave Atque Vale*: In Memory of Charles
Baudelaire', 500–6.
[138] *Adieu* lit. 'I commend you to God' (French); farewell.
[139] *sepulchral* of sepulchres, tombs.
[140] *catacombs* underground burial places.
[141] *crypts* rooms constructed in foundations of churches,
often used as burial places.

And put thy harsher moods aside,[142]　　　　　　　　　　1135
If thou wilt have me wise and good.[143]

My centred passion cannot move,
　Nor will it lessen from to-day;
　But I'll have leave at times to play
As with the creature of my love;　　　　　　　　　　　1140

And set thee forth, for thou art mine,
　With so much hope for years to come,
　That, howsoe'er I know thee, some
Could hardly tell what name were thine.

60

He past; a soul of nobler tone:　　　　　　　　　　　1145
　My spirit loved and loves him yet,
　Like some poor girl whose heart is set
On one whose rank exceeds her own.

He mixing with his proper sphere,
　She finds the baseness of her lot,　　　　　　　　　1150
　Half jealous of she knows not what,
And envying all that meet him there.

The little village looks forlorn;
　She sighs amid her narrow days,
　Moving about the household ways,　　　　　　　　　1155
In that dark house where she was born.

The foolish neighbours come and go,
　And tease her till the day draws by:
　At night she weeps, 'How vain am I!
How should he love a thing so low?'　　　　　　　　1160

61

If, in thy second state sublime,[144]
　Thy ransom'd[145] reason change replies
　With all the circle of the wise,
The perfect flower of human time;

And if thou cast thine eyes below,　　　　　　　　　1165
　How dimly character'd and slight,
　How dwarf'd a growth of cold and night,
How blanch'd with darkness must I grow!

Yet turn thee to the doubtful shore,
　Where thy first form was made a man;　　　　　　1170

---

[142] *harsher . . . aside* Tennyson said, 'A time has now elapsed & he treats sorrow in a more familiar and less dreading way'.
[143] *O Sorrow . . . good* Tennyson alludes gently, and ironically, to the wedding service from the Book of Common Prayer: 'Wilte thou have this woman to thy wedded wife, to live together after Goddes ordeinaunce in the holy estate of matrimonie? Wilt thou love her,

coumforte her, honor, and kepe her in sickenesse and in health? And forsaking all other kepe thee only to her, so long as you both shall live?'
[144] *second . . . sublime* in heaven, transformed.
[145] *ransom'd* redeemed, like all people in Christian theology, through Jesus's death.

I loved thee, Spirit, and love, nor can
The soul of Shakspeare[146] love thee more.

62

Tho' if an eye that's downward cast
Could make thee somewhat blench[147] or fail,
    Then be my love an idle tale,   1175
    And fading legend of the past;

And thou, as one that once declined,
When he was little more than boy,
    On some unworthy heart with joy,
    But lives to wed an equal mind;   1180

And breathes a novel world, the while
His other passion wholly dies,
    Or in the light of deeper eyes
    Is matter for a flying smile.

63

Yet pity for a horse o'er-driven,   1185
And love in which my hound has part,
    Can hang no weight upon my heart
    In its assumptions up to heaven;[148]

And I am so much more than these,
As thou, perchance, art more than I,   1190
    And yet I spare them sympathy,
    And I would set their pains at ease.

So mayst thou watch me where I weep,
As, unto vaster motions bound,
    The circuits of thine orbit round   1195
    A higher height, a deeper deep.

64

Dost thou look back on what hath been,
As some divinely gifted man,
    Whose life in low estate began
    And on a simple village green;   1200

Who breaks his birth's invidious[149] bar,
And grasps the skirts of happy chance,
    And breasts the blows of circumstance,
    And grapples with his evil star;

Who makes by force his merit known   1205
And lives to clutch the golden keys,

---

[146] *Shakspeare* a favourite author of Hallam's, who called him 'the most universal mind that ever existed'.

[147] *blench* flinch, shrink away.

[148] *Yet pity . . . heaven* Tennyson said, 'Man can love below as well as above himself; So surely it cannot be a weight on the Spirit [of Hallam] to remember the writer [of *In Memoriam*]'.

[149] *invidious* that which incites ill-feeling, evil.

To mould a mighty state's decrees,
And shape the whisper of the throne;

And moving up from high to higher,
Becomes on Fortune's crowning slope   1210
The pillar of a people's hope,
The centre of a world's desire;

Yet feels, as in a pensive dream,
When all his active powers are still,
A distant dearness in the hill,   1215
A secret sweetness in the stream,

The limit of his narrower fate,
While yet beside its vocal springs
He play'd at counsellors and kings.
With one that was his earliest mate;   1220

Who ploughs with pain his native lea[150]
And reaps the labour of his hands,
Or in the furrow musing stands;
'Does my old friend remember me?'

65
Sweet soul, do with me as thou wilt;   1225
I lull a fancy trouble-tost
With 'Love's too precious to be lost,
A little grain shall not be spilt.'

And in that solace can I sing,
Till out of painful phases wrought   1230
There flutters up a happy thought,
Self-balanced on a lightsome wing:

Since we deserved the name of friends,
And thine effect so lives in me,
A part of mine may live in thee   1235
And move thee on to noble ends.

66
You[151] thought my heart too far diseased;
You wonder when my fancies play
To find me gay among the gay,
Like one with any trifle pleased.   1240

The shade by which my life was crost,
Which makes a desert in the mind,
Has made me kindly with my kind,
And like to him whose sight is lost;

Whose feet are guided thro' the land,   1245
Whose jest among his friends is free,

---

[150] *lea* meadow.   [151] *You* Tennyson said 'the auditor'.

Who takes the children on his knee,
And winds their curls about his hand:

He plays with threads, he beats his chair
For pastime, dreaming of the sky;   1250
His inner day can never die,
His night of loss is always there.

67

When on my bed the moonlight falls,
I know that in thy place of rest
By that broad water of the west,[152]   1255
There comes a glory on the walls;

Thy marble bright in dark appears,
As slowly steals a silver flame
Along the letters of thy name,
And o'er the number of thy years.   1260

The mystic glory swims away;
From off my bed the moonlight dies;
And closing eaves of wearied eyes
I sleep till dusk is dipt in gray:

And then I know the mist is drawn   1265
A lucid veil from coast to coast,
And in the dark church[153] like a ghost
Thy tablet glimmers to the dawn.

68

When in the down[154] I sink my head,
Sleep, Death's twin-brother, times my breath;   1270
Sleep, Death's twin-brother, knows not Death,
Nor can I dream of thee as dead:

I walk as ere I walk'd forlorn,
When all our path was fresh with dew,
And all the bugle breezes blew   1275
Reveillée[155] to the breaking morn.

But what is this? I turn about,
I find a trouble in thine eye,
Which makes me sad I know not why,
Nor can my dream resolve the doubt: 1280

But ere the lark hath left the lea
I wake, and I discern the truth;
It is the trouble of my youth
That foolish sleep transfers to thee.

---

[152] *broad water . . . west* Bristol Channel.
[153] *dark church* Clevedon, where Hallam lies buried.
[154] *down* i.e., pillow of feathers.

[155] *Reveillée* reveille (UK pron. ree-valley), the morning bugle call in the British Army.

69

I dream'd there would be Spring no more,   1285
That Nature's ancient power was lost:
The streets were black with smoke and frost,
They chatter'd trifles at the door:

I wander'd from the noisy town,
I found a wood with thorny boughs: 1290
I took the thorns to bind my brows,
I wore them like a civic crown:

I met with scoffs, I met with scorns
From youth and babe and hoary[156] hairs:
They call'd me in the public squares   1295
The fool that wears a crown of thorns:[157]

They call'd me fool, they call'd me child:
I found an angel of the night;
The voice was low, the look was bright;
He look'd upon my crown and smiled: 1300

He reach'd the glory of a hand,
That seem'd to touch it into leaf:
The voice was not the voice of grief,
The words were hard to understand.

70

Captivating

I cannot see the features right,   1305
When on the gloom I strive to paint
The face I know; the hues are faint
And mix with hollow masks of night;

Cloud-towers by ghostly masons wrought,
A gulf that ever shuts and gapes,   1310
A hand that points, and pallèd[158] shapes
In shadowy thoroughfares of thought;

And crowds that stream from yawning doors,
And shoals of pucker'd faces drive;
Dark bulks that tumble half alive,
And lazy lengths on boundless shores;   1315

Till all at once beyond the will
I hear a wizard music roll,
And thro' a lattice on the soul
Looks thy fair face and makes it still.   1320

71

Sleep, kinsman thou to death and trance
And madness, thou hast forged at last

---

[156] *hoary* grey with age.

[157] *crown of thorns* Tennyson said, 'To write poems about death and grief is "to wear a crown of thorns," which the people say ought to be laid aside'.

[158] *pallèd* wearing palls, funeral cloths placed over coffins.

A night-long Present of the Past
In which we went thro' summer France.[159]

Hadst thou such credit with the soul?   1325
Then bring an opiate trebly strong,
Drug down the blindfold sense of wrong
That so my pleasure may be whole;

While now we talk as once we talk'd
Of men and minds, the dust of change,   1330
The days that grow to something strange,
In walking as of old we walk'd

Beside the river's wooded reach,
The fortress, and the mountain ridge,
The cataract flashing from the bridge,   1335
The breaker breaking on the beach.

72
Risest thou thus, dim dawn,[160] again,
And howlest, issuing out of night,
With blasts that blow the poplar white,
And lash with storm the streaming pane?   1340

Day, when my crown'd estate[161] begun
To pine in that reverse of doom,[162]
Which sicken'd every living bloom,
And blurr'd the splendour of the sun;

Who usherest in the dolorous[163] hour   1345
With thy quick tears that make the rose
Pull sideways, and the daisy close
Her crimson fringes to the shower;

Who might'st have heaved a windless flame
Up the deep East, or, whispering, play'd   1350
A chequer-work of beam and shade
Along the hills, yet look'd the same.

As wan,[164] as chill, as wild as now;
Day, mark'd as with some hideous crime,
When the dark hand struck down thro' time,   1355
And cancell'd nature's best: but thou,

Lift as thou may'st thy burthen'd brows
Thro' clouds that drench the morning star,
And whirl the ungarner'd[165] sheaf afar,
And sow the sky with flying boughs,   1360

---

[159] *summer France* Tennyson and Hallam had toured the south of France in 1830.
[160] *dim dawn* anniversary of Hallam's death (15 September).
[161] *estate* he imagines himself as the possessor of royal lands.

[162] *reverse of doom* reversal of life ordained by fate, the death of Hallam.
[163] *dolorous* sad, sorrowful.
[164] *wan* pale.
[165] *ungarner'd* ungathered.

And up thy vault[166] with roaring sound
Climb thy thick noon, disastrous day;
Touch thy dull goal of joyless gray,
And hide thy shame[167] beneath the ground.

73

So many worlds, so much to do,   1365
So little done, such things to be,
How know I what had need of thee,
For thou wert strong as thou wert true?

The fame is quench'd that I foresaw,
The head hath miss'd an earthly wreath: 1370
I curse not nature, no, nor death;
For nothing is that errs from law.

We pass; the path that each man trod
Is dim, or will be dim, with weeds:
What fame is left for human deeds   1375
In endless age? It rests with God.

O hollow wraith[168] of dying fame,
Fade wholly, while the soul exults,
And self-infolds the large results
Of force that would have forged a name.   1380

74

As sometimes in a dead man's face,
To those that watch it more and more,
A likeness, hardly seen before,
Comes out – to some one of his race:

So, dearest, now thy brows are cold,   1385
I see thee what thou art, and know
Thy likeness to the wise below,
Thy kindred with the great of old.

But there is more than I can see,
And what I see I leave unsaid,   1390
Nor speak it, knowing Death has made
His darkness beautiful with thee.[169]

75

I leave thy praises unexpress'd
In verse that brings myself relief,
And by the measure of my grief   1395
I leave thy greatness to be guess'd;

What practice howsoe'er expert
In fitting aptest words to things,

---

[166] *vault* of the sky.
[167] *shame* of having been the day on which Hallam died.
[168] *wraith* spectre, apparition of a dead person.

[169] *His darkness . . . thee* Hallam had written an essay including Petrarch's line on the dead Laura: 'Death appeared lovely in that lovely face'.

Or voice the richest-toned that sings,
Hath power to give thee as thou wert?   1400

I care not in these fading days
To raise a cry that lasts not long,
And round thee with the breeze of song
To stir a little dust of praise.

Thy leaf has perish'd in the green,   1405
And, while we breathe beneath the sun,
The world which credits what is done
Is cold to all that might have been.

So here shall silence guard thy fame;
But somewhere, out of human view,   1410
Whate'er thy hands are set to do
Is wrought with tumult of acclaim.

76
Take wings of fancy, and ascend,
And in a moment set thy face
Where all the starry heavens of space   1415
Are sharpen'd to a needle's end;

Take wings of foresight; lighten thro'
The secular abyss[170] to come,
And lo, thy deepest lays are dumb
Before the mouldering of a yew,[171]   1420

And if the matin[172] songs, that woke
The darkness of our planet, last,
Thine[173] own shall wither in the vast,
Ere half the lifetime of an oak.

Ere these have clothed their branchy bowers   1425
With fifty Mays, thy songs are vain;
And what are they when these remain
The ruin'd shells of hollow towers?

77
What hope is here for modern rhyme
To him, who turns a musing eye   1430
On songs, and deeds, and lives, that lie
Foreshorten'd in the tract of time?

These mortal lullabies of pain
May bind a book,[174] may line a box,
May serve to curl a maiden's locks;[175]   1435
Or when a thousand moons shall wane

---

[170] *secular abyss* the future.
[171] *mouldering of a yew* (on Hallam's grave).
[172] *matin* morning; Tennyson said 'matin songs' referred to 'the great early poets'.

[173] *Thine* Tennyson addresses himself.
[174] *bind a book* unwanted printed material was often used in the binding of books in the nineteenth century.
[175] *curl . . . locks* paper was used to help curl hair.

A man upon a stall may find,
And, passing, turn the page that tells
A grief, then changed to something else.
Sung by a long-forgotten mind.   1440

But what of that? My darken'd ways
Shall ring with music all the same;
To breathe my loss is more than fame,
To utter love more sweet than praise.

78
Again at Christmas did we weave   1445
The holly round the Christmas hearth;
The silent snow possess'd the earth,
And calmly fell our Christmas-eve:

The yule-clog[176] sparkled keen with frost,
No wing of wind the region swept,   1450
But over all things brooding slept
The quiet sense of something lost.

As in the winters left behind,
Again our ancient games had place,
The mimic picture's breathing grace,[177]   1455
And dance and song and hoodman-blind.[178]

Who show'd a token of distress?
No single tear, no mark of pain:
O sorrow, then can sorrow wane?
O grief, can grief be changed to less?   1460

O last regret, regret can die!
No – mixt with all this mystic frame.
Her deep relations are the same,
But with long use her tears are dry.

79[179]
'More than my brothers are to me,' – [180]   1465
Let this not vex thee, noble heart!
I know thee of what force thou art
To hold the costliest love in fee.[181]

But thou and I are one in kind,
As moulded like in Nature's mint;   1470
And hill and wood and field did print
The same sweet forms in either mind.

For us the same cold streamlet curl'd
Thro' all his eddying coves;[182] the same

[176] *yule-clog* log placed on the fire at Christmas Eve, its burning a reminder of the returning sun.
[177] *mimic . . . grace tableaux vivants*, stationary mimes of scenes, a Victorian entertainment.
[178] *hoodman-blind* blind man's buff, a party game.

[179] *lyric 79* addressed to Tennyson's brother Charles Tennyson Turner.
[180] *'More . . . me,'* cf. l. 220.
[181] *fee* i.e., on condition of homage and service.
[182] *coves* bays, inlets.

All winds that roam the twilight came 1475
In whispers of the beauteous world.

At one dear knee we proffer'd vows,
One lesson from one book we learn'd,
Ere childhood's flaxen ringlet turn'd
To black and brown on kindred brows. 1480

And so my wealth[183] resembles thine,[184]
But he[185] was rich where I was poor,
And he supplied my want the more
As his unlikeness fitted mine.

80
If any vague desire should rise, 1485
That holy Death ere Arthur died
Had moved me kindly from his side,
And dropt the dust on tearless eyes;

Then fancy shapes, as fancy can,
The grief my loss in him had wrought, 1490
A grief as deep as life or thought,
But stay'd in peace with God and man.

I make a picture in the brain;
I hear the sentence that he speaks;
He bears the burthen[186] of the weeks 1495
But turns his burthen into gain.

His credit thus shall set me free;
And, influence rich to soothe and save,
Unused example from the grave
Reach out dead hands to comfort me. 1500

81
Could I have said while he was here,[187]
'My love shall now no further range;
There cannot come a mellower change,
For now is love mature in ear.'

Love, then, had hope of richer store: 1505
What end is here to my complaint?
This haunting whisper makes me faint,
'More years had made me love thee more.'

But Death returns an answer sweet:
'My sudden frost was sudden gain, 1510
And gave all ripeness to the grain,
It might have drawn from after-heat.'

---

[183] *wealth* Hallam.
[184] *thine* Charles Tennyson Turner was more prosperous than Tennyson.
[185] *he* Hallam.

[186] *burthen* burden.
[187] *Could I have said* Tennyson said this meant 'Would that I could have said'.

82

I wage not any feud with Death
For changes wrought on form and face;
No lower life that earth's embrace
May breed with him, can fright my faith.   1515

Eternal process moving on,
From state to state the spirit walks;
And these are but the shatter'd stalks,
Or ruin'd chrysalis of one.   1520

Nor blame I Death, because he bare
The use of virtue out of earth:
I know transplanted human worth
Will bloom to profit, otherwhere.

For this alone on Death I wreak   1525
The wrath that garners in my heart;
He put our lives so far apart
We cannot hear each other speak.

83

Dip down upon the northern shore,
O sweet new-year delaying long;   1530
Thou doest expectant nature wrong;
Delaying long, delay no more.

What stays thee from the clouded noons,
Thy sweetness from its proper place?
Can trouble live with April days,   1535
Or sadness in the summer moons?

Bring orchis,[188] bring the foxglove spire,
The little speedwell's[189] darling blue,
Deep tulips dash'd with fiery dew,
Laburnums,[190] dropping-wells of fire.   1540

O thou, new-year, delaying long,
Delayest the sorrow in my blood,
That longs to burst a frozen bud
And flood a fresher throat with song.

84

When I contemplate all alone   1545
The life that had been thine below,
And fix my thoughts on all the glow
To which thy crescent would have grown;

I see thee sitting crown'd with good,
A central warmth diffusing bliss   1550
In glance and smile, and clasp and kiss,
On all the branches of thy blood;

[188] *orchis* orchids.
[189] *speedwell* small plant with blue flowers.

[190] *Laburnum* small tree that produces long pendulous yellow flowers.

Thy blood, my friend, and partly mine;[191]
For now the day was drawing on,
When thou should'st link thy life with one   1555
Of mine own house, and boys of thine

Had babbled 'Uncle' on my knee;
But that remorseless iron hour
Made cypress[192] of her orange flower,
Despair of Hope, and earth of thee.   1560

I seem to meet their least desire,
To clap their cheeks, to call them mine.
I see their unborn faces shine
Beside the never-lighted fire.

I see myself an honour'd guest,   1565
Thy partner in the flowery walk
Of letters, genial table-talk,
Or deep dispute, and graceful jest:

While now thy prosperous labour fills
The lips of men with honest praise,   1570
And sun by sun the happy days
Descend below the golden hills

With promise of a morn as fair;
And all the train of bounteous hours
Conduct by paths of growing powers,   1575
To reverence and the silver hair;

Till slowly worn her earthly robe,
Her lavish mission richly wrought,
Leaving great legacies of thought,
Thy spirit should fail from off the globe;   1580

What time mine own might also flee,
As link'd with thine in love and fate,
And, hovering o'er the dolorous strait
To the other shore, involved in thee,

Arrive at last the blessed goal,   1585
And He[193] that died in Holy Land
Would reach us out the shining hand,
And take us as a single soul.

What reed was that on which I leant?
Ah, backward fancy, wherefore wake   1590
The old bitterness again, and break
The low beginnings of content.

[191] *partly mine* Hallam had been engaged to Emily,
Tennyson's sister; see headnote, 88.

[192] *cypress* tree associated with death and burial.
[193] *He* Jesus.

85

This truth came borne with bier[194] and pall,
I felt it, when I sorrow'd most,
'Tis better to have loved and lost,
Than never to have loved at all – [195]   1595

O true in word, and tried in deed,
Demanding, so to bring relief
To this which is our common grief,
What kind of life is that I lead;   1600

And whether trust in things above
Be dimm'd of sorrow, or sustain'd;
And whether love for him have drain'd
My capabilities of love;

Your words have virtue such as draws   1605
A faithful answer from the breast,
Thro' light reproaches, half exprest,
And loyal unto kindly laws.

My blood an even tenor kept,
Till on mine ear this message falls,   1610
That in Vienna's fatal walls[196]
God's finger touch'd him, and he slept.

The great Intelligences fair
That range above our mortal state,
In circle round the blessed gate,   1615
Received and gave him welcome there;

And led him thro' the blissful climes,
And show'd him in the fountain fresh
All knowledge that the sons of flesh
Shall gather in the cycled times.   1620

But I remain'd, whose hopes were dim,
Whose life, whose thoughts were little worth,
To wander on a darken'd earth,
Where all things round me breathed of him.

O friendship, equal-poised control,   1625
O heart, with kindliest motion warm,
O sacred essence, other form,
O solemn ghost, O crowned soul!

Yet none could better know than I,
How much of act at human hands   1630
The sense of human will demands
By which we dare to live or die.

---

[194] *bier* stand for a coffin or corpse before burial.   [196] *Vienna's fatal walls* Hallam died in Vienna.
[195] *'Tis better . . . at all* cf. ll.567–8.

Whatever way my days decline,
I felt and feel, tho' left alone,
His being working in mine own,   1635
    The footsteps of his life in mine;

A life that all the Muses deck'd
With gifts of grace, that might express
All-comprehensive tenderness,
    All-subtilising intellect: 1640

And so my passion hath not swerved
To works of weakness, but I find
An image comforting the mind,
    And in my grief a strength reserved.

Likewise the imaginative woe,   1645
That loved to handle spiritual strife
Diffused the shock thro' all my life,
    But in the present broke the blow.

My pulses therefore beat again
For other friends that once I met;   1650
    Nor can it suit me to forget
The mighty hopes that make us men.

I woo your love: I count it crime
To mourn for any overmuch;
    I, the divided half of such   1655
A friendship as had master'd Time;

Which masters Time indeed, and is
Eternal, separate from fears:
The all-assuming months and years
    Can take no part away from this: 1660

But Summer on the steaming floods,
And Spring that swells the narrow brooks,
And Autumn, with a noise of rooks,
    That gather in the waning woods,

And every pulse of wind and wave   1665
Recalls, in change of light or gloom,
    My old affection of the tomb,
And my prime passion in the grave:

My old affection of the tomb,
A part of stillness, yearns to speak;   1670
    'Arise, and get thee forth and seek
A friendship for the years to come.

'I watch thee from the quiet shore;
Thy spirit up to mine can reach;
But in dear words of human speech   1675
    We two communicate no more.'

And I, 'Can clouds of nature stain
The starry clearness of the free?
How is it? Canst thou feel for me
Some painless sympathy with pain?'   1680

And lightly does the whisper fall;
'Tis hard for thee to fathom this;
I triumph in conclusive bliss,
And that serene result of all.'

So hold I commerce with the dead;   1685
Or so methinks the dead would say;
Or so shall grief with symbols play
And pining life be fancy-fed.

Now looking to some settled end,
That these things pass, and I shall prove   1690
A meeting somewhere, love with love,
I crave your pardon, O my friend;

If not so fresh, with love as true,
I, clasping brother-hands, aver
I could not, if I would, transfer   1695
The whole I felt for him to you.

For which be they that hold apart
The promise of the golden hours?
First love, first friendship, equal powers,
That marry with the virgin heart.   1700

Still mine, that cannot but deplore,
That beats within a lonely place,
That yet remembers his embrace,
But at his footstep leaps no more,

My heart, tho' widow'd, may not rest   1705
Quite in the love of what is gone,
But seeks to beat in time with one
That warms another living breast.[197]

Ah, take the imperfect gift I bring,
Knowing the primrose yet is dear,   1710
The primrose of the later year,
As not unlike to that of Spring.

86

Sweet after showers, ambrosial[198] air,
That rollest from the gorgeous gloom

---

[197] *But seeks . . . living breast* Tennyson said this referred to 'a friend', unnamed. Other commentators have thought it may refer to Emily Sellwood, whom Tennyson later married.

[198] *ambrosial* of ambrosia, legendary food of gods and immortals in Greek mythology.

Of evening over brake[199] and bloom
And meadow, slowly breathing bare   1715

The round of space, and rapt below
Thro' all the dewy-tassell'd wood,
And shadowing down the hornèd flood[200]
In ripples, fan my brows and blow   1720

The fever from my cheek, and sigh
The full new life that feeds thy breath
Throughout my frame, till Doubt and Death,
I'll brethren, let the fancy fly

From belt to belt of crimson seas   1725
On leagues[201] of odour streaming far,
To where in yonder orient star
A hundred spirits whisper 'Peace.'[202]

87   College

I past beside the reverend walls[203]
In which of old I wore the gown;[204]   1730
I roved at random thro' the town,
And saw the tumult of the halls;[205]

And heard once more in college fanes[206]
The storm their high-built organs[207] make,
And thunder-music, rolling, shake   1735
The prophet blazon'd on the panes;[208]

And caught once more the distant shout,
The measured pulse of racing oars
Among the willows;[209] paced the shores
And many a bridge, and all about   1740

The same gray flats[210] again, and felt
The same, but not the same; and last
Up that long walk of limes I past
To see the rooms in which he dwelt.

Another name was on the door;[211]   1745
I linger'd; all within was noise
Of songs, and clapping hands, and boys
That crash'd the glass and beat the floor;

---

[199] *brake* undergrowth, bracken.
[200] *hornèd flood* 'between two promontories', Tennyson said.
[201] *leagues* measurement at sea, 3 nautical miles.
[202] *From belt . . . 'Peace'* Tennyson said, 'The west wind rolling to the Eastern seas till its meets the evening star'.
[203] *reverend walls* Trinity College Cambridge, where Tennyson and Hallam had been undergraduates.
[204] *gown* undergraduate academic gown.
[205] *halls* dining halls.
[206] *fanes* see note 133.

[207] *high-built organs* high built because often on the choir screen between nave and chancel (e.g., at Trinity College [Tennyson's college] and King's College).
[208] *prophet . . . panes* figure of Biblical prophet on stained-glass chapel windows.
[209] *willows* the River Cam, on which undergraduate rowing takes place, has willows on its banks.
[210] *gray flats* Cambridge is situated amid the flat fenland of Cambridgeshire.
[211] *Another . . . door* college rooms had their occupant's name on their doors.

Where once we held debate, a band
Of youthful friends, on mind and art,
And labour, and the changing mart,[212]
And all the framework of the land;

1750

When one would aim an arrow fair,
But send it slackly from the string;
And one would pierce an outer ring,[213]
And one an inner, here and there;

1755

And last the master-bowman, he,
Would cleave the mark. A willing ear
We lent him. Who, but hung to hear
The rapt oration flowing free

1760

From point to point, with power and grace
And music in the bounds of law,
To those conclusions when we saw
The God within him light his face,

And seem to lift the form, and glow
In azure orbits heavenly-wise;
And over those ethereal eyes
The bar of Michael Angelo.[214]

1765

88

Wild bird, whose warble, liquid sweet,
Rings Eden[215] thro' the budded quicks,[216]
O tell me where the senses mix,
O tell me where the passions meet,

1770

Whence radiate: fierce extremes employ
Thy spirits in the darkening leaf,
And in the midmost heart of grief
Thy passion clasps a secret joy:

1775

And I – my harp would prelude woe –
I cannot all command the strings;
The glory of the sum of things
Will flash along the chords and go.[217]

1780

89

Witch-elms that counterchange[218] the floor
Of this flat lawn with dusk and bright;
And thou, with all thy breadth and height
Of foliage, towering sycamore;

---

[212] *mart* market.
[213] *outer ring* of an archery target.
[214] *bar of Michael Angelo* Tennyson said, 'the broad bar of frontal bone over the eyes of Michael Angelo' (Hallam himself, rather egotistically, had said, 'surely I have the bar of Michael Angelo!'). Michelangelo Buonarroti (1475–1564) was a great Italian Renaissance sculptor, painter, architect and poet.

[215] *Eden* paradise.
[216] *quicks* couch grasses, field grasses.
[217] *Wild bird . . . and go* on this section, cf. Hardy's 'The Darkling Thrush', 512–13.
[218] *counterchange* chequer.

How often, hither wandering down,
My Arthur found your shadows fair,
And shook to all the liberal air
The dust and din and steam of town:

1785

He brought an eye for all he saw;
He mixt in all our simple sports;
They pleased him, fresh from brawling courts
And dusty purlieus[219] of the law.

1790

O joy to him in this retreat,
Immantled in ambrosial dark,
To drink the cooler air, and mark
The landscape winking thro' the heat:

1795

O sound to rout the brood of cares,
The sweep of scythe in morning dew,
The gust that round the garden flew,
And tumbled half the mellowing pears!

1800

O bliss, when all in circle drawn
About him, heart and ear were fed
To hear him, as he lay and read
The Tuscan[220] poets on the lawn:

Or in the all-golden afternoon
A guest, or happy sister, sung,
Or here she brought the harp and flung
A ballad to the brightening moon:

1805

Nor less it pleased in livelier moods,
Beyond the bounding hill to stray,
And break the livelong summer day
With banquet in the distant woods;

1810

Whereat we glanced from theme to theme,
Discuss'd the books to love or hate,
Or touch'd the changes of the state,
Or threaded some Socratic[221] dream;

1815

But if I praised the busy town,
He loved to rail against it still,
For 'ground in yonder social mill
We rub each other's angles down,

1820

'And merge' he said 'in form and gloss
The picturesque of man and man.'
We talk'd: the stream beneath us ran,
The wine-flask lying couch'd in moss,

---

[219] *purlieus* outskirts.
[220] *Tuscan* of Tuscany, area in northern Italy.

[221] *Socratic* literally, of Socrates (469–399 BC), Greek philosopher, but Tennyson means more generally 'philosophical'.

Or cool'd within the glooming[222] wave;   1825
And last, returning from afar,
Before the crimson-circled star
Had fall'n into her father's grave,[223]

And brushing ankle-deep in flowers,
We heard behind the woodbine[224] veil   1830
The milk that bubbled in the pail,
And buzzings of the honied hours.

90

He tasted love with half his mind,
Nor ever drank the inviolate spring
Where nighest heaven, who first could fling   1835
This bitter seed among mankind;

That could the dead, whose dying eyes
Were closed with wail, resume their life,
They would but find in child and wife
An iron welcome when they rise: 1840

'Twas well, indeed, when warm with wine,
To pledge them with a kindly tear,
To talk them o'er, to wish them here,
To count their memories half divine;

But if they came who past away,   1845
Behold their brides in other hands;
The hard heir strides about their lands,
And will not yield them for a day.

Yea, tho' their sons were none of these,
Not less the yet-loved sire would make   1850
Confusion worse than death, and shake
The pillars of domestic peace.

Ah dear, but come thou back to me:
Whatever change the years have wrought,
I find not yet one lonely thought   1855
That cries against my wish for thee.

91

When rosy plumelets[225] tuft the larch,
And rarely pipes the mounted thrush;
Or underneath the barren bush
Flits by the sea-blue bird of March;[226]   1860

Come, wear the form by which I know
Thy spirit in time among thy peers;

---

[222] *glooming* dark, but perhaps with its more obscure, dialectal sense of gleaming, shining.
[223] *Before . . . grave* Tennyson noted, 'Before Venus, the evening star, had dipt into the sunset'.
[224] *woodbine* honeysuckle (Tennyson pronounced it 'wood bin').
[225] *plumelets* minute plumes.
[226] *sea-blue . . . March* kingfisher.

The hope of unaccomplish'd years
Be large and lucid round thy brow.

When summer's hourly-mellowing change   1865
May breathe, with many roses sweet,
Upon the thousand waves of wheat,
That ripple round the lonely grange;

Come: not in watches of the night,
But where the sunbeam broodeth warm,   1870
Come, beauteous in thine after form,[227]
And like a finer light in light.

92

If any vision should reveal
Thy likeness, I might count it vain
As but the canker[228] of the brain;   1875
Yea, tho' it spake and made appeal

To chances where our lots were cast
Together in the days behind,
I might but say, I hear a wind
Of memory murmuring the past.   1880

Yea, tho' it spake and bared to view
A fact within the coming year;
And tho' the months, revolving near,
Should prove the phantom-warning true,

They might not seem thy prophecies,   1885
But spiritual presentiments,
And such refraction of events
As often rises ere they rise.

93

I shall not see thee. Dare I say
No spirit ever brake the band   1890
That stays him from the native land
Where first he walk'd when claspt in clay?[229]

No visual shade of some one lost,
But he, the Spirit himself, may come
Where all the nerve of sense is numb;   1895
Spirit to Spirit, Ghost to Ghost.

O, therefore from thy sightless[230] range
With gods in unconjectured bliss,
O, from the distance of the abyss
Of tenfold-complicated change,[231]   1900

---

[227] *after form* form adopted after death.
[228] *canker* cancer, gangrenous corruption.
[229] *clay* flesh.

[230] *sightless* invisible.
[231] *tenfold-complicated change* the ten heavens of Dante's *Paradiso*, Hallam Tennyson said.

Descend, and touch, and enter; hear
The wish too strong for words to name;
That in this blindness of the frame
My Ghost may feel that thine is near.

94

How pure at heart and sound in head,
    With what divine affections bold
Should be the man whose thought would hold
    An hour's communion with the dead.   1905

In vain shalt thou, or any, call
    The spirits from their golden day,   1910
Except, like them, thou too canst say,
    My spirit is at peace with all.

They haunt the silence of the breast,
    Imaginations calm and fair,
    The memory like a cloudless air,   1915
The conscience as a sea at rest:

But when the heart is full of din,
And doubt beside the portal[232] waits,
    They can but listen at the gates,
And hear the household jar[233] within.   1920

95

By night we linger'd on the lawn,
    For underfoot the herb was dry;
And genial warmth; and o'er the sky
    The silvery haze of summer drawn;

And calm that let the tapers burn   1925
    Unwavering: not a cricket chirr'd:
The brook alone far-off was heard,
    And on the board the fluttering urn:

And bats went round in fragrant skies,
    And wheel'd or lit the filmy shapes[234]   1930
That haunt the dusk, with ermine[235] capes
    And woolly breasts and beaded eyes;

While now we sang old songs that peal'd
From knoll to knoll, where, couch'd at ease,
The white kine[236] glimmer'd, and the trees   1935
    Laid their dark arms about the field.

But when those others, one by one,
Withdrew themselves from me and night,

---

[232] *portal* gate.
[233] *jar* make a discordant noise.
[234] *filmy shapes* moths.
[235] *ermine* stoat, with fur that is reddish brown in summer, but in winter wholly white, except the tip of the tail, which is always black. Ermine has long been a much-prized, lordly fur.
[236] *kine* cows.

And in the house light after light
Went out, and I was all alone,   1940

A hunger seized my heart; I read
Of that glad year which once had been,
In those fall'n leaves which kept their green,
The noble letters of the dead:

And strangely on the silence broke   1945
The silent-speaking words, and strange
Was love's dumb cry defying change
To test his[237] worth; and strangely spoke

The faith, the vigour, bold to dwell
On doubts that drive the coward back,   1950
And keen thro' wordy snares to track
Suggestion to her inmost cell.

So word by word, and line by line,
The dead man touch'd me from the past,
And all at once it seem'd at last   1955
The living soul was flash'd on mine,[238]

And mine in this was wound, and whirl'd
About empyreal[239] heights of thought,
And came on that which is, and caught
The deep pulsations of the world,   1960

Æonian[240] music measuring out
The steps of Time – the shocks of Chance –
The blows of Death. At length my trance
Was cancell'd, stricken thro' with doubt.

Vague words! but ah, how hard to frame   1965
In matter-moulded forms of speech,
Or ev'n for intellect to reach
Thro' memory that which I became:

Till now the doubtful dusk reveal'd
The knolls once more where, couch'd at ease,   1970
The white kine glimmer'd, and the trees
Laid their dark arms about the field:

And suck'd from out the distant gloom
A breeze began to tremble o'er
The large leaves of the sycamore,   1975
And fluctuate all the still perfume,

---

[237] *his* 'its', said Tennyson.
[238] *The . . . mine* 'The deity, maybe', Tennyson said (he changed the first word to 'The' from 'His', feeling that it perhaps gave 'a wrong impression').

[239] *empyreal* highest heaven.
[240] *Æonian* see note 93.

And gathering freshlier overhead,
Rock'd the full-foliaged elms, and swung
The heavy-folded rose, and flung
    The lilies to and fro, and said   1980

'The dawn, the dawn,' and died away;
And East and West, without a breath,
Mixt their dim lights, like life and death,
    To broaden into boundless day.

96

You[241] say, but with no touch of scorn,   1985
Sweet-hearted, you, whose light-blue eyes
    Are tender over drowning flies,
    You tell me, doubt is Devil-born.

I know not: one[242] indeed I knew
In many a subtle question versed,   1990
    Who touch'd a jarring lyre at first,
    But ever strove to make it true:

Perplext in faith, but pure in deeds,
    At last he beat his music out.
There lives more faith in honest doubt,   1995
    Believe me, than in half the creeds.

He fought his doubts and gather'd strength,
He would not make his judgment blind,
    He faced the spectres of the mind
    And laid them: thus he came at length   2000

To find a stronger faith his own;
And Power was with him in the night,
    Which makes the darkness and the light,
    And dwells not in the light alone,

But in the darkness and the cloud,   2005
    As over Sinaï's[243] peaks of old,
    While Israel made their gods of gold,
    Altho' the trumpet blew so loud.[244]

97

My love has talk'd with rocks and trees;
He finds on misty mountain-ground   2010
    His own vast shadow glory-crown'd;
    He sees himself in all he sees.

---

[241] *You* insofar as anyone in particular is addressed, this is probably intended for Emily Sellwood, whose engagement to Tennyson had been delayed partly because of her anxieties about his religious beliefs.

[242] *one* Hallam.

[243] *Sinaï* Mount Sinai, where Moses received the Ten Commandments.

[244] *While Israel . . . loud* Tennyson drew attention to Exodus 19.16, just before Moses receives the Ten Commandments: 'And it came to passe on the third day in the morning, that there were thunders and lightnings, and a thicke cloud vpon the mount, and the voyce of the trumpet exceeding lowd, so that all the people that was in the campe, trembled.'

Two partners of a married life[245] –
I look'd on these and thought of thee
    In vastness and in mystery,
And of my spirit as of a wife.   2015

These two – they dwelt with eye on eye,
Their hearts of old have beat in tune,
Their meetings made December June
    Their every parting was to die.   2020

    Their love has never past away;
    The days she never can forget
Are earnest[246] that he loves her yet,
    Whate'er the faithless people say.

    Her life is lone, he sits apart,   2025
He loves her yet, she will not weep,
Tho' rapt in matters dark and deep
He seems to slight her simple heart.

He thrids[247] the labyrinth of the mind,
    He reads the secret of the star,   2030
    He seems so near and yet so far,
He looks so cold: she thinks him kind.

She keeps the gift of years before,
    A wither'd violet is her bliss:
She knows not what his greatness is,   2035
For that, for all, she loves him more.

For him she plays, to him she sings
Of early faith and plighted vows;
She knows but matters of the house,
And he, he knows a thousand things.   2040

Her faith is fixt and cannot move,
She darkly feels him great and wise,
She dwells on him with faithful eyes,
    'I cannot understand: I love.'

98
You[248] leave us: you will see the Rhine,[249]   2045
And those fair hills I sail'd below,
When I was there with him; and go
By summer belts of wheat and vine

To where he breathed his latest breath,
That City.[250] All her splendour seems   2050

[245] *My love . . . life* Tennyson said, 'The relation of one on
earth to one in the other and higher world. Not my relation
to him here. He looked up to me as I looked up to him.'
[246] *Are earnest* are a promise.
[247] *thrids* threads.

[248] *You* Tennyson said cagily this addressee was imaginary,
but Hallam Tennyson suggested it referred to the
honeymoon of Charles, Tennyson's brother, on the Rhine.
[249] *Rhine* major German river.
[250] *City* Vienna.

No livelier than the wisp that gleams[251]
On Lethe in the eyes of Death.

Let her great Danube rolling fair
Enwind her isles, unmark'd of me:
I have not seen, I will not see   2055
Vienna; rather dream that there,

A treble darkness, Evil haunts
The birth, the bridal; friend from friend
Is oftener parted, fathers bend
Above more graves, a thousand wants   2060

Gnarr[252] at the heels of men, and prey
By each cold hearth, and sadness flings
Her shadow on the blaze of kings:
And yet myself have heard him say,

That not in any mother town   2065
With statelier progress to and fro
The double tides of chariots flow
By park and suburb under brown

Of lustier leaves; nor more content,
He told me, lives in any crowd,   2070
When all is gay with lamps, and loud
With sport and song, in booth and tent,

Imperial halls, or open plain;
And wheels the circled dance, and breaks
The rocket molten into flakes   2075
Of crimson or in emerald rain.

99

Risest thou thus, dim dawn, again,
So loud with voices of the birds,
So thick with lowings of the herds,
Day,[253] when I lost the flower of men;   2080

Who tremblest thro' thy darkling red
On yon swoll'n brook that bubbles fast
By meadows breathing of the past,
And woodlands holy to the dead;

Who murmurest in the foliaged eaves   2085
A song that slights the coming care,
And Autumn laying here and there
A fiery finger on the leaves;

Who wakenest with thy balmy breath
To myriads[254] on the genial earth,   2090

---

[251] *wisp that gleams* Tennyson said 'the ghosts'.

[252] *Gnarr* snarl.

[253] *Day* another anniversary of Hallam's death.

[254] *myriads* tens of thousands.

Memories of bridal, or of birth,
And unto myriads more, of death.

O wheresoever those may be,
Betwixt the slumber of the poles,
To-day they count as kindred souls;   2095
They know me not, but mourn with me.

100
I climb the hill: from end to end
Of all the landscape underneath,
I find no place that does not breathe
Some gracious memory of my friend;   2100

No gray old grange, or lonely fold,
Or low morass and whispering reed,
Or simple stile from mead to mead,
Or sheepwalk up the windy wold;

Nor hoary knoll of ash and haw   2105
That hears the latest linnet trill,
Nor quarry trench'd along the hill
And haunted by the wrangling daw;[255]

Nor runlet tinkling from the rock;
Nor pastoral rivulet that swerves   2110
To left and right thro' meadowy curves,
That feed the mothers of the flock;

But each has pleased a kindred eye,
And each reflects a kindlier day;
And, leaving these,[256] to pass away,   2115
I think once more he seems to die.

101
Unwatch'd, the garden bough shall sway,
The tender blossom flutter down,
Unloved, that beech will gather brown,
This maple burn itself away;   2120

Unloved, the sun-flower, shining fair,
Ray round with flames her disk of seed,
And many a rose-carnation feed
With summer spice the humming air;

Unloved, by many a sandy bar,   2125
The brook shall babble down the plain,
At noon or when the lesser wain[257]
Is twisting round the polar star;

---

[255] *daw* jackdaw, cawing crow-like bird.
[256] *leaving these* lyrics 100–103 refer to Tennyson's move from the Lincolnshire hamlet of Somersby, his home, in 1837.

[257] *lesser wain* group of seven stars in the Little Bear.

Uncared for, gird[258] the windy grove,
And flood the haunts of hern[259] and crake;[260]   2130
Or into silver arrows break
The sailing moon in creek and cove;

Till from the garden and the wild
A fresh association blow,
And year by year the landscape grow   2135
Familiar to the stranger's child;

As year by year the labourer tills
His wonted glebe,[261] or lops the glades;
And year by year our memory fades
From all the circle of the hills.   2140

102

We leave the well-beloved place
Where first we gazed upon the sky;
The roofs, that heard our earliest cry,
Will shelter one of stranger race.

We go, but ere we go from home,   2145
As down the garden-walks I move,
Two spirits of a diverse love
Contend for loving masterdom.

One whispers, 'Here thy boyhood sung
Long since its matin song, and heard   2150
The low love-language of the bird
In native hazels tassel-hung.'

The other answers, 'Yea, but here
Thy feet have stray'd in after hours
With thy lost friend among the bowers,   2155
And this hath made them trebly dear.'

These two have striven half the day,
And each prefers his separate claim,
Poor rivals in a losing game,
That will not yield each other way.   2160

I turn to go: my feet are set
To leave the pleasant fields and farms;
They mix in one another's arms
To one pure image of regret.

103

On that last night before we went   2165
From out the doors where I was bred,
I dream'd a vision of the dead,
Which left my after-morn content.

---

[258] *gird* with the medieval sense of blow, strike.
[259] *hern* heron.

[260] *crake* corn-crake (bird) or, dialectally, a crow or raven.
[261] *glebe* field.

Methought I dwelt within a hall, Near
And maidens with me: distant hills 2170
From hidden summits fed with rills
 A river sliding by the wall. Far

The hall with harp and carol rang.
They sang of what is wise and good
And graceful. In the centre stood 2175
A statue veil'd, to which they sang;

And which, tho' veil'd, was known to me,
The shape of him I loved, and love
For ever: then flew in a dove
And brought a summons from the sea:[262] 2180

And when they learnt that I must go
They wept and wail'd, but led the way
To where a little shallop[263] lay
At anchor in the flood below;

And on by many a level mead, 2185
And shadowing bluff that made the banks,
We glided winding under ranks
Of iris, and the golden reed;

And still as vaster grew the shore[264]
And roll'd the floods in grander space, 2190
The maidens gather'd strength and grace
And presence, lordlier than before;

And I myself, who sat apart
And watch'd them, wax'd in every limb;
I felt the thews[265] of Anakim,[266] Giant 2195
The pulses of a Titan's[267] heart;

As one would sing the death of war,
And one would chant the history
Of that great race, which is to be,
And one the shaping of a star; 2200

Until the forward-creeping tides
Began to foam, and we to draw
From deep to deep, to where we saw
A great ship lift her shining sides.

The man we loved was there on deck, 2205
But thrice as large as man he bent
To greet us. Up the side I went,
And fell in silence on his neck:

[262] *sea* 'eternity', said Tennyson.
[263] *shallop* small boat.
[264] *vaster . . . shore* 'The progress of the Age', Tennyson said.
[265] *thews* strength.

[266] *Anakim* cf. Deuteronomy 2.10–11: 'The Emims dwelt therein in times past, a people great, and many, and tall, as the Anakims: Which also were accounted giants.'
[267] *Titan* giants overthrown by the Olympian gods in Greek mythology.

Whereat those maidens with one mind
Bewail'd their lot; I did them wrong: 2210
'We served thee here,' they said, 'so long,
And wilt thou leave us now behind?'

So rapt I was, they could not win
An answer from my lips, but he
Replying, 'Enter likewise ye   2215
And go with us:' they enter'd in.

And while the wind began to sweep
A music out of sheet and shroud,[268]
We steer'd her toward a crimson cloud
That landlike slept along the deep.   2220

104

The time draws near the birth of Christ;
The moon is hid, the night is still;
A single church below the hill
Is pealing, folded in the mist.

A single peal of bells below,   2225
That wakens at this hour of rest
A single murmur in the breast,
That these are not the bells I know.

Like strangers' voices here they sound,
In lands where not a memory strays,   2230
Nor landmark breathes of other days,
But all is new unhallow'd ground.

105

To-night ungather'd let us leave
This laurel, let this holly stand:
We live within the stranger's land,   2235
And strangely falls our Christmas-eve.

Our father's dust[269] is left alone
And silent under other snows:
There in due time the woodbine blows,
The violet comes, but we are gone.   2240

No more shall wayward grief abuse
The genial hour with mask and mime;
For change of place, like growth of time,
Has broke the bond of dying use.

Let cares that petty shadows cast,   2245
By which our lives are chiefly proved,
A little spare the night I loved,
And hold it solemn to the past.

---

[268] *sheet and shroud* sails.
[269] *father's dust* Tennyson's father, the Rev. Dr George

Tennyson, had died in 1831 and is buried in the
churchyard at Somersby.

But let no footstep beat the floor,
Nor bowl of wassail[270] mantle warm;
For who would keep an ancient form
Thro' which the spirit breathes no more?

2250

Be neither song, nor game, nor feast;
Nor harp be touch'd, nor flute be blown;
No dance, no motion, save alone
What lightens in the lucid east

2255

Of rising worlds by yonder wood.
Long sleeps the summer in the seed;
Run out your measured arcs,[271] and lead
The closing cycle rich in good.

2260

106

Ring out, wild bells, to the wild sky,
The flying cloud, the frosty light:
The year is dying in the night;
Ring out, wild bells, and let him[272] die.

Ring out the old, ring in the new,
Ring, happy bells, across the snow:
The year is going, let him go;
Ring out the false, ring in the true.

2265

Ring out the grief that saps the mind,
For those that here we see no more;
Ring out the feud of rich and poor,
Ring in redress to all mankind.

2270

Ring out a slowly dying cause,
And ancient forms of party strife;
Ring in the nobler modes of life,
With sweeter manners, purer laws.

2275

Ring out the want, the care, the sin,
The faithless coldness of the times;
Ring out, ring out my mournful rhymes,
But ring the fuller minstrel in.

2280

Ring out false pride in place and blood,
The civic slander and the spite;
Ring in the love of truth and right,
Ring in the common love of good.

Ring out old shapes of foul disease;
Ring out the narrowing lust of gold;
Ring out the thousand wars of old,
Ring in the thousand years of peace.

2285

---

[270] *wassail* spiced Christmas ale.
[271] *arcs* of the sun's movement across the sky.

[272] *him* the old year.

Ring in the valiant man and free,
The larger heart, the kindlier hand;
Ring out the darkness of the land,
Ring in the Christ that is to be.[273]

2290

107

It is the day when he[274] was born,[275]
A bitter day that early sank
Behind a purple-frosty bank
Of vapour, leaving night forlorn.

2295

The time admits not flowers or leaves
To deck the banquet. Fiercely flies
The blast of North and East, and ice
Makes daggers at the sharpen'd eaves,

2300

And bristles all the brakes and thorns
To yon hard crescent, as she hangs
Above the wood which grides[276] and clangs
Its leafless ribs and iron horns

Together, in the drifts that pass
To darken on the rolling brine
That breaks the coast. But fetch the wine,
Arrange the board and brim the glass;

2305

Bring in great logs and let them lie,
To make a solid core of heat;
Be cheerful-minded, talk and treat
Of all things ev'n as he were by;

2310

We keep the day. With festal cheer,
With books and music, surely we
Will drink to him, whate'er he be,
And sing the songs he loved to hear.

2315

108

I will not shut me from my kind,
And, lest I stiffen into stone,
I will not eat my heart alone,
Nor feed with sighs a passing wind:

2320

What profit lies in barren faith,
And vacant yearning, tho' with might
To scale the heaven's highest height,
Or dive below the wells of Death?

What find I in the highest place,
But mine own phantom chanting hymns?
And on the depths of death there swims
The reflex[277] of a human face.

2325

---

[273] *Ring in the Christ that is to be* 'The broader Christianity of the future', Tennyson said.
[274] *he* Hallam.

[275] *It is . . . born* 1 February 1811.
[276] *grides* grates.
[277] *reflex* reflection.

I'll rather take what fruit may be
Of sorrow under human skies: 2330
 'Tis held that sorrow makes us wise,
Whatever wisdom sleep with thee.

109
Heart-affluence[278] in discursive talk
From household fountains never dry;
 The critic clearness of an eye,   2335
That saw thro' all the Muses' walk;

Seraphic intellect and force
To seize and throw the doubts of man;
 Impassion'd logic, which outran
The hearer in its fiery course;   2340

High nature amorous of the good,
But touch'd with no ascetic gloom;
 And passion pure in snowy bloom
Thro' all the years of April blood;

A love of freedom rarely felt,   2345
 Of freedom in her regal seat
Of England; not the schoolboy heat,
 The blind hysterics of the Celt;[279]

And manhood fused with female grace
In such a sort, the child would twine   2350
 A trustful hand, unask'd, in thine,
And find his comfort in thy face;

All these have been, and thee mine eyes
Have look'd on: if they look'd in vain,
 My shame is greater who remain,   2355
Nor let thy wisdom make me wise.

110
Thy converse drew us with delight,
The men of rathe[280] and riper years:
 The feeble soul, a haunt of fears,
Forgot his weakness in thy sight.   2360

On thee the loyal-hearted hung,
The proud was half disarm'd of pride,
 Nor cared the serpent[281] at thy side
To flicker with his double tongue.

The stern were mild when thou wert by,   2365
The flippant put himself to school

---

[278] *Heart-affluence* richness, generosity of heart.
[279] *blind . . . Celt* cf. 'Yet fear that passion may convulse / Thy judgment: fear the neighbourhood / Of that unstable Celtic blood / That never keeps an equal pulse' ('Hail Briton!', written 1831–3).

[280] *rathe* early.
[281] *serpent* temptation, evil.

And heard thee, and the brazen fool
Was soften'd, and he knew not why;

While I, thy nearest, sat apart,
And felt thy triumph was as mine;   2370
And loved them more, that they were thine,
The graceful tact, the Christian art;

Nor mine the sweetness or the skill,
But mine the love that will not tire,
And, born of love, the vague desire   2375
That spurs an imitative will.

111

The churl[282] in spirit, up or down
Along the scale of ranks, thro' all,
To him who grasps a golden ball,[283]
By blood a king, at heart a clown;   2380

The churl in spirit, howe'er he veil
His want in forms for fashion's sake,
Will let his coltish nature break
At seasons thro' the gilded pale:

For who can always act? but he,   2385
To whom a thousand memories call,
Not being less but more than all
The gentleness he seem'd to be,

Best seem'd the thing he was, and join'd
Each office of the social hour   2390
To noble manners, as the flower
And native growth of noble mind;

Nor ever narrowness or spite,
Or villain fancy fleeting by,
Drew in the expression of an eye,   2395
Where God and Nature met in light;

And thus he bore without abuse
The grand old name of gentleman,
Defamed by every charlatan,[284]
And soil'd with all ignoble use.   2400

112

High wisdom holds my wisdom less,
That I, who gaze with temperate eyes
On glorious insufficiencies,
Set light by narrower perfectness.

But thou, that fillest all the room   2405
Of all my love, art reason why

---

[282] *churl* low man, serf.
[283] *golden ball* sceptre, symbol of kingship.

[284] *charlatan* pretender, quack. Tennyson pronounced it
with an accent on the final syllable.

I seem to cast a careless eye
On souls, the lesser lords of doom.[285]

For what wert thou? some novel power
   Sprang up for ever at a touch,   2410
And hope could never hope too much,
   In watching thee from hour to hour,

Large elements in order brought,
   And tracts of calm from tempest made,
And world-wide fluctuation sway'd   2415
   In vassal[286] tides that follow'd thought.

113
'Tis held that sorrow makes us wise;
   Yet how much wisdom sleeps with thee
   Which not alone had guided me,
But served the seasons that may rise;   2420

For can I doubt, who knew thee keen
   In intellect, with force and skill
   To strive, to fashion, to fulfil –
I doubt not what thou wouldst have been:

   A life in civic action warm,   2425
   A soul on highest mission sent,
   A potent voice of Parliament,
   A pillar steadfast in the storm,

Should licensed boldness gather force,
   Becoming, when the time has birth,   2430
   A lever to uplift the earth
   And roll it in another course,

With thousand shocks that come and go,
   With agonies, with energies,
   With overthrowings, and with cries.   2435
   And undulations to and fro.

114 *Knowledge*
Who loves not Knowledge? Who shall rail
   Against her beauty? May she mix
   With men and prosper! Who shall fix
Her pillars? Let her work prevail.   2440

But on her forehead sits a fire:
   She sets her forward countenance
   And leaps into the future chance,
Submitting all things to desire.

Half-grown as yet, a child, and vain –   2445
   She cannot fight the fear of death.

---

[285] *souls, the lesser lords of doom* 'Those that have free-will, but less intellect', Tennyson said.   [286] *vassal* bondsman, slave.

What is she, cut from love and faith,
But some wild Pallas[287] from the brain

Of Demons? fiery-hot to burst
All barriers in her onward race   2450
For power. Let her know her place;
She is the second, not the first.

A higher hand must make her mild,
If all be not in vain; and guide
Her footsteps, moving side by side   2455
With wisdom, like the younger child:

For she is earthly of the mind,
But Wisdom heavenly of the soul.
O, friend, who camest to thy goal
So early, leaving me behind,   2460

I would the great world grew like thee,
Who grewest not alone in power
And knowledge, but by year and hour
In reverence and in charity.

115

Now fades the last long streak of snow,   2465
Now burgeons[288] every maze of quick[289]
About the flowering squares, and thick
By ashen roots the violets blow.

Now rings the woodland loud and long,
The distance takes a lovelier hue,   2470
And drown'd in yonder living blue
The lark becomes a sightless song.

Now dance the lights on lawn and lea,
The flocks are whiter down the vale,
And milkier every milky sail   2475
On winding stream or distant sea;

Where now the seamew[290] pipes, or dives
In yonder greening gleam, and fly
The happy birds, that change their sky
To build and brood; that live their lives   2480

From land to land; and in my breast
Spring wakens too; and my regret
Becomes an April violet,[291]
And buds and blossoms like the rest.

---

[287] *Pallas* Pallas Athena, Greek goddess of war. Tennyson means 'a wild, violent force'.
[288] *burgeons* buds, sprouts.
[289] *quick* 'quickset thorn', Tennyson said.

[290] *seamew* common gull.
[291] *violet* the metre demands a diaresis: vi-o-let. The sound of the word is transformed, as is Tennyson's regret.

116

Is it, then, regret for buried time   2485
  That keenlier in sweet April wakes,
  And meets the year, and gives and takes
    The colours of the crescent prime?[292]

  Not all: the songs, the stirring air,
    The life re-orient out of dust,   2490
    Cry thro' the sense to hearten trust
  In that which made the world so fair.

  Not all regret: the face will shine
    Upon me, while I muse alone;
  And that dear voice, I once have known,   2495
    Still speak to me of me and mine:

    Yet less of sorrow lives in me
  For days of happy commune dead;
  Less yearning for the friendship fled,
    Than some strong bond which is to be.   2500

117

O days and hours, your work is this
  To hold me from my proper place,
    A little while from his embrace,
    For fuller gain of after bliss:

  That out of distance might ensue   2505
  Desire of nearness doubly sweet;
  And unto meeting when we meet,
    Delight a hundredfold accrue,

  For every grain of sand that runs,
  And every span of shade that steals,[293]   2510
  And every kiss of toothed wheels,[294]
    And all the courses of the suns.

118

Contemplate all this work of Time,
  The giant labouring in his youth;
  Nor dream of human love and truth,   2515
    As dying Nature's earth and lime;

  But trust that those we call the dead
    Are breathers of an ampler day
    For ever nobler ends. They say,
  The solid earth whereon we tread   2520

    In tracts of fluent heat began,
  And grew to seeming-random forms,[295]

[292] *crescent prime* 'growing spring', said Tennyson.

[293] *span . . . steals* reference to a sundial, said Tennyson.

[294] *kiss . . . wheels* cogs of a clock.

[295] *In tracts . . . forms* reference to cataclysmic theory of earth's beginning.

The seeming prey of cyclic storms,
Till at the last arose the man;

Who throve and branch'd from clime to clime,[296]   2525
The herald of a higher race,
And of himself in higher place,
If so he type this work of time

Within himself, from more to more;
Or, crown'd with attributes of woe   2530
Like glories, move his course, and show
That life is not as idle ore,

But iron dug from central gloom,
And heated hot with burning fears,
And dipt in baths of hissing tears,   2535
And batter'd with the shocks of doom

To shape and use. Arise and fly
The reeling Faun,[297] the sensual feast;
Move upward, working out the beast,
And let the ape and tiger die.   2540

119

Doors, where my heart was used to beat
So quickly, not as one that weeps
I come once more; the city sleeps;
I smell the meadow in the street;

I hear a chirp of birds; I see   2545
Betwixt the black fronts long-withdrawn
A light-blue lane of early dawn,
And think of early days and thee,

And bless thee, for thy lips are bland,
And bright the friendship of thine eye;   2550
And in my thoughts with scarce a sigh
I take the pressure of thine hand.

120

I trust I have not wasted breath:
I think we are not wholly brain,
Magnetic mockeries;[298] not in vain,   2555
Like Paul with beasts, I fought with Death;[299]

Not only cunning casts in clay:
Let Science prove we are, and then

---

[296] *Who throve and branched . . . clime* this sounds as if it is approaching a pre-Darwinian theory of the mutability of species.
[297] *Faun* part-man, part-goat; here, thought of as sensual and indulgent.
[298] *Magnetic mockeries* i.e., like machines, things worked through material forces.

[299] *Like Paul . . . death* cf. 1 Corinthians 15.32, 'If after the maner of men I haue fought with beasts at Ephesus, what aduantageth it me, if the dead rise not? let vs eate and drinke, for to morrowe wee die'.

What matters Science unto men,
At least to me? I would not stay.   2560

Let him, the wiser man who springs
Hereafter, up from childhood shape
His action like the greater ape,[300]
But I was born to other things.

121

Sad Hesper[301] o'er the buried sun   2565
And ready, thou, to die with him,
Thou watchest all things ever dim
And dimmer, and a glory done:

The team is loosen'd from the wain,[302]
The boat is drawn upon the shore;   2570
Thou listenest to the closing door,
And life is darken'd in the brain.

Bright Phosphor,[303] fresher for the night,
By thee the world's great work is heard
Beginning, and the wakeful bird;   2575
Behind thee comes the greater light:

The market boat is on the stream,
And voices hail it from the brink;
Thou hear'st the village hammer[304] clink,
And see'st the moving of the team.   2580

Sweet Hesper-Phosphor, double name
For what is one,[305] the first, the last,
Thou, like my present and my past,
Thy place is changed; thou art the same.

122

Oh, wast thou with me, dearest, then,   2585
While I rose up against my doom,
And yearn'd to burst the folded gloom,
To bare the eternal Heavens again,

To feel once more, in placid awe,
The strong imagination roll   2590
A sphere of stars about my soul,
In all her motion one with law;

If thou wert with me, and the grave
Divide us not, be with me now,
And enter in at breast and brow,   2595
Till all my blood, a fuller wave,

---

[300] *Let him . . . ape* 'Spoken ironically against mere
materialism, not against evolution', said Tennyson.
[301] *Hesper* the evening star.
[302] *wain* waggon.

[303] *Phosphor* see note 29.
[304] *village hammer* of the blacksmith.
[305] *one* morning and evening stars are both the planet Venus.

Be quicken'd with a livelier breath,
And like an inconsiderate boy,
As in the former flash of joy,
I slip the thoughts of life and death;   2600

And all the breeze of Fancy blows,
And every dew-drop paints a bow,[306]
The wizard lightnings deeply glow,
And every thought breaks out a rose.

123

There rolls the deep where grew the tree.[307]   2605
O earth, what changes hast thou seen!
There where the long street roars, hath been
The stillness of the central sea.

The hills are shadows, and they flow
From form to form, and nothing stands;   2610
They melt like mist, the solid lands,
Like clouds they shape themselves and go.

But in my spirit will I dwell,
And dream my dream, and hold it true;
For tho' my lips may breathe adieu,   2615
I cannot think the thing farewell.

124

That which we dare invoke to bless;
Our dearest faith; our ghastliest doubt;
He, They, One, All; within, without;
The Power in darkness whom we guess;   2620

I found Him not in world or sun,
Or eagle's wing, or insect's eye;
Nor thro' the questions men may try,
The petty cobwebs we have spun:

If e'er when faith had fall'n asleep,   2625
I heard a voice 'believe no more'
And heard an ever-breaking shore
That tumbled in the Godless deep;

A warmth within the breast would melt
The freezing reason's colder part,   2630
And like a man in wrath the heart
Stood up and answer'd 'I have felt.'

No, like a child in doubt and fear:
But that blind clamour made me wise;
Then was I as a child that cries,   2635
But, crying, knows his father near;

---

[306] *every dew-drop . . . bow* 'Every dew-drop turns into a miniature rainbow', said Tennyson.
[307] *There rolls . . . tree* lyric influenced by Tennyson's knowledge of modern geology (including Charles Lyell's *Principles of Geology*, which he read in 1836).

And what I am beheld again
What is, and no man understands;
And out of darkness came the hands
That reach thro' nature, moulding men.   2640

125

Whatever I have said or sung,
Some bitter notes my harp would give,
Yea, tho' there often seem'd to live
A contradiction on the tongue,

Yet Hope had never lost her youth;   2645
She did but look through dimmer eyes;
Or Love but play'd with gracious lies,
Because he felt so fix'd in truth:

And if the song were full of care,
He breathed the spirit of the song;   2650
And if the words were sweet and strong
He set his royal signet[308] there;

Abiding with me till I sail
To seek thee on the mystic deeps,
And this electric force,[309] that keeps   2655
A thousand pulses dancing, fail.

126

Love is and was my Lord and King,
And in his presence I attend
To hear the tidings of my friend,
Which every hour his couriers bring.   2660

Love is and was my King and Lord,
And will be, tho' as yet I keep
Within his court on earth, and sleep
Encompass'd by his faithful guard,

And hear at times a sentinel   2665
Who moves about from place to place,
And whispers to the worlds of space,
In the deep night, that all is well.

127

And all is well, tho' faith and form
Be sunder'd in the night of fear;   2670
Well roars the storm to those that hear
A deeper voice across the storm,

Proclaiming social truth shall spread,
And justice, ev'n tho' thrice again
The red fool-fury of the Seine[310]   2675
Should pile her barricades with dead.

[308] *royal signet* seal (of approval).
[309] *electric force* life force.

[310] *Seine* river running through Paris: Tennyson refers to the French revolutions of 1789 and 1830.

But ill for him that wears a crown,
  And him, the lazar,[311] in his rags:
  They tremble, the sustaining crags;
  The spires of ice are toppled down,　　　　　　2680

And molten up, and roar in flood;
  The fortress crashes from on high,
  The brute earth lightens to the sky,
  And the great Æon[312] sinks in blood,

And compass'd by the fires of Hell;　　　　　　2685
  While thou, dear spirit, happy star,
  O'erlook'st the tumult from afar,
  And smilest, knowing all is well.

128

The love that rose on stronger wings,
  Unpalsied when he met with Death,　　　　　　2690
  Is comrade of the lesser faith
  That sees the course of human things.

No doubt vast eddies in the flood
  Of onward time shall yet be made,
  And throned races may degrade;　　　　　　2695
  Yet O ye mysteries of good,

Wild Hours[313] that fly with Hope and Fear,
  If all your office had to do
  With old results that look like new;
  If this were all your mission here,　　　　　　2700

To draw, to sheathe a useless sword,
  To fool the crowd with glorious lies,
  To cleave a creed in sects and cries,
  To change the bearing of a word,

To shift an arbitrary power,　　　　　　2705
  To cramp the student at his desk,
  To make old bareness picturesque
  And tuft with grass a feudal tower;

Solomon

Why then my scorn might well descend
  On you and yours. I see in part　　　　　　2710
  That all, as in some piece of art,
  Is toil cöoperant to an end.

129

Dear friend, far off, my lost desire,
  So far, so near in woe and weal;[314]
  O loved the most, when most I feel　　　　　　2715
  There is a lower and a higher;

---

[311] *lazar* poor man (reference to the story of Dives and Lazarus, Luke 16.20–31).
[312] *Æon* an age of the universe, a vast period of time.

[313] *Wild Hours* time – the rest of the lyric is built around questions of time's agency.
[314] *weal* happiness, prosperity.

Known and unknown; human, divine;
Sweet human hand and lips and eye;
Dear heavenly friend that canst not die,
Mine, mine, for ever, ever mine;

Compared to God? 2720

His friend?
Time?

Strange friend, past, present, and to be;
Loved deeplier, darklier understood;
Behold, I dream a dream of good,
And mingle all the world with thee.

130
Thy voice is on the rolling air;   2725
I hear thee where the waters run;
Thou standest in the rising sun,
And in the setting thou art fair.

What art thou then? I cannot guess;
But tho' I seem in star and flower   2730
To feel thee some diffusive power,
I do not therefore love thee less:

My love involves the love before;
My love is vaster passion now;
Tho' mix'd with God and Nature thou,   2735
I seem to love thee more and more.

Far off thou art, but ever nigh;
I have thee still, and I rejoice;
I prosper, circled with thy voice;
I shall not lose thee tho' I die.   2740

131
O living will[315] that shalt endure
When all that seems shall suffer shock,
Rise in the spiritual rock,
Flow thro' our deeds and make them pure,[316]

That we may lift from out of dust   2745
A voice as unto him that hears,
A cry above the conquer'd years
To one that with us works, and trust,

With faith that comes of self-control,
The truths that never can be proved   2750
Until we close with all we loved,
And all we flow from, soul in soul.

---

[315] *O living will* 'That which we know as Free-will in man', said Tennyson.
[316] *Rise . . . pure* cf. 1 Corinthians 10.4, 'And did all drinke the same spirituall drinke: (for they dranke of that spirituall Rocke that followed them: and that Rocke was Christ)'.

[Epilogue]

O true and tried, so well and long,
Demand not thou a marriage lay;[317]
    In that it is thy marriage day   2755
    Is music more than any song.

    Nor have I felt so much of bliss
    Since first he told me that he loved
A daughter of our house;[318] nor proved
    Since that dark day a day like this;   2760

    Tho' I since then have number'd o'er
Some thrice three years:[319] they went and came,
Remade the blood and changed the frame,
    And yet is love not less, but more;

      No longer caring to embalm   2765
      In dying songs a dead regret,
      But like a statue solid-set,
    And moulded in colossal calm.

      Regret is dead, but love is more
    Than in the summers that are flown,   2770
    For I myself with these have grown
    To something greater than before;

Which makes appear the songs I made
    As echoes out of weaker times,
    As half but idle brawling rhymes,   2775
The sport of random sun and shade.

    But where is she, the bridal flower,
That must be made a wife ere noon?
    She enters, glowing like the moon
      Of Eden on its bridal bower: 2780

    On me she bends her blissful eyes
And then on thee; they meet thy look
And brighten like the star that shook
    Betwixt the palms of paradise.

    O when her life was yet in bud,   2785
    He too foretold the perfect rose.
For thee she grew, for thee she grows
    For ever, and as fair as good.

    And thou art worthy; full of power;
    As gentle; liberal-minded, great,   2790

---

[317] *lay* song. The 'Epilogue' refers to the marriage of Tennyson's sister Cecilia to Edmund Lushington on 10 October 1842.

[318] *Since . . . house* since Arthur Hallam told Tennyson of his love for Emily.

[319] *thrice three years* the nine between Arthur Hallam's death and Cecilia's wedding.

Consistent; wearing all that weight
Of learning lightly like a flower.

But now set out: the noon is near,
And I must give away[320] the bride;
She fears not, or with thee beside   2795
And me behind her, will not fear.

For I that danced her on my knee,
That watch'd her on her nurse's arm,
That shielded all her life from harm
At last must part with her to thee;   2800

Now waiting to be made a wife,
Her feet, my darling, on the dead;[321]
Their pensive tablets round her head,[322]
And the most living words of life

Breathed in her ear. The ring is on,   2805
The 'wilt thou' answer'd, and again
The 'wilt thou' ask'd, till out of twain
Her sweet 'I will' has made you one.[323]

Now sign your names,[324] which shall be read,
Mute symbols of a joyful morn,   2810
By village eyes as yet unborn;
The names are sign'd, and overhead

Begins the clash and clang that tells
The joy to every wandering breeze;
The blind wall rocks, and on the trees   2815
The dead leaf trembles to the bells.

O happy hour, and happier hours
Await them. Many a merry face
Salutes them – maidens of the place,
That pelt us in the porch with flowers.   2820

O happy hour, behold the bride
With him to whom her hand I gave.[325]
They leave the porch, they pass the grave
That has to-day its sunny side.

---

[320] *give away* Tennyson's father being dead, the task of 'giving away' the bride during the marriage service falls to Tennyson himself.

[321] *Her feet . . . dead* she stands on the gravestones of those interred in the chancel of the church.

[322] *pensive tablets . . . head* memorial stones on the walls of the church.

[323] *wilt thou . . . I will* references to the marriage service in the Book of Common Prayer. Both bride and groom are asked by the priest whether they accept the conditions of marriage. The question to the woman is, 'Wilt thou have

this man to thy wedded housband, to lyve together after Goddes ordynaunce in the holy estate of matrimony? wilt thou obey hym and serve him, love, honour, and kepe him, in sycknes and in health? And forsakynge al other, kepe the onely to him so long as ye bothe shal live?' The woman's answer is, 'I will'.

[324] *Now sign your names* in the official register of marriages.

[325] *her hand I gave* the Church of England's ceremony here involved Tennyson literally giving Cecilia's hand to her future husband.

To-day the grave is bright for me,
For them the light of life increased,
Who stay to share the morning feast,
Who rest to-night beside the sea.

2825

Let all my genial spirits advance
To meet and greet a whiter sun;
My drooping memory will not shun
The foaming grape of eastern France.[326]

2830

It circles round, and fancy plays,
And hearts are warm'd and faces bloom,
As drinking health to bride and groom
We wish them store of happy days.

2835

Nor count me all to blame if I
Conjecture of a stiller guest,
Perchance, perchance, among the rest,
And, tho' in silence, wishing joy.

2840

But they must go, the time draws on,
And those white-favour'd[327] horses wait;
They rise, but linger; it is late;
Farewell, we kiss, and they are gone.

A shade falls on us like the dark
From little cloudlets on the grass,
But sweeps away as out we pass
To range the woods, to roam the park,

2845

Discussing how their courtship grew,
And talk of others that are wed,
And how she look'd, and what he said,
And back we come at fall of dew.

2850

Again the feast, the speech, the glee,
The shade of passing thought, the wealth
Of words and wit, the double health,[328]
The crowning cup, the three-times-three,[329]

2855

And last the dance; – till I retire:
Dumb is that tower which spake so loud,
And high in heaven the streaming cloud,
And on the downs a rising fire:

2860

And rise, O moon, from yonder down,
Till over down and over dale
All night the shining vapour sail
And pass the silent-lighted town,

---

[326] *foaming grape . . . France* champagne.
[327] *white-favour'd* a favour is a small gift at a wedding; here, some ribbon, perhaps.

[328] *double health* toast to both bride and groom.
[329] *three-times-three* cheers.

The white-faced halls, the glancing rills,   2865
  And catch at every mountain head,
And o'er the friths[330] that branch and spread
  Their sleeping silver thro' the hills;

And touch with shade the bridal doors,
  With tender gloom the roof, the wall;   2870
And breaking let the splendour fall
  To spangle all the happy shores

By which they rest, and ocean sounds,
  And, star and system[331] rolling past,
A soul shall draw from out the vast   2875
  And strike his being into bounds,

And, moved thro' life of lower phase,
  Result in man, be born and think,
And act and love, a closer link
  Betwixt us and the crowning race   2880

Of those that, eye to eye, shall look
On knowledge; under whose command
Is Earth and Earth's, and in their hand
  Is Nature like an open book;[332]

No longer half-akin to brute,   2885
  For all we thought and loved and did,
And hoped, and suffer'd, is but seed
  Of what in them is flower and fruit;

Whereof the man, that with me trod
  This planet, was a noble type[333]   2890
Appearing ere the times were ripe,
  That friend of mine who lives in God,

That God, which ever lives and loves,
  One God, one law, one element,
And one far-off divine event,   2895
  To which the whole creation moves.

[330] *friths* trees.
[331] *system* constellations.
[332] *book* perhaps Tennyson recalls the supposed etymology of *book* and its assumed link with the name of the beech tree, *bóc*, *béce*, in Old English. The idea behind this was that beech bark, it was thought, had been written on. If Tennyson does have this in mind, he would be playing on the idea that, once, an open book *was* nature.
[333] *type* something which prefigures.

The Charge of the Light Brigade

Tennyson wrote widely on the subject of war, human heroism *in extremis* and violent death. His first major poem after *In Memoriam*, 88–165, *Maud: A Monodrama* (1855), considered among other things the response of a man of uncertain sanity to the Crimean War (1853–6); Tennyson's long Arthuriad *The Idylls of the King* (1859–85) was an extensive treatment of questions of heroic masculinity in conflict and national identity. 'The Charge of the Light Brigade', written, the poet said, in a 'few minutes', and published in 1854, was a brief reflection on how violent death that was the result of maladministration could be recuperated as heroic.

Tennyson's prompt for the poem was a report in *The Times* – the Crimean was the first war to be covered by newspaper reporters and photographers – recounting what rapidly became known as one of the British Army's most infamous errors. Indeed, Tennyson's poem is indebted for its images to journalistic reports. The Crimean War was fought between an alliance of Great Britain, the Ottoman Empire, France and later Sardinia against Russia. On 25 October 1854, the British officer Lord Lucan, it seems, misunderstood an order from his commanding officer, Lord Raglan, believing he should order a cavalry charge into a valley directly in the face of Russian artillery. Out of 673 British soldiers believed to have charged, only some 195 returned fit for service with their horses; 113 had been killed, and of the rest, 247 were wounded. Around 475 horses were lost. Tennyson's poem, more focused on vivid male action, on movement and pace, than is usual in his work, celebrated the Brigade, finding heroism amid what it constructs as dreadful failure. (Modern military scholarship points out that the losses at Balaclava were not, in the wider context

of massacres, absolutely calamitous.) 'The Charge of the Light Brigade' is careful to accept error but not to be specific about blame. Apparently answering a national need for patriotic poetry – as Felicia Hemans (1793–1835) had answered an earlier one – Tennyson's poem was hugely popular: multiple copies were requested even from the Crimean frontline.

Given Tennyson's earlier engagement with the pleasurable allure of death and with retreat from the responsibilities of life (cf. 'The Lotos-Eaters', 66–71), some have discerned an uneasy sub-theme in 'The Charge of the Light Brigade': a focus on men who have escaped from the demands of present existence but done so gloriously. They had perhaps found a way – to put it bluntly – of committing suicide without opprobrium. None of the moral question marks raised in 'The Lotos-Eaters' about abandoning the familiar world is to be found here. The apparently galloping rhythms of the poem seem to invite a swiftly paced delivery. But Tennyson recorded the text himself in 1890 – he and Robert Browning both made still-extant wax cylinder recordings – delivering it as a slow, half-sung incantation.

Text: *The Examiner*, 9 December 1854.

> Half a league,[1] half a league,
> Half a league onward,
> All in the valley of Death
> Rode the six hundred.
> 'Forward, the Light Brigade!   5
> Charge for the guns!' he said:
> Into the valley of Death
> Rode the six hundred.
>
> 2
> 'Forward, the Light Brigade!'
> Was there a man dismay'd?   10
> Not tho' the soldier knew
> Some one had blunder'd:
> Their's not to make reply,
> Their's not to reason why,
> Their's but to do and die: 15
> Into the valley of Death
> Rode the six hundred.
>
> 3
> Cannon to right of them,
> Cannon to left of them,
> Cannon in front of them   20

---

[1] *league* unit of distance, approximately 3 miles.

Volley'd and thunder'd;
Storm'd at with shot and shell,
Boldly they rode and well,
Into the jaws of Death,
Into the mouth of Hell   25
Rode the six hundred.

4

Flash'd all their sabres[2] bare,
Flash'd as they turn'd in air
Sabring the gunners there,
Charging an army, while   30
All the world wonder'd:
Plunged in the battery[3]-smoke
Right thro' the line they broke;
Cossack[4] and Russian
Reel'd from the sabre-stroke   35
Shatter'd and sunder'd.
Then they rode back, but not
Not the six hundred.

5

Cannon to right of them,
Cannon to left of them,   40
Cannon behind them
Volley'd and thunder'd;
Storm'd at with shot and shell,
While horse and hero fell,
They that had fought so well   45
Came thro' the jaws of Death,
Back from the mouth of Hell,
All that was left of them,
Left of six hundred.

6

When can their glory fade?   50
O the wild charge they made!
All the world wonder'd.
Honour the charge they made!
Honour the Light Brigade,
Noble six hundred!   55

---

[2] *sabres* cavalry swords.
[3] *battery* successive series of cannon fire.

[4] *Cossack* Turkish people occupying the parts north of the Black Sea; their horsemen served with the Russian Army.

To the Marquis of Dufferin and Ava

Tennyson suffered two grievous personal bereavements overseas. Arthur Hallam, commemorated in *In Memoriam A.H.H.*, 88–165, died in Vienna. Tennyson's younger son Lionel (b. 1854) died in April 1886 of fever onboard ship. He was returning from India through the Red Sea where he had been the guest of the Governor-General, Frederick Temple Hamilton-Temple, first Marquis of Dufferin and Ava (1826–1902), an old friend of the poet's. The movement across water became profoundly associated for Tennyson with the passage of death, an association that reached its climax in 'Crossing the Bar', 169–70.

The achieved monosyllabic severity of 'To the Marquis of Dufferin and Ava' (1889) and its employment of well-worn phrases – the poem deliberately foregrounds the cliché as a poetic resource – marks a difference from the affective lyricism of *In Memoriam* though the same stanza form is used (see the headnote to *In Memoriam*, 89). Here, under similar conditions of bereavement, Tennyson tests the expressive limit of verbal austerity, the capacity of poetry to communicate through lines chiselled like epitaphs or spare inscriptions. The poem's recollection of Lionel's last words, in stanza 9, dramatically reorientates the emotional direction, releasing power that is all the stronger for having been restrained. Tennyson's private grief,

made public in the marmoreal language of the elegy, is bound up with imperial discourse. Although Dufferin and Ava's rule of India is solemnly celebrated, a subtle counter-theme emerges in the poem's domestic narrative of Lionel's life and its inscription of imperial contact with India as deadly. The poem offers a suggestively double response to British imperial involvement in the subcontinent (cf. Thomas Hardy's 'Drummer Hodge', 511–12).

Text: *Demeter and Other Poems* (1889).

At times our Britain cannot rest,
At times her steps are swift and rash;
She moving,[1] at her girdle clash
The golden keys of East and West.

2
Not swift or rash, when late she lent   5
The sceptres of her West, her East,[2]
To one, that ruling has increased
Her greatness and her self-content.

3
Your rule has made the people love
Their ruler. Your viceregal[3] days   10
Have added fulness to the phrase
Of 'Gauntlet in the velvet glove.'[4]

4
But since your name will grow with Time,
Not all,[5] as honouring your fair fame
Of Statesman, have I made the name   15
A golden portal[6] to my rhyme:

5
But more, that you and yours may know
From me and mine, how dear a debt
We owed you, and are owing yet
To you and yours, and still would owe.   20

6
For he – your India was his Fate,
And drew him over sea to you –

---

[1] *She moving* as she moves.
[2] *her West, her East* Dufferin had been Governor-General of Canada before moving to India.
[3] *viceregal* adjective from viceroy, one acting in the name of the monarch.
[4] *Gauntlet ... glove* Dufferin was a strong ruler in India and his policies of railway development and military expansion strengthened British authority.
[5] *Not all* with the sense of 'Not only'.
[6] *portal* gateway.

He fain[7] had ranged her thro' and thro',
To serve her myriads[8] and the State, –

7

A soul that, watch'd from earliest youth,   25
And on thro' many a brightening year,
Had never swerved for craft or fear,
By one side-path, from simple truth;

8

Who might have chased and claspt Renown
And caught her chaplet[9] here – and there   30
In haunts of jungle-poison'd air
The flame of life went wavering down;

9

But ere he left your fatal shore,
And lay on that funereal boat,
Dying, 'Unspeakable' he wrote   35
'Their kindness,' and he wrote no more;

10

And sacred is the latest[10] word;
And now the Was, the Might-have-been,
And those lone rites[11] I have not seen,
And one drear sound I have not heard,   40

11

Are dreams that scarce will let me be,
Not there to bid my boy farewell,
When That within the coffin fell,
Fell – and flash'd into the Red Sea,

12

Beneath a hard Arabian moon   45
And alien stars. To question, why
The sons before the fathers die,
Not mine! and I may meet him soon;

13

But while my life's late eve endures,
Nor settles into hueless gray,   50
My memories of his briefer day
Will mix with love for you and yours.

[7] *fain* gladly.
[8] *myriads* countless number.
[9] *chaplet* wreath.

[10] *latest* last.
[11] *lone rites* Lionel's burial at sea.

Crossing the Bar

Written, in 20 minutes, while sailing over the Solent in October 1889, 'Crossing the Bar' brought into concise form one of the themes that had preoccupied Tennyson throughout his life: the question of life's continuance after death. (The Solent is a narrow stretch of sea on the south coast of England between the mainland and the Isle of Wight, where Tennyson lived at Freshwater.) The poem deploys the literal journey across water – evoking the Greek myth of crossing the Styx on the way to the underworld – to figure the movement of the soul after its departure from the body (cf. 'To the Marquis of Dufferin and Ava', 167–9). Characteristically, however, Tennyson remains guarded about what precisely awaits that soul: the poem is inconclusive about modes of existence beyond the grave, even though it is confident in the continuation of that existence. The nautical image of the pilot (one who steers a boat) offers only an intrigu-ingly open metaphor for powers beyond earthly knowledge. Tennyson was conscious of the poem's clinching expression of his peculiar mixture of faith and uncertainty, and asked that 'Crossing the Bar', first published in 1889, be placed always at the end of any edition of his collected poetry. Like much of Tennyson's work, the poem is a narrative that dramatizes an idea.

Text: *Demeter and Other Poems* (1889).

which love penis working?

Sunset and evening star,
And one clear call[1] for me!
And may there be no moaning of the bar,[2]
When I put out to sea,

2

But such a tide as moving seems asleep,   5
Too full for sound and foam,
When that which drew from out the boundless deep
Turns again home.

3

Twilight and evening bell,
And after that the dark!   10
And may there be no sadness of farewell,
When I embark;

4

For tho' from out our bourne[3] of Time and Place
The flood may bear me far,
I hope to see my Pilot face to face   15
When I have crost the bar.[4]

[1] *call* a word that can refer to a summons to duty on a ship.
[2] *moaning of the bar* perhaps the low sound of deep waters meeting over a sand bar.
[3] *bourne* limit.
[4] *crost the bar* nautical phrase meaning 'put out to sea' from a harbour or inland shelter.

Robert Browning (1812–1889)

The most intellectually arresting of the Victorian poets, Robert Browning was born in Camberwell in London in 1812, the son of Robert Browning Snr, a banker who had left the family plantation at St Kitts because of his objections to slavery, and Sarah Anna Wiedemann. Browning's father possessed an outstanding, eclectic library of some 6,000 books, which provided the basis of his son's education and the foundation of his extensive learning. Robert Browning, like John Ruskin, who grew up in the same area, briefly attended the new London University, 1827–8, and learned about art first hand in the Dulwich Gallery. Browning was excluded – though it didn't matter as he found his own reading more conducive – from the ancient universities of Oxford and Cambridge because he was a Dissenter not an Anglican. This faith he seems to have maintained throughout his life, to the puzzlement of some of his contemporaries; it is certainly difficult to discern in his searching poems about history, knowledge, certainty, uncertainty, belief. In 1833, Browning published a long dramatic work – halfway between a Byronic confessional poem and his own later dramatic monologues – entitled *Pauline: A Fragment of a Confession* (Shelley eventually eclipsed Byron in this admiration). *Paracelsus* (1835) was more of a success and secured him an *entrée* into important literary circles, but *Sordello* (1840) was infamously difficult, helping secure a reputation for the arcane and obscure that Browning always had some problem in throwing off. But he was peculiarly sensitive to criticism of his work, and tried nothing of the challenge of this poem again. Well-known, and more accessible, early dramatic monologues included 'Porphyria's Lover' (1836) and 'My Last Duchess' (1842). 'The Bishop Orders his Tomb at St Praxed's Church' appeared in 1845 in *Dramatic Romances and Lyrics*, and that same year he began his correspondence with Elizabeth Barrett, whom he would marry in secret in September the following year. She was the more well-known poet at this point, and certainly Browning regarded her, always, as his superior. They had one son, Robert Weidemann Browning, 'Pen', who, understandably, had some difficulty in living up to the expectations that pressed on the offspring of two of the century's finest writers.

Browning published an important statement about poetry in a post-Romantic climate in 1852 – which defined the 'objective' and 'subjective' poets – in what was intended to be an introduction to some new Shelley letters (they turned out to be fakes), and in 1855 came *Men and Women*, containing a number of his most memorable monologues from the first stage of his maturity as a poet. Browning picked up an 'Old Yellow Book' on a market stall in Florence in 1860 – where he and his wife had moved after their marriage – which was to provide the narrative basis for his multiple monologue work, a kind of crime novel in verse, *The Ring and the Book* (1868–9), which followed *Dramatis Personae*, another collection of monologues, published in 1864. By the time *The Ring and the Book* appeared, Browning had achieved enormous popularity, particularly among the discerning, as a brilliantly inventive writer who had brought a new mode of psychological exploration to poetry, a probing intellect, and introduced a fresh language into the nineteenth century with the gutsy diction of a host of dramatic speakers. Browning, sadly, was unable to share the change in his fortunes with his wife, who had died in 1861. His invention continued to the end: *The Inn Album* (1875), *Dramatic Idyls* (1879), *Jocoseria* (1883), *Parleyings with Certain People of Importance* (1887) and *Asolando*, published on the day of his death in 1889. Browning, who died in his daughter-in-law's *palazzo* in Venice, was buried, like Tennyson, in Westminster Abbey.

Porphyria's Lover ✓

Robert Browning's early dramatic monologue tests an extreme: the capacity of the newly minted genre to permit a reader's understanding of a murderer (cf. 'My Last Duchess', 173–5). Its ethics are audacious. Determined to preserve the 'good minute' of his relationship with Porphyria, the speaker strangles her and persuades himself that she has obtained what she desired (for a different meditation on the good minute in a relationship, see 'Two in the Campagna', 204–6).

'Porphyria's Lover', initially simply 'Porphyria' in its first publication in the *Monthly Repository* in January 1836, appeared as one of two 'Madhouse Cells' in its 1842 publication, which made clear its focus on the diseased (but internally coherent) logic of a disturbed mind. It gained its present title in 1849. The monologue may, perhaps, be seen as an uncomfortable reflection about what happens to beauty and life itself when art attempts to secure a permanent representation of it (this is a particularly important question for the monologist, seeking to create the illusion of real life in real time in a poetic form that disguises its identity as text). Like 'Two in the Campagna', its narrative carries displaced concerns with the aesthetic and of the artist's/monologist's struggle to distil a particular temporal moment, dramatized here as an act that brings death. In a post-Romantic context, 'Porphyria's Lover' is a provocative challenge to the Romantic-period notion of confessional poetry, to the idea that the sincere self articulates its own mind in the textures of verse. It may also be read, along with its companion 'Johannes Agricola', as an ironic comment on John Stuart Mill's distinction in his 1833 essay 'What is Poetry?' (published

earlier in the *Monthly Repository*) between eloquence and poetry. The first, he said, is heard, the second, overheard. Poetry 'is the natural fruit of meditation; eloquence, of intercourse with the world'. These are the terms that Browning ironizes, figuring the *moral* consequences of poetic utterance divorced from 'intercourse with the world' in the overheard solitary musings of a man separated from all normal principles of ethical behaviour who believes even God silent about his murderous deed. Emotion expressed privately here is delusion, paranoia, obsessiveness, insanity.

Text: *Dramatic Lyrics* (1842), but with its more familiar title.

> The rain set early in to-night,
> The sullen wind was soon awake,
> It tore the elm-tops down for spite,
> And did its worst to vex the lake:
> I listened with heart fit to break.   5
> When glided in Porphyria; straight
> She shut the cold out and the storm,
> And kneeled and made the cheerless grate
> Blaze up, and all the cottage warm;
> Which done, she rose, and from her form   10
> Withdrew the dripping cloak and shawl,
> And laid her soiled gloves by, untied
> Her hat and let the damp hair fall,
> And, last, she sat down by my side
> And called me. When no voice replied,   15
> She put my arm about her waist,
> And made her smooth white shoulder bare,
> And all her yellow hair displaced,
> And, stooping, made my cheek lie there,
> And spread, o'er all, her yellow hair,   20
> Murmuring how she loved me – she
> Too weak, for all her heart's endeavour,
> To set its struggling passion free
> From pride, and vainer ties dissever,
> And give herself to me for ever.   25
> But passion sometimes would prevail,
> Nor could to-night's gay feast restrain
> A sudden thought of one so pale
> For love of her, and all in vain:
> So, she was come through wind and rain.   30
> Be sure I looked up at her eyes
> Happy and proud; at last I knew
> Porphyria worshipped me; surprise
> Made my heart swell, and still it grew
> While I debated what to do.   35
> That moment she was mine, mine, fair,
> Perfectly pure and good: I found
> A thing to do, and all her hair

Handwritten annotations:

- pathetic fallacy (?)
- Speaker waiting & he is in torment
- Denotes her power, autonomy agency – Action words
- Lines 1–21? has all the power.
- shift here
- speaker "rises up"
- shift in power
- Shift
- Realizes there's been a shift in power – she "worshipped" him & he wants to capture this moment "forever" to gain back his masculinity.
- heart's passion
- Too proud to lose her face to socially status to a "lower man"
- he is pale / weak for love of her
- She left upper society to be w/ him & was happy. Not usual, for he was "surprised"

In one long yellow string I wound
Three times her little throat around, 40
And strangled her. No pain felt she;
I am quite sure she felt no pain.
As a shut bud that holds a bee,
I warily oped her lids: again
Laughed the blue eyes without a stain.[1] 45
And I untightened next the tress[2]
About her neck; her cheek once more
Blushed bright beneath my burning kiss:
I propped her head up as before,
Only, this time my shoulder bore 50
Her head, which droops upon it still:
The smiling rosy little head,
So glad it has its utmost will,
That all it scorned at once is fled,
And I, its love, am gained instead! 55
Porphyria's love: she guessed not how
Her darling one wish would be heard.
And thus we sit together now,
And all night long we have not stirred,
And yet God has not said a word! 60

[1] *without a stain* cf. 'Thou art all faire, my loue, there is no spot in thee', Song of Solomon 4.7.

[2] *tress* plait of hair.

Handwritten annotations: "After dead he has the power and speaks w/ 'I' voice. Action" · "What is her utmost will? He says 'it' not 'her'" · "B4 she was standing / 'tall'" · "1st instance/use of 'we'" · "Perhaps a twisted excuse / in his mind for why God has not said a word – b/c the male in his society should be dominant, and now he finally is – using God's 'silence' as a perverse way of approval. Since God has not stopped me this must be so."

My Last Duchess

Ferrara

'My Last Duchess' (1842), like 'Porphyria's Lover', 171–3, shows Robert Browning's early interests in human extremes – murderers in particular – and in the exploration of the dramatic monologue's capacity to provide a window into complex and disturbed psychology. This poem also muses on the haunting of the present by the past, a particular post-Romantic anxiety.

The proud speaker of the poem was probably modelled on Alfonso II, fifth Duke of Ferrara (a city in northeastern Italy), who married Lucrezia de' Medici when she was 14. Poison was suspected at her death three years later. Browning imagines his Duke entertaining an emissary from another court, through whom a new marriage is being arranged. The Duke – far more (guiltily?) preoccupied with his past than with his future alliance – points to a picture of his previous wife and in describing her reveals a disposition unnaturally jealous and vain. His chilling words 'I gave commands; / Then all smiles stopped together' seem to implicate him in her death.

Browning characteristically invites the reader to see more in the speaker's words than the speaker sees himself. As the reader perceives the Duke's murderous jealousy and his regard for women as objects, the ironies of his words become apparent. The Duke notices nothing peculiar in his declaration that the Count's 'fair daughter' is his 'object', but he is revealing his view of women as possessions (the title does not distinguish between art object and human being). Ironies abound, and are clinched in the final 'rare' bronze he points out at the end, which – though he naturally does not recognize it – comments on his relationship with his dead wife and his disproportionate expression of power. The Neptune of the statue is taming a sea horse: but sea horses need no taming. The poem is an excellent example of the kind of reading the new genre of the dramatic monologue, in Browning's hands, required and rewarded.

Text: *Dramatic Lyrics* (1842).

That's my last Duchess painted on the wall,
Looking as if she were alive. I call
That piece a wonder, now: Frà Pandolf's[1] hands
Worked busily a day, and there she stands.
Will't please you sit and look at her? I said   5
'Frà Pandolf' by design, for never read
Strangers like you that pictured countenance,
The depth and passion of its earnest glance,
But to myself they turned (since none puts by
The curtain I have drawn for you, but I)   10
And seemed as they would ask me, if they durst,[2]
How such a glance came there; so, not the first
Are you to turn and ask thus. Sir, 't was not
Her husband's presence only, called that spot
Of joy into the Duchess' cheek: perhaps   15
Frà Pandolf chanced to say 'Her mantle laps
'Over my lady's wrist too much,' or 'Paint
'Must never hope to reproduce the faint
'Half-flush that dies along her throat:' such stuff
Was courtesy, she thought, and cause enough   20
For calling up that spot of joy. She had
A heart – how shall I say? – too soon made glad,
Too easily impressed; she liked whate'er
She looked on, and her looks went everywhere.
Sir, 't was all one! My favour[3] at her breast,   25
The dropping of the daylight in the West,
The bough of cherries some officious fool
Broke in the orchard for her, the white mule
She rode with round the terrace – all and each
Would draw from her alike the approving speech,   30
Or blush, at least. She thanked men, – good! but thanked
Somehow – I know not how – as if she ranked
My gift of a nine-hundred-years-old name
With anybody's gift. Who'd stoop to blame
This sort of trifling? Even had you skill   35
In speech – (which I have not) – to make your will
Quite clear to such an one, and say, 'Just this
'Or that in you disgusts me; here you miss,
'Or there exceed the mark' – and if she let
Herself be lessoned so, nor plainly set   40
Her wits to yours, forsooth, and made excuse,
– E'en then would be some stooping; and I choose
Never to stoop. Oh sir, she smiled, no doubt,
Whene'er I passed her, but who passed without
Much the same smile? This grew; I gave commands;   45
Then all smiles stopped together. There she stands
As if alive. Will't please you rise? We'll meet
The company below, then. I repeat,
The Count your master's known munificence[4]
Is ample warrant that no just pretence   50

---

[1] *Frà Pandolf* imaginary painter.
[2] *durst* dared.
[3] *favour* love gift.
[4] *munificence* splendid liberality in giving.

Of mine for dowry[5] will be disallowed;
Though his fair daughter's self, as I avowed
At starting, is my object. Nay, we'll go
Together down, sir. Notice Neptune,[6] though,
Taming a sea-horse, thought a rarity,   55
Which Claus of Innsbruck[7] cast in bronze for me!

---

[5] *dowry* money brought with a bride for her husband.
[6] *Neptune* god of the sea.

[7] *Claus of Innsbruck* another invented figure (though Innsbruck was known for its bronze sculpting in the sixteenth century).

The Bishop Orders his Tomb at St Praxed's Church

Rome, 15 –

The central interest of Browning's early monologues 'Porphyria's Lover', 171–3, and 'My Last Duchess', 173–5, was pathologized psychology. In poems shortly afterwards, including 'The Bishop Orders his Tomb', Browning began to consider other themes that would occupy him throughout his career. Chiefly, here, the patterns of history, the way a speaker may be both individual and representative of the temper of an age, and the 'turning point' in historical process (cf. 'Fra Lippo Lippi', 179–88, for another monologue on a turning point). The speaker of 'The Bishop Orders his Tomb' (1845) is an Italian Renaissance prelate on his deathbed. Trying to make his sons – which of course as a Catholic priest he should not have – listen to his requests for a grand tomb in the Basilica di Santa Prassede, in Rome (a real church), he reveals his appetitive but oddly engaging personality, secular desires, hazy grasp of the Christian religion and personal animosities.

The poem contributes to a Victorian debate about the relationship between art and morality, particularly as it applies to the idea, early tested by Alexis François Rio in *De la poésie Chrétienne* (1836), that the high Italian Renaissance was a period of moral and spiritual decline, however rich its artistic achievement. The art and social critic John Ruskin (1819–1900) would declare his version of the moral decadence of the Renaissance in *The Stones of Venice* (1851–3), and he saw in Browning's work a suggestive forebear. He remarked in 1856: 'I know no other piece of modern English, prose or poetry, in which there is so much told, as in these lines, of the Renaissance spirit, – its worldliness, inconsistency, pride, hypocrisy, ignorance of itself, love of art, of luxury, and of good Latin. It is nearly all that I said of the central Renaissance in thirty pages of the *Stones of Venice* put into as many lines, Browning's being also the antecedent work.' Ruskin saw the poem addressing a fault line in European culture between the Christian sincerity of the Middle Ages and the debased values of the Renaissance (cf. 'Fra Lippo Lippi').

But however much Ruskin sought to co-opt this poem into his own paradigm of European culture's decline, Browning does not invite the reader simply to condemn his speaker and what he stands for. The Bishop's enthusiasm for physical experience is appealingly narrated, his honesty, and the pathos of his position – his sons pay little heed to him – deserve some sympathy, and, at a more general level, the poem works within the terms of comedy. Its colloquial energy is arresting, characteristic of Browning's monologues that would inject new verbal vigour into the diction of nineteenth-century poetry.

Where 'My Last Duchess' considered the haunting of the present by the past, 'The Bishop Orders his Tomb' is interested in how the present may endure in the future. Its obvious preoccupation with audience and with forms of survival in posterity can be seen to be expressive of displaced anxieties about poetic reception and the possibilities of authorial legacy (cf. 'A Toccata of Galuppi's', 202–4). The poem was first published in *Hood's Magazine* in March 1845, then in *Dramatic Romances and Lyrics* (1845).

Text: *Dramatic Romances and Lyrics* (1845).

Vanity, saith the preacher, vanity![1]
Draw round my bed: is Anselm keeping back?
Nephews – sons mine[2] . . . ah God, I know not! Well –
She, men would have to be your mother once,
    Old Gandolf envied me, so fair she was!   5
What's done is done, and she is dead beside,
    Dead long ago, and I am Bishop since,
And as she died so must we die ourselves,
And thence ye may perceive the world's a dream.
    Life, how and what is it? As here I lie   10
    In this state-chamber, dying by degrees,
Hours and long hours in the dead night, I ask
'Do I live, am I dead?' Peace, peace seems all.
Saint Praxed's[3] ever was the church for peace;
    And so, about this tomb of mine. I fought   15
With tooth and nail to save my niche, ye know:
– Old Gandolf cozened[4] me, despite my care;
Shrewd was that snatch from out the corner South
He graced his carrion with, God curse the same!
Yet still my niche is not so cramped but thence   20
    One sees the pulpit o' the epistle-side,[5]
And somewhat of the choir, those silent seats,
    And up into the aery dome where live
The angels, and a sunbeam's sure to lurk:
And I shall fill my slab of basalt[6] there,   25
    And 'neath my tabernacle[7] take my rest,
With those nine columns round me, two and two,
The odd one at my feet where Anselm stands:
Peach-blossom marble all, the rare, the ripe
    As fresh-poured red wine of a mighty pulse.   30
– Old Gandolf with his paltry onion-stone,[8]
Put me where I may look at him! True peach,
Rosy and flawless: how I earned the prize!
Draw close: that conflagration of my church
– What then? So much was saved if aught were missed!   35
My sons, ye would not be my death? Go dig
The white-grape vineyard where the oil-press stood,
    Drop water gently till the surface sink,
And if ye find . . . Ah God, I know not, I! . . .
    Bedded in store of rotten fig-leaves soft,   40
    And corded up in a tight olive-frail,[9]
Some lump, ah God, of lapis lazuli,[10]
Big as a Jew's head cut off at the nape,
Blue as a vein o'er the Madonna's[11] breast . . .

---

[1] *Vanity . . . vanity!* cf. Ecclesiastes 1.2, 'Uanitie of vanities, saith the Preacher, vanitie of vanities, all is vanitie'.

[2] *Nephews . . . mine* 'nephews' was often adopted euphemistically for 'sons' in discussions of the medieval and Renaissance Catholic priests (whom Church law meant to be celibate and chaste).

[3] *St Praxed* Santa Prassede, virgin and martyr of the second century.

[4] *cozened* tricked.

[5] *epistle-side* south side of the church from which the Epistle – one of the letters from the New Testament – is read.

[6] *basalt* greenish or brownish-black rock.

[7] *tabernacle* canopy.

[8] *onion-stone* stone of poor quality.

[9] *olive-frail* basket made of rushes.

[10] *lapis lazuli* semi-precious bright blue stone.

[11] *Madonna* Virgin Mary.

Sons, all have I bequeathed you, villas, all,   45
  That brave Frascati[12] villa with its bath,
So, let the blue lump poise between my knees,
Like God the Father's globe on both his hands
Ye worship in the Jesu Church[13] so gay,
For Gandolf shall not choose but see and burst!   50
  Swift as a weaver's shuttle fleet our years:[14]
Man goeth to the grave, and where is he?[15]
Did I say basalt for my slab, sons? Black –
'T was ever antique-black I meant! How else
Shall ye contrast my frieze to come beneath?   55
The bas-relief[16] in bronze ye promised me,
Those Pans and Nymphs[17] ye wot[18] of, and perchance
Some tripod,[19] thyrsus,[20] with a vase or so,
The Saviour at his sermon on the mount,[21]
  Saint Praxed in a glory, and one Pan   60
Ready to twitch the Nymph's[22] last garment off,
And Moses with the tables[23] . . . but I know
Ye mark me not! What do they whisper thee,
Child of my bowels,[24] Anselm? Ah, ye hope
  To revel down my villas while I gasp   65
Bricked o'er with beggar's mouldy travertine[25]
Which Gandolf from his tomb-top chuckles at!
Nay, boys, ye love me – all of jasper,[26] then!
'T is jasper ye stand pledged to, lest I grieve.
  My bath must needs be left behind, alas!   70
One block, pure green as a pistachio-nut,
There's plenty jasper somewhere in the world –
And have I not Saint Praxed's ear to pray
Horses for ye, and brown Greek manuscripts,
And mistresses with great smooth marbly limbs?   75
  – That's if ye carve my epitaph aright,
Choice Latin, picked phrase, Tully's[27] every word,
No gaudy ware like Gandolf's second line –
Tully, my masters? Ulpian[28] serves his need
And then how I shall lie through centuries,   80

---

[12] *Frascati* town close to Rome dominated by the Villa Aldobrandini.

[13] *Jesu Church* Rome's Chiesa del Gesù.

[14] *Swift . . . years* cf. Job 7.6, 'My dayes are swifter then a weauers shuttle, and are spent without hope'.

[15] *Man . . . he* cf. Job 7.9, 'As the cloud is consumed and vanisheth away: so he that goeth downe to the graue, shall come vp no more', and Job 14.10, 'But man dyeth, and wasteth away; yea, man giueth vp the ghost, and where is hee?'

[16] *bas-relief* sculpture or carving where the figures project less than one half of their true proportions.

[17] *Pans and Nymphs* figures from Classical mythology. Their conjunction with Christian iconography was a familiar trait of Renaissance tomb work. Pan, Greek god of the field and forest, was associated with licentiousness.

[18] *wot* know.

[19] *tripod* three-legged vessel used for votive offering in Classical religious rites.

[20] *thyrsus* staff or spear tipped with an ornament like a pine-cone borne by Dionysus – god of wine and orgies – and his followers.

[21] *sermon on the mount* for Jesus's Sermon on the Mount, see Matthew 5–7.

[22] *Nymph* minor deity in Classical mythology.

[23] *tables* stones on which the Ten Commandments were engraved (see Exodus 20).

[24] *bowels* seat of emotions, 'heart'.

[25] *travertine* white limestone.

[26] *jasper* precious stone, usually red.

[27] *Tully* Marcus Tullius Cicero (106–43 BC), masterly Roman orator and statesman, who set the standard for formal Latin eloquence.

[28] *Ulpian* Domitius Ulpianus, fl. 212–23 AD, a jurist: here, a lesser writer than Cicero (Tully).

And hear the blessed mutter of the mass,
And see God made and eaten all day long,
And feel the steady candle-flame, and taste
Good strong thick stupefying incense-smoke!
For as I lie here, hours of the dead night,   85
Dying in state and by such slow degrees,
I fold my arms as if they clasped a crook,[29]
And stretch my feet forth straight as stone can point,
And let the bedclothes, for a mortcloth,[30] drop
Into great laps and folds of sculptor's-work: 90
And as yon tapers dwindle, and strange thoughts
Grow, with a certain humming in my ears,
About the life before I lived this life,
And this life too, popes, cardinals and priests,
Saint Praxed at his sermon on the mount,[31]   95
Your tall pale mother with her talking eyes,
And new-found agate[32] urns as fresh as day,
And marble's language, Latin pure, discreet,
– Aha, *elucescebat*[33] quoth our friend?
No Tully, said I, Ulpian at the best!   100
Evil and brief hath been my pilgrimage.[34]
All lapis, all, sons! Else I give the Pope
My villas! Will ye ever eat my heart?
Ever your eyes were as a lizard's quick,
They glitter like your mother's for my soul,   105
Or ye would heighten my impoverished frieze,[35]
Piece out its starved design, and fill my vase
With grapes, and add a vizor[36] and a Term,[37]
And to the tripod ye would tie a lynx[38]
That in his struggle throws the thyrsus down,   110
To comfort me on my entablature[39]
Whereon I am to lie till I must ask
'Do I live, am I dead?' There, leave me, there!
For ye have stabbed me with ingratitude
To death – ye wish it – God, ye wish it! Stone –   115
Gritstone,[40] a-crumble! Clammy squares which sweat
As if the corpse they keep were oozing through –
And no more lapis to delight the world!
Well go! I bless ye. Fewer tapers there,
But in a row: and, going, turn your backs   120
– Ay, like departing altar-ministrants,
And leave me in my church, the church for peace,

[29] *crook* pastoral staff of a bishop.
[30] *mortcloth* funeral pall.
[31] *Saint . . . mount* the Bishop's mind is going: St Praxed was female, and Jesus delivered the Sermon on the Mount (see note 21).
[32] *agate* multi-coloured precious stone.
[33] *elucescebat* 'He was illustrious' (Ciceronian Latin = *elucebat*).
[34] *Evil . . . pilgrimage* cf. Genesis 47.9, 'And Iacob said vnto Pharaoh, The dayes of the yeeres of my pilgrimage are an hundred & thirtie yeres: few and euill haue the dayes of the yeeres of my life bene, and haue not attained vnto the dayes

of the yeeres of the life of my fathers, in the dayes of their pilgrimage'.
[35] *frieze* band of painted or sculptured decoration.
[36] *vizor* mask.
[37] *Term* statue representing the upper part of the body, sometimes without the arms, and terminating below in a pedestal.
[38] *lynx* lynxes, panthers and other wild cats often accompany representations of Dionysius.
[39] *entablature* the Bishop means, loosely, that which is above the frieze, but the word is not accurately used.
[40] *Gritstone* cheap sandy stone.

That I may watch at leisure if he leers –
Old Gandolf, at me, from his onion-stone,
As still he envied me, so fair she was!

125

[handwritten margin notes: Davinci : 1452-1519 / Michelangelo : 1475-1564 / RAPHAEL: 1483-1520]

Fra Lippo Lippi   *[handwritten: Renaissance 1300-1700]*

Fra Lippo Lippi (properly Filippo Lippi) was an important Renaissance Florentine painter (1406–69). Browning, in this poem from *Men and Women* (1855), takes details of his life from a book he particularly admired: Vasari's *Le Vite de' più eccelenti Pittori, Scultori, et Architettori* (1550/68), usually known in English as Vasari's *Lives of the Artists*, a collection of short biographies of major painters, sculptors and architects of Renaissance Italy. Vasari's account of Lippo includes the narrative of his escape from the house of his famous patron, Cosimo de' Medici (1389–1464), which forms the basic narrative of Browning's poem: '[The painter's] lust was so violent that when it took hold of him he could never concentrate on his work. And because of this, one time or other when he was doing something for Cosimo de' Medici in Cosimo's house, Cosimo had him locked in so that he wouldn't wander away and waste time. After he had been confined for a few days, Fra Filippo's amorous or rather his animal desires drove him one night to seize a pair of scissors, make a rope from his bed-sheets and escape through a window to pursue his own pleasures for days on end. When Cosimo discovered that he was gone, he searched for him and eventually got him back to work. And after that he always allowed him to come and go as he liked, having regretted the way he had shut him up before and realizing how dangerous it was for such a madman to be confined. Cosimo determined for the future to keep hold on him by affection and kindness and, being served all the more readily, he used to say that artists of genius were to be treated with respect, not used as hacks.'

Lippi is at once a figure from the Italian *quattrocento* (fifteenth century) and a contributor to various aesthetic discussions of relevance to Browning himself, and to the mid-nineteenth century more generally. Firstly, Browning uses Fra Lippo's life (the 'Fra' signifies he is a monastic brother) to stage a debate pertinent for his own poetry, since there is a close relationship between Lippo's aesthetic of the material world and Browning's (cf. 'Two in the Campagna', 204–6, '"Childe Roland to the Dark Tower

Came"', 195–202). Secondly, the poem contributes more widely to mid-nineteenth-century artistic culture because its concerns reflect discussions about the idealist legacy of Sir Joshua Reynolds (1723–92), John Ruskin's naturalist aesthetics and his denunciation of the Renaissance in *The Stones of Venice* (1851–3), and the realist principles of the new art of the Pre-Raphaelite Brotherhood (formed 1848). The key general issues explored here include whether the first aim of art is to idealize or to represent material reality accurately.

One of the major questions to linger over Lippo's art derives from Alexis Rio's *De la poésie Chrétienne* (1836) and Ruskin's later, related critique of the achievement of the Renaissance and its identity as a period of immorality and faithlessness (cf. 'The Bishop Orders his Tomb', 175–9). Is the immoral Lippo's naturalistic art the beginning of cultural decline, a 'grey beginning', as the painter ambiguously says at the end, or of new life? Does the poem, in mapping a transition from medieval aesthetics to Renaissance, chart the fault line, as Ruskin would have it, of European civilization? Or is Lippi's humanistic art, contrary to Ruskin, a defining step forward in the history of representation and in the liberation of the mind from the narrowing strictures of the Middle Ages? Like 'Andrea del Sarto', 189–95, 'Fra Lippo Lippi' exemplifies Browning's engagement with visual art as a creative stimulus for poetry (cf. 'Eurydice to Orpheus', 214–15), as a way of dramatizing Victorian aesthetic and moral debates, and as part of an investigation in contrasting forms of artistic masculinity.

The colloquial colour of the speaker is appealing, however awkwardly it suits a monk. Making Lippi live so vividly, Browning is perhaps continuing to muse on the question of the artist's – or writer's – endurance into posterity, the artistic afterlife, which is an important theme generally of *Men and Women*.

Text: *Men and Women* (1855).

I am poor brother Lippo, by your leave!
You need not clap your torches to my face.
Zooks,[1] what's to blame? you think you see a monk!

---

[1] *Zooks* an oath.

What, 'tis past midnight, and you go the rounds,
    And here you catch me at an alley's end   5
Where sportive ladies leave their doors ajar?
    The Carmine's[2] my cloister: hunt it up,
Do, – harry out, if you must show your zeal,
Whatever rat, there, haps[3] on his wrong hole,
And nip each softling of a wee white mouse,   10
Weke, weke, that's crept to keep him company!
Aha, you know your betters! Then, you'll take
Your hand away that's fiddling on my throat,
And please to know me likewise. Who am I?
    Why, one, sir, who is lodging with a friend   15
Three streets off – he's a certain . . . how d'ye call?
    Master – a . . . Cosimo of the Medici,[4]
I' the house that caps the corner. Boh! you were best!
Remember and tell me, the day you're hanged,
    How you affected such a gullet's-gripe![5]   20
But you, sir, it concerns you that your knaves
    Pick up a manner[6] nor discredit you:
Zooks, are we pilchards, that they sweep the streets
And count fair prize what comes into their net?
    He's Judas[7] to a tittle,[8] that man is!   25
Just such a face! Why, sir, you make amends.
Lord, I'm not angry! Bid your hangdogs go
Drink out this quarter-florin[9] to the health
Of the munificent House[10] that harbours me
(And many more beside, lads! more beside!)   30
And all's come square[11] again. I'd like his face –
    His, elbowing on his comrade in the door
With the pike and lantern, – for the slave that holds
    John Baptist's head a-dangle by the hair[12]
With one hand ('Look you, now,' as who should say)   35
And his weapon in the other, yet unwiped!
It's not your chance to have a bit of chalk,
A wood-coal or the like? or you should see!
Yes, I'm the painter, since you style me so.
What, brother Lippo's doings, up and down,   40
You know them and they take you?[13] like enough!
    I saw the proper twinkle in your eye –
'Tell you, I liked your looks at very first.
Let's sit and set things straight now, hip to haunch.
Here's spring come, and the nights one makes up bands   45
    To roam the town and sing out carnival,
And I've been three weeks shut within my mew,[14]

[Handwritten margin note: Locked up by Medici to paint]

[2] *Carmine* Carmelite Convent where Vasari says Lippo was placed aged 8.
[3] *haps* happens.
[4] *Cosimo of the Medici* Cosimo de' Medici (the Elder) (1389–1464), Florentine statesman and patron of arts.
[5] *gullet's-gripe* 'grip of the gullet'.
[6] *pick . . . manner* learn good manners.
[7] *Judas* disciple who betrays Jesus (see Luke 22). (Lippi is looking for a model.)
[8] *to a tittle* to the last detail.
[9] *quarter-florin* the gold florin was a coin in circulation in Florence from the thirteenth century.
[10] *House* of the Medici.
[11] *square* right.
[12] *I'd like . . . hair* Lippi is thinking of another model, this time for a painting of the martyrdom of John the Baptist, see Mark 6.21–9.
[13] *they take you?* you like them?
[14] *mew* cage for fattening fowl.

A-painting for the great man, saints and saints
And saints again. I could not paint all night –
Ouf! I leaned out of window for fresh air.   50
There came a hurry of feet and little feet,
A sweep of lute-strings, laughs, and whifts of song, –
          Flower o' the broom,[15]
Take away love, and our earth is a tomb!
          Flower o' the quince,   55
I let Lisa go, and what good in life since?
Flower o' the thyme – and so on. Round they went.
Scarce had they turned the corner when a titter
Like the skipping of rabbits by moonlight, – three slim shapes,
And a face that looked up . . . zooks, sir, flesh and blood,   60
That's all I'm made of! Into shreds it went,
          Curtain and counterpane and coverlet,
          All the bed-furniture – a dozen knots,
There was a ladder! Down I let myself,
Hands and feet, scrambling somehow, and so dropped,   65
And after them. I came up with the fun
Hard by Saint Laurence,[16] hail fellow, well met,[17] –
          Flower o' the rose,
If I've been merry, what matter who knows?
          And so as I was stealing back again   70
          To get to bed and have a bit of sleep
          Ere I rise up to-morrow and go work
On Jerome knocking at his poor old breast
With his great round stone to subdue the flesh,[18]
          You snap me of the sudden. Ah, I see!   75
Though your eye twinkles still, you shake your head –
Mine's shaved – a monk, you say – the sting's in that!
          If Master Cosimo announced himself,
          Mum's the word naturally; but a monk!
Come, what am I a beast for? tell us, now!   80
          I was a baby when my mother died
          And father died and left me in the street.
I starved there, God knows how, a year or two
On fig-skins, melon-parings, rinds and shucks,[19]
          Refuse and rubbish. One fine frosty day,   85
          My stomach being empty as your hat,
The wind doubled me up and down I went.
Old Aunt Lapaccia trussed me with one hand,
          (Its fellow was a stinger as I knew)
          And so along the wall, over the bridge,   90
By the straight cut to the convent. Six words there,
While I stood munching my first bread that month:
'So, boy, you're minded,' quoth the good fat father
Wiping his own mouth, 'twas refection-time,[20] –

[15] *broom* yellow flowering shrub.
[16] *Saint Laurence* S. Lorenzo, church in central Florence.
[17] *hail . . . met* conventional greeting.
[18] *Jerome . . . flesh* St Jerome (340/2–420), cardinal, hermit

and translator of the Bible, often depicted as a penitent
beating his breast with a stone. The reference is ironic.
[19] *shucks* husks, pods.
[20] *refection-time* meal time.

'To quit this very miserable world?   95
Will you renounce' . . . 'the mouthful of bread?' thought I;
By no means! Brief, they made a monk of me;
I did renounce the world, its pride and greed,
Palace, farm, villa, shop and banking-house,
Trash, such as these poor devils of Medici   100
Have given their hearts to – all at eight years old.
Well, sir, I found in time, you may be sure,
'Twas not for nothing – the good bellyful,
The warm serge[21] and the rope that goes all round,
And day-long blessed idleness beside!   105
'Let's see what the urchin's fit for' – that came next.
Not overmuch their way, I must confess.
Such a to-do! They tried me with their books:
Lord, they'd have taught me Latin in pure waste!
    Flower o' the clove,   110
    All the Latin I construe is, 'amo' I love!
But, mind you, when a boy starves in the streets
    Eight years together, as my fortune was,
    Watching folk's faces to know who will fling
The bit of half-stripped grape-bunch he desires,   115
And who will curse or kick him for his pains, –
    Which gentleman processional and fine,
    Holding a candle to the Sacrament,
Will wink and let him lift a plate and catch
    The droppings of the wax to sell again,   120
Or holla for the Eight[22] and have him whipped, –
How say I? – nay, which dog bites, which lets drop
His bone from the heap of offal in the street, –
Why, soul and sense of him grow sharp alike,
He learns the look of things, and none the less   125
For admonition from the hunger-pinch.
I had a store of such remarks, be sure,
Which, after I found leisure, turned to use.
    I drew men's faces on my copy-books,
Scrawled them within the antiphonary's marge,[23]   130
Joined legs and arms to the long music-notes,
Found eyes and nose and chin for A's and B's,
And made a string of pictures of the world
Betwixt the ins and outs of verb and noun,
On the wall, the bench, the door. The monks looked black.   135
'Nay,' quoth the Prior, 'turn him out, d' ye say?
In no wise. Lose a crow and catch a lark.
What if at last we get our man of parts,
We Carmelites, like those Camaldolese[24]
And Preaching Friars,[25] to do our church up fine   140
And put the front on it that ought to be!'

---

[21] *serge* durable woollen fabric of a monk's habit.
[22] *Eight* Council of Eight, magistrates of Florence.
[23] *antiphonary's marge* margin of a book of liturgical chants.
[24] *Camaldolese* order of hermits and cenobites (those who live in a monastic community) founded in the eleventh century.
[25] *Preaching Friars* Dominicans (religious order).

And hereupon he bade me daub away.
Thank you! my head being crammed, the walls a blank,
Never was such prompt disemburdening.
First, every sort of monk, the black and white,[26]   145
I drew them, fat and lean: then, folk at church,
From good old gossips waiting to confess
Their cribs[27] of barrel-droppings, candle-ends, –
To the breathless fellow at the altar-foot,
Fresh from his murder, safe[28] and sitting there   150
With the little children round him in a row
Of admiration, half for his beard and half
For that white anger of his victim's son
Shaking a fist at him with one fierce arm,
Signing himself with the other because of Christ   155
(Whose sad face on the cross sees only this
After the passion[29] of a thousand years)
Till some poor girl, her apron o'er her head,
(Which the intense eyes looked through) came at eve
On tiptoe, said a word, dropped in a loaf,   160
Her pair of earrings and a bunch of flowers
(The brute took growling), prayed, and so was gone.
I painted all, then cried "Tis ask and have;
Choose, for more's ready!' – laid the ladder flat,
And showed my covered bit of cloister-wall   165
The monks closed in a circle and praised loud
Till checked, taught what to see and not to see,
Being simple bodies, – 'That's the very man!
Look at the boy who stoops to pat the dog!
That woman's like the Prior's niece[30] who comes   170
To care about his asthma: it's the life!'
But there my triumph's straw-fire flared and funked;[31]
Their betters took their turn to see and say:
The Prior and the learned pulled a face
And stopped all that in no time. 'How? what's here?   175
Quite from the mark of painting, bless us all!
Faces, arms, legs and bodies like the true
As much as pea and pea! it's devil's-game!
Your business is not to catch men with show,
With homage to the perishable clay,   180
But lift them over it, ignore it all,
Make them forget there's such a thing as flesh.
Your business is to paint the souls of men –
Man's soul, and it's a fire, smoke . . . no, it's not . . .
It's vapour done up like a new-born babe –   185
(In that shape when you die it leaves your mouth)[32]
It's . . . well, what matters talking, it's the soul!
Give us no more of body than shows soul!

---

[26] *black and white* from the colour of their habits, the Dominicans are popularly known as Black Friars, the Carmelites as White Friars.

[27] *cribs* petty thefts.

[28] *safe* a church sanctuary, in accordance with medieval law, was not under the jurisdiction of secular authorities.

[29] *passion* Jesus's Passion is his suffering on the cross that, Christians believe, continues throughout subsequent ages of sinful human history.

[30] *niece* euphemism for mistress.

[31] *funked* smoked, caused an offensive smell.

[32] *mouth* reference to the traditional notion that the soul could be seen leaving the mouth on death.

Here's Giotto,[33] with his Saint a-praising God,
That sets us praising, – why not stop with him?   190
Why put all thoughts of praise out of our head
With wonder at lines, colours, and what not?
Paint the soul, never mind the legs and arms!
    Rub all out, try at it a second time.
Oh, that white smallish female with the breasts,   195
She's just my niece . . . Herodias,[34] I would say, –
Who went and danced and got men's heads cut off!
    Have it all out!' Now, is this sense, I ask?
    A fine way to paint soul, by painting body
So ill, the eye can't stop there, must go further   200
And can't fare worse! Thus, yellow does for white
When what you put for yellow's simply black,
    And any sort of meaning looks intense
When all beside itself means and looks nought.
    Why can't a painter lift each foot in turn,   205
    Left foot and right foot, go a double step,
Make his flesh liker and his soul more like,
Both in their order? Take the prettiest face,
The Prior's niece . . . patron-saint – is it so pretty
    You can't discover if it means hope, fear,   210
    Sorrow or joy? won't beauty go with these?
Suppose I've made her eyes all right and blue,
Can't I take breath and try to add life's flash,
And then add soul and heighten them threefold?
    Or say there's beauty with no soul at all –   215
    (I never saw it – put the case the same –)
If you get simple beauty and nought else,
    You get about the best thing God invents:
That's somewhat: and you'll find the soul you have missed,
    Within yourself, when you return him thanks.   220
'Rub all out!' Well, well, there's my life, in short,
    And so the thing has gone on ever since.
I'm grown a man no doubt, I've broken bounds:
    You should not take a fellow eight years old
    And make him swear to never kiss the girls.   225
I'm my own master, paint now as I please –
Having a friend, you see, in the Corner-house![35]
Lord, it's fast holding by the rings in front[36] –
Those great rings serve more purposes than just
    To plant a flag in, or tie up a horse!   230
And yet the old schooling sticks, the old grave eyes
    Are peeping o'er my shoulder as I work,
The heads shake still – 'It's art's decline, my son!
    You're not of the true painters, great and old;
    Brother Angelico's[37] the man, you'll find;   235
    Brother Lorenzo[38] stands his single peer:

---

[33] *Giotto* (1267–1337), early Renaissance Italian painter.
[34] *Herodias* in most versions, it is the daughter of Herodias who asks for the head of John the Baptist (see Matthew 14.6).
[35] *Corner-house* see l. 18.

[36] *rings in front* rings that provide the means for securing horses.
[37] *Angelico* Fra Angelico (1400–55), monastic Florentine painter.
[38] *Lorenzo* Lorenzo Monaco (c.1370–c.1423), Florentine painter.

Fag[39] on at flesh, you'll never make the third!'
    Flower o' the pine,
You keep your mistr . . . manners, and I'll stick to mine!
I'm not the third, then: bless us, they must know!   240
Don't you think they're the likeliest to know,
They with their Latin? So, I swallow my rage,
Clench my teeth, suck my lips in tight, and paint
To please them – sometimes do and sometimes don't;
    For, doing most, there's pretty sure to come   245
A turn, some warm eve finds me at my saints –
A laugh, a cry, the business of the world –
    (Flower o' the peach,
Death for us all, and his own life for each!)
And my whole soul revolves, the cup runs over,[40]   250
The world and life's too big to pass for a dream,
And I do these wild things in sheer despite,
    And play the fooleries you catch me at,
In pure rage! The old mill-horse, out at grass
After hard years, throws up his stiff heels so,   255
Although the miller does not preach to him
The only good of grass is to make chaff.
What would men have? Do they like grass or no –
May they or mayn't they? all I want's the thing
    Settled for ever one way. As it is,   260
You tell too many lies and hurt yourself:
You don't like what you only like too much,
You do like what, if given you at your word,
    You find abundantly detestable.
For me, I think I speak as I was taught;   265
I always see the garden and God there
A-making man's wife:[41] and, my lesson learned,
    The value and significance of flesh,
I can't unlearn ten minutes afterwards,

You understand me: I'm a beast, I know.   270
    But see, now – why, I see as certainly
As that the morning-star's about to shine,
What will hap[42] some day. We've a youngster here
    Comes to our convent, studies what I do,
Slouches and stares and lets no atom drop: 275
His name is Guidi[43] – he'll not mind the monks –
They call him Hulking Tom,[44] he lets them talk –
He picks my practice up – he'll paint apace,
    I hope so – though I never live so long,
I know what's sure to follow. You be judge!   280
    You speak no Latin more than I, belike,

[39] *Fag* work.
[40] *the cup runs over* cf. Psalm 23.5, 'Thou preparest a table before me, in the presence of mine enemies: thou anointest my head with oyle, my cuppe runneth ouer'.
[41] *I always . . . wife* cf. Genesis 2.21–2, 'And the LORD God caused a deepe sleepe to fall vpon Adam, and hee slept; and he tooke one of his ribs, and closed vp the flesh in stead thereof. And the rib which the LORD God had taken from man, made hee a woman, & brought her vnto the man.'
[42] *hap* happen.
[43] *Guidi* paternal name of Tommaso di Giovanni (1401–28) – in fact, Lippo's teacher, not his pupil.
[44] *Hulking Tom* Vasari thought Tommaso di Giovanni clumsy.

However, you're my man, you've seen the world
– The beauty and the wonder and the power,
The shapes of things, their colours, lights and shades,
Changes, surprises, – and God made it all!   285
– For what? Do you feel thankful, ay or no,
For this fair town's face, yonder river's line,
The mountain round it and the sky above,
Much more the figures of man, woman, child,
These are the frame to? What's it all about?   290
To be passed over, despised? or dwelt upon,
Wondered at? oh, this last of course! – you say.
But why not do as well as say, – paint these
Just as they are, careless what comes of it?
God's works – paint anyone, and count it crime   295
To let a truth slip. Don't object, 'His works
Are here already; nature is complete:
Suppose you reproduce her – (which you can't)
There's no advantage! you must beat her, then.'
For, don't you mark? we're made so that we love   300
First when we see them painted, things we have passed
Perhaps a hundred times nor cared to see;
And so they are better, painted – better to us,
Which is the same thing. Art was given for that;
God uses us to help each other so,   305
Lending our minds out. Have you noticed, now,
Your cullion's[45] hanging face? A bit of chalk,
And trust me but you should, though! How much more,
If I drew higher things with the same truth!
That were to take the Prior's pulpit-place,   310
Interpret God to all of you! Oh, oh,
It makes me mad to see what men shall do
And we in our graves! This world's no blot for us,
Nor blank; it means intensely, and means good:
To find its meaning is my meat and drink.   315
'Ay, but you don't so instigate to prayer!'
Strikes in the Prior: 'when your meaning's plain
It does not say to folk – remember matins,[46]
Or, mind you fast next Friday!' Why, for this
What need of art at all? A skull and bones,   320
Two bits of stick nailed crosswise, or, what's best,
A bell to chime the hour with, does as well.
I painted a Saint Laurence six months since
At Prato,[47] splashed the fresco in fine style:
'How looks my painting, now the scaffold's down?'   325
I ask a brother: 'Hugely,' he returns –
'Already not one phiz[48] of your three slaves
Who turn the Deacon off his toasted side,[49]
But's scratched and prodded to our heart's content,
The pious people have so eased their own   330

[45] *cullion* rascal.
[46] *matins* early morning service of the monks'
day.
[47] *Saint . . . Prato* St Lawrence was a Roman deacon,
martyred in 258. No picture of him is known in Prato (city

in Tuscany) now but, as we find out, Lippi describes the
fresco being swiftly destroyed.
[48] *phiz* face.
[49] *Who . . . side* tradition ascribes to Lawrence martyrdom
on a red hot grid iron.

With coming to say prayers there in a rage:
We get on fast to see the bricks beneath.
Expect another job this time next year,
For pity and religion grow i'the crowd –
Your painting serves its purpose!' Hang the fools! 335

– That is – you'll not mistake an idle word
Spoke in a huff by a poor monk, Got wot,[50]
Tasting the air this spicy night which turns
The unaccustomed head like Chianti wine![51]
Oh, the church knows! don't misreport me, now! 340
It's natural a poor monk out of bounds
Should have his apt word to excuse himself:
And hearken how I plot to make amends.
I have bethought me: I shall paint a piece
. . . There's for you! Give me six months, then go, see 345
Something in Sant' Ambrogio's![52] Bless the nuns!
They want a cast o' my office. I shall paint
God in the midst, Madonna and her babe,
Ringed by a bowery flowery angel-brood,
Lilies and vestments and white faces, sweet 350
As puff on puff of grated orris-root[53]
When ladies crowd to Church at midsummer.
And then i' the front, of course a saint or two –
Saint John, because he saves the Florentines,[54]
Saint Ambrose,[55] who puts down in black and white 355
The convent's friends and gives them a long day,
And Job,[56] I must have him there past mistake,
The man of Uz[57] (and Us without the z,
Painters who need his patience). Well, all these
Secured at their devotion, up shall come 360
Out of a corner when you least expect,
As one by a dark stair into a great light,
Music and talking, who but Lippo![58] I! –
Mazed, motionless and moonstruck – I'm the man!
Back I shrink – what is this I see and hear? 365
I, caught up with my monk's-things by mistake,
My old serge gown and rope that goes all round,
I, in this presence, this pure company!
Where's a hole, where's a corner for escape?
Then steps a sweet angelic slip of a thing 370
Forward, puts out a soft palm – 'Not so fast!'
– Addresses the celestial presence, 'nay –
He made you and devised you, after all,
Though he's none of you! Could Saint John there draw –

---

[50] *Got wot* God knows.
[51] *Chianti wine* from a region of Tuscany.
[52] *Sant' Ambrogio's* the painting, *Coronation of the Virgin* (1441–7), is now in the Uffizi in Florence (see plate 3).
[53] *orris-root* iris-root, known for its oil.
[54] *Saint John . . . Florentines* John the Baptist, patron saint of Florence.
[55] *Saint Ambrose* (c.340–97), Bishop of Milan, Doctor of the Church.

[56] *Job* see the Book of Job in the Old Testament.
[57] *man of Uz* Job ('There was a man in the land of Uz, whose name was Iob', Job 1.1).
[58] *who but Lippo!* Browning may have read that Lippi portrayed himself in the painting, but there is no scholarly agreement about this.

His camel-hair[59] make up a painting-brush?   375
We come to brother Lippo for all that,
    Iste perfecit opus![60] So, all smile –
I shuffle sideways with my blushing face
Under the cover of a hundred wings
Thrown like a spread of kirtles[61] when you're gay   380
And play hot cockles,[62] all the doors being shut,
Till, wholly unexpected, in there pops
The hothead husband! Thus I scuttle off
To some safe bench behind, not letting go
    The palm of her, the little lily thing   385
That spoke the good word for me in the nick,[63]
Like the Prior's niece . . . Saint Lucy[64] I would say.
And so all's saved for me, and for the church
A pretty picture gained. Go, six months hence!
Your hand, sir, and good-bye: no lights, no lights!   390
The street's hushed, and I know my own way back,
Don't fear me! There's the grey beginning. Zooks!

[59] *camel-hair* 'And the same Iohn had his raiment of camels haire, and a leatherne girdle about his loynes, and his meate was locusts and wilde hony', Mark 3.4.

[60] *Iste . . . opus* 'he completed the work' (Latin). The tag is visible on a small banner in the *Coronation*.

[61] *kirtles* clothes, petticoats.

[62] *hot cockles* rustic game in which one player lies face downwards, or kneels down with his eyes covered, and, being struck on the back by the others in turn, guesses who hit him.

[63] *in the nick* just before time ran out.

[64] *Saint Lucy* virgin and martyr (d. 303), who died after being saved from enforced prostitution.

Plate 3   Filippo Lippi, *Coronation of the Virgin* (1441–7), Uffizi, Florence/photo Bridgeman Art Library, London.

Andrea del Sarto

(Called 'The Faultless Painter')

Browning's dramatic monologue, set in 1525, published in 1855, makes a natural comparison with 'Fra Lippo Lippi', 179–88, to complete a diptych of sharply contrasting forms of artistic manliness. Once again, Browning's chief source for this representation of Andrea del Sarto (1486–1530), a Florentine Renaissance painter, is Vasari's *Lives* (see the headnote to 'Fra Lippo Lippi', 179). Vasari was in no doubt that Andrea's abilities were great, but he saw him hampered by a weakness of mind and a demanding wife. He wrote that the painter was one 'in whom art and nature combined to show all that may be done in painting, when design, colouring, and invention unite in one and the same person. Had this master possessed a somewhat bolder and more elevated mind, had be been as much distinguished for higher qualifications as he was for genius and depth of judgment in the art he practised, he would beyond all doubt, have been without an equal. But there was a certain timidity of mind, a sort of diffidence and want of force in his nature, which rendered it impossible that those evidences of ardour and animation, which are proper to the more exalted character, should ever appear in him; nor did he at any time display one particle of that elevation which, could it be have been added to the advantage wherewith he was endowed, would have rendered him a truly divine painter.'

From this, it was natural that Browning's central interest in Andrea's life – and the poem is particularly devoted to the exploration of *character* – should be moral failure. The painter is possessed of a flawless technique, but lacks the capacity of exertion, either in his painting or in his private life. In declaring that 'a man's reach should exceed his grasp, / Or what's a heaven for?' Andrea condemns himself in words that have a close relationship to Browning's own ethical principles. The question of the moral value of failure – part of Browning's Protestant inheritance – is also considered in '"Childe Roland to the Dark Tower Came"', 195–202, 'Two in the Campagna', 204–6, and, from a different angle, in 'Eurydice to Orpheus',

214–15. Sexuality and creativity were productively related in 'Fra Lippo Lippi'; for 'Andrea del Sarto', marriage has brought – so he claims – grave problems. He looks with envy at those great painters who are unmarried or homosexual. But what the reader sees is Andrea searching for excuses. The enervated pace and diction of this monologue help define Andrea against the energies of 'Fra Lippo Lippi'. Its first line is, apparently, a statement to restore calm but, once the monologue has been read, the reader realizes it has no real expectation behind it but a weary acceptance of failing that marks Andrea throughout; the last three words of the poem are deeply ironic.

'Andrea del Sarto' was probably written in 1853, the same year that Matthew Arnold published the volume of *Poems* with its important Preface in which he repudiated verse that dwelt on unresolved human problems. No poetical pleasure was to be found, Arnold said, in works 'in which . . . suffering finds no vent in action; in which a continuous state of mental distress is prolonged'. The 'eternal objects of poetry' were, claimed the author of the now spurned 'Empedocles on Etna', 268–95, 'actions; human actions; possessing an inherent interest in themselves, and which are to be communicated in an interesting manner by the art of the poet'. Browning's monologue provides a sharp comment on such a preference, a comment that, by its publication in 1855, may have become part of its intention. 'Andrea del Sarto' explores the 'inherent interest' of human *in*action, an enthralling dramatic moment is made from domestic suffering and the beguiling impotence of inertia. It was nicely appropriate, given this contest between alternative views of the poetic possibilities of inaction, that it was Robert Browning who, in due course, encouraged Arnold to restore 'Empedocles on Etna' to print, the poem that had seemed to its author the quintessence of stalled deed.

Text: *Men and Women* (1855).

> But do not let us quarrel any more,
> No, my Lucrezia;[1] bear with me for once:
> Sit down and all shall happen as you wish.
> You turn your face, but does it bring your heart?
> I'll work then for your friend's friend, never fear,   5
> Treat his own subject after his own way,

---

[1] *Lucrezia* Andrea's wife.

Fix his own time, accept too his own price,
And shut the money into this small hand
When next it takes mine. Will it? tenderly?
Oh, I'll content him, – but to-morrow, Love!   10
I often am much wearier than you think,
This evening more than usual, and it seems
As if – forgive now – should you let me sit
Here by the window with your hand in mine
And look a half-hour forth on Fiesole,[2]   15
Both of one mind, as married people use,
Quietly, quietly the evening through,
I might get up to-morrow to my work
Cheerful and fresh as ever. Let us try.
To-morrow, how you shall be glad for this!   20
Your soft hand is a woman of itself,
And mine the man's bared breast she curls inside.
Don't count the time lost, neither; you must serve
For each of the five pictures we require:
It saves a model.[3] So! keep looking so –   25
My serpentining beauty, rounds on rounds!
– How could you ever prick those perfect ears,
Even to put the pearl there! oh, so sweet –
My face, my moon, my everybody's moon,
Which everybody looks on and calls his,   30
And, I suppose, is looked on by in turn,
While she looks – no one's: very dear, no less.
You smile? why, there's my picture ready made,
There's what we painters call our harmony!
A common greyness silvers everything, –   35
All in a twilight, you and I alike
– You, at the point of your first pride in me
(That's gone you know), – but I, at every point;
My youth, my hope, my art, being all toned down
To yonder sober pleasant Fiesole.[4]   40
There's the bell clinking from the chapel-top;
That length of convent-wall across the way
Holds the trees safer, huddled more inside;
The last monk leaves the garden; days decrease,
And autumn grows, autumn in everything.   45
Eh? the whole seems to fall into a shape
As if I saw alike my work and self
And all that I was born to be and do,
A twilight-piece. Love, we are in God's hand.
How strange now, looks the life he makes us lead;   50
So free we seem, so fettered fast we are!
I feel he laid the fetter: let it lie!
This chamber for example – turn your head –
All that's behind us! You don't understand
Nor care to understand about my art,   55
But you can hear at least when people speak:

---

[2] *Fiesole* elegant hill town close to Florence.
[3] *saves a model* Vasari remarked how frequently Andrea used his wife as a model.

[4] *My youth . . . Fiesole* Vasari noted that Andrea would have benefited from longer in Rome.

And that cartoon,[5] the second from the door
– It is the thing, Love! so such things should be –
Behold Madonna![6] – I am bold to say.
I can do with my pencil what I know,   60
What I see, what at bottom of my heart
I wish for, if I ever wish so deep –
Do easily, too – what I say, perfectly,
I do not boast, perhaps: yourself are judge,
Who listened to the Legate's[7] talk last week,   65
And just as much they used to say in France.
At any rate 'tis easy, all of it!
No sketches first, no studies, that's long past:
I do what many dream of, all their lives,
– Dream? strive to do, and agonize to do,   70
And fail in doing. I could count twenty such
On twice your fingers, and not leave this town,
Who strive – you don't know how the others strive
To paint a little thing like that you smeared
Carelessly passing with your robes afloat, –   75
Yet do much less, so much less, Someone says,[8]
(I know his name, no matter) – so much less!
Well, less is more, Lucrezia: I am judged.
There burns a truer light of God in them,
In their vexed beating stuffed and stopped-up brain,   80
Heart, or whate'er else, than goes on to prompt
This low-pulsed forthright craftsman's hand of mine.
Their works drop groundward, but themselves, I know,
Reach many a time a heaven that's shut to me,
Enter and take their place there sure enough,   85
Though they come back and cannot tell the world.
My works are nearer heaven, but I sit here.
The sudden blood of these men! at a word –
Praise them, it boils, or blame them, it boils too.
I, painting from myself and to myself,   90
Know what I do, am unmoved by men's blame
Or their praise either. Somebody remarks
Morello's[9] outline there is wrongly traced,
His hue mistaken; what of that? or else,
Rightly traced and well ordered; what of that?   95
Speak as they please, what does the mountain care?
Ah, but a man's reach should exceed his grasp,
Or what's a heaven for? All is silver-grey
Placid and perfect with my art: the worse!
I know both what I want and what might gain,   100
And yet how profitless to know, to sigh
'Had I been two, another and myself,
'Our head would have o'erlooked the world!' No doubt.
Yonder's a work now, of that famous youth

---

[5] *cartoon* drawing on stout paper, made as a design for a
painting of the same size as the final version.
[6] *Madonna* the Virgin Mary.
[7] *Legate* Papal representative; here, the Legate was
commending Andrea's work.

[8] *Someone* Michelangelo Buonarroti (1475–1564), Italian
Renaissance painter, sculptor and architect.
[9] *Morello* Mount Morello in the Apennines, north of
Florence.

The Urbinate[10] who died five years ago.   105
('Tis copied, George Vasari[11] sent it me.)
Well, I can fancy how he did it all,
Pouring his soul, with kings and popes to see,
Reaching, that heaven might so replenish him,
Above and through his art – for it gives way;   110
That arm is wrongly put – and there again –
A fault to pardon in the drawing's lines,
Its body, so to speak: its soul is right,
He means right – that, a child may understand.
Still, what an arm! and I could alter it: 115
But all the play, the insight and the stretch –
Out of me, out of me! And wherefore out?
Had you enjoined them on me, given me soul,
We might have risen to Rafael, I and you!
Nay, Love, you did give all I asked, I think –   120
More than I merit, yes, by many times.
But had you – oh, with the same perfect brow,
And perfect eyes, and more than perfect mouth,
And the low voice my soul hears, as a bird
The fowler's pipe, and follows to the snare –   125
Had you, with these the same, but brought a mind!
Some women do so. Had the mouth there urged
'God and the glory! never care for gain.
'The present by the future, what is that?
'Live for fame, side by side with Agnolo![12]   130
'Rafael is waiting: up to God, all three!'
I might have done it for you. So it seems:
Perhaps not. All is as God over-rules.
Beside, incentives come from the soul's self;
The rest avail not. Why do I need you?   135
What wife had Rafael, or has Agnolo?[13]
In this world, who can do a thing, will not;
And who would do it, cannot, I perceive:
Yet the will's somewhat – somewhat, too, the power –
And thus we half-men struggle. At the end,   140
God, I conclude, compensates, punishes.
'Tis safer for me, if the award be strict,
That I am something underrated here,
Poor this long while, despised, to speak the truth.
I dared not, do you know, leave home all day,   145
For fear of chancing on the Paris lords.[14]
The best is when they pass and look aside;
But they speak sometimes; I must bear it all.
Well may they speak! That Francis, that first time,
And that long festal year at Fontainebleau![15]   150

---

[10] *Urbinate* Raphael (Raffaello Sanzio) (1483–1520), Italian Renaissance painter and architect, born at Urbino.
[11] *Vasari* Giorgio Vasari (1511–74), author of the *Vite*, painter and architect, a friend of Andrea: see headnote, 189, and the headnote, 179, to 'Fra Lippo Lippi'.
[12] *Agnolo* Michelangelo.
[13] *What wife . . . Agnolo* Raphael had mistresses but did not marry; Michelangelo did not marry, and was probably homosexual.

[14] *Paris lords* see l. 214.
[15] *That Francis . . . Fontainebleau* François I (1494–1547), King of France, who admired Andrea and was, at first, a generous patron to him. The *château* of Fontainebleau was François's favourite residence, which he had designed to rival an Italian Renaissance *palazzo*. Among others, he invited Leonardo da Vinci and Benvenuto Cellini to work on it.

I surely then could sometimes leave the ground,
        Put on the glory, Rafael's daily wear,
    In that humane great monarch's golden look, –
        One finger in his beard or twisted curl
Over his mouth's good mark that made the smile,   155
        One arm about my shoulder, round my neck,
    The jingle of his gold chain in my ear,
    I painting proudly with his breath on me,
All his court round him, seeing with his eyes,
Such frank French eyes, and such a fire of souls   160
Profuse, my hand kept plying by those hearts, –
    And, best of all, this, this, this face beyond,
This in the background, waiting on my work,
        To crown the issue with a last reward!
    A good time, was it not, my kingly days?   165
And had you not grown restless[16] . . . but I know –
'T is done and past; 't was right, my instinct said;
    Too live the life grew, golden and not grey,
And I'm the weak-eyed bat no sun should tempt
Out of the grange whose four walls make his world.   170
        How could it end in any other way?
You called me, and I came home to your heart.
The triumph was – to reach and stay there; since
    I reached it ere the triumph, what is lost?
Let my hands frame your face in your hair's gold,   175
        You beautiful Lucrezia that are mine!
    'Rafael did this, Andrea painted that;
    'The Roman's[17] is the better when you pray,
    'But still the other's Virgin was his wife – '
        Men will excuse me. I am glad to judge   180
Both pictures in your presence; clearer grows
        My better fortune, I resolve to think.
    For, do you know, Lucrezia, as God lives,
        Said one day Agnolo, his very self,
    To Rafael . . . I have known it all these years . . .   185
(When the young man[18] was flaming out his thoughts
        Upon a palace-wall for Rome to see,
        Too lifted up in heart because of it)
    'Friend, there's a certain sorry little scrub[19]
    'Goes up and down our Florence, none cares how,   190
        'Who, were he set to plan and execute
    'As you are, pricked on by your popes and kings,
    'Would bring the sweat into that brow of yours!'[20]
    To Rafael's! – And indeed the arm is wrong.
        I hardly dare . . . yet, only you to see,   195
Give the chalk here – quick, thus the line should go!
        Ay, but the soul! he's Rafael! rub it out!
        Still, all I care for, if he spoke the truth,

---

[16] *restless* Vasari notes that Lucrezia 'wrote with bitter complaints to Andrea, declaring that she never ceased to weep, and was in perpetual affliction at his absence'.
[17] *Roman's* Raphael, who died in Rome after working for the last years of his life on St Peter's, the Sistine Chapel and the Vatican apartments.

[18] *young man* Raphael.
[19] *scrub* person of little account or poor appearance.
[20] *Friend . . . of yours* Michelangelo is said to have remarked to Raphael that 'there is in Florence a mannikin who, if he were employed on great matters, as Raphael himself was, would have brought sweat to his brow'.

(What he? why, who but Michel Agnolo?
Do you forget already words like those?)   200
If really there was such a chance, so lost, –
Is, whether you're – not grateful – but more pleased.
Well, let me think so. And you smile indeed!
This hour has been an hour! Another smile?
If you would sit thus by me every night   205
I should work better, do you comprehend?
I mean that I should earn more, give you more.
See, it is settled dusk now; there's a star;
Morello's gone, the watch-lights show the wall,
The cue-owls[21] speak the name we call them by,   210
Come from the window, love, – come in, at last,
Inside the melancholy little house
We built to be so gay with. God is just.
King Francis may forgive me:[22] oft at nights
When I look up from painting, eyes tired out,   215
The walls become illumined, brick from brick
Distinct, instead of mortar, fierce bright gold,
That gold of his I did cement them with!
Let us but love each other. Must you go?
That Cousin[23] here again? he waits outside?   220
Must see you – you, and not with me? Those loans?
More gaming debts to pay? you smiled for that?
Well, let smiles buy me! have you more to spend?
While hand and eye and something of a heart
Are left me, work's my ware, and what's it worth?   225
I'll pay my fancy. Only let me sit
The grey remainder of the evening out,
Idle, you call it, and muse perfectly
How I could paint, were I but back in France,
One picture, just one more – the Virgin's face,   230
Not yours this time! I want you at my side
To hear them – that is, Michel Agnolo –
Judge all I do and tell you of its worth.
Will you? To-morrow, satisfy your friend.
I take the subjects for his corridor,[24]   235
Finish the portrait out of hand – there, there,
And throw him in another thing or two
If he demurs; the whole should prove enough
To pay for this same Cousin's freak. Beside,
What's better and what's all I care about,   240

---

[21] *cue-owl* Scops-owl, common around the Mediterranean.
[22] *King . . . me* Vasari notes that the King allowed Andrea to
go back to his wife in Florence on condition that he return
with works of art: 'The king, confiding in these promises,
gave him money for the purchase of those pictures and
sculptures. Andrea, taking an oath on the gospels to return
within the space of a few months, and that done he
departed to his native city. He arrived safely in Florence,
enjoying the society of his beautiful wife and that of his
friends, with the sight of his native city during several
months; but when the period specified by the kind . . . had
come and passed, he found himself at the end, not only of

his own money, but what with building, indulging himself
in various pleasures and doing no work, of that belonging
to the French monarch also, the whole of which he has
consumed. He was nevertheless determined to return to
France, but the prayers and tears of his wife had more
power than his own necessities, or the faith which he had
pledged to the king: he remained therefore in Florence, and
the French monarch was so greatly angered thereby, that
for a long time after he would not look at the paintings of
Florentine masters.'
[23] *Cousin* lover, clearly.
[24] *his corridor* that is, where he displays his paintings.

Get you the thirteen scudi[25] for the ruff!
Love, does that please you? Ah, but what does he,
The Cousin! what does he to please you more?

I am grown peaceful as old age to-night.
I regret little, I would change still less.   245
Since there my past life lies, why alter it?
The very wrong to Francis! – it is true
I took his coin, was tempted and complied,
And built this house and sinned, and all is said.
My father and my mother died of want.[26]   250
Well, had I riches of my own? you see
How one gets rich! Let each one bear his lot.
They were born poor, lived poor, and poor they died:
And I have laboured somewhat in my time
And not been paid profusely. Some good son   255
Paint my two hundred pictures[27] – let him try!
No doubt, there's something strikes a balance. Yes,
You loved me quite enough, it seems to-night.
This must suffice me here. What would one have?
In heaven, perhaps, new chances, one more chance –   260
Four great walls in the New Jerusalem,
Meted[28] on each side by the angel's reed,[29]
For Leonard,[30] Rafael, Agnolo and me
To cover – the three first without a wife,[31]
While I have mine! So – still they overcome   265
Because there's still Lucrezia, – as I choose.

Again the Cousin's whistle! Go, my Love.

---

[25] *scudi* plural of *scudo*, coin used widely in Renaissance Italian states.

[26] *My father . . . want* Vasari notes of Lucrezia that she had 'as much pride and haughtiness as beauty and fascination. She delighted in trapping the hearts of men, and among others ensnared the unlucky Andrea, whose immoderate love for her soon caused him to neglect the studies demanded by his art, and in great measure to discontinue the assistance which he had given to his parents.'

[27] *two hundred pictures* Andrea was a prolific painter, though only about 90 of his works are known to survive today.

[28] *Meted* measured.

[29] *Four great . . . reed* 'And hee that talked with mee, had a golden reede to measure the citie, and the gates thereof, and the wall thereof. And the city lieth foure square, and the length is as large as the breadth: and he measured the city with the reed, twelue thousand furlongs: the length, and the breadth, and the height of it are equall', Revelation 21.15–16.

[30] *Leonard* Leonardo da Vinci (1452–1519), Italian Renaissance painter, architect, designer and engineer.

[31] *without a wife* Leonardo was probably also homosexual.

'Childe Roland to the Dark Tower Came'

(See Edgar's song in Lear)

This is Browning's most enigmatic essay in the medievalist mode, and a particularly open-ended meditation on the morality of failure (for other examples of Victorian medievalism, see Tennyson's 'Morte d'Arthur', 76–84, and William Morris's 'The Defence of Guenevere', 428–38, 'Concerning Geffray Teste Noire', 438–45, and 'The Haystack in the Floods', 423–7; for other Browning poems that consider issues of failure, see 'Andrea del Sarto', 189–95, and 'Two in the Campagna', 204–6). Browning invoked a myth of Romantic authorship when recounting the genesis of this mysterious piece, saying that '"Childe Roland to the Dark Tower Came"' (1855) began 'as a kind of dream' that he felt compelled to write down. 'I did not know then what I meant,' he said, '. . . and I'm sure I don't know now. But I am very fond of it.' He provocatively distanced the text from authorial intention. And he was speaking of a dramatic monologue, a form that already involved, as a key property, the desynonymization of speaker and poet.

'"Childe Roland to the Dark Tower Came"' is, in part, an anti-romance, the story of a quest evacuated of a sense of noble adventure, clear moral purpose and chivalric clarity (a 'Childe' is a medieval title for a youth of gentle birth). It follows a dream-like, or rather nightmare-like, logic as a study in the grotesque that maps, perhaps, an internal mindscape as much as an imagined landscape. '"Childe Roland to the Dark Tower Came"' exploits the gothic mode to create an imaginary world of extraordinary malevolence, in which the details of the Childe's journey are depicted in gruesome close-focus. That same fidelity to physical form that Fra Lippo Lippi articulates as a central feature of his aesthetic (ll. 199–220) is here applied to the representation of the diseased. On the role of the particular – the vividly realized facts of nature – in Victorian poetry, see also D. G. Rossetti's 'Song 8: The Woodspurge', 368–9.

Browning's conclusion particularly challenges the reader seeking closure. Does the dauntless blowing of the slug-horn mean that the Childe – if indeed it is he who speaks the poem – has succeeded, and if so, in what? Has he managed to wring some form of heroic action, some kind of conquest, despite the legacy of his peers? Or is his act one of terrible folly? Is there something morally tainted about his achievement? Whatever the case, the reader must fall back on the few facts he or she can establish: the speaker, at least, lives long enough to recount the tale. The title of the poem comes from Shakespeare's *King Lear* (folio) 3.4.170, and is a line spoken by Edgar while pretending to be the insane Poor Tom. The Shakespearian reference already invites the reader to think of a discourse that involves a mixture of uncertain meaning and sense, of clarity with suggestive bafflement. The imaginative force of this intriguing poem lies in its dark energies and its constant refusal to satisfy with certainty.

Text: *Men and Women* (1855).

My first thought was, he lied in every word,
That hoary cripple, with malicious eye
Askance[1] to watch the working of his lie
On mine, and mouth scarce able to afford
Suppression of the glee, that pursed and scored   5
Its edge, at one more victim gained thereby.

2
What else should he be set for, with his staff?
What, save to waylay with his lies, ensnare
All travellers who might find him posted there,
And ask the road? I guessed what skull-like laugh   10
Would break, what crutch 'gin write my epitaph
For pastime in the dusty thoroughfare,

3
If at his counsel I should turn aside
Into that ominous tract which, all agree,[2]
Hides the Dark Tower. Yet acquiescingly   15
I did turn as he pointed: neither pride
Nor hope rekindling at the end descried,[3]
So much as gladness that some end might be

4
For, what with my whole world-wide wandering,
What with my search drawn out thro' years, my hope   20

[1] *Askance* sidewise.
[2] *all agree* the Childe is indirectly and ironically quoting the words of the hoary cripple.
[3] *descried* caught sight of.

Dwindled into a ghost not fit to cope
With that obstreperous[4] joy success would bring, –
I hardly tried now to rebuke the spring
My heart made, finding failure in its scope.[5]

5

As when a sick man very near to death   25
Seems dead indeed, and feels begin and end
The tears and takes the farewell of each friend,
And hears one bid the other go, draw breath
Freelier outside, ('since all is o'er,' he saith,
'And the blow fallen no grieving can amend;')   30

6

While some discuss if near the other graves
Be room enough for this, and when a day
Suits best for carrying the corpse away,
With care about the banners, scarves and staves:[6]
And still the man hears all, and only craves   35
He may not shame such tender love and stay.

7

Thus, I had so long suffered in this quest,[7]
Heard failure prophesied so oft, been writ
So many times among 'The Band' – to wit,[8]
The knights who to the Dark Tower's search addressed   40
Their steps – that just to fail as they, seemed best,
And all the doubt was now – should I be fit?

8

So, quiet as despair, I turned from him,
That hateful cripple, out of his highway
Into the path he pointed. All the day   45
Had been a dreary one at best, and dim
Was settling to its close, yet shot one grim
Red leer to see the plain catch its estray.[9]

9

For mark! no sooner was I fairly found
Pledged to the plain,[10] after a pace or two,   50
Than, pausing to throw backward a last view[11]
O'er the safe road, 'twas gone; grey plain all round:
Nothing but plain to the horizon's bound.
I might go on; nought else remained to do.

10

So, on I went. I think I never saw   55
Such starved ignoble nature; nothing throve:

[4] *obstreperous* noisy, clamorous.
[5] *in its scope* in its reach.
[6] *staves* perhaps ceremonial batons for a funeral procession.
[7] *quest* adventure undertaken by a knight of medieval
romance.

[8] *to wit* that is.
[9] *estray* strayed animal (the last red light of the sun
illuminates those lost on the plain).
[10] *Pledged to the plain* committed to taking this direction.
[11] *view* look.

For flowers – as well expect a cedar grove!
But cockle,[12] spurge,[13] according to their law
Might propagate their kind, with none to awe,
You'd think; a burr[14] had been a treasure-trove.   60

11

No! penury,[15] inertness and grimace,
In some strange sort, were the land's portion. 'See
'Or shut your eyes,' said Nature peevishly,
'It nothing skills:[16] I cannot help my case:
''T is the Last Judgment's fire[17] must cure this place,   65
'Calcine[18] its clods and set my prisoners free.'

12

If there pushed any ragged thistle-stalk
Above its mates, the head was chopped; the bents[19]
Were jealous else. What made those holes and rents
In the dock's[20] harsh swarth[21] leaves, bruised as to baulk[22]   70
All hope of greenness? 't is a brute must walk
Pashing[23] their life out, with a brute's intents.

13

As for the grass, it grew as scant as hair
In leprosy;[24] thin dry blades pricked the mud
Which underneath looked kneaded up with blood.   75
One stiff blind horse, his every bone a-stare,
Stood stupefied, however he came there:
Thrust out past service from the devil's stud!

14

Alive? he might be dead for aught I know,
With that red gaunt and colloped[25] neck a-strain,   80
And shut eyes underneath the rusty mane;
Seldom went such grotesqueness with such woe;
I never saw a brute I hated so;
He must be wicked to deserve such pain.

15

I shut my eyes and turned them on my heart.   85
As a man calls for wine before he fights,
I asked one draught of earlier, happier sights,

---

[12] *cockle* reddish-purple flower that grows in cornfields (i.e., a weed).

[13] *spurge* those plants characterized by an acrid milky juice.

[14] *burr* rough or prickly seed-vessel of a plant.

[15] *penury* poverty, destitution.

[16] *It nothing skills* it achieves nothing, it makes no difference.

[17] *Last Judgment's fire* cf. 'But the heauens and the earth which are now, by the same word are kept in store, reserued vnto fire against the day of Iudgement, and perdition of vngodly men', 2 Peter 3.7.

[18] *Calcine* to reduce to quick-lime by burning.

[19] *bent* grass of a reedy or rush-like habit, or which has persistent stiff stems.

[20] *dock* common weedy plant.

[21] *swarth* blackish (the leaves of dock are dark green: these are clearly diseased).

[22] *baulk* refuse.

[23] *Pashing* breaking into tiny pieces or atoms.

[24] *leprosy* infectious bacterial disease which slowly eats away the body and forms shining white scales on the skin; common in medieval Europe.

[25] *colloped* collop can mean a piece of flesh: the horse's neck is red and raw (there is also an anti-pun on 'collop' meaning a thick fold of flesh on the body as evidence of a well-fed condition).

Ere fitly I could hope to play my part.
Think first, fight afterwards – the soldier's art:
One taste of the old time sets all to rights.   90

16

Not it! I fancied Cuthbert's[26] reddening face
Beneath its garniture[27] of curly gold,
Dear fellow, till I almost felt him fold
An arm in mine to fix me to the place,
That way he used. Alas, one night's disgrace!   95
Out went my heart's new fire and left it cold.

17

Giles[28] then, the soul of honour – there he stands
Frank as ten years ago when knighted first.
What honest man should dare (he said) he durst.[29]
Good – but the scene shifts – faugh! what hangman-hands   100
Pin to his breast a parchment? His own bands[30]
Read it. Poor traitor, spit upon and curst!

18

Better this present than a past like that;
Back therefore to my darkening path again!
No sound, no sight as far as eye could strain.   105
Will the night send a howlet[31] or a bat?
I asked: when something on the dismal flat
Came to arrest my thoughts and change their train.

19

A sudden little river crossed my path
As unexpected as a serpent comes.   110
No sluggish tide congenial to the glooms;
This, as it frothed by, might have been a bath
For the fiend's glowing hoof – to see the wrath
Of its black eddy bespate[32] with flakes and spumes.[33]

20

So petty yet so spiteful! All along,   115
Low scrubby alders[34] kneeled down over it;
Drenched willows flung them headlong in a fit
Of mute despair, a suicidal throng:
The river which had done them all the wrong,
Whate'er that was, rolled by, deterred no whit.[35]   120

21

Which, while I forded,[36] – good saints, how I feared
To set my foot upon a dead man's cheek,

---

[26] *Cuthbert* one of Roland's peers, who disgraced himself.

[27] *garniture* ornaments, embellishment.

[28] *Giles* another of Roland's peers who was a traitor to his vows.

[29] *durst* would dare.

[30] *bands* companions.

[31] *howlet* owl or owlet (onomatopoeic).

[32] *bespate* spat upon.

[33] *spumes* foam and froth.

[34] *alder* kind of birch tree that lives in wet places.

[35] *no whit* not at all.

[36] *forded* crossed through the water.

Each step, or feel the spear I thrust to seek
For hollows, tangled in his hair or beard!
– It may have been a water-rat I speared,   125
But, ugh! it sounded like a baby's shriek.

22

Glad was I when I reached the other bank.
Now for a better country.[37] Vain presage![38]
Who were the strugglers, what war did they wage,
Whose savage trample thus could pad[39] the dank   130
Soil to a plash?[40] Toads in a poisoned tank,
Or wild cats in a red-hot iron cage –

23

The fight must so have seemed in that fell cirque.[41]
What penned them there, with all the plain to choose?
No foot-print leading to that horrid mews,[42]   135
None out of it. Mad brewage set to work
Their brains, no doubt, like galley-slaves the Turk
Pits for his pastime, Christians against Jews.

24

And more than that – a furlong[43] on – why, there!
What bad use was that engine for, that wheel,   140
Or brake,[44] not wheel – that harrow[45] fit to reel
Men's bodies out like silk? with all the air
Of Tophet's tool,[46] on earth left unaware,
Or brought to sharpen its rusty teeth of steel.

25

Then came a bit of stubbed[47] ground, once a wood,   145
Next a marsh, it would seem, and now mere earth
Desperate and done with; (so a fool finds mirth,
Makes a thing and then mars it,[48] till his mood
Changes and off he goes!) within a rood[49] –
Bog, clay and rubble, sand and stark black dearth.   150

26

Now blotches rankling, coloured gay and grim,
Now patches where some leanness of the soil's
Broke into moss or substances like boils;
Then came some palsied oak, a cleft in him
Like a distorted mouth that splits its rim   155
Gaping at death, and dies while it recoils.

---

[37] *country* area of land.
[38] *Vain presage* Roland's initial hope of a better country was misplaced.
[39] *pad* beat down.
[40] *plash* marshy pool, puddle.
[41] *fell cirque* deadly circle.
[42] *mews* cages, prisons.
[43] *furlong* eighth part of an English mile.
[44] *brake* rack, instrument of torture.

[45] *harrow* instrument of torture.
[46] *Tophet's tool* Tophet was Isaiah's symbol of Hell ('For Tophet is ordained of olde; yea, for the king it is prepared, he hath made it deepe and large: the pile thereof is fire and much wood, the breath of the Lord, like a streame of brimstone, doeth kindle it', Isaiah 30.33).
[47] *stubbed* with trees cut off near the ground.
[48] *fool . . . mars it* proverbial.
[49] *rood* linear measurement of 6 to 8 yards/metres.

27

And just as far as ever from the end!
Nought in the distance but the evening, nought
To point my footstep further! At the thought,
A great black bird, Apollyon's[50] bosom-friend,   160
Sailed past, nor beat his wide wing dragon-penned[51]
That brushed my cap – perchance the guide I sought.

28

For, looking up, aware I somehow grew,
'Spite of the dusk, the plain had given place
All round to mountains – with such name to grace   165
Mere ugly heights and heaps now stolen in view.
How thus they had surprised me, – solve it, you!
How to get from them was no clearer case.

29

Yet half I seemed to recognize some trick
Of mischief happened to me, God knows when –   170
In a bad dream perhaps. Here ended, then,
Progress this way. When, in the very nick
Of giving up, one time more, came a click
As when a trap shuts – you're inside the den!

30

Burningly it came on me all at once,   175
This was the place! those two hills on the right,
Crouched like two bulls locked horn in horn in fight;
While to the left, a tall scalped[52] mountain . . . Dunce,
Dotard, a-dozing at the very nonce,[53]
After a life spent training for the sight!   180

31

What in the midst lay but the Tower itself?
The round squat turret, blind as the fool's heart,[54]
Built of brown stone, without a counterpart
In the whole world. The tempest's mocking elf[55]
Points to the shipman thus the unseen shelf   185
He strikes on, only when the timbers start.[56]

32

Not see? because of night perhaps? – why, day
Came back again for that! before it left,
The dying sunset kindled through a cleft:
The hills, like giants at a hunting, lay,   190
Chin upon hand, to see the game at bay, –
'Now stab and end the creature – to the heft![57]

---

[50] *Apollyon* cf. 'And they [the damned] had a king ouer them, which is the Angel of the bottomlesse pit, whose name in the Hebrew tongue is Abaddon, but in the Greeke tongue hath his name Apollyon', Revelation 9.11.
[51] *dragon-penned* with dragon's wings.
[52] *scalped mountain* tree-less summit.
[53] *at the very nonce* at the very moment.

[54] *blind as the fool's heart* cf. Psalm 14.1, 'The foole hath sayd in his heart, There is no God'.
[55] *tempest's mocking elf* it has been suggested that Browning may have been inspired by one of the small figures blowing the winds in the corners of antique maps.
[56] *start* shudder.
[57] *heft* haft: handle, hilt.

33

Not hear? when noise was everywhere! it tolled
Increasing like a bell. Names in my ears
Of all the lost adventurers my peers, –   195
How such a one was strong, and such was bold,
And such was fortunate, yet each of old
Lost, lost! one moment knelled the woe of years.

34

There they stood, ranged along the hill-sides, met
To view the last of me, a living frame   200
For one more picture! in a sheet of flame
I saw them and I knew them all. And yet
Dauntless the slug-horn[58] to my lips I set,
And blew. *'Childe Roland to the Dark Tower came.'*

[58] *slug-horn* trumpet.

A Toccata of Galuppi's

Robert Browning was particularly interested in the relation between visual art and word art, and he wrote a number of dramatic monologues about painters (see, in this anthology, 'Fra Lippo Lippi', 179–88, and 'Andrea del Sarto', 189–95). But he was also a musician and intrigued by relations between music and words as expressive arts. In 'A Toccata of Galuppi's' (1855), Browning considers, among other things, how a human being reacts to and 'interprets' music, and how legitimate such interpretative procedures are. Is the speaker's understanding of non-programmatic music – his assumption that it can be translated into rational sense – acceptable, or erroneous and a sign of his limited mind?

Baldassare Galuppi (1706–85) was an important Venetian instrumentalist and composer, much admired by the English musician and music historian Dr Charles Burney (1726–1814). In Browning's poem, an unnamed speaker – a provincial Englishman who has never been abroad – listens to one of Galuppi's toccatas. (A toccata is usually a fast-moving show piece, but the Italian keyboard toccatas, including those by Galuppi, were in a wide range of styles, sometimes even slow: it is not clear that this poem refers to a specific piece.) From the playing of the work, the speaker imagines a version of eighteenth-century Venice, assembled from a set of clichés of carnival, and populated by 'lives that came to nothing'. (Venice in the eighteenth century had indeed reached a nadir both in terms of political power and moral

identity: the Venetian Republic was finally extinguished by Napoleon Bonaparte in 1797, and the city's fortunes would then increasingly depend on tourism.) From stanza 11, a new element appears. The speaker, who has interests in natural history and science, admits that Galuppi's music has had a more uncomfortable effect, making him think of his own mortality. By the end, he feels some sympathy for the 'Dear dead women' whose lives the music had imaginatively created for him; beginning with the superficial, the poem moves into the authentically elegiac.

'A Toccata of Galuppi's' suggests commonalities that underlie national differences, and raises a question about how the mid-nineteenth century responds to and constructs the eighteenth century. It also processes ideas about how an art form is interpreted and what its life is like once it has left the custody of its creator. This is a theme variously treated in Browning's *Men and Women* (1855), from where 'A Toccata' is taken, and is perhaps revealing of Browning's anxieties about the endurance and comprehension of his own work in posterity (cf. 'The Bishop Orders his Tomb at St Praxed's Church', 175–9, 'Cleon' and 'A Grammarian's Funeral' in *Men and Women*). Browning suggests from the start the limits of the speaker's mind by the naive sing-song rhythms of the first stanza; certainly, his – the speaker's – grasp on the technicalities of music is weak.

Text: *Men and Women* (1855).

Oh Galuppi, Baldassaro,[1] this is very sad to find!
I can hardly misconceive you; it would prove me deaf and blind;
But although I take your meaning, 't is with such a heavy mind!

2

Here you come with your old music, and here's all the good it brings.
What, they lived once thus at Venice where the merchants were the kings,[2] 5
Where Saint Mark's[3] is, where the Doges used to wed the sea with rings?[4]

3

Ay, because the sea's the street there; and 't is arched by . . . what you call
. . . Shylock's bridge[5] with houses on it, where they kept the carnival:[6]
I was never out of England – it's as if I saw it all.

4

Did young people take their pleasure when the sea was warm in May? 10
Balls and masks begun at midnight, burning ever to midday,
When they made up fresh adventures for the morrow, do you say?

5

Was a lady such a lady, cheeks so round and lips so red, –
On her neck the small face buoyant, like a bell-flower[7] on its bed,
O'er the breast's superb abundance where a man might base his head? 15

6

Well, and it was graceful of them – they'd break talk off and afford
– She, to bite her mask's black velvet – he, to finger on his sword,
While you sat and played Toccatas, stately at the clavichord?[8]

7

What? Those lesser thirds[9] so plaintive, sixths diminished,[10] sigh on sigh,
Told them something? Those suspensions, those solutions[11] – 'Must we die?'[12] 20
Those commiserating sevenths[13] – 'Life might last! we can but try!'

---

[1] *Baldassaro* the speaker misremembers the composer's name.
[2] *merchants were the kings* Venice's wealth was achieved through international trade.
[3] *Saint Mark's* basilica of Venice, where Galuppi served as director of music.
[4] *sea with rings* reference to the ceremony on Ascension Day of the symbolic marriage of the Doge – the leader of the Venetian Republic – to the sea, signifying the city's superiority over the waves. The Doge cast a gold ring into the Adriatic.
[5] *Shylock's bridge* Rialto Bridge, with shops, is the central crossing point of the Grand Canal. The speaker calls it Shylock's bridge because of Shylock's question in *The Merchant of Venice* 1.3.36, 'What news on the Rialto?'
[6] *carnival* the Venetian carnival is held before Lent (and is not specifically associated with Rialto).
[7] *bell-flower* common name of the *Campanula*, with striking bell-shaped flowers.

[8] *clavichord* small keyboard instrument.
[9] *lesser thirds* minor thirds (an interval – distance in pitch – between two notes in music).
[10] *sixths diminished* inaccuracy on the speaker's part: this is not an accepted interval.
[11] *suspensions . . . solutions* a suspension is the holding of a note from one chord discordantly into the next; the solution (resolution) is when the suspended note falls to one appropriate for the new chord, thus resolving the discord.
[12] *'Must we die?'* the speaker interprets the resolution of a suspension as a musical expression of inevitability. The ear, hearing a suspension, knows that it must change and be 'resolved'.
[13] *commiserating sevenths* presumably minor sevenths, a milder discord than the major seventh.

8

'Were you happy?' – 'Yes.' – 'And are you still as happy?' – 'Yes. And you?'
– 'Then, more kisses!' – 'Did *I* stop them, when a million seemed so few?'
Hark, the dominant's persistence till it must be answered to![14]

9

So, an octave struck the answer.[15] Oh, they praised you, I dare say!   25
'Brave[16] Galuppi! that was music! good alike at grave and gay!
I can always leave off talking when I hear a master play!'

10

Then they left you for their pleasure: till in due time, one by one,
Some with lives that came to nothing, some with deeds as well undone,
Death stepped tacitly and took them where they never see the sun.   30

11

But when I sit down to reason, think to take my stand nor swerve,
While I triumph o'er a secret wrung from nature's close reserve,[17]
In you come with your cold music till I creep thro' every nerve.

12

Yes, you, like a ghostly cricket, creaking where a house was burned:
'Dust and ashes, dead and done with, Venice spent what Venice earned.   35
The soul, doubtless, is immortal – where a soul can be discerned.

13

'Yours for instance: you know physics, something of geology,
Mathematics are your pastime; souls shall rise in their degree;[18]
Butterflies may dread extinction, – you'll not die, it cannot be!

14

'As for Venice and her people, merely born to bloom and drop,   40
Here on earth they bore their fruitage, mirth and folly were the crop:
What of soul was left, I wonder, when the kissing had to stop?

15

'Dust and ashes!' So you creak it, and I want the heart to scold.
Dear dead women, with such hair, too – what's become of all the gold
Used to hang and brush their bosoms? I feel chilly and grown old.   45

[14] *dominant's persistence . . . too* the insistent sounding of the
dominant (the fifth note of the scale) portends the end of
the music in a perfect cadence (the musical 'full stop'
comprising the progression from the dominant to the tonic,
the key chord of the scale).
[15] *octave struck the answer* the speaker means the tonic,
completing the perfect cadence, and ending the Toccata.

[16] *Brave* worthy, excellent.
[17] *a secret wrung . . . reserve* while engaged in natural history
or scientific investigation of nature; a suggestion of
vivisection?
[18] *souls . . . degree* in the next life, souls will be in a
hierarchy.

Two in the Campagna

Robert Browning's dramatic monologues privilege the
exploration of individual character. 'Two in the Campagna' – a dramatic lyric in which speaker and poet
are not individuated – involves an investigation of a
relationship, a meditation not on a single speaker but
on the nature of love between two people (though, to
be sure, from one lover's perspective only). As in 'Porphyria's Lover', 171–3, Browning's interest is in the
'good minute', the precious moment of closeness
between two human beings that does not endure. As
in 'Porphyria's Lover' also, this meditation on the
pattern of human experience subtly encodes a reflec-

tion on the kind of knowledge that art offers. The struggle to sustain the good minute is a displaced version of the artist's struggle with representation (particularly in the dramatic monologue with its effort to capture the *moment*).

The Roman Campagna is a large expanse of open country that includes the crumbling remains of ancient Roman settlements. The Brownings had visited it – they had lived in Rome from November 1853 to the end of May 1854 – but this lyric poem is not simply autobiographical. Like 'Andrea del Sarto', 189–95, and '"Childe Roland to the Dark Tower Came"', 195–202, it offers a perspective on the nature and place of human failure and its inevitability. In describing a universalized human yearning for union, Browning also implicitly muses on the challenges of art to catch the full meaning of human events, or to represent the essence (a subject considered at greater length in 'Fra Lippo Lippi', 179–88). Such striving

for togetherness, and the sense of human dislocation from community, is addressed in the context of the divine scheme in Matthew Arnold's 'To Marguerite – Continued', 267–8, and 'The Buried Life', 296–8. In 'Two in the Campagna', the poet's desire to know the beloved's consciousness and to become one with her – 'I would I could adopt your will, /See with your eyes' – forms a contrast with the sexual politics of Elizabeth Barrett Browning's *Sonnets from the Portuguese*, 52–5, where the preservation of the self in love, through recollection of its own melancholy history, is emphasized. Stanza 4 has often been read as a good example of Browning's aesthetic of particularity – to use Carol Christ's term – his engagement with the closely observed details of the natural world and their representational potential/limits; cf. D. G. Rossetti's 'Song 8: The Woodspurge', 368–9.

Text: *Men and Women* (1855).

I wonder do you feel to–day
As I have felt since, hand in hand,
We sat down on the grass, to stray
In spirit better through the land,
This morn of Rome and May?　　　　5

2
For me, I touched a thought, I know,
Has tantalized me many times,
(Like turns of thread the spiders throw
Mocking across our path) for rhymes
To catch at and let go.　　　　10

3
Help me to hold it! First it left
The yellowing fennel,[1] run to seed
There, branching from the brickwork's cleft,
Some old tomb's ruin: yonder weed
Took up the floating weft,[2]　　　　15

4
Where one small orange cup amassed
Five beetles, – blind and green they grope
Among the honey-meal: and last,
Everywhere on the grassy slope
I traced it. Hold it fast!　　　　20

5
The champaign[3] with its endless fleece
Of feathery grasses everywhere!

[1] *fennel* fragrant, aniseed-like plant.
[2] *weft* threads.
[3] *champaign* plain of land.

Silence and passion, joy and peace,
An everlasting wash of air –
Rome's ghost[4] since her decease.

6

Such life here, through such lengths of hours,
Such miracles performed in play,
Such primal naked forms of flowers,
Such letting nature have her way
While heaven looks from its towers!

7

How say you? Let us, O my dove,
Let us be unashamed of soul,
As earth lies bare to heaven above!
How is it under our control
To love or not to love?

8

I would that you were all to me,
You that are just so much, no more.
Nor yours nor mine, nor slave nor free!
Where does the fault lie? What the core
O' the wound, since wound must be?

9

I would I could adopt your will,
See with your eyes, and set my heart
Beating by yours, and drink my fill
At your soul's springs, – your part my part
In life, for good and ill.

10

No. I yearn upward, touch you close,
Then stand away. I kiss your cheek,
Catch your soul's warmth, – I pluck the rose
And love it more than tongue can speak –
Then the good minute goes.

11

Already how am I so far
Out of that minute? Must I go
Still like the thistle-ball, no bar,
Onward, whenever light winds blow
Fixed by no friendly star?

12

Just when I seemed about to learn!
Where is the thread now? Off again!
The old trick! Only I discern –
Infinite passion, and the pain
Of finite hearts that yearn.

25

30

35

40

45

50

55

60

---

[4] *Rome's ghost* the Campagna di Roma is dotted with ruins.

Caliban upon Setebos; or, Natural Theology in the Island

'Thou thoughtest that I was altogether such a one as thyself.'[1]

One of Robert Browning's interests in *Men and Women* (1855) had been the history of religious faith (part of a wider interest in the patterns of history generally). In his next collection, *Dramatis Personae* (1864), questions of religious belief and history increased in significance. 'Caliban upon Setebos' is one example of this, a poem that imaginatively responds to a major issue of mid-nineteenth-century theology. As the title epigraph indicates, Browning's concern is in the way ideas of God are determined by individual consciousnesses. Genesis declares that 'God created man in his owne Image' (1.27); 'Caliban upon Setebos' tests the idea that gods are shaped by believers and, in doing so, asks for the reader's sympathy for the non-/sub-human.

The poem can be seen as an imaginative engagement with the new German Biblical scholarship that was beginning to have a subversive effect on English theology in the mid-century: its important representatives included Ludwig Feuerbach's *Das Wesen des Christentums* (*The Essence of Christianity*, 1841). Feuerbach – whose work was translated into English by George Eliot in 1854 – proposed, centrally, that Christianity was an expression of human need, not a statement of objective truth. Browning's speaker, constructing a god in response to his own circumstances, seems to be a kind of Feuerbachian creature.

Yet while the poem takes its imaginative inspiration from Feuerbach, it does not simply accept the legitimacy of his argument about Christianity. Rather, it can perhaps be understood as proposing the limits of natural theology – the dominant eighteenth- and nineteenth-century practice of deducing truths about the mind of God from the wonders of the natural world – unassisted by revelation. Caliban has no Bible and no inner light to guide him; accordingly his conception of the divine, based simply on his experience of the island, is far from Christian (for a later, radical assault on natural theology, see Swinburne's 'A Forsaken Garden', 506–9).

The poem draws energy from another significant challenge to natural theology in the middle of the nineteenth century: Darwinian evolution. In concentrating on a speaker who is neither human nor animal, but a kind a transitional species between the two, a suggestive 'missing link', Browning's poem – perhaps written in 1859–60 – is in creative exchange with Darwin's *The Origin of Species* (1859) and its theory of the evolution of all species from primordial forms and archetypes.

The specific literary context of the poem is, obviously, Shakespeare's *The Tempest*. 'Caliban upon Setebos' is set on Prospero's island, to where the witch Sycorax was banished. Her misshapen son, Caliban, was the island's sole inhabitant prior to the arrival of Prospero, ousted Duke of Milan. Prospero is an enchanter whose servant, released from Sycorax's spell, is the sylph-like Ariel; Prospero's daughter is Miranda. Largely due to the contemporary interests of post-colonialism, Caliban has become a figure of consequence in modern readings of *The Tempest*. Browning's poem is prescient in choosing to give life to this marginalized character (cf. other monologues that allow voices to those historically on the outside, such as Amy Levy's 'Xantippe: A Fragment', 630–6, and Augusta Webster's 'Circe', 450–5).

Caliban's uncertain sense of identity is suggested in the curious absence of pronouns. He often speaks of himself in the implied third pronoun ('[he] will') and only infrequently uses 'I'. The initial and final sections in parentheses are Caliban's thoughts. The rest of his monologue is spoken aloud (disastrously, as he believes at the end).

Text: *Dramatis Personae* (1864).

['Will sprawl,[2] now that the heat of day is best,
   Flat on his belly in the pit's much mire,[3]
With elbows wide, fists clenched to prop his chin.
And, while he kicks both feet in the cool slush,
And feels about his spine small eft-things[4] course,   5
   Run in and out each arm, and make him laugh:

---

[1] The epigraph is from Psalm 50.21: 'thou thoughtest that I was altogether such a one as thy selfe: but I will reproue thee, and set them in order before thine eyes'.

[2] *'Will sprawl* Caliban refers to himself in the third person: 'will sprawl = he will sprawl = I will sprawl.
[3] *much mire* large amount of mire.
[4] *eft-things* small lizards, newts, etc.

And while above his head a pompion-plant,[5]
Coating the cave-top as a brow its eye,
Creeps down to touch and tickle hair and beard,
And now a flower drops with a bee inside,   10
And now a fruit to snap at, catch and crunch, –
He looks out o'er yon sea which sunbeams cross
And recross till they weave a spider-web
(Meshes of fire, some great fish breaks at times)
And talks to his own self, howe'er he please,   15
Touching that other, whom his dam[6] called God.
Because to talk about Him, vexes – ha,
Could He but know! and time to vex is now,
When talk is safer than in winter-time.
Moreover Prosper and Miranda sleep   20
In confidence he drudges at their task,
And it is good to cheat the pair, and gibe,
Letting the rank[7] tongue blossom into speech.]

Setebos, Setebos, and Setebos!
'Thinketh, He dwelleth i'the cold o'the moon.   25
'Thinketh He made it, with the sun to match,
But not the stars;[8] the stars came otherwise;
Only made clouds, winds, meteors, such as that:
Also this isle, what lives and grows thereon,
And snaky sea which rounds and ends the same.   30

'Thinketh, it came of being ill at ease:
He hated that He cannot change His cold,
Nor cure its ache. 'Hath spied an icy fish
That longed to 'scape the rock-stream where she lived,
And thaw herself within the lukewarm brine   35
O' the lazy sea her stream thrusts far amid,
A crystal spike 'twixt two warm walls of wave;
Only, she ever sickened, found repulse
At the other kind of water, not her life,
(Green-dense and dim-delicious, bred o' the sun)   40
Flounced back from bliss she was not born to breathe,
And in her old bounds buried her despair,
Hating and loving warmth alike: so He.

'Thinketh, He made thereat the sun, this isle,
Trees and the fowls here, beast and creeping thing.   45
Yon otter, sleek-wet, black, lithe as a leech;
Yon auk,[9] one fire-eye in a ball of foam,
That floats and feeds; a certain badger brown
He hath watched hunt with that slant white-wedge eye
By moonlight; and the pie[10] with the long tongue   50
That pricks deep into oakwarts[11] for a worm,
And says a plain word when she finds her prize,
But will not eat the ants; the ants themselves

---

[5] *pompion-plant* pumpkin.
[6] *dam* mother (Sycorax).
[7] *rank* rebellious (with the added association of foul smell).
[8] *not the stars* see ll. 137–9.

[9] *auk* name of a family of seabirds.
[10] *pie* magpie or other pied bird.
[11] *oakwarts* oak galls.

That build a wall of seeds and settled stalks
About their hole – He made all these and more, 55
Made all we see, and us, in spite: how else?
He could not, Himself, make a second self
To be His mate; as well have made Himself:[12]
He would not make what he mislikes or slights,
An eyesore to Him, or not worth His pains: 60
But did, in envy, listlessness or sport,
Make what Himself would fain,[13] in a manner, be –
Weaker in most points, stronger in a few,
Worthy, and yet mere playthings all the while,
Things He admires and mocks too, – that is it. 65
Because, so brave, so better though they be,
It nothing skills if He begin to plague.
Look now, I melt a gourd-fruit into mash,
Add honeycomb and pods, I have perceived,
Which bite like finches when they bill and kiss, – 70
Then, when froth rises bladdery, drink up all,
Quick, quick, till maggots scamper through my brain;[14]
Last, throw me on my back i' the seeded thyme,
And wanton, wishing I were born a bird.
Put case, unable to be what I wish, 75
I yet could make a live bird out of clay:
Would not I take clay, pinch my Caliban
Able to fly? – for, there, see, he hath wings,
And great comb like the hoopoe's[15] to admire,
And there, a sting to do his foes offence, 80
There, and I will that he begin to live,
Fly to yon rock-top, nip me off the horns
Of grigs[16] high up that make the merry din,
Saucy their veined wings, and mind me not.
In which feat, if his leg snapped, brittle clay, 85
And he lay stupid-like, – why, I should laugh;
And if he, spying me, should fall to weep,
Beseech me to be good, repair his wrong,
Bid his poor leg smart less or grow again, –
Well, as the chance were, this might take or else 90
Not take my fancy: I might hear his cry,
And give the mankin[17] three sound legs for one,
Or pluck the other off, leave him like an egg,
And lessoned he was mine and merely clay.
Were this no pleasure, lying in the thyme, 95
Drinking the mash, with brain become alive,
Making and marring clay at will? So He.

'Thinketh, such shows nor right nor wrong in Him,
Nor kind, nor cruel: He is strong and Lord.
'Am strong myself compared to yonder crabs 100

[12] *as well . . . Himself* 'He could as easily have made
Himself'.
[13] *fain* gladly.
[14] *till maggots . . . brain* Caliban's appropriately materialistic
description of the alcoholic effects of the drink, though the
expression was a colloquial one in the nineteenth century to
describe animal thought. Cf. the discussion of harpooning
in chapter 9 of Elizabeth Gaskell's *Sylvia's Lovers* (1863):

' "At last a thinks to mysel' a can't get free o' t' line, and t'
line is fast to t' harpoon, and t' harpoon is fast to t' whale;
and t' whale may go down fathoms deep wheniver t'
maggot stirs i'her head." '
[15] *hoopoe* south European bird conspicuous with variegated
plumage and large crest standing upright.
[16] *grigs* grasshoppers, crickets.
[17] *mankin* puny man.

That march now from the mountain to the sea,
   'Let twenty pass, and stone the twenty-first,
   Loving not, hating not, just choosing so.
'Say, the first straggler that boasts purple spots
   Shall join the file, one pincer twisted off;   105
'Say, this bruised fellow shall receive a worm,
And two worms he whose nippers end in red;
   As it likes me each time, I do: so He.

Well then, 'supposeth He is good i' the main,
   Placable if His mind and ways were guessed,   110
   But rougher than His handiwork, be sure!
Oh, He hath made things worthier than Himself,
And envieth that, so helped, such things do more
Than He who made them! What consoles but this?
That they, unless through Him, do nought at all,   115
   And must submit: what other use in things?
      'Hath cut a pipe of pithless elder-joint
That, blown through, gives exact the scream o' the jay[18]
When from her wing you twitch the feathers blue:
   Sound this, and little birds that hate the jay   120
Flock within stone's throw, glad their foe is hurt:
Put case such pipe could prattle and boast forsooth
   'I catch the birds, I am the crafty thing,
   'I make the cry my maker cannot make
'With his great round mouth; he must blow through mine!'   125
   Would not I smash it with my foot? So He.

But wherefore rough, why cold and ill at ease?
      Aha, that is a question! Ask, for that,
      What knows, – the something over Setebos
That made Him, or He, may be, found and fought,   130
Worsted,[19] drove off and did to nothing, perchance.
There may be something quiet o'er His head,
   Out of His reach, that feels nor joy nor grief,
   Since both derive from weakness in some way.
I joy because the quails[20] come; would not joy   135
Could I bring quails here when I have a mind:
   This Quiet,[21] all it hath a mind to, doth.
   'Esteemeth stars the outposts of its couch,
But never spends much thought nor care that way.
It may look up, work up, – the worse for those   140
      It works on! 'Careth but for Setebos
      The many-handed as a cuttle-fish,[22]
Who, making Himself feared through what He does,
   Looks up, first, and perceives he cannot soar
      To what is quiet and hath happy life;   145
   Next looks down here, and out of very spite
   Makes this a bauble-world to ape yon real,
These good things to match those as hips do grapes.
   'T is solace making baubles, ay, and sport.
   Himself peeped late, eyed Prosper at his books   150

[18] *jay* chattering arboreal bird, like a strikingly coloured magpie.
[19] *Worsted* defeated.
[20] *quail* small bird, like a partridge.
[21] *Quiet* undefined power Caliban imagines above Setebos.
[22] *cuttle-fish* edible marine creature.

Careless and lofty, lord now of the isle:
Vexed, 'stitched[23] a book of broad leaves, arrow-shaped,
Wrote thereon, he knows what, prodigious words;
Has peeled a wand and called it by a name;
Weareth at whiles for an enchanter's robe 155
The eyed skin of a supple oncelot;[24]
And hath an ounce[25] sleeker than youngling mole,
A four-legged serpent he makes cower and couch,
Now snarl, now hold its breath and mind his eye,
And saith she is Miranda and my wife: 160
'Keeps for his Ariel[26] a tall pouch-bill crane[27]
He bids go wade for fish and straight disgorge;
Also a sea-beast, lumpish, which he snared,
Blinded the eyes of, and brought somewhat tame,
And split its toe-webs, and now pens the drudge 165
In a hole o' the rock and calls him Caliban;
A bitter heart that bides its time and bites.
'Plays thus at being Prosper in a way,
Taketh his mirth with make-believes: so He.

His dam held that the Quiet made all things 170
Which Setebos vexed only: 'holds not so.
Who made them weak, meant weakness He might vex.
Had He meant other, while His hand was in,
Why not make horny eyes no thorn could prick,
Or plate my scalp with bone against the snow, 175
Or overscale my flesh 'neath joint and joint,
Like an orc's[28] armour? Ay, – so spoil His sport!
He is the One now: only He doth all.

'Saith, He may like, perchance, what profits Him.
Ay, himself loves what does him good; but why? 180
'Gets good no otherwise. This blinded beast
Loves whoso places flesh-meat on his nose,
But, had he eyes, would want no help, but hate
Or love, just as it liked him: He hath eyes.
Also it pleaseth Setebos to work, 185
Use all His hands, and exercise much craft,
By no means for the love of what is worked.
'Tasteth, himself, no finer good i' the world
When all goes right, in this safe summer-time,
And he wants little, hungers, aches not much, 190
Than trying what to do with wit and strength.
'Falls to make something: 'piled yon pile of turfs,
And squared and stuck there squares of soft white chalk,
And, with a fish-tooth, scratched a moon on each,
And set up endwise certain spikes of tree, 195
And crowned the whole with a sloth's[29] skull a-top,
Found dead i' the woods, too hard for one to kill.
No use at all i' the work, for work's sole sake;
'Shall some day knock it down again: so He.

---

[23] *'stitched* Caliban is referring to Prospero.

[24] *oncelot* an ocelot?

[25] *ounce* lynx, cheetah or snow-leopard.

[26] *Ariel* Prospero's air-like servant in *The Tempest*.

[27] *crane* bird with long neck, legs and bill.

[28] *orc* Caliban means a sea-monster.

[29] *sloth* slow-moving mammal living among trees.

'Saith He is terrible: watch His feats in proof!   200
One hurricane will spoil six good months' hope.
  He hath a spite against me, that I know,
Just as He favours Prosper, who knows why?
    So it is, all the same, as well I find.
'Wove wattles[30] half the winter, fenced them firm   205
  With stone and stake to stop she-tortoises
Crawling to lay their eggs here: well, one wave,
  Feeling the foot of Him upon its neck,
Gaped as a snake does, lolled out its large tongue,
And licked the whole labour flat: so much for spite.   210
  'Saw a ball[31] flame down late (yonder it lies)
Where, half an hour before, I slept i' the shade:
  Often they scatter sparkles: there is force![32]
'Dug up a newt He may have envied once
And turned to stone, shut up inside a stone.[33]   215
Please Him and hinder this? – What Prosper does?
  Aha, if He would tell me how! Not He!
  There is the sport: discover how or die!
All need not die, for of the things o' the isle
  Some flee afar, some dive, some run up trees;   220
Those at His mercy, – why, they please Him most
When . . . when . . . well, never try the same way twice!
Repeat what act has pleased, He may grow wroth.
You must not know His ways, and play Him off,
  Sure of the issue. 'Doth the like himself: 225
  'Spareth a squirrel that it nothing fears
But steals the nut from underneath my thumb,
  And when I threat, bites stoutly in defence:
  'Spareth an urchin[34] that contrariwise,
  Curls up into a ball, pretending death   230
For fright at my approach: the two ways please.
But what would move my choler[35] more than this,
  That either creature counted on its life
To-morrow and next day and all days to come,
  Saying, forsooth,[36] in the inmost of its heart,   235
    'Because he did so yesterday with me,
  And otherwise with such another brute,
So must he do henceforth and always.' – Ay?
Would teach the reasoning couple what 'must' means!
'Doth as he likes, or wherefore Lord? So He.   240

  'Conceiveth all things will continue thus,
  And we shall have to live in fear of Him
So long as He lives, keeps His strength: no change,
  If He have done His best, make no new world[37]
To please Him more, so leave off watching this, –   245
  If He surprise not even the Quiet's self
Some strange day, – or, suppose, grow into it

---

[30] *wattle* rods or stakes, interlaced with twigs or branches of trees.
[31] *ball* fire-ball: a meteor.
[32] *force* with the Victorian sense of 'energy'.
[33] *'Dug up . . . stone* referring to a fossil.

[34] *urchin* hedgehog.
[35] *choler* temper.
[36] *forsooth* in truth.
[37] *new world* cf. Miranda's 'O brave new world / That has such people in't!', *The Tempest* 5.1.186–7.

As grubs[38] grow butterflies: else, here are we,
And there is He, and nowhere help at all.
'Believeth with the life, the pain shall stop.   250
His dam held different, that after death
He both plagued enemies and feasted friends:
Idly! He doth His worst in this our life,
Giving just respite lest we die through pain,
Saving last pain for worst, – with which, an end.   255
Meanwhile, the best way to escape His ire
Is, not to seem too happy. 'Sees, himself,
Yonder two flies, with purple films and pink,
Bask on the pompion-bell above: kills both.
'Sees two black painful beetles roll their ball   260
On head and tail as if to save their lives:
Moves them the stick away they strive to clear.
Even so, 'would have Him misconceive, suppose
This Caliban strives hard and ails no less,
And always, above all else, envies Him;   265
Wherefore he mainly dances on dark nights,
Moans in the sun, gets under holes to laugh,
And never speaks his mind save housed as now:
Outside, 'groans, curses. If He caught me here,
O'erheard this speech, and asked 'What chucklest at?'   270
'Would, to appease Him, cut a finger off,
Or of my three kid yearlings[39] burn the best,
Or let the toothsome apples rot on tree,
Or push my tame beast for the orc to taste:
While myself lit a fire, and made a song   275
And sung it, 'What I hate, be consecrate
To celebrate Thee and Thy state, no mate
For Thee; what see for envy in poor me?'
Hoping the while, since evils sometimes mend,
Warts rub away and sores are cured with slime,   280
That some strange day, will either the Quiet catch
And conquer Setebos, or likelier He
Decrepit may doze, doze, as good as die.

[What, what? A curtain[40] o'er the world at once!
Crickets stop hissing; not a bird – or, yes,   285
There scuds His raven that has told Him all!
It was fool's play, this prattling! Ha! The wind
Shoulders the pillared dust, death's house o' the move,
And fast invading fires begin![41] White blaze –
A tree's head snaps – and there, there, there, there, there,   290
His thunder follows! Fool to gibe at Him!
Lo! 'Lieth flat and loveth Setebos!
'Maketh his teeth meet through his upper lip,
Will let those quails fly, will not eat this month
One little mess[42] of whelks,[43] so he may 'scape!]   295

---

[38] *grubs* caterpillars.
[39] *kid yearlings* year-old goats.
[40] *curtain* thunder cloud.
[41] *invading fires* bolts of lightning: there is a storm that
Caliban imagines is Setebos's wrath.

[42] *mess* meal.
[43] *whelks* unappetizing sea molluscs.

Eurydice to Orpheus: A Picture by Leighton

The dramatic monologue – which was not, in fact, a term used until the late Victorian period – naturally prioritized speech, inviting the reader to consider the poem as a transcript of spontaneous utterance. But Browning also worked with speech in more concise forms, and outside the terms of the dramatic monologue. Here, his subject is not historical, as in the great monologues, but mythical. In ancient Greek legend, the musician Orpheus married the nymph Eurydice, but she died from a snakebite. Overcome with grief, Orpheus determined to rescue her from the underworld. After charming its guardians with his beautiful singing, he persuaded the King and Queen of the underworld to allow Eurydice to return to the earth; they set as their only conditions the requirement that he must lead the way and that he must not look behind him. Overwhelmed with desire to see Eurydice, Orpheus did turn round, and at that instant lost his wife a second time.

Browning's poem, like Sir Frederick Leighton's *Orpheus and Eurydice* (plate 4) which it illustrates, modifies the original myth. Both poet and painter, in fact, illustrate, as Catherine Maxwell has argued, a later form of the story, such as that in Gluck's opera *Orfeo ed Euridice* (1792). Here, Orpheus is forbidden not only to look at his wife but also to explain why he cannot. Eventually, he yields to her entreaties. But for Browning's text, as for Leighton's painting, this is not a matter of tragedy. Eurydice is confident that one look from her husband is enough for eternity, and the poem movingly transforms what Greek mythology knew as unutterable grief (with an emphasis on male grief) into female erotic triumph. 'Eurydice to Orpheus' was one of Browning's many responses in verse to his wife's death in 1861 (Leighton helped design her tomb). It originally appeared, mistakenly set out as prose, in the catalogue of the Royal Academy Exhibition (1864) in which Leighton's picture was shown, and then, as verse, in *Selections* (1865).

Text: *Selections* (1865).

Plate 4   Sir Frederick Leighton, *Orpheus and Eurydice* (c.1864), Leighton House, London.

But give them me, the mouth, the eyes, the brow!
Let them once more absorb me! One look now
Will lap me round for ever, not to pass
Out of its light, though darkness lie beyond:
Hold me but safe again within the bond   5
Of one immortal look! All woe that was,
Forgotten, and all terror that may be,
Defied, – no past is mine, no future: look at me!

Inapprehensiveness

Browning's final volume of poetry, *Asolando: Fancies and Facts* (1889), was published on the day of his death. Although the work of a hugely productive and now old man, it was remarkable for its inventiveness and energy. 'Inapprehensiveness', from the collection, is not a monologue like 'Andrea del Sarto', 189–95, which invites the reader to make moral judgements about the speaker, but it does nevertheless place emphasis on the reader's interpretative powers to discern the dynamics beneath the situation it portrays.

The male speaker is in love with his companion, and knows that his strong feelings would be expressed if she looked with realization at him. But she does not – her 'inapprehensiveness' is presumably strategic – and he, elegantly, returns to their ordinary conversation, his passion unarticulated. His final words indicate, one assumes, a willingness to accept her terms for the friendship.

Browning's early psychological interests had been in extremes (see 'Porphyria's Lover', 171–3, and 'My Last Duchess', 173–5). Here, he maps far more subtle situations and the delicate negotiations of human relationships. His own love for the widow Katherine de Kay Bronson, who lived in the northern Italian town of Asolo, and who was the dedicatee of *Asolando*, lies in the background of the poem. There is also an element of personal revision, of retrospect at the end of a career. 'Inapprehensiveness' recalls details of 'Love Among the Ruins', the first poem in *Men and Women* (1855), and offers a more complex consideration of the challenges of human love and the dynamics of heterosexual relations than that earlier poem.

Text: *Asolando* (1889).

We two stood simply friend-like side by side,
Viewing a twilight country far and wide,[1]
Till she at length broke silence. 'How it towers
Yonder, the ruin o'er this vale of ours!
The West's faint flare behind it so relieves   5
Its rugged outline – sight perhaps deceives,
Or I could almost fancy that I see
A branch wave plain – belike some wind-sown tree
Chance-rooted where a missing turret was.
What would I give for the perspective glass[2]   10
At home, to make out if 't is really so!
Has Ruskin[3] noticed here at Asolo
That certain weed-growths on the ravaged wall
Seem' . . . something that I could not say at all,
My thought being rather – as absorbed she sent   15

[1] *We two . . . wide* cf. the rhythms of 'Love Among the Ruins' (1855): 'Where the quiet-coloured end of evening smiles, / Miles and miles / On the solitary pastures where our sheep / Half-asleep'.

[2] *perspective glass* telescope.

[3] *Ruskin* John Ruskin (1819–1900), English art and social critic: his works on northern Italy, including *The Stones of Venice* (1851–3), played an important role in the English conception of Italy in the second half of the century. He published nothing on Asolo.

Look onward after look from eyes distent[4]
With longing to reach Heaven's gate left ajar –
'Oh, fancies that might be, oh, facts that are![5]
What of a wilding?[6] By you stands, and may
So stand unnoticed till the Judgment Day,   20
One who, if once aware that your regard
Claimed what his heart holds, – woke, as from its sward[7]
The flower, the dormant passion, so to speak –
Then what a rush of life would startling wreak
Revenge on your inapprehensive stare   25
While, from the ruin and the West's faint flare,
You let your eyes meet mine, touch what you term
Quietude – that's an universe in germ –
The dormant passion needing but a look
To burst into immense life!'   30

'No, the book
Which noticed how the wall-growths wave' said she
'Was not by Ruskin.'

I said 'Vernon Lee?'[8]

---

[4] *distent* stretched, expanded.
[5] *Oh . . . are* cf. the subtitle of the volume: *Asolando: Fancies and Facts.*
[6] *wilding* wild plant.

[7] *sward* surface soil covered with grass.
[8] *Vernon Lee* pseudonym of Violet Paget (1856–1935), English essayist, novelist and travel writer who lived mostly in Florence and wrote widely on northern Italy.

Emily (Jane) Brontë (1818–1848)

Emily Brontë was born in Thornton, near Bradford in Yorkshire, and moved, when she was 2, to the parsonage at Haworth where her father was perpetual curate (Maria Branwell, her mother, died when she was 3). Briefly educated at Roe Head in 1835, she returned to Haworth due, she said, to homesickness; she served briefly as a governess at Law Hill near Halifax in 1837 and visited her sister Charlotte (1816–55) in Brussels. But Haworth was where her heart was. Here, too, she and her sister Anne (1820–49) invented the Gondal stories of an imaginary kingdom that remained important to Emily's creative imagination throughout her short life. In 1845, Charlotte 'discovered' her sister's poetry and some

was included in the *Poems of Currer, Ellis, and Acton Bell* (that is, Charlotte, Emily and Anne Brontë) in 1846. In 1847, Emily Brontë's only novel, *Wuthering Heights*, was published, an extraordinary work of gothic imagination, violence, human desire and grim comedy rooted in a hyperbolized vision of the landscape around Haworth. Emily Brontë, who left behind few records of her life and thought aside from her literary writing, died painfully of consumption in 1848 and the full extent of her ability as a poet – a writer of visionary lyricism, spare and stoic, preoccupied with the interior life of the mind – became clear only afterwards. She was buried in the family vault in Haworth church.

High waving heather

A driven poem of nature and the elements, 'High waving heather' portrays a stormy natural world as blending darkness and light, earth and heaven, 'shining and lowering'. The pattern of ceaseless change recalls the ideas of the Greek philosopher Heraclitus (*c.*540–*c.*480 BC), who famously declared that 'all things are in a state of flux'. For him, the world's unity existed in a constant effort to secure a balance between opposites that resulted in continual universal movement (Walter Pater was to find such ideas suggestive in his important contribution to the English Aesthetic movement, *The Renaissance* [1873]). The energy of the storm is connected in Brontë's first stanza, in a Shelleyan movement, with the freedom of the mind. Such mental freedom is often a topic of

Brontë's poetry, and is most conspicuous in 'The Prisoner: A Fragment', 223–5. The poem's meditation on disruptive forces and their connection with liberty tempts a political reading, while the first stanza's emphasis on the conjunction of opposites hints at an alchemical or mystical context. The poem has a high concentration of present participles – bend*ing*, shin*ing* – acting adjectivally and adverbially, giving it energy and movement like a verbal *moto perpetuo*. It is dated in MS as 13 December 1836 – a day when a very high south-west wind and much rain was recorded at Keighley, near the Brontës' home at Haworth – and was first published in 1902.

Text: MS with standardized spelling and punctuation.

High waving heather 'neath stormy blasts bending
Midnight and moonlight and bright shining stars
Darkness and glory rejoicingly blending
Earth rising to heaven and heaven descending
Man's spirit away from its drear dungeon sending   5
Bursting the fetters and breaking the bars

2

All down the mountain sides wild forests lending
One mighty voice to the life giving wind
Rivers their banks in the jubilee rending
Fast through the valleys a reckless course wending   10
Wider and deeper their waters extending
Leaving a desolate desert behind

3

Shining and lowering[1] and swelling and dying
Changing forever from midnight to noon
Roaring like thunder like soft music sighing   15
Shadows on shadows advancing and flying
Lightning bright flashes the deep gloom defying
Coming as swiftly and fading as soon

[1] *lowering* gloomy, threatening.

The Night-Wind

Natural powers and human desire conjoin throughout the turbulent narrative of Emily Brontë's only novel, *Wuthering Heights* (1847). In 'The Night-Wind', the ungendered voice of the wind, like one of Shelley's natural spirits, woos the poet in terms both erotic and threatening. Part of the tension of the verse – which looks forward in its combination of the sexual with the natural, kept under tight metrical control, to W. B. Yeats – comes from the potential violence that lies beneath the exchange. The absence of a final response from the poet, whose position uncomfortably recalls those figures from Classical myth impregnated by divinities disguised in non-human form, creates an unsettling absence of certainty. Emily Brontë may have wanted this poem to precede 'Shall Earth no more inspire thee', 219–20. The poem's MS is dated to 11 September 1840, and it was printed first in 1850.

Text: MS.

In summer's mellow midnight
A cloudless moon shone through
Our open parlour[1] window
And rosetrees wet with dew –

2

I sat in silent musing –   5
The soft wind waved my hair
It told me Heaven was glorious
And sleeping Earth was fair –

3

I needed not its breathing
To bring such thoughts to me   10
But still it whispered lowly
'How dark the woods[2] will be! –

4

'The thick leaves in my murmur
Are rustling like a dream,
And all their myriad[3] voices   15
Instinct[4] with spirit seem'

5

I said, 'Go gentle singer,
Thy wooing voice is kind

[1] *parlour* sitting room; there was a full moon on the night of 11 September 1840.
[2] *woods* the valleys of Haworth – the Brontës' Yorkshire home – were still surrounded by woods in the mid-nineteenth century.
[3] *myriad* ten thousand, a large number.
[4] *Instinct with* imbued or charged with.

But do not think its music
Has power to reach my mind –   20

6
'Play with the scented flower,
The young tree's supple bough –
And leave my human feelings
In their own course to flow'

7
The Wanderer would not leave me   25
Its kiss grew warmer still –
'O come,' it sighed so sweetly
'I'll win thee 'gainst thy will –

8
'Have we not been from childhood friends?
Have I not loved thee long?   30
As long as thou hast loved the night
Whose silence wakes my song?

9
'And when thy heart is laid at rest
Beneath the church-yard stone
I shall have time enough to mourn   35
And thou to be alone' –

Shall Earth no more inspire thee[?]

A spirit of nature was the subject of Brontë's 'The Night-Wind', 218–19. 'Shall Earth no more inspire thee' similarly concerns a voice of nature, here directly addressing one of nature's disciples. Charlotte Brontë said of the poem: 'the following little piece has no title; but in it the Genius [presiding spirit] of a solitary region seems to address his wandering and wayward votary, and to recall within his influence the proud mind which rebelled at times against what it most loved'. The voice of nature endeavours to guide the addressee back to accustomed devotions (nature is divinity here), but without the sense of threat apparent in 'The Night-Wind'.

'Shall Earth no more inspire thee' proclaims, even in its title, that it is in negotiation with Wordsworthian Romanticism. The emphasis of Brontë's poem is not on Wordsworth's belief in nature's capacity to signify the divine but on the possession of the earth itself: 'none would ask a Heaven / More like this Earth than thine'. Catherine Earnshaw's dream in Book 1, chapter 9 of Emily Brontë's only novel, *Wuthering Heights* (1847), is relevant: '"This is nothing," cried she; "I was only going to say that heaven did not seem to be my home; and I broke my heart with weeping to come back to earth; and the angels were so angry that they flung me out, into the middle of the heath on the top of Wuthering Heights; where I woke sobbing for joy."' The poem, written in 1841, was first published in 1850.

Text: MS (with standardized spelling).

Shall Earth no more inspire thee,
Thou lonely dreamer now?
Since passion may not fire thee
Shall Nature cease to bow?

2
Thy mind is ever moving
In regions dark to thee;
Recall its useless roving –
Come back and dwell with me –   5

3
I know my mountain breezes
Enchant and soothe thee still –
I know my sunshine pleases   10
Despite thy wayward will –

4
When day with evening blending
Sinks from the summer sky,
I've seen thy spirit bending
In fond idolatry –   15

5
I've watched thee every hour –
I know my mighty sway –
I know my magic power
To drive thy griefs away –   20

6
Few hearts to mortals given
On earth so wildly pine
Yet none would ask a Heaven
More like this Earth than thine –

7
Then let my winds caress thee –   25
Thy comrade let me be –
Since nought beside can bless thee
Return and dwell with me –

To Imagination

Emily Brontë's poetry is in persistent negotiation with its Romantic inheritance. Here, she writes of the restorative powers of the imagination in a subtle response to both Wordsworth's 'Intimations of Immortality' ode and Coleridge's 'Dejection', both poems about the vicissitudes of the imaginative faculty. As in 'The Prisoner: A Fragment', 223–5, and 'No coward soul is mine', 225–6, Brontë's focus is on the enabling power of the life within. The poem contributes significantly to Brontë's self-fashioning as solitary poet whose gift is individual and private, and whose art is one of inspiration. She offers herself cut off from the social, and a model of her mind as one sustained by the spontaneous and quasi-supernatural rather than as involved in the intellectual and political culture of her environment. This idea of the decontextualized writer dominated readings of Brontë's poetry and fiction well into the twentieth century. Like much of Brontë's poetry, 'To Imagination' is characterized by a pared-down diction, where every word counts, and adjectives and nouns in particular have an austere authenticity. The MS is dated 3 September 1844.

Text: revised text of 1846 (with standardized spelling).

When weary with the long day's care
And earthly change from pain to pain
And lost and ready to despair
Thy kind voice calls me back again –
Oh my true friend, I am not lone   5
While thou canst speak with such a tone!

2

So hopeless is the world without
The world within I doubly prize
Thy world, where guile and hate and doubt
And cold suspicion never rise –   10
Where thou and I and Liberty
Have undisputed sovereignty.

3

What matters it that all around
Danger and guilt and darkness lie
If but within our bosom's bound   15
We hold a bright untroubled sky,
Warm with ten thousand mingled rays
Of suns that know no winter days –

4

Reason indeed may oft complain
For Nature's sad reality   20
And tell the suffering heart how vain
Its cherished dreams must always be
And Truth may rudely trample down
The flowers of fancy[1] newly blown:

5

But thou art ever there to bring   25
The hovering vision back, and breathe
New glories o'er the blighted spring
And call a lovelier life from death
And whisper with a voice divine
Of real worlds as bright as thine.   30

6

I trust not to thy phantom bliss
Yet still, in evening's quiet hour
With Never failing thankfulness[2]
I welcome thee benignant[3] Power
Sure Solacer of human cares,   35
And sweeter hope when hope despairs –

---

[1] *fancy* distinguished from the Imagination as a less substantial and more fanciful power (see Brontë's 'How Clear She Shines', a poem concerning the fancy).

[2] *Never failing thankfulness* words that deliberately suggest Christian devotion, but the object of the poet's gratitude is her own imagination.
[3] *benignant* benign.

Remembrance

Like 'The Prisoner: A Fragment', 223–5, the context of 'Remembrance' is the Gondal narratives. Gondal was the imaginary land, a development, sometime before November 1834, of childhood games, which was shared between Emily and her sister Anne. It became the focus of much of their creativity, though the narratives of it have not survived intact. Titled in the manuscript 'R. Alcona to J. Brenzaida' (Gondal characters), it was conceived as the lament of the imaginary Rosina Alcona for her dead husband or lover Prince Julius Brenzaida (who was perhaps assassinated). Its affective power, strengthened by its slow rhythms ('the slowest rhythm I know in English poetry', said C. Day Lewis) and complex, twisting syntax, comes partly from the tension between the speaker's declaration that she 'Dare not indulge in Memory's rapturous pain' and the fact that the poem continually recollects her dead lover. The MS is dated 3 March 1845.

Text: revised text of 1846 (with standardized spelling).

Cold in the earth and the deep snow piled above thee!
Far, far removed, cold in the dreary grave!
Have I forgot, my Only Love, to love thee,
Severed at last by Time's all-severing wave?

2
Now, when alone, do my thoughts no longer hover   5
Over the mountains, on that northern shore,[1]
Resting their wings where heath and fern-leaves cover
Thy noble heart for ever, ever more?

3
Cold in the earth – and fifteen wild Decembers,[2]
From those brown hills, have melted into spring –   10
Faithful indeed is the spirit that remembers
After such years of change and suffering!

4
Sweet Love of youth, forgive, if I forget thee
While the World's tide is bearing me along
Other desires and other Hopes beset me   15
Hopes which obscure, but cannot do thee wrong –

5
No later light has lightened up my heaven:
No second morn has ever shone for me
All my life's bliss from thy dear life was given –
All my life's bliss is in the grave with thee   20

6
But when the days of golden dreams had perished
And even Despair was powerless to destroy
Then did I learn how existence could be cherished,
Strengthened and fed without the aid of joy.

---

[1] *northern shore* of Angora, one of the kingdoms of Gondal. Originally, Brontë wrote 'on Angora's shore'.

[2] *fifteen wild Decembers* Gondal chronology.

7

Then did I check the tears of useless passion,   25
Weaned my young soul from yearning after thine;
Sternly denied its burning wish to hasten
Down to that tomb already more than mine!

8

And even yet, I dare not let it languish,
Dare not indulge in Memory's rapturous pain   30
Once drinking deep of that divinest anguish³
How could I seek the empty world again?

³ *drinking . . . anguish* cf. Jesus's words during the Agony in the Garden of Gethsemane: 'And he went a little further, and fell on his face, and prayed, saying, O my father, if it be possible, let this cup passe from me: neuerthelesse, not as I will, but as thou wilt', Matthew 26.39.

The Prisoner: A Fragment

Emily Brontë's engagement with mysticism and the liberty possible to the mind receives its amplest treatment in this poem, originally entitled 'Julian M. and A. G. Rochelle' (characters from the Gondal stories, see headnote to 'Remembrance', 222). Brontë extracted 'The Prisoner' from a longer piece that has the date 9 October 1845 to produce, none the less, a poem whole in itself (the subtitle 'A Fragment' recalls her debt to Romantic period forms). Focusing on the powers of the individual mind to transcend material existence (cf. 'To Imagination', 220–1), the poem is distinctive in presenting an account of female mystical experience: the mind escaping from a prison to contact the 'Invisible'. The poem sexualizes mystical experience, and mimics elements of Christian vocab-

ulary, but only to keep a guarded distance from the religious. Its literary roots are in Byron (*The Prisoner of Chillon* [1816]) and in Shelley's preoccupation with imaginative liberty and resistance to tyranny. The Royalist–Republican war of the Gondal narratives is presumably the literal political context. Once again, Brontë's pace is slow, and the austerity of her diction makes each word resonate. Lines are often syntactically divided into two – such as the chiasmic 'Then dawns the Invisible; the Unseen its truth reveals' – intensifying the poem's formal poise, its balanced solidity.

Text: 1846, with MS additions.

In the dungeon-crypts, idly did I stray,
Reckless of the lives wasting there away;
'Draw the ponderous¹ bars! open, Warder stern!'
He dared not say me nay – the hinges harshly turn.

2

'Our guests are darkly lodged,' I whisper'd, gazing through   5
The vault, whose grated eye showed heaven more grey than blue;
(This was when glad spring laughed in awaking pride;)
'Aye, darkly lodged enough!' returned my sullen guide.

3

Then, God forgive my youth; forgive my careless tongue;
I scoffed, as chill chains on the damp flag-stones rung: 10
'Confined in triple walls, art thou so much to fear,
That we must bind thee down and clench thy fetters here?'

¹ *ponderous* of great weight.

4

The captive raised her face, it was as soft and mild
As sculptured marble saint, or slumbering unwean'd child;
It was so soft and mild, it was so sweet and fair,   15
Pain could not trace a line, nor grief a shadow there!

5

The captive raised her hand and pressed it to her brow;
'I have been struck,' she said, 'and I am suffering now;
Yet these are little worth, your bolts and irons strong,
And, were they forged in steel, they could not hold me long.'   20

6

Hoarse laughed the jailer grim: 'Shall I be won to hear;
Dost think, fond,[2] dreaming wretch, that *I* shall grant thy prayer?
Or, better still, wilt melt my master's heart with groans?
Ah! sooner might the sun thaw down these granite stones.

7

'My master's voice is low, his aspect bland and kind,   25
But hard as hardest flint, the soul that lurks behind;
And I am rough and rude, yet not more rough to see
Than is the hidden ghost[3] that has its home in me.'

8

About her lips there played a smile of almost scorn,
'My friend,' she gently said, 'you have not heard me mourn;   30
When you my kindred's lives, *my* lost life, can restore,
Then may I weep and sue,[4] – but never, friend, before!

9

'Still, let my tyrants[5] know, I am not doomed to wear[6]
Year after year in gloom, and desolate despair;
A messenger of Hope, comes every night to me,   35
And offers for short life, eternal liberty.

10

'He comes with western winds, with evening's wandering airs,
With that clear dusk of heaven that brings the thickest stars.
Winds take a pensive tone, and stars a tender fire,
And visions rise, and change, that kill me with desire.   40

11

'Desire for nothing known in my maturer years,
When Joy grew mad with awe, at counting future tears.
When, if my spirit's sky was full of flashes warm,
I knew not whence they came, from sun, or thunder storm.

12

'But,[7] first, a hush of peace – a soundless calm descends;   45
The struggle of distress, and fierce impatience ends.

---

[2] *fond* silly, foolishly credulous.
[3] *hidden ghost* soul (the Warder is as rough inside as out).
[4] *sue* petition for redress.
[5] *tyrants* those who imprison her.

[6] *wear* lose strength, wear out.
[7] *But* . . . she returns to narrating the mystical experiences in prison.

Mute music soothes my breast, unuttered harmony,
That I could never dream, till Earth was lost to me.

13
'Then dawns the Invisible; the Unseen its truth reveals;
My outward sense is gone, my inward essence feels:
Its wings are almost free – its home, its harbour found,
Measuring the gulf, it stoops, and dares[8] the final bound.

50

14
'Oh, dreadful is the check – intense the agony –
When the ear begins to hear, and the eye begins to see;
When the pulse begins to throb, the brain to think again,
The soul to feel the flesh, and the flesh to feel the chain.

55

15
'Yet I would lose no sting, would wish no torture less,
The more that anguish racks, the earlier it will bless;
And robed in fires of hell, or bright with heavenly shine,
If it but herald death, the vision is divine!'

60

16
She ceased to speak, and we, unanswering, turned to go –
We had no further power to work the captive woe:
Her cheek, her gleaming eye, declared that man had given
A sentence, unapproved, and overruled by Heaven.

[8] *dares* challenges (but does not actually take the final bound).

No coward soul is mine

'The Prisoner: A Fragment', 223–5, and 'To Imagination', 220–1, reflect on the internal resources of the mind, the 'world within' that is 'doubly prize[d]'. In 'No coward soul is mine', Emily Brontë takes a step further to describe an inner power as an immortal 'God within my breast'. (For the relationship between Brontë's concentration on inner powers and her fashioning of an idea of authorship, see the headnote to 'To Imagination', 220.)

Brontë's reading of the Stoic philosopher Epictetus (*c.*50–*c.*120 AD) may have influenced this poem that boldly defies the fear of death, armed from within. Brontë perhaps knew Elizabeth Carter's popular translation of Epictetus (1758), including these words: 'Why, do you not know, then, that the origin of all human evils and of the mean-spiritedness and cowardice is not death, but rather the fear of death? Fortify yourself, therefore, against this. Hither let all your discourses, readings, exercises tend. And then you will know that thus alone are all men made free.' Suggestively, Carter's translation was prefixed with a poem by Hester Chapone (1727–1801), beginning 'No more repine, my coward Soul!' Brontë's text has the courage of someone standing on the edge: Charlotte, Emily's sister, thought these the last lines Emily wrote, and one can see why. The MS is dated 2 January 1846, and the poem was printed first in 1850.

Text: MS.

No coward soul is mine
No trembler in the world's storm troubled sphere
I see Heaven's glories shine
And Faith shines equal arming me from Fear

2

O God within my breast[1]   5
Almighty ever-present Deity
Life, that in me hast rest
As I, – Undying Life, have power in thee

3

Vain are the thousand creeds[2]
That move men's hearts, unutterably vain,   10
Worthless as withered weeds
Or idlest froth amid the boundless main[3]

4

To waken doubt in one
Holding so fast by thy infinity
So surely anchored on   15
The steadfast rock of Immortality

5

With wide-embracing love
Thy Spirit animates eternal years
Pervades and broods above,
Changes, sustains, dissolves, creates and rears   20

6

Though Earth and moon were gone
And suns and universes ceased to be
And Thou wert left alone
Every Existence would exist in thee

7

There is not room for Death   25
Nor atom that his might could render void
Since Thou art Being and Breath
And what thou art may never be destroyed

[1] *O God . . . breast* cf. Epictetus, *Discourses*, 'God himself is   [2] *creeds* beliefs.
within you, and hears and sees all'.   [3] *main* sea.

Arthur Hugh Clough (1819–1861)

Born in Liverpool to a cotton trader, Arthur Hugh Clough was taken to Charleston, South Carolina, in 1822 when the family emigrated in search of better times. He returned for an English education in 1828. Clough was sent to Rugby School in 1829, which was being turned around by its new, increasingly eminent, disciple-attracting headmaster, Thomas Arnold (the father of Matthew). The inspiring but also oppressive model of Thomas Arnold's moral rectitude, certainty and self-possession lies behind many of Clough's meditations on and ironizations of masculine identity, including Claude in *Amours de Voyage*. In 1837, Clough went up to Balliol College Oxford where he became friendly with Matthew Arnold (who commemorated him in 'Thyrsis'). Clough involved himself in the ecclesiastical debates surrounding the Oxford Movement, the centre of common room discussion, and missed the expected First ('I have failed,' he said memorably of his second class) probably as a consequence. None the less, he obtained a prestigious fellowship at Oriel College – right at the heart of the Oxford Movement – but gradually became wracked with doubts about his religious commitment, doubts that, in due course, left him distinctly post-Christian. In 1848, he felt himself unable to sign assent to the 39 Articles, the tenets of Anglicanism's Protestant identity, then a requirement of Oxford Fellows, and resigned his position. Many believed him far too fastidious in taking such a stand (Matthew Arnold, on

the other hand, wrote, 'Live by thy light, and earth will live by hers!' ['Religious Isolation']). Just afterwards, his epistolary poem of politics and love on an Oxford vacation reading tour, *The Bothie of Tober-na-Vuolich* (1848), was issued (originally *The Bothie of Toper-na-Fuosich*). The following year came the collection *Ambarvalia*, which included some poems by Thomas Burbidge (a Rugby friend), and the writing of *Amours de Voyage* while Clough was in Rome during the Siege. *Amours* appeared only in the United States, serialized in the Boston periodical the *Atlantic Monthly*. In 1849, Clough became Principal of University Hall, London – founded by Dissenters, he hoped the atmosphere would be more tolerant – and a Professor of English Literature there. But his unorthodox religious opinions were too much even for them, and he resigned in 1852. In the summer of 1850, Clough had begun to draft *Dipsychus*, a Faustian dialogue set in Venice and only published, posthumously, in 1865. After the problems of London, he took himself to Boston, Massachusetts, then to London again, where he became an Examiner at the Education Office and seemingly more settled. By this stage, he had stopped writing poetry altogether. He married Blanche Smith in 1854, whose cousin was Florence Nightingale, and exerted – over-exerted – himself in aiding her medical and charity work. He died in Florence of malaria, where he had been trying to recover his broken health.

Say not the struggle nought availeth

Arthur Hugh Clough's *Amours de Voyage*, 228–62, considers a protagonist unwilling to commit himself wholeheartedly and who is fraught with uncertainty. The hymn-like 'Say not the struggle nought availeth' (which has, in fact, been set to music as a hymn) offers a more decisive position. This is Clough at his most optimistic, and the many negatives of the poem serve only an affirmative purpose. Changing metaphors from the battlefield to the ocean tide to the dawn, the poem gives reassurance to an unindividuated but dispirited listener, encouraging him that failure may be apparent but not real (cf. Claude's preoccupation with the illusory and factitious in *Amours*). 'Say not the struggle nought availeth', which keeps returning

to images of physical spaces in the process of redefinition, is without irony, unlike another later poem of encouragement, Rudyard Kipling's 'If – ', 654–5. It was probably written during the Siege of Rome in 1849, in which *Amours de Voyage* is set (cf. Matthew Arnold's 'Consolation', which he claimed was 'Written during the siege of Rome'). 'Say not' was first published in *The Crayon* in 1855, and exists in various MSS with different titles: 'In Profundis' ('in the depths') and 'Dum Spiro' from the Latin tag 'Dum spiro spero', 'while I breathe I hope'.

Text: MS.

Say not the struggle nought availeth,
The labour and the wounds are vain,
The enemy faints not, nor faileth,
And as things have been, things remain.

2

If hopes were dupes, fears may be liars;   5
It may be, in yon smoke concealed,
Your comrades chase e'en now the fliers,[1]
And, but for you, possess the field.

3

For while the tired waves, vainly breaking,
Seem here no painful inch to gain,   10
Far back through creeks and inlets making
Came, silent, flooding in, the main,[2]

4

And not by eastern windows only,
When daylight comes, comes in the light,
In front the sun climbs slow, how slowly,   15
But westward, look, the land is bright.

---

[1] *fliers* enemy retreating from the battlefield.   [2] *main* open sea.

Amours de Voyage

Epistolary poems (poems comprising letters) are rare in the Victorian period. Arthur Hugh Clough's *Amours de Voyage*, first published in *Atlantic Monthly* in 1858, is a notable exception, a major mid-century text about the relationship between national and sexual politics, as original in its handling of subject matter as in form (cf. Clough's epistolary *Bothie of Tober-na-Vuolich* [1848]). In the person of the poem's hero – hero is hardly the word – Clough dramatizes the conflictual middle-class Victorian intellectual male, offering a sustained study in the pressures of mid-century masculinity and a figure who bears a number of Clough's own displaced dilemmas.

Amours de Voyage – the title can mean 'love on a journey'/'travelling romances'/'travelling liaisons'/ 'itinerant love (affairs)'/'love of travel' (French) – is set during one of the key stages in the build-up to Italian unification, a major event in the history of nineteenth-century European nationalism (the united Kingdom of Italy was proclaimed in 1861). A number of mid-century English poets in addition to Clough were interested in Italy's struggle for unification – Italy, prior to unification, comprised a large number of separate areas controlled by different local and foreign powers – and Robert Browning and Elizabeth Barrett Browning, whose affection for Italy was

considerable, were prominent among them (see Elizabeth Barrett Browning's *Casa Guidi Windows* [1851] and *Poems Before Congress* [1860]).

The historical setting of *Amours de Voyage* is as follows. On 9 February 1849, a Roman revolutionary council declared the end of the Pope's temporal authority (his authority at this point included significant political as well as spiritual power as he had authority over the Italian Papal States) and the rebirth of the long extinct Roman Republic. The Pope – Pius IX – had already escaped to Naples, where he urged sympathetic Catholic powers to restore him to his former position. In Rome, Giuseppe Mazzini (1805–72), to become a crucial figure in the movement for Italian unification, established himself as a political leader with appealing moral conviction, while Giuseppe Garibaldi (1807–82) was placed in command of the army, including volunteers and members of the National Guard. With a determined but irregular force, they commenced the defence of the city.

The first to respond to Pius's call for assistance was France. On 25 April, an expeditionary force under General Oudinot landed at Civita Vecchia and marched to Rome. The French and Roman armies clashed first on 30 April, and the French were – to their surprise – beaten. They had misjudged the energy of the Roman defenders. Meanwhile, anti-revolutionary forces from Naples were moving towards Rome. The next major engagement between the city's defenders and the French was on 3 June. Here, Oudinot inflicted heavy losses on the Italians, and the next few weeks of siege were grim. Perceiving that defeat was inevitable, Garibaldi and his volunteers made a risky escape from the city. The victorious French entered Rome on 3 July. *Amours de Voyage* plots these events as the background to Claude's sojourn in Rome and his unfulfilled love affair.

The Siege of Rome was one of failure in the longer, but eventually successful, story of the struggle for Italian unification. Against this backdrop, Clough offers a narrative of failed human togetherness. Claude, the bookish and hesitating protagonist, fails, despite his busy search, to catch up with Mary Trevellyan with whom he has, to his surprise, fallen in love. The poem maps political failure against personal and union is secured in neither. Carlylean faith in sincerity is scrutinized in *Amours de Voyage*, a poem variously engaged with questions of dissident masculinity. In his Oxford diary in the summer of 1848, Clough wrote: 'The sincere man, most easily too in neglect &

unobservance – will among the counters of vanity detect the ringing coin of self-knowledge – he will in the end, & ere the end, find his work and do it.' *Amours de Voyage* dramatizes and ironizes such a conviction, testing Claude's self-knowledge, sincerity and capacity for action. The idea of fissured identity is supplemented in the poem's extensive consideration of Rome, which is presented as a city of layers, with one identity imposed on another (cf. Goethe's *Roman Elegies*, which may have influenced *Amours*).

There may also be a private context. Clough's friend Matthew Arnold wrote a series of poems eventually entitled *Switzerland*, of which 'To Marguerite – Continued', 267–8, was one. Marguerite may not have been a real person, but Park Honan has suggested that her real-life counterpart was a woman named Mary Claude. Arnold planned to visit her in Switzerland only to discover that he had missed her. Claude's love for Mary in *Amours de Voyage* suggests Clough had a cheeky purpose in writing the poem, making a joke at the expense of his friend (the fact that his central characters are called *Claude* and *Mary* seems some confirmation of this).

Text: *The Poems of Arthur Hugh Clough* (1974).

Oh, you are sick of self-love, Malvolio,
And taste with a distempered appetite!
Shakspeare.[1]

Il doutait de tout, même de l'amour.
French Novel.[2]

Solvitur ambulando.
Solutio Sophismatum.[3]

Flevit amores
Non elaboratum ad pedem.
Horace.[4]

CANTO 1.

Over the great windy waters, and over the clear-crested summits,
Unto the sun and the sky, and unto the perfecter earth,
Come, let us go, – to a land wherein gods of the old time wandered,
Where every breath even now changes to ether[5] divine.
Come, let us go; though withal a voice whisper, 'The world that we live in,   5
Whithersoever we turn, still is the same narrow crib;

[1] *Oh you . . . Shakspeare*, from *Twelfth Night* 1.5.86–7.
[2] *Il doutait . . . l'amour* 'He doubted everything, even love.' The 'French Novel' is unidentified.
[3] *Solvitur ambulando* 'It is solved by walking': a Sophist's solution. This faith in action is not Claude's.

[4] *Flevit . . . pedem* adapted from Horace's *Epodes* 14.10–11. '[They say that Teian Anacreon], who very often in simple measures deplored his loves'. Clough makes Horace's word 'love' plural.
[5] *ether* clear sky, medium filling upper regions of space.

'Tis but to prove limitation, and measure a cord, that we travel;
    Let who would 'scape and be free go to his chamber and think;
      'Tis but to change idle fancies for memories wilfully falser;
      'Tis but to go and have been.' – Come, little bark![6] let us go.   10

1. Claude to Eustace.

Dear Eustatio,[7] I write that you may write me an answer,
    Or at the least to put us again *en rapport*[8] with each other.
Rome disappoints me much, – St. Peter's,[9] perhaps, in especial;
Only the Arch of Titus[10] and view from the Lateran[11] please me:
    This, however, perhaps is the weather, which truly is horrid.   15
    Greece must be better, surely; and yet I am feeling so spiteful,
That I could travel to Athens, to Delphi, and Troy, and Mount Sinai,[12]
    Though but to see with my eyes that these are vanity also.

Rome disappoints me much; I hardly as yet understand, but
    Rubbishy seems the word that most exactly would suit it.   20
    All the foolish destructions, and all the sillier savings,
    All the incongruous things of past incompatible ages,
Seem to be treasured up here to make fools of present and future.
Would to Heaven the old Goths[13] had made a cleaner sweep of it!
Would to Heaven some new ones would come and destroy these churches!   25
    However, one can live in Rome as also in London.
    It is a blessing, no doubt, to be rid, at least for a time, of
All one's friends and relations, – yourself (forgive me!) included, –
    All the *assujettissement*[14] of having been what one has been,
    What one thinks one is, or thinks that others suppose one;   30
    Yet, in despite of all, we turn like fools to the English.
Vernon has been my fate; who is here the same that you knew him, –
Making the tour, it seems, with friends of the name of Trevellyn.

2. Claude to Eustace.

Rome disappoints me still; but I shrink and adapt myself to it.
    Somehow a tyrannous sense of a superincumbent[15] oppression   35
      Still, wherever I go, accompanies ever, and makes me
Feel like a tree (shall I say?) buried under a ruin of brickwork.
Rome, believe me, my friend, is like its own Monte Testaceo,[16]
Merely a marvellous mass of broken and castaway wine-pots.
    Ye gods! what do I want with this rubbish of ages departed,   40
Things that nature abhors, the experiments that she has failed in?
What do I find in the Forum?[17] An archway and two or three pillars.
Well, but St. Peter's? Alas, Bernini[18] has filled it with sculpture!

---

[6] *bark* little boat (also referring to the poem).
[7] *Eustatio* gesture towards Italian.
[8] *en rapport* in relation (with).
[9] *St. Peter's* basilica of the Vatican (built 1450–1626).
[10] *Arch of Titus* triumphal arch, built in 81 AD.
[11] *Lateran* St John Lateran is the oldest of the basilicas of Rome.
[12] *Athens . . . Sinai* three major Classical sites and the mountain where God gave the Law to Moses.

[13] *old Goths* Alaric and his Goths sacked Rome in 410 AD.
[14] *assujettissement* subjection.
[15] *superincumbent* lying upon.
[16] *Monte Testaceo* (Monte Testaccio) artificial hill outside Rome made from ancient heaps of broken *amphorae*.
[17] *Forum* ancient centre of Rome.
[18] *Bernini* Giovanni Lorenzo Bernini (1598–1680), sculptor, architect: his contributions to St Peter's include the piazza.

No one can cavil, I grant, at the size of the great Coliseum.[19]
Doubtless the notion of grand and capacious and massive amusement,   45
This the old Romans had; but tell me, is this an idea?
Yet of solidity much, but of splendour little is extant:[20]
'Brickwork I found thee, and marble I left thee!'[21] their Emperor vaunted;
'Marble I thought thee, and brickwork I find thee!' the Tourist[22] may answer.

3. Georgina Trevellyn to Louisa.

At last, dearest Louisa, I take up my pen to address you.   50
Here we are, you see, with the seven-and-seventy boxes,
Courier, Papa and Mamma, the children, and Mary and Susan:
Here we all are at Rome, and delighted of course with St. Peter's,
And very pleasantly lodged in the famous Piazza di Spagna.[23]
Rome is a wonderful place, but Mary shall tell you about it;   55
Not very gay, however; the English are mostly at Naples;[24]
There are the A.'s, we hear, and most of the W. party.
George, however, is come; did I tell you about his mustachios?
Dear, I must really stop, for the carriage, they tell me, is waiting;
Mary will finish; and Susan is writing, they say, to Sophia.   60
Adieu, dearest Louise, – evermore your faithful Georgina.
Who can a Mr. Claude be whom George has taken to be with?
Very stupid, I think, but George says so very clever.

4. Claude to Eustace.

No, the Christian faith, as at any rate I understood it,
With its humiliations and exaltations combining,   65
Exaltations sublime, and yet diviner abasements,
Aspirations from something most shameful here upon earth and
In our poor selves to something most perfect above in the heavens, –
No, the Christian faith, as I, at least, understood it,
Is not here, O Rome, in any of these thy churches;   70
Is not here, but in Freiburg, or Rheims, or Westminster Abbey.[25]
What in thy Dome[26] I find, in all thy recenter efforts,
Is a something, I think, more *rational* far, more earthly,
Actual, less ideal, devout not in scorn and refusal,
But in a positive, calm, Stoic-Epicurean[27] acceptance.   75
This I begin to detect in St. Peter's and some of the churches,
Mostly in all that I see of the sixteenth-century masters;
Overlaid of course with infinite gauds and gewgaws,[28]
Innocent, playful follies, the toys and trinkets of childhood,

---

[19] *Coliseum* huge ruined arena in the centre of Rome for gladiators and other sports built *c.*70 to 82 AD.
[20] *splendour . . . extant* the walls of the Coliseum have long lost their marble cladding.
[21] *'Brickwork . . . thee!'* famous statement attributed to Augustus, first emperor of Rome, 63 BC–14 AD.
[22] *Tourist* a relatively new term and notion of identity. *OED*'s first instance is 1780.
[23] *Piazza di Spagna* Murray's handbook to Rome, which Claude uses (see note 109), indicated there were two good hotels here.

[24] *Naples* fashionable city for the English tourist and a safe distance from the conflict that looked about to break out in Rome.
[25] *Freiburg, or Rheims, or Westminster Abbey* cities with famous cathedrals and the historic abbey church of Westminster (London).
[26] *Dome* of St Peter's.
[27] *Stoic-Epicurean* composite of two ancient philosophical systems: the fusion of calm endurance with a rejection of ideas of the divine or supernatural.
[28] *gewgaws* gaudy trifles, ornaments.

Forced on maturer years, as the serious one thing needful,[29]   80
By the barbarian will of the rigid and ignorant Spaniard.[30]

Curious work, meantime, re-entering society: how we
Walk a livelong[31] day, great Heaven, and watch our shadows!
What our shadows seem, forsooth, we will ourselves be.
Do I look like that? you think me that: then I am that.   85

5. Claude to Eustace.

Luther,[32] they say, was unwise; like a half-taught German, he could not
See that old follies were passing most tranquilly out of remembrance;
Leo the Tenth was employing all efforts to clear out abuses;[33]
Jupiter, Juno, and Venus, Fine Arts, and Fine Letters, the Poets,
Scholars, and Sculptors, and Painters, were quietly clearing away the   90
Martyrs, and Virgins, and Saints,[34] or at any rate Thomas Aquinas:[35]
He must forsooth make a fuss and distend his huge Wittenberg[36] lungs, and
Bring back Theology once yet again in a flood upon Europe:
Lo you, for forty days[37] from the windows of heaven it fell; the
Waters prevail on the earth yet more for a hundred and fifty;   95
Are they abating at last? the doves that are sent to explore are
Wearily fain[38] to return, at the best with a leaflet of promise, –
Fain to return, as they went, to the wandering wave-tost vessel, –
Fain to re-enter the roof which covers the clean and the unclean, –
Luther, they say, was unwise; he didn't see how things were going;   100
Luther was foolish, – but, O great God! what call you Ignatius?[39]
O my tolerant soul, be still! but you talk of barbarians,
Alaric, Attila, Genseric;[40] – why, they came, they killed, they
Ravaged, and went on their way; but these vile, tyrannous Spaniards,[41]
These are here still, – how long, O ye heavens, in the country of Dante?[42]   105
These, that fanaticized Europe, which now can forget them, release not
This, their choicest of prey, this Italy; here you see them, –
Here, with emasculate pupils and gimcrack churches of Gesu,[43]
Pseudo-learning and lies, confessional-boxes and postures, –
Here, with metallic beliefs and regimental devotions, –   110
Here, overcrusting with slime, perverting, defacing, debasing,

---

[29] *one thing needful* cf. 'But one thing is needefull, and Mary hath chosen that good part, which shall not bee taken away from her', Luke 10.42.

[30] *Spaniard* Ignatius Loyola (1491–1556), founder of the Jesuit order, championed the Catholic Church against the Reformers. Claude objects to the activities of the Counter-Reformation.

[31] *livelong* intensifier of 'long'.

[32] *Luther* Martin Luther (1483–1546), leader of the Reformation in Germany.

[33] *Leo . . . abuses* ironic: Pope Leo X (1475–1521) was not a reformer.

[34] *Jupiter . . . Saints* 'the Renaissance with its revival of Classical antiquity was clearing away the medieval forms of Catholicism' (ironic).

[35] *Aquinas* St Thomas Aquinas (*c.*1225–74), the most important of the medieval Scholastic philosophers whose

work here signifies the intellectual preoccupations of the pre-Reformation Catholic Church.

[36] *Wittenberg* Luther was popularly believed to have nailed his 95 *Theses* objecting to Catholic practices on the door of the castle church of Wittenberg in 1517.

[37] *forty days* Claude begins to allude to the story of Noah's ark in Genesis 6–8.

[38] *fain* glad.

[39] *Ignatius* see note 30.

[40] *Alaric, Attila, Genseric* Alaric led the Goths in the sack of Rome in 410; Attila attacked Italy in 452; Genseric led the Vandals in their assault on Rome in 455.

[41] *Spaniards* Jesuits; see note 30.

[42] *Dante* Dante Alighieri (1265–1321), supreme medieval Italian poet, author of *Divina Commedia*.

[43] *Gesu* churches of the Jesuits including the Gesù in Rome, where Ignatius Loyola lies buried.

Michael Angelo's dome,[44] that had hung the Pantheon in heaven,[45]
Raphael's[46] Joys and Graces, and thy clear stars, Galileo![47]

6. Claude to Eustace.

Which of three Misses Trevellyn it is that Vernon shall marry
Is not a thing to be known; for our friend is one of those natures   115
Which have their perfect delight in the general tender-domestic;
So that he trifles with Mary's shawl, ties Susan's bonnet,
Dances with all, but at home is most, they say, with Georgina,
Who is, however, *too* silly in my apprehension for Vernon.
  I, as before when I wrote, continue to see them a little;   120
Not that I like them much or care a *bajocco*[48] for Vernon,
But I am slow at Italian, have not many English acquaintance,
And I am asked, in short, and am not good at excuses.
Middle-class people these, bankers very likely, not wholly
Pure of the taint of the shop; will at *table d'hôte*[49] and restaurant   125
Have their shilling's worth, their penny's pennyworth even:
Neither man's aristocracy this, nor God's, God knoweth!
Yet they are fairly descended, they give you to know, well connected;
Doubtless somewhere in some neighbourhood have, and are careful to keep, some
  Threadbare-genteel relations, who in their turn are enchanted   130
Grandly among county people to introduce at assemblies
To the unpennied cadets[50] our cousins with excellent fortunes.
Neither man's aristocracy this, nor God's, God knoweth!

7. Claude to Eustace.

Ah, what a shame, indeed, to abuse these most worthy people!
Ah, what a sin to have sneered at their innocent rustic pretensions!   135
  Is it not laudable really, this reverent worship of station?
Is it not fitting that wealth should tender this homage to culture?
Is it not touching to witness these efforts, if little availing,
Painfully made, to perform the old ritual service of manners?
Shall not devotion atone for the absence of knowledge? and fervour   140
  Palliate, cover, the fault of a superstitious observance?
Dear, dear, what do I say? but, alas! just now, like Iago,[51]
  I can be nothing at all, if it is not critical wholly;
So in fantastic height, in coxcomb[52] exultation,
Here in the garden I walk, can freely concede to the Maker   145
That the works of His hand are all very good:[53] His creatures,
Beast of the field and fowl, He brings them before me; I name them;[54]

[44] *Michael Angelo's dome* painter, sculptor and architect Michelangelo Buonarroti (1475–1564) was appointed chief architect to St. Peter's, Rome, in 1546. He designed the dome but it was not completed until after his death.
[45] *Pantheon . . . heaven* Michelangelo is reported to have said that he would suspend the dome of the Pantheon in air above St Peter's grave.
[46] *Raphael* Raphael (Raffaello Sanzio) (1483–1520), appointed the chief architect of St Peter's in 1514.
[47] *Galileo* Galileo Galilei (1564–1642), Italian astronomer and physicist, who fell foul of the Church authorities.
[48] *bajocco* small copper coin of little value.
[49] *table d'hôte* lodgings that provide food.
[50] *cadets* younger members of the family.

[51] *like Iago* cf. 'O, gentle Lady, do not put me to't, / For I am nothing if not critical', *Othello* 2.1.121–2.
[52] *coxcomb* foolish, conceited, showy person.
[53] *Here . . . good* cf. Biblical creation narrative where God approves His work: 'And the earth brought foorth grasse, and herbe yeelding seed after his kinde, and the tree yeelding fruit, whose seed was in it selfe, after his kinde: and God saw that it was good', Genesis 1.12.
[54] *His creatures . . . name them* cf. 'And out of ye ground the LORD God formed euery beast of the field, and euery foule of the aire, and brought them vnto Adam, to see what he would call them: and whatsoeuer Adam called euery liuing creature, that was the name thereof', Genesis 2.19.

That which I name them, they are, – the bird, the beast, and the cattle.
But for Adam, – alas, poor critical coxcomb Adam!
But for Adam there is not found an help-meet for him.[55]   150

8. Claude to Eustace.

No, great Dome of Agrippa,[56] thou art not Christian! canst not,
Strip and replaster and daub and do what they will with thee, be so!
Here underneath the great porch of colossal Corinthian columns,[57]
Here as I walk, do I dream of the Christian belfries above them;
Or, on a bench as I sit and abide for long hours, till thy whole vast   155
Round grows dim as in dreams to my eyes, I repeople thy niches,
Not with the Martyrs, and Saints, and Confessors, and Virgins, and children,
But with the mightier forms of an older, austerer worship;
And I recite to myself,[58] how
Eager for battle here   160
Stood Vulcan,[59] here matronal Juno,[60]
And with the bow to his shoulder faithful
He who with pure dew laveth of Castaly[61]
His flowing locks, who holdeth of Lycia[62]
The oak forest and the wood that bore him,   165
Delos'[63] and Patara's[64] own Apollo.

9. Claude to Eustace.

Yet it is pleasant, I own it, to be in their company; pleasant,
Whatever else it may be, to abide in the feminine presence.
Pleasant, but wrong, will you say? But this happy, serene coexistence
Is to some poor soft souls, I fear, a necessity simple,   170
Meat and drink and life, and music, filling with sweetness,
Thrilling with melody sweet, with harmonies strange overwhelming,
All the long-silent strings of an awkward, meaningless fabric.
Yet as for that, I could live, I believe, with children; to have those
Pure and delicate forms encompassing, moving about you,   175
This were enough, I could think; and truly with glad resignation
Could from the dream of Romance, from the fever of flushed adolescence,
Look to escape and subside into peaceful avuncular[65] functions.
Nephews and nieces! alas, for as yet I have none! and, moreover,
Mothers are jealous, I fear me, too often, too rightfully; fathers   180
Think they have title exclusive to spoiling their own little darlings;
And by the law of the land, in despite of Malthusian doctrine,[66]

[55] *Adam . . . help-meet for him* cf. Genesis 2.18, 'And the
LORD God said, It is not good that the man should be alone:
I will make him an helpe meet for him'.
[56] *Dome of Agrippa* the Pantheon in Rome was built as a
pre-Christian temple but converted to a Christian church in
608 AD.
[57] *Corinthian columns* one of the three major Greek orders
of columns (Doric, Ionic, Corinthian). The Corinthian is
the lightest and most ornate, having a bell-shaped capital
adorned with acanthus leaves.
[58] *recite to myself* Claude, imagining himself in the Pantheon
when it was a pre-Christian temple, recalls a translation of
Horace, *Odes* 3.4.58–64 in the next 7 lines as if he is taking
part in the 'austerer worship' of the past.

[59] *Vulcan* Roman god of fire and forge.
[60] *Juno* Queen of Heaven, wife and sister of Jupiter.
[61] *Castaly* Castalian spring near Delphi, sacred to the
Muses.
[62] *Lycia* territory in Asia Minor.
[63] *Delos* island where Apollo, Greek god of the arts, was
born.
[64] *Patara* in Lycia where Apollo had an oracle.
[65] *avuncular* of an uncle.
[66] *Malthusian doctrine* Thomas Malthus's *An Essay on the
Principle of Population* (1798) argued that populations
increase, unless checked, beyond the means to support
them.

No sort of proper provision is made for that most patriotic,
   Most meritorious subject, the childless and bachelor uncle.

10. Claude to Eustace.

Ye, too, marvellous Twain,[67] that erect on the Monte Cavallo   185
Stand by your rearing steeds in the grace of your motionless movement,
   Stand with your upstretched arms and tranquil regardant faces,
   Stand as instinct[68] with life in the might of immutable manhood, –
   O ye mighty and strange, ye ancient divine ones of Hellas.[69]
Are ye Christian too? to convert and redeem and renew you,   190
Will the brief form have sufficed, that a Pope has set up on the apex
   Of the Egyptian stone that o'ertops you, the Christian symbol?[70]
   And ye, silent, supreme in serene and victorious marble,
   Ye that encircle the walls of the stately Vatican chambers,
   Juno and Ceres, Minerva, Apollo, the Muses and Bacchus,[71]   195
Ye unto whom far and near come posting the Christian pilgrims,
   Ye that are ranged in the halls of the mystic Christian Pontiff,[72]
   Are ye also baptized; are ye of the kingdom of Heaven?
Utter, O some one, the word that shall reconcile Ancient and Modern?
Am I to turn me from this unto thee, great Chapel of Sixtus?[73]   200

11. Claude to Eustace.

These are the facts. The uncle, the elder brother, the squire (a
   Little embarrassed, I fancy), resides in the family place in
   Cornwall, of course; 'Papa is in business,' Mary informs me;
   He's a good sensible man, whatever his trade is. The mother
   Is – shall I call it fine? – herself she would tell you refined, and   205
Greatly, I fear me, looks down on my bookish and maladroit[74] manners;
   Somewhat affecteth the blue;[75] would talk to me often of poets;
Quotes, which I hate, Childe Harold;[76] but also appreciates Wordsworth;
   Sometimes adventures on Schiller;[77] and then to religion diverges;
Questions me much about Oxford;[78] and yet, in her loftiest flights still   210
   Grates the fastidious ear with the slightly mercantile accent.
   Is it contemptible, Eustace – I'm perfectly ready to think so, –
   Is it, – the horrible pleasure of pleasing inferior people?
   I am ashamed my own self; and yet true it is, if disgraceful,
That for the first time in life I am living and moving with freedom.   215
   I, who never could talk to the people I meet with my uncle, –
   I, who have always failed, – I, trust me, can suit the Trevellyns;

---

[67] *marvellous Twain* huge Roman statues of horse tamers and their horses in the Piazza del Quirinale. They confront Claude with a model of manliness from which he is excluded.

[68] *instinct* ready.

[69] *Hellas* Murray thought the statues of Greek origin.

[70] *Egyptian . . . symbol* an obelisk stands between the horse tamers, with a cross on the top, put there by Pope Pius VI in 1786.

[71] *Juno . . . Bacchus* Claude refers to the Graeco-Roman pagan figures on Christian buildings in the Vatican.

[72] *halls of the mystic Christian Pontiff* Vatican.

[73] *Chapel of Sixtus* Sistine Chapel in the Vatican, built during the papacy of Sixtus IV and dedicated in 1483.

[74] *maladroit* awkward, bungling.

[75] *Somewhat affecteth the blue* Claude's cumbersome way of saying she is a 'blue-stocking' (the term often applied disparagingly to women in the nineteenth century who had or affected literary or intellectual interests).

[76] *Childe Harold* Byron's poem *Childe Harold's Pilgrimage* was published 1812–18.

[77] *Schiller* Johann Christoph Friedrich von Schiller (1759–1805), German dramatist and lyric poet.

[78] *Oxford* she perhaps wants to know about the aftermath of John Henry Newman's conversion to Roman Catholicism in 1845, which dealt a blow to the Oxford Movement. Clough had been heavily involved in Oxford Movement controversies.

I, believe me, – great conquest, am liked by the country bankers.
And I am glad to be liked, and like in return very kindly.
So it proceeds; *Laissez faire, laissez aller,*[79] – such is the watchword.   220
Well, I know there are thousands as pretty and hundreds as pleasant,
Girls by the dozen as good, and girls in abundance with polish
Higher and manners more perfect than Susan or Mary Trevellyn.
Well, I know, after all, it is only juxtaposition, –
Juxtaposition, in short; and what is juxtaposition?   225

12. Claude to Eustace.

But I am in for it now, – *laissez faire*, of a truth, *laissez aller*.
Yes, I am going, – I feel it, I feel and cannot recall it, –
Fusing with this thing and that, entering into all sorts of relations,
Tying I know not what ties, which, whatever they are, I know one thing,
Will, and must, woe is me, be one day painfully broken, –   230
Broken with painful remorses, with shrinkings of soul, and relentings,
Foolish delays, more foolish evasions, most foolish renewals.
But I have made the step, have quitted the ship of Ulysses;[80]
Quitted the sea and the shore, passed into the magical island;[81]
Yet on my lips is the *moly*,[82] medicinal, offered of Hermes.   235
I have come into the precinct, the labyrinth[83] closes around me,
Path into path rounding slyly; I pace slowly on, and the fancy,
Struggling awhile to sustain the long sequences weary, bewildered,
Fain must collapse in despair; I yield, I am lost, and know nothing;
Yet in my bosom unbroken remaineth the clue; I shall use it.   240
Lo, with the rope on my loins I descend through the fissure; I sink, yet
Inly secure in the strength of invisible arms up above me;
Still, wheresoever I swing, wherever to shore, or to shelf, or
Floor of cavern untrodden, shell sprinkled, enchanting, I know I
Yet shall one time feel the strong cord tighten about me, –   245
Feel it, relentless, upbear me from spots I would rest in; and though the
Rope sway wildly, I faint, crags wound me, from crag unto crag re-
Bounding, or, wide in the void, I die ten deaths, ere the end I
Yet shall plant firm foot on the broad lofty spaces I quit, shall
Feel underneath me again the great massy strengths of abstraction,   250
Look yet abroad from the height o'er the sea whose salt wave I have tasted.

13. Georgina Trevellyn to Louisa – .

Dearest Louisa, – Inquire, if you please, about Mr. Claude – .
He has been once at R., and remembers meeting the H.'s.
Harriet L., perhaps, may be able to tell you about him.
It is an awkward youth, but still with very good manners;   255
Not without prospects, we hear; and, George says, highly connected.
Georgy declares it absurd, but Mamma is alarmed, and insists he has
Taken up strange opinions, and may be turning a Papist.

---

[79] *Laissez faire, laissez aller* literally 'Let do, let go', or 'let things happen, let things go by'.
[80] *Ulysses* hero of Homer's *Odyssey*.
[81] *magical island* Circe's island of Aeaea. Circe was the enchantress who turned Odysseus's men into pigs (cf. Augusta Webster, 'Circe', 450–5).

[82] *moly* legendary herb: in the *Odyssey*, Hermes gave it to Odysseus as a charm against Circe's sorceries (Book 10).
[83] *labyrinth* Claude now associates himself with Theseus, who entered King Minos of Crete's labyrinth to slay the monstrous Minotaur.

Certainly once he spoke of a daily service[84] he went to.
'Where?' we asked, and he laughed and answered, 'At the Pantheon.'   260
This was a temple, you know, and now is a Catholic church; and
Though it is said that Mazzini[85] has sold it for Protestant service,[86]
Yet I suppose this change can hardly as yet be effected.
Adieu again, – evermore, my dearest, your loving Georgina.

P.S. by Mary Trevellyn.

I am to tell you, you say, what I think of our last new acquaintance.   265
Well, then, I think that George has a very fair right to be jealous.
I do not like him much, though I do not dislike being with him.
He is what people call, I suppose, a superior man, and
Certainly seems so to me; but I think he is terribly selfish.

Alba,[87] *thou findest me still, and, Alba, thou findest me ever,*   270
Now from the Capitol[88] *steps, now over Titus's Arch,*
Here from the large grassy spaces that spread from the Lateran portal,
Towering o'er aqueduct lines lost in perspective between,
Or from a Vatican window, or bridge, or the high Coliseum,
Clear by the garlanded line cut of the Flavian ring.[89]   275
Beautiful can I not call thee, and yet thou hast power to o'ermaster,
Power of mere beauty; in dreams, Alba, thou hauntest me still.
Is it religion? I ask me; or is it a vain superstition?
Slavery abject and gross? service, too feeble, of truth?
Is it an idol I bow to, or is it a god that I worship?   280
Do I sink back on the old, or do I soar from the mean?
So through the city I wander and question, unsatisfied ever,
Reverent so I accept, doubtful because I revere.

CANTO 2.

Is it illusion? or does there a spirit from perfecter ages,
Here, even yet, amid loss, change, and corruption, abide?   285
Does there a spirit we know not, though seek, though we find, comprehend not,
Here to entice and confuse, tempt and evade us, abide?
Lives in the exquisite grace of the column disjointed and single,
Haunts the rude masses of brick garlanded gaily with vine,
E'en in the turret fantastic surviving that springs from the ruin,   290
E'en in the people itself? is it illusion or not?
Is it illusion or not that attracteth the pilgrim transalpine,[90]
Brings him a dullard and dunce hither to pry and to stare?
Is it illusion or not that allures the barbarian stranger,
Brings him with gold to the shrine, brings him in arms to the gate?   295

[84] *daily service* indication of Tractarian (Oxford Movement/High Church) sympathies.
[85] *Mazzini* see headnote, 228.
[86] *sold . . . service* the story of the sale was a joke in Rome, but Georgina naively believes it.
[87] *Alba* Alba Longa, a city of ancient Latium, in the Alban Hills near Lake Albano.
[88] *Capitol* site of great temple on the Capitoline Hill in Rome.
[89] *Flavian ring* Coliseum.
[90] *transalpine* across the Alps.

1. Claude to Eustace.

What do the people say, and what does the government do? – you
Ask, and I know not at all. Yet fortune will favour your hopes; and
    I, who avoided it all, am fated, it seems, to describe it.
I, who nor meddle nor make in politics, – I who sincerely
    Put not my trust in leagues nor any suffrage by ballot,[91]   300
    Never predicted Parisian millenniums,[92] never beheld a
New Jerusalem coming down dressed like a bride out of heaven
    Right on the Place de la Concorde,[93] – I, nevertheless, let me say it,
Could in my soul of souls, this day, with the Gaul[94] at the gates shed
    One true tear for thee, thou poor little Roman Republic;   305
What, with the German restored, with Sicily safe to the Bourbon,[95]
    Not leave one poor corner for native Italian exertion?
France, it is foully done! and you, poor foolish England, –
You, who a twelvemonth ago said nations must choose for themselves, you
Could not, of course, interfere, – you, now, when a nation has chosen –   310
Pardon this folly! *The Times* will, of course, have announced the occasion,
Told you the news of to-day; and although it was slightly in error
    When it proclaimed as a fact the Apollo was sold to a Yankee,[96]
You may believe when it tells you the French are at Civita Vecchia.[97]

2. Claude to Eustace.

Dulce it is, and *decorum*, no doubt,[98] for the country to fall, – to   315
Offer one's blood an oblation[99] to Freedom, and die for the Cause; yet
    Still, individual culture is also something, and no man
Finds quite distinct the assurance that he of all others is called on,
    Or would be justified even, in taking away from the world that
Precious creature, himself. Nature sent him here to abide here;   320
    Else why send him at all? Nature wants him still, it is likely;
On the whole, we are meant to look after ourselves; it is certain
    Each has to eat for himself, digest for himself, and in general
Care for his own dear life, and see to his own preservation;
    Nature's intentions, in most things uncertain, in this are decisive;   325
Which, on the whole, I conjecture the Romans will follow, and I shall.
    So we cling to our rocks like limpets; Ocean may bluster,
Over and under and round us; we open our shells to imbibe our
Nourishment, close them again, and are safe, fulfilling the purpose
Nature intended, – a wise one, of course, and a noble, we doubt not.   330
Sweet it may be and decorous, perhaps, for the country to die; but,
    On the whole, we conclude the Romans won't do it, and I sha'n't.

---

[91] *Put not . . . ballot* gesture towards Biblical syntax: cf. Psalm 147.10, 'Hee delighteth not in the strength of the horse: he taketh not pleasure in the legs of a man'.

[92] *Parisian millenniums* French revolutionaries' aspirations in 1848 for an epoch of content and benign government.

[93] *Never beheld . . . Concorde* cf. 'And I Iohn saw the holy City, new Hierusalem comming down from God out of heauen, prepared as a bride adorned for her husband', Revelation 21.2. The Place de la Concorde is the major square in the heart of Paris.

[94] *Gaul* French. Oudinot landed at Civita Vecchia on 25 April 1849.

[95] *Bourbon* ancient royal house of Europe (chiefly French), which ruled the Kingdom of the Two Sicilies until unification.

[96] *Apollo . . . Yankee* a peculiar story reported in *The Times*, 9 April 1849.

[97] *Civita Vecchia* west coast port near Rome (see note 94).

[98] *Dulce . . . doubt* cf. Horace, *Odes* 3.2.12: '*Dulce et decorum est pro patria mori*' (it is sweet and right to die for one's country).

[99] *oblation* offering (often in a religious context).

3. Claude to Eustace.

Will they fight? They say so. And will the French? I can hardly,
Hardly think so; and yet – He is come, they say, to Palo,
He is passed from Monterone, at Santa Severa[100]   335
He hath laid up his guns. But the Virgin, the Daughter of Roma,
She hath despised thee and laughed thee to scorn, – the Daughter of Tiber,
She hath shaken her head and built barricades against thee![101]
Will they fight? I believe it. Alas! 'tis ephemeral folly,
Vain and ephemeral folly, of course, compared with pictures,   340
Statues, and antique gems! – Indeed: and yet indeed too,
Yet methought, in broad day did I dream, – tell it not in St. James's,[102]
Whisper it not in thy courts, O Christ Church![103] – yet did I, waking,
Dream of a cadence that sings, *Si tombent nos jeunes héros, la*
Terre en produit de nouveaux contre vous tous prêts à se battre;[104]   345
Dreamt of great indignations and angers transcendental,
Dreamt of a sword at my side and a battle-horse underneath me.[105]

4. Claude to Eustace.

Now supposing the French or the Neapolitan soldier
Should by some evil chance come exploring the Maison Serny[106]
(Where the family English are all to assemble for safety),   350
Am I prepared to lay down my life for the British female?
Really, who knows? One has bowed and talked, till, little by little,
All the natural heat has escaped of the chivalrous spirit.
Oh, one conformed, of course; but one doesn't die for good manners,
Stab or shoot, or be shot, by way of graceful attention.   355
No, if it should be at all, it should be on the barricades there;
Should I incarnadine[107] ever this inky pacifical finger,
Sooner far should it be for this vapour of Italy's freedom,
Sooner far by the side of the d — d and dirty plebeians.
Ah, for a child in the street I could strike; for the full-blown lady –   360
Somehow, Eustace, alas! I have not felt the vocation.
Yet these people of course will expect, as of course, my protection,
Vernon in radiant arms stand forth for the lovely Georgina,
And to appear, I suppose, were but common civility. Yes, and
Truly I do not desire they should either be killed or offended.   365
Oh, and of course, you will say, 'When the time comes, you will be ready.'

[100] *Palo . . . Santa Severa* towns on the way to Rome from Civita Vecchia.
[101] *But the Virgin . . . thee!* cf. Isaiah 37.21–23, 'Then Isaiah the sonne of Amoz sent vnto Hezekiah, saying, Thus saith the Lord God of Israel, Wheras thou hast prayed to me against Sennacherib king of Assyria: This is the worde which the Lord hath spoken concerning him: The virgin, the daughter of Zion hath despised thee, and laughed thee to scorne, the daughter of Ierusalem hath shaken her head at thee'.
[102] *St. James's*: St James's Palace, influential centre of political power: British ambassadors serve the 'Court of St James'.
[103] *Christ Church* aristocratic Oxford college. Cf. 'Tell it not in Gath, publish it not in the streetes of Askelon', 2 Samuel 1.20.
[104] *Si tombent . . . battre* from the French revolutionary marching song, the *Marseillaise*: 'If our young heroes fall, the earth will produce new, ready to fight against you all'.
[105] *Dreamt of great . . . me* Claude does not specify whose side he is on.
[106] *Maison Serny* special house to which the English were allowed to retire.
[107] *incarnadine* literally, to dye with incarnadine (pink carnation): Claude means redden with blood. He alludes ironically to Shakespeare's *Macbeth* 2.2.58–61: 'Will all great Neptune's ocean wash this blood / Clean from my hand? No, this hand will rather / The multitudinous seas incarnadine, / Making the green one red.'

Ah, but before it comes, am I to presume it will be so?
What I cannot feel now, am I to suppose that I shall feel?
Am I not free to attend for the ripe and indubious[108] instinct?
Am I forbidden to wait for the clear and lawful perception?   370
Is it the calling of man to surrender his knowledge and insight,
For the mere venture of what may, perhaps, be the virtuous action?
Must we, walking our earth, discern a little, and hoping
Some plain visible task shall yet for our hands be assigned us, –
Must we abandon the future for fear of omitting the present,   375
Quit our own fireside hopes at the alien call of a neighbour,
To the mere possible shadow of Deity offer the victim?
And is all this, my friend, but a weak and ignoble refining,
Wholly unworthy the head or the heart of Your Own Correspondent?

5. Claude to Eustace.

Yes, we are fighting at last, it appears. This morning, as usual,   380
Murray,[109] as usual, in hand, I enter the Caffè Nuovo;[110]
Seating myself with a sense as it were of a change in the weather,
Not understanding, however, but thinking mostly of Murray,
And, for to-day is their day, of the Campidoglio Marbles;[111]
Caffè-latte![112] I call to the waiter, – and *Non c' è latte*,[113]   385
This is the answer he makes me, and this is the sign of a battle.
So I sit; and truly they seem to think anyone else more
Worthy than me of attention. I wait for my milkless *nero*,[114]
Free to observe undistracted all sorts and sizes of persons,
Blending civilian and soldier in strangest costume, coming in, and   390
Gulping in hottest haste, still standing, their coffee, – withdrawing
Eagerly, jangling a sword on the steps, or jogging a musket
Slung to the shoulder behind. They are fewer, moreover, than usual,
Much and silenter far; and so I begin to imagine
Something is really afloat. Ere I leave, the Caffè is empty,   395
Empty too the streets, in all its length the Corso[115]
Empty, and empty I see to my right and left the Condotti.[116]
Twelve o'clock, on the Pincian Hill,[117] with lots of English,
Germans, Americans, French, – the Frenchmen, too, are protected, –
So we stand in the sun, but afraid of a probable shower;   400
So we stand and stare, and see, to the left of St. Peter's,
Smoke, from the cannon, white, – but that is at intervals only, –
Black, from a burning house,[118] we suppose, by the Cavalleggieri;[119]
And we believe we discern some lines of men descending
Down through the vineyard-slopes, and catch a bayonet gleaming.   405
Every ten minutes, however, – in this there is no misconception, –
Comes a great white puff from behind Michel Angelo's dome, and

---

[108] *indubious* feeling no doubt.
[109] *Murray* Claude has with him the standard early
Victorian guide to Rome and its environs: Octavian
Blewitt's *Handbook for Travellers in Central Italy, including
the Papal States, Rome, and the Cities of Etruria* (London:
Murray, 1843).
[110] *Caffè Nuovo* New Café, a political centre during
Oudinot's occupation.
[111] *Campidoglio Marbles* in the museum on the Capitoline
Hill.
[112] *Caffè-latte* coffee with milk.

[113] *Non c' è latte* there is no milk.
[114] *nero* black (coffee).
[115] *Corso* Via del Corso, on which the Caffè Nuovo stood.
[116] *Condotti* Via Condotti, major thoroughfare in the heart
of Rome.
[117] *Pincian Hill* famously advantageous viewing point.
[118] *Smoke . . . house* ironic glance at the procedure for
electing popes where black smoke from the College of
Cardinals signifies that no election has been made and
white that a new pope has been chosen and has accepted.
[119] *Cavalleggieri* Porta Cavalleggieri, a gate.

After a space the report of a real big gun, – not the Frenchman's! –
That must be doing some work. And so we watch and conjecture.
Shortly, an Englishman comes, who says he has been to St. Peter's, 410
   Seen the Piazza and troops, but that is all he can tell us;
So we watch and sit, and, indeed, it begins to be tiresome. –
   All this smoke is outside; when it has come to the inside,
It will be time, perhaps, to descend and retreat to our houses.
   Half-past one, or two. The report of small arms frequent, 415
   Sharp and savage indeed; that cannot all be for nothing:
   So we watch and wonder; but guessing is tiresome, very.[120]
Weary of wondering, watching, and guessing, and gossiping idly,
   Down I go, and pass through the quiet streets with the knots of
National Guards patrolling, and flags hanging out at the windows, 420
   English, American, Danish, – and, after offering to help an
   Irish family moving *en masse*[121] to the Maison Serny,
After endeavouring idly to minister balm to the trembling
   Quinquagenarian[122] fears of two lone British spinsters,
Go to make sure of my dinner before the enemy enter. 425
But by this there are signs of stragglers returning; and voices
Talk, though you don't believe it, of guns and prisoners taken;
And on the walls you read the first bulletin of the morning. –
   This is all that I saw, and all I know of the battle.

6. Claude to Eustace.

Victory! Victory! – Yes! ah, yes, thou republican Zion,[123] 430
   Truly the kings of the earth are gathered and gone by together;
Doubtless they marvelled to witness such things, were astonished, and so forth.
   Victory! Victory! Victory! – Ah, but it is, believe me,
   Easier, easier far, to intone the chant of the martyr
   Than to indite any pæan[124] of any victory. Death may 435
Sometimes be noble; but life, at the best, will appear an illusion.
   While the great pain is upon us, it is great; when it is over,
   Why, it is over. The smoke of the sacrifice rises to heaven,
   Of a sweet savour, no doubt, to Somebody; but on the altar,
Lo, there is nothing remaining but ashes and dirt and ill odour. 440
So it stands, you perceive; the labial muscles[125] that swelled with
   Vehement evolution of yesterday Marseillaises,[126]
   Articulations sublime of defiance and scorning, to-day col-
Lapse and languidly mumble, while men and women and papers
Scream and re-scream to each other the chorus of Victory. Well, but 445
I am thankful they fought, and glad that the Frenchmen were beaten.

7. Claude to Eustace.

So, I have seen a man killed! An experience that, among others!
   Yes, I suppose I have; although I can hardly be certain,

---

[120] *very* linguistic trademark of Dickens's Mr Jingle in *Pickwick Papers* (1836–7), e.g., ' "Ha! ha!" said Jingle, "good fellow, Pickwick – fine heart – stout old boy – but must *not* be passionate – bad thing, very" '.
[121] *en masse* altogether.
[122] *Quinquagenarian* person aged between 50 and 59.
[123] *Zion* one of the hills of Jerusalem, on which the city of

David was built; here, Rome as the centre of the Catholic faith made 'republican' by the ousting of the Pope.
[124] *pæan* song of triumph.
[125] *labial muscles* lips.
[126] *Marseillaises* accepted as the French national anthem by order of the revolutionaries on 14 July 1795.

And in a court of justice could never declare I had seen it.
But a man was killed, I am told, in a place where I saw   450
Something; a man was killed, I am told, and I saw something.
I was returning home from St. Peter's; Murray, as usual,
Under my arm, I remember; had crossed the St. Angelo bridge;[127] and
Moving towards the Condotti, had got to the first barricade, when
Gradually, thinking still of St. Peter's, I became conscious   455
Of a sensation of movement opposing me, – tendency this way
(Such as one fancies may be in a stream when the wave of the tide is
Coming and not yet come, – a sort of noise and retention);
So I turned, and, before I turned, caught sight of stragglers
Heading a crowd, it is plain, that is coming behind that corner.   460
Looking up, I see windows filled with heads; the Piazza,
Into which you remember the Ponte St. Angelo enters,
Since I passed, has thickened with curious groups; and now the
Crowd is coming, has turned, has crossed that last barricade, is
Here at my side. In the middle they drag at something. What is it?   465
Ha! bare swords in the air, held up? There seem to be voices
Pleading and hands putting back; official, perhaps; but the swords are
Many, and bare in the air. In the air? they descend; they are smiting,
Hewing, chopping – At what? In the air once more upstretched? And –
Is it blood that's on them? Yes, certainly blood! Of whom, then?   470
Over whom is the cry of this furor of exultation?
While they are skipping and screaming, and dancing their caps on the points of
Swords and bayonets, I to the outskirts back, and ask a
Mercantile-seeming bystander, 'What is it?' and he, looking always
That way, makes me answer, 'A Priest, who was trying to fly to   475
The Neapolitan army,'[128] – and thus explains the proceeding.
You didn't see the dead man? No; – I began to be doubtful;
I was in black myself,[129] and didn't know what mightn't happen, –
But a National Guard close by me, outside of the hubbub,
Broke his sword with slashing a broad hat covered with dust, – and   480
Passing away from the place with Murray under my arm, and
Stooping, I saw through the legs of the people the legs of a body.
You are the first, do you know, to whom I have mentioned the matter.
Whom should I tell it to else? – these girls? – the Heavens forbid it! –
Quidnuncs[130] at Monaldini's?[131] – idlers upon the Pincian?[132]   485
If I rightly remember, it happened on that afternoon when
Word of the nearer approach of a new Neapolitan army
First was spread. I began to bethink me of Paris Septembers,
Thought I could fancy the look of that old 'Ninety-two.[133] On that evening
Three or four, or, it may be, five, of these people were slaughtered.   490
Some declared they had, one of them, fired on a sentinel; others
Say they were only escaping; a Priest, it is currently stated,
Stabbed a National Guard[134] on the very Piazza Colonna:[135]

[127] *St Angelo* second-century AD bridge.
[128] *Neapolitan army* Pius IX had taken refuge in the Kingdom of Naples.
[129] *black myself* and thus in danger of being confused for a priest in a black cassock.
[130] *Quidnuncs* those constantly asking: 'What now?' 'What's the news?', gossipers.
[131] *Monaldini's* English reading room at Rome.
[132] *Pincian* see note 117.

[133] *Paris . . . 'Ninety-two* Claude is thinking of the September Massacres in Paris in 1792 when the revolutionaries organized the execution of priests (hence the event comes to Claude's mind) and aristocrats held in prison.
[134] *National Guard* pro-Republican militia.
[135] *Piazza Colonna* piazza at the midpoint of the Via del Corso.

History, Rumour of Rumours, I leave it to thee to determine!
But I am thankful to say the government seems to have strength to 495
Put it down; it has vanished, at least; the place is most peaceful.
Through the Trastevere[136] walking last night, at nine of the clock, I
Found no sort of disorder; I crossed by the Island-bridges,
So by the narrow streets to the Ponte Rotto,[137] and onwards
Thence by the Temple of Vesta,[138] away to the great Coliseum, 500
Which at the full of the moon is an object worthy a visit.[139]

8. Georgina Trevellyn to Louisa – .

Only think, dearest Louisa, what fearful scenes we have witnessed! –

* * *

George has just seen Garibaldi, dressed up in a long white cloak, on
Horseback, riding by, with his mounted negro behind him:[140]
This is a man, you know, who came from America with him,[141] 505
Out of the woods, I suppose, and uses a lasso in fighting,
Which is, I don't quite know, but a sort of noose, I imagine;
This he throws on the heads of the enemy's men in a battle,
Pulls them into his reach, and then most cruelly kills them:
Mary does not believe, but we heard it from an Italian. 510
Mary allows she was wrong about Mr. Claude *being selfish*;
He was *most* useful and kind on the terrible thirtieth of April.[142]
Do not write here any more; we are starting directly for Florence:
We should be off to-morrow, if only Papa could get horses;
All have been seized everywhere for the use of this dreadful Mazzini. 515

P.S.

Mary has seen thus far. – I am really so angry, Louisa, –
Quite out of patience, my dearest! What can the man be intending?
I am quite tired; and Mary, who might bring him to in a moment,
Lets him go on as he likes, and neither will help nor dismiss him.

9. Claude to Eustace.

It is most curious to see what a power a few calm words (in 520
Merely a brief proclamation) appear to possess on the people.
Order is perfect, and peace; the city is utterly tranquil;
And one cannot conceive that this easy and *nonchalant* crowd, that
Flows like a quiet stream through street and market-place, entering
Shady recesses and bays of church, *osteria*,[143] and *caffè*, 525
Could in a moment be changed to a flood as of molten lava,
Boil into deadly wrath and wild homicidal delusion.

[136] *Trastevere* area of Rome on the right bank of the Tiber.
[137] *Ponte Rotto* bridge.
[138] *Temple of Vesta* marble building from the late second century BC, later transformed into the Christian church Santo Stefano delle Carrozze. From the fifteenth century, it was also called Santa Maria del Sole.
[139] *full . . . visit* Clough had visited parts of Rome by moonlight.
[140] *mounted . . . him* André de Aguyar, Garibaldi's companion and bodyguard.
[141] *from America with him* from South America: Aguyar was from Montevideo.
[142] *thirtieth of April* day of Garibaldi's surprise victory. See headnote, 228–9.
[143] *osteria* guest house.

Ah, 'tis an excellent race, – and even in old degradation,
Under a rule that enforces to flattery, lying, and cheating,
E'en under Pope and Priest, a nice and natural people.   530
Oh, could they but be allowed this chance of redemption! – but clearly
That is not likely to be. Meantime, notwithstanding all journals,
Honour for once to the tongue and the pen of the eloquent writer!
Honour to speech! and all honour to thee, thou noble Mazzini!

10. Claude to Eustace.

I am in love, meantime, you think; no doubt you would think so.   535
I am in love, you say; with those letters, of course, you would say so.
I am in love, you declare. I think not so; yet I grant you
It is a pleasure indeed to converse with this girl. Oh, rare gift,
Rare felicity, this! she can talk in a rational way, can
Speak upon subjects that really are matters of mind and of thinking,   540
Yet in perfection retain her simplicity; never, one moment,
Never, however you urge it, however you tempt her, consents to
Step from ideas and fancies and loving sensations to those vain
Conscious understandings that vex the minds of mankind.
No, though she talk, it is music; her fingers desert not the keys; 'tis   545
Song, though you hear in the song the articulate vocables[144] sounded,
Syllabled singly and sweetly the words of melodious meaning.
I am in love, you say; I do not think so, exactly.

11. Claude to Eustace.

There are two different kinds, I believe, of human attraction:
One which simply disturbs, unsettles, and makes you uneasy,   550
And another that poises, retains, and fixes and holds you.
I have no doubt, for myself, in giving my voice for the latter.
I do not wish to be moved, but growing where I was growing,
There more truly to grow, to live where as yet I had languished.
I do not like being moved: for the will is excited; and action   555
Is a most dangerous thing; I tremble for something factitious,[145]
Some malpractice of heart and illegitimate process;
We are so prone to these things, with our terrible notions of duty.

12. Claude to Eustace.

Ah, let me look, let me watch, let me wait, unhurried, unprompted!
Bid me not venture on aught that could alter or end what is present!   560
Say not, Time flies, and Occasion, that never returns, is departing!
Drive me not out, ye ill angels with fiery swords, from my Eden,[146]
Waiting, and watching, and looking! Let love be its own inspiration!
Shall not a voice, if a voice there must be, from the airs that environ,
Yea, from the conscious heavens, without our knowledge or effort,   565
Break into audible words? And love be its own inspiration?

---

[144] *vocables* words.
[145] *factitious* artificial.
[146] *Drive me . . . Eden* see Genesis 3.23–4: 'Therefore the LORD God sent him [Adam] foorth from the garden of Eden, to till the ground, from whence he was taken. So he droue out the man: and he placed at the East of the garden of Eden, Cherubims, and a flaming sword, which turned euery way, to keepe the way of the tree of life.'

13. Claude to Eustace.

Wherefore and how I am certain, I hardly can tell; but it is so.
She doesn't like me, Eustace; I think she never will like me.
Is it my fault, as it is my misfortune, my ways are not her ways?[147]
Is it my fault, that my habits and modes are dissimilar wholly? 570
'Tis not her fault; 'tis her nature, her virtue, to misapprehend them:
'Tis not her fault; 'tis her beautiful nature, not ever to know me.
Hopeless it seems, – yet I cannot, though hopeless, determine to leave it:
She goes – therefore I go; she moves, – I move, not to lose her.[148]

14. Claude to Eustace.

Oh, 'tisn't manly, of course, 'tisn't manly, this method of wooing; 575
'Tisn't the way very likely to win. For the woman, they tell you,
Ever prefers the audacious, the wilful, the vehement hero;
She has no heart for the timid, the sensitive soul; and for knowledge, –
Knowledge, O ye Gods! – when did they appreciate knowledge?
Wherefore should they, either? I am sure I do not desire it. 580
Ah, and I feel too, Eustace, she cares not a tittle[149] about me!
(Care about me, indeed! and do I really expect it?)
But my manner offends; my ways are wholly repugnant;
Every word that I utter estranges, hurts, and repels her;
Every moment of bliss that I gain, in her exquisite presence, 585
Slowly, surely, withdraws her, removes her, and severs her from me.
Not that I care very much! – any way I escape from the boy's own
Folly, to which I am prone, of loving where it is easy.
Not that I mind very much! Why should I? I am not in love, and
Am prepared, I think, if not by previous habit, 590
Yet in the spirit beforehand for this and all that is like it;
It is an easier matter for us contemplative creatures,
Us upon whom the pressure of action is laid so lightly;
We, discontented indeed with things in particular, idle,
Sickly, complaining, by faith, in the vision of things in general, 595
Manage to hold on our way without, like others around us,
Seizing the nearest arm to comfort, help, and support us.
Yet, after all, my Eustace, I know but little about it.
All I can say for myself, for present alike and for past, is,
Mary Trevellyn, Eustace, is certainly worth your acquaintance. 600
You couldn't come, I suppose, as far as Florence, to see her?

15. Georgina Trevellyn to Louisa – .

. . . To-morrow we're starting for Florence,
Truly rejoiced, you may guess, to escape from republican terrors;
Mr. C. and Papa to escort us; we by *vettura*[150]
Through Siena,[151] and Georgy to follow and join us by Leghorn.[152] 605
Then – Ah, what shall I say, my dearest? I tremble in thinking!

---

[147] *ways* cf. Isaiah 55.8, 'For my thoughts are not your thoughts, neither are your wayes my wayes, saith the Lord'.
[148] *lose her* cf. Ruth 1.16, 'And Ruth said, Intreate mee not to leaue thee, or to returne from following after thee: for whither thou goest, I will goe; and where thou lodgest, I will lodge'.

[149] *tittle* tiny thing.
[150] *vettura* hired carriage.
[151] *Siena* historic city south of Florence.
[152] *Leghorn* Livorno, large port on the Tuscan coast.

You will imagine my feelings, – the blending of hope and of sorrow!
How can I bear to abandon Papa and Mamma and my Sisters?
Dearest Louise, indeed it is very alarming; but, trust me
Ever, whatever may change, to remain your loving Georgina.   610

P.S. by Mary Trevellyn.

. . . 'Do I like Mr. Claude any better?'
I am to tell you, – and, 'Pray, is it Susan or I that attract him?'
This he never has told, but Georgina could certainly ask him.
All I can say for myself is, alas! that he rather repels me.
There! I think him agreeable, but also a little repulsive.   615
So be content, dear Louisa; for one satisfactory marriage
Surely will do in one year for the family you would establish;
Neither Susan nor I shall afford you the joy of a second.

P.S. by Georgina Trevellyn.

Mr. Claude, you must know, is behaving a little bit better;
He and Papa are great friends; but he really is too *shilly-shally*,[153] –   620
So unlike George! Yet I hope that the matter is going on fairly.
I shall, however, get George, before he goes, to say something.
Dearest Louise, how delightful to bring young people together!

Is it to Florence we follow, or are we to tarry yet longer,
E'en amid clamour of arms, here in the city of old,   625
Seeking from clamour of arms in the Past and the Arts to be hidden,
Vainly 'mid Arts and the Past seeking one life to forget?
Ah, fair shadow,[154] scarce seen, go forth! for anon[155] he shall follow, –
He that beheld thee, anon, whither thou leadest must go!
Go, and the wise, loving Muse, she also will follow and find thee!   630
She, should she linger in Rome, were not dissevered from thee!

CANTO 3.

Yet to the wondrous St. Peter's, and yet to the solemn Rotonda,[156]
Mingling with heroes and gods, yet to the Vatican Walls,
Yet may we go, and recline, while a whole mighty world seems above us,
Gathered and fixed to all time into one roofing supreme;[157]   635
Yet may we, thinking on these things, exclude what is meaner around us;
Yet, at the worst of the worst, books and a chamber remain;
Yet may we think, and forget, and possess our souls in resistance.[158] –
Ah, but away from the stir, shouting, and gossip of war,
Where, upon Apennine[159] slope, with the chestnut the oak-trees immingle,   640
Where, amid odorous copse bridle-paths wander and wind,
Where, under mulberry-branches, the diligent rivulet sparkles,
Or amid cotton and maize peasants their water-works ply,
Where, over fig-tree and orange in tier upon tier still repeated,

[153] *shilly-shally* irresolute, undecided.
[154] *fair shadow* Mary.
[155] *anon* at once.
[156] *Rotonda* Pantheon.
[157] *Yet may we go . . . supreme* refers to lying on one's back to look at the Sistine roof.
[158] *possess our souls in resistance* maintain ourselves as resistant.
[159] *Apennine* mountain range that runs the length of Italy.

> *Garden on garden upreared, balconies step to the sky, –*   645
> *Ah, that I were far away from the crowd and the streets of the city,*
> *Under the vine-trellis laid, O my beloved, with thee!*

1. Mary Trevellyn to Miss Roper, – *on the way to Florence*.

Why doesn't Mr. Claude come with us? you ask. – We don't know.
You should know better than we. He talked of the Vatican marbles;[160]
    But I can't wholly believe that this was the actual reason, –   650
He was so ready before, when we asked him to come and escort us.
    Certainly he is odd, my dear Miss Roper. To change so
    Suddenly, just for a whim, was not quite fair to the party, –
    Not quite right. I declare, I really almost am offended:
    I, his great friend, as you say, have doubtless a title to be so.   655
    Not that I greatly regret it, for dear Georgina distinctly
Wishes for nothing so much as to show her adroitness.[161] But, oh, my
Pen will not write any more; – let us say nothing further about it.

             *   *   *

    Yes, my dear Miss Roper, I certainly called him repulsive;
    So I think him, but cannot be sure I have used the expression   660
    Quite as your pupil should; yet he does most truly repel me.
Was it to you I made use of the word? or who was it told you?
    Yes, repulsive; observe, it is but when he talks of ideas
    That he is quite unaffected, and free, and expansive, and easy;
    I could pronounce him simply a cold intellectual being. –   665
When does he make advances? – He thinks that women should woo him;
    Yet, if a girl should do so, would be but alarmed and disgusted.
She that should love him must look for small love in return, – like the ivy
On the stone wall, must expect but a rigid and niggard[162] support, and
E'en to get that must go searching all round with her humble embraces.   670

2. Claude to Eustace, – *from Rome*.

Tell me, my friend, do you think that the grain would sprout in the furrow,
    Did it not truly accept as its *summum* and *ultimum bonum*[163]
    That mere common and may-be indifferent soil it is set in?
    Would it have force to develop and open its young cotyledons,[164]
Could it compare, and reflect, and examine one thing with another?   675
    Would it endure to accomplish the round of its natural functions,
Were it endowed with a sense of the general scheme of existence?
While from Marseilles[165] in the steamer we voyage to Civita Vecchia,
    Vexed in the squally seas as we lay by Capraja and Elba,[166]
    Standing, uplifted, alone on the heaving poop of the vessel,   680
    Looking around on the waste of the rushing incurious billows,
'This is Nature,' I said: 'we are born as it were from her waters;
    Over her billows that buffet and beat us, her offspring uncared-for,
    Casting one single regard of a painful victorious knowledge,
Into her billows that buffet and beat us we sink and are swallowed.'   685

---

[160] *Vatican marbles* treasures of the Vatican museum.
[161] *adroitness* skill, cleverness.
[162] *niggard* mean, stingy.
[163] *summum and ultimum bonum* highest and ultimate good.

[164] *cotyledons* primary leaves of plants.
[165] *Marseilles* major port on the south coast of France.
[166] *Capraja and Elba* Elba is the largest island in the Tuscan Archipelago; Capraja is a small satellite island to its north.

This was the sense in my soul, as I swayed with the poop of the steamer;
And as unthinking I sat in the hall of the famed Ariadne,[167]
Lo, it looked at me there from the face of a Triton[168] in marble.
It is the simpler thought, and I can believe it the truer.
Let us not talk of growth; we are still in our Aqueous Ages.[169]   690

3. Claude to Eustace.

Farewell, Politics, utterly! What can I do? I cannot
Fight, you know; and to talk I am wholly ashamed.[170] And although I
Gnash my teeth when I look in your French or your English papers,
What is the good of that? Will swearing, I wonder, mend matters?
Cursing and scolding repel the assailants? No, it is idle;   695
No, whatever befalls, I will hide, will ignore or forget it.
Let the tail shift for itself; I will bury my head. And what's the
Roman Republic to me, or I to the Roman Republic?[171]
Why not fight? – In the first place, I haven't so much as a musket;[172]
In the next, if I had, I shouldn't know how I should use it;   700
In the third, just at present I'm studying ancient marbles;
In the fourth, I consider I owe my life to my country;
In the fifth – I forget, but four good reasons are ample.
Meantime, pray let 'em fight, and be killed. I delight in devotion.
So that I 'list[173] not, hurrah for the glorious army of martyrs![174]   705
Sanguis martyrum semen Ecclesiæ;[175] though it would seem this
Church is indeed of the purely Invisible, Kingdom-come[176] kind:
Militant here on earth! Triumphant, of course, then, elsewhere![177]
Ah, good Heaven, but I would I were out far away from the pother![178]

4. Claude to Eustace.

Not, as we read in the words of the olden-time inspiration,   710
Are there two several trees in the place we are set to abide in;
But on the apex most high of the Tree of Life in the Garden,[179]
Budding, unfolding, and falling, decaying and flowering ever,
Flowering is set and decaying the transient blossom of Knowledge, –
Flowering alone, and decaying, the needless unfruitful blossom.   715

---

[167] *famed Ariadne* the Vatican museum includes the *Sleeping Ariadne*, a statue believed to be a Roman copy of a Greek original.

[168] *Triton* sea deity.

[169] *Aqueous Ages* early stage of development.

[170] *wholly ashamed* cf. 'Then the Steward said within himselfe, What shall I doe, for my lord taketh away from mee the Stewardship? I cannot digge, to begge I am ashamed', Luke 16.3.

[171] *what's the . . . Republic?* cf. 'What's Hecuba to him, or he to Hecuba, / That he should weep for her? What would he do, / Had he the motive and the cue for passion / That I have?' *Hamlet* 2.2.561–4.

[172] *musket* handgun, superseded by the rifle.

[173] *'list* enlist.

[174] *glorious army of martyrs* cf. the *Te Deum*, ancient Christian hymn of praise, which includes the lines 'The glorious company of the apostles praise thee' and 'the noble of army of martyrs praise thee'.

[175] *Sanguis . . . Ecclesiæ* 'The blood of the martyrs is the seed of the Church.'

[176] *Kingdom-come* cf. the end of the Lord's Prayer, 'Thy kingdom come'.

[177] *Militant . . . elsewhere* two forms of the Church recognized in Christian literature: the *Church militant*, the Church on earth considered as warring against the powers of evil; and the *Church triumphant*, the portion of the Church that has overcome the world and entered into glory.

[178] *pother* literally choking smoke, atmosphere of dust.

[179] *two several . . . Garden* cf. Genesis 2.9, 'And out of the ground made the LORD God to grow euery tree that is pleasant to the sight, and good for food: the tree of life also in the midst of the garden, and the tree of knowledge of good and euill'.

Or as the cypress-spires by the fair-flowing stream Helles-pontine,[180]
Which from the mythical tomb of the godlike Protesilaüs
Rose sympathetic in grief to his love-lorn Laodamia,
Evermore growing, and, when in their growth to the prospect attaining,
    Over the low sea-banks, of the fatal Ilian city,[181]   720
Withering still at the sight which still they upgrow to encounter.
Ah, but ye that extrude[182] from the ocean your helpless faces,
    Ye over stormy seas leading long and dreary processions,
Ye, too, brood of the wind, whose coming is whence we discern not,
Making your nest on the wave, and your bed on the crested billow,[183]   725
Skimming rough waters, and crowding wet sands that the tide shall return to,
    Cormorants, ducks, and gulls, fill ye my imagination!
Let us not talk of growth; we are still in our Aqueous Ages.

5. Mary Trevellyn to Miss Roper, – *from Florence.*

Dearest Miss Roper, – Alas! we are all at Florence quite safe, and
    You, we hear, are shut up! indeed, it is sadly distressing!   730
We were most lucky, they say, to get off when we did from the troubles.
    Now you are really besieged;[184] they tell us it soon will be over;
    Only I hope and trust without any fight in the city.
Do you see Mr. Claude? – I thought he might do something for you.
    I am quite sure on occasion he really would wish to be useful.   735
    What is he doing? I wonder; – still studying Vatican marbles?
Letters, I hope, pass through. We trust your brother is better.

6. Claude to Eustace.

    Juxtaposition, in fine; and what is juxtaposition?
Look you, we travel along in the railway carriage or steamer,
And, *pour passer le temps*,[185] till the tedious journey be ended,   740
Lay aside paper or book, to talk with the girl that is next one;
And, *pour passer le temps*, with the terminus all but in prospect,
    Talk of eternal ties and marriages made in heaven.
Ah, did we really accept with a perfect heart the illusion!
Ah, did we really believe that the Present indeed is the Only!   745
Or through all transmutation, all shock and convulsion of passion,
Feel we could carry undimmed, unextinguished, the light of our knowledge!
But for his funeral train which the bridegroom sees in the distance,
Would he so joyfully, think you, fall in[186] with the marriage procession?
But for that final discharge,[187] would he dare to enlist in that service?   750
But for that certain release, ever sign to that perilous contract?

[180] *cypress . . . Helles-pontine* Protesilaus was the first Greek to land at Troy before the assault on the city, and, in accordance with the Delphic oracle, the first to die. The gods brought him back from the world of the dead to visit his grieving wife, Laodamia, for three hours. When he died for a second time, so did she. Trees were planted around his grave (these are sometimes described as cypresses): they flourished till they were high enough to catch sight of Troy, then they withered, giving place to fresh foliage that grew from the roots. Wordsworth wrote a version of the story in 'Laodamia' (1815). Hellespont is the ancient name for the Strait of the Dardanelles.

[181] *Ilian city* Troy.
[182] *extrude* thrust out.
[183] *Making . . . billow* allusion to the myth of the halcyon, a bird believed to breed about the time of the winter solstice in a nest floating on the sea: it charmed the wind and waves to calm.
[184] *besieged* the Siege of Rome began early in the morning of 3 June.
[185] *pour passer le temps* in order to pass the time.
[186] *fall in* join.
[187] *final discharge* death (Claude's metaphor is a military one).

But for that exit secure, ever bend to that treacherous doorway? –
Ah, but the bride, meantime, – do you think she sees it as he does?
But for the steady fore-sense of a freer and larger existence,
Think you that man could consent to be circumscribed here into action?   755
But for assurance within of a limitless ocean divine, o'er
Whose great tranquil depths unconscious the wind-tost surface
Breaks into ripples of trouble that come and change and endure not, –
But that in this, of a truth, we have our being, and know it,
Think you we men could submit to live and move as we do here?   760
Ah, but the women, – God bless them! they don't think at all about it.
Yet we must eat and drink, as you say. And as limited beings
Scarcely can hope to attain upon earth to an Actual Abstract,[188]
Leaving to God contemplation, to His hands knowledge confiding,
Sure that in us if it perish, in Him it abideth and dies not,   765
Let us in His sight accomplish our petty particular doings, –
Yes, and contented sit down to the victual[189] that He has provided.
Allah is great, no doubt, and Juxtaposition his prophet.[190]
Ah, but the women, alas! they don't look at it in that way.
Juxtaposition is great; – but, my friend, I fear me, the maiden   770
Hardly would thank or acknowledge the lover that sought to obtain her,
Not as the thing he would wish, but the thing he must even put up with, –
Hardly would tender her hand to the wooer that candidly told her
That she is but for a space, an *ad-interim*[191] solace and pleasure, –
That in the end she shall yield to a perfect and absolute something,   775
Which I then for myself shall behold, and not another,[192] –
Which, amid fondest endearments, meantime I forget not, forsake not.
Ah, ye feminine souls, so loving and so exacting,
Since we cannot escape, must we even submit to deceive you?
Since, so cruel is truth, sincerity shocks and revolts you,   780
Will you have us your slaves to lie to you, flatter and – leave you?

7. Claude to Eustace.

Juxtaposition is great, – but, you tell me, affinity greater.
Ah, my friend, there are many affinities, greater and lesser,
Stronger and weaker; and each, by the favour of juxtaposition,
Potent, efficient, in force, – for a time; but none, let me tell you,   785
Save by the law of the land and the ruinous force of the will, ah,
None, I fear me, at last quite sure to be final and perfect.
Lo, as I pace in the street, from the peasant-girl to the princess,
Homo sum, nihil humani a me alienum puto,[193] –
Vir sum, nihil fæminei,[194] – and e'en to the uttermost circle,   790
All that is Nature's is I, and I all things that are Nature's.
Yes, as I walk, I behold, in a luminous, large intuition,
That I can be and become anything that I meet with or look at:
I am the ox in the dray,[195] the ass with the garden stuff panniers;[196]

---

[188] *Abstract* ideal.
[189] *victual* food, provisions.
[190] *Allah . . . prophet* cf. Islamic declaration of faith: 'There is but one God and Mohammed is His prophet. Allah is great and Mohammed is His prophet.'
[191] *ad-interim* temporary.
[192] *Which I . . . another* cf. Job 19.26–7, 'Whom I shal see for my selfe, and mine eyes shall beholde, and not another'.

[193] *Homo . . . puto* 'I am a man, nothing that is human is alien to me' (Terence).
[194] *Vir . . . fæminei* 'I am a man, nothing female [is alien to me].' Claude's adjustment to the line.
[195] *dray* low cart.
[196] *panniers* baskets.

I am the dog in the doorway, the kitten that plays in the window,   795
    On sunny slab of the ruin the furtive and fugitive lizard,
  Swallow above me that twitters, and fly that is buzzing about me;
    Yea, and detect, as I go, by a faint, but a faithful assurance,
E'en from the stones of the street, as from rocks or trees of the forest,
  Something of kindred, a common, though latent vitality, greets me;   800
And, to escape from our strivings, mistakings, misgrowths, and perversions,
  Fain could demand to return to that perfect and primitive silence,
    Fain be enfolded and fixed, as of old, in their rigid embraces.

8. Claude to Eustace.

And as I walk on my way, I behold them consorting and coupling;
  Faithful it seemeth, and fond, very fond, very probably faithful,   805
    All as I go on my way, with a pleasure sincere and unmingled.
Life is beautiful, Eustace, entrancing, enchanting to look at;
  As are the streets of a city we pace while the carriage is changing,
    As a chamber filled-in with harmonious, exquisite pictures,
      Even so beautiful Earth; and could we eliminate only   810
This vile hungering impulse, this demon within us of craving,
  Life were beatitude, living a perfect divine satisfaction.

9. Claude to Eustace.

Mild monastic faces in quiet collegiate cloisters:
  So let me offer a single and celibatarian[197] phrase, a
    Tribute to those whom perhaps you do not believe I can honour.   815
But, from the tumult escaping, 'tis pleasant, of drumming and shouting,
  Hither, oblivious awhile, to withdraw, of the fact or the falsehood,
    And amid placid regards and mildly courteous greetings
Yield to the calm and composure and gentle abstraction that reign o'er
  Mild monastic faces in quiet collegiate cloisters: 820
Terrible word, Obligation! You should not, Eustace, you should not,
  No, you should not have used it. But, oh, great Heavens, I repel it!
    Oh, I cancel, reject, disavow, and repudiate wholly
Every debt in this kind, disclaim every claim, and dishonour,
  Yea, my own heart's own writing, my soul's own signature! Ah, no!   825
    I will be free in this; you shall not, none shall, bind me.
No, my friend, if you wish to be told, it was this above all things,
  This that charmed me, ah, yes, even this, that she held me to nothing.
No, I could talk as I pleased; come close; fasten ties, as I fancied;
  Bind and engage myself deep; – and lo, on the following morning   830
    It was all e'en as before, like losings in games played for nothing.
Yes, when I came, with mean fears in my soul, with a semi-performance
  At the first step breaking down in its pitiful rôle of evasion,
    When to shuffle I came, to compromise, not meet, engagements,
Lo, with her calm eyes there she met me and knew nothing of it, –   835
  Stood unexpecting, unconscious. *She* spoke not of obligations,
    Knew not of debt – ah, no, I believe you, for excellent reasons.

---

[197] *celibatarian* celibate.

10. Claude to Eustace.

Hang this thinking, at last! what good is it? oh, and what evil!
Oh, what mischief and pain! like a clock in a sick man's chamber,
Ticking and ticking, and still through each covert of slumber pursuing.   840
What shall I do to thee, O thou Preserver of men?[198] Have compassion;
Be favourable, and hear! Take from me this regal[199] knowledge;
Let me, contented and mute, with the beasts of the fields, my brothers,
Tranquilly, happily lie, – and eat grass, like Nebuchadnezzar![200]

11. Claude to Eustace.

Tibur[201] is beautiful, too, and the orchard slopes, and the Anio[202]   845
Falling, falling yet, to the ancient lyrical cadence;
Tibur and Anio's tide; and cool from Lucretilis[203] ever,
With the Digentian[204] stream, and with the Bandusian fountain,[205]
Folded in Sabine recesses, the valley and villa of Horace: –
So not seeing I sang;[206] so seeing and listening say I,   850
Here as I sit by the stream, as I gaze at the cell of the Sibyl,[207]
Here with Albunea's[208] home and the grove of Tiburnus[209] beside me;
Tivoli beautiful is, and musical, O Teverone,[210]
Dashing from mountain to plain, thy parted impetuous waters!
Tivoli's waters and rocks; and fair unto Monte Gennaro[211]   855
(Haunt even yet, I must think, as I wander and gaze, of the shadows,
Faded and pale, yet immortal, of Faunus,[212] the Nymphs, and the Graces),[213]
Fair in itself, and yet fairer with human completing creations,
Folded in Sabine recesses the valley and villa of Horace: –
So not seeing I sang; so now – Nor seeing, nor hearing,   860
Neither by waterfall lulled, nor folded in sylvan[214] embraces,
Neither by cell of the Sibyl, nor stepping the Monte Gennaro,
Seated on Anio's bank, nor sipping Bandusian waters,
But on Montorio's[215] height, looking down on the tile-clad streets, the
Cupolas, crosses, and domes, the bushes and kitchen-gardens,   865
Which, by the grace of the Tibur, proclaim themselves Rome of the Romans, –
But on Montorio's height, looking forth to the vapoury mountains,
Cheating the prisoner Hope with illusions of vision and fancy, –

[198] *Preserver of men* cf. Job 7.20, 'I haue sinned, what shall I doe vnto thee, O thou preseruer of men? why hast thou set me as a mark against thee, so that I am a burden to my selfe?'

[199] *regal* Claude asks God to take away the vexing power of thought. It is 'regal' in the sense that the capacity to think signifies, for him, the sovereignty of man over animals. He would happily do without it and live like a grazing beast.

[200] *eat grass . . . Nebuchadnezzar* cf. Daniel 4.33, 'The same houre was the thing fulfilled vpon Nebuchad-nezzar, and he was driuen from men, and did eate grasse as oxen'.

[201] *Tibur* Tivoli, near Rome. Claude, frustrated with his thoughts and with the confines imposed by the conflict, imagines a visit to Horace's Sabine farm, which Horace celebrated as a paradise of rural simplicity and content. Seventeenth-century scholarship fixed its location as probably in the hills to the north-east of Tivoli.

[202] *Anio* river that flows into the Tiber.

[203] *Lucretilis* mountain near the Sabine farm.

[204] *Digentian* stream that flowed into the Anio.

[205] *Bandusian fountain* spring near the farm, addressed by Horace in *Odes* 3.13.

[206] *not seeing . . . sang* conflict in Rome makes an actual visit difficult.

[207] *Sibyl* one of the attractions of Tivoli for the ancient Romans was that it had its own oracle, the Sybil Albunea.

[208] *Albunea* the Sybil.

[209] *Tiburnus* Tivoli.

[210] *Teverone* River Anio.

[211] *Monte Gennaro* hill above Horace's farm.

[212] *Faunus* Roman god of fields and shepherds.

[213] *Nymphs, and the Graces* minor deities.

[214] *sylvan* belonging to the woods.

[215] *Montorio's height* platform in front of S. Pietro in Montorio in Rome, which gave good views of the city to the distant hills around Tivoli.

But on Montorio's height, with these weary soldiers[216] by me,
Waiting till Oudinot enter, to reinstate Pope and Tourist.   870

12. Mary Trevellyn to Miss Roper.

Dear Miss Roper, – It seems, George Vernon, before we left Rome, said
Something to Mr. Claude about what they call his attentions.
Susan, two nights ago, for the first time, heard this from Georgina.
It is so disagreeable and *so* annoying to think of!
If it could only be known, though we never may meet him again, that   875
It was all George's doing, and we were entirely unconscious,
It would extremely relieve – Your ever affectionate Mary.

P.S. (1)

Here is your letter arrived this moment, just as I wanted.
So you have seen him, – indeed, – and guessed, – how dreadfully clever!
What did he really say? and what was your answer exactly?   880
Charming! – but wait for a moment, I haven't read through the letter.

P.S. (2)

Ah, my dearest Miss Roper, do just as you fancy about it.
If you think it sincerer to tell him I know of it, do so.
Though I should most extremely dislike it, I know I could manage.
It is the simplest thing, but surely wholly uncalled for.   885
Do as you please; you know I trust implicitly to you.
Say whatever is right and needful for ending the matter.
Only don't tell Mr. Claude, what I will tell you as a secret,
That I should like very well to show him myself I forget it.

P.S. (3)

I am to say that the wedding is finally settled for Tuesday.   890
Ah, my dear Miss Roper, you surely, surely can manage
Not to let it appear that I know of that odious matter.
It would be pleasanter far for myself to treat it exactly
As if it had not occurred; and I do not think he would like it.
I must remember to add, that as soon as the wedding is over   895
We shall be off, I believe, in a hurry, and travel to Milan;
There to meet friends of Papa's, I am told, at the Croce di Malta;[217]
Then I cannot say whither, but not at present to England.

13. Claude to Eustace.

Yes, on Montorio's height for a last farewell of the city, –
So it appears; though then I was quite uncertain about it.   900
So, however, it was. And now to explain the proceeding.
I was to go, as I told you, I think, with the people to Florence.
Only the day before, the foolish family Vernon
Made some uneasy remarks, as we walked to our lodging together,

[216] *weary soldiers* forces defending Rome during the siege.

[217] *Croce di Malta* hotel in Milan.

As to intentions, forsooth, and so forth. I was astounded, 905
Horrified quite; and obtaining just then, as it happened, an offer
(No common favour) of seeing the great Ludovisi collection,[218]
Why, I made this a pretence, and wrote that they must excuse me.
How could I go? Great Heavens! to conduct a permitted flirtation
Under those vulgar eyes, the observed of such observers! 910
Well, but I now, by a series of fine diplomatic inquiries,
Find from a sort of relation, a good and sensible woman,
Who is remaining at Rome with a brother too ill for removal,
That it was wholly unsanctioned, unknown, – not, I think, by Georgina:
She, however, ere this, – and that is the best of the story, – 915
She and the Vernon, thank Heaven, are wedded and gone – honeymooning.
So – on Montorio's height for a last farewell of the city.
Tibur I have not seen, nor the lakes that of old I had dreamt of;
Tibur I shall not see, nor Anio's waters, nor deep en-
Folded in Sabine recesses the valley and villa of Horace; 920
Tibur I shall not see; – but something better I shall see.
Twice I have tried before, and failed in getting the horses;
Twice I have tried and failed: this time it shall not be a failure.

Therefore farewell, ye hills, and ye, ye envineyarded ruins!
Therefore farewell, ye walls, palaces, pillars, and domes! 925
Therefore farewell, far seen, ye peaks of the mythic Albano,
Seen from Montorio's height, Tibur and Æsula's hills![219]
Ah, could we once, ere we go, could we stand, while, to ocean descending,
Sinks o'er the yellow dark plain slowly the yellow broad sun,
Stand, from the forest emerging at sunset, at once in the champaign,[220] 930
Open, but studded with trees, chestnuts umbrageous[221] *and old,*
E'en in those fair open fields that incurve to thy beautiful hollow,
Nemi, imbedded in wood, Nemi, inurned in the hill![222] *–*
Therefore farewell, ye plains, and ye hills, and the City Eternal![223]
Therefore farewell! We depart, but to behold you again! 935

CANTO 4.

Eastward, or Northward, or West? I wander and ask as I wander,
Weary, yet eager and sure, Where shall I come to my love?
Whitherward hasten to seek her? Ye daughters of Italy, tell me,[224]
Graceful and tender and dark, is she consorting with you?
Thou that out-climbest the torrent, that tendest thy goats to the summit, 940
Call to me, child of the Alp, has she been seen on the heights?
Italy, farewell I bid thee! for whither she leads me, I follow.
Farewell the vineyard! for I, where I but guess her, must go.
Weariness welcome, and labour, wherever it be, if at last it
Bring me in mountain or plain into the sight of my love. 945

[218] *Ludovisi collection* major collection of Greek and Roman antiquities, including the world-famous Ludovisi Throne of *c.*460 BC.
[219] *Æsula's hills* around Tivoli.
[220] *champaign* open level land.
[221] *umbrageous* shady.

[222] *Nemi . . . hill* Nemi is a small crater lake in the Alban Hills, south-east of Rome.
[223] *City Eternal* Rome is the 'Eternal City'.
[224] *Ye daughters . . . me* cf. Song of Solomon 5.8, 'I charge you, O daughters of Ierusalem, if ye find my beloued, that yee tell him, that I am sicke of loue'.

1. Claude to Eustace, – *from Florence*.

Gone from Florence; indeed! and that is truly provoking; –
Gone to Milan, it seems; then I go also to Milan.
Five days now departed; but they can travel but slowly; –
I quicker far; and I know, as it happens, the house they will go to. –
Why, what else should I do? Stay here and look at the pictures,   950
Statues, and churches? Alack, I am sick of the statues and pictures! –
No, to Bologna, Parma, Piacenza, Lodi, and Milan,
Off go we to-night, – and the Venus go to the Devil![225]

2. Claude to Eustace, – *from Bellaggio*.[226]

Gone to Como, they said; and I have posted[227] to Como.
There was a letter left; but the *cameriere*[228] had lost it.   955
Could it have been for me? They came, however, to Como,
And from Como went by the boat, – perhaps to the Splügen,[229] –
Or to the Stelvio,[230] say, and the Tyrol;[231] also it might be
By Porlezza[232] across to Lugano,[233] and so to the Simplon
Possibly, or the St. Gothard,[234] – or possibly, too, to Baveno,   960
Orta, Turin, and elsewhere. Indeed, I am greatly bewildered.

3. Claude to Eustace, – *from Bellaggio*.

I have been up the Splügen, and on the Stelvio also:
Neither of these can I find they have followed; in no one inn, and
This would be odd, have they written their names. I have been to Porlezza;
There they have not been seen, and therefore not at Lugano.   965
What shall I do? Go on through the Tyrol, Switzerland, Deutschland,[235]
Seeking, an inverse Saul, a kingdom, to find only asses?[236]
There is a tide, at least, in the *love* affairs of mortals,
Which, when taken at flood, leads on to the happiest fortune,[237] –
Leads to the marriage-morn and the orange-flowers[238] and the altar,   970
And the long lawful line of crowned joys to crowned joys succeeding. –
Ah, it has ebbed with me! Ye gods, and when it was flowing,
Pitiful fool that I was, to stand fiddle-faddling[239] in that way!

4. Claude to Eustace, – *from Bellaggio*.

I have returned and found their names in the book at Como.
Certain it is I was right, and yet I am also in error.   975
Added in feminine hand, I read, *By the boat to Bellaggio*. –

[225] *Venus go to the Devil* both 'Classical antiquities' (and especially the Venus de' Medici in the Uffizi, Florence) and 'love' 'go to the devil'.
[226] *Bellagio* town on the southern shore of Lake Como.
[227] *posted* travelled express.
[228] *cameriere* servant.
[229] *Splügen* mountain pass in the Alps.
[230] *Stelvio* area of particular beauty in the Alps and pass into Austria.
[231] *Tyrol* another Alpine tourist area.
[232] *Porlezza* town at the head of Lake Lugano.
[233] *Lugano* lake on the modern Italian border.

[234] *Simplon . . . St. Gothard* two Alpine passes.
[235] *Deutschland* Germany.
[236] *inverse . . . asses* cf. 1 Samuel 9, in which 'Saul seeking asses, is by Samuel anointed king'.
[237] *There is a tide . . . fortune* Claude alludes to Shakespeare, *Julius Caesar* 4.2.270–1, 'There is a tide in the affairs of men / Which, taken at the flood, leads on to fortune'.
[238] *orange-flowers* Queen Victoria revived a fashion for wearing orange blossom as a bride at her marriage on 10 February 1840 to Prince Albert.
[239] *fiddle-faddling* trifling.

So to Bellaggio again, with the words of her writing to aid me.
Yet at Bellagio I find no trace, no sort of remembrance.
So I am here, and wait, and know every hour will remove them.

5. Claude to Eustace, – *from Bellaggio.*

I have but one chance left, – and that is going to Florence.   980
But it is cruel to turn. The mountains seem to demand me, –
Peak and valley from far to beckon and motion me onward.
Somewhere amid their folds she passes whom fain I would follow;
Somewhere among those heights she haply calls me to seek her.
Ah, could I hear her call! could I catch the glimpse of her raiment!   985
Turn, however, I must, though it seem I turn to desert her;
For the sense of the thing is simply to hurry to Florence,
Where the certainty yet may be learnt, I suppose, from the Ropers.

6. Mary Trevellyn, *from Lucerne,*[240] to Miss Roper, *at Florence.*

Dear Miss Roper, – By this you are safely away, we are hoping,
Many a league from Rome; ere long we trust we shall see you.   990
How have you travelled? I wonder; – was Mr. Claude your companion?
As for ourselves, we went from Como straight to Lugano;
So by the Mount St. Gothard; we meant to go by Porlezza,
Taking the steamer, and stopping, as you had advised, at Bellaggio,
Two or three days or more; but this was suddenly altered,   995
After we left the hotel, on the very way to the steamer.
So we have seen, I fear, not one of the lakes in perfection.
Well, he is not come, and now, I suppose, he will not come.
What will you think, meantime? – and yet I must really confess it; –
What will you say? I wrote him a note. We left in a hurry,   1000
Went from Milan to Como, three days before we expected.
But I thought, if he came all the way to Milan, he really
Ought not to be disappointed; and so I wrote three lines to
Say I had heard he was coming, desirous of joining our party; –
If so, then I said, we had started for Como, and meant to   1005
Cross the St. Gothard, and stay, we believed, at Lucerne, for the summer.
Was it wrong? and why, if it was, has it failed to bring him?
Did he not think it worth while to come to Milan? He knew (you
Told him) the house we should go to. Or may it, perhaps, have miscarried?
Any way, now, I repent, and am heartily vexed that I wrote it.   1010

There is a home on the shore of the Alpine sea,[241] *that upswelling*
High up the mountain-sides spreads in the hollow between;
Wilderness, mountain, and snow from the land of the olive conceal it;
Under Pilatus's hill[242] *low by its river it lies:*
Italy, utter the word, and the olive and vine will allure not, –   1015
Wilderness, forest, and snow will not the passage impede;
Italy, unto thy cities receding, the clue to recover,
Hither, recovered the clue, shall not the traveller haste?

---

[240] *Lucerne* city in the heart of Switzerland.
[241] *Alpine sea* Lake Lucerne.

[242] *Pilatus's hill* more of a mountain than a hill, Pilatus looms over Lucerne.

CANTO 5.

> There is a city,[243] upbuilt on the quays of the turbulent Arno,[244]
>   Under Fiesole's[245] heights, – thither are we to return?   1020
> There is a city[246] that fringes the curve of the inflowing waters,
>   Under the perilous hill fringes the beautiful bay, –
> Parthenope,[247] do they call thee? – the Siren,[248] Neapolis,[249] seated
>   Under Vesevus's hill,[250] – are we receding to thee? –
> Sicily, Greece, will invite, and the Orient; – or are we to turn to   1025
>   England, which may after all be for its children the best?

1. Mary Trevellyn, *at Lucerne*, to Miss Roper, *at Florence*.

> So you are really free, and living in quiet at Florence;
>   That is delightful news; you travelled slowly and safely;
>   Mr. Claude got you out; took rooms at Florence before you;
>   Wrote from Milan to say so; had left directly for Milan,   1030
> Hoping to find us soon; – *if he could, he would, you are certain.* –
> Dear Miss Roper, your letter has made me exceedingly happy.
> You are quite sure, you say, he asked you about our intentions;
> You had not heard as yet of Lucerne, but told him of Como. –
>   Well, perhaps he will come; – however, I will not expect it.   1035
> Though you say you are sure, – *if he can, he will, you are certain.*
> O my dear, many thanks from your ever affectionate Mary.

2. Claude to Eustace.

Florence.

> *Action will furnish belief,* – but will that belief be the true one?
> This is the point, you know. However, it doesn't much matter.
>   What one wants, I suppose, is to predetermine the action,   1040
> So as to make it entail, not a chance belief, but the true one.
> *Out of the question,* you say; *if a thing isn't wrong, we may do it.*
> Ah! but this *wrong,* you see – but I do not know that it matters.
> Eustace, the Ropers are gone, and no one can tell me about them.

Pisa.[251]

> Pisa, they say they think; and so I follow to Pisa,   1045
>   Hither and thither inquiring. I weary of making inquiries.
>   I am ashamed, I declare, of asking people about it. –
> Who are your friends? You said you had friends who would certainly know them.

Florence.

> But it is idle, moping, and thinking, and trying to fix her
>   Image more and more in, to write the old perfect inscription   1050
>   Over and over again upon every page of remembrance.

---

[243] *city* Florence.
[244] *Arno* river running through Florence.
[245] *Fiesole* hill town overlooking Florence.
[246] *city* Naples.
[247] *Parthenope* ancient name for Naples, see note 248.
[248] *Siren* Parthenope was the Siren who drowned herself after unsuccessfully attempting to seduce Ulysses. Her body was washed ashore at the point where the ancient city of Naples was founded.
[249] *Neapolis* Naples.
[250] *Vesevus's hill* the fearful volcano Mount Vesuvius is close to Naples.
[251] *Pisa* major city, west of Florence.

I have settled to stay at Florence to wait for your answer.
Who are your friends? Write quickly and tell me. I wait for your answer.

3. Mary Trevellyn to Miss Roper, – *at Lucca*[252] *Baths*.

You are at Lucca baths, you tell me, to stay for the summer;
Florence was quite too hot; you can't move further at present.   1055
Will you not come, do you think, before the summer is over?
Mr. C. got you out with very considerable trouble;
And he was useful and kind, and seemed so happy to serve you.
Didn't stay with you long, but talked very openly to you;
Made you almost his confessor, without appearing to know it, –   1060
What about? – and you say you didn't need his confessions.
O my dear Miss Roper, I dare not trust what you tell me!
Will he come, do you think? I am really so sorry for him
They didn't give him my letter at Milan, I feel pretty certain.
You had told him Bellagio. We didn't go to Bellagio;   1065
So he would miss our track, and perhaps never come to Lugano,
Where we were written in full, *To Lucerne across the St. Gothard.*
But he could write to you; – you would tell him where you were going.

4. Claude to Eustace.

Let me, then, bear to forget her. I will not cling to her falsely;
Nothing factitious or forced shall impair the old happy relation.   1070
I will let myself go, forget, not try to remember;
I will walk on my way, accept the chances that meet me,
Freely encounter the world, imbibe these alien airs, and
Never ask if new feelings and thoughts are of her or of others.
Is she not changing herself? – the old image would only delude me.   1075
I will be bold, too, and change, – if it must be. Yet if in all things,
Yet if I do but aspire evermore to the Absolute only,
I shall be doing, I think, somehow, what she will be doing; –
I shall be thine, O my child, some way, though I know not in what way,
Let me submit to forget her; I must; I already forget her.   1080

5. Claude to Eustace.

Utterly vain is, alas! this attempt at the Absolute, – wholly!
I, who believed not in her, because I would fain believe nothing,
Have to believe as I may, with a wilful, unmeaning acceptance.
I, who refused to enfasten the roots of my floating existence
In the rich earth, cling now to the hard, naked rock that is left me, –   1085
Ah! she was worthy, Eustace, – and that, indeed, is my comfort, –
Worthy a nobler heart than a fool such as I could have given her.
Yes, it relieves me to write, though I do not send, and the chance that
Takes may destroy my fragments. But as men pray, without asking
Whether One really exist to hear or do anything for them, –   1090
Simply impelled by the need of the moment to turn to a Being
In a conception of whom there is freedom from all limitation, –

---

[252] *Lucca* historic city north-east of Pisa.

So in your image I turn to an *ens rationis*[253] of friendship,
Even so write in your name I know not to whom nor in what wise.

* * *

There was a time, methought it was but lately departed,   1095
When, if a thing was denied me, I felt I was bound to attempt it;
Choice alone should take, and choice alone should surrender.
There was a time, indeed, when I had not retired thus early,
Languidly thus, from pursuit of a purpose I once had adopted.
But it is over, all that! I have slunk from the perilous field in   1100
Whose wild struggle of forces the prizes of life are contested.
It is over, all that! I am a coward, and know it.
Courage in me could be only factitious, unnatural, useless.

* * *

Comfort has come to me here in the dreary streets of the city,
Comfort – how do you think? – with a barrel-organ[254] to bring it.   1105
Moping along the streets, and cursing my day as I wandered,
All of a sudden my ear met the sound of an English psalm-tune.
Comfort me it did, till indeed I was very near crying.
Ah, there is some great truth, partial, very likely, but needful,
Lodged, I am strangely sure, in the tones of the English psalm-tune: 1110
Comfort it was at least; and I must take without question
Comfort, however it come, in the dreary streets of the city.

* * *

What with trusting myself, and seeking support from within me,
Almost I could believe I had gained a religious assurance,
Formed in my own poor soul a great moral basis to rest on.   1115
Ah, but indeed I see, I feel it factitious entirely;
I refuse, reject, and put it utterly from me;
I will look straight out, see things, not try to evade them;
Fact shall be fact for me, and the Truth the Truth as ever,
Flexible, changeable, vague, and multiform, and doubtful. –   1120
Off, and depart to the void, thou subtle, fanatical tempter?

* * *

I shall behold thee again (is it so?) at a new visitation,
O ill genius thou! I shall, at my life's dissolution
(When the pulses are weak, and the feeble light of the reason
Flickers, an unfed flame retiring slow from the socket),   1125
Low on a sick-bed laid, hear one, as it were, at the doorway,
And, looking up, see thee standing by, looking emptily at me;
I shall entreat thee then, though now I dare to refuse thee, –
Pale and pitiful now, but terrible then to the dying. –
Well, I will see thee again, and while I can, will repel thee.   1130

---

[253] *ens rationis* entity of reason, being that has no existence outside the mind.   [254] *barrel-organ* street musical instrument.

6. Claude to Eustace.

Rome is fallen,[255] I hear, the gallant Medici taken,[256]
Noble Manara slain,[257] and Garibaldi has lost *il Moro*;[258] –
Rome is fallen; and fallen, or falling, heroical Venice.[259]
I, meanwhile, for the loss of a single small chit[260] of a girl, sit
Moping and mourning here, – for her, and myself much smaller.   1135
Whither depart the souls of the brave that die in the battle,
Die in the lost, lost fight, for the cause that perishes with them?
Are they upborne from the field on the slumberous pinions of angels
Unto a far-off home, where the weary rest from their labour,
And the deep wounds are healed, and the bitter and burning moisture   1140
Wiped from the generous eyes? or do they linger, unhappy,
Pining, and haunting the grave of their by-gone hope and endeavour?
All declamation, alas! though I talk, I care not for Rome nor
Italy; feebly and faintly, and but with the lips, can lament the
Wreck of the Lombard[261] youth, and the victory of the oppressor.   1145
Whither depart the brave? – God knows; I certainly do not.

7. Mary Trevellyn to Miss Roper.

He has not come as yet; and now I must not expect it.
You have written, you say, to friends at Florence, to see him,
If he perhaps should return; – but that is surely unlikely.
Has he not written to you? – he did not know your direction.   1150
Oh, how strange never once to have told him where you were going!
Yet if he only wrote to Florence, that would have reached you.
If what you say he said was true, why has he not done so?
Is he gone back to Rome, do you think, to his Vatican marbles? –
O my dear Miss Roper, forgive me! do not be angry! –   1155
You have written to Florence; – your friends would certainly find him.
Might you not write to him? – but yet it is so little likely!
I shall expect nothing more. – Ever yours, your affectionate Mary.

8. Claude to Eustace.

I cannot stay at Florence, not even to wait for a letter.
Galleries only oppress me. Remembrance of hope I had cherished   1160
(Almost more than as hope, when I passed through Florence the first time)
Lies like a sword in my soul. I am more a coward than ever,
Chicken-hearted, past thought. The *caffès* and waiters distress me.
All is unkind, and, alas! I am ready for any one's kindness.
Oh, I knew it of old, and knew it, I thought, to perfection,   1165
If there is any one thing in the world to preclude all kindness,
It is the need of it, – it is this sad, self-defeating dependence.
Why is this, Eustace? Myself, were I stronger, I think I could tell you.
But it is odd when it comes. So plumb I the deeps of depression,

[255] *Rome is fallen* the French entered Rome on 3 July.
[256] *Medici taken* Giacomo Medici, the commander of
Lombard forces, was, in fact, not captured here.
[257] *Manara slain* Major Luciano Manara joined Garibaldi's
forces on 28 April with 600 men from Lombardy. He was
killed on 30 June.

[258] *il Moro* (the Moor) Aguyar was killed in the conflict on
30 June.
[259] *Venice* last Italian city to surrender (to the Austrians)
after the 1848 revolts.
[260] *chit* person no better than a child.
[261] *Lombard* see notes 256–7.

Daily in deeper, and find no support, no will, no purpose.   1170
All my old strengths are gone. And yet I shall have to do something.
Ah, the key of our life, that passes all wards,[262] opens all locks,
Is not *I will*, but *I must*. I must, – I must, – and I do it.

After all, do I know that I really cared so about her?
Do whatever I will, I cannot call up her image;   1175
For when I close my eyes, I see, very likely, St. Peter's,
Or the Pantheon façade, or Michel Angelo's figures,[263]
Or, at a wish, when I please, the Alban hills and the Forum, –
But that face, those eyes, – ah, no, never anything like them;
Only, try as I will, a sort of featureless outline,   1180
And a pale blank orb, which no recollection will add to.
After all, perhaps there was something factitious about it;
I have had pain, it is true: I have wept, and so have the actors.

At the last moment I have your letter, for which I was waiting;
I have taken my place, and see no good in inquiries.   1185
Do nothing more, good Eustace, I pray you. It only will vex me.
Take no measures. Indeed, should we meet, I could not be certain;
All might be changed, you know. Or perhaps there was nothing to be changed.
It is a curious history, this; and yet I foresaw it;
I could have told it before. The Fates, it is clear, are against us;   1190
For it is certain enough I met with the people you mention;
They were at Florence the day I returned there, and spoke to me even;
Stayed a week, saw me often; departed, and whither I know not.
Great is Fate, and is best. I believe in Providence partly.
What is ordained is right,[264] and all that happens is ordered.   1195
Ah, no, that isn't it. But yet I retain my conclusion.
I will go where I am led, and will not dictate to the chances.
Do nothing more, I beg. If you love me, forbear interfering.

9. Claude to Eustace.

Shall we come out of it all, some day, as one does from a tunnel?
Will it be all at once, without our doing or asking,   1200
We shall behold clear day, the trees and meadows about us,
And the faces of friends, and the eyes we loved looking at us?
Who knows? Who can say? It will not do to suppose it.

10. Claude to Eustace, – *from Rome*.

Rome will not suit me, Eustace; the priests[265] and soldiers possess it;
Priests and soldiers: – and, ah! which is the worst, the priest or the soldier?   1205
Politics farewell, however! For what could I do? with inquiring,
Talking, collating the journals, go fever my brain about things o'er
Which I can have no control. No, happen whatever may happen,
Time, I suppose, will subsist; the earth will revolve on its axis;
People will travel; the stranger will wander as now in the city;   1210
Rome will be here, and the Pope the *custode*[266] of Vatican marbles.

[262] *ward* ridge projecting from the inside plate of a lock, stopping any incorrect key.
[263] *figures* paintings in the Sistine Chapel.
[264] *is right* cf. Pope's *An Essay on Man* (1733–4), I.294: 'One truth is clear, Whatever is, is RIGHT.'
[265] *priests* the end of the siege naturally brought the restoration of the Pope's temporal power.
[266] *custode* custodian.

I have no heart, however, for any marble or fresco;
I have essayed it in vain; 'tis in vain as yet to essay it:
But I may haply resume some day my studies in this kind;
Not as the Scripture says, is, I think, the fact. Ere our death-day,   1215
Faith, I think, does pass, and Love; but Knowledge abideth.[267]
Let us seek Knowledge; – the rest may come and go as it happens.
Knowledge is hard to seek, and harder yet to adhere to.
Knowledge is painful often; and yet when we know, we are happy.
Seek it, and leave mere Faith and Love to come with the chances.   1220
As for Hope, – to-morrow I hope to be starting for Naples.
Rome will not do, I see, for many very good reasons.
Eastward, then, I suppose, with the coming of winter, to Egypt.

11. Mary Trevellyn to Miss Roper.

You have heard nothing; of course, I know you can have heard nothing.
Ah, well, more than once I have broken my purpose, and sometimes,   1225
Only too often, have looked for the little lake-steamer to bring him.
But it is only fancy, – I do not really expect it.
Oh, and you see I know so exactly how he would take it:
Finding the chances prevail against meeting again, he would banish
Forthwith every thought of the poor little possible hope, which   1230
I myself could not help, perhaps, thinking only too much of;
He would resign himself, and go. I see it exactly.
So I also submit, although in a different manner.
Can you not really come? We go very shortly to England.
So go forth to the world, to the good report and the evil!   1235
Go, little book![268] thy tale, is it not evil and good?
Go, and if strangers revile, pass quietly by without answer.
Go, and if curious friends ask of thy rearing and age,
Say, 'I am flitting about many years from brain unto brain of
Feeble and restless youths born to inglorious days: 1240
But,' so finish the word, 'I was writ in a Roman chamber,
When from Janiculan heights[269] thundered the cannon of France.'

---

[267] *Ere . . . abideth* see 1 Corinthians 13.13, 'And now abideth faith, hope, charitie, these three, but the greatest of these is charitie'.
[268] *So go forth . . . book!* form of *envoi* (closing stanza), favoured among medieval poets. Cf. the end of Chaucer's

Troilus and Criseyde, another poem about a relationship's failure: 'Go, litel book, go litel myn tregedie.'
[269] *Janiculan heights* the French captured these on 21–2 June, and their guns therefore commanded the city.

The Latest Decalogue

Satire in the Victorian period is often assumed to be the territory of fiction, making its appearance with pungent effect in, say, Dickens's, Thackeray's or Trollope's novels rather than in verse. But Victorian satirical poetry did exist and Clough's modern version of the Ten Commandments (the 'Decalogue' is another name for the Ten Commandments, the foundational laws of Judaeo-Christian morality) is a powerful example, directed at the moral standards of competitive capitalism and at hypocritical and cynical attitudes generally. For a satirical poem on evolutionary theory understood as progessive in this anthology, see May Kendall, 'Lay of the Trilobite', 627–9. Even Clough's title is satirical insofar as it suggests that the Ten Commandments can be revised when more up-to-date versions are required. The poem, written in 1849, was first published in 1862.

Text: *The Poems of Arthur Hugh Clough* (1974).

Thou shalt have one God only;[1] who
Would be at the expense of two?
No graven images may be
Worshipped,[2] except the currency:
Swear not at all;[3] for, for thy curse   5
Thine enemy is none the worse:
At church on Sunday to attend[4]
Will serve to keep the world thy friend:
Honour thy parents;[5] that is, all
From whom advancement may befall: 10
Thou shalt not kill;[6] but needst not strive
Officiously to keep alive:
Do not adultery commit;[7]
Advantage rarely comes of it:
Thou shalt not steal;[8] an empty feat,   15
When it's so lucrative to cheat:
Bear not false witness;[9] let the lie
Have time on its own wings to fly:
Thou shalt not covet;[10] but tradition
Approves all forms of competition.   20
The sum of all is, thou shalt love,
If any body, God above:
At any rate shall never labour
More than yourself to love your neighbour.[11]

[1] *Thou . . . only* cf. 'Thou shalt haue no other Gods before me', Exodus 20.3.

[2] *No . . . worshipped* cf. 'Thou shalt not make vnto thee any grauen Image', Exodus 20.4.

[3] *Swear . . . all* cf. 'Thou shalt not take the Name of the Lord thy God in vaine', Exodus 20.7.

[4] *At . . . attend* cf. 'Remember the Sabbath day, to keepe it holy', Exodus 20.8.

[5] *Honour . . . parents* cf. 'Honour thy father and thy mother', Exodus 20.12.

[6] *Thou . . . kill* cf. 'Thou shalt not kill', Exodus 20.13.

[7] *Do not . . . commit* cf. 'Thou shalt not commit adultery', Exodus 20.14.

[8] *Thou . . . steal* cf. 'Thou shalt not steale', Exodus 20.15.

[9] *Bear . . . witness* cf. 'Thou shalt not beare false witnes against thy neighbour', Exodus 20.16.

[10] *covet* cf. 'Thou shalt not couet thy neighbours house, thou shalt not couet thy neighbours wife, nor his man seruant, nor his maid seruant, nor his oxe, nor his asse, nor any thing that is thy neighbours', Exodus 20.17.

[11] *The sum . . . neighbour* cf. Matthew 22.37–40, 'Iesus sayd vnto him, Thou shalt loue the Lord thy God with all thy heart, and with all thy soule, and with all thy minde. This is the first and great Commandement. And the second is like vnto it, Thou shalt loue thy neighbour as thy selfe. On these two Commandements hang all the Law and the Prophets.' The last four lines are not included in one MS version and were not published until 1951.

Matthew Arnold (1822–1888)

Matthew Arnold was the eldest son of Dr Thomas Arnold (1795–1842), the great headmaster of Rugby School and later Regius Professor of Modern History at Oxford who was a significant influence on Matthew's friend A. H. Clough. Arnold negotiated with the shade of his father – altruistic, dutiful, morally certain, possessed of compelling masculine fortitude – throughout his life. Educated at Winchester, then Rugby, Arnold took a Classical Scholarship to Balliol College Oxford where he won the University's Newdigate prize for poetry. He took a second-class degree – disappointing his supporters – but successfully obtained a Fellowship at Oriel College, then a teaching job at Rugby, and then a position as private secretary to Lord Lansdowne in swift succession. In 1851, he became an Inspector of Schools – no sinecure – which he maintained for 35 years. The position required much travel, but he found time to write. In 1849, Arnold published his first collection of poems, *The Strayed Reveller and Other Poems*, followed by *Empedocles on Etna, and Other Poems* (1852); in 1851, he married Frances Wightman, the daughter of a prominent judge. The 'Preface' to the 1853 edition of *Poems* was a key statement of Arnold's conception of poetry. He expressed dissatisfaction at the productions of modernity – chiefly his own 'Empedocles on Etna', 268–95 – as failing to offer anything but doubt and discouragement. The contemporary moment was characterized, he said, by disarray: 'The confusion of the present times is great, the multitude of voices counselling different things bewildering.' Poetry should be a guide, an inspiring presence. It should certainly not offer the introspective anxieties of a man on the verge of suicide – Empedocles – but take as its subject human actions that have universal interest, nobility, intensity. Arnold's 'Sohrab and Rustum' (1853) was the closest he came to exemplifying these principles, a poem that covertly processed more of the poet's thoughts about the legacy of his father (who had died in 1842).

In 1857, Arnold began a 10-year office as Oxford's (elected) Professor of Poetry, though his own work was increasingly in prose. *Essays in Criticism* came out in 1865, *Culture and Anarchy* in 1869, *Literature and Dogma* in 1873, and many other volumes on education, the Bible, literature and English intellectual life that helped establish Arnold's reputation as a leading cultural critic. *Essays in Criticism* included the influential essay 'The Function of Criticism at the Present Time' where Arnold articulated his claim for the properly 'disinterested' nature of criticism that should try to know 'the best that is known and thought in the world, irrespectively of practice, politics and everything of the kind'. He championed the idea of a liberal culture against the Philistinism and narrow-mindedness of the present. England needed more intellectual energy, curiosity, contact with the great works of the past, international awareness (especially in education), clear-mindedness and *criticism*. Christianity was becoming ossified; 'culture', with the 'sweetness and light' of unprejudiced thinking and knowledge of the best that had been thought and said in the world, would replace it. Arnold's influence on the foundational principles of English literature as a university and school discipline at the end of the nineteenth and beginning of the twentieth centuries was – to say nothing of his wider legacies – substantial. He published *New Poems* in 1867, including 'Thyrsis', an elegy for his friend A. H. Clough that recalled 'The Scholar-Gipsy'. Matthew Arnold, who retired as Chief Inspector of Schools in 1886, the same year as he undertook his second lecture tour of the United States, died suddenly of heart failure in 1888. He had been hastening to catch a tram so that he could meet his daughter Lucy, returning to Liverpool docks from New York.

A Summer Night

'A Summer Night' (1852), like 'Dover Beach', 312–13, and 'To Marguerite – Continued', 267–8, moves from autobiographical experience, with a conversational quality to its narration, to universalized reflection on what human beings have lost or do not possess. Arnold presents himself, as he often does, as representative of a historical moment and as a figure dislocated from community and distinctive in his failure to be as others or to derive comfort from that difference. As in the 'Stanzas from the Grande Chartreuse', 305–12 – also a poem in which a physical space precipitates the poem's debate – Arnold's position is unresolved and stalled between two possibilities (or impossibilities). In 'The Scholar-Gipsy' (published 1853), 298–305, Arnold would celebrate – albeit regretfully – the man who had escaped from the mainstream of his community to live on its edges, under the more enabling dispensation of a counter-culture. But 'A Summer Night' has none of the same optimism in the fortunes of the rebel. The intrepid man who breaks away from the common life is here without sanity and disastrously self-destructive, doomed to a failure more inglorious than those who doggedly stay in the rigid spaces their culture has provided them. The contrast between these two poems reminds the reader that Arnold's poetry, taken as a whole, dramatizes multiple stages of a changing mind and, like his friend A. H. Clough's *Amours de Voyage*, 228–62, tests the possibilities of Carlylean sincerity in the modern world.

With its bleak diagnosis of modern life, 'A Summer Night' considers Carlyle's legacy in an additional way. Carlyle, maintaining that each man 'must find his work and do it', offered a powerful transformation of the Protestant belief in the value of labour to insist that daily work was a source of personal redemption. Work in this poem brings nothing of the sort, and the text finds optimism in neither labour nor faith, but only and not entirely innocently in a prospect of the natural world. The conclusion of the poem – which is an important text in the developing representations of the Victorian city that would reach a desolate climax in the work of James Thomson and John Davidson – offers an image, a representation of a natural space, as a focus of human possibility. Like John Keats's 'To Autumn', or Arnold's 'Sohrab and Rustum' (1853), 'A Summer Night' concludes with a spatially represented sense of potential. But Arnold's image here perhaps hovers dangerously close to irony. The poem's spoken manner makes it formally akin to 'The Buried Life', 296–8.

Text: *Empedocles on Etna, and Other Poems* (1852).

In the deserted, moon-blanched street,
How lonely rings the echo of my feet!
Those windows, which I gaze at, frown,
Silent and white, unopening down,
Repellent as the world; – but see, 5
A break between the housetops shows
The moon! and, lost behind her, fading dim
Into the dewy dark obscurity
Down at the far horizon's rim,
Doth a whole tract of heaven disclose! 10
And to my mind the thought
Is on a sudden brought
Of a past night, and a far different scene.
Headlands stood out into the moonlit deep
As clearly as at noon; 15
The spring-tide's brimming flow
Heaved dazzlingly between;
Houses, with long white sweep,
Girdled the glistening bay;
Behind, through the soft air, 20
The blue haze-cradled mountains spread away.
That night was far more fair –
But the same restless pacings to and fro,
And the same vainly throbbing heart was there,
And the same bright, calm moon. 25

And the calm moonlight seems to say:

Hast thou then still the old unquiet breast,
Which neither deadens into rest,
Nor ever feels the fiery glow
That whirls the spirit from itself away, 30
But fluctuates to and fro,
Never by passion quite possess'd

And never quite benumbed by the world's sway? –
And I, I know not if to pray
Still to be what I am, or yield and be   35
Like all the other men I see.
For most men in a brazen[1] prison live,
Where, in the sun's hot eye,
With heads bent o'er their toil, they languidly
Their lives to some unmeaning taskwork give,   40
Dreaming of nought beyond their prison-wall.
And as, year after year,
Fresh products of their barren labour fall
From their tired hands, and rest
Never yet comes more near,   45
Gloom settles slowly down over their breast;
And while they try to stem
The waves of mournful thought by which they are pressed,
Death in their prison reaches them,
Unfreed, having seen nothing, still unblest.   50

And the rest, a few,
Escape their prison and depart
On the wide ocean of life anew.
There the freed prisoner, where'er his heart
Listeth,[2] will sail;   55
Nor doth he know how there prevail,
Despotic on that sea,
Trade-winds which cross it from eternity.
Awhile he holds some false way, undebarred
By thwarting signs, and braves   60
The freshening wind and blackening waves.
And then the tempest strikes him; and between
The lightning-bursts is seen
Only a driving wreck,
And the pale master on his spar-strewn deck   65
With anguished face and flying hair
Grasping the rudder hard,
Still bent[3] to make some port he knows not where,
Still standing for some false, impossible shore.
And sterner comes the roar   70
Of sea and wind, and through the deepening gloom
Fainter and fainter wreck and helmsman loom,
And he too disappears, and comes no more.

Is there no life, but these alone?
Madman or slave, must man be one?   75

Plainness and clearness without shadow of stain!
Clearness divine!
Ye heavens, whose pure dark regions have no sign
Of languor,[4] though so calm, and, though so great,
Are yet untroubled and unpassionate;   80

---

[1] *brazen* made from brass, strong as brass.
[2] *Listeth* chooses.
[3] *bent* intending.
[4] *languor* disease, mental suffering.

Who, though so noble, share in the world's toil,
And, though so tasked, keep free from dust and soil!
I will not say that your mild deeps retain
A tinge, it may be, of their silent pain
Who have longed deeply once, and longed in vain –   85
But I will rather say that you remain
A world above man's head, to let him see
How boundless might his soul's horizons be,
How vast, yet of what clear transparency!
How it were good to abide there, and breathe free;   90
How fair a lot to fill
Is left to each man still!

To Marguerite – Continued

As for A. C. Swinburne, the sea provided Arnold with a range of referential possibilities. In this poem, originally entitled 'To Marguerite, in returning a volume of the Letters of Ortis', Arnold's characteristic movement from the autobiographical to the universal is clear. The poem's trajectory is from local experience to general and, as in 'Stanzas from the Grande Chartreuse', 305–12, and 'The Buried Life', 296–8, the physical setting of the poem – here, islands separated by the ocean – provides a compelling possibility for metaphor. Arnold's post-Romantic condition (on which he explicitly meditates in 'Stanzas from the Grande Chartreuse' and implicitly in 'Empedocles on Etna', 268–95) is partly defined by the impossibility of imagining Wordsworthian forms of spiritualized union with the natural world (cf. the proto-Wordsworthian Callicles in 'Empedocles on Etna'). Here, nature is available to him only in its sharply realized materiality, brilliantly represented in Arnold's last line, with its finely judged rhythmic economy.

'To Marguerite – Continued', first published in 1852, became part of the group of poems that Arnold finally completed in 1877 under the title *Switzerland*. The sequence belongs with Elizabeth Barrett Browning's *Sonnets from the Portuguese*, 52–5, George Meredith's *Modern Love*, 328–49, A. H. Clough's *Amours de Voyage*, 228–62, and Coventry Patmore's *The Angel in the House* (1854–63) as a poetic meditation from the mid-century on the nature of modern love, its meaning, possibilities and peculiar problems. 'To Marguerite – Continued' diagnoses 'a God' as the root cause of human isolation but, characteristically, pushes its analysis no further, leaving a fuller sense of causality open. For another differently generalist diagnosis of the modern moment – Arnold repeatedly constructs a view of a 'modern spirit', a peculiar quality of the present that radically distinguishes itself from the past – see 'Dover Beach', 312–13.

Text: *Poems* (1877).

Yes! in the sea of life enisled,
With echoing straits between us thrown,
Dotting the shoreless watery wild,
We mortal millions live *alone*.
The islands feel the enclasping flow,   5
And then their endless bounds they know.

2
But when the moon their hollows lights,
And they are swept by balms of spring,
And in their glens, on starry nights,
The nightingales divinely sing;   10
And lovely notes, from shore to shore,
Across the sounds and channels pour –

3
Oh! then a longing like despair
Is to their farthest caverns sent;

For surely once, they feel, we were   15
Parts of a single continent!
Now round us spreads the watery plain –
Oh might our marges meet again!

4
Who ordered, that their longing's fire
Should be, as soon as kindled, cooled?   20
Who renders vain their deep desire? –
A God, a God their severance rul'd!
And bade betwixt their shores to be
The unplumbed, salt, estranging sea.

Empedocles on Etna: A Dramatic Poem

The dramatic monologue – albeit a term employed only at the end of the nineteenth century – was the dominant form of Victorian dramatic poetry. But other more extensive dramatic forms were explored too. These include Tennyson's *Maud: A Monodrama* (1855) and Arnold's 'dramatic poem', 'Empedocles on Etna' (pronounced 'Empedoclees'). Arnold presents himself in other poems – 'To Marguerite – Continued', 267–8, 'A Summer Night', 264–7, 'Stanzas from the Grande Chartreuse', 305–12 – as both individual and representative, as a spokesman for broader, universal conditions. But it is through the figure of a real ancient Greek philosopher that 'Empedocles on Etna' explores, in a transhistorical movement, the precariousness of the sensitive thinking man amid the intellectual uncertainties and alienations of post-Romantic Europe.

Learned but sensuous, the poem presents a speaker who perceives no comfort in communication with others, who is conscious that he has outlived his time, who is unable to take consolation in the pleasures of the natural world, and whose belief that man must 'moderate desire' in order to secure earthly content finally does not satisfy him. Like Arnold himself in 'Stanzas from the Grande Chartreuse', this poem – in which, Arnold said plainly, 'modern problems have presented themselves' – offers a conflicted protagonist, dislocated from his age and the securities that once supported him. It is a portrait of the modern thinker and of modern feeling.

Empedocles (*c.*495–*c.*435 BC) was a Pre-Socratic philosopher, healer, scientist and mystic. He saw Love and Strife as the two important principles of the Universe, and perceived the latter gaining ascendancy during the time in which he lived. In Simon Karsten's *Philosophorum Graecorum Veterum* (1838), Arnold found the specific information he used in the poem. That material may be summarized as follows: Empedocles cured a woman named Panthea who had lain in a trance; he was a lyre player; he lived for some time

in the house of P(e)isianax, a friend; Pausanias, a physician, was a follower; at the end of his life Empedocles's influence dwindled as the Sophists (a class of professional philosophy instructors) extended their power among the Greeks. From the life and death of this eloquently melancholy ancient philosopher, Arnold fashions a poem that dramatizes a myth of the modern and, as for many of his poems, deliberately invites the reader to see it as emblematic of the age. Empedocles was usually thought to have died after throwing himself into Mount Etna, an active volcano.

Arnold's comment on the poem – which, like 'Stanzas', is engaged with a moment of transition in European history – was that Empedocles 'has not the religious consolations of other men . . . He sees things as they are – the world as it is – God as he is.' He is 'clouded, oppressed, dispirited, without hope & energy. Before he comes the victim of depression & overtension of mind, to the utter deadness to joy, grandeur, spirit, and animated life, he desires to die; to be reunited with the universe, before by exaggerating his human side he has become utterly estranged from it.' Empedocles's suicidal leap is a parody of the Wordsworthian relationship with nature, where perceiver and perceived are united by a common spirit (Callicles may be seen as a Wordsworthian figure, finding joy in the mountain environment). But there is still something triumphant about Empedocles's plunge, as if something has, after all, been achieved.

Arnold famously rejected this poem, first published in 1852, from his 1853 collection of *Poems*, because it no longer fitted his sense of poetry's universal obligations. He declared in the 1853 Preface that 'Empedocles' had failed to address the fundamental requirements of poetry to interest and to 'inspirit and rejoice the reader'. Here instead, he remarked, 'suffering finds no vent in action [and . . .] everything is to be endured, nothing to be done'. He replaced it with the more Classical 'Sohrab and Rustum'. But in charting the mental turmoil of the suffering philosopher, Arnold had provided a potent model for mid-century intellectual crisis and, at the

request of Robert Browning, he republished the poem in 1867.

Text: *Empedocles on Etna, and Other Poems* (1852).

Persons.
Empedocles; Pausanias, *a Physician*; Callicles, *a young Harp-player*.

The Scene of the Poem is on Mount Etna;[1] *at first in the forest region, afterwards on the summit of the mountain.*

ACT 1. SCENE 1.

Morning. A Pass in the forest region of Etna.

Callicles. (*Alone, resting on a rock by the path.*)
The mules, I think, will not be here this hour;
They feel the cool wet turf under their feet
By the stream-side, after the dusty lanes
In which they have toiled all night from Catana,[2]
And scarcely will they budge a yard.[3] O Pan,[4]   5
How gracious is the mountain at this hour!
A thousand times have I been here alone,
Or with the revellers from the mountain-towns,
But never on so fair a morn; – the sun
Is shining on the brilliant mountain-crests,   10
And on the highest pines; but farther down,
Here in the valley, is in shade; the sward[5]
Is dark, and on the stream the mist still hangs;
One sees one's footprints crushed in the wet grass,
One's breath curls in the air; and on these pines   15
That climb from the stream's edge, the long grey tufts,
Which the goats love, are jewelled thick with dew.
Here will I stay till the slow litter[6] comes.
I have my harp too – that is well. – Apollo!
What mortal could be sick or sorry here?   20
I know not in what mind Empedocles,
Whose mules I followed, may be coming up,
But if, as most men say, he is half mad
With exile, and with brooding on his wrongs,
Pausanias, his sage friend, who mounts with him,   25
Could scarce have lighted on a lovelier cure.
The mules must be below, far down. I hear
Their tinkling bells, mixed with the song of birds,
Rise faintly to me – now it stops! Who's here?
Pausanias! and on foot? alone?   30

[1] *Etna* still-active volcano on the east coast of Sicily.
[2] *Catana* Catania, city on the east coast of Sicily, 25 km south of Etna.
[3] *yard* unit of measurement: a little less than a metre.
[4] *Pan* Greek god of field and forest; half man, half goat.
[5] *sward* top soil covered with grass.
[6] *litter* frame containing a couch with curtains.

Pausanias.
And thou, then?
I left thee supping with Peisianax,
With thy head full of wine, and thy hair crowned,
Touching thy harp as the whim came on thee,
And praised and spoiled by master and by guests   35
Almost as much as the new dancing-girl.
Why hast thou followed us?

Callicles.
The night was hot,
And the feast past its prime; so we slipped out,
Some of us, to the portico to breathe –   40
Peisianax, thou know'st, drinks late; and then,
As I was lifting my soiled garland off,
I saw the mules and litter in the court,
And in the litter sate[7] Empedocles;
Thou, too, wast with him. Straightway I sped home;   45
I saddled my white mule, and all night long
Through the cool lovely country followed you,
Passed you a little since as morning dawned,
And have this hour sate by the torrent here,
Till the slow mules should climb in sight again.   50
And now?

Pausanias.
And now, back to the town with speed!
Crouch in the wood first, till the mules have passed;
They do but halt, they will be here anon.
Thou must be viewless[8] to Empedocles;   55
Save mine, he must not meet a human eye.
One of his moods is on him that thou know'st;
I think, thou wouldst not vex him.

Callicles.
No – and yet
I would fain[9] stay, and help thee tend him. Once   60
He knew me well, and would oft notice me;
And still, I know not how, he draws me to him,
And I could watch him with his proud sad face,
His flowing locks and gold-encircled brow
And kingly gait,[10] for ever; such a spell   65
In his severe looks, such a majesty
As drew of old the people after him,
In Agrigentum[11] and Olympia,[12]
When his star reigned, before his banishment,
Is potent still on me in his decline.   70

---

[7] *sate* sat.
[8] *viewless* invisible.
[9] *fain* gladly.
[10] *gait* manner of walking.
[11] *Agrigentum* modern Agrigento, centre of the south coast of Sicily. As the ancient city of Akragas, it was the home of Empedocles.
[12] *Olympia* ancient city near the west coast of the Peloponnese, west of Athens.

But oh! Pausanias, he is changed of late;
There is a settled trouble in his air
Admits no momentary brightening now,
And when he comes among his friends at feasts,
'Tis as an orphan among prosperous boys.   75
Thou know'st of old he loved this harp of mine,
When first he sojourned[13] with Peisianax;
He is now always moody, and I fear him;
But I would serve him, soothe him, if I could,
Dared one but try.   80

Pausanias.
Thou wast a kind child ever!
He loves thee, but he must not see thee now.
Thou hast indeed a rare touch on thy harp,
He loves that in thee, too; – there was a time
(But that is passed), he would have paid thy strain[14]   85
With music to have drawn the stars from heaven.
He hath his harp and laurel with him still,
But he has laid the use of music by,
And all which might relax his settled gloom.
Yet thou may'st try thy playing, if thou wilt –   90
But thou must keep unseen; follow us on,
But at a distance! in these solitudes,
In this clear mountain-air, a voice will rise,
Though from afar, distinctly; it may soothe him.
Play when we halt, and, when the evening comes   95
And I must leave him (for his pleasure is
To be left musing these soft nights alone
In the high unfrequented mountain-spots),
Then watch him, for he ranges swift and far,
Sometimes to Etna's top, and to the cone;   100
But hide thee in the rocks a great way down,
And try thy noblest strains, my Callicles,
With the sweet night to help thy harmony!
Thou wilt earn my thanks sure, and perhaps his.

Callicles.
More than a day and night, Pausanias,   105
Of this fair summer-weather, on these hills,
Would I bestow to help Empedocles.
That needs no thanks; one is far better here
Than in the broiling city in these heats.
But tell me, how hast thou persuaded him   110
In this his present fierce, man-hating mood,
To bring thee out with him alone on Etna?

Pausanias.
Thou hast heard all men speaking of Pantheia,[15]
The woman who at Agrigentum lay
Thirty long days in a cold trance of death,   115
And whom Empedocles called back to life.

---

[13] *sojourned* stayed.
[14] *strain* music.

[15] *Pantheia* see headnote, 268.

Thou art too young to note it, but his power
Swells with the swelling evil of this time,
And holds men mute to see where it will rise.
He could stay swift diseases in old days,   120
Chain madmen by the music of his lyre,
Cleanse to sweet airs the breath of poisonous streams,
And in the mountain-chinks inter the winds.[16]
This he could do of old; but now, since all
Clouds and grows daily worse in Sicily,   125
Since broils tear us in twain, since this new swarm
Of sophists[17] has got empire in our schools
Where he was paramount, since he is banished
And lives a lonely man in triple gloom –
He grasps the very reins of life and death.   130
I asked him of Pantheia yesterday,
When we were gathered with Peisianax,
And he made answer, I should come at night
On Etna here, and be alone with him,
And he would tell me, as his old, tried friend,   135
Who still was faithful, what might profit me;
That is, the secret of this miracle.

Callicles.

Bah! Thou a doctor! Thou art superstitious.
Simple Pausanias, 'twas no miracle!
Pantheia, for I know her kinsmen well,   140
Was subject to these trances from a girl.
Empedocles would say so, did he deign;[18]
But he still lets the people, whom he scorns,
Gape and cry wizard at him, if they list.[19]
But thou, thou art no company for him!   145
Thou art as cross, as soured as himself!
Thou hast some wrong from thine own citizens,
And then thy friend is banished, and on that,
Straightway thou fallest to arraign[20] the times,
As if the sky was impious not to fall.   150
The sophists are no enemies of his;
I hear, Gorgias,[21] their chief, speaks nobly of him,
As of his gifted master, and once friend.
He is too scornful, too high-wrought, too bitter.
'Tis not the times, 'tis not the sophists vex him;   155
There is some root of suffering in himself,
Some secret and unfollowed vein of woe,
Which makes the time look black and sad to him.
Pester him not in this his sombre mood
With questionings about an idle tale,   160
But lead him through the lovely mountain-paths,
And keep his mind from preying on itself,
And talk to him of things at hand and common,

---

[16] *And in . . . winds* allusion to Aeolus, guardian of the winds, which he kept in a cave on his island.
[17] *sophists* see headnote, 268.
[18] *deign* think it worthy of himself.

[19] *list* please.
[20] *arraign* accuse.
[21] *Gorgias* (*c.*483–*c.*385), most influential of the Greek Sophists.

Not miracles! thou art a learned man,
But credulous of fables as a girl. 165

Pausanias.
And thou, a boy whose tongue outruns his knowledge,
And on whose lightness blame is thrown away.
Enough of this! I see the litter wind
Up by the torrent-side, under the pines.
I must rejoin Empedocles. Do thou 170
Crouch in the brushwood till the mules have passed;
Then play thy kind part well. Farewell till night!

SCENE 2.

Noon. A Glen on the highest skirts of the woody region of Etna.
Empedocles – Pausanias.

Pausanias.
The noon is hot. When we have crossed the stream,
We shall have left the woody tract, and come
Upon the open shoulder of the hill. 175
See how the giant spires of yellow bloom
Of the sun-loving gentian,[22] in the heat,
Are shining on those naked slopes like flame!
Let us rest here; and now, Empedocles,
Pantheia's history! 180

A harp-note below is heard.

Empedocles.
Hark! what sound was that
Rose from below? If it were possible,
And we were not so far from human haunt,
I should have said that some one touched a harp.
Hark! there again! 185

Pausanias.
'Tis the boy Callicles,
The sweetest harp-player in Catana.
He is for ever coming on these hills,
In summer, to all country-festivals,
With a gay revelling band; he breaks from them 190
Sometimes, and wanders far among the glens.
But heed him not, he will not mount to us;
I spoke with him this morning. Once more, therefore,
Instruct me of Pantheia's story, Master,
As I have prayed thee. 195

Empedocles.
That? and to what end?

[22] *gentian* common blue mountain plant.

Pausanias.
It is enough that all men speak of it.
But I will also say, that when the Gods
Visit us as they do with sign and plague,
To know those spells of thine which stay their hand   200
Were to live free from terror.

Empedocles.
Spells? Mistrust them!
Mind is the spell which governs earth and heaven.
Man has a mind with which to plan his safety;
Know that, and help thyself!   205

Pausanias.
But thine own words?
'The wit and counsel of man was never clear,
Troubles confound the little wit he has.'
Mind is a light which the Gods mock us with,
To lead those false who trust it.   210

The harp sounds again.

Empedocles.
Hist![23] once more!
Listen, Pausanias! – Ay, 'tis Callicles;
I know these notes among a thousand. Hark!

Callicles. (*Sings unseen, from below.*)
The track winds down to the clear stream,
To cross the sparkling shallows; there   215
The cattle love to gather, on their way
To the high mountain-pastures, and to stay,
Till the rough cow-herds drive them past,
Knee-deep in the cool ford; for 'tis the last
Of all the woody, high, well-watered dells   220
On Etna; and the beam
Of noon is broken there by chestnut-boughs
Down its steep verdant[24] sides; the air
Is freshened by the leaping stream, which throws
Eternal showers of spray on the mossed roots   225
Of trees, and veins of turf, and long dark shoots
Of ivy-plants, and fragrant hanging bells
Of hyacinths, and on late anemonies,
That muffle its wet banks; but glade,
And stream, and sward, and chestnut-trees,   230
End here; Etna beyond, in the broad glare
Of the hot noon, without a shade,
Slope behind slope, up to the peak, lies bare;
The peak, round which the white clouds play.

In such a glen, on such a day,   235
On Pelion,[25] on the grassy ground,

---

[23] *Hist!* exclamation: pay attention!
[24] *verdant* green.

[25] *Pelion* Mount Pelion, legendary home of the centaur: half man, half horse.

Chiron,[26] the aged Centaur lay,
The young Achilles[27] standing by.
The Centaur taught him to explore
The mountains; where the glens are dry   240
And the tired Centaurs come to rest,
And where the soaking springs abound
And the straight ashes grow for spears,
And where the hill-goats come to feed,
And the sea-eagles build their nest.   245
He showed him Phthia[28] far away,
And said: O boy, I taught this lore
To Peleus,[29] in long distant years!
He told him of the Gods, the stars,
The tides; – and then of mortal wars,   250
And of the life which heroes lead
Before they reach the Elysian[30] place
And rest in the immortal mead;[31]
And all the wisdom of his race.

The music below ceases, and Empedocles speaks, accompanying himself in a solemn manner on his harp.

Empedocles
The out-spread world to span   255
A cord the Gods first slung,
And then the soul of man
There, like a mirror, hung,
And bade the winds through space impel the gusty toy.

Hither and thither spins   260
The wind-borne, mirroring soul,
A thousand glimpses wins,
And never sees a whole;
Looks once, and drives elsewhere, and leaves its last employ.

The Gods laugh in their sleeve   265
To watch man doubt and fear,
Who knows not what to believe
Since he sees nothing clear,
And dares stamp nothing false where he finds nothing sure.

Is this, Pausanias, so?   270
And can our souls not strive,
But with the winds must go,
And hurry where they drive?
Is fate indeed so strong, man's strength indeed so poor?

---

[26] *Chiron* wise centaur, tutor of a number of Greek heroes including Achilles, the greatest warrior of the Trojan war.

[27] *Achilles* see note 26.

[28] *Phthia* town in Thessaly.

[29] *Peleus* hero, king of Phthia, allowed the privilege of marrying a goddess: he was the father of Achilles. Peleus was saved from death by Chiron.

[30] *Elysian* of Elysium, an island where a small number of the blessed lived in bliss after death.

[31] *mead* meadow.

I will not judge. That man,   275
Howbeit, I judge as lost,
Whose mind allows a plan,
Which would degrade it most;
And he treats doubt the best who tries to see least ill.

Be not, then, fear's blind slave!   280
Thou art my friend; to thee,
All knowledge that I have,
All skill I wield, are free.
Ask not the latest news of the last miracle,

Ask not what days and nights   285
In trance Pantheia lay,
But ask how thou such sights
May'st see without dismay;
Ask what most helps when known, thou son of Anchitus!

What? hate, and awe, and shame   290
Fill thee to see our time;
Thou feelest thy soul's frame
Shaken and out of chime?
What? life and chance go hard with thee too, as with us;

Thy citizens, 'tis said,   295
Envy thee and oppress,
Thy goodness no men aid,
All strive to make it less;
Tyranny, pride, and lust, fill Sicily's abodes;

Heaven is with earth at strife,   300
Signs make thy soul afraid,
The dead return to life,
Rivers are dried, winds stayed;
Scarce can one think in calm, so threatening are the Gods;

And we feel, day and night,   305
The burden of ourselves –
Well, then, the wiser wight[32]
In his own bosom delves,
And asks what ails him so, and gets what cure he can.

The sophist sneers: Fool, take   310
Thy pleasure, right or wrong.
The pious wail: Forsake
A world these sophists throng.
Be neither saint nor sophist-led, but be a man!

These hundred doctors try   315
To preach thee to their school.
We have the truth! they cry;
And yet their oracle,
Trumpet it as they will, is but the same as thine.

[32] *wight* creature.

Once read thy own breast right,   320
And thou hast done with fears;
Man gets no other light,
Search he a thousand years.
Sink in thyself! there ask what ails thee, at that shrine!

What makes thee struggle and rave?   325
Why are men ill at ease? –
'Tis that the lot they have
Fails their own will to please;
For man would make no murmuring, were his will obeyed.

And why is it, that still   330
Man with his lot thus fights? –
'Tis that he makes this will
The measure of his rights,
And believes Nature outraged if his will's gainsaid.[33]

Couldst thou, Pausanias, learn   335
How deep a fault is this;
Couldst thou but once discern
Thou hast no right to bliss,
No title from the Gods to welfare and repose;

Then thou wouldst look less mazed[34]   340
Whene'er of bliss debarred,
Nor think the Gods were crazed
When thy own lot went hard.
But we are all the same – the fools of our own woes!

For, from the first faint morn   345
Of life, the thirst for bliss
Deep in man's heart is born;
And, sceptic as he is,
He fails not to judge clear if this be quenched or no.

Nor is the thirst to blame.   350
Man errs not that he deems
His welfare his true aim,
He errs because he dreams
The world does but exist that welfare to bestow.

We mortals are no kings   355
For each of whom to sway
A new-made world up-springs,
Meant merely for his play;
No, we are strangers here; the world is from of old.

In vain our pent wills fret,   360
And would the world subdue.
Limits we did not set
Condition all we do;
Born into life we are, and life must be our mould.

[33] *gainsaid* denied.   [34] *mazed* confused.

Born into life! man grows   365
Forth from his parents' stem,
And blends their bloods, as those
Of theirs are blent[35] in them;
So each new man strikes root into a far fore-time.

Born into life! we bring   370
A bias with us here,
And, when here, each new thing
Affects us we come near;
To tunes we did not call our being must keep chime.

Born into life! in vain,   375
Opinions, those or these,
Unaltered to retain
The obstinate mind decrees;
Experience, like a sea, soaks all-effacing in.

Born into life! who lists[36]   380
May what is false hold dear,
And for himself make mists
Through which to see less clear:
The world is what it is, for all our dust and din.

Born into life! 'tis we,   385
And not the world, are new;
Our cry for bliss, our plea,
Others have urged it too –
Our wants have all been felt, our errors made before.

No eye could be too sound   390
To observe a world so vast,
No patience too profound
To sort what's here amassed;
How man may here best live no care too great to explore.

But we – as some rude[37] guest   395
Would change, where'er he roam,
The manners there professed
To those he brings from home –
We mark not the world's course, but would have *it* take *ours*.

The world's course proves the terms   400
On which man wins content;
Reason the proof confirms –
We spurn it, and invent
A false course for the world, and for ourselves, false powers.

Riches we wish to get,   405
Yet remain spendthrifts still;
We would have health, and yet

---

[35] *blent* mingled.   [37] *rude* unlearned, inexperienced, as well as impolite.
[36] *lists* chooses.

Still use our bodies ill;
Bafflers of our own prayers, from youth to life's last scenes.

We would have inward peace,   410
Yet will not look within;
We would have misery cease,
Yet will not cease from sin;
We want all pleasant ends, but will use no harsh means;

We do not what we ought,   415
What we ought not, we do,
And lean upon the thought
That chance will bring us through;
But our own acts, for good or ill, are mightier powers.

Yet, even when man forsakes   420
All sin, – is just, is pure,
Abandons all which makes
His welfare insecure, –
Other existences there are, that clash with ours.

Like us, the lightning-fires   425
Love to have scope and play;
The stream, like us, desires
An unimpeded way;
Like us, the Libyan wind delights to roam at large.

Streams[38] will not curb their pride   430
The just man not to entomb,
Nor lightnings go aside
To give his virtues room;
Nor is that wind less rough which blows a good man's barge.

Nature, with equal mind,   435
Sees all her sons at play;
Sees man control the wind,
The wind sweep man away;
Allows the proudly-riding and the foundering bark.[39]

And, lastly, though of ours   440
No weakness spoil our lot,
Though the non-human powers
Of Nature harm us not,
The ill deeds of other men make often *our* life dark.

What were the wise man's plan?   445
Through this sharp, toil-set life,
To work as best he can,
And win what's won by strife.
But we an easier way to cheat our pains have found.

Scratched by a fall, with moans   450
As children of weak age

---

[38] *Streams* of mud or lava.   [39] *bark* small boat.

Lend life to the dumb stones
Whereon to vent their rage,
And bend their little fists, and rate[40] the senseless ground;

So, loath to suffer mute,   455
We, peopling the void air,
Make Gods to whom to impute
The ills we ought to bear;[41]
With God and Fate to rail at, suffering easily.

Yet grant – as sense long missed   460
Things that are now perceived,
And much may still exist
Which is not yet believed –
Grant that the world were full of Gods we cannot see;

All things the world which fill   465
Of but one stuff are spun,
That we who rail are still,
With what we rail at, one;
One with the o'erlaboured Power that through the breadth and length

Of earth, and air, and sea,   470
In men, and plants, and stones,
Hath toil perpetually,
And travails, pants, and moans;
Fain would do all things well, but sometimes fails in strength.

And patiently exact   475
This universal God
Alike to any act
Proceeds at any nod,
And quietly declaims the cursings of himself.

This is not what man hates,   480
Yet he can curse but this.
Harsh Gods and hostile Fates
Are dreams! this only *is*[42] –
Is everywhere; sustains the wise, the foolish elf.

Nor only, in the intent   485
To attach blame elsewhere,
Do we at will invent
Stern Powers who make their care
To embitter human life, malignant Deities;

But, next, we would reverse   490
The scheme ourselves have spun,
And what we made to curse
We now would lean upon,
And feign[43] kind Gods who perfect what man vainly tries.

[40] *rate* berate.
[41] *So, loath . . . bear* cf. the ideas of Feuerbach discussed in
the headnote to Browning's 'Caliban upon Setebos', 207.
[42] *this only is* the life that we know is all there is.
[43] *feign* invent.

Look, the world tempts our eye,   495
And we would know it all!
We map the starry sky,
We mine this earthen ball,
We measure the sea-tides, we number the sea-sands;

We scrutinise the dates   500
Of long-past human things,
The bounds of effaced states,
The lines of deceased kings;
We search out dead men's words, and works of dead men's hands;

We shut our eyes, and muse   505
How our own minds are made,
What springs of thought they use,
How rightened, how betrayed –
And spend our wit to name what most employ unnamed.

But still, as we proceed   510
The mass swells more and more
Of volumes yet to read,
Of secrets yet to explore.
Our hair grows grey, our eyes are dimmed, our heat is tamed;

We rest our faculties,   515
And thus address the Gods:
'True science if there is,
It stays in your abodes!
Man's measures cannot mete[44] the immeasurable All.

'You only can take in   520
The world's immense design.
Our desperate search was sin,
Which henceforth we resign,
Sure only that your mind sees all things which befall.'

Fools! That in man's brief term   525
He cannot all things view,
Affords no ground to affirm
That there are Gods who do;
Nor does being weary prove that he has where to rest.

Again. Our youthful blood   530
Claims rapture as its right;
The world, a rolling flood
Of newness and delight,
Draws in the enamoured gazer to its shining breast;

Pleasure, to our hot grasp,   535
Gives flowers after flowers;
With passionate warmth we clasp
Hand after hand in ours;
Now do we soon perceive how fast our youth is spent.

---

[44] *mete* ascertain the dimensions of.

At once our eyes grow clear!   540
We see, in blank dismay,
Year posting after year,
Sense after sense decay;
Our shivering heart is mined by secret discontent;

Yet still, in spite of truth,   545
In spite of hopes entombed,
That longing of our youth
Burns ever unconsumed,
Still hungrier for delight as delights grow more rare.

We pause; we hush our heart,   550
And thus address the Gods:
'The world hath failed to impart
The joy our youth forebodes,
Failed to fill up the void which in our breasts we bear.

'Changeful till now, we still   555
Looked on to something new;
Let us, with changeless will,
Henceforth look on to you,
To find with you the joy we in vain here require!'

Fools! That so often here   560
Happiness mocked our prayer,
I think, might make us fear
A like event elsewhere;
Make us, not fly to dreams, but moderate desire.

And yet, for those who know   565
Themselves, who wisely take
Their way through life, and bow
To what they cannot break,
Why should I say that life need yield but *moderate* bliss?

Shall we, with temper spoiled,   570
Health sapped by living ill,
And judgment all embroiled
By sadness and self-will,
Shall *we* judge what for man is not true bliss or is?

Is it so small a thing   575
To have enjoyed the sun,
To have lived light in the spring,
To have loved, to have thought, to have done;
To have advanced true friends, and beat down baffling foes –

That we must feign a bliss   580
Of doubtful future date,
And, while we dream on this,
Lose all our present state,
And relegate to worlds yet distant our repose?

Not much, I know, you prize   585
What pleasures may be had,
Who look on life with eyes
Estranged, like mine, and sad;
And yet the village-churl[45] feels the truth more than you,

Who's loth to leave this life   590
Which to him little yields –
His hard-tasked sunburnt wife,
His often-laboured fields,
The boors[46] with whom he talked, the country-spots he knew.

But thou, because thou hear'st   595
Men scoff at Heaven and Fate,
Because the Gods thou fear'st
Fail to make blest thy state,
Tremblest, and wilt not dare to trust the joys there are!

I say: Fear not! Life still   600
Leaves human effort scope.
But, since life teems with ill,
Nurse no extravagant hope;
Because thou must not dream, thou need'st not then despair!

A long pause. At the end of it the notes of a harp below
are again heard, and Callicles sings: –

Far, far from here,   605
The Adriatic[47] breaks in a warm bay
Among the green Illyrian[48] hills; and there
The sunshine in the happy glens is fair,
And by the sea, and in the brakes.[49]
The grass is cool, the sea-side air   610
Buoyant and fresh, the mountain flowers
More virginal and sweet than ours.
And there, they say, two bright and aged snakes,
Who once were Cadmus[50] and Harmonia,[51]
Bask in the glens or on the warm sea-shore,   615
In breathless quiet, after all their ills;[52]
Nor do they see their country,[53] nor the place
Where the Sphinx[54] lived among the frowning hills,
Nor the unhappy palace of their race,
Nor Thebes, nor the Ismenus,[55] any more.   620
There those two live, far in the Illyrian brakes!

---

[45] *village-churl* ordinary villager.
[46] *boors* peasants.
[47] *Adriatic* sea between the east coast of Italy and the west coasts of Croatia, Montenegro, etc.
[48] *Illyrian* of Illyria, ancient name for the Balkan territories on the Adriatic coast.
[49] *brakes* undergrowth.
[50] *Cadmus* legendary founder of the city of Thebes.
[51] *Harmonia* bride of Cadmus, daughter of the gods Ares and Aphrodite. After an anguished period of marriage, she

and her husband were mercifully turned into snakes and allowed to live forever in Elysium. Arnold, however, associates them with Illyria.
[52] *their ills* see note 56.
[53] *country* that around Thebes.
[54] *Sphinx* Thebes had the most famous Sphinx – a deadly creature with the head of a woman, body of a lion and wings of a bird, possessed of a riddle that Oedipus finally answered – who lived on Mount Thikion, outside the city.
[55] *Ismenus* river running through Thebes.

They had stayed long enough to see,
In Thebes, the billow of calamity
Over their own dear children rolled,
Curse upon curse, pang upon pang,[56]
For years, they sitting helpless in their home,   625
A grey old man and woman; yet of old
The Gods had to their marriage come,[57]
And at the banquet all the Muses[58] sang.

Therefore they did not end their days
In sight of blood; but were rapt, far away,   630
To where the west-wind plays,
And murmurs of the Adriatic come
To those untrodden mountain-lawns; and there
Placed safely in changed forms, the pair
Wholly forget their first sad life, and home,   635
And all that Theban woe, and stray
For ever through the glens, placid and dumb.

Empedocles.

That was my harp-player again! – where is he?
Down by the stream?
                                                                   640

Pausanias.

Yes, Master, in the wood.

Empedocles.

He ever loved the Theban story well!
But the day wears. Go now, Pausanias,
For I must be alone. Leave me one mule;
Take down with thee the rest to Catana.
And for young Callicles, thank him from me;   645
Tell him, I never failed to love his lyre –
But he must follow me no more to-night.

Pausanias.

Thou wilt return to-morrow to the city?

Empedocles.

Either to-morrow or some other day,
In the sure revolutions of the world,   650
Good friend, I shall revisit Catana.
I have seen many cities in my time,
Till mine eyes ache with the long spectacle,
And I shall doubtless see them all again;
Thou know'st me for a wanderer from of old.   655
Meanwhile, stay me not now. Farewell, Pausanias!

---

[56] *curse . . . pang* Cadmus and Harmonia had four daughters (Autonoe, Ino, Semele and Agave) and a son (Polydorus). Semele was killed by Zeus's thunderbolt; Ino went mad, killing her child then herself; Autonoe's son was torn to pieces by hounds; Agave's son, Pentheus, was ripped apart by worshippers of Dionysius, including Agave.

[57] *Gods . . . come* the gods attended the wedding as it was the union of a mortal with divinity.
[58] *Muses* divinities associated with the arts, thought and writing, on whom mortals relied for inspiration.

He departs on his way up the mountain.

Pausanias. (*alone*).

I dare not urge him further – he must go;
But he is strangely wrought! I will speed back
And bring Peisianax to him from the city; 660
His counsel could once soothe him. But, Apollo![59]
How his brow lightened as the music rose!
Callicles must wait here, and play to him;
I saw him through the chestnuts far below,
Just since, down at the stream. – Ho! Callicles! 665

He descends, calling.

* * *

ACT 2.

Evening. The Summit of Etna.

Empedocles.

Alone! –
On this charred, blackened, melancholy waste,
Crowned by the awful peak, Etna's great mouth,
Round which the sullen vapour rolls – alone!
Pausanias is far hence, and that is well, 670
For I must henceforth speak no more with man.
He hath his lesson too, and that debt's paid;
And the good, learned, friendly, quiet man,
May bravelier front his life, and in himself
Find henceforth energy and heart. But I – 675
The weary man, the banished citizen,
Whose banishment is not his greatest ill,
Whose weariness no energy can reach,
And for whose hurt courage is not the cure –
What should I do with life and living more? 680

No, thou art come too late, Empedocles![60]
And the world hath the day, and must break thee,
Not thou the world. With men thou canst not live,
Their thoughts, their ways, their wishes, are not thine;
And being lonely thou art miserable, 685
For something has impaired thy spirit's strength,
And dried its self-sufficing fount of joy.
Thou canst not live with men nor with thyself –
O sage! O sage! – Take then the one way left;
And turn thee to the elements, thy friends, 690
Thy well-tried friends, thy willing ministers,
And say: Ye helpers, hear Empedocles,
Who asks this final service at your hands!
Before the sophist-brood hath overlaid

---

[59] *Apollo* god of prophecy, patron of the arts, leader of the Muses.

[60] *too late, Empedocles!* cf. Empedocles's views of Strife in the headnote, 268.

The last spark of man's consciousness with words –   695
Ere quite the being of man, ere quite the world
Be disarrayed of their divinity[61] –
Before the soul lose all her solemn joys,
And awe be dead, and hope impossible,
And the soul's deep eternal night come on –   700
Receive me, hide me, quench me, take me home!

*He advances to the edge of the crater. Smoke and fire break forth with a loud noise, and
Callicles is heard below singing: –*

The lyre's voice is lovely everywhere;
In the court of Gods, in the city of men,
And in the lonely rock-strewn mountain-glen,
In the still mountain air.   705

Only to Typho[62] it sounds hatefully;
To Typho only, the rebel o'erthrown,
Through whose heart Etna drives her roots of stone,
To imbed them in the sea.

Wherefore dost thou groan so loud?   710
Wherefore do thy nostrils flash,
Through the dark night, suddenly,
Typho, such red jets of flame?[63]
Is thy tortured heart still proud?
Is thy fire-scathed arm still rash?   715
Still alert thy stone-crushed frame?
Doth thy fierce soul still deplore
Thine ancient rout by the Cilician hills,[64]
And that curst treachery on the Mount of Gore?[65]
Do thy bloodshot eyes still weep   720
The fight which crowned thine ills,
Thy last mischance on this Sicilian deep?
Hast thou sworn, in thy sad lair,
Where erst the strong sea-currents sucked thee down,
Never to cease to writhe, and try to rest,   725
Letting the sea-stream wander through thy hair?
That thy groans, like thunder prest,
Begin to roll, and almost drown
The sweet notes whose lulling spell
Gods and the race of mortals love so well,   730
When through thy caves thou hearest music swell?
But an awful pleasure bland
Spreading o'er the Thunderer's[66] face,
When the sound climbs near his seat,

---

[61] *divinity* wonder.
[62] *Typho* Typhon was a great monster, composed partly of snakes, who was the last challenger to the power of Zeus. Zeus pursued him, hurling Mount Etna at him and burying him beneath it.
[63] *flame* snakes on Typhon's body had eyes that flashed fire.
[64] *Cicilian hills* Typhon was born in the Corycian cave in Cilicia, north of Cyprus. In one version of the story, he was routed by Zeus there and flung into the lowest region of the underworld.
[65] *Mount of Gore* as he was pursued by Zeus, in some versions of the story, Typhon threw whole mountains at him. One of these bounced back and wounded Typhon: it was named Mount Haemus from being stained with his blood (Greek *haima*).
[66] *Thunderer* Zeus, king of the gods.

735

The Olympian[67] council sees;
As he lets his lax right hand,
Which the lightnings doth embrace,[68]
Sink upon his mighty knees.
And the eagle,[69] at the beck
Of the appeasing, gracious harmony,
Droops all his sheeny, brown, deep-feathered neck,
Nestling nearer to Jove's[70] feet;
While o'er his sovran eye
The curtains of the blue films slowly meet.[71]
And the white Olympus-peaks
Rosily brighten, and the soothed Gods smile
At one another from their golden chairs,
And no one round the charmed circle speaks.
Only the loved Hebe[72] bears
The cup about, whose draughts beguile
Pain and care, with a dark store
Of fresh-pulled violets wreathed and nodding o'er;
And her flushed feet glow on the marble floor.

Empedocles.

He fables, yet speaks truth!
The brave, impetuous heart yields everywhere
To the subtle, contriving head;
Great qualities are trodden down,
And littleness united
Is become invincible.
These rumblings are not Typho's groans, I know!
These angry smoke-bursts
Are not the passionate breath
Of the mountain-crushed, tortured, intractable Titan[73] king –
But over all the world
What suffering is there not seen
Of plainness oppressed by cunning,
As the well-counselled Zeus oppressed
That self-helping son of earth![74]
What anguish of greatness,
Railed and hunted from the world,
Because its simplicity rebukes
This envious, miserable age!

I am weary of it.
– Lie there, ye ensigns[75]
Of my unloved preëminence
In an age like this!

740 745 750 755 760 765 770 775

---

[67] *Olympian* the gods dwelt on Mount Olympus.
[68] *lightnings doth embrace* Zeus's weapon was the thunderbolt.
[69] *eagle* Zeus was accompanied by an eagle, symbol of his power.
[70] *Jove* Zeus.
[71] *curtains . . . meet* dawn.
[72] *Hebe* goddess of Youth, cupbearer for the other gods on Olympus.
[73] *Titan* older generation of gods, overthrown by the Olympians.
[74] *earth* Typhon was the son of Gaia, the earth. The dispirited Empedocles feels some sympathy for the crushed Typhon. See note 64.
[75] *ensigns* clothes and symbols of his authority.

Among a people of children,
Who thronged me in their cities,
Who worshipped me in their houses,
And asked, not wisdom,   780
But drugs to charm with,
But spells to mutter –
All the fool's-armoury of magic! Lie there,
My golden circlet,
My purple robe!   785

Callicles. (*from below*).
As the sky-brightening south-wind clears the day,
And makes the massed clouds roll,
The music of the lyre blows away
The clouds which wrap the soul.
Oh! that Fate had let me see   790
That triumph of the sweet persuasive lyre,
That famous, final victory,
When jealous Pan with Marsyas did conspire;[76]

When, from far Parnassus'[77] side,
Young Apollo, all the pride   795
Of the Phrygian[78] flutes to tame,
To the Phrygian highlands came;
Where the long green reed-beds sway
In the rippled waters grey
Of that solitary lake   800
Where Mæander's[79] springs are born;
Whence the ridged pine-wooded roots
Of Messogis[80] westward break,
Mounting westward, high and higher.
There was held the famous strife;   805
There the Phrygian brought his flutes,
And Apollo brought his lyre;
And, when now the westering sun
Touched the hills, the strife was done,
And the attentive Muses said: 810
'Marsyas, thou art vanquished!'
Then Apollo's minister
Hanged upon a branching fir
Marsyas, that unhappy Faun,[81]
And began to whet his knife.   815
But the Mænads,[82] who were there,
Left their friend, and with robes flowing
In the wind, and loose dark hair
O'er their polished bosoms blowing,
Each her ribboned tambourine   820
Flinging on the mountain-sod,

[76] *jealous . . . conspire* Marsyas was a Phrygian Satyr who played the pipes so well (hence the pipe-playing Pan's jealousy) that he challenged Apollo. Apollo, playing his lyre, won unfairly and had Marsyas hung on a pine tree and flayed alive.
[77] *Parnassus* mountain home of Apollo and the Muses.
[78] *Phrygian* of Phrygia, country in Asia Minor.
[79] *Mæander* river flowing from Phrygia into the Aegean.
[80] *Messogis* mountain in the valley of the Mæander.
[81] *Faun* a Satyr, half man and half goat.
[82] *Mænads* 'frenzied women', they followed Dionysius, god of wine and intoxication, and danced wildly at his rites.

With a lovely frightened mien[83]
Came about the youthful God.[84]
But he turned his beauteous face
    Haughtily another way,   825
From the grassy sun-warmed place
    Where in proud repose he lay,
    With one arm over his head,
    Watching how the whetting sped.

    But aloof, on the lake-strand,   830
    Did the young Olympus[85] stand,
        Weeping at his master's end;
For the Faun had been his friend.
For he taught him how to sing,
And he taught him flute-playing.   835
Many a morning had they gone
To the glimmering mountain-lakes,
    And had torn up by the roots
    The tall crested water-reeds
With long plumes and soft brown seeds, 840
    And had carved them into flutes,
        Sitting on a tabled stone
Where the shoreward ripple breaks.
And he taught him how to please
The red-snooded[86] Phrygian girls,   845
    Whom the summer evening sees
    Flashing in the dance's whirls
    Underneath the starlit trees
        In the mountain-villages.
Therefore now Olympus stands,   850
    At his master's piteous cries
Pressing fast with both his hands
    His white garment to his eyes,
    Not to see Apollo's scorn; –
Ah, poor Faun, poor Faun! ah, poor Faun! 855

Empedocles.

And lie thou there,
    My laurel bough!
Scornful Apollo's ensign,[87] lie thou there!
Though thou hast been my shade in the world's heat –
Though I have loved thee, lived in honouring thee – 860
    Yet lie thou there,
    My laurel bough!
I am weary of thee.
I am weary of the solitude
Where he who bears thee must abide –   865
    Of the rocks of Parnassus,

---

[83] *mien* air, bearing or manner of a person.
[84] *God* Apollo.
[85] *Olympus* pupil of Marsyas.

[86] *snooded* with a band or ribbon confining the hair.
[87] *laurel . . . ensign* the wreath of laurels is a sign of Apollo's supremacy as a musician and his leadership of the Muses.

Of the gorge of Delphi,[88]
Of the moonlit peaks, and the caves.
Thou guardest them, Apollo!
Over the grave of the slain Pytho,[89]   870
Though young, intolerably severe!
Thou keepest aloof the profane,
But the solitude oppresses thy votary![90]
The jars of men reach him not in thy valley –
But can life reach him?   875
Thou fencest him from the multitude –
Who will fence him from himself?
He hears nothing but the cry of the torrents,
And the beating of his own heart.
The air is thin, the veins swell,   880
The temples tighten and throb there –
Air! air!

Take thy bough, set me free from my solitude;
I have been enough alone!

Where shall thy votary fly then? back to men? –   885
But they will gladly welcome him once more,
And help him to unbend his too tense thought,
And rid him of the presence of himself,
And keep their friendly chatter at his ear,
And haunt him, till the absence from himself,   890
That other torment, grow unbearable;
And he will fly to solitude again,
And he will find its air too keen for him,
And so change back; and many thousand times
Be miserably bandied to and fro   895
Like a sea-wave, betwixt the world and thee,
Thou young, implacable God![91] and only death
Can cut his oscillations short, and so
Bring him to poise. There is no other way.

And yet what days were those, Parmenides!   900
When we were young, when we could number friends
In all the Italian cities like ourselves,
When with elated hearts we joined your train,
Ye Sun-born Virgins! on the road of truth.[92]
Then we could still enjoy, then neither thought   905
Nor outward things were closed and dead to us;
But we received the shock of mighty thoughts
On simple minds with a pure natural joy;
And if the sacred load oppressed our brain,
We had the power to feel the pressure eased,   910
The brow unbound, the thoughts flow free again,

---

[88] *Delphi* on the southern slopes of Mount Parnassus, Delphi was the home of the Delphic oracle, the most important of the ancient oracles, dedicated to Apollo.
[89] *Pytho* Python was the monstrous she-dragon who originally lived at Delphi before the coming of Apollo.
[90] *votary* follower.

[91] *young, implacable God* Apollo was always represented as a type of youthful male beauty. He was also implacable: he punished slights violently, as the story of Marsyas shows.
[92] *Sun-born . . . truth* cf. Parmenides, *Karsten*, 1.2.28: 'The maidens of the sun, leaving the halls of night, led the way to the light.'

In the delightful commerce of the world.
We had not lost our balance then, nor grown
Thought's slaves, and dead to every natural joy.
The smallest thing could give us pleasure then[93] –   915
    The sports of the country-people,
    A flute-note from the woods,
        Sunset over the sea;
        Seed-time and harvest,
        The reapers in the corn,   920
    The vinedresser in his vineyard,
    The village-girl at her wheel.

    Fulness of life and power of feeling, ye
    Are for the happy, for the souls at ease,
    Who dwell on a firm basis of content!   925
But he, who has outlived his prosperous days –
But he, whose youth fell on a different world
From that on which his exiled age is thrown –
Whose mind was fed on other food, was trained
    By other rules than are in vogue to-day –   930
Whose habit of thought is fixed, who will not change,
    But, in a world he loves not, must subsist
    In ceaseless opposition, be the guard
Of his own breast, fettered to what he guards,
    That the world win no mastery over him –   935
Who has no friend, no fellow left, not one;
Who has no minute's breathing space allowed
    To nurse his dwindling faculty of joy –
Joy and the outward world must die to him,
        As they are dead to me.   940

A long pause, during which Empedocles remains motionless,
plunged in thought. The night deepens.
He moves forward and gazes round him, and proceeds: –

        And you, ye stars,
    Who slowly begin to marshal,
    As of old, in the fields of heaven,
        Your distant, melancholy lines!
    Have you, too, survived yourselves?   945
    Are you, too, what I fear to become?
        You, too, once lived;
        You too moved joyfully
        Among august companions,
    In an older world, peopled by Gods,   950
        In a mightier order,
The radiant, rejoicing, intelligent Sons of Heaven.
        But now, ye kindle
    Your lonely, cold-shining lights,
        Unwilling lingerers   955
    In the heavenly wilderness,
    For a younger, ignoble world;

---

[93] *smallest . . . then* cf. Act 1, ll. 575–9.

And renew, by necessity,
Night after night your courses,
In echoing, unneared silence,   960
Above a race you know not –
Uncaring and undelighted,
Without friend and without home;
Weary like us, though not
Weary with our weariness.   965

No, no, ye stars! there is no death with you,
No languor, no decay! languor and death,
They are with me, not you! ye are alive –
Ye, and the pure dark ether[94] where ye ride
Brilliant above me! And thou, fiery world,   970
That sapp'st the vitals of this terrible mount
Upon whose charred and quaking crust I stand –
Thou, too, brimmest with life! – the sea of cloud,
That heaves its white and billowy vapours up
To moat this isle of ashes from the world,   975
Lives; and that other fainter sea, far down,
O'er whose lit floor a road of moonbeams leads
To Etna's Liparëan[95] sister-fires
And the long dusky line of Italy[96] –
That mild and luminous floor of waters lives,   980
With held-in joy swelling its heart; I only,
Whose spring of hope is dried, whose spirit has failed,
I, who have not, like these, in solitude
Maintained courage and force, and in myself
Nursed an immortal vigour – I alone   985
Am dead to life and joy, therefore I read
In all things my own deadness.

A long silence. He continues: –

Oh, that I could glow like this mountain!
Oh, that my heart bounded with the swell of the sea!
Oh, that my soul were full of light as the stars!   990
Oh, that it brooded over the world like the air!

But no, this heart will glow no more; thou art
A living man no more, Empedocles!
Nothing but a devouring flame of thought –
But a naked, eternally restless mind!   995

After a pause: –

To the elements it came from
Everything will return –
Our bodies to earth,
Our blood to water,
Heat to fire,   1000

---

[94] *ether* clear sky beyond the clouds.
[95] *Liparëan* of Lipari, island off the Sicilian coast due north
of Etna, notable for its volcanoes.
[96] *long . . . Italy* visible parts of the eastern coast of Italy.

Breath to air.
They were well born, they will be well entombed –
But mind? . . .

And we might gladly share the fruitful stir
Down in our mother earth's miraculous womb;   1005
Well would it be
With what rolled of us in the stormy main;
We might have joy, blent with the all-bathing air,
Or with the nimble, radiant life of fire.

But mind, but thought –   1010
If these have been the master part of us –
Where will *they* find their parent element?
What will receive *them*, who will call *them* home?
But we shall still be in them, and they in us,
And we shall be the strangers of the world,   1015
And they will be our lords, as they are now;
And keep us prisoners of our consciousness,
And never let us clasp and feel the All
But through their forms, and modes, and stifling veils.
And we shall be unsatisfied as now;   1020
And we shall feel the agony of thirst,
The ineffable[97] longing for the life of life
Baffled for ever; and still thought and mind
Will hurry us with them on their homeless march,
Over the unallied unopening earth,   1025
Over the unrecognising sea; while air
Will blow us fiercely back to sea and earth,
And fire repel us from its living waves.
And then we shall unwillingly return
Back to this meadow of calamity,[98]   1030
This uncongenial place, this human life;
And in our individual human state
Go through the sad probation all again,
To see if we will poise our life at last,
To see if we will now at last be true   1035
To our own only true, deep-buried selves,
Being one with which we are one with the whole world;
Or whether we will once more fall away
Into some bondage of the flesh or mind,
Some slough[99] of sense, or some fantastic maze   1040
Forged by the imperious lonely thinking-power.
And each succeeding age in which we are born
Will have more peril for us than the last;
Will goad our senses with a sharper spur,
Will fret our minds to an intenser play,   1045
Will make ourselves harder to be discerned.
And we shall struggle awhile, gasp and rebel –
And we shall fly for refuge to past times,
Their soul of unworn youth, their breath of greatness;

[97] *ineffable* too great for words.
[98] *return . . . calamity* reference to the doctrine of reincarnation.
[99] *slough* bog or mire.

And the reality will pluck us back,   1050
Knead us in its hot hand, and change our nature.
And we shall feel our powers of effort flag,
And rally them for one last fight – and fail;
And we shall sink in the impossible strife,
            And be astray for ever.   1055

            Slave of sense
I have in no wise been; – but slave of thought? . . .
And who can say: I have been always free,
Lived ever in the light of my own soul? –
I cannot; I have lived in wrath and gloom,   1060
Fierce, disputatious, ever at war with man,
Far from my own soul, far from warmth and light.
But I have not grown easy in these bonds –
But I have not denied what bonds these were.
            Yea, I take myself to witness,   1065
            That I have loved no darkness,
            Sophisticated no truth,[100]
            Nursed no delusion,
            Allowed no fear!

And therefore, O ye elements! I know –   1070
Ye know it too – it hath been granted me
Not to die wholly, not to be all enslaved.
I feel it in this hour. The numbing cloud
Mounts off my soul; I feel it, I breathe free.

            Is it but for a moment?   1075
            – Ah, boil up, ye vapours!
            Leap and roar, thou sea of fire!
            My soul glows to meet you.
            Ere it flag, ere the mists
            Of despondency and gloom   1080
            Rush over it again,
            Receive me, save me!

He plunges into the crater.

Callicles (*from below*).
Through the black, rushing smoke-bursts,
Thick breaks the red flame;
            All Etna heaves fiercely   1085
            Her forest-clothed frame.
            Not here, O Apollo!
            Are haunts meet for thee.
But, where Helicon[101] breaks down
            In cliff to the sea,   1090

Where the moon-silvered inlets
Send far their light voice

---

[100] *Sophisticated no truth* not constructed as an intellectual truth something false.

[101] *Helicon* mountain in Boeotia, north of the Gulf of Corinth in Greece, a favourite haunt of the Muses.

Up the still vale of Thisbe,[102]
O speed, and rejoice!

On the sward at the cliff-top   1095
Lie strewn the white flocks,
On the cliff-side the pigeons
Roost deep in the rocks.

In the moonlight the shepherds,
Soft lulled by the rills,   1100
Lie wrapt in their blankets
Asleep on the hills.

– What forms are these coming
So white through the gloom?
What garments out-glistening   1105
The gold-flowered broom?[103]

What sweet-breathing presence
Out-perfumes the thyme?
What voices enrapture
The night's balmy prime?   1110

'Tis Apollo comes leading
His choir, the Nine.[104]
– The leader is fairest,
But all are divine.

They are lost in the hollows!   1115
They stream up again!
What seeks on this mountain
The glorified train? –

They bathe on this mountain,
In the spring by their road;   1120
Then on to Olympus,
Their endless abode.

– Whose praise do they mention?
Of what is it told?
What will be for ever;   1125
What was from of old.

First hymn they the Father
Of all things; and then,
The rest of immortals,
The action of men.   1130

The day in his hotness,
The strife with the palm;
The night in her silence,
The stars in their calm.

---

[102] *Thisbe* town between Helicon and the Gulf of Corinth.   [104] *Nine* the Muses.
[103] *broom* common shrub with large yellow flowers.

✕ The Buried Life

Matthew Arnold's 'To Marguerite – Continued', 267–8, brooded gloomily on human isolation, using the context of sexual desire (the poet's love for Marguerite) to figure a universalized condition of solitariness. But 'The Buried Life' (written *c.*1849–52, published 1852) is more optimistic about what human connection can achieve and it identifies sexual love – of a domesticated form – as a potential alternative to the alienating experience of the contemporary. The poem does not celebrate human love as something that bonds two people together against the swirling uncertainties of the world, as is momentarily suggested in 'Dover Beach', 312–13. Love's value is not social here but individual for it facilitates – or rather, occasionally has the possibility of facilitating – self-knowledge. Domestic relations may allow a sense of calm and certainty amid the 'thousand nothings of the hour'. Arnold's Scholar-Gipsy – see 298–305 – possessed a unitary desire and singleness of purpose; in this poem,

the presence of the beloved allows, in those precious moments, an individual to sense his own identity and purposes, or at least to *think* he does (see ll. 96–8). If Thomas Carlyle had defined labour as the route to a man's salvation, 'The Buried Life' continues Arnold's resistance to Carlylean diagnosis – cf. 'A Summer Night', 264–7 – by constructing human life as a search for *rest*. The monologue maps mental turmoil and emotional predicament, characteristically resisting precise definition in preference for the representation of a more nebulous state, a 'nameless sadness' that is the sensation of the displaced intellectual. Diction and syntax imitate the spoken, catching the changing pace and mood of the poet's reflections in a movement towards a glowing climax that finds in poetic exultation, if in nothing else, a state of mind that transcends the 'war of mocking words'.

Text: *Empedocles on Etna, and Other Poems* (1852).

Light flows our war of mocking words, and yet,
Behold, with tears mine eyes are wet!
I feel a nameless sadness o'er me roll.
    Yes, yes, we know that we can jest,
    We know, we know that we can smile!   5
    But there's a something in this breast,
    To which thy light words bring no rest,
    And thy gay smiles no anodyne.[1]
    Give me thy hand, and hush awhile,
    And turn those limpid[2] eyes on mine,   10
And let me read there, love! thy inmost soul.

    Alas! is even love too weak
    To unlock the heart, and let it speak?
    Are even lovers powerless to reveal
    To one another what indeed they feel?   15
    I knew the mass of men concealed
    Their thoughts, for fear that if revealed
    They would by other men be met
With blank indifference, or with blame reproved;
    I knew they lived and moved   20
    Trick'd in disguises, alien to the rest
Of men, and alien to themselves – and yet
The same heart beats in every human breast!

But we, my love! – doth a like spell benumb
Our hearts, our voices? must we too be dumb?   25

---

[1] *anodyne* medicine to relieve pain.   [2] *limpid* clear.

Ah! well for us, if even we,
Even for a moment, can get free
Our heart, and have our lips unchained;
For that which seals them hath been deep-ordained![3]

Fate, which foresaw   30
How frivolous a baby man would be –
By what distractions he would be possessed,
How he would pour himself in every strife,
And well-nigh change his own identity –
That it might keep from his capricious play   35
His genuine self, and force him to obey

Even in his own despite his being's law,
Bade through the deep recesses of our breast
The unregarded river of our life
Pursue with indiscernible flow its way;   40
And that we should not see
The buried stream, and seem to be
Eddying at large in blind uncertainty,
Though driving on with it eternally.

But often, in the world's most crowded streets,   45
But often, in the din of strife,
There rises an unspeakable desire
After the knowledge of our buried life;
A thirst to spend our fire and restless force[4]
In tracking out our true, original course;   50

A longing to inquire
Into the mystery of this heart which beats
So wild, so deep in us – to know
Whence our lives come and where they go.
And many a man in his own breast then delves,   55
But deep enough, alas! none ever mines.
And we have been on many thousand lines,
And we have shown, on each, spirit and power;
But hardly have we, for one little hour,
Been on our own line, have we been ourselves –   60
Hardly had skill to utter one of all
The nameless feelings that course through our breast,
But they course on for ever unexpressed.
And long we try in vain to speak and act
Our hidden self, and what we say and do   65
Is eloquent, is well – but 'tis not true!
And then we will no more be racked
With inward striving, and demand
Of all the thousand nothings of the hour
Their stupefying power;   70
Ah yes, and they benumb us at our call!
Yet still, from time to time, vague and forlorn,
From the soul's subterranean depth upborne

---

[3] *For that . . . deep-ordained* cf. Arnold's 'To Marguerite –   [4] *force* energy.
Continued', 267–8, ll. 22–4.

As from an infinitely distant land,
Come airs, and floating echoes, and convey   75
A melancholy into all our day.
Only – but this is rare –
When a belovèd hand is laid in ours,
When, jaded with the rush and glare
Of the interminable hours,   80
Our eyes can in another's eyes read clear,
When our world-deafened ear
Is by the tones of a loved voice caressed –
A bolt is shot back somewhere in our breast,
And a lost pulse of feeling stirs again.   85
The eye sinks inward, and the heart lies plain,
And what we mean, we say, and what we would, we know.
A man becomes aware of his life's flow,
And hears its winding murmur; and he sees
The meadows where it glides, the sun, the breeze.   90
And there arrives a lull in the hot race
Wherein he doth for ever chase
That flying and elusive shadow, rest.
An air of coolness plays upon his face,
And an unwonted[5] calm pervades his breast.   95
And then he thinks he knows
The hills where his life rose,
And the sea where it goes.

[5] *unwonted* unaccustomed.

✗ The Scholar-Gipsy

Echo to Keats Ode to Nightingale

Matthew Arnold found in autobiography, in a parody of the spiritual journey, and in ventriloquization through the voice of an ancient Greek philosopher, distinctive poetic modes for his own cultural diagnosis (see 'Dover Beach', 312–13, 'Stanzas from the Grande Chartreuse', 305–12, and 'Empedocles on Etna', 268–95, respectively). In 'The Scholar-Gipsy', he takes an English folk legend as the starting point for his probing of the uncertainty of the present and scrutiny of a society dislocated from purpose, authority and tranquillity. In 'A Summer Night', 264–7, Arnold had mused on the folly of escaping from the constraints of daily life and the doomed nature of any effort to rebel. 'The Scholar-Gipsy', published first in 1853, takes a different view, celebrating one romantic rebel who does successfully break away from institutional life – Oxford University is both itself and a metaphor of establishment values in the poem – to live on his own terms. Rooted in fondly recalled memories of Oxford and its countryside (Arnold was an undergraduate at Balliol College), the poem places a luminous sense of rural Englishness against a picture of fretful, contemporary life.

Arnold took the outline of his story from Joseph Glanvill's *The Vanity of Dogmatizing: or Confidence in Opinions Manifested in a Discourse of the Shortness and Uncertainty of our Knowledge, and its Causes* (1661), not entirely an inappropriate title for the concerns of the poem. Glanvill tells the story of a young man who 'very lately' left the University of Oxford because he was too poor. Wandering freely, he was at last forced 'to joyn himself to a company of *Vagabond Gypsies*'. Becoming well regarded by them in due course, he learns a power of imagination that allows him to control the conversation of others out of his sight by mental force. He demonstrates this faculty to two of his former University friends, and undertakes, when he has fully learned the gipsies' law, 'to give the world an account of what he had learned'. Arnold's Scholar-Gipsy is not close, it seems, to learning anything, but his spectral presence on its continual quest reminds the reader that it was once possible to live without the divided aims of Victorian society. None the less, the scholar's integrity is of limited use to those actually caught in the present moment. He offers confirmation – such confirmation that a fragile, ghostly figure of the seventeenth century can offer to modernity – that the only thing to do is to escape, if not literally, then into myth and nostalgia. The final image – an epic simile – is revealingly problematic. It is offered in lieu of reconciliation between the Scholar's world and the divided aims of modernity, but it has a life of its own, it becomes a brief independent narrative in its own right, ironically affirming its inability to achieve harmony between the two elements of the text. The unusual stanzaic form, original to Arnold, is influenced by Keats's stanzas for the 'Ode to a Nightingale'.

Text: *Poems* (1853).

Go, for they call you, shepherd, from the hill;
Go, shepherd, and untie the wattled cotes![1]
No longer leave thy wistful flock unfed,
Nor let thy bawling fellows rack their throats,
Nor the cropped herbage shoot another head.   5
But when the fields are still,
And the tired men and dogs all gone to rest,
And only the white sheep are sometimes seen
Cross and recross the strips of moon-blanched green,
Come, shepherd, and again begin the quest!   10

2

Here, where the reaper was at work of late –
In this high field's dark corner, where he leaves
His coat, his basket, and his earthen cruise,[2]
And in the sun all morning binds the sheaves,
Then here, at noon, comes back his stores to use –   15
Here will I sit and wait,
While to my ear from uplands far away
The bleating of the folded flocks is borne,
With distant cries of reapers in the corn –
All the live murmur of a summer's day.   20

3

Screen'd is this nook o'er the high, half-reap'd field,
And here till sun-down, shepherd! will I be.
Through the thick corn the scarlet poppies peep,
And round green roots and yellowing stalks I see
Pale pink convolvulus[3] in tendrils creep;   25
And air-swept lindens[4] yield
Their scent, and rustle down their perfumed showers
Of bloom on the bent grass where I am laid,
And bower me from the August sun with shade;
And the eye travels down to Oxford's towers.   30

4

And near me on the grass lies Glanvil's book[5] –
Come, let me read the oft-read tale again!
The story of the Oxford scholar poor,
Of pregnant[6] parts and quick inventive brain,

---

[1] *wattled cotes* wattling is the interlacing of twigs or branches of trees to form fences and walls; cotes are small constructions for sheltering animals.
[2] *cruise* (cruse) small earthen vessel for liquids.
[3] *convolvulus* bindweed.

[4] *lindens* lime trees.
[5] *Glanvil's book* see headnote, 298.
[6] *pregnant parts* fertile and fruitful mind. Glanvill calls the 'Scholar-Gipsy' 'of very pregnant and ready parts'.

Who, tired of knocking at preferment's door,[7]   35
        One summer-morn forsook
His friends, and went to learn the gipsy-lore,
And roamed the world with that wild brotherhood,
And came, as most men deemed, to little good,
    But came to Oxford and his friends no more.   40

                            5
But once, years after, in the country-lanes,
Two scholars, whom at college erst[8] he knew,
    Met him, and of his way of life enquired;
    Whereat he answered, that the gipsy-crew,
    His mates, had arts to rule as they desired   45
        The workings of men's brains,
And they can bind them to what thoughts they will.
    'And I,' he said, 'the secret of their art,
    When fully learned, will to the world impart;
    But it needs heaven-sent moments for this skill.'   50

                            6
This said, he left them, and returned no more. –
    But rumours hung about the country-side,
    That the lost Scholar long was seen to stray,
Seen by rare glimpses, pensive and tongue-tied,
    In hat of antique shape, and cloak of grey,   55
        The same the gipsies wore.
Shepherds had met him on the Hurst[9] in spring;
At some lone alehouse in the Berkshire[10] moors,
On the warm ingle-bench,[11] the smock-frocked boors[12]
    Had found him seated at their entering,   60

                            7
But, 'mid their drink and clatter, he would fly.
And I myself seem half to know thy looks,
    And put the shepherds, wanderer! on thy trace;
And boys who in lone wheatfields scare the rooks
    I ask if thou hast passed their quiet place;   65
        Or in my boat I lie
Moored to the cool bank in the summer-heats,
'Mid wide grass meadows which the sunshine fills,
And watch the warm, green-muffled Cumner[13] hills,
    And wonder if thou haunt'st their shy retreats.   70

                            8
For most, I know, thou lov'st retired ground!
    Thee at the ferry Oxford riders blithe,
Returning home on summer-nights, have met
Crossing the stripling Thames at Bab-lock-hithe,[14]

[7] *preferment's door* cf. Glanvill: 'yet wanting the encouragement of preferment; was by poverty forc'd to leave his studies [at Oxford]'.
[8] *erst* previously.
[9] *Hurst* Hurst Hill, less than a mile east of Cumnor village, west of Oxford.
[10] *Berkshire* county abutting Oxfordshire.
[11] *ingle-bench* bench beside the fire.
[12] *boors* peasants (not necessarily with a pejorative sense).
[13] *Cumner* (Cumnor) village outside Oxford.
[14] *Bab-lock-hithe* Bablock Hythe, point on the river west of Cumnor; there was a ferry there in the nineteenth century.

Trailing in the cool stream thy fingers wet,   75
    As the punt's[15] rope chops round;
And leaning backward in a pensive dream,
And fostering in thy lap a heap of flowers
Plucked in shy fields and distant Wychwood[16] bowers,
    And thine eyes resting on the moonlit stream.   80

9

And then they land, and thou art seen no more!
    Maidens, who from the distant hamlets come
To dance around the Fyfield[17] elm in May,
Oft through the darkening fields have seen thee roam,
    Or cross a stile into the public way.   85
    Oft thou hast given them store
Of flowers – the frail-leaf'd, white anemony,[18]
Dark bluebells drench'd with dews of summer eves,
And purple orchises[19] with spotted leaves –
    But none hath words she can report of thee.   90

10

And, above Godstow Bridge,[20] when hay-time's here
    In June, and many a scythe in sunshine flames,
Men who through those wide fields of breezy grass
Where black-winged swallows haunt the glittering Thames,
    To bathe in the abandoned lasher[21] pass,   95
    Have often passed thee near
Sitting upon the river bank o'ergrown;
Marked thine outlandish garb, thy figure spare,
Thy dark vague eyes, and soft abstracted air –
    But, when they came from bathing, thou wast gone!   100

11

At some lone homestead in the Cumner hills,
    Where at her open door the housewife darns,
Thou hast been seen, or hanging on a gate
To watch the threshers in the mossy barns.
    Children, who early range these slopes and late   105
    For cresses[22] from the rills,
Have known thee eying, all an April-day,
The springing pastures and the feeding kine;[23]
And marked thee, when the stars come out and shine,
    Through the long dewy grass move slow away.   110

12

In autumn, on the skirts of Bagley Wood[24] –
    Where most the gipsies by the turf-edged way

---

[15] *punt* flat-bottomed river boat powered by levering the river bottom with a long pole, favoured on the Thames.
[16] *Wychwood* ancient wood, south-west of Charlbury in Oxfordshire.
[17] *Fyfield* village south-west of Oxford.
[18] *anemony* (anemone), small field flower.
[19] *orchises* orchids, exotic field flowers.
[20] *Godstow Bridge* crossing the Thames near Wolvercote, just outside Oxford.

[21] *lasher* local word on the Thames meaning the body of water that lashes or rushes over an opening in a barrier or weir.
[22] *cresses* water cress.
[23] *kine* cows.
[24] *Bagley Wood* wood south of Oxford.

Pitch their smoked tents, and every bush you see
With scarlet patches tagg'd and shreds of grey,
Above the forest-ground called Thessaly[25] –   115
The blackbird, picking food,
Sees thee, nor stops his meal, nor fears at all;
So often has he known thee past him stray,
Rapt, twirling in thy hand a withered spray,
And waiting for the spark from heaven to fall.   120

13

And once, in winter, on the causeway chill
Where home through flooded fields foot-travellers go,
Have I not passed thee on the wooden bridge,
Wrapt in thy cloak and battling with the snow,
Thy face tow'rd Hinksey[26] and its wintry ridge?   125
And thou hast climb'd the hill,
And gain'd the white brow of the Cumner range;
Turned once to watch, while thick the snowflakes fall,
The line of festal light in Christ-Church hall[27] –
Then sought thy straw in some sequestered[28] grange.   130

14

But what – I dream! Two hundred years are flown
Since first thy story ran through Oxford halls,
And the grave Glanvil did the tale inscribe
That thou wert wandered from the studious walls
To learn strange arts, and join a gipsy-tribe;   135
And thou from earth art gone
Long since, and in some quiet churchyard laid –
Some country-nook, where o'er thy unknown grave
Tall grasses and white flowering nettles wave,
Under a dark, red-fruited yew-tree's shade.[29]   140

15

– No, no, thou hast not felt the lapse of hours!
For what wears out the life of mortal men?
'Tis that from change to change their being rolls;
'Tis that repeated shocks, again, again,
Exhaust the energy of strongest souls   145
And numb the elastic powers.
Till having used our nerves with bliss and teen,[30]
And tired upon a thousand schemes our wit,
To the just-pausing Genius[31] we remit
Our worn-out life, and are – what we have been.   150

16

Thou hast not lived, why should'st thou perish, so?
Thou hadst *one* aim, *one* business, *one* desire;

---

[25] *Thessaly* unknown. But there are still a number of places in Oxford known by fanciful names – Jericho, Mesopotamia – and this was clearly another, nineteenth-century, studentish nickname, now lost.

[26] *Hinksey* either South or North Hinksey, villages outside the southwestern edge of Oxford.

[27] *Christ-Church hall* the dining hall of Christ Church, large and aristocratic Oxford college.

[28] *sequestered* far removed, set apart.

[29] *yew-tree's shade* yews commonly grow in English churchyards.

[30] *teen* vexation, grief.

[31] *Genius* spirit that presides over each human life.

Else wert thou long since numbered with the dead!
Else hadst thou spent, like other men, thy fire!
    The generations of thy peers are fled,   155
        And we ourselves shall go;
But thou possessest an immortal lot,
And we imagine thee exempt from age
And living as thou liv'st on Glanvil's page,
    Because thou hadst – what we, alas! have not.   160

17

For early didst thou leave the world, with powers
    Fresh, undiverted to the world without,
Firm to their mark, not spent on other things;
Free from the sick fatigue, the languid doubt,
Which much to have tried, in much been baffled, brings.   165
        O life unlike to ours!
Who fluctuate idly without term or scope,
Of whom each strives, nor knows for what he strives,
And each half lives a hundred different lives;
    Who wait like thee, but not, like thee, in hope.   170

18

Thou waitest for the spark from heaven! and we,
    Light half-believers of our casual creeds,[32]
Who never deeply felt, nor clearly willed,
Whose insight never has borne fruit in deeds,
Whose vague resolves never have been fulfilled;   175
        For whom each year we see
Breeds new beginnings, disappointments new;
    Who hesitate and falter life away,
And lose to-morrow the ground won to-day –
    Ah! do not we, wanderer! await it too?   180

19

Yes, we await it! – but it still delays,
And then we suffer! and amongst us one,[33]
Who most has suffer'd, takes dejectedly
His seat upon the intellectual throne;[34]
And all his store of sad experience he   185
    Lays bare of wretched days;[35]
Tells us his misery's birth and growth and signs,
And how the dying spark of hope was fed,
And how the breast was soothed, and how the head,
    And all his hourly varied anodynes.[36]   190

[32] *creeds* beliefs.
[33] *one* sometimes thought to be Goethe, but surely
Tennyson is intended.
[34] *intellectual throne* cf. Tennyson's 'The Palace of Art'
(1832): 'Full oft the riddle of the painful earth /
Flash'd thro' her as she sat alone, / Yet not the less
held she her solemn mirth, / And intellectual
throne.'

[35] *wretched days* cf. Tennyson's *In Memoriam A.H.H.*
(1850), 88–165, about the loss of the poet's friend A. H.
Hallam.
[36] *anodynes* cf. Tennyson's *In Memoriam*: 'But, for the
unquiet heart and brain, / A use in measured language lies;
/ The sad mechanic exercise, / Like dull narcotics,
numbing pain.'

20

This for our wisest! and we others pine,
And wish the long unhappy dream would end,
And waive all claim to bliss, and try to bear;
With close-lipped patience for our only friend,
Sad patience, too near neighbour to despair –   195
But none has hope like thine!
Thou through the fields and through the woods dost stray,
Roaming the country-side, a truant boy,
Nursing thy project in unclouded joy,
And every doubt long blown by time away.   200

21

O born in days when wits were fresh and clear,
And life ran gaily as the sparkling Thames;
Before this strange disease of modern life,
With its sick hurry, its divided aims,
Its heads o'ertaxed, its palsied hearts, was rife –   205
Fly hence, our contact fear!
Still fly, plunge deeper in the bowering wood!
Averse, as Dido[37] did with gesture stern
From her false friend's approach in Hades turn,
Wave us away, and keep thy solitude!   210

22

Still nursing the unconquerable hope,
Still clutching the inviolable shade,
With a free, onward impulse brushing through,
By night, the silvered branches of the glade –
Far on the forest-skirts, where none pursue,   215
On some mild pastoral slope
Emerge, and resting on the moonlit pales
Freshen thy flowers as in former years
With dew, or listen with enchanted ears,
From the dark dingles, to the nightingales!   220

23

But fly our paths, our feverish contact fly!
For strong the infection of our mental strife,
Which, though it gives no bliss, yet spoils for rest;
And we should win thee from thy own fair life,
Like us distracted, and like us unblest.   225
Soon, soon thy cheer would die,
Thy hopes grow timorous,[38] and unfixed thy powers,
And thy clear aims be cross and shifting made;
And then thy glad perennial youth would fade,
Fade, and grow old at last, and die like ours.   230

[37] *Dido* cf. Virgil, *Aeneid*, Book 6, where Dido, who has died out of grief for the loss of Aeneas, is met by him, visiting the underworld: Aeneas speaks to her mournfully, but 'She, with averted face, held her gaze fixed on earth; and her countenance was no more stirred by his faltered speech, than had she stood a pillar of stubborn flint or a cliff of Marpesian rock. At length she tore herself away, and, unreconciled, fled again to the shady grove, where her old-time lord responded to her sorrow.'
[38] *timorous* fearful.

Essay on Criticism

24

Then fly our greetings, fly our speech and smiles!
– As some grave Tyrian[39] trader, from the sea,
Descried at sunrise an emerging prow
Lifting the cool-haired creepers stealthily,
The fringes of a southward-facing brow   235
Among the Ægæan[40] isles;
And saw the merry Grecian coaster[41] come,
Freighted with amber grapes, and Chian[42] wine,
Green, bursting figs, and tunnies[43] steeped in brine –
And knew the intruders on his ancient home,   240

25

The young light-hearted masters of the waves –
And snatched his rudder, and shook out more sail;
And day and night held on indignantly
O'er the blue Midland waters with the gale,
Betwixt the Syrtes[44] and soft Sicily,[45]   245
To where the Atlantic raves[46]
Outside the western straits; and unbent sails
There, where down cloudy cliffs, through sheets of foam,
Shy traffickers, the dark Iberians[47] come;
And on the beach undid his corded bales.   250

[39] *Tyrian* from Tyre (Sūr) in Lebanon.
[40] *Ægæan* sea between the west coast of Turkey and east coast of Greece.
[41] *coaster* vessel employed in sailing along the coast, or in trading from port to port of the same country.
[42] *Chian* from the island of Khios in the Ægean, anciently famed for its wine.

[43] *tunnies* kind of large edible fish.
[44] *Syrtes* Gulf of Sirte, the centre of the Libyan coast.
[45] *Sicily* large Italian Mediterranean island.
[46] *Atlantic raves* i.e., at the mouth of the Mediterranean, the Strait of Gibraltar.
[47] *Iberians* those from the Iberian peninsular (Spain and Portugal).

✗ Stanzas from the Grande Chartreuse

A journey to a high wooded monastery as the subject of a poem might seem a natural analogue to a spiritual quest: the ardours of the expedition equating to the struggles of the soul, the arrival signifying a point of spiritual attainment and a climax of religious experience. Arnold's 'Stanzas from the Grande Chartreuse' – published first in *Fraser's Magazine*, 1855 – invites this analogy with the *paysage pèlerinage* only to push it away. The journey mapped here brings not renewed faith but lament for its passing. The encounter with a space set apart from the movements of history generates intense post-Romantic uncertainty as to the principles of modernity by which a human being might securely live.

Matthew Arnold visited the Grande Chartreuse, at Saint Pierre de Chartreuse in France, in September 1851. It is the chief monastery of the Carthusian monks, a solitary Catholic order founded by St Bruno and formally constituted in the twelfth century. As a

particularly austere community, they suitably contribute to Arnold's myth – powerfully articulated in this poem – of the difference between the commitment and conviction of the ancient age of faith and the fractured state of the present. For other poems that meditate on the relationship between the faith of modernity and an earlier age, see Arnold, 'Dover Beach', 312–13, and 'The Scholar-Gipsy', 298–305, and D. G. Rossetti, 'The Burden of Nineveh', 350–6; see also Thomas Carlyle, *Past and Present* (1843), and John Ruskin, *The Stones of Venice* (1851–3).

Arnold, like Browning and Swinburne, is interested in points of historical transition, but his personal investment in what is lost is central (cf. Browning's 'Fra Lippo Lippi', 179–88, Swinburne's 'Hymn to Proserpine', 476–9, and Arnold's 'Empedocles on Etna', 268–95). The Carthusian community represents the Christian faith seemingly on the verge of extinction. Arnold's teachers, he admits, have made him doubtful of Christianity, but he cannot respond to the monastery in only intellectual terms. The emotional attraction of the systems of thought he has cast aside remains. He perceives himself – and the poem foregrounds the poet as temptingly representative of a whole generation – caught between the fading certainties of the past and what may be the new, as yet unborn certainties of the future. In what asks to be read as a classic definition of mid-nineteenth-century intellectual and spiritual dislocation, Arnold memorably depicts himself as 'Wandering between two worlds, one dead, / The other powerless to be born'. 'Stanzas from the Grande Chartreuse' dramatizes a split between reason and the affections, proposing a

model of conflictual masculinity that continually haunts Arnold's verse (cf. 'A Summer Night', 264–7, and, in contrast, 'The Scholar-Gipsy'). In its reflections on the 'bootless' legacy of the Romantics, 'Stanzas from the Grande Chartreuse' is also fraught with uncertainty about what kind of poetry is now possible and what role the poet might assume after the generation of Byron and Shelley. For another later perspective on history after the Romantic generation, see Thomas Hardy's 'The Darkling Thrush', 512–13.

Text: *Fraser's Magazine* (1855).

Through Alpine meadows soft-suffused
With rain, where thick the crocus[1] blows,
Past the dark forges long disused,
The mule-track from Saint Laurent[2] goes.
The bridge is crossed, and slow we ride, 5
Through forest, up the mountain-side.

2
The autumnal evening darkens round,
The wind is up, and drives the rain;
While, hark! far down, with strangled sound
Doth the Dead Guier's stream[3] complain, 10
Where that wet smoke, among the woods,
Over his boiling cauldron broods.

3
Swift rush the spectral vapours white
Past limestone scars with ragged pines,
Showing – then blotting from our sight! 15
Halt – through the cloud-drift something shines!
High in the valley, wet and drear,
The huts of Courrerie[4] appear.

4
Strike leftward! cries our guide; and higher
Mounts up the stony forest-way. 20
At last the encircling trees retire;
Look! through the showery twilight grey
What pointed roofs[5] are these advance?
A palace of the Kings of France?

5
Approach, for what we seek is here! 25
Alight, and sparely sup, and wait

[1] *crocus* the autumn crocus (see l. 7).
[2] *Saint Laurent* St Laurent-du-Pont, village north-west of the Grande Chartreuse.
[3] *Dead Guier's stream* Guier Mort river, on the way to the Grande Chartreuse.
[4] *Courrerie* La Correrie: outbuildings of the monastery.
[5] *roofs* the roofs of the Grande Chartreuse are steeply pitched.

For rest in this outbuilding near;
Then cross the sward[6] and reach that gate.
Knock; pass the wicket![7] Thou art come
To the Carthusians' world-famed home.   30

6

The silent courts, where night and day
Into their stone-carved basins cold
The splashing icy fountains play –
The humid corridors behold!
Where, ghostlike in the deepening night,   35
Cowled forms brush by in gleaming white.[8]

7

The chapel, where no organ's peal
Invests the stern and naked prayer –
With penitential cries they kneel
And wrestle; rising then, with bare   40
And white uplifted faces stand,
Passing the Host[9] from hand to hand;

8

Each takes, and then his visage wan
Is buried in his cowl once more.
The cells! – the suffering Son of Man   45
Upon the wall[10] – the knee-worn floor –
And where they sleep, that wooden bed,
Which shall their coffin be, when dead![11]

9

The library, where tract and tome
Not to feed priestly pride are there,
To hymn the conquering march of Rome,   50
Nor yet to amuse, as ours are!
They paint of souls the inner strife,
Their drops of blood, their death in life.

10

The garden, overgrown – yet mild,   55
See, fragrant herbs are flowering there!
Strong children of the Alpine wild
Whose culture is the brethren's care;
Of human tasks their only one,
And cheerful works beneath the sun.[12]   60

---

[6] *sward* surface soil covered with grass.

[7] *wicket* small gate.

[8] *white* Carthusians wear monastic habits of white serge.

[9] *Host* consecrated bread signifying the body of Jesus. The Carthusians do not pass the Host between them at Mass, but a Pax, a small plaque of metal, wood or ivory, kissing its carved sacred image in turn.

[10] *suffering . . . wall* crucifix.

[11] *wooden . . . dead* Carthusians are, in fact, buried in their habits on a simple plank of wood.

[12] *fragant herb . . . sun* reference to the manufacture of Chartreuse, the liqueur. The Carthusians acquired the secret recipe in the seventeenth century.

11

Those halls, too, destined to contain
Each its own pilgrim-host of old,
From England, Germany, or Spain –
All are before me! I behold
The House, the Brotherhood austere!   65
– And what am I, that I am here?

12

For rigorous teachers[13] seized my youth,
And purged its faith, and trimmed its fire,
Showed me the high, white star of Truth,
There bade me gaze, and there aspire.   70
Even now their whispers pierce the gloom:
What dost thou in this living tomb?

13

Forgive me, masters of the mind!
At whose behest I long ago
So much unlearnt, so much resigned –   75
I come not here to be your foe!
I seek these anchorites,[14] not in ruth,[15]
To curse and to deny your truth;

14

Not as their friend, or child, I speak!
But as, on some far northern strand,   80
Thinking of his own Gods, a Greek
In pity and mournful awe might stand
Before some fallen Runic stone[16] –
For both were faiths, and both are gone.[17]

15

Wandering between two worlds, one dead,   85
The other powerless to be born,
With nowhere yet to rest my head,[18]
Like these, on earth I wait forlorn.
Their faith, my tears, the world deride –
I come to shed them at their side.   90

16

Oh, hide me in your gloom profound,
Ye solemn seats of holy pain!
Take me, cowled forms, and fence me round,
Till I possess my soul again;
Till free my thoughts before me roll,   95
Not chafed by hourly false control!

---

[13] *rigorous teachers* writers who early disturbed Arnold's religious beliefs, including Carlyle, Goethe and Spinoza.
[14] *anchorites* religious recluses, hermits.
[15] *ruth* repentance.
[16] *Runic stone* stone carved with runes, letters or characters extensively used by pagan Scandinavians. They often had mysterious or magical powers attributed to them.

[17] *faiths . . . gone* i.e., neither the faith of those who carved the runes nor the Christianity of the monks is any longer credible.
[18] *head* ironic recollection of Jesus's words: 'The Foxes haue holes, and the birds of the ayre haue nests: but the sonne of man hath not where to lay his head', Matthew 8.20.

17

[handwritten: Faith believed to be lost]

For the world cries your faith is now
But a dead time's exploded dream;
My melancholy, sciolists[19] say,
Is a passed mode, an outworn theme –
As if the world had ever had
A faith, or sciolists been sad!

100

18

Ah, if it *be* passed, take away,
At least, the restlessness, the pain;
Be man henceforth no more a prey
To these out-dated stings again!
The nobleness of grief is gone –
Ah, leave us not the fret alone!

105

[handwritten: Feels that the "faith" of these people has been food for monks or of the faith generally]

19

[handwritten: Who?]

But – if you cannot give us ease –
Last of the race of them who grieve
Here leave us to die out with these
Last of the people who believe!
Silent, while years engrave the brow;
Silent – the best are silent now.

110

20

Achilles ponders in his tent,[20]
The kings of modern thought are dumb;
Silent they are, though not content,
And wait to see the future come.
They have the grief men had of yore,
But they contend and cry no more.

115

120

21

Our fathers watered with their tears
This sea of time whereon we sail,
Their voices were in all men's ears
Who passed within their puissant hail.[21]
Still the same ocean round us raves,
But we stand mute, and watch the waves.

125

22

For what availed it, all the noise
And outcry of the former men?
Say, have their sons achieved more joys,
Say, is life lighter now than then?
The sufferers died, they left their pain –
The pangs which tortured them remain.

130

[handwritten: Feels that faith was of no use - people still suffer the same]

[19] *sciolists* superficial pretenders to knowledge.
[20] *Achilles . . . tent* Homer's *Iliad* begins with Achilles's argument with Agamemnon at the siege of Troy, after which Achilles withdraws to his tent in anger. Unlike Arnold in this poem, Achilles eventually rejoins the battle.
[21] *puissant hail* strong (voices) declaring greetings.

23

What helps it now, that Byron[22] bore,
With haughty scorn which mocked the smart,
Through Europe to the Ætolian shore[23]   135
The pageant of his bleeding heart?[24]
That thousands counted every groan,
And Europe made his woe her own?

24

What boots it,[25] Shelley![26] that the breeze
Carried thy lovely wail away,   140
Musical through Italian trees
Which fringe thy soft blue Spezzian bay?[27]
Inheritors of thy distress
Have restless hearts one throb the less?

25

Or are we easier, to have read,   145
O Obermann![28] the sad, stern page,
Which tells us how thou hidd'st thy head
From the fierce tempest of thine age
In the lone brakes[29] of Fontainebleau,[30]
Or chalets near the Alpine snow?   150

26

Ye slumber in your silent grave!
The world, which for an idle day
Grace to your mood of sadness gave,
Long since hath flung her weeds[31] away.
The eternal trifler breaks your spell;   155
But we – we learnt your lore too well!

27

Years hence, perhaps, may dawn an age,
More fortunate, alas! than we,
Which without hardness will be sage,
And gay without frivolity.   160
Sons of the world, oh, speed those years;
But, while we wait, allow our tears!

28

Allow them! We admire with awe
The exulting thunder of your race;[32]
You give the universe your law,   165

---

[22] *Byron* English poet (1788–1824).
[23] *Ætolian shore* Byron died at Mesolóngion, a major port in Aetolia, Greece, in 1824.
[24] *heart* cf. Byron's *Don Juan* (1819–24).
[25] *What boots it* what does it matter.
[26] *Shelley* English poet (1792–1822).
[27] *Spezzian bay* Shelley was drowned while sailing in the bay of La Spezia on 8 July 1822.
[28] *Obermann* Arnold refers to Étienne Pivert de Senancour (1770–1846), who published *Oberman* in 1804 (retitled *Obermann* in 1833), a series of letters from a melancholy recluse staying in an Alpine valley.
[29] *brakes* brackens or thickets.
[30] *Fontainebleau* celebrated deep forest south-west of Paris.
[31] *weeds* widow's garments, clothes of sorrow.
[32] *your race* the sons of the world, i.e., those more at home in it than Arnold.

You triumph over time and space!
Your pride of life, your tireless powers,
We laud them, but they are not ours.

29

We are like children reared in shade
Beneath some old-world abbey wall,   170
Forgotten in a forest-glade,
And secret from the eyes of all.
Deep, deep the greenwood round them waves,
Their abbey, and its close of graves!

30

But, where the road runs near the stream,   175
Oft through the trees they[33] catch a glance
Of passing troops in the sun's beam –
Pennon,[34] and plume, and flashing lance!
Forth to the world those soldiers fare,
To life, to cities, and to war!   180

31

And through the wood, another way,
Faint bugle-notes from far are borne,
Where hunters gather, staghounds bay,
Round some fair forest-lodge at morn.
Gay dames are there, in sylvan[35] green;   185
Laughter and cries – those notes between!

32

The banners flashing through the trees
Make their blood dance and chain their eyes;
That bugle-music on the breeze
Arrests them with a charmed surprise.   190
Banner by turns and bugle woo:
Ye shy recluses, follow too!

33

O children, what do ye reply? –
'Action and pleasure, will ye roam
Through these secluded dells to cry   195
And call us? – but too late ye come!
Too late for us your call ye blow,
Whose bent was taken long ago.

34

'Long since we pace this shadowed nave;
We watch those yellow tapers shine,   200
Emblems of hope over the grave,
In the high altar's depth divine;
The organ[36] carries to our ear
Its accents of another sphere.

---

[33] *they* children reared in an abbey's shade.
[34] *Pennon* long narrow flag at head of a lance.
[35] *sylvan* of the forest.

[36] *organ* it is worth being reminded that Arnold is, of course, speaking here of the 'old-world abbey', not the Grande Chartreuse (which has no organ).

35

'Fenced early in this cloistral[37] round   205
Of reverie, of shade, of prayer,
How should we grow in other ground?
How can we flower in foreign air?
– Pass, banners, pass, and bugles, cease;
And leave our forest to its peace!'   210

[37] *cloistral* of a monastic cloister, covered passageway around
an open square.

✗ Dover Beach

The generalist terms of 'Dover Beach', with its description of the sea of faith's withdrawal from the nineteenth century, secured its talismanic position in histories of mid-nineteenth-century belief. Its terms are broad, its representation of the culture deliberately generalized while attentive to the particularities of physical place. The poem has consistently been taken as representative of a whole phase of Victorian thought because it refuses to ground itself exactly: it has, intriguingly, neither specific focus on what kind of faith it considers nor on the causes of its decay. Modernity here is puzzling, but the poem tells us how it *feels*.

The chief sources of 'Dover Beach' are in Wordsworth. Arnold recalls lines in particular from the sonnets 'It is a beauteous evening' (1807) and 'At Dover' (1838). But he radically transforms Wordsworth's belief in nature's capacity to reveal God. In 'At Dover', Wordsworth writes of 'the dread Voice that speaks from out the sea / Of God's eternal Word' (ll. 11–12). Arnold erases this Romantic faith, replacing it with a statement that the waves insist on faith's loss. Like 'Stanzas from the Grande Chartreuse', 305–12, the poem debates with its Romantic predecessors, marking a sharp break between them and the new uncertainties of the later nineteenth century. Milton's *Paradise Lost* is recalled in l. 31 for the same purpose of making clear the differential between a period mythologized as one of conviction and one without.

Yet the faith to which Arnold refers is not only religious. 'Dover Beach' most obviously invites such an interpretation, more explicitly addressed in

'Stanzas from the Grande Chartreuse', but Arnold's 'faith' may refer to the condition of contemporary England as one without secure principles generally. 'The Scholar-Gipsy', 298–305, can be compared as a poem that deals with a fantasy of sincerity, musing on a man possessed of purpose and who has credible belief by which he can live. 'Dover Beach' constructs a world where the Gipsy could not endure.

Arnold maps universal problems of human isolation in terms of sexual relations in 'To Marguerite – Continued', 267–8, and 'The Buried Life', 296–8, as well as in 'Dover Beach'. But where, in 'The Buried Life', Arnold finds human affection a potential source of self-knowledge – 'And then he thinks he knows / The hills where his life rose, / And the sea where it goes' – its achievement in 'Dover Beach' is much less certain. The poem initially offers romance as the bulwark against modernity, but modernity, Arnold swiftly admits, does not allow of real love.

Arnold visited the major English port of Dover on his honeymoon in 1851, when he may have drafted this poem (not published till 1867). Certainly, Dover is a peculiarly appropriate setting for a text that concludes with a vision of the modern world as one of armies in conflict. Attack and defence dominate Dover's violent history, and England's traditional enemy, France, lies closest to the port than to anywhere else on the English coast. The opening scene of two historically antagonistic countries facing each other prepares neatly for the clinching metaphor of the close.

Text: *New Poems* (1867).

The sea is calm to-night.
The tide is full, the moon lies fair
Upon the straits; – on the French coast[1] the light
Gleams and is gone; the cliffs of England[2] stand,

Simple
tranquil
calm

[1] *French coast* Dover is a major British port that faces Calais on the French mainland: on clear days, France is distinct.

[2] *cliffs of England* Dover's famous white chalk cliffs.

Glimmering and vast, out in the tranquil bay.   5
Come to the window, sweet is the night-air!
Only, from the long line of spray
Where the sea meets the moon-blanched land,
Listen! you hear the grating roar
Of pebbles which the waves draw back, and fling,   10
At their return, up the high strand,
Begin, and cease, and then again begin,
With tremulous cadence slow, and bring
The eternal note of sadness in.

Sophocles[3] long ago
Heard it on the Ægæan,[4] and it brought   15
Into his mind the turbid[5] ebb and flow
Of human misery; we
Find also in the sound a thought,
Hearing it by this distant northern sea.[6]   20

The Sea of Faith
Was once, too, at the full, and round earth's shore
Lay like the folds of a bright girdle furled.
But now I only hear
Its melancholy, long, withdrawing roar,   25
Retreating, to the breath
Of the night-wind, down the vast edges drear
And naked shingles of the world.

Ah, love, let us be true
To one another! for the world, which seems   30
To lie before us[7] like a land of dreams,
So various, so beautiful, so new,
Hath really neither joy, nor love, nor light,
Nor certitude, nor peace, nor help for pain;
And we are here as on a darkling[8] plain   35
Swept with confused alarms of struggle and flight,
Where ignorant armies clash by night.

---

[3] *Sophocles* (496–406 BC), Arnold's favourite Greek dramatist. See the third chorus of *Antigone*: 'Blest are those whose days have not tasted of evil. For when a house has once been shaken by the gods, no form of ruin is lacking, but it spreads over the bulk of the race, just as, when the surge is driven over the darkness of the deep by the fierce breath of Thracian sea-winds, it rolls up the black sand from the depths, and the wind-beaten headlands that front the blows of the storm give out a mournful roar.'

[4] *Ægæan* sea between the east coast of Greece and the west coast of Turkey.

[5] *turbid* cloudy, muddy.

[6] *northern sea* English Channel.

[7] *before us* cf. Milton's *Paradise Lost*, 12.646, where, as Adam and Eve leave the Garden of Eden, 'The world was all before them'.

[8] *darkling* lying in darkness.

Adelaide Anne Procter (1825–1864)

Adelaide Procter was born in London into a literary family: her father Bryan Waller Procter (1787–1874) was a friend of Leigh Hunt, Charles Lamb and eventually of Dickens. Under the name 'Barry Cornwall', he had achieved some success with *Dramatic Scenes* (1819) and *Marcian Collona* (1820). Her mother, Anne Benson Skepper, was admired for her wit and intelligence. Adelaide, her parents' first child, was privately educated and encouraged in literature from the beginning. She published 'Ministering Angels' in a woman's annual – a form of literary publication much condemned by the higher strata of publishing as frivolous and feminine – in 1843 and most of her verse appeared in Dickens's two periodicals, *Household Words* and *All the Year Round*, under the name 'Miss Mary Berwick' (she didn't want to trade on the family name). Procter audaciously converted to Roman Catholicism at the mid-century; her sister Agnes also converted and became, to the even greater surprise of her family, a nun. Procter published her first solo volume of verse, *Legends and Lyrics*, in 1858 but devoted much of her time to the sick and poor, and to women's employment; a friend of the prominent feminists Bessie Rayner Parkes and Barbara Leigh Smith Bodichon, she was a minor member of the Langham Place Group, an influential gathering of feminists, journalists and educationalists. A second book of *Legends and Lyrics* followed in 1861, and Procter edited *The Victoria Regia: A Volume of Original Contributions in Poetry and Prose* the same year. This was an effort to promote the Victoria Press, a publishing outfit that Bessie Parkes and Emily Faithfull had established to train women as compositors. Procter's *A Chaplet of Verses* (1861) was sold to benefit a Catholic refuge for homeless women and children. But she was already dying by the time it was issued. Never married, Adelaide Anne Procter died of consumption in 1864 after more than a year confined to bed.

Philip and Mildred

One of the ways in which mid-nineteenth-century writing, both fiction and poetry, may seem alien to the contemporary reader is in its use of what some have come to call 'sentimentality'. The great set-piece scenes of sentiment in Dickens's fiction – most famously the death of Little Nell in *The Old Curiosity Shop* (1841) or the death of Jo the crossing sweeper in *Bleak House* (1852–3) – appear to some, looking from a modern perspective, insufficiently self-conscious. But it would be wrong, as it would be hubristic, to dismiss 'sentimentality', a judgemental term for language that has a palpable emotional intention, the affective aesthetic of Victorian poetry and prose, merely as a defect of nineteenth-century taste. Reading the past requires cherishing the idea of difference. 'Sentimentality' – like the practices of melodrama – plays an important role in the complex patterns of Victorian aesthetics and its occasions deserve our understanding as they require our imaginative sympathy.

Adelaide Anne Procter's 'Philip and Mildred' (1861) deploys affective rhetoric with peculiar strength. It asks the reader to be moved as a central part of its ambitions. The poem is unified from the first stanza with a sense of emotional pressure that reaches a final, Dickensian climax in a deathbed scene with angels. However forceful, its investment in stock tropes and strong emotions is certainly never crude. The intricate ironies of 'Philip and Mildred', its unfolding of a complex human situation and its reluctance to over-simplify the position and psychology of either of its protagonists mean that its emotional energy is set against complications and nuances.

In narrating the story of a man who leaves his fiancée to seek fame in London, the poem probes and gently critiques the notion of 'separate spheres', the idea of private–public worlds as female–male, mapping the damage done to a human relationship partly by the confines in which Mildred lives. Philip may seek his fortune in the public world; Mildred has only her 'weary duties, cold and formal' back at home. Procter, none the less, is careful not to make the poem a merely blunt or monologic attack on the curtailing demands of such domesticity.

Dramatizing questions of gender politics through their effect on two individual lives, placed on either side of a town and country split, the poem offers the city as a space where identities may change, and the countryside as one of stasis. It also raises questions about the constraining power of vows, of past agreements that bind people together forever, a theme that would later receive devastating treatment in Thomas Hardy's *Jude the Obscure* (1894–5). Cast in language of unaffected simplicity and with reassuringly regular metricality, 'Philip and Mildred' engages with politi- cized ideas of human relations and gender roles and invites its reader to *feel* their force.

Text: *Legends and Lyrics* (second book, 1861).

Lingering fade the rays of daylight, and the listening air is chilly;
Voice of bird and forest murmur, insect hum and quivering spray,
Stir not in that quiet hour: through the valley, calm and stilly,
All in hushed and loving silence watch the slow departing Day.

2
Till the last faint western cloudlet, faint and rosy, ceases blushing, 5
And the blue grows deep and deeper where one trembling planet shines,
And the day has gone for ever – then, like some great ocean rushing,
The sad night wind wails lamenting, sobbing through the moaning pines.

3
Such, of all day's changing hours, is the fittest and the meetest
For a farewell hour – and parting looks less bitter and more blest; 10
Earth seems like a shrine for sorrow, Nature's mother voice is sweetest,
And her hand seems laid in chiding on the unquiet throbbing breast.

4
Words are lower, for the twilight seems rebuking sad repining,
And wild murmur and rebellion, as all childish and in vain;
Breaking through dark future hours clustering starry hopes seem shining, 15
Then the calm and tender midnight folds her shadow round the pain.

5
So they paced the shady lime-walk[1] in that twilight dim and holy,
Still the last farewell deferring, she could hear or he should say;
Every word, weighed down by sorrow, fell more tenderly and slowly –
This, which now beheld their parting, should have been their wedding-day. 20

6
Should have been: her dreams of childhood, never straying, never faltering,
Still had needed Philip's image to make future life complete;
Philip's young hopes of ambition, ever changing, ever altering,
Needed Mildred's gentle presence even to make successes sweet.

7
This day should have seen their marriage; the calm crowning and assurance 25
Of two hearts, fulfilling rather, and not changing, either life:
Now they must be rent asunder, and her heart must learn endurance,
For he leaves their home, and enters on a world of work and strife.

8
But her gentle spirit long had learnt, unquestioning, submitting,
To revere his youthful longings, and to marvel at the fate 30

[1] *lime-walk* pathway with lime trees on either side; a conventional middle-class/aristocratic space in mid-nineteenth-century literature.

That gave such a humble office, all unworthy and unfitting,
To the genius of the village, who was born for something great.

9

When the learnèd Traveller came there who had gained renown at college,
Whose abstruse research had won him even European fame,
Questioned Philip, praised his genius, marvelled at his self-taught knowledge,   35
Could she murmur if he called him up to London and to fame?

10

Could she waver when he bade her take the burden of decision,
Since his troth to her was plighted, and his life was now her own?
Could she doom him to inaction? could she, when a newborn vision
Rose in glory for his future, check it for her sake alone?   40

11

So her little trembling fingers, that had toiled with such fond pleasure,
Paused, and laid aside, and folded the unfinished wedding gown;
Faltering earnestly assurance, that she too could, in her measure,
Prize for him the present honour, and the future's sure renown.

12

Now they pace the shady lime-walk, now the last words must be spoken,   45
Words of trust, for neither dreaded more than waiting and delay;
Was not love still called eternal – could a plighted vow be broken? –
See the crimson light of sunset fades in purple mist away.

13

'Yes, my Mildred,' Philip told her, 'one calm thought of joy and blessing,
Like a guardian spirit by me, through the world's tumultuous stir,   50
Still will spread its wings above me, and now urging, now repressing,
With my Mildred's voice will murmur thoughts of home, and love, and her.

14

'It will charm my peaceful leisure, sanctify my daily toiling,
With a right none else possesses, touching my heart's inmost string;
And to keep its pure wings spotless I shall fly the world's touch, soiling   55
Even in thought this Angel Guardian of my Mildred's Wedding Ring.

15

'Take it, dear; this little circlet is the first link, strong and holy,
Of a life-long chain, and holds me from all other love apart;
Till the day when you may wear it as my wife – my own – mine wholly –
Let me know it rests for ever near the beating of your heart.'   60

16

Dawn of day saw Philip speeding on his road to the Great City,
Thinking how the stars gazed downward just with Mildred's patient eyes;
Dreams of work, and fame, and honour, struggling with a tender pity,
Till the loving Past receding saw the conquering Future rise.

17

Daybreak still found Mildred watching, with the wonder of first sorrow,   65
How the outward world unaltered shone the same this very day;

How unpitying and relentless busy life met this new morrow,
Earth, and sky, and man unheeding that her joy had passed away.

18
Then the round of weary duties, cold and formal, came to meet her,
With the life within departed that had given them each a soul; 70
And her sick heart even slighted gentle words that came to greet her;
For Grief spread its shadowy pinions,[2] like a blight, upon the whole.

19
Jar one chord, the harp is silent; move one stone, the arch is shattered;
One small clarion-cry of sorrow bids an armèd host awake;
One dark cloud can hide the sunlight; loose one string, the pearls are scattered; 75
Think one thought, a soul may perish; say one word, a heart may break!

20
Life went on, the two lives running side by side; the outward seeming,
And the truer and diviner hidden in the heart and brain;
Dreams grow holy, put in action; work grows fair through starry dreaming;
But where each flows on unmingling, both are fruitless and in vain. 80

21
Such was Mildred's life; her dreaming lay in some far-distant region,
All the fairer, all the brighter, that its glories were but guessed;
And the daily round of duties seemed an unreal, airy legion –
Nothing true save Philip's letters and the ring upon her breast.

22
Letters telling how he struggled, for some plan or vision aiming, 85
And at last how he just grasped it as a fresh one spread its wings;
How the honour or the learning, once the climax, now were claiming,
Only more and more, becoming merely steps to higher things.

23
Telling her of foreign countries: little store had she of learning,
So her earnest, simple spirit answered as he touched the string; 90
Day by day, to these bright fancies all her silent thoughts were turning,
Seeing every radiant picture framed within her golden Ring.

24
Oh, poor heart – love, if thou willest; but, thine own soul still possessing,
Live thy life: not a reflection or a shadow of his own:
Lean as fondly, as completely, as thou willest – but confessing 95
That thy strength is God's, and therefore can, if need be, stand alone.

25
Little means were there around her to make farther, wider ranges,
Where her loving gentle spirit could try and stronger flight;
And she turned aside, half fearing that fresh thoughts were fickle changes –
That she *must* stay as he left her on that farewell summer night. 100

[2] *pinions* wings.

26

Love should still be guide and leader, like a herald should have risen,
Lighting up the long dark vistas, conquering all opposing fates;
But new claims, new thoughts, new duties found her heart a silent prison,
And found Love, with folded pinions, like a jailer by the gates.

27

Yet why blame her? it had needed greater strength than she was given   105
To have gone against the current that so calmly flowed along;
Nothing fresh came near the village save the rain and dew of heaven,
And her nature was too passive, and her love perhaps too strong.

28

The great world of thought, that rushes down the years, and onward sweeping
Bears upon its mighty billows in its progress each and all,   110
Flowed so far away, its murmur did not rouse them from their sleeping;
Life and Time and Truth were speaking, but they did not hear their call.

29

Years flowed on; and every morning heard her prayer grow lower, deeper,
As she called all blessings on him, and bade every ill depart,
And each night when the cold moonlight shone upon that quiet sleeper,   115
It would show her ring that glittered with each throbbing of her heart.

30

Years passed on. Fame came for Philip in a full, o'erflowing measure;
He was spoken of and honoured through the breadth of many lands,
And he wrote it all to Mildred, as if praise were only pleasure,
As if fame were only honour, when he laid them in her hands.   120

31

Mildred heard it without wonder, as a sure result expected,
For how could it fail, since merit and renown go side by side:
And the neighbours who first fancied genius ought to be suspected,
Might at last give up their caution, and could own him now with pride.

32

Years flowed on. These empty honours led to others they called better,   125
He had saved some slender fortune, and might claim his bride at last:
Mildred, grown so used to waiting, felt half startled by the letter
That now made her future certain, and would consecrate her past.

33

And he came: grown sterner, older – changed indeed: a grave reliance
Had replaced his eager manner, and the quick short speech of old: 130
He had gone forth with a spirit half of hope and half defiance;
He returned with proud assurance half disdainful and half cold.

34

Yet his old self seemed returning while he stood some-times, and listened
To her calm soft voice, relating all the thoughts of these long years;
And if Mildred's heart was heavy, and at times her blue eyes glistened,   135
Still in thought she would not whisper aught of sorrow or of fears.

35

Autumn with its golden corn-fields, autumn with its storms and showers,
    Had been there to greet his coming with its forests gold and brown;
And the last leaves still were falling, fading still the year's last flowers,
    When he left the quiet village, and took back his bride to town.   140

36

Home – the home that she had pictured many a time in twilight, dwelling
    On that tender gentle fancy, folded round with loving care;
Here was home – the end, the haven; and what spirit voice seemed telling,
    That she only held the casket, with the gem no longer there?

37

Sad it may be to be longing, with a patience faint and weary,   145
    For a hope deferred – and sadder still to see it fade and fall;
Yet to grasp the thing we long for, and, with sorrow sick and dreary,
    Then to find how it can fail us, is the saddest pain of all.

38

What was wanting? He was gentle, kind, and generous still, deferring
    To her wishes always; nothing seemed to mar their tranquil life: 150
There are skies so calm and leaden that we long for storm-winds stirring,
    There is peace so cold and bitter, that we almost welcome strife.

39

Darker grew the clouds above her, and the slow conviction clearer,
    That he gave her home and pity, but that heart, and soul, and mind
Were beyond her now; he loved her, and in youth he had been near her,   155
    But he now had gone far onward, and had left her there behind.

40

Yes, beyond her: yes, quick-hearted, her Love helped her in revealing
    It was worthless, while so mighty; was too weak, although so strong;
There were courts she could not enter; depths she could not sound; yet feeling
    It was vain to strive or struggle, vainer still to mourn or long.   160

41

He would give her words of kindness, he would talk of home, but seeming
    With an absent look, forgetting if he held or dropped her hand;
And then turn with eager pleasure to his writing, reading, dreaming,
    Or to speak of things with others that she could not understand.

42

He had paid, and paid most nobly, all he owed; no need of blaming;   165
    It had cost him something, may be, that no future could restore:
In her heart of hearts she knew it; Love and Sorrow, not complaining,
    Only suffered all the deeper, only loved him all the more.

43

Sometimes then a stronger anguish, and more cruel, weighed upon her,
    That through all those years of waiting, he had slowly learnt the truth;   170
He had known himself mistaken, but that, bound to her in honour,
    He renounced his life, to pay her for the patience of her youth.

44

But a star was slowly rising from that mist of grief, and brighter
Grew her eyes, for each slow hour surer comfort seemed to bring;
And she watched with strange sad smiling, how her trembling hands grew slighter,   175
And how thin her slender finger, and how large her wedding-ring.

45

And the tears dropped slowly on it, as she kissed that golden token
With a deeper love, it may be, than was in the far off past;
And remembering Philip's fancy, that so long ago was spoken,
Thought her Ring's bright angel guardian had stayed near her to the last.   180

46

Grieving sorely, grieving truly, with a tender care and sorrow,
Philip watched the slow, sure fading of his gentle, patient wife;
Could he guess with what a yearning she was longing for the morrow,
Could he guess the bitter knowledge that had wearied her of life?

47

Now with violets strewn upon her, Mildred lies in peaceful sleeping;   185
All unbound her long, bright tresses, and her throbbing heart at rest,
And the cold, blue rays of moonlight, through the open casement[3] creeping,
Show the Ring upon her finger, and her hands crossed on her breast.

48

Peace at last. Of peace eternal is her calm sweet smile a token.
Has some angel lingering near her let a radiant promise fall?   190
Has he told her Heaven unites again the links that Earth has broken?
For on Earth so much is needed, but in Heaven Love is all!

[3] *casement* window, or part of a window.

A Legend of Provence

A significant poem in mid-century debates about the fallen woman, Adelaide Anne Procter's 'A Legend of Provence' (1858) offers its reader both a comforting restoration of the status quo, and the suggestion of cautious boundary-testing. The poem begins in a gothic atmosphere in which a painting is central: it places in the foreground the notion of image, of external representation, which Procter will later thematize as a story of the Virgin Mary's appearance in the place of the ordinary novice, Angela. Like W. B. Yeats's later retelling of the Irish folk story of an exhausted priest served by one of God's angels in 'The Ballad of Father Gilligan' in *The Rose* (1893), 'A Legend of Provence' is a tale of divine intervention in humble human life. Its obvious moral concerns the limitless nature of God's forgiveness in distinction to the qualified forgiveness of human beings (cf. the more problematized 'obvious' moral at the end of Christina G. Rossetti's 'Goblin Market', 373–85). Like Rossetti's text, however, 'A Legend of Provence' is a poem of sexual transgression that concludes with restoration

and redemption. In this, the plot of Angela's salvation, and also of 'Goblin Market', differs sharply from Augusta Webster's treatment of the fallen woman theme in 'A Castaway', 456–71, which determinedly eschews such closure.

The divinely aided restoration of Angela might well be read as the effect – displaced, certainly – of a cultural suspicion of female sexuality and a rejection of a woman's self-determination beyond the bounds of domestic life, covertly figured in the daily life of the convent (cf. 'Philip and Mildred', 314–20). None the less, the poem has a double relationship with the structures of gender politics it seems to affirm. In making its ideological weighting so visible, the text serves, at a subtle level, to expose it, quietly making gender ideology available for critique. At another level, the poem also suggests the tentative exploration of cultural boundaries in the mid-century. Although the borders are reinforced at the close, and explicitly given authorial sanction, 'A Legend of Provence' brings into the open a suggestive narrative of their testing as if registering the cultural moment in which challenge is becoming familiar.

The writerly device of retelling a legend modestly disclaims any authorial power of creation (as well as banishing a narrative of sexual fall to the remoteness of a Catholic community in the south of France [Provence is the picturesque area of southern France on the Mediterranean coast]). But it also inscribes the poet as part of a community, transmitting a narrative that had become a collective possession. The poet figure gains some of her moral authority from associating herself with a legend that has endured through time. This sympathetic engagement with the terms of history is resisted by other woman writers in this period: the torsion of Amy Levy's 'Xantippe: A Fragment', 630–6, for instance, comes partly from its contest with historical tradition and its explicit thematization of the question of history's authority. As a legend retold, Procter's poem can be contrasted with the very different narrative of defiant female behaviour in Elizabeth Barrett Browning's 'Rime of the Duchess May', 29–44, which reveals further the plural possibilities of historical themes for gender debate in women's poetry of legend and ballad in the period.

Text: *Legends and Lyrics* (second book, 1861).

The lights extinguished, by the hearth I leant,
   Half weary with a listless discontent.
The flickering giant-shadows, gathering near,
   Closed round me with a dim and silent fear.
All dull, all dark; save when the leaping flame,   5
   Glancing, lit up a Picture's ancient frame.
Above the hearth it hung. Perhaps the night,
   My foolish tremors, or the gleaming light,
Lent power to that Portrait dark and quaint –
   A Portrait such as Rembrandt[1] loved to paint –   10
The likeness of a Nun. I seemed to trace
   A world of sorrow in the patient face,
     In the thin hands folded across her breast –
Its own and the room's shadow hid the rest.
I gazed and dreamed, and the dull embers stirred,   15
   Till an old legend that I once had heard
Came back to me; linked to the mystic gloom
Of that dark Picture in the ghostly room.

In the far south, where clustering vines are hung;
   Where first the old chivalric lays[2] were sung,   20
Where earliest smiled that gracious child of France,
   Angel and knight and fairy, called Romance,[3]
I stood one day. The warm blue June was spread
   Upon the earth; blue summer overhead,
Without a cloud to fleck its radiant glare,   25
   Without a breath to stir its sultry air.
All still, all silent, save the sobbing rush
   Of rippling waves, that lapsed in silver hush
Upon the beach; where, glittering towards the strand,
   The purple Mediterranean kissed the land.   30

All still, all peaceful; when a convent chime
   Broke on the mid-day silence for a time,

[1] *Rembrandt* (1606–69), Dutch painter whose work included many portraits.

[2] *chivalric lays* songs of chivalry (Provence was home to many troubadours – wandering lyric poets – in the eleventh to thirteenth centuries).

[3] *Romance* medieval quest narrative.

Then trembling into quiet, seemed to cease,
In deeper silence and more utter peace.
So as I turned to gaze, where gleaming white,   35
Half hid by shadowy trees from passers' sight,
The Convent lay, one who had dwelt for long
In that fair home of ancient tale and song,
Who knew the story of each cave and hill,
And every haunting fancy lingering still   40
Within the land, spake thus to me, and told
The Convent's treasured Legend, quaint and old:

Long years ago, a dense and flowering wood,
Still more concealed where the white convent stood,
Borne on its perfumed wings the title came: 45
'Our Lady of the Hawthorns'[4] is its name.
Then did that bell, which still rings out to-day,
Bid all the country rise, or eat, or pray.
Before that convent shrine, the haughty knight
Passed the lone vigil of his perilous fight;   50
For humbler cottage strife or village brawl,
The Abbess listened, prayed, and settled all.
Young hearts that came, weighed down by love or wrong,
Left her kind presence comforted and strong.
Each passing pilgrim, and each beggar's right   55
Was food, and rest, and shelter for the night.
But, more than this, the Nuns could well impart
The deepest mysteries of the healing art;
Their store of herbs and simples[5] was renowned,
And held in wondering faith for miles around.   60
Thus strife, love, sorrow, good and evil fate,
Found help and blessing at the convent gate.

Of all the nuns, no heart was half so light,
No eyelids veiling glances half as bright,
No step that glided with such noiseless feet,   65
No face that looked so tender or so sweet,
No voice that rose in choir so pure, so clear,
No heart to all the others half so dear,
So surely touched by others' pain or woe,
(Guessing the grief her young life could not know,)   70
No soul in childlike faith so undefiled,
As Sister Angela's,[6] the 'Convent Child.'
For thus they loved to call her. She had known
No home, no love, no kindred, save their own.
An orphan, to their tender nursing given,   75
Child, plaything, pupil, now the Bride of Heaven.[7]
And she it was who trimmed the lamp's red light
That swung before the altar, day and night;
Her hands it was whose patient skill could trace

---

[4] *'Our Lady . . . Hawthorns'* in Catholic veneration, the Virgin Mary is often associated with particular places or attributes (e.g., Our Lady of Rocamadour).
[5] *simples* medicines.

[6] *Angela* the name, appropriately, comes from 'angel', messenger of God.
[7] *Bride of Heaven* the nun is, like all nuns, symbolically wedded to Jesus.

The finest broidery, weave the costilest lace;   80
But most of all, her first and dearest care,
The office she would never miss or share,
Was every day to weave fresh garlands sweet,
To place before the shrine at Mary's feet.
    Nature is bounteous in that region fair,   85
For even winter has her blossoms there.
Thus Angela loved to count each feast[8] the best,
By telling with what flowers the shrine was dressed
In pomp supreme the countless Roses passed,
    Battalion on battalion thronging fast.   90
Each with a different banner, flaming bright,
Damask,[9] or striped, or crimson, pink, or white,
Until they bowed before a new born queen,
    And the pure virgin Lily[10] rose serene.
Though Angela always thought the Mother blest   95
Must love the time of her own hawthorn best,
Each evening through the year, with equal care,
She placed her flowers; then kneeling down in prayer
As their faint perfume rose before the shrine,
    So rose her thoughts, as pure and as divine.   100
She knelt until the shades grew dim without,
Till one by one the altar lights shone out,
Till one by one the Nuns, like shadows dim,
Gathered around to chant their vesper[11] hymn;
    Her voice then led the music's wingèd flight,   105
And 'Ave, Maris Stella'[12] filled the night.
But wherefore linger on those days of peace?
When storms draw near, then quiet hours must cease
War, cruel war, defaced the land, and came
    So near the convent with its breath of flame,   110
That, seeking shelter, frightened peasants fled,
Sobbing out tales of coming fear and dread.
Till after a fierce skirmish, down the road,
One night came straggling soldiers, with their load
    Of wounded, dying comrades; and the band,   115
Half pleading, yet as if they could command,
Summoned the trembling Sisters, craved their care,
Then rode away, and left the wounded there.
But soon compassion bade all fear depart,
    And bidding every Sister do her part,   120
Some prepare simples, healing salves,[13] or bands,
The Abbess chose the more experienced hands,
To dress the wounds needing most skilful care;
Yet even the youngest Novice[14] took her share
    To Angela, who had but ready will   125
    And tender pity, yet no special skill,
Was given the charge of a young foreign Knight,
Whose wounds were painful, but whose danger slight

---

[8] *feast* day of celebration in the Church's calendar.
[9] *Damask* deep plum colour of the damask rose.
[10] *Lily* flower of the Virgin Mary.
[11] *vesper*[s] evening service in the Catholic liturgy.

[12] *'Ave, Maris Stella'* ancient Catholic prayer to the Virgin Mary: 'Hail, Star of the sea'.
[13] *salves* restorative ointments.
[14] *Novice* one preparing to become a nun.

Day after day she watched beside his bed,
And first in hushed repose the hours fled: 130
His feverish moans alone the silence stirred,
Or her soft voice, uttering some pious word.
At last the fever left him; day by day
The hours, no longer silent, passed away.
What could she speak of? First, to still his plaints,   135
She told him legends of the martyred Saints;
Described the pangs, which, through God's plenteous grace,
Had gained their souls so high and bright a place.
This pious artifice soon found success –
Or so she fancied – for he murmured less.   140
So she described the glorious pomp sublime,
In which the chapel shone at Easter time,
The Banners, Vestments,[15] gold, and colours bright,
Counted how many tapers gave their light;
Then, in minute detail went on to say,   145
How the High Altar looked on Christmas-day:
The kings and shepherds, all in green and red,
And a bright star of jewels overhead.
Then told the sign by which they all had seen,
How even nature loved to greet her Queen,   150
For, when Our Lady's last procession went
Down the long garden, every head was bent,
And, rosary[16] in hand, each Sister prayed;
As the long floating banners were displayed,
They struck the hawthorn boughs, and showers and showers   155
Of buds and blossoms strewed her way with flowers.
The Knight unwearied listened; till at last,
He too described the glories of his past;
Tourney,[17] and joust, and pageant bright and fair,
And all the lovely ladies who were there.   160
But half incredulous she heard. Could this –
This be the world? this place of love and bliss!
Where then was hid the strange and hideous charm,
That never failed to bring the gazer harm?
She crossed herself, yet asked, and listened still,   165
And still the Knight described with all his skill
The glorious world of joy, all joys above,
Transfigured in the golden mist of love.
Spread, spread your wings, ye angel guardians bright,
And shield these dazzling phantoms from her sight!   170
But no; days passed, matins[18] and vespers rang,
And still the quiet Nuns toiled, prayed, and sang,
And never guessed the fatal, coiling net
Which every day drew near, and nearer yet,
Around their darling; for she went and came   175
About her duties, outwardly the same.
The same? ah, no! even when she knelt to pray,
Some charmèd dream kept all her heart away.

---

[15] *Vestments* ecclesiastical garments of the clergy.
[16] *rosary* string of 165 prayer beads for use in prayers to the Virgin in Catholic practice.
[17] *Tourney* tournament, jousting competition.
[18] *matins* morning service.

So days went on, until the convent gate
Opened one night. Who durst go forth so late?   180
Across the moonlit grass, with stealthy tread,
Two silent, shrouded figures passed and fled.
And all was silent, save the moaning seas,
That sobbed and pleaded, and a wailing breeze
That sighed among the perfumed hawthorn trees.   185

What need to tell that dream so bright and brief,
Of joy unchequered by a dread of grief?
What need to tell how all such dreams must fade,
Before the slow, foreboding, dreaded shade,
That floated nearer, until pomp and pride,   190
Pleasure and wealth, were summoned to her side,
To bid, at least, the noisy hours forget,
And clamour down the whispers of regret.
Still Angela strove to dream, and strove in vain;
Awakened once, she could not sleep again.   195
She saw, each day and hour, more worthless grown
The heart for which she cast away her own;
And her soul learnt, through bitterest inward strife,
The slight, frail love for which she wrecked her life,
The phantom for which all her hope was given,   200
The cold bleak earth for which she bartered heaven
But all in vain; would even the tenderest heart
Now stoop to take so poor an outcast's part?

Years fled, and she grew reckless more and more,
Until the humblest peasant closed his door,   205
And where she passed, fair dames, in scorn and pride,
Shuddered, and drew their rustling robes aside.
At last a yearning seemed to fill her soul,
A longing that was stronger than control:
Once more, just once again, to see the place   210
That knew her young and innocent; to retrace
The long and weary southern path; to gaze
Upon the haven of her childish days;
Once more beneath the convent roof to lie;
Once more to look upon her home – and die!   215

Weary and worn – her comrades, chill remorse
And black despair, yet a strange silent force
Within her heart, that drew her more and more –
Onward she crawled, and begged from door to door.
Weighed down with weary days, her failing strength   220
Grew less each hour, till one day's dawn at length,
As first its rays flooded the world with light,
Showed the broad waters, glittering blue and bright,
And where, amid the leafy hawthorn wood,
Just as of old the quiet cloister stood.   225
Would any know her? Nay, no fear. Her face
Had lost all trace of youth, of joy, of grace,
Of the pure happy soul they used to know –
The novice Angela – so long ago.
She rang the convent bell. The well-known sound   230

Smote on her heart, and bowed her to the ground,
And she, who had not wept for long dry years,
Felt the strange rush of unaccustomed tears;
Terror and anguish seemed to check her breath,
And stop her heart. Oh God! could this be death?   235
Crouching against the iron gate, she laid
Her weary head against the bars, and prayed:
But nearer footsteps drew, then seemed to wait;
And then she heard the opening of the grate,
And saw the withered face, on which awoke   240
Pity and sorrow, as the portress spoke,
And asked the stranger's bidding: 'Take me in,'
She faltered, 'Sister Monica, from sin,
And sorrow, and despair, that will not cease;
Oh, take me in, and let me die in peace!'   245
With soothing words the Sister bade her wait,
Until she brought the key to unbar the gate.
The beggar tried to thank her as she lay,
And heard the echoing footsteps die away.
But what soft-voice was that which sounded near,   250
And stirred strange trouble in her heart to hear?
She raised her head; she saw – she seemed to know –
A face that came from long, long years ago:
Herself; yet not as when she fled away,
The young and blooming novice, fair and gay,   255
But a grave woman, gentle and serene:
The outcast knew it – *what she might have been.*
But, as she gazed and gazed, a radiance bright
Filled all the place with strange and sudden light;
The Nun was there no longer, but instead,   260
A figure with a circle round its head,
A ring of glory; and a face, so meek,
So soft, so tender . . . Angela strove to speak,
And stretched her hands out, crying, 'Mary mild,
Mother of mercy, help me! – help your child!'   265
And Mary answered, 'From thy bitter past,
Welcome, my child! oh, welcome home at last!
I filled thy place. Thy flight is known to none,
For all thy daily duties I have done;
Gathered thy flowers, and prayed, and sung, and slept;   270
Didst thou not know, poor child, *thy place was kept?*
Kind hearts are here; yet would the tenderest one
Have limits to its mercy: God has none.
And man's forgiveness may be true and sweet,
But yet he stoops to give it. More complete   275
Is Love that lays forgiveness at thy feet,
And pleads with thee to raise it. Only Heaven
Means *crowned*, not *vanquished*, when it says "Forgiven!"'
Back hurried Sister Monica; but where
Was the poor beggar she left lying there?   280
Gone; and she searched in vain, and sought the place
For that wan[19] woman, with the piteous face:
But only Angela at the gateway stood,

[19] *wan* pale.

Laden with hawthorn blossoms from the wood
And never did a day pass by again, 285
But the old portress, with a sigh of pain,
Would sorrow for her loitering: with a prayer
That the poor beggar, in her wild despair,
Might not have come to any ill; and when
She ended, 'God forgive her!' humbly then 290
Did Angela bow her head, and say 'Amen!'
How pitiful her heart was! all could trace
Something that dimmed the brightness of her face
After that day, which none had seen before;
Not trouble – but a shadow – nothing more. 295

Years passed away. Then, one dark day of dread
Saw all the sisters kneeling round a bed,
Where Angela lay dying; every breath
Struggling beneath the heavy hand of death.
But suddenly a flush lit up her cheek, 300
She raised her wan right hand, and strove to speak.
In sorrowing love they listened; not a sound
Or sigh disturbed the utter silence round.
The very tapers' flames were scarcely stirred,
In such hushed awe the sisters knelt and heard. 305
And through that silence Angela told her life:
Her sin, her flight; the sorrow and the strife,
And the return; and then clear, low and calm,
'Praise God for me, my sisters;' and the psalm
Rang up to heaven, far and clear and wide, 310
Again and yet again, then sank and died;
While her white face had such a smile of peace,
They saw she never heard the music cease;
And weeping sisters laid her in her tomb,
Crowned with a wreath of perfumed hawthorn bloom. 315

And thus the Legend ended. It may be
Something is hidden in the mystery,
Besides the lesson of God's pardon shown,
Never enough believed, or asked, or known.
Have we not all, amid life's petty strife, 320
Some pure ideal of a noble life
That once seemed possible? Did we not hear
The flutter of its wings, and feel it near,
And just within our reach? It was. And yet
We lost it in this daily jar and fret, 325
And now live idle in a vague regret.
But still *our place is kept*, and it will wait,
Ready for us to fill it, soon or late:
No star is ever lost we once have seen,
We always may be what we might have been 330
Since Good, though only thought, has life and breath,
God's life – can always be redeemed from death;
And evil, in its nature, is decay,
And any hour can blot it all away;
The hopes that lost in some far distance seem, 335
May be the truer life, and this the dream.

George Meredith (1828–1909)

Meredith was born the son and grandson of a tailor and naval outfitter. The family was increasingly reduced to impoverished circumstances, though Meredith received some school education both locally and, briefly, in Germany at a Moravian institution in Neuwied. In 1845, he was articled to a solicitor in London but started writing at the same time in an effort to boost his miserable income. Meredith's first poem was published in 1849, the same year as he married Mary Ellen Nicolls, a writer and widowed daughter of the satirist and poet Thomas Love Peacock (1785–1866). Meredith's *Poems* appeared in 1851, dedicated to Peacock (he later disowned the volume and would be regarded in his lifetime as primarily a writer of fiction). The improbably named novel *The Shaving of Shagpat* (1856) was well received but brought few of the needed shillings. That same year, he modelled for Henry Wallis's painting *The Death of Chatterton*, but domestic upset waited: in 1857, his wife left him for Wallis, and they ran off to the Italian island of Capri. Meredith's first important novel, *The Ordeal of Richard Feverel* (1859), was both admired and scandalous: Mudie's, the great Lending Library and self-appointed guardian of bourgeois morals, cancelled its order, a financially calamitous thing for any Victorian novelist. Mary Ellen subse-quently fell ill and died, and the whole messy business lies somewhere behind *Modern Love* (1862). Journalism just about sustained Meredith, and he served for more than three decades as a reader of manuscripts for the publishers Chapman and Hall. But he could not secure the level of financial success for which he hoped. Perhaps his most significant novel, *The Egoist*, appeared in 1879, and *Poems and Lyrics of the Joy of Earth* in 1883; *Diana of the Crossways* followed in 1885, a novel that sold unusually well. Gradually, his reputation, if not his finances, turned a corner: by his death in 1909, he had received the Order of Merit (1905), an Oxford honorary doctorate, and had been made president of the Society of Authors in 1892. Thomas Hardy said of him (in the poem 'George Meredith [1828–1909]'): 'His note was trenchant, turning kind. / He was of those whose wit can shake / And riddle to the very core / The counterfeits that Time will break.' Others had little patience with the difficulties of his over-elaborate prose, his egotism and his gender politics. Certainly, his novels have few admirers today. *Modern Love*, however, remains a startlingly convincing work, innovative in theme and manner, shocking in its exploration of disaster, and searching in its depiction of what the twentieth century would know as the psychological.

Modern Love

From the sixteenth century, the sonnet sequence, drawing on its rich Petrarchan inheritance, has been a traditional medium of love poetry in England. George Meredith's *Modern Love* (1862) resists, as it calls to mind, the form of the sonnet (each poem here is 16 lines), just as it bears a revisionary relationship with the conventional thematics of the sonnet sequence. In presenting instead of a lover's declaration to his beloved the anatomy of a failing marriage, it denies the familiar terrain of the poetic form it so narrowly avoids.

[margin note: Anti-Sonnet]

The poems dwell on particular moments or moods, sustained by an underlying narrative of marital double infidelity. Focusing on discrete occasions that are embedded in an implied broader history, *Modern Love* formally relates to the Romantic-period song cycle such as those by Franz Schubert (1797–1828) or Robert Schumann (1810–56). The process might also be thought cinematographic. Within the broad terms of the narrative, Meredith tests the capacity of single events, gestures or verbal exchanges to bear momentous meaning in a crumbling human relationship. Other experimental forms of narrative in poetry or poems with a creative relationship with linearity in the period include Robert Browning's *The Ring and the Book* (1868–9), A. H. Clough's *Amours de Voyage* (1858), 228–62, W. E. Henley's *In Hospital* (1875/88), 571–86, and Alfred Tennyson's *Idylls of the King* (1859–85), texts that variously explore the possibility of occupying territory normally possessed by fiction.

The underlying narrative of *Modern Love* begins with an extended account of the husband's response to his wife's infidelity. In poem 20, he admits to his own past transgressions; in 27 he confesses to his relationship with the golden-haired 'Lady' (he refers to his wife as 'Madam'). His feelings of desire, jealousy and guilt are picked over, and we learn that the two women meet (poem 36). However, the wife is distraught by her husband's betrayal (poem 42), and although there is an unexpected, brief period of apparently recovered affection (a 'little moment mercifully [given]'), in poem 47, she poisons herself, Chatterton-like, in poem 49. The final 16 lines are left to an apparently omniscient narrator's rumination on the dark forces that lie beneath human lives.

Modern Love takes a little of its painful subject matter from Meredith's own life and Mary Ellen's elopement with Wallis. But the events narrated do not conform to the autobiographical facts, nor do the feelings presented relate to Meredith's actual response to his wife's adultery (so far as it can be recovered). *Modern Love*'s painfully depicted emotional disasters are more the product of Meredith's ambition to make a general statement about what he perceives as the nature of modern desire, and the fraught dynamics of contemporary sexual politics located in a generalized middle-class environment. For later poems examining the *lower* middle class as it emerged as a distinct class position in the Victorian period, see John Davidson's 'The Crystal Palace', 618–26, and 'Thirty Bob a Week', 606–9.

Modern Love resists the ideals of the sonnet sequence as it resists the sonnet form. In doing so, it defines the modern experience of sexual relations against the familiar conventions of literary history. It exposes the distance between the language of ideals and the turbulence of the actual, the pain and messiness of lived experience. The poem did not please its first reviewers, who found it sordid and 'unworthy of the name of art'. But it is remarkable for its honesty, darkness and spoken vigour, and its treatment of female sexuality (the speaker is misogynistic, but peculiarly alert to his wife's emotional life). It is a distinctive probing of a sexual triangle that involves contradictory responses. There is no God here to blame for the calamities, merely human passion.

Frankly accepting the contradictory nature of emotional logic, *Modern Love* is mostly narrated by the husband. His consciousness is changeful, by turns bitter, satirical, aloof, guilty, witty and tender, and frequently undercut by ironic self-awareness. But a narrator using the third person occasionally emerges (e.g. in the first two poems). This may or may not be the husband, distancing himself from his wretched story. Certainly, it is only a more remote voice that could speak the final poem with its movement away from the particular to general Hardyesque/Zola-esque reflection on what 'moves dark' under earthly existence. Offering an arresting study of a male psychology that presents itself as caught in an inevitable trajectory of tragedy, *Modern Love* is an important indication of a mid-Victorian sense of the emergence and identity of the 'modern' as well as a provocative redefinition of 'tragedy' itself. It is an early text to admit the influence of nineteenth-century French literature, especially Charles Baudelaire (1821–67), a relationship that would prove of consequence for the poetry of later English radicals and Decadents.

First published, a few months after Mary Nicolls' death, in *Modern Love and Poems of the English Roadside with Poems and Ballads* (1862).

Text: *The Complete Poetical Works of George Meredith* (1912).

[*This is not meat*
For little people or for fools
Book of the Sages[1]]

By this he knew she wept with waking eyes:
That, at his hand's light quiver by her head,
The strange low sobs that shook their common bed
Were called into her with a sharp surprise,
And strangled mute, like little gaping snakes,
Dreadfully venomous to him. She lay
Stone-still, and the long darkness flowed away
With muffled pulses. Then, as midnight makes
Her giant heart of Memory and Tears
Drink the pale drug of silence, and so beat
Sleep's heavy measure, they from head to feet
Were moveless, looking through their dead black years,
By vain regret scrawled over the blank wall.
Like sculptured effigies they might be seen

5

10

---

[1] *This is . . . Sages* epigraph invented by Meredith. It was included in the first edition, then omitted thereafter.

[handwritten: Vivid and excellent but so sad !!]   Upon their marriage-tomb,[2] the sword between;   15
Each wishing for the sword that severs all.

2

It ended, and the morrow brought the task.
[handwritten: good description]   Her eyes were guilty gates, that let him in
By shutting all too zealous for their sin:
Each sucked a secret, and each wore a mask.   20
But, oh, the bitter taste her beauty had!
He sickened as at breath of poison-flowers:[3]
[handwritten: ?]   A languid humour stole among the hours,
And if their smiles encountered, he went mad,
And raged deep inward, till the light was brown   25
Before his vision, and the world, forgot,
Looked wicked as some old dull murder-spot.
A star with lurid beams, she seemed to crown
The pit of infamy: and then again
He fainted on his vengefulness, and strove   30
To ape the magnanimity[4] of love,
And smote himself, a shuddering heap of pain.

3

This was the woman; what now of the man?
But pass him. If he comes beneath a heel,
He shall be crushed until he cannot feel,[5]   35
Or, being callous, haply till he can.
But he is nothing: – nothing? Only mark
The rich light striking out from her on him!
Ha! what a sense it is when her eyes swim
Across the man she singles, leaving dark   40
All else! Lord God, who mad'st the thing so fair,
See that I am drawn to her even now!
It cannot be such harm on her cool brow
To put a kiss? Yet if I meet him there!
But she is mine! Ah, no! I know too well   45
I claim a star whose light is overcast:
I claim a phantom-woman in the Past.
The hour has struck, though I heard not the bell!

4   *[handwritten: – who]*

All other joys of life [*handwritten: he*] strove to warm,
And magnify, and catch them to his lip: 50
But they had suffered shipwreck with the ship,

---

[2] *marriage-tomb* the poet is thinking of a medieval tomb surmounted with the effigies of knight and lady.
[3] *poison-flowers* cf. Charles Baudelaire's *Les Fleurs du mal* [the flowers of sickness] (1857), a collection of poems that caused a scandal for its representation of sexuality, evil and vice. The *Saturday Review* thought *Modern Love* was itself a product of French influence. It was 'no doubt [Meredith's] conviction, derived from French authorities,' the reviewer said, 'that there is a species of nineteenth-century infidelity, more recondite, more interesting, more intellectual, forsooth, than those which have gone before, and that this novelty was not undeserving of a bard'. Cf. Swinburne's '*Ave Atque Vale*', 500–6.
[4] *magnanimity* generosity.
[5] *If he . . . feel* cf. Genesis 3.15, where God addresses the serpent who has tempted Eve: 'And I will put enmitie betweene thee and the woman, and betweene thy seed and her seed: it shal bruise thy head, and thou shalt bruise his heele.'

And gazed upon him sallow from the storm.
Or if Delusion came, 'twas but to show
The coming minute mock the one that went.
Cold as a mountain in its star-pitched tent, 55
Stood high Philosophy, less friend than foe:
Whom self-caged Passion, from its prison-bars,
Is always watching with a wondering hate.[6]
Not till the fire is dying in the grate,
Look we for any kinship with the stars. 60
Oh, wisdom never comes when it is gold,
And the great price we pay for it full worth:
We have it only when we are half earth.
Little avails that coinage to the old!

5

A message from her set his brain aflame. 65
A world of household matters filled her mind,
Wherein he saw hypocrisy designed:[7]
She treated him as something that is tame,
And but at other provocation bites.
Familiar was her shoulder in the glass, 70
Through that dark rain: yet it may come to pass
That a changed eye finds such familiar sights
More keenly tempting than new loveliness.
The 'What has been' a moment seemed his own:
The splendours, mysteries, dearer because known, 75
Nor less divine: Love's inmost sacredness
Called to him, 'Come!' – In his restraining start,
Eyes nurtured to be looked at scarce could see
A wave of the great waves of Destiny
Convulsed at a checked impulse of the heart. 80

6

It chanced his lips did meet her forehead cool.
She had no blush, but slanted down her eye.
Shamed nature, then, confesses love can die:
And most she punishes the tender fool
Who will believe what honours her the most! 85
Dead! is it dead? She has a pulse, and flow
Of tears, the price of blood-drops, as I know,
For whom the midnight sobs around Love's ghost,
Since then I heard her, and so will sob on.
The love is here; it has but changed its aim. 90
O bitter barren woman! what's the name?
The name, the name, the new name thou hast won?
Behold me striking the world's coward stroke
That will I not do, though the sting is dire.
– Beneath the surface this, while by the fire 95
They sat, she laughing at a quiet joke.

---

[6] *Whom self-caged . . . hate* Passion watches Reason with a 'wondering hate'.

[7] *hypocrisy designed* he thinks she is concerning herself with household matters to avoid considering the relationship.

7

[Handwritten left margin: Reminds me of Angelo when he sees Isabella Measure for Measure] [Interesting paradox]

She issues radiant from her dressing-room,
Like one prepared to scale an upper sphere:[8]
 – By stirring up a lower, much I fear! *[Handwritten: ?]*
How deftly that oiled barber[9] lays his bloom!   100
That long-shanked dapper Cupid[10] with frisked curls
    Can make known women torturingly fair; *[Handwritten: women not virgins?]*
The gold-eyed serpent dwelling in rich hair
Awakes beneath his magic whisks and twirls.
His art can take the eyes from out my head,   105
    Until I see with eyes of other men;
While deeper knowledge crouches in its den,
And sends a spark up: – is it true we are wed?
    [Handwritten: Such powerful language –] Yea! filthiness of body is most vile,
But faithlessness of heart I do hold worse.   110
    The former, it were not so great a curse
To read on the steel-mirror[11] of her smile.

8

Yet it was plain she struggled, and that salt
    Of righteous feeling made her pitiful.
Poor twisting worm, so queenly beautiful! *[Handwritten: ?]*   115
[Handwritten: Who's to blame?] Where came the cleft between us? whose the fault?
    My tears are on thee, that have rarely dropped
As balm for any bitter wound of mine:
My breast will open for thee at a sign!
But, no: we are two reed-pipes, coarsely stopped: 120
The God[12] once filled them with his mellow breath;
    And they were music till he flung them down,
Used! used! Hear now the discord-loving clown
Puff his gross spirit in them, worse than death!
I do not know myself without thee more: 125
    In this unholy battle I grow base:
If the same soul be under the same face,
Speak, and a taste of that old time restore![13]

9

He felt the wild beast in him betweenwhiles
So masterfully rude, that he would grieve   130
    To see the helpless delicate thing receive
His guardianship through certain dark defiles.[14]
[Handwritten: Angry at her infidelity but still "spared" her?] Had he not teeth to rend, and hunger too?
But still he spared her. Once: 'Have you no fear?

---

[8] *Like one . . . upper sphere* dressed like someone from a wealthier class, but also, as if about to enter an angelic realm.
[9] *oiled barber* hairdresser.
[10] *Cupid* god of love; here, partly a satirical reference to the barber.
[11] *steel-mirror* both a mirror made from polished steel, and the steeliness of her expression.
[12] *God* Pan, mischievous sexually active Greek god who played panpipes (cf. Elizabeth Barrett Browning, 'A Musical Instrument', 57–9).
[13] *a taste . . . restore* cf. Wordsworth's 'Surprised by joy' (1815), a sonnet recalling his dead daughter, Catherine: 'I stood forlorn, / Knowing my heart's best treasure was no more; / That neither present time, nor years unborn / Could to my sight that heavenly face restore.'
[14] *defiles* narrow ways or passages.

Beautiful
languery
Imagery

He said: 'twas dusk; she in his grasp; none near.   135
She laughed: 'No, surely; am I not with you?'
And uttering that soft starry 'you,' she leaned
    Her gentle body near him, looking up;
    And from her eyes, as from a poison-cup,
He drank until the flittering eyelids screened.   140
Devilish malignant witch! and oh, young beam
    Of heaven's circle-glory! Here thy shape
    To squeeze like an intoxicating grape –
I might, and yet thou goest safe,[15] supreme.

10

But where began the change; and what's my crime?   145
The wretch condemned, who has not been arraigned,[16]
    Chafes at his sentence. Shall I, unsustained,
    Drag on Love's nerveless body thro' all time?
I must have slept, since now I wake. Prepare,
    You lovers, to know Love a thing of moods: 150
Not, like hard life, of laws. In Love's deep woods,
    I dreamt of loyal Life: – the offence is there!
Love's jealous woods about the sun are curled;
At least, the sun far brighter there did beam. –
    My crime is, that the puppet of a dream,   155
    I plotted to be worthy of the world.
Oh, had I with my darling helped to mince
    The facts of life, you still had seen me go
    With hindward feather and with forward toe,
Her much-adored delightful Fairy Prince!   160

11

Out in the yellow meadows, where the bee
Hums by us with the honey of the Spring,
And showers of sweet notes from the larks on wing
    Are dropping like a noon-dew, wander we.
    Or is it now? or was it then? for now,   165
As then, the larks from running rings[17] pour showers:
    The golden foot of May is on the flowers,
    And friendly shadows dance upon her brow.
What's this, when Nature swears there is no change
    To challenge eyesight? Now, as then, the grace   170
    Of heaven seems holding earth in its embrace.
Nor eyes, nor heart, has she to feel it strange?
Look, woman, in the West. There wilt thou see
    An amber cradle near the sun's decline:
    Within it, featured even in death divine,   175
Is lying a dead infant,[18] slain by thee.

---

[15] *Here thy shape . . . safe* despite his feelings, he does nothing.
[16] *arraigned* called to answer criminal charge.
[17] *larks . . . rings* the skylark ascends by stages as Shelley portrays it in his ode, and the effect seen from below can be that the bird describes a series of circles or loops as it progresses upwards to the peak of its song.
[18] *dead infant* love? their future?

12

Not solely that the Future she destroys,
And the fair life which in the distance lies
For all men, beckoning out from dim rich skies:
Nor that the passing hour's supporting joys   180
Have lost the keen-edged flavour, which begat
Distinction in old times, and still should breed
Sweet Memory, and Hope, – earth's modest seed,
And heaven's high-prompting: not that the world is flat
Since that soft-luring creature I embraced   185
Among the children of Illusion went:
Methinks with all this loss I were content,
If the mad Past, on which my foot is based,
Were firm, or might be blotted: but the whole
Of life is mixed: the mocking Past will stay: 190
And if I drink oblivion of a day,
So shorten I the stature of my soul.[19]

13

'I play for Seasons; not Eternities!'
Says Nature, laughing on her way. 'So must
All those whose stake is nothing more than dust!'   195
And lo, she wins, and of her harmonies
She is full sure! Upon her dying rose
She drops a look of fondness, and goes by,
Scarce any retrospection in her eye;
For she the laws of growth[20] most deeply knows,   200
Whose hands bear, here, a seed-bag – there, an urn.[21]
Pledged she herself to aught, 'twould mark her end!
This lesson of our only visible friend
Can we not teach our foolish hearts to learn?
Yes! yes! – but, oh, our human rose is fair   205
Surpassingly! Lose calmly Love's great bliss,
When the renewed for ever of a kiss
Whirls life within the shower of loosened hair!

14

What soul would bargain for a cure that brings
Contempt the nobler agony to kill?   210
Rather let me bear on the bitter ill,
And strike this rusty bosom with new stings!
It seems there is another veering fit,
Since on a gold-haired lady's eyeballs pure
I looked with little prospect of a cure,   215
The while her mouth's red bow loosed shafts of wit.
Just heaven! can it be true that jealousy
Has decked the woman thus? and does her head
Swim somewhat for possessions forfeited?

---

[19] *And if I drink . . . soul* if he does anything to blot out the memory of the past such as drink himself into stupor, then he is ignoble, and the lesser man for it.
[20] *laws of growth* Darwin's recently published *The Origin of*
Species (1859) gave such a formulation a peculiarly contemporary edge.
[21] *seed-bag – there, an urn* one a symbol of life, the other of death.

Madam, you teach me many things that be. 220
I open an old book,[22] and there I find
That 'Women still may love whom they deceive.'
Such love I prize not, madam: by your leave,
The game you play at is not to my mind.[23]

15

I think she sleeps: it must be sleep, when low 225
Hangs that abandoned arm toward the floor;
The face turned with it.[24] Now make fast the door.
Sleep on: it is your husband, not your foe.
The Poet's black stage-lion of wronged love
Frights not our modern dames:[25] – well if he did! 230
Now will I pour new light upon that lid,
Full-sloping like the breasts beneath. 'Sweet dove,
Your sleep is pure. Nay, pardon: I disturb.
I do not? good!' Her waking infant-stare
Grows woman to the burden my hands bear: 235
Her own handwriting to me when no curb
Was left on Passion's tongue. She trembles through;
A woman's tremble – the whole instrument: –
I show another letter lately sent.
The words are very like: the name is new.[26] 240

16

In our old shipwrecked days there was an hour,
When in the firelight steadily aglow,
Joined slackly, we beheld the red chasm grow
Among the clicking coals. Our library-bower
That eve was left to us: and hushed we sat 245
As lovers to whom Time is whispering.
From sudden-opened doors we heard them sing:
The nodding elders mixed good wine with chat.
Well knew we that Life's greatest treasure lay
With us, and of it was our talk. 'Ah, yes! 250
Love dies!' I said: I never thought it less.
She yearned to me that sentence to unsay.
Then when the fire domed blackening, I found
Her cheek was salt against my kiss, and swift
Up the sharp scale of sobs her breast did lift: – 255
Now am I haunted by that taste! that sound!

17

At dinner, she is hostess, I am host.
Went the feast ever cheerfuller? She keeps
The Topic over intellectual deeps
In buoyancy afloat. They see no ghost. 260
With sparkling surface-eyes we ply the ball:

---

[22] *old book* unidentified.

[23] *The game . . . mind* a peculiarly ironic sentence.

[24] *Hangs . . . it* exactly the pose Meredith adopted for Wallis's fateful picture, *The Death of Chatterton* (see biographical headnote, 328).

[25] *The Poet's . . . dames* dramatic expressions of jealousy do not work; more specifically, the black stage lion is perhaps Shakespeare's murderously jealous lover Othello.

[26] *Her own handwriting . . . is new* he shows her a letter she wrote to him, and another written more recently to the other man.

It is in truth a most contagious game:
Hiding the Skeleton, shall be its name.
Such play as this the devils might appal!
But here's the greater wonder; in that we,   265
Enamoured of an acting nought can tire,
Each other, like true hypocrites, admire;
Warm-lighted looks, Love's ephemerioe,[27]
Shoot gaily o'er the dishes and the wine.
We waken envy of our happy lot.   270
Fast, sweet, and golden, shows the marriage-knot.
Dear guests, you now have seen Love's corpse-lightshine.[28]

18

Here Jack and Tom are paired with Moll and Meg.[29]
Curved open to the river-reach is seen
A country merry-making on the green.   275
Fair space for signal shakings of the leg.
That little screwy fiddler from his booth,
Whence flows one nut-brown stream, commands the joints
Of all who caper here at various points.
I have known rustic revels in my youth: 280
The May-fly[30] pleasures of a mind at ease.
An early goddess was a country lass:
A charmed Amphion[31]-oak she tripped the grass.
What life was that I lived? The life of these?
Heaven keep them happy! Nature they seem near   285
They must, I think, be wiser than I am;
They have the secret of the bull and lamb.
'Tis true that when we trace its source, 'tis beer.

19

No state is enviable.[32] To the luck alone
Of some few favoured men I would put claim.   290
I bleed, but her who wounds I will not blame.
Have I not felt her heart as 'twere my own
Beat thro' me? could I hurt her? heaven and hell!
But I could hurt her cruelly! Can I let
My Love's old time-piece[33] to another set,   295
Swear it can't stop, and must for ever swell?
Sure, that's one way Love drifts into the mart[34]
Where goat-legged[35] buyers throng. I see not plain: –
My meaning is, it must not be again.
Great God! the maddest gambler throws his heart.   300
If any state be enviable on earth,
'Tis yon born idiot's, who, as days go by,
Still rubs his hands before him, like a fly,
In a queer sort of meditative mirth.

[27] *ephemerioe* winged insects that live for only one day.
[28] *corpse-lightshine* mysterious light in a churchyard thought to foretell death.
[29] *Jack and Tom . . . with Moll and Meg* names signifying ordinary country people.
[30] *May-fly* insect with a very short lifespan.
[31] *Amphion* brilliant musician in Greek legend whose skill made animals, birds and trees follow him. The drunk rustic mistakes his lover for a charmed tree dancing to the music of the violinist.
[32] *No state . . . enviable* cf. this poem with Shakespeare's Sonnet 29.
[33] *time-piece* clock, watch.
[34] *mart* market.
[35] *goat-legged* lustful.

20

I am not of those miserable males   305
Who sniff at vice and, daring not to snap,
Do therefore hope for heaven. I take the hap[36]
Of all my deeds. The wind that fills my sails
Propels; but I am helmsman. Am I wrecked,
    I know the devil has sufficient weight   310
    To bear: I lay it not on him, or fate.
Besides, he's damned. That man I do suspect
A coward, who would burden the poor deuce[37]
With what ensues from his own slipperiness.
    I have just found a wanton-scented tress[38]   315
    In an old desk, dusty for lack of use.
Of days and nights it is demonstrative,
That, like some aged star, gleam luridly.
If for those times I must ask charity,
    Have I not any charity to give?   320

21

We three are on the cedar-shadowed lawn;
My friend being third. He who at love once laughed
    Is in the weak rib by a fatal shaft
Struck through, and tells his passion's bashful dawn
    And radiant culmination, glorious crown,   325
When 'this' she said: went 'thus': most wondrous she.
Our eyes grow white, encountering: that we are three,
    Forgetful; then together we look down.
    But he demands our blessing; is convinced
That words of wedded lovers must bring good.   330
    We question; if we dare! or if we should!
And pat him, with light laugh. We have not winced.
Next, she has fallen. Fainting points the sign
To happy things in wedlock.[39] When she wakes,
    She looks the star that thro' the cedar shakes: 335
Her lost moist hand clings mortally to mine.

22

What may the woman labour[40] to confess?
There is about her mouth a nervous twitch.
'Tis something to be told, or hidden: – which?
    I get a glimpse of hell in this mild guess.   340
    She has desires of touch, as if to feel
That all the household things are things she knew.
She stops before the glass. What sight in view?
    A face that seems the latest[41] to reveal!
    For she turns from it hastily, and tossed   345
Irresolute steals shadow-like to where
I stand; and wavering pale before me there,
Her tears fall still as oak-leaves after frost.
She will not speak. I will not ask. We are

---

[36] *hap* chance, whatever happens.
[37] *deuce* devil.
[38] *tress* plait or braid of hair; evidence of his own infidelity.

[39] *Fainting . . . wedlock* it may indicate pregnancy.
[40] *labour* a pun, in the light of the previous poem.
[41] *latest* last, least likely.

League-sundered by the silent gulf between.   350
You burly lovers on the village green,
Yours is a lower, and a happier star!

23
'Tis Christmas weather, and a country house
Receives us: rooms are full: we can but get
An attic-crib.[42] Such lovers will not fret   355
At that, it is half-said. The great carouse[43]
Knocks hard upon the midnight's hollow door,
But when I knock at hers, I see the pit.
Why did I come here in that dullard[44] fit?
I enter, and lie couched upon the floor.   360
Passing, I caught the coverlet's quick beat: –
Come, Shame, burn to my soul! and Pride, and Pain –
Foul demons that have tortured me, enchain!
Out in the freezing darkness the lambs bleat.
The small bird stiffens in the low starlight.   365
I know not how, but shuddering as I slept,
I dreamed a banished angel to me crept:
My feet were nourished on her breasts all night.[45]

24
The misery is greater, as I live!
To know her flesh so pure, so keen her sense,   370
That she does penance now for no offence,
Save against Love. The less can I forgive!
The less can I forgive, though I adore
That cruel lovely pallor which surrounds
Her footsteps; and the low vibrating sounds   375
That come on me, as from a magic shore.
Low are they, but most subtle to find out
The shrinking soul. Madam, 'tis understood
When women play upon their womanhood,
It means, a Season gone. And yet I doubt   380
But I am duped. That nun-like look waylays
My fancy. Oh! I do but wait a sign!
Pluck out the eyes of pride! thy mouth to mine!
Never! though I die thirsting. Go thy ways!

25
You like not that French novel?[46] Tell me why.   385
You think it quite unnatural. Let us see.
The actors are, it seems, the usual three:
Husband, and wife, and lover. She – but fie!
In England we'll not hear of it. Edmond,
The lover, her devout chagrin[47] doth share;   390

---

[42] *'Tis Christmas . . . attic-crib* cf. the Christian nativity narrative where Mary lays the newborn Jesus in a manger 'because there was no roome for them in the Inne' (Luke 2.7).
[43] *carouse* drinking party.
[44] *dullard* dull, stupid person.

[45] *I dreamed . . . night* ambiguous dream, suggesting both reunion with one lost and a fantasy of power.
[46] *French novel* associated in the Victorian period with the sordid, sexual or vicious.
[47] *chagrin* shame.

Blanc-mange and absinthe[48] are his penitent fare,
  Till his pale aspect makes her over-fond:
So, to preclude fresh sin, he tries rosbif.[49]
  Meantime the husband is no more abused:
  Auguste forgives her ere the tear is used.   395
Then hangeth all on one tremendous *If:* –
  If she will choose between them. She does choose;
  And takes her husband, like a proper wife.
Unnatural? My dear, these things are life:
And life, some think, is worthy of the Muse.   400

26

Love ere he bleeds, an eagle in high skies,
  Has earth beneath his wings: from reddened eve
  He views the rosy dawn. In vain they weave
The fatal web below while far he flies.
But when the arrow strikes him, there's a change.   405
  He moves but in the track of his spent pain,
  Whose red drops are the links of a harsh chain,
Binding him to the ground, with narrow range.
  A subtle serpent then has Love become.
    I had the eagle in my bosom erst: 410
    Henceforward with the serpent I am cursed.
  I can interpret where the mouth is dumb.
  Speak, and I see the side-lie of a truth.
Perchance my heart may pardon you this deed:
But be no coward: – you that made Love bleed,   415
  You must bear all the venom of his tooth!

27

Distraction is the panacea,[50] Sir!
  I hear my oracle of Medicine say.
  Doctor! that same specific yesterday
I tried, and the result will not deter   420
A second trial. Is the devil's line[51]
  Of golden hair, or raven black, composed?
  And does a cheek, like any sea-shell rosed,
Or clear as widowed sky, seem most divine?
  No matter, so I taste forgetfulness.   425
  And if the devil snare me, body and mind,
  Here gratefully I score:[52] – he[53] seemëd kind,
When not a soul would comfort my distress!
O sweet new world, in which I rise new made!
  O Lady,[54] once I gave love: now I take!   430
Lady, I must be flattered. Shouldst thou wake
  The passion of a demon, be not afraid.

---

[48] *absinthe* addictive and powerful alcoholic liqueur originally distilled from wine mixed with wormwood, associated in France in the nineteenth century with decadence and sexual transgression. Cf. Arthur Symons, 'The Absinthe Drinker', 658–9.

[49] *rosbif* 'roast beef' with a French accent: in cooking, beef roasted in the English manner.

[50] *panacea* universal cure. In this poem, the speaker admits to his own infidelity with the 'Lady'. Poems 27–33 are concerned with her.

[51] *line* fishing-line, something on which one is caught.

[52] *score* write.

[53] *he* the devil.

[54] *Lady* his mistress.

28

I must be flattered. The imperious
Desire speaks out. Lady, I am content
To play with you the game of Sentiment,   435
And with you enter on paths perilous;
But if across your beauty I throw light,
To make it threefold, it must be all mine.
First secret; then avowed. For I must shine
Envied, – I, lessened in my proper sight!   440
Be watchful of your beauty, Lady dear!
How much hangs on that lamp you cannot tell.
Most earnestly I pray you, tend it well:
And men shall see me as a burning sphere;
And men shall mark you eyeing me, and groan   445
To be the God of such a grand sunflower![55]
I feel the promptings of Satanic power,
While you do homage unto me alone.

29

Am I failing? For no longer can I cast
A glory round about this head of gold.   450
Glory she wears, but springing from the mould;
Not like the consecration of the Past!
Is my soul beggared? Something more than earth
I cry for still: I cannot be at peace
In having Love upon a mortal lease.   455
I cannot take the woman at her worth!
Where is the ancient wealth wherewith I clothed
Our human nakedness, and could endow
With spiritual splendour a white brow
That else had grinned at me the fact I loathed?   460
A kiss is but a kiss now! and no wave
Of a great flood that whirls me to the sea.
But, as you will! we'll sit contentedly,
And eat our pot of honey on the grave.

30

What are we first? First, animals; and next   465
Intelligences at a leap;[56] on whom
Pale lies the distant shadow of the tomb,
And all that draweth on the tomb for text.[57]
Into which state comes Love, the crowning sun:
Beneath whose light the shadow loses form.   470
We are the lords of life, and life is warm.
Intelligence and instinct now are one.
But nature says: 'My children most they seem
When they least know me: therefore I decree
That they shall suffer.' Swift doth young Love flee,   475
And we stand wakened, shivering from our dream.

---

[55] *sunflower* she has golden hair.
[56] *animals . . . at a leap* glance at evolutionary theory.
[57] *for text* in the religious sense of a passage from scripture

that provides the basis of a belief or the subject of an
interpretation.

Then if we study Nature we are wise.
Thus do the few who live but with the day:[58]
The scientific animals are they. –
Lady, this is my sonnet to your eyes.[59]

480

31

This golden head has wit in it. I live
Again, and a far higher life, near her.
Some women like a young philosopher;
Perchance because he is diminutive.[60]
For woman's manly god must not exceed

485

Proportions of the natural nursing size.
Great poets and great sages draw no prize
With women: but the little lap-dog breed,
Who can be hugged, or on a mantel-piece
Perched up for adoration, these obtain

490

Her homage. And of this we men are vain?
Of this! 'Tis ordered for the world's increase!
Small flattery! Yet she has that rare gift
To beauty, Common Sense. I am approved.
It is not half so nice as being loved,

495

And yet I do prefer it. What's my drift?

32

Full faith I have she holds that rarest gift
To beauty, Common Sense. To see her lie
With her fair visage[61] an inverted sky
Bloom-covered, while the underlids uplift,

500

Would almost wreck the faith; but when her mouth
(Can it kiss sweetly? sweetly!) would address
The inner me that thirsts for her no less,
And has so long been languishing in drouth,[62]
I feel that I am matched; that I am man!

505

One restless corner of my heart or head,
That holds a dying something never dead,
Still frets, though Nature giveth all she can.
It means, that woman is not, I opine,[63]
Her sex's antidote. Who seeks the asp[64]

510

For serpents' bites? 'Twould calm me could I clasp
Shrieking Bacchantes[65] with their souls of wine!

33

'In Paris, at the Louvre,[66] there have I seen
The sumptuously-feathered angel pierce

---

[58] *with the day* unassumingly, for the moment.

[59] *sonnet to your eyes* cf. sonnet convention of paying tribute to the beloved's features and person, e.g., Sidney's *Astrophil and Stella* (1591), Sonnet 7: 'When nature made her chiefe worke, *Stellas* eyes, / In collour blacke, why wrapt she beames so bright?'

[60] *diminutive* some have suggested – not very convincingly – that these lines refer to Count Joseph Boruwlaski (1739–1837), a Polish dwarf exiled in Durham, who was a well-known musician and writer of sonnets.

[61] *visage* face.

[62] *drouth* drought.

[63] *opine* express an opinion.

[64] *asp* snake – Cleopatra was killed by one.

[65] *Bacchantes* frenzied women who followed Bacchus, Greek god of wine and intoxication, and celebrated his rites in ecstatic frenzy.

[66] *Louvre* main art gallery in Paris.

Plate 5   Raphael, *St Michael trampling Satan* (1518), Louvre. Photo © RMN, R.G. Ojeda/P. Néri.

Prone Lucifer,[67] descending. Looked he fierce,   515
  Showing the fight a fair one? Too serene!
The young Pharsalians[68] did not disarray
  Less willingly their locks of floating silk:
  That suckling mouth of his upon the milk
Of heaven might still be feasting through the fray.   520
Oh, Raphael![69] when men the Fiend do fight,
  They conquer not upon such easy terms.
Half serpent in the struggle grow these worms.
  And does he grow half human, all is right.'
    This to my Lady in a distant spot,   525
  Upon the theme: *While mind is mastering clay,*
    Gross clay invades it. If the spy you play,
My wife, read this! Strange love-talk, is it not?

[67] *Prone Lucifer* refers to Raphael's *Saint Michael Trampling Satan* (1518) in the Louvre, Paris. There, the devil is represented in human form, scorched, and St Michael, with rich feathered wings, is confidently serene in defeating him. See plate 5.

[68] *Pharsalians* Classical people, of great reknown for their cavalry, here imagined as persistently preserving the elegance of their physical appearance; or perhaps those who fought at the Battle of Pharsalia and who similarly did not want to be disarrayed.

[69] *Raphael* Italian Renaissance painter (1483–1520). See note 67.

34

Madam would speak with me. So, now it comes:
The Deluge or else Fire![70] She's well; she thanks   530
My husbandship. Our chain on silence clanks.
Time leers between, above his twiddling thumbs.
Am I quite well? Most excellent in health!
The journals, too, I diligently peruse.
Vesuvius is expected to give news:[71]   535
Niagara[72] is no noisier. By stealth
Our eyes dart scrutinizing snakes. She's glad
I'm happy, says her quivering under-lip.
'And are not you?' 'How can I be?' 'Take ship!
For happiness is somewhere to be had.'   540
'Nowhere for me!' Her voice is barely heard.
I am not melted, and make no pretence.
With commonplace I freeze her, tongue and sense.
Niagara or Vesuvius is deferred.

35

It is no vulgar nature I have wived.   545
Secretive, sensitive, she takes a wound
Deep to her soul, as if the sense had swooned,
And not a thought of vengeance had survived.
No confidences has she: but relief
Must come to one whose suffering is acute.   550
O have a care of natures that are mute!
They punish you in acts: their steps are brief.
What is she doing? What does she demand
From Providence or me? She is not one
Long to endure this torpidly,[73] and shun   555
The drugs that crowd about a woman's hand.
At Forfeits[74] during snow we played, and I
Must kiss her. 'Well performed!' I said: then she:
''Tis hardly worth the money, you agree?'
Save her? What for? To act this wedded lie!   560

36

My Lady unto Madam makes her bow.
The charm of women is, that even while
You're probed by them for tears, you yet may smile,
Nay, laugh outright, as I have done just now.
The interview was gracious: they anoint   565
(To me aside) each other with fine praise:
Discriminating compliments they raise,
That hit with wondrous aim on the weak point:
My Lady's nose of Nature might complain.
It is not fashioned aptly to express   570

[70] *Deluge or else Fire* i.e., the Deluge from which God preserved Noah and the Ark (Genesis 6–9) and the eternal fires of Hell.
[71] *Vesuvius . . . news* famous volcano above the Bay of Naples in Italy, active in the nineteenth century. It erupted in 1822, 1834, 1839, 1850, 1855 and 1861, a year before the poem's publication.
[72] *Niagara* great waterfall on the New York state/Ontario border.
[73] *torpidly* deprived of the power of motion or feeling.
[74] *Forfeits* game in which an article (usually something carried on the person) is given up by the player by way of penalty for making some mistake, and which he or she afterwards redeems by performing some ludicrous task.

Her character of large-browed steadfastness.[75]
But Madam says: Thereof she may be vain!
Now, Madam's faulty feature is a glazed
And inaccessible eye, that has soft fires,
Wide gates, at love-time, only. This admires   575
My Lady. At the two I stand amazed.

37

Along the garden terrace, under which
A purple valley (lighted at its edge
By smoky torch-flame on the long cloud-ledge
Whereunder dropped the chariot) glimmers rich,   580
A quiet company we pace, and wait
The dinner-bell in prae-digestive[76] calm.
So sweet up violet banks the Southern balm
Breathes round, we care not if the bell[77] be late:
Though here and there grey seniors question Time   585
In irritable coughings. With slow foot
The low rosed moon, the face of Music mute,
Begins among her silent bars to climb.
As in and out, in silvery dusk, we thread,
I hear the laugh of Madam, and discern   590
My Lady's heel before me at each turn.
Our tragedy, is it alive or dead?

38

Give to imagination some pure light
In human form to fix it, or you shame
The devils with that hideous human game: –   595
Imagination urging appetite!
Thus fallen have earth's greatest Gogmagogs,[78]
Who dazzle us, whom we can not revere:
Imagination is the charioteer
That, in default of better, drives the hogs.   600
So, therefore, my dear Lady, let me love!
My soul is arrowy[79] to the light in you.
You know me that I never can renew
The bond that woman broke:[80] what would you have?
'Tis Love, or Vileness! not a choice between,   605
Save petrifaction![81] What does Pity here?
She killed a thing, and now it's dead, 'tis dear.
Oh, when you counsel me, think what you mean!

---

[75] *large-browed steadfastness* allusion to nineteenth-century science of phrenology by which facial features and skull shape were thought to declare character.

[76] *prae-digestive* before dinner.

[77] *bell* for dinner.

[78] *Gogmagogs* Gog and Magog, a king and supposed kingdom mentioned in the Old and New Testaments; mighty powers. The name Gogmagog then passed to a giant who inhabited Britain in the earliest times before being slain by the Cornish hero Corineus.

[79] *arrowy* 'drawn like an arrow'; ironic reference to the notion that without womanly help, man cannot be virtuous.

[80] *bond . . . broke* speaker's misogyny; he refers both to the fact that his wife has transgressed and to Eve succumbing to the serpent in the Garden of Eden (Genesis 2–3).

[81] *petrifaction* decay.

39

She yields: my Lady in her noblest mood
 Has yielded:[82] she, my golden-crownëd rose!   610
The bride of every sense! more sweet than those
 Who breathe the violet breath of maidenhood.
   O visage of still music in the sky!
  Soft moon! I feel thy song, my fairest friend!
   True harmony within can apprehend   615
  Dumb harmony without. And hark! 'tis nigh!
  Belief has struck the note of sound: a gleam
   Of living silver shows me where she shook
Her long white fingers down the shadowy brook,
 That sings her song, half waking, half in dream.   620
What two come here to mar this heavenly tune?
 A man is one: the woman bears my name,
And honour. Their hands touch! Am I still tame?[83]
God, what a dancing spectre seems the moon!

40

I bade my Lady think what she might mean.   625
  Know I my meaning, I? Can I love one,
  And yet be jealous of another? None
Commits such folly. Terrible Love, I ween,[84]
Has might, even dead, half sighing to upheave
 The lightless seas of selfishness amain:[85]   630
 Seas that in a man's heart have no rain
 To fall and still them. Peace can I achieve,
By turning to this fountain-source of woe,
This woman, who's to Love as fire to wood?
 She breathed the violet breath of maidenhood   635
  Against my kisses once! but I say, No!
  The thing is mocked at! Helplessly afloat,
  I know not what I do, whereto I strive.
 The dread that my old love may be alive
Has seized my nursling new love by the throat.   640

41

How many a thing which we cast to the ground,
 When others pick it up becomes a gem!
 We grasp at all the wealth it is to them;
And by reflected light its worth is found.
 Yet for us still 'tis nothing! and that zeal   645
  Of false appreciation quickly fades.
  This truth is little known to human shades,
  How rare from their own instinct 'tis to feel!
  They waste the soul with spurious desire,
 That is not the ripe flame upon the bough.   650
  We two have taken up a lifeless vow
 To rob a living passion: dust for fire!
Madam is grave, and eyes the clock that tells

---

[82] *yielded* their relationship has become more physically
intimate. Cf. poem 43.

[83] *tame* tolerant, not likely to become angry.

[84] *ween* think, believe.

[85] *amain* vehemently, violently.

Approaching midnight. We have struck despair
Into two hearts. O, look we like a pair   655
Who for fresh nuptials[86] joyfully yield all else?

42

I am to follow her. There is much grace
In women when thus bent on martyrdom.
They think that dignity of soul may come,
Perchance, with dignity of body. Base!   660
But I was taken by that air of cold
And statuesque sedateness, when she said
'I'm going'; lit a taper, bowed her head,
And went, as with the stride of Pallas[87] bold.
Fleshly indifference horrible! The hands   665
Of Time now signal: O, she's safe from me!
Within those secret walls what do I see?
Where first she set the taper down she stands:
Not Pallas: Hebe[88] shamed! Thoughts black as death
Like a stirred pool in sunshine break. Her wrists   670
I catch: she faltering, as she half resists,
'You love . . . ? love . . . ? love . . . ?' all on an indrawn breath.

43

Mark where the pressing wind shoots javelin-like
Its skeleton shadow on the broad-backed wave!
Here is a fitting spot to dig Love's grave;   675
Here where the ponderous breakers plunge and strike,
And dart their hissing tongues high up the sand:
In hearing of the ocean, and in sight
Of those ribbed wind-streaks running into white.
If I the death of Love had deeply planned,   680
I never could have made it half so sure,
As by the unblest kisses which upbraid
The full-waked sense; or failing that, degrade!
'Tis morning: but no morning can restore
What we have forfeited. I see no sin: 685
The wrong is mixed. In tragic life, God wot,[89]
No villain need be! Passions spin the plot:
We are betrayed by what is false within.

44

They say, that Pity in Love's service dwells,
A porter at the rosy temple's gate.   690
I missed him going: but it is my fate
To come upon him now beside his wells;
Whereby I know that I Love's temple leave,
And that the purple doors have closed behind.
Poor soul! if, in those early days unkind,   695
Thy power to sting had been but power to grieve,
We now might with an equal spirit meet,

---

[86] *nuptials* marriages.
[87] *Pallas* title given to Athena, Greek virgin goddess of
war.

[88] *Hebe* goddess of youthful beauty, wife of Hercules,
cupbearer of the gods.
[89] *wot* knows.

And not be matched like innocence and vice.
She for the Temple's worship has paid price,
  And takes the coin of Pity as a cheat.   700
She sees through simulation to the bone:
What's best in her impels her to the worst:
Never, she cries, shall Pity soothe Love's thirst,
  Or foul hypocrisy for truth atone!

45

It is the season of the sweet wild rose,   705
  My Lady's emblem in the heart of me!
So golden-crownèd shines she gloriously,
And with that softest dream of blood she glows:
Mild as an evening heaven round Hesper[90] bright!
  I pluck the flower, and smell it, and revive   710
  The time when in her eyes I stood alive.
I seem to look upon it out of Night.
Here's Madam, stepping hastily. Her whims
Bid her demand the flower, which I let drop.
  As I proceed, I feel her sharply stop,   715
And crush it under heel with trembling limbs.
She joins me in a cat-like way, and talks
  Of company, and even condescends
  To utter laughing scandal of old friends.
These are the summer days, and these our walks.   720

46

At last we parley:[91] we so strangely dumb
  In such a close communion! It befell
  About the sounding of the Matin-bell,[92]
And lo! her place was vacant, and the hum
Of loneliness was round me. Then I rose,   725
And my disordered brain did guide my foot
To that old wood where our first love-salute
Was interchanged: the source of many throes!
  There did I see her, not alone. I moved
  Toward her, and made proffer of my arm.   730
She took it simply, with no rude alarm;
And that disturbing shadow passed reproved.
I felt the pained speech coming, and declared
  My firm belief in her, ere she could speak.
  A ghastly morning came into her cheek,   735
While with a widening soul on me she stared.

47

We saw the swallows gathering in the sky,[93]
And in the osier-isle[94] we heard them noise.
We had not to look back on summer joys,
  Or forward to a summer of bright dye: 740
But in the largeness of the evening earth

---

[90] *Hesper* evening star.
[91] *parley* converse.
[92] *Matin-bell* matins, morning service in the Church of England.

[93] *swallows . . . sky* cf. Keats's 'To Autumn' (1819): 'And gathering swallows twitter in the skies'.
[94] *osier-isle* osier = species of willow.

Our spirits grew as we went side by side.
The hour became her husband and my bride.
Love, that had robbed us so, thus blessed our dearth!
The pilgrims of the year waxed very loud   745
In multitudinous chatterings, as the flood
Full brown came from the West, and like pale blood
Expanded to the upper crimson cloud.
Love, that had robbed us of immortal things,
This little moment mercifully gave,   750
Where I have seen across the twilight wave
The swan sail with her young beneath her wings.

48

Their sense is with their senses all mixed in,
Destroyed by subtleties these women are!
More brain, O Lord, more brain! or we shall mar   755
Utterly this fair garden we might win.[95]
Behold! I looked for peace, and thought it near.
Our inmost hearts had opened, each to each.
We drank the pure daylight of honest speech.
Alas! that was the fatal draught, I fear.   760
For when of my lost Lady came the word,
This woman, O this agony of flesh!
Jealous devotion bade her break the mesh,
That I might seek that other like a bird.
I do adore the nobleness! despise   765
The act! She has gone forth, I know not where.
Will the hard world my sentience of her share?
I feel the truth; so let the world surmise.

49

He found her by the ocean's moaning verge,
Nor any wicked change in her discerned;   770
And she believed his old love had returned,
Which was her exultation, and her scourge.
She took his hand, and walked with him, and seemed
The wife he sought, though shadow-like and dry.
She had one terror, lest her heart should sigh,   775
And tell her loudly she no longer dreamed.
She dared not say, 'This is my breast: look in.'
But there's a strength to help the desperate weak.
That night he learned how silence best can speak
The awful things when Pity pleads for Sin.   780
About the middle of the night her call
Was heard, and he came wondering to the bed.
'Now kiss me, dear! it may be, now!' she said.
Lethe[96] had passed those lips, and he knew all.

50

Thus piteously Love closed what he begat: 785
The union of this ever-diverse pair!

[95] *this fair garden we might win* more of the speaker's misogyny: he alludes again to the loss of the Garden of Eden (Genesis 2–3) through Eve's yielding to temptation.

[96] *Lethe* river of forgetfulness: she has taken poison. Meredith's wife did not poison herself, of course. But Chatterton – whom Meredith was modelling for Wallis – did.

These two were rapid falcons in a snare,
Condemned to do the flitting of the bat.
Lovers beneath the singing sky of May,
They wandered once; clear as the dew on flowers: 790
But they fed not on the advancing hours:
Their hearts held cravings for the buried day.
Then each applied to each that fatal knife,
Deep questioning, which probes to endless dole.[97]
Ah, what a dusty answer gets the soul   795
When hot for certainties in this our life! –
In tragic hints here see what evermore
Moves dark as yonder midnight ocean's force,
Thundering like ramping hosts of warrior horse,
To throw that faint thin line upon the shore!   800

[97] *dole* sorrow.

Dante Gabriel Rossetti (1828–1882)
[Gabriel Charles Dante Rossetti]

Born in central London (just behind what is now Broadcasting House), Dante Gabriel Rossetti was the son of the Italian poet, patriot and scholar Gabriele Rossetti, Professor of Italian at King's College London, and Frances Polidori, sister of Byron's doctor. Rossetti left school at 14, having obtained a better education at home. He studied painting with William Holman Hunt (1827–1910) and John Everett Millais (1829–96) and in 1848 joined forces with them to lead the formation of the Pre-Raphaelite Brotherhood, espousing a return to realist aesthetics, medievalism, Christian symbolism, craftsmanship, draughtsmanship, and seeking to reject the values of the Royal Academy (the group was not a coherent one). He exhibited his first major painting, *The Girlhood of Mary Virgin*, rich in religious symbolism, in 1849 and published verse in the short-lived Pre-Raphaelite journal *The Germ* in 1850. That year, he also met Lizzie Siddal who, along with Janey Morris, William Morris's wife, would provide the face for many a Pre-Raphaelite picture; he married Lizzie in 1860, but she died – probably by her own choice – from an overdose of laudanum (opium and alcohol) in 1862. Rossetti, in a self-defeating gesture to a departed muse, had some of his poems in manuscript buried in her coffin in Highgate cemetery. He started the picture *Found* – a fallen woman image – in 1854 and the controversial, provocatively sexual painting *Bocca Baciata* – 'kissed mouth' – in 1859. Rossetti shared a house briefly with Swinburne and Meredith, and, during the 1850s, his friendship with the art critic John Ruskin grew, then steadily deteriorated into acrimony (Rossetti) and disappointment (Ruskin). By 1869, he was seriously regretting the loss of his poems in Lizzie's coffin and arranged for them to be recovered in the most macabre incident in the history of Victorian poetry. He did not attend the exhumation but was able to bring out the volume *Poems* in 1870. The following year came Robert Buchanan's great attack in the *Contemporary Review* on Rossetti as the chief representative of the 'Fleshly School' of poetry. 'In poems like "Nuptial Sleep",' Buchanan said (writing as Thomas Maitland), 'the man who is too sensitive to exhibit his pictures, and so modest that it takes him years to make up his mind to publish his poems, parades his private sensations before a coarse public, and is gratified by their applause.' Rossetti, he said, was *trashy*. The painter-poet replied in the *Athenaeum* in December 1872 with 'The Stealthy School of Criticism', but the whole business brought about a mental breakdown. Ill health continued to overshadow Rossetti's life and he became increasingly troublesome to manage. His sonnet sequence *The House of Life* appeared complete in 1881 (half of it had been in the 1870 volume), but he died in April 1882, one of the most provocative, resourceful and erotic poets of the period, and a peculiarly difficult man.

The Burden of Nineveh

Robert Buchanan's 'The Fleshly School of Poetry' controversy in 1871 – and Rossetti's reply, 'The Stealthy School of Criticism' (1872) – overshadowed his poetic achievement, convincing many readers then and now that his art was persistently sexually transgressive, that he was defined as a poet dangerously entangled with scenes and desires which were both corrupt and corrupting. But there were other sides to Rossetti's poetry, including the prophetic, the public poetry of quasi-satirical national statement. 'The Burden of Nineveh' (1856) is an example, many years before the 'Fleshly School' scandal; a striking text in which an autobiographical moment of observation is extrapolated into a provocative, half-playful, half-serious query about the nature of Englishness.

'The Burden of Nineveh' commences with a record of a real event, the arrival at the British Museum in London of an enormous Winged Bull excavated in 1847 by Austen Henry Layard (1817–94), one of the most important and successful of Victorian archaeologists. The bull came from Nimroud, a site in modern Iraq, which Layard first believed was the Biblical city of Nineveh. Nineveh had been the ancient capital of the Assyrian empire, which reached its peak under Sennacherib and Assurbanipal. It continued to be the leader of the ancient world until it fell victim to an alliance of Babylonians, Medes and Scythians in 612 BC. The city's fall meant the end of the Assyrian empire. As the capital of a vast empire, Nineveh obviously offered Rossetti a comparison to modern London, the centre of the new imperial power. The bull reached the British Museum – where it is still – at the end of September 1850. As it happens, Nimroud, Layard shortly afterwards discovered, was the ancient Kahlu: Nineveh was at Mosul. But this does not matter for the poem.

Rossetti follows the model of cultural criticism offered by John Ruskin in *The Stones of Venice* (1851–3). Where Ruskin read in the ruins of Venice important lessons for modern England and the condition of her faith, Rossetti uses an ancient artefact, a fragment of a lost culture, also to probe the spiritual condition of the present. 'The Burden of Nineveh' – the title comes from the Book of Nahum 1.1, and 'burden' means both 'message' and 'arduous weight'

– may be compared to other texts in this anthology that test modern England against the past, using history or myth to produce contemporary critique (e.g., Matthew Arnold, 'Empedocles on Etna', 268–95, Augusta Webster, 'Circe', 450–5, Amy Levy, 'Xantippe', 630–6, and Christina G. Rossetti, 'Babylon the Great', 393).

Text: *The Collected Works of Dante Gabriel Rossetti* (1886).

> In our Museum[1] galleries
> To-day I lingered o'er the prize
> Dead Greece vouchsafes to living eyes, –
> Her Art for ever in fresh wise
> From hour to hour rejoicing me.
> Sighing I turned at last to win
> Once more the London dirt and din;
> And as I made the swing-door spin
> And issued, they were hoisting in
> A wingèd beast from Nineveh.

5

10

> 2
> A human face the creature wore,
> And hoofs behind and hoofs before,
> And flanks with dark runes[2] fretted o'er.
> 'Twas bull, 'twas mitred[3] Minotaur,[4]
> A dead disbowelled mystery:
> The mummy of a buried faith
> Stark from the charnel[5] without scathe,
> Its wings stood for the light to bathe, –
> Such fossil cerements[6] as might swathe
> The very corpse of Nineveh.

15

20

> 3
> The print of its first rush-wrapping,
> Wound ere it dried, still ribbed the thing.
> What song did the brown maidens sing,
> From purple mouths alternating,
> When that was woven languidly?
> What vows, what rites, what prayers preferr'd,
> What songs has the strange image heard?
> In what blind vigil stood interr'd
> For ages, till an English word
> Broke silence first at Nineveh?

25

30

---

[1] *Museum* British Museum, London; then (and still) the most important museum of antiquities in Great Britain.

[2] *runes* mystical system of writing.

[3] *mitred* the bull wears an Assyrian layered crown which looks a little like an English bishop's mitre.

[4] *Minotaur* monster of Greek myth: half man, half bull, kept in a labyrinth and fed on human flesh.

[5] *charnel* burial place. In fact the bull was not 'stark from the charnel' – it had been much interrupted in its journey to England.

[6] *cerements* grave clothes.

4

Oh when upon each sculptured court,[7]
Where even the wind might not resort, –
O'er which Time passed, of like import
With the wild Arab boys at sport, –
    A living face looked in to see: –   35
Oh seemed it not – the spell once broke –
As though the carven warriors woke,
As though the shaft the string forsook,
The cymbals clashed, the chariots shook,
    And there was life in Nineveh?   40

5

On London stones our sun anew
The beast's recovered shadow threw.
(No shade that plague of darkness knew,
No light, no shade, while older grew
    By ages the old earth and sea.)   45
Lo thou! could all thy priests have shown
Such proof to make thy godhead known?
From their dead Past thou liv'st alone;
And still thy shadow is thine own,
    Even as of yore in Nineveh.   50

6

That day whereof we keep record,
When near thy city-gates the Lord
Sheltered His Jonah with a gourd,[8]
This sun, (I said) here present, pour'd
    Even thus this shadow that I see.   55
This shadow has been shed the same
From sun and moon, – from lamps which came
For prayer, – from fifteen days of flame,[9]
The last, while smouldered to a name
    Sardanapalus'[10] Nineveh.   60

7

Within thy shadow, haply, once
Sennacherib[11] has knelt, whose sons
Smote him between the altar-stones:[12]
Or pale Semiramis[13] her zones
    Of gold, her incense brought to thee,   65
In love for grace, in war for aid: . . .
Ay, and who else? . . . till 'neath thy shade

---

[7] *court* Layard's main excavations were in the palace complex of Nimroud.

[8] *When near . . . gourd* see Jonah 4.6, where God sends a gourd to protect Jonah from the sun.

[9] *fifteen days of flame* see note 10.

[10] *Sardanapalus* ancient but probably mythical Assyrian monarch who lived in luxury at Nineveh. He was besieged by the Medes for two years, finally setting fire to his palace, destroying himself and his court in the flames: cf. Byron's *Saradanapalus* (1821).

[11] *Sennacherib* King of Assyria (705–681 BC) who built his palace at Nineveh.

[12] *altar-stones* cf. 'So Sennacherib king of Assyria departed, and went and returned, and dwelt at Nineueh. And it came to passe as hee was worshipping in the house of Nisroch his god, that Adramelech, and Sharezer his sonnes, smote him with the sword', 2 Kings 19.36–7.

[13] *Semiramis* mythical Assyrian queen, famous for her beauty and wisdom; she supposedly conquered many lands and founded Babylon.

Within his trenches newly made
Last year the Christian knelt and pray'd[14] –
Not to thy strength – in Nineveh.   70

8

Now, thou poor god, within this hall
Where the blank windows blind the wall
From pedestal to pedestal,
The kind of light shall on thee fall
Which London takes the day to be: 75
While school-foundations in the act
Of holiday, three files compact,
Shall learn to view thee as a fact
Connected with that zealous tract:
'Rome, – Babylon and Nineveh.'[15]   80

9

Deemed they of this, those worshippers,
When, in some mythic chain of verse
Which man shall not again rehearse,
The faces of thy ministers
Yearned pale with bitter ecstasy?   85
Greece, Egypt, Rome, – did any god
Before whose feet men knelt unshod
Deem that in this unblest abode
Another scarce more unknown god
Should house with him, from Nineveh?   90

10

Ah! in what quarries lay the stone
From which this pillared pile has grown,
Unto man's need how long unknown,
Since those thy temples, court and cone,
Rose far in desert history?   95
Ah! what is here that does not lie
All strange to thine awakened eye?
Ah! what is here can testify
(Save that dumb presence of the sky)
Unto thy day and Nineveh?   100

11

Why, of those mummies in the room
Above, there might indeed have come
One out of Egypt to thy home,
An alien. Nay, but were not some
Of these thine own 'antiquity'?   105
And now, – they and their gods and thou
All relics here together, – now
Whose profit? whether bull or cow,

---

[14] *knelt . . . pray'd* 'During the excavations, the Tiyari workmen held their services in the shadow of the great bulls. (Layard)' [Rossetti's note].

[15] *Rome, – Babylon and Nineveh* school parties will be encouraged to see the artefacts of Nineveh as a reminder of three cities that have been sacked or destroyed.

Isis[16] or Ibis,[17] who or how,
Whether of Thebes[18] or Nineveh?   110

12

The consecrated metals found,
And ivory tablets, underground,
Winged teraphim[19] and creatures crown'd.
When air and daylight filled the mound,[20]
Fell into dust immediately.   115
And even as these, the images
Of awe and worship, – even as these, –
So, smitten with the sun's increase,
Her glory mouldered and did cease
From immemorial Nineveh.   120

13

The day her builders made their halt,
Those cities of the lake of salt[21]
Stood firmly 'stablished without fault,
Made proud with pillars of basalt,[22]
With sardonyx[23] and porphyry.[24]   125
The day that Jonah bore abroad
To Nineveh the voice of God,[25]
A brackish lake lay in his road,
Where erst Pride fixed her sure abode,
As then in royal Nineveh.   130

14

The day when he,[26] Pride's lord and Man's,
Showed all the kingdoms at a glance
To Him before whose countenance
The years recede, the years advance,
And said, Fall down and worship me:[27] –   135
'Mid all the pomp beneath that look,
Then stirred there, haply, some rebuke,
Where to the wind the Salt Pools shook,
And in those tracts, of life forsook,
That knew thee not, O Nineveh!   140

15

Delicate harlot! On thy throne
Thou with a world beneath thee prone

[16] *Isis* ancient Egyptian goddess.
[17] *Ibis* sacred bird in ancient Egypt.
[18] *Thebes* not the principal city of Boeotia in Greece but the Greek name for the city on which Luxor now stands in Upper Egypt: capital of Egypt from *c.*2000 BC.
[19] *teraphim* idol, image, household god.
[20] *mound* Layard discovered the bull in excavations in a giant mound that covered the palace complex.
[21] *lake of salt* Dead Sea, famous for its saltiness, which crosses the borders of Israel and Jordan. Rossetti refers chiefly to Jerusalem.
[22] *basalt* greenish or brownish-black rock.
[23] *sardonyx* rock, variety of onyx.
[24] *porphyry* valuable and highly polished purple stone.

[25] *The day . . . God* cf. 'Now the word of the Lord came vnto Ionah the sonne of Amittai, saying, Arise, goe to Nineueh that great citie, and cry against it: for their wickednes is come vp before me', Jonah 1.1–2.
[26] *he* Satan.
[27] *The day when . . . me* cf. third temptation of Jesus in the wilderness: 'Againe the Deuill taketh him vp into an exceeding high mountaine, and sheweth him all the kingdomes of the world, and the glory of them: And saith vnto him, All these things will I giue thee, if thou wilt fall downe and worship me. Then saith Iesus vnto him, Get thee hence, Satan: for it is written, Thou shalt worship the Lord thy God, and him onely shalt thou serue', Matthew 4.8–10.

In state for ages sat'st alone;
And needs were years and lustres flown
Ere strength of man could vanquish thee: 145
Whom even thy victor foes must bring,
Still royal, among maids that sing
As with doves' voices, taboring[28]
Upon their breasts, unto the King, –
A kingly conquest, Nineveh!   150

16

. . . Here woke my thought. The wind's slow sway
Had waxed; and like the human play
Of scorn that smiling spreads away,
The sunshine shivered off the day:
The callous wind, it seemed to me,   155
Swept up the shadow from the ground:
And pale as whom the Fates astound,
The god forlorn stood winged and crown'd:
Within I knew the cry lay bound
Of the dumb soul of Nineveh.   160

17

And as I turned, my sense half shut
Still saw the crowds of kerb and rut
Go past as marshalled to the strut
Of ranks in gypsum[29] quaintly cut.
It seemed in one same pageantry   165
They followed forms which had been erst;[30]
To pass, till on my sight should burst
That future of the best or worst
When some may question which was first,
Of London or of Nineveh.   170

18

For as that Bull-god[31] once did stand
And watched the burial-clouds of sand,
Till these at last without a hand
Rose o'er his eyes, another land,
And blinded him with destiny: –   175
So may he stand again; till now,
In ships of unknown sail and prow,
Some tribe of the Australian plough
Bear him afar, – a relic now
Of London, not of Nineveh!   180

19

Or it may chance indeed that when
Man's age is hoary[32] among men, –
His centuries threescore and ten,[33] –

---

[28] *taboring* beating (as if on a drum [tabor]).

[29] *gypsum* hydrous calcium sulphate.

[30] *had been erst* had existed before them.

[31] *Bull-god* Layard suggested that the human-headed bull represented, in the symbolic system of Assyria, 'the union of the greatest intellectual and physical powers'.

[32] *hoary* grey with age.

[33] *threescore and ten* traditional duration of human life (see Psalm 90.10).

His furthest childhood shall seem then
More clear than later times may be: 185
Who, finding in this desert place
This form, shall hold us for some race
That walked not in Christ's lowly ways,
But bowed its pride and vowed its praise
Unto the God of Nineveh.   190

20

The smile rose first, – anon[34] drew nigh
The thought: . . . Those heavy wings spread high,[35]
So sure of flight, which do not fly;
That set gaze never on the sky;
Those scriptured flanks it cannot see;   195
Its crown, a brow-contracting load;
Its planted feet which trust the sod: . . .
(So grew the image as I trod:)
O Nineveh, was this thy God, –
Thine also, mighty Nineveh?   200

[34] *anon* immediately.
[35] *spread high* the bull's wings are not so much spread as
folded back.

Sestina. Of the Lady Pietra degli Scrovigni

This poem is a translation of a *sestina* of 'great and peculiar beauty', Rossetti said, by Dante Alighieri (1265–1321), the supreme medieval Italian poet and author of the *Divina Commedia*. Rossetti was named after Dante by his Italian patriot father, and in this poem, first published in *Early Italian Poets* (1861), he silently lays claim to his own position as the inheritor and guardian of medieval Italy's poetic traditions. A *sestina* is an involved verse form first worked out by the troubadours of medieval France consisting of six stanzas of six lines each, with an *envoi* – final stanza – of three lines. Rossetti, who admits the Paduan lady of the title is only included as a gesture, does not reproduce the demanding rhyme scheme of the original form. But the verbal economy of his poem is remarkable, as is its exploitation of the limited number of material components (grass, stones, hills) to produce a highly concentrated, radiant love poem.

Where Rossetti's 'The Woodspurge', 368–9, presents natural form shorn of meaning beyond itself, the 'Sestina' continually exploits the capacity of nature to signify more. The poem moves between the natural world and the 'lady', between physical space and human identity, so that the barriers between them become indistinct. The English painter-poet Charles Tomlinson (1927–) thought this text, with its extraordinary static, formal but concentrated quality, the greatest poem of the nineteenth century – a remarkable statement about a translation.

Text: *The Collected Works of Dante Gabriel Rossetti* (1886).

To the dim light and the large circle of shade
I have clomb,[1] and to the whitening of the hills,
There where we see no colour in the grass.

Rossetti's note to this poem reads: 'I have translated this piece both on account of its great and peculiar beauty, and also because it affords an example of a form of composition which I have met with in no Italian writer before Dante's time, though it is not uncommon among the Provençal poets . . . I have headed it with the name of a Paduan lady, to whom it is surmised by some to have been addressed during Dante's exile; but this must be looked upon as a rather doubtful conjecture. I have adopted the name chiefly to mark it at once as not referring to Beatrice [Dante's beloved in the *Vita Nuova* and the *Divina Commedia*].'
[1] *clomb* climbed.

Nathless[2] my longing loses not its green,
    It has so taken root in the hard stone   5
Which talks and hears as though it were a lady.

2
    Utterly frozen is this youthful lady,
Even as the snow that lies within the shade;
    For she is no more moved than is the stone
By the sweet season which makes warm the hills   10
    And alters them afresh from white to green,
Covering their sides again with flowers and grass.

3
When on her hair she sets a crown of grass
    The thought has no more room for other lady;
Because she weaves the yellow with the green   15
    So well that Love sits down there in the shade, –
Love who has shut me in among low hills
    Faster[3] than between walls of granite-stone.

4
    She is more bright than is a precious stone;
The wound she gives may not be healed with grass:[4]   20
    I therefore have fled far o'er plains and hills
For refuge from so dangerous a lady;
    But from her sunshine nothing can give shade, –
Not any hill, nor wall, nor summer-green.

5
    A while ago, I saw her dressed in green, –   25
So fair, she might have wakened in a stone
    This love which I do feel even for her shade;
And therefore, as one woos a graceful lady,
    I wooed her in a field that was all grass
Girdled about with very lofty hills.   30

6
Yet shall the streams turn back and climb the hills
Before Love's flame in this damp wood and green
    Burn, as it burns within a youthful lady,
For my sake, who would sleep away in stone
My life, or feed like beasts upon the grass,   35
    Only to see her garments cast a shade.

7
How dark soe'er the hills throw out their shade,
    Under her summer-green the beautiful lady
Covers it, like a stone covered in grass.

[2] *Nathless* nevertheless.
[3] *Faster* more secure.

[4] *healed with grass* grass will grow over a scar on a hillside.

Jenny

The 'fallen woman' poem – as well as the novel and picture – was a well-recognized genre in the mid-nineteenth century. Elizabeth Barrett Browning's *Aurora Leigh* (1857), Christina G. Rossetti's 'Goblin Market', 373–85, Augusta Webster's 'A Castaway', 456–71 (which may be a direct response to Rossetti's 'Jenny'), and Adelaide Anne Procter's 'A Legend of Provence', 320–7, are examples of poems or authors included in this anthology. G. F. Watts's *Found Drowned* (1848–50) is a peculiarly bleak image of the fate of many a London prostitute; Dante Gabriel Rossetti's own picture *Found* (1854) is another representation in Victorian visual culture of the prostitution narrative. Rossetti's 'Jenny' (*Poems*, 1870), an example of this form of pornography, in the original sense of the term as 'writing about prostitutes', provides a provocatively open-ended text, sparked by the serious mid-century problem of sexual commerce, and an instance of Rossetti's radical poetics that prompted Robert Buchanan's notorious rebuke in 'The Fleshly School of Poetry' (1871/2).

Where Swinburne's controversial, radical, dissenting aesthetic had come from a mixture of pagan themes, non-normative sexuality and enthusiasm for the French Decadents such as Charles Baudelaire, the provocative nature of Rossetti's poetic voice here derives from its engagement with English sexual vice. 'Jenny' creatively responds to a mid-period debate about prostitutes, evidenced, for instance, in William Acton's *Prostitution, Considered in its Moral, Social and Sanitary Aspects, in London and Other Large Cities: with Proposals for the Mitigation and Prevention of its Attendant Evils*, published first in 1857 and in a second edition the same year as 'Jenny' was issued. The three Contagious Diseases Acts, of 1864, 1866 and 1869, had attempted to regulate prostitution in the decade before and had caused major social controversy (some thought them effectively legitimizing prostitution, others regarded them as brutal).

Rossetti's poem, intervening in this high-profile public debate, addresses itself, in part, to the same contemporary questions as Augusta Webster's 'A Castaway': what kind of person is a prostitute? What does she think about, and what kind of life does she lead? Is she radically unlike others? And what is the relationship between her 'fall' and societal degeneration? Like 'A Castaway', 'Jenny' is intrigued by the contrast between the prostitute and the unfallen woman. But unlike Webster, Rossetti does not allow her to speak for herself and the persistent issue of the poem's narration – and hence of how the reader approaches it – is the speaker's fairness. The speaker reveals, perhaps, far more about himself and his own mental templates than about Jenny. The poem provokes its reader to recognize the way in which prostitutes generally fall victim to societal assumptions and ready-made categories of identity (cf. Webster's 'Faded', 471–5).

Robert Buchanan complained of the poet's harshness though not of the subject matter: 'What we object to in this poem is not the subject, which any writer may be fairly left to choose for himself; nor anything particularly vicious in the poetic treatment of it . . . But the whole tone, without being more than usually coarse, seems heartless. There is not a drop of piteousness in Mr. Rossetti.' Yet 'Jenny' requires the reader to distinguish between the speaker and the poet, however uncertain the final result. While the reader perceives more of the speaker's character than he intends, 'Jenny' is not a dramatic monologue in the tradition of Tennyson and Browning. Its generic boundaries are more challengingly fluid.

Text: *The Collected Works of Dante Gabriel Rossetti* (1886).

Vengeance of Jenny's case! Fie on her! Never name her, child!
– (Mrs. Quickly.)[1]

Lazy laughing languid Jenny,
Fond of a kiss and fond of a guinea,[2]
Whose head upon my knee to-night
Rests for a while, as if grown light
With all our dances and the sound   5
To which the wild tunes spun you round:

---

[1] *Vengeance . . . child!* Shakespeare, *The Merry Wives of Windsor* 4.1.56–7, 'Vengeance of Jenny's case! Fie on her! Never name her, child, if she be a whore'.

[2] *guinea* gold coin worth 21 shillings (£1.05).

Fair Jenny mine, the thoughtless queen
Of kisses which the blush between
Could hardly make much daintier;
Whose eyes are as blue skies, whose hair   10
Is countless gold incomparable:
Fresh flower, scarce touched with signs that tell
Of Love's exuberant hotbed: – Nay,
Poor flower left torn since yesterday
Until to-morrow leave you bare;   15
Poor handful of bright spring-water
Flung in the whirlpool's shrieking face;
Poor shameful Jenny, full of grace³
Thus with your head upon my knee; –
Whose person or whose purse⁴ may be   20
The lodestar⁵ of your reverie?

This room of yours, my Jenny, looks
A change from mine so full of books,
Whose serried⁶ ranks hold fast, forsooth,
So many captive hours of youth, –   25
The hours they thieve from day and night
To make one's cherished work come right,
And leave it wrong for all their theft,
Even as to-night my work was left:
Until I vowed that since my brain   30
And eyes of dancing seemed so fain,⁷
My feet should have some dancing too: –
And thus it was I met with you.
Well, I suppose 'twas hard to part,
For here I am. And now, sweetheart,   35
You seem too tired to get to bed.

It was a careless life I led
When rooms like this were scarce so strange
Not long ago. What breeds the change, –
The many aims or the few years?   40
Because to-night it all appears
Something I do not know again.

The cloud's not danced out of my brain –
The cloud that made it turn and swim
While hour by hour the books grew dim.   45
Why, Jenny, as I watch you there, –
For all your wealth of loosened hair,
Your silk ungirdled and unlac'd
And warm sweets open to the waist,
All golden in the lamplight's gleam, –   50
You know not what a book you seem,
Half-read by lightning in a dream!
How should you know, my Jenny? Nay,

---

³ *full of grace* cf. the Catholic prayer 'Hail Mary, full of grace, the Lord is with thee'.

⁴ *purse* pun on the Victorian slang meaning = scrotum.

⁵ *lodestar* star that reveals the way.

⁶ *serried* shoulder to shoulder, in close order.

⁷ *fain* glad.

And I should be ashamed to say: –
Poor beauty, so well worth a kiss!   55
But while my thought runs on like this
With wasteful whims more than enough,
I wonder what you're thinking of.

If of myself you think at all,
What is the thought? – conjectural   60
On sorry matters best unsolved? –
Or inly is each grace revolved
To fit me with a lure? – or (sad
To think!) perhaps you're merely glad
That I'm not drunk or ruffianly   65
And let you rest upon my knee.

For sometimes, were the truth confess'd,
You're thankful for a little rest, –
Glad from the crush to rest within,
From the heart-sickness and the din   70
Where envy's voice at virtue's pitch
Mocks you because your gown is rich;
And from the pale girl's dumb rebuke,
Whose ill-clad grace and toil-worn look
Proclaim the strength that keeps her weak,   75
And other nights than yours bespeak;
And from the wise unchildish elf,
To schoolmate lesser than himself
Pointing you out, what thing you are: –
Yes, from the daily jeer and jar,   80
From shame and shame's outbraving too,
Is rest not sometimes sweet to you? –
But most from the hatefulness of man,
Who spares not to end what he began,
Whose acts are ill and his speech ill,   85
Who, having used you at his will,
Thrusts you aside, as when I dine
I serve the dishes and the wine.

Well, handsome Jenny mine, sit up:
I've filled our glasses, let us sup,   90
And do not let me think of you,
Lest shame of yours suffice for two.
What, still so tired? Well, well then, keep
Your head there, so you do not sleep;
But that the weariness may pass   95
And leave you merry, take this glass.
Ah! lazy lily hand, more bless'd
If ne'er in rings it had been dress'd
Nor ever by a glove conceal'd!

Behold the lilies of the field,   100
They toil not neither do they spin;[8]

---

[8] *Behold . . . spin* cf. 'Consider the lillies of the field, how they grow: they toile not, neither doe they spinne. And yet I say vnto you, that euen Solomon in all his glory, was not arayed like one of these', Matthew 6.28–9.

(So doth the ancient text begin, –
Not of such rest as one of these
Can share.) Another rest and ease
Along each summer-sated path   105
From its new lord the garden hath,
Than that whose spring in blessings ran
Which praised the bounteous husbandman,[9]
Ere yet, in days of hankering[10] breath,
The lilies sickened unto death.   110

What, Jenny, are your lilies dead?
Aye, and the snow-white leaves are spread
Like winter on the garden-bed.
But you had roses left in May, –
They were not gone too. Jenny, nay,   115
But must your roses die, and those
Their purfled[11] buds that should unclose?
Even so; the leaves are curled apart,
Still red as from the broken heart,
And here's the naked stem of thorns.   120

Nay, nay, mere words. Here nothing warns
As yet of winter. Sickness here
Or want alone could waken fear, –
Nothing but passion wrings a tear.
Except when there may rise unsought   125
Haply at times a passing thought
Of the old days which seem to be
Much older than any history
That is written in any book;
When she would lie in fields and look   130
Along the ground through the blown grass
And wonder where the city was,
Far out of sight, whose broil and bale[12]
They told her then for a child's tale.

Jenny, you know the city now.   135
A child can tell the tale there, how
Some things which are not yet enroll'd
In market-lists are bought and sold
Even till the early Sunday light,
When Saturday night is market-night   140
Everywhere, be it dry or wet,
And market-night in the Haymarket.[13]
Our learned London children know,
Poor Jenny, all your pride and woe;
Have seen your lifted silken skirt   145
Advertise dainties through the dirt;
Have seen your coach-wheels splash rebuke
On virtue; and have learned your look

[9] *husbandman* cultivator of soil.
[10] *hankering* longing.
[11] *purfled* bordered, fringed.
[12] *bale* evil.
[13] *Haymarket* area of central London.

When, wealth and health slipped past, you stare
    Along the streets alone, and there,   150
Round the long park, across the bridge,
The cold lamps at the pavement's edge
    Wind on together and apart,
    A fiery serpent for your heart.

Let the thoughts pass, an empty cloud!   155
    Suppose I were to think aloud, –
    What if to her all this were said?
    Why, as a volume seldom read
    Being opened halfway shuts again,
    So might the pages of her brain   160
Be parted at such words, and thence
    Close back upon the dusty sense.
    For is there hue or shape defin'd
        In Jenny's desecrated mind,
Where all contagious currents meet,   165
A Lethe[14] of the middle street?[15]
    Nay, it reflects not any face,
    Nor sound is in its sluggish pace,
    But as they coil those eddies clot,
    And night and day remember not.   170

Why, Jenny, you're asleep at last! –
Asleep, poor Jenny, hard and fast, –
    So young and soft and tired; so fair,
    With chin thus nestled in your hair,
    Mouth quiet, eyelids almost blue[16]   175
As if some sky of dreams shone through!

Just as another woman sleeps!
Enough to throw one's thoughts in heaps
    Of doubt and horror, – what to say
    Or think, – this awful secret sway,   180
    The potter's power over the clay!
Of the same lump (it has been said)
    For honour and dishonour made,
    Two sister vessels. Here is one.

    My cousin Nell is fond of fun,   185
And fond of dress, and change, and praise,
    So mere a woman in her ways:
    And if her sweet eyes rich in youth
    Are like her lips that tell the truth,
    My cousin Nell is fond of love.   190
    And she's the girl I'm proudest of.
Who does not prize her, guard her well?
    The love of change, in cousin Nell,
    Shall find the best and hold it dear:
    The unconquered mirth turn quieter   195

---

[14] *Lethe* river of forgetfulness in Greek mythology.   [16] *eyelids almost blue* a sign of illness, perhaps.
[15] *middle street* gutters ran down the centre of the street.

Not through her own, through others' woe:
The conscious pride of beauty glow
Beside another's pride in her,
One little part of all they share.
For Love himself shall ripen these
In a kind soil to just increase
Through years of fertilizing peace.

Of the same lump (as it is said)
For honour and dishonour made,
Two sister vessels. Here is one.

It makes a goblin of the sun.

So pure, – so fall'n! How dare to think
Of the first common kindred link?
Yet, Jenny, till the world shall burn
It seems that all things take their turn:
And who shall say but this fair tree[17]
May need, in changes that may be,
Your children's children's charity?
Scorned then, no doubt, as you are scorn'd!
Shall no man hold his pride forewarn'd
Till in the end, the Day of Days,
At Judgment, one of his own race,
As frail and lost as you, shall rise, –
His daughter, with his mother's eyes?

How Jenny's clock ticks on the shelf!
Might not the dial scorn itself
That has such hours to register?
Yet as to me, even so to her
Are golden sun and silver moon,
In daily largesse[18] of earth's boon,[19]
Counted for life – coins to one tune.
And if, as blindfold fates are toss'd,
Through some one man this life be lost,
Shall soul not somehow pay for soul?

Fair shines the gilded aureole[20]
In which our highest painters place
Some living woman's simple face.
And the stilled features thus descried
As Jenny's long throat droops aside, –
The shadows where the cheeks are thin,
And pure wide curve from ear to chin, –
With Raffael's,[21] Leonardo's[22] hand
To show them to men's souls, might stand,

200

205

210

215

220

225

230

235

---

[17] *this fair tree* Nell.
[18] *largesse* bountifulness.
[19] *boon* favour, gift.
[20] *aureole* gold disc surrounding the head in paintings, denoting the glory of the person represented. The speaker thinks chiefly of depictions of the Virgin Mary.

[21] *Raffael* Raphael (1483–1520), Italian painter.
[22] *Leonardo* Leonardo da Vinci (1452–1519), Florentine painter, scientist and thinker.

Whole ages long, the whole world through,
    For preachings of what God can do.   240
What has man done here? How atone,
Great God, for this which man has done?
  And for the body and soul which by
  Man's pitiless doom must now comply
    With lifelong hell, what lullaby   245
    Of sweet forgetful second birth[23]
Remains? All dark.[24] No sign on earth
What measure of God's rest endows
The many mansions of his house.[25]

  If but a woman's heart might see   250
    Such erring heart unerringly
  For once! But that can never be.

    Like a rose shut in a book
  In which pure women may not look,
    For its base pages claim control   255
  To crush the flower within the soul;
Where through each dead rose-leaf that clings,
  Pale as transparent Psyche-wings,[26]
  To the vile text, are traced such things
  As might make lady's cheek indeed   260
  More than a living rose to read;
  So nought save foolish foulness may
  Watch with hard eyes the sure decay;
  And so the life-blood of this rose,
  Puddled with shameful knowledge, flows   265
Through leaves no chaste hand may unclose:
  Yet still it keeps such faded show
  Of when 'twas gathered long ago,
  That the crushed petals' lovely grain,
  The sweetness of the sanguine[27] stain,   270
  Seen of a woman's eyes, must make
  Her pitiful heart, so prone to ache,
  Love roses better for its sake: –
  Only that this can never be: –
  Even so unto her sex is she.   275

  Yet, Jenny, looking long at you,
  The woman almost fades from view.
  A cipher[28] of man's changeless sum
  Of lust, past, present, and to come,
  Is left. A riddle that one shrinks   280
To challenge from the scornful sphinx.[29]

---

[23] *second birth* following forgiveness (see John 3.3, 'Iesus answered, and said vnto him, Uerily, verily I say vnto thee, except a man be borne againe, he cannot see the kingdome of God').

[24] *All dark* cf. the blinded Gloucester in Shakespeare's *King Lear* (folio) 3.7.83: 'All dark and comfortless?'

[25] *many mansions of his house* cf. Jesus's words in John 14.2, 'In my Fathers house are many mansions; if it were not so, I would haue told you: I goe to prepare a place for you'.

[26] *Psyche-wings* wings of the soul.

[27] *sanguine* blood-coloured.

[28] *cipher* symbol or character (with the additional sense of worthless person).

[29] *sphinx* hybrid monster with a riddle, usually described as having the head of a woman and the winged body of a lion, which infested Thebes until the riddle was solved by Oedipus.

Like a toad within a stone[30]
Seated while Time crumbles on;
Which sits there since the earth was curs'd
For Man's transgression at the first;[31]   285
Which, living through all centuries,
Not once has seen the sun arise;
Whose life, to its cold circle charmed,
The earth's whole summers have not warmed;
Which always – whitherso the stone   290
Be flung – sits there, deaf, blind, alone; –
Aye, and shall not be driven out
Till that which shuts him round about
Break at the very Master's stroke,[32]
And the dust thereof vanish as smoke,   295
And the seed of Man vanish as dust: –
Even so within this world is Lust.

Come, come, what use in thoughts like this?
Poor little Jenny, good to kiss, –
You'd not believe by what strange roads   300
Thought travels, when your beauty goads
A man to-night to think of toads!
Jenny, wake up . . . Why, there's the dawn!

And there's an early waggon drawn
To market, and some sheep that jog   305
Bleating before a barking dog;
And the old streets come peering through
Another night that London knew;
And all as ghostlike as the lamps.

So on the wings of day decamps   310
My last night's frolic. Glooms begin
To shiver off as lights creep in
Past the gauze curtains half drawn-to,
And the lamp's doubled shade grows blue, –
Your lamp, my Jenny, kept alight,   315
Like a wise virgin's,[33] all one night!
And in the alcove coolly spread
Glimmers with dawn your empty bed;
And yonder your fair face I see

---

[30] *toad . . . stone* reference to the popular belief that toads could live permanently in stones.
[31] *Man's transgression at the first* the Fall (Genesis 2–3).
[32] *Master's stroke* the Last Day.
[33] *like a wise virgin's* ironic reference to Matthew 25.1–13: 'Then shall the kingdome of heauen be likened vnto ten Uirgins, which tooke their lamps, & went forth to meet the bridegrome. And fiue of them were wise, and fiue were foolish. They that were foolish tooke their lampes, and tooke no oyle with them: But the wise tooke oyle in their vessels with their lampes. While the bridegrome taried, they all slumbred and slept. And at midnight there was a cry made, Behold, the bridegrome commeth, goe ye out to meet him. Then all those virgins arose, and trimmed their lampes. And the foolish said vnto the wise, Giue vs of your oyle, for our lampes are gone out. But the wise answered, saying, Not so, lest there be not ynough for vs and you, but goe ye rather to them that sell, and buy for your selues. And while they went to buy, the bridegrome came, and they that were ready, went in with him to the marriage, and the doore was shut. Afterward came also the other virgines, saying, Lord, Lord, open to vs. But he answered, and said, Uerely I say vnto you, I know you not. Watch therefore, for ye know neither the day, nor the houre, wherein the Sonne of man commeth.'

Reflected lying on my knee,   320
Where teems with first foreshadowings
Your pier-glass[34] scrawled with diamond rings:[35]
And on your bosom all night worn
Yesterday's rose now droops forlorn,
But dies not yet this summer morn.   325

And now without,[36] as if some word
Had called upon them that they heard,
The London sparrows far and nigh
Clamour together suddenly;
And Jenny's cage-bird grown awake   330
Here in their song his part must take,
Because here too the day doth break.

And somehow in myself the dawn
Among stirred clouds and veils withdrawn
Strikes greyly on her. Let her sleep.   335
But will it wake her if I heap
These cushions thus beneath her head
Where my knee was? No, – there's your bed,
My Jenny, while you dream. And there
I lay among your golden hair,   340
Perhaps the subject of your dreams,
These golden coins.

For still one deems
That Jenny's flattering sleep confers
New magic on the magic purse, –   345
Grim web,[37] how clogged with shrivelled flies!
Between the threads fine fumes arise
And shape their pictures in the brain.
There roll no streets in glare and rain,
Nor flagrant man-swine whets his tusk;[38]   350
- But delicately sighs in musk[39]
The homage of the dim boudoir;[40]
Or like a palpitating star
Thrilled into song, the opera-night
Breathes faint in the quick pulse of light;   355
Or at the carriage-window shine
Rich wares for choice; or, free to dine,
Whirls through its hour of health (divine
For her) the concourse of the Park.[41]
And though in the discounted dark   360

---

[34] *pier-glass* large tall mirror.
[35] *diamond rings* the early light on the pier-glass reveals its highly scratched surface. Cf. chapter 27 of George Eliot's *Middlemarch* (1871–2): 'Your pier-glass or extensive surface of polished steel made to be rubbed by a housemaid, will be minutely and multitudinously scratched in all directions; but place now against it a lighted candle as a centre of illumination, and lo! the scratches will seem to arrange themselves in a fine series of concentric circles round that little sun.'

[36] *without* outside.
[37] *Grim web* her purse, full of money made through trading sex.
[38] *flagrant man-swine whets his tusk* in Jenny's dream, as the speaker imagines it, there are no lustful men requiring sex.
[39] *musk* expensive perfume.
[40] *boudoir* small elegantly furnished room, often for women to retire to alone or with private friends.
[41] *Park* some fashionable place in which to be seen.

Her functions there and here are one,
Beneath the lamps and in the sun
There reigns at least the acknowledged belle[42]
Apparelled beyond parallel.
Ah Jenny, yes, we know your dreams.   365

For even the Paphian Venus[43] seems
A goddess o'er the realms of love,
When silver-shrined in shadowy grove:
Aye, or let offerings nicely plac'd
But hide Priapus[44] to the waist,   370
And whoso looks on him shall see
An eligible deity.[45]

Why, Jenny, waking here alone
May help you to remember one,[46]
Though all the memory's long outworn   375
Of many a double-pillowed morn.
I think I see you when you wake,
And rub your eyes for me, and shake
My gold, in rising, from your hair,
A Danaë[47] for a moment there.   380

Jenny, my love rang true! for still
Love at first sight is vague, until
That tinkling makes him audible.

And must I mock you to the last,
Ashamed of my own shame, – aghast   385
Because some thoughts not born amiss
Rose at a poor fair face like this?
Well, of such thoughts so much I know:
In my life, as in hers, they show,
By a far gleam which I may near,   390
A dark path I can strive to clear.
Only one kiss. Good-bye, my dear.

---

[42] *belle* beauty.
[43] *Paphian Venus* Venus is the Roman Aphrodite, the goddess of love: Paphian is one of her epithets (born of the sea, some thought she come ashore first at Paphos). Tacitus records in Book 2 of the *Histories* that the image of the Paphian Venus in her temple was not a human shape. Rossetti, recalling Tacitus, is making the point that, in shade and with ornamentation, this figure might indeed be taken for the beautiful goddess of love.
[44] *Priapus* god of sexuality and fertility represented with a grotesquely huge phallus.

[45] *deity* cf. note 44. If Priapus's huge sexual appetite (and organ) are covered, he appears perfectly attractive.
[46] *one* the speaker.
[47] *Danaë* daughter of the King of Argos and Eurydice, her father was told she would bear a son who would slay him. He kept her in a bronze chamber or tower, but Zeus, the king of the gods, made love to her as a shower of golden rain pouring into her lap.

Nuptial Sleep

A sonnet from the first part of Rossetti's *The House of Life* (published in 1870), 'Nuptial Sleep' was the especial target of Robert Buchanan's 'The Fleshly School of Poetry' article in the *Contemporary Review* (1871): 'Here is a full-grown man, presumably intelligent and cultivated, putting on record for other full-grown men to read, the most secret mysteries of sexual connection, and that with so sickening a desire to reproduce the sensual mood, so careful a choice of epithet to convey mere animal sensations, that we merely shudder at the shameless nakedness. We are no purists in such matters. We hold the sensual part of our nature to be as holy as the spiritual or intellectual part, and we believe that such things must find their equivalent in all; but it is neither poetic, nor manly, nor even human, to obtrude such things as the themes of whole poems. It is simply nasty.' Rossetti, much affected by the 'Fleshly School' controversy, excluded this 'nasty' poem from the final version of *The House of Life* (1881).

As Buchanan – publishing under the name of Thomas Maitland – recognized, the poem's distinctiveness lies in its making public the private, its foregrounding of sexual experience as an appropriate subject for poetry (its gesture towards legitimization

is the 'nuptial' of the title). Redefining the accepted terrain of the sonnet – long associated with ideal/idealized love – Rossetti's poem is remarkable not least for its inscription of female sexual desire. At the close of 'Nuptial Sleep', the woman occupies the culturally familiar female position as the object of a man's erotic gaze. But prior to that, Rossetti writes her as an equal, as inseparable from her partner in desire and sexual action. The final line's emphasis on the wondrous *fact* of the woman's body might be compared to 'Song 8: The Woodspurge', 368–9, with its rather different valorization of material existence and 'real presence'.

Text: *The Collected Works of Dante Gabriel Rossetti* (1886).

At length their long kiss severed, with sweet smart:
And as the last slow sudden drops are shed
From sparkling eaves when all the storm has fled,
So singly flagged the pulses of each heart.
Their bosoms sundered, with the opening start   5
Of married flowers to either side outspread
From the knit stem; yet still their mouths, burnt red,
Fawned on each other where they lay apart.

Sleep sank them lower than the tide of dreams,
And their dreams watched them sink, and slid away.   10
Slowly their souls swam up again, through gleams
Of watered light and dull drowned waifs of day;
Till from some wonder of new woods and streams
He woke, and wondered more: for there she lay.

Song 8: The Woodspurge

Robert Browning's 'Fra Lippo Lippi', 179–88, debated the role of materiality in representation, the use and meaning of physical reality in providing knowledge of the non-physical. The role of the material in the semantic economy of verse continues to be a theme in Rossetti's 'Woodspurge' – a song from the first version of his *House of Life* sonnet sequence (this was initially published in 1870 as *Sonnets and Songs Towards a Work to be called 'The House of Life'*; in 1881, it was completed and reorganized to consist solely of sonnets). Like 'Fra Lippo Lippi', the poem comments on the aesthetic of particularity, the concentrated focus on material nature, which was a key component of the art of the two other painters who, with Rossetti, led the formation of the Pre-Raphaelite Brotherhood in 1848: William Holman Hunt and John Everett Millais (see headnote, 350). In Hunt's art, as it matured, natural form was used in a system of symbolic reference, a procedure this poem implicitly contests.

'The Woodspurge' disputes Romantic ideas that nature speaks of God or, as Wordsworth would have it, offers consolation to the dejected. The woodspurge here – a common greenish-yellow plant, *Euphorbia amygdaloides*, used ornamentally today – stands out to the grieving poet in sharply realized natural detail. It provides an image that remains in his mind but only as itself, resisting emotional association, metaphor or symbolization. It has none of the power that Wordsworth attributed to the memory of nature. The poet of 'The Woodspurge' does nothing with the 'weed' – an un-Romantic denotation anyway – other than to observe it, sloughing off any cultural association between poetry and prophetic insight, and suggesting a more limited conception of the work of the imagination.

Text: *The Collected Works of Dante Gabriel Rossetti* (1886).

The wind flapped loose, the wind was still,
Shaken out dead from tree and hill:
I had walked on at the wind's will, –
I sat now, for the wind was still.

2

Between my knees my forehead was, –
My lips, drawn in, said not Alas!
My hair was over in the grass,
My naked ears heard the day pass.

3

My eyes, wide open, had the run
Of somea ten weeds to fix upon;
Among those few, out of the sun,
The woodspurge flowered, three cups in one.

4

From perfect grief there need not be
Wisdom or even memory:
One thing then learnt remains to me, –
The woodspurge has a cup of three.

Christina G. Rossetti (1830–1894)

Christina Rossetti – Christina G. Rossetti as she preferred – was born in London, daughter of the Italian poet, patriot and scholar Gabriele Rossetti, Professor of Italian at King's College London, and Frances Polidori, sister of Byron's doctor. With her brother Dante Gabriel, she made full use of the cultural and literary opportunities provided by her family though was plagued by ill health (this may have been strategic at first, but became increasingly serious and eventually fatal). It cut short her attempts to work as a governess, and she retired to a largely quiet indoor life, the devotions of her High Anglicanism, and writing (she did, none the less, travel through France [1861] and Italy [1865], which is more than can be said for her brother who, despite his Italian roots, fascination with Dante, Italian translations and artistic preferences for the pre-Renaissance, never made it to his father's country). Christina also worked for many years with fallen women at the Highgate Penitentiary. She contributed to *The Germ*, the short-lived Pre-Raphaelite magazine, but made her name properly with the publication of *Goblin Market and Other Poems* in 1862 and *The Prince's Progress and Other Poems* in 1866. Her enigmatic writing, its plotted dissatisfactions, expressive range, concern with isolation, occupation of positions of weakness as sources of strength, masterly use of the sonnet, and sudden erotic power, has been steadily recognized, and she now stands as one of the major poets of the Victorian period, increasingly anthologized and debated. Christina Rossetti turned down offers of marriage – largely on religious grounds – and remained single. Much verse and prose including nursery rhymes and a substantial amount of devotional writing followed the first two successful volumes (e.g., *Annus Domini: A Prayer for Each Day of the Year* [1874]; *A Pageant and Other Poems* [1881]; *Called to be Saints: The Minor Festivals Devotionally Studied* [1881]; *Time Flies: A Reading Diary* [1885]; *The Face of the Deep: A Devotional Commentary on the Apocalypse* [1892]). Her five books on religious and devotional subjects were all published by the Society for the Promotion of Christian Knowledge. She was friendly with other women poets despite her lifestyle, but fell out with Augusta Webster over women's suffrage, which Rossetti could not accept. She died in agony of breast cancer in December 1894; her brother William Michael Rossetti edited her *Poetical Works* in 1904.

In an Artist's Studio

Exploring a relationship between what is represented in art and its material model, a question, that is, of the kind of knowledge art provides, Christina G. Rossetti's poem contributes to a debate to which Browning's 'Fra Lippo Lippi', 179–88, Dante Gabriel Rossetti's 'Song 8: The Woodspurge', 368–9, and Michael Field's 'La Gioconda', 558–9, and 'A Portrait: Bartolommeo Veneto', 560–2, also responded. As with Christina Rossetti's 'Sonnet: In life our absent friend is far away', 391–2, 'In an Artist's Studio' meditates on the different identities a human being has once he or she enters the social order and is the object of another's gaze (cf. Augusta Webster's 'Faded', 471–5, a poem preoccupied with female identity). Rossetti had first-hand knowledge of the artist's studio, since she sat as a model for her brother Dante Gabriel. But she was thinking in this poem primarily of Elizabeth Siddall (1834–62), first Dante Gabriel's model and later his wife. Christina Rossetti wrote 'In an Artist's Studio' after a visit to her brother's apartment on 24 December 1856 where there were many drawings of Lizzie on show, and it is their ultimately tragic relationship that lies behind this sonnet's concern with a recurrent, reiterated image. 'In an Artist's Studio' muses on the politics of female representation and the ideals of heterosexual relationships, hinting at a calamitous narrative. It belongs among a group of poems, unpublished during Rossetti's life, that were critical of the Pre-Raphaelites. With measured pace, the poem exploits characteristically lean diction, its sestet comprised almost entirely of monosyllables clustering around simple, sad negatives. It was published first in 1896.

Text: *The Complete Poems of Christina Rossetti: A Variorum Edition* (1979–90).

One face looks out from all his canvasses,
One selfsame figure sits or walks or leans;
We found her hidden just behind those screens,
That mirror gave back all her loveliness.
A queen in opal[1] or in ruby dress,   5
A nameless girl in freshest summer greens,
A saint, an angel; – every canvass means
The same one meaning, neither more nor less.
He feeds upon her face by day and night,
And she with true kind eyes looks back on him   10
Fair as the moon and joyful as the light:
Not wan[2] with waiting, not with sorrow dim;
Not as she is, but was when hope shone bright;
Not as she is, but as she fills his dream.

[handwritten notes in left margin:]
All positive but "distant" images
what the "ideal" woman looks like? Literally or in the painting?
Unrealistic paintings "ideal" woman

[1] *opal* delicately coloured quartz-like gemstone.   [2] *wan* pale.

An Apple-Gathering

Influenced by English ballad and folksong, 'An Apple-Gathering' (1861) stages a narrative about physical desire and temptation around the possession of ripe fruit. The natural world here, as so often in Christina Rossetti's work, provides material of symbolic significance, moving fluidly between its material self and meanings beyond while resisting the full clarity of allegory. Like 'Goblin Market', 373–85, 'An Apple-Gathering' meditates on transgression – it is a curious kind of fallen woman poem. The figure of the solitary poet at the end, loitering alone, is a familiar subject position for Rossetti as marginalized (cf. 'Shut Out', 388–9). Tenderly, the poem offers a scene of English rurality. Like 'A Christmas Carol', 390–1, it is quietly involved in constructing an idea of a nation – here, its rural labour and pre-industrial social dynamics. 'An Apple-Gathering' first appeared in *Macmillan's Magazine*, 4 (1861).

Text: *Goblin Market and Other Poems* (1862).

[handwritten note:] b4 apples appeared

I plucked pink blossoms from mine apple tree
And wore them all that evening in my hair:
Then in due season when I went to see
I found no apples there.

2
With dangling basket all along the grass   5
As I had come I went the selfsame track:
My neighbours mocked me while they saw me pass
So empty-handed back.

3
Lilian and Lilias smiled in trudging by,
Their heaped-up basket teazed me like a jeer;   10
Sweet-voiced they sang beneath the sunset sky,
Their mother's home was near.

4
Plump Gertrude passed me with her basket full,
A stronger hand than hers helped it along;
A voice talked with her thro' the shadows cool   15
More sweet to me than song.

5

Ah Willie, Willie, was my love less worth
Than apples with their green leaves piled above?
I counted rosiest apples on the earth
    Of far less worth than love.   20

6

So once it was with me you stooped to talk
Laughing and listening in this very lane:
To think that by this way we used to walk
    We shall not walk again!

7

I let my neighbours pass me, ones and twos   25
And groups; the latest said the night grew chill,
And hastened: but I loitered, while the dews
    Fell fast I loitered still.

A Birthday

Christina G. Rossetti's poem is about the coming of a lover, not a real birthday: life begins properly (a metaphorical *birth* day) with the lover's arrival. Although 'A Birthday' (*Macmillan's Magazine*, 3 [1861]) is occasioned by the appearance of the lover, its focus is not, as perhaps one might expect, on togetherness or on arrival. It concentrates instead on the singleness and singularity of the lover's inner life (cf. other poems in which Rossetti foregrounds the solitary speaker, e.g., 'Shut Out', 388–9, 'An Apple-Gathering', 371–2, 'When I am dead', 385–6). 'A Birthday' opens up the speaker's mind to reveal his or her own private thoughts and self-representation (the speaker is non-gendered). It offers an instance of self-dramatization, an extraordinary self-projection, in the second stanza, into a kind of camp baroque fantasy. As an account of feeling, moreover, Rossetti produces a poem that is intriguingly double. 'A Birthday' is apparently joyful; gladness is the speaker's obvious response to the coming of love. But details of the diction – richer than her customary simplicity – query this. The images of the first stanza are precarious (a nest in a stream, an over-weighted apple bough, a halcyon sea), while the second, with its silks, purples and pomegranates, has a funereal weightiness and covert allusions to death.

Text: *Goblin Market and Other Poems* (1862).

My heart is like a singing bird
Whose nest is in a watered shoot;
My heart is like an apple tree
Whose boughs are bent with thickset fruit;
My heart is like a rainbow shell   5
That paddles in a halcyon[1] sea;
My heart is gladder than all these
Because my love is come to me.

Raise me a dais[2] of silk and down;
Hang it with vair[3] and purple dyes;   10

[handwritten: Who is he/she talking to?]
[handwritten: Commands]

---

[1] *halcyon* fabled bird that breeds around the winter solstice in a nest floating on the sea, having charmed the wind and waves. Halcyon days are therefore calm but short.

[2] *dais* raised platform.

[3] *vair* fur from grey and white squirrel used ornamentally.

Carve it in doves and pomegranates,[4] *Also Bible*
And peacocks with a hundred eyes;
Work it in gold and silver grapes,
In leaves and silver fleurs-de-lys;[5]
Because the birthday of my life   15
Is come, my love is come to me.

[4] *pomegranates* fruit of the dual-natured goddess Proserpine, Queen of the Dead. She ate a few pomegranate seeds while in the underworld and was obliged to spend some months (the same number as the seeds she ate – versions differ as to the number) there each year.
[5] *fleurs-de-lys* heraldic lily.

Goblin Market

Capitalism
Market
Drug Pushing/Selling

'Goblin Market' (1862) is a profoundly intriguing poem, susceptible to a diversity of readings, yet remaining enigmatic. If the unsolved is a particular feature of Christina Rossetti's verse (cf. 'Winter: My Secret', 386–7), then this poem remains aloof from resolution in an exceptionally sustained way. Like Elizabeth Barrett Browning's 'Rime of the Duchess May', 29–44, it is a narrative poem that debates a question of gender politics; like Dante Gabriel Rossetti's 'Jenny', 358–67, and Augusta Webster's 'A Castaway', 456–71, it is a fallen woman poem, though one that narrativizes redemption. It offers precisely the kind of closure Webster eschews. Like Webster's 'Circe', 450–5, 'Goblin Market' considers the topic of female sexual desire, but here a virginal purity is restored through a sister's love, and heteronormativity (re)inscribed at the close. Such heteronormativity, however, is intriguingly without husbands. (The poem's final bland lines ironically sharpen, as perhaps they are intended to do, the reader's sense of the poem's earlier vitality, the violence and eroticism of its language that lingers longer in the mind than the 'moral' of the close.) Again, like Barrett Browning's 'Rime', 'Goblin Market' considers the nature of female heroism, musing on how to represent the heroine as a distinct literary category. It can be read in relation to Macaulay's 'Horatius', 1–17, to form a diptych of male and female redemptory heroic action.

'Goblin Market' presents a narrative of a girl saved from calamity by the generosity of her sister, who suffers physical assault to provide an antidote for her seemingly fatal desires. As a poem about consumerism and the near fatal entry into a system of economic exchange, it seems to be a reflection on modern capitalism and commerce. On the other hand, while the poem implies an anxious view of consumerism, it also finds in the act of consumption – Laura's orgiastic absorption of the juices on her sister's body – a source of redemption. In the physical suffering Lizzie endures, some feminist scholars have seen a brutal enactment of oppressive gender politics, a scene, as it were, from 'patriarchy' but one in which, finally, the female triumphs. Yet the poem finally slips beyond determinedly allegorical readings. Lush, sexual, but not far from a child's moral fable, 'Goblin Market' exploits an obvious Biblical connotation of fruit eating as sinful. It certainly affirms female redemptive power celebrating woman-to-woman relations as peculiarly constructive and life giving (cf. the affirmation of female love in 'A Christmas Carol', 390–1).

Rossetti's Tractarian faith included belief in a typological understanding of the Old Testament. This was read as offering 'types' or symbolic prefigurings of events of the Christian gospels. 'Goblin Market', like much of Rossetti's poetry, may in turn be seen investing in the typological. She once said that she agreed wholly with the notion that 'All the world over, visible things typify things invisible'. Such a view may lie behind 'Goblin Market', a poem which acts out, perhaps, a version of the redemption, Jesus's suffering at the hands of humanity that, in Christian theology, takes away the sins of the world. Rossetti's Christ-figure is, significantly, female. Some have suggested that the poem was written to be read at the Highgate Penitentiary where Rossetti worked with former prostitutes – an environment that would have given it particular resonance. (For other poems that invite a typological reading, cf. 'The World', 389–90, 'The Lambs of Grasmere', 387–8, and 'Babylon the Great', 393.)   *Interesting*

Like Lord Macaulay's poem, 'Goblin Market' offers also, at a plainer level, the pleasures of narrative and pace, together with arresting verbal energy. It makes an unsettling connection between the enthralment of exuberant language and transgressive, dangerous, sexual desire.

Text: *Goblin Market and Other Poems* (1862).

Morning and evening
Maids heard the goblins cry:
'Come buy our orchard fruits,
Come buy, come buy:
Apples and quinces,   5
Lemons and oranges,
Plump unpecked cherries,
Melons and raspberries,
Bloom-down-cheeked peaches,
Swart[1]-headed mulberries,   10
Wild free-born cranberries,
Crab-apples, dewberries,
Pine-apples, blackberries,
Apricots, strawberries; –
All ripe together   15
In summer weather, –
Morns that pass by,
Fair eves that fly;
Come buy, come buy:
Our grapes fresh from the vine,   20
Pomegranates full and fine,
Dates and sharp bullaces,[2]
Rare pears and greengages,
Damsons and bilberries,
Taste them and try: 25
Currants and gooseberries,
Bright-fire-like barberries,[3]
Figs to fill your mouth,
Citrons[4] from the South,
Sweet to tongue and sound to eye;   30
Come buy, come buy.'

Evening by evening
Among the brookside rushes,
Laura bowed her head to hear,
Lizzie veiled her blushes: 35
Crouching close together
In the cooling weather,
With clasping arms and cautioning lips,
With tingling cheeks and finger tips.
'Lie close,' Laura said,   40
Pricking up her golden head:
'We must not look at goblin men,
We must not buy their fruits:
Who knows upon what soil they fed
Their hungry thirsty roots?'   45
'Come buy,' call the goblins
Hobbling down the glen.
'Oh,' cried Lizzie, 'Laura, Laura,
You should not peep at goblin men.'
Lizzie covered up her eyes,   50

---

[1] *swart* dark in colour, black.
[2] *bullaces* wild plums.
[3] *barberries* acidic berries of a European shrub.

[4] *Citrons* acid juicy tree-fruit (sometimes the term includes lemons).

Covered close lest they should look;
Laura reared her glossy head,
And whispered like the restless brook:
'Look, Lizzie, look, Lizzie,
Down the glen tramp little men.   55
One hauls a basket,
One bears a plate,
One lugs a golden dish
Of many pounds weight.
How fair the vine must grow   60
Whose grapes are so luscious;
How warm the wind must blow
Thro' those fruit bushes.'
'No,' said Lizzie: 'No, no, no;
Their offers should not charm us,   65
Their evil gifts would harm us.'
She thrust a dimpled finger
In each ear, shut eyes and ran:
Curious Laura chose to linger
Wondering at each merchant man.   70
One had a cat's face,
One whisked a tail,
One tramped at a rat's pace,
One crawled like a snail,
One like a wombat prowled obtuse and furry, 75
One like a ratel[5] tumbled hurry skurry.
She heard a voice like voice of doves
Cooing all together:
They sounded kind and full of loves
In the pleasant weather.   80

Laura stretched her gleaming neck
Like a rush-imbedded swan,
Like a lily from the beck,[6]
Like a moonlit poplar branch,
Like a vessel at the launch   85
When its last restraint is gone.

Backwards up the mossy glen
Turned and trooped the goblin men,
With their shrill repeated cry,
'Come buy, come buy.'   90
When they reached where Laura was
They stood stock still upon the moss,
Leering at each other,
Brother with queer brother;
Signalling each other,   95
Brother with sly brother.
One set his basket down,
One reared his plate;
One began to weave a crown
Of tendrils, leaves and rough nuts brown 100

[5] *ratel* honey badger, native to Africa and southern Asia.   [6] *beck* brook, stream.

(Men sell not such in any town);
One heaved the golden weight
Of dish and fruit to offer her:
'Come buy, come buy,' was still their cry.
Laura stared but did not stir,   105
Longed but had no money:
The whisk-tailed merchant bade her taste
In tones as smooth as honey,
The cat-faced purr'd,
The rat-paced spoke a word   110
Of welcome, and the snail-paced even was heard;
One parrot-voiced and jolly
Cried 'Pretty Goblin' still for 'Pretty Polly;' –
One whistled like a bird.

But sweet-tooth Laura spoke in haste: *– Uncalculated*   115
'Good folk, I have no coin;   *Inconsiderate*
To take were to purloin:[7]
I have no copper in my purse,
I have no silver either,
And all my gold is on the furze[8]   120
That shakes in windy weather
Above the rusty heather.'
'You have much gold upon your head,'   *NB, just sell us*
They answered all together: *your soul–your head*
'Buy from us with a golden curl.'   125
She clipped a precious golden lock,
She dropped a tear more rare than pearl,
Then sucked their fruit globes fair or red:
Sweeter than honey from the rock.[9]
Stronger than man-rejoicing wine,   130
Clearer than water flowed that juice;
She never tasted such before,
How should it cloy with length of use?
Bewildered,   She sucked and sucked and sucked the more
after hasty   Fruits which that unknown orchard bore;   135
feverish   She sucked until her lips were sore;
enjoyment   Then flung the emptied rinds away
But gathered up one kernel-stone,
And knew not was it night or day   *– In a daze;*
As she turned home alone.   *bewildered*   140

Lizzie met her at the gate
Full of wise upbraidings:
'Dear, you should not stay so late,
Twilight is not good for maidens;   *– women*
Should not loiter in the glen   145
In the haunts of goblin men.
Do you not remember Jeanie,   *other friend*
How she met them in the moonlight,   *fallen woman*
Took their gifts both choice and many,

---

[7] *purloin* steal.
[8] *furze* spiny evergreen shrub with yellow flowers (hence the 'gold').

[9] *honey . . . rock* cf. 'Hee should haue fedde them also with the finest of the wheat: and with honie out of the rocke, should I haue satisfied thee', Psalm 81.16.

Ate their fruits and wore their flowers
Plucked from bowers
Where summer ripens at all hours?
But ever in the noonlight
She pined and pined away;
Sought them by night and day,
Found them no more but dwindled and grew grey;
Then fell with the first snow,
While to this day no grass will grow
Where she lies low:
I planted daisies there a year ago   160
That never blow.
You should not loiter so.'
'Nay, hush,' said Laura:
'Nay, hush, my sister:
I ate and ate my fill,   165
Yet my mouth waters still;
Tomorrow night I will
Buy more:' and kissed her:
'Have done with sorrow;
I'll bring you plums tomorrow   170
Fresh on their mother twigs,
Cherries worth getting;
You cannot think what figs
My teeth have met in,
What melons icy-cold   175
Piled on a dish of gold
Too huge for me to hold,
What peaches with a velvet nap,
Pellucid[10] grapes without one seed:
Odorous indeed must be the mead[11]   180
Whereon they grow, and pure the wave they drink
With lilies at the brink,
And sugar-sweet their sap.'

Golden head by golden head,
Like two pigeons in one nest   185
Folded in each other's wings,
They lay down in their curtained bed:[12]
Like two blossoms on one stem,
Like two flakes of new-fall'n snow,
Like two wands of ivory   190
Tipped with gold for awful[13] kings.
Moon and stars gazed in at them,
Wind sang to them lullaby,
Lumbering owls forbore to fly,
Not a bat flapped to and fro   195
Round their rest:
Cheek to cheek and breast to breast
Locked together in one nest.

---

[10] *Pellucid* allowing the passage of light, translucent.
[11] *mead* meadow.
[12] *Golden head . . . bed* it was common for sisters to sleep in the same bed in the Victorian period, though these lines are, certainly, teasingly erotic.
[13] *awful* as in 'awe-ful'.

Early in the morning
When the first cock crowed his warning,   200
Neat like bees, as sweet and busy,
Laura rose with Lizzie:
Fetched in honey, milked the cows,
Aired and set to rights the house,
Kneaded cakes of whitest wheat,   205
Cakes for dainty mouths to eat,
Next churned butter, whipped up cream,
Fed their poultry, sat and sewed;
Talked as modest maidens should:
Lizzie with an open heart,   210
Laura in an absent dream,
One content, one sick in part;
One warbling for the mere bright day's delight,
One longing for the night.

At length slow evening came: 215
They went with pitchers to the reedy brook;
Lizzie most placid in her look,
Laura most like a leaping flame.
They drew the gurgling water from its deep;
Lizzie plucked purple and rich golden flags,[14]   220
Then turning homewards said: 'The sunset flushes
Those furthest loftiest crags;
Come, Laura, not another maiden lags,
No wilful squirrel wags,
The beasts and birds are fast asleep.'   225
But Laura loitered still among the rushes
And said the bank was steep.

And said the hour was early still,
The dew not fall'n, the wind not chill:
Listening ever, but not catching   230
The customary cry,
'Come buy, come buy,'
With its iterated jingle
Of sugar-baited words:
Not for all her watching   235
Once discerning even one goblin
Racing, whisking, tumbling, hobbling;
Let alone the herds
That used to tramp along the glen,
In groups or single,   240
Of brisk fruit-merchant men.
Till Lizzie urged, 'O Laura, come;
I hear the fruit-call but I dare not look:
You should not loiter longer at this brook:
Come with me home.   245
The stars rise, the moon bends her arc,
Each glowworm winks her spark,
Let us get home before the night grows dark:

---

[14] *flag* tall violet or blue rush-like plant, some with yellow
petal markings, usually growing near water; an iris.

For clouds may gather
Tho' this is summer weather,   250
Put out the lights and drench us thro';
Then if we lost our way what should we do?'

Laura turned cold as stone
To find her sister heard that cry alone,
That goblin cry,   255
'Come buy our fruits, come buy.'
Must she then buy no more such dainty fruit?
Must she no more such succous[15] pasture find,
Gone deaf and blind?
Her tree of life drooped from the root: 260
She said not one word in her heart's sore ache;
But peering thro' the dimness, nought discerning,
Trudged home, her pitcher dripping all the way;
So crept to bed, and lay
Silent till Lizzie slept;   265
Then sat up in a passionate yearning,
And gnashed her teeth for baulked desire, and wept
As if her heart would break.

[handwritten margin note: Biblical terms "weeping & gnashing of teeth."]

Day after day, night after night,
Laura kept watch in vain   270
In sullen silence of exceeding pain.
She never caught again the goblin cry:
'Come buy, come buy;' –
She never spied the goblin men
Hawking their fruits along the glen: 275
But when the noon waxed bright
Her hair grew thin and gray;
She dwindled, as the fair full moon doth turn
To swift decay and burn
Her fire away.   280

[handwritten margin note: Addiction]

[handwritten margin note: Wages of sin death w/ its by-products: aging, decay]

One day remembering her kernel-stone
She set it by a wall that faced the south;
Dewed it with tears, hoped for a root,
Watched for a waxing shoot,
But there came none;   285
It never saw the sun,
It never felt the trickling moisture run:
While with sunk eyes and faded mouth
She dreamed of melons, as a traveller sees
False waves in desert drouth[16]   290
With shade of leaf-crowned trees,
And burns the thirstier in the sandful breeze.

[handwritten margin note: Addicts save a little something for themselves.]

[handwritten margin note: effect of drugs]

She no more swept the house,
Tended the fowls or cows,
Fetched honey, kneaded cakes of wheat,   295
Brought water from the brook:

[handwritten margin note: couldn't function w/out drug]

---

[15] *succous* juicy.   [16] *drouth* drought.

But sat down listless in the chimney-nook
And would not eat.

Tender Lizzie could not bear
To watch her sister's cankerous[17] care   300
Yet not to share.
She night and morning
Caught the goblins' cry:
'Come buy our orchard fruits,
Come buy, come buy:' –   305
Beside the brook, along the glen,
She heard the tramp of goblin men,
The voice and stir
Poor Laura could not hear;
Longed to buy fruit to comfort her,   310
But feared to pay too dear.
She thought of Jeanie in her grave,
Who should have been a bride;
But who for joys brides hope to have
Fell sick and died   315
In her gay prime,
In earliest Winter time,
With the first glazing rime,[18]
With the first snow-fall of crisp Winter time.

Till Laura dwindling   320
Seemed knocking at Death's door:
Then Lizzie weighed no more
Better and worse;
But put a silver penny in her purse,
Kissed Laura, crossed the heath with clumps of furze   325
At twilight, halted by the brook:
And for the first time in her life
Began to listen and look.

Laughed every goblin
When they spied her peeping: 330
Came towards her hobbling,
Flying, running, leaping,
Puffing and blowing,
Chuckling, clapping, crowing,
Clucking and gobbling,   335
Mopping and mowing,
Full of airs and graces,
Pulling wry faces,
Demure grimaces,
Cat-like and rat-like,   340
Ratel- and wombat-like,
Snail-paced in a hurry,
Parrot-voiced and whistler,
Helter skelter, hurry skurry,

[Handwritten annotations: "Was not a bride b/c of premature pleasure?"; "fallen woman?"; "Redemption Bible"; "dying"; "x weighed the cost"; "Like Satan tempting x."]

---

[17] *cankerous* ulcerous, cancerous.   [18] *rime* frozen mist.

Chattering like magpies,   345
Fluttering like pigeons,
Gliding like fishes, –
Hugged her and kissed her,
Squeezed and caressed her:
Stretched up their dishes,   350
Panniers, and plates:
'Look at our apples
Russet and dun,
Bob at our cherries,
Bite at our peaches,   355
Citrons and dates,
Grapes for the asking,
Pears red with basking
Out in the sun,
Plums on their twigs;   360
Pluck them and suck them,
Pomegranates, figs.' –

'Good folk,' said Lizzie,
  Mindful of Jeanie:
'Give me much and many:' –   365
Held out her apron,
Tossed them her penny.
'Nay, take a seat with us,
Honour and eat with us,'
They answered grinning: 370
'Our feast is but beginning.
Night yet is early,
Warm and dew-pearly,
Wakeful and starry:
Such fruits as these   375
No man can carry;
Half their bloom would fly,
Half their dew would dry,
Half their flavour would pass by.
Sit down and feast with us,   380
Be welcome guest with us,
Cheer you and rest with us.' –
'Thank you,' said Lizzie: 'But one waits
  At home alone for me:
So without further parleying,[19]   385
If you will not sell me any
Of your fruits tho' much and many,
Give me back my silver penny
I tossed you for a fee.' –
They began to scratch their pates,[20]   390
No longer wagging, purring,
But visibly demurring,
Grunting and snarling.
One called her proud,
Cross-grained, uncivil;   395
Their tones waxed loud,

[19] *parleying* conversation.   [20] *pates* heads.

Their looks were evil.
Lashing their tails
They trod and hustled her,
Elbowed and jostled her,   400
Clawed with their nails,
Barking, mewing, hissing, mocking,
Tore her gown and soiled her stocking,
Twitched her hair out by the roots,
Stamped upon her tender feet,   405
Held her hands and squeezed their fruits
Against her mouth to make her eat.

White and golden Lizzie stood,
Like a lily in a flood, –
Like a rock of blue-veined stone   410
Lashed by tides obstreperously, –
Like a beacon left alone
In a hoary roaring sea,
Sending up a golden fire, –
Like a fruit-crowned orange-tree   415
White with blossoms honey-sweet
Sore beset by wasp and bee, –
Like a royal virgin town
Topped with gilded dome and spire
Close beleaguered by a fleet   420
Mad to tug her standard down.

One may lead a horse to water,
Twenty cannot make him drink.
Tho' the goblins cuffed and caught her,
Coaxed and fought her,   425
Bullied and besought her,
Scratched her, pinched her black as ink,
Kicked and knocked her,
Mauled and mocked her,
Lizzie uttered not a word;   430
Would not open lip from lip
Lest they should cram a mouthful in:
But laughed in heart to feel the drip
Of juice that syrupped all her face,
And lodged in dimples of her chin,   435
And streaked her neck which quaked like curd.[21]
At last the evil people
Worn out by her resistance
Flung back her penny, kicked their fruit
Along whichever road they took,   440
Not leaving root or stone or shoot;
Some writhed into the ground,
Some dived into the brook
With ring and ripple,
Some scudded on the gale without a sound,   445
Some vanished in the distance.

---

[21] *curd* cheese-like substance made from milk.

Strange phrase... In a smart, ache, tingle,
        Lizzie went her way;
    Knew not was it night or day;
Sprang up the bank, tore thro' the furze,   450
        Threaded copse and dingle,
        And heard her penny jingle
        Bouncing in her purse,
    Its bounce was music to her ear.
        She ran and ran   455
    As if she feared some goblin man
    Dogged her with gibe or curse
        Or something worse:
    But not one goblin skurried after,
        Nor was she pricked by fear;   460
    The kind heart made her windy-paced
That urged her home quite out of breath with haste
        And inward laughter.

    She cried 'Laura,' up the garden,
        'Did you miss me?   465
        Come and kiss me.
        Never mind my bruises,
    Hug me, kiss me, suck my juices
    Squeezed from goblin fruits for you,
        Goblin pulp and goblin dew.   470
    Eat me, drink me, love me;[22]   —— *"Savior-like"*
        Laura, make much of me:
    For your sake I have braved the glen
    And had to do with goblin merchant men.'

        Laura started from her chair,   475
        Flung her arms up in the air,
            Clutched her hair:
    'Lizzie, Lizzie, have you tasted
    For my sake the fruit forbidden?[23]
    Must your light like mine be hidden,   480
    Your young life like mine be wasted,
        Undone in mine undoing
        And ruined in my ruin,
    Thirsty, cankered, goblin-ridden?' –
        She clung about her sister,   485
        Kissed and kissed and kissed her:
        Tears once again
        Refreshed her shrunken eyes,
        Dropping like rain
        After long sultry drouth;   490
    Shaking with aguish[24] fear, and pain,
    She kissed and kissed her with a hungry mouth.

---

[22] *Eat me . . . love me* cf. the Last Supper in Luke 22.19–20, 'And hee [Jesus] tooke bread, and gaue thankes, and brake it, and gaue vnto them, saying, This is my body which is giuen for you, this doe in remembrance of me. Likewise also the cup after supper, saying, This cup is the New Testament in my blood, which is shed for you.'

[23] *fruit forbidden* cf. 'And the LORD God commanded the man, saying, Of euery tree of the garden thou mayest freely eate. But of the tree of the knowledge of good and euill, thou shalt not eate of it: for in the day that thou eatest thereof, thou shalt surely die', Genesis 2.16–17.
[24] *aguish* having an ague (acute or violent fever).

Her lips began to scorch,
That juice was wormwood[25] to her tongue,
She loathed the feast: 495
Writhing as one possessed she leaped and sung,
Rent[26] all her robe, and wrung
Her hands in lamentable haste,
And beat her breast.
Her locks streamed like the torch   500
Borne by a racer at full speed,
Or like the mane of horses in their flight,
Or like an eagle when she stems the light
Straight toward the sun,
Or like a caged thing freed,   505
Or like a flying flag when armies run.

Swift fire spread thro' her veins, knocked at her heart,
Met the fire smouldering there
And overbore its lesser flame;
She gorged on bitterness without a name: 510
Ah! fool, to choose such part
Of soul-consuming care!
Sense failed in the mortal strife:
Like the watch-tower of a town
Which an earthquake shatters down,   515
Like a lightning-stricken mast,
Like a wind-uprooted tree
Spun about,
Like a foam-topped waterspout
Cast down headlong in the sea,   520
She fell at last;
Pleasure past and anguish past,
Is it death or is it life?

Life out of death.
That night long Lizzie watched by her,   525
Counted her pulse's flagging stir,
Felt for her breath,
Held water to her lips, and cooled her face
With tears and fanning leaves:
But when the first birds chirped about their eaves,   530
And early reapers plodded to the place
Of golden sheaves,
And dew-wet grass
Bowed in the morning winds so brisk to pass,
And new buds with new day   535
Opened of cup-like lilies on the stream,
Laura awoke as from a dream,
Laughed in the innocent old way,
Hugged Lizzie but not twice or thrice;
Her gleaming locks showed not one thread of grey,   540
Her breath was sweet as May
And light danced in her eyes.

[25] *wormwood* bitter-tasting plant.   [26] *Rent* tore.

Days, weeks, months, years
Afterwards, when both were wives
With children of their own;
Their mother-hearts beset with fears,   545
Their lives bound up in tender lives;
Laura would call the little ones
And tell them of her early prime,
Those pleasant days long gone   550
Of not-returning time:
Would talk about the haunted glen,
The wicked, quaint fruit-merchant men,
Their fruits like honey to the throat
But poison in the blood;   555
(Men sell not such in any town:)
Would tell them how her sister stood
In deadly peril to do her good,
And win the fiery antidote:
Then joining hands to little hands   560
Would bid them cling together,
'For there is no friend like a sister
In calm or stormy weather;
To cheer one on the tedious way,
To fetch one if one goes astray,   565
To lift one if one totters down,
To strengthen whilst one stands.'

[handwritten annotation: Restored to society's standard?]

[handwritten annotation: A call to women's role to women?]

Song ('When I am dead, my dearest')

Christina Rossetti's 'Song' (1862), obliquely a fretful meditation of a poet's relationship with posterity, complicates a commonplace idea. In Shelley's 'Adonais' on the death of Keats, and in the final stanza of Swinburne's elegy for Charles Baudelaire, '*Ave Atque Vale*', 500–6, death is offered, in a secularist discourse, as a welcome release from earthly pain. Used by Rossetti, however, the idea is in tension with the general mood of the poem. In enumerating elements of life that the poet will not encounter after her death – shadows, rain – the 'Song' seems more regretful than relieved. The poet's self-dramatization involves the cultivation of apparent indifference, but her weighty rhythms and negatives insist more on lament. One other paradox is clear: in the act of asking to be forgotten, the poet is helping secure the continuation of her memory (like the final letter of Michael Henchard at the end of Hardy's *The Mayor of Casterbridge* [1886]). Indeed, the poem has become one of Christina Rossetti's most famous. It draws on Shakespeare's Sonnet 71:

No longer mourn for me when I am dead
Than you shall hear the surly sullen bell
Give warning to the world that I am fled
From this vile world with vilest worms to dwell.
Nay, if you read this line, remember not
The hand that writ it; for I love you so
That I in your sweet thoughts would be forgot . . .

Text: *Goblin Market and Other Poems* (1862).

When I am dead, my dearest,
Sing no sad songs for me;
Plant thou no roses at my head,
Nor shady cypress tree:[1]

---

[1] *cypress tree* associated with death and burial.

Be the green grass above me
With showers and dewdrops wet;
And if thou wilt, remember,
And if thou wilt, forget.   5

2

I shall not see the shadows,
I shall not feel the rain;   10
I shall not hear the nightingale
Sing on, as if in pain:[2]
And dreaming through the twilight
That doth not rise nor set,
Haply[3] I may remember,   15
And haply may forget.

> *Still Conciousness* [handwritten annotation]

[2] *nightingale . . . pain* in the Roman version of the myth of
Tereus and Procne, Philomela, having been raped and
mutilated by Tereus, is turned into a nightingale by the
gods, hence the sorrow of her song.

[3] *Haply* perhaps.

Winter: My Secret

Christina Rossetti's poetry often remains enigmatic, and the withholding of knowledge from the reader, the investment in partial disclosure, is an important part of her aesthetic (cf. 'Goblin Market', 373–85, 'An Apple-Gathering', 371–2). The whole question of secrecy and the reader's deprivation is thematized in 'Winter: My Secret' (1862), where strategic anti-climax lies at the heart of the poem's purposes. The speaker – whose identity is suggestively androgynous – teases the listener with a secret that he or she will not tell, and which may not exist (the poem was originally entitled 'Nonsense', which gives it a very different feel). The poem's concern with keeping back invites a question about the relationship between poetry and autobiography, between writing and confessing the self. 'Winter: My Secret' contests a Romantic assumption about the nature of poetry as self-revelatory. This act of disguise is simultaneously one of self-renunciation and of self-empowerment/preservation. The fresh conversational style of the poem suggests intimacy – but that is precisely what it does not offer.

Text: *Goblin Market and Other Poems* (1862).

I tell my secret? No indeed, not I:
Perhaps some day, who knows?
But not today; it froze, and blows, and snows,
And you're too curious: fie![1]
You want to hear it? well: 5
Only, my secret's mine, and I won't tell.

Or, after all, perhaps there's none:
Suppose there is no secret after all,
But only just my fun.
Today's a nipping day, a biting day;   10
In which one wants a shawl,
A veil, a cloak, and other wraps:
I cannot ope[2] to every one who taps,

[1] *fie!* exclamation expressing, not fully seriously, disgust or
indignant reproach.

[2] *ope* open.

And let the draughts come whistling thro' my hall;
Come bounding and surrounding me, 15
Come buffeting, astounding me,
Nipping and clipping thro' my wraps and all.
I wear my mask for warmth: who ever shows
His nose to Russian snows
To be pecked at by every wind that blows? 20
You would not peck? I thank you for good will,
Believe, but leave that truth untested still.

Spring's an expansive time: yet I don't trust
March with its peck[3] of dust,
Nor April with its rainbow-crowned brief showers, 25
Nor even May, whose flowers
One frost may wither thro' the sunless hours.

Perhaps some languid summer day,
When drowsy birds sing less and less,
And golden fruit is ripening to excess, 30
If there's not too much sun nor too much cloud,
And the warm wind is neither still nor loud,
Perhaps my secret I may say,
Or you may guess.

[3] *peck* dot, tiny amount.

The Lambs of Grasmere, 1860

In 'Goblin Market', 373–85, Rossetti emphasized the healing, life-giving power of love and the personal cost of loving. In 'The Lambs of Grasmere, 1860' (1862), she considers a very different scenario in which life is preserved through personal generosity and affection. The poem is based on a real incident – an unusual example of Christina Rossetti's reference to contemporary events. In saving the starving lambs of Grasmere (a town and area in the English Lake District), the shepherds fulfil a female role as life-giver (they explicitly take the place of mothers). Tractarian typology may be as significant here as it was for 'Goblin Market' since the narrative acts out another type of (feminized) redemption. But there is the continual possibility of irony. The unspoken of the poem, as in William Blake's 'The Lamb' (1789), may be the role of the lambs in a system of economic exchange. The poem may suggest the possibilities of harmony between economic needs and benign action: saving the lambs, in this reading, would be the coordination of humane principle with the imperatives of the rural economy that keep the *shepherds* alive.

But equally, the poem perhaps subtly challenges the discourse of sentiment that it seems overtly to validate, and invites a suspicious reading. This would expose the narrator's views as idealistic, suggesting that he or she is imposing an interpretation foolishly innocent of the economic conditions that help motivate the scene. 'The Lambs of Grasmere' disputes a Wordsworthian sacramental view of nature (Wordsworth had lived at Grasmere) and suggests the way in which the imagination can easily omit the starker truths of rural existence. The final line mimics and ironizes the Wordsworthian procedure of recalling nature's lessons through memory, for the speaker's memory here continues to efface determining commercial forces that are, perhaps, the absent-present of the poem.

Text: *Goblin Market and Other Poems* (1862).

The upland flocks grew starved and thinned:
Their shepherds scarce could feed the lambs
Whose milkless mothers butted them,
Or who were orphaned of their dams.[1]

[1] *dams* mothers.

The lambs athirst for mother's milk   5
Filled all the place with piteous sounds:
Their mothers' bones made white for miles
The pastureless wet pasture grounds.

2
Day after day, night after night,
From lamb to lamb the shepherds went,   10
With teapots for the bleating mouths
Instead of nature's nourishment.
The little shivering gaping things
Soon knew the step that brought them aid,
And fondled the protecting hand,   15
And rubbed it with a woolly head.

3
Then, as the days waxed on to weeks,
It was a pretty sight to see
These lambs with frisky heads and tails
Skipping and leaping on the lea,[2]   20
Bleating in tender, trustful tones,
Resting on rocky crag or mound,
And following the beloved feet
That once had sought for them and found.

4
These very shepherds of their flocks,   25
These loving lambs so meek to please,
Are worthy of recording words
And honour in their due degrees:
So I might live a hundred years,
And roam from strand to foreign strand,   30
Yet not forget this flooded spring
And scarce-saved lambs of Westmoreland.[3]

[2] *lea* meadow.
[3] *Westmoreland* English rural area between Cumbria and
Yorkshire.

Shut Out

The symbolic or allegoric possibilities of the natural world are explored in 'Shut Out' (1862), a poem that contributed to an enduring model of Rossetti-as-poet. Taking inspiration from the work of the seventeenth-century Anglican poet George Herbert (1593–1633), 'Shut Out' helps affirm the figure of Rossetti as isolated, deprived and unable to achieve real content. It may be read as a drama of the Christian soul, separated from heaven, or an account of the poet's suffering subjectivity more generally. The 'outcast state' represented, insofar as it refers to contemporary gender politics, is explored more combatively in Amy Levy's 'Xantippe', 630–6, and is an opposite of the harmony and nurturing community celebrated in 'Goblin Market', 373–85, or 'A Christmas Carol', 390–1. 'Shut Out' may convincingly be read as an Eve poem, as if spoken by Eve after her banishment with Adam from the Garden of Eden. The poem is characterized by lexical simplicity, a frugality of diction (especially where adjectives are concerned) that creates a texture none the less capable of subtle expressiveness. The last two lines are as perfectly judged as they are balanced: day-to-day language articulates the most nuanced of feelings.

Text: *Goblin Market and Other Poems* (1862).

The door was shut. I looked between
Its iron bars; and saw it lie,
My garden, mine, beneath the sky,
Pied[1] with all flowers bedewed and green:

2

From bough to bough the song-birds crossed,   5
From flower to flower the moths and bees;
With all its nests and stately trees
It had been mine, and it was lost.

3

A shadowless spirit kept the gate,
Blank and unchanging like the grave.   10
I peering thro' said: 'Let me have
Some buds to cheer my outcast state.'

4

He answered not. 'Or give me, then,
But one small twig from shrub or tree;
And bid my home remember me   15
Until I come to it again.'

5

The spirit was silent; but he took
Mortar and stone to build a wall;
He left no loophole great or small
Thro' which my straining eyes might look: 20

6

So now I sit here quite alone
Blinded with tears; nor grieve for that,
For nought is left worth looking at
Since my delightful land is gone.

7

A violet bed is budding near,   25
Wherein a lark has made her nest:
And good they are, but not the best;
And dear they are, but not so dear.

---

[1] *Pied* two or three colours together.

The World

Gothic forms lay close to the heart of Christina Rossetti's moral imagination as potent representations of transgressive energies. In the sonnet 'The World' (1862), the poet's disgust with what life offers her, and the temptations that it involves, are expressed through the vivid construction of a leprous woman shaped by the same imaginative forces that fashioned the city in 'Babylon the Great', 393. Bringing into a single representation the threefold Christian antagonist of 'the world, the flesh and the devil', the gothic dimension of Rossetti's religious imagination evident here, its powerful sense of conflict and moral challenge, has often been overlooked in the history of her reception in preference for the tranquil, feminized devotional spirit of 'A Christmas Carol', 390–1. Another version of the fallen woman poem – cf. 'Goblin Market', 373–85, 'An Apple-Gathering', 371–2 – 'The World' sustains the Judaeo-Christian myth of the peculiar link between Satan and woman. Its meditation on the split self – a relationship presented in terms of the homoerotic – can be compared to Gerard M. Hopkins's 'My own heart let me more have pity on', 544, Michael Field's 'A Girl', 562–3, and 'Sometimes

I do despatch my heart', 563–4, and Lionel Johnson's 'The Dark Angel', 677–9.

Text: *Goblin Market and Other Poems* (1862).

By day she wooes me, soft, exceeding fair:
But all night as the moon so changeth she;
Loathsome and foul with hideous leprosy[1]
And subtle serpents gliding in her hair.
By day she wooes me to the outer air,   5
Ripe fruits, sweet flowers, and full satiety:[2]
But thro' the night, a beast she grins at me,
A very monster void of love and prayer.
By day she stands a lie: by night she stands
In all the naked horror of the truth   10
With pushing horns and clawed and clutching hands.
Is this a friend indeed; that I should sell
My soul to her, give her my life and youth,
Till my feet, cloven[3] too, take hold on hell?

[1] *leprosy* disease that slowly eats away the body, forming white scales on the skin.

[2] *satiety* fully gratified, satisfied (perhaps to excess).

[3] *cloven* with divided hoofs (like the devil's).

A Christmas Carol

Unlike her brother's, Christina Rossetti's poetry was sustained by a religious devotion, the 'all-important topic of Christianity', as she said. One well-known result was this lucidly simple meditation on the birth of Jesus (Luke 3.1–20). With crisply plain diction, she exploits the expressive possibilities of the most economical of language ('Snow had fallen, snow on snow, / Snow on snow'). Rossetti locates the nativity in an English winter scene, emphasizing the universal nature of Jesus's ministry (each nation, the poem implies, can reimagine Jesus as if born within its borders). Likewise, 'A Christmas Carol' (*Scribner's Monthly*, 3 [1872]) collapses time, similarly affirming Jesus's universal presence, by offering a modern speaker using modern imagery ('Earth stood hard as iron') in the historical tableau of the nativity. The poem contributes to what would become a powerful myth, constructing a visual image of the snowy English Christmas scene, increasingly to be marketed and commercialized. Here, it is preserved for the purposes of devotion.

Where 'Goblin Market', 373–85, places in the foreground the redemptive activity of the female, this poem raises a mother's love to the centre. 'A Christmas Carol' – which is still widely sung as a carol in settings by Harold Darke and Gustav Holst – emphasizes the priority of the Virgin's affection, the centrality of her motherly love, over the adoration of all the ranks of the heavenly orders. It interestingly erases the figure of Joseph from the scene, just as the husbands were removed from the end of 'Goblin Market'. Affection, the giving of devotion, which is an obvious theme of 'Goblin Market', is explicitly valorized for the Christian believer. For other Victorian hymns, see 566–70; for other examples of Rossetti's religious poetry not in the tranquil mood of 'A Christmas Carol', see 'The World', 389–90, 'Babylon the Great', 393, and 'Resurgam', 392–3.

Text: *Goblin Market, The Prince's Progress and Other Poems* (1875).

In the bleak mid-winter
Frosty wind made moan,
Earth stood hard as iron,
Water like a stone;

Snow had fallen, snow on snow,   5
Snow on snow,
In the bleak mid-winter
Long ago.

2
Our God, Heaven cannot hold Him
Nor earth sustain;   10
Heaven and earth shall flee away
When He comes to reign:[1]
In the bleak mid-winter
A stable-place sufficed
The Lord God Almighty   15
Jesus Christ.

3
Enough for Him whom cherubim[2]
Worship night and day,
A breastful of milk
And a mangerful of hay;   20
Enough for Him whom angels
Fall down before,
The ox and ass and camel
Which adore.

4
Angels and archangels   25
May have gathered there,
Cherubim and seraphim[3]
Throng'd the air,
But only His mother
In her maiden bliss   30
Worshipped the Beloved
With a kiss.

5
What can I give Him,
Poor as I am?
If I were a shepherd   35
I would bring a lamb,
If I were a wise man
I would do my part, –
Yet what I can I give Him,
Give my heart.   40

[1] *comes to reign* Second Coming of Jesus at the end of the
world.

[2] *cherubim* class of angel.
[3] *seraphim* another class of angel.

Sonnet: 'In life our absent friend is far away'

In unexpectedly proposing that death may bring a
friend closer than mere absence, Rossetti produces a
poem – the last in her sequence *Later Life: A Double
Sonnet of Sonnets* (from *A Pageant and Other Poems*
[1881]) – freshly hopeful of a form of love's continuation beyond death. This was an issue that Tennyson
anxiously contemplated in *In Memoriam A.H.H.*,
88–165, but without Rossetti's optimism. The sonnet,

quite different from the intimate conversational mode of Elizabeth Barrett Browning's sonnets (see 'Hiram Powers' *Greek Slave*', 51–2, and *Sonnets from the Portuguese*, 52–5), is formally distinctive in being an argument precipitated by its first line. Repetition and a gentle simplicity of lexis characterize the close that attains a glowing climax with the plainest of material. 'In life our absent friend' concludes a sequence generally restless about the self, brooding on dark thoughts. The immediately preceding sonnet provides pertinent contextualization as it is a meditation on the narrator's own death:

> . . . Too dulled, it may be, for a last good-bye,
> Too comfortless for any one to soothe,
> A helpless charmless spectacle of ruth
> Through long last hours.

'In life our absent friend', offering a kind of gothicism, a theory of ghosts, an idea of benign haunting, is cathartic, peaceful, reassuring; it replaces the uncomforted deathbed scene with an image of enduring friendship.

Text: *A Pageant and Other Poems* (1881).

In life our absent friend is far away:
But death may bring our friend exceeding near,
Show him familiar faces long so dear
And lead him back in reach of words we say.
He only cannot utter yea or nay   5
In any voice accustomed to our ear;
He only cannot make his face appear
And turn the sun back on our shadowed day.
The dead may be around us, dear and dead;
The unforgotten dearest dead may be   10
Watching us with unslumbering eyes and heart;
Brimful of words which cannot yet be said,
Brimful of knowledge they may not impart,
Brimful of love for you and love for me.

Resurgam

In 'Resurgam' (first published *Athenaeum*, 2831 [1882]), the natural world provides the basis for an allegory of Christian endurance that takes some of its inspiration from the New Testament injunction: 'let vs runne with patience vnto the race that is set before vs' (Hebrews 12.1). For a contrast, see the sonnet 'Rend hearts and rend not garments' (1881). Unlike Rossetti's other poems in this anthology that exploit the signification possibilities of the natural world, such as 'Shut Out', 388–9, the boundaries of meaning in 'Resurgam' are reasonably clear. The title means 'I shall rise again' in Latin, and usually refers to the general resurrection of the world's dead at the Last

Day (part of Christian theology of the End). Life in this allegorical mountain climb is figured as arduous and as one that involves loss and deprivation, familiar aspects of Rossetti's own self-construction. As in 'Shut Out', it is also solitary. Where 'The World', 389–90, diagnoses the *terms* of a struggle, 'Resurgam', portraying another struggle, concludes with achievement. The sonnet drives the reader onwards to the resolution of the final line, the climax characteristically expressed in remarkably ordinary language.

Text: *Poems* (1888).

From depth to height, from height to loftier height,
The climber sets his foot and sets his face,
Tracks lingering sunbeams to their halting-place,
And counts the last pulsations of the light.
Strenuous thro' day and unsurprised by night   5
He runs a race with Time and wins the race,[1]

---

[1] *race* see headnote.

Emptied and stripped of all save only Grace,
Will, Love, a threefold panoply[2] of might.
Darkness descends for light he toiled to seek:
He stumbles on the darkened mountain-head,
Left breathless in the unbreathable thin air,   10
Made freeman[3] of the living and the dead: –
He wots[4] not he has topped the topmost peak,
But the returning sun will find him there.

---

[2] *panoply* complete armour for spiritual or mental warfare.   [4] *wots* knows.
[3] *freeman* cf. the award of the freedom of a city.

Babylon the Great

Ancient Biblical cities provided various models for national admonishment in the Victorian period. John Ruskin in *The Stones of Venice* (1851–3) compared the fortunes of Venice (and the possible fortunes of England) to the fallen cities of Tyre and Sidon; Dante Gabriel Rossetti's 'The Burden of Nineveh', 350–6, muddied boundaries between modern London and the ancient capital of the Assyrian empire to produce a satirical reflection on the moral life of the modern metropolis. Christina Rossetti's severe public mode is heard in her sonnet 'Babylon the Great' (1893), in which the fate of the Biblical city of Babylon provides a way of denouncing sexual sin, ancient and contemporary, in a manner paradoxically energized by the extravagance and wealth of the burnt city it describes.

Rossetti takes her cue from the book of Revelation: 'And there followed another Angel, saying, Babylon is fallen, is fallen, that great citie, because she made all

nations drinke of the wine of the wrath of her fornication' (Revelation 18.8). The poem's depiction of the 'unutterable' filth of Babylon's insatiable desire, figured as a foul and wanton woman, contrasts with the drama of 'Goblin Market', 373–85, where it is precisely such disfiguring lust for transgression that is healed by love. The aggressive voice of this poem, hammering out words on an anvil, is also in contrast with the tender voice of 'A Christmas Carol', 390–1, a poem that has often been assumed representative of Rossetti's religious writing. 'Babylon the Great' might be compared to Dante Gabriel Rossetti's 'Jenny', 358–67, as a text that associates the city with the sexual (cf. also the poetry of Arthur Symons, 657–66, and Ernest Dowson, 667–71).

Text: *Verses* (1893).

Foul is she and ill-favoured, set askew:
Gaze not upon her till thou dream her fair,
Lest she should mesh thee in her wanton hair,[1]
Adept in arts grown old yet ever new.
Her heart lusts not for love, but thro' and thro'   5
For blood, as spotted panther lusts in lair;
No wine is in her cup, but filth is there
Unutterable, with plagues hid out of view.
Gaze not upon her, for her dancing whirl
Turns giddy the fixed gazer presently: 10
Gaze not upon her, lest thou be as she
When, at the far end of her long desire,
Her scarlet vest and gold and gem and pearl
And she amid her pomp are set on fire.

---

[1] *wanton hair* cf. Dante Gabriel Rossetti's 'Lilith' and his painting *Lady Lilith* (1864–73). The sonnet, on the woman traditionally believed to have been Adam's first wife, dwells on her enchanted 'strangling golden hair'.

James Thomson, 'B. V.' (1834–1882)

James Thomson was born the son of a poor and disabled merchant seaman, James Thomson Snr, and Sarah Kennedy, his wife, a member of the Edward Irving's Catholic Apostolic Church. He was educated at the Royal Caledonian Asylum School for the sons of poor Scottish sailors and soldiers in London when the family moved there in 1842. In 1850, he began to train as an army schoolmaster in Chelsea and served in Cork, Ireland, where he met Charles Bradlaugh (1833–91), social reformer, advocate of contraception, free thinker and eventual proprietor of the secularist/atheist *National Reformer* in which much of Thomson's work appeared. During this period, Thomson fell in love with the young Matilda Weller, who shortly afterwards died; she was to be an important symbolic figure in his work. He was dishonourably discharged from the army – drink was probably at the bottom of it – and became increasingly dependent on alcohol thereafter. He lodged with Bradlaugh and wrote for the *National Reformer* under the name 'B. V.' (B for Percy Bysshe Shelley's middle name, and V for Vanolis, an anagram of Novalis, the pseudonym of the German poet, novelist and mystic Friedrich Leopold von Hardenberg [1772–1810], whose *Hymnen an die Nacht* [1800], with which Thomson felt an obvious connection, laments the death of his young fiancée Sophie von Kuhn). For some of 1872, Thomson laboured with a gold company in Colorado and the following year was in Spain as a reporter on the civil war for the *New York World*. In 1874 came the serialization of *The City of Dreadful Night*, which was well received, and admired by George Eliot; *The City of Dreadful Night and Other Poems* (1880) sold well, and its dedication expressed Thomson's regard for the Italian pessimist philosopher Giacomo Leopardi, the 'younger brother of Dante', he wrote, 'a spirit as lofty[,] a genius as intense[,] with a yet more tragic doom'. *Vane's Story and Other Poems* (1881) was less well regarded. By now, however, drink was destroying this peculiarly depressive, sporadically brilliant atheist, the Victorian 'laureate of pessimism'. He was sent to prison for two weeks for arson, and, shattered both physically and mentally, died in June 1882.

The City of Dreadful Night 1870; 1874

Published first in 1874, James Thomson's *The City of Dreadful Night* is a key poem in defining the new urban experience of the great Victorian city as godless and hopeless. It set terms from which *fin de siècle* themes of pessimism and degeneration grew, and its probing of the conditions of human life and belief in city spaces would be developed in the work of John Davidson (cf. 606-26). The brooding meditation of *Dreadful Night* on the wasted city and its lost souls would also form part of the imaginative context from which Modernism would emerge in the twentieth century (cf. T. S. Eliot's *The Waste Land* [1922]).

Thomson had been working on the pessimistic Italian essayist and poet Giacomo Leopardi (1798–1837), publishing translations in the secularist *National Reformer*, before he began *The City of Dreadful Night*. He admired the Italian's recognition of human hopelessness, saying that 'the facts of the world do not sanction the belief in a good tendency. Leopardi's greatness [lay] in steadfastly acknowledging these facts, so terrible and mysterious for us poor human kind; [in] his heroic self-restraint from all the frailties of vain hope which seduce even the best intellects.' Thomson's understanding of Leopardi lay the foundations for his bleakest work, also published in the *National Reformer*.

Drawing partly on Matthew Arnold's 'Empedocles on Etna', 268-95, as a poem which debates the human fashioning of gods, Thomson's account of the aftermath of the sea of faith's withdrawal finds its chief source in the *Inferno* from Dante's *Divine Comedy*, one of the central works of the European Middle Ages. Dante journeys into hell in the *Inferno*, accompanied by the poet Virgil, encountering stage by stage its wretched inhabitants. Likewise, the poet figure of *The City of Dreadful Night* moves through the hellish spaces of a vast city, stumbling upon some of its tormented souls. The whole poem is introduced with words from the *Inferno* – 'through me is the way to the city of pain'. To enter the poem is to enter hell. The radical difference from Dante's masterpiece is, of course, the sufficiency of Thomson's hell: for him, there is no corresponding *Paradiso* because there is no over-arching frame of Christian redemption. His vision is of a materialist world in which faith is dead, and belief in God or Providence lost in the squalid materialism of the despairing city. The preacher in the atheist cathedral articulates the darkest moment of the poem, the climax of its *terribilità*:

> I find no hint throughout the Universe
> Of good or ill, of blessing or of curse;
> I find alone Necessity Supreme;
> With infinite Mystery, abysmal, dark,
> Unlighted ever by the faintest spark
> For us the flitting shadows of a dream

Virgil in the *Inferno* accompanies Dante; the poet of *The City of Dreadful Night* is alone, a position expressive of the human isolation he repeatedly finds. 'Community' and 'society' no longer seem words that refer to the modern city, and the poem uses neither of them. The account of human isolation in Arnold's 'To Marguerite – Continued', 267-8, is reconceived by Thomson as the despairing condition of modern urban life (not, however, that there is any sense in the poem of the *country* life beyond it that escapes contamination: the rural is merely erased in Thomson's vision).

The poem, rooted in reference to the particularities of a terrible city, especially its river, summons Darwinian ideas of evolution (see section 14) to express its sense of the doomed nature of humanity. Ruskin's devastating critique of the moral nature of the modern is also evoked. His *The Stones of Venice* (1851–3) considered what the fall of Venice told England about her potential destiny if she continued to disregard the spiritual principles of her society. Thomson's meditation on a 'Venice of the Black Sea', as he calls it, likewise uses a wasted city to diagnose – and, of course, to fashion – the spiritual and intellectual condition of contemporary Britain.

Text: *The City of Dreadful Night and Other Poems*, 2nd edn (1888).

> '*Per me si va nella città dolente.*'[1]
> – Dante.

> '*Poi di tanto adoprar, di tanti moti*
> *D'ogni celeste, ogni terrena cosa,*
> *Girando senza posa,*
> *Per tornar sempre là donde son mosse;*
> *Uso alcuno, alcun frutto*
> *Indovinar non so.*'[2]

> '*Sola nel mondo eterna, a cui si volve*
> *Ogni creata cosa,*
> *In te, morte, si posa*
> *Nostra ignuda natura;*
> *Lieta no, ma sicura*
> *Dell' antico dolor . . .*
> *Però ch' esser beato*
> *Nega ai mortali e nega a' morti il fato.*'[3]
> – Leopardi.

PROEM.[4]

> Lo, thus, as prostrate, 'In the dust I write
> My heart's deep languor and my soul's sad tears.'
> Yet why evoke the spectres of black night
> To blot the sunshine of exultant years?

---

[1] *Per . . . dolente* 'through me is the way to the city of pain', Dante, *Inferno* 3.1.

[2] *Poi . . . so* 'Then out of such endless working, so many movements of everything in heaven and earth, revolving incessantly, only to return to the point from which they were moved: from all this I can imagine neither purpose nor gain', Giacomo Leopardi, *Canti* 23.

[3] *Sola . . . fato* 'Eternal alone in the world, received of all created things, in you, death, our naked being comes to rest; joyful no, but safe from the age-old pain . . . For happiness is denied by fate to the living and denied to the dead', Leopardi, *Poerette Morali*, 'Coro di morti', from 'Dialogo di Federico Ruysch e delle sue mummie'.

[4] *Proem* preface, introduction.

Why disinter dead faith from mouldering hidden?   5
Why break the seals of mute despair unbidden,
And wail life's discords into careless ears?

Because a cold rage seizes one at whiles
To show the bitter old and wrinkled truth
Stripped naked of all vesture that beguiles,   10
False dreams, false hopes, false masks and modes of youth;
Because it gives some sense of power and passion
In helpless impotence to try to fashion
Our woe in living words howe'er uncouth.

Surely I write not for the hopeful young,   15
Or those who deem their happiness of worth,
Or such as pasture and grow fat among
The shows of life and feel nor doubt nor dearth,
Or pious spirits with a God above them
To sanctify and glorify and love them,   20
Or sages who foresee a heaven on earth.

For none of these I write, and none of these
Could read the writing if they deigned[5] to try:
So may they flourish, in their due degrees,
On our sweet earth and in their unplaced sky.   25
If any cares for the weak words here written,
It must be some one desolate, Fate-smitten,
Whose faith and hope are dead, and who would die.

Yes, here and there some weary wanderer
In that same city of tremendous night,   30
Will understand the speech, and feel a stir
Of fellowship in all-disastrous fight;
'I suffer mute and lonely, yet another
Uplifts his voice to let me know a brother
Travels the same wild paths though out of sight.'   35

O sad Fraternity,[6] do I unfold
Your dolorous[7] mysteries shrouded from of yore?
Nay, be assured; no secret can be told
To any who divined it not before:
None uninitiate by many a presage   40
Will comprehend the language of the message,
Although proclaimed aloud for evermore.

1

The City is of Night; perchance of Death,
But certainly of Night; for never there
Can come the lucid morning's fragrant breath   45
After the dewy dawning's cold grey air;
The moon and stars may shine with scorn or pity;
The sun has never visited that city,
For it dissolveth in the daylight fair.

---

[5] *deigned* thought fit.   [7] *dolorous* painful, sorrowful.
[6] *Fraternity* (religious) brotherhood.

Dissolveth like a dream of night away; 50
Though present in distempered gloom of thought
And deadly weariness of heart all day.
But when a dream night after night is brought
Throughout a week, and such weeks few or many
Recur each year for several years, can any 55
Discern that dream from real life in aught?

For life is but a dream whose shapes return,
Some frequently, some seldom, some by night
And some by day, some night and day: we learn,
The while all change and many vanish quite, 60
In their recurrence with recurrent changes
A certain seeming order; where this ranges
We count things real; such is memory's might.

A river girds the city west and south,
The main north channel of a broad lagoon, 65
Regurging[8] with the salt tides from the mouth;
Waste marshes shine and glister to the moon
For leagues,[9] then moorland black, then stony ridges;
Great piers and causeways, many noble bridges,
Connect the town and islet suburbs strewn. 70

Upon an easy slope it lies at large,
And scarcely overlaps the long curved crest
Which swells out two leagues from the river marge.
A trackless wilderness rolls north and west,
Savannahs,[10] savage woods, enormous mountains, 75
Bleak uplands, black ravines with torrent fountains;
And eastward rolls the shipless sea's unrest.

The city is not ruinous, although
Great ruins of an unremembered past,
With others of a few short years ago 80
More sad, are found within its precincts vast.
The street-lamps always burn; but scarce a casement
In house or palace front from roof to basement
Doth glow or gleam athwart[11] the mirk[12] air cast.

The street-lamps burn amidst the baleful[13] glooms, 85
Amidst the soundless solitudes immense
Of rangèd mansions dark and still as tombs.
The silence which benumbs or strains the sense
Fulfils with awe the soul's despair unweeping:
Myriads[14] of habitants are ever sleeping, 90
Or dead, or fled from nameless pestilence!

Yet as in some necropolis[15] you find
Perchance one mourner to a thousand dead,

---

[8] *Regurging* turning again and again, becoming a whirlpool.
[9] *league* measurement of distance, about 3 miles.
[10] *Savannahs* treeless plains.
[11] *athwart* across.
[12] *mirk* murky.
[13] *baleful* unhappy, wretched.
[14] *Myriads* tens of thousands.
[15] *necropolis* city of the dead.

So there; worn faces that look deaf and blind
Like tragic masks of stone. With weary tread,   95
Each wrapt in his own doom, they wander, wander,
Or sit foredone[16] and desolately ponder
Through sleepless hours with heavy drooping head.

Mature men chiefly, few in age or youth,
A woman rarely, now and then a child: 100
A child! If here the heart turns sick with ruth[17]
To see a little one from birth defiled,
Or lame or blind, as preordained to languish
Through youthless life, think how it bleeds with anguish
To meet one erring in that homeless wild.   105

They often murmur to themselves, they speak
To one another seldom, for their woe
Broods maddening inwardly and scorns to wreak
Itself abroad; and if at whiles it grow
To frenzy which must rave, none heeds the clamour,   110
Unless there waits some victim of like glamour,
To rave in turn, who lends attentive show.

The City is of Night, but not of Sleep;
There sweet sleep is not for the weary brain;
The pitiless hours like years and ages creep,   115
A night seems termless[18] hell. This dreadful strain
Of thought and consciousness which never ceases,
Or which some moments' stupor but increases,
This, worse than woe, makes wretches there insane.

They leave all hope behind who enter there:[19]   120
One certitude while sane they cannot leave,
One anodyne[20] for torture and despair;
The certitude of Death, which no reprieve
Can put off long; and which, divinely tender,
But waits the outstretched hand to promptly render   125
That draught whose slumber nothing can bereave.[21]

2

Because he seemed to walk with an intent
I followed him; who, shadowlike and frail,
Unswervingly though slowly onward went,
Regardless, wrapt in thought as in a veil: 130
Thus step for step with lonely sounding feet
We travelled many a long dim silent street.

At length he paused: a black mass in the gloom,
A tower that merged into the heavy sky;

[16] *foredone* already done for.
[17] *ruth* pity.
[18] *termless* endless.
[19] *They . . . there* cf. Dante, *Inferno* 3.9, 'Leave hope behind, all ye who enter here' (Thomson's translation): the words above the gate of hell.

[20] *anodyne* relief for pain.
[21] *. . . bereave* 'Though the Garden of thy Life be wholly waste, the sweet flowers withered, the fruit-trees barren, over its wall hang ever the rich dark clusters of the Vine of Death, within easy reach of thy hand, which may pluck of them when it will' (Thomson).

Around, the huddled stones of grave and tomb: 135
Some old God's-acre now corruption's sty:
He murmured to himself with dull despair,
Here Faith died, poisoned by this charnel[22] air.

Then turning to the right went on once more,
And travelled weary roads without suspense; 140
And reached at last a low wall's open door,
Whose villa gleamed beyond the foliage dense:
He gazed, and muttered with a hard despair,
Here Love died, stabbed by its own worshipped pair.

Then turning to the right resumed his march, 145
And travelled streets and lanes with wondrous strength,
Until on stooping through a narrow arch
We stood before a squalid house at length:
He gazed, and whispered with a cold despair,
Here Hope died, starved out in its utmost lair. 150

When he had spoken thus, before he stirred,
I spoke, perplexed by something in the signs
Of desolation I had seen and heard
In this drear pilgrimage to ruined shrines:
When Faith and Love and Hope[23] are dead indeed, 155
Can Life still live?[24] By what doth it proceed?

As whom his one intense thought overpowers,
He answered coldly, Take a watch, erase
The signs and figures of the circling hours,
Detach the hands, remove the dial-face; 160
The works proceed until run down; although
Bereft of purpose, void of use, still go.
Then turning to the right paced on again,
And traversed squares and travelled streets whose glooms

Seemed more and more familiar to my ken;[25] 165
And reached that sullen temple of the tombs;
And paused to murmur with the old despair,
Here Faith died, poisoned by this charnel air.
I ceased to follow, for the knot of doubt
Was severed sharply with a cruel knife: 170
He circled thus for ever tracing out
The series of the fraction left of Life;
Perpetual recurrence in the scope
Of but three terms, dead Faith, dead Love, dead Hope.

3

Although lamps burn along the silent streets; 175
Even when moonlight silvers empty squares

---

[22] *charnel* burial place, cemetery.
[23] *Faith . . . Hope* cf. 1 Corinthians 13.13, 'And now abideth faith, hope, charitie [love], these three, but the greatest of these is charitie'.

[24] *When Faith . . . live* cf. Wordsworth, 'We live by Admiration, Hope, and Love', *Excursion* (1814), Book 4, 763.
[25] *ken* perception.

The dark holds countless lanes and close retreats;
But when the night its sphereless mantle wears
The open spaces yawn with gloom abysmal,
The sombre mansions loom immense and dismal,   180
The lanes are black as subterranean lairs.

And soon the eye a strange new vision learns:
The night remains for it as dark and dense,
Yet clearly in this darkness it discerns
As in the daylight with its natural sense;   185
Perceives a shade in shadow not obscurely,
Pursues a stir of black in blackness surely,
Sees spectres also in the gloom intense.

The ear, too, with the silence vast and deep
Becomes familiar though unreconciled;   190
Hears breathings as of hidden life asleep,
And muffled throbs as of pent passions wild,
Far murmurs, speech of pity or derision;
But all more dubious than the things of vision,
So that it knows not when it is beguiled.   195

No time abates the first despair and awe,
But wonder ceases soon; the weirdest thing
Is felt least strange beneath the lawless law
Where Death-in-Life is the eternal king;
Crushed impotent beneath this reign of terror,   200
Dazed with such mysteries of woe and error,
The soul is too outworn for wondering.

4

He stood alone within the spacious square
Declaiming from the central grassy mound,
With head uncovered and with streaming hair,   205
As if large multitudes were gathered round:
A stalwart[26] shape, the gestures full of might,
The glances burning with unnatural light: –
As I came through the desert thus it was,
As I came through the desert: All was black,   210
In heaven no single star, on earth no track;
A brooding hush without a stir or note,
The air so thick it clotted in my throat;
And thus for hours; then some enormous things
Swooped past with savage cries and clanking wings: 215
But I strode on austere;
No hope could have no fear.

As I came through the desert thus it was,
As I came through the desert: Eyes of fire
Glared at me throbbing with a starved desire;   220
The hoarse and heavy and carnivorous breath
Was hot upon me from deep jaws of death;

---

[26] *stalwart* robust, sturdy.

Sharp claws, swift talons, fleshless fingers cold
Plucked at me from the bushes, tried to hold:
    But I strode on austere;   225
    No hope could have no fear.

As I came through the desert thus it was,
As I came through the desert: Lo you, there,
    That hillock burning with a brazen glare;
Those myriad dusky flames with points a-glow   230
Which writhed and hissed and darted to and fro;
A Sabbath of the Serpents, heaped pell-mell
For Devil's roll-call and some *fête*[27] of Hell:
    Yet I strode on austere;
    No hope could have no fear.   235

As I came through the desert thus it was,
As I came through the desert: Meteors ran
And crossed their javelins[28] on the black sky-span;
    The zenith opened to a gulf of flame,
The dreadful thunderbolts jarred earth's fixed frame;   240
The ground all heaved in waves of fire that surged
And weltered round me sole there unsubmerged:
    Yet I strode on austere;
    No hope could have no fear.
                            245

As I came through the desert thus it was,
As I came through the desert: Air once more,
    And I was close upon a wild sea-shore;
    Enormous cliffs arose on either hand,
The deep tide thundered up a league-broad strand;
White foambelts seethed there, wan[29] spray swept and flew;   250
The sky broke, moon and stars and clouds and blue:
    And I strode on austere;
    No hope could have no fear.

As I came through the desert thus it was,
As I came through the desert: On the left   255
    The sun arose and crowned a broad crag-cleft;
There stopped and burned out black, except a rim,
    A bleeding eyeless socket, red and dim;
Whereon the moon fell suddenly south-west,
And stood above the right-hand cliffs at rest: 260
    Still I strode on austere;
    No hope could have no fear.

As I came through the desert thus it was,
As I came through the desert: From the right
    A shape came slowly with a ruddy light;   265
    A woman with a red lamp in her hand,
Bareheaded and barefooted on that strand;
    O desolation moving with such grace!
    O anguish with such beauty in thy face!

[27] *fête* pron. 'fet' – festival.
[28] *javelins* spear-like tail of meteors.
[29] *wan* pale.

I fell as on my bier,[30]   270
Hope travailed[31] with such fear.

As I came through the desert thus it was,
As I came through the desert: I was twain,
Two selves distinct that cannot join again;
One stood apart and knew but could not stir,   275
And watched the other stark in swoon[32] and her;
And she came on, and never turned aside,
Between such sun and moon and roaring tide:
And as she came more near
My soul grew mad with fear.   280

As I came through the desert thus it was,
As I came through the desert: Hell is mild
And piteous matched with that accursèd wild;
A large black sign was on her breast that bowed,
A broad blackband ran down her snow-white shroud;   285
That lamp she held was her own burning heart,
Whose blood-drops trickled step by step apart:
The mystery was clear;
Mad rage had swallowed fear.

As I came through the desert thus it was,   290
As I came through the desert: By the sea
She knelt and bent above that senseless me;
Those lamp-drops fell upon my white brow there,
She tried to cleanse them with her tears and hair;
She murmured words of pity, love, and woe,   295
She heeded not the level rushing flow:
And mad with rage and fear,
I stood stonebound so near.

As I came through the desert thus it was,
As I came through the desert: When the tide   300
Swept up to her there kneeling by my side,
She clasped that corpse-like me, and they were borne
Away, and this vile me was left forlorn;
I know the whole sea cannot quench that heart,
Or cleanse that brow, or wash those two apart: 305
They love; their doom is drear,
Yet they nor hope nor fear;
But I, what do I here?

5

How he arrives there none can clearly know:
Athwart the mountains and immense wild tracts,   310
Or flung a waif[33] upon that vast sea-flow,
Or down the river's boiling cataracts:
To reach it is as dying fever-stricken;
To leave it, slow faint birth intense pangs quicken;
And memory swoons in both the tragic acts.   315

---

[30] *bier* a stand for a corpse.
[31] *travailed* laboured.

[32] *swoon* faint.
[33] *waif* person without home or friends.

But being there one feels a citizen;
Escape seems hopeless to the heart forlorn:
Can Death-in-Life be brought to life again?
And yet release does come; there comes a morn
When he awakes from slumbering so sweetly   320
That all the world is changed for him completely,
And he is verily as if new-born.

He scarcely can believe the blissful change,
He weeps perchance who wept not while accurst;
Never again will he approach the range   325
Infected by that evil spell now burst:
Poor wretch! who once hath paced that dolent[34] city
Shall pace it often, doomed beyond all pity,
With horror ever deepening from the first.

                                                             330
Though he possess sweet babes and loving wife,
A home of peace by loyal friendships cheered,
And love them more than death or happy life,
They shall avail not; he must dree his weird;[35]
Renounce all blessings for that imprecation,[36]
Steal forth and haunt that builded desolation,   335
Of woe and terrors and thick darkness reared:

6
I sat forlornly by the river-side,
And watched the bridge-lamps glow like golden stars
Above the blackness of the swelling tide,
Down which they struck rough gold in ruddier bars;   340
And heard the heave and plashing of the flow
Against the wall a dozen feet below.

Large elm-trees stood along that river-walk;
And under one, a few steps from my seat,
I heard strange voices join in stranger talk,   345
Although I had not heard approaching feet:
These bodiless voices in my waking dream
Flowed dark words blending with the sombre stream: –

And you have after all come back; come back.
I was about to follow on your track.   350
And you have failed: our spark of hope is black.
That I have failed is proved by my return:
The spark is quenched, nor ever more will burn.
But listen; and the story you shall learn.

I reached the portal[37] common spirits fear,   355
And read the words above it, dark yet clear,
'Leave hope behind, all ye who enter here:'[38]
And would have passed in, gratified to gain
That positive eternity of pain,

[34] *dolent* sorrowing, grieving.
[35] *dree his weird* endure his fate.
[36] *imprecation* curse.

[37] *portal* gate.
[38] *'Leave . . . here'* see note 19.

Instead of this insufferable inane.[39]   360

A demon warder clutched me, Not so fast;
First leave your hopes behind! – But years have passed
Since I left all behind me, to the last:[40]

You cannot count for hope, with all your wit,
This bleak despair that drives me to the Pit:[41]   365
How could I seek to enter void of it?

He snarled, What thing is this which apes a soul,
And would find entrance to our gulf of dole[42]
Without the payment of the settled toll?

Outside the gate he showed an open chest: 370
Here pay their entrance fees the souls unblest;
Cast in some hope, you enter with the rest.

This is Pandora's box;[43] whose lid shall shut,
And Hell-gate too, when hopes have filled it; but
They are so thin that it will never glut.   375

I stood a few steps backwards, desolate;
And watched the spirits pass me to their fate,
And fling off hope, and enter at the gate.

When one casts off a load he springs upright,
Squares back his shoulders, breathes with all his might,   380
And briskly paces forward strong and light:

But these, as if they took some burden, bowed;
The whole frame sank; however strong and proud
Before, they crept in quite infirm and cowed.

And as they passed me, earnestly from each   385
A morsel of his hope I did beseech,
To pay my entrance; but all mocked my speech.

Not one would cede[44] a tittle[45] of his store,
Though knowing that in instants three or four
He must resign the whole for evermore.   390

So I returned. Our destiny is fell;[46]
For in this Limbo[47] we must ever dwell,
Shut out alike from Heaven and Earth and Hell.

---

[39] *inane* void.
[40] *A demon . . . last* Thomson gestures to the three-line verse
form (*terza rima*) of Dante's *Divine Comedy*, though
without its distinctive rhyme scheme.
[41] *Pit* hell.
[42] *dole* sorrow.
[43] *Pandora's box* Pandora was the first woman in Greek
mythology: her box contained all the evils of the world.
[44] *cede* grant.
[45] *tittle* tiny amount.
[46] *fell* savage, cruel.
[47] *Limbo* region on the border of hell, not earth, heaven, or
hell.

The other sighed back, Yea; but if we grope
With care through all this Limbo's dreary scope,
We yet may pick up some minute lost hope;   395

And, sharing it between us, entrance win,
In spite of fiends so jealous for gross sin:
Let us without delay our search begin.

7

Some say that phantoms haunt those shadowy streets,   400
And mingle freely there with sparse mankind;
And tell of ancient woes and black defeats,
And murmur mysteries in the grave enshrined:
But others think them visions of illusion,
Or even men gone far in self-confusion;   405
No man there being wholly sane in mind.

And yet a man who raves, however mad,
Who bares his heart and tells of his own fall,
Reserves some inmost secret good or bad:
The phantoms have no reticence at all: 410
The nudity of flesh will blush though tameless,
The extreme nudity of bone grins shameless,
The unsexed skeleton mocks shroud and pall.[48]

I have seen phantoms there that were as men
And men that were as phantoms flit and roam;   415
Marked shapes that were not living to my ken,
Caught breathings acrid as with Dead Sea[49] foam:
The City rests for man so weird and awful,
That his intrusion there might seem unlawful,
And phantoms there may have their proper home.   420

8

While I still lingered on that river-walk,
And watched the tide as black as our black doom,
I heard another couple join in talk,
And saw them to the left hand in the gloom
Seated against an elm bole[50] on the ground,   425
Their eyes intent upon the stream profound.

'I never knew another man on earth
But had some joy and solace in his life,
Some chance of triumph in the dreadful strife:
My doom has been unmitigated dearth.'   430

'We gaze upon the river, and we note
The various vessels large and small that float,
Ignoring every wrecked and sunken boat.'

'And yet I asked no splendid dower,[51] no spoil
Of sway or fame or rank or even wealth;   435

---

[48] *pall* rich cloth spread over a coffin.   [50] *bole* trunk.
[49] *Dead Sea* famous for its saltiness, in which little can live.   [51] *dower* endowment.

But homely love with common food and health,
And nightly sleep to balance daily toil.'

'This all-too humble soul would arrogate[52]
Unto itself some signalising hate
From the supreme indifference of Fate!'   440

'Who is most wretched in this dolorous place?
I think myself; yet I would rather be
My miserable self than He, than He
Who formed such creatures to His own disgrace.

'The vilest thing must be less vile than Thou   445
From whom it had its being, God and Lord!
Creator of all woe and sin! abhorred,
Malignant and implacable! I vow

'That not for all Thy power furled and unfurled,
For all the temples to Thy glory built,   450
Would I assume the ignominious guilt
Of having made such men in such a world.'

'As if a Being, God or Fiend, could reign,
At once so wicked, foolish, and insane,
As to produce men when He might refrain!   455

'The world rolls round for ever like a mill;
It grinds out death and life and good and ill;
It has no purpose, heart or mind or will.

'While air of Space and Time's full river flow
The mill must blindly whirl unresting so: 460
It may be wearing out, but who can know?

'Man might know one thing were his sight less dim;
That it whirls not to suit his petty whim,
That it is quite indifferent to him.

'Nay, does it treat him harshly as he saith?   465
It grinds him some slow years of bitter breath,
Then grinds him back into eternal death.'

9

It is full strange to him who hears and feels,
When wandering there in some deserted street,
The booming and the jar of ponderous wheels,   470
The trampling clash of heavy ironshod feet:
Who in this Venice[53] of the Black Sea[54] rideth?
Who in this city of the stars abideth
To buy or sell as those in daylight sweet?

---

[52] *arrogate* lay claim to (without reason or justice).   [54] *Black Sea* i.e., cursed sea.
[53] *Venice* see headnote, 395.

The rolling thunder seems to fill the sky 475
As it comes on; the horses snort and strain,
The harness jingles, as it passes by;
The hugeness of an overburthened wain:[55]
A man sits nodding on the shaft or trudges
Three parts asleep beside his fellow-drudges: 480
And so it rolls into the night again.

What merchandise? whence, whither, and for whom?
Perchance it is a Fate-appointed hearse,
Bearing away to some mysterious tomb
Or Limbo of the scornful universe 485
The joy, the peace, the life-hope, the abortions
Of all things good which should have been our portions,
But have been strangled by that City's curse.

10
The mansion stood apart in its own ground;
In front thereof a fragrant garden-lawn, 490
High trees about it, and the whole walled round:
The massy[56] iron gates were both withdrawn;
And every window of its front shed light,
Portentous[57] in that City of the Night.

But though thus lighted it was deadly still 495
As all the countless bulks of solid gloom:
Perchance a congregation to fulfil
Solemnities of silence in this doom,
Mysterious rites of dolour and despair
Permitting not a breath of chant or prayer? 500

Broad steps ascended to a terrace broad
Whereon lay still light from the open door;
The hall was noble, and its aspect awed,
Hung round with heavy black from dome to floor;
And ample stairways rose to left and right 505
Whose balustrades were also draped with night.

I paced from room to room, from hall to hall,
Nor any life throughout the maze discerned;
But each was hung with its funereal pall,
And held a shrine, around which tapers burned, 510
With picture or with statue or with bust,
All copied from the same fair form of dust:

A woman very young and very fair;
Beloved by bounteous life and joy and youth,
And loving these sweet lovers, so that care 515
And age and death seemed not for her in sooth:[58]
Alike as stars, all beautiful and bright,
These shapes lit up that mausoléan[59] night.

---

[55] *wain* open vehicle for carrying heavy loads.
[56] *massy* weighty, heavy.
[57] *Portentous* ominous.

[58] *sooth* truth.
[59] *mausoléan* of a mausoleum, tomb.

At length I heard a murmur as of lips,
    And reached an open oratory[60] hung   520
With heaviest blackness of the whole eclipse;
Beneath the dome a fuming censer swung;
And one lay there upon a low white bed,
With tapers burning at the foot and head:

    The Lady of the images: supine,[61]   525
Deathstill, lifesweet, with folded palms she lay:
    And kneeling there as at a sacred shrine
A young man wan and worn who seemed to pray:
    A crucifix of dim and ghostly white
Surmounted the large altar left in night: –   530

The[62] chambers of the mansion of my heart,
    In every one whereof thine image dwells,
    Are black with grief eternal for thy sake.
    The inmost oratory of my soul,
Wherein thou ever dwellest quick[63] or dead,   535
    Is black with grief eternal for thy sake.

I kneel beside thee and I clasp the cross,
    With eyes for ever fixed upon that face,
    So beautiful and dreadful in its calm.

I kneel here patient as thou liest there;   540
    As patient as a statue carved in stone,
        Of adoration and eternal grief.

While thou dost not awake I cannot move;
And something tells me thou wilt never wake,
    And I alive feel turning into stone.   545

Most beautiful were Death to end my grief,
    Most hateful to destroy the sight of thee,
    Dear vision better than all death or life.

But I renounce all choice of life or death,
    For either shall be ever at thy side,   550
    And thus in bliss or woe be ever well. –

He murmured thus and thus in monotone,
    Intent upon that uncorrupted face,
    Entranced except his moving lips alone:
I glided with hushed footsteps from the place.   555
    This was the festival that filled with light
    That palace in the City of the Night.

---

[60] *oratory* place of prayer, chapel.
[61] *supine* lying on one's back.
[62] *The* . . . the following words are spoken by the 'young
man wan and worn'.

[63] *quick* living.

11

What men are they who haunt these fatal glooms,
And fill their living mouths with dust of death,
　　And make their habitations in the tombs,　　　　　　560
And breathe eternal sighs with mortal breath,
And pierce life's pleasant veil of various error
To reach that void of darkness and old terror
　　Wherein expire the lamps of hope and faith?

They have much wisdom yet they are not wise,　　　　565
They have much goodness yet they do not well,
　　(The fools we know have their own Paradise,
　　The wicked also have their proper Hell);
They have much strength but still their doom is stronger,
Much patience but their time endureth longer,　　　　570
Much valour but life mocks it with some spell.

They are most rational and yet insane:
An outward madness not to be controlled;
　　A perfect reason in the central brain,
Which has no power, but sitteth wan and cold,　　　　575
And sees the madness, and foresees as plainly
　　The ruin in its path, and trieth vainly
　　To cheat itself refusing to behold.

And some are great in rank and wealth and power,
　　And some renowned for genius and for worth;　　　580
And some are poor and mean, who brood and cower
And shrink from notice, and accept all dearth
Of body, heart and soul, and leave to others
All boons[64] of life: yet these and those are brothers,
　　The saddest and the weariest men on earth.　　　　585

12

Our isolated units could be brought
To act together for some common end?
For one by one, each silent with his thought,
I marked a long loose line approach and wend
Athwart the great cathedral's cloistered square,　　　590
And slowly vanish from the moonlit air.

Then I would follow in among the last:
And in the porch a shrouded figure stood,
Who challenged each one pausing ere he passed,
With deep eyes burning through a blank white hood:　595
Whence come you in the world of life and light
To this our City of Tremendous Night? –

From pleading in a senate of rich lords
For some scant justice to our countless hordes
Who toil half-starved with scarce a human right:　　600
I wake from daydreams to this real night.

[64] *boons* rewards, gifts.

From wandering through many a solemn scene
Of opium visions, with a heart serene
And intellect miraculously bright:
I wake from daydreams to this real night.   605

From making hundreds laugh and roar with glee
By my transcendent feats of mimicry,
And humour wanton as an elfish sprite:
I wake from daydreams to this real night.

From prayer and fasting in a lonely cell,   610
Which brought an ecstasy ineffable[65]
Of love and adoration and delight:
I wake from daydreams to this real night.

From ruling on a splendid kingly throne
A nation which beneath my rule has grown   615
Year after year in wealth and arts and might:
I wake from daydreams to this real night.

From preaching to an audience fired with faith
The Lamb[66] who died to save our souls from death,
Whose blood hath washed our scarlet sins wool-white:[67]   620
I wake from daydreams to this real night.

From drinking fiery poison in a den
Crowded with tawdry[68] girls and squalid men,
Who hoarsely laugh and curse and brawl and fight:
I wake from daydreams to this real night.   625

From picturing with all beauty and all grace
First Eden and the parents of our race,[69]
A luminous rapture unto all men's sight:
I wake from daydreams to this real night.

From writing a great work with patient plan   630
To justify the ways of God to man,[70]
And show how ill must fade and perish quite:
I wake from daydreams to this real night.

From desperate fighting with a little band
Against the powerful tyrants of our land,   635
To free our brethren in their own despite:
I wake from daydreams to this real night.

Thus, challenged by that warder sad and stern,
Each one responded with his countersign,
Then entered the cathedral; and in turn   640
I entered also, having given mine;

[65] *ineffable* too great for words.
[66] *Lamb* Lamb of God, Jesus.
[67] *blood . . . white* cf. Revelation 7.14, 'These are they which came out of great tribulation, and haue washed their robes, and made them white in the blood of the Lambe'.

[68] *tawdry* cheap, showy.
[69] *parents . . . race* Adam and Eve.
[70] *justify . . . man* cf. Milton, *Paradise Lost* 1.26, 'And justify the ways of God to men'.

But lingered near until I heard no more,
And marked the closing of the massive door.

13

Of all things human which are strange and wild
This is perchance the wildest and most strange,   645
  And showeth man most utterly beguiled,
  To those who haunt that sunless City's range;
That he bemoans himself for aye,[71] repeating
How time is deadly swift, how life is fleeting,
  How naught is constant on the earth but change.   650

The hours are heavy on him and the days;
The burden of the months he scarce can bear;
  And often in his secret soul he prays
  To sleep through barren periods unaware,
Arousing at some longed-for date of pleasure;   655
Which having passed and yielded him small treasure,
  He would outsleep another term of care.

Yet in his marvellous fancy he must make
Quick wings for Time, and see it fly from us;
  This Time which crawleth like a monstrous snake,   660
  Wounded and slow and very venomous;
Which creeps blindwormlike round the earth and ocean,
Distilling poison at each painful motion,
  And seems condemned to circle ever thus.

And since he cannot spend and use aright   665
The little time here given him in trust,
  But wasteth it in weary undelight
  Of foolish toil and trouble, strife and lust
He naturally claimeth to inherit
The everlasting Future, that his merit   670
  May have full scope; as surely is most just.

O length of the intolerable hours,
O nights that are as æons[72] of slow pain,
  O Time, too ample for our vital powers,
  O Life, whose woeful vanities remain   675
Immutable for all of all our legions
Through all the centuries and in all the regions,
  Not of your speed and variance we complain.

We do not ask a longer term of strife,
Weakness and weariness and nameless woes;   680
  We do not claim renewed and endless life
  When this which is our torment here shall close,
An everlasting conscious inanition![73]
We yearn for speedy death in full fruition,
  Dateless[74] oblivion and divine repose.   685

---

[71] *aye* ever.
[72] *æons* immeasurable periods of time.
[73] *inanition* condition of being empty.
[74] *Dateless* endless.

14

Large glooms were gathered in the mighty fane,[75]
With tinted moongleams slanting here and there;
And all was hush: no swelling organ-strain,
No chant, no voice or murmuring of prayer;
No priests came forth, no tinkling censers fumed,   690
And the high altar space was unillumed.

Around the pillars and against the walls
Leaned men and shadows; others seemed to brood
Bent or recumbent in secluded stalls.
Perchance they were not a great multitude   695
Save in that city of so lonely streets
Where one may count up every face he meets.

All patiently awaited the event
Without a stir or sound, as if no less
Self-occupied, doomstricken, while attent.[76]   700
And then we heard a voice of solemn stress
From the dark pulpit, and our gaze there met
Two eyes which burned as never eyes burned yet:

Two steadfast and intolerable eyes
Burning beneath a broad and rugged brow;   705
The head behind it of enormous size.
And as black fir-groves in a large wind bow,
Our rooted congregation, gloom-arrayed,
By that great sad voice deep and full were swayed: –

O melancholy Brothers, dark, dark, dark!   710
O battling in black floods without an ark![77]
O spectral wanderers of unholy Night!
My soul hath bled for you these sunless years,
With bitter blood-drops running down like tears:
Oh, dark, dark, dark, withdrawn from joy and light!   715

My heart is sick with anguish for your bale;[78]
Your woe hath been my anguish; yea, I quail
And perish in your perishing unblest.
And I have searched the highths and depths, the scope
Of all our universe, with desperate hope   720
To find some solace for your wild unrest.

And now at last authentic word I bring,
Witnessed by every dead and living thing;
Good tidings of great joy for you,[79] for all:
There is no God; no Fiend with names divine   725
Made us and tortures us; if we must pine,
It is to satiate no Being's gall.

[75] *fane* temple.
[76] *attent* full of attention.
[77] *battling . . . ark* cf. the story of Noah and the ark, in which God saved animals and people from the Flood (Genesis 6–9).
[78] *bale* woe, injury.

[79] *Good tidings . . . you* ironic allusion to words said to shepherds about the birth of Jesus in Luke 2.10: 'And the Angel said vnto them, Feare not: For behold, I bring you good tidings of great ioy, which shall be to all people'.

It was the dark delusion of a dream,
That living Person conscious and supreme,
Whom we must curse for cursing us with life;[80]   730
Whom we must curse because the life He gave
Could not be buried in the quiet grave,
Could not be killed by poison or by knife.

This little life is all we must endure,
The grave's most holy peace is ever sure,   735
We fall asleep and never wake again;
Nothing is of us but the mouldering flesh,
Whose elements dissolve and merge afresh
In earth, air, water, plants, and other men.

We finish thus; and all our wretched race   740
Shall finish with its cycle, and give place
To other beings, with their own time-doom:
Infinite æons ere our kind began;
Infinite æons after the last man
Has joined the mammoth in earth's tomb and womb.   745

We bow down to the universal laws,
Which never had for man a special clause
Of cruelty or kindness, love or hate:
If toads and vultures are obscene to sight,
If tigers burn with beauty and with might,[81]   750
Is it by favour or by wrath of fate?

All substance lives and struggles evermore[82]
Through countless shapes continually at war,
By countless interactions interknit:
If one is born a certain day on earth,   755
All times and forces tended to that birth,
Not all the world could change or hinder it.

I find no hint throughout the Universe
Of good or ill, of blessing or of curse;
I find alone Necessity Supreme;   760
With infinite Mystery, abysmal, dark,
Unlighted ever by the faintest spark
For us the flitting shadows of a dream.

O Brothers of sad lives! they are so brief;
A few short years must bring us all relief: 765
Can we not bear these years of labouring breath?
But if you would not this poor life fulfil,

[80] *must curse . . . life* cf. Job 3.1–3, 'After this, opened Iob his mouth, and cursed his day. And Iob spake, and said, Let the day perish, wherein I was borne, and the night in which it was said, There is a man-childe conceiued.'
[81] *If tigers . . . might* cf. Blake, 'The Tyger', in *Songs of Experience* (1795), 'Tyger! Tyger! burning bright / In the forests of the night'.
[82] *All substance . . . evermore* cf. the subtitle of Charles Darwin's *The Origin of Species by Means of Natural Selection, or the Preservation of Favoured Races in the Struggle for Life* (1859).

Lo, you are free to end it when you will,
Without the fear of waking after death. –

The organ-like vibrations of his voice   770
Thrilled through the vaulted aisles and died away;
The yearning of the tones which bade rejoice
Was sad and tender as a requiem[83] lay:
Our shadowy congregation rested still
As brooding on that 'End it when you will.'   775

15
Wherever men are gathered, all the air
Is charged with human feeling, human thought;[84]
Each shout and cry and laugh, each curse and prayer,
Are into its vibrations surely wrought;
Unspoken passion, wordless meditation,   780
Are breathed into it with our respiration;
It is with our life fraught and overfraught.

So that no man there breathes earth's simple breath,
As if alone on mountains or wide seas;
But nourishes warm life or hastens death   785
With joys and sorrows, health and foul disease,
Wisdom and folly, good and evil labours,
Incessant of his multitudinous neighbours;
He in his turn affecting all of these.

That City's atmosphere is dark and dense,   790
Although not many exiles wander there,
With many a potent evil influence,
Each adding poison to the poisoned air;
Infections of unutterable sadness,
Infections of incalculable madness,   795
Infections of incurable despair.

16
Our shadowy congregation rested still,
As musing on that message we had heard
And brooding on that 'End it when you will;'
Perchance awaiting yet some other word;   800
When keen as lightning through a muffled sky
Sprang forth a shrill and lamentable cry: –

The man speaks sooth, alas! the man speaks sooth:
We have no personal life beyond the grave;
There is no God; Fate knows nor wrath nor ruth: 805
Can I find here the comfort which I crave?

In all eternity I had one chance,
One few years' term of gracious human life:

---

[83] *requiem* mass for the dead.
[84] *Wherever . . . thought* secular version of Jesus's
words: 'For where two or three are gathered together

in my Name, there am I in the midst of them', Matthew
18.20.

The splendours of the intellect's advance,
The sweetness of the home with babes and wife;   810

The social pleasures with their genial wit;
The fascination of the worlds of art,
The glories of the worlds of nature, lit
By large imagination's glowing heart;

The rapture of mere being, full of health;   815
The careless childhood and the ardent youth,
The strenuous manhood winning various wealth,
The reverend age serene with life's long truth:

All the sublime prerogatives of Man;
The storied memories of the times of old,   820
The patient tracking of the world's great plan
Through sequences and changes myriadfold.[85]

This chance was never offered me before;
For me the infinite Past is blank and dumb:
This chance recurreth never, nevermore;   825
Blank, blank for me the infinite To-come.

And this sole chance was frustrate from my birth,
A mockery, a delusion; and my breath
Of noble human life upon this earth
So racks me that I sigh for senseless death.   830

My wine of life is poison mixed with gall,[86]
My noonday passes in a nightmare dream,
I worse than lose the years which are my all:
What can console me for the loss supreme?

Speak not of comfort where no comfort is,   835
Speak not at all: can words make foul things fair?
Our life's a cheat, our death a black abyss:
Hush and be mute envisaging despair. –

This vehement voice came from the northern aisle
Rapid and shrill to its abrupt harsh close;   840
And none gave answer for a certain while,
For words must shrink from these most wordless woes;
At last the pulpit speaker simply said,
With humid eyes and thoughtful drooping head: –

My Brother, my poor Brothers, it is thus;   845
This life itself holds nothing good for us,
But it ends soon and nevermore can be;
And we knew nothing of it ere our birth,
And shall know nothing when consigned to earth:
I ponder these thoughts and they comfort me.   850

---

[85] *myriadfold* multiple.
[86] *My wine . . . gall* cf. Matthew 27.34 describing Jesus on the cross: 'They gaue him vineger to drinke, mingled with gall: and when hee had tasted thereof, hee would not drinke'; gall = type of intensely bitter substance.

17

How the moon triumphs through the endless nights!
How the stars throb and glitter as they wheel
Their thick processions of supernal[87] lights
Around the blue vault obdurate[88] as steel!
And men regard with passionate awe and yearning   855
The mighty marching and the golden burning,
And think the heavens respond to what they feel.

Boats gliding like dark shadows of a dream,
Are glorified from vision as they pass
The quivering moonbridge on the deep black stream;   860
Cold windows kindle their dead glooms of glass
To restless crystals; cornice,[89] dome, and column
Emerge from chaos in the splendour solemn;
Like faëry[90] lakes gleam lawns of dewy grass.

With such a living light these dead eyes shine,   865
These eyes of sightless heaven, that as we gaze
We read a pity, tremulous, divine,
Or cold majestic scorn in their pure rays:
Fond man! they are not haughty, are not tender;
There is no heart or mind in all their splendour,   870
They thread mere puppets all their marvellous maze.

If we could near them with the flight unflown,
We should but find them worlds as sad as this,
Or suns all self-consuming like our own
Enringed by planet worlds as much amiss: 875
They wax and wane through fusion and confusion;
The spheres eternal are a grand illusion,
The empyréan[91] is a void abyss.

18

I wandered in a suburb of the north,
And reached a spot whence three close lanes led down,   880
Beneath thick trees and hedgerows winding forth
Like deep brook channels, deep and dark and lown:[92]
The air above was wan with misty light,
The dull grey south showed one vague blur of white.

I took the left-hand lane and slowly trod   885
Its earthen footpath, brushing as I went
The humid leafage; and my feet were shod
With heavy languor, and my frame downbent,
With infinite sleepless weariness outworn,
So many nights I thus had paced forlorn.   890

After a hundred steps I grew aware
Of something crawling in the lane below;

[87] *supernal* that which exists in the heavens.
[88] *obdurate* hardened, impervious to sympathy.
[89] *cornice* horizontal moulded projection in a building.
[90] *faëry* fairy.

[91] *empyréan* visible heavens, the whole extent of cosmic space.
[92] *lown* gentle, still.

It seemed a wounded creature prostrate there
That sobbed with pangs in making progress slow,
The hind limbs stretched to push, the fore limbs then   895
To drag; for it would die in its own den.

But coming level with it I discerned
That it had been a man; for at my tread
It stopped in its sore travail[93] and half-turned,
Leaning upon its right, and raised its head,   900
And with the left hand twitched back as in ire[94]
Long grey unreverend locks befouled with mire.[95]

A haggard filthy face with bloodshot eyes,
An infamy for manhood to behold.
He gasped all trembling, What, you want my prize?   905
You leave, to rob me, wine and lust and gold
And all that men go mad upon, since you
Have traced my sacred secret of the clue?

You think that I am weak and must submit;
Yet I but scratch you with this poisoned blade,   910
And you are dead as if I clove with it
That false fierce greedy heart. Betrayed! betrayed!
I fling this phial[96] if you seek to pass,
And you are forthwith shrivelled up like grass.

And then with sudden change, Take thought! take thought!   915
Have pity on me! it is mine alone.
If you could find, it would avail you naught;
Seek elsewhere on the pathway of your own:
For who of mortal or immortal race
The lifetrack of another can retrace?   920

Did you but know my agony and toil!
Two lanes diverge up yonder from this lane;
My thin blood marks the long length of their soil;
Such clue I left, who sought my clue in vain:
My hands and knees are worn both flesh and bone;   925
I cannot move but with continual moan.

But I am in the very way at last
To find the long-lost broken golden thread
Which reunites my present with my past,
If you but go your own way. And I said,   930
I will retire as soon as you have told
Whereunto leadeth this lost thread of gold.

And so you know it not! he hissed with scorn;
I feared you, imbecile! It leads me back

---

[93] *travail* labour.

[94] *ire* anger.

[95] *been a man . . . mire* Thomson is alluding to William Blake's *Nebuchadnezzar* (1795), a picture of the long-bearded king crawling as if half animal. Thomson's crawling man, struggling to find 'Eden innocence in Eden's clime', is a parody and metonymic rejection of Blake's ideas, which Thomson had earlier admired.

[96] *phial* small container for liquid.

From this accursed night without a morn,   935
And through the deserts which have else no track,
And through vast wastes of horror-haunted time,
    To Eden innocence in Eden's clime:

    And I become a nursling soft and pure,
    An infant cradled on its mother's knee,   940
Without a past, love-cherished and secure;
Which if it saw this loathsome present Me,
Would plunge its face into the pillowing breast,
    And scream abhorrence hard to lull to rest.

    He turned to grope; and I retiring brushed   945
Thin shreds of gossamer[97] from off my face,
And mused, His life would grow, the germ uncrushed;
    He should to antenatal[98] night retrace,
    And hide his elements in that large womb
Beyond the reach of man-evolving Doom.   950

And even thus, what weary way were planned,
    To seek oblivion through the far-off gate
Of birth, when that of death is close at hand!
    For this is law, if law there be in Fate:
What never has been, yet may have its when;   955
The thing which has been, never is again.

19

    The mighty river flowing dark and deep,
With ebb and flood from the remote sea-tides
Vague-sounding through the City's sleepless sleep,
    Is named the River of the Suicides;[99]   960
For night by night some lorn wretch overweary,
And shuddering from the future yet more dreary,
    Within its cold secure oblivion hides.

    One plunges from a bridge's parapet,
    As by some blind and sudden frenzy hurled;   965
    Another wades in slow with purpose set
    Until the waters are above him furled;
    Another in a boat with dreamlike motion
    Glides drifting down into the desert ocean,
To starve or sink from out the desert world.   970

They perish from their suffering surely thus,
    For none beholding them attempts to save,
The while each thinks how soon, solicitous,
    He may seek refuge in the self-same wave;
Some hour when tired of ever-vain endurance   975
Impatience will forerun the sweet assurance
    Of perfect peace eventual in the grave.

---

[97] *gossamer* fine filmy cobweb.
[98] *antenatal* before birth.

[99] *River of the Suicides* cf. the River Thames in London, which became peculiarly associated with suicide in the nineteenth century.

When this poor tragic-farce has palled us long,
  Why actors and spectators do we stay? –
To fill our so-short *rôles* out right or wrong;   980
  To see what shifts are yet in the dull play
For our illusion; to refrain from grieving
Dear foolish friends by our untimely leaving:
  But those asleep at home, how blest are they!

    Yet it is but for one night after all: 985
What matters one brief night of dreary pain?
  When after it the weary eyelids fall
  Upon the weary eyes and wasted brain;
And all sad scenes and thoughts and feelings vanish
In that sweet sleep no power can ever banish,   990
  That one best sleep which never wakes again.

20
    I sat me weary on a pillar's base,
And leaned against the shaft; for broad moonlight
O'erflowed the peacefulness of cloistered space,
  A shore of shadow slanting from the right: 995
The great cathedral's western front stood there,
  A wave-worn rock in that calm sea of air.

    Before it, opposite my place of rest,
  Two figures faced each other, large, austere;
A couchant[100] sphinx[101] in shadow to the breast,   1000
  An angel standing in the moonlight clear;
  So mighty by magnificence of form,
They were not dwarfed beneath that mass enorm.[102]

    Upon the cross-hilt of a naked sword
The angel's hands, as prompt to smite, were held;   1005
  His vigilant intense regard was poured
  Upon the creature placidly unquelled,
Whose front was set at level gaze which took
No heed of aught, a solemn trance-like look.

    And as I pondered these opposèd shapes   1010
  My eyelids sank in stupor, that dull swoon
Which drugs and with a leaden mantle drapes
  The outworn to worse weariness. But soon
A sharp and clashing noise the stillness broke,
    And from the evil lethargy I woke.   1015

    The angel's wings had fallen, stone on stone,
And lay there shattered; hence the sudden sound:
  A warrior leaning on his sword alone
Now watched the sphinx with that regard profound;
The sphinx unchanged looked forthright, as aware   1020
    Of nothing in the vast abyss of air.

---

[100] *couchant* (heraldic) lying down.   [102] *enorm* enormous.
[101] *sphinx* mythological monster with the head of a woman
and the winged body of a lion.

Again I sank in that repose unsweet,
Again a clashing noise my slumber rent;
The warrior's sword lay broken at his feet:
An unarmed man with raised hands impotent   1025
Now stood before the sphinx, which ever kept
Such mien[103] as if with open eyes it slept.

My eyelids sank in spite of wonder grown;
A louder crash upstartled me in dread:
The man had fallen forward, stone on stone,   1030
And lay there shattered, with his trunkless head
Between the monster's large quiescent[104] paws,
Beneath its grand front changeless as life's laws.

The moon had circled westward full and bright,
And made the temple-front a mystic dream,   1035
And bathed the whole enclosure with its light,
The sworded angel's wrecks, the sphinx supreme:
I pondered long that cold majestic face
Whose vision seemed of infinite void space.

21

Anear the centre of that northern crest   1040
Stands out a level upland bleak and bare,
From which the city east and south and west
Sinks gently in long waves; and thronèd there
An Image sits, stupendous, superhuman,
The bronze colossus[105] of a wingèd Woman,   1045
Upon a graded granite base foursquare.

Low-seated she leans forward massively,
With cheek on clenched left hand, the forearm's might
Erect, its elbow on her rounded knee;
Across a clasped book in her lap the right   1050
Upholds a pair of compasses; she gazes
With full set eyes, but wandering in thick mazes
Of sombre thought beholds no outward sight.

Words cannot picture her; but all men know
That solemn sketch the pure sad artist wrought   1055
Three centuries and threescore years ago,[106]
With phantasies of his peculiar thought:
The instruments of carpentry and science
Scattered about her feet, in strange alliance
With the keen wolf-hound sleeping undistraught;   1060

Scales, hour-glass, bell, and magic-square[107] above;
The grave and solid infant perched beside,
With open winglets that might bear a dove,

---

[103] *mien* bearing, manner of carrying self.
[104] *quiescent* motionless.
[105] *colossus* vast statue, something gigantic.
[106] *Words cannot . . . ago* the 'sketch' referred to is *Melencolia*
I (1514) by Albrecht Dürer (1471–1528); see plate 6.

[107] *magic-square* diagram consisting of a square divided into
smaller squares, in each of which a number is written, their
position being so arranged that the sum of the figures in a
row, vertical, horizontal or diagonal, is always the same.

Plate 6 Albrecht Dürer, *Melencolia* I (1514), engraving. Photo ARG Images.

Intent upon its tablets, heavy-eyed;
Her folded wings as of a mighty eagle,   1065
But all too impotent to lift the regal
Robustness of her earth-born strength and pride;

And with those wings, and that light wreath which seems
To mock her grand head and the knotted frown
Of forehead charged with baleful thoughts and dreams,   1070
The household bunch of keys, the housewife's gown
Voluminous, indented, and yet rigid
As if a shell of burnished metal frigid,
The feet thick shod to tread all weakness down;

The comet hanging o'er the waste dark seas,   1075
The massy rainbow curved in front of it,
Beyond the village with the masts and trees;
The snaky imp,[108] dog-headed, from the Pit,
Bearing upon its batlike leathern pinions[109]
Her name unfolded in the sun's dominions,   1080
The 'MELENCOLIA' that transcends all wit.

---

[108] *imp* devil.
[109] *pinion* the end segment of a bird's wing or, more
generally, the wing as a whole.

Thus has the artist copied her, and thus
Surrounded to expound her form sublime,
Her fate heroic and calamitous;
Fronting the dreadful mysteries of Time,   1085
Unvanquished in defeat and desolation,
Undaunted in the hopeless conflagration[110]
Of the day setting on her baffled prime.

Baffled and beaten back she works on still,
Weary and sick of soul she works the more,   1090
Sustained by her indomitable will:
The hands shall fashion and the brain shall pore
And all her sorrow shall be turned to labour,
Till death the friend-foe piercing with his sabre[111]
That mighty heart of hearts ends bitter war.   1095

But as if blacker night could dawn on night,
With tenfold gloom on moonless night unstarred,
A sense more tragic than defeat and blight,
More desperate than strife with hope debarred,
More fatal than the adamantine[112] Never   1100
Encompassing her passionate endeavour,
Dawns glooming in her tenebrous[113] regard:

The sense that every struggle brings defeat
Because Fate holds no prize to crown success;
That all the oracles are dumb[114] or cheat   1105
Because they have no secret to express;
That none can pierce the vast black veil uncertain
Because there is no light beyond the curtain;[115]
That all is vanity and nothingness.

Titanic[116] from her high throne in the north,   1110
That City's sombre Patroness and Queen,
In bronze sublimity she gazes forth
Over her Capital of teen[117] and threne,[118]
Over the river with its isles and bridges,
The marsh and moorland, to the stern rock-ridges,   1115
Confronting them with a coëval[119] mien.

The moving moon and stars from east to west
Circle before her in the sea of air;
Shadows and gleams glide round her solemn rest.
Her subjects often gaze up to her there: 1120
The strong to drink new strength of iron endurance,
The weak new terrors; all, renewed assurance
And confirmation of the old despair.

---

[110] *conflagration* great fire.
[111] *sabre* form of sword.
[112] *adamantine* immovable, impregnable.
[113] *tenebrous* full of darkness.
[114] *the oracles are dumb* cf. Milton, 'Ode on the Morning of Christ's Nativity' (1629), 'The oracles are dumb'.
[115] *no light . . . curtain* cf. Tennyson, *In Memoriam A.H.H.*,

lyric 56, 'O life as futile, then, as frail! / O for thy voice to soothe and bless! / What hope of answer, or redress? / Behind the veil, behind the veil.'
[116] *Titanic* vast; Titans were giants in Greek mythology.
[117] *teen* injury, affliction.
[118] *threne* song of lamentation.
[119] *coëval* of the same age, equally old.

William Morris (1834–1896)

Born near Walthamstow, William Morris was the son of a businessman and grew up in an Evangelical environment of wealth and books. In 1848, he went to Marlborough College, then in 1853, after private tuition, to Exeter College Oxford where he formed a lasting friendship with the Pre-Raphaelite painter Edward Burne-Jones. Morris was articled to the gothic revivalist ecclesiastical architect G. E. Street, through whom he met his life-long friend Philip Webb, who was to design Morris's home, the Red House, at Bexleyheath, Kent. Morris, at this stage, was an enthusiast for the Pre-Raphaelites, joining them in their medievalism and preference for the gothic, natural forms and high-quality craftsmanship. He contributed verse to the *Oxford and Cambridge Magazine* which he helped found in 1856 and pay for. In 1858, he issued his *The Defence of Guenevere and Other Poems*, which contained some of his most striking medievalist verse – 'The Haystack in the Floods', 'Concerning Geffray Teste Noire' – with its probing of the dark histories of chivalry, its destructive human passions and radiant beauties. In 1859, he married Jane Burden, whose face, together with Lizzie Siddal's, dominated Pre-Raphaelite iconography for a time. With Webb, D. G. Rossetti, Madox Brown and others, Morris founded Morris, Marshall, Faulkner & Co., dedicated to interior decoration and furniture manufacture using hand labour. It was a central part of Morris's medieval revivalist approach to industrialism – a key part of the so-called Arts and Crafts Movement – and an effort to make high-quality, aesthetically pleasing products at reasonable prices.

In 1867, Morris published *The Life and Death of Jason*, a long poem on Jason, Medea and the Argonauts, followed by *The Earthly Paradise* (1868–70). In 1871, he visited Iceland, which was to have a significant consequence on his work, prompting him to cast off his earlier Pre-Raphaelite preferences for Arthurian legend in favour of the heroic themes of ancient Icelandic writing. *Love is Enough* came out in 1872, after Morris had rented Kelmscott Manor in Lechlade (where D. G. Rossetti's affair with Janey Morris continued, with Morris's knowledge, perhaps his agreement). *Three Northern Love Stories* was issued in 1875; *The Story of Sigurd the Volsung and the Fall of the Niblungs* in 1876. Morris's energy was extraordinary and he continued throughout his life to develop new skills – dyeing, carpet weaving, tapestry making – and extending the scope of the Company, which moved to Merton Abbey near Wimbledon in 1881. He founded the Society for the Protection of Ancient Buildings in 1877 ('Anti-Scrape') and became more and more involved in political reform, socialism and communism, lecturing on the radical circuits and writing on political subjects. He was enormously influential as a political figure in his own time and well into the twentieth century. *Chants for Socialists* appeared in 1885, *The House of the Wolfings* in 1889, and *News from Nowhere*, a socialist, medievalist utopia, in 1891. In 1890, Morris founded the Kelmscott Press to print high-quality books with its own ornamental typefaces, most memorably the *Works of Geoffrey Chaucer Newly Augmented*, including illustrations by Burne-Jones, in 1896. William Morris died in October that year and is buried in the ancient churchyard at Kelmscott beneath a Viking-style tomb designed by Webb.

The Haystack in the Floods

William Morris's medievalist poetry frequently explores the calamities of human exchange, the dark side of chivalry, the apparent brutality of the Middle Ages, the failure of romance ideals, the complexity of human choice in a knightly setting. Typically, Morris's texts challenge a romanticized conception of the Middle Ages as an age of ideals, the locus of pure faith, devout sincerity and true knightliness. Such a challenge is most obvious in 'Concerning Geffray Teste Noire', 438–45. But it is also apparent in 'The Haystack in the Floods' (1858), a poem that offers itself as a fragment of an epic, plunging the reader bewilderingly into the middle of a story, and depriving him/her – or so it first seems – of the contexts that he or she might initially want to make sense of it. The broken fragments of epic that Morris offers serve to reinforce, subtly, a point about the fracturing of ideals and the heroic ethos.

'The Haystack in the Floods' erases the notion of the Victorian poet as creator, as Morris gestures instead towards a balladic, medievalist sense of the poet as the re-teller of narratives already in cultural circulation (cf. Adelaide Anne Procter, 'A Legend of Provence', 320–7, and Amy Levy, 'Xantippe', 630–6). The poem draws on a story about the aftermath of the Battle at Poi[c]tiers in September 1356 – a key military engagement early in the Hundred Years' War between France and England – where English forces under Edward the Black Prince defeated a larger French army led by John II of France (who was captured). The English knight in the poem is Sir Robert de Marny, who has fallen in love with a French woman, Jehane. As he attempts to escape with her to the safety of English-held Gascony, they are intercepted by a French knight, Godmar, together with his thuggish retinue, in French territory. Godmar offers Jehane an impossible choice: either become Godmar's paramour and save Sir Robert's life, or refuse Godmar and cause Robert's death. The poem painfully unpicks the limits of idealism in a conflicted society and continues the brooding of 'The Defence of Guenevere', 428–38, on the disastrous consequences of love and sexual desire. Depicting the representative English man as overcome by a combination of French brutality and French integrity, 'The Haystack' also sustains a construction of France as the traditional enemy of England, defined by barbarous cruelty for which Jehane's love insufficiently compensates.

Morris employs a high degree of verbal concision and the minimum number of dramatic events and visual details to dramatize a situation of emotional pain. The mode is not one of realism – the characters are stylized and the poem eschews the terms of psychology that, for instance, Robert Browning probed in his dramatic monologues. It creates a peculiarly stark sense of tragedy that looks towards nihilism.

Text: *The Defence of Guenevere and Other Poems* (1858).

Had she come all the way for this,
To part at last without a kiss?
Yea, had she borne the dirt and rain
That her own eyes might see him slain
Beside the haystack in the floods?   5

Along the dripping leafless woods,
The stirrup touching either shoe,
She rode astride as troopers do;
With kirtle[1] kilted to her knee,
To which the mud splash'd wretchedly;   10
And the wet dripp'd from every tree
Upon her head and heavy hair,
And on her eyelids broad and fair;
The tears and rain ran down her face.
By fits and starts they rode apace,   15
And very often was his place
Far off from her; he had to ride
Ahead, to see what might betide
When the roads cross'd; and sometimes, when
There rose a murmuring from his men,   20
Had to turn back with promises;
Ah me! she had but little ease;
And often for pure doubt and dread
She sobb'd, made giddy in the head
By the swift riding; while, for cold,   25
Her slender fingers scarce could hold
The wet reins; yea, and scarcely, too,
She felt the foot within her shoe
Against the stirrup: all for this,
To part at last without a kiss   30
Beside the haystack in the floods.

[1] *kirtle* gown.

For when they near'd that old soak'd hay,
　　　　They saw across the only way
　　　That Judas,[2] Godmar, and the three
　　　　Red running lions dismally　　　　　　　　　　35
　　Grinn'd from his pennon,[3] under which
　　In one straight line along the ditch,
　　　　　They counted thirty heads.

　　　　　　So then,
　While Robert turn'd round to his men,　　　　　　40
　　She saw at once the wretched end,
And, stooping down, tried hard to rend
Her coif[4] the wrong way from her head,
And hid her eyes; while Robert said:
　'Nay, love, 'tis scarcely two to one,　　　　　　　45
At Poictiers[5] where we made them run
So fast – why, sweet my love, good cheer,
　The Gascon[6] frontier is so near,
　　　　　Nought after this.'

　　　　　But, 'O!' she said,　　　　　　　　　50
'My God! my God! I have to tread
The long way back without you; then
The court at Paris; those six men;[7]
　The gratings of the Chatelet;[8]
The swift Seine[9] on some rainy day　　　　　　　55
Like this, and people standing by
And laughing, while my weak hands try
　To recollect how strong men swim.
All this, or else a life with him,[10] — *Godmar*
For which I should be damned at last.　　　　　　60
Would God that this next hour were past!'

He answer'd not, but cried his cry,
'St. George for Marny!'[11] cheerily;
　And laid his hand upon her rein.
　Alas! no man of all his train　　　　　　　　　65
　Gave back that cheery cry again;
And, while for rage his thumb beat fast
Upon his sword-hilts, some one cast
　About his neck a kerchief[12] long,
　　　　　And bound him.　　　　　　　　70

　　　　Then they went along
　To Godmar; who said: 'Now, Jehane,
　Your lover's life is on the wane

---

[2] *Judas* traitor (Judas betrayed Jesus).
[3] *pennon* flag or streamer, usually on a lance.
[4] *coif* cap.
[5] *Poictiers* see headnote, 423–4.
[6] *Gascon* Gascony, under English control, see headnote, 423–4.
[7] *six men* judges.
[8] *Chatelet* Paris court and prison, known for its brutality.

[9] *Seine* river running through Paris. Jehane refers to the trial by water whereby a prisoner was cast into water: only if he or she did not surface was the prisoner believed innocent.
[10] *him* Godmar.
[11] *'St. George for Marny!'* exclamation of encouragement (St George is the patron saint of England).
[12] *kerchief* piece of fabric around the neck.

So fast, that, if this very hour
You yield not as my paramour,[13]   75
He will not see the rain leave off –
Nay, keep your tongue from gibe and scoff,
      Sir Robert, or I slay you now.'

      She laid her hand upon her brow,
      Then gazed upon the palm, as though   80
She thought her forehead bled, and – 'No!'
She said, and turn'd her head away,
As there were nothing else to say,
And everything were settled: red
Grew Godmar's face from chin to head: 85
'Jehane, on yonder hill there stands
My castle, guarding well my lands:
What hinders me from taking you,
      And doing that I list[14] to do
      To your fair wilful body, while   90
      Your knight lies dead?'

                  A wicked smile
      Wrinkled her face, her lips grew thin,
      A long way out she thrust her chin:
'You know that I should strangle you   95
While you were sleeping; or bite through
Your throat, by God's help – ah!' she said,
'Lord Jesus, pity your poor maid!
For in such wise[15] they hem me in,
      I cannot choose but sin and sin,   100
      Whatever happens: yet I think
      They could not make me eat or drink,
      And so should I just reach my rest.' — *Jane*
            — 'Nay, if you do not my behest,[16]
God
mar
      O Jehane! though I love you well,'   105
      Said Godmar, 'would I fail to tell
All that I know?' 'Foul lies,' she said.
'Eh? lies, my Jehane? by God's head,
At Paris folks would deem them true!
Do you know, Jehane, they cry for you: 110
"Jehane the brown! Jehane the brown!
Give us Jehane to burn or drown!" –
Eh – gag me Robert! – sweet my friend,
      This were indeed a piteous end
      For those long fingers, and long feet,   115
And long neck, and smooth shoulders sweet;
An end that few men would forget
That saw it – So, an hour yet:
      Consider, Jehane, which to take
      Of life or death!'   120

            So, scarce awake,
      Dismounting, did she leave that place,

And totter some yards: with her face
Turn'd upward to the sky she lay,
Her head on a wet heap of hay,   125
And fell asleep: and while she slept,
And did not dream, the minutes crept
Round to the twelve again; but she,
Being waked at last, sigh'd quietly,
And strangely childlike came, and said: 130
— 'I will not.' Straightway Godmar's head,
As though it hung on strong wires, turn'd
Most sharply round, and his face burn'd.

For Robert – both his eyes were dry,
He could not weep, but gloomily   135
He seem'd to watch the rain; yea, too,
His lips were firm; he tried once more
To touch her lips; she reach'd out, sore
And vain desire so tortured them,
The poor grey lips, and now the hem   140
Of his sleeve brush'd them.

With a start
Up Godmar rose, thrust them apart;
From Robert's throat he loosed the bands
Of silk and mail; with empty hands   145
Held out, she stood and gazed, and saw
The long bright blade without a flaw
Glide out from Godmar's sheath, his hand
In Robert's hair; she saw him bend
Back Robert's head; she saw him send   150
The thin steel down; the blow told well,
Right backward the knight Robert fell,
And moaned as dogs do, being half dead,
Unwitting, as I deem: so then
Godmar turn'd grinning to his men,   155
Who ran, some five or six, and beat
His head to pieces at their feet.   *O Lord...*

Then Godmar turn'd again and said:
'So, Jehane, the first fitte[17] is read!
Take note, my lady, that your way   160
Lies backward to the Chatelet!'
She shook her head and gazed awhile
At her cold hands with a rueful smile,   *She could be pretending*
As though this thing had made her mad.

This was the parting that they had   165
Beside the haystack in the floods.

[17] *fitte* division of a medieval poem, canto.

The Defence of Guenevere

The chivalric subject matter of 'The Defence of Guenevere' (1858) links it obviously with the romance interests of the Pre-Raphaelites, with whom William Morris was connected. More generally, the poem relates to the mid-century medieval revivalism – cf. Pugin's *Contrasts or a Parallel between the Noble Edifices of the Fourteenth and Fifteenth centuries and similar Buildings of the present day; shewing the present Decay of Taste* (1836), Carlyle's *Past and Present* (1843) – that left its mark, in this collection, on, for instance, Tennyson's 'Morte d'Arthur', 76–84, and Robert Browning's '"Childe Roland to the Dark Tower Came"', 195–202. Morris's approach to the Middle Ages in the 'Defence' – as with 'Concerning Geffray Teste Noire', 438–45, and 'The Haystack by the Floods', 423–7 – is to emphasize human suffering in the chivalric context and the fracturing of ideals. The 'Defence' is also a fallen woman poem, cognate with Augusta Webster's 'A Castaway', 456–71, in giving the protagonist a voice. One of the important elements of Morris's poem is the fact that it leaves the reader uncertain of the nature of the Queen's guilt: the question of where to apportion blame and responsibility is deliberately murky, and Morris offers a portrait of a situation of human desire in which clarity could only be reductive (cf. 'The Haystack by the Floods' for another approach to the problematics of human love).

The story of the poem, like Tennyson's 'Morte d'Arthur', comes from the Arthuriad, the tales of King Arthur and his knights of the Round Table. Morris's preference for the Arthuriad – prior to his discovery of the Icelandic sagas that preoccupied him from the 1870s (cf. 'Iceland First Seen', 445–7) – was shared with Pre-Raphaelite painters such as John Everett Millais (1829–96), Edward Burne-Jones (1833–98) and William Holman Hunt (1827–1910). Queen Guenevere (more usually spelt Guinevere) was the wife of Arthur. Her adultery with Sir Lancelot, Arthur's finest knight, helped spread corruption through the standards of Camelot, and was a factor in the final destruction of the Round Table. Morris took the basis for his unusual version of this popular story from Sir Thomas Malory's *Morte d'Arthur* (1485). But he changed many elements. Here, for a start,

Guenevere defends herself, which she is not allowed to do in Malory.

Guenevere's defence involves various strategies, and she discards one in favour of another in order to repel Sir Gauwaine's accusation of infidelity. She suggests the unfairness of her fate and its arbitrariness; she accuses Arthur of having 'little love', and she uses the story of Mellyagraunce's accusation to remind her listeners – somewhat disingenuously – that she has been cleared of a charge of adultery before. Guenevere repeatedly denies Gauwaine's version, though we are not told exactly what this is, being left to imagine that, perhaps, Gauwaine would misconstrue whatever she said. She also returns on several occasions to the luminous fact of her beauty to aid her defence. Morris's poem extends a scene of anxious suspense, but unlike in the characteristic mode of delay in Tennyson's poetry, such as 'Ulysses', 85–7, action ultimately concludes it. Lancelot finally saves her from further interrogation.

Tennyson concentrated in his long poem on the Queen's adultery – 'Guinevere' from the *Idylls of the King* (1859–91) – on the Queen's public role and the consequences of her infidelity for the community: his poem is ultimately about *shame* more than *guilt.* Tennyson's Guinevere is partially redeemed by the fact that, in her shame, she learns something of the importance of social duty and is at last able to assume leadership of the convent, a poor replacement for the realm, but a sign of her maturation none the less. Morris's Queen, however, is detached from the wider realm of Camelot; the questions of moral and political consequence that so exercise Tennyson are both far from her mind and, it seems, her accusers'. What is important is the quality of her life, rather than her social role, and she leaves a vivid impression of her passion and presence. The original first page of the poem was omitted – it seems unlikely that this was, as is often said, accidental – making the opening a bracingly abrupt plunge into the middle of events.

Text: *The Defence of Guenevere and Other Poems* (1858).

> *public*
>
> ~~~~ *where are they?*
>
> But, knowing now that they would have her speak,
> She threw her wet hair backward from her brow,
> Her hand close to her mouth touching her cheek,

2

As though she had had there a shameful blow,   *did he hit her?*
And feeling it shameful to feel aught but shame
All through her heart, yet felt her cheek burned so,

5

3

She must a little touch it; like one lame
She walked away from Gauwaine,[1] with her head
Still lifted up; and on her cheek of flame

4

The tears dried quick; she stopped at last and said: 10
'O knights and lords, it seems but little skill
To talk of well-known things past now and dead.

5

'God wot[2] I ought to say, I have done ill,
And pray you all forgiveness heartily!
Because you must be right, such great lords – still   15

6

'Listen, suppose your time were come to die,
And you were quite alone and very weak;
Yea, laid a dying while very mightily

7

'The wind was ruffling up the narrow streak
Of river through your broad lands running well: 20
Suppose a hush should come, then some one speak:

8

'"One of these cloths is heaven, and one is hell,
Now choose one cloth for ever; which they be,
I will not tell you, you must somehow tell

9

'"Of your own strength and mightiness; here, see!"   25
Yea, yea, my lord, and you to ope your eyes,
At foot of your familiar bed to see

10

'A great God's angel standing, with such dyes,
Not known on earth, on his great wings, and hands
Held out two ways, light from the inner skies   30

11

'Showing him well, and making his commands
Seem to be God's commands, moreover, too,
Holding within his hands the cloths on wands;

12

'And one of these strange choosing cloths was blue,
Wavy and long, and one cut short and red;   35
No man could tell the better of the two.

---

[1] *Gauwaine* knight of Arthur's Round Table (usually said to
be Arthur's nephew).   [2] *wot* knows.

13
'After a shivering half-hour you said:
"God help! heaven's colour, the blue;" and he said: "hell."
Perhaps you then would roll upon your bed,

14
'And cry to all good men that loved you well,   40
"Ah Christ! if only I had known, known, known;"
—— Launcelot went away, then I could tell,

after he left
she knew it
was wrong?

15
'Like wisest man how all things would be, moan,
And roll and hurt myself, and long to die,
And yet fear much to die for what was sown.   45

16
'Nevertheless you, O Sir Gauwaine, lie,
Whatever may have happened through these years,
God knows I speak truth, saying that you lie.'

17
Her voice was low at first, being full of tears,
But as it cleared, it grew full loud and shrill,   50
Growing a windy shriek in all men's ears,

18
A ringing in their startled brains, until
She said that Gauwaine lied, then her voice sunk,
And her great eyes began again to fill,

19
Brave
glorious
Though still she stood right up, and never shrunk,   55
But spoke on bravely, glorious lady fair!
Whatever tears her full lips may have drunk,

20
Bold   She stood, and seemed to think, and wrung her hair,
no shame Spoke out at last with no more trace of shame,
With passionate twisting of her body there: 60

21
'It chanced upon a day that Launcelot came
To dwell at Arthur's court: at Christmas-time
This happened; when the heralds sung his name,

22
'"Son of King Ban of Benwick,"[3] seemed to chime
Along with all the bells that rang that day,   65
O'er the white roofs, with little change of rhyme.

23
'Christmas and whitened winter passed away,
And over me the April sunshine came,
Made very awful with black hail-clouds, yea

---

[3] '"*Son . . . Benwick*"['] Lancelot.

24

'And in the Summer I grew white with flame,   70
And bowed my head down – Autumn, and the sick
Sure knowledge things would never be the same,

25

'However often Spring might be most thick
Of blossoms and buds, smote on me, and I grew
Careless of most things, let the clock tick, tick,   75

26

'To my unhappy pulse, that beat right through
My eager body; while I laughed out loud,
And let my lips curl up at false or true,

27

'Seemed cold and shallow without any cloud.
Behold my judges, then the cloths were brought;   80
While I was dizzied thus, old thoughts would crowd,

28

'Belonging to the time ere I was bought
By Arthur's great name and his little love;
Must I give up for ever then, I thought,

29

'That which I deemed would ever round me move   85
Glorifying all things; for a little word,
Scarce ever meant at all, must I now prove

30

'Stone-cold for ever? Pray you, does the Lord
Will that all folks should be quite happy and good?
I love God now a little, if this cord   90

31

'Were broken, once for all what striving could
Make me love anything in earth or heaven?
So day by day it grew, as if one should

32

'Slip slowly down some path worn smooth and even,
Down to a cool sea on a summer day;   95
Yet still in slipping there was some small leaven

33

'Of stretched hands catching small stones by the way,
Until one surely reached the sea at last,
And felt strange new joy as the worn head lay

34

'Back, with the hair like sea-weed; yea all past   100
Sweat of the forehead, dryness of the lips,
Washed utterly out by the dear waves o'ercast,

35

'In the lone sea, far off from any ships!
Do I not know now of a day in Spring?
No minute of that wild day ever slips   105

36

'From out my memory; I hear thrushes sing,
And wheresoever I may be, straightway
Thoughts of it all come up with most fresh sting:

Begins   ### 37

'I was half mad with beauty on that day,
And went without my ladies all alone,   110
In a quiet garden walled round every way;

38

'I was right joyful of that wall of stone,
That shut the flowers and trees up with the sky,
And trebled all the beauty: to the bone,

39

'Yea right through to my heart, grown very shy   115
With weary thoughts, it pierced, and made me glad;
Exceedingly glad, and I knew verily,[4]

40

'A little thing just then had made me mad;
I dared not think, as I was wont[5] to do,
Sometimes, upon my beauty; if I had   120

41

'Held out my long hand up against the blue,
And, looking on the tenderly darken'd fingers,
Thought that by rights one ought to see quite through,

42

'There, see you, where the soft still light yet lingers,
Round by the edges; what should I have done,   125
If this had joined with yellow spotted singers,[6]

43

'And startling green drawn upward by the sun?
But shouting, loosed out, see now! all my hair,
And trancedly stood watching the west wind run

44

'With faintest half-heard breathing sound – why there   130
I lose my head e'en now in doing this;
But shortly listen – In that garden fair

---

[4] *verily* truly.
[5] *wont* accustomed.

[6] *yellow . . . singers* birds, presumably song thrushes.

45

'Came Launcelot walking; this is true, the kiss
Wherewith we kissed in meeting that spring day,
I scarce dare talk of the remember'd bliss, 135

46

'When both our mouths went wandering in one way,
And aching sorely, met among the leaves;
Our hands being left behind strained far away. 7

47

'Never within a yard of my bright sleeves
Had Launcelot come before – and now, so nigh! 140
After that day why is it Guenevere grieves?

48

[*Why does she accuse him of lying?*]
'Nevertheless you, O Sir Gauwaine, lie,
Whatever happened on through all those years,
God knows I speak truth, saying that you lie.

49

'Being such a lady could I weep these tears 145
If this were true? A great queen such as I
Having sinn'd this way, straight her conscience sears;

50

'And afterwards she liveth hatefully,
Slaying and poisoning, certes[7] never weeps, –
Gauwaine, be friends now, speak me lovingly. 150

51

'Do I not see how God's dear pity creeps
All through your frame, and trembles in your mouth?
Remember in what grave your mother sleeps,

[*Don't get...*]

52

'Buried in some place far down in the south,
Men are forgetting as I speak to you; 155
By her head sever'd in that awful drouth[8]

53

'Of pity that drew Agravaine's[9] fell blow,
I pray your pity! let me not scream out
For ever after, when the shrill winds blow

54

'Through half your castle-locks! let me not shout 160
For ever after in the winter night
When you ride out alone! in battle-rout

[7] *certes* certainly.
[8] *drouth* drought.
[9] *Agravaine* according to Malory, Gauwaine's brother Gaheris, not Agravaine, beheaded their mother Margawse on finding her *in fragrante*.

55

'Let not my rusting tears make your sword light!
Ah! God of mercy, how he turns away!
So, <u>ever must I dress me to the fight;</u>   165

56

'So – let God's justice work! Gauwaine, I say,
See me hew down your proofs: yea, all men know
Even as you said how Mellyagraunce[10] one day,

57

'One bitter day in *la Fausse Garde*,[11] for so
All good knights held it after, saw –   170
Yea, sirs, by cursed unknightly outrage; though

58

'You, Gauwaine, held his word without a flaw,
This Mellyagraunce saw blood upon my bed –
Whose blood then pray you? is there any law

59

'To make a queen say why some spots of red   175
Lie on her coverlet? or will you say:
'Your hands are white, lady, as when you wed,

60

'"Where did you bleed?" and must I stammer out: "Nay,
I blush indeed, fair lord, only to rend
My sleeve up to my shoulder, where there lay   180

61

'"A knife-point last night:" so must I defend
The honour of the lady Guenevere?
Not so, fair lords, even if the world should end

62

'This very day, and you were judges here
Instead of God. Did you see Mellyagraunce   185
When Launcelot stood by him? what white fear

63

'Curdled his blood, and how his teeth did dance,
His side sink in? as my knight cried and said:
"Slayer of unarm'd men, here is a chance!

---

[10] *Mellyagraunce* knight who claimed evidence of Guenevere's adultery; slain by Lancelot. In 'The Knight of the Cart' section of Malory, Mellyagraunce abducts the Queen, though her 10 knights fight hard against him. She insists, however, that they stay with her over night in the chamber to which she is confined while she tends their wounds. During the night, Lancelot forces his way in through her window. Mellyagraunce, entering the room later, sees (Lancelot's) blood on the Queen's bed: but he mistakes the nature of her infidelity: 'he demed in her that she was false to the kynge and that som of the wounded knyghtes had lyene by her all that nyght.' Lancelot is given an occasion legitimately to defend the Queen's honour against a false charge. He slays Mellyagraunce in the lists at her wish. Guenevere is recalling a similar occasion to her present predicament when she was charged with adultery – and, if only technically, vindicated.

[11] *la Fausse Garde* Mellyagraunce's castle.

64

'"Setter of traps, I pray you guard your head,   190
By God I am so glad to fight with you,
Stripper of ladies, that my hand feels lead

65

'"For driving weight; hurrah now! draw and do,
For all my wounds are moving in my breast,
And I am getting mad with waiting so."   195

66

'He struck his hands together o'er the beast,
Who fell down flat and grovell'd at his feet,
And groan'd at being slain so young – "at least."

67

'My knight said: "Rise you, sir, who are so fleet
At catching ladies, half-arm'd will I fight,   200
My left side all uncovered!" then I weet,[12]

68

'Up sprang Sir Mellyagraunce with great delight
Upon his knave's face; not until just then
Did I quite hate him, as I saw my knight

69

'Along the lists[13] look to my stake and pen   205
With such a joyous smile, it made me sigh
From agony beneath my waist-chain, when

70

'The fight began, and to me they drew nigh;
Ever Sir Launcelot kept him on the right,
And traversed warily, and ever high   210

71

'And fast leapt caitiff's[14] sword, until my knight
Sudden threw up his sword to his left hand,
Caught it, and swung it; that was all the fight,

72

'Except a spout of blood on the hot land;
For it was hottest summer; and I know   215
I wonder'd how the fire, while I should stand,

73

'And burn, against the heat, would quiver so,
Yards above my head; thus these matters went;
Which things were only warnings of the woe

---

[12] *weet* know.

[13] *lists* barriers enclosing a space set apart for tournaments.

[14] *caitiff* poor wretch.

74

'That fell on me. Yet Mellyagraunce was shent,[15]   220
For Mellyagraunce had fought against the Lord;
Therefore, my lords, take heed lest you be blent[16]

Threat?

75

'With all this wickedness; say no rash word
Against me, being so beautiful; my eyes,
Wept all away to grey, may bring some sword   225

76

'To drown you in your blood; see my breast rise,
Like waves of purple sea, as here I stand;
And how my arms are moved in wonderful wise,

77

'Yea also at my full heart's strong command,
See through my long throat how the words go up   230
In ripples to my mouth; how in my hand

78

'The shadow lies like wine within a cup
Of marvellously colour'd gold; yea now
This little wind is rising, look you up,

79

'And wonder how the light is falling so   235
Within my moving tresses: will you dare,
When you have looked a little on my brow,

80

'To say this thing is vile? or will you care
For any plausible lies of cunning woof,[17]
When you can see my face with no lie there   240

81

'For ever? am I not a gracious proof –
"But in your chamber Launcelot was found" –
Is there a good knight then would stand aloof,

82

'When a queen says with gentle queenly sound:
'O true as steel, come now and talk with me,   245
I love to see your step upon the ground

83

'"Unwavering, also well I love to see
That gracious smile light up your face, and hear
Your wonderful words, that all mean verily

[15] *shent* ruined.   [17] *woof* texture, referring to a woven fabric.
[16] *blent* mixed.

84

' "The thing they seem to mean: good friend, so dear 250
   To me in everything, come here to-night,
Or else the hours will pass most dull and drear;

85

' "If you come not, I fear this time I might
   Get thinking over much of times gone by,
When I was young, and green hope was in sight: 255

86

' "For no man cares now to know why I sigh;
   And no man comes to sing me pleasant songs,
Nor any brings me the sweet flowers that lie

87

' "So thick in the gardens; therefore one so longs
   To see you, Launcelot; that we may be 260
Like children once again, free from all wrongs

88

' "Just for one night." Did he not come to me?
   What thing could keep true Launcelot away
If I said, "Come?" There was one less than three

89

'In my quiet room that night, and we were gay; 265
   Till sudden I rose up, weak, pale, and sick,
Because a bawling broke our dream up, yea

90

'I looked at Launcelot's face and could not speak,
   For he looked helpless too, for a little while;
Then I remember how I tried to shriek, 270

91

'And could not, but fell down; from tile to tile
   The stones they threw up rattled o'er my head
And made me dizzier; till within a while

92

'My maids were all about me, and my head
   On Launcelot's breast was being soothed away 275
From its white chattering, until Launcelot said –

93

'By God! I will not tell you more to-day,
   Judge any way you will – what matters it?
You know quite well the story of that fray,

94

'How Launcelot still'd their bawling, the mad fit 280
   That caught up Gauwaine – all, all, verily,
But just that which would save me; these things flit.

95

'Nevertheless you, O Sir Gauwaine, lie,
Whatever may have happen'd these long years,
God knows I speak truth, saying that you lie!   285

96

'All I have said is truth, by Christ's dear tears.'
She would not speak another word, but stood
Turn'd sideways; listening, like a man who hears

97

His brother's trumpet sounding through the wood
Of his foes' lances. She lean'd eagerly,   290
And gave a slight spring sometimes, as she could

98

At last hear something really; joyfully
Her cheek grew crimson, as the headlong speed
Of the roan[18] charger drew all men to see,
The knight who came was Launcelot at good need.   295

---

[18] *roan* horse with coat in which the prevailing colour is thickly interspersed with another.

Concerning Geffray Teste Noire

With Pre-Raphaelite visual clarity, William Morris's 'Concerning Geffray Teste Noire' (1858) muses on the violence of the Middle Ages. Brutality, including that to women, punctures chivalric ideals in this poem, just as the potentially heroic narrative of the defeat of a savage thief – Geffray Teste Noire – ends bathetically with the swift announcement that the narrator did not succeed. The narrative occurs during the time of the Hundred Years' War (1337–1453), a prolonged dispute between England and France (Morris's 'The Haystack in the Floods', 423–7, is set just after the Battle of Poitiers, an important early engagement in the same conflict). Geoffroy Tête Noire – to use the name by which he is now remembered – was, historically, a brigand during the war, believed to be in the pay of the English, who seized the castle of Ventadour through treachery in 1379 and pillaged the surrounding areas for the next 10 years. Ventadour was finally taken back by the armies of the Duc de Berry in 1389.

The narrator of Morris's poem – one John of Castel Neuf (New Castle), a French knight – tells the story of an attempt to ambush Teste Noire and put an end to his activities. While hiding in undergrowth in preparation, however, he discovers two skeletons, one of which, he is told by his comrade, is that of a woman. The sight of this body – depicted with disturbing precision – reminds him briefly of a time when he was 15 and involved in the vicious repression by the nobles of the Jacquerie, the peasants' rebellion

in northern France in 1358. There, he saw many of the rebellious women burned to death. Thinking about the woman's skeleton now before him, he imagines what she would have been like, recreating a chivalric ideal of a courtly woman. Presently, his reverie is broken by the call to arms, but his planned assault on Teste Noire fails. The poem concludes not with the celebration of the eventual slaughter of the 'Gascon thief', but merely with a statement of the narrator's own mortality, and an implicit question about what his knightly life has achieved.

'Concerning Geffray Teste Noire' thematizes the practice of imagining the Middle Ages in seductively idealized terms, as the speaker dreamily fashions the lady as a figure belonging to a thoroughly different world from his own experience of aristocratic violence. Morris would later cast off medievalist writing that was immersed in the bloodshed of European history – this poem is imagined as a footnote for the 'official' historian of the Hundred Years' War – in preference for what he saw as the stranger, starker narratives of Icelandic sagas (cf. 'Iceland First Seen', 445–7). But in both stages of his medievalist writing, he made transparently original contributions to the corpus of Victorian medievalism. As with 'The Haystack in the Floods', Morris's technique is to plunge the reader straight into the midst of a situation, and here he recalls the kind of opening used by Robert Browning for his dramatic monologues in, say, his 1855 collection *Men and Women* (cf. 'Andrea del Sarto', 189–95, and 'Fra Lippo Lippi', 179–88). An annotated edition does not allow the reader to experience the bewilderment that 'Concerning Geffray Teste Noire' – lacking explicit statements of context

and moving from one subject to another without warning – must have originally induced.

Text: *The Defence of Guenevere and Other Poems* (1858).

And if you[1] meet the Canon of Chimay,[2]
As going to Ortaise you well may do,
Greet him from John of Castel Neuf, and say,
All that I tell you, for all this is true.

2

This Geffray Teste Noire was a Gascon[3] thief,   5
Who, under shadow of the English name,[4]
Pilled all such towns and countries as were lief[5]
To King Charles[6] and St. Denis;[7] thought it blame

3

If anything escaped him; so my lord
The Duke of Berry[8] sent Sir John Bonne Lance,   10
And other knights, good players with the sword,
To check this thief and give the land a chance.

4

Therefore we set our bastides[9] round the tower
That Geffray held, the strong thief! like a king,
High perch'd upon the rock of Ventadour,[10]   15
Hopelessly strong by Christ! It was mid spring,

5

When first I joined the little army there
With ten good spears; Auvergne[11] is hot, each day
We sweated armed before the barrier;
Good feats of arms were done there often – eh?   20

6

Your brother was slain there? I mind me now,
A right good man-at-arms, God pardon him!
I think 'twas Geffray smote him on the brow
With some spiked axe, and while he totter'd, dim

---

[1] *you* auditor (whose name, we later discover, is Alleyne).
[2] *Canon of Chimay* i.e., Jean Froissart (c.1337–c.1410), French historian and poet, author of *Chronicles* that recorded the activities of English and French knights from 1325 to 1410 during the Hundred Years' War; he was vicar of Estinnes-au-Mont, canon of Chimay and chaplain to the Comte de Blois.
[3] *Gascon* of Gascony, area of English-held France.
[4] *English name* see headnote, 438.
[5] *lief* feudal property.
[6] *King Charles* Charles V, King of France 1364–80, called 'Charles the Wise'.

[7] *St. Denis* patron saint of France.
[8] *Duke of Berry* historically, it was the Duc de Berry who finally ousted Geffray from Ventadour in 1389; see headnote, 438.
[9] *bastides* temporary huts for besieging purposes.
[10] *Ventadour* castle Geffray seized through treachery in 1379; see headnote, 438.
[11] *Auvergne* used loosely to mean 'area in the south of France'.

7

About the eyes, the spear of Alleyne Roux   25
Slipped through his camaille[12] and his throat; well, well!
Alleyne is paid now; your name Alleyne too?
Mary! how strange – but this tale I would tell –

8

For spite of all our bastides, damned Blackhead
Would ride abroad whene'er he chose to ride,   30
We could not stop him; many a burgher[13] bled
Dear gold all round his girdle; far and wide

9

The villaynes[14] dwelt in utter misery
'Twixt us and thief Sir Geffray; hauled this way
By Sir Bonne Lance at one time, he gone by,   35
Down comes this Teste Noire on another day,

10

And therefore they dig up the stone, grind corn,
Hew wood, draw water, yea, they lived, in short,
As I said just now, utterly forlorn,
Till this our knave and Blackhead was out-fought.   40

11

So Bonne Lance fretted, thinking of some trap
Day after day, till on a time he said:
'John of Newcastle,[15] if we have good hap,[16]
We catch our thief in two days.' 'How?' I said.

12

'Why, Sir, to-day he rideth out again,   45
Hoping to take well certain sumpter mules[17]
From Carcassonne,[18] going with little train,
Because, forsooth,[19] he thinketh us mere fools;

13

'But if we set an ambush in some wood,
He is but dead: so, Sir, take thirty spears   50
To Verville forest, if it seem you good.'
Then felt I like the horse in Job, who hears

14

The dancing trumpet sound,[20] and we went forth;
And my red lion on the spear-head flapped,

---

[12] *camaille* strong chain mesh attached to helmet and protecting throat.
[13] *burgher* citizen.
[14] *villaynes* ordinary people.
[15] *John of Newcastle* i.e., the narrator, 'John of Castel Neuf'.
[16] *hap* fortune, chance.
[17] *sumpter mules* beasts of burden, pack mules.
[18] *Carcassonne* medieval city in the south of France.
[19] *forsooth* in truth.

[20] *like the horse . . . sound* cf. Job 39.19–24, 'Hast thou giuen the horse strength? hast thou clothed his necke with thunder? Canst thou make him afraid as a grashopper? the glory of his nostrils is terrible. He paweth in the valley, and reioyceth in his strength: hee goeth on to meet the armed men. He mocketh at feare, and is not affrighted: neither turneth he backe from the sword. The quiuer ratleth against him, the glittering speare and the shield. He swalloweth the ground with fiercenesse and rage: neither beleeueth he that it is the sound of the trumpet.'

As faster than the cool wind we rode north,   55
Towards the wood of Verville; thus it happed.

15

We rode a soft pace on that day, while spies
Got news about Sir Geffray; the red wine
Under the road-side bush was clear; the flies,
The dragon-flies I mind me most, did shine   60

16

In brighter arms than ever I put on;
So – 'Geffray,' said our spies, 'would pass that way
Next day at sundown:' then he must be won;
And so we enter'd Verville wood next day,

17

In the afternoon; through it the highway runs,   65
'Twixt copses of green hazel, very thick,
And underneath, with glimmering of suns,
The primroses are happy; the dews lick

18

The soft green moss. 'Put cloths about your arms,[21]
Lest they should glitter; surely they will go   70
In a long thin line, watchful for alarms,
With all their carriages of booty; so –

19

'Lay down my pennon[22] in the grass – Lord God!
What have we lying here? will they be cold,
I wonder, being so bare, above the sod,   75
Instead of under? This was a knight too, fold

20

'Lying on fold of ancient rusted mail;
No plate at all, gold rowels[23] to the spurs,
And see the quiet gleam of turquoise pale
Along the ceinture;[24] but the long time blurs   80

21

'Even the tinder of his coat to nought,
Except these scraps of leather; see how white
The skull is, loose within the coif![25] He fought
A good fight, maybe, ere he was slain quite.

22

'No armour on the legs too; strange in faith –   85
A little skeleton for a knight, though – ah!
This one is bigger, truly without scathe
His enemies escaped not – ribs driven out far –

[21] *arms* weapons.
[22] *pennon* narrow flag at the top of a lance.
[23] *rowels* small stellar wheels at the end of spurs.

[24] *ceinture* girdle.
[25] *coif* close-fitting skull cap, often of leather, worn beneath the helmet.

23

'That must have reach'd the heart, I doubt – how now,
What say you, Aldovrand – a woman? why?'   90
'Under the coif a gold wreath on the brow,
Yea, see the hair not gone to powder, lie,

24

'Golden, no doubt, once – yea, and very small
This for a knight; but for a dame, my lord,
These loose-hung bones seem shapely still, and tall, –   95
Didst ever see a woman's bones, my lord?'

25

Often, God help me! I remember when
I was a simple boy, fifteen years old,
The Jacquerie[26] froze up the blood of men
With their fell deeds, not fit now to be told: 100

26

God help again! we enter'd Beauvais[27] town,
Slaying them fast, whereto I help'd, mere boy
As I was then; we gentles cut them down,
These burners and defilers, with great joy.

27

Reason for that, too: in the great church there   105
These fiends had lit a fire, that soon went out,
The church at Beauvais being so great and fair –
My father, who was by me, gave a shout

28

Between a beast's howl and a woman's scream,
Then, panting, chuckled to me: 'John, look! look!   110
Count the dames' skeletons!' from some bad dream
Like a man just awaked, my father shook;

29

And I, being faint with smelling the burnt bones,
And very hot with fighting down the street,
And sick of such a life, fell down, with groans   115
My head went weakly nodding to my feet.

30

– An[28] arrow had gone through her tender throat,
And her right wrist was broken; then I saw
The reason why she had on that war-coat,
Their story came out clear without a flaw;   120

---

[26] *Jacquerie* peasant rebellion in France in 1358, partly motivated by the widespread poverty consequent on the Hundred Years' War. It was brutally crushed by the nobles (the narrator was part of this counter-assault).

[27] *Beauvais* cathedral city of northern France, where the Jacquerie rebellion began.
[28] *An* . . . he returns to the present moment and the woman's skeleton beneath the undergrowth.

31

For when he knew that they were being waylaid,
    He threw it over her, yea, hood and all;
Whereby he was much hack'd, while they were stay'd
    By those their murderers; many an one did fall

32

Beneath his arm, no doubt, so that he clear'd   125
    Their circle, bore his death-wound out of it;
But as they rode, some archer least afear'd
    Drew a strong bow, and thereby she was hit.

33

Still as he rode he knew not she was dead,
    Thought her but fainted from her broken wrist,   130
He bound with his great leathern belt – she bled?
    Who knows! he bled too, neither was there miss'd

34

The beating of her heart, his heart beat well
    For both of them, till here, within this wood,
He died scarce sorry; easy this to tell;   135
    After these years the flowers forget their blood. –

35

How could it be? never before that day,
    However much a soldier I might be,
Could I look on a skeleton and say
    I care not for it, shudder not – now see,   140

36

Over those bones I sat and pored for hours,
And thought, and dream'd, and still I scarce could see
    The small white bones that lay upon the flowers,
        But evermore I saw the lady; she

37

With her dear gentle walking leading in,   145
    By a chain of silver twined about her wrists,
Her loving knight, mounted and arm'd to win
    Great honour for her, fighting in the lists.

38

O most pale face, that brings such joy and sorrow
    Into men's hearts – yea, too, so piercing sharp   150
That joy is, that it marcheth nigh[29] to sorrow
    For ever – like an overwinded harp. –

39

Your face must hurt me always; pray you now,
    Doth it not hurt you too? seemeth some pain
To hold you always, pain to hold your brow   155
    So smooth, unwrinkled ever; yea again,

---

[29] *nigh* next.

40

Your long eyes where the lids seem like to drop,
Would you not, lady, were they shut fast, feel
Far merrier? there so high they will not stop,
They are most sly to glide forth and to steal   160

41

Into my heart; I kiss their soft lids there,
And in green gardens scarce can stop my lips
From wandering on your face, but that your hair
Falls down and tangles me, back my face slips.

42

Or say your mouth – I saw you drink red wine   165
Once at a feast; how slowly it sank in,
As though you fear'd that some wild fate might twine
Within that cup, and slay you for a sin.

43

And when you talk your lips do arch and move
In such wise that a language new I know   170
Besides their sound; they quiver, too, with love
When you are standing silent; know this, too,

44

I saw you kissing once, like a curved sword
That bites with all its edge, did your lips lie,
Curled gently, slowly, long time could afford   175
For caught-up breathings; like a dying sigh

45

They gather'd up their lines and went away,
And still kept twitching with a sort of smile,
As likely to be weeping presently, –
Your hands too – how I watch'd them all the while!   180

46

'Cry out St.Peter now,' quoth Aldovrand;
I cried, 'St.Peter!' broke out from the wood
With all my spears; we met them hand to hand,
And shortly slew them; natheless,[30] by the rood,[31]

47

We caught not Blackhead then, or any day;   185
Months after that he died at last in bed,
From a wound pick'd up at a barrier-fray;
That same year's end a steel bolt in the head,

48

And much bad living kill'd Teste Noire at last;
John Froissart[32] knoweth he is dead by now,   190

---

[30] *natheless* nevertheless.
[31] *rood* representation of the Crucifixion.

[32] *John Froissart* see note 2.

No doubt, but knoweth not this tale just past;[33]
Perchance then you can tell him what I show.

49

In my new castle, down beside the Eure,
There is a little chapel of squared stone,
Painted inside and out; in green nook pure   195
There did I lay them, every wearied bone;

50

And over it they lay, with stone-white hands
Clasped fast together, hair made bright with gold;
This Jaques Picard,[34] known through many lands,
Wrought cunningly; he's dead now – I am old.   200

[33] *but . . . past* the story of Teste Noire is not in Froissart.   [34] *Jaques Picard* imaginary funerary sculptor.

Iceland First Seen

Morris's Pre-Raphaelite medievalist verse – e.g., 'The Haystack in the Floods', 423–7 – typically offers narratives of human disasters that challenge an idealist discourse of the Middle Ages. 'Iceland First Seen' meditates on a land in which, seemingly, dreams and ideals of the ancient past still have currency. William Morris's first visit to Iceland was in 1871, though he was already familiar with some of its saga literature. His medievalism thereafter was to become distinct in its indebtedness to northern saga tradition, and he threw off his earlier Pre-Raphaelite style and preoccupation with the Arthuriad and southern European sources, in preference for the boldness of the sagas, a 'good corrective', he said, 'to the maundering side of mediaevalism'. Inspired by Iceland and its ancient literature, he produced, for instance, the popular adaptation of the epic *Sigurd the Volsung* in 1876.

In 'Iceland First Seen', Morris reveals what expectations he brought to the country before even arriving: *a priori* he expected it to prove a place rich with evidence of heroes and gods. What appeals to him is, partly, the otherness of the country, its radical difference from England. The landscape is strange – possessed, Morris said, of 'terrific and melancholy beauty'. And Iceland challenges English identity through what Morris fantasizes as the continuous if spectral presence of her past. Critical writing in Victorian England often returned to the idea that the nation was now incapable of producing heroes. Morris's use of epic fragments in 'The Haystack' and 'The Defence of Guenevere', 428–38, subtly implied the impossibility of epic ideals in modern Britain; Matthew Arnold's 'Dover Beach', 312–13, dramatized the modern condition as one in which there was struggle but no glory; and Arthur Hugh Clough's *Amours de Voyage*, 228–62, ironized the whole notion of conventional masculine heroism in the mid-century. But Iceland, for Morris in the early 1870s, is an imagined place saturated with memories of a heroic past and still possessing a quality of human experience and feeling on the grand scale of epic: Iceland is the queen of 'grief without knowledge, of the courage that may not avail, / Of the longing that may not attain, of the love that shall never forget'. Keeping faith with her ancient past, Iceland still belongs, unlike modern England, within the terms of myth and legend, here presented in long, stretched lines that acknowledge Swinburne.

Text: *Poems by the Way* (1891).

Lo from our loitering ship a new land at last to be seen;
Toothed rocks down the side of the firth[1] on the east guard a weary wide lea,[2]
And black slope the hillsides above, striped adown with their desolate green:
And a peak rises up on the west from the meeting of cloud and of sea,

[1] *firth* estuary.   [2] *lea* meadow, open ground.

Foursquare from base unto point like the building of Gods that have been,   5
The last of that waste of the mountains all cloud-wreathed and snow-flecked and grey,
And bright with the dawn that began just now at the ending of day.[3]

2

Ah! what came we forth for to see[4] that our hearts are so hot with desire?
Is it enough for our rest, the sight of this desolate strand,
And the mountain-waste voiceless as death but for winds that may sleep not nor tire?   10
Why do we long to wend forth through the length and breadth of a land,
Dreadful with grinding of ice, and record of scarce hidden fire,[5]
But that there 'mid the grey grassy dales sore scarred by the ruining streams
Lives the tale of the Northland of old and the undying glory of dreams?

3

O land, as some cave by the sea where the treasures of old have been laid,   15
The sword it may be of a king whose name was the turning of fight;[6]
Or the staff of some wise of the world that many things made and unmade,
Or the ring of a woman maybe whose woe is grown wealth and delight.[7]
No wheat and no wine grows above it, no orchard for blossom and shade;
The few ships that sail by its blackness but deem it the mouth of a grave;   20
Yet sure when the world shall awaken, this too shall be mighty to save.[8]

4

Or rather, O land, if a marvel it seemeth that men ever sought
Thy wastes for a field and a garden fulfilled of all wonder and doubt,
And feasted amidst of the winter when the fight of the year had been fought,
Whose plunder all gathered together was little to babble about;   25
Cry aloud from thy wastes, O thou land, 'Not for this nor for that was I wrought.
Amid waning of realms and of riches and death of things worshipped and sure,
I abide here the spouse of a God, and I made and I make and I endure.'

5

O Queen[9] of the grief without knowledge, of the courage that may not avail,
Of the longing that may not attain, of the love that shall never forget,   30
More joy than the gladness of laughter thy voice hath amidst of its wail:
More hope than of pleasure fulfilled amidst of thy blindness is set;
More glorious than gaining of all thine unfaltering hand that shall fail:
For what is the mark on thy brow but the brand[10] that thy Brynhild[11] doth bear?
Love once, and loved and undone by a love that no ages outwear.   35

---

[3] *And bright . . . day* at a time when the sun barely sets in Iceland.

[4] *what . . . see* cf. Matthew 11.7–8, 'And as they departed, Iesus began to say vnto the multitudes concerning Iohn [the Baptist], what went ye out into the wildernesse to see? a reede shaken with the winde? But what went ye out for to see? A man clothed in soft raiment?'

[5] *scarce . . . fire* volcanoes.

[6] *The sword . . . fight* generalist mythological fantasy (ancient Iceland was, apart from anything else, a republic).

[7] *staff . . . delight* Morris continues his impressionistic sense of Iceland's mythic remains.

[8] *mighty to save* cf. Isaiah 63.1, 'Who is this that commeth from Edom, with died garments from Bozrah? this that is glorious in his apparel, trauelling in the greatnesse of his strength? I that speake in righteousnesse, mightie to saue.'

[9] *Queen* Iceland herself.

[10] *brand* sword.

[11] *Brynhild* again, Morris is impressionistic and is not referring to a specific event. Brynhild is a Valkyrie (woman warrior) from the *Völsunga Saga*.

6

Ah! when thy Balder[12] comes back, and bears from the heart of the Sun
Peace and the healing of pain, and the wisdom that waiteth no more;
And the lilies are laid on thy brow 'mid the crown of the deeds thou hast done;
And the roses spring up by thy feet that the rocks of the wilderness wore:
Ah! when thy Balder comes back and we gather the gains he hath won,   40
Shall we not linger a little to talk of thy sweetness of old,
Yea, turn back awhile to thy travail whence the Gods stood aloof to behold?

[12] *Balder* Norse god of the sunlight who, after his murder, was bound in Hell forever. His return was something to be hoped for, but impossible. Balder's story, well known in Victorian England (cf. Matthew Arnold's 'Balder Dead'), was also associated with the cycle of the seasons and the coming of spring.

Alfred Austin (1835–1913)

Born into a Roman Catholic family, Alfred Austin was educated at Stonyhurst and Oscott College but in due course abandoned his faith. Originally intending to be a barrister, he inherited a fortune from his uncle and gave up the law in preference for life as a writer. With W. J. Courthope, he became an editor of the Tory *National Review* (sole editor 1887–95). Ardently pro-imperialist, he was made Poet Laureate in 1896 to widespread amazement and disapproval (he was always subject to parody and lampoon). George Meredith scathingly observed that 'it will suit little Alfred to hymn the babies of the house of Hanover'. Austin's writing offered an intemperate challenge to the Decadent poets of the *fin de siècle*, but he earned little respect from his fellow poets, to say nothing of the anti-imperialists. None the less, his work is a suggestive indicator of one spirited element of late Victorian poetry and its embeddedness in the politics of patriotism. Austin published 20 volumes of verse and a popular prose work, *The Garden that I Love* (1894).

Henry Bartle Edward Frere

Born A.D. 1815. Died A.D. 1884

Alfred Austin's angry pro-imperialism is exemplified in this elegy for Sir Bartle Frere (as he was usually known), administrator in India, Governor of Bombay, and later Governor of the Cape Colony in South Africa. Frere, a prominent opponent of slavery, was charged with implementing the disastrous policy of confederation when he was sent to South Africa, an effort to unite the British colonies and the Afrikaner (Boer) republics into a single nation under British rule. Frere believed that the destruction of Zulu military forces was a crucial step towards this and his policy led to the beginning of a war with the Zulus in 1879. The British defeat at the Battle of Isandhlwana (22 January) by Zulu forces under Chief Cetewayo (as the Victorians spelt his name) was the first dire result for Frere (the celebrated defence of Rorke's Drift followed). Confederation was abandoned and, although the Battle of Ulundi on 4 July 1879 saw the British reverse their losses and end the war, Frere's position was unsustainable as far as government back at home was concerned. Fiercely criticized by Parliament, he was recalled to London in July 1880 as Gladstone, an old enemy, returned to the premiership after the general election. The novelist Anthony Trollope, who had visited Frere in South Africa in 1877, wrote of him in 1879: 'Frere, for whom personally I have both respect and regard, is a man who thinks it is England's duty to carry English civilization and English Christianity among all the Savages. Consequently, having the chance, he has waged war against these unfortunates, – who [have] lived side by side with us in Natal for 25 years without ever having raised a hand against us! The consequence is that we have already slaughtered 10,000 of them, and rejoice in having done so. To me it seems like civilization gone mad!' Frere had his supporters – he was a selfless man who believed he was acting in the interests of laudable aims – and his entry in the *Dictionary of National Biography* was stout in his defence. But for many his name had become synonymous with failure and the unacceptable face of empire.

Austin's poem (written in 1884, included in *English Lyrics* [1890]) has not a shred of patience with views such as Trollope's, with the new prime minister, or with the hostile post-Third Reform Act Houses of Parliament who criticized Frere's actions. Instead, Austin uncompromisingly hails the former governor as a hero, whose only mistake is to be born the son of a land no longer heroic. The elegy is suffused with a stern late Victorian imperialist's sense that true manliness is decaying in the wake of national feminization and that great men no longer have a place in the destiny of the nation (cf. Rudyard Kipling, 'Recessional, A Victorian Ode', 650–2, 'The White Man's Burden', 652–3, and 'The Way through the Woods', 655–6). Making no claims to be a great poem – certainly a sincere and stately one – it is nevertheless representative of a historical moment and an anxiety that united a tranche of Tories and ardent pro-imperialists towards the end of the century. The distrust of cultural feminization here may be compared to fearfulness that Decadence was emasculating poetry, poets and readers in the 1890s.

Text: *English Lyrics* (1890).

Bend down and read[1] – the birth, the death, the name.
    Born in the year that Waterloo[2] was won,
  And died in this, whose days are not yet run,
  But which, because a year conceived in shame,
    No noble need will christen or will claim.   5
And yet this dead man, England, was Thy son,
  And at his grave we ask what had he done,
  Bred to be famous, to be foiled of Fame.
    Be the reply his epitaph: That he,
In years as youth, the unyielding spirit bore   10
He got from Thee, but Thou hast got no more;
    And that it is a bane[3] and bar to be
A child of Thine, now the adventurous sea
All vainly beckons to a shrinking shore.

2

    Therefore, great soul, within your marble bed   15
Sleep sound, nor hear the useless tears we weep.
Why should you wake, when England is asleep,
    Or care to live, since England now is dead?
    Forbidden are the steeps where glory led;
  No more from furrowed danger of the deep   20
We harvest greatness; to our hearths we creep,
  Count and recount our coin, and nurse our dread.
The sophist's[4] craft hath grown a prosperous trade,
  And womanish Tribunes[5] hush the manly drum:
    The very fear of Empire strikes us numb,   25
Fumbling with pens, who brandished once the blade.
Therefore, great soul, sleep sound where you are laid,
  Blest in being deaf when Honour now is dumb.

[1] *Bend down and read* Henry Bartle Edward Frere is buried in St Paul's Cathedral, London.
[2] *Waterloo* the Battle of Waterloo, 18 June 1815, the final defeat of Napoleon Bonaparte by the British Army with Prussian reinforcements.
[3] *bane* curse, hapless fate.

[4] *sophist* false reasoner.
[5] *Tribunes* title of Roman politicians; here, Gladstone and members of the British Parliament who chastised and recalled Frere after the disasters in South Africa.

(Julia) Augusta Webster (1837–1894)

Julia Augusta Webster (née Davies) was born in Dorset, the daughter of Vice-Admiral George Davies, later Chief Constable of Cambridgeshire. She took courses at the Cambridge School of Art and married Thomas Webster, lecturer in law at Trinity College Cambridge, in 1863. She learned Greek, Italian and Spanish, and perfected her French while living in Paris and Geneva. She had one child, celebrated in her *Mother and Daughter: An Uncompleted Sonnet-Sequence* (1895). Her first volumes of verse appeared under the name 'Cecil Home', but later she used her own. In the 1860s, the family moved to London where Webster became active, with Frances Power Cobbe and John Stuart Mill, in the woman's suffrage movement (she fell out with Christina Rossetti about this). Her articles for the *Examiner* were collected as *A Housewife's Opinions* in 1879. Here, she wrote about the limits of middle-class education, argued for women to be awarded university degrees, for female suffrage, on the problems of teaching children through games, and on the necessity of good domestic service. But we should be careful not to assume entire coincidence between Victorian and contemporary radicalism. Webster also wrote in favour of 'Mrs Grundy' – the representational figure of moral probity – remarking that 'We look to her to store the mind of adolescence with manners and morality, and well does she repay our trust[;] . . . in nine cases out of ten . . . Mrs Grundy's golden rule is the best for us'. Augusta Webster was a member of the London School Board, 1879–92. Her major collections of poetry, *Dramatic Studies* (1866) and *Portraits* (1870), employed the dramatic monologue for feminist purposes, involving searching exploration of female speakers – historical, mythological and contemporary – and their relation to modern gender politics. Webster published verse drama in the 1870s and 1880s, and *Parliamentary Franchise for Women Ratepayers* (1878), arguing the injustice of denying the vote to women ratepayers while allowing it to men. She died relatively young at Kew, London, in September 1894.

Circe

The Victorians' relationship with the ancient Greeks was both enduring and diverse. For women poets, writing on Greek myths was helpfully transgressive – culturally, Greek language and literature was the preserve of men for much of the century – enabling intervention in contemporary gender and sexual politics (cf. Elizabeth Barrett Browning, 'A Musical Instrument', 57–9, Amy Levy, 'Xantippe', 630–6, and Michael Field, 'Maids, not to you my mind doth change', 557–8). Like Amy Levy's 'Xantippe', Augusta Webster's 'Circe' (1870) allows a Greek female's voice, marginalized by traditional history/myth, to be imaginatively recreated. Engaging with Greek epic poetry and the Homeric figure of Circe, the enchantress of the mythical island of Aeaea, Webster tests commonplace nineteenth-century ideas about female identity and sexual politics. But she does so with a degree of ambivalence.

In Book 10 of Homer's *Odyssey*, Odysseus and his men arrive at Circe's island. He dispatches them to investigate the terrain, but they are all, save Eurylochus, turned to pigs after consuming a mixture of drugs, food and wine. Eurylochus runs back to Odysseus to tell him about the disaster, and he immediately sets out to confront Circe. Meeting Hermes, the messenger of the gods, Odysseus is given a herb – moly – that will guard him against Circe's powers.

The moly works and Circe is amazed: 'How firmly seated must be your indomitable mind!' (Circe is unaware that Odysseus is protected, a point to which Webster refers ironically, ll. 190–3.) Circe invites him to her bed and, after she has sworn an oath not to harm him, Odysseus accepts. She restores his crew to human form, and he stays her lover for a year.

Augusta Webster draws on the Homeric story but her poem is in a mysterious relationship with it. Is the vessel descried in this poem Odysseus's ship? Is the lover that she is waiting for the hero of the *Odyssey*? To what extent should knowledge of the Homeric story – with its outcome – inflect the reading of this poem? The question of a woman poet's relationship to an historical source – what issues of authenticity and authority are involved – is an explicit theme of Levy's 'Xantippe' and an implicit one here.

Circe speaks a forceful denunciation of male lust, upturning her habitual place in western art and literature as herself a symbol of unbridled desires and swinish pleasures. Men in this poem are already animalistic and Circe remarks that she merely makes the truth visible. None the less, the poem preserves the notion of the heterosexual ideal insofar as Circe still hopes for the perfect lover. Her vocalization of sexual desire is a striking instance of Webster's redefinition of womanhood – albeit in the antique – and insistence on the recognition of a woman's sexual nature (cf. Elizabeth Barrett Browning, 'Rime of the Duchess May', 29–44).

In Circe's voice might be heard, at least initially, an oblique representation of the confining tedium of middle-class women's lives bound to a changeless routine (cf. Tennyson's 'Mariana', 64–6). But the gender questions of the final section are less certain. *Is* Circe a strong-minded woman, bold in denouncing male folly, or a heartless enchantress merely trying to justify mercilessness? At the root of this question is a generic one about Webster's use of the dramatic monologue (which in any case is distinctive in its handling of the auditor). In the form as practised by Tennyson and Browning, the defining quality of reader response was the tension between sympathy and judgement in what Wolfgang Iser calls the 'esthetic', the reader's construction, of the poem. Women poets in the Victorian period handled the form differently, and the reader is interestingly uncertain at the end of 'Circe' about how to read her words and whether they invite sympathy *or* judgement. There is an arrestingly erotic poem on the same subject, also entitled 'Circe', by the North American poet Madison Julius Cawein (1865–1914), which forms a powerful contrast with the gender politics of Webster's monologue. Cf. also the paintings *Circe Offering the Cup to Ulysses* (1891) and *Circe Invidiosa* (1895) by J. W. Waterhouse (1849–1917), and *Circe and Scylla* (1886) by John Melhuish Strudwick (1849–1937). Perhaps the most extraordinary picture of the enchantress in a late Victorian idiom is that by the British artist Wright Barker (1863–1941) now hanging in the Bradford City Art Gallery, again called *Circe* (no date of painting).

Text: *Portraits* (1870, but the first letter of each line has been capitalized).

The sun drops luridly into the west;
Darkness has raised her arms to draw him down
Before the time, not waiting as of wont[1]
Till he has come to her behind the sea;
And the smooth waves grow sullen in the gloom   5
And wear their threatening purple; more and more
The plain of waters sways and seems to rise
Convexly from its level of the shores;
And low dull thunder rolls along the beach:
There will be storm at last, storm, glorious storm!   10
Oh welcome, welcome, though it rend my bowers,
Scattering my blossomed roses like the dust,
Splitting the shrieking branches, tossing down
My riotous vines with their young half-tinged grapes
Like small round amethysts[2] or beryls[3] strung   15
Tumultuously in clusters; though it sate[4]
Its ravenous spite among my goodliest pines
Standing there round and still against the sky
That makes blue lakes between their sombre tufts,
Or harry[5] from my silvery olive slopes   20
Some hoary king whose gnarled fantastic limbs
Wear rugged armour of a thousand years;
Though it will hurl high on my flowery shores
The hostile wave that rives[6] at the poor sward[7]
And drags it down the slants, that swirls its foam   25
Over my terraces, shakes their firm blocks
Of great bright marbles into tumbled heaps,

[1] *wont* habit, custom.
[2] *amethyst* precious stone of clear purple or bluish-violet colour.
[3] *beryl* transparent precious stone of a pale-green colour.
[4] *sate* satisfy.
[5] *harry* molest.
[6] *rive* tear apart.
[7] *sward* grassy turf.

And makes my pleached[8] and mossy labyrinths,
Where the small odorous blossoms grow like stars
    Strewn in the milky way,[9] a briny marsh.
What matter? let it come and bring me change,
    Breaking the sickly sweet monotony.

    I am too weary of this long bright calm;
    Always the same blue sky, always the sea
    The same blue perfect likeness of the sky,
One rose to match the other that has waned,
To-morrow's dawn the twin of yesterday's;
And every night the ceaseless crickets chirp
The same long joy and the late strain of birds
    Repeats their strain of all the even month;
And changelessly the petty plashing surfs
Bubble their chiming burden round the stones;
Dusk after dusk brings the same languid trance
    Upon the shadowy hills, and in the fields
The waves of fireflies come and go the same,
    Making the very flash of light and stir
Vex one like dronings of the shuttles[10] at task.

    Give me some change. Must life be only sweet,
All honey-pap as babes would have their food?
    And, if my heart must always be adrowse
In a hush of stagnant sunshine, give me, then,
Something outside me stirring; let the storm
    Break up the sluggish beauty, let it fall
Beaten below the feet of passionate winds,
    And then to-morrow waken jubilant
    In a new birth; let me see subtle joy
Of anguish and of hopes, of change and growth.

    What fate is mine, who, far apart from pains
And fears and turmoils of the cross-grained world,
    Dwell like a lonely god in a charmed isle
    Where I am first and only, and, like one
Who should love poisonous savours more than mead,[11]
    Long for a tempest on me and grow sick
    Of rest and of divine free carelessness!
    Oh me, I am a woman, not a god;
Yea, those who tend me, even, are more than I,
My nymphs who have the souls of flowers and birds
    Singing and blossoming immortally.

    Ah me! these love a day and laugh again,
    And loving, laughing, find a full content;
But I know nought of peace, and have not loved.

30

35

40

45

50

55

60

65

70

---

[8] *pleached* interlaced.
[9] *milky way* galaxy including earth.
[10] *shuttle* moving part of loom, carrying threads to be woven.

[11] *mead* alcoholic drink made from fermenting mixture of honey and water.

Where is my love? Does someone cry for me
Not knowing whom he calls? Does his soul cry
For mine to grow beside it, grow in it?
Does he beseech the gods to give him me,   75
The one unknown rare woman by whose side
No other woman thrice as beautiful
Could once seem fair to him; to whose voice heard
In any common tones no sweetest sound
Of love made melody on silver lutes,[12]   80
Or singing like Apollo's[13] when the gods
Grow pale with happy listening, might be peered
For making music to him; whom once found
There will be no more seeking anything?

Oh love, oh love, oh love, art not yet come   85
Out of the waiting shadows into life?
Art not yet come after so many years
That I have longed for thee? Come! I am here.

Not yet. For surely I should feel a sound
Of his far answer if now in the world   90
He sought me who will seek me – Oh, ye gods,
Will he not seek me? Is it all a dream?
Will there be only these, these bestial things[14]
Who wallow in their styes, or mop and mow
Among the trees, or munch in pens and byres,   95
Or snarl and filch[15] behind their wattled[16] coops;
These things who had believed that they were men?

Nay, but he *will* come. Why am I so fair,
And marvellously minded, and with sight
Which flashes suddenly on hidden things,   100
As the gods see, who do not need to look?
Why wear I in my eyes that stronger power
Than basilisks,[17] whose gaze can only kill,
To draw men's souls to me to live or die
As I would have them? Why am I given pride   105
Which yet longs to be broken, and this scorn,
Cruel and vengeful, for the lesser men
Who meet the smiles I waste for lack of him,
And grow too glad? Why am I who I am?
But for the sake of him whom fate will send   110
One day to be my master utterly,
That he should take me, the desire of all,
Whom only he in the world could bow to him.

Oh, sunlike glory of pale glittering hairs,
Bright as the filmy wires my weavers take   115
To make me golden gauzes – Oh, deep eyes,

---

[12] *lute* early stringed musical instrument, related to modern guitar.

[13] *Apollo* Greek god of music and poetry, leader of the Muses.

[14] *bestial things* men Circe has turned into animals.

[15] *filch* steal.

[16] *wattled* made from wattle: rods or stakes interlaced with twigs or branches of trees.

[17] *basilisk* fabulous reptile whose hissing drove away all other snakes and whose breath, or even look, was fatal.

Darker and softer than the bluest dusk
Of August violets, darker and deep
Like crystal fathomless lakes in summer noons –
Oh, sad sweet longing smile – Oh, lips that tempt   120
My very self to kisses – oh, round cheeks
Tenderly radiant with the even flush
Of pale smoothed coral – perfect lovely face
Answering my gaze from out this fleckless pool –
Wonder of glossy shoulders, chiselled limbs –   125
Should I be so your lover as I am,
Drinking an exquisite joy to watch you thus
In all a hundred changes through the day,
But that I love you for him till he comes,
But that my beauty means his loving it?   130

Oh, look! a speck on this side of the sun,
Coming – yes, coming with the rising wind
That frays the darkening cloud-wrack on the verge
And in a little while will leap abroad,
Spattering the sky with rushing blacknesses,   135
Dashing the hissing mountainous waves at the stars.
'Twill drive me that black speck a shuddering hulk
Caught in the buffeting waves, dashed impotent
From ridge to ridge, will drive it in the night
With that dull jarring crash upon the beach,   140
And the cries for help and the cries of fear and hope.

And then to-morrow they will thoughtfully,
With grave low voices, count their perils up,
And thank the gods for having let them live
And tell of wives and mothers in their homes,   145
And children, who would have such loss in them
That they must weep (and maybe I weep too)
With fancy of the weepings had they died.
And the next morrow they will feel their ease
And sigh with sleek content, or laugh elate,   150
Tasting delight of rest and revelling,
Music and perfumes, joyaunce[18] for the eyes
Of rosy faces and luxurious pomps,
The savour of the banquet and the glow
And fragrance of the wine-cup; and they'll talk   155
How good it is to house in palaces
Out of the storms and struggles, and what luck
Strewed their good ship on our accessless coast.
Then the next day the beast in them will wake,
And one will strike and bicker, and one swell   160
With puffed-up greatness, and one gibe and strut
In apish pranks, and one will line his sleeve
With pilfered booties, and one snatch the gems
Out of the carven goblets as they pass,
One will grow mad with fever of the wine,   165
And one will sluggishly besot himself,

---

[18] *joyaunce* archaic: happiness.

And one be lewd, and one be gluttonous;
And I shall sickly look and loathe them all.
Oh my rare cup! my pure and crystal cup,
With not one speck of colour to make false 170
The entering lights, or flaw to make them swerve!
My cup of Truth! How the lost fools will laugh
And thank me for my boon,[19] as if I gave
Some momentary flash of the gods' joy,
To drink where I have drunk and touch the touch 175
Of my lips with their own! Aye, let them touch.

Too cruel, am I? And the silly beasts,
Crowding around me when I pass their way,
Glower on me and, although they love me still,
(With their poor sorts of love such as they could) 180
Call wrath and vengeance to their humid eyes
To scare me into mercy, or creep near
With piteous fawnings, supplicating bleats.
Too cruel? Did I choose them what they are?
Or change them from themselves by poisonous charms? 185
But any draught, pure water, natural wine,
Out of my cup, revealed them to themselves
And to each other. Change? there was no change;
Only disguise gone from them unawares:
And had there been one true right man of them 190
He would have drunk the draught as I had drunk,
And stood unharmed and looked me in the eyes,
Abashing me before him.[20] But these things –
Why, which of them has even shown the kind
Of some one nobler beast? Pah! yapping wolves, 195
And pitiless stealthy wild-cats, curs,[21] and apes,
And gorging swine, and slinking venomous snakes –
All false and ravenous and sensual brutes
That shame the Earth that bore them, these they are.

Lo, lo! the shivering blueness darting forth 200
On half the heavens, and the forked thin fire
Strikes to the sea: and hark, the sudden voice
That rushes through the trees before the storm,
And shuddering of the branches. Yet the sky
Is blue against them still, and early stars 205
Sparkle above the pine-tops; and the air
Clings faint and motionless around me here.

Another burst of flame – and the black speck
Shows in the glare, lashed onwards. It were well
I bade make ready for our guests to-night. 210

---

[19] *boon* gift.

[20] *And had there been . . . before him* not a description of
what happens to Odysseus, who is assisted by moly to avoid
Circe's dangers – see headnote, 450.

[21] *cur* worthless, low-bred, snappish dog.

A Castaway

Augusta Webster's 'A Castaway' is an audacious fallen woman poem that asks its reader to reconsider commonplaces about the Victorian sex trade. The publication of the second edition of William Acton's *Prostitution, Considered in its Moral, Social and Sanitary Aspect* in the same year as 'A Castaway' (1870) indicates the poem's timeliness as an intervention into a culturally prominent debate. The monologue is spoken not, as the title might suggest to us, by a wrecked sailor, but by a prostitute, adrift from polite society (she is a reasonably well-off woman whose clients are more upmarket than those of 'my likenesses / Of the humbler kind').

The poem is an implicit and possibly intentional reply to Dante Gabriel Rossetti's 'Jenny', 358–67, which Webster perhaps saw in manuscript shortly before writing her text. Rossetti's speaker has a silent prostitute asleep on his knee and he imagines what goes on in her mind ungenerously. In 'A Castaway', the prostitute speaks for herself, providing a long account of her life, her feelings about her innocent past, and her views on the politics of prostitution. All this is precipitated by the fact that she has reread part of her childhood diary. Unlike Christina G. Rossetti's fallen woman poem 'Goblin Market', 373–85, Webster eschews any restoration of innocence at the close. It would be a false imposition on the complexity of the text and would undermine the power of its social critique.

A reviewer in the *Nonconformist* (1870) thought 'A Castaway' unrealistic in its depiction of a prostitute: '[so] high a moral tone', the reviewer said, 'could not have survived such degradation; the cynicism of vice is wanting. The woman who had resolution enough to subject herself to so keen a torture as all this remembrance and self-judgment involve, would have been

able to break away from her entanglements, and could have borne the discipline of "the Refuge".' The force of the poem is, however, to question assumptions about what a prostitute *should* be like and what her responses *ought* to be. This is Webster's challenge to Rossetti's 'Jenny', whose speaker is so sure of the prostitute's identity.

Eulalie – the speaker's name – suggests a range of justifications for her life and explanations as to what drove her to it. She admits a personal hatred for a quiet conventional life, but also bitterly discusses the economic forces that keep prostitution alive. The speaker has extremely mixed feelings about her life now, and sometimes, perhaps, she is trying to argue herself out of her residual 'homesickness' for a lost innocent past. But the poem's social critique is extensive and relates to Webster's own views of middle-class values in essays collected together as *A Housewife's Opinions* (1879). 'A Castaway' articulates astringent complaint about the superficialities of a bourgeois woman's education – a theme of *A Housewife's Opinions*. It is also scathing on the domestic ideal of heterosexual life as merely 'nursery logic' and on the polite middle-class society that has so comprehensively rejected the speaker. Augusta Webster's supple language deftly catches the feisty but troubled mood of Eulalie, whose name recalls the doomed poet of Letitia Elizabeth Landon's melancholy 'A History of the Lyre'. The quality of the text's exploration of character and voice – the *printed voice* of Victorian poetry in Eric Griffiths's term – and its provocative investigation of a key social theme make it a major mid-period poem.

Text: *Portraits* (1870, but the first letter of each line has been capitalized).

Poor little diary, with its simple thoughts,
Its good resolves, its 'Studied French an hour,'
'Read Modern History,' 'Trimmed up my grey hat,'
'Darned stockings,' 'Tatted,'[1] 'Practised my new song,'[2]
'Went to the daily service,' 'Took Bess[3] soup,'   5
'Went out to tea.' Poor simple diary!
And did *I* write it? Was I this good girl,
This budding colourless young rose of home?

[1] *Tatted* made a kind of knotted lace, netted with a small flat shuttle-shaped instrument from stout sewing-thread; used for edging or trimming, and sometimes for doyley and parasol covers.
[2] *Practised . . . song* cf. 'Pianist and Martyr' in *A Housewife's Opinions*: 'In our days there are many maidens, young and doubtless heavenly, who are perseveringly flattening their

finger-tips with a view to becoming musical. They pursue their art of measured sounds ascetically, not to gratify a taste but to perform a duty. Left to their own instinctive aspirations, they would have been as likely to wish to learn bricklaying as instrumental music.'
[3] *Bess* standard name for a servant, housekeeper (clearly sick here).

Did I so live content in such a life,
    Seeing no larger scope, nor asking it,   10
Than this small constant round – old clothes to mend,
New clothes to make, then go and say my prayers,
    Or carry soup, or take a little walk
And pick the ragged-robins[4] in the hedge?
    Then, for ambition, (was there ever life   15
That could forego that?) to improve my mind
And know French better and sing harder songs;
    For gaiety, to go, in my best white
Well washed and starched and freshened with new bows,
    And take tea out to meet the clergyman.   20
No wishes and no cares, almost no hopes,
Only the young girl's hazed and golden dreams
    That veil the Future from her.

    So long since:
And now it seems a jest to talk of me   25
As if I could be one with her, of me
    Who am . . . me.

And what is that? My looking-glass
Answers it passably; a woman sure,
No fiend, no slimy thing out of the pools,   30
A woman with a ripe and smiling lip
That has no venom in its touch I think,
With a white brow on which there is no brand;
A woman none dare call not beautiful,
Not womanly in every woman's grace.   35

Aye, let me feed upon my beauty thus,
Be glad in it like painters when they see
At last the face they dreamed but could not find
Look from their canvas on them, triumph in it,
    The dearest thing I have. Why, 'tis my all,   40
    Let me make much of it: is it not this,
This beauty, my own curse at once and tool
To snare men's souls, (I know what the good say
    Of beauty in such creatures) is it not this
That makes me feel myself a woman still,   45
With still some little pride, some little –
        Stop!
'Some little pride, some little' –

    Here's a jest!
What word will fit the sense but modesty?   50
    A wanton I, but modest!

    Modest, true;
I'm not drunk in the streets, ply not for hire
At infamous corners with my likenesses
Of the humbler kind;[5] yes, modesty's my word –   55

---

[4] *ragged-robins* popular English hedge-flowers.   [5] *likenesses . . . kind* lower-class prostitutes.

'Twould shape my mouth well too, I think I'll try:
'Sir, Mr. What-you-will, Lord Who-knows-what,
My present lover or my next to come,
Value me at my worth, fill your purse full,
For I am modest; yes, and honour me   60
As though your schoolgirl sister or your wife
Could let her skirts brush mine or talk of me;
For I am modest.'

Well, I flout myself:
But yet, but yet –   65

Fie, poor fantastic fool,
Why do I play the hypocrite alone,
Who am no hypocrite with others by?
Where should be my 'But yet'? I am that thing
Called half a dozen dainty names, and none   70
Dainty enough to serve the turn and hide
The one coarse English worst that lurks beneath:
Just that, no worse, no better.

And, for me,
I say let no one be above her trade;   75
I own my kindredship with any drab[6]
Who sells herself as I, although she crouch
In fetid[7] garrets and I have a home
All velvet and marqueterie[8] and pastilles,[9]
Although she hide her skeleton in rags   80
And I set fashions and wear cobweb lace:
The difference lies but in my choicer ware,
That I sell beauty and she ugliness;
Our traffic's one – I'm no sweet slaver-tongue[10]
To gloze[11] upon it and explain myself   85
A sort of fractious[12] angel misconceived –
Our traffic's one: I own it. And what then?
I know of worse that are called honourable.
Our lawyers, who with noble eloquence
And virtuous outbursts lie to hang a man,   90
Or lie to save him, which way goes the fee:
Our preachers, gloating on your future hell
For not believing what they doubt themselves:
Our doctors, who sort poisons out by chance
And wonder how they'll answer,[13] and grow rich: 95
Our journalists, whose business is to fib
And juggle truths and falsehoods to and fro:
Our tradesmen, who must keep unspotted names
And cheat the least like stealing that they can:
Our – all of them, the virtuous worthy men   100

[6] *drab* prostitute.
[7] *fetid* stinking.
[8] *marqueterie* inlaid work, especially as decoration of furniture.
[9] *pastilles* either small rolls of aromatic paste prepared to be burnt as a perfume, or an error for *pastels*, soft tints of material, subdued shades used generally in textiles, interior decoration.
[10] *slaver-tongue* flattering tongue.
[11] *gloze* expound, discourse.
[12] *fractious* unruly.
[13] *how they'll answer* how they will work.

Who feed on the world's follies, vices, wants,
And do their businesses of lies and shams
Honestly, reputably, while the world
Claps hands and cries 'good luck,' which of their trades,
Their honourable trades, barefaced like mine,   105
All secrets brazened out, would shew more white?

And whom do I hurt more than they? as much?
The wives? Poor fools, what do I take from them
Worth crying for or keeping? If they knew
What their fine husbands look like seen by eyes   110
That may perceive there are more men than one!
But, if they can, let them just take the pains
To keep them: 'tis not such a mighty task
To pin an idiot to your apron-string;
And wives have an advantage over us,   115
(The good and blind ones have) the smile or pout
Leaves them no secret nausea at odd times.
Oh, they could keep their husbands if they cared,
But 'tis an easier life to let them go,
And whimper at it for morality.   120

Oh! those shrill carping virtues, safely housed
From reach of even a smile that should put red
On a decorous cheek, who rail[14] at us
With such a spiteful scorn and rancorousness,[15]
(Which maybe is half envy at the heart)   125
And boast themselves so measurelessly good
And us so measurelessly unlike them,
What is their wondrous merit that they stay
In comfortable homes whence not a soul
Has ever thought of tempting them, and wear   130
No kisses but a husband's upon lips
There is no other man desires to kiss –
Refrain in fact from sin impossible?
How dare they hate us so? what have they done,
What borne, to prove them other than we are?   135
What right have they to scorn us – glass-case saints,
Dianas[16] under lock and key – what right
More than the well-fed helpless barn-door fowl
To scorn the larcenous[17] wild-birds?

Pshaw,[18] let be!   140
Scorn or no scorn, what matter for their scorn?
I have outfaced my own – that's harder work.
Aye, let their virtuous malice dribble on –
Mock snowstorms on the stage – I'm proof long since:
I have looked coolly on my what and why,   145
And I accept myself.

---

[14] *rail* utter abusive language.
[15] *rancorousness* bitter ill-feeling.
[16] *Diana* goddess of wild nature, hunting and women.
[17] *larcenous* thievish.
[18] *Pshaw* exclamation expressing contempt, impatience, disgust.

Oh I'll endorse
The shamefullest revilings mouthed at me,
Cry 'True! Oh perfect picture! Yes, that's I!'
And add a telling blackness here and there,   150
And then dare swear you, every nine of ten,
My judges and accusers, I'd not change
My conscience against yours, you who tread out
Your devil's pilgrimage along the roads
That take in church and chapel, and arrange   155
A roundabout and decent way to hell.

Well, mine's a short way and a merry one:
So says my pious hash[19] of ohs and ahs,
Choice texts and choicer threats, appropriate names,
(Rahabs[20] and Jezebels[21]) some fierce Tartuffe[22]   160
Hurled at me through the post. We had rare fun
Over that tract[23] digested with champagne.
Where is it? where's my rich repertory
Of insults Biblical? '*I prey on souls*' –
Only my men have oftenest none I think: 165
'*I snare the simple ones*' – but in these days
There seem to be none simple and none snared
And most men have their favourite sinnings planned
To do them civilly and sensibly:
'*I braid[24] my hair*' – but braids are out of date: 170
'*I paint my cheeks*' – I always wear them pale:
'*I* –'

Pshaw! the trash is savourless to-day:
One cannot laugh alone. There, let it burn.
What, does the windy dullard think one needs   175
His wisdom dove-tailed on to Solomon's,[25]
His threats out-threatening God's, to teach the news
That those who need not sin have safer souls?
We know it, but we've bodies to save too;
And so we earn our living.   180

Well lit, tract!
At least you've made me a good leaping blaze.
Up, up, how the flame shoots! and now 'tis dead.
Oh proper finish, preaching to the last –
No such bad omen either; sudden end,   185
And no sad withering horrible old age.
How one would clutch at youth to hold it tight!
And then to know it gone, to see it gone,
Be taught its absence by harsh careless looks,
To live forgotten, solitary, old –   190
The cruellest word that ever woman learns.

---

[19] *hash* medley, mess.
[20] *Rahab* prostitute in the Book of Joshua.
[21] *Jezebel* infamous wife of Ahab, King of Israel (e.g., 2 Kings 9.30–7).
[22] *Tartuffe* hypocritical pretender to religion (after Molière's *Tartuffe* [1664]).

[23] *tract* short (usually propagandist) pamphlet on a moral, religious or political theme.
[24] *braid* plait, decoratively twine.
[25] *Solomon* Old Testament king famed for wisdom.

Old – that's to be nothing, or to be at best
A blurred memorial that in better days
There was a woman once with such a name.
No, no, I could not bear it: death itself   195
Shows kinder promise . . . even death itself,
Since it must come one day –

Oh this grey gloom!
This rain, rain, rain, what wretched thoughts it brings!
Death: I'll not think of it.   200

Will no one come?
'Tis dreary work alone.

Why did I read
That silly diary? Now, sing-song, ding-dong,
Come the old vexing echoes back again,   205
Church bells and nursery good-books, back again
Upon my shrinking ears that had forgotten –
I hate the useless memories: 'tis fools' work
Singing the hacknied dirge of 'better days':
Best take Now kindly, give the past good-bye,   210
Whether it were a better or a worse.

Yes, yes, I listened to the echoes once,
The echoes and the thoughts from the old days.
The worse for me: I lost my richest friend,
And that was all the difference. For the world,   215
I would not have that flight known. How they'd roar:
'What! Eulalie,[26] when she refused us all,
"Ill" and "away," was doing Magdalene,[27]
Tears, ashes, and her Bible, and then off
To hide her in a Refuge[28] . . . for a week!'   220

A wild whim that, to fancy I could change
My new self for my old because I wished!
Since then, when in my languid days there comes
That craving, like homesickness, to go back
To the good days, the dear old stupid days,   225
To the quiet and the innocence, I know
'Tis a sick fancy and try palliatives.[29]

What is it? You go back to the old home,
And 'tis not *your* home, has no place for you,
And, if it had, you could not fit you in it.   230
And could I fit me to my former self?
If I had had the wit, like some of us,

---

[26] *Eulalie* the name means 'fair speech'.
[27] *Magdalene* i.e., acting as repentant: Mary Magdalene is traditionally identified as the repentant sinner who appears in Luke 7.37–44; tradition also holds that she was a prostitute or sexually transgressive.

[28] *Refuge* for former prostitutes such as that founded by Angela Burdett Coutts (1814–1906), 'Urania Cottage', which was supported from 1847 by Charles Dickens.
[29] *palliatives* things which give temporary relief.

To sow my wild-oats into three per cents,[30]
Could I not find me shelter in the peace
Of some far nook where none of them would come,   235
Nor whisper travel from this scurrilous world
(That gloats, and moralizes through its leers)
To blast me with my fashionable shame?
There I might – oh my castle in the clouds!
And where's its rent? – but there, were there a there,   240
I might again live the grave blameless life
Among such simple pleasures, simple cares:
But could they be my pleasures, be my cares?
The blameless life, but never the content –
Never. How could I henceforth be content   245
With any life but one that sets the brain
In a hot merry fever with its stir?
What would there be in quiet rustic days,
Each like the other, full of time to think,
To keep one bold enough to live at all?   250
Quiet is hell, I say – as if a woman
Could bear to sit alone, quiet all day,
And loathe herself and sicken on her thoughts.

They tried it at the Refuge, and I failed:
I could not bear it. Dreary hideous room,   255
Coarse pittance, prison rules, one might bear these
And keep one's purpose; but so much alone,
And then made faint and weak and fanciful
By change from pampering to half-famishing –
Good God, what thoughts come! Only one week more   260
And 'twould have ended: but in one day more
I must have killed myself. And I loathe death,
The dreadful foul corruption with who knows
What future after it.

                    Well, I came back,   265
Back to my slough.[31] Who says I had my choice?
Could I stay there to die of some mad death?
And if I rambled out into the world
Sinless but penniless, what else were that
But slower death, slow pining shivering death   270
By misery and hunger? Choice! what choice
Of living well or ill? could I have that?
And who would give it me? I think indeed
If some kind hand, a woman's – I hate men –
Had stretched itself to help me to firm ground,   275
Taken a chance and risked my falling back,
I could have gone my way not falling back:
But, let her be all brave, all charitable,
How could she do it? Such a trifling boon –
A little work to live by, 'tis not much –   280
And I might have found will enough to last:

[30] *three per cents* popular mid-nineteenth-century form of financial investment.   [31] *slough* mire, mud.

But where's the work? More sempstresses[32] than shirts;
    And defter hands at white work than are mine
    Drop starved at last: dressmakers, milliners,[33]
    Too many too they say; and then their trades   285
    Need skill, apprenticeship. And who so bold
      As hire me for their humblest drudgery?
    Not even for scullery[34] slut; not even, I think,
    For governess although they'd get me cheap.
    And after all it would be something hard,   290
    With the marts[35] for decent women overfull,
      If I could elbow in and snatch a chance
    And oust some good girl so, who then perforce
Must come and snatch her chance among our crowd.

    Why, if the worthy men who think all's done   295
If we'll but come where we can hear them preach,
      Could bring us all, or any half of us,
    Into their fold, teach all us wandering sheep,
      Or only half of us, to stand in rows
    And baa them hymns and moral songs, good lack,   300
    What would they do with us? what could they do?
    Just think! with were't but half of us on hand
    To find work for . . . or husbands. Would they try
      To ship us to the colonies for wives?

    Well, well, I know the wise ones talk and talk: 305
'Here's cause, here's cure:' 'No, here it is, and here:'
      And find society to blame, or law,
The Church, the men, the women, too few schools,
    Too many schools, too much, too little taught:
    Somewhere or somehow someone is to blame: 310
      But I say all the fault's with God himself
    Who puts too many women in the world.[36]
    We ought to die off reasonably and leave
    As many as the men want, none to waste.
      Here's cause; the woman's superfluity: 315
    And for the cure, why, if it were the law,
      Say, every year, in due percentages,
    Balancing them with males as the times need,
    To kill off female infants, 'twould make room;
    And some of us would not have lost too much,   320
      Losing life ere we know what it *can* mean.

    The other day I saw a woman weep
    Beside her dead child's bed: the little thing
    Lay smiling, and the mother wailed half mad,
      Shrieking to God to give it back again.   325
    I could have laughed aloud: the little girl
    Living had but her mother's life to live;
    There she lay smiling, and her mother wept
      To know her gone!

---

[32] *sempstresses* women who seam or sew.
[33] *milliners* women who make fancy wear, bonnets, gloves, etc.
[34] *scullery* where washing up is done.
[35] *marts* markets.
[36] *But I . . . world* she becomes bitterly ironic.

My mother would have wept.   330

Oh, mother, mother, did you ever dream,
You good grave simple mother, you pure soul
No evil could come nigh,[37] did you once dream
In all your dying cares for your lone girl
Left to fight out her fortune helplessly   335
That there would be *this* danger? – for *your* girl,
Taught by you, lapped in a sweet ignorance,
Scarcely more wise of what things sin could be
Than some young child a summer six months old,
Where in the north the summer makes a day,   340
Of what is darkness . . . darkness that will come
To-morrow suddenly. Thank God at least
For this much of my life, that when you died,
That when you kissed me dying, not a thought
Of this made sorrow for you, that I too   345
Was pure[38] of even fear.

Oh yes, I thought,
Still new in my insipid treadmill life,
(My father so late dead), and hopeful still,
There might be something pleasant somewhere in it,   350
Some sudden fairy come, no doubt, to turn
My pumpkin to a chariot,[39] I thought then
That I might plod and plod and drum the sounds
Of useless facts into unwilling ears,
Tease children with dull question half the day   355
Then con[40] dull answers in my room at night
Ready for next day's questions, mend quill pens[41]
And cut my fingers, add up sums done wrong
And never get them right; teach, teach, and teach –
What I half knew, or not at all – teach, teach   360
For years, a lifetime – *I!*

And yet, who knows?
It might have been, for I was patient once,
And willing, and meant well; it might have been
Had I but still clung on in my first place –   365
A safe dull place, where mostly there were smiles
But never merry-makings; where all days
Jogged on sedately busy, with no haste;
Where all seemed measured out, but margins broad:
A dull home but a peaceful, where I felt   370
My pupils would be dear young sisters soon,
And felt their mother take me to her heart,
Motherly to all lonely harmless things.
But I must have a conscience, must blurt out
My great discovery of my ignorance!   375
And who required it of me? And who gained?

---

[37] *nigh* near.
[38] *pure* innocent.
[39] *pumpkin . . . chariot* fairytale transformation from
Cinderella.

[40] *con* study, learn.
[41] *quill pens* nibs attached to goose feathers and dipped in
ink to form pens.

What did it matter for a more or less
The girls learnt in their schoolbooks, to forget
In their first season? We did well together:
They loved me and I them: but I went off   380
To housemaid's pay, six crossgrained brats to teach,
Wrangles and jangles, doubts, disgrace . . . then this;
And they had a perfection[42] found for them,
Who has all ladies' learning in her head
Abridged and scheduled, speaks five languages,   385
Knows botany and conchology[43] and globes,[44]
Draws, paints, plays, sings, embroiders, teaches all
On a patent method never known to fail:
And now they're finished and, I hear, poor things,
Are the worst dancers and worst dressers out.   390
And where's their profit of those prison years
All gone to make them wise in lesson-books?
Who wants his wife to know weeds' Latin names?
Who ever chose a girl for saying dates?
Or asked if she had learned to trace a map?   395

Well, well, the silly rules this silly world
Makes about women! This is one of them.
Why must there be pretence of teaching them
What no one ever cares that they should know,
What, grown out of the schoolroom, they cast off   400
Like the schoolroom pinafore,[45] no better fit
For any use of real grown-up life,
For any use to her who seeks or waits
The husband and the home, for any use,
For any shallowest pretence of use,   405
To her who has them? Do I not know this,
I, like my betters, that a woman's life,
Her natural life, her good life, her one life,
Is in her husband, God on earth to her,
And what she knows and what she can and is   410
Is only good as it brings good to him?

Oh God, do I not know it? I the thing
Of shame and rottenness, the animal
That feed men's lusts and prey on them, I, I,
Who should not dare to take the name of wife   415
On my polluted lips, who in the word
Hear but my own reviling, I know that.
I could have lived by that rule, how content:
My pleasure to make him some pleasure, pride
To be as he would have me, duty, care,   420
To fit all to his taste, rule my small sphere
To his intention; then to lean on him,
Be guided, tutored, loved – no not that word,

---

[42] *perfection* i.e., the new governess.
[43] *conchology* study of shells.
[44] *globes* geography, use of globes that are models of the earth.

[45] *pinafore* sleeveless, apron-like garment.

That *loved* which between men and women means
All selfishness, all cloying talk, all lust,   425
All vanity, all idiocy – not loved,
But cared for. I've been loved myself, I think,
Some once or twice since my poor mother died,
But *cared for*, never: – that's a word for homes,
Kind homes, good homes, where simple children come   430
And ask their mother is this right or wrong,
Because they know she's perfect, cannot err;
Their father told them so, and he knows all,
Being so wise and good and wonderful,
Even enough to scold even her at times   435
And tell her everything she does not know.
Ah the sweet nursery logic!

Fool! thrice fool!
Do I hanker after that too? Fancy me
Infallible nursery saint, live code of law!   440
Me preaching! teaching innocence to be good! –
A mother!

Yet the baby thing that woke
And wailed an hour or two, and then was dead,
Was mine, and had he lived . . . why then my name   445
Would have been mother. But 'twas well he died:
I could have been no mother, I, lost then
Beyond his saving. Had he come before
And lived, come to me in the doubtful days
When shame and boldness had not grown one sense,   450
For his sake, with the courage come of him,
I might have struggled back.

But how? But how?
His father would not then have let me go:
His time had not yet come to make an end   455
Of my 'for ever' with a hireling's fee
And civil light dismissal. None but him
To claim a bit of bread of if I went,
Child or no child: would he have given it me?
He! no; he had not done with me. No help,   460
No help, no help. Some ways can be trodden back,
But never our way, we who one wild day
Have given goodbye to what in our deep hearts
The lowest woman still holds best in life,
Good name – good name though given by the world   465
That mouths and garbles with its decent prate,[46]
And wraps it in respectable grave shams,
And patches conscience partly by the rule
Of what one's neighbour thinks, but something more
By what his eyes are sharp enough to see.   470

---

[46] *prate* chatter.

How I could scorn it with its Pharisees,[47]
If it could not scorn me: but yet, but yet –
Oh God, if I could look it in the face!

Oh I am wild, am ill, I think, to-night:
Will no one come and laugh with me? No feast,   475
No merriment to-night. So long alone!
          Will no one come?

          At least there's a new dress
To try, and grumble at – they never fit
To one's ideal. Yes, a new rich dress,   480
With lace like this too, that's a soothing balm
For any fretting woman, cannot fail;
I've heard men say it . . . and they know so well
What's in all women's hearts, especially
          Women like me.   485

          No help! no help! no help!
How could it be? It was too late long since –
Even at the first too late. Whose blame is that?
There are some kindly people in the world,
But what can they do? If one hurls oneself   490
Into a quicksand, what can be the end,
But that one sinks and sinks? Cry out for help?
Ah yes, and, if it came, who is so strong
To strain from the firm ground and lift one out?
And how, so firmly clutching the stretched hand   495
As death's pursuing terror bids, even so,
How can one reach firm land, having to foot
The treacherous crumbling soil that slides and gives
And sucks one in again? Impossible path!
No, why waste struggles, I or any one?   500
What is must be. What then? I where I am,
Sinking and sinking; let the wise pass by
And keep their wisdom for an apter use,
          Let me sink merrily as I best may.

Only, I think my brother – I forgot;   505
He stopped his brotherhood[48] some years ago –
But if he had been just so much less good
As to remember mercy. Did he think
How once I was his sister, prizing him
As sisters do, content to learn for him   510
The lesson girls with brothers all must learn,
          To do without?

          I have heard girls lament
That doing so without all things one would,
But I saw never aught to murmur at,   515
For men must be made ready for their work

<hr>

[47] *Pharisees* ancient Jewish sect distinguished by their strict observance of oral and written law, traditionally thought to have pretensions to superior sanctity.

[48] *stopped his brotherhood* denied he was her brother.

And women all have more or less their chance
Of husbands to work for them, keep them safe
Like summer roses in soft greenhouse air
That never guess 'tis winter out of doors: 520
No, I saw never aught to murmur at,
Content with stinted fare and shabby clothes
And cloistered silent life to save expense,
Teaching myself out of my borrowed books,
While he for some one pastime, (needful, true,   525
To keep him of his rank; 'twas not his fault)
Spent in a month what could have given me
My teachers for a year.

'Twas no one's fault:
For could he be launched forth on the rude sea   530
Of this contentious world and left to find
Oars and the boatman's skill by some good chance?
'Twas no one's fault: yet still he might have thought
Of our so different youths and owned at least
'Tis pitiful when a mere nerveless girl   535
Untutored must put forth upon that sea,
Not in the woman's true place, the wife's place,
To trust a husband and be borne along,
But impotent blind pilot to herself.

Merciless, merciless – like the prudent world   540
That will not have the flawed soul prank itself
With a hoped second virtue, will not have
The woman fallen once lift up herself . . .
Lest she should fall again. Oh how his taunts,
His loathing fierce reproaches, scarred and seared   545
Like branding iron hissing in a wound!
And it was true – *that* killed me: and I felt
A hideous hopeless shame burn out my heart,
And knew myself for ever that he said,
That which I was – Oh it was true, true, true.   550

No, not true then. I was not all that then.
Oh, I have drifted on before mad winds
And made ignoble shipwreck; not to-day
Could any breeze of heaven prosper me
Into the track again, nor any hand   555
Snatch me out of the whirlpool I have reached;
But then?

Nay, he judged very well: he knew
Repentance was too dear a luxury
For a beggar's buying, knew it earns no bread –   560
And knew me a too base and nerveless thing
To bear my first fault's sequel and just die.
And how could he have helped me? Held my hand,
Owned me for his, fronted the angry world
Clothed with my ignominy?[49] Or maybe   565

---

[49] *ignominy* dishonour, disgrace.

Taken me to his home to damn him worse?
What did I look for? for what less would serve
That he could do, a man without a purse?
He meant me well, he sent me that five pounds,
Much to him then; and, if he bade me work   570
And never vex him more with news of me,
We both knew him too poor for pensioners.
I see he did his best; I could wish now
Sending it back I had professed some thanks.

But there! I was too wretched to be meek: 575
It seemed to me as if he, every one,
The whole great world, were guilty of my guilt,
Abettors[50] and avengers: in my heart
I gibed them back their gibings; I was wild.

I see clear now and know one has one's life   580
In hand at first to spend or spare or give
Like any other coin; spend it, or give,
Or drop it in the mire, can the world see
You get your value for it, or bar off
The hurrying of its marts to grope it up   585
And give it back to you for better use?
And if you spend or give, that is your choice;
And if you let it slip, that's your choice too,
You should have held it firmer. Yours the blame,
And not another's, not the indifferent world's   590
Which goes on steadily, statistically,
And count by censuses not separate souls –
And if it somehow needs to its worst use
So many lives of women, useless else,
It buys us of ourselves; we could hold back,   595
Free all of us to starve, and some of us,
(Those who have done no ill, and are in luck)
To slave their lives out and have food and clothes
Until they grow unserviceably old.

Oh, I blame no one – scarcely even myself.   600
It was to be: the very good in me
Has always turned to hurt; all I thought right
At the hot moment, judged of afterwards,
Shows reckless.

Why, look at it, had I taken   605
The pay my dead child's father offered me
For having been its mother, I could then
Have kept life in me – many have to do it,
That swarm in the back alleys, on no more,
Cold sometimes, mostly hungry, but they live –   610
I could have gained a respite trying it,
And maybe found at last some humble work
To eke the pittance out. Not I, forsooth,[51]

---

[50] *Abettors* instigators, supporters, promoters.   [51] *forsooth* in truth.

I must have spirit, must have womanly pride,
Must dash back his contemptuous wages, I   615
Who had not scorned to earn them, dash them back
The fiercer that he dared to count our boy
In my appraising: and yet now I think
I might have taken it for my dead boy's sake;
It would have been *his* gift.   620

But I went forth
With my fine scorn, and whither did it lead?
Money's the root of evil do they say?
Money is virtue, strength: money to me
Would then have been repentance: could I live   625
Upon my idiot's pride?

Well, it fell soon.
I had prayed Clement[52] might believe me dead,
And yet I begged of him – That's like me too,
Beg of him and then send him back his alms![53]   630
What if he gave as to a whining wretch
That holds her hand and lies? I am less to him
Than such a one; her rags do him no wrong,
But I, I wrong him merely that I live,
Being his sister. Could I not at least   635
Have still let him forget me? But 'tis past:
And naturally he may hope I am long dead.
Good God! to think that we were what we were

One to the other . . . and now!
He has done well;   640

Married a sort of heiress, I have heard,
A dapper little madam dimple cheeked
And dimple brained, who makes him a good wife –
No doubt she'd never own but just to him,
And in a whisper, she can even suspect   645
That we exist, we other women things:
What would she say if she could learn one day
She has a sister-in-law? So he and I
Must stand apart till doomsday.

But the jest,   650
To think how she would look! – Her fright, poor thing!
The notion! – I could laugh outright . . . or else,
For I feel near it, roll on the ground and sob.

Well, after all, there's not much difference
Between the two sometimes.[54]   655
Was that the bell?
Someone at last, thank goodness. There's a voice,

---

[52] *Clement* the brother; ironically, his name means merciful, lenient.
[53] *alms* gifts of charity.
[54] *Well . . . sometimes* cf. Rossetti's 'Jenny', ll. 177–219.

And that's a pleasure. Whose though? Ah, I know.
Why did she come alone, the cackling goose?
Why not have brought her sister? – she tells more   660
And titters less. No matter; half a loaf
Is better than no bread.

Oh, is it you?
Most welcome, dear: one gets so moped[55] alone.

[55] *moped* dejected, low-spirited.

Faded

Memory for William Wordsworth was a source of joy and a form of salvation; for the speaker of 'Faded', there is little consolation in recalling the past. The experience of growing old for Matthew Arnold, in the poem 'Growing Old' (*c.*1864–7), was the wretched loss of feeling and the awful sense that being old 'is to spend long days / And not once feel that we were ever young'. But for the old lady who is the speaker of 'Faded', it is the memory of youth that is precisely the problem. The poem offers, through the speaker's sustained meditation on a portrait of herself as a young woman, a female perspective on the Romantic conception of memory as redemptory. In doing so, it expresses impatience with the gender politics of age, vexation with the differences in cultural perception of male and female courage in fighting against the inevitable, and a statement of frustration with the privileging of youth in the wider social perception of

middle-class women. 'Faded' places in the foreground the problem of how identity – particularly a woman's identity – is socially constructed, and how that identity relates to the individual's own self-perception as she is caught up in society's assumptions and prejudices. The lines (102–31) in which the speaker presents marriage as 'a woman's destiny and sole hope' are carefully poised on the edge of bitter irony. For other texts that involve contemplation of the female as *image*, see Robert Browning, 'My Last Duchess', 173–5, Christina G. Rossetti, 'In an Artist's Studio', 370–1, and Michael Field, 'A Portrait: Bartolommeo Veneto', 560–2. 'Faded' was written in 1870 but only published in 1893; it had originally been intended for *Portraits* of 1870 but somehow was missed out.

Text: *Portraits*, 3rd edn (1893).

Ah face, young face, sweet with unpassionate joy,
Possessful joy of having all to hope –
Rich, measureless, nameless, formless, *all* to hope –
Fair, happy, face with the girl's questioning smile
Expectant of an answer from the days,   5
Fair, happy, morning, face who wast myself,
Talk with me, with this later drearier self.
Oftenest I dare not see thee: but alone,
Thou and I in the quiet, while, without,
Dim eve goes dwindling her hushed, hueless, light   10
And makes the leaden dusk before the stars –
While, if my duller eyes through envious tears
Reply to thine, there's none at hand to note,
Not yet thyself, in the sad and pensive calm,
Wilt flout me for my faded look of thee,   15
As when thou mock'st me in the untender noon –
While now we two a little time are one,
Elder and girl, the blossoming and the sere,[1]

[1] *sere* dry and withered.

One blended, dateless, woman for an hour –
Thou and I thus alone, I read from thee   20
My lesson what I was; which (ah, poor heart!)
Means trulier my lesson, bitter to learn,
    Of what I cease to be.

    Fie, cruel face!
Too comely, thou. Thy round curves shame my cheeks;   25
Thy gloss of almond-bloom in the March sun
Affronts my hardened reds; thy satiny brow,
Like smooth magnolia[2] petals warmly white,
    Enforces all my tale of fretted lines;
The quivering woof[3] of sunshine through thy hairs   30
Shows mine's spent russets[4] deader. All in thee
That's likest me to-day is proof of the more
Of my to-day's unlikeness. Ah! I have waned.
As every summer wanes, that, all the while,
Seems to grow still more summer, till, one day,   35
The first dead leaves are falling and all's past.
    Myself has faded from me; I am old.

Well, well, what's that to fret for? Yet, indeed,
    'Tis pity for a woman to be old.
Youth going lessens us of more than youth: 40
    We lose the very instinct of our lives –
Song-birds left voiceless, diswinged flies of the air.
And the loss comes so soon; and ere we know:
    We have so many many after years,
    To use away (the unmarried ones at least)   45
    In only withering leisurely. Ah me!
    Men jeer us clinging, clinging pitiably,
To that themselves account whole all for us:
Aye, but what man of them could bear, as we must,
    To live life's worth a stinted dozen years.   50
And the long sequel all for learning age.
Why, if we try to cheat the merciless world
That bids us grow old meekly and to the hour,
(Like babes that must not cry when bed-time comes)
    And, being old, be nothing – try, maybe,   55
To cheat our lingering selves as if Time lingered –
    Is our fault other than the toil in vain
Of any shipwrecked swimmer who, miles from land,
    No sail in sight, breasts the resistless sea,
And perishing will not perish? Oh, 'tis known   60
How bankrupt men will hopelessly, impotent,
    Battle each inch with unforgiving ruin,
Waste their tired brains on schemes a child should laugh at,
Befool their hearts with more unbodied hopes
    Than shadows flung by momentary spray,   65

[2] *magnolia* tree with striking foliage, cultivated for the beauty of its pink-white flowers.
[3] *woof* threads that cross from side to side of a loom.

[4] *russets* coarse homespun woollen cloth of a reddish-brown: the speaker refers to the colour of her hair and its health, sustaining the metaphor of woven fabrics from the previous line.

Tease their unwilling faces into smiles
And loathingly look contentment – but, at best,
To gain some futile hour from certainty:
But we in our utter loss, outlawed from life,
Irretrievable bankrupts of our very selves,   70
We must give ruin welcome, blaze our fact
Of nothingness – 'good friends, perceive I am old;
Pray laugh and leave me.' We are fools, we sin,
Abjectly, past all pardon, past all pity,
We women, if we linger, if, maybe,   75
We use our petty melancholy arts
And are still women some filched[5] year or two –
Still women and not ghosts, not lifeless husks,
Spent memories that slink through the world and breathe,
As if they lived, and yet they know they are dead.   80

Once, long ago, I dreamed I had truly died:
My numb void body, in its winding-sheet,[6]
Lay ignorant, but I, grown viewlessness,[7]
Met my home's dear ones still; I spoke, methought,
Words which they marked not, smiled unanswered smiles,   85
And then I wept, and clung about their necks,
Closer, with vain embracing; and one said
(Another ghost, a voice, I searched not what)
'Thou art all dead for them; they cannot know,'
And still replied 'They felt not,' or 'They heard not,'   90
'They cannot, thou being dead,' until ere long
The anguish of it waked me – to be thus,
With them yet so forlorn of sense of theirs!
'Twas in my happiest days, when, like new fronds
Uncurling coil by coil on ferns in May   95
And widening to the light and dews and air,
The girl grows woman gladly, but, untold,
That dream clung like a sorrow, and, for pity,
I hoped the poor lone dead should bide apart,
Never among their living. Like that dream,   100
Lost and alone, I haunt our world to-day.

How strange life is! – a woman's – if, I mean,
One miss a woman's destiny and sole hope,
The wife's dear service with its round of tasks
And sweet humilities and glad fatigues,   105
And anxious joy of mothers – strange indeed!
To wait and wait, like the flower upon its stalk,
For nothing save to wither! And the while
Knows she that she is waiting? Maybe, yes:
And maybe, no. That new-made shallow lake,   110
Asleep there in the park, knows not, asleep,
It waits the brook next rain-fall shall let loose

---

[5] *filched* stolen.

[6] *winding-sheet* shroud, wrapped around a dead body for
burial.

[7] *viewlessness* invisible.

To brim it with full waters, bear it on
Filling its further channel: girls so wait,
Careless and calm, not judging what shall be;   115
Only they know life has not reached them yet,
And till life come they'll dream and laugh in the sun.
And the sun shines, and the dumb days flit by
And make no sign for working . . . till, at time,
To her whom life and love need the voice comes   120
Which names her wife among the happier many:
And till to her, maybe, who not again
Shall know rest and sweet dreams, nor in the world
Call anywhere her home, nor laugh at ease,
Nor spend her toils on those who'll love her for them,   125
Dawns change and the hour of wonder while she wakes
Alone in the eastwinds of a barren world:
And till to her to whom life never comes,
Whether by joy or sorrows or by toil,
The sunshine has grown drought, the calm, decay;   130
And there's the woman old.
        Poor imaged mock,[8]
Thou art more than I to-day; thou hast my right,
My womanhood's lost right to meet pleased eyes
And please by being happy. Many a time   135
I note, forgotten, how thy youth, that lasts,
Earns thee companionship of lingering looks,[9]
Thy smile a tenderness whereof nought's mine.
Thou hast a being still; but what am I?
A shadow and an echo – one that was.   140

Well, Time's thy tyrant too: there waits for thee
In the sure end the day thou wilt have faded.
Carelessly thou'lt be lifted from thy place,[10]
Too long usurped, where there'll, room being given,
Bloom some such other face, nor thine be missed –   145
As a newer rose, alike as roses are,
Makes us the self-same sweet as yesterday's –
As in the river's stream an on-come wave,
That is to pass, fills all the other filled
That took the drift before it and has passed –   150
As we have our succession, woman to woman,
And so no smiles are missed, there being enough.
I shall not know it: winters of many years
Before then long may have annulled my grave,
My date may be so back past household talk   155
'Tis out of guess whose the vague counterfeit
That on the canvas has past memory
Smiled peering through the dirt-crust and the cracks.
Yes; after me thou'lt years and years be thus,
Be young, be fair, be, dumb unconscious toy,   160

---

[8] *imaged mock* the portrait she addresses.
[9] *I note . . . looks* 'I often note that, while I am overlooked in the flesh, my picture draws people's attention and they linger over its beauty.'

[10] *lifted . . . place* in due course, the portrait will be changed.

Beloved for youth and fairness; but at the end
Age and decay for thee too. Face of mine,
Forgotten self, thou art woman after all:
   Sooner or later we are one again:
Both shall have had our fate . . . decay, neglect,   165
Loneliness, and then die and never a one
In the busy world the poorer for our loss.

How dusk it is! Have I sat indeed so long?
I had not marked. Time to have been long since
In the merry drawing-room with its lights and talk   170
And my young sisters' music. Hark! that's sweet.
Maudie's clear voice sends me my favourite song,
   Filling my stillness here. She sings it well.

                                        [Exit.]

Algernon Charles Swinburne (1837–1909)

Born in London, the son of an admiral and an earl's daughter, Swinburne's childhood was cultured and comfortable. He spent much of his time on the Isle of Wight, where his love of the sea and sea-swimming flourished. At Eton, where he was a pupil, Swinburne was distinguished by his wide reading and love of the sexual pleasures of flogging. Leaving the College for some unspecified misdemeanour, he entered Balliol College Oxford, where he was known as a magnetic talker. He picked up an enthusiasm for Italian republican politics, and cast off the Anglo-Catholicism he had inherited from his parents. He left Balliol without a degree and moved to London, where he lived a truly wild lifestyle. His first successful volume was *Atalanta in Calydon* (1865), a poetic drama of exceptional rhythmic fluency. In 1866 came *Poems and Ballads*, from where 'Laus Veneris', 'Anactoria' and 'Hymn to Proserpine' are taken. It stirred controversy for its representation of transgressive sexuality (lesbianism, necrophilia, sado-masochism), paganism, and its anti-Christian poems (Swinburne is another target, along with Dante Gabriel Rossetti, of Buchanan's 'Fleshly School' article in 1871; see headnote, 350). Throughout his career, Swinburne prompted strong reaction, and not just for provocative or offensive themes. Robert Browning disputed his abilities as a poet *tout court*. 'Swinburne's verses', Browning said, '. . . are "florid impotence", to my taste, the *minimum* of thought and idea in the *maximum* of words and phraseology. Nothing said and nothing done with, left to stand alone and trust for its effect in its own worth.' The subtlety of Swinburne's *thinking* – which an annotated edition helps make clearer – has taken many years to be recognized. But he is now beginning to be properly admired as a remarkable and original Victorian voice, a serious poet of ideas as well as a writer possessed of extraordinary verbal fluency.

Swinburne was a versatile man whose output included poetry, verse drama, criticism, translations and two novels (now known as *Love's Cross Currents* and *Lesbia Brandon*); he was a scholar of Elizabethan drama and an early advocate of the work of William Blake, who was little known during the Victorian period. The volumes *A Song of Italy* (1867) and *Songs Before Sunrise* (1871) were followed by *Poems and Ballads, Second Series*, published in 1878, including 'A Forsaken Garden'. In 1879, Swinburne, by then a formidable drinker, was taken under the wing of Theodore Watts-Dunton, a somewhat prosy figure who managed to wean Swinburne from the bottle. Many more volumes were the result, including *Tristram of Lyonesse and Other Poems* (1882) and *Marino Faliero* (1885), a play on the only Venetian doge to be executed for treason. Swinburne died in April 1909 and was buried on the Isle of Wight.

Hymn to Proserpine: After the Proclamation in Rome of the Christian Faith

Swinburne's critique of Christianity took many forms. 'A Forsaken Garden', 506–9, gains some of its energy from a parodic relationship with Christian imagery and vocabulary. The 'Hymn to Proserpine', from *Poems and Ballads* (1866), looks at Christianity as an impoverished faith from the point of view of an ancient pagan. Swinburne took the epigraph for this poem – meaning 'You have conquered, Galilean' (i.e., Jesus) – from the supposed dying words of Julian the Apostate, Emperor of Rome 360–3 AD. Julian had unsuccessfully tried to restore paganism. Swinburne's poem takes the epigraph as a starting point but is not set during Julian's reign, and considers not the revival but the fall of paganism under the advance of a 'pale' Christianity. It tests how differently Christianity could look when perceived from an unfamiliar historical vantage point and from a cultural context distant from the Victorian.

And yet, the poem ultimately suggests, not that distant. The fourth-century speaker is also partly a nineteenth-century one, impatient with the nature of Christianity, its gloom, distaste for the body and colourlessness. 'Hymn to Proserpine', inscribing the arrival of Christianity as retrogressive, proposes a relationship between historical periods that challenges a simple notion of progress or of continual difference between one age and another.

The speaker's personal devotion is to the Roman goddess Proserpine, a divinity of dual nature. She was abducted by Pluto, king of the underworld. Ceres, her mother, pleaded for her, and she was allowed back to earth, but not permanently. Because she had eaten while in the land of the dead, she had to return there for a portion of the year. Her absence from earth was winter; her return, spring. For the speaker of the 'Hymn', the retreating paganism involves sensual pleasures that Christianity does not tolerate. It means the loss of the pleasuring body.

Swinburne's use of the monologue to investigate historical speakers who are at once individual and representative of a phase of history, and to explore transitional moments in the history of faith, can be compared to Robert Browning's handling of the form. 'Hymn to Proserpine' could be read specifically in relation to Browning's 'An Epistle Containing the Strange Medical Experience of Karshish, the Arab Physician' (1855), a poem about a pagan man of medicine's encounter with Christianity. Swinburne's sympathies, unlike in Browning's more even-handed monologue, are clearly with the routed paganism and its suggestive relationship with the modern.

The position of Victorian Classical studies and the place of myth in the period provide other contexts for the 'Hymn'. Where the disciplines of Greek and Latin were associated in the mid-century with establishment values – the male preserves of the public schools, the ancient universities of Oxford and Cambridge, the law, the clergy – Swinburne's approach to Roman history is to emphasize the subversive potential of pagan religion to critique the authority of Christianity. Myth here – the religion of Proserpine – is valued for its radical possibilities. For another dimension to Swinburne's approach to the Classical world and its myths, see '*Ave Atque Vale*: In Memory of Charles Baudelaire', 500–6. On the association between the pagan and the sexual, see 'Anactoria', 480–6. Swinburne returned to the subject of 'Hymn to Proserpine' in 'The Last Oracle', from *Poems and Ballads, Second Series* (1878), a volume variously concerned with forms of endurance and survival, not least the continuance of the poet's words.

Text: *Poems and Ballads* (1866).

Vicisti, Galilæe[1]

I have lived long enough,[2] having seen one thing, that love hath an end;
Goddess and maiden and queen,[3] be near me now and befriend.
Thou art more than the day or the morrow, the seasons that laugh or that weep;
For these give joy and sorrow; but thou, Proserpina, sleep.
Sweet is the treading of wine, and sweet the feet of the dove; 5
But a goodlier gift is thine than foam of the grapes or love.
Yea, is not even Apollo,[4] with hair and harpstring of gold,
A bitter God to follow,[5] a beautiful God to behold?
I am sick of singing: the bays[6] burn deep and chafe: I am fain[7]
To rest a little from praise and grievous pleasure and pain. 10
For the Gods we know not of, who give us our daily breath,
We know they are cruel as love or life, and lovely as death.
O Gods dethroned and deceased, cast forth, wiped out in a day!
From your wrath is the world released, redeemed from your chains, men say.
New Gods are crowned in the city; their flowers have broken your rods; 15
They are merciful, clothed with pity, the young compassionate Gods.
But for me their new device[8] is barren, the days are bare;
Things long past over suffice, and men forgotten that were.
Time and the Gods are at strife; ye dwell in the midst thereof,
Draining a little life from the barren breasts of love. 20
I say to you, cease, take rest; yea, I say to you all, be at peace,
Till the bitter milk of her breast and the barren bosom shall cease.
Wilt thou yet take all, Galilean? but these thou shalt not take,

[1] *Vicisti, Galilæe* see headnote, 476.
[2] *I have lived long enough* cf. 'I have lived long enough. My way of life / Is fall'n into the sere, the yellow leaf', *Macbeth* 5.3.24–5.
[3] *queen* note the internal rhyme at the end of the third foot throughout.
[4] *Apollo* one of the 12 great Olympian gods, god of

prophecy, patron of music and arts. He is associated with the lyre, a form of handheld harp.
[5] *bitter God to follow* because so ideal, and quick to avenge slights.
[6] *bays* laurel crown he wears as a singer.
[7] *fain* content, willing.
[8] *device* emblematic figure or design for a heraldic bearing.

The laurel, the palms and the pæan,[9] the breasts of the nymphs[10] in the brake;[11]
    Breasts more soft than a dove's, that tremble with tenderer breath;   25
    And all the wings of the Loves, and all the joy before death;
        All the feet of the hours that sound as a single lyre,
    Dropped and deep in the flowers, with strings that flicker like fire.
    More than these wilt thou give, things fairer than all these things?
        Nay, for a little we live, and life hath mutable wings.   30
        A little while and we die; shall life not thrive as it may?
    For no man under the sky lives twice, outliving his day.
And grief is a grievous thing, and a man hath enough of his tears:
    Why should he labour, and bring fresh grief to blacken his years?
Thou hast conquered, O pale Galilean; the world has grown grey from thy breath;   35
    We have drunken of things Lethean,[12] and fed on the fullness of death.
        Laurel is green for a season, and love is sweet for a day;
    But love grows bitter with treason, and laurel outlives not May.
Sleep, shall we sleep after all? for the world is not sweet in the end;
    For the old faiths loosen and fall, the new years ruin and rend.   40
Fate is a sea without shore, and the soul is a rock that abides;[13]
But her[14] ears are vexed with the roar and her face with the foam of the tides.
O lips that the live blood faints in, the leavings of racks and rods![15]
    O ghastly glories of saints, dead limbs of gibbeted Gods![16]
——— Though all men abase them before you[17] in spirit, and all knees bend,[18]   45
    I kneel not neither adore you, but standing, look to the end.
All delicate days and pleasant, all spirits and sorrows are cast
Far out with the foam of the present that sweeps to the surf of the past:
    Where beyond the extreme sea-wall, and between the remote sea-gates,
    Waste water washes, and tall ships founder, and deep death waits: 50
Where, mighty with deepening sides, clad about with the seas as with wings,
    And impelled of invisible tides, and fulfilled[19] of unspeakable things,
    White-eyed and poisonous-finned, shark-toothed and serpentine-curled,
Rolls, under the whitening wind of the future, the wave of the world.
    The depths stand naked in sunder behind it, the storms flee away;   55
    In the hollow before it the thunder is taken and snared as a prey;
    In its sides is the north-wind bound; and its salt is of all men's tears;
    With light of ruin, and sound of changes, and pulse of years:
    With travail[20] of day after day, and with trouble of hour upon hour;
And bitter as blood is the spray; and the crests are as fangs that devour: 60
And its vapour and storm of its steam as the sighing of spirits to be;
And its noise as the noise in a dream; and its depth as the roots of the sea:
And the height of its heads as the height of the utmost stars of the air:
And the ends of the earth at the might thereof tremble, and time is made bare.
Will ye bridle the deep sea with reins, will ye chasten the high sea with rods?   65

---

[9] *pæan* hymn to Apollo.
[10] *nymphs* semi-divine figures, often represented as beautiful women, and associated with particular places, streams, trees.
[11] *brake* bushes, bracken.
[12] *Lethean* Lethe is the river of forgetfulness in Classical mythology.
[13] *rock that abides* cf. Jesus's words: 'Therefore, whosoeuer heareth these sayings of mine, and doeth them, I wil liken him vnto a wise man, which built his house vpon a rocke: And the raine descended, and the floods came, and the windes blew, and beat vpon that house: and it fell not, for it was founded vpon a rocke', Matthew 7.24–5.

[14] *her* the soul.
[15] *racks and rods* instruments of torture for the Christians.
[16] *O ghastly . . . Gods* martyrs and the crucified Jesus.
[17] *you* Jesus.
[18] *knees bend* cf. 'Wherefore God also hath highly exalted him, and giuen him a Name which is aboue euery name: That at the Name of Iesus euery knee should bow', Philippians 2.9–10.
[19] *fulfilled* filled full.
[20] *travail* labour.

Will ye take her to chain her with chains, who is older than all ye Gods?
   All ye as a wind shall go by, as a fire shall ye pass and be past;
Ye are Gods, and behold, ye shall die, and the waves be upon you at last.
   In the darkness of time, in the deeps of the years, in the changes of things,
Ye shall sleep as a slain man sleeps, and the world shall forget you for kings.   70
Though the feet of thine high priests tread where thy lords and our forefathers trod,
   Though these that were Gods are dead, and thou being dead[21] art a God,
Though before thee the throned Cytherean[22] be fallen, and hidden her head,
   Yet thy kingdom shall pass, Galilean, thy dead shall go down to thee dead.
Of the maiden thy mother[23] men sing as a goddess with grace clad around;   75
   Thou art throned where another was king; where another was queen she is crowned.
Yea, once we had sight of another: but now she is queen, say these.
   Not as thine, not as thine was our mother,[24] a blossom of flowering seas,
Clothed round with the world's desire as with raiment, and fair as the foam,
   And fleeter than kindled fire, and a goddess, and mother of Rome.[25]   80
For thine came pale and a maiden, and sister to sorrow;[26] but ours,
   Her deep hair heavily laden with odour and colour of flowers,
   White rose of the rose-white water, a silver splendour, a flame,
Bent down unto us that besought her, and earth grew sweet with her name.
   For thine came weeping, a slave among slaves, and rejected; but she   85
Came flushed from the full-flushed wave, and imperial, her foot on the sea.[27]
   And the wonderful waters knew her, the winds and the viewless ways,
   And the roses grew rosier, and bluer the sea-blue stream of the bays.
Ye are fallen, our lords, by what token? we wist[28] that ye should not fall.
   Ye were all so fair that are broken; and one more fair than ye all.   90
But I turn to her still, having seen she shall surely abide in the end;
   Goddess and maiden and queen, be near me now and befriend.
O daughter of earth,[29] of my mother, her crown and blossom of birth,
   I am also, I also, thy brother; I go as I came unto earth.
In the night where thine eyes are as moons are in heaven, the night where thou art,   95
   Where the silence is more than all tunes, where sleep overflows from the heart,
Where the poppies[30] are sweet as the rose in our world, and the red rose is white,
   And the wind falls faint as it blows with the fume of the flowers of the night,
And the murmur of spirits that sleep in the shadow of Gods from afar
   Grows dim in thine ears and deep as the deep dim soul of a star,   100
In the sweet low light of thy face, under heavens untrod by the sun,
Let my soul with their souls find place, and forget what is done and undone.
Thou art more than the Gods who number the days of our temporal breath;
   For these give labour and slumber; but thou, Proserpina, death.
Therefore now at thy feet I abide for a season in silence. I know   105
   I shall die as my fathers died, and sleep as they sleep; even so.
For the glass of the years is brittle wherein we gaze for a span;
   A little soul for a little bears up this corpse which is man.
So long I endure, no longer; and laugh not again, neither weep.
For there is no God found stronger than death; and death is a sleep.[31]   110

---

[21] *being dead* Jesus's death at Calvary.
[22] *Cytherean* Venus, goddess of beauty, sexual attraction and erotic love.
[23] *maiden thy mother* Virgin Mary.
[24] *our mother* Venus, who, as Aphrodite, was the mother of Aeneas, the legendary founder of the Roman race.
[25] *mother of Rome* see note 24.
[26] *sister to sorrow* Simeon told Mary: 'Yea a sword shall pearce thorow thy owne soule also', Luke 2.35.
[27] *but she . . . sea* Venus, born of the sea, was the product of contact between her father's dismembered genitals and the

foam (*aphros*) of the ocean into which they had been thrown.
[28] *wist* know.
[29] *daughter of earth* Proserpine's mother, Ceres, goddess of corn and the sustainer of life, was associated with the earth itself.
[30] *poppies* bringers of sleep, symbols of Proserpine.
[31] *death is a sleep* irony lies in the fact that the speaker's words are close to Christian theology: Jesus's resurrection made death a sleep, to be followed by eternal life (see, for instance, 1 Thessalonians 4.13–14).

Anactoria

The work of the Greek female lyric poet Sappho (b. late seventh century BC) survives, but only in fragments. It attracted a wide range of poets throughout the Victorian period, including Matthew Arnold, Robert Browning, Elizabeth Barrett Browning, Christina G. Rossetti and Tennyson: Michael Field, at the end of the century, found inspiration in her work for their poetry of woman–woman love in *Long Ago* (1889), a poem from which is included in the present anthology, 557–8. Swinburne regarded Sappho as a writer of genius, the 'supreme head of song', as he said in '*Ave Atque Vale*: In Memory of Charles Baudelaire', 500–6. She is the speaker of 'Anactoria' (*Poems and Ballads*, 1866). As for other poets, Swinburne is particularly interested in Sappho and posterity, the fortune of poetic survival. Sappho's confidence that her reputation will endure expresses both something of Swinburne's regard for her, and displaced anxieties and aspirations about his own legacy (cf. '*Ave Atque Vale*' as another consideration of poetic legacy).

Anactoria was a woman loved by Sappho, and Swinburne's erotic poem uses a Classical setting to investigate lesbian desire (Sappho lived on the isle of Lesbos, from where the term derives). Indeed, 'Anactoria' was the first important poetic representation in English of Sappho – hitherto edited into heterosexuality – as a lesbian. As with 'Hymn to Proserpine', 476–9, Swinburne's approach to Classical subjects enables controversial representations. In its engagement with sado-masochism, 'Anactoria' reveals the influence of Swinburne's reading of the Marquis de Sade's *La nouvelle Justine; ou, Les Malheurs de la vertu* (usually translated as *The New Justine; or Good Conduct Well Chastised*) (1797) in 1862. The poem is one of the most prominent instances of de Sade's legacy in Victorian poetry. Swinburne also uses fragments from Sappho's own 'Ode to Anactoria' ('To a Beloved Woman'), a poem that expresses Sappho's fierce jealousy.

The sexual nature of 'Anactoria', its driven and intense eroticism, is its most obvious feature, but it is also a meditation on poetic fame and an outburst against divine governance of the world. Like 'Hymn to Proserpine', it is a poem concerned with the changing nature of religious faith. Swinburne recreates a moment in the history of human belief when the gods are accepted as real personalities: the difficulty of tracking the pronouns in the poem indicates how, in this radically different religious society, living human beings and gods/goddesses are readily confused. Swinburne's poem explores the dense textures of impassioned speech, its language abundant, excessive, intoxicated, though, as the surviving drafts of the poem indicate, also most carefully worked out. For another response to Anactoria, see 'Anaktoria' in Frederick Tennyson's *The Isles of Greece: Sappho and Alcæus* (1890).

Text: *Poems and Ballads* (1866).

τίνος αὐ τύ πειθοῖ μὰψ σαγηνεύσας φιλότατα Sappho[1]

My life is bitter with thy love; thine eyes
Blind me, thy tresses[2] burn me, thy sharp sighs
Divide my flesh and spirit with soft sound,
And my blood strengthens, and my veins abound.
I pray thee sigh not, speak not, draw not breath;   5
Let life burn down, and dream it is not death.
I would the sea had hidden us, the fire
(Wilt thou fear that, and fear not my desire?)
Severed the bones that bleach, the flesh that cleaves,
And let our sifted ashes drop like leaves.   10
I feel thy blood against my blood: my pain
Pains thee, and lips bruise lips, and vein stings vein.
Let fruit be crushed on fruit, let flower on flower,

---

[1] τίνος αὐ τύ πειθοῖ μὰψ σαγηνεύσας φιλότατα 'Whose love have you caught in vain by persuasion?'

[2] *tresses* braids of hair.

Breast kindle breast, and either burn one hour.
Why wilt thou follow lesser loves?[3] are thine   15
Too weak to bear these hands and lips of mine?
I charge thee for my life's sake, O too sweet
To crush love with thy cruel faultless feet,
I charge thee keep thy lips from hers or his,
Sweetest, till theirs be sweeter than my kiss: 20
Lest I too lure, a swallow for a dove,
Erotion[4] or Erinna[5] to my love.

I would my love could kill thee; I am satiated
With seeing the live, and fain[6] would have thee dead.
I would earth had thy body as fruit to eat,   25
And no mouth but some serpent's found thee sweet.
I would find grievous ways to have thee slain,
Intense device, and superflux of pain;
Vex thee with amorous agonies, and shake
Life at thy lips, and leave it there to ache;   30
Strain out thy soul with pangs too soft to kill,
Intolerable interludes, and infinite ill;
Relapse and reluctation[7] of the breath,
Dumb tunes and shuddering semitones[8] of death.
I am weary of all thy words and soft strange ways,   35
Of all love's fiery nights and all his days,
And all the broken kisses salt as brine
That shuddering lips make moist with waterish wine,
And eyes the bluer for all those hidden hours
That pleasure fills with tears and feeds from flowers,   40
Fierce at the heart with fire that half comes through,
But all the flowerlike white stained round with blue;
The fervent underlid, and that above
Lifted with laughter or abashed with love;
Thine amorous girdle, full of thee and fair,   45
And leavings of the lilies in thine hair.
Yea, all sweet words of thine and all thy ways,
And all the fruit of nights and flower of days,
And stinging lips wherein the hot sweet brine
That Love was born of burns and foams like wine,   50
And eyes insatiable of amorous hours,
Fervent as fire and delicate as flowers,
Coloured like night at heart, but cloven through
Like night with flame, dyed round like night with blue,
Clothed with deep eyelids under and above –   55
Yea, all thy beauty sickens me with love;
Thy girdle empty of thee and now not fair,
And ruinous lilies in thy languid hair.
Ah, take no thought for Love's[9] sake; shall this be,

[3] *lesser loves* in one of her fragments, Sappho suggests
Anactoria married.
[4] *Erotion* little cupid, male lover.
[5] *Erinna* Greek woman poet, probably of fourth century BC,
often (and clearly wrongly) thought in the Victorian period
to have been one of Sappho's lovers; cf. Simeon Solomon's
Sappho and Erinna in a Garden at Mytilene (1864).

[6] *fain* gladly.
[7] *reluctation* struggle, resistance.
[8] *semitone* smallest interval between two notes in western
music.
[9] *Love* Aphrodite, Greek goddess of erotic love.

And she who loves thy lover not love thee?[10]   60
Sweet soul, sweet mouth of all that laughs and lives,
 Mine is she, very mine; and she forgives.
 For I beheld in sleep the light that is
 In her high place in Paphos,[11] heard the kiss
Of body and soul that mix with eager tears   65
And laughter stinging through the eyes and ears;
Saw Love, as burning flame from crown to feet,
 Imperishable, upon her storied seat;
Clear eyelids lifted toward the north and south,
 A mind of many colours, and a mouth   70
 Of many tunes and kisses; and she bowed,
 With all her subtle face laughing aloud,
Bowed down upon me, saying, 'Who doth thee wrong,
 Sappho?' but thou – thy[12] body is the song,
 Thy mouth the music; thou art more than I,   75
Though my voice die not till the whole world die;
Though men that hear it madden; though love weep,
Though nature change, though shame be charmed to sleep.
 Ah, wilt thou slay me lest I kiss thee dead?
Yet the queen laughed from her sweet heart and said: 80
 'Even she that flies shall follow for thy sake,
 And she shall give thee gifts that would not take,
Shall kiss that would not kiss thee' (yca, kiss me)[13]
'When thou wouldst not' – when I would not kiss thee!

 Ah, more to me than all men as thou[14] art,   85
 Shall not my songs assuage her[15] at the heart?
 Ah, sweet to me as life seems sweet to death,
Why should her wrath fill thee with fearful breath?
 Nay, sweet, for is she[16] God alone? hath she
 Made earth and all the centuries of the sea,   90
Taught the sun ways to travel, woven most fine
The moonbeams, shed the starbeams forth as wine,
Bound with her myrtles,[17] beaten with her rods,
The young men and the maidens and the gods?
Have we not lips to love with, eyes for tears,   95
And summer and flower of women and of years?
 Stars for the foot of morning, and for noon
 Sunlight, and exaltation of the moon;
 Waters that answer waters, fields that wear
 Lilies, and languor of the Lesbian[18] air?   100
 Beyond those flying feet of fluttered doves,
 Are there not other gods for other loves?
Yea, though she scourge thee, sweetest, for my sake,
Blossom not thorns and flowers not blood should break.
 Ah that my lips were tuneless lips, but pressed   105
To the bruised blossom of thy scourged white breast!

[10] *she who . . . thee* with the sense that she [Sappho] who loves a follower of Aphrodite [Anactoria] must also love Aphrodite herself.

[11] *Paphos* in Cyprus, where Aphrodite was thought to have come ashore (she was born from the sea).

[12] *thy* Sappho addresses Anactoria.

[13] *yea, kiss me* aside addressed by Sappho to Anactoria.

[14] *thou* Anactoria.

[15] *her* Aphrodite.

[16] *she* Aphrodite.

[17] *myrtles* common south European shrubs, sacred to Aphrodite.

[18] *Lesbian* of the isle of Lesbos, Sappho's home.

Ah that my mouth for Muses'[19] milk were fed
On the sweet blood thy sweet small wounds had bled!
That with my tongue I felt them, and could taste
    The faint flakes from thy bosom to the waist!   110
That I could drink thy veins as wine, and eat
Thy breasts like honey! that from face to feet
    Thy body were abolished and consumed,
    And in my flesh thy very flesh entombed!

    Ah, ah, thy beauty! like a beast it bites,   115
    Stings like an adder, like an arrow smites.
Ah sweet, and sweet again, and seven times sweet,
    The paces and the pauses of thy feet!
    Ah sweeter than all sleep or summer air
    The fallen fillets[20] fragrant from thine hair!   120
Yea, though their alien kisses do me wrong,
Sweeter thy lips than mine with all their song;
Thy shoulders whiter than a fleece of white,
And flower-sweet fingers, good to bruise or bite
    As honeycomb of the inmost honey-cells,   125
With almond-shaped and roseleaf-coloured shells
    And blood like purple blossom at the tips
    Quivering; and pain made perfect in thy lips
    For my sake when I hurt thee; O that I
    Durst crush thee out of life with love, and die,   130
    Die of thy pain and my delight, and be
    Mixed with thy blood and molten into thee!
    Would I not plague thee dying overmuch?
    Would I not hurt thee perfectly? not touch
Thy pores of sense with torture, and make bright   135
Thine eyes with bloodlike tears and grievous light?
Strike pang from pang as note is struck from note,
    Catch the sob's middle music in thy throat,
Take thy limbs living, and new-mould with these
    A lyre[21] of many faultless agonies?   140
Feed thee with fever and famine and fine drouth,[22]
    With perfect pangs convulse thy perfect mouth,
    Make thy life shudder in thee and burn afresh,
    And wring thy very spirit through the flesh?
Cruel? but love makes all that love him well   145
    As wise as heaven and crueller than hell.
    Me hath love made more bitter toward thee
Than death toward man; but were I made as he[23]
Who hath made all things to break them one by one,
    If my feet trod upon the stars and sun   150
    And souls of men as his have alway trod,
    God knows I might be crueller than God.
For who shall change with prayers or thanksgivings
    The mystery of the cruelty of things?
    Or say what God above all gods and years   155

---

[19] *Muses* divinities on whom mortals depend for inspiration.
[20] *fillets* headbands.
[21] *lyre* early form of harp, associated with poetry.
[22] *drouth* drought.
[23] *he* Zeus, king of gods.

With offering and blood-sacrifice of tears,
With lamentation from strange lands, from graves
Where the snake pastures, from scarred mouths of slaves,
From prison, and from plunging prows of ships
Through flamelike foam of the sea's closing lips –   160
With thwartings of strange signs, and wind-blown hair
Of comets, desolating the dim air,
When darkness is made fast with seals and bars,
And fierce reluctance of disastrous stars,
Eclipse, and sound of shaken hills, and wings   165
Darkening, and blind inexpiable[24] things –
With sorrow of labouring moons, and altering light
And travail[25] of the planets of the night,
And weeping of the weary Pleiads seven,[26]
Feeds the mute melancholy lust of heaven?   170
Is not his incense bitterness, his meat
Murder? his hidden face and iron feet
Hath not man known, and felt them on their way
Threaten and trample all things and every day?
Hath he not sent us hunger? who hath cursed   175
Spirit and flesh with longing? filled with thirst
Their lips who cried unto him? who bade exceed
The fervid[27] will, fall short the feeble deed,
Bade sink the spirit and the flesh aspire,
Pain animate the dust of dead desire,   180
And life yield up her flower to violent fate?
Him would I reach, him smite, him desecrate,
Pierce the cold lips of God with human breath,
And mix his immortality with death.
Why hath he made us? what had all we done   185
That we should live and loathe the sterile sun,
And with the moon wax paler as she wanes,
And pulse by pulse feel time grow through our veins?
Thee[28] too the years shall cover; thou shalt be
As the rose born of one same blood with thee,   190
As a song sung, as a word said, and fall
Flower-wise, and be not any more at all,
Nor any memory of thee anywhere;
For never Muse has bound above thine hair
The high Pierian[29] flower[30] whose graft outgrows   195
All summer kinship of the mortal rose
And colour of deciduous[31] days, nor shed
Reflex and flush of heaven about thine head,
Nor reddened brows made pale by floral grief
With splendid shadow from that lordlier leaf.   200
Yea, thou shalt be forgotten like spilt wine,
Except these kisses of my lips on thine
Brand them with immortality; but me –

---

[24] *inexpiable* unpardonable.

[25] *travail* labour.

[26] *Pleiads seven* the mournful daughters of Atlas, metamorphosed into the star cluster, the Pleiades.

[27] *fervid* passionate, zealous.

[28] *Thee* Anactoria.

[29] *Pierian* of Pieria, where the Muses were born.

[30] *Pierian flower* tribute from the Muses.

[31] *deciduous* fleeting, transitory.

Men shall not see bright fire nor hear the sea,
Nor mix their hearts with music, nor behold 205
Cast forth of heaven, with feet of awful gold
And plumeless wings that make the bright air blind,
Lightning, with thunder for a hound behind
Hunting through fields unfurrowed and unsown,
But in the light and laughter, in the moan 210
And music, and in grasp of lip and hand
And shudder of water that makes felt on land
The immeasurable tremor of all the sea,
Memories shall mix and metaphors of me.
Like me shall be the shuddering calm of night, 215
When all the winds of the world for pure delight
Close lips that quiver and fold up wings that ache;
When nightingales are louder for love's sake,
And leaves tremble like lute-strings or like fire;
Like me the one star swooning with desire 220
Even at the cold lips of the sleepless moon,
As I at thine; like me the waste white noon,
Burnt through with barren sunlight; and like me
The land-stream and the tide-stream in the sea.
I am sick with time as these with ebb and flow, 225
And by the yearning in my veins I know
The yearning sound of waters; and mine eyes
Burn as that beamless fire which fills the skies
With troubled stars and travailing things of flame;
And in my heart the grief consuming them 230
Labours, and in my veins the thirst of these,
And all the summer travail of the trees
And all the winter sickness; and the earth,
Filled full with deadly works of death and birth,
Sore spent with hungry lusts of birth and death, 235
Has pain like mine in her divided breath;
Her spring of leaves is barren, and her fruit
Ashes; her boughs are burdened, and her root
Fibrous and gnarled with poison; underneath
Serpents have gnawn it through with tortuous teeth 240
Made sharp upon the bones of all the dead,
And wild birds rend her branches overhead.
These, woven as raiment for his word and thought,
These hath God made, and me as these, and wrought
Song, and hath lit it at my lips; and me 245
Earth shall not gather though she feed on thee.

As a shed tear shalt thou be shed; but I –
Lo, earth may labour, men live long and die,
Years change and stars, and the high God devise
New things, and old things wane before his eyes 250
Who wields and wrecks them, being more strong than they –
But, having made me, me he shall not slay.
Nor slay nor satiate, like those herds of his
Who laugh and live a little, and their kiss
Contents them, and their loves are swift and sweet, 255
And sure death grasps and gains them with slow feet,
Love they or hate they, strive or bow their knees –

And all these end; he hath his will of these.
Yea, but albeit he slay me, hating me –
Albeit he hide me in the deep dear sea[32]   260
And cover me with cool wan foam, and ease
This soul of mine as any soul of these,
And give me water and great sweet waves, and make
The very sea's name lordlier for my sake,
The whole sea sweeter – albeit I die indeed   265
And hide myself and sleep and no man heed,
Of me the high God hath not all his will.
Blossom of branches, and on each high hill
Clear air and wind, and under in clamorous vales
Fierce noises of the fiery nightingales,   270
Buds burning in the sudden spring like fire,
The wan washed sand and the waves' vain desire,
Sails seen like blown white flowers at sea, and words
That bring tears swiftest, and long notes of birds
Violently singing till the whole world sings –   275
I Sappho shall be one with all these things,
With all high things for ever; and my face
Seen once, my songs once heard in a strange place,
Cleave to men's lives, and waste the days thereof
With gladness and much sadness and long love.   280
Yea, thcy shall say, earth's womb has borne in vain
New things, and never this best thing again;
Borne days and men, borne fruits and wars and wine,
Seasons and songs, but no song more like mine.
And they shall know me as ye who have known me here,   285
Last year when I loved Atthis,[33] and this year
When I love thee; and they shall praise me, and say
'She hath all time as all we have our day,
Shall she not live and have her will' – even I?
Yea, though thou diest, I say I shall not die.   290
For these shall give me of their souls, shall give
Life, and the days and loves wherewith I live,
Shall quicken me with loving, fill with breath,
Save me and serve me, strive for me with death.
Alas, that neither moon nor snow nor dew   295
Nor all cold things can purge me wholly through,
Assuage me nor allay me nor appease,
Till supreme sleep shall bring me bloodless ease;
Till time wax faint in all his periods;
Till fate undo the bondage of the gods,   300
And lay, to slake and satiate me all through,
Lotus[34] and Lethe[35] on my lips like dew,
And shed around and over and under me
Thick darkness and the insuperable sea.[36]

---

[32] *Yea, but . . . sea* allusion to the heterosexual tradition, derived largely from Ovid's *Heroides*, that Sappho threw herself off the Leucadian cliffs for love of Phaon, a ferryman.

[33] *Atthis* Athenian woman to whom Sappho addressed a number of poems.

[34] *Lotus* plant inducing dreamy forgetfulness (cf. Tennyson, 'The Lotos-Eaters', 66–71).

[35] *Lethe* river of forgetfulness.

[36] *insuperable sea* cf. the sea into which Sappho jumps in the Ovidian version of her story (see note 32).

Laus Veneris

Swinburne's choice of the Tannhäuser story (pronounced 'Tanhoyser') as the basis for 'Laus Veneris', from *Poems and Ballads* (1866), enabled him to deal with a provocative narrative of sexual desire, corporeality and the rejection of Christianity without the narrowness of a modern setting. The mythic status of the hero relieved the need for psychological realism and meant that Swinburne could investigate human passion on a scale that belonged to the realms of legend (and which had already attracted the composer Richard Wagner, whose music drama *Tannhäuser* was first performed in 1845). The Tannhäuser story, found in the sixteenth-century German poem *Tannhäuserlied*, concerns a poet (Swinburne makes him simply a knight) who is, one day, entranced by a beautiful woman. She is Venus and entices him to her grotto in the heart of a mountain where he spends the next seven years in revelry. On leaving her, he makes for Rome to seek the forgiveness of the Pope. But the Pope replies that it is no more possible for Tannhäuser to be forgiven than for his (the Pope's) staff to blossom. Three days later, the staff does break into flower and the Pope urgently sends for the unforgiven man. But he is not to be found. Tannhäuser has returned to Venus.

Swinburne's poem – its title means 'in praise of Venus' – weaves sexual desire, guilt and a longing for death into highly patterned lyricism that at once distracts from close reading and rewards it. The poem is not a dramatic monologue in the manner of Tennyson and Browning, as it hardly involves their classic dynamic of sympathy and judgement, but rather a dramatic poem in which a particular extreme of emotion and spiritual anxiety is made available for scrutiny. The poem hyperbolizes Keats's sensuous language and transforms his meditation on the link between pain and pleasure in the 'Melancholy' ode into an extended eroticism bound up with a sense of sin – Swinburne's first line signifies the poem's Keatsian inheritance at once by recalling the last line of 'Ode to a Nightingale'. Swinburne's stanza form recalls Edward Fitzgerald's sensuous translation of *The Rubáiyát of Omar Khayyám* (1859). The powerful sexuality of 'Laus Veneris' invites comparison with the sadism of Swinburne's 'Anactoria', 480–6. Edward Burne Jones's controversial painting *Laus Veneris* (1868) concerned the same subject; William Morris's *The Earthly Paradise* (1868–70) included a version of the Tannhäuser narrative as 'The Hill of Venus'. The story is sharp-edged in the context of early and mid-Victorian medievalism. Where Pugin and Ruskin and many others had admired the Middle Ages as the period of intense Christian faith, the *Tannhäuserlied* insists on the continuation of pagan divinity – Venus – into the heart of the medieval. Other nineteenth-century poets who wrote on this legend include John Davidson in 'A New Ballad of Tannhäuser', the New York Jewish poet Emma Lazarus's 'Tannhäuser' and Eugene Lee-Hamilton's 'Tannhäuser to Venus', from his *Imaginary Sonnets* (see 553–6 for other poems from this volume included in the present anthology).

Text: *Poems and Ballads* (1866; I omit the long French epigraph which narrates the Tannhäuser story).

Asleep or waking is it? for her neck,
Kissed over close, wears yet a purple speck
Wherein the pained blood falters and goes out;
Soft, and stung softly – fairer for a fleck.

2

But though my lips shut sucking on the place,   5
There is no vein at work upon her face;
Her eyelids are so peaceable, no doubt
Deep sleep has warmed her blood through all its ways.

3

Lo, this is she that was the world's delight;
The old grey years were parcels of her might;   10
The strewings of the ways wherein she trod
Were the twain seasons of the day and night.

4

Lo, she was thus when her clear limbs enticed
All lips that now grow sad with kissing Christ,
Stained with blood fallen from the feet of God,
The feet and hands[1] whereat our souls were priced.[2]   15

5

Alas, Lord, surely thou art great and fair.
But lo her wonderfully woven hair!
And thou didst heal us with thy piteous kiss;
But see now, Lord; her mouth is lovelier.   20

6

She is right fair; what hath she done to thee?
Nay, fair Lord Christ, lift up thine eyes and see;
Had now thy mother[3] such a lip – like this?
Thou knowest how sweet a thing it is to me.

7

Inside the Horsel[4] here the air is hot;   25
Right little peace one hath for it, God wot;[5]
The scented dusty daylight burns the air,
And my heart chokes me till I hear it not.

8

Behold, my Venus, my soul's body, lies
With my love laid upon her garment-wise,   30
Feeling my love in all her limbs and hair
And shed between her eyelids through her eyes.

9

She holds my heart in her sweet open hands
Hanging asleep; hard by her head there stands,
Crowned with gilt thorns and clothed with flesh like fire,   35
Love, wan[6] as foam blown up the salt burnt sands –

10

Hot as the brackish waifs of yellow spume[7]
That shift and steam – loose clots of arid fume
From the sea's panting mouth of dry desire;
There stands he,[8] like one labouring at a loom.   40

11

The warp[9] holds fast across; and every thread
That makes the woof[10] up has dry specks of red;
Always the shuttle cleaves clean through, and he
Weaves with the hair of many a ruined head.

---

[1] *feet and hands* injured at the Crucifixion.
[2] *souls were priced* Jesus's death redeemed humankind from its sins.
[3] *mother* the Virgin Mary.
[4] *Horsel* the Hörselberg, mountain in Thuringia where Venus's grotto was.
[5] *wot* knows.
[6] *wan* pale.
[7] *spume* foam.
[8] *he* i.e., Love.
[9] *warp* threads which are extended lengthwise in the loom.
[10] *woof* threads that cross from side to side of a web, at right angles to the warp.

12

Love is not glad nor sorry, as I deem;   45
Labouring he dreams, and labours in the dream,
Till when the spool is finished, lo I see
His web, reeled off, curls and goes out like steam.

13

Night falls like fire; the heavy lights run low,
And as they drop, my blood and body so   50
Shake as the flame shakes, full of days and hours
That sleep not neither weep they as they go.

14

Ah yet would God this flesh of mine might be
Where air might wash and long leaves cover me,
Where tides of grass break into foam of flowers,   55
Or where the wind's feet shine along the sea.

15

Ah yet would God that stems and roots were bred
Out of my weary body and my head,
That sleep were sealed upon me with a seal,
And I were as the least of all his dead.   60

16

Would God my blood were dew to feed the grass,
Mine ears made deaf and mine eyes blind as glass,
    My body broken as a turning wheel,
And my mouth stricken ere it saith Alas!

17

Ah God, that love were as a flower or flame,   65
That life were as the naming of a name,
That death were not more pitiful than desire,
That these things were not one thing and the same!

18

Behold now, surely somewhere there is death:
For each man hath some space of years, he saith,   70
    A little space of time ere time expire,
    A little day, a little way of breath.

19

And lo, between the sundawn and the sun,
His day's work and his night's work are undone;
And lo, between the nightfall and the light,   75
He is not, and none knoweth of such an one.

20

Ah God, that I were as all souls that be,
    As any herb or leaf of any tree,
As men that toil through hours of labouring night,
    As bones of men under the deep sharp sea.   80

21

Outside it must be winter among men;
For at the gold bars of the gates again
I heard all night and all the hours of it
The wind's wet wings and fingers drip with rain.

22

Knights gather, riding sharp for cold; I know
The ways and woods are strangled with the snow;
And with short song the maidens spin and sit
Until Christ's birthnight, lily-like, arow.[11]

85

23

The scent and shadow shed about me make
The very soul in all my senses ache;
The hot hard night is fed upon my breath,
And sleep beholds me from afar awake.

90

24

Alas, but surely where the hills grow deep,
Or where the wild ways of the sea are steep,
Or in strange places somewhere there is death,
And on death's face the scattered hair of sleep.

95

25

There lover-like with lips and limbs that meet
They lie, they pluck sweet fruit of life and eat;
But me the hot and hungry days devour,
And in my mouth no fruit of theirs is sweet.

100

26

No fruit of theirs, but fruit of my desire,
For her love's sake whose lips through mine respire;
Her eyelids on her eyes like flower on flower,
Mine eyelids on mine eyes like fire on fire.

27

So lie we, not as sleep that lies by death,
With heavy kisses and with happy breath;
Not as man lies by woman, when the bride
Laughs low for love's sake and the words he saith.

105

28

For she lies, laughing low with love; she lies
And turns his kisses on her lips to sighs,
To sighing sound of lips unsatisfied,
And the sweet tears are tender with her eyes.

110

29

Ah, not as they, but as the souls that were
Slain in the old time, having found her fair;
Who, sleeping with her lips upon their eyes,
Heard sudden serpents hiss across her hair.

115

[11] *arow* in a row.

30
Their blood runs round the roots of time like rain:
She casts them forth and gathers them again;
With nerve and bone she weaves and multiplies
Exceeding pleasure out of extreme pain. 120

31
Her little chambers drip with flower-like red,
Her girdles, and the chaplets[12] of her head,
Her armlets and her anklets; with her feet
She tramples all that winepress of the dead.

32
Her gateways smoke with fume of flowers and fires, 125
With loves burnt out and unassuaged[13] desires;
Between her lips the steam of them is sweet,
The languor in her ears of many lyres.[14]

33
Her beds are full of perfume and sad sound,
Her doors are made with music, and barred round 130
With sighing and with laughter and with tears,
With tears whereby strong souls of men are bound.

34
There is the knight Adonis[15] that was slain;
With flesh and blood she chains him for a chain;
The body and the spirit in her ears 135
Cry, for her lips divide him vein by vein.

35
Yea, all she slayeth; yea, every man save me;
Me, love, thy lover that must cleave to thee
Till the ending of the days and ways of earth,
The shaking of the sources of the sea. 140

36
Me, most forsaken of all souls that fell;[16]
Me, satiated with things insatiable;
Me, for whose sake the extreme hell makes mirth,
Yea, laughter kindles at the heart of hell.

37
Alas thy beauty! for thy mouth's sweet sake 145
My soul is bitter to me, my limbs quake
As water, as the flesh of men that weep,
As their heart's vein whose heart goes nigh to break.

38
Ah God, that sleep with flower-sweet finger-tips
Would crush the fruit of death upon my lips; 150

---

[12] *chaplets* wreaths for the head.
[13] *unassuaged* unsatisfied.
[14] *lyre* harp-like musical instrument.

[15] *Adonis* name suggestive of the Greek god of vegetation and fertility, who was remarkably beautiful.
[16] *most forsaken . . . fell* because refused pardon by the Pope.

Ah God, that death would tread the grapes of sleep
And wring their juice upon me as it drips.

39

There is no change of cheer for many days,
But change of chimes high up in the air, that sways
    Rung by the running fingers of the wind;   155
    And singing sorrows heard on hidden ways.

40

Day smiteth day in twain, night sundereth night,
    And on mine eyes the dark sits as the light;
Yea, Lord, thou knowest I know not, having sinned,
    If heaven be clean or unclean in thy sight.   160

41

Yea, as if earth were sprinkled over me,
Such chafed harsh earth as chokes a sandy sea,
Each pore doth yearn, and the dried blood thereof
    Gasps by sick fits, my heart swims heavily,

42

There is a feverish famine in my veins;   165
Below her bosom, where a crushed grape stains
The white and blue, there my lips caught and clove
    An hour since, and what mark of me remains?

43

I dare not always touch her, lest the kiss
Leave my lips charred. Yea, Lord, a little bliss,   170
    Brief bitter bliss, one hath for a great sin;
Nathless[17] thou knowest how sweet a thing it is.

44

Sin, is it sin whereby men's souls are thrust
    Into the pit? yet had I a good trust
    To save my soul before it slipped therein,   175
    Trod under by the fire-shod feet of lust.

45

For if mine eyes fail and my soul takes breath,
    I look between the iron sides of death
Into sad hell where all sweet love hath end,
    All but the pain that never finisheth.   180

46

There are the naked faces of great kings,
The singing folk with all their lute[18]-playings;
There when one cometh he shall have to friend
The grave that covets and the worm that clings.

---

[17] *Nathless* nevertheless.   [18] *lute* early guitar-like musical instrument.

47

There sit the knights that were so great of hand,   185
The ladies that were queens of fair green land,
Grown grey and black now, brought unto the dust,
Soiled, without raiment, clad about with sand.

48

There is one end for all of them; they sit
Naked and sad, they drink the dregs of it,   190
Trodden as grapes in the wine-press of lust,
Trampled and trodden by the fiery feet.

49

I see the marvellous mouth[19] whereby there fell
Cities and people whom the gods loved well,
Yet for her sake on them the fire gat hold,   195
And for their sakes on her the fire of hell.

50

And softer than the Egyptian lote-leaf[20] is,
The queen[21] whose face was worth the world to kiss,
Wearing at breast a suckling snake of gold;
And large pale lips of strong Semiramis,[22]   200

51

Curled like a tiger's that curl back to feed;
Red only where the last kiss made them bleed;
Her hair most thick with many a carven gem,
Deep in the mane, great-chested, like a steed.

52

Yea, with red sin the faces of them shine;   205
But in all these there was no sin like mine;
No, not in all the strange great sins of them
That made the wine-press froth and foam with wine.

53

For I was of Christ's choosing, I God's knight,
No blinkard[23] heathen stumbling for scant light;   210
I can well see, for all the dusty days
Gone past, the clean great time of goodly fight.

54

I smell the breathing battle sharp with blows,
With shriek of shafts and snapping short of bows;
The fair pure sword smites out in subtle ways,   215
Sounds and long lights are shed between the rows

---

[19] *marvellous mouth* of Helen of Troy, in legend the most beautiful woman in the world, whose abduction by Paris prompted the Trojan war.
[20] *lote-leaf* lotus leaf.

[21] *queen* Cleopatra, Queen of Egypt.
[22] *Semiramis* legendary Queen of Assyria.
[23] *blinkard* reproachful name for one who has imperfect sight.

55

Of beautiful mailed men; the edged light slips,
Most like a snake that takes short breath and dips
Sharp from the beautifully bending head,
With all its gracious body lithe as lips   220

56

That curl in touching you; right in this wise
My sword doth, seeming fire in mine own eyes,
Leaving all colours in them brown and red
And flecked with death; then the keen breaths like sighs,

57

The caught-up choked dry laughters following them,   225
When all the fighting face is grown a flame
For pleasure, and the pulse that stuns the ears,
And the heart's gladness of the goodly game.

58

Let me think yet a little; I do know
These things were sweet, but sweet such years ago,   230
Their savour is all turned now into tears;
Yea, ten years since, where the blue ripples blow,

59

The blue curled eddies of the blowing Rhine,[24]
I felt the sharp wind shaking grass and vine
Touch my blood too, and sting me with delight   235
Through all this waste and weary body of mine

60

That never feels clear air; right gladly then
I rode alone, a great way off my men,
And heard the chiming bridle smite and smite,
And gave each rhyme thereof some rhyme again,   240

61

Till my song shifted to that iron one;
Seeing there rode up between me and the sun
Some certain of my foe's men, for his three
White wolves across their painted coats did run.

62

The first red-bearded, with square cheeks – alack,   245
I made my knave's blood turn his beard to black;
The slaying of him was a joy to see:
Perchance too, when at night he came not back,

63

Some woman fell a-weeping, whom this thief
Would beat when he had drunken; yet small grief   250

---

[24] *Rhine* major German river.

Hath any for the ridding of such knaves;
Yea, if one wept, I doubt[25] her teen[26] was brief.

64
This bitter love is sorrow in all lands,
Draining of eyelids, wringing of drenched hands,
  Sighing of hearts and filling up of graves;   255
A sign across the head of the world he[27] stands,

65
An one that hath a plague-mark on his brows;
Dust and spilt blood do track him to his house
Down under earth; sweet smells of lip and cheek,
Like a sweet snake's breath made more poisonous   260

66
With chewing of some perfumed deadly grass,
Are shed all round his passage if he pass,
And their quenched savour leaves the whole soul weak,
Sick with keen guessing whence the perfume was.

67
As one who hidden in deep sedge and reeds   265
Smells the rare scent made where a panther feeds,
And tracking ever slotwise[28] the warm smell
Is snapped upon by the sweet mouth and bleeds,

68
His head far down the hot sweet throat of her –
So one tracks love, whose breath is deadlier,   270
And lo, one springe[29] and you are fast in hell,
Fast as the gin's[30] grip of a wayfarer.

69
I think now, as the heavy hours decease
One after one, and bitter thoughts increase
One upon one, of all sweet finished things;   275
The breaking of the battle; the long peace

70
Wherein we sat clothed softly, each man's hair
Crowned with green leaves beneath white hoods of vair;[31]
The sounds of sharp spears at great tourneyings,[32]
And noise of singing in the late sweet air.   280

71
I sang of love too, knowing nought thereof;
'Sweeter,' I said, 'the little laugh of love

---

[25] *I doubt* 'I have no doubt'.
[26] *teen* suffering, grief.
[27] *he* bitter love.
[28] *slotwise* track or trail of an animal, as shown by the marks of the foot; here misapplied to the scent of an animal.

[29] *springe* snare, trap.
[30] *gin's* trap's.
[31] *vair* fur from grey and white squirrel used ornamentally.
[32] *tourneyings* tournaments, jousts.

Than tears out of the eyes of Magdalen,[33]
Or any fallen feather of the Dove.

72

'The broken little laugh that spoils a kiss,   285
The ache of purple pulses, and the bliss
Of blinded eyelids that expand again –
Love draws them open with those lips of his,

73

'Lips that cling hard till the kissed face has grown
Of one same fire and colour with their own;   290
Then ere one sleep, appeased with sacrifice,
Where his lips wounded, there his lips atone.'

74

I sang these things long since and knew them not;
'Lo, here is love, or there is love, God wot,
This man and that finds favour in his eyes,'   295
I said, 'but I, what guerdon[34] have I got?

75

'The dust of praise that is blown everywhere
In all men's faces with the common air;
The bay-leaf that wants chafing to be sweet
Before they wind it in a singer's hair.'[35]   300

76

So that one dawn I rode forth sorrowing;
I had no hope but of some evil thing,
And so rode slowly past the windy wheat
And past the vineyard and the water-spring,

77

Up to the Horsel. A great elder-tree   305
Held back its heaps of flowers to let me see
The ripe tall grass, and one that walked therein,
Naked, with hair shed over to the knee.

78

She walked between the blossom and the grass;
I knew the beauty of her, what she was,   310
The beauty of her body and her sin,
And in my flesh the sin of hers, alas!

79

Alas! for sorrow is all the end of this.
O sad kissed mouth, how sorrowful it is!
O breast whereat some suckling sorrow clings,   315
Red with the bitter blossom of a kiss!

---

[33] *Magdalen* Mary Magdalene has been traditionally identified as the repentant sinner in Luke 7.37–44, whose sins are equally traditionally believed to be sexual.

[34] *guerdon* reward, recompense.
[35] *wind it . . . singer's hair* a wreath of bay is one of the traditional crowns of a poet.

80

Ah, with blind lips I felt for you, and found
About my neck your hands and hair enwound,
   The hands that stifle and the hair that stings,
I felt them fasten sharply without sound.   320

81

Yea, for my sin I had great store of bliss:
Rise up, make answer for me, let thy kiss
   Seal my lips hard from speaking of my sin,
Lest one go mad to hear how sweet it is.

82

Yet I waxed faint with fume of barren bowers,   325
And murmuring of the heavy-headed hours;
   And let the dove's beak fret and peck within
My lips in vain, and Love shed fruitless flowers.

83

So that God looked upon me when your hands
Were hot about me; yea, God brake my bands   330
   To save my soul alive, and I came forth
Like a man blind and naked in strange lands

84

That hears men laugh and weep, and knows not whence
Nor wherefore, but is broken in his sense;
   Howbeit I met folk riding from the north   335
Towards Rome, to purge them of their souls' offence,[36]

85

And rode with them, and spake to none; the day
Stunned me like lights upon some wizard way,
   And ate like fire mine eyes and mine eyesight;
So rode I, hearing all these chant and pray,   340

86

And marvelled; till before us rose and fell
White cursed hills, like outer skirts of hell
   Seen where men's eyes look through the day to night,
Like a jagged shell's lips, harsh, untunable,

87

Blown in between by devils' wrangling breath;   345
Nathless we won well past that hell and death,
   Down to the sweet land where all airs are good,
Even unto Rome where God's grace tarrieth.[37]

88

Then came each man and worshipped at his knees
Who in the Lord God's likeness bears the keys   350

[36] *to purge . . . offence* i.e., seek the Pope's forgiveness in
Rome.

[37] *God's grace tarrieth* i.e., in the person of the Pope.

To bind or loose,[38] and called on Christ's shed blood,
And so the sweet-souled father gave him ease.

89
But when I came I fell down at his feet,
Saying, 'Father, though the Lord's blood be right sweet,
The spot it takes not off the panther's skin,   355
Nor shall an Ethiop's stain[39] be bleached with it.

90
'Lo, I have sinned and have spat out at God,
Wherefore his hand is heavier and his rod
More sharp because of mine exceeding sin,
And all his raiment redder than bright blood   360

91
'Before mine eyes; yea, for my sake I wot
The heat of hell is waxen seven times hot
Through my great sin.' Then spake he some sweet word,
Giving me cheer; which thing availed me not;

92
Yea, scarce I wist if such indeed were said;   365
For when I ceased – lo, as one newly dead
Who hears a great cry out of hell, I heard
The crying of his voice across my head.

93
'Until this dry shred staff, that hath no whit
Of leaf nor bark, bear blossom and smell sweet,   370
Seek thou not any mercy in God's sight,
For so long shalt thou be cast out from it.'

94
Yea, what if dried-up stems wax red and green,
Shall that thing be which is not nor has been?
Yea, what if sapless bark wax green and white,   375
Shall any good fruit grow upon my sin?

95
Nay, though sweet fruit were plucked of a dry tree,
And though men drew sweet waters of the sea,
There should not grow sweet leaves on this dead stem,
This waste wan body and shaken soul of me.   380

96
Yea, though God search it warily enough,
There is not one sound thing in all thereof;

---

[38] *bears . . . loose* Catholics believe the Pope is the successor of St Peter who received Jesus's charge to lead the Church: 'And I say also vnto thee, that thou art Peter, and vpon this rocke I will build my Church: and the gates of hell shall not preuaile against it. And I will giue vnto thee the keyes of the kingdome of heauen: and whatsoeuer thou shalt bind on earth, shall be bound in heauen: whatsoeuer thou shalt loose on earth, shall be loosed in heauen', Matthew 16.18–19.

[39] *Ethop's stain* black skin of an Ethiopian (proverbial).

Though he search all my veins through, searching them
He shall find nothing whole therein but love.

97

For I came home right heavy, with small cheer,   385
And lo my love, mine own soul's heart, more dear
Than mine own soul, more beautiful than God,
Who hath my being between the hands of her –

98

Fair still, but fair for no man saving me,
As when she came out of the naked sea   390
Making the foam as fire whereon she trod,
And as the inner flower of fire was she.

99

Yea, she laid hold upon me, and her mouth
Clove unto mine as soul to body doth,
And, laughing, made her lips luxurious;   395
Her hair had smells of all the sunburnt south,

100

Strange spice and flower, strange savour of crushed fruit,
And perfume the swart[40] kings tread underfoot
For pleasure when their minds wax amorous,
Charred frankincense[41] and grated sandal-root.[42]   400

101

And I forgot fear and all weary things,
All ended prayers and perished thanksgivings,
Feeling her face with all her eager hair
Cleave to me, clinging as a fire that clings

102

To the body and to the raiment, burning them;   405
As after death I know that such-like flame
Shall cleave to me for ever; yea, what care,
Albeit I burn then, having felt the same?

103

Ah love, there is no better life than this;
To have known love, how bitter a thing it is,   410
And afterward be cast out of God's sight;
Yea, these that know not, shall they have such bliss

104

High up in barren heaven before his face
As we twain in the heavy-hearted place,
Remembering love and all the dead delight,   415
And all that time was sweet with for a space?

---

[40] *swart* dark, black.
[41] *frankincense* aromatic gum burnt as incense.
[42] *sandal-root* aromatic root.

105

For till the thunder in the trumpet be,[43]
Soul may divide from body, but not we
One from another; I hold thee with my hand,
I let mine eyes have all their will of thee,   420

106

I seal myself upon thee with my might,
Abiding alway out of all men's sight
Until God loosen over sea and land
The thunder of the trumpets of the night.

EXPLICIT LAUS VENERIS.[44]

[43] *thunder . . . trumpet be* the Last Day.   [44] *EXPLICIT LAUS VENERIS* here ends the praise of Venus.

Ave Atque Vale: In Memory of Charles Baudelaire

Swinburne's lament on the death (or rather supposed death) of the French poet Charles Baudelaire (1821–67) has something of the grandeur of Classical tragedy. (Like many English elegies, it gestures to the pastoral 'Lament for Bion', traditionally ascribed to Moschus and rendered in English, for instance, by John Oldham [1653–83] as *A Pastoral, In Imitation of the Greek of Moschus*). Its energies are pagan, its definition of poetic line, the lineage of poetic genius, one that has as its tutelary authority the god Apollo (stanza 14) (for more of Swinburne's handling of Classical material, see 'Hymn to Proserpine', 476–9, and 'Anactoria', 480–6). Swinburne's rhythms are restrained, and the poem has a taut control, a disciplined diction, which chooses precise individual images over a more generalized texture.

Charles Baudelaire's volume of poems *Les Fleurs du mal* [the flowers of sickness] (1857) contained controversial lyrics that explored vice, evil and the degradations of Paris life, endeavouring to find beauty and order there. Like George Meredith, Swinburne responded to Baudelaire's poetry positively – *Les Fleurs du mal* was influential on later English Decadent culture widely – and his embrace of French themes helped distinguish his poetic radicalism from that of Dante Gabriel Rossetti (see 350–69). Swinburne, who recalls a succession of Baudelaire's poems, is at once speaking of the author of *Les Fleurs du mal* and of his own poetic persona. The discussion of the dead poet is, centrally, self-reflexive, and reveals features that connect Swinburne and Baudelaire: 'fierce' loves, the 'strange flowers' of vision, vices and powerful desires. Swinburne is concerned with the establishment of a canon and silently inscribes himself as Baudelaire's successor, as a 'brother' poet (stanza 3),

worthy to mourn him as Orestes mourned his father Agamemnon (stanza 10).

Death itself is also a preoccupation, and the distinctive form of self-perpetuation that poetry provides. The nature of what, if anything, lies beyond the grave is the subject of stanzas 6–8, as Swinburne admits the limits of the poet's vision to see beyond life's margin. The conclusion of the elegy, which at this point echoes Shelley's 1821 poem 'Adonais' on the death of John Keats, takes what consolation it can – it is an elegy that does not seek consolation as a primary aim – from the fact that Baudelaire, now dead, is no longer subject to the troublous shocks of earthly existence. As it happens, the rumour that Swinburne had heard in May 1867 that Baudelaire was dead, and which prompted this poem, turned out not to be true. Baudelaire, none the less, really did die later the same year. The poem was included in *Poems and Ballads, Second Series* (1878). The title reference is to Catullus, '*Accipe fraterno multum manantia fletu, / atque in perpetuum, frater, ave atque vale*' ('Take them, wet with many tears of a brother, and for ever, O my brother, hail and farewell!'). Tennyson said of these lines that no 'modern elegy, so long as men retain the least hope in the after-life of those whom they loved, equal in pathos the desolation of that everlasting farewell'. Included in the second series of *Poems and Ballads* were many other poems on dead poets, such as 'Memorial Verses' for Théophile Gautier and 'In Memory of Barry Cornwall' (Adelaide Anne Procter's father), a poem buoyantly confident about the endurance of art after death.

Text: *Poems and Ballads, Second Series* (1878).

Nous devrions pourtant lui porter quelques fleurs;
Les morts, les pauvres morts, ont de grandes douleurs,
Et quand Octobre souffle, émondeur des vieux arbres
Son vent mélancolique à l'entour de leurs marbres,
Certes, ils doivent trouver les vivants bien ingrats.[1]
Les Fleurs du mal

Shall I strew on thee rose or rue or laurel,[2]
Brother, on this that was the veil of thee?
Or quiet sea-flower moulded by the sea,
Or simplest growth of meadow-sweet or sorrel,[3]
Such as the summer-sleepy Dryads[4] weave,   5
Waked up by snow-soft sudden rains at eve?
Or wilt thou rather, as on earth before,
Half-faded fiery blossoms, pale with heat
And full of bitter summer, but more sweet
To thee than gleanings of a northern shore   10
Trod by no tropic feet?

2

For always thee the fervid languid[5] glories
Allured of heavier suns in mightier skies;
Thine ears knew all the wandering watery sighs
Where the sea sobs round Lesbian[6] promontories,   15
The barren kiss of piteous wave to wave
That knows not where is that Leucadian grave[7]
Which hides too deep the supreme head of song.
Ah, salt and sterile as her kisses were,
The wild sea winds her and the green gulfs bear   20
Hither and thither, and vex and work her wrong,
Blind gods that cannot spare.

3

Thou sawest, in thine old singing season, brother,
Secrets and sorrows unbeheld of us:
Fierce loves, and lovely leaf-buds poisonous,   25
Bare to thy subtler eye, but for none other
Blowing by night in some unbreathed-in clime;
The hidden harvest of luxurious time,
Sin without shape, and pleasure without speech;
And where strange dreams in a tumultuous sleep   30
Make the shut eyes of stricken spirits weep;

[1] *Nous devrions . . . ingrats* 'We ought to be taking her some flowers; the dead, the poor dead, have great griefs, and when October blows, the pruner of the old trees, its melancholy wind around their marble tombs, they must certainly think that the dead are truly ungrateful', from Baudelaire's *Les Fleurs du mal*, poem 100.
[2] *rose or rue or laurel* rose for love, rue for sorrow, laurel for praise.
[3] *sorrel* small, sour-tasting plant.
[4] *Dryads* tree nymphs.
[5] *fervid languid* an oxymoron.

[6] *Lesbian* i.e., of Lesbos, island in the east Aegean, where Sappho, the Greek poet whom Swinburne thought the greatest of lyric poets, was born in the mid-seventh century BC. Cf. 'Anactoria', 480–6.
[7] *Leucadian grave* Sappho was supposed in some (heterosexual) versions of her story – largely deriving from Ovid's *Heroides* – to have thrown herself from the Leucadian rock because of unrequited love for the youth Phaon. Swinburne alludes to Baudelaire's poem 'Lesbos', which includes a meditation on Sappho at the rock, and on her lost body.

And with each face thou sawest the shadow on each,
Seeing as men sow men reap.

4

O sleepless heart and sombre soul unsleeping,
That were athirst for sleep and no more life   35
And no more love, for peace and no more strife!
Now the dim gods of death have in their keeping
Spirit and body and all the springs of song,
Is it well now where love can do no wrong,
Where stingless pleasure has no foam or fang   40
Behind the unopening closure of her lips?
Is it not well where soul from body slips
And flesh from bone divides without a pang
As dew from flower-bell drips?

5

It is enough;[8] the end and the beginning   45
Are one thing to thee,[9] who art past the end.
O hand unclasped of unbeholden friend,[10]
For thee no fruits to pluck, no palms for winning,
No triumph and no labour and no lust,
Only dead yew-leaves[11] and a little dust.   50
O quiet eyes wherein the light saith nought,
Whereto the day is dumb, nor any night
With obscure finger silences your sight,
Nor in your speech the sudden soul speaks thought,
Sleep, and have sleep for light.   55

6

Now[12] all strange hours and all strange loves are over,
Dreams and desires and sombre songs and sweet,
Hast thou found place at the great knees and feet
Of some pale Titan-woman[13] like a lover,
Such as thy vision here solicited,   60
Under the shadow of her fair vast head,
The deep division of prodigious breasts,
The solemn slope of mighty limbs asleep,
The weight of awful tresses that still keep
The savour and shade of old-world pine-forests   65
Where the wet hill-winds weep?

[8] *It is enough* cf. Baudelaire's poem 'Sed non satiata' ['never satisfied'].
[9] *the end . . . to thee* i.e., nothing now matters to Baudelaire in death.
[10] *unbeholden friend* Swinburne had not met Baudelaire.
[11] *yew-leaves* yew trees traditionally grow in English churchyards.
[12] *Now . . . hill-winds weep* cf. Baudelaire's poem 'La Géante': 'In the old days when nature in her lusty strength conceived each day monstrous infants, I would happily have lived next to some young giantess, like a voluptuous cat at the feet of a queen. I would have liked to watch her body flowering with her soul and freely developing in her terrible games; and to think whether she was hiding in her heart some tragic passion, as I saw the humid mists float in her eyes. I would have loved to explore her magnificent form at leisure; climb the slopes of her enormous knees and sometimes, when the sickly mists of summer made her wearily stretch out across the fields, to sleep with trust in the shadow of her breasts, like a peaceable hamlet at the foot of a mountain.'
[13] *Titan-woman* Titans were the older generation of gods whom the Olympians, led by Zeus, overthrew.

7

Hast thou found any likeness for thy vision?
O gardener of strange flowers,[14] what bud, what bloom,
Hast thou found sown, what gathered in the gloom?
What of despair, of rapture, of derision,   70
What of life is there, what of ill or good?
Are the fruits grey like dust or bright like blood?
Does the dim ground grow any seed of ours,
The faint fields quicken any terrene[15] root,
In low lands where the sun and moon are mute   75
And all the stars keep silence? Are there flowers
At all, or any fruit?

8

Alas, but though my flying song flies after,
O sweet strange elder singer, thy more fleet
Singing, and footprints of thy fleeter feet,   80
Some dim derision of mysterious laughter
From the blind tongueless warders of the dead,
Some gainless glimpse of Proserpine's[16] veiled head,
Some little sound of unregarded tears
Wept by effaced unprofitable eyes,   85
And from pale mouths some cadence of dead sighs –
These only, these the hearkening spirit hears,
Sees only such things rise.

9

Thou art far too far for wings of words to follow,
Far too far off for thought or any prayer.   90
What ails us with thee, who art wind and air?
What ails us gazing where all seen is hollow?
Yet with some fancy, yet with some desire,
Dreams pursue death as winds a flying fire,
Our dreams pursue our dead and do not find.   95
Still, and more swift than they, the thin flame flies,
The low light fails us in elusive skies,
Still the foiled earnest ear is deaf, and blind
Are still the eluded eyes.

10

Not thee, O never thee, in all time's changes,   100
Not thee, but this the sound of thy sad soul,
The shadow of thy swift spirit, this shut scroll[17]
I lay my hand on, and not death estranges
My spirit from communion of thy song –[18]
These memories and these melodies that throng   105
Veiled porches of a Muse[19] funereal –
These I salute, these touch, these clasp and fold

---

[14] *strange flowers* cf. *Les Fleurs du mal*, the flowers of sickness.
[15] *terrene* belonging to the earth.
[16] *Proserpine* goddess who spent part of her life in Hades, the world of the dead, and the rest on earth. See Swinburne's 'Hymn to Proserpine', 476–9.

[17] *scroll* Baudelaire's poems.
[18] *Not thee . . . song* the sense is: 'Swinburne will never now commune with Baudelaire himself, but can at least read his poems'.
[19] *Muse* Muses were the Greek divinities on whom artists and thinkers depended for inspiration.

As though a hand were in my hand to hold,
Or through mine ears a mourning musical
        Of many mourners rolled.   110

11

I among these, I also, in such station
As when the pyre was charred, and piled the sods,
And offering to the dead made, and their gods,
The old mourners had, standing to make libation,[20]
        I stand, and to the gods and to the dead   115
Do reverence without prayer or praise, and shed
Offering to these unknown, the gods of gloom,
And what of honey and spice my seedlands bear,
    And what I may of fruits in this chilled air,
        And lay, Orestes-like,[21] across the tomb   120
        A curl of severed hair.

12

But by no hand nor any treason stricken,
Not like the low-lying head of Him, the King,[22]
The flame that made of Troy a ruinous thing,[23]
Thou liest, and on this dust no tears could quicken[24]   125
There fall no tears like theirs that all men hear
    Fall tear by sweet imperishable tear
Down the opening leaves of holy poets' pages.
    Thee not Orestes, not Electra[25] mourns;
        But bending us-ward with memorial urns   130
    The most high Muses that fulfil all ages
        Weep, and our God's heart yearns.

13

For, sparing of his sacred strength, not often
Among us darkling here the lord of light[26]
    Makes manifest his music and his might   135
In hearts that open and in lips that soften
With the soft flame and heat of songs that shine.
    Thy lips indeed he touched with bitter wine,
And nourished them indeed with bitter bread;
Yet surely from his hand thy soul's food came,   140
    The fire that scarred thy spirit at his flame
Was lighted, and thine hungering heart he fed
        Who feeds our hearts with fame.

14

Therefore he too now at thy soul's sunsetting,
God of all suns and songs,[27] he too bends down   145

[20] *libation* drink-offering to a god.
[21] *Orestes-like* Orestes was the son of the murdered Agamemnon: he laid a lock of his own hair on his father's tomb in the Prologue of *Libation Bearers* in Aeschylus's trilogy *The Oresteia*.
[22] *King* Agamemnon, treacherously murdered by his wife, Clytemnestra.
[23] *The flame . . . ruinous thing* Agamemnon was the victor of the Trojan war.

[24] *quicken* bring to life.
[25] *Electra* Orestes's sister, who also mourns her father in *Libation Bearers*.
[26] *lord of light* Apollo, one of the Olympian gods, leader of the Muses, god of the sun.
[27] *suns and songs* Apollo as god of the sun and of music.

To mix his laurel with thy cypress crown,
And save thy dust from blame and from forgetting.
Therefore he too, seeing all thou wert and art,
Compassionate, with sad and sacred heart,
Mourns thee of many his children the last dead,   150
And hallows with strange tears and alien sighs
Thine unmelodious mouth and sunless eyes,
And over thine irrevocable head
Sheds light from the under skies.

                                    15
And one weeps with him in the ways Lethean,[28]   155
And stains with tears her changing bosom chill:
That obscure Venus of the hollow hill,[29]
That thing transformed which was the Cytherean,[30]
With lips that lost their Grecian laugh divine
Long since, and face no more called Erycine;[31]   160
A ghost, a bitter and luxurious god.
Thee also with fair flesh and singing spell
Did she, a sad and second prey,[32] compel
Into the footless places once more trod,
And shadows hot from hell.   165

                                    16
And now no sacred staff shall break in blossom,[33]
No choral salutation lure to light
A spirit sick with perfume and sweet night
And love's tired eyes and hands and barren bosom.
There is no help for these things; none to mend   170
And none to mar; not all our songs, O friend,
Will make death clear or make life durable.
Howbeit with rose and ivy and wild vine
And with wild notes about this dust of thine
At least I fill the place where white dreams dwell   175
And wreathe an unseen shrine.

                                    17
Sleep; and if life was bitter to thee, pardon,
If sweet, give thanks; thou hast no more to live;
And to give thanks is good, and to forgive.
Out of the mystic and the mournful garden   180
Where all day through thine hands in barren braid[34]
Wove the sick flowers of secrecy and shade,
Green buds of sorrow and sin, and remnants grey,
Sweet-smelling, pale with poison, sanguine-hearted,[35]

[28] *Lethean* of Lethe, river of forgetfulness.
[29] *Venus of the hollow hill* the stanza refers to the Venus of the Tannhäuser legend. Venus, goddess of erotic love, dwelt in a mountain: Tannhäuser spent seven years in debauched revelry there. The story is treated in 'Laus Veneris', 487–500.
[30] *Cytherean* epithet of Venus (having been born of the sea, she was sometimes thought to have come ashore first on the island of Cythera).
[31] *Erycine* another epithet of Venus: she had a temple on Mount Eryx in Sicily.

[32] *second prey* the first being Tannhäuser.
[33] *And now . . . blossom* after Tannhäuser emerged from Venus's mountain he sought absolution from the Pope, who refused, saying that it was as impossible for him to be forgiven as for the Pope's staff to flower. After three days, the staff broke into blossom (but Tannhäuser had returned to Venus).
[34] *braid* plait.
[35] *sanguine-hearted* 'with blood at the heart', sick.

Passions that sprang from sleep and thoughts that started,   185
Shall death not bring us all as thee one day
Among the days departed?

18

For thee, O now a silent soul, my brother,
Take at my hands this garland, and farewell.
Thin is the leaf, and chill the wintry smell,   190
And chill the solemn earth, a fatal mother,
With sadder than the Niobean[36] womb,
And in the hollow of her breasts a tomb.
Content thee, howsoe'er, whose days are done;
There lies not any troublous thing before,   195
Nor sight nor sound to war against thee more,[37]
For whom all winds are quiet as the sun,
All waters as the shore.

---

[36] *Niobean womb* Niobe was the wife of Amphion, King of Thebes. She had many children, but Apollo and Artemis killed them all. In her grief, she turned into a rock on Mount Sipylus to become an image of everlasting sorrow with water running down her face in perpetual weeping.
[37] *war against thee more* cf. Shelley's 'Adonais' (1821) on the

death of Keats: 'He has outsoared the shadow of our night; / Envy and calumny and hate and pain, / And that unrest which men miscall delight, / Can touch him not and torture not again; / From the contagion of the world's slow stain / He is secure.'

A Forsaken Garden

As Edward Elgar endeavoured to depict silence in music (in *The Dream of Gerontius* [1900]), so Swinburne looks to depict a space in which time no longer has purchase through the medium of poetry that cannot exist outside time. 'A Forsaken Garden' (*Athenaeum*, July 1876, then *Poems and Ballads, Second Series* [1878]) is an extended description of an abandoned patch near the sea – always a richly suggestive element for Swinburne – and most obviously a reflection on the forces of decay, an hyperbolization of Tennyson's most familiar preoccupation with change and the passage of time. Swinburne's poetry may be seen as frequently in negotiation with Tennyson's, whose art, he once said, is a church into which 'we were all in my time born and baptized'.

As a meditation on the nature of history – or, in this case, on a space where history is no longer possible – 'A Forsaken Garden' can be compared to 'Hymn to Proserpine', 476–9. At a subtler level, the poem also relates to the 'Hymn' and its resistance to Christianity. Choosing a familiar *topos* of Judaeo-Christian religion – the garden – Swinburne crafts a discourse that subtly challenges familiar certainties of the Christian theology of death and resurrection. He reflects on the utter mystery of death (stanza 7), offering no clear hope of life beyond it, and thinks of the apocalypse

(stanzas 9 and 10) separately from any sense of Second Coming or Christian Last Judgement. In the final stanza, Swinburne presents the decayed garden as a place in which 'Death lies dead', provocatively borrowing the Christian idea of Jesus's conquest over death only in the context of a garden in which *everything* is dead. 'A Forsaken Garden' may be thought, as an elegy contesting forms of religious consolation, a comment on Tennyson's *In Memoriam A.H.H.*, 88–165, and a radical challenge to the assumptions of natural theology.

The poem's acoustic patterning is typically sophisticated. Consider the chiming simply in the first two lines:

In a co*ig*n *o*f the **c**liff betwEEn low**land** and
                                                    high**land**,
At the **sea**-**down's edge** betwEEn windward and
                                                    lEE

The poem's control of time, its subtly modulating rhythms, adds to the irony of the depiction of a garden where the clock has stopped. *Poems and Ballads, Second Series* is dominated by retrospective poems, elegies and reflections on death and loss (cf. '*Ave Atque Vale*', 500–6). In the original ordering of the volume, 'A Forsaken Garden' was followed by

'Relics', a poem both parodic of and indebted to the characteristic posture of Tennysonian lament for 'dear times dead to me'. Swinburne's debt in 'A Forsaken Garden' to Thomas Campbell's 'Lines Written on Visiting a Scene in Argyleshire', another poem about a remote ruined garden, has been recognized.

Text: *Poems and Ballads, Second Series* (1878).

In a coign[1] of the cliff between lowland and highland,
At the sea-down's edge between windward[2] and lee,[3]
Walled round with rocks as an inland island,
The ghost of a garden fronts the sea.
A girdle of brushwood and thorn encloses   5
The steep square slope of the blossomless bed
Where the weeds that grew green from the graves of its roses
Now lie dead.

2
The fields fall southward, abrupt and broken,
To the low last edge of the long lone land.   10
If a step should sound or a word be spoken,
Would a ghost not rise at the strange guest's hand?
So long have the grey bare walks lain guestless,
Through branches and briars if a man make way,
He shall find no life but the sea-wind's, restless   15
Night and day.

3
The dense hard passage is blind and stifled
That crawls by a track none turn to climb
To the strait waste place that the years have rifled
Of all but the thorns that are touched not of time.   20
The thorns he spares when the rose is taken;
The rocks are left when he wastes the plain.
The wind that wanders, the weeds wind-shaken,
These remain.

4
Not a flower to be pressed of the foot that falls not;   25
As the heart of a dead man the seed-plots are dry;
From the thicket of thorns whence the nightingale calls not,
Could she call, there were never a rose to reply.
Over the meadows that blossom and wither
Rings but the note of a sea-bird's song;   30
Only the sun and the rain come hither
All year long.

5
The sun burns sere[4] and the rain dishevels
One gaunt bleak blossom of scentless breath.
Only the wind here hovers and revels   35

---

[1] *coign* place (often a projecting corner).
[2] *windward* towards the wind.
[3] *lee* (as in 'leeward') turned away from the wind.
[4] *sere* dry, withered.

In a round where life seems barren as death.
Here there was laughing of old, there was weeping,
Haply,[5] of lovers none ever will know,
Whose eyes went seaward a hundred sleeping
    Years ago.   40

6

Heart handfast in heart as they stood, 'Look thither,'
Did he whisper? 'look forth from the flowers to the sea;
For the foam-flowers endure when the rose-blossoms wither,
And men that love lightly may die – but we?'
And the same wind sang and the same waves whitened,   45
And or ever the garden's last petals were shed,
In the lips that had whispered, the eyes that had lightened,
    Love was dead.

7

Or they loved their life through, and then went whither?
And were one to the end – but what end who knows?   50
Love deep as the sea as a rose must wither,
As the rose-red seaweed that mocks the rose.
Shall the dead take thought for the dead to love them?
What love was ever as deep as a grave?
They are loveless now as the grass above them   55
    Or the wave.

8

All are at one now, roses and lovers,
Not known of the cliffs and the fields and the sea.
Not a breath of the time that has been hovers
In the air now soft with a summer to be.   60
Not a breath shall there sweeten the seasons hereafter
Of the flowers or the lovers that laugh now or weep,
When as they that are free now of weeping and laughter
    We shall sleep.

9

Here death may deal not again for ever;   65
Here change may come not till all change end.[6]
From the graves they have made they shall rise up never,
Who have left nought living to ravage and rend.
Earth, stones, and thorns of the wild ground growing,
While the sun and the rain live, these shall be;   70
Till a last wind's breath upon all these blowing
    Roll the sea.

10

Till the slow sea rise and the sheer cliff crumble,
Till terrace and meadow the deep gulfs drink,
Till the strength of the waves of the high tides humble   75

[5] *Haply* perhaps.

[6] *till all change end* the end of the world, the apocalypse described in the last stanza.

The fields that lessen, the rocks that shrink,
Here now in his triumph where all things falter,
Stretched out on the spoils that his own hand spread,
As a god self-slain on his own strange altar,
Death lies dead.   80

Thomas Hardy (1840–1928)

The son of a stonemason, Hardy was born near Dorchester in Dorset. He learned the violin from his father (his family were locally respected musicians) and went to school in Dorchester before being articled to John Hicks, a local architect. He later moved to London to work for another architect, Arthur Blomfield, and continued to pursue a course of wide reading (he had learned the Classical languages). Losing his religious faith – he blamed *The Origin of Species* (1859) for this – he gave up on an idea to take holy orders. Returning to Dorset to work for Hicks again, Hardy began writing fiction (his first, unpublished, novel was given the rather untempting title *The Poor Man and the Lady: A Story with no Plot; Containing some Original Verses* [1868]). *Desperate Remedies* was, however, published in 1871, followed by *Under the Greenwood Tree* (1872), *A Pair of Blue Eyes* (1873) and, the novel that marked the turn in his fortunes, *Far from the Madding Crowd* (1874). He married Emma Gifford that same year, having met her while on an architectural mission to St Juliot, Cornwall. The marriage was increasingly unhappy. Hardy's career as a novelist bloomed, but the controversies over *Tess of the D'Urbervilles* (1891) and *Jude the Obscure* (1894–5) left him, he claimed, disillusioned with fiction (though there were many positive reviews). He turned back to poetry (which he had been writing on and off throughout) and began a new career. *Wessex Poems and Other Verses* was published in 1898; *Poems of the Past and the Present* in 1901 (with 1902 on the title page), using much work written many years before; six further volumes would follow, ending with *Winter Words* (1928). In 1912, Emma died (prompting guilt-laden poems) and Hardy married Florence Dugdale in 1914. Thomas Hardy's poetry, his exploration of the potential of ungainly syntax and seemingly inelegant diction, his rejection of anything like Swinburnean smoothness of rhythm, brought a newly expressive conversational idiom to lyric verse but it was one that took some time before it was appreciated. His dominant themes of indifference, time's ironies and what Laurence Binyon called 'the implanted crookedness of things' remained remarkably consistent across his whole career. Thomas Hardy died in January 1928; his ashes were interred in Westminster Abbey, his heart in Dorset.

Hap

In the colloquial syntax and with the rhythms of speech, Hardy probes universal questions of purpose. 'Hap' (written in 1866, published in 1898) offers a view of the poet as indistinguishable from all other men in his sufferings, and possessed of prophetic insight that serves only to reveal the blindness of forces that determine earth's fate, all the more dispiriting for being associated with individual personalities. 'Hap' means chance or fortune; Hardy's meditation on the governance of the world sees chance at its heart. The sonnet, despite its mere regulatory 14 lines, is an anti-theodicy, a reply to systems of faith that find a benign divine plan at work in the universe. Matthew Arnold's eponymous speaker in 'Empedocles on Etna', 268–95, had leapt into a volcano at the end of his long diagnosis of distress: at once suicide, it was also a quasi-triumphant reunion with the forces of nature. Hardy offers no action to follow the poem's conclusion, implicitly figuring human powerlessness before the 'purblind Doomsters' that determine human life. The diction is quintessential Hardy – colloquial, eclectic, with a peculiar angularity or expressive ungainliness of syntax that eschews the decorum of the Tennyson tradition.

Text: *The Complete Poetical Works of Thomas Hardy* (1982).

If but some vengeful god would call to me
From up the sky, and laugh: 'Thou suffering thing,
Know that thy sorrow is my ecstasy,
That thy love's loss is my hate's profiting!'

2

Then would I bear it, clench myself, and die,   5
Steeled by the sense of ire[1] unmerited;

---

[1] *ire* anger.

Half-eased in that a Powerfuller than I
Had willed and meted[2] me the tears I shed.

3

But not so. How arrives it joy lies slain,
And why unblooms the best hope ever sown?   10
– Crass Casualty obstructs the sun and rain,
And dicing Time for gladness casts a moan. . . .
These purblind[3] Doomsters had as readily strown
Blisses about my pilgrimage as pain.

1866
16 Westbourne Park Villas.[4]

[2] *meted* given.
[3] *purblind* with defective vision.

[4] *16 . . . Villas* in Bayswater, where Hardy moved in 1863.

Drummer Hodge

Hardy's imagination is frequently drawn to the isolated and solitary. Here his subject is a man alienated by time and space who none the less, through the literal transformation of his body, will become a permanent part of a foreign land. The concentration on the union of the body with the soil in the final stanza – the only future life the poem allows – invokes and secularizes Tennyson's meditations in *In Memoriam A.H.H.*, 88–165, on the metamorphosis of Arthur Hallam's body beneath the yews of Clevedon. 'Drummer Hodge' (first published in *Literature*, 25 November 1899) is set during the second Anglo–Boer War (1899–1902), during which the British Army fought to keep the two breakaway Boer states, the Orange Free State and the Transvaal, under British influence. The poem reminds us that sympathy for the suffering soldier at war was not achieved for the first time in English poetry by the writers of the Great War (1914–18).

Drummer Hodge, a deliberately ordinary name, is an imaginary young army musician, killed during the campaign and indecorously laid to rest in the veldt. Buried in an alien space – alienation is introduced into the reading experience as Hardy's Afrikaans nouns set the English reader at a distance – after failing to understand the meaning of the land in which he was to die, Hodge's life suggests the fate of ordinary British soldiers in the Boer War. The landscape's final apotheosis of his remains elevates him, none the less, to dignity and almost epic stature. Hodge's death, and the concentration on his misplacedness, invites a broader question, a subtle critique of the imperialist project, about British presence in South Africa anyway (cf. Tennyson, 'To the Marquis of Dufferin and Ava', 167–9).

Text: *The Complete Poetical Works of Thomas Hardy* (1982).

They throw in Drummer Hodge, to rest
Uncoffined – just as found:
His landmark is a kopje[1]-crest
That breaks the veldt[2] around;
And foreign constellations west   5
Each night above his mound.

[1] *kopje* in South Africa, small hill.

[2] *veldt* in South Africa, plain.

2

Young Hodge the Drummer never knew –
Fresh from his Wessex[3] home –
The meaning of the broad Karoo,[4]
The Bush, the dusty loam,[5]   10
And why uprose to nightly view
Strange stars amid the gloam.[6]

3

Yet portion of that unknown plain
Will Hodge for ever be;
His homely Northern breast and brain   15
Grow to some Southern tree,
And strange-eyed constellations reign
His stars eternally.

[3] *Wessex* name Hardy gave to the area of southern England from Exeter in the west to Aldershot in the east, the Isle of Wight in the south to Oxford in the north, and which formed the geographical terrain of much of his fiction and verse.

[4] *Karoo* in South Africa, barren tract of soil comprising extensive, elevated and arid plateaux.
[5] *loam* clay, soil.
[6] *gloam* twilight.

The Darkling Thrush

Rewriting the bird poems of the Romantic period offered a number of Victorian poets a distinctive form of self-definition and a way of defining the peculiar character of their age against the past. Hardy's 'The Darkling Thrush' (first published in the *Graphic*, 29 December 1900) alludes to Keats's 'To a Nightingale' – from where perhaps it takes the word 'darkling' in its title – and Shelley's 'To a Skylark' to mark the shift from one end of the century to the other. Hardy suggests the radical contrast between the Romantic-period myth of the poet as prophet and the baffled, 'unaware' late Victorian poet, unable to grasp the hope that the bird seemingly offers at the close of this bleak piece. 'The Darkling Thrush' is preoccupied with movement away from previous generations, both in literary history and in history more generally, for it is also a meditation on the shift from the nineteenth to the twentieth centuries, as the date Hardy deliberately adds at the end indicates (31 December 1900 is, properly, the last day of the nineteenth century).

An idea for the poem came probably from W. H. Hudson's *Nature in Downland* (1900), which refers to the winter song of the thrush: 'The sound is beauti-

ful in quality, but the singer has no art, and flings out his notes anyhow; the song is an outburst, a cry of happiness.' Hardy reconceives this entirely.

Shelley's skylark was more spirit than bird. Hardy's songbird is a frail creature like an aged man. Romantic transcendence is replaced by a fragile sense of earthly mortality. 'The Darkling Thrush' registers not only personal unease – it is part of Hardy's sustained self-dramatization as miserable, disappointed, alone – but wider concerns about cultural degeneration and the withering of healthy human stock. In its late Darwinian and eugenicist context, the poem poses the question of whether the nineteenth is capable of producing a new twentieth century that will be vigorous. Given this preoccupation with the diseased nature of late Victorianism and its inability to procreate healthily, it is no accident that the bird at the centre of the poem should bear a name that is also that of a sexually transmitted fungal disease.

Text: *The Complete Poetical Works of Thomas Hardy* (1982).

I leant upon a coppice[1] gate
When Frost was spectre-gray,[2]
And Winter's dregs made desolate

[1] *coppice* small wood, thicket.

[2] *spectre-gray* cf. Keats's 'To a Nightingale', 'Where youth grows pale, and spectre-thin, and dies'.

The weakening eye of day.[3]
The tangled bine-stems[4] scored the sky   5
Like strings of broken lyres,[5]
And all mankind that haunted nigh[6]
Had sought their household fires.

2

The land's sharp features seemed to be
The Century's corpse outleant,   10
His crypt[7] the cloudy canopy,
The wind his death-lament.
The ancient pulse of germ and birth
Was shrunken hard and dry,
And every spirit upon earth   15
Seemed fervourless[8] as I.

3

At once a voice arose among
The bleak twigs overhead
In a full-hearted evensong[9]
Of joy illimited;[10]   20
An aged thrush, frail, gaunt, and small,
In blast-beruffled plume,
Had chosen thus to fling his soul
Upon the growing gloom.

4

So little cause for carolings[11]   25
Of such ecstatic sound[12]
Was written on terrestrial things
Afar or nigh around,
That I could think there trembled through
His happy good-night air   30
Some blessed Hope, whereof he knew
And I was unaware.

31 December 1900.

[3] *eye of day* the sun.
[4] *bine-stems* stems of the hedge bindweed.
[5] *lyre* early form of harp.
[6] *nigh* near.
[7] *crypt* burial place beneath a church.
[8] *fervourless* without heat.
[9] *evensong* evening service in the Anglican liturgy. Cf. Keats's 'full-throated ease' in the 'Nightingale' ode.

[10] *illimited* unlimited, unbounded (though it is appropriate in the context of the poem that Hardy's word includes 'ill').
[11] *carolings* singing.
[12] *Had chosen . . . ecstatic sound* cf. Keats, 'While thou art pouring forth thy soul abroad / In such an ecstacy!' ('Nightingale').

In the Old Theatre, Fiesole

April 1887

What intrigues Hardy in this poem is the *pastness* of the past. Preoccupied elsewhere with the reprises and repetitions of time – cf. 'The Revisitation', 520–4 – he is here faced with evidence of a whole mighty

culture lost. The Romans modified the west central Italian city of Fiesole from 80 BC, making it an important community on the Cassian Way, the major route north from Rome through Etruria. The ruins of their theatre – built in the customary design of tiered seats around part of a circle – were discovered in 1792.

'In the Old Theatre, Fiesole' (first published in *Academy*, 1901) responds to a feature of Victorian imaginative life given fresh impetus by the New Geology at the beginning of the period and, later, by the work of Charles Darwin and T. H. Huxley. As scientists pondered the implications of fossils, they discerned the great antiquity of the earth and the enormous number and diversity of species that once inhabited the past and were now lost forever. Tennyson in *In Memoriam A.H.H.*, 88–165, observed in lyric 56 nature's apparent reckless regard for species: '"So careful of the type?" but no. / From scarpèd cliff and quarried stone / She cries, "A thousand types are gone: / I care for nothing, all shall go."' Hardy's imagination is shaped in 'In the Old Theatre, Fiesole' by a cognate fascination with the vastness of the lost past that is political rather than biological, its traces recoverable not by fossils but by the signs of human industry. 'In the Old Theatre' also implicitly considers the provisional nature of Englishness. What is 'English loam' now was once the soil of a different nation and culture, suggesting the constructed nature of modern national identity and historical tradition. The spoken quality of the syntax disguises the highly worked sound patterns where consonants and vowels answer each other across the sonnet's rich texture.

Text: *The Complete Poetical Works of Thomas Hardy* (1982).

I traced the Circus[1] whose gray stones incline
Where Rome and dim Etruria[2] interjoin,
Till came a child who showed an ancient coin
That bore the image of a Constantine.[3]

She lightly passed; nor did she once opine[4]   5
How, better than all books, she had raised for me
In swift perspective Europe's history
Through the vast years of Csar's sceptred line.[5]

For in my distant plot of English loam[6]
'Twas but to delve, and straightway there to find   10
Coins of like impress. As with one half blind
Whom common simples[7] cure, her act flashed home
In that mute moment to my opened mind
The power, the pride, the reach of perished Rome.

[1] *Circus* the Roman theatre at Fiesole is, as is customary, in the form of an incomplete ring.
[2] *Etruria* ancient area that included Fiesole in west central Italy: see headnote.
[3] *Constantine* the most famous emperor of this name was Constantine I, *c.*285–337.
[4] *opine* express an opinion.

[5] *Caesar's sceptred line* usually, all the Roman emperors down to the fall of Constantinople, but Hardy presumably means all the emperors of the Roman empire in the west, the last of whom was Romulus Augustulus, 475–6.
[6] *loam* clay. Roman remains had been found at Max Gate, Hardy's home in Dorchester.
[7] *simples* medicines.

The Ruined Maid

Thomas Hardy's dialogue text – deliberately removing any sense of authorial commentary – wittily parodies the common subject of the fallen woman poem in the mid-Victorian period. For some of the versions of this in the present edition, see D. G. Rossetti's 'Jenny', 358–67, Christina G. Rossetti's 'Goblin Market', 373–85, Augusta Webster's 'A Castaway', 456–71, and Adelaide Anne Procter's 'A Legend of Provence', 320–7. Hardy upturns the expected sense of a 'ruined maid'. Amelia is ruined not through sexual violation and a consequent decline into prostitution, but by being assimilated, presumably by marriage, into the middle class. The poem, neatly articulating social difference through linguistic difference, makes a transparently ironic comment on mid-nineteenth-century social progress into the new middle classes. It also muses on how a woman's body and behaviour are situated and read within the discourse of class. 'The Ruined Maid' was first published in *Poems of the Past and the Present* (1902).

Text: *The Complete Poetical Works of Thomas Hardy* (1982).

'O 'Melia,[1] my dear, this does everything crown!
Who could have supposed I should meet you in Town?
And whence such fair garments, such prosperi-ty?' –
'O didn't you know I'd been ruined?' said she.

2

– 'You left us in tatters, without shoes or socks,   5
Tired of digging potatoes, and spudding[2] up docks;[3]
And now you've gay bracelets and bright feathers three!' –
'Yes: that's how we dress when we're ruined,' said she.

3

– 'At home in the barton[4] you said "thee" and "thou,"
And "thik oon," and "theäs oon," and "t'other"; but now   10
Your talking quite fits 'ee for high compa-ny!' –
'Some polish is gained with one's ruin,' said she.

4

– 'Your hands were like paws then, your face blue and bleak
But now I'm bewitched by your delicate cheek,
And your little gloves fit as on any la-dy!' –   15
'We never do work when we're ruined,' said she.

5

– 'You used to call home-life a hag-ridden dream,
And you'd sigh, and you'd sock;[5] but at present you seem
To know not of megrims[6] or melancho-ly!' –
'True. One's pretty lively when ruined,' said she.   20

6

– 'I wish I had feathers, a fine sweeping gown,
And a delicate face, and could strut about Town!' –
'My dear – a raw country girl, such as you be,
Cannot quite expect that. You ain't ruined,' said she.

Westbourne Park Villas, 1866.[7]

---

[1] *'Melia* i.e., Amelia.
[2] *spudding* digging with a spud, a spade-type instrument with a chisel-shaped blade.
[3] *dock* common name of a coarse weed.
[4] *barton* farmyard.

[5] *sock* in nineteenth-century Dorset dialect, to 'sigh with a loudish sound'.
[6] *megrims* nervous or sick headaches.
[7] *Westbourne . . . 1866* in Bayswater, where Hardy moved in 1863.

The Self Unseeing

Always acutely conscious of the patterns of time, its reprises and continuations, Hardy considers a revisitation to an old house in this brief poem (cf. 'Lausanne: In Gibbon's Old Garden', 519–20, and 'The Revisitation', 520–4, as other poems on the movement and continuations of the temporal, and on forms of haunting). Here, the poet remembers a party years earlier in which, it seemed, all things 'glowed with a gleam'. Hardy is recalling dancing to his father's fiddle when he was a child. Hardy Snr had died in 1892 and the final line speaks of the calamity then unknown. 'The Self Unseeing' (*Poems of the Past and the Present* [1902]) is self-conscious about forms of textual representation, even from the first two words – 'Here is' – which so overtly invite participation in a representational illusion. Hardy's language is spare, colloquial, with a characteristic eclecticism of register in the sudden change to 'emblazoned'.

Text: *The Complete Poetical Works of Thomas Hardy* (1982).

Here is the ancient floor,
Footworn and hollowed and thin,
Here was the former door
Where the dead feet walked in.

2

She sat here in her chair,   5
Smiling into the fire;
He who played[1] stood there,
Bowing it higher and higher.

3

Childlike, I danced in a dream;
Blessings emblazoned[2] that day;   10
Everything glowed with a gleam;
Yet we were looking away!

[1] *played* (on the violin).

[2] *emblazoned* from heraldry: adorned, inscribed.

In Tenebris I

The Romantic-period conception of the male poet as a writer possessed of greater sensitivity to the world than others is reconfigured in this dark poem. Here, the poet is precisely the man who claims he can no longer feel (though of course the grief of his words betrays him). He is no prophetic seer either, but a figure deprived of any sense of the future or of knowledge beyond his own condition: he waits merely in 'unhope'. Hardy's title means 'in darkness' (Latin) and the poem, like a fragment from an autobiography, is an instance of the poet's powerful self-dramatization as bereaved and isolated (cf. 'The Darkling Thrush', 512–13, which, contrastingly, moves from the poet's outcast predicament to national statement). 'In Tenebris I' (*Poems of the Past and the Present* [1902]) is saved from utter despair only by the formality of the verse form, and the economy of its tightly worked language that parries any sense of indulgence. The austere diction, with its monosyllabic severity, marks a contrast to the more colloquial reflections on the indifference of universal forces such as 'Hap', 510–11.

Text: *The Complete Poetical Works of Thomas Hardy* (1982).

'Percussus sum sicut foenum, et aruit cor meum.'[1]

Wintertime nighs;[2]
But my bereavement-pain
It cannot bring again:
Twice no one dies.

2
Flower-petals flee;   5
But, since it once hath been,
No more that severing scene
Can harrow me.

3
Birds faint in dread:
I shall not lose old strength   10
In the lone frost's black length:
Strength long since fled!

4
Leaves freeze to dun;[3]
But friends can not turn cold
This season as of old   15
For him with none.

5
Tempests may scath;[4]
But love can not make smart
Again this year his heart
Who no heart hath.   20

6
Black is night's cope;[5]
But death will not appal[6]
One who, past doubtings all,
Waits in unhope.

[1] *Percussus . . . meum* 'my heart is smitten, and withered like grasse', Psalm 102.4. Although by this stage Hardy had rejected Christianity, the Bible still had resonance for him.
[2] *nighs* approaches.
[3] *dun* dingy brown colour.
[4] *scath* (scathe) injure, damage.
[5] *cope* ecclesiastical robe.
[6] *appal* pun on 'pall', fabric covering a coffin.

Shelley's Skylark

(The neighbourhood of Leghorn: March 1887)

Percy Bysshe Shelley's 'To a Skylark' (1820) saluted the singing bird as a spirit in touch with heavenly joys, a divine poet with prophetic insight. It was a key statement of Shelley's conception of the work of poetry. Hardy's double-edged poem on his precursor continues his negotiations with Romanticism, defining complicatedly the late Victorian poet's enterprise against that of the generation of Shelley and Keats (cf. the repositioning in 'The Darkling Thrush', 512–13, a text directly contesting Romantic-period bird-poet poems).

The unresolved tension of 'Shelley's Skylark' (*Poems of the Past and the Present* [1902]) comes from the reader's uncertainty of where its sincerity lies. It is a compelling mixture of parody and nostalgia. Romanticism is defeated here by mimicking the discourse of sincerity, by the use of a bathetic sentimentalism, a parody of Romanticism's hieratic view of the poet, and an impersonation of Romantic-period gestures to the supernatural – 'Go find it, faeries' – to almost comic effect. None the less, there remains wistfulness about the confidence of Shelley's generation, so sharply different from the present.

The poem's intertext is richer still. It transacts with the work of Robert Browning, whose poem 'Memorabilia' (1855) suggested Hardy's. Hardy complicated and half satirized the reverent adulation of Browning's poem – the young Browning much admired Shelley. 'Memorabilia' commemorated the experience of meeting a man who had known the Romantic:

> Ah, did you once see Shelley plain,
> And did he stop and speak to you
> And did you speak to him again?
> How strange it seems and new!

> But you were living before that,
> And also you are living after;
> And the memory I started at –
> My starting moves your laughter

> I crossed a moor, with a name of its own
> And a certain use in the world no doubt,
> Yet a hand's-breadth of it shines alone
> 'Mid the blank miles round about:

> For there I picked up on the heather
> And there I put inside my breast
> A moulted feather, an eagle-feather!
> Well, I forget the rest.

Shelley's superiority is figured in the cherished eagle-feather. Hardy's thoughts about Shelley's legacy are far more ambivalent. 'Leghorn' – Livorno – is where Shelley wrote the 'Skylark', and near the bay of La Spezia where he drowned.

Text: *The Complete Poetical Works of Thomas Hardy* (1982).

> Somewhere afield here something lies
> In Earth's oblivious eyeless trust
> That moved a poet to prophecies –
> A pinch of unseen, unguarded dust:

> 2
> The dust of the lark that Shelley heard,   5
> And made immortal through times to be; –
> Though it only lived like another bird,
> And knew not its immortality:

> 3
> Lived its meek life; then, one day, fell –
> A little ball of feather and bone;   10
> And how it perished, when piped farewell,
> And where it wastes, are alike unknown.

> 4
> Maybe it rests in the loam[1] I view,
> Maybe it throbs in a myrtle's[2] green,
> Maybe it sleeps in the coming hue   15
> Of a grape on the slopes of yon inland scene.

> 5
> Go find it, faeries, go and find
> That tiny pinch of priceless dust,
> And bring a casket silver-lined,
> And framed of gold that gems encrust;   20

[1] *loam* clay, soil.

[2] *myrtle* evergreen shrub growing abundantly in Italy.

6
And we will lay it safe therein,
And consecrate it to endless time;
For it inspired a bard to win
Ecstatic heights in thought and rhyme.

Lausanne: In Gibbon's Old Garden: 11–12p.m. June 27, 1897

The 110th anniversary of the completion of the Decline and Fall at the same hour and place

This poem is dated at the exact location and time when Edward Gibbon (1737–94), 110 years before, had written the final words of the monumental *The History of the Decline and Fall of the Roman Empire* (in 1787), a defining text in English Classicism and European historiography. It is an example of Hardy's abiding preoccupation with anniversaries, repetitions and commemorations, and his engagement with questions of what endures through time. 'Lausanne' (*Poems of the Past and the Present* [1902]) is also, perhaps, a rueful reflection on what Hardy chose to see as the tumultuous reception of *Jude the Obscure* (1894–5).

'It was on the night of the 27th of June 1787,' wrote Gibbon, the greatest of England's historians of ancient Rome, 'between the hours of eleven and twelve, that I wrote the last line of the last page in a summer-house in my garden. After laying down my pen, I took several turns in a *berceau*, or covered walk of acacias . . . I will not dissemble the first emotions of joy on recovery of my freedom, and, perhaps, the establishment of my fame. But my pride was soon humbled, and a sober melancholy was spread over my mind, by the idea that I had taken an everlasting leave of an old and agreeable companion, and that whatsoever might be the future fate of my History, the life of the historian must be short and precarious.' Hardy makes Gibbon's ghost return – cf. a different kind of return in 'The Revisitation', 520–4 – to meditate not on life's brevity but on the endurance of error. Hardy's response to Gibbon's ghost is unspoken, but the poem's seemingly predetermined answer is 'yes', rupturing any sense of progress from Gibbon's generation to Hardy's. Alternatively, the poem might be seen as offering a pessimist who, in *mimicking* Hardy's own textual persona, ironizes it.

Text: *The Complete Poetical Works of Thomas Hardy* (1982).

A spirit seems to pass,
Formal in pose, but grave withal and grand:
He contemplates a volume in his hand,
And far lamps fleck him through the thin acacias.[1]

2
Anon[2] the book is closed, 5
With 'It is finished!'[3] And at the alley's end
He turns, and when on me his glances bend
As from the Past comes speech – small, muted, yet composed.

3
'How fares the Truth now? – Ill?
– Do pens but slily further her advance? 10
May one not speed her but in phrase askance?
Do scribes aver the Comic to be Reverend still?

---

[1] *acacias* shrub or tree, found in warmer parts of Europe.
[2] *Anon* directly, immediately.
[3] *'It is finished!'* cf. 'When Iesus therefore had receiued the vineger, he said, It is finished, and he bowed his head, and gaue vp the ghost', John 19.30; now proverbial.

4
'Still rule those minds on earth
At whom sage Milton's wormwood[4] words were hurled:
"*Truth like a bastard comes into the world*   15
Never without ill-fame to him who gives her birth"?'[5]

[4] *wormwood* plant renowned for bitter taste.
[5] *Truth . . . birth* see Milton's *Doctrine and Discipline of Divorce* (first published 1643), 'for Truth is as impossible to be soil'd by any outward touch, as the Sunbeam; though this ill hap wait on her Nativity, that she never comes into the World, but like a Bastard, to the ignominy of him that brought her forth; till Time, the Midwife rather than the Mother of Truth, have washt and salted the Infant, [and] declar'd her legitimate'.

The Revisitation

A short narrative poem of Wessex, 'The Revisitation' (*Fortnightly Review* [1904], then in *Time's Laughing-stocks* [1909]) has a ballad-like interest in the actions of rural men and women (Wessex was Hardy's imaginary county in the south of England). The poem, with its themes of lost love, ageing, human emotional cruelty and the bitter consequences of coincidence, implies the repetitive patterns of history in a human life span. Set in a landscape marked by prehistory, 'The Revisitation' – originally subtitled 'A Summer Romance' – confronts the tragic potential of time's repetitions. It gains some of its force from bleak Biblical parody. The title invites association with the narrative of the Visitation (Luke 1), the arrival of the angel Gabriel to the young Virgin Mary to announce her pregnancy by the Holy Spirit. But in Hardy's *re*visitation, the woman is at the close of middle age and is met by her long-abandoned lover only to re-enact a separation. No divine schemes of salvation are manifested here.

The sense of the impotence of age and of the dissipation of energies through time connects the poem with Hardy's meditation on the enervation of the whole nineteenth century in 'The Darkling Thrush', 512–13. Late Victorian science had mused on the dissipation of useful energies in the universe. Work by William Thomson, later Lord Kelvin (1824–1907), suggested in a key interpretation of the Second Law of Thermodynamics that the sun was gradually cooling and that life on earth would, in due course, cease. Hardy's text – which ironically finds in the *rising* of the sun its own bleak climax – dramatizes a local, human version of this ominous narrative of entropy.

Text: *The Complete Poetical Works of Thomas Hardy* (1982).

As I lay awake at night-time
In an ancient country barrack known to ancient cannoneers,
And recalled the hopes that heralded each seeming brave and bright time
Of my primal purple[1] years,

2
Much it haunted me that, nigh[2] there,   5
I had borne my bitterest loss – when One who went, came not again;
In a joyless hour of discord, in a joyless-hued July there –
A July just such as then.

3
And as thus I brooded longer,
With my faint eyes on the feeble square of wan-lit[3] window frame,   10
A quick conviction sprung within me, grew, and grew yet stronger
That the month-night was the same,

[1] *purple* colloq. splendid.
[2] *nigh* near.
[3] *wan-lit* dimly lit.

4
Too, as that which saw her leave me
On the rugged ridge of Waterstone, the peewits[4] plaining round:
And a lapsing twenty years had ruled that – as it were to grieve me –   15
I should near the once-loved ground.

5
Though but now a war-worn stranger
Chance had quartered here, I rose up and descended to the yard.
All was soundless, save the troopers' horses tossing at the manger,
And the sentry keeping guard.   20

6
Through the gateway I betook me
Down the High Street and beyond the lamps, across the battered bridge,
Till the country darkness clasped me and the friendly shine forsook me,
And I bore towards the Ridge,

7
With a dim unowned emotion   25
Saying softly: 'Small my reason, now at midnight, to be here . . .
Yet a sleepless swain[5] of fifty with a brief romantic notion
May retrace a track so dear.'

8
Thus I walked with thoughts half-uttered
Up the lane I knew so well, the grey, gaunt, lonely Lane of Slyre;[6]   30
And at whiles behind me, far at sea, a sullen thunder muttered
As I mounted high and higher.

9
Till, the upper roadway quitting,
I adventured on the open drouthy[7] downland thinly grassed,
While the spry white scuts of conies[8] flashed before me, earthward flitting,   35
And an arid wind went past.

10
Round about me bulged the barrows[9]
As before, in antique silence – immemorial funeral piles –
Where the sleek herds trampled daily the remains of flint-tipt arrows
Mid the thyme and chamomiles;[10]   40

11
And the Sarsen stone[11] there, dateless,
On whose breast we had sat and told the zephyrs[12] many a tender vow,
Held the heat of yester sun, as sank thereon one fated mateless   45
From those far fond hours till now.

---

[4] *peewits* lapwings.
[5] *swain* countryman (with ironic recollection of its sense as rustic lover).
[6] *Slyre* fine linen, lawn.
[7] *drouthy* arid, dry.
[8] *scuts of conies* rabbit tails.
[9] *barrows* prehistoric grave mounds.
[10] *chamomile* (camomile) aromatic creeping herb.
[11] *Sarsen stone* large sandstone boulder found on chalk downs.
[12] *zephyrs* light winds.

12

Maybe flustered by my presence   50
Rose the peewits, just as all those years back, wailing soft and loud,
And revealing their pale pinions[13] like a fitful phosphorescence
Up against the cope[14] of cloud,

13

Where their dolesome exclamations
Seemed the voicings of the self-same throats I had heard when life was green,   55
Though since that day uncounted frail forgotten generations
Of their kind had flecked the scene. –

14

And so, living long and longer
In a past that lived no more, my eyes discerned there, suddenly,
That a figure broke the skyline – first in vague contour, then stronger,   60
And was crossing near to me.

15

Some long-missed familiar gesture,
Something wonted,[15] struck me in the figure's pause to list[16] and heed,
Till I fancied from its handling of its loosely wrapping vesture
That it might be She indeed.   65

16

'Twas not reasonless: below there
In the vale, had been her home; the nook might hold her even yet,
And the downlands were her father's fief;[17] she still might come and go there; –
So I rose, and said, 'Agnette!'

17

With a little leap, half-frightened,   70
She withdrew some steps; then letting intuition smother fear
In a place so long-accustomed, and as one whom thought enlightened,
She replied: 'What – that voice? – here!'

18

'Yes, Agnette! – And did the occasion
Of our marching hither make you think I might walk where we two – '   75
'O, I often come,' she murmured with a moment's coy evasion,
'('Tis not far), – and – think of you.'

19

Then I took her hand, and led her
To the ancient people's stone whereon I had sat. There now sat we;
And together talked, until the first reluctant shyness fled her,   80
And she spoke confidingly.

---

[13] *pinions* wings.
[14] *cope* ecclesiastical robe.
[15] *wonted* accustomed.

[16] *list* listen.
[17] *fief* feudal estate.

20

'It is just as ere we parted!'
Said she, brimming high with joy. – 'And when, then, came you here, and why?'
' – Dear, I could not sleep for thinking of our trystings[18] when twin-hearted.'
She responded, 'Nor could I.   85

21

'There are few things I would rather
Than be wandering at this spirit-hour – lone-lived, my kindred dead –
On this wold[19] of well-known feature I inherit from my father:
Night or day, I have no dread . . .

22

'O I wonder, wonder whether   90
Any heartstring bore a signal-thrill between us twain or no? –
Some such influence can, at times, they say, draw severed souls together.'
I said, 'Dear, we'll dream it so.'

23

Each one's hand the other's grasping,
And a mutual forgiveness won, we sank to silent thought,   95
A large content in us that seemed our rended lives reclasping,
And contracting years to nought.

24

Till I, maybe overweary
From the lateness, and a wayfaring so full of strain and stress
For one no longer buoyant, to a peak so steep and eery,   100
Sank to slow unconsciousness . . .

25

How long I slept I knew not,
But the brief warm summer night had slid when, to my swift surprise,
A red upedging sun, of glory chambered mortals view not,
Was blazing on my eyes,   105

26

From the Milton Woods to Dole-Hill[20]
All the spacious landscape lighting, and around about my feet
Flinging tall thin tapering shadows from the meanest mound and mole-hill,
And on trails the ewes had beat.

27

She was sitting still beside me,   110
Dozing likewise; and I turned to her, to take her hanging hand;
When, the more regarding, that which like a spectre shook and tried me
In her image then I scanned;

28

That which Time's transforming chisel
Had been tooling night and day for twenty years, and tooled too well,   115

---

[18] *trystings* lovers' meetings.   [20] *Dole-Hill* dole means 'grief', 'sorrow'.
[19] *wold* piece of open country.

In its rendering of crease where curve was, where was raven,[21] grizzle[22] –
Pits, where peonies[23] once did dwell.

29
She had wakened, and perceiving
(I surmise) my sigh and shock, my quite involuntary dismay,
Up she started, and – her wasted figure all throughout it heaving –   120
Said, 'Ah, yes: I am thus by day!

30
'Can you really wince and wonder
That the sunlight should reveal you such a thing of skin and bone,
As if unaware a Death's-head[24] must of need lie not far under
Flesh whose years out-count your own?   125

31
'Yes: that movement was a warning
Of the worth of man's devotion! – Yes, Sir, I am old,' said she,
'And the thing which should increase love turns it quickly into scorning –
And your new-won heart from me!'

32
Then she went, ere I could call her,   130
With the too proud temper ruling that had parted us before,
And I saw her form descend the slopes, and smaller grow and smaller,
Till I caught its course no more . . .

33
True; I might have dogged her downward;
– But it may be (though I know not) that this trick on us of Time   135
Disconcerted and confused me. – Soon I bent my footsteps townward,
Like to one who had watched a crime.

34
Well I knew my native weakness,
Well I know it still. I cherished her reproach like physic-wine,[25]
For I saw in that emaciate shape of bitterness and bleakness   140
A nobler soul than mine.

35
Did I not return, then, ever? –
Did we meet again? – mend all? – Alas, what greyhead perseveres! –
Soon I got the Route elsewhither. – Since that hour I have seen her never:
Love is lame at fifty years.

---

[21] *raven* rich black.
[22] *grizzle* grey.
[23] *peonies* plants with large handsome flowers of red and white.

[24] *Death's-head* human skull used as emblem of mortality.
[25] *physic-wine* wine taken as medicine.

Gerard M[anley] Hopkins (1844–1889)

Gerard Manley Hopkins (who usually used the form Gerard M. Hopkins) was born in Stratford, east London, into a middle-class, High Anglican family. He was taught by the poet and church historian Richard Watson Dixon at Highgate School and then entered Balliol College Oxford. At Oxford, he became friends with the future Poet Laureate Robert Bridges (1844–1930) and wrote poetry himself, some of which survived. He was influenced by the Oxford Movement but, like John Henry Newman, eventually abandoned the Church of England; he was received into the Catholic Church in 1866. Resolving to become a Jesuit – the major Catholic teaching order – in 1868, he symbolically destroyed his poetic manuscripts (it was symbolic because he had sent copies to Bridges). He trained in Roehampton, Stonyhurst and St Bueno's in Wales (where he returned to writing poetry with 'The Wreck of the *Deutschland*') before serving as priest in London, Oxford and then Liverpool. During 1877, Hopkins wrote some of his best-known work ('The Windhover', 'Pied Beauty'); he taught at Stonyhurst between 1881 and 1884 and was then appointed to a professorship in Greek and Latin at University College Dublin. The administrative and academic labour overwhelmed him and other personal feelings of isolation led to the 'Dark' or 'Terrible' sonnets (including 'No worst, there is none' and 'My own heart let me more have pity on'). Hopkins died of typhoid in Dublin in June 1889 at the age of 44, perhaps the most original poet of the age and one almost totally unknown. Robert Bridges inherited his papers and brought out the *Poems of Gerard Manley Hopkins* in 1918.

The Wreck of the *Deutschland*

To the happy memory of five Franciscan Nuns exiles by the Falk Laws drowned between midnight and morning of Dec. 7th. 1875

If the Romantic-period poets, chiefly Shelley, associated liberty with creativity, freedom of body and mind with freedom of poetic imagination, Gerard M. Hopkins found vitality in constraint, pressure, confinement, anguish and suffering. The energy of 'The Wreck of the *Deutschland*' is partly the product of a mind that takes nothing easily. Poetry is born of strain, and the extraordinarily compacted language of this shaken mosaic bears witness to the poet's (and, at a more general level, the Christian's) efforts to master the meaning of torment and to accommodate the knowledge that God Himself is present in suffering.

'The Wreck of the *Deutschland*' was written in December 1875. In *The Times* and *Illustrated London News*, Hopkins, then studying for ordination at a Jesuit college in Wales, read reports of the wreck of the passenger ship the *Deutschland*, a German vessel bound for New York with more than a hundred passengers. In a fierce storm on 6 December 1875, the captain of the *Deutschland* lost direction and the vessel foundered on a sandbank at the mouth of the Thames. Help was slow to come (perhaps deliberately, so that a plunder of cargo could be made) and when it did, 30 hours later, more than 60 passengers and crew were dead. Conditions were ferocious. *The Times* reported

on 11 December in words that lie behind some of the substance and urgency of the poem: 'Five German nuns, whose bodies are now in the dead-house here, clasped hands and were drowned together, the chief sister, a gaunt woman 6ft. high, calling out loudly and often "O Christ, come quickly" till the end came. The shrieks and sobbing of women and children are described by the survivors as agonising. One brave sailor, who was safe in the rigging, went down to try and save a child or woman who was drowning on deck. He was secured by a rope to the rigging, but a wave dashed him against the bulwarks, and when daylight dawned his headless body, detained by the rope, was swaying to and fro with the waves. In the dreadful excitement of these hours one man hung himself behind the wheelhouse, another hacked at his wrist with a knife, hoping to die a comparatively painless death by bleeding.'

The first part of Hopkins's poem, the most extensive of his major achievements as a writer, concerns the role of violence in the Catholic's experience of God. Hopkins, privileging the anguish and disturbance of the Christian life, asserts that God masters the individual believer, who will find Him through terrifying but merciful conquest, the 'anvil-ding' of

Grace. This section sets the context for the poem's exploration of the question of death and disaster in human experience, and its binding of apparent calamity into the logic of the divine scheme.

The second part of 'The Wreck' gives, as it were, a case study of this theology of the violence of Grace by focusing on the wreck itself. In the person of the tall nun, Hopkins sees his principle of God's presence in tumult expressed with peculiar force, affirming at the same time that the ordinary faithful life can be transformed by God and made heroic. Doomed by the storm, the tall nun towers over the catastrophe with her rock-sure faith. Hopkins's language for her meeting with Jesus in heaven, the reward of faith through torment and violent death, is ecstatic and erotic, drawing on a long tradition of assimilating the language of religious and sexual ecstasy. In stanza 31, the poet speculates that the shipwreck might be part of God's way of revealing His presence to non-Catholics too. But it is the reconversion of England as a nation to Catholicism to which Hopkins looks at the conclusion of the poem, asking for the nun's intercessory assistance. On 29 September 1850, Pope Pius IX, with the document *Universalis Ecclesiae*, had restored the Catholic ecclesiastical hierarchy in England: Hopkins, in 1875, aspires to a more complete re-embrace of the faith of Pre-Reformation England.

The poem, limitedly circulated in Hopkins's lifetime, was greeted with bafflement: the Catholic periodical the *Month* would not publish it. But Hopkins's efforts to make syntax and vocabulary articulate his meaning through violent reconfiguration generated an extraordinary new language for Victorian poetry, a discourse suggestive of that to which the Modernists would return in the twentieth century. Its challenges remain, however, and 'The Wreck of the *Deutschland*', with its experimental rhythmic effects and unexpected verbal collocations, speaks most clearly if read aloud. Hopkins carefully marks the stresses of his distinctive use of rhythm, guiding the poem's performance. As the poet's most vivid effort to insist on the sense that violence made, it can be compared with Tennyson's debate about the death of Arthur Hallam in *In Memoriam A.H.H.*, 88–165, and with Hopkins's other considerations of divine violence, e.g., 'The Windhover', 538–9.

Text: *The Poems of Gerard Manley Hopkins* (1918).

PART THE FIRST

Thou mastering me
God! giver of breath and bread;
World's strand, sway of the sea;
Lord of living and dead;
Thou hast bound bones and veins in me, fastened me flesh,   5
And after it almost unmade, what with dread,
  Thy doing: and dost thou touch me afresh?
  Over again I feel thy finger and find thee.

2

I did say yes[1]
O at lightning and lashed rod;   10
Thou heardst me truer than tongue confess
Thy terror, O Christ, O God;
Thou knowest the walls, altar and hour and night:
The swoon of a heart that the sweep and the hurl of thee trod
  Hard down with a horror of height: 15
And the midriff astrain with leaning of, laced with fire of stress.

3

The frown of his face
Before me, the hurtle of hell
Behind, where, where was a, where was a place?
I whirled out wings that spell   20

[1] *yes* saying 'Yes' to God is Hopkins's acceptance of His authority.

And fled with a fling of the heart to the heart of the Host.[2]
My heart, but you were dovewinged, I can tell,
Carrier-witted,[3] I am bold to boast,
To flash from the flame to the flame[4] then, tower from the grace to the grace.[5]

4

I am soft sift   25
In an hourglass[6] – at the wall
Fast, but mined with a motion, a drift,
And it crowds and it combs to the fall;
I steady as a water in a well, to a poise, to a pane,[7]
But roped with,[8] always, all the way down from the tall   30
Fells or flanks of the voel,[9] a vein
Of the gospel proffer, a pressure, a principle, Christ's gift.

5

I kiss my hand
To the stars, lovely-asunder
Starlight, wafting him out of it; and   35
Glow, glory in thunder;
Kiss my hand to the dappled-with-damson west:
Since, tho' he is under the world's splendour and wonder,
His mystery must be instressed,[10] stressed;
For I greet him the days I meet him, and bless when I understand.   40

6

Not out of his bliss
Springs the stress felt
Nor first from heaven (and few know this)
Swings the stroke dealt –
Stroke and a stress that stars and storms deliver,   45
That guilt is hushed by, hearts are flushed by and melt –
But it rides time like riding a river
(And here the faithful waver, the faithless fable and miss).

7

It dates from day
Of his going in Galilee;[11]   50
Warm-laid grave of a womb-life grey;
Manger,[12] maiden's knee;
The dense and the driven Passion,[13] and frightful sweat;

---

[2] *Host* sacred bread of the mass, signifying the body of Jesus.
[3] *carrier-witted* Hopkins's heart knew where it belonged, like a carrier-pigeon.
[4] *flame to the flame* from pain and fear to the flame of God.
[5] *grace to the grace* from the grace of God working on Hopkins himself to God as the source of all Grace.
[6] *hourglass* timing device using the slow pouring of sand (hence 'soft sift').
[7] *pane* the water in the well is as smooth as a pane of glass.
[8] *roped with* Hopkins thinks of himself as like a hill 'roped' with streams (that look like straggling ropes down the hillside): the streams come from the vein of God and are Grace.

[9] *voel* bare hill or mountain in Welsh (Hopkins was in Wales when he wrote the poem). Pronounced 'voil'.
[10] *instressed* Hopkins defined 'instress' both as the force of being that holds the individual and unique characteristics of something together, and the power that communicates this to the beholder.
[11] *It . . . Galilee* the violence that brings God into human hearts – which has been described in the previous stanzas – is an enactment of the first violence against Jesus, his life on earth (in Galilee) leading to his death that redeemed humankind.
[12] *Manger* the baby Jesus was laid to rest in a manger (Luke 2.7).
[13] *Passion* suffering and crucifixion of Jesus (Mark 14–16).

Thence the discharge of it, there its swelling to be,
Though felt before, though in high flood yet –   55
What none would have known of it, only the heart, being hard at bay,

8

Is out with it![14] Oh,
We lash with the best or worst
Word last! How a lush-kept plush-capped sloe[15]
Will, mouthed to flesh-burst,   60
Gush! – flush the man, the being with it, sour or sweet,
Brim, in a flash, full! – Hither then, last or first,
To hero of Calvary,[16] Christ's feet –
Never ask if meaning it, wanting it, warned of it – men go.

9

Be adored among men,   *Donne*   65
God, three-numberèd form;[17]
Wring thy rebel, dogged in den,
Man's malice, with wrecking and storm.
Beyond saying sweet, past telling of tongue,
Thou art lightning and love, I found it, a winter and warm;   70
Father and fondler of heart thou hast wrung:
Hast thy dark descending and most art merciful then.

10

With an anvil-ding
And with fire in him forge thy will
Or rather, rather then, stealing as Spring   75
Through him, melt him but master him still:
Whether at once, as once at a crash Paul,[18]
Or as Austin,[19] a lingering-out swéet skíll,
Make mercy in all of us, out of us all
Mastery, but be adored, but be adored King.   80

PART THE SECOND

11   *Death*

'Some find me a sword; some
The flange[20] and the rail; flame,
Fang, or flood' goes Death on drum,
And storms bugle his fame.[21]
But wé dream we are rooted in earth – Dust!   85
Flesh falls within sight of us, we, though our flower the same,
Wave with the meadow, forget that there must
The sour scythe cringe, and the blear share come.[22]

---

[14] *hard at bay . . . it* only the suffering/hard-pressed heart comprehends the meaning of Jesus's death.

[15] *sloe* berry, the fruit of the blackthorn with sharp sour taste. It is only under pressure that the sloe yields, just as it is only under pressure that a human moves closer to God.

[16] *Calvary* place of Jesus's crucifixion (Luke 23.33).

[17] *three-numberèd form* God the Trinity: Father, Son and Holy Spirit.

[18] *Paul* St Paul was converted to Christianity in an instant on the road to Damascus (Acts 9.3).

[19] *Austin* St Augustine (354–430), whose conversion to Christianity was, unlike St Paul's, a gradual one.

[20] *flange* projecting rim from an object; here, a suggestion of an instrument of torture?

[21] *Some find . . . fame* death comes in different forms including war, fire and flood: storms bring death also.

[22] *But wé dream . . . come* we think we are rooted to earth and forget about death.

12   *Nuns*

On Saturday sailed from Bremen,[23]
American-outward-bound,[24]   90
Take settler and seamen, tell men with women,
Two hundred souls[25] in the round –
O Father, not under thy feathers nor ever as guessing
The goal was a shoal, of a fourth the doom to be drowned;[26]
Yet did the dark side of the bay of thy blessing   95
Not vault them, the million of rounds of thy mercy not reeve[27] even them in?

13

Into the snows she sweeps,
Hurling the haven behind,
The Deutschland, on Sunday; and so the sky keeps,
For the infinite air is unkind,   100
And the sea flint-flake, black-backed in the regular blow,
Sitting Eastnortheast, in cursed quarter, the wind;
Wiry and white-fiery and whirlwind-swivellèd snow
Spins to the widow-making unchilding unfathering deeps.

14

She drove in the dark to leeward,[28]   105
She struck – not a reef or a rock
But the combs of a smother of sand: night drew her
Dead to the Kentish Knock;[29]
And she beat the bank down with her bows and the ride of her keel:
The breakers rolled on her beam with ruinous shock;   110
And canvas and compass, the whorl[30] and the wheel
Idle for ever to waft her or wind her with, these she endured.

15

Hope had grown grey hairs,
Hope had mourning on,
Trenched with tears, carved with cares,   115
Hope was twelve hours gone;
And frightful a nightfall folded rueful a day
Nor rescue, only rocket and lightship, shone,
And lives at last were washing away:
To the shrouds[31] they took, – they shook in the hurling and horrible airs.   120

16

One stirred from the rigging to save
The wild woman-kind below,
With a rope's end round the man, handy and brave –
He was pitched to his death at a blow,
For all his dreadnought breast and braids[32] of thew:[33]   125

[23] *Bremen* major city of northern Germany with access through the River Weser to the North Sea.
[24] *American-outward-bound* the *Deutschland* was bound for New York.
[25] *Two hundred souls* an over-estimate (see headnote, 525).
[26] *fourth . . . drowned* a fourth of the ship's complement – who were not Catholics – would drown on the journey.
[27] *reeve* with the nautical sense of passing a rope through a ring or block to secure something.

[28] *leeward* away from the wind.
[29] *Kentish Knock* sandbank at the mouth of the River Thames.
[30] *whorl* spiral structure.
[31] *shrouds* clothing of death.
[32] *braid* plait or woven string.
[33] *thew* strength, sinews, muscles.

They could tell him for hours, dandled the to and fro
Through the cobbled foam-fleece. What could he do
With the burl of the fountains of air, buck and the flood of the wave?

17

They fought with God's cold –
And they could not and fell to the deck   130
(Crushed them) or water (and drowned them) or rolled
With the sea-romp over the wreck.
Night roared, with the heart-break hearing a heart-broke rabble,
The woman's wailing, the crying of child without check –
Turn   Till a lioness[34] arose breasting the babble,   135
A prophetess towered in the tumult, a virginal tongue told.

18

Ah, touched in your bower of bone
Are you! turned for an exquisite smart,
Have you! make words break from me here all alone,
Do you![35] – mother of being in me, heart.   140
O unteachably after evil, but uttering truth,[36]
Why, tears! is it? tears; such a melting, a madrigal[37] start!
Never-eldering revel and river of youth,
What can it be, this glee? the good you have there of your own?

19

Sister, a sister calling   145
A master, her master and mine! –
And the inboard seas run swirling and hawling;[38]
The rash smart sloggering brine
Blinds her; but she that weather sees one thing, one;
Has one fetch in her: she rears herself to divine   150
Ears, and the call of the tall nun
To the men in the tops and the tackle rode over the storm's brawling.

20

She was first of a five and came
Of a coifèd[39] sisterhood.
(O Deutschland, double a desperate name![40]   155
O world wide of its good!
But Gertrude,[41] lily,[42] and Luther,[43] are two of a town,
Christ's lily and beast of the waste wood:

DOESN'T LIKE L.
COMPARES L
& GETRUDE
TO CAIN & ABEL

---

[34] *lioness* the nun who takes control.

[35] *make words . . . Do you!* thought of the nun makes
Hopkins, far away from the events, exclaim.

[36] *mother of being . . . truth* despite his fallen nature,
Hopkins recognizes the truth for which the nun stands.

[37] *madrigal* early form of English part song, here meaning, I
think, that Hopkins is moved as if by music in
contemplation of the nun.

[38] *hawling* neologism: a compound, presumably, of hauling
and sprawling.

[39] *coifèd* a coif is a close-fitting cap covering the top, back
and sides of the head.

[40] *double a desperate name* Deutschland refers both to the
country and the ship: one has cast out its religious (and was
the birthplace of the hated Reformer Luther, see note 41),
the other is wrecked.

[41] *Gertrude* thirteenth-century German saint (there is
disagreement as to her dates), often thought to have been
born in Eisleben. See note 43.

[42] *lily* St Gertrude is like a lily, a flower associated, through
its whiteness, with Mary and Jesus.

[43] *Luther*, Martin Luther (1438–1546), leader of the
German Reformation, also born in Eisleben. Hopkins, the
Jesuit, thinks of Luther as the opposite of St Gertrude, a
'beast of the waste wood'.

From life's dawn it is drawn down,
Abel is Cain's brother[44] and breasts they have sucked the same.)   160

21

Loathed for a love men knew in them,
Banned by the land of their birth,[45]
Rhine[46] refused them. Thames would ruin them;[47]
Surf, snow, river and earth
Gnashed: but thou art above, thou Orion[48] of light;   165
Thy unchancelling[49] poising palms were weighing the worth,
Thou martyr-master: in thy sight
Storm flakes were scroll-leaved flowers, lily showers – sweet heaven was astrew in them.

[handwritten marginal note: others understood this kind of love / Could not be Cath.]

22

Five! the finding and sake
And cipher of suffering Christ.[50]   170
Mark, the mark is of man's make
And the word of it Sacrificed.
But he scores it in scarlet himself on his own bespoken,
Before-time-taken, dearest prizèd and priced –
Stigma,[51] signal, cinquefoil[52] token   175
For lettering of the lamb's fleece,[53] ruddying of the rose-flake.

23

Joy fall to thee, father Francis,
Drawn to the Life that died;
With the gnarls of the nails in thee, niche of the lance, his
Lovescape crucified   180
And seal of his seraph-arrival![54] and these thy daughters
And five-livèd and leavèd favour and pride,
Are sisterly sealed in wild waters,
To bathe in his fall-gold mercies, to breathe in his all-fire glances.

24

Away in the loveable west,   185
On a pastoral forehead of Wales,[55]

---

[44] *Abel is Cain's brother* Cain and Abel were both sons of Adam and Eve: Cain slew Abel from jealousy (Genesis 4.1–17). As the children of the same mother they represent a similar pairing of good and evil born of the same parents as Gertrude and Luther, both born in the same country and town.

[45] *Banned . . . birth* under the Falck Laws (from 1872), Catholic schools were brought under state control, religious orders were forbidden to teach and Jesuits (eventually all orders) were expelled from Germany.

[46] *Rhine* central river of northwestern Germany, here, representative of the nation.

[47] *Thames would ruin them* there was some indication that English sailors on boats in the area deliberately waited for the *Deutschland* to break up so they could pillage her. First reports indicated that the dead had all been stripped of valuables.

[48] *Orion* large and brilliant constellation south of the zodiac, figured as a hunter with belt and sword.

[49] *unchancelling* neologism: presumably it means leaving nothing to chance. It also has the resonance of 'being outside a chancel', i.e., outside (though still in the hands of God).

[50] *Five . . . Christ* five wounds of Jesus at the crucifixion.

[51] *Stigma* recalling 'stigmata', crucifixion wounds.

[52] *cinquefoil* architectural term referring to five divisions in a pointed arch or ring.

[53] *lamb's fleece* cf. red dye used to mark the fleece of lambs and sheep; the line also recalls that Jesus is the Lamb of God.

[54] *And seal of his seraph-arrival* St Francis (1181/1182–1226), Italian saint and founder of the Franciscans, miraculously received the stigmata – the five wounds of Jesus.

[55] *Wales* Hopkins was at the Jesuit community at St Beuno's in Wales, continuing his theological education in the winter of 1875.

I was under a roof here, I was at rest,
And they the prey of the gales;
She to the black-about air, to the breaker, the thickly
Falling flakes, to the throng that catches and quails   190
Was calling 'O Christ, Christ, come quickly':[56]
The cross to her she calls Christ to her, christens her wild-worst Best.[57]

25

The majesty! what did she mean?
Breathe, arch and original Breath.[58]
Is it love in her of the being as her lover had been?   195
Breathe, body of lovely Death.
They were else-minded then, altogether, the men
Woke thee with a *We are perishing* in the weather of Gennesareth.[59]
Or is it that she cried for the crown then,
The keener to come at the comfort for feeling the combating keen?[60]   200

26

For how to the heart's cheering
The down-dugged ground-hugged grey
Hovers off, the jay-blue heavens appearing
Of pied and peeled May!
Blue-beating and hoary-glow height; or night, still higher,   205
With belled fire and the moth-soft Milky Way,[61]
What by your measure is the heaven of desire,
The treasure never eyesight got, nor was ever guessed what for the hearing?

27

No, but it was not these.
The jading and jar of the cart,   210
Time's tasking, it is fathers that asking for ease
Of the sodden-with-its-sorrowing heart,
Not danger, electrical horror; then further it finds
——— The appealing of the Passion is tenderer in prayer apart:
Other, I gather, in measure her mind's   215
Burden, in wind's burly and beat of endragonèd seas.[62]

28

But how shall I . . . make me room there:
Reach me a . . . Fancy, come faster –
Strike you the sight of it? look at it loom there,
Thing that she . . . there then! the Master,   220

---

[56] 'O Christ, Christ, come quickly' cf. Revelation 22.20: 'Surely, I come quickly. Amen. Euen so, Come Lord Iesus' (and headnote, 525). The words are part of the Church's liturgy for the season of Advent, the penitential period that is the preparation for the coming of Jesus at Christmas. The *Deutschland* sank during Advent.
[57] *christens her wild-worst Best* the storm is the nun's worst moment, but she 'christens' it the best because it unites her with God.
[58] *Breath* God.
[59] *Gennesareth* cf. Mark 4.37–41, where Jesus calms a storm:

'And hee arose, and rebuked the winde, and said vnto the sea, Peace, be still: and the winde ceased, and there was a great calme' (4.39).
[60] *The keener to come at the comfort for feeling the combating keen?* nearly a chiasmus: the verbal form that marks out a cross. Even syntax gestures to the Christian theology of the poem.
[61] *Milky Way* galaxy that includes earth.
[62] *then further it finds . . . seas* God's Passion is known in prayer, but also this 'Other', the nun, knew it in the midst of the raging sea.

Latin (himself)

Ipse,[63] the only one, Christ, King, Head:
He was to cure the extremity where he had cast her;
Do, deal, lord it with living and dead;
Let him ride, her pride, in his triumph, despatch and have done with his doom there.

29

Ah! there was a heart right!   225
There was single eye!
Read the unshapeable shock night
And knew the who and the why;
Wording it how but by him that present and past,
Heaven and earth are word of, worded by? –   230
The Simon Peter[64] of a soul! to the blast
Tarpeian-fast,[65] but a blown beacon of light.

30

Jesu, heart's light,
Jesu, maid's son,
What was the feast followed the night   235
Thou hadst glory of this nun? –
Feast of the one woman without stain.[66]
For so conceivèd, so to conceive thee is done;
But here was heart-throe, birth of a brain,
Word, that heard and kept thee and uttered thee outright.   240

31

Well, she has thee for the pain, for the
Patience; but pity of the rest of them!
Heart, go and bleed at a bitterer vein for the
Comfortless unconfessed of them[67] –
No not uncomforted: lovely-felicitous Providence   245
Finger of a tender of, O of a feathery delicacy, the breast of the
Maiden could obey so, be a bell to, ring of it, and
Startle the poor sheep back! is the shipwreck then a harvest, does tempest carry the grain for
thee?[68]

---

[63] *Ipse* himself (Jesus).

[64] *Simon Peter* Peter, one of Jesus's disciples (a fisherman, and therefore associated with the sea). Hopkins thinks of his confession of faith (in Luke 9.20): '[Jesus] said vnto them, But whom say yee that I am? Peter answering, said, The Christ of God.' Hopkins is referring to the nun's belief in God in the midst of the storm.

[65] *Tarpeian-fast* cf. the Tarpeian Rock on the Capitoline Hill at Rome over which those convicted of treason to the state were thrown headlong. Hopkins stresses the violence of the storm, but also sees the nun as like a 'beacon of light', a lighthouse surviving through it.

[66] *without stain* i.e., the Virgin Mary. The *Deutschland* struck a sandbank on 6 December, and lay there all day: most of the deaths occurred the following night, 6–7 December. 7 December is the eve of the Church's feast of the Immaculate Conception on 8 December ('feast' meaning day of celebration), a festival of the Virgin Mary's conception without the burden of original sin. This doctrine had been made an official dogma of the Catholic Church only with Pope Pius IX's *Ineffabilis Deus* of 8 December 1854. Hopkins's reference expresses assent to Pius's authority. The poet is partly implying that the sinking of the *Deutschland* reveals the divine scheme that Pius had – to the shock of many English Protestants – enshrined as dogma. Hopkins thinks of Jesus welcoming the nun into heaven at the time the Church celebrates his mother's purity.

[67] *Comfortless unconfessed of them* those who were not Catholics.

[68] *is the shipwreck . . . for thee* Hopkins wonders if the shipwreck was God's way of leading non-Catholics back to God.

32

I admire thee, master of the tides,
Of the Yore-flood,[69] of the year's fall;   250
The recurb and the recovery of the gulf's sides,
The girth of it and the wharf of it and the wall;
Stanching, quenching ocean of a motionable mind;
Ground of being, and granite of it: past all
Grasp God, throned behind   255
Death with a sovereignty that heeds but hides, bodes but abides;

33

With a mercy that outrides
The all of water, an ark[70]
For the listener; for the lingerer with a love glides
Lower than death and the dark;   260
A vein for the visiting of the past-prayer, pent in prison,
The-last-breath penitent spirits – the uttermost mark
Our passion-plungèd giant risen,
The Christ of the Father compassionate, fetched in the storm of his strides.

34

Now burn, new born to the world,   265
Doubled-naturèd name,[71]
The heaven-flung, heart-fleshed, maiden-furled
Miracle-in-Mary-of-flame,
Mid-numbered He in three of the thunder-throne![72]
Not a dooms-day dazzle in his coming nor dark as he came;   270
Kind, but royally reclaiming his own;
A released shower, let flash to the shire, not a lightning of fire hard-hurled.

35

Dame, at our door
Drowned, and among our shoals,
Remember us in the roads, the heaven-haven of the Reward: 275
Our King back, oh, upon English souls![73]
Let him easter[74] in us, be a dayspring to the dimness of us, be a crimson-cresseted east,
More brightening her, rare-dear Britain, as his reign rolls,
Pride, rose, prince, hero of us, high-priest,
Our hearts' charity's hearth's fire, our thoughts' chivalry's throng's Lord.   280

[69] *Yore-flood* colloquialism for the Biblical flood (Genesis 6–9).
[70] *ark* cf. the Biblical flood, from which God preserved Noah and the ark.
[71] *Doubled-naturèd name* Jesus is both man and God, both 'heaven-flung' and 'heart-fleshed'.

[72] *Mid-numbered He in three of the thunder-throne* Jesus is the central Person of the Trinity: Father, Son and Holy Ghost.
[73] *Remember us . . . souls* Hopkins asks the drowned nun ('Dame') to pray for the restoration of the Catholic faith in England.
[74] *easter* be reborn.

Spring and Fall: to a young child

'Spring and Fall' is dated from 1880, but its seductively fluid rhythms are less experimental than the extraordinary manipulations of the earlier 'Wreck of the *Deutschland*', 525–34. The few neologisms and expressively irregular syntax only just hint at verbal and syntactical innovations elsewhere. In exploring a correspondence between the events of the natural world and the journey of the soul, Hopkins moves from the familiar to the theological, a sermon-like procedure. Margaret's sorrow at autumn (the literal meaning of 'fall') becomes her sorrow for original sin (the Christian sense of 'fall'). A priestly, Catholic response to Wordsworth's 'Immortality Ode', 'Spring and Fall' maps the child's life and growth away from the first fresh perceptions of nature in accordance with the Judaeo-Christian concept of humanity's innate sinfulness. It is without explicit comment on redemption (cf. the later 'That Nature is a Heraclitean fire and of the Comfort of the Resurrection', 540–1) but subtle allusions to the Bible suggest the hope of consolation under the poem's breath. Hopkins's rhythms and syntax catch the patterns of the speaking voice, while the certainties of the rhyme scheme and the chiming of assonance and alliteration foreground the artifice of the art and hold firmly in check the mourning the poem describes.

Hopkins may have taken the idea for the poem from a work of popular fiction which it seems he knew, Sylvester Judd's *Margaret: A Tale of the Real and Ideal, Blight and Bloom, Including Sketches of a Place not Before Described, Called Mons Christi* (1845). This includes, early on, a description of Margaret's first encounter with death when she goes hunting bees with other children: 'Margaret, looking in, and seeing the beautiful well-constructed house of the bees, seemed struck with remorse.' Judd's account of the incident and of the 'Blight and Bloom' of Margaret's life may lay distantly behind Hopkins's meditation.

Text: *The Poems of Gerard Manley Hopkins* (1918).

Márgarét, áre you gríeving
Over Goldengrove[1] unleaving?[2]
Leáves, líke the things of man, you
With your fresh thoughts care for, can you?
Áh! ás the heart grows older   5
It will come to such sights colder
By and by, nor spare a sigh
Though worlds of wanwood[3] leafmeal[4] lie;
And yet you *wíll* weep and know why.
Now no matter, child, the name: 10
Sórrow's spríngs áre the same.
Nor mouth had, no nor mind, expressed
What heart heard of, ghost[5] guessed:[6]
It ís the blight man was born for,
It is Margaret you mourn for.   15

[1] *Goldengrove* perhaps an imaginary place, certainly one with a sense of the 'golden age'/Eden. Jeremy Taylor (1613–67), the divine, wrote a book which Hopkins may have known called *The Golden Grove: A Choice Manual Containing What is to be Believed, Practised, and Desired or Prayed for* (there were a number of Victorian publications of this).
[2] *unleaving* losing its leaves.
[3] *wanwood* fading or decayed woodland.
[4] *leafmeal* with leaves fallen one by one.

[5] *ghost* spirit, soul.
[6] *ghost guessed* cf. Isaiah 64.4, 'For since the beginning of the world men haue not heard, nor perceiued by the eare, neither hath the eye seene, O God, besides thee, what hee hath prepared for him that waiteth for him' and 1 Corinthians 2.9, 'But as it is written, Eye hath not seene, nor eare heard, neither haue entred into the heart of man, the things which God hath prepared for them that loue him'.

As kingfishers catch fire

Hopkins created two important terms to describe the elements of individual identity. 'Inscape', he said, was the individual's distinctive form, the oneness or uniqueness of a natural thing. 'Instress' was the natural energy that upheld and determined 'inscape'. Both terms affirmed Hopkins's concern with the uniqueness of life and form, and 'As kingfishers catch fire' expresses this central preoccupation. The poem defines an individual creature's unique identity and

purpose, as well as that of each human being. This might appear to be a theory of individuality at the expense of community – a problematic relationship much debated, apart from anywhere else, in Victorian political economy – but Hopkins sees all individuality bound together in the divine plan. It is God who lies behind creation's multiplicity, just as Christ, in the diversity of human life, 'plays in ten thousand places', affirming man's difference and oneness with God.

Hopkins's preoccupation with unique individuality in relation to the broader community is partly to do with his own position as a poet: this issue is treated subtly in 'Pied Beauty', 537–8. In nature he persistently discerns the convincing signs of teleology – ultimate purpose – and human society is rarely his explicit subject. He has often, as a result, been read as apolitical. But his work can be seen in broad terms as *related* to political and economic circumstances. The determined focus on the consuming human subject, the self as absorber of nature and God, for instance, relates to, or, rather, belongs within the same cultural frame as the major change in Victorian economic theory from production to consumption principles, from an emphasis on man as producer to a conception of man as consumer. This modulation informs the individualist priorities of Paterian Aestheticism – marking a link between the secular principles of Walter Pater and the Catholic poetics of Hopkins – and lies behind Pater's definition of the first question of Aesthetic criticism in *The Renaissance* (1873): 'What is this song or picture, this engaging personality presented in life or in a book, to *me*?' Hopkins asks the same question, with its consumerist core, of nature.

Text: *The Poems of Gerard Manley Hopkins* (1918).

As kingfishers catch fire, dragonflies dráw fláme;
    As tumbled over rim in roundy wells
Stones ring; like each tucked string[1] tells, each hung bell's
Bow swung finds tongue to fling out broad its name;
Each mortal thing does one thing and the same: 5
    Deals out that being indoors each one dwells;
Selves – goes itself; *myself* it speaks and spells,
    Crying *Whát I do is me: for that I came.*

    I say móre: the just man justices;
Kéeps gráce: thát keeps all his goings graces;   10
Acts in God's eye what in God's eye he is –
    Chríst – for Christ plays in ten thousand places,
Lovely in limbs, and lovely in eyes not his
To the Father through the features of men's faces.

[1] *string* bell rope.

God's Grandeur

Hopkins's perception of the presence of God in nature is electrifyingly expressed here. As in 'The Windhover', 538–9, it is imagined partly in terms of violence, troped in 'God's Grandeur' as the crushing of seeds and berries to produce oil. While articulating a conception of divinity's omnipresence, Hopkins's language remains deeply rooted in the physical details of the material world. The poem – like much of Hopkins's work, it is a theological *argument* – addresses the problem of why, when God is so compellingly present, human beings take little account of Him. Human ignorance is imagined as the muddying and denudation of the soil. But nature offers evidence of heartening reassurance: it 'is never spent' because the Holy Ghost is within it and over it everlastingly. The answer to the sonnet's question, then, is already in the first line.

The notion of nature's infinite capacity to replenish itself, which is Christianized in 'God's Grandeur', is a Victorian assumption sharply alien to the twenty-first century. It lies at the heart of many nineteenth-century attitudes to the natural world including hunting, marine collecting, natural history museum displays of stuffed animals and birds, and still life painting. Hopkins considers contrastingly nature's permanent state of change – its endless destructiveness – in 'That Nature is a Heraclitean Fire and of the Comfort of the Resurrection', 540–1. Where Hopkins hinted at the androgynous power of God in 'Pied Beauty', 537–8, 'God's Grandeur' suggests more explicitly God's male and female energies as it moves from the masculine figure of God as immanent power to a feminized image of the Holy Ghost's motherhood.

Text: *The Poems of Gerard Manley Hopkins* (1918).

The world is charged[1] with the grandeur of God.
It will flame out, like shining from shook foil;
It gathers to a greatness, like the ooze of oil
Crushed.[2] Why do men then now not reck[3] his rod?
Generations have trod, have trod, have trod;   5
And all is seared with trade; bleared, smeared with toil;
And wears man's smudge and shares man's smell: the soil
Is bare now, nor can foot feel, being shod.

And for all this, nature is never spent;
There lives the dearest freshness deep down things;   10
And though the last lights off the black West[4] went
Oh, morning, at the brown brink eastward, springs –
Because the Holy Ghost over the bent
World broods with warm breast and with ah![5] bright wings.[6]

[handwritten marginalia: men w/ their industry over the years have lost sight of ¿]

[handwritten marginalia: although man has damaged the world, God always sets & rises the sun]

[handwritten marginalia: Reference to Gen 1:2 and the E became waste & emptiness darkness covered surface of deep & Spirit was brooding over surface of water]

[1] *charged* a quasi-scientific/electrical image. Cf. 'like shining from shook foil'.
[2] *ooze . . . Crushed* the image is one of a crushed olive.
[3] *reck* take heed.
[4] *black West* i.e., after the sun has set.
[5] *ah!* cf. George Herbert's 'ah my dear,' in 'Love III', a poem celebrating the generosity of divine love.

[6] *Because . . . wings* cf. Jesus's words: 'O Hierusalem, Hierusalem, thou that killest the Prophets, and stonest them which are sent vnto thee, how often would I haue gathered thy children together, euen as a hen gathereth her chickens vnder her wings, and yee would not?' Matthew 23.37.

Pied Beauty

'Pied Beauty' is an example of one of Hopkins's 'curtal' sonnets (a sonnet structure but of only 10 lines). This irregular sonnet praises irregularity. John Ruskin had celebrated the Gothic as architecture of natural form that eschewed symmetries and the artificial order imposed by neo-classicism, the Renaissance and the laws of mathematics (see 'The Nature of Gothic', from *The Stones of Venice*, vol. 2 [1853]). Here, Hopkins – who absorbed much from Ruskin – concentrates on the irregularities of natural form itself, insisting that there is a place, at a more abstract level, for the unorthodox, unusual and 'original' in God's creational scheme. The poem may be compared to 'As kingfishers catch fire', 535–6, as a meditation on the relationship between individuality and community, a version of the ancient philosophical conundrum of the One and the Many.

In insisting on the origin of all forms in divine creation, even the 'dappled things', Hopkins is partly producing an argument about himself and his art. The poem implicitly allows space for his innovative, difficult and 'counter' poetry, which does not easily fit into literary tradition. At a more private level, Hopkins's consideration of God's acceptance of the irregular speaks to his position as a homosexual. Although inscribing himself as 'counter' in terms of normative sexuality, Hopkins affirms, in the celebratory generosity of this text, that even such as he is by no means excluded from God. Hopkins figures God in suggestively androgynous terms – he does so more plainly in 'God's Grandeur', 536–7 – emphasizing the wholeness of the divine as including all that is human. God 'fathers-forth' beauty at the end of this poem, but as the generator of life He is mother as well as father.

Text: *The Poems of Gerard Manley Hopkins* (1918).

Glory be to God for dappled things –
For skies of couple-colour as a brinded[1] cow;
For rose-moles all in stipple[2] upon trout that swim;
Fresh-firecoal chestnut-falls; finches' wings;
Landscape plotted and pieced – fold, fallow, and plough;   5
And áll trádes, their gear and tackle and trim.

[1] *brinded* of a tawny or brownish colour, marked with bars or streaks of a different colour.
[2] *stipple* dots.

All things counter, original, spare, strange;
Whatever is fickle, freckled (who knows how?)
With swift, slow; sweet, sour; adazzle, dim;
He fathers-forth whose beauty is past change:
Praise him.   10

The Windhover

To Christ Our Lord

Where Romantic-period poets – Coleridge, Keats, Shelley, Charlotte Smith – wrote of encounters with birds as a way of dramatizing debates about poetry, Hopkins's finds Christ in the early morning experience of watching a bird of prey. The force of the experience described in 'The Windhover' (a local name for a kestrel) is that of a man who senses God through the masterly behaviour of a wild creature. As in 'The Wreck of the *Deutschland*', 525–34, Hopkins utilizes the language of violence and eroticism in an effort to articulate in words the staggering extreme of the event. The sexual undertone may be amplified by taking into account the fact that Hopkins was likely to have known the other popular country name for the kestrel – the windfucker. Hopkins added the subtitle 'To Christ Our Lord' some six years after the poem was written, partly, perhaps, to help tone down its sexual suggestiveness.

The peculiar pressure under which the poet places language and syntax convincingly suggests the energy of the encounter: words buckle and strain, syntax stretches beyond its habitual limits. Like Hopkins's work more generally, the poem aspires towards the spoken word, to the rhythms and pace of language that is declared aloud.

Hopkins's sustained preoccupation with his own singleness (and, elsewhere, singularity) is noticeable as the poem foregrounds the solitary observer (evident from the first word) in private communion with the kestrel/Christ. Poetry becomes a mode for establishing a community between writer and audience, even though it persistently figures the uniqueness of individual experience. The last three lines of this sonnet focus on the way forms of violence – treading ploughed soil and the breaking apart of embers after a fall – release beauty and energy. This prioritizing of violence connects with the theology of 'The Wreck of the *Deutschland*'. The reference to 'Fall' in the final line gives a clue to its meaning. 'Fall' suggests the fall of human beings in the Garden of Eden, reminding one that the 'gash[ing]' of Jesus – the brutality of the crucifixion – secured human redemption. As the violent fall of an apparently dull and dying ember will reveal a blazing glory, so Jesus restored glory to sinful humanity by enduring the violence of bloody death. The lines are an excellent example of Hopkins's thinking at its most compacted. Yielding its meaning only after struggle, Hopkins's language, like his theology, celebrates the productive nature of strain and exertion.

Text: *The Poems of Gerard Manley Hopkins* (1918).

I caught this morning morning's minion,[1] king-
dom of daylight's dauphin,[2] dapple-dawn-drawn Falcon, in his riding
Of the rolling level underneath him steady air, and striding
High there, how he rung upon the rein of a wimpling[3] wing
In his ecstacy! then off, off forth on swing,   5
As a skate's[4] heel sweeps smooth on a bow-bend: the hurl and gliding
Rebuffed the big wind. My heart in hiding
Stirred for a bird, – the achieve[5] of, the mastery of the thing!

Brute beauty and valour and act, oh, air, pride, plume, here
Buckle![6] AND the fire that breaks from thee then, a billion   10

[1] *minion* loved one, darling.
[2] *dauphin* title of the eldest son of the King of France; here, the royal son of the morning.
[3] *wimpling* usually of streams: meandering, wandering.
[4] *skate's* the image is of an ice skater.
[5] *achieve* Hopkins intensifies the poem's sense of action by making a verbal form from the noun 'achievement'.
[6] *Buckle* both 'secure together' and 'give under pressure'.

Violent severe / holiness / powerful

No surprise. / that Hell / told again and / again.

Times told lovelier, more dangerous, O my chevalier![7]   Nobleman, horse rider

No wonder of it: shéer plód makes plough down sillion)   — coined by Hopkins

Shine,[8] and blue-bleak embers, ah my dear,[9]

Fall, gall themselves, and gash gold-vermillion.[10]

Knight

[7] *chevalier* noble man, horse rider (cf. l. 2).

[8] *sheer plod . . . shine* mere walking compacts ploughed soil (sillion) so that it shines.

[9] *ah my dear* recalling George Herbert's 'ah my dear,' in 'Love III', a poem celebrating the generosity of divine love.

[10] *blue-bleak . . . vermillion* nearly extinguished embers that fall from a fire will break open to reveal a hot gold-red centre.

Inversnaid

Alert to the uniqueness and individuality of language, form and identity, Hopkins captures a distinctive voice of place here. The poem mimics a speaker whose life is bound up with Inversnaid (a hamlet on the north-east shore of Loch Lomond in Scotland, famous for its waterfall). Diction – dialectal features, possible folk-legend reference, apparently local names – invites the reader to assume the poet's familiarity with and affection for every detail of a cherished landscape. 'Inversnaid' glances back to William Wordsworth's 'To the Highland Girl of Inversnaid' but replaces his tribute to a 'Sweet Highland Girl, a very shower / Of beauty' with celebration of the place itself. The final stanza's employment of standard English suggests the broader audience to whom the appeal for the preservation of 'wildness' is made. Hopkins champions the uniqueness of wild, unregulated places, asking for them to be safe-guarded against the unnamed threat in the last four lines. This acknowledgement of uniqueness, free growth and indeed of 'weeds', the irregular and potentially rejected, is self-reflexive and bound up with Hopkins's sense of himself as poet and human being (cf. 'Pied Beauty', 537–8, as another meditation on the place of the irregular in the divine scheme).

Text: *The Poems of Gerard Manley Hopkins* (1918).

This darksome burn,[1] horseback brown,

His rollrock highroad[2] roaring down,

In coop[3] and in comb[4] the fleece of his foam

Flutes and low to the lake falls home.

2

A windpuff-bonnet of fáwn-fróth[5]   5

Turns and twindles[6] over the broth

Of a pool so pitchblack, féll[7]-fról wning,

It rounds and rounds Despair to drowning.[8]

3

Degged[9] with dew, dappled with dew

Are the groins of the braes[10] that the brook treads through,   10

Wiry heathpacks,[11] flitches[12] of fern,

And the beadbonny[13] ash that sits over the burn.

[1] *burn* stream.

[2] *rollrock highroad* the stream's route is rolling over rocks.

[3] *coop* hollow place (perhaps where the edges of stream are trapped and turned to foam).

[4] *comb* crest.

[5] *fawn-froth* light brown froth; also, perhaps, fine, elegant like a fawn (young deer).

[6] *twindles* compound word suggesting 'dwindles', 'twists', 'twines'.

[7] *fell* moor land. The pitch-black pool adds a frown to the landscape.

[8] *It rounds . . . drowning* reference to a local legend?

[9] *Degged* dampened (Lancashire dialect).

[10] *braes* steeps, banks, hillsides.

[11] *heathpacks* heathers.

[12] *flitches* tufts, clumps.

[13] *beadbonny* handsome as if with beads (the dark buds of the ash).

4
What would the world be, once bereft
Of wet and of wildness? Let them be left,
O let them be left, wildness and wet;   15
Long live the weeds and the wilderness yet.

That Nature is a Heraclitean Fire and of the Comfort of the Resurrection

Gerard Hopkins's religious poetry is habitually built around a proposition; it negotiates an argument and moves towards statement. Even the title of 'That Nature is a Heraclitean Fire and of the Comfort of the Resurrection' belongs to a philosophical essay, bespeaking clearly Hopkins's investment in the poetry of debate, which, here, moves to triumphant conclusion.

The ancient Greek philosopher Heracl(e)itus (*c.*540–*c.*480 BC) maintained that all things, throughout the whole universe, were in a state of permanent flux. He believed that the essential element of the cosmos was fire. At death, Heraclitus thought the souls of the virtuous, themselves made of fire, joined the great cosmic conflagration. In 'That Nature is a Heraclitean Fire', Hopkins takes Heraclitus's philosophy to construct a Christian argument. He considers the continual movement of the clouds and wind and the 'Million-fuelèd' quality of nature's multiplicity. Man, situated in this everlasting condition of changefulness, leaves no permanent mark and, on his own, is lost in 'an enormous dark'.

But Jesus's resurrection means that humanity is not merely consumed: the pre-Christian philosophy of Heraclitus naturally omits the great truth of the Christian faith. While everything else is burnt up and transformed to carbon, the human soul is, by God's grace, saved. Human salvation is figured at the close of the poem as man's metamorphosis to a radically different form of carbon: immortal diamond. 'That Nature is a Heraclitean Fire' is remarkable throughout for its verbal exuberance, the tumbling of words over each other in mimicry of the universal flux. Its climax – the last words – is achieved through the simplest device of repetition. But *repeating* words, in showing they are not mutated through time, Hopkins brilliantly mirrors at the level of lexical choice God's power to resist the continual changefulness of nature's ceaseless transformations.

Hopkins is at the heart of the text, and it is in his own transformation – from 'poor potsherd' to diamond – that he represents the salvation of all believers. For other poems in which Hopkins implicitly meditates on his place within the greater scheme, cf. 'Pied Beauty', 537–8, and 'Inversnaid', 539–40.

Text: *The Poems of Gerard Manley Hopkins* (1918).

Cloud-puffball, torn tufts, tossed pillows ⎮flaunt forth, then chevy[1] on an air-
built thoroughfare: heaven-roysterers, in gay-gangs ⎮they throng; they glitter in marches.
Down roughcast, down dazzling whitewash, ⎮wherever an elm arches,
Shivelights[2] and shadowtackle in long ⎮lashes lace, lance, and pair.
Delightfully the bright wind boisterous ⎮ropes, wrestles, beats earth bare   5
Of yestertempest's creases; ⎮in pool and rut peel parches
Squandering ooze to squeezed ⎮dough, crust, dust; stanches,[3] starches
Squadroned masks and manmarks ⎮treadmire toil there
Footfretted in it. Million-fuelèd, ⎮nature's bonfire burns on.
But quench her bonniest, dearest ⎮to her, her clearest-selvèd spark   10
Man, how fast his firedint,[4] ⎮his mark on mind, is gone!
Both are in an unfathomable, all is in an enormous dark
Drowned. O pity and indig⎮nation! Manshape, that shone
Sheer off, disseveral,[5] a star, ⎮death blots black out; nor mark

---

[1] *chevy* chase.
[2] *Shivelights* slivers of light.
[3] *stanches* stops the flow.

[4] *firedint* mark made by fire; cf. Heraclitus's belief in the human soul as fire (headnote, above).
[5] *disseveral* not together.

Is any of him at all so stark 15
But vastness blurs and time |beats level. Enough! the Resurrection,
A heart's-clarion![6] Away grief's gasping, |joyless days, dejection.
Across my foundering deck shone
A beacon, an eternal beam. |Flesh fade, and mortal trash
Fall to the residuary worm; |world's wildfire, leave but ash: 20
In a flash, at a trumpet crash,
I am all at once what Christ is, |since he was what I am, and
This Jack,[7] joke, poor potsherd,[8] |patch, matchwood, immortal diamond,
Is immortal diamond.

[6] *clarion* shrill, bright trumpet.　　　　　　　　[8] *potsherd* fragment of earthenware pot.
[7] *Jack* colloquial expression for 'ordinary man'.

Harry Ploughman

'Harry Ploughman' is a celebration in muscular vocabulary of a strong man performing his appointed manual labour. The ploughman (who ploughs by hand, without a horse) is an exemplum of Hopkins's sense of teleology. In 'As kingfishers catch fire', 535–6, Hopkins dramatizes the natural world as replete with species declaring their uniqueness: *'Whát I do is me: for that I came.'* Harry Ploughman possesses a similar unitary purpose, of the kind Matthew Arnold found impossible in the nineteenth century (cf. 'Stanzas from the Grande Chartreuse', 305–12, 'The Scholar-Gipsy', 298–305).

Hopkins stresses various elements of Harry's diverse completeness: he is at one with his labour, but also a union of man and boy, a fusion of the ordinary with the extraordinary, both statuesque and in motion;

he possesses masculinized power but also feminized 'wind-lilylocks-laced'. Politically, the poem is a meditation on unalienated pre-industrial rural labour, where man and his work are undivided (cf. Tennyson's 'The Lotos-Eaters', 66–71, as a stark contrast). Hopkins's neologisms express Harry's muscular power, gracefulness and sexual appeal: the poem is energized by a homoeroticism that turns the plough-man into someone almost edible. Violence and effort are eroticized, but the poet is still alone. He gazes and admires – his words exuberantly describe the *thisness* of the labourer, making him vividly present to the reader's mind – but there is still no real connection between the gazer and gazed at.

Text: *The Poems of Gerard Manley Hopkins* (1918).

[handwritten: Like Meat]

[handwritten, left margin: A man deeply engaged physically with his work.]

Hard as hurdle arms, with a broth of goldish flue[1]
Breathed round; the rack of ribs; the scooped flank; lank
Rope-over thigh; knee-nave;[2] and barrelled shank –
Head and foot, shoulder and shank –
By a grey eye's heed[3] steered well, one crew, fall to;[4] 5
Stand at stress.[5] Each limb's barrowy brawn, his thew[6]
That onewhere[7] curded,[8] onewhere sucked or sank –
Soared ór sánk – ,
Though as a beechbole[9] firm, finds his, as at a rollcall,[10] rank
And features, in flesh, what deed he each must do – 10
His sinew-service where do.

[1] *flue* down, downy hair.
[2] *knee-nave* perhaps bent and imitating the shape of a Gothic church nave (the main body of a church building).
[3] *heed* attention, care.
[4] *fall to* begin work.
[5] *Stand at stress* inversion of the usual military 'Stand at ease'.

[6] *thew* strength.
[7] *onewhere* [for] someone somewhere (i.e., not for Harry).
[8] *curded* weakened, as if it had curd forming on it.
[9] *beechbole* beech trunk, beech tree.
[10] *rollcall* military register taking.

He leans to it, Harry bends, look. Back, elbow, and liquid waist
In him, all quail to the wallowing o' the plough. 'S[11] cheek crimsons; curls
Wag or crossbridle, in a wind lifted, windlaced –
See his wind-lilylocks-laced;   15
Churlsgrace,[12] too, child of Amansstrength, how it hangs or hurls
Them – broad in bluff hide his frowning feet lashed! raced
With, along them, cragiron[13] under and cold furls –
With-a-fountain's shining-shot furls.[14]

[11] *'S* His.
[12] *Churlsgrace* grace of an ordinary man.
[13] *cragiron* i.e., the iron plough Harry pulls.

[14] *With . . . furls* with a fountain of soil emerging from the rear of the moving plough blade.

Binsey Poplars felled 1879

Violence, such as that considered in 'The Wreck of the *Deutschland*', 525–34, and 'The Windhover', 538–9, was for Hopkins an integral part of God's scheme and the believer's knowledge of Him. 'Binsey Poplars' mourns violence that is not God's, but destructive of that through which God is revealed. Here, human beings chop down aspen trees near Binsey village, now part of west Oxford. In doing so, they destroy the individual *thisness* of the elegant, slender forms, changing a scene forever (the title solemnly includes the date from which the scene is lost). Hopkins's poem stresses the *visual* loss as particularly important, partly through the image of a punctured eye and partly in the repeated 'scene' of the final lines, emphasizing the relationship between *seeing* nature and *knowing* God that lies behind all Hopkins's poems on nature's reve-lation. 'Binsey Poplars' affirms the close affective bond between the poet and the natural world – '*My* aspens dear' – almost in the language of a lover, framing other human beings as destructive of that private relationship. Hopkins fashions the poet as isolated and deprived, a man possessed of greater sensibility than those around him, and a victim, like the trees, of ignorant others. Cf. Charlotte Mew's 'The Trees are Down', 687–9, where violated nature and the self are associated. There is a bitter modern environmentalist response to this poem's earlier regret for human treatment of the natural world in Maxine Kumin's 'Homage to Binsey Poplars', included in her 1997 *Selected Poems*.

Text: *The Poems of Gerard Manley Hopkins* (1918).

My aspens[1] dear, whose airy cages quelled,
Quelled or quenched in leaves the leaping sun,
All felled, felled, are all felled;
Of a fresh and following folded rank
Not spared, not one   5
That dandled a sandalled[2]
Shadow that swam or sank
On meadow and river and wind-wandering weed-winding bank.

O if we but knew what we do
When we delve or hew –   10
Hack and rack the growing green!
Since country is so tender
To touch, her being só slender,
That, like this sleek and seeing ball[3]
But a prick will make no eye at all,   15
Where we, even where we mean
To mend her we end her,
When we hew or delve:

[1] *aspens* trees of the poplar family.
[2] *sandalled* lightfooted.

[3] *ball* eyeball.

After-comers[4] cannot guess the beauty been.
  Ten or twelve, only ten or twelve   20
    Strokes of havoc unselve — "thisness"
    The sweet especial scene,
    Rural scene, a rural scene,
    Sweet especial rural scene.

[4] *after-comers* those who come afterwards.

No worst, there is none

The meaning of violence in Hopkins's theology and poetics takes a new form in this sonnet, one of the 'Terrible' or 'Dark' sonnets, which record the poet's spiritual desolation. The group is part of a long tradition of Christian mystical writings that document the 'dark night of the soul'. Deprived of the comfort of the Holy Ghost and the Virgin Mary, Hopkins in 'No worst, there is none' suffers the 'fell' violence of spiritual wretchedness, troping it in terms of a mountainous mental landscape. Persistently constructing himself as solitary throughout his work, 'No worst, there is none' marks a transformation of Hopkins's characteristic isolation into spiritual – perhaps also sexual and personal – desolation (cf. the internal dialogue of 'My own heart let me more have pity on', 544). The final lines of the sonnet offer not consolation but, at least, a little calm, a plainer syntax, in contrast to the turbulence of the beginning. This poem and 'My own heart' comprise the densest poetic representation of male inner conflict in this anthology. Hopkins's allusions to Shakespeare's *King Lear* and *The Tempest* suggest a broadening of perspective, an opening out into a wider world than the claustrophobic confines of the lone, suffering mind.

Text: *The Poems of Gerard Manley Hopkins* (1918).

No worst, there is none. Pitched past pitch of grief,
More pangs will, schooled at forepangs, wilder wring.
  Comforter,[1] where, where is your comforting?
  Mary, mother of us, where is your relief?
My cries heave, herds-long; huddle in a main, a chief   5
Woe, world-sorrow; on an age-old anvil wince and sing –
  Then lull, then leave off. Fury had shrieked 'No ling-
  ering! Let me be fell:[2] force[3] I must be brief'.
O the mind, mind has mountains; cliffs of fall
Frightful, sheer, no-man-fathomed. Hold them cheap   10
May who ne'er hung there.[4] Nor does long our small
Durance[5] deal with that steep or deep. Here! creep,
Wretch, under a comfort serves in a whirlwind:[6] all
Life death does end and each day dies with sleep.[7]

[1] *Comforter* Holy Ghost.
[2] *fell* terrible, ruthless.
[3] *force* perforce.
[4] *Hold them . . . there* those who have not been there, hold them cheap.
[5] *Durance* endurance.

[6] *Wretch . . . whirlwind* cf. King Lear's meeting with Poor Tom on the stormy heath, *King Lear* (folio) 3.4.
[7] *each day . . . sleep* cf. Prospero in *The Tempest* 4.1.156–7: 'We are such stuff / As dreams are made on, and our little life / Is rounded with a sleep.'

My own heart let me more have pity on

Belonging with 'No worst, there is none', 543, this sonnet signifies some progress in the poet's wretched condition, and in his sense of isolation. (The sonnet has a long tradition as a mode of argument, during which *change* takes place: Hopkins's use of the sonnet form has already within it a sign of hope.) The poet's circular syntax – 'not live this tormented mind / With this tormented mind tormenting yet' – figures the spiritual and emotional turmoil from which the poems grows. The poet advises himself to have more compassion on his own being, though the emotional subtlety and verbal challenge of the poem excludes mere *self-pity*.

The text records the mind's dialogue with itself. That self that is at the centre of Hopkins's poems here becomes bifurcated: its entry into an apparent community of exchange merely an indication of its own duality. For Matthew Arnold, the inner dialogue of the self was the beginning of despair, and in 'Empedocles on Etna', 268–95, it led to self-destruction. For Hopkins, it marks the possibility of peace and the beginning of a spiritual restoration, appropriately suggested in the recovery of the natural scene, the observed world, described with touchingly childlike vocabulary, beyond the tormented consciousness. The final gesture towards the open skies – an expanding of possibilities – is perhaps a textual salute to Matthew Arnold's 'A Summer Night', 264–7.

Text: *The Poems of Gerard Manley Hopkins* (1918).

My own heart let me more have pity on; let
Me live to my sad self hereafter kind,
Charitable; not live this tormented mind
With this tormented mind tormenting yet.

I cast for comfort I can no more get   5
By groping round my comfortless,[1] than blind
Eyes in their dark can day or thirst can find
Thirst's all-in-all[2] in all a world of wet.

Soul, self; come, poor Jackself,[3] I do advise
You, jaded, let be; call off thoughts awhile   10
Elsewhere; leave comfort root-room; let joy size[4]

At God knows when to God knows what; whose smile
's not wrung, see you; unforeseen times rather[5] – as skies
Betweenpie[6] mountains – lights a lovely mile.

[1] *comfortless* adjective working as a noun.
[2] *Thirst's all-in-all* water, refreshment.
[3] *Jackself* ordinary self.
[4] *size* grow.

[5] *whose smile . . . rather* God's smile is not wrung from him, it comes unforeseen.
[6] *Betweenpie* made from 'between' and 'pied': the sky and the mountains create a gently pied, or two-coloured, scene.

Eugene (Jacob) Lee-Hamilton (1845–1907)

Eugene Lee-Hamilton was born in London but brought up in France by his mother after his father's death. In 1864, he returned to England to attend Oriel College Oxford though left without taking a degree. He worked as a diplomat in embassies in France, Switzerland and Portugal until a curious, and possibly strategic, nervous breakdown in 1865 left him bedridden for the next two decades (modern physicians have speculated that it may have been, or may have become, ME). He stayed in Florence with his mother and half-sister Violet Paget (who, as Vernon Lee [1856–1935], was an important novelist, critic and travel writer) and was visited by many figures of the literary world. From his bed, he wrote widely, pro- ducing volumes including *Apollo and Marsyas and Other Poems* (1884), *Imaginary Sonnets* (1888) and *The Fountain of Youth: A Fantastic [Verse] Tragedy, in Five Acts* (1891). By the mid-1890s he had recovered, and in 1898 married Annie E. Holdsworth, the feminist novelist and author of, among other things, *Joanna Traill, Spinster* (1894) and *The Gods Arrive* (1897). Lee-Hamilton's translation of Dante's *Inferno* was published in 1898. But the death of the couple's only child – commemorated in the posthumous *Mimma Bella: In Memory of a Little Life* (1909), originally published in the *Fortnightly Review* for November 1907 – cast a dark shadow over his last days. He died in Lucca in September 1907.

The New Medusa

A.D. 1620

Gothic writing reached a climax in the nineteenth century. While it is often thought confined to fiction – the work of Sheridan Le Fanu (1814–73), Bram Stoker's *Dracula* (1897) – Eugene Lee-Hamilton's 'The New Medusa' (1882) exploits the mode in poetry to produce a monologue that plays its horror against the narrator's unsettling sense of doubt. Like Henry James's *The Turn of the Screw* (1898), the tension of this poem resides in the unresolved question of the speaker's grasp of the real. The poem challenges the reader to assess the relation between seeing and knowing in its philosophical excursion at ll. 280–97, but the question is one at the heart of the narrator's experience. Set at the beginning of the seventeenth century, its wonderfully grim events are located beyond English shores in Venice and Sicily, and involve Turkey. Sicily and Turkey are coded as non-rational places where civilization has yet to banish the darkest forces; Englishness is defined against this, but uncertainly. The poem offers English national identity, represented in the narrator, as reasoned, possessed of conscience and acting to banish evil, but also as unstable, prey to the irrational fears of the subconscious, and perhaps murderous.

Lee-Hamilton's narrator is a traveller of the seventeenth century, though the tale responds to a late nineteenth-century conception of human knowledge of the world. It teases the reader with the idea of forces unknown to empirical science, so prominent in Victorian culture as the increasingly dominant mode for understanding nature. 'Who shall dare to call / That unsubstantial form a madman's dream?', the narrator says, as the poem flirts with the existence of a world outside the apprehension of the self-proclaimed rational terrain of empirical science (the Society for Psychical Research was founded in the same year as 'The New Medusa' was published). At another level, the poem powerfully encodes female sexuality as threatening. The passionate Medusa-figure is a highly sexualized woman and her desires – always visible in bed – cannot be accommodated in the male speaker's worldview. He accordingly demonizes her. But the speaker's doubts about the truth of what he saw add an important qualification. 'The New Medusa', deliberately inviting the question of whether the male narrator is reliable or not, queries precisely that anxious view of female sexuality that the poem might, *prima facie*, be thought to express (cf. Dante Gabriel Rossetti's 'Jenny', 358–67, and Augusta Webster's 'Circe', 450–5, as poems about female sexuality, one from the point of view of a man, the other, a woman).

The Classical narrative behind Lee-Hamilton's monologue is the story of Medusa, one of the three Gorgons of Greek myth, whose heads were entwined with a mass of writhing snakes and whose glance could turn men to stone. Polydectes, King of Seriphos, intended to kill the hero Perseus, and so sent him to bring the head of Medusa knowing that her glance would petrify him. Perseus protected himself against her fatal gaze with a highly polished bronze shield and cut off her head. Putting it in a bag, he later employed its power against his enemies. Basic elements of this myth obviously underlie the 'new' Medusa – the improbably named Joan – of Lee-Hamilton's gothic tale, and there is irony in the speaker's relationship to Perseus as Medusa's doom.

Amy Levy and Augusta Webster gave voices to figures marginalized from ancient Greek history and Homeric narrative (cf. 'Xantippe', 630–6, and

'Circe'), just as Lee-Hamilton recovered lost historical perspectives in *Imaginary Sonnets*, 553–6. Even Medusa found her champion in the nineteenth century. The minor poet Lady Charlotte Elliot (1839–80) published a volume called *Medusa and Other Poems* in 1878, which contained a sympathetic monologue spoken by the Gorgon, insisting on her 'unspeakable woe' and expressing gratitude to Perseus for delivering her from agony. That monologue put another side to her history, suggesting the heartless (and perhaps misogynistic) forces controlling the shape of her myth.

Text: *The New Medusa and Other Poems* (1882).

Grown strangely pale? Grown silent and morose
In my three years of travel? Brother John,
Oh, once for all, why watch me thus so close?
When since my childhood was my cheek not wan,[1]
My soul not moody, and my speech not short?   5
As Nature made me, let me then live on.
Spare me thy questions; seek such noisy sport
As suits thy stronger frame and happier mood,
And cease thy preaching of this irksome sort.
It suits my whim to hold aloof and brood;   10
Go, medler, go! Forgive me, I recall
The word; it was too harsh, for thou art good.
O cruel Heaven, shall I tell him all?
God knows I need a hand to cling to tight,
For on my path all Horror's shadows fall.   15
I am like one who's dogged, and who, as night
Is closing in, must cross a lonely spot,
And needs some staunch companion in his flight.

My enemy is Madness: I have got
His stealthy step behind me, ever near,   20
And he will clutch me if thou help me not.
Oh, I have sailed across a sea of fear,
And met new lands to add to Horror's realms,
And shores of Guilt whence none may scatheless[2] steer.
A very world of jarring thoughts o'erwhelms   25
My cowering soul when I would tell what's been
Since last I saw this Hall, these English elms.
Yet must the tale be told, and every scene
Gone o'er again. I fear some monstrous thing
From my own self, and on thy strength must lean.   30

So listen. I had spent the early spring
In Venice, till Ascension Feast[3] – the day
On which the Doge casts in his bridal ring;[4]

[1] *wan* pale.
[2] *scatheless* uninjured.
[3] *Ascension Feast* commemoration of the Ascension of Jesus from earth to heaven (see Acts 1.1–12).

[4] *the day ... ring* Venice celebrated her historical naval supremacy with the ceremony of the Doge's marriage to the sea each Ascension Day. The Doge – the chief figure of the Venetian Republic – cast a gold ring into the lagoon.

And had embarked, with pleasant winds of May
  And gentle seas, on a Venetian ship   35
Bound for Palermo,[5] where I meant to stay.
  All gave us promise of a prosperous trip;
  Yet, by the second day, mishap began,
And 'tween two Turkish[6] sail we had to slip.
  From dawn to dusk before the Turk we ran,   40
  Till, safe and breathless off Illyria's[7] coast,

We each thanked God to be a chainless man.
  'Twas but the respite of an hour at most;
  The weather changed with dread rapidity.
  As in rebuke of Safety's hasty boast,   45
  God laid His mighty hand upon the sea,
  Moulding at once a million liquid peaks
That ever round us tossed more furiously.
For three whole days the tempest blanched the cheeks
  Of men whom years of storm had ill enriched,   50
  And long familiar with the petrel's[8] shrieks.
  It was as if the maddened ocean itched
  Beneath the ship; so desperately it tried
To shake it off, and bounded, roared, and pitched,
  And, like a lion in whose quivering hide   55
An insect burrows, wasted strength and wrath,
    In rush on rush, by littleness defied.
At last, like one who no more hoping hath,
  It ceased the strife; and we, at dawn of day,
  Had set the helm to seek our long-lost path,   60
  When in the offing,[9] on the lurid grey,
Where tossed black waves, as if of ire[10] still full,
  We saw a something looming far away.
  It proved to be a small dismasted hull,
  To all appearance empty, which remained   65
  Upon one spot, just like a sea-rocked gull.
  On closer search we found that it contained
  A woman, lashed to remnants of a mast,
Who seemed a corpse, but, slowly, life regained.
  Her black, wet, rope-like locks she backward cast,   70
  And in her troubled memory seemed to seek;
  Then strangely, doggedly, concealed the past.
  Her garb, her features, said she was a Greek,
But Tuscan[11] she spoke well; and 'tis that tongue
  Which she and I in aftertimes did speak.   75
And as she stood amid the wondering throng,
  And no account of home or kindred gave,
  A murmur 'mong the sailors ran along.
'Keep her,' they cried; 'we'll sell her as a slave;
  She owns no kin that she should be exempt;   80
She's common prize tossed up by wind and wave.'

---

[5] *Palermo* city on northern coast of Sicily.
[6] *Turkish* Turkey was a long-standing enemy of Venice.
[7] *Illyria* eastern shore of the Adriatic sea.
[8] *petrel* small sea bird.

[9] *offing* part of the visible sea beyond the area in which the ship is anchored.
[10] *ire* anger.
[11] *Tuscan* from Tuscany, area of north central Italy.

She caught the words, but made no vain attempt
To melt their hearts by prayer and sobs and sighs,
And looked around her with a queen's contempt.
    And then it was that suddenly her eyes,   85
    Singling me out, were fastened upon mine
    So searchingly, that all felt huge surprise;
    And that, like one who by some secret sign
Knows that a strange command will be obeyed,
She cried, 'Lord, buy me;' and I paid her fine.   90
    So she my slave, and I her slave was made,
    She taking eager bondage from that hour,
    And binding me in chains that never weighed.
    She seemed contented with a latent power,
    Keeping slave garb, and took small gifts alone,   95
    As might an empress from some love below her.
She bade me name her, and I named her Joan,
    Feeling no wish to pry within her breast,
    Or learn what name her former life might own.
    With all the strong lithe beauty, she possessed   100
    The noiseless tread of a tame leopardess,
    Docile, majestic, holding strength repressed.
With wondrous insight soon she learned to guess
    My gloomy temper's ever-shifting mood,
    And, fierce in love, was chary of caress.   105
Now wisely silent, she would let me brood
    Until the fit was over; now she cheered
    With such fantastic tales as tribes still rude
Delight to hear, the night till dawn appeared;
    Now sang unto the lute some old Greek air,   110
Like gusts of moaning tempest wild and weird.
    And other gifts she had, and arts more rare;
    For when at Syracuse[12] I once fell ill
    Of a malignant fever, and her care
Preserved my life, she showed a leech's[13] skill   115
    In mingling drugs, and knew how to extract
From long-sought herbs a juice for ague's[14] cure.
    Oh she was strangely dowered, and she lacked
    Nought that can rivet man to woman's side,
    Nought that can win, or on the senses act.   120
But there were moments when a fear would glide
    Across my heart, I knew not well of what,
    And on the secret which her life might hide
My mind would work; and yet she daily got
    A firmer tenure of the love she'd won,   125
And felt each day my kisses grow more hot,
    Even as those of the Sicilian sun,
Which made of winter spring, with fiery love,
Long ere the thaw had in our clime begun.

    She loved, like me, from place to place to move,   130
    And seldom we long lingered where mere chance
    Had made us stop, but sought some lovelier grove,

---

[12] *Syracuse* city of south-east Sicily.   [14] *ague* ache.
[13] *leech* doctor, apothecary.

Where, from deep shade, we saw the sunshine dance
On the blue sea which lapped the tideless coast,
And watched the sails which specked the blue expanse.   135
But when that happened which I dread to reach,
    We were abiding where the owlet made
The night oft sleepless with his lonesome screech.
It was a sea-girt castle much decayed,
    Belonging to an old Sicilian prince   140
With whom, when at Palermo, I had stayed.
He loathed the place, would go to no expense
    To keep it up; but, loving town resorts,
Had left it in his youth, nor seen it since.
It suited well my mood. The weird reports,   145
The legends which the peasants loved to tell
About its empty halls and grass-grown courts;
Its garden paths where unpicked flowers fell;
    Its silent rooms where many echoes woke
And fancies came – all made me love it well.   150
Its furniture of carved and blackened oak
Looked ghostly in the twilight; while the walls
Were hung with shields and swords of mighty stroke.
Of mighty stroke? Ay, ay, my tongue forestalls
    My hesitating thoughts as I relate,   155
    And every item that I name appals,
As I retread in mind where monstrous Fate
Changed love to horror; every look I cast
Makes me all love, all horror, re-create.

One night – O John, I come to it at last -   160
One night I had a nightmare in my sleep
    For vividness and terror unsurpassed.
Methought I felt a snake's cold body creep
About my hand and throat, entwine them tight,
    And o'er my breast a hideous mastery keep.   165
    Awhile I lay all-helpless, in despite
Of agony, and felt the pressed veins swell,
Then forced a smothered cry into the night.
    My cry awoke me, waking Joan as well,
When, panting still with nightmare fear, I found   170
That the black locks that on her bosom fell
Had crept about my throat and girt it round
    So tightly as awhile to stop the breath,
While other locks about my arms had wound.
We laughed away my ugly dream of death,   175
    And in the silence of the night that waned
We heaped up kisses, burying fear beneath.
I gave the thing no thought; but Hell ordained
That this same dream, before a week was cut,
    Should be repeated, and its horror strained.   180
Once more the snakes encompassed me about,
Once more I woke her with my strangled cry,
Once more I found her locks around my throat.

Then I began to brood; and by and by
Strange things of God's strong chastisement of crime   185

Recurred all vaguely to my memory.
I seemed to recollect from olden rhymes
Some tale about the hair of those who take
A many lives through poison; how at times,
When guilt haunts sleep, each lock becomes a snake,   190
While they remain unconscious of the change;
And turns again to hair so soon they wake.
Smile not, or I will throttle thee. The range
Of Nature is so vast that it hath room
For things more strange than what we call most strange.   195
I am not mad. I thought with growing gloom
How we had met her, tossed alone at sea,
And how the Turks who rule those coasts oft doom
Their women to strange punishments. Might she,
For some great crime, not have been made to brave   200
The winds and waves by some such strange decree?
And then I thought what proof she often gave
Of skill in medicine and botanic lore;
And how that serves to kill that serves to save.
I struggled with these thoughts – I struggled sore: 205
With shame and self-contempt I cast them out,
And, looking on her beauty, loved her more.
But listen, John. A month or thereabout
Went by unmarked, and then there came a night
Which seemed to put an end to every doubt.   210

I was awake; there was no sound, no light.
Yes, there was sound: her breathing met my ear,
The breath of dreamless sleep – low, smooth, and slight.
But suddenly it quickened, as in fear,
And broken words whose sense I could not tell   215
Escaped her lips; my name I seemed to hear.
Now listen, John. Methought she lay not well,
I stretched my hand to slightly raise her head;
But what my hand encountered was, O hell!
No locks of silky hair: it met instead   220
A something cold which whipt around my wrist
Unholdable, and through my fingers fled.
I groped again and felt two others twist
About my arm; – a score of vipers twined
Beneath my hand, and, as I touched them, hissed.   225
There is a horror which leaves free the mind
But glues the tongue. Without a word I slipt
From out the bed, and struck a light behind
Its ample curtain; then, unheard, I crept
Close up and let the light's faint radiance hover   230
Over the Gorgon's features as she slept.
The snakes were gone. But long I bent me over
Her placid face with searching, sickened glance,
Like one who in deep waters would discover
A corpse, and can see nothing save, perchance,   235
The landscape's fair reflected shapes, which keep
Balking[15] the vision with their endless dance.

---

[15] *Balking* rejecting, refusing.

It seemed to me that in that placid sleep,
Beneath that splendid surface lay concealed
    Unutterable horror sunken deep.   240
And, seeking not to have the whole revealed,
    I fled that fatal room without a sound,
And sought the breeze of night with brain that reeled.

    How long I wandered 'mid the rocks around,
Like some priced outlaw – whether one, or two,   245
    Or three whole days I know not – fever bound
A veil across my brain, and I've no clue
To guide my memory through those days accurst,
    Or show me what my misery found to do.
        I recollect intolerable thirst,   250
    And nothing more; until the night again
Enwrapped the earth, and with it brought the worst.
    A mighty wish, with which I fought in vain,
Came o'er my soul to see once more her face,
    And dragged me back, as by an unseen chain.   255
Where love and horror struggle, there is place
    For countless fierce and contradict'ry tides
Of Will and Sense within one short day's space.
    With every hour the gale has shifted sides;
The needle of Thought's compass will have leapt   260
    From pole to pole, and chance at last decides.
    So I returned, and like a thief I crept
Into the house, where every light was out,
    And sought the silent chamber where she slept.

    O brother, brother! I'm in awful doubt.   265
If what I saw, and what shall now be told,
    Was a mere figment of the brain throughout,
Then will the sickened Heaven ne'er behold
A deed more monstrous than the deed I've done,
    Though this old earth should grow again as old. 270
        But if the thing was real, if 'twas one
    Of hell's corroborations of great guilt,
    My hand was an avenger's hand alone.
So wonder not, if, with the blood I've spilt
Still on my hand, I fain[16] would have thee think 275
That the great wall, which God Himself hath built
Between this world and hell, may have a chink
Through which some horror, yet unknown to earth,
    And over great for us, may sometimes slink.
May not such strays from Hell have given birth 280
    To poets' fancies which the wise deride,
And olden saws[17] of which we now make mirth.
    Oh who shall have the courage to decide
Between the things that are and those that seem,
    And tell the spirit that the eyes have lied?   285
    Watch thy own face reflected in the stream;
    Is that a figment? Who shall dare to call

---

[16] *fain* gladly.   [17] *saws* sayings, or wise men of superstitious cultures.

That unsubstantial form a madman's dream?
Or watch the shadow on the sunlit wall,
If thou could'st clutch it great would be thy skill;   290
Thou'lt feel a chilly spot – and that is all.
So may the spectres which, more subtle still,
    Elude the feeble intellect of man,
And leave us empty-handed with a chill,
    Be just as much reality. We spend   295
Life 'mid familiar spectres, while the soul
In fear denies the rest. But hear the end.

The moon was at the full; but o'er the whole
Vast vault of heaven was stretched a fleecy tent,
Through which her baffled light but dimly stole,   300
Save where the breezes of the night had rent
On some few points that subtle woof[18] o'erhead,
That men might catch her glances as she went.
And as once more I trod with stealthy tread
    Each silent, vast, and solitary room,   305
Where, through the tiny panes, encased in lead,
Of Gothic windows, moonlight broke the gloom
So dimly that I scarce could thread my way,
    I seemed a ghost returning to its tomb.
    I neared the fatal bed in which she lay;   310
Its sculptured columns had a ghostly look;
    Its heavy daïs,[19] of faded silk by day,
Looked stony in its tintlessness, and took
    The semblance of the marble canopy
Above some Templar's[20] tomb. Yea, every nook   315
Of this strange room bred awe, I know not why,
While dim mysterious gleamings seemed to thrill
From swords and shields that decked the walls on high.
With soundless step, approaching nearer still,
I touched the sculptured oak, while love and fear   320
    Contesting in my breast suspended will.
    I saw her shape but vaguely, but could hear
Her placid breath attesting, if aught could,
A dreamless sleep and conscience wholly clear.
    Love in my breast was winning, as I stood   325
And watched her thus some moments in her sleep;
    Her tranquil breathing seemed to do me good.
    But suddenly it quickened with a leap,
    Becoming like the fierce and panting breath
Of one in flight, who climbs a rocky steep.   330
The soul seemed struggling with the fear of death,
    While broken utterings in a tongue unknown
Escaped at moments through her tightened teeth.
    I was about to wake her, when the moon
    Lit up the bed, and let me see a sight   335
Which for a while changed flesh and blood to stone.
All round the face, convulsed in sleep and white,

---

[18] *woof* fabric, threads.
[19] *daïs* here with the rare sense of 'canopy'.

[20] *Templar* order of Christian knights founded in 1118: their original role, ironically, was as the protector of pilgrims.

Innumerable snakes – some large and slow,
Some lithe and small – writhed bluish in the light,
   Each striving with a sort of ceaseless flow   340
   To quit the head, and groping as in doubt;
   Then, fast retained, returning to the brow.
     They glided on her pillow; all about
The moonlit sheet in endless turn and coil,
   And all about her bosom, in and out;   345
While round her temples, pale as leaden foil,
And fast closed lids, live curls of vipers twined,
   Whose endless writhe had made all hell recoil.
Long I stood petrified; both limbs and mind
    Refusing in the presence of that face   350
   The customary work to each assigned.
    But, all at once, I felt a fire replace
My frozen blood, and unseen spirits seemed
    To call for an Avenger, and to brace
My arm for one great blow. Above me gleamed   355
   A double-handed sword upon the wall,
Whose weight, till then, beyond my strength I deemed.
   I seized it, swung it high, and let it fall
Like thunder on the sleeping Gorgon's[21] neck
Before her eye could see or tongue could call.   360
   And, O my God! as if herself a snake
   Which, stricken of a sudden in its sleep,
Coils up and writhes all round the injuring stake,
   She coiled about the weapon in a heap,
But gave no sound, while all the sheet soaked red,   365
   Except a sort of gurgle hoarse and deep,
   Which made me strike again, until the head,
Whose beauty death's convulsion seemed to spare,
   Rolled like a heavy ball from off the bed.
   I held the dripping trophy by the hair,[22]   370
Which now no more was snakes, but long black locks,
   And scanned the features with a haggard stare.
   And, like to one around whose spirit flocks
Too great a crowd of thoughts for thought to act,
   I fled once more along the moonlit rocks.   375
Then Doubt, with his tormentors, came and racked.

[21] *Gorgon's* Medusa was one of the three Gorgon sisters; see headnote, 545–6.

[22] *I held . . . hair* common posture for representations of Perseus after slaying Medusa; see headnote, 545–6.

Sonnets from *Imaginary Sonnets* (1888)

Laura to Petrarch (1345)

The Italian poet and humanist Petrarch – Francesco Petrarca (1304–74) – wrote his celebrated love poetry to a woman he named Laura (pronounced so the first syllable rhymes with the *show* in shower). But her exact identity is not known (some scholars think her the wife of Hugues de Sade of Avignon; others believe her imaginary). Eugene Lee-Hamilton gives Laura a voice, tantalizingly offering the reader a few clues to a great literary puzzle. The poem provides a surprising perspective on Petrarch's poetry – an important influence on Renaissance sonnet sequences and on the history of the European sonnet altogether – because

Laura here regards it as merely an addition to a life already content with husband and children. Great art and one of western Europe's most famous loves are charmingly domesticated as Lee-Hamilton explores the unexpected hidden history behind familiar names. The sonnet gently reminds its reader that Petrarch's love was adulterous.

Sweet Florentine[1] that sitteth by the hearth
When hums my spinning, and the shadows leap
As leaps the fire and with its stealthy creep,
The winter twilight hushes all the earth:

A husband's love besunning my life's girth,   5
Warms me like grain that ripens for the reap;
And children, my life's jewels, stand and peep
Behind my chair, and leave my heart no dearth.

But who would scorn to add another hour
To glorious summer's ampleness, or scorn   10
Bright gems of thought, though sparkling be her dower?[2]

So let thy fondness warm me and adorn,
Sweet Florentine, though Love already shower
Its ripening rays like sunshine on the corn.

[1] *Florentine* Petrarch was born in Arezzo, but his father was an exile from Florence.

[2] *dower* gifts, possessions, especially those given on marriage.

Carmagnola to the Republic of Venice (1432)

Lee-Hamilton was peculiarly interested in isolated figures in *Imaginary Sonnets*, drawn to moments of life under pressure, often in broader narratives of the failed hero. 'Carmagnola to the Republic of Venice' lends voice to a man on the verge of execution as a traitor. Francesco Bussone da Carmagnola (*c.*1380?–1432) was a great Italian *condottiere* or hired commander. He fought for Filippo Maria Visconti, Duke of Milan, in wars against Florence and Venice. But he later fell foul of the Duke and swapped sides in the service of Venice. After 1425 he led Florentine and Venetian armies against Milan, but the Venetians suspected him of treason and he was tried and exe-cuted. His story has been seen as a parable of a *state's* treachery to one of its faithful sons. To be sure there has never been final certainty of Carmagnola's guilt. In the Victorian period, the novelist Margaret Oliphant was intrigued by his fate and the dreadful reversal of fortune from celebrated hero to traitor in her *The Makers of Venice* (1887). Here, Lee-Hamilton makes Carmagnola prophetic, foreseeing the collapse of the Venetian Republic. Venice's fortunes did indeed drastically decline from the fifteenth century, and Napoleon finally abolished the Republic in 1797. The poem suggests what dignity, power and capacity for prophecy can be summoned *in extremis*.

I hear my death-bell tolling in the square;[1]
And I am ready, ye Venetian Ten![2]
But God at times reveals to dying men
The Future's depths, and what the years prepare:

[1] *square* Piazza di San Marco, the central square of Venice.

[2] *Venetian Ten* the Council of Ten were the chief magistrates of the Republic who largely controlled the actions of the Doge, the nominal head of state.

And, through Time's veil, I see, as through thick air,   5
　　A day of doom beyond your finite ken,[3]
　　When this strong Venice – old and feeble then –
In vain, like me, shall call on men to spare.

The day shall come when she shall drink of gall,[4]   10
　　And when the same blind fear that makes you take
　　My life to-day, shall consummate her fall;

When she shall take the noise her own troops make
　　For the strong foe, and, in this very hall,
　　In her wild fear, her old sea-sceptre[5] break.

[3] *ken* knowledge.
[4] *gall* bitterness.
[5] *sea-sceptre* Venice's wealth came from maritime trade and she celebrated her dominance over the waters in an annual ritual where the Doge cast a wedding ring into the lagoon to signify the bond of city and sea. Cf. Browning's 'A Toccata of Galuppi's', l. 6 and n. 4.

Fallopius to his Dissecting Knife (1550)

The question of animal vivisection generated controversy in Victorian England involving writers including Robert and Elizabeth Barrett Browning, John Ruskin, Michael Field and John Davidson. Lee-Hamilton's poem on the Italian anatomist Gabriello Fallopius (1523–62), who gave his name to the fallopian tubes, distantly echoes the sounds of that modern debate. But it does so all the more provocatively because Lee-Hamilton's sonnet concerns vivisection on human beings. The Duke of Tuscany permitted Fallopius to use prisoners for his experiments and this poem disturbingly offers the anatomist's thoughts just before he begins his awful investigations on live men. Fallopius's words suggest the foundation of suffering on which modern science is built, and the sonnet is another example of Lee-Hamilton's preoccupation with history's hidden pains. The poem obliquely registers Victorian questions about the moral nature of the empirical investigator, the proper limits of scientific knowledge and the issue of how far vivisection corrupts the vivisector.

Now shalt thou have thy way, thou little blade,
　　So bright and keen; now shalt thou have thy way,
　　And plod no more through bodies cold as clay,
But through quick flesh, by fiery pulses swayed.

A glorious and munificent duke hath made   5
　　Thee a great gift: live convicts; and to-day,
　　Though Nature shudder, thou shalt say thy say
On Life's deep springs where God so long forbade.

Fear not lest Mercy blunt thy edge, or make
　　The hand that holds thee o'er the living man   10
　　With any human hesitation shake;

But thou shalt tell me why his life-blood ran
　　Thus in his veins; what Life is; and shalt slake
The thirst of thirsts that makes my cheek so wan.[1]

[1] *wan* pale.

Charles Edward to his Last Friend (1777)

Charles Edward Stuart (1720–88) was the claimant to the British throne known as the Young Pretender or, more usually, Bonnie Prince Charlie. A romantic figure of charm and good looks, he led the Jacobites in their great uprising of 1745 but was defeated at the Battle of Culloden Moor in 1746. Charles fled, roaming Europe and drinking heavily. From 1766 he lived in Rome, where he finally died a broken alcoholic, all his dreams of the throne shattered. Lee-Hamilton's sonnet dwells, like 'Carmagnola to the Republic of Venice', on another bleak moment of human isolation. Where Carmagnola prophesies the end of the republic, however, Bonnie Prince Charlie can take no comfort from the future. The poem extends Hamilton's preoccupation with the underside of romantic history, the bleaker personal stories of those known as heroes. The glimpse of Charles's dismal life here is all the more gloomy because, at the time the poem is set, he has 11 more years to live.

Text: *Imaginary Sonnets* (1888).

Thou bottle, thou last comrade that is worth
My love, thou sole Prime Minister[1] I have,
Thou art the last adherent[2] who can save
Thy master still some woe in his heart's dearth.

The table thou art on is my realm's girth, 5
Instead of that broad England which God gave:
And with thy help I shuffle to the grave,
Besotten, gouty,[3] left by all on earth.

Hark, hark! I hear above the trees that sigh
A sound of Highland[4] music wild and sweet, 10
Like gusts from Falkirk,[5] gusts of victory!

My heart contracts and doubles in its beat;
I shiver in the sun I know not why:
'Twas but the Roman[6] pipers in the street.

[1] *Prime Minister* as British monarch, Charles's prime minister would have been accountable directly to him.
[2] *adherent* follower.
[3] *gouty* gout is a painful disease of the circulatory system, common to heavy wine and port drinkers.
[4] *Highland* mountainous area of northern Scotland whose inhabitants supported Charles's claim to the throne.
[5] *Falkirk* Charles won the Battle of Falkirk in January 1746 in the build-up to Culloden.
[6] *Roman* see headnote.

Michael Field (Katherine Harris Bradley [1846–1914] and Edith Emma Cooper [1862–1913])

Katherine Bradley was the daughter of a Birmingham tobacco manufacturer; she was educated at home, in Paris, and then at Newnham College Cambridge. She brought up from childhood her niece, Edith Cooper, when her mother became an invalid. In 1878, they both took classes at Bristol University and, from around this time, became lovers. Katherine had been a member of Ruskin's Guild of St George, but her frank admission of atheism led to her expulsion. Both women were active in support of female suffrage and the anti-vivisection movement. In 1881, their first joint volume appeared, *Bellerophon* by 'Arran and Isla Leigh'; with *Calirrhoe and Fair Rosamund* (1884), 'Michael Field' was born and remained thereafter their collective pseudonym. In 1889, they published their first collection of verse, *Long Ago*, inspired by Henry Wharton's openly lesbian edition of Sappho (1885). *Sight and Song* followed in 1892, then *Underneath the Bough* (1893) and *Wild Honey from Various Thyme* (1908). The two travelled Europe widely, attempted to hear Pater lecturing (he was inaudible), made friends with Robert Browning (who had helped with the manuscript of *Long Ago*), and knew Vernon Lee and the vegetarian sexologist Havelock Ellis.

Famously, however, they acquired a Chow dog – called Whym Chow – whose adored presence stopped the travelling as they could not face leaving him behind. Katherine and Edith distanced themselves from what they saw as the depravity of much of 1890s writing, loathing Zola, Huysmans and Beardsley, and withdrawing a poem from John Lane's *Yellow Book*, the central organ of Decadent poetry, in 1894. In 1906, Whym Chow died, which led firstly to the extraordinary volume of love lyrics, *Whym Chow: Flame of Love*, and also, so Edith would have it, their conversion to Catholicism. Their poetry thereafter gave up the sensuousness of their previous work and became devotional. Edith died of cancer in 1913 (she refused drugs so she could keep her mind clear till the end) and Katherine, who wrote several volumes of verse alone (still under the name Michael Field), died, also of cancer, in September 1914. Their early verse mingled *fin de siècle* sensuousness with pagan themes and a fondness for crisp images that anticipated Imagism; they boldly associated lyricism with lesbian love, making a link between innovative poetics and same-sex desire that would be significant for Modernism.

Maids, not to you my mind doth change [XXXIII][1]

Sappho, born in the late seventh century BC, was a Greek lyric poet whose subjective, personal lyrics, almost all about love, survive only in fragments. She exerted fascination for the Victorians who came to mythologize her as the founding voice of lyricism. Swinburne thought her the 'greatest poet who ever was at all' (cf. Swinburne's 'Anactoria', 480–6). In the early period, from Ovid onwards, she was constructed as heterosexual and her same-sex desires disguised. But Michael Field, at the end of the century, knew her, as Swinburne did, as a lesbian muse (she lived on the isle of Lesbos, giving the name to female homosexuality). The publication of Henry Wharton's *Sappho: Memoir, Text, Selected Renderings, and a Literal Translation* (1885), which restored the feminine pronouns to the verse, was the chief inspiration behind Michael Field's first collection of poetry, *Long Ago* (1889), from which 'Maids, not to you my mind

doth change' is taken. *Long Ago* celebrated the possibilities of a Sapphic identity and her capacity to continue engendering poetry in an afterlife of translation and inspiration (cf. Field's 'A Girl', 562–3, as another poem on a female muse).

Long Ago is a complex Sapphic text in that it offers poetic responses, like this one, to fragments of Sappho's verse written by two female lesbian poets writing as the unitary male 'Michael Field'. The Sapphic signature – Sappho-as two women writers-as one man – becomes, as Yopie Prins argues, remarkably permissive (all the more so as Robert Browning made some changes to their initial manuscript too). 'Maids, not to you my mind doth change' celebrates female sexuality and companionship over male, particularly valuing the healing quality of femininity (cf. Christina G. Rossetti's 'Goblin Market', 373–85, on the therapeutic possibilities of the sister–sister relationship).

---

[1] *XXXIII* Michael Field's poems from *Long Ago* are simply numbered – here, '33' – in the original rather than given formal titles.

Hellenic studies were, at the beginning of the century, associated with the prestigious male domains of public schools, Oxford and Cambridge Universities, the clergy and the law; later, in the 1870s, Greek literature became bound up with discourses of male homosexuality through the figure of Plato. Michael Field redefines Victorian Hellenism further in their Sapphic work at the end of the 1880s, appropriating the authority of Classical antiquity to produce poetry conscious of lesbian desire and of the Sapphic inheritance of modern lyricism.

Text: *Long Ago* (1889).

" The poets as translators make an "effort" to be objective and yet that force of "individuality" is still an inevitable component in the poets' aesthetic experience or "impression".

Ταὶς καλαις ὑμμιν [τὸ] νόημα τώμον ου διάμειπτον.[2]

Maids, not to you my mind doth change;
Men I defy, allure, estrange,
Prostrate, make bond or free:
Soft as the stream beneath the plane[3]
To you I sing my love's refrain;[4]   5
Between us is no thought of pain, peril, satiety.[5]

2

Soon doth a lover's[6] patience tire,
But ye to manifold desire
Can yield response, ye know
When for long, museful[7] days I pine,   10
The presage[8] at my heart divine;
To you I never breathe a sign
Of inward want or woe.

3

When injuries my spirit bruise,
Allaying virtue[9] ye infuse   15
With unobtrusive skill:
And if care frets ye come to me
As fresh as nymph[10] from stream or tree,
And with your soft vitality
My weary bosom fill.   20

[2] Ταὶς καλαις ὑμμιν [τὸ] νόημα τώμον ου διάμειπτον
'To you lovely women my mind does not change.'
[3] *plane* tree.
[4] *refrain* chorus, repeated part of a song.
[5] *satiety* state of being glutted.
[6] *lover's* [male] lover's.
[7] *museful* days when the muse is with her; when she is able to write.

[8] *presage* something that portends or foreshadows.
[9] *virtue* medicine.
[10] *nymph* one of the semi-divine beautiful women of Classical mythology, often imagined as associated with places, rivers, trees.

La Gioconda

Leonardo da Vinci: The Louvre

Walter Pater had written memorably of Leonardo da Vinci's *La Gioconda* (*Mona Lisa* – plate 7), in his foundational text in the development of the English Aesthetic movement, *The Renaissance* (1873). Pater's rhapsodic description of Leonardo's most famous painting set terms that helped define Aesthetic criticism as a creative not an analytical art, as one rooted in individual subjectivity. For Pater, La Gioconda was a mythical and timeless figure, touched with the gothic: she was 'older than the rocks among which she sits; like the vampire, she has been dead many times, and learned the secrets of the grave'. Michael Field's response to the same image affirms the subjectivity at the heart of Aesthetic criticism by presenting a sharply different view of the painting as engagingly erotic, and suggestive of cruelty and violence. Like 'A Girl', 562–3, 'La Gioconda' (1892) is a meditation on an enthralling, mysterious woman, rich with homo-erotic potential. Another of Michael Field's considerations of a painting, 'A Portrait: Bartolommeo Veneto', 560–2, makes explicit the tension perhaps implicit here between the enduring image and the woman represented, now long dead, unknowable.

Text: *Sight and Song* (1892).

> Historic, side-long, implicating eyes;
> A smile of velvet's lustre on the cheek;
> Calm lips the smile leads upward; hand that lies
> Glowing and soft, the patience in its rest
> Of cruelty that waits and doth not seek
> For prey; a dusky[1] forehead and a breast   5
> Where twilight touches ripeness amorously:
> Behind her, crystal rocks, a sea and skies
> Of evanescent[2] blue on cloud and creek;
> Landscape that shines suppressive of its zest
> For those vicissitudes[3] by which men die.   10

[1] *dusky* dark.
[2] *evanescent* fading.

[3] *vicissitudes* changes.

Plate 7   Leonardo da Vinci, *La Gioconda*, Louvre. Photo © RMN, R.G. Ojeda.

A Portrait: Bartolommeo Veneto

The Städel'sche Institut at Frankfurt

'A Portrait' (1892), a particularly complex example of Michael Field's preoccupation with female form, character and identity, concerns the image of a woman whose smile offers 'The gazer . . . no tidings from the face'. The poem focuses on the difference between that strange, erotic image and the self that lies behind it, unrepresented. The image of the 'flawless beauty' has conquered time, but the woman it represents is long dead; the sitter gave a 'fair, blank form' to art, but the canvas did not capture the real personality who dramatized herself as moral emblem in a picture 'unverified by life'.

'A Portrait' demonstrates a sharp sense of the limits and fictiveness of representation – a perspective to which the Modernists would return – and Michael Field's sustained interest in self-construction, the adopting of public roles and the doubleness of a woman's identity (cf. Augusta Webster, 'Faded', 471–5, as a poem about representations of the female built around a tension between a painting and its real subject). Although 'A Portrait' – which debates issues of art and immortality considered in Keats's 'Ode on a Grecian Urn' – concludes with the triumphant exclamation that 'she has conquered death!', such conquest has only been accomplished through the preservation of an unbreathing image. The painting referred to is *Portrait of a Woman* by Bartolomeo Veneto, an Italian painter who was active in Venice between 1502 and 1555. It still hangs in the Städelsches Kunstinstitut, Frankfurt (see plate 8).

Both 'A Portrait' and 'La Gioconda', 558–9, are taken from Field's *Sight and Song* (1892), a volume that includes many poems on pictures including those by Giorgione, Botticelli and Tintoretto. In the 'Preface',

Plate 8 Bartolomeo Veneto, *Portrait of a Woman*, Städelsches Kunstinstitut, Frankfurt.

Michael Field remarks: 'The aim of this little volume is, as far as may be, to translate into verses what the lines and colours of certain chosen pictures sing in themselves; to express not so much what these pictures are to the poet, but rather what poetry they objectively incarnate. Such an attempt demands patient, continuous sight as pure as the gazer can refine it of theory, fancies, or his mere subjective enjoyment.'

Text: *Sight and Song* (1892).

A crystal, flawless beauty on the brows
Where neither love nor time has conquered space
On which to live; her leftward smile endows
The gazer with no tidings from the face;
About the clear mounds of the lip it winds with silvery pace   5
And in the umber[1] eyes it is a light
Chill as a glowworm's when the moon embrowns an August night.

2
She saw her beauty often in the glass,
Sharp on the dazzling surface, and she knew
The haughty custom of her grace must pass: 10
Though more persistent in all charm it grew
As with a desperate joy her hair across her throat she drew
In crinkled locks stiff as dead, yellow snakes . . .
Until at last within her soul the resolution wakes

3
She will be painted, she who is so strong   15
In loveliness, so fugitive in years:
Forth to the field she goes and questions long
Which flowers to choose of those the summer bears;
She plucks a violet larkspur,[2] – then a columbine[3] appears
Of perfect yellow, – daisies choicely wide;   20
These simple things with finest touch she gathers in her pride.

4
Next on her head, veiled with well-bleachen white
And bound across the brow with azure-blue,
She sets the box-tree leaf and coils it tight
In spiky wreath of green, immortal[4] hue;   25
Then, to the prompting of her strange, emphatic insight true,
She bares one breast, half-freeing it of robe,
And hangs green-water gem and cord beside the naked globe.

5
So was she painted and for centuries
Has held the fading field-flowers in her hand   30
Austerely as a sign. O fearful eyes
And soft lips of the courtesan[5] who planned
To give her fragile shapeliness to art, whose reason spanned[6]
Her doom, who bade her beauty in its cold
And vacant eminence persist for all men to behold!   35

---

[1] *umber* brown.
[2] *larkspur* blue delphinium.
[3] *columbine* flower of the genus *Aquilegia*.

[4] *immortal* box is evergreen.
[5] *courtesan* court mistress, prostitute.
[6] *reason spanned* thought as far ahead as.

6

She had no memories save of herself
And her slow-fostered graces, naught to say
Of love in gift or boon;[7] her cruel pelf[8]
Had left her with no hopes that grow and stay;
She found default[9] in everything that happened night or day,   40
Yet stooped in calm to passion's dizziest strife
And gave to art a fair, blank form, unverified by life.

7

Thus has she conquered death: her eyes are fresh,
Clear as her frontlet[10] jewel, firm in shade
And definite as on the linen mesh   45
Of her white hood the box-tree's sombre braid,[11]
That glitters leaf by leaf and with the year's waste will not fade.
The small, close mouth, leaving no room for breath,
In perfect, still pollution smiles – Lo,[12] she has conquered death!

[7] *boon* request, gift.
[8] *pelf* fortune.
[9] *default* fault.
[10] *frontlet* band worn on the forehead.

[11] *braid* plaited or interwoven work.
[12] *Lo* word usually used in a religious context (meaning look, see, behold).

A Girl

Another of Field's poems about a powerful, magnetizing woman, 'A Girl' (1893) is a modern version of a Classical apostrophe (address) to the muse (one of the divinities on whom mortals depend, in Classical myth, for inspiration). This muse, however, is not ethereally supernatural but possessed of a temptingly erotic corporeality and a mysterious 'tempestuous heart'. Her real identity – is she imaginary or actual? – remains undisclosed. Like 'Sometimes I do despatch my heart', 563–4, and 'La Gioconda', 558–9, 'A Girl' is preoccupied with the knowableness of identities, the aura of a woman's intriguing selfhood.

'A Girl' associates poetry with enigmatic but sexualized female power, as the Sapphic poems of *Long Ago* (1889) linked lyricism with the female more gen-

erally through the originating figure of Sappho (see 'Maids, not to you my mind doth change', 557–8). Involving a mysterious, sexualized, perhaps internalized muse, Michael Field defines the source of their inspiration as fundamentally female, affirming a link between lyric poetry and women suggested across the Victorian period (cf. Tennyson's 'The Dying Swan', 62–4, and 'The Lady of Shalott', 71–6, Swinburne's '*Ave Atque Vale*: In Memory of Charles Baudelaire', 500–6). 'A Girl' is distinctive as another innovative sonnet, a sonnet deconstructed or unravelled, with free line lengths (cf. 'Sometimes I do despatch my heart').

Text: *Underneath the Bough* (1893).

        A girl,
    Her soul a deep-wave pearl
Dim, lucent[1] of all lovely mysteries;
    A face flowered for heart's ease,[2]
    A brow's grace soft as seas   5
    Seen through faint forest-trees:
    A mouth, the lips apart,
Like aspen[3]-leaflets trembling in the breeze
    From her tempestuous heart.

[1] *lucent* luminous.
[2] *flowered for heart's ease* pun, heartsease = pansy.

[3] *aspen* form of poplar, its leaves liable to tremulous motion.

Such: and our souls so knit,   10
I leave a page half-writ –
The work begun   ˎ
Will be to heaven's conception done,
If she come to it.

⊹ Cyclamens

The brief clarity of this poem and its focus on a single visual image link it with the Imagists, the group of poets including Ezra Pound (1885–1972), T. E. Hulme (1883–1917) and H. D. ([Hilda Doolittle], 1886–1961) at the beginning of the twentieth century, who believed in the necessity of sharp, clear images in poetic discourse. In 'Cyclamens', Michael Field takes the Romantic conception of being 'struck to the heart' by the natural world but not as a prophetic event. The *meaning* of the flowers, more artificial in their *fin de siècle* 'chiselled white' than natural, remains private. The poet is the sensitive spectator of nature, but her complete relationship with it is kept from the reader's knowledge. What we have first and foremost is the crisp image, syntax moving from the simple to the complex as the personal element deepens, and the luminous presence of the white flowers themselves.

Text: *Underneath the Bough* (1893).

They are terribly white:
There is snow on the ground,
And a moon on the snow at night;
The sky is cut by the winter light;
Yet I, who have all these things in ken,[1]   5
Am struck to the heart by the chiselled white
Of this handful of cyclamen.[2]

[1] *ken* sight.

[2] *cyclamen* plant of the genus *Primulaceæ*, cultivated for its early-blooming, handsome flowers.

Sometimes I do despatch my heart

Michael Field's preoccupation with the complexities and divisions of the self is evident in this poem, at once about a lost part of the self and love for the dead. 'Sometimes I do despatch my heart' (1893) dramatizes bereavement, as the poet's heart wanders through a space of uncertain identity, both perhaps a real grave-yard and a metaphor of her interior consciousness. Like 'A Portrait: Bartolommeo Veneto', 560–2, 'Sometimes I do despatch my heart' focuses on the multiplicity of identity. It fractures notions of the self's unity and marks a shift in assumptions about selfhood that would be given most conspicuous prominence in the work of Sigmund Freud (1856–1939). The poem is an innovative version of the sonnet, which achieves its devastating climax with the simplest of statements and the poignant dissatisfaction of half-rhyme (cf. 'A Girl', 562–3).

Text: *Underneath the Bough* (1893).

Sometimes I do despatch my heart
Among the graves to dwell apart:
On some the tablets[1] are erased,
Some earthquake-tumbled, some defaced,
And some that have forgotten lain   5
A fall of tears makes green again;

[1] *tablets* of stone, tombstones.

And my brave heart can overtread
Her brood of hopes, her infant dead,
And pass with quickened[2] footsteps by
The headstone of hoar[3] memory,   10
Till she hath found
One swelling mound
With just her name writ and beloved;
From that she cannot be removed.

---

[2] *quickened* with a pun on 'quick' = alive.   [3] *hoar* grey with age.

It was deep April

Sappho provided many Victorian women poets with a figure imaginatively associated with versions of themselves. At the beginning of the century, the popular poet 'L. E. L.' (Letitia Elizabeth Landon [1802–38]) found in Sappho a model of the disappointed and doomed figure who exemplified some of her feelings about the difficulties of being a woman poet. In 'Sappho's Song' from L. E. L.'s *The Improvisatrice and Other Poems* (1824), Sappho declares, moments before she commits suicide, that she was doomed by an 'evil star' and betrayed by a faithless lover who had destroyed her art. It was this incompatibility between sexual desire and art – domestic life and professional life, as we might say – that Elizabeth Barrett Browning sought to heal in the conclusion of *Aurora Leigh* (1857).

Michael Field's 'It was deep April' needs to be read against the Sapphic tradition represented by L. E. L. While the poem does not explicitly invoke Sappho, the Classical context naturally invites recollection of the figure Michael Field had buoyantly celebrated in

Long Ago (1889) (cf. 'Maids, not to you my mind doth change', 557–8). 'It was deep April' redefines the Sapphic voice of poetry as a joyful, erotic collaborative venture between two lovers. Poetry and love, unlike for L. E. L., are productively bound together. Although most first readers would not have known it, the fact that 'It was deep April' celebrates lesbian love 'against the world' as inextricable from the creation of poetry adds to the radical redefinition of the woman poet here. Poetry and desire are connected with pagan energies and set against Christianity: in their rapturous, confident state, the poets declare themselves 'Indifferent to heaven and hell'. This Baudelairean paganism – which can be compared with the mid-period paganism of Swinburne's poetry, 476–509 – comprised an important element of Michael Field's early work. The volume from where 'It was deep April' comes, *Underneath the Bough* (1893), was dedicated to Apollo, the Greek god of poetry.

Text: *Underneath the Bough* (1893).

It was deep April, and the morn
Shakspere was born;[1]
The world was on us, pressing sore;[2]
My Love and I took hands and swore,
Against the world, to be   5
Poets and lovers evermore,[3]
To laugh and dream on Lethe's shore,[4]
To sing to Charon[5] in his boat,

---

[1] *morn / Shakspere was born* traditionally 23 April.
[2] *The world . . . sore* cf. Wordsworth's sonnet 'The world is too much with us' that includes these lines: 'Great God! I'd rather be / A Pagan suckled in a creed outworn; / So might I, standing on this pleasant lea, / Have glimpses that would make me less forlorn; / Have sight of Proteus rising from the sea; / Or hear old Triton blow his wreathed horn.'
[3] *evermore* there is perhaps some irony in the fact that the poem which follows 'It was deep April' in *Underneath the*

Bough is about a dying woman: 'There comes a change in her breath, / A change that saith / She is breathing in her sleep, / Breathing, breathing and yet so low: / O life at ebb, O life at flow, / Her life, her breath!'
[4] *Lethe's shore* river of forgetfulness in Greek mythology.
[5] *Charon* old ferryman of Greek mythology who guided the souls of the dead to the underworld across the River Styx.

Heartening the timid souls afloat;
Of judgment never to take heed,
But to those fast-locked souls to speed,
Who never from Apollo[6] fled,
Who spent no hour among the dead;
Continually
With them to dwell,
Indifferent to heaven and hell.[7]

10

15

[6] *Apollo* Greek god of prophecy and the arts, leader of the Muses.

[7] *Indifferent . . . hell* cf. Baudelaire's 'Lesbos' from *Les Fleurs du mal* (1857), 'Et l'amour se rira de l'Enfer et du Ciel!', 'And love will laugh at hell and heaven!'.

Nests in Elms

'Nests in Elms' (1908) refuses Christian reassurance about death. But it does not make death without God seem terrifying or imagine it in nihilistic terms. The sonnet elegantly proposes a secular version of the deathbed scene that bespeaks consolation even at life's end. The rooks are chosen partly because they are not birds saluted in the poetic tradition; they have an ordinariness that is precious. Vocalizing a life that continues beyond the individual's cessation, the sound of the rooks' homely, outdoor cawing is the agnostic's or atheist's comfort. Death here occurs by 'open doors' – it is both welcomed and an opening up of possibilities. Michael Field's final line is striking for the way it invites then repels irony.

The late Victorian secularism of 'Nests in Elms' and its total resistance to natural theology can be compared with James Thomson, *The City of Dreadful Night*, 394–422, A. C. Swinburne, 'A Forsaken Garden', 506–9, and John Davidson, 'A Woman and her Son', 609–15. Within Michael Field's own work, 'Nests in Elms' is a recantation of 'Elvan Justice' from *Underneath the Bough* (1893), a harsh poem about bird life:

The rooks have their nests,
And the rooks we do not love.
The man who will break their eggs
Shall have half-a-crown
In the midst of the ring, where we twirl our legs,
Laid every morning down,
As white as any he ever saw,
Or shall ever see.
Ha, ha, hi, hi!
Caw, caw!

Text: *Wild Honey from Various Thyme* (1908).

The rooks are cawing up and down the trees!
Among their nests they caw. O sound I treasure,
Ripe as old music is, the summer's measure,[1]
Sleep at her gossip, sylvan[2] mysteries,
With prate[3] and clamour to give zest of these –
In rune[4] I trace the ancient law of pleasure,
Of love, of all the busy-ness of leisure,
With dream on dream of never-thwarted ease.
O homely birds, whose cry is harbinger[5]
Of nothing sad, who know not anything
Of sea-birds' loneliness, of Procne's[6] strife,
Rock round me when I die! So sweet it were
To die by open doors, with you on wing
Humming the deep security of life.

5

10

[1] *measure* in its musical sense: the rhythm or time signature of a piece of music.

[2] *sylvan* of woods.

[3] *prate* chatter.

[4] *rune* ancient form of alphabet.

[5] *harbinger* one that goes before to announce an arrival.

[6] *Procne* wife of Tereus, her sister Philomela was raped by Tereus and he cut her tongue out to silence her. In revenge, Procne killed and cooked her son Itys and served him to his father. The gods turned all three adults into birds: a nightingale, a swallow and a hoopoe: none of them, in other words, became a rook.

Four Victorian Hymns

The day thou gavest, Lord, is ended

For those countless Victorian churchgoers for whom published volumes of poetry by contemporary writers were unknown, the hymn was the most important form of poetic language available to them. In a period that saw the composition of an enormous number of hymns and hymn tunes – most prominently for the Revd Sir H. W. Baker's *Hymns Ancient and Modern* (1861) – it was a practice of writing that reached a triumphant peak in the nineteenth century. The Victorian hymn is an important window on nineteenth-century faith, and it offers glimpses of the cultural history and intellectual world of the ordinary worshipper. The hymn was sometimes an important mode of self-expression for writers whose work did not appear in the public market of verse, and, of course, a form of poetry with its own rules, decorum and expressive force.

John Ellerton (1826–93) was a clergyman and vicar of St Nicholas, Brighton, and then of Crewe Green, Cheshire. He was the author of many hymns and a contributor to *Hymns Ancient and Modern*. 'The day thou gavest', still an enormously popular hymn, was originally written for missionary meetings in 1870 (revised for *Church Hymns* [1871]) and demonstrates some of the qualities of a good hymn: consistent in theme, but not repetitive; progressive in the development of ideas (and moving towards a climax) but not confusingly rapid or overweighted with thought, and with a clear meaning to each line, even if enjambement is used (and, of course, absolutely metrical). 'The day thou gavest', set for evening time, reveals a suggestive coordination of Christian discourse with the language of contemporary politics, as the last verse imagines Christianity as an empire that will endure beyond earthly ones. Queen Victoria appointed this hymn as one of those to be sung in churches throughout the world on the occasion of her Diamond Jubilee in 1897 (celebrating 60 years on the throne). With its admission that 'earth's proud empires' will 'pass away', it can be compared with Rudyard Kipling's admonishing Jubilee poem 'Recessional', 650–2, and the fourth verse of 'Onward, Christian Soldiers' (N.B., hymns are divided into *verses*; poems into *stanzas*).

> The day thou gavest, Lord, is ended,
> The darkness falls at thy behest;
> To thee our morning hymns ascended,
> Thy praise shall sanctify our rest.
>
> 2
> We thank thee that thy Church, unsleeping   5
> While earth rolls onward into light,
> Through all the world her watch is keeping
> And rests not now by day nor night.
>
> 3
> As o'er each continent and island
> The dawn leads on another day,   10
> The voice of prayer is never silent,
> Nor dies the strain of praise away.
>
> 4
> The sun that bids us rest is waking
> Our brethren 'neath the western sky,
> And hour by hour fresh lips are making   15
> Thy wondrous doings heard on high.
>
> 5
> So be it, Lord; thy throne shall never,
> Like earth's proud empires, pass away;
> Thy kingdom stands, and grows for ever,
> Till all thy creatures own thy sway.   20

Take my life, and let it be

(Consecration Hymn)

Frances Ridley Havergal (1836–79) was an exceptionally intelligent young woman who received little formal education but developed precociously, writing verse fluently from the age of 7. Her hymns and poetry, including *Under the Surface* (poems, 1874) and *Loyal Responses* (hymns, 1878, from where 'Take my life' comes), obtained a large Evangelical following. The intensity of her religious nature is clear from her work, and she emphasized, throughout her confident writing, the strong emotions of the believer. Her 'Consecration Hymn', still popular in the Anglican Church, appropriates the conventional language of a woman's self-sacrifice to the will of a man and transforms it into a joyful, perhaps erotic, acceptance of divine power. 'Take my life' offers self-giving as infinite gain. Its insistent anaphora – the repetition of the same word or phrase in several successive clauses – is its most striking formal feature. Havergal's own account of its genesis gives a taste of Evangelical fervour surviving into the 1870s: 'There were ten persons in the house, some unconverted and long prayed for, some converted by not rejoicing Christians. He gave me the prayer "Lord give me ALL in this house". And He just did. Before I left the house every one had got a blessing. The last night of my visit, after I had retired, the governess asked me to go to the two daughters. They were crying. Then and there both of them trusted and rejoiced. I was too happy to sleep, and passed most of the night in praise and renewal of my own consecration; and these little couplets formed themselves in my heart one after the other, till they finished with "Ever, ONLY, ALL for Thee!"'

Take my life, and let it be consecrated, Lord, to Thee.
Take my moments and my days; let them flow in ceaseless praise.
Take my hands, and let them move at the impulse of Thy love.
Take my feet, and let them be swift and beautiful for Thee.

2
Take my voice, and let me sing always, only, for my King. 5
Take my lips, and let them be filled with messages from Thee.
Take my silver and my gold; not a mite[1] would I withhold.
Take my intellect, and use every power as Thou shalt choose.

3
Take my will, and make it Thine; it shall be no longer mine.
Take my heart, it is Thine own; it shall be Thy royal throne. 10
Take my love, my Lord, I pour at Thy feet its treasure store.
Take myself, and I will be ever, only, all for Thee.

[1] *mite* tiny coin.

Onward, Christian soldiers

The stirring confidence of the Revd Sabine Baring-Gould's 'Onward, Christian Soldiers' (1865) expressed the triumphalist element of Victorian Anglicanism with a peculiar vigour that made it one of the most popular of nineteenth-century hymns. Written for a Whit Sunday school festival in Yorkshire for children to sing as they processed from village to village led by a cross bearer – Baring-Gould was in charge of a mission at Horbury Bridge, near Wakefield – it illustrates with lucidity the assimilation of military vocabulary into Christian declaration, producing a heavily masculinized vision of the Church militant. Sabine Baring-Gould (1834–1924), a graduate of Clare College Cambridge, was a prolific author including novels and devotional works.

Onward, Christian soldiers, marching as to war,
With the cross of Jesus going on before.
Christ, the royal Master, leads against the foe;
Forward into battle see His banners go![1]

Refrain
Onward, Christian soldiers, marching as to war,   5
With the cross of Jesus going on before.

2
At the sign of triumph Satan's host doth flee;
On then, Christian soldiers, on to victory!
Hell's foundations quiver at the shout of praise;
Brothers lift your voices, loud your anthems raise.   10

Refrain

3
Like a mighty army moves the church of God;
Brothers, we are treading where the saints have trod.
We are not divided, all one body we,[2]
One in hope and doctrine, one in charity.

Refrain

4
What the saints established that I hold for true.[3]   15
What the saints believed, that I believe too.
Long as earth endureth, men the faith will hold,
Kingdoms, nations, empires, in destruction rolled.

Refrain

5
Crowns and thrones may perish, kingdoms rise and wane,
But the church of Jesus constant will remain.   20
Gates of hell can never 'gainst that church prevail;
We have Christ's own promise, and that cannot fail.

Refrain

6
Onward then, ye people, join our happy throng,
Blend with ours your voices in the triumph song.
Glory, laud and honour unto Christ the King,   25
This through countless ages men and angels sing.

Refrain

[1] *Forward . . . go!* cf. the ancient Latin hymn 'Vexilla regis prodeunt', usually sung in English as 'The royal banners forward go'.
[2] *We are not divided . . . we* this Pauline sentiment was sometimes regarded as a provocative statement since the Victorian Church was by no means undivided. But perhaps it should be remembered that Baring-Gould was writing for a specific occasion and has the cheery band of children in procession at the forefront of his mind.
[3] *What the saints . . . true* this Oxford Movement verse – linking modern Anglicanism with the ancient faith of the saints, martyrs and Church fathers – is usually omitted from modern printed versions of the hymn.

My God, how wonderful Thou art

['The Eternal Father']

The Oxford Movement – that influential group of Anglicans, beginning in 1833, who sought to return the Church of England to its Catholic roots – made an important contribution to Victorian hymnology, not least through the work of the translator John Mason Neale (1818–66), whose translations included the hymns 'Blessed city, heavenly Salem' and 'A great and mighty wonder'. Frederick William Faber (1814–63) matriculated at Balliol College Oxford and was later a Fellow of University College; having been a supporter of the Oxford Movement, however, he then converted to Catholicism, was ordained priest, and served as Warden of the Brompton Oratory in London, founded by John Henry Newman (1801–90). His most well-known hymn, 'My God, how wonderful Thou art', offers a glimpse of the fervent devotion, the strongly affective piety, of the 'new' Catholic at a point in English ecclesiastical history when Catholicism was still regarded with much suspicion by the Protestant majority. In the 'Preface' to Faber's *Jesus and Mary: or Catholic Hymns* (1849) from where this hymn comes, Faber remarked that he wanted to provide English Catholics with hymns for their own faith as they were having to make do with Protestant ones which did not 'contain the mysteries of the faith in easy verse' (not that 'My God, how wonderful' is peculiarly Catholic in doctrine, however). The language of intense devotion and exclamation may be compared to the Catholic Gerard M. Hopkins later in the century (cf. 'The Wreck of the *Deutschland*', 525–34, and 'The Windhover', 538–9). Hopkins's contribution to hymnology, one might add, included his translation of the Latin 'Adoro Te Devote' as the hymn of the Blessed Sacrament: 'Godhead here in hiding, whom I do adore'.

'My God, how wonderful' is usually printed with seven verses, but I give here the original nine from *Jesus and Mary*.

My God, how wonderful Thou art,
Thy majesty, how bright;
How beautiful Thy Mercy Seat
In depths of burning light!

2
How dread are Thine eternal years,   5
O everlasting Lord,
By prostrate spirits day and night
Incessantly adored!

3
How wonderful, how beautiful,
The sight of Thee must be;   10
Thy endless wisdom, boundless power,
And awful purity!

4
O how I fear Thee, Living God!
With deepest, tenderest fear;
And worship Thee with trembling hope,   15
And penitential tears.

5
Yet I may love Thee too, O Lord!
Almighty as Thou art;
For Thou hast stooped to ask of me
The love of my poor heart.   20

6

O then the worse than worthless heart
In pity deign to take,
And make it love Thee, for Thyself
And for Thy glory's sake.[1]

7

No earthly father loves like Thee,   25
No mother half so mild,
Bears and forbears, as Thou hast done,
With me Thy sinful child.

8

Only to sit and think of God –
Oh what a joy it is!   30
To think the thought, to breathe the Name –
Earth has no higher bliss![2]

9

Father of Jesus, love's Reward!
What rapture it will be
Prostrate before Thy Throne to lie,   35
And gaze and gaze on Thee!

[1] *O then . . . sake* usually omitted.   [2] *Only . . . bliss!* usually omitted.

W[illiam] E[rnest] Henley (1849–1903)

Henley was born in Gloucester, the eldest son of a bookseller; his mother was a descendant of the Warton family who numbered an eighteenth-century Poet Laureate among them (Thomas Warton [1728–90]). He was educated at the Gloucester Crypt Grammar School but suffered from some kind of tubercular arthritis from boyhood and had to have a foot amputated. In 1873, he was sent to Edinburgh for treatment by Joseph Lister ([1827–1912], an important pioneer of antiseptics after whom the commercial brand Listerine has been named) in an effort – happily successful – to save his other foot. In hospital over a year and a half, he sent the verses written during the period to the *Cornhill Magazine* and some were published in 1875. While in the infirmary he was visited by Robert Louis Stevenson, who became a close friend; they collaborated on the largely unsuccessful plays *Deacon Brodie* (1880), *Admiral Guinea* (1884), *Beau Austin* (1884) and *Macaire* (1885). Leaving hospital, Henley worked for *Encyclopaedia Britannica* then edited the weekly *London*. In 1878, he married Anna Boyle and wrote much miscellaneous journalism; he edited the *Magazine of Art* (1882–6) and the *Scots Observer*, later

the *National Observer*. From 1894 to 1898 he took charge of the *New Review*. He was responsible during this busy career for publishing important work by, among others, J. M. Barrie, Thomas Hardy, Rudyard Kipling, Arthur Morrison, R. L. Stevenson, H. G. Wells, W. B. Yeats, his old headmaster T. E. Brown, and Alice Meynell. He compiled anthologies including the popular *Lyra Heroica: A Book of Verse for Boys* (1892) and a co-authored historical dictionary of slang; the *In Hospital* sequence came out completed in *A Book of Verses* (1888). *The Song of the Sword and Other Verses* followed in 1892, *London Voluntaries* in 1893, and his patriotic, Boer War volume *For England's Sake: Verses and Songs in Time of War* was issued in 1900 including 'Pro Rege Nostro' ('Where shall the watchful Sun, / England, my England, / Match the master-work you've done, / England, my own? / When shall he rejoice agen / Such a breed of mighty men / As come forward, one to ten, / To the Song on your bugles blown, / England – / Down the years on your bugles blown?'). W. E. Henley, the inspiration behind Stevenson's Long John Silver in *Treasure Island* (1881–2/1883), died in Woking in 1903

In Hospital 1873–1875

William Ernest Henley's *In Hospital* was first published in a shorter version in the *Cornhill Magazine* in 1875. It was subsequently expanded for *A Book of Verses* (1888), which is the version reproduced here. *In Hospital* is crucial as a new direction in poetic realism in the second half of the Victorian period, setting terms that would be developed, most importantly, by John Davidson (see 606–26). Henley provides an account of his own 20-week period in hospital during 1873, during which he had a foot amputated. The grim hospital setting, the suffering of impoverished men and women on the wards, the account of a desperate suicide who failed, the sheer pain of the operation are recorded with frankness and without self-pity. This terrible personal experience is new territory for Victorian poetry, just as the hospital operation with anaesthetic is a relatively new experience of modern medicine. Popular culture is embraced; human vulnerability is here, and a new preoccupation with the body in pain. Historical reference increases the painful torsion as one of Henley's speakers recalls the plight of the poorest foot soldiers of the Confederacy in the American Civil War to make a provocative comparison with the condition of the hospital patients.

In Hospital centralizes the unlovely, but not unremittingly. There is generosity too, and the natural world, dreams and self-giving human beings offer alternatives. Henley perceives the heroism and achievement of some of the day-to-day men and women memorialized in the verse, including those employed in the hospital, and especially of the lowest of them all. The scrubber – sonnet 19 – is admired without sentimentality, her ordinariness accepted as much as her gift, neatly exemplified in the balanced line 'No rougher, quainter speech, nor kinder heart'. *In Hospital* is not a noisy indictment in its depiction of the suffering body as necessarily passive, deprived of individuality. Henley's language is for the most part of striking plainness, with the transparency of ordinary speech – 'Here comes the basket? Thank you. I am ready' – but he secures particularly telling effects with the clinching single line or half line. Exploiting spare, demotic resources, Henley creates a work of pungent realism, wit, affection, irony, simple horror and, at last, merciful, grateful triumph.

Text: *In Hospital: Rhymes and Rhythms* (1903).

On ne saurait dire à quel point un homme,
seul dans son lit et malade, devient personnel. – Balzac[1]

Enter Patient

The morning mists still haunt the stony street;
The northern summer air is shrill and cold;
And lo, the Hospital, grey, quiet, old,
Where Life and Death like friendly chafferers[2] meet.
Thro' the loud spaciousness and draughty gloom   5
A small, strange child – so aged yet so young! –
Her little arm besplinted and beslung,
Precedes me gravely to the waiting-room.
I limp behind, my confidence all gone.
The grey-haired soldier-porter waves me on,   10
And on I crawl, and still my spirits fail:
A tragic meanness seems so to environ
These corridors and stairs of stone and iron,
Cold, naked, clean – half-workhouse[3] and half jail.

2
Waiting

A square, squat room (a cellar on promotion),   15
Drab to the soul, drab to the very daylight;
Plasters astray in unnatural-looking tinware;
Scissors and lint and apothecary's[4] jars.
Here, on a bench a skeleton would writhe from,
Angry and sore, I wait to be admitted: 20
Wait till my heart is lead upon my stomach,
While at their ease two dressers do their chores.
One has a probe – it feels to me a crowbar.
A small boy sniffs and shudders after bluestone.[5]
A poor old tramp explains his poor old ulcers.   25
Life is (I think) a blunder and a shame.

3
Interior

The gaunt brown walls
Look infinite in their decent meanness.
There is nothing of home in the noisy kettle,
The fulsome fire.   30

The atmosphere
Suggests the trail of a ghostly druggist.
Dressings and lint on the long, lean table –
Whom are they for ?

---

[1] *On ne saurait dire à quel point un homme, seul dans son lit et malade, devient personnel* 'one could not say at which point a man, alone in his bed and ill, becomes an individual'.
[2] *chafferers* dealers, bargainers.
[3] *workhouse* statutory provision: a communal building providing poor men and women basic necessities in return for manual labour. A much-criticized form of nineteenth-century institutional welfare.
[4] *apothecary* early form of medical man, herbalist.
[5] *bluestone* copper sulphate, used as a medical treatment.

The patients yawn,   35
Or lie as in training for shroud and coffin.
A nurse in the corridor scolds and wrangles.
It's grim and strange.

Far footfalls clank.
The bad burn waits with his head unbandaged.   40
My neighbour chokes in the clutch of chloral[6] . . .
O, a gruesome world!

4
Before

Behold me waiting – waiting for the knife.
A little while, and at a leap I storm
The thick, sweet mystery of chloroform,[7]   45
The drunken dark, the little death-in-life.
The gods are good to me: I have no wife,
No innocent child, to think of as I near
The fateful minute; nothing all-too dear
Unmans me for my bout of passive strife.   50
Yet am I tremulous and a trifle sick,
And, face to face with chance, I shrink a little:
My hopes are strong, my will is something weak.
Here comes the basket?[8] Thank you. I am ready.
But, gentlemen my porters, life is brittle: 55
You carry Caesar[9] and his fortunes – steady!

5
Operation

You are carried in a basket,
Like a carcase from the shambles,[10]
To the theatre, a cockpit
Where they stretch you on a table.   60

Then they bid you close your eyelids,
And they mask you with a napkin,
And the anaesthetic reaches
Hot and subtle through your being.

And you gasp and reel and shudder   65
In a rushing, swaying rapture,
While the voices at your elbow
Fade – receding – fainter – farther.

Lights about you shower and tumble,
And your blood seems crystallising –   70
Edged and vibrant, yet within you
Racked and hurried back and forward.

[6] *chloral* early form of anaesthetic.
[7] *chloroform* an anaesthetic.
[8] *basket* basket chair, a wheeled chair.

[9] *Caesar* honorary name for a Roman emperor.
[10] *shambles* that part of a city or town where animals were slaughtered.

Then the lights grow fast and furious,
And you hear a noise of waters,
And you wrestle, blind and dizzy,   75
In an agony of effort,

Till a sudden lull accepts you,
And you sound an utter darkness . . .
And awaken . . . with a struggle . . .
On a hushed, attentive audience.   80

6
After

Like as a flamelet blanketed in smoke,
So through the anaesthetic shows my life;
So flashes and so fades my thought, at strife
With the strong stupor that I heave and choke
And sicken at, it is so foully sweet.   85
Faces look strange from space – and disappear.
Far voices, sudden loud, offend my ear –
And hush as sudden. Then my senses fleet:
All were a blank, save for this dull, new pain
That grinds my leg and foot; and brokenly   90
Time and the place glimpse on to me again;
And, unsurprised, out of uncertainty,
I wake – relapsing – somewhat faint and fain,
To an immense, complacent dreamery.

7
Vigil

Lived on one's back,   95
In the long hours of repose
Life is a practical nightmare –
Hideous asleep or awake.

Shoulders and loins
Ache - - - !   100
Ache, and the mattress,
Run into boulders and hummocks,
Glows like a kiln, while the bedclothes –
Tumbling, importunate, daft –
Ramble and roll, and the gas,[11]   105
Screwed to its lowermost,
An inevitable atom of light,
Haunts, and a stertorous[12] sleeper
Snores me to hate and despair.

All the old time   110
Surges malignant before me;
Old voices, old kisses, old songs
Blossom derisive about me;

---

[11] *gas* the ward is lit by low gas lighting.   [12] *stertorous* snoring.

While the new days
Pass me in endless procession: 115
A pageant of shadows
Silently, leeringly wending
On . . . and still on . . . still on!

Far in the stillness a cat
Languishes loudly. A cinder   120
Falls, and the shadows
Lurch to the leap of the flame. The next man to me
Turns with a moan; and the snorer,
The drug like a rope at his throat,
Gasps, gurgles, snorts himself free, as the night-nurse,   125
Noiseless and strange,
Her bull's eye[13] half-lanterned in apron,[14]
(Whispering me, 'Are ye no sleepin' yet?')
Passes, list-slippered[15] and peering,
Round . . . and is gone.   130

Sleep comes at last –
Sleep full of dreams and misgivings –
Broken with brutal and sordid
Voices and sounds that impose on me,
Ere I can wake to it,   135
The unnatural, intolerable day.

8
Staff-Nurse: Old Style

The greater masters of the commonplace,
REMBRANDT[16] and good SIR WALTER[17] – only these
Could paint her all to you: experienced ease
And antique liveliness and ponderous grace;   140
The sweet old roses of her sunken face;
The depth and malice of her sly, grey eyes;
The broad Scots tongue that flatters, scolds, defies,
The thick Scots wit that fells you like a mace.
These thirty years has she been nursing here,   145
Some of them under SYME,[18] her hero still.
Much is she worth, and even more is made of her.
Patients and students hold her very dear.
The doctors love her, tease her, use her skill.
They say 'The Chief' himself is half-afraid of her.   150

---

[13] *bull's eye* lens in the side of a lantern.
[14] *half-lanterned in apron* the lantern with the bull's eye is half surrounded by her apron.
[15] *list-slippered* wearing footwear that muffled sound.
[16] REMBRANDT (1606–69), Dutch painter and portrait artist.
[17] SIR WALTER Scott (1771–1832), Scottish historical novelist whose novels include many ordinary men and women.
[18] SYME James Syme (1799–1870), Professor of Surgery at the University of Edinburgh from 1833. Significantly, he was known for his speed with amputations before anaesthetics, and perfected a technique called *Syme's Amputation* in 1842 for amputation of the foot at the ankle.

9
Lady-Probationer

Some three, or five, or seven, and thirty years;
A Roman nose; a dimpling double-chin;
Dark eyes and shy that, ignorant of sin,
Are yet acquainted, it would seem, with tears;
A comely shape; a slim, high-coloured hand,   155
Graced, rather oddly, with a signet ring;
A bashful air, becoming everything;
A well-bred silence always at command.
Her plain print gown, prim cap, and bright steel chain
Look out of place on her, and I remain   160
Absorbed in her, as in a pleasant mystery.
Quick, skilful, quiet, soft in speech and touch . . .
'Do you like nursing?' 'Yes, Sir, very much.'
Somehow, I rather think she has a history.

10
Staff-Nurse: New Style

Blue-eyed and bright of face but waning fast   165
Into the sere[19] of virginal decay,
I view her as she enters, day by day,
As a sweet sunset almost overpast.
Kindly and calm, patrician[20] to the last,
Superbly falls her gown of sober gray,   170
And on her chignon's[21] elegant array
The plainest cap is somehow touched with caste.
She talks BEETHOVEN; frowns disapprobation
At BALZAC's[22] name, sighs it at 'poor GEORGE SAND's';[23]
Knows that she has exceeding pretty hands;   175
Speaks Latin with a right accentuation;
And gives at need (as one who understands)
Draught, counsel, diagnosis, exhortation.

11
Clinical

Hist?[24] . . .
Through the corridor's echoes   180
Louder and nearer
Comes a great shuffling of feet.
Quick, every one of you,
Straighten your quilts, and be decent!
Here's the Professor.   185

In he comes first
With the bright look we know,

---

[19] *sere* dryness, witheredness.

[20] *patrician* noble, as if of aristocratic birth.

[21] *chignon* coil of hair, worn around a pad. It was particularly fashionable in 1870.

[22] *BALZAC* Honoré de Balzac (1799–1850), prolific French novelist.

[23] *GEORGE SAND* pseudonym of Amandine-Aurore Lucille Dupin, Baronne Dudevant (1804–76), French woman writer, lover of Chopin.

[24] *Hist?* exclamation: 'is someone there?'

From the broad, white brows the kind eyes
Soothing yet nerving you. Here at his elbow,
White-capped, white-aproned, the Nurse,   190
Towel on arm and her inkstand
Fretful with quills.[25]
Here in the ruck,[26] anyhow,
Surging along,
Louts, duffers, exquisites, students, and prigs –   195
Whiskers and foreheads, scarf-pins and spectacles –
Hustles the Class! And they ring themselves
Round the first bed, where the Chief
(His dressers and clerks at attention),
Bends in inspection already.   200

So shows the ring
Seen, from behind, round a conjurer
Doing his pitch in the street.
High shoulders, low shoulders, broad shoulders, narrow ones,
Round, square, and angular, serry[27] and shove;   205
While from within a voice,
Gravely and weightily fluent,
Sounds; and then ceases; and suddenly
(Look at the stress of the shoulders!)
Out of a quiver of silence,   210
Over the hiss of the spray,
Comes a low cry, and the sound
Of breath quick intaken through teeth
Clenched in resolve. And the Master
Breaks from the crowd, and goes,   215
Wiping his hands.
To the next bed, with his pupils
Flocking and whispering behind him.

Now one can see.
Case Number One   220
Sits (rather pale) with his bedclothes
Stripped up, and showing his foot
(Alas for God's Image!)[28]
Swaddled in wet, white lint
Brilliantly hideous with red.   225

12
Etching

Two and thirty is the ploughman.
He's a man of gallant inches,
And his hair is close and curly,
And his beard;
But his face is wan[29] and sunken,   230
And his eyes are large and brilliant,

[25] *quills* quill pens.
[26] *ruck* multitude, crowd.
[27] *serry* press close together.

[28] *God's Image* human beings, cf. 'So God created man in his owne Image, in the Image of God created hee him', Genesis 1.27.
[29] *wan* pale.

And his shoulder-blades are sharp,
And his knees.

He is weak of wits, religious,
Full of sentiment and yearning,   235
Gentle, faded – with a cough
And a snore.
When his wife (who was a widow,
And is many years his elder)
Fails to write, and that is always,   240
He desponds.

Let his melancholy wander,
And he'll tell you pretty stories
Of the women that have wooed him
Long ago;   245
Or he'll sing of bonnie lasses
Keeping sheep among the heather,
With a crackling, hackling click
In his voice.

13
Casualty

As with varnish red and glistening   250
Dripped his hair; his feet looked rigid;
Raised, he settled stiffly sideways:
You could see his hurts were spinal.

He had fallen from an engine,
And been dragged along the metals.   255
It was hopeless, and they knew it;
So they covered him, and left him.

As he lay, by fits half sentient,
Inarticulately moaning,
With his stockinged soles protruded   260
Stark and awkward from the blankets,

To his bed there came a woman,
Stood and looked and sighed a little,
And departed without speaking,
As himself a few hours after.   265

I was told it was his sweetheart.
They were on the eve of marriage.
She was quiet as a statue,
But her lip was grey and writhen.[30]

---

[30] *writhen* twisted out of regular shape, contorted.

14
Ave, Cæsar!³¹

From the winter's grey despair,   270
From the summer's golden languor,
Death, the lover of Life,
Frees us for ever.

Inevitable, silent, unseen,
Everywhere always,   275
Shadow by night and as light in the day,
Signs she at last to her chosen;
And, as she waves them forth,
Sorrow and Joy
Lay by their looks and their voices,   280
Set down their hopes, and are made
One in the dim Forever.

Into the winter's grey delight,
Into the summer's golden dream,
Holy and high and impartial,   285
Death, the mother of Life,
Mingles all men for ever.

15
'The Chief'

His brow spreads large and placid, and his eye
Is deep and bright, with steady looks that still.
Soft lines of tranquil thought his face fulfill –   290
His face at once benign and proud and shy.
If envy scout, if ignorance deny,
His faultless patience, his unyielding will,
Beautiful gentleness and splendid skill,
Innumerable gratitudes reply.   295
His wise, rare smile is sweet with certainties
And seems in all his patients to compel
Such love and faith as failure cannot quell.
We hold him for another Herakles,³²
Battling with custom, prejudice, disease,   300
As once the son of Zeus³³ with Death and Hell.

16
House-Surgeon

Exceeding tall, but built so well his height
Half-disappears in flow of chest and limb;
Moustache and whisker trooper-like in trim;
Frank-faced, frank-eyed, frank-hearted; always bright   305
And always punctual – morning, noon, and night;

---

³¹ *Ave, Cæsar!* Hail, Caesar!
³² *Herakles* Hercules, the most famous strongman of Greek legend.

³³ *Zeus* leader of the gods in Greek religion (Hercules *was* the son of Zeus).

Bland as a Jesuit,[34] sober as a hymn;
Humorous, and yet without a touch of whim;
Gentle and amiable, yet full of fight.
His piety, though fresh and true in strain,   310
Has not yet whitewashed up his common mood
To the dead blank of his particular Schism.[35]
Sweet, unaggressive, tolerant, most humane,
Wild artists like his kindly elderhood,
And cultivate his mild Philistinism.[36]   315

17
Interlude

O the fun, the fun and frolic
That *The Wind that Shakes the Barley*[37]
Scatters through a penny-whistle
Tickled with artistic fingers!

Kate the scrubber (forty summers,   320
Stout but sportive) treads a measure,
Grinning, in herself a ballet,
Fixed as fate upon her audience.

Stumps are shaking, crutch-supported;
Splinted fingers tap the rhythm;   325
And a head all helmed with plasters
Wags a measured approbation.

Of their mattress-life oblivious,
All the patients, brisk and cheerful,
Are encouraging the dancer,   330
And applauding the musician.

Dim the gas-lights in the output
Of so many ardent smokers,
Full of shadow lurch the corners,
And the doctor peeps and passes.   335

There are, maybe, some suspicions
Of an alcoholic presence . . .
'Tak' a sup of this, my wumman! . . .
New Year comes but once a twelve-month.

18
Children: Private Ward

Here, in this dim, dull, double-bedded room,   340
I play the father to a brace[38] of boys,

---

[34] *Jesuit* member of the Catholic order of the Society of Jesus (hardly known for being bland).
[35] *Schism* division in the Christian Church.
[36] *Philistinism* a Philistine is traditionally one deficient in liberal culture and enlightenment, whose interests are material and commonplace.

[37] *The Wind that Shakes the Barley* popular reel with words by Robert Dwyer Joyce (1830–83).
[38] *brace* pair.

Ailing, but apt for every sort of noise,
Bedfast but brilliant yet with health and bloom.
Roden, the Irishman, is 'sieven past,'
Blue-eyed, snub-nosed, chubby, and fair of face.　　345
Willie's but six, and seems to like the place,
A cheerful little collier to the last.
They eat, and laugh and sing, and fight, all day;
All night they sleep like dormice. See them play
At operations – Roden, the Professor,　　350
Saws, lectures, takes the artery up, and ties;
Willie, self-chloroformed, with half-shut eyes,
Holding the limb and moaning – Case and Dresser.

19
Scrubber

She's tall and gaunt, and in her hard, sad face
With flashes of the old fun's animation　　355
There lowers the fixed and peevish resignation
Bred of a past where troubles came apace.
She tells me that her husband, ere he died,
Saw seven of their children pass away,
And never knew the little lass at play　　360
Out on the green, in whom he's deified.
Her kin dispersed, her friends forgot and gone,
All simple faith her honest Irish mind,
Scolding her spoiled young saint, she labours on
Telling her dreams, taking her patients' part,　　365
Trailing her coat sometimes: and you shall find
No rougher, quainter speech, nor kinder heart.

20
Visitor

Her little face is like a walnut shell
With wrinkling lines; her soft, white hair adorns
Her withered brows in quaint, straight curls, like horns;　　370
And all about her clings an old, sweet smell.
Prim is her gown and quakerlike[39] her shawl.
Well might her bonnets have been born on her.
Can you conceive a Fairy Godmother
The subject of a strong religious call?　　375
In snow or shine, from bed to bed she runs,
All twinkling smiles and texts and pious tales,
Her mittened hands, that ever give or pray,
Bearing a sheaf of tracts,[40] a bag of buns:
A wee old maid that sweeps the Bridegroom's[41] way,　　380
Strong in a cheerful trust that never fails.

[39] *quakerlike* Quakers were distinguished in the nineteenth century by their plain clothes.
[40] *tracts* documents of a polemical nature (usually religious).

[41] *Bridegroom* Jesus Christ, as the Bridegroom of the Church (the Bride) at the Second Coming.

21

Romance

'Talk of pluck!'[42] pursued the Sailor,
 Set at euchre[43] on his elbow,
'I was on the wharf at Charleston,[44]
 Just ashore from off the runner.   385

'It was grey and dirty weather,
 And I heard a drum go rolling,
Rub-a-dubbing in the distance,
 Awful dourlike and defiant.

'In and out among the cotton,[45]   390
Mud, and chains, and stores, and anchors,
Tramped a squad of battered scarecrows –
 Poor old Dixie's bottom dollar![46]

'Some had shoes, but all had rifles,
 Them that wasn't bald was beardless,   395
And the drum was rolling *Dixie*,[47]
 And they stepped to it like men, sir!

'Rags and tatters, belts and bayonets,
 On they swung, the drum a-rolling,
Mum and sour.[48] It looked like fighting,   400
 And they meant it too, by thunder!'

22

Pastoral

It's the Spring.
Earth has conceived, and her bosom,
Teeming with summer, is glad.

Vistas of change and adventure,   405
Thro' the green land
The grey roads go beckoning and winding,
Peopled with wains,[49] and melodious
With harness-bells jangling:
Jangling and twangling rough rhythms   410
To the slow march of the stately, great horses
Whistled and shouted along.

White fleets of cloud,
Argosies[50] heavy with fruitfulness,

---

[42] *pluck* courage.
[43] *euchre* game of cards, originally from the United States, which was popular in Victorian Britain.
[44] *Charleston* in South Carolina, Confederate stronghold much besieged by Federal forces during the American Civil War (1861–5): it finally fell in the last year of the war.
[45] *cotton* South Carolina is a major cotton-growing state.

[46] *Dixie's bottom dollar* the lowest, poorest lives of the southern states (Dixieland).
[47] *Dixie* popular song, written by D. D. Emmett in 1859.
[48] *Mum and sour* silent and bitter.
[49] *wains* wagons.
[50] *Argosies* largest forms of merchant vessels.

Sail the blue peacefully. Green flame the hedgerows.   415
Blackbirds are bugling, and white in wet winds
Sway the tall poplars.
Pageants of colour and fragrance,
Pass the sweet meadows, and viewless[51]
Walks the mild spirit of May,   420
Visibly blessing the world.

O, the brilliance of blossoming orchards!
O, the savour and thrill of the woods,
When their leafage is stirred
By the flight of the Angel of Rain!   425
Loud lows the steer;[52] in the fallows
Rooks are alert; and the brooks
Gurgle and tinkle and trill. Thro' the gloaming,[53]
Under the rare, shy stars,
Boy and girl wander   430
Dreaming in darkness and dew.

It's the Spring.
A sprightliness feeble and squalid
Wakes in the ward, and I sicken,
Impotent, winter at heart.   435

23
Music

Down the quiet eve,
Thro' my window, with the sunset
Pipes to me a distant organ
Foolish ditties;

And, as when you change   440
Pictures in a magic lantern,[54]
Books, beds, bottles, floor, and ceiling
Fade and vanish,

And I'm well once more. . . .
August flares adust and torrid,   445
But my heart is full of April
Sap and sweetness.

In the quiet eve
I am loitering, longing, dreaming . . .
Dreaming, and a distant organ   450
Pipes me ditties.

I can see the shop,
I can smell the sprinkled pavement,
Where she serves – her chestnut chignon
Thrills my senses!   455

---

[51] *viewless* invisible.

[52] *steer* cattle.

[53] *gloaming* twilight.

[54] *magic lattern* early form of projector for visual images.

O, the sight and scent,
Wistful eve and perfumed pavement!
In the distance pipes an organ . . .
The sensation

Comes to me anew,   460
And my spirit, for a moment
Thro' the music breathes the blessèd
Airs of London.

24
Suicide

Staring corpselike at the ceiling,
See his harsh, unrazored features,   465
Ghastly brown against the pillow,
And his throat – so strangely bandaged!

Lack of work and lack of victuals,[55]
A debauch of smuggled whisky,
And his children in the workhouse   470
Made the world so black a riddle

That he plunged for a solution;
And, although his knife was edgeless,
He was sinking fast towards one,
When they came, and found, and saved him.   475

Stupid now with shame[56] and sorrow,
In the night I hear him sobbing.
But sometimes he talks a little.
He has told me all his troubles.

In his broad face, tanned and bloodless,   480
White and wild his eyeballs glisten;
And his smile, occult[57] and tragic,
Yet so slavish, makes you shudder!

25
Apparition[58]

Thin-legged, thin-chested, slight unspeakably,
Neat-footed and weak-fingered: in his face –   485
Lean, large-boned, curved of beak, and touched with race,
Bold-lipped, rich-tinted, mutable as the sea,
The brown eyes radiant with vivacity –
There shines a brilliant and romantic grace,
A spirit intense and rare, with trace on trace   490
Of passion and impudence and energy.
Valiant in velvet, light in ragged luck,

---

[55] *victuals* provisions, food.
[56] *shame* suicide was illegal in the nineteenth century.
[57] *occult* mysterious.

[58] *Apparition* this sonnet is about Robert Louis Stevenson (1850–94), who visited Henley in hospital.

Most vain, most generous, sternly critical,
Buffoon and poet, lover and sensualist:
A deal of Ariel,[59] just a streak of Puck,[60]   495
Much Antony,[61] of Hamlet[62] most of all,
And something of the Shorter-Catechist.[63]

26
Anterotics

Laughs the happy April morn
Thro' my grimy, little window,
And a shaft of sunshine pushes   500
Thro' the shadows in the square.

Dogs are tracing thro' the grass,
Crows are cawing round the chimneys,
In and out among the washing
Goes the west at hide-and-seek.   505

Loud and cheerful clangs the bell
Here the nurses troop to breakfast.
Handsome, ugly, all are women . . .
O, the Spring – the Spring – the Spring!

27
Nocturn[64]

At the barren heart of midnight,   510
When the shadow shuts and opens
As the loud flames pulse and flutter,
I can hear a cistern leaking.

Dripping, dropping, in a rhythm,
Rough, unequal, half-melodious,   515
Like the measures aped from nature
In the infancy of music;

Like the buzzing of an insect,
Still, irrational, persistent.
I must listen, listen, listen   520
In a passion of attention;

Till it taps upon my heartstrings,
And my very life goes dripping,
Dropping, dripping, drip-drip-dropping,
In the drip-drop of the cistern.   525

[59] *Ariel* airy spirit of Shakespeare's *The Tempest*.
[60] *Puck* mischievous fairy from Shakespeare's *A Midsummer Night's Dream*.
[61] *Antony* noble but doomed hero of Shakespeare's *Antony and Cleopatra*.
[62] *Hamlet* eponymous hero – thoughtful, procrastinating – of Shakespeare's *Hamlet*.
[63] *Shorter-Catechist* Presbyterian catechism (catechism = elementary text for the instruction of basic Christian principles in the form of questions and answers).
[64] *Nocturn* of night time, a musical form.

28
Discharged

Carry me out
Into the wind and the sunshine,
Into the beautiful world.

O the wonder, the spell of the streets!
The stature and strength of the horses,   530
The rustle and echo of footfalls,
The flat roar and rattle of wheels!
A swift tram floats huge on us . . .
It's a dream?
The smell of the mud in my nostrils   535
Blows brave – like a breath of the sea!

As of old,
Ambulant, undulant[65] drapery,
Vaguely and strangely provocative,
Flutters and beckons. O yonder –   540
Scarlet? – the gleam of a stocking!
Sudden a spire
Wedged in the mist! O the houses,
The long lines of lofty, gray houses,
Cross-hatched with shadow and light!   545

These are the streets. . . .
Each is an avenue leading
Whither I will!

Free . . .!
Dizzy, hysterical, faint,   550
I sit, and the carriage rolls on with me
Into the wonderful world.

The Old Infirmary, Edinburgh, 1873–75

---

[65] *undulant* in waves.

Oscar (Fingal O'Flahertie Wills) Wilde (1854–1900)

Oscar Wilde was born in Dublin to distinguished parents – his father was an eminent surgeon, his mother, a poet and literary hostess who published under the name 'Speranza'. He was educated at the Protestant Portora Royal School in Enniskillen then at Trinity College Dublin, graduating in Classics in 1874. He won a scholarship to Magdalen College Oxford (pronounced Maudlin) and took a double first in Classics, won the Newdigate poetry prize (for 'Ravenna'), and cultivated an aesthetic pose, conversational wittiness and a Paterian dedication to '*l'art pour l'art*' (art for art's sake). Wilde went on a lecture tour of the United States in 1882 after the publication of his *Poems* in 1881; he married Constance Lloyd in 1884, and published a collection of fairy-stories, *The Happy Prince and Other Tales*, in 1888 for his children. In 1890 came the magazine version of *The Picture of Dorian Gray* (issued as a book in 1891): a novel that controversially half moralized about, and half celebrated, the aesthetic life. *Lady Windermere's Fan* (1892) was his first theatrical success – there had been several previous dramatic flops – and was followed by *A Woman of No Importance* (1893), *An Ideal Husband* (1895) and the enormously popular *The Importance of Being Earnest* (1895). In 1895, the Marquess of Queensberry accused Wilde of improper relations with his (Queensberry's) son, Lord Alfred Douglas. This began a succession of events that concluded in Wilde's imprisonment with hard labour for homosexual offences, a brutal conclusion to the flamboyance that Wilde's earlier life had symbolized, and a defining moment in the history both of the Aesthetic movement and of western homosexuality. His prison letter to Lord Alfred ('Bosie') was published in a heavily edited version in 1905 as *De Profundis*. Released, bankrupt, in 1897, Wilde went to France under the name Sebastian Melmoth where he wrote *The Ballad of Reading Gaol* (1898). But his health had been destroyed by incarceration; he died in Paris in 1900. His remains were eventually moved to the Parisian cemetery of Père Lachaise.

Fantaisies Décoratives: II. Les Ballons

An enamelled decorative fantasy, Wilde's 'Les Ballons' ('the balloons') revels in a curious natural scene made unnatural, artificial, theatrical. Emphasizing the Aesthete's preference for art over nature, for the illusion over the actual, the pose over the sincere, 'Les Ballons' (1887) presents a texture of similes, concentrating on what the balloons are *like*, not what they are (cf. 'Symphony in Yellow', 588). The French title and the sumptuous comparisons make up part of Wilde's *fin de siècle* exoticism: turquoise was a particular favourite. *The Ballad of Reading Gaol*, 588–605, dramatically reorientated Wilde's poetics away from the Decadent writing represented by this poem and 'Symphony'.

Text: *The Poems of Oscar Wilde* (1908).

Against these turbid turquoise skies
The light and luminous balloons
Dip and drift like satin moons,
Drift like silken butterflies;

2
Reel with every windy gust,
Rise and reel like dancing girls,
Float like strange transparent pearls,
Fall and float like silver dust.

3
Now to the low leaves they cling,
Each with coy fantastic pose,
Each a petal of a rose
Straining at a gossamer string.

5

10

[handwritten annotations: "Hypey Catalectic trochaic feet"; "flaky"]

4
Then to the tall trees they climb,
Like thin globes of amethyst,[1]
Wandering opals[2] keeping tryst[3]
With the rubies[4] of the lime.

15

[1] *amethyst* clear purple or bluish-violet precious stone.
[2] *opals* quartz-like gemstones.
[3] *tryst* lovers' meeting.
[4] *rubies* deep crimson to rose-red precious stones.

Symphony in Yellow

Like 'Les Ballons', 587–8, 'Symphony in Yellow' (1889) prioritizes the image, both in the sense of the visual and in the rhetorical sense of simile. The poem appeals to the senses and it focuses on how the perceived world is made different by translating the actual into other, so that an omnibus is transformed when it ceases to be its quotidian self and becomes a yellow butterfly. The world of the unlike, the staged, alternative vision of the aesthetic imagination, is more precious and appealing. Wilde's synaesthetic title is fashionable, as he intended. It is a compliment to the American painter James Abbott McNeill Whistler (1834–1903), much admired by the Aesthetes for his impressionistic canvases and fascination with form and colour. His paintings include *Symphony in White No. 1: The White Girl* (1862) and *Symphony in White No 2: The Little White Girl* (1864).

Text: *The Poems of Oscar Wilde* (1908).

An omnibus across the bridge
Crawls like a yellow butterfly,
And, here and there, a passer-by
Shows like a little restless midge.

2
Big barges full of yellow hay
Are moved against the shadowy wharf,
And, like a yellow silken scarf,
The thick fog hangs along the quay.

5

3
The yellow leaves begin to fade
And flutter from the Temple[1] elms,
And at my feet the pale green Thames[2]
Lies like a rod of rippled jade.[3]

10

[1] *Temple* area in London.
[2] *Thames* river running through London.
[3] *jade* translucent green stone.

The Ballad of Reading Gaol

In Memoriam C. T. W. Sometime Trooper of the Royal Horse Guards
Obiit [died] H. M. Prison, Reading, Berkshire, July 7, 1896.

In 1895, Oscar Wilde was sentenced to two years' imprisonment with hard labour for illegal homosexual acts. Most of his sentence was served in Reading Gaol, built in 1844, and now a young offenders institution and remand centre (non-UK readers will want to know that Reading, a town in Berkshire in southern England, is pronounced 'redding'). The *Ballad* – published in 1898 – was written in 1897 after Wilde's release from the torment of the late Victorian penal system, which was dedicated to wearing away the prisoners' mental and physical health in an effort to purge their moral corruption (crime here being understood as the result of personal moral weakness). In a single text, the *Ballad* blew away the Decadence of the 1890s, the sensual pleasures, *ennui*, the yearning for beauty, to insist on human brutality that could not be disguised behind the artifices and masks that *fin de siècle* aesthetics had privileged. Against excess and exuberance, it places monotony, repetition, human wretchedness, and mental and physical violence. In the rings of the exercise yard, Wilde silently alludes to Dante's circles of hell, figuring the modern British penal system as the new Inferno. (Cf. James Thomson's use of Dante to represent modernity in *The City of Dreadful Night*, 394–422).

Stark in its account of prison life and death, the *Ballad* centres on the execution for murder of Charles Thomas Wooldridge. It challenges the cruel and absurd regime of British prisons – 'The vilest deeds like poison weeds, / Bloom well in prison-air; / It is only what is good in Man / That wastes and withers there' – and compassionately admits that the executed man no more deserved to die than any other. Indeed, Wilde provocatively finds something morally courageous in his action, since 'each man kills the thing he loves', but most do it merely in cowardly ways. Charles Thomas Wooldridge, executed on 7 July 1896, had slit the throat of his wife Laura in a jealous rage in March that year: she was 23. Wilde's poem finds hope for him and for all sinners in the generosity of divine love. But God's ministers on earth are condemned with especial bitterness for their involvement in the brutalities of the prison system. *The Ballad of Reading Gaol* was published first in 1898 under the name of C.3.3, Wilde's prison-cell number. It moves W. E. Henley's realist poetics – cf. *In Hospital*, 571–86 – into more brutal territory.

Text: *The Poems of Oscar Wilde* (1908).

He did not wear his scarlet coat,[1]
For blood and wine are red,
And blood and wine were on his hands
When they found him with the dead,
The poor dead woman whom he loved,   5
And murdered in her bed.

He walked amongst the Trial Men[2]
In a suit of shabby gray;
A cricket cap was on his head,
And his step seemed light and gay;   10
But I never saw a man who looked
So wistfully at the day.

I never saw a man who looked
With such a wistful eye
Upon that little tent of blue   15
Which prisoners call the sky,
And at every drifting cloud that went
With sails of silver by.

I walked, with other souls in pain,
Within another ring,   20
And was wondering if the man had done
A great or little thing,
When a voice behind me whispered low,
'That fellow's got to swing.'

Dear Christ! the very prison walls   25
Suddenly seemed to reel,

---

[1] *scarlet coat* uniform as a British soldier. But the Royal Horse Guards uniform was dark blue trimmed with red. 'I could hardly have written "He did not wear his azure coat, for blood and wine are blue",' Wilde remarked.

[2] *Trial Men* those awaiting trial.

And the sky above my head became
Like a casque[3] of scorching steel;
And, though I was a soul in pain,
My pain I could not feel.   30

I only knew what hunted thought
Quickened his step, and why
He looked upon the garish[4] day
With such a wistful eye;
The man had killed the thing he loved,   35
And so he had to die.

* * *

Yet each man kills the thing he loves,
By each let this be heard,
Some do it with a bitter look,
Some with a flattering word,
The coward does it with a kiss,[5]   40
The brave man with a sword!

Some kill their love when they are young,
And some when they are old;
Some strangle with the hands of Lust,
Some with the hands of Gold: 45
The kindest use a knife, because
The dead so soon grow cold.

Some love too little, some too long,
Some sell, and others buy;
Some do the deed with many tears,   50
And some without a sigh:
For each man kills the thing he loves,
Yet each man does not die.

Those in prison
do yet all the
other killers"
are free

He does not die a death of shame   55
On a day of dark disgrace,
Nor have a noose about his neck,
Nor a cloth upon his face,
Nor drop feet foremost through the floor
Into an empty space.[6]   60

* * *

He does not sit with silent men
Who watch him night and day;
Who watch him when he tries to weep,

---

[3] *casque* helmet.
[4] *garish* excessively bright.
[5] *The coward . . . kiss* cf. the betrayal of Jesus: 'And while he yet spake, behold, a multitude, and hee that was called Iudas, one of the twelue, went before them, and drewe neere vnto Iesus, to kisse him. But Iesus said vnto him, Iudas, betrayest thou the sonne of man with a kisse?' Luke 22.47–8.

[6] *noose . . . space* British judicial executions, until their abolition in 1965, involved hanging. In 1861, the Criminal Law Consolidation Act had reduced the large number of capital crimes to four: murder, high treason, arson in a royal dockyard and piracy.

And when he tries to pray;
Who watch him lest himself should rob
   The prison of its prey.

       65

He does not wake at dawn to see
   Dread figures throng his room,
The shivering Chaplain robed in white,
   The Sheriff stern with gloom,
And the Governor all in shiny black,
   With the yellow face of Doom.

       70

He does not rise in piteous haste
   To put on convict-clothes,
While some coarse-mouthed Doctor gloats, and notes
   Each new and nerve-twitched pose,
Fingering a watch whose little ticks
   Are like horrible hammer-blows.

       75

He does not know that sickening thirst
   That sands one's throat, before
The hangman with his gardener's gloves
   Slips through the padded door,
And binds one with three leathern thongs,
   That the throat may thirst no more.

       80

He does not bend his head to hear
   The Burial Office[7] read,
Nor, while the terror of his soul
   Tells him he is not dead,
Cross his own coffin, as he moves
   Into the hideous shed.

       85

       90

He does not stare upon the air
   Through a little roof of glass:
He does not pray with lips of clay
   For his agony to pass;[8]
Nor feel upon his shuddering cheek
   The kiss of Caiaphas.[9]

       95

2

Six weeks our guardsman walked the yard,
   In the suit of shabby grey:
His cricket cap was on his head,
   And his step seemed light and gay,
But I never saw a man who looked
   So wistfully at the day.

       100

---

[7] *Burial Office* Christian funeral liturgy.
[8] *pray . . . agony to pass* cf. Jesus before his betrayal at the Mount of Olives: 'Father, if thou be willing, remooue this cup from me: neuerthelesse, not my will, but thine be done. And there appeared an Angel vnto him from heauen, strengthening him. And being in an agonie, he prayed more earnestly, and his sweat was as it were great drops of blood falling downe to the ground', Luke 22.42–4.
[9] *Caiaphas* high priest before whom Jesus was tried (see Luke 26). The betraying kiss, however, was Judas's. Wilde said the figure stood for 'any priest who assists at the cruel and unjust punishments of men'.

I never saw a man who looked
With such a wistful eye
Upon that little tent of blue
Which prisoners call the sky,
And at every wandering cloud that trailed
Its ravelled fleeces by.   105

He did not wring his hands, as do
Those witless men who dare
To try to rear the changeling[10] Hope
In the cave of black Despair: 110
He only looked upon the sun,
And drank the morning air.

He did not wring his hands nor weep,   115
Nor did he peek[11] or pine,
But he drank the air as though it held
Some healthful anodyne;[12]
With open mouth he drank the sun
As though it had been wine!   120

And I and all the souls in pain,
Who tramped the other ring,
Forgot if we ourselves had done
A great or little thing,
And watched with gaze of dull amaze   125
The man who had to swing.

And strange it was to see him pass
With a step so light and gay,
And strange it was to see him look
So wistfully at the day,   130
And strange it was to think that he
Had such a debt to pay.

* * *

For oak and elm have pleasant leaves
That in the spring-time shoot:
But grim to see is the gallows-tree,   135
With its adder-bitten root,
And, green or dry, a man must die
Before it bears its fruit!

The loftiest place is that seat of grace
For which all worldlings try: 140
But who would stand in hempen[13] band
Upon a scaffold high,
And through a murderer's collar take
His last look at the sky?

---

[10] *changeling* child secretly substituted for another in infancy.
[11] *peek* utter slight sounds, speak thinly.
[12] *anodyne* something that assuages pain.
[13] *hempen* made from hemp, a tough, fibrous plant.

It is sweet to dance to violins 145
When Love and Life are fair:
To dance to flutes, to dance to lutes
Is delicate and rare:
But it is not sweet with nimble feet
To dance upon the air![14] 150

So with curious eyes and sick surmise
We watched him day by day,
And wondered if each one of us
Would end the self-same way,
For none can tell to what red Hell 155
His sightless soul may stray.

At last the dead man walked no more
Amongst the Trial Men,
And I knew that he was standing up
In the black dock's dreadful pen, 160
And that never would I see his face
In God's sweet world again.

Like two doomed ships that pass in storm
We had crossed each other's way:
But we made no sign, we said no word, 165
We had no word to say;
For we did not meet in the holy night,
But in the shameful day.

A prison wall was round us both,
Two outcast men we were: 170
The world had thrust us from its heart,
And God from out His care:
And the iron gin[15] that waits for Sin
Had caught us in its snare.

3

In Debtors' Yard the stones are hard, 175
And the dripping wall is high,
So it was there he took the air
Beneath the leaden sky,
And by each side a Warder walked,
For fear the man might die. 180

Or else he sat with those who watched
His anguish night and day;
Who watched him when he rose to weep,
And when he crouched to pray;
Who watched him lest himself should rob 185
Their scaffold of its prey.

The Governor was strong upon
The Regulations Act:

---

[14] *dance . . . air* the prisoner involuntarily kicking as he dies
at the end of the rope.   [15] *gin* trap.

The Doctor said that Death was but
A scientific fact:
And twice a day the Chaplain called,   190
And left a little tract.[16]

Chaplain
or
Doctor?

And twice a day he smoked his pipe,
And drank his quart[17] of beer:
His soul was resolute, and held   195
No hiding-place for fear;
He often said that he was glad
The hangman's hands were near.

But why he said so strange a thing
No Warder dared to ask: 200
For he to whom a watcher's doom
Is given as his task,
Must set a lock upon his lips,
And make his face a mask.

Or else he might be moved, and try   205
To comfort or console:
And what should Human Pity do
Pent up in Murderers' Hole?
What word of grace in such a place
Could help a brother's soul?   210

*   *   *

Very
bleak

With slouch and swing around the ring
We trod the Fools' Parade!
We did not care: we knew we were
The Devil's Own Brigade:
And shaven head and feet of lead   215
Make a merry masquerade.

We tore the tarry rope to shreds[18]
With blunt and bleeding nails;
We rubbed the doors, and scrubbed the floors,
And cleaned the shining rails: *odd, ironic*   220
And, rank by rank, we soaped the plank,
And clattered with the pails.

We sewed the sacks,[19] we broke the stones,[20]
We turned the dusty drill:[21]
We banged the tins, and bawled the hymns,   225
And sweated on the mill:[22]

---

[16] *tract* polemical publication, usually religious.
[17] *quart* two pints.
[18] *tore . . . shreds* traditional prison labour of unpicking old ropes for the loose fibre, which was then sold to the navy or other ship-builders; mixed with tar, it was used for caulking – sealing – wooden ships. This and the other tasks Wilde lists are all the result of being sentenced to prison *with hard labour*.
[19] *sacks* mailbags – more demeaning prison labour.

[20] *broke . . . stones* stone breaking was a further traditional prison task; the broken stones were used for road making.
[21] *drill* the meaningless task of turning a crank handle to scoop and then release sand.
[22] *mill* treadmill, invented by Sir William Cubitt (1785–1861) to employ prisoners without taking away actual work from needy labourers outside. It was non-productive and exhausting.

But in the heart of every man
Terror was lying still.

So still it lay that every day
Crawled like a weed-clogged wave: 230
And we forgot the bitter lot
That waits for fool and knave,
Till once, as we tramped in from work,
We passed an open grave.

With yawning mouth the yellow hole   235
Gaped for a living thing;
The very mud cried out for blood
To the thirsty asphalte[23] ring:
And we knew that ere one dawn grew fair
Some prisoner had to swing.   240

Right in we went, with soul intent
On Death and Dread and Doom:
The hangman, with his little bag,
Went shuffling through the gloom:
And each man trembled as he crept   245
Into his numbered tomb.

*   *   *

That night the empty corridors
Were full of forms of Fear,
And up and down the iron town
Stole feet we could not hear,   250
And through the bars that hide the stars
White faces seemed to peer.

who?

He lay as one who lies and dreams
In a pleasant meadow-land,
The watchers watched him as he slept,   255
And could not understand
How one could sleep so sweet a sleep
With a hangman close at hand.

But there is no sleep when men must weep
Who never yet have wept: 260
So we – the fool, the fraud, the knave –
That endless vigil kept,
And through each brain on hands of pain
Another's terror crept.

Alas! it is a fearful thing   265
To feel another's guilt!
For, right within, the sword of Sin
Pierced to its poisoned hilt,
And as molten lead were the tears we shed
For the blood we had not spilt.   270

---

[23] *asphalte* asphalt, composition of bitumen, pitch and sand.

The Warders with their shoes of felt
Crept by each padlocked door,
And peeped and saw, with eyes of awe,
Grey figures on the floor,
And wondered why men knelt to pray   275
Who never prayed before.

All through the night we knelt and prayed,
Mad mourners of a corse![24]
The troubled plumes of midnight were
The plumes upon a hearse: 280
And bitter wine upon a sponge
Was the savour of Remorse.[25]

*   *   *

The grey cock crew, the red cock crew,
But never came the day:
And crooked shapes of Terror crouched,   285
In the corners where we lay:
And each evil sprite that walks by night
Before us seemed to play.

They glided past, they glided fast,
Like travellers through a mist: 290
They mocked the moon in a rigadoon[26]
Of delicate turn and twist,
And with formal pace and loathsome grace
The phantoms kept their tryst.[27]

With mop and mow,[28] we saw them go,   295
Slim shadows hand in hand:
About, about, in ghostly rout
They trod a saraband:[29]
And the damned grotesques made arabesques,
Like the wind upon the sand!   300
With the pirouettes of marionettes,[30]

They tripped on pointed tread:
But with flutes of Fear they filled the ear,
As their grisly masque they led,
And loud they sang, and long they sang, 305
For they sang to wake the dead.

'*Oho!*' they cried, '*The world is wide,*
But fettered limbs go lame!

---

[24] *corse* corpse.
[25] *bitter wine . . . Remorse* cf. Jesus on the cross: 'And about the ninth houre, Iesus cried with a loud voyce, saying, Eli, Eli, Lamasabachthani, that is to say, My God, my God, why hast thou forsaken mee? Some of them that stood there, when they heard that, said, This man calleth for Elias. And straightway one of them ran, and tooke a spunge, and filled it with vineger, and put it on a reede, and gaue him to drinke', Luke 27.46–8.

[26] *rigadoon* lively and complicated dance for two.
[27] *tryst* lovers' meeting.
[28] *mop and mow* colloquial phrase: grimaces.
[29] *About . . . saraband* cf. Coleridge, 'The Rime of the Ancient Mariner', 'About, about, in reel and rout / The death-fires danced at night'. Saraband = slow, stately dance.
[30] *marionettes* puppets.

And once, or twice, to throw the dice
    Is a gentlemanly game,
But he does not win who plays with Sin
    In the secret House of Shame.'

310

No things of air these antics were,
    That frolicked with such glee:
To men whose lives were held in gyves,[31]
    And whose feet might not go free,
Ah! wounds of Christ! they were living things,
    Most terrible to see.

315

Around, around, they waltzed and wound;
    Some wheeled in smirking pairs;
With the mincing step of a demirep[32]
    Some sidled up the stairs:
And with subtle sneer, and fawning leer,
    Each helped us at our prayers.

320

The morning wind began to moan,
    But still the night went on:
Through its giant loom the web of gloom
    Crept till each thread was spun:
And, as we prayed, we grew afraid
    Of the Justice of the Sun.

325
330

The moaning wind went wandering round
    The weeping prison-wall:
Till like a wheel of turning steel
    We felt the minutes crawl:
O moaning wind! what had we done
    To have such a seneschal?[33]

335

At last I saw the shadowed bars,
    Like a lattice wrought in lead,
Move right across the whitewashed wall
    That faced my three-plank bed,
And I knew that somewhere in the world
    God's dreadful dawn was red.

340

At six o'clock we cleaned our cells,
    At seven all was still,
But the sough[34] and swing of a mighty wing
    The prison seemed to fill,
For the Lord of Death with icy breath
    Had entered in to kill.

345

He did not pass in purple pomp,
    Nor ride a moon-white steed.
Three yards of cord and a sliding board

350

[31] *gyves* shackles (also instrument of torture).
[32] *demirep* woman whose character is only half reputable.

[33] *seneschal* administrator charged with justice and domestic arrangements in a royal or noble household.
[34] *sough* murmuring.

Are all the gallows' need:
So with rope of shame the Herald came
To do the secret deed.

We were as men who through a fen   355
Of filthy darkness grope:
We did not dare to breathe a prayer,
Or to give our anguish scope:
Something was dead in each of us,
And what was dead was Hope.   360

For Man's grim Justice goes its way,
And will not swerve aside:
It slays the weak, it slays the strong,
It has a deadly stride:
With iron heel it slays the strong,   365
The monstrous parricide![35]

We waited for the stroke of eight:
Each tongue was thick with thirst:
For the stroke of eight is the stroke of Fate
That makes a man accursed,   370
And Fate will use a running noose
For the best man and the worst.

We had no other thing to do,
Save to wait for the sign to come:
So, like things of stone in a valley lone,   375
Quiet we sat and dumb:
But each man's heart beat thick and quick,
Like a madman on a drum!

With sudden shock the prison-clock
Smote on the shivering air,   380
And from all the gaol rose up a wail
Of impotent despair,
Like the sound that frightened marshes hear
From some leper in his lair.

And as one sees most fearful things   385
In the crystal of a dream,
We saw the greasy hempen rope
Hooked to the blackened beam,
And heard the prayer the hangman's snare
Strangled into a scream.   390

And all the woe that moved him so
That he gave that bitter cry,
And the wild regrets, and the bloody sweats,
None knew so well as I:

---

[35] *parricide* murderer of any one whose person is specially
sacred: parents, close relatives, the ruler of the country or
someone in a position of trust.

For he who lives more lives than one   395
More deaths than one must die.

4

There is no chapel on the day
On which they hang a man:
The Chaplain's heart is far too sick,
Or his face is far too wan,[36]   400
Or there is that written in his eyes
Which none should look upon.

So they kept us close till nigh on noon,
And then they rang the bell,
And the Warders with their jingling keys   405
Opened each listening cell,
And down the iron stair we tramped,
Each from his separate Hell.

Out into God's sweet air we went,
But not in wonted[37] way,   410
For this man's face was white with fear,
And that man's face was grey,
And I never saw sad men who looked
So wistfully at the day.

I never saw sad men who looked   415
With such a wistful eye
Upon that little tent of blue
We prisoners called the sky,
And at every careless cloud that passed
In happy freedom by.   420

But there were those amongst us all
Who walked with downcast head,
And knew that, had each got his due,
They should have died instead:
He had but killed a thing that lived,   425
Whilst they had killed the dead.

For he who sins a second time
Wakes a dead soul to pain,
And draws it from its spotted shroud,
And makes it bleed again,   430
And makes it bleed great gouts[38] of blood,
And makes it bleed in vain!

*   *   *

Like ape or clown, in monstrous garb
With crooked arrows starred,[39]

---

[36] *wan* pale.
[37] *wonted* accustomed, usual.
[38] *gouts* streams of liquid. Cf. Macbeth's entranced preoccupation with the dagger he sees before his eyes in Act 2 scene 1 of Shakespeare's play. 'I see thee still,' Macbeth says, 'And on thy blade and dudgeon gouts of blood / Which was not so before', 2.1.45–7.
[39] *crooked arrows starred* British prison uniform.

Silently we went round and round,   435
    The slippery asphalte yard;
Silently we went round and round
    And no man spoke a word.

Silently we went round and round,
    And through each hollow mind   440
The Memory of dreadful things
    Rushed like a dreadful wind,
And Horror stalked before each man,
    And Terror crept behind.

*   *   *

The Warders strutted up and down,   445
    And kept their herd of brutes,
Their uniforms were spick and span,
    And they wore their Sunday suits,
But we knew the work they had been at,
    By the quicklime on their boots.[40]   450

For where a grave had opened wide,
    There was no grave at all:
Only a stretch of mud and sand
    By the hideous prison-wall,
And a little heap of burning lime,   455
    That the man should have his pall.[41]

For he has a pall, this wretched man,
    Such as few men can claim:
Deep down below a prison-yard,
    Naked for greater shame,   460
He lies, with fetters on each foot,
    Wrapt in a sheet of flame!

And all the while the burning lime
    Eats flesh and bone away,
It eats the brittle bone by night,   465
    And the soft flesh by day,
It eats the flesh and bone by turns,
    But it eats the heart alway.

*   *   *

For three long years they will not sow
    Or root or seedling there: 470
For three long years the unblessed spot
    Will sterile be and bare,
And look upon the wondering sky
    With unreproachful stare.

---

[40] *work . . . boots* they have disposed of the executed man's   [41] *pall* grave cloth, covering for a coffin.
body by covering it in quicklime to speed decomposition.

They think a murderer's heart would taint   475
  Each simple seed they sow.
It is not true! God's kindly earth
  Is kindlier than men know,
And the red rose would but blow more red,
  The white rose whiter blow.   480

Out of his mouth a red, red rose!
  Out of his heart a white!
For who can say by what strange way,
  Christ brings His will to light,
Since the barren staff the pilgrim bore   485
  Bloomed in the great Pope's sight?[42]

But neither milk-white rose nor red
  May bloom in prison air;
The shard, the pebble, and the flint,
  Are what they give us there: 490
For flowers have been known to heal
  A common man's despair.

So never will wine-red rose or white,
  Petal by petal, fall
On that stretch of mud and sand that lies   495
  By the hideous prison-wall,
To tell the men who tramp the yard
  That God's Son died for all.

*   *   *

Yet though the hideous prison-wall
  Still hems him round and round,   500
And a spirit may not walk by night
  That is with fetters bound,
And a spirit may but weep that lies
  In such unholy ground,

He is at peace – this wretched man –   505
  At peace, or will be soon:
There is no thing to make him mad,
  Nor does Terror walk at noon,
For the lampless Earth in which he lies
  Has neither Sun nor Moon.   510

They hanged him as a beast is hanged:
  They did not even toll
A requiem that might have brought
  Rest to his startled soul,
But hurriedly they took him out,   515
  And hid him in a hole.

---

[42] *barren staff . . . sight* ironic allusion to the Tannhäuser
story. See the headnote to Swinburne's 'Laus Veneris', 487.

They stripped him of his canvas clothes,
And gave him to the flies:
They mocked the swollen purple throat,
And the stark and staring eyes: 520
And with laughter loud they heaped the shroud
In which their convict lies.

The Chaplain would not kneel to pray
By his dishonoured grave:
Nor mark it with that blessed Cross   525
That Christ for sinners gave,
Because the man was one of those
Whom Christ came down to save.

Yet all is well; he has but passed
To life's appointed bourne:[43]   530
And alien tears will fill for him
Pity's long-broken urn,
For his mourners will be outcast men,
And outcasts always mourn.

5

I know not whether Laws be right,   535
Or whether Laws be wrong;
All that we know who lie in gaol
Is that the wall is strong;
And that each day is like a year,
A year whose days are long.   540

But this I know, that every Law
That men have made for Man,
Since first Man took his brother's life,[44]
And the sad world began,
But straws the wheat and saves the chaff   545
With a most evil fan.

This too I know – and wise it were
If each could know the same –
That every prison that men build
Is built with bricks of shame,   550
And bound with bars lest Christ should see
How men their brothers maim.

With bars they blur the gracious moon,
And blind the goodly sun:
And they do well to hide their Hell,   555
For in it things are done
That Son of God nor son of Man
Ever should look upon!

*   *   *

---

[43] *bourne* destination.

[44] *Man took his brother's life* Cain's murder of Abel in Genesis 4.

The vilest deeds like poison weeds,
    Bloom well in prison-air;   *Repeat*   560
  It is only what is good in Man
    That wastes and withers there:
  Pale Anguish keeps the heavy gate,
    And the Warder is Despair.

For they starve the little frightened child   565
    Till it weeps both night and day:
  And they scourge the weak, and flog the fool,
    And gibe the old and grey,
  And some grow mad, and all grow bad,
    And none a word may say.   570

Each narrow cell in which we dwell
    Is a foul and dark latrine,
  And the fetid[45] breath of living Death
    Chokes up each grated screen,
  And all, but Lust, is turned to dust   575
    In Humanity's machine.

The brackish[46] water that we drink
    Creeps with a loathsome slime,
  And the bitter bread they weigh in scales
    Is full of chalk and lime,   580
  And Sleep will not lie down, but walks
    Wild-eyed, and cries to Time.

                    *   *   *

But though lean Hunger and green Thirst
    Like asp with adder fight,
  We have little care of prison fare,   585
    For what chills and kills outright
  Is that every stone one lifts by day
    Becomes one's heart by night.

With midnight always in one's heart,
    And twilight in one's cell,   590
  We turn the crank, or tear the rope,
    Each in his separate Hell,
  And the silence is more awful far
    Than the sound of a brazen[47] bell.

And never a human voice comes near   595
    To speak a gentle word:
  And the eye that watches through the door
    Is pitiless and hard:
  And by all forgot, we rot and rot,
    With soul and body marred.   600

---

[45] *fetid* stinking.   [47] *brazen* brass.
[46] *brackish* partly fresh, partly salty.

And thus we rust Life's iron chain
Degraded and alone:
And some men curse, and some men weep,
And some men make no moan:
But God's eternal Laws are kind   605
And break the heart of stone.

* * *

And every human heart that breaks,
In prison-cell or yard,
Is as that broken box that gave
Its treasure to the Lord,   610
And filled the unclean leper's house
With the scent of costliest nard.[48]

Mary's
spikenard
ointment

Ah! happy they whose hearts can break
And peace of pardon win!
How else may man make straight his plan   615
And cleanse his soul from Sin?
How else but through a broken heart
May Lord Christ enter in?

And he of the swollen purple throat,
And the stark and staring eyes,   620
Waits for the holy hands that took
The Thief to Paradise;[49]
And a broken and a contrite heart
The Lord will not despise.[50]

So
sad

The man in red who reads the Law   625
Gave him three weeks of life,
Three little weeks in which to heal
His soul of his soul's strife,
And cleanse from every blot of blood
The hand that held the knife.   630

And with tears of blood he cleansed the hand,
The hand that held the steel:
For only blood can wipe out blood,
And only tears can heal:

[48] *Is as . . . nard* cf. Luke 7.37–48, 'And behold, a woman in the citie which was a sinner, when shee knew that Iesus sate at meat in the Pharisees house, brought an Alabaster boxe of ointment, And stood at his feet behind him, weeping, and began to wash his feete with teares, and did wipe them with the haires of her head, and kissed his feet, and anointed them with the ointment . . . And he said vnto her, Thy sinnes are forgiuen.'

[49] *Thief to Paradise* cf. the account of Jesus's crucifixion in Luke 23.39–43, 'And one of ye malefactors, which were hanged, railed on him, saying, If thou be Christ, saue thy selfe and vs. But the other answering, rebuked him, saying, Doest not thou feare God, seeing thou art in the same condemnation? And we indeed iustly; for we receiue the due reward of our deeds, but this man hath done nothing amisse. And he said vnto Iesus, Lord, remember me when thou commest into thy kingdome. And Iesus said vnto him, Uerily, I say vnto thee, to day shalt thou be with me in Paradise.'

[50] *a broken . . . despise* cf. Psalm 15.17, 'The sacrifices of God are a broken spirit: a broken and a contrite heart, O God, thou wilt not despise'.

And the crimson stain that was of Cain[51]   635
Became Christ's snow–white seal.[52]

6

In Reading gaol by Reading town
There is a pit of shame,
And in it lies a wretched man
Eaten by teeth of flame,   640
In a burning winding-sheet[53] he lies,
And his grave has got no name.

And there, till Christ call forth the dead,
In silence let him lie:
No need to waste the foolish tear,   645
Or heave the windy sigh:
The man had killed the thing he loved,
And so he had to die.

And all men kill the thing they love,   650
By all let this be heard,
Some do it with a bitter look,
Some with a flattering word,
The coward does it with a kiss,
The brave man with a sword!

[51] *Cain* the first murderer – see Genesis 4.
[52] *Christ's . . . seal* cf. Revelation 7.13–15, 'And one of the Elders answered, saying vnto mee, What are these which are arayed in white robes? and whence came they? And I said vnto him, Sir, thou knowest. And he said to me, These are they which came out of great tribulation, and haue washed their robes, and made them white in the blood of the Lambe. Therefore are they before the throne of God, and serue him day and night in his Temple.'
[53] *winding-sheet* burial cloth. But Wilde means the quicklime, which burns.

John Davidson (1857–1909)

Davidson was born at Barrhead, Renfrewshire, into an impoverished Evangelical family. Irregularly educated, he worked on and off as a schoolteacher, trying to write poetry. He married Margaret McArthur in 1885 after the publication in Glasgow of his novel, *The North Wall*. In 1890, the family moved to London, and Davidson appeared on the edge of the Yeatsian Rhymers' Club, but his own writing was darker, more starkly realist than the Rhymers' preferred mode. *Fleet Street Eclogues* was published in 1893, *Ballads and Songs* in 1894; *A Second Series of Fleet Street Eclogues* (1896), *New Ballads* (1897) and *The Last Ballad and Other Poems* (1899) followed. Thereafter came a series of materialist, Nietzschean 'Testaments'

('The Testament of a Vivisector' [1901], 'The Testament of a Man Forbid' [1901], 'The Testament of an Empire-builder' [1902], 'The Testament of a Prime Minister' [1904]). The dingy images of urban life and the angular colloquialism of Davidson's poetry (some poems started as prose) increasingly presented the unappealing sides of downmarket modern life. In 1896, Davidson suffered a mental breakdown (mental illness ran in the family); he endeavoured to recuperate at Shoreham then moved to Cornwall. *The Theatrocrat: A Tragic Play of Church and Stage* was issued in 1905, but Davidson killed himself in 1909 – his decaying body was found at sea.

Thirty Bob a Week

John Davidson's 'Thirty Bob a Week' (1894), highly conscious of class divisions and the unglamorous life of labour, reflects a shift in the last years of the nineteenth century towards the literature of the working man, often trapped by a system. In fiction, this was the terrain of George Gissing (1857–1903) and later, from a rather different perspective, of Arnold Bennett (1867–1931). In poetry, Rudyard Kipling's exploration of the voices of the ordinary soldier in 'Tommy', 649–50, or 'Gunga Din', 646–8, compares with this monologue's demotic intentions. W. E. Henley's *In Hospital* sequence, 571–86, lies behind it too. Like Kipling and Henley, Davidson catches the slang and idiom of the ordinary speaker, figuring class identity in non-standard English. 'Thirty Bob a Week' is spoken by a poorly paid clerk such as would be represented in E. M. Forster's Leonard Bast in *Howards End* (1910).

Davidson's poetry is persistently interested in the conditions of the modern and its distance from the high Victorian. 'Thirty Bob a Week' effects this through a radical break with the Carlylean conviction that labour is redemptory to consider instead the drudgery and human cost of unrewarding work, the 'dull official round', and life on a meagre wage. 'Thirty Bob a Week' expresses the difficulties and ambiguous stoicism of the relatively new class of commuting worker at the end of the nineteenth century,

here, travelling to work on the recently built London Underground.

'Thirty Bob a Week' addresses itself to the conditions of life in the major new growth area of city residence: suburbia. If the experience of the great city *per se* had been a topic of literature at the beginning of the century – cf. Wordsworth's 'On Westminster Bridge' (1802) – it was the new geographical/classed division in the city, the residential areas of its margins, neither countryside nor city centre, which became prominent subjects at the other end. So familiar was the theme in this period, indeed, it was comically treated in George and Weedon Grossmith's *Diary of a Nobody* (1892). 'Thirty Bob a Week' is spoken to an educated 'silver-tongued' man from a higher class. The speaker's understanding of individual will as self-determining suggests Davidson's interest in the work of the German philosopher Friedrich Nietzsche (1844–1900), and his belief in the central importance of will/desire in human development (cf. 'Snow', 616–18). Davidson's rhyming monologue highlights the mental anxiety of life for a clerk on a knife-edge wage and the gaps between one class's understanding of another. The speaker's final image is poised between stoic fortitude and a sense of utter waste.

Text: *Yellow Book*, 1894.

I couldn't touch a stop[1] and turn a screw,
And set the blooming[2] world a-work for me,
Like such as cut their teeth – I hope, like you –
On the handle of a skeleton gold key;
I cut mine on a leek, which I eat it every week: 5
I'm a clerk at thirty bob[3] as you can see.

2
But I don't allow it's luck and all a toss;
There's no such thing as being starred and crossed;[4]
It's just the power of some to be a boss,
And the bally[5] power of others to be bossed: 10
I face the music, sir; you bet I ain't a cur;[6]
Strike me lucky if I don't believe I'm lost!

3
For like a mole I journey in the dark,
A-travelling along the underground[7]
From my Pillar'd Halls and broad Suburbean Park,   15
To come the daily dull official round;
And home again at night with my pipe all alight,
A-scheming how to count ten bob a pound.[8]

4
And it's often very cold and very wet,
And my missis stitches towels for a hunks;[9]   20
And the Pillar'd Halls is half of it to let –
Three rooms about the size of travelling trunks.
And we cough, my wife and I, to dislocate a sigh,
When the noisy little kids are in their bunks.

5
But you never hear her do a growl or whine,   25
For she's made of flint and roses, very odd;
And I've got to cut my meaning rather fine,
Or I'd blubber, for I'm made of greens and sod:
So p'r'aps we are in Hell for all that I can tell,
And lost and damn'd and served up hot to God.   30

6
I ain't blaspheming, Mr Silver-tongue;
I'm saying things a bit beyond your art:
Of all the rummy[10] starts you ever sprung,
Thirty bob a week's the rummiest start!
With your science and your books and your the'ries about spooks,   35
Did you ever hear of looking in your heart?

---

[1] *touch a stop* make things stop.
[2] *blooming* at the end of the nineteenth century, new slang for 'bloody'.
[3] *bob* slang for 'shilling'. 30 shillings = £1.50.
[4] *starred and crossed* cf. 'star-crossed lovers', *Romeo and Juliet*, Prologue, 6.
[5] *bally* euphemism for 'bloody'.

[6] *cur* worthless, snappish dog.
[7] *underground* railway in London, first section opened in 1863.
[8] *ten bob a pound* 20 shillings made one pound.
[9] *hunks* (Scot. dialect) indolent woman.
[10] *rummy* bad.

7

I didn't mean your pocket, Mr., no:
I mean that having children and a wife,
With thirty bob on which to come and go,
Isn't dancing to the tabor[11] and the fife:[12]   40
When it doesn't make you drink, by Heaven! it makes you think,
And notice curious items about life.

8

I step into my heart and there I meet
A god-almighty devil singing small,
Who would like to shout and whistle in the street,   45
And squelch the passers flat against the wall;
If the whole world was a cake he had the power to take,
He would take it, ask for more, and eat it all.

9

And I meet a sort of simpleton beside,
The kind that life is always giving beans;   50
With thirty bob a week to keep a bride
He fell in love and married in his teens:
At thirty bob he stuck; but he knows it isn't luck:
He knows the seas are deeper than tureens.[13]

10

And the god-almighty devil and the fool   55
That meet me in the High Street on the strike,
When I walk about my heart a-gathering wool,
Are my good and evil angels if you like.
And both of them together in every kind of weather
Ride me like a double-seated bike.   60

11

That's rough a bit and needs its meaning curled.
But I have a high old hot un in my mind –
A most engrugious[14] notion of the world,
That leaves your lightning 'rithmetic behind:
I give it at a glance when I say 'There ain't no chance,   65
Nor nothing of the lucky-lottery kind.'

12

And it's this way that I make it out to be:
No fathers, mothers, countries, climates – none;
Not Adam[15] was responsible for me,
Nor society, nor systems, nary[16] one: 70
A little sleeping seed, I woke – I did, indeed –
A million years before the blooming sun.

13

I woke because I thought the time had come;
Beyond my will there was no other cause;

---

[11] *tabor* early form of drum.
[12] *fife* shrill-toned flute-like instrument.
[13] *tureens* receptacles for serving soup.

[14] *engrugious* neologism: egregious, shocking.
[15] *Adam* the first man, according to Genesis.
[16] *nary* not any.

And everywhere I found myself at home, 75
Because I chose to be the thing I was;
And in whatever shape of mollusc or of ape
I always went according to the laws.

14

I was the love that chose my mother out;
I joined two lives and from the union burst; 80
My weakness and my strength without a doubt
Are mine alone for ever from the first:
It's just the very same with a difference in the name
As 'Thy will be done.'[17] You say it if you durst![18]

15

They say it daily up and down the land 85
As easy as you take a drink, it's true;
But the difficultest go to understand,
And the difficultest job a man can do,
Is to come it brave and meek with thirty bob a week,
And feel that that's the proper thing for you. 90

16

It's naked child against a hungry wolf;
It's playing bowls upon a splitting wreck;
It's walking on a string across a gulf
With millstones fore-and-aft about your neck;
But the thing is daily done by many and many a one; 95
And we fall, face forward, fighting, on the deck.

---

[17] *'Thy will be done'* God's will be done: from the Lord's Prayer (Matthew 6.9–13). [18] *durst* dare.

A Woman and Her Son

Conscious of the ending of the century, 'A Woman and her Son' (written in 1896) marks the transition from the Victorian to the modern through a grotesque domestic drama. With dingy comedy and savage irony, the poem caricatures the high Victorian past in the figure of the mother, a religious bigot, and the modern secular spirit in the person of the hard-hearted son. This free verse dialogue is a dark, parodic enactment of the relationship between the new thinking of the contemporary world and the decades of Victoria's reign that gave it birth. Cf. Thomas Hardy's 'The Darkling Thrush', 512–13, on the degenerate offspring of the high Victorian.

Davidson transforms the genre of Robert Browning's dramatic monologues. Offering a dialogue between two speakers, 'A Woman and her Son' has little room for the readerly sympathy and understanding that Browning exploited. Presenting a man and a woman profoundly separated by opinion, 'A Woman and her Son' makes the reader the spectator of a bleak scene of failure that is not – as failure often is for Browning – energizing or the root of moral achievement. Davidson's speakers are at last damned in a way Browning's never are by the narrator's intrusive judgement.

As with 'Thirty Bob a Week', 606–9, 'A Woman and her Son' probes the bleak conditions of lower-middle-class suburbia. It is social documentation, a form of unsentimental realism first conspicuous in nineteenth-century English poetry in W. E. Henley's *In Hospital*, 571–86. Davidson wrote 'A Woman and her Son' (also, of course, set in a hospital) shortly before his own mother's death in Edinburgh in September 1896, though the poem is – self-evidently – not straightforwardly autobiographical.

Text: *New Ballads* (1897).

'Has he come yet?' the dying woman asked.
'No,' said the nurse. 'Be quiet.'
'When he comes
Bring him to me: I may not live an hour.'

'Not if you talk. Be quiet.'   5

'When he comes
Bring him to me.'

'Hush, will you!'

Night came down.
The cries of children playing in the street   10
Suddenly rose more voluble and shrill;
Ceased, and broke out again; and ceased and broke
In eager prate;[1] then dwindled and expired.

'Across the dreary common once I saw
The moon rise out of London like a ghost.   15
Has the moon risen? Is he come?'

'Not yet.
Be still, or you will die before he comes.'

The working-men with heavy iron tread,
The thin-shod clerks, the shopmen neat and plump   20
Home from the city came. On muddy beer
The melancholy mean suburban street
Grew maudlin[2] for an hour; pianos waked
In dissonance from dreams of rusty peace,
And unpitched voices quavered[3] tedious songs   25
Of sentiment infirm or nerveless mirth.

'Has he come yet?'

'Be still or you will die!'

And when the hour of gaiety had passed,
And the poor revellers were gone to bed,   30
The moon among the chimneys wandering long
Escaped at last, and sadly overlooked
The waste raw land where doleful suburbs thrive.

Then came a firm quick step – measured but quick;
And then a triple knock that shook the house   35
And brought the plaster down.

'My son!' she cried.
'Bring him to me!'

---

[1] *prate* chatter.
[2] *maudlin* melancholy, especially that induced by alcohol.

[3] *quavered* pun: both 'trembled' and 'sang in quavers', rhythmic units in music.

He came; the nurse went out.

'Mother, I thought to spare myself this pain,'   40
He said at once, 'but that was cowardly.
And so I come to bid you try to think,
    To understand at last.'

        'Still hard, my son?'

    'Hard as the nether millstone.'   45

        'But I hope
To soften you,' she said, 'before I die.'

'And I to see you harden with a hiss
As life goes out in the cold bath of death.
Oh, surely now your creed will set you free   50
 'For one great moment, and the universe
Flash on your intellect as power, power, power,
    Knowing not good or evil, God or sin,
    But only everlasting yea and nay.⁴
Is weakness greatness? No, a thousand times!   55
    Is force the greatest? Yes, for ever yes!
Be strong, be great, now you have come to die.'

    'My son, you seem to me a kind of prig.'

'How can I get it said? Think, mother, think!
    Look back upon your fifty wretched years   60
And show me anywhere the hand of God.
Your husband saving souls – O, paltry souls
That need salvation! – lost the grip of things,
    And left you penniless with none to aid
    But me the prodigal. Back to the start!   65
    An orphan girl, hurt, melancholy, frail,
Before you learned to play, your toil began:
That might have been your making, had the weight
    Of drudgery, the unsheathed fire of woe
Borne down and beat on your defenceless life: 70
    Souls shrivel up in these extremes of pain,
    Or issue diamonds to engrave the world;
But yours before it could be made or marred,
Plucked from the burning, saved by faith, became
    Inferior as a thing of paste that hopes   75
To pass for real in heaven's enduring light.
    You married then a crude evangelist,
Whose soul was like a wafer that can take
    One single impress only.'⁵

        'Oh, my son!   80
    Your father!'

⁴ *everlasting yea and nay* terms from Carlyle's *Sartor Resartus* (1833–4): here, they signify the son's secularism and Nietzschean belief in individual will (cf. 'Thirty Bob a Week', 606–9, and 'Snow', 616–18).

⁵ *wafer . . . only* cf. small wafers used for communion, often embossed with a cross or other religious symbol.

'He, my father! These are times
When all must to the crucible – no thought,
Practice, or use, or custom sacro-sanct
But shall be violable now. And first   85
If ever we evade the wonted[6] round,
The stagnant vortex of the eddying years,
The child must take the father by the beard,
And say, "What did you in begetting me?"'

'I will not listen!'   90

'But you shall, you must –
You cannot help yourself. Death in your eyes
And voice, and I to torture you with truth,
Even as your preachers for a thousand years
Pestered with falsehood souls of dying folk.   95
Look at the man, your husband. Of the soil;
Broad, strong, adust;[7] head, massive; eyes of steel;
Yet some way ailing, for he understood
But one idea, and he married you.'

The dying woman sat up straight in bed;   100
A ghastly blush glowed on her yellow cheek,
And flame broke from her eyes, but words came not.

The son's pent wrath burnt on. 'He married you;
You were his wife, his servant; cheerfully
You bore him children; and your house was hell.   105
Unwell, half-starved, and clad in cast-off clothes,
We had no room, no sport; nothing but fear
Of our evangelist, whose little purse
Opened to all save us; who squandered smiles
On wily proselytes,[8] and gloomed at home.   110
You had eight children; only three grew up:
Of these, one died bedrid, and one insane,[9]
And I alone am left you. Think of it!
It matters nothing if a fish, a plant
Teem with waste offspring, but a conscious womb!   115
Eight times you bore a child, and in fierce throes,
For you were frail and small: of all your love,
Your hopes, your passion, not a memory steals
To smooth your dying pillow, only I
Am here to rack you. Where does God appear?'   120

'God shall appear,' the dying woman said.
'God has appeared; my heart is in his hand.
Were there no God, no Heaven! – Oh, foolish boy!
You foolish fellow! Pain and trouble here
Are God's benignest providence – the whip   125
And spur to Heaven. But joy was mine below –
I am unjust to God – great joy was mine:

[6] *wonted* accustomed.
[7] *adust* gloomy.
[8] *proselytes* converts.

[9] *insane* Davidson's brother Thomas had spent 6 months in Morningside Asylum, Edinburgh, after a mental breakdown in 1893.

Which makes Heaven sweeter too; because if earth
  Afford such pleasure in mortality
    What must immortal happiness be like! 130

  Eight times I was a mother. Frail and small?
    Yes; but the passionate, courageous mate
  Of a strong man. Oh, boy! You paltry boy!
Hush! Think! Think – you! Eight times I bore a child,
Eight souls for God! In Heaven they wait for me – 135
  My husband and the seven. I see them all!
  And two are children still – my little ones!
While I have sorrowed here, shrinking sometimes
  From that which was decreed, my Father, God,
Was storing Heaven with treasure for me. Hush! 140
  My dowry in the skies! God's thoughtfulness!
  I see it all! Lest Heaven might, unalloyed,
  Distress my shy soul, I leave earth in doubt
Of your salvation: something to hope and fear
    Until I get accustomed to the peace 145
That passeth understanding.[10] When you come –
    For you will come, my son. . . .'

    Her strength gave out;
She sank down panting, bathed in tears and sweat.

  'Could I but touch your intellect,' he cried, 150
  'Before you die! Mother, the world is mad:
This castle in the air, this Heaven of yours,
  Is the lewd dream of morbid vanity.
    For each of us death is the end of all;
And when the sun goes out the race of men 155
  Shall cease for ever. It is ours to make
  This farce of fate a splendid tragedy:
Since we must be the sport of circumstance,
We should be sportsmen, and produce a breed
Of gallant creatures, conscious of their doom, 160
Marching with lofty brows, game[11] to the last.
  Oh good and evil, heaven and hell are lies!
But strength is great: there is no other truth:
This is the yea-and-nay that makes men hard.
  Mother, be hard and happy in your death.' 165

  'What do you say? I hear the waters roll . . .'
Then, with a faint cry, striving to arise –
    'After I die I shall come back to you,
And then you must believe; you must believe,
For I shall bring you news of God and Heaven!' 170

  He set his teeth, and saw his mother die.
    Outside a city-reveller's tipsy tread
  Severed the silence with a jagged rent;

---

[10] *peace . . . understanding* cf. Philippians 4.7, 'And the peace
of God which passeth all vnderstanding, shall keepe your
hearts & minds through Christ Iesus'.

[11] *game* plucky, spirited.

The tall lamps flickered through the sombre street,
    With yellow light hiding the stainless stars: 175
    In the next house a child awoke and cried;
    Far off a clank and clash of shunting trains
Broke out and ceased, as if the fettered world
    Started and shook its irons in the night;
        Across the dreary common citywards,   180
The moon, among the chimneys sunk again,
Cast on the clouds a shade of smoky pearl.

And when her funeral day had come, her son,
    Before they fastened down the coffin lid,
    Shut himself in the chamber, there to gaze   185
    Upon her dead face, hardening his heart.
But as he gazed, into the smooth wan cheek
    Life with its wrinkles shot again; the eyes
    Burst open, and the bony fingers clutched
    The coffin sides; the woman raised herself,   190
And owl-like in her shroud blinked on the light.

'Mother, what news of God and Heaven?' he asked.

Feeble and strange, her voice came from afar:
    'I am not dead: I must have been asleep.'

    'Do not imagine that. You lay here dead –   195
Three days and nights, a corpse.[12] Life has come back:
    Often it does, although faint-hearted folk
    Fear to admit it: none of those who die,
        And come to life again, can ever tell
Of any bourne[13] from which they have returned: 200
Therefore they were not dead, your casuists[14] say.
    The ancient jugglery that tricks the world!
You lay here dead, three days and nights. What news?
        "After I die I shall come back to you,
And then you must believe" – these were your words –   205
    "For I shall bring you news of God and Heaven."'

    She cast a look forlorn about the room:
    The door was shut; the worn venetian,[15] down;
    And stuffy sunlight through the dusty slats
Spotted the floor, and smeared the faded walls.   210
    He with his strident voice and eyes of steel
        Stood by relentless.

        'I remember, dear,'
She whispered, 'very little. When I died
I saw my children dimly bending down,   215
    The little ones in front, to beckon me,
    A moment in the dark; and that is all.'

---

[12] *Three . . . corpse* ironically, the amount of time between Jesus's death and resurrection.
[13] *bourne* limit of a race or journey.

[14] *casuist* suspicious person who supposedly resolves cases of conscience or difficult questions of theology.
[15] *venetian* Venetian blind, horizontally louvred blind to control light.

'That was before you died – the last attempt
Of fancy to create the heart's desire.
Now mother, be courageous; now, be hard.'   220

'What must I say or do, my dearest son?
Oh me, the deep discomfort of my mind!
Come to me, hold me, help me to be brave,
And I shall make you happy if I can,
For I have none but you – none anywhere . . .   225
Mary, the youngest, whom you never saw
Looked out of Heaven first: her little hands . . .
Three days and nights, dead, and no memory! . . .
A poor old creature dying a second death,
I understand the settled treachery,   230
The plot of love and hope against the world.
Fearless, I gave myself at nature's call;
And when they died, my children, one by one,
All sweetly in my heart I buried them.
Who stole them while I slept? Where are they all?   235
My heart is eerie, like a rifled grave
Where silent spiders spin among the dust,
And the wind moans and laughs under its breath.
But in a drawer . . . What is there in the drawer?
No pressure of a little rosy hand   240
Upon a faded cheek – nor anywhere
The seven fair stars I made. Oh love the cheat!
And hope, the radiant devil pointing up,
Lest men should cease to give the couple sport
And end the world at once! For three days dead –   245
Here in my coffin; and no memory!
Oh, it is hard! But I – I, too, am hard . . .
Be hard, my son, and steep your heart of flesh
In stony waters till it grows a stone,
Or love and hope will hack it with blunt knives   250
As long as it can feel.'

He, holding her,
With sobs and laughter spoke: his mind had snapped
Like a frayed string o'erstretched: 'Mother, rejoice;
For I shall make you glad. There is no heaven   255
Your children are resolved to dust and dew:
But, mother, I am God. I shall create
The heaven of your desires. There must be heaven
For mothers and their babes. Let heaven be now!'

They found him conjuring chaos with mad words   260
And brandished hands across his mother's corpse.

Thus did he see her harden with a hiss
As life went out in the cold bath of death;
Thus did she soften him before she died:
For both were bigots – fateful souls that plague   265
The gentle world.

Snow

In 'Thirty Bob a Week', 606–9, Davidson's speaker champions a Nietzschean individual will as the guiding force of human progress and evolutionary history. In 'Snow', based on an article he wrote in the *Glasgow Herald* for 5 January 1907 and published posthumously in 1909, Davidson muses on the identity of a physical, apparently inert form. The snowflake is imagined as part of the great chain of all things struggling up to consciousness and self-consciousness. Such is its powerful will – seeking to maintain the angles of its crystallization – that it might be thought alive.

Davidson's poetry repeatedly draws attention to the shift from the high Victorian to the modern. 'A Woman and her Son', 609–15, for instance, dramatizes the division through a confrontation between two generations of a family. In its secular materialism, 'Snow' – playful, parodic, ironic – marks out the contemporary as freed from the last vestiges of natural theology (cf. A. C. Swinburne, 'A Forsaken Garden', 506–9, and Michael Field, 'Nests in Elms', 565).

The audience for modern technology is scruti-nized in 'The Crystal Palace', 618–26; in 'Snow' the activity of the investigative empirical scientist, a peculiarly modern form of identity, is quirkily examined. The poem parodies the practice of vivisection in the martyred snowflake on the microscope glass, inviting comparison with experimentation on living creatures that is provocatively without clear moral coordinates. Davidson's staggeringly brutal 'Testament of a Vivisector' is his most controversial handling of this important Victorian issue (cf. Eugene Lee-Hamilton, 'Fallopius to his Dissecting Knife', 555–6). Davidson's poem is prickly and undercut by ironies, but it also manages to preserve a sense of authentic wonder at the natural world in its final radiant stanza.

For other poems reflecting on the metamorphosis from Victorian to modern, see Thomas Hardy, 'The Darkling Thrush', 512–13, Amy Levy, 'A Ballad of Religion and Marriage', 642–3, and Rudyard Kipling, 'The Way through the Woods', 655–6.

Text: *Fleet Street, and Other Poems* (1909).

'Who affirms that crystals are alive?'
I affirm it, let who will deny: –
Crystals are engendered, wax and thrive,
Wane and wither; I have seen them die.

Trust me, masters, crystals have their day,　　　　5
Eager to attain the perfect norm,
Lit with purpose, potent to display
Facet, angle, colour, beauty, form.

2
Water-crystals need for flower and root
Sixty clear degrees,[1] no less, no more;　　　　10
Snow, so fickle, still in this acute
Angle[2] thinks, and learns no other lore:

Such its life, and such its pleasure is,
Such its art and traffic, such its gain,
Evermore in new conjunctions this　　　　15
Admirable angle to maintain.

Crystalcraft in every flower and flake
Snow exhibits, of the welkin[3] free:
Crystalline are crystals for the sake,
All and singular, of crystalry.　　　　20

[1] *Sixty clear degrees* a well-formed snow crystal has six main arms that are 60 degrees apart.
[2] *acute / Angle* one less than 90 degrees.
[3] *welkin* sky.

Yet does every crystal of the snow
Individualise, a seedling sown
Broadcast, but instinct with power to grow
Beautiful in beauty of its own.

Every flake with all its prongs and dints   25
Burns ecstatic as a new-lit star:
Men are not more diverse, finger-prints[4]
More dissimilar than snow-flakes are.

Worlds of men and snow endure, increase,
Woven of power and passion to defy   30
Time and travail: only races cease,
Individual men and crystals die.

3

Jewelled shapes of snow whose feathery showers,
Fallen or falling wither at a breath,
All afraid are they, and loth as flowers   35
Beasts and men to tread the way to death.

Once I saw upon an object-glass,[5]
Martyred underneath a microscope,
One elaborate snow-flake slowly pass,
Dying hard, beyond the reach of hope.   40

Still from shape to shape the crystal changed,
Writhing in its agony; and still,
Less and less elaborate, arranged
Potently the angle of its will.

Tortured to a simple final form,   45
Angles six and six divergent beams,
Lo, in death it touched the perfect norm[6]
Verifying all its crystal dreams!

4

Such the noble tragedy of one
Martyred snow-flake. Who can tell the fate   50
Heinous[7] and uncouth of showers undone,
Fallen in cities! – showers that expiate

Errant lives from polar worlds adrift
Where the great millennial[8] snows abide;
Castaways from mountain-chains that lift   55
Snowy summits in perennial pride;

---

[4] *finger-prints* cf. the increasing interest in the late Victorian period in finger prints as a form of personal identification. Francis Galton's *Finger Prints* (1892) was the first major public discussion of the issue in England.
[5] *object-glass* lens in a microscope, situated nearest to the object, which receives the rays of light directly from it.
[6] *perfect norm* basic form of snowflake, with six arms.
[7] *Heinous* hateful, odious.
[8] *millennial* i.e. snows that will only melt at Jesus's second coming.

Nomad snows, or snows in evil day
Born to urban ruin, to be tossed,
Trampled, shovelled, ploughed and swept away
Down the seething sewers: all the frost   60

Flowers of heaven melted up with lees,[9]
Offal, recrement,[10] but every flake
Showing to the last in fixed degrees
Perfect crystals for the crystal's sake.

5

Usefulness of snow is but a chance[11]   65
Here in temperate climes with winter sent,
Sheltering earth's prolonged hibernal trance:
All utility is accident.

Sixty clear degrees the joyful snow,
Practising economy of means,   70
Fashions endless beauty in, and so
Glorifies the universe with scenes

Arctic and antarctic: stainless shrouds,
Ermine[12] woven in silvery frost, attire
Peaks in every land among the clouds   75
Crowned with snows to catch the morning's fire.

---

[9] *lees* dregs.
[10] *recrement* refuse, dross.
[11] *chance* i.e., not evidence of God's plan.

[12] *Ermine* valuable fur from the ermine (stoat, weasel-like creature that is almost wholly white in winter).

The Crystal Palace

John Davidson's 'The Crystal Palace' (*Westminster Gazette*, 28 November 1908 and 23 January 1909) diagnoses the condition of modernity with chaotic, unsympathetic, dazzling energy. Like 'Snow', 616–18, 'A Woman and her Son', 609–15, and 'Thirty Bob a Week', 606–9, it reflects on the break between the Victorian and the present. Davidson describes a visit to the Crystal Palace, the giant exhibition hall in Sydenham, south London (destroyed by fire in 1936), containing material from the Great Exhibition of 1851 and many other items from overseas. A temple to technology, science and industry, it also included many copies of art works. The Queen and Prince Albert opened the new Crystal Palace on 10 June 1854. Its ideals were high. The art and social critic John Ruskin (1819–1900) thought it offered a unique chance for improving the education of the labouring classes. Positioned, he said, in 'close neighbourhood of a metropolis overflowing with a population weary of labour, yet thirsting for knowledge, where contemplation may be consistent with rest, and instruction with enjoyment', it might have an extensive influence 'on the minds of the working-classes' (1854). Davidson's poem ironizes such Victorian ideals – which, in fact, Ruskin did not believe fulfilled in the Palace – in an important pre-Modernist exploration of urban culture and attitudes of mind.

'The Crystal Palace' presents a vast Mob – the modern phenomenon of the crowd animated as a monster – invading the building and expressing a mixture of ignorance, pretentiousness, idleness and the shallow desire to be fashionable. The haughtiness of the poet's view of the crowd defines a relationship between contemporary forms of culture that characterized Modernism in the later twentieth century. 'The Crystal Palace' poet is aloofly superior to what he observes.

The poem identifies consumerism – the consumerism of the spectator's gaze – as the dominant human identity of the modern. Europe's first department store had opened in Paris in 1852; Debenhams opened its first in England in 1905. The spectators of the Crystal Palace in Davidson's poem mimic the consumerist behaviour of this new and symptomatic mode of urban experience. High and low culture jostle and the dislocation/displacedness that Davidson sees defining the mob, with its divergent aims, is mirrored in the enormously eclectic vocabulary of the poem. 'The Crystal Palace' brings together slang, classicisms, colloquialisms, pretentious circumlocutions, references to high art and literature, Biblical allusion and the diction of modern technology to create a linguistic mêlée persistently ironizing the culture and crowd it describes. Artifice and showiness are emphasized and the fact that the Palace is full of *imitations* of great art confirms the shallowness of the 'stupid' crowd whom Davidson depicts with such bravura impatience in this foundational text of literary Modernism.

Text: *Fleet Street, and Other Poems* (1909).

Contraption,[1] – that's the bizarre, proper slang,
Eclectic word, for this portentous[2] toy,
The flying-machine, that gyrates stiffly, arms
A-kimbo, so to say, and baskets slung
From every elbow, skating in the air.   5
Irreverent, we;[3] but Tartars[4] from Thibet[5]
May deem Sir Hiram[6] the Grandest Lama,[7] deem
His volatile machinery best, and most
Magnific, rotatory engine, meant
For penitence and prayer combined, whereby   10
Petitioner as well as orison[8]
Are spun about in space: a solemn rite
Before the portal of that fane[9] unique,
Victorian temple of commercialism,
Our very own eighth wonder of the world,[10]   15
The Crystal Palace.

So sublime! Like some
Immense crustacean's gannoid[11] skeleton,
Unearthed, and cleansed, and polished! Were it so
Our paleontological[12] respect   20
Would shield it from derision; but when a shed,
Intended for a palace, looks as like
The fossil of a giant myriapod![13] . . .
'Twas Isabey[14] – sarcastic wretch! – who told
A young aspirant, studying tandem art   25

---

[1] *Contraption OED* gives the first reference to this word as 1825. In 1863, William Barnes glossed its use in Dorset dialect with the sense that Davidson has here: a contrivance. It is, for Davidson, a slang term.
[2] *portentous* ominous, threatening.
[3] *Irreverent, we* Davidson and the critic and caricaturist Max Beerbohm, who visited the Crystal Palace in June 1906.
[4] *Tartars* native inhabitants of the region of Central Asia extending eastward from the Caspian Sea.
[5] *Thibet* Tibet.
[6] *Sir Hiram* Sir Hiram Maxim (1840–1916) developed the machine-gun that bore his name (Maxim gun), unveiling it in 1884, and also, as here, flying machines. Davidson wrote in the prose article that formed the basis of the poem ('Automatic Augury and the Crystal Palace', *Glasgow Herald*, 18 March 1905): 'In the grounds Sir Hiram Maxim's flying machines are whirling seriously, and gyrate there all day earnestly occupied. The wandering Lama from Thibet doubtless conceives this to be a brilliant,

magnificent rotatory praying machine in which the petitioner as well as the orison is spun about in space.'
[7] *Lama* title given to the Buddhist priests of Mongolia and Tibet.
[8] *orison* prayer.
[9] *fane* temple.
[10] *eighth wonder of the world* the seven ancient wonders of the world were the Great Pyramid of Giza, the Hanging Gardens of Babylon, the Statue of Zeus at Olympia, the Temple of Artemis at Ephesus, the Mausoleum at Halicarnassus, the Colossus of Rhodes and the Lighthouse of Alexandria.
[11] *gannoid* more usually 'ganoid': covered with polished bony plates or scales, normally an epithet of fish.
[12] *paleontological* palaeontology is the department of geology or biology that treats of fossil animals and plants.
[13] *myriapod* having many legs.
[14] *Isabey* Jean Baptiste Isabey (1767–1855), French portrait painter.

And medicine, that he certainly was born
To be a surgeon: 'When you try', he said,
'To paint a boat you paint a tumour'.[15]

No
Idea of its purpose, and no word
Can make your glass and iron beautiful.   30
Colossal ugliness may fascinate
If something be expressed; and time adopts
Ungainliest stone and brick and ruins them
To beauty; but a building lacking life,
A house that must not mellow or decay? –   35
'Tis nature's outcast. Moss and lichen? Stains
Of weather? From the first Nature said 'No!
Shine there unblessed, a witness of my scorn!
I love the ashlar[16] and the well-baked clay;
My seasons can adorn them sumptuously: 40
But you shall stand rebuked till men ashamed,
Abhor you, and destroy you and repent!'

But come: here's crowd; here's mob; a gala day!
The walks are black with people: no one hastes;
They all pursue their purpose business-like –   45
The polo-ground, the cycle-track; but most
Invade the palace glumly once again.
It is 'again'; you feel it in the air –
Resigned habitués[17] on every hand:
And yet agog;[18] abandoned, yet concerned!   50
They can't tell why they come; they only know
They must shove through the holiday[19] somehow.

In the main floor the fretful multitude
Circulates from the north nave to the south
Across the central transept – swish and tread   55
And murmur, like a seaboard's[20] mingled sound.
About the sideshows eddies swirl and swing:
Distorting mirrors; waltzing-tops – wherein
Couples are wildly spun contrariwise
To your revolving platform; biographs,[21]   60
Or rifle-ranges; panoramas:[22] choose!

As stupid as it was last holiday?
They think so, – every whit! Outside, perhaps?
A spice of danger in the flying-machine?
A few who passed that whirligig,[23] their hopes   65

---

[15] *'When you . . . tumour'* source of anecdote unidentified.
[16] *ashlar* square hewn stone for building purposes.
[17] *habitués* habitual visitor or resident.
[18] *agog* in eager readiness.
[19] *holiday* the growing demand for more leisure time in the Victorian period led to the Bank Holiday Act of 1871 (which increased the number of holidays to 8 a year) and the Holidays Extension Act of 1875. Davidson uses the term 'holiday' with a sense of its modernity.
[20] *seaboard* coastline, seashore.
[21] *biograph* earlier form of cinema, introduced from the United States.
[22] *panorama* another visual device comprising a picture of a landscape or other scene unrolled or unfolded and made to pass before the viewer and showing the various parts in succession.
[23] *whirligig* any mechanical contrivance with a whirling movement.

On higher things, return disconsolate
To try the Tartar's volant[24] oratory.[25]
Others again, no more anticipant
Of any active business in their own
Diversion, joining stalwart folk who sought 70
At once the polo-ground, the cycle-track,
Accept the ineludible;[26] while some
(Insidious anti-climax here) frequent
The water-entertainments – shallops,[27] chutes
And rivers subterrene:[28] – thus, passive, all, 75
Like savages bewitched, submit at last
To be the dupes of pleasure, sadly gay –
Victims, and not companions, of delight!

Not all! The garden-terrace: – hark, behold,
Music and dancing! People by themselves 80
Attempting happiness! A box of reeds –
Accordion,[29] concertina,[30] seraphine[31] –
And practised fingers charm advertent[32] feet!
The girls can dance, but, O their heavy-shod
Unwieldy swains![33] – No matter: – hatless heads, 85
With hair undone, eyes shut and cheeks aglow
On blissful shoulders lie: – such solemn youths
Sustaining ravished donahs![34] Round they swing,
In time or out, but unashamed and all
Enchanted with the glory of the world. 90
And look! – Among the laurels on the lawns
Torn coats and ragged skirts, starved faces flushed
With passion and with wonder! – hid away
Avowedly; but seen – and yet not seen!
None laugh; none point; none notice; multitude 95
Remembers and forgives; unwisest love
Is sacrosanct upon a holiday.
Out of the slums, into the open air
Let loose for once, their scant economies
Already spent, what was there left to do? 100
O sweetly, tenderly, devoutly think,
Shepherd and Shepherdess in Arcady![35]

A heavy shower; the Palace fills; begins
The business and the office of the day,
The eating and the drinking – only real 105
Enjoyment to be had, they tell you straight
Now that the shifty[36] weather fails them too.

---

[24] *volant* moving rapidly or flying.
[25] *oratory* place of prayer.
[26] *ineludible* that which cannot be escaped.
[27] *shallops* small boats used in shallow waters.
[28] *subterrene* underground.
[29] *Accordion* portable musical hand-instrument invented in 1829.
[30] *concertina* related instrument invented in 1829.
[31] *seraphine* another reed musical instrument, invented in 1833.

[32] *advertent* attentive.
[33] *swains* lovers, usually in a pastoral context (and thus ironic).
[34] *donahs* Victorian slang: sweethearts.
[35] *Shepherd and Shepherdess in Arcady* ironic use of pastoral language: Arcady is Arcadia, literally the wide central region of the mountainous Peloponnese, but mythically the idealized setting of pastoral poetry and the locus of simple rural life.
[36] *shifty* with Victorian sense of changeable.

But what's the pother[37] here, the blank dismay?
Money has lost its value at the bars:
Like tavern–tokens[38] when the Boar's Head rang   110
With laughter and the Mermaid[39] swam in wine,
Tickets are now the only currency.
Before the buffets, metal tables packed
As closely as mosaic, with peopled chairs
Cementing them, where damsels in and out   115
Attend with food, like disembodied things
That traverse rock as easily as air –
These are the havens, these the happy isles![40]
A dozen people fight for every seat –
Without a quarrel, unturbently:[41] O,   120
A peaceable, a tame, a timorous crowd!
And yet relentless: this they know they need;
Here have they money's worth – some food, some drink;
And so alone, in couples, families, groups,
Consuming and consumed – for as they munch   125
Their victuals all their vitals ennui[42] gnaws –
They sit and sit, and fain[43] would sit it out
In tedious gormandize[44] till firework-time.
But business beats them: those who sit must eat.
Tickets are purchased at besieged kiosks,   130
And when their value's spent – with such a grudge! –
They rise to buy again, and lose their seats;
For this is Mob, unhappy locust-swarm,
Instinctive, apathetic, ravenous.

Beyond a doubt a most unhappy crowd!   135
Some scores of thousands searching up and down
The north nave and the south nave hungrily
For space to sit and rest to eat and drink:
Or captives in a labyrinth,[45] or herds
Imprisoned in a vast arena;[46] here   140
A moment clustered; there entangled; now
In reaches sped and now in whirlpools spun
With noises like the wind and like the sea,
But silent vocally: they hate to speak:
Crowd; Mob; a blur of faces featureless,   145
Of forms inane; a stranded shoal of folk.

Astounding in the midst of this to meet
Voltaire, the man who worshipped first, who made
Indeed, the only god men reverence now,
Public Opinion. There he sits alert –   150

[37] *pother* choking atmosphere of dust, commotion.
[38] *tavern-tokens* tokens given in change by a tavern-keeper, which he will again accept in payment.
[39] *Boar's Head* and *Mermaid* typical names of English pubs.
[40] *happy isles* isles of the blessed in Classical myth.
[41] *unturbently* contraction of 'unturbulently'.
[42] *ennui* boredom.
[43] *fain* gladly.
[44] *gormandize* gluttonous eating.
[45] *labyrinth* allusion to ancient Greek myth adds irony to Davidson's description of the uncultured crowd. The labyrinth was the complex maze-like prison in which the Minotaur, half man, half bull, was kept until being slain by Theseus.
[46] *arena* with Roman sense of a space for entertainments (usually cruel).

A cast of Houdon's smiling philosophe.[47]
Old lion-fox, old tiger-ape – what names
They gave him! – better charactered by one
Who was his heir: 'The amiable and gay'.
So said the pessimist who called life sour   155
And drank it to the dregs.[48] Enough: Voltaire –
About to speak: hands of a mummy[49] clutch
The fauteuil's[50] arms; he listens to the last
Before reply; one foot advanced; a new
Idea radiant in his wrinkled face.   160

Lunch in the grill-room for the well-to-do,
The spendthrifts and the connoisseurs of food –
Gourmet,[51] gourmand,[52] bezonian,[53] epicure.[54]
Reserved seats at the window? – Surely; you
And I must have the best place everywhere.   165
A deluge smudges out the landscape. Watch
The waiters since the scenery's not on view.
A harvest-day with them, our Switzers[55] – knights
Of the napkin! How they balance loaded trays
And though they push each other spill no drop!   170
And how they glare at lazy lunchers, snatch
Unfinished plates sans[56] 'by your leave', and fling
The next dish down, before the dazzled lout
(The Switzer knows his man) has time to con[57]
The menu, every tip precisely gauged,   175
Precisely earned, no service thrown away.
Sign of an extra douceur,[58] reprimand
Is welcomed, and the valetudinous[59]
Voluptuary served devoutly: he
With cauteries[60] on his cranium;[61] dyed moustache;   180
Teeth like a sea-wolf's,[62] each a work of art
Numbered and valued singly; copper skin;
And nether eyelids pouched: – why he alone
Is worth a half-day's wage! Waiters for him
Are pensioners of indigestion, paid   185
As secret criminals disburse[63] blackmail,
As Attic[64] gluttons sacrificed a cock

[47] *Houdon's smiling philosophe* Jean Antoine Houdon (1741–1828) was a French sculptor. Davidson is thinking of Houdon's *Voltaire* (1781), the original of which is in the Musée Fabre, Montpellier, France. Voltaire, depicted as a smiling elderly man, leans slightly forward in his chair, the arms of which he grips, as if listening to a speaker. The *philosophes* were the French Enlightenment philosophers who helped create the intellectual climate that fostered revolution.

[48] *pessimist . . . dregs* perhaps pessimistic German philosopher Arthur Schopenhauer (1788–1860); quotation unidentified.

[49] *mummy* Houdon's Voltaire looks emaciated.

[50] *fauteuil* armchair.

[51] *Gourmet* connoisseur of food.

[52] *gourmand* glutton.

[53] *bezonian* needy beggar, base person.

[54] *epicure* here, one who has given himself up to eating well.

[55] *Switzers* he thinks of the waiters as his own Switzers or personal guards.

[56] *sans* without (French).

[57] *con* examine.

[58] *douceur* tip.

[59] *valetudinous* invalid, weakly.

[60] *cauteries* scars sealed with heat.

[61] *cranium* skull.

[62] *sea-wolf's* pirate's.

[63] *disburse* pay out.

[64] *Attic* Greek.

To sculapius to propitiate
Hygeia[65] – if the classic flourish serves!

'Grilled soles?' – for us: – Kidneys to follow. – Now,   190
Your sole, sir; eat it with profound respect.
A little salt with one side; – scarce a pinch!
The other side with lemon; – tenderly!
Don't crush the starred bisection;[66] – count the drops!
Those who begin with lemon miss the true   195
Aroma: quicken sense with salt, and then
The subtle, poignant, citric savour tunes
The delicate texture of the foam-white fish,
Evolving palatable harmony
That music might by happy chance express.   200
A crust of bread – (eat slowly: thirty chews,
Gladstonian[67] rumination) – to change the key.
And now the wine – a well-decanted, choice
Chateau,[68] *bon per*;[69] a decade old; not more;
A velvet claret,[70] piously unchilled.   205
A boiled potato with the kidney . . . No!
Barbarian! Vandal! Sauce? 'Twould ruin all!
The kidney's the potato's sauce. Perpend:[71]
You taste the esoteric attribute
In food; and know that all necessity   210
Is beauty's essence. Fill your glass: salute
The memory of the happy neolith[72]
Who had the luck to hit on roast and boiled.
Finish the claret. – Now the rain has gone
The clouds are winnowed by the sighing south,   215
And hidden sunbeams through a silver woof[73]
A warp[74] of pallid bronze in secret ply.

Cigars and coffee in the billiard-room.
No soul here save the marker,[75] eating chops;
The waiter and the damsel at the bar,   220
In listless talk. A most uncanny thing,
To enter suddenly a desolate cave
Upon the margent[76] of the sounding Mob!
A hundred thousand people, class and mass,
In and about the palace, and not a pair   225
To play a hundred up! The billiard-room's
The smoking-room; and spacious too, like all
The apartments of the Palace: – why
Unused on holidays? The marker: aged;

[65] *sacrificed . . . Hygeia* Aesculapius is the Roman god of healing; Hygeia is the Greek personification of health. The traditional sacrifice for a cure was a cock to the god (Socrates's last words, according to Plato, were that he owed a cock to Aesculapius).
[66] *starred bisection* slice of lemon (centre looking like a star).
[67] *Gladstonian* William Ewart Gladstone (1809–98), four times Liberal prime minister of England: an intellectual imagined here as characteristically thoughtful.
[68] *choice / Chateau* i.e., French wine from a good vineyard.
[69] *bon per* (French) 'good for', i.e., 'good/fine as usual', 'as good as ever'.
[70] *claret* English name for red wine imported from Bordeaux in France.
[71] *Perpend* consider.
[72] *neolith* person of the later Stone Age.
[73] *woof* threads that cross from side to side of a web.
[74] *warp* threads at right angles to the woof.
[75] *marker* for the billiards.
[76] *margent* margin.

Short, broad, but of a presence; reticent   230
And self-respecting; not at all the type: –
'O well', says he; 'the business of the room
Fluctuates very little, year in, year out.
My customers are seasons mostly'. One
On the instant enters: a curate, very much   235
At ease in Zion[77] – and in Sydenham.[78]
He tells two funny stories – not of the room;
And talks about the stage. 'In London now',
He thinks, 'the play's the thing.[79] He undertakes
To entertain and not to preach: you see,   240
It's with the theatre and the music-hall,
Actor and artiste, the parson must compete.
Every bank-holiday and special day
The Crystal Palace sees him. Yes; he feels
His hand's upon the public pulse on such   245
Occasions'. O, a sanguine[80] clergyman!

Heard in the billiard-room the sound of Mob,
Occult[81] and ominous, besets the mind:
Something gigantic, something terrible
Passes without; repasses; lingers; goes;   250
Returns and on the threshold pants in doubt
Whether to knock and enter, or burst the door
In hope of treasure and a living prey.
The vainest fantasy! Rejoin the crowd:
At once the sound depreciates. Up and down   255
The north nave and the south nave hastily
Some tens of thousands walk, silent and sad,
A most unhappy people. – Hereabout
Cellini's Perseus[82] ought to be. Not that;
That's stucco[83] – and Canova's:[84] a stupid thing;   260
The face and posture of a governess –
A nursery governess who's had the nerve
To pick a dead mouse up.[85] It used to stand
Beside the billiard-room, against the wall,
A cast of Benvenuto's masterpiece –   265
That came out lame, as he foretold, despite
His dinner dishes in the foundry flung.
They shift their sculpture here haphazard. – That?
King Francis – by Clesinger[86] – on a horse.
Absurd: most mounted statues are. – And this?   270
Verrochio's Coleone.[87] Not absurd:

---

[77] *very . . . Zion* cf. Amos 6.1, 'Woe to them that are at ease in Zion [the house of God]'.
[78] *Sydenham* the new Crystal Palace, moved from Hyde Park, was opened at Sydenham, south London, by Queen Victoria in June 1854.
[79] *the play's the thing* Davidson makes the curate refer to Shakespeare's *Hamlet* 2.2.606–7: 'The play's the thing / Wherein I'll catch the conscience of the king.'
[80] *sanguine* hopeful.
[81] *Occult* not visible.
[82] *Cellini's Perseus* Benvenuto Cellini (1500–71), Florentine goldsmith, sculptor and autobiographer. His bronze *Perseus* (1545–54) is in the Loggia dei Lanzi, Florence.

[83] *stucco* fine plaster.
[84] *Canova's* Antonio Canova (1757–1822), Italian sculptor.
[85] *mouse up* Perseus holds the severed head of Medusa high in his left hand.
[86] *Clesinger* Jean-Baptiste Clesinger (1814–83), French sculptor.
[87] *Verrochio's Coleone* one of the most famous of all equestrian statues, standing in the campo beside San Giovanni e Paolo in Venice. Andrea del Verrocchio (1433–88) was a Florentine sculptor, Bartolomeo Colleoni (1400–75), a famous Venetian *condottiere* or hired commander.

Grotesque and strong, the battle-harlot rides
A stallion; fore and aft, his saddle, peaked
Like a mitre, grips him as in a vice.
In heavy armour mailed; his lifted helm   275
Reveals his dreadful look; his brows are drawn;
Four wrinkles deeply trench his muscular face;
His left arm half-extended, and the reins
Held carelessly, although the gesture's tense;
His right hand wields a sword invisible;   280
Remorseless pressure of his lips protrudes
His mouth; he would decapitate the world.

The light is artificial now; the place
Phantasmal like a beach in hell where souls
Are ground together by an unseen sea.   285
A dense throng in the central transept, wedged
So tightly they can neither clap nor stamp,
Shouting applause at something, goad themselves
In sheer despair to think it rather fine:
'We came here to enjoy ourselves. Bravo,   290
Then! Are we not?' Courageous folk beneath
The brows of Michael Angelo's Moses[88] dance
A cakewalk[89] in the dim Renascence Court.[90]
Three people in the silent Reading-room
Regard us darkly as we enter: three   295
Come in with us, stare vacantly about,
Look from the window and withdraw at once.
A drama; a balloon; a Beauty Show: –
People have seen them doubtless; but none of those
Deluded myriads[91] walking up and down   300
The north nave and the south nave anxiously –
And aimlessly, so silent and so sad.

The day wears; twilight ends; the night comes down.
A ruddy targelike[92] moon in a purple sky,
And the crowd waiting on the fireworks. Come: 305
Enough of Mob for one while. This way out –
Past Linacre[93] and Chatham,[94] the second Charles,[95]
Venus[96] and Victory[97] – and Sir William Jones[98]
In placid contemplation of a State! –
Down the long corridor to the district train.   310

---

[88] *Michael Angelo* Michelangelo Buonarroti (1475–1564), Italian High Renaissance painter and sculptor. His *Moses* (1515) is from the base of his *Tomb of Julius II* (1545).
[89] *cakewalk* modern dance, derived from the black communities of the southern United States.
[90] *Renascence Court* area of the Exhibition devoted to the Renaissance.
[91] *myriads* tens of thousands.
[92] *targelike* like a shield.

[93] *Linacre* statue of Thomas Linacre (*c.*1460–1524), founder of the Royal College of Physicians.
[94] *Chatham* statue of William Pitt the Elder, Earl of Chatham (1708–78).
[95] *second Charles* Charles II, King of England (1660–85).
[96] *Venus* statue of the Roman goddess of love.
[97] *Victory* statue of Nike, Greek goddess of victory.
[98] *Sir William Jones* (1746–94), English orientalist, pioneer of comparative philology, student of eastern languages.

May Kendall (1861–?1943)

May Kendall (Emma Goldworth Kendall) was born the daughter of a Wesleyan minister in Bridlington, Yorkshire. She published a collection of satiric verse and essays of social satire as *That Very Mab* in 1885, nominally with the joint authorship of the poet, historian, anthropologist and fairy-tale writer Andrew Lang (1844–1912). *Dreams to Sell* (1887) was her first explicitly solo volume of verse including work – satirical, reformist – that she had previously issued in magazines. *Songs from Dreamland* appeared in 1894 and a collection of stories on the side of the Armenians massacred by the Turks (and a variety of Ottoman irregulars) in 1895 entitled *Turkish Bonds* (1898). With this publication, Kendall gave up writing to dedicate herself to social reform, particularly helping the Quaker Rowntree family in York, where she lived for most of her life (10 Monkgate). She none the less discreetly assisted with others' publications including B. Seebohm Rowntree's book on the minimum wage, *The Human Needs of Labour* (1918). She refused any salary, and clearly had independent means. It is not known when this self-effacing woman died – sometime between 1931 and the usually given 1943.

Lay of the Trilobite

There is a healthy tradition of comic poetry in the Victorian period, most memorably in the work of Edward Lear (1812–88) and Charles Lutwidge Dodgson ('Lewis Carroll', 1832–98). May Kendall's 'Lay of the Trilobite' ('lay' = song) turns comedy to satiric purposes in considering the 'advance' of evolution and the 'supremacy' of man. Victorian satire is often assumed confined to fiction – Dickens, Thackeray, Samuel Butler – and spurned by nineteenth-century poets. But the public mode of satire did appeal to some; cf., in this edition, A. H. Clough's 'The Latest Decalogue', 262–3, D. G. Rossetti, 'The Burden of Nineveh', 350–6, and John Davidson's 'Snow', 616–18.

Exploiting the Victorian fascination with fossils, Kendall produces witty but devastating satire on modern pretensions to superiority in its consideration of the lessons of a trilobite, an extinct marine creature, like a three-lobed crab, whose remains are often found in rocks from the ancient Silurian period. The creature's cheerful account of his life in prehistoric seas is in sharp contrast to the depiction of modern human existence and its intellectual and artistic achievements. The chief victims of this poem are those who thought the Darwinian conception of evolution meant simply progress and that the pattern of earth's development was upwards towards the creation of human beings, earth's finest achievement. (Charles Darwin [1809–82] himself was consistently ambiguous in equating evolution with progress, but popular versions of his theory found no difficulty in making the association.) The 'Lay' (1887) is also a satire on the kind of faith in progress that consoled Tennyson (in his case a pre-Darwinian one) in *In Memoriam A.H.H.*, 88–165, for the loss of Hallam, the 'higher' species of human being.

Text: *Dreams to Sell* (1887).

A mountain's giddy height I sought,
Because I could not find
Sufficient vague and mighty thought
To fill my mighty mind;
And as I wandered ill at ease,
There chanced upon my sight
A native of Silurian[1] seas,
An ancient Trilobite.

5

---

[1] *Silurian* name given to the ancient period during which the Silurian system of Palaeozoic rocks was formed (period of trilobites).

2

So calm, so peacefully he lay,
I watched him even with tears: 10
I thought of Monads[2] far away
In the forgotten years.
How wonderful it seemed and right,
The providential plan,
That he should be a Trilobite,   15
And I should be a Man!

3

And then, quite natural and free
Out of his rocky bed,
That Trilobite he spoke to me
And this is what he said: 20
'I don't know how the thing was done,
Although I cannot doubt it;
But Huxley[3] – he if anyone
Can tell you all about it;

4

'How all your faiths are ghosts and dreams,   25
How in the silent sea
Your ancestors were Monotremes[4] –
Whatever these may be;
How you evolved your shining lights
Of wisdom and perfection   30
From Jelly-Fish and Trilobites
By Natural Selection.[5]

5

'You've Kant[6] to make your brains go round,
Hegel[7] you have to clear them,
You've Mr Browning[8] to confound,   35
And Mr Punch[9] to cheer them!
The native of an alien land
You call a man and brother,
And greet with hymn-book in one hand
And pistol in the other![10]   40

6

'You've Politics to make you fight
As if you were possessed:

---

[2] *Monad* hypothetical simple organism, assumed in evolutionary speculations as the first term in the genealogy of living beings.
[3] *Huxley* Thomas Henry Huxley (1825–95), evolutionary biologist and influential proponent of Darwinian theory.
[4] *Monotremes* non-complex creatures with only one opening for the genital, urinary and digestive organs.
[5] *Natural Selection* Darwinian theory of evolution by natural selection: creatures born with natural accidental advantages are more successful in the struggle for existence and thus 'naturally selected' to continue the existence of their species.

[6] *Kant* Immanuel Kant (1724–1804), German philosopher (whose work is famously difficult).
[7] *Hegel* G. W. F. Hegel (1770–1831), German philosopher (whose work is also famously difficult).
[8] *Browning* Robert Browning (1812–89), English poet (see 171–216): known as challengingly obscure in the period.
[9] *Mr Punch* the comic periodical *Punch, or The London Charivari* was first published in 1841.
[10] *The native . . . other!* satirical reference to the activities of English missionaries.

You've cannon and you've dynamite
To give the nations rest:
The side that makes the loudest din   45
Is surest to be right,
And oh, a pretty fix you're in!'
Remarked the Trilobite.

7

'But gentle, stupid, free from woe
I lived among my nation,   50
I didn't care – I didn't know
That I was a Crustacean.[11]
I didn't grumble, didn't steal,
I *never* took to rhyme:
Salt water was my frugal meal,   55
And carbonate of lime.'

8

Reluctantly I turned away,
No other word he said;
An ancient Trilobite, he lay
Within his rocky bed.   60
I did not answer him, for that
Would have annoyed my pride:
I merely bowed, and raised my hat,
But in my heart I cried: –

9

'I wish our brains were not so good,   65
I wish our skulls were thicker,
I wish that Evolution could
Have stopped a little quicker;
For oh, it was a happy plight,
Of liberty and ease,   70
To be a simple Trilobite
In the Silurian seas!'

---

[11] *Crustacean* 'He was not a Crustacean. He has since discovered that he was an Arachnid, or something similar. But he says it does not matter. He says they told him wrong once, and they may again' (Kendall's note). The classification of the trilobite remains doubtful. They are usually classed as crustaceans, but also sometimes as arachnids.

Amy Levy (1861–1889)

Amy Levy was born in Clapham, London, educated in Brighton, and was the first Jewish student to be admitted to Newnham College Cambridge (founded in 1871 for women only). She had published a poem at the age of 13, and continued to write while at university. Her first volume, *Xantippe and Other Verse*, was issued in 1881, its title poem an oblique discussion of modern Cambridge. After a relatively short period, however, Levy abandoned her studies (it is not clear why) and returned to her parents' house in London. She continued writing, publishing poems and stories in, for instance, *Woman's World* and the *Jewish Chronicle*. Her second volume, *A Minor Poet and Other Verse*, came out in 1884, and the following year, Levy and her friend Clementina Black visited Italy, where she met Vernon Lee (Violet Paget), the essayist, novelist and travel writer. Returning to England, she acted as secretary to the Beaumont Trust, raising funds for education in London's East End, and came to know the socialist, writer and theatre enthusiast Eleanor Marx (1855–98). Marx translated Levy's second novel – *Rueben Sachs* (1888) – into German (prior to this Levy had written *The Romance of a Shop* [1888] and after it, *Miss Meredith* [1889]). Levy was known to suffer from 'fits of extreme depression', as Clementina Black described it, and, after correcting the proofs of her final volume, *A London Plane-Tree and Other Verse* (1889), she killed herself, at the age of 27, by inhaling charcoal fumes.

Xantippe: A Fragment

Other earlier Victorian women poets including Elizabeth Barrett Browning ('Rime of the Duchess May', 29–44) and Augusta Webster ('Circe', 450–5) had used figures of history, myth and literature to intervene in contemporary debates about gender identity and politics. Amy Levy's 'Xantippe' (pronounced 'Zantipay') is a peculiarly rich example of the later feminist appropriation of history. It is an anxious protest about the opportunities of modern female education displaced onto an historical scene. Amy Levy takes a woman from the prestigious male world of ancient Greek philosophy to articulate a claim about the nature of female experience and to express impatience with cultural perceptions of femininity, opportunities for education and the closed male circles of contemporary intellectual culture (for another perspective on exclusion from intellectual circles, see 'A Minor Poet', 636–42).

Xantippe was, historically, the wife of the great Greek philosopher Socrates (469–399 BC), whose thought inspired Plato and helped define ancient Athenian philosophy. Xantippe is represented throughout English literature as a shrew. Her most infamous incarnation is in Chaucer's *The Canterbury Tales*. Iankin, the husband of the Wife of Bath in the *Wife of Bath's Prologue*, includes Xantippe in his list of miscreant women: 'Nothing forgat he,' the Wife recalls:

> the penaunce and wo
> That Socrates had with hise wyves two;
> How Xantippa caste pisse up-on his heed;

> This sely [silly] man sat stille, as he were deed;
> He wyped his heed, namore dorste he seyn
> But 'er that thonder stinte [stops], comth a reyn'.

Levy writes her version of Xantippe against the misogyny of a long historical tradition of which Chaucer's Iankin is only the most spritely representative. The poem is revisionary in intent, and tackles the whole question of the authority of history not only by rewriting Xantippe's story – though it does not allow her anything other than ultimate failure – but also by staging a debate that explicitly involves the consideration of the ownership of history and the kind of authority the past possesses. After Xantippe has declared her views on the condition of women, Socrates replies: 'From what high source, from what philosophies / Didst cull the sapient notion of thy words?' But the poem itself answers Socrates, for its substance challenges the legitimacy of history as an authority by showing how it has yielded to misogynistic forces (cf. the headnote to Eugene Lee-Hamilton's 'The New Medusa', 545–53).

'Xantippe' first appeared in the *University Magazine* for May 1880 and is a comment indirectly on Oxford and Cambridge Universities: it implicitly expresses support for the foundations of the women's colleges there (e.g., Newnham at Cambridge, founded in 1871, and Lady Margaret Hall and Somerville Hall Oxford, founded in 1878 and 1879, respectively). None the less, the poem is riven with guilt and gloom about defiance, and refuses to rewrite history to the extent of allowing Xantippe the same apparent success as Aspasia, the mistress of Pericles, who is in shadowy conflict with her throughout her monologue. Xantippe's final words – 'give me light!' – are in ironic relationship with her defeated desires for intellectual enlightenment. Some readers have felt that Levy's use of an historical figure impedes as much as it enables her critique of the contemporary. But the effect of Xantippe's story is still a powerful one that escapes from the bounds of its historical context. The polemic use of the monologue form can be compared with Webster's 'Circe' and 'Faded', 471–5.

Text: *Xantippe and Other Verse* (1881).

What, have I waked again? I never thought
To see the rosy dawn, or ev'n this grey,
Dull, solemn stillness, ere the dawn has come.
The lamp burns low; low burns the lamp of life:
The still morn stays expectant, and my soul,   5
All weighted with a passive wonderment,
Waiteth and watcheth, waiteth for the dawn.
Come hither, maids; too soundly have ye slept
That should have watched me; nay, I would not chide –
Oft have I chidden, yet I would not chide   10
In this last hour; – now all should be at peace.
I have been dreaming in a troubled sleep
Of weary days I thought not to recall;
Of stormy days, whose storms are hushed long since;
Of gladsome days, of sunny days; alas   15
In dreaming, all their sunshine seem'd so sad,
As though the current of the dark To-Be
Had flow'd, prophetic, through the happy hours.
And yet, full well, I know it was not thus;
I mind me sweetly of the summer days,   20
When, leaning from the lattice, I have caught
The fair, far glimpses of a shining sea;
And, nearer, of tall ships which thronged the bay,
And stood out blackly from a tender sky
All flecked with sulphur, azure, and bright gold;   25
And in the still, clear air have heard the hum
Of distant voices; and methinks there rose
No darker fount to mar or stain the joy
Which sprang ecstatic in my maiden breast
Than just those vague desires, those hopes and fears,   30
Those eager longings, strong, though undefined,
Whose very sadness makes them seem so sweet.
What cared I for the merry mockeries
Of other maidens sitting at the loom?
Or for sharp voices, bidding me return   35
To maiden labour? Were we not apart –
I and my high thoughts, and my golden dreams,
My soul which yearned for knowledge, for a tongue
That should proclaim the stately mysteries
Of this fair world, and of the holy gods?   40
Then followed days of sadness, as I grew
To learn my woman-mind had gone astray,
And I was sinning in those very thoughts –
For maidens, mark, such are not woman's thoughts –
(And yet, 'tis strange, the gods who fashion us   45

Have given us such promptings) . . .
Fled the years,
Till seventeen had found me tall and strong,
And fairer, runs it, than Athenian[1] maids
Are wont to seem; I had not learnt it well –   50
My lesson of dumb patience – and I stood
At Life's great threshold with a beating heart,
And soul resolved to conquer and attain . . .
Once, walking 'thwart[2] the crowded market-place,
With other maidens, bearing in the twigs   55
White doves for Aphrodite's[3] sacrifice,
I saw him, all ungainly and uncouth,
Yet many gathered round to hear his words,
Tall youths and stranger-maidens – Sokrates[4] –
I saw his face and marked it, half with awe,   60
Half with a quick repulsion at the shape . . .
The richest gem lies hidden furthest down,
And is the dearer for the weary search;
We grasp the shining shells which strew the shore,
Yet swift we fling them from us; but the gem   65
We keep for aye[5] and cherish. So a soul,
Found after weary searching in the flesh
Which half repelled our senses, is more dear,
For that same seeking, than the sunny mind
Which lavish Nature marks with thousand hints   70
Upon a brow of beauty. We are prone
To overweigh such subtle hints, then deem,
In after disappointment, we are fooled . . .
And when, at length, my father told me all,
That I should wed me with great Sokrates,   75
I, foolish, wept to see at once cast down
The maiden image of a future love,
Where perfect body matched the perfect soul.
But slowly, softly did I cease to weep;
Slowly I 'gan to mark the magic flash   80
Leap to the eyes, to watch the sudden smile
Break round the mouth, and linger in the eyes;
To listen for the voice's lightest tone –
Great voice, whose cunning modulations seemed
Like to the notes of some sweet instrument.   85
So did I reach and strain, until at last
I caught the soul athwart the grosser flesh.
Again of thee, sweet Hope, my spirit dreamed!
I, guided by his wisdom and his love,
Led by his words, and counselled by his care,   90
Should lift the shrouding veil from things which be,
And at the flowing fountain of his soul
Refresh my thirsting spirit . . .
And indeed,
In those long days which followed that strange day   95

---

[1] *Athenian* Xantippe is from Athens, capital of Greece and centre of Socratic/Platonic thought.
[2] *'thwart* across.
[3] *Aphrodite* Greek goddess of beauty and sexual attraction.
[4] *Sokrates* Socrates (469–399 BC), Greek philosopher, who, though he wrote nothing, strongly influenced Plato.
[5] *aye* ever.

When rites and song, and sacrifice and flow'rs,
Proclaimed that we were wedded, did I learn,
In sooth, a-many lessons; bitter ones
Which sorrow taught me, and not love inspired,
Which deeper knowledge of my kind impressed   100
With dark insistence on reluctant brain; –
But that great wisdom, deeper, which dispels
Narrowed conclusions of a half-grown mind,
And sees athwart the littleness of life
Nature's divineness and her harmony,   105
Was never poor Xantippe's . . .
I would pause
And would recall no more, no more of life,
Than just the incomplete, imperfect dream
Of early summers, with their light and shade,   110
Their blossom-hopes, whose fruit was never ripe;
But something strong within me, some sad chord
Which loudly echoes to the later life,
Me to unfold the after-misery
Urges, with plaintive wailing in my heart.   115
Yet, maidens, mark; I would not that ye thought
I blame my lord departed,[6] for he meant
No evil, so I take it, to his wife.
'Twas only that the high philosopher,
Pregnant with noble theories and great thoughts,   120
Deigned not to stoop to touch so slight a thing
As the fine fabric of a woman's brain –
So subtle as a passionate woman's soul.
I think, if he had stooped a little, and cared,
I might have risen nearer to his height,   125
And not lain shattered, neither fit for use
As goodly household vessel, nor for that
Far finer thing which I had hoped to be . . .
Death, holding high his retrospective lamp,
Shows me those first, far years of wedded life,   130
Ere I had learnt to grasp the barren shape
Of what the Fates had destined for my life
Then, as all youthful spirits are, was I
Wholly incredulous that Nature meant
So little, who had promised me so much.   135
At first I fought my fate with gentle words,
With high endeavours after greater things;
Striving to win the soul of Sokrates,
Like some slight bird, who sings her burning love
To human master, till at length she finds   140
Her tender language wholly misconceived,
And that same hand whose kind caress she sought,
With fingers flippant flings the careless corn . . .
I do remember how, one summer's eve,
He, seated in an arbour's leafy shade,   145
Had bade me bring fresh wine-skins[7] . . .

---

[6] *lord departed* Socrates was sentenced to death for introducing strange gods and corrupting youth; see note 24.

[7] *wine-skins* receptacles of animal skin for the storage of wine.

As I stood
Ling'ring upon the threshold, half concealed
By tender foliage, and my spirit light
With draughts of sunny weather, did I mark   150
An instant the gay group before mine eyes.
Deepest in shade, and facing where I stood,
Sat Plato,[8] with his calm face and low brows
Which met above the narrow Grecian eyes,
The pale, thin lips just parted to the smile,   155
Which dimpled that smooth olive of his cheek.
His head a little bent, sat Sokrates,
With one swart[9] finger raised admonishing,
And on the air were borne his changing tones.
Low lounging at his feet, one fair arm thrown   160
Around his knee (the other, high in air
Brandish'd a brazen[10] amphor,[11] which yet rained
Bright drops of ruby on the golden locks
And temples with their fillets[12] of the vine),
Lay Alkibiades[13] the beautiful.   165
And thus, with solemn tone, spake Sokrates:
'This fair Aspasia,[14] which our Perikles[15]
Hath brought from realms afar, and set on high
In our Athenian city, hath a mind,
I doubt not, of a strength beyond her race;   170
And makes employ of it, beyond the way
Of women nobly gifted: woman's frail –
Her body rarely stands the test of soul;
She grows intoxicate with knowledge; throws
The laws of custom, order, 'neath her feet,   175
Feasting at life's great banquet with wide throat.'
Then sudden, stepping from my leafy screen,
Holding the swelling wine-skin o'er my head,
With breast that heaved, and eyes and cheeks aflame,
Lit by a fury and a thought, I spake: 180
'By all great powers around us! can it be
That we poor women are empirical?[16]
That gods who fashioned us did strive to make
Beings too fine, too subtly delicate,
With sense that thrilled response to ev'ry touch   185
Of nature's, and their task is not complete?
That they have sent their half-completed work
To bleed and quiver here upon the earth?
To bleed and quiver, and to weep and weep,
To beat its soul against the marble walls   190
Of men's cold hearts, and then at last to sin!'

---

[8] *Plato* Greek philosopher (*c.*428–*c.*348 BC), friend and
admirer of Socrates.
[9] *swart* dark.
[10] *brazen* brass.
[11] *amphor* (amphora) two-handled ancient vessel for holding
wine or oil.
[12] *fillets* a band, as for hair: the drops falling on Socrates's
head are like a kind of hairband made of spilt wine.
[13] *Alkibiades* (Alcibiades) (*c.*450–404 BC), friend of Socrates,
statesman and general.

[14] *Aspasia* (470–410 BC), mistress of Pericles, whose
intellectual eminence led to her acquaintance with Socrates.
[15] *Perikles* (Pericles) (495–429 BC), great Athenian
statesman, rebuilder of Athens.
[16] *empirical* in matters of art or practice, guided by mere
experience, without scientific knowledge; here with the
opprobrious sense meaning ignorantly presumptuous.

I ceased, the first hot passion stayed and stemmed
And frighted by the silence: I could see,
Framed by the arbour[17] foliage, which the sun
   In setting softly gilded with rich gold,   195
Those upturned faces, and those placid limbs;
Saw Plato's narrow eyes and niggard[18] mouth,
Which half did smile and half did criticise,
One hand held up, the shapely fingers framed
   To gesture of entreaty – 'Hush, I pray,   200
   Do not disturb her; let us hear the rest;
Follow her mood, for here's another phase
   Of your black-browed Xantippe . . .'
         Then I saw
   Young Alkibiades, with laughing lips   205
And half-shut eyes, contemptuous shrugging up
Soft, snowy shoulders, till he brought the gold
Of flowing ringlets round about his breasts.
   But Sokrates, all slow and solemnly,
Raised, calm, his face to mine, and sudden spake: 210
   'I thank thee for the wisdom which thy lips
Have thus let fall among us: prythee[19] tell
From what high source, from what philosophies
Didst cull the sapient[20] notion of thy words?'
   Then stood I straight and silent for a breath,   215
Dumb, crushed with all that weight of cold contempt;
   But swiftly in my bosom there uprose
   A sudden flame, a merciful fury sent
   To save me; with both angry hands I flung
   The skin upon the marble, where it lay   220
Spouting red rills and fountains on the white;
   Then, all unheeding faces, voices, eyes,
   I fled across the threshold, hair unbound –
White garment stained to redness – beating heart
   Flooded with all the flowing tide of hopes   225
Which once had gushed out golden, now sent back
Swift to their sources, never more to rise . . .
   I think I could have borne the weary life,
   The narrow life within the narrow walls,
   If he had loved me; but he kept his love   230
   For this Athenian city and her sons;
And, haply, for some stranger-woman,[21] bold
With freedom, thought, and glib philosophy . . .
Ah me! the long, long weeping through the nights,
   The weary watching for the pale-eyed dawn   235
Which only brought fresh grieving: then I grew
Fiercer, and cursed from out my inmost heart
The Fates which marked me an Athenian maid.
   Then faded that vain fury; hope died out;
   A huge despair was stealing on my soul,   240
   A sort of fierce acceptance of my fate, –

---

[17] *arbour* shady retreat formed of intertwining trees and shrubs.
[18] *niggard* mean, stingy.

[19] *prythee* please.
[20] *sapient* wise.
[21] *stranger-woman* Aspasia.

He wished a household vessel – well 'twas good,
For he should have it! He should have no more
The yearning treasure of a woman's love,
But just the baser treasure which he sought.   245
I called my maidens, ordered out the loom,
And spun unceasing from the morn till eve;
Watching all keenly over warp[22] and woof,[23]
Weighing the white wool with a jealous hand.
I spun until, methinks, I spun away   250
The soul from out my body, the high thoughts
From out my spirit; till at last I grew
As ye have known me, – eye exact to mark
The texture of the spinning; ear all keen
For aimless talking when the moon is up,   255
And ye should be a-sleeping; tongue to cut
With quick incision, 'thwart the merry words
Of idle maidens . . .
Only yesterday
My hands did cease from spinning; I have wrought   260
My dreary duties, patient till the last.
The gods reward me! Nay, I will not tell
The after years of sorrow; wretched strife
With grimmest foes – sad Want and Poverty; –
Nor yet the time of horror, when they bore   265
My husband from the threshold; nay, nor when
The subtle weed had wrought its deadly work.[24]
Alas! alas! I was not there to soothe
The last great moment; never any thought
Of her that loved him – save at least the charge,   270
All earthly, that her body should not starve . . .
You weep, you weep; I would not that ye wept;
Such tears are idle; with the young, such grief
Soon grows to gratulation,[25] as, 'her love
Was withered by misfortune; mine shall grow   275
All nurtured by the loving,' or, 'her life
Was wrecked and shattered – mine shall smoothly sail.'
Enough, enough. In vain, in vain, in vain!
The gods forgive me! Sorely have I sinned
In all my life. A fairer fate befall   280
You all that stand there.
Ha! the dawn has come;
I see a rosy glimmer – nay! it grows dark;
Why stand ye so in silence? throw it wide,
The casement, quick; why tarry? – give me air –   285
O fling it wide, I say, and give me light!

[22] *warp* threads which are extended lengthwise in the loom.
[23] *woof* threads that cross from side to side.

[24] *subtle weed . . . work* Socrates died by being forced to drink liquid containing hemlock, a deadly poisonous plant.
[25] *gratulation* joy.

A Minor Poet

Amy Levy's interest in this poem with a suicidal minor poet indicates her move away from the gender issues that concerned her in the earlier 'Xantippe', 630–6. Choosing a male speaker to forestall a reading prioritizing feminist critique, her focus is more generally on the psychology of a writer unsuited to the world. The Romantic myth of the poet-genius is ousted in this presentation of the depressing realities of life as a *minor* author. As in 'Xantippe', 'A Minor Poet' (1884) considers the individual excluded from intellectual circles, with their potential to support suffering minds. Xantippe failed to break into Socrates's closed circle; the minor poet's books are a sadly parodic version of a sustaining cadre of literary allies.

'A Minor Poet' comments bleakly on some earlier texts from the period, reflecting darkly on the male legacy Levy inherited as a late Victorian writer but creatively transforming it for her own purposes. The poem perhaps offers, for instance, an etiolated version of Goethe's *Die Leiden des jungen Werthers* (1774), usually translated as *The Sorrows of Young Werther*. Closer to its own time, it is also a subtle rewriting of Matthew Arnold's 'Empedocles on Etna', 268–95. Levy's text replaces the intellectual ruminations of Arnold's philosopher with those of the desperate second-rate writer, who, we finally learn, has been unlucky in love. The relationship of 'A Minor Poet' to 'Empedocles' is deeply bathetic and it implies the historical decline that has occurred from the ancient period to the 'world of woe' that constitutes the present. Levy's minor poet recalls Empedocles's end

the moment before his own suicide, but he possesses none of the same tragic stature. The low world in which *he* lives does not permit it.

'A Minor Poet' is also a gloomy reply to Robert Browning's conception of authorship and the necessity of failure for human moral and aesthetic advancement (cf. Browning's 'Andrea del Sarto', 189–95, and Levy's 'Xantippe' as another poem about failure). Failure in 'A Minor Poet' does not inspire new endeavour, but disastrously overwhelms. It is not an agent for moral advance, but a brutal reality of an unsuccessful life. Levy's interest in the plight of a struggling man in the dismal city can be compared to John Davidson's figures clinging to their lives, such as the speaker of 'Thirty Bob a Week', 606–9, and the bleaker canvas of James Thomson's *The City of Dreadful Night*, 394–422. Levy sees the monologue as ideal for the representation of conflicted consciousnesses and in this she shares her approach with Charlotte Mew (cf. 'The Forest Road', 680–2). In writing of the poet's lonely suicide, Levy seemed somehow to be fantasizing about the nature of her death.

Text: *A Minor Poet and Other Verse* (1884).

> '*What should such fellows as I do,*
> *Crawling between earth and heaven?*'[1]

Here is the phial;[2] here I turn the key
Sharp in the lock. Click! – there's no doubt it turned.
This is the third time;[3] there is luck in threes –
Queen Luck, that rules the world, befriend me now
And freely I'll forgive you many wrongs!   5
Just as the draught began to work, first time,
Tom Leigh, my friend (as friends go in the world),
Burst in, and drew the phial from my hand,
(Ah, Tom! ah, Tom! that was a sorry turn!)
And lectured me a lecture, all compact   10
Of neatest, newest phrases, freshly culled
From works of newest culture: 'common good;'
'The world's great harmonies;' 'must be content
With knowing God works all things for the best,
And Nature never stumbles.' Then again,   15
'The common good,' and still, 'the common, good;'
And what a small thing was our joy or grief
When weigh'd with that of thousands. Gentle Tom,
But you might wag your philosophic tongue
From morn till eve, and still the thing's the same: 20
I am myself, as each man is himself –
Feels his own pain, joys his own joy, and loves
With his own love, no other's. Friend, the world

---

[1] '*What . . . heaven?*' from *Hamlet* 3.1.129–30.
[2] *phial* small vessel for holding liquids.
[3] *third time* third attempt to commit suicide.

Is but one man; one man is but the world.
And I am I, and you are Tom, that bleeds   25
When needles prick your flesh (mark, yours, not mine).
I must confess it; I can feel the pulse
A-beating at my heart, yet never knew
The throb of cosmic pulses. I lament
The death of youth's ideal in my heart;   30
And, to be honest, never yet rejoiced
In the world's progress – scarce, indeed, discerned;
(For still it seems that God's a Sisyphus[4]
With the world for stone).
You shake your head. I'm base,   35
Ignoble? Who is noble – you or I?
I was not once thus? Ah, my friend, we are
As the Fates make us.
This time is the third;
The second time the flask fell from my hand,   40
Its drowsy juices spilt upon the board;
And there my face fell flat, and all the life
Crept from my limbs, and hand and foot were bound
With mighty chains, subtle, intangible;
While still the mind held to its wonted[5] use,   45
Or rather grew intense and keen with dread,
An awful dread – I thought I was in Hell.
In Hell, in Hell! Was ever Hell conceived
By mortal brain, by brain Divine devised,
Darker, more fraught with torment, than the world   50
For such as I? A creature maimed and marr'd
From very birth. A blot, a blur, a note
All out of tune in this world's instrument.
A base thing, yet not knowing to fulfil
Base functions. A high thing, yet all unmeet[6]   55
For work that's high. A dweller on the earth,
Yet not content to dig with other men
Because of certain sudden sights and sounds
(Bars of broke music; furtive, fleeting glimpse
Of angel faces 'thwart[7] the grating seen)   60
Perceived in Heaven. Yet when I approach
To catch the sound's completeness, to absorb
The faces' full perfection, Heaven's gate,
Which then had stood ajar, sudden falls to,
And I, a-shiver in the dark and cold,   65
Scarce hear afar the mocking tones of men:
'He would not dig, forsooth; but he must strive
For higher fruits than what our tillage yields;
Behold what comes, my brothers, of vain pride!'
Why play with figures? trifle prettily   70
With this my grief which very simply's said,
'There is no place for me in all the world'?
The world's a rock, and I will beat no more

---

[4] *Sisyphus* one of the four great sinners of ancient Greece, set to the eternal punishment of rolling a great stone to the top of a hill, only for it to roll down again.

[5] *wonted* accustomed.

[6] *unmeet* unsuited.

[7] *'thwart* athwart, across.

A breast of flesh and blood against a rock . . .
A stride across the planks for old time's sake.   75
Ah, bare, small room that I have sorrowed in;
    Ay, and on sunny days, haply, rejoiced;
    We know some things together, you and I!
Hold there, you rangèd row of books! In vain
You beckon from your shelf. You've stood my friends   80
    Where all things else were foes; yet now I'll turn
    My back upon you, even as the world
    Turns it on me. And yet – farewell, farewell!
You, lofty Shakespere, with the tattered leaves
And fathomless great heart, your binding's bruised   85
    Yet did I love you less? Goethe,[8] farewell;
    Farewell, triumphant smile and tragic eyes,
        And pitiless world-wisdom!
            For all men
These two. And 'tis farewell with you, my friends,   90
    More dear because more near: Theokritus;[9]
Heine[10] that stings and smiles; Prometheus' bard;[11]
    (I've grown too coarse for Shelley latterly:)
And one wild singer of to-day,[12] whose song
    Is all aflame with passionate bard's blood   95
Lash'd into foam by pain and the world's wrong.
    At least, he has a voice to cry his pain;
    For him, no silent writhing in the dark,
    No muttering of mute lips, no straining out
Of a weak throat a-choke with pent-up sound,   100
    A-throb with pent-up passion . . .
        Ah, my sun!
That's you, then, at the window, looking in
To beam farewell on one who's loved you long
    And very truly. Up, you creaking thing,   105
    You squinting, cobwebbed casement![13]
        So, at last,
I can drink in the sunlight. How it falls
    Across that endless sea of London roofs,
Weaving such golden wonders on the grey,   110
    That almost, for the moment, we forget
        The world of woe beneath them.
            Underneath,
    For all the sunset glory, Pain is king.
Yet, the sun's there, and very sweet withal;   115
    And I'll not grumble that it's only sun,
    But open wide my lips – thus – drink it in;
    Turn up my face to the sweet evening sky
    (What royal wealth of scarlet on the blue
So tender toned, you'd almost think it green)   120
And stretch my hands out – so – to grasp it tight.

---

[8] *Goethe* Johann Wolfgang von Goethe (1749–1832), German Enlightenment and Romantic poet, dramatist and novelist.

[9] *Theokritus* (Theocritus) (*c.*308–*c.*240 BC), Greek pastoral poet.

[10] *Heine* Heinrich Heine (1797–1856), German poet.

[11] *Prometheus' bard* Shelley (1792–1822), English poet, author of *Prometheus Unbound* (1820).

[12] *wild singer of to-day* perhaps a composite of Swinburne, Tennyson and Ruskin.

[13] *casement* frame or sash, forming part of a window.

Ha, ha! 'tis sweet awhile to cheat the Fates,
And be as happy as another man.
The sun works in my veins like wine, like wine!
'Tis a fair world: if dark, indeed, with woe,   125
Yet having hope and hint of such a joy,
That a man, winning, well might turn aside,
Careless of Heaven . . .
O enough; I turn
From the sun's light, or haply[14] I shall hope.   130
I have hoped enough; I would not hope again:
'Tis hope that is most cruel.
Tom, my friend,
You very sorry philosophic fool;
'Tis you, I think, that bid me be resign'd,   135
Trust, and be thankful.
Out on you! Resign'd?
I'm not resign'd, not patient, not school'd in
To take my starveling's[15] portion and pretend
I'm grateful for it. I want all, all, all;   140
I've appetite for all. I want the best:
Love, beauty, sunlight, nameless joy of life.
There's too much patience in the world, I think.
We have grown base with crooking of the knee.
Mankind – say – God has bidden to a feast;   145
The board is spread, and groans with cates[16] and drinks;
In troop the guests; each man with appetite
Keen-whetted with expectance.
In they troop,
Struggle for seats, jostle and push and seize.   150
What's this? what's this? There are not seats for all!
Some men must stand without[17] the gates; and some
Must linger by the table, ill-supplied
With broken meats. One man gets meat for two,
The while another hungers. If I stand   155
Without the portals,[18] seeing others eat
Where I had thought to satiate the pangs
Of mine own hunger; shall I then come forth
When all is done, and drink my Lord's good health
In my Lord's water? Shall I not rather turn   160
And curse him, curse him for a niggard[19] host?
O, I have hungered, hungered, through the years,
Till appetite grows craving, then disease;
I am starved, wither'd, shrivelled.
Peace, O peace!   165
This rage is idle; what avails to curse
The nameless forces, the vast silences
That work in all things.
This time is the third,
I wrought before in heat, stung mad with pain,   170
Blind, scarcely understanding; now I know

---

[14] *haply* maybe.   [17] *without* outside.
[15] *starveling* starved person.   [18] *portals* gates, doors.
[16] *cates* provisions, dainties.   [19] *niggard* stingy, mean.

What thing I do.
There was a woman once;
Deep eyes she had, white hands, a subtle smile,
Soft speaking tones: she did not break my heart,   175
Yet haply had her heart been otherwise
Mine had not now been broken. Yet, who knows?
My life was jarring discord from the first:
Tho' here and there brief hints of melody,
Of melody unutterable, clove[20] the air.   180
From this bleak world, into the heart of night,
The dim, deep bosom of the universe,
I cast myself.[21] I only crave for rest;
Too heavy is the load. I fling it down.

EPILOGUE.

We knocked and knocked; at last, burst in the door,   185
And found him as you know – the outstretched arms
Propping the hidden face. The sun had set,
And all the place was dim with lurking shade.
There was no written word to say farewell,
Or make more clear the deed.   190
I search'd and search'd;
The room held little: just a row of books
Much scrawl'd and noted; sketches on the wall,
Done rough in charcoal; the old instrument
(A violin, no Stradivarius[22])   195
He played so ill on; in the table drawer
Large schemes of undone work. Poems half-writ;
Wild drafts of symphonies; big plans of fugues;[23]
Some scraps of writing in a woman's hand:
No more – the scattered pages of a tale,   200
A sorry tale that no man cared to read.
Alas, my friend, I lov'd him well, tho' he
Held me a cold and stagnant-blooded fool,
Because I am content to watch, and wait
With a calm mind the issue of all things.   205
Certain it is my blood's no turbid[24] stream;
Yet, for all that, haply I understood
More than he ever deem'd; nor held so light
The poet in him. Nay, I sometimes doubt
If they have not, indeed, the better part –   210
These poets, who get drunk with sun, and weep
Because the night or a woman's face is fair.
Meantime there is much talk about my friend.
The women say, of course, he died for love;
The men, for lack of gold, or cavilling[25]   215
Of carping critics. I, Tom Leigh, his friend

---

[20] *clove* cleaved.
[21] *From this . . . myself* cf. Arnold's 'Empedocles on Etna'
(see ll. 1070–82).
[22] *Stradivarius* Antonio Stradivari (1644–1737), violin maker
of Cremona, Italy: his instruments are the most celebrated
of violins.

[23] *fugues* highly disciplined musical forms involving strict
counterpoint.
[24] *turbid* cloudy, muddy.
[25] *cavilling* disputing without good reason.

I have no word at all to say of this.
Nay, I had deem'd him more philosopher;
For did he think by this one paltry²⁶ deed
To cut the knot of circumstance, and snap   220
The chain which binds all being?

²⁶ *paltry* petty, trifling.

A Ballad of Religion and Marriage

Amy Levy's 'Ballad of Religion and Marriage' (published 1915) is an assault on the institutional regularization of heterosexual life of a rare boldness and grimness of humour. Presumably because of its extremity, the poem was not offered for publication during Levy's lifetime. The cheery metrical regularity and the poem's flippancy deliberately chafe against the seriousness of its vexation with a woman's place in marriage as a dreary 'Domestic round of boiled and roast' and its impatience with heterosexual monogamy as the natural state for human beings. The 'Ballad' dis-

plays an unqualified atheism, an acceptance that God has already been disposed of, which is of a piece with James Thomson's sense of late Victorian society as transparently post-Christian in *The City of Dreadful Night*, 394–422. The polemical nature of Levy's writing on gender politics can be compared with 'Xantippe', 630–6.

Text: from the pamphlet *A Ballad of Religion and Marriage* (1915), of which only 12 copies were printed 'for private circulation'.

Swept into limbo¹ is the host
Of heavenly angels, row on row;
The Father, Son, and Holy Ghost,
Pale and defeated, rise and go.
The great Jehovah² is laid low,   5
Vanished his burning bush³ and rod⁴ –
Say, are we doomed to deeper woe?
Shall marriage go the way of God?

2
Monogamous, still at our post,
Reluctantly we undergo   10
Domestic round of boiled and roast,
Yet deem the whole proceeding slow.
Daily the secret murmurs grow;
We are no more content to plod
Along the beaten paths – and so   15
Marriage must go the way of God.

¹ *limbo* transitional space, including that between death and heaven or hell.
² *Jehovah* the Old Testament name of God.
³ *burning bush* cf. 'And the Angel of the Lord appeared vnto him, in a flame of fire out of the midst of a bush, and he looked, and behold, the bush burned with fire, and the bush was not consumed. And Moses saide, I will nowe turne aside, and see this great sight, why the bush is not burnt. And when the Lord sawe that he turned aside to see, God

called vnto him out of the midst of the bush, and said, Moses, Moses. And he saide, Here am I', Exodus 3.2–4.
⁴ *rod* cf. 'And the Lord said vnto him, What is that in thine hand? and he said, A rod. And he said, Cast it on the ground: And he cast it on the ground, and it became a serpent: and Moses fled from before it. And the Lord said vnto Moses, Put forth thine hand, and take it by the taile: And he put foorth his hand, and caught it, and it became a rod in his hand', Exodus 4.2–4.

3

Soon, before all men, each shall toast
The seven strings unto his bow,
Like beacon fires along the coast,
The flames of love shall glance and glow.   20
Nor let[5] nor hindrance man shall know,
From natal bath[6] to funeral sod;
Perennial shall his pleasures flow
When marriage goes the way of God.

4

Grant, in a million years at most,   25
Folk shall be neither pairs nor odd –
Alas! we sha'n't be there to boast
'Marriage has gone the way of God!'

[5] *let* impediment. Cf. the priest's declaration in the 1662 Book of Common Prayer when issuing banns of marriage: 'If any of you know cause, or just impediment, why these two persons should not be joined together in holy Matrimony, ye are to declare it'.

[6] *natal bath* bath after birth.

Rudyard Kipling (1865–1936)

Rudyard Kipling was the first child of John Lockwood Kipling, author and illustrator of *Beast and Man in India* (1891), and Alice MacDonald, who had connections to English aesthetic circles; one sister married Edward Burne-Jones, the other Edward Poynter; a third was to be the mother of Stanley Baldwin, three times British prime minister. Born in Bombay, Kipling and his sister Trix (Alice) were taken to England in 1871 and left in the care of dour foster parents while they attended a small private school in Southsea. Kipling stayed more than five years at what he called 'the House of Desolation', and this period of his life was bitterly commemorated in the short story 'Baa, Baa, Black Sheep' (1888) and the novel *The Light that Failed* (1890). From 1878 to 1882 he was not much happier at the United Services College at Westward Ho! in Devon, later to be represented in *Stalky & Co.* (1899). In 1882, Kipling began work as a journalist in Lahore, India, and many of his poems and stories were published first in newspapers and journals. *Departmental Ditties* (1886) was his first proper collection of verse; *Plain Tales from the Hills* and *Soldiers Three* were issued in 1888. *Barrack-Room Ballads*, containing memorable pieces such as 'Gunga Din' and 'Tommy', was published in 1892 and became a great success, a powerful masculinized antidote to the effeminacies of the *fin de siècle*. Married to Caroline Balestier that same year, Kipling lived for some time in Vermont, where he wrote the two *Jungle Books* (1894–5); he visited South Africa and witnessed the Boer War at first hand, before eventually returning to England to settle at Bateman's – a large Jacobean house – in Sussex in 1902, a year after the publication of the novel *Kim* (1901). His daughter Josephine died in 1899, and more gloom followed in 1915 with the death of his only son John in the Battle of Loos in France. A friend of the ardent imperialist Cecil Rhodes (1853–1902), Kipling was no merely uncritical advocate of imperialism, though he has often been represented as such. His incomplete autobiography *Something of Myself* was published in 1937, the year after his death in London.

Fuzzy-Wuzzy

(Soudan Expeditionary Force)

Kipling's 'Fuzzy-Wuzzy' is a lively essay in the demotic (cf. 'Tommy', 649–50, and 'Gunga Din', 646–8) that brings a working-class voice speaking non-standard English into the poetry of the 1890s. The poem's monologist is an ordinary soldier who offers opinions not associated with any official point of view and whose story would not form the subject of official biographies or histories. The poem is dramatic – there is no necessary correlation between the speaker's views and the poet's – and, like others in *Barrack-Room Ballads* (1892), recovers one of the potentially lost perspectives of imperial history's common scenes.

'Fuzzy-Wuzzy' describes successions of violent engagements between white and non-white with colloquial ease and rhythmic vigour that partly defuses their horror (cf. 'Tommy' and the inescapability of violence). But its central point is to express respect for the 'Fuzzy-Wuzzy', the nickname for the Sudanese warriors who wore their hair in wild disorder, and against whom the British Army fought on many occasions during Victorian imperial expansion. More particularly, Kipling's poem memorializes the Mahdi warriors who broke the British square – the suppos-edly impregnable military formation of foot soldiers – during the Battle of Abu Klea in 1885. This battle occurred during the effort of the British Nile Expeditionary Force to relieve General Charles Gordon (1833–85) at Khartoum, later to be celebrated as one of imperial Britain's most eminent martyrs. Much of the force travelled by steamer, but a Camel Corps of about 2,000 men moved directly cross-country. Half the soldiers of a Royal Artillery Battery, subsequently named 176th (Abu Klea) Battery Royal Artillery, were sent to support the Corps; they encountered Mahdi warriors at Abu Klea in the northern Sudan on 16 January 1885. A bloody battle followed. Eventually, the British succeeded in routing their opponents after savage hand-to-hand fighting.

The quality of being a 'first-class fightin' man' in this poem is a descriptor of masculinity that crosses the racial and religious borders crucial in Kipling's understanding of human hierarchies (cf. his 'The Ballad of East and West' [1889]). The poem, which works to fashion a myth of the 'noble enemy', celebrates the transcultural identity of the 'fightin' man' in discourse that in other ways persistently constructs what we now see as racial/racist barriers between the speaker and his enemies. The identity politics of 'Fuzzy-Wuzzy' may be compared with those of 'Gunga Din', with its racist perspective but eventual recognition of the native water-carrier's superiority as a human being (if only when dead).

Text: *Barrack-Room Ballads* (1892).

We've fought with many men acrost the seas,
An' some of 'em was brave an' some was not:
The Paythan[1] an' the Zulu an' Burmese;
But the Fuzzy was the finest o' the lot.
We never got a ha'porth's[2] change of 'im: 5
'E squatted in the scrub an' 'ocked[3] our 'orses,
'E cut our sentries up at Sua*kim*,[4]
An' 'e played the cat an' banjo[5] with our forces.
So 'ere's *to* you,[6] Fuzzy-Wuzzy, at your 'ome in the Soudan;
You're a pore benighted 'eathen but a first-class fightin' man;   10
We gives you your certificate, an' if you want it signed
We'll come an' 'ave a romp with you whenever you're inclined.

2

We took our chanst among the Kyber 'ills,[7]
The Boers[8] knocked us silly at a mile,
The Burman give us Irriwaddy chills,[9]   15
An' a Zulu *impi*[10] dished us up in style:
But all we ever got from such as they
Was pop to what the Fuzzy made us swaller;
We 'eld our bloomin'[11] own, the papers say,
But man for man the Fuzzy knocked us 'oller.   20
Then 'ere's *to* you, Fuzzy-Wuzzy, an' the missis and the kid;
Our orders was to break you, an' of course we went an' did.
We sloshed you with Martinis,[12] an' it wasn't 'ardly fair;
But for all the odds agin' you, Fuzzy-Wuz, you broke the square.[13]

3

'E 'asn't got no papers of 'is own.   25
'E 'asn't got no medals nor rewards,
So we must certify the skill 'e's shown

---

[1] *Paythan* African black man (derog.).

[2] *ha'porth's* halfpenny worth's ('halfpenny' always pronounced 'haypenny').

[3] *'ocked* hocked, disabled by cutting the tendons of the ham or hock.

[4] *Suakim* south of Port Sudan on the Red Sea.

[5] *cat an' banjo* game.

[6] *'ere's to you* drinking toast.

[7] *Kyber 'ills* Khyber Pass, steep-sided mountain pass on the Pakistan–Afghanistan border that was of strategic importance to Britain during the Afghan Wars (1st Afghan War, 1839–42; 2nd, 1878–80).

[8] *Boers* those living in the Transvaal or beyond British dominions in South Africa. The first Anglo-Boer War was fought 1880–1.

[9] *Irriwaddy chills* Iradwadi is the principal river of Burma.

The British Army fought in three Anglo-Burmese wars during the nineteenth century, the last in 1885.

[10] *impi* the British Army was annihilated at Isandlwana in January 1879 by Zulu impi warriors; the garrison at Rorke's Drift nearly followed but famously defended itself with great heroism (cf. the headnote to Macaulay's 'Horatius', 1–2, and Alfred Austin, 'Henry Bartle Edward Frere', 448–9).

[11] *bloomin'* at the end of the nineteenth century, this was a new slang term for 'bloody'.

[12] *Martinis* rifles used in the British Army from 1871 to 1891.

[13] *square* military formation. At the Battle of Abu Klea (1885), Mahdists briefly broke into the supposedly impregnable British square. See headnote, 644.

In usin' of 'is long two-'anded swords:
When 'e's 'oppin' in an' out among the bush
With 'is coffin-'eaded shield an' shovel-spear,   30
An 'appy day with Fuzzy on the rush
Will last an 'ealthy Tommy[14] for a year.

4

So 'ere's *to* you, Fuzzy-Wuzzy, an' your friends which are no more,
If we 'adn't lost some messmates[15] we would 'elp you to deplore.
But give an' take's the gospel, an' we'll call the bargain fair,   35
For if you 'ave lost more than us,[16] you crumpled up the square!

5

'E rushes at the smoke when we let drive,
An', before we know, 'e's 'ackin' at our 'ead;
'E's all 'ot sand an' ginger when alive,
An' 'e's generally shammin' when 'e's dead.   40
'E's a daisy, 'e's a ducky, 'e's a lamb!
'E's a injia-rubber idiot on the spree,
'E's the on'y thing that doesn't give a damn
For a Regiment o' British Infantree!
So 'ere's *to* you, Fuzzy-Wuzzy, at your 'ome in the Soudan;   45
You're a pore benighted 'eathen but a first-class fightin' man;
An' 'ere's *to* you, Fuzzy-Wuzzy, with your 'ayrick 'ead of 'air –
You big black boundin' beggar – for you broke a British square!

[14] *Tommy* ordinary British soldier (see 'Tommy', 649–50).
[15] *lost some messmates* the British Army had some 170 casualties from Abu Klea.
[16] *more than us* the Mahdists lost 1,100; many inside the square.

Gunga Din

Based on a real incident, or an amalgam of real incidents, from the Siege of Delhi, India, in 1857, 'Gunga Din' captures, like 'Tommy', 649–50, the distinctive verbal features of an ordinary fighting soldier. In giving the Private – the lowest rank in the British Army – a voice, it reveals that aspect of Kipling's realism that was grounded in ordinary male perspectives, expressed in the virile language of slang (cf. John Davidson on slang in 'The Crystal Palace', 618–26, and W. E. Henley's dictionary of slang [see biographical headnote to *In Hospital*, 571]). 'Gunga Din' suggests Kipling's development from earlier Victorian preoccupations with self-representation in monologue form, chiefly in the work of Robert Browning, 171–216. Kipling's monologues differed sharply from much of the poetry of his own time. The scruffy realist poetics of *Barrack-Room Ballads* (1892) – from which 'Gunga Din' comes – could hardly be further from the sensuous Decadent poetics of *ennui* and artifice that characterized the work of Arthur Symons, 657–66, Ernest Dowson, 667–71, and Oscar Wilde before 1895.

The hero celebrated in 'Gunga Din' is, like its speaker, no officer, but the native water-carrier Gunga Din. The soldier-narrator thinks mostly of Gunga Din's heroism in what we now see as deeply racist terms, attributing his goodness to metaphorical identification with the supposedly superior colour: he is 'white, clear white, inside'. But the final line suggestively escapes the heavily laden discourse of race.

The poem omits any clear sense of history and suggests some hidden uncertainties about the nature of British imperial conflicts. Set in India, the exact circumstances of the siege in which the actions occur are effaced, hinting at the speaker's own ignorance of the larger political dramas in which he serves. 'Gunga Din' does not define what is politically at stake, nor does it even make clear who is the enemy: the ammunition flies from and into nowhere. The poem, which, like 'Tommy', had a long afterlife in working-class culture in the twentieth century, catches the innocence of the ordinary fighting soldier dutifully engaged, even to death, in campaigns not fully understood. The unspokens of the poem are significant too. The text invites us to ask but does not reply to the question of what Gunga Din himself thinks of his role among the embattled English forces.

Text: *Barrack-Room Ballads* (1892).

You may talk o' gin and beer
When you're quartered[1] safe out 'ere,
An' you're sent to penny-fights[2] an' Aldershot[3] it;
But when it comes to slaughter
You will do your work on water,   5
An' you'll lick the bloomin'[4] boots of 'im that's got it.
Now in Injia's sunny clime,
Where I used to spend my time
A-servin' of 'Er Majesty the Queen,
Of all them blackfaced crew   10
The finest man I knew
Was our regimental bhisti,[5] Gunga Din.
He was 'Din! Din! Din!
You limpin' lump o' brick-dust, Gunga Din!
Hi! slippery *hitherao*![6]   15
Water, get it! *Panee lao*![7]
You squidgy-nosed old idol,[8] Gunga Din.'

                                2

The uniform 'e wore
Was nothin' much before,
An' rather less than 'arf o' that be'ind,   20
For a piece o' twisty rag
An' a goatskin water-bag
Was all the field-equipment 'e could find.
When the sweatin' troop-train lay
In a sidin' through the day,   25
Where the 'eat would make your bloomin' eyebrows crawl,
We shouted 'Harry By!'[9]
Till our throats were bricky-dry,
Then we wopped[10] 'im 'cause 'e couldn't serve us all.
It was 'Din! Din! Din!   30
You 'eathen, where the mischief 'ave you been?
You put some *juldee*[11] in it
Or I'll *marrow*[12] you this minute
If you don't fill up my helmet, Gunga Din!'

                                3

'E would dot an' carry one[13]   35
Till the longest day was done;
An' 'e didn't seem to know the use o' fear.
If we charged or broke or cut,
You could bet your bloomin' nut,[14]
'E'd be waitin' fifty paces right flank rear.   40
With 'is mussick[15] on 'is back,

---

[1] *quartered* accommodated.
[2] *penny-fights* military engagements of little consequence.
[3] *Aldershot* major British Army base.
[4] *bloomin'* at the end of the nineteenth century, this was a new slang term for 'bloody'.
[5] *bhisti* native water-carrier.
[6] *hitherao* come here.
[7] *Panee lao* bring water quickly.
[8] *idol* unsympathetic reference to the notion that, as an Indian native, Gunga Din must have worshipped idols.

[9] *Harry By!* Kipling's note says 'Mr. Atkins's equivalent for "O brother"', but this is ironic: the exclamation is usually applied to horses, urging them onwards.
[10] *wopped* hit.
[11] *juldee* be quick.
[12] *marrow* beat you.
[13] *dot an' carry one* expression from school mathematics, referring to the process of working out a sum. The speaker uses the phrase as slang for 'continue the process'.
[14] *nut* head.
[15] *mussick* water skin.

'E would skip with our attack,
An' watch us till the bugles made 'Retire',[16]
An' for all 'is dirty 'ide
'E was white, clear white, inside   45
When 'e went to tend the wounded under fire!
It was 'Din! Din! Din!'
With the bullets kickin' dust-spots on the green.
When the cartridges ran out,
You could hear the front-files shout,   50
'Hi! ammunition-mules[17] an' Gunga Din!'

4

I sha'n't forgit the night
When I dropped be'ind the fight
With a bullet where my belt-plate should 'a' been.
I was chokin' mad with thirst,   55
An' the man that spied me first
Was our good old grinnin', gruntin' Gunga Din.
'E lifted up my 'ead,
An' he plugged me where I bled,
An' 'e guv me 'arf-a-pint o' water-green: 60
It was crawlin' and it stunk,
But of all the drinks I've drunk,
I'm gratefullest to one from Gunga Din.
It was 'Din! Din! Din!
'Ere's a beggar with a bullet through 'is spleen;   65
'E's chawin' up the ground,
An' 'e's kickin' all around:
For Gawd's sake git the water, Gunga Din!'

5

'E carried me away
To where a dooli[18] lay,   70
An' a bullet come an' drilled the beggar clean.
'E put me safe inside,
An' just before 'e died,
'I 'ope you liked your drink', sez Gunga Din.
So I'll meet 'im later on   75
At the place where 'e is gone –
Where it's always double drill and no canteen;[19]
'E'll be squattin' on the coals
Givin' drink to poor damned souls,
An' I'll get a swig in hell from Gunga Din!   80
Yes, Din! Din! Din!
You Lazarushian-leather[20] Gunga Din!
Though I've belted you and flayed you,
By the livin' Gawd that made you,
You're a better man than I am, Gunga Din!   85

[16] *'Retire'* bugle call for retreat.
[17] *ammunition-mules* bearers of ammunition.
[18] *dooli* stretcher.
[19] *always double . . . canteen* hell.
[20] *Lazarushian-leather* the speaker's neologism. In Jesus's parable (Luke 16), Lazarus is a beggar who sits at the gate of a rich man. When both die, Lazarus goes to heaven, the rich man to hell. From hell, he calls out 'Father Abraham, haue mercy on mee, and send Lazarus, that he may dip the tip of his finger in water, and coole my tongue, for I am tormented in this flame' (Luke 16.24). The speaker of Kipling's poem thinks of Gunga Din as Lazarus, bringing water ('leather' refers to his water carrier).

Tommy

The mistreatment of the defenders of empire – the ordinary British soldiers – back at home was a key theme of Kipling's *Barrack-Room Ballads* (first series, 1892) from where this poem comes. The volume's dedicatory poem to 'T[ommy] A[tkins]' – the representative British soldier – looked forward to a time when the military and civilians were better integrated:

> O there'll surely come a day
> When they'll give you all your pay,
> And treat you as a Christian ought to do;
> So, until that day comes round,
> Heaven keep you safe and sound,
> And, Thomas, here's my best respects to you!

Here was Kipling's vexation with British civvy-street treatment of its most needed imperial players who were, he believed, helping the nation fulfil its God-given duty. (On imperial duties of white nations, cf. 'Recessional', 650–2, and 'The White Man's Burden',

652–3; for more late Victorian poetry of the ordinary man's complaint, cf. John Davidson, 'Thirty Bob a Week', 606–9, and Oscar Wilde, *Ballad of Reading Gaol*, 588–605).

Kipling's 'Tommy', characteristic of the radical nature of the poet's realism, gives a voice to the ordinary fighter, resisting the expectation that officers' views and experiences are the only ones suitable for public expression. Poorly regarded in peacetime, the speaker of 'Tommy' reveals the overlooked struggles in his homeland. The poem suggests the regularity of conflict, assuming that England's role as leading imperial nation is of necessity a ceaseless return to war after brief, and in Tommy's case, difficult, periods of peace. Imperial identity and conflict are inseparable (cf. a different reflection on the relationship between violence and empire in 'The Way through the Woods', 655–6).

Text: *Barrack-Room Ballads* (1892).

I went into a public-'ouse to get a pint o' beer,
The publican 'e up an' sez, 'We serve no red-coats[1] here.'
The girls be'ind the bar they laughed an' giggled fit to die,
I outs into the street again an' to myself sez I:
O it's Tommy[2] this, an' Tommy that, an' 'Tommy, go away';   5
But it's 'Thank you, Mister Atkins', when the band begins to play,[3]
The band begins to play, my boys, the band begins to play,
O it's 'Thank you, Mister Atkins', when the band begins to play.

2
I went into a theatre as sober as could be,
They gave a drunk civilian room, but 'adn't none for me;   10
They sent me to the gallery or round the music-'alls,
But when it comes to fightin', Lord! they'll shove me in the stalls!
For it's Tommy this, an' Tommy that, an' 'Tommy, wait outside';
But it's 'Special train for Atkins' when the trooper's[4] on the tide,
The troopship's on the tide, my boys, the troopship's on the tide,   15
O it's 'Special train for Atkins' when the trooper's on the tide.

3
Yes, makin' mock o' uniforms that guard you while you sleep
Is cheaper than them uniforms, an' they're starvation cheap;
An' hustlin' drunken soldiers when they're goin' large[5] a bit
Is five times better business than paradin' in full kit.   20
Then it's Tommy this, an' Tommy that, an' 'Tommy, 'ow's yer soul?'

---

[1] *red-coats* soldiers in the British Army.
[2] *Tommy* the use of 'Tommy Atkins' as a nickname for the ordinary British private dates from 1815, when the War Office introduced a soldier's Account Book, using 'Thomas Atkins' as a specimen name in its sample material.

[3] *band begins to play* when preparations are being made for military action.
[4] *trooper* ship for carrying troops.
[5] *goin' large* getting out of order.

But it's 'Thin red line[6] of 'eroes' when the drums begin to roll,
  The drums begin to roll, my boys, the drums begin to roll,
  O it's 'Thin red line of 'eroes' when the drums begin to roll.

4

We aren't no thin red 'eroes, nor we aren't no blackguards[7] too,   25
  But single men in barricks, most remarkable like you;
  An' if sometimes our conduck isn't all your fancy paints,
  Why, single men in barricks don't grow into plaster saints;
While it's Tommy this, an' Tommy that, an' 'Tommy, fall be'ind',[8]
  But it's 'Please to walk in front, sir', when there's trouble in the wind,   30
  There's trouble in the wind, my boys, there's trouble in the wind,
  O it's 'Please to walk in front, sir', when there's trouble in the wind.

5

You talk o' better food for us, an' schools, an' fires, an' all:
  We'll wait for extry rations if you treat us rational.
Don't mess about the cook-room slops, but prove it to our face   35
  The Widow's Uniform is not the soldier-man's disgrace.[9]
For it's Tommy this, an' Tommy that, an' 'Chuck him out, the brute!'
  But it's 'Saviour of 'is country' when the guns begin to shoot;
An' it's Tommy this, an' Tommy that, an' anything you please;
  An' Tommy ain't a bloomin'[10] fool – you bet that Tommy sees!   40

---

[6] *thin red line* William Russell, war correspondent for *The Times* during the Crimean War, referred to British troops before the Battle of Balaclava (October 1854) as a 'thin red line tipped with steel', and the first three words passed into the language as a proverbial description of the British Army.
[7] *blackguards* vagabonds or, in a military sense, camp followers.

[8] *fall be'ind* marching command.
[9] *The Widow's . . . disgrace* the Widow is Queen Victoria, widowed in 1861, hence 'fighting for the Queen is no disgraceful thing'.
[10] *bloomin'* at the end of the nineteenth century, a new slang term for 'bloody'.

Recessional, A Victorian Ode

The public voice of this poem is that of the preacher, and Kipling's diction is replete with Biblical reference, firmly insisting on the fact that Britain's imperial role is divinely appointed. 'Recessional' was written for Queen Victoria's diamond jubilee in 1897 (celebrating 60 years on the throne) and published in *The Times* that year (and later included in *The Five Nations* [1903]). It was intended to act as a counter to the triumphalism of the official celebrations and to serve, Kipling said, 'in the nature of a *nuzzur-wattu* (an averter of the Evil Eye)'. The poem – in which Kipling as poet adopts the role of guardian of the national spirit – solemnly admonishes England against forgetting her responsibilities and ethical identity as an imperial power with 'Dominion over palm and pine'. England is, characteristically, the chosen nation, having a special covenant with God at the head of empire (cf. 'The White Man's

Burden', 652–3, on the responsibilities of white imperialists).

A 'Recessional' is a hymn (or other piece of music) sung or played at the end of a church service as the procession of clergy and choir leave. In the case of this poem, the title ironically also suggests a decline – a recession – in the religious and moral standards of those involved in the development and administration of the empire. Kipling's lines ironize a real hymn (in fact, 'Recessional' itself has served as a real hymn), 'God of our fathers' (1876) by Daniel Roberts. This includes the following stanzas, to which Kipling's are a reply:

> God of our fathers, whose almighty hand
> Leads forth in beauty all the starry band
> Of shining worlds in splendor through the skies,
> Our grateful songs before thy throne arise.

Thy love divine hath led us in the past,
In this free land by thee our lot is cast;
Be thou our ruler, guardian, guide, and stay,
Thy word our law, thy paths our chosen way.

For another text associated with the jubilee and the empire, see 'The day thou gavest' included as one of the 'Four Victorian Hymns', 566.

Text: *The Five Nations* (1903).

God of our fathers,[1] known of old,
Lord of our far-flung battle-line,
Beneath whose awful[2] Hand we hold
Dominion over palm and pine[3] –
Lord God of Hosts,[4] be with us yet,   5
Lest we forget – lest we forget![5]

2
The tumult and the shouting dies;
The Captains and the Kings depart:
Still stands Thine ancient sacrifice,
An humble and a contrite heart.[6]   10
Lord God of Hosts, be with us yet,
Lest we forget – lest we forget!

3
Far-called, our navies melt away;
On dune and headland sinks the fire:
Lo, all our pomp of yesterday   15
Is one with Nineveh and Tyre![7]
Judge of the Nations, spare us yet,
Lest we forget – lest we forget!

4
If, drunk with sight of power, we loose
Wild tongues that have not Thee in awe,   20
Such boastings as the Gentiles use,
Or lesser breeds without the Law[8] –
Lord God of Hosts, be with us yet,
Lest we forget – lest we forget!

5
For heathen heart that puts her trust   25
In reeking tube and iron shard,[9]

---

[1] *God of our fathers* traditional Judaeo-Christian form of address to God.
[2] *awful* awe-ful.
[3] *palm and pine* south and north.
[4] *Lord God of Hosts* another traditional form of Judaeo-Christian address to God.
[5] *Lest we . . . forget!* cf. 'Then beware lest thou forget the Lord which brought thee forth out of the land of Egypt, from the house of bondage', Deuteronomy 6.12.
[6] *An humble . . . heart* cf. 'The sacrifices of God are a broken spirit: a broken and a contrite heart, O God, thou wilt not despise', Psalm 51.17.

[7] *Nineveh and Tyre* proverbially corrupt but once splendid Biblical cities now lost. Cf. D. G. Rossetti's 'The Burden of Nineveh', 350–6.
[8] *If, drunk . . . Law* much-discussed lines: Kipling refers to the idea of the Jews as the Chosen People, associating this with England's sense of herself as the chosen imperial nation. The stanza asks God to withhold England from forgetting what she is required to do, and behaving like Gentiles (non-Jews) or those 'beneath the Law'. The 'lesser breeds' must include those white nations who spurned imperialism, and non-white races who had still not been shown the benefit of the white law.
[9] *reeking tube and iron shard* guns and bullets.

All valiant dust that builds on dust,
And guarding, calls not Thee to guard,
For frantic boast and foolish word –
Thy mercy on Thy People, Lord!   30

The White Man's Burden

(The United States and the Philippine Islands)

Nowhere did Kipling make so clear the lofty responsibilities of empire as in this poem, the title of which became a commonplace to describe the self-denying duties of white imperial rule (cf. 'Recessional', 650–2, for an earlier concern that England might forget her international responsibilities). The white man is imagined as preordained to the double identity of the imperialist: ruler and server. Framing those peoples governed and brought out of 'darkness' as persistently ungrateful and blameful, the poem avoids any other perspective on the native inhabitants of imperial territories (and certainly does not allow them a voice within the poem itself). 'The White Man's Burden' first appeared in *The Times*, *The New York Tribune* and *McClure's Magazine* in 1899.

In its confidence about the moral dignity of white destiny, 'The White Man's Burden' offers potent expression of Kipling's belief in the civilizing force of empire and of the centrality of *giving*. To early twenty-first-century minds, the poem also reveals racist assumptions and a rhetoric that confuses political and economic domination with the language of moral righteousness.

The poem comments on white imperialism generally, but it also has a specific focus that its subtitle makes obvious. In 1898, after a prolonged campaign by Cuba for independence from Spain, the United States entered the war and defeated the Spanish forces. In the Treaty of Paris (1898), Spain agreed to free Cuba and ceded Puerto Rico, Guam and the Philippines to the United States, marking the USA's emergence as an imperial power. It is this that Kipling commemorates in 'The White Man's Burden' (1899), acknowledging what he sees as the USA's maturation, its role as imperialist signifying that it has left behind its 'childish days'. This was not a description the Americans welcomed, but Kipling's sense of imperial responsibility as the destiny of mature white nations was firm. For another poem in which growing up and the possession of territories are also linked, see 'If – ', 654–5. 'The White Man's Burden', with its resonant reiterations, its rhetorical gestures imbued with the language of the Bible, exploits the sermonic diction of national statement (cf. 'Recessional').

Text: *The Five Nations* (1903).

Take up the White Man's burden –
Send forth the best ye breed –
Go bind your sons to exile
To serve your captives' need;
To wait in heavy harness   5
On fluttered folk and wild –
Your new-caught, sullen peoples,
Half devil and half child.

2
Take up the White Man's burden –
In patience to abide,   10
To veil the threat of terror
And check the show of pride;
By open speech and simple,
An hundred times made plain,
To seek another's profit,   15
And work another's gain.

3

Take up the White Man's burden –
The savage wars of peace –
Fill full the mouth of Famine
And bid the sickness cease;   20
And when your goal is nearest
The end for others sought,
Watch Sloth and heathen Folly
Bring all your hope to nought.

4

Take up the White Man's burden –   25
No tawdry[1] rule of kings,
But toil of serf[2] and sweeper –
The tale of common things.
The ports ye shall not enter,
The roads ye shall not tread,   30
Go make them with your living,
And mark them with your dead!

5

Take up the White Man's burden –
And reap his old reward:
The blame of those ye better,   35
The hate of those ye guard –
The cry of hosts ye humour
(Ah, slowly!) toward the light: –
'Why brought ye us from bondage,
'Our loved Egyptian night?'[3]   40

6

Take up the White Man's burden –
Ye dare not stoop to less –
Nor call too loud on Freedom
To cloak your weariness;
By all ye cry or whisper,   45
By all ye leave or do,
The silent, sullen peoples
Shall weigh your Gods and you.

7

Take up the White Man's burden –
Have done with childish days –   50
The lightly proffered laurel,[4]
The easy, ungrudged praise.
Comes now, to search your manhood
Through all the thankless years,
Cold-edged with dear-bought wisdom,   55
The judgment of your peers!

[1] *tawdry* cheaply adorned.
[2] *serf* slave, bondman.
[3] *Our . . . night* cf. Exodus 16.2–3 where Moses is criticized by the Israelites for leading them out of bondage in Egypt: 'And the whole Congregation of the children of Israel murmured against Moses and Aaron in the wildernesse. And the children of Israel saide vnto them, Would to God wee had died by the hand of the Lord in the land of Egypt, when wee sate by the flesh pots, and when we did eate bread to the full: for ye haue brought vs forth into this wildernesse, to kill this whole assembly with hunger.'
[4] *laurel* victor's wreath.

If –

The definition and celebration of heroic manliness was a preoccupation of Kipling's verse. It is, for instance, a theme of 'Fuzzy-Wuzzy', 644–6. 'If – ' (*American Magazine*, 1910), however, has explicit instructional ambitions. It offers the reader a series of requirements for stout manhood (though it is only at the end that the gender dimension is certain). Integrity and self-possession are centrally valued, together with a strand of pragmatism, and a hint of anti-intellectualism ('don't . . . talk too wise'). Against a rough world, the ideal hero will endeavour to maintain a rugged sense of self and purpose. Poetry here functions as the plain discourse of moral instruction.

Or at least, so it seems. The text has entered popular culture as a convincing ethical guide and is now one of England's favourite poems. But the persistent conditionality of Kipling's stanzas, the possibilities of parody and irony and the relativism suggested by its context continually chip away at the ideal. 'If – ' is, perhaps, best seen as brilliantly poised between an innocent salutation of heroic fortitude and its ironization. As the text moves on, its conditional mode becomes apparent. The 'Ifs' increasingly suggest the unreachableness of the ideal, mounting up a stock of requirements that is forbiddingly large.

Kipling seems to parody the giving of moral instruction at one point in offering an example of reckless irresponsibility to suggest the admirable ability to endure setbacks: 'If you can make one heap of all your winnings / And risk it on one turn of pitch-and-toss'. The fact that 'If – ' *has* a speaker hints at qualification too. The conclusion introduces the personal element, revealing that the poem is not, as the reader is first invited to believe, a general statement sanctioned by an invisible god-like author (cf. 'Recessional', 650–2), but a speech by one person to another, perhaps father to son. In introducing the idea that an individual in a particular, unknown context utters the poem, Kipling challenges the reader's sense of it as universal statement. And of course, the confirmation of the gender specificity at the end, the poem's concern with the nature of manliness, challenges it even more. 'If – ' mimics the language of the older, wise adviser, the moral sage like the Lama in Kipling's *Kim* (1901), but also subtly escapes from it. The poem's penultimate line suggests the assimilation of the idea of maturation with the acquisition of territory; cf. 'The White Man's Burden', 652–3.

Text: *Rewards and Fairies* (1910).

If you can keep your head when all about you
    Are losing theirs and blaming it on you,
If you can trust yourself when all men doubt you,
    But make allowance for their doubting too;
If you can wait and not be tired by waiting,   5
    Or being lied about, don't deal in lies,
    Or being hated, don't give way to hating,
And yet don't look too good, nor talk too wise:

2

If you can dream – and not make dreams your master;
If you can think – and not make thoughts your aim;   10
    If you can meet with Triumph and Disaster
    And treat those two impostors just the same;
If you can bear to hear the truth you've spoken
    Twisted by knaves to make a trap for fools,
Or watch the things you gave your life to, broken,   15
    And stoop and build 'em up with worn-out tools:

3

If you can make one heap of all your winnings
    And risk it on one turn of pitch-and-toss,[1]
    And lose, and start again at your beginnings

---

[1] *pitch-and-toss* game involving coins, associated with the working classes.

And never breathe a word about your loss;   20
If you can force your heart and nerve and sinew
To serve your turn long after they are gone,
And so hold on when there is nothing in you
Except the Will which says to them: 'Hold on!'

4

If you can talk with crowds and keep your virtue,   25
Or walk with Kings – nor lose the common touch,
If neither foes nor loving friends can hurt you,
If all men count with you, but none too much;
If you can fill the unforgiving minute
With sixty seconds' worth of distance run,   30
Yours is the Earth and everything that's in it,
And – which is more – you'll be a Man, my son!

The Way through the Woods

Rudyard Kipling had grumbled loudly about the dangers of British hubris and the corrupting lure of imperial power in 'Recessional', 650–2, stressing that the responsibilities of empire must not be forgotten. Empire for Kipling was always about *responsibility*. 'The Way through the Woods', first published in 1910 in *Rewards and Fairies*, can be seen, perhaps, to register a different climate of feeling, and a different phase of history, over a decade later. The poem's Georgian idiom is markedly unlike the demotic energies of *Barrack-Room Ballads* (1892), and particularly anticipates the elegiac lyric poetry of Edward Thomas (1878–1917). In its original context, it relates to the short story with which it is paired, 'Marklake Witches', and another poem, 'Brookland Road'. Read outside this frame, 'The Way through the Woods' suggests a delicate reflection on the fact that England in the new century has lost her way as an imperial power.

Rich with allegorical possibility, the poem exemplifies a Bakhtinian understanding of literature as discourse in which competing ideological positions can be simultaneously present. Mixed with the dominant tones of nostalgia and regret for the lost way – for the imperial project of Victorian England – 'The Way through the Woods' also offers silent recognition of the peace that is its consequence. In the now secure and unthreatened creatures of the forest, who 'fear not men . . . / Because they see so few', is oblique acknowledgement of empire as the bringer of violence and dread. 'The Way through the Woods' considers the new century haunted by the ghost of the previous. As a meditation on the close of the Victorian (and on a particular construction *of* the Victorian), it can be compared to Thomas Hardy's threnody for the nineteenth century, 'The Darkling Thrush', 512–13, and to John Davidson's poetry reproduced in this anthology, 606–26

Text: *Rewards and Fairies* (1910).

They shut the road through the woods
Seventy years ago.
Weather and rain have undone it again,
And now you would never know
There was once a road through the woods   5
Before they planted the trees.
It is underneath the coppice[1] and heath,
And the thin anemones.[2]
Only the keeper sees

---

[1] *coppice* small wood, thicket.

[2] *anemones* probably the wood anemone, plant with small whitish five-petalled flowers.

That, where the ring-dove[3] broods,   10
And the badgers roll at ease,
There was once a road through the woods.

2

Yet, if you enter the woods
Of a summer evening late,
When the night-air cools on the trout-ringed pools   15
Where the otter whistles[4] his mate.
(They fear not men in the woods,[5]
Because they see so few)
You will hear the beat of a horse's feet,
And the swish of a skirt in the dew,   20
Steadily cantering through
The misty solitudes,
As though they perfectly knew
The old lost road through the woods. . . .
But there is no road through the woods.   25

[3] *ring-dove* woodpigeon.
[4] *whistles* otters make many noises, including a high-pitched whistle.

[5] *They fear . . . woods* otter hunting with hounds was a popular blood sport in England well into the twentieth century: otters became a protected species in England and Wales only in 1978.

Arthur (William) Symons (1865–1945)

Symons was born into a Cornish Wesleyan family (his father was a Wesleyan minister), but he was quickly to abandon what he saw as the narrow rural life in preference for the freedom and cultural dynamism of the city. He rapidly became a representative rootless, urban Decadent, a spokesman for the 1890s *par excellence*. A scholar and critic as well as poet, Symons's 'The Decadent Movement in Literature' (1893) and *The Symbolist Movement in Literature* (1899) established his reputation as a leading theorist of his culture. He became a friend of W. B. Yeats while he was in London, and a member of the Rhymers' Club, an informal gathering of poets who met at the Cheshire Cheese on Fleet Street from 1891 to read their work to each other. Symons's first volume of verse, *Days and Nights*, appeared in 1889 and was followed by *Silhouettes* (1892), *London Nights* (1895/7), *Images of Good and Evil* (1899), *The Fool of the World and Other Poems* (1906) and *Love's Cruelty* (1923). His *Collected Works* was issued in 1924 in nine volumes, including three volumes of poetry and two of tragedies. Symons was an enthusiastic champion of Blake, Yeats and contemporary French writing, bringing Paul Verlaine to England in 1893 and translating Verlaine, Gautier and Mallarmé. He suffered a serious nervous breakdown in 1908, spending the next two years in asylums. Although he lived to the last year of the Second World War, Symons's place in literary history is centrally in the poetry and culture of the last years of Victorian England.

From Théophile Gautier: Posthumous Coquetry

The influence of French poetry – particularly Charles Baudelaire (1821–67), Paul Verlaine (1844–96) and Théophile Gautier (1811–72) – was decisive for English Decadent verse of the 1890s. Its critics thought France was responsible for the 1890s' morbidity, degeneration and unhealthy interest in sexual experience. But the poets themselves celebrated their Gallic inheritance as Symons does here through this intense, erotic translation with its *frisson* of death.

The poet, journalist and historian of Romanticism, Théophile Gautier was closely associated with the principle of *l'art pour l'art* (art for art's sake), the reigning idea among English Aesthetes in the later years of the nineteenth century. Gautier's main discussion of *l'art pour l'art* is to be found in the 'Preface' to his novel *Mademoiselle de Maupin* (1835–6). '*L'art pour l'art*' became shorthand in England for the Aesthetic philosophy that believed there was a radical separation between art and morality. Aesthetes thought the fashioning of beautiful art objects a sufficient end in itself. Oscar Wilde's epigram in the 'Preface' to *The Picture of Dorian Gray* (1890–1) – 'There is no such thing as a moral or an immoral book. Books are well written, or badly written. That is all' – expressed the principle with typical concision and teasing flippancy.

Arthur Symons's translation of Gautier's 'Coquetterie posthume' takes a poem from Gautier's collection *Émaux et camées* (1852). Symons omits the three final stanzas, heavy with death and loss, in which the speaker talks of her Catholic faith and the Pope's blessing. Gautier's eroticized dying woman, made secular in the translation, is preoccupied with appearance, how she will be seen after death. Symons said of Gautier that the sensory, and particularly the visual, world was all in all: he 'absorbed . . . this visible world with the hardly discriminating impartiality of the retina . . . The five senses made [him] for themselves, that they might become articulate.' Symons's image in the last line – implied rather than explicit in Gautier's original – clinches the translation's delicate engagement with the physical world, with that which can be known through the senses, especially the eyes.

Text: *The Collected Works of Arthur Symons* (1924).

Let there be laid, when I am dead,
Ere 'neath the coffin-lid I lie,
Upon my cheek a little red,
A little black about the eye.

2

For I in my close bier would fain,[1]   5
As on the night his vows were made,
Rose-red eternally remain,
With khol[2] beneath my blue eye laid.

3

Wind me no shroud of linen down
My body to my feet, but fold   10
The white folds of my muslin[3] gown
With thirteen flounces,[4] as of old.

4

This shall go with me where I go:
I wore it when I won his heart;
His first look hallowed it, and so,   15
For him, I laid the gown apart.

5

No immortelles,[5] no broidered grace
Of tears upon my cushion be;
Lay me on my own pillow's lace,
My hair across it, like a sea.[6]   20

[1] *fain* gladly.
[2] *khol* ebony black eyeliner (usually 'kohl' in English but perhaps Symons is thinking of the French *khôl*; alternatively, it may be a typographical error in the first edition).
[3] *muslin* woven cotton fabric.
[4] *flounce* ornamental appendage to the skirt of a lady's dress, consisting of a strip gathered and sewed on by its upper edge around the skirt, and left hanging and waving.
[5] *immortelles* name for various composite flowers of papery texture that retain their colour after being dried.
[6] *My hair . . . sea* the original reads 'De ma chevelure inondé', 'flooded with my hair'.

The Absinthe Drinker

This dreamy, inward-looking sonnet revels in the pleasures of absinthe, a powerful green liqueur originally made with wormwood, which is hallucinogenic. Imported into late Victorian English culture from France, where Parisian society's *'l'heure verte'* (green hour) had given the drink peculiar notoriety, it became closely associated with Decadence and that favoured 1890s figure of the passive, partially incapacitated poet. Edgar Degas's painting *The Absinthe Drinkers* (1876, plate 9), controversially shown in London in 1893, offered an image of a melancholy woman lost in her private world in front of a glass of the drink. The poet of 'The Absinthe Drinker' (1892) is self-absorbed, narcissistic too. Decadent motifs of intense, dangerous sensual pleasures, introspection and detachment from the 'visible world' are evident (for another relevant image, see Félicien Rops [1833–98], 'The Absinthe Drinker', an etching *c.*1890). Symons's language is remarkably ordinary, the syntax indolently spread across lines, with sentences ceasing in the middle of them as if they have run out of energy. 'The Absinthe Drinker' provocatively suggests that the Romantic perception of the beauty of the world is available for the 1890s poet only through the perilous indulgence of hallucinogenic alcohol.

The poem is taken from the section 'Masks and Faces' in Symons's *Silhouettes*. In the 'Preface' to this volume, the poet remarked, 'I claim only an equal liberty for the rendering of every mood of that variable and inexplicable and contradictory creature which we call ourselves, of every aspect under which we are gifted or condemned to apprehend the beauty and strangeness and curiosity of the visible world'.

Text: *Silhouettes* (1892).

Gently I wave the visible world away.
Far off, I hear a roar, afar yet near,
Far off and strange, a voice is in my ear,
And is the voice my own? the words I say
Fall strangely, like a dream, across the day;   5
And the dim sunshine is a dream. How clear,
New as the world to lovers' eyes, appear
The men and women passing on their way!

The world is very fair. The hours are all
Linked in a dance of mere forgetfulness.   10
I am at peace with God and man. O glide,
Sands of the hour-glass that I count not, fall
Serenely: scarce I feel your soft caress,
Rocked on this dreamy and indifferent tide.

Javanese Dancers

Dance appealed to Decadent writers as an ideal aesthetic expression in which life and art became one. 'Poetry is first of all an art,' Symons said, 'and, in art, there must be a complete marriage or interpenetration of substance and form.' W. B. Yeats's later question in 'Among School Children' (from *The Tower* [1928]) expresses the unity the art form offered exactly: 'How can we know the dancer from the dance?' Arthur Symons offers an impression of exotic performers first seen in Paris in 1889. Movement and stillness are

Plate 9   Edgar Degas, *The Absinthe Drinkers* (1876), Musée d'Orsay, Paris. Photo © RMN, H. Lewardavski.

unified in the pleasing artifice of the dancers' delicate gestures. Here is the Decadent's preference for the staged, theatrical, artificial.

The poem's focus on the dancer also indicates Symons's concentration on the image, on a 'symbol' that is sufficient in itself, not susceptible to rational paraphrase (cf. Michael Field, 'Cyclamens', 563). Symons observed in his essay 'The World as Ballet' (1898) that 'something in the particular elegance of the dancer, the scenery; the avoidance of emphasis, the evasive, winding turn of things; and, above all, the intellectual as well as sensuous appeal of a living symbol, which can but reach the brain through the

eyes, in the visual, concrete, imaginative way; has seemed to make the ballet concentrate in itself a good deal of the modern ideal in matters of artistic expression'. The French painter and sculptor Edgar Degas (1834–1917) created many images of dancers that, like this poem, capture the doubleness of motion in stillness in a graceful symbol of aesthetic union (cf. Edgar Degas, *L'étoile* [*La danseuse sur la scène*] (*The Star* [*Dancer on Stage*]) (1878), plate 10). 'Javanese Dancers' was first published in 1892 in *Silhouettes* in the section 'Masks and Faces'.

Text: *Silhouettes* (1892).

Twitched strings, the clang of metal, beaten drums,
Dull, shrill, continuous, disquieting;
And now the stealthy dancer comes
Undulantly with cat-like steps that cling;

2

Smiling between her painted lids a smile,   5
Motionless, unintelligible, she twines
Her fingers into mazy lines,
Twining her scarves across them all the while.

3

One, two, three, four step forth, and, to and fro,
Delicately and imperceptibly,   10
Now swaying gently in a row,
Now interthreading slow and rhythmically,

4

Still with fixed eyes, monotonously still,
Mysteriously, with smiles inanimate,
With lingering feet that undulate,   15
With sinuous fingers, spectral hands that thrill

5

The little amber-coloured dancers move,
Like little painted figures on a screen,
Or phantom-dancers haply seen
Among the shadows of a magic grove.[1]   20

---

[1] *The little . . . magic grove* a later version of this stanza reads: 'In measure while the gnats of music whirr, / The

little amber-coloured dancers move, / Like painted idols seen to stir / By the idolators in a magic grove.'

Prologue ['My life is like a music-hall']

Poets of the 1890s often located themselves in relation to city spaces, cross-class meeting (cf. 'Stella Maris', 664–6), and in the sordid venues of downmarket bars, rooms, streets and places of public entertainment (cf. 'The Absinthe Drinker', 658–9). In the 'Prologue' to

London Nights – Symons's volume of verse of 1895 dedicated to the French writer Paul Verlaine (1844–96) – the poet is seated vacantly in the stalls of a music hall, where popular forms of musical entertainment were staged in late Victorian cities. The

Plate 10 Edgar Degas, *L'étoile* [*La danseuse sur la scène*] (*The Star* [*Dancer on Stage*]) (1878), Musée d'Orsay, Paris. Photo © RMN/Jean Schormans.

speaker is deeply narcissistic, seeing only versions of himself, sometimes a pathetic version, enacted on the stage ('The Absinthe Drinker' is another 1890s poem of narcissistic subjectivity). Offering the poet as purposeless, spending long hours 'lounging' in boredom (*ennui*), 'Prologue' suggests another facet of the Decadent writer's persona as unhealthy idler, desultory wanderer. Max Nordau's *Degeneration* (English translation 1895), a volume highly critical of the culture of the 1890s, had remarked tellingly that 'incapacity for action' and 'predilection for inane reveries' characterized all too obviously the modern degener-

ates. Like 'Javanese Dancers', 659–60, the 'Prologue' reflects the persistent Decadent interest in masks, illusion and artifice, for the poet presents himself acting out a life that is an achieved deception, a 'make-believe of holiday'. Deliberately employing – to match its downmarket setting – a kind of staged sloppiness in language, 'Prologue' cheekily mixes male and female rhyme and includes the provocative chiming of 'pathetically gay / holiday' and 'weary us / riotous' among its indolent rhymes.

Text: *London Nights* (1895).

My life is like a music-hall,
Where, in the impotence of rage,
Chained by enchantment to my stall,
I see myself upon the stage
Dance to amuse a music-hall.   5

2

'Tis I that smoke this cigarette,
Lounge here, and laugh for vacancy,
And watch the dancers turn; and yet
It is my very self I see
Across the cloudy cigarette.   10

3

My very self that turns and trips,
Painted, pathetically gay,
An empty song upon the lips
In make-believe of holiday:
I, I, this thing that turns and trips!   15

4

The light flares in the music-hall,
The light, the sound, that weary us;
Hour follows hour, I count them all,
Lagging, and loud, and riotous:
My life is like a music-hall.   20

Paris

The possibilities of the city, its peculiar forms of relationships, are familiar themes of 1890s writing. English poets often acknowledged the influence on this of Baudelaire's *Les Fleurs du mal* (1857) and his steamy portrait of Paris. (On Baudelaire, see A. C. Swinburne's '*Ave Atque Vale*: In Memory of Charles Baudelaire', 500–6). Paris was the quintessential *fin de siècle* city, erotic, dangerous, self-indulgent, alluring, the home of the *flâneur*.

Symons said, in a discussion of the French novelist Honoré de Balzac (1799–1850), that cities were places of continual possibility: 'There is a particular kind of excitement inherent in the very aspect of a modern city, of London or Paris; in the mere sensation of being in its midst, in the sight of all those active and fatigued faces which pass so rapidly; of those long and endless streets, full of houses, each of which is like the body of a multiform soul, looking out through the eyes of many windows. There is something intoxicating in the lights, the movement of shadows under the lights, the vast and billowy sound of that shadowy movement. And there is something more than this mere unconscious action upon the nerves. Every step in a great city is a step into an unknown world. A new future is possible at every street corner. I never know, when I go out into one of those crowded streets, but that the whole course of my life may be changed before I return to the house I have quitted.'

In 'Paris' (1895), Symons concentrates on the sexual magnetism of the great metropolis, constructing a fantasy of erotic opportunity. Paris appears in Whistler-like colours, touched with violence and the pleasures of the evanescent (for more on Whistler, see Oscar Wilde's 'Symphony in Yellow', 588). For another poem about the fleeting sexual encounters of the city, see 'Stella Maris', 664–6.

Text: *London Nights* (1895).

My Paris is a land where twilight days
Merge into violent nights of black and gold;
Where, it may be, the flower of dawn is cold:
Ah, but the gold nights, and the scented ways!

2

Eyelids of women, little curls of hair,   5
A little nose curved softly, like a shell,
A red mouth like a wound, a mocking veil:
Phantoms, before the dawn, how phantom-fair!

3

And every woman with beseeching eyes,
Or with enticing eyes, or amorous,
Offers herself, a rose, and craves of us
A rose's place among our memories.

10

Hands. To Marcelle

A poem of spooky fetishism, 'Hands' (1895) involves another brief encounter with a woman, perhaps a prostitute (cf. 'Stella Maris', 664–6, and Ernest Dowson's *'Non sum qualis eram bonae sub regno Cynarae'*, 670–1). It records the finite moment of sexual experience, the passing meeting with another human being that forms no lasting connection. Such transitoriness is peculiarly associated with the city in 1890s writing (cf. 'Paris', 662–3, and the *flâneur* of Charles Baudelaire's *Les Fleurs du mal* [1857]). Sensory experience is foregrounded and the woman is not seen fully; she is able only to touch and be touched. The image of 'white . . . morbid hands'

arises from Symons's continual sense of sickness and mortality – the 'fading flowers' too (Baudelaire's flowers of sickness) – and introduces a provocative *frisson* of necrophilia to Decadent themes of transgressive sexuality. As with 'White Heliotrope', below, 'Hands' anticipates nostalgia and a time when recollection will be possible, transforming the Tennysonian posture of lament for a lost past. The memory of the encounter – its ghost or image – is as important as the event itself, smudging the borders between the real and the imagined.

Text: *London Nights* (1895).

The little hands too soft and white
To have known more laborious hours
Than those which die upon a night
Of kindling wine and fading flowers;

2

The little hands that I have kissed,
Finger by finger, to the tips,
And delicately about each wrist
Have set a bracelet with my lips;

5

3

Dear soft white little morbid hands,
Mine all one night, with what delight
Shall I recall in other lands,
Dear hands, that you were mine one night!

10

White Heliotrope

In the 'Preface' to the second edition of *London Nights* (1897), the volume from which this poem comes, Arthur Symons declared his commitment to poetry that sought simply to capture a moment's feeling. 'The moods of men!', he wrote, 'There I find my subject, there the region over which art rules; and whatever has once been a mood of mine, though it has been no more than a ripple on the sea, and had no longer than that ripple's duration, I claim the right to rend, if I can, in verse.' An impression poem of this

sort, fixing a moment of sensory experience and anticipating the capacity of the senses to recall it vividly, 'White Heliotrope' is preoccupied with the slippage between the actual and the image, the real and the spectral (cf. 'Hands', above). It also muses on a mysterious, alluring, perhaps Eastern woman of the sort that flits through other Decadent writing (cf. 'Javanese Dancers', 659–60), while its 'feverish' setting and disorderly room provide the ideal space for the distracted 1890s poet and his erotic encounters.

White heliotrope is a plant with fragrant, pure-white flowers, having a strong, talc-like smell. For other Decadent poems of the senses, see 'From Théophile Gautier: Posthumous Coquetry', 657–8, and Ernest Dowson, 'Extreme Unction', 668–9, and '*Non sum qualis eram bonae sub regno Cynarae*', 670–1; scent plays a significant part in the sensory explorations of *London Nights* altogether.

Text: *London Nights* (1895).

The feverish room and that white bed,
The tumbled skirts upon a chair,
The novel flung half-open, where
Hat, hair-pins, puffs, and paints, are spread;

2
The mirror that has sucked your face   5
Into its secret deep of deeps,
And there mysteriously keeps
Forgotten memories of grace;

3
And you, half dressed and half awake,
Your slant eyes strangely watching me,   10
And I, who watch you drowsily,
With eyes that, having slept not, ache;

4
This (need one dread? nay, dare one hope?)
Will rise, a ghost of memory, if
Ever again my handkerchief   15
Is scented with White Heliotrope.

Stella Maris

D. G. Rossetti's 'Jenny', 358–67, lies behind this poem, paying tribute to the connection between that mid-period poet's work and the full flourishing of Decadent writing at the end of the century. Provoking a torrent of criticism, Symons's 'Stella Maris' (1895, revised for 1897) is an account, like 'Jenny', of a night with a prostitute, a 'chance romance of the streets', which recalls Rossetti's poem in subject, language and rhythm. Here, however, the sexual experience is aestheticized and mythologized as one of adoration, fashioned as a moment of authentic passion snatched from oblivion. The poet's self-projection as random 'wayfare[r]' of the city and casual visitor of prostitutes, as a man who is convinced of the emptiness of life and who forms no lasting relationships with others, contributes powerfully to a potent idea of the Decadent persona as *flâneur* (city wanderer). Fleeting (sexual) encounters were particular features of modern city life as Symons's imagined it: cf. 'Paris', 662–3, and Baudelaire's *Les Fleurs du mal* (1857).

The emphasis of 'Stella Maris' on physicality, its description of the woman's body, and their orgasm – discrete enough to our eyes – seemed to some critics the quintessence of the sordid, French-inspired corruption of verse at the end of the century. One said: 'We know that the younger poets make art independent of morals, and certainly the two have no necessary connection; but why should poetic art be employed to celebrate common fornication?' Symons increased the provocation with his title, which means 'Star of the Sea' and is an ancient title of the Virgin Mary from the Latin prayer *Ave maris stella*. Symons not only aestheticizes his experience with the prostitute but subtly dramatizes it: in thinking of the lovers as ironic versions of Shakespeare's Romeo and Juliet, he adds a layer of theatricality to the poem, a characteristic Decadent preference for artifice over the real.

Text: *London Nights*, 2nd edn (1897).

Why is it I remember yet
You, of all women one has met
In random wayfare, as one meets
The chance romances of the streets,
    The Juliet of a night? I know   5
Your heart holds many a Romeo.
And I, who call to mind your face
  In so serene a pausing-place,
Where the bright pure expanse of sea,
    The shadowy shore's austerity,   10
Seems a reproach to you and me,
  I too have sought on many a breast
    The ecstasy of love's unrest,
I too have had my dreams, and met
    (Ah me!) how many a Juliet.   15
    Why is it, then, that I recall
    You, neither first nor last of all?
    For, surely as I see tonight
The glancing of the lighthouse light,
    Against the sky, across the bay,   20
Fade, and return, and fade away,
    So surely do I see your eyes
    Out of the empty night arise,
  Child, you arise and smile to me
Out of the night, out of the sea,   25
The Nereid[1] of a moment there,
    And is it seaweed in your hair?
O lost and wrecked, how long ago,
Out of the drowning past, I know,
You come to call me, come to claim   30
My share of your delicious shame.
  Child, I remember, and can tell,
One night we loved each other well;
And one night's love, at least or most,
    Is not so small a thing to boast.   35
    You were adorable, and I
    Adored you to infinity,
That nuptial night[2] too briefly borne
    To the oblivion of morn.
    Ah! no oblivion, for I feel   40
    Your lips deliriously steal
Along my neck and fasten there;
  I feel the perfume of your hair,
And feel your breast that heaves and dips,
    Desiring my desirous lips,   45
    And that ineffable delight
When souls turn bodies, and unite
    In the intolerable, the whole
    Rapture of the embodied soul.

That joy was ours, we passed it by;   50
    You have forgotten me, and I

---

[1] *Nereid* one of the sea nymphs in Classical myth, renowned for their beauty.

[2] *nuptial night* wedding night, the first time they sleep together (ironic).

Remember you thus strangely, won
An instant from oblivion.
And I, remembering, would declare
That joy, not shame, is ours to share,   55
Joy that we had the frank delight
To choose the chances of one night,
Out of vague nights, and days at strife,
So infinitely full of life.
What shall it profit me to know   60
Your heart holds many a Romeo?
Why should I grieve, though I forget
How many another Juliet?
Let us be glad to have forgot
That roses fade, and loves are not,   65
As dreams, immortal, though they seem
Almost as real as a dream.
It is for this I see you rise,
A wraith,[3] with starlight in your eyes,
Where calm hours move, for such a mood   70
Solitude out of solitude;
For this, for this, you come to me
Out of the night, out of the sea.

[3] *wraith* apparition of a dead person.

Ernest (Christopher) Dowson (1867–1900)

Born into a poor family, the son of a dry-dock owner in Limehouse, Dowson was informally educated but spent much time with his sick parents on the Riviera and in Italy. He went up to Queen's College Oxford in 1886 where he read widely and met Lionel Johnson (see 672–9). But he left without taking a degree. He worked for his father's faltering business, then threw himself into London literary society, the Rhymers' Club, friendships with Aubrey Beardsley, Richard Le Gallienne, Oscar Wilde, and so on. He contributed poems to the *Yellow Book*, the main journal of Decadence, and to the *Book of the Rhymers' Club* (1892, 1894). He fell in love with Adelaide Foltinow-icz ('Missie'), who was 12, and she haunts some of his verse as a symbol of lost love. Dowson's only volume of poems, *Verses*, was published in 1896 with fashion-able attention to its physical appearance: the cover design was by Aubrey Beardsley; there were 300 small paper copies on expensive handmade paper, 30 large paper copies on even more expensive Japanese vellum. He translated Laclos's *Les Liaisons dangereuses* and fairy-tales from the French. By now, however, after the suicide of both his parents and the loss of Missie (she had gone off with another man), he was living a reck-less and intemperate life, travelling between England, Ireland and Paris. He managed to produce two novels (*A Comedy of Masks* [1896], *Adrian Rome: A Tale* [1899], both with Arthur Moore), visited Oscar Wilde, who had moved to France after release from prison, but died a broken alcoholic in London in February 1900, for many the embodiment of the nineties' poet, passionate and doomed.

Nuns of the Perpetual Adoration

For The Countess Sobieska von Platt

If escaping into art is a familiar Decadent trope – Oscar Wilde's Dorian Gray and Huysman's Des Esseintes in *A Rebours* (1884) are the obvious examples – Ernest Dowson's 'Nuns of the Perpetual Adoration' (1896) concerns the retreat from the weari-ness and sickness of the world to an aestheticized image of a religious community. The poet is intrigu-ingly on the margins, neither wholly immersed in the world nor able to share the consolations of religious solitude. A passive spectator, he wistfully regards the nuns as a spectacle, but they do not make him act. Here is a subtle form of Decadent *ennui* and enervation.

The Sisters of the Perpetual Adoration are nuns devoted to the continual adoration of the Blessed Sacrament – the bread and wine of the eucharist signifying the body and blood of Jesus. The *fin de siècle* entanglement of eroticism and Catholicism – cf. Lionel Johnson's 'The Dark Angel', 677–9, and Charlotte Mew's 'Madeleine in Church', 682–7 – is joined with an 1890s preoccupation with the life of the senses.

Dowson's nuns have left the 'wild' world behind them for a half-pleasurable, half-melancholy solitude. They have become part of a dream as if absorbed into art or theatrical spectacle (cf. other 1890s poems on the theatrical such as Symons's 'Javanese Dancers', 659–60, and 'Prologue', 660–2). The poet is uncon-vinced by their decision: 'Surely their choice of vigil is the best?' has doubt in its first word. Unobtrusive dissatisfaction characterizes the poet's position. 'Perpetual Adoration' is slow paced, weighted with heavy rhythms, and employing styl-ized, almost ritualistic, syntactic repetitions, mimick-ing the liturgies of the convent life it describes.

Text: *Verses* (1896).

Calm, sad, secure; behind high convent walls,
These watch the sacred lamp,[1] these watch and pray:[2]
And it is one with them when evening falls,
And one with them the cold return of day.

---

[1] *sacred lamp* signifying the presence of the Host, the consecrated bread of the eucharist, in a church.

[2] *watch and pray* cf. Matthew 26.41, 'Watch and pray, that yee enter not into temptation'.

2

These heed not time; their nights and days they make   5
Into a long, returning rosary,[3]
Whereon their lives are threaded for Christ's sake:
Meekness and vigilance and chastity.

3

A vowed patrol, in silent companies,
Life-long they keep before the living Christ: 10
In the dim church, their prayers and penances
Are fragrant incense to the Sacrificed.[4]

4

Outside, the world is wild and passionate;
Man's weary laughter and his sick despair
Entreat at their impenetrable gate: 15
They heed no voices in their dream of prayer.

5

They saw the glory of the world displayed;
They saw the bitter of it, and the sweet;
They knew the roses of the world should fade,
And be trod under by the hurrying feet.   20

6

Therefore they rather put away desire,
And crossed their hands and came to sanctuary;[5]
And veiled their heads and put on coarse attire:
Because their comeliness was vanity.

7

And there they rest; they have serene insight   25
Of the illuminating dawn to be:
Mary's sweet Star[6] dispels for them the night,
The proper darkness of humanity.

8

Calm, sad, secure; with faces worn and mild:
Surely their choice of vigil is the best?   30
Yea! for our roses fade, the world is wild;
But there, beside the altar, there, is rest.

[3] *rosary* string of 165 beads used by Catholics for a cycle of prayer to the Virgin Mary.
[4] *Sacrificed* Jesus.
[5] *sanctuary* both a safe place away from the world, and the sanctuary – sacred space containing high altar – of the convent church.
[6] *Star* cf. ancient Catholic prayer: '*Ave maris stella*' ('Hail, Star of the sea, God's own dear Mother').

Extreme Unction. For Lionel Johnson

'Extreme Unction' (1896), written for the Catholic convert, poet and fellow member of the Rhymers' Club Lionel Johnson (see 672–9), brings together a number of broader themes of the 1890s. Early death, the idea of endings, Catholicism, guilt, the life of the senses are each here. The Catholic sacrament of extreme unction – the priest's anointing of the dying with holy oil – is the final forgiveness available on earth. But the speaker thinks partly of its power to refresh the senses. Dowson, who had converted to

Catholicism before he wrote this poem, was inspired by the account of Emma Bovary receiving the last sacrament in Flaubert's *Madame Bovary* (1857):

The priest recited the *Misereatur* and the *Indulgentiuam*; then he dipped his right thumb into the oil and began the unctions: firstly on the eyes, that had so coveted all the splendours of the earth; then on the nostrils, that had loved warm breezes and amorous perfumes; then on the mouth, that had opened for falsehood, had groaned with pride and cried out in lust; then on the hands, that had revelled in delicious contacts; lastly on the soles of the feet, that once had run so swiftly to the assuaging of her desires, and now would walk no more.

'Extreme Unction' considers the appealing possibility of returned innocence, fashioning an image of the sinful man on the verge of escape from vanity and 'troublous sights and sounds'. There is none of Tennyson's anxiety about withdrawal from the world (cf. 'The Lotos-Eaters', 66–71). An implicit world-weariness, another familiar Decadent posture, defines the poet's response to the aestheticized spectacle of death. Dowson's diction is heavily weighted, the poem's rhythmic movements solemn; he insists on the specificity of the nouns, 'Upon the eyes, the lips, the feet', with a delicate precision. Compare with Gerard M. Hopkins's early poem 'The Habit of Perfection'.

Text: *Verses* (1896).

Upon the eyes, the lips, the feet,
On all the passages of sense,
The atoning oil is spread with sweet
Renewal of lost innocence.

2
The feet, that lately ran so fast
To meet desire, are soothly[1] sealed;
The eyes, that were so often cast
On vanity, are touched and healed.

3
From troublous sights and sounds set free;
In such a twilight hour of breath,
Shall one retrace his life, or see,
Through shadows, the true face of death?

4
Vials[2] of mercy! Sacring[3] oils!
I know not where nor when I come,
Nor through what wanderings and toils,
To crave of you Viaticum.[4]

5
Yet, when the walls of flesh grow weak,
In such an hour, it well may be,
Through mist and darkness, light will break,
And each anointed sense will see.

5

10

15

20

---

[1] *soothly* truly.
[2] *Vials* small vessels for holding liquid.

[3] *Sacring* consecrating.
[4] *Viaticum* the eucharist, as received by one who is dying.

Non sum qualis eram bonae sub regno Cynarae

Oscar Wilde's hero in *The Picture of Dorian Gray* (1890), once inspired by Henry Wotton, seeks more and more intense experience. He becomes the Decadent figure *par excellence* in his desire to consume pleasure but failure to attain satisfaction. The poet of '*Non sum qualis eram bonae sub regno Cynarae*' (1896) is similarly appetitive, a passionate consumer of experience, calling for 'madder music and for stronger wine'. But consumption does not satisfy either, and the poet – as, in a milder form, in 'Nuns of the Perpetual Adoration', 667–8 – is restlessly lacking.

Arthur Symons (see 657–66) observed of Dowson that the 'curious love of the sordid, so common an affectation of the modern decadent, and with him so genuine, grew upon him, and dragged him into more and more sorry corners of a life which was never exactly "gay" to him'. '*Non sum qualis*' is an arresting account of the sordid, transformed into driven poetry, headlong, unresolved.

The title of '*Non sum qualis eram bonae sub regno Cynarae*' – usually simply known as 'Cynara' – is taken from Horace and means 'I am not as I was under the reign of the good Cynara'. As this suggests, it is preoccupied with decline and the insufficiency of the present against the past. Notions of disintegration dominate the *fin de siècle*, most famously in Max Nordau's angry study of cultural corruption, *Degeneration* (1892). Here, degeneration is figured in terms of an individual's sexual guilt and desolation.

'Cynara' offers itself as representative of a whole cultural moment. Arthur Symons certainly believed it distilled exactly a quality of the *fin de siècle*. He called it 'one of the greatest lyrical poems of our time; in it he has for once said everything, and he has said it to an intoxicating and perhaps immortal music'. Its mode of composition was quintessentially of the 1890s too, being largely written in the bar of the Cock pub in London while, supposedly, drinking absinthe (cf. Arthur Symons, 'The Absinthe Drinker', 658–9).

Text: *Verses* (1896).

Last night, ah, yesternight, betwixt her lips and mine
There fell thy shadow, Cynara! thy breath was shed
Upon my soul between the kisses and the wine;
And I was desolate and sick of an old passion,
    Yea, I was desolate and bowed my head: 5
I have been faithful to thee, Cynara! in my fashion.

2

All night upon mine heart I felt her warm heart beat,
Night-long within mine arms in love and sleep she lay;
Surely the kisses of her bought red mouth were sweet;
But I was desolate and sick of an old passion,   10
    When I awoke and found the dawn was gray:
I have been faithful to thee, Cynara! in my fashion.

3

I have forgot much, Cynara! gone with the wind,[1]
Flung roses, roses riotously with the throng,
Dancing, to put thy pale, lost lilies out of mind;   15
But I was desolate and sick of an old passion,
    Yea, all the time, because the dance was long:
I have been faithful to thee, Cynara! in my fashion.

4

I cried for madder music and for stronger wine,
But when the feast is finished and the lamps expire,   20

---

[1] *gone with the wind* Margaret Mitchell did indeed find the title for her 1936 novel in this line.

Then falls thy shadow, Cynara! the night is thine;
And I am desolate and sick of an old passion,
Yea hungry for the lips of my desire:
I have been faithful to thee, Cynara! in my fashion.

Vitae summa brevis spem nos vetat incohare longam

Transience, life as a dream-like state, dissatisfaction and the impossibility of satisfaction are Decadent motifs clinched in this short, famous meditation on temporality that takes pleasure in the melancholy contemplation of beauty's and pleasure's insubstantiality. The poem's aestheticization of loss and death – its turning of life into art – is a quintessential element of 1890s culture and poetics. Dowson's title – '*Vitae summa brevis spem nos vetat incohare longam*' – means 'The brevity of life forbids us to entertain hopes of long duration' in Latin. In suggesting the poem's roots in Classical culture, as if it is restating what ancient poets already knew, Dowson subtly reminds his reader of cultures lost, preserved only in their common recognition of the inescapability of death. That sense of ending, another common *fin de siècle* theme, is differently present in Charlotte Mew's 'The Forest Road', 680–2, Michael Field's 'Nests in Elms', 565, and Thomas Hardy's 'The Darkling Thrush', 512–13. '*Vitae summa*' appears as the epigraph before the contents page of Dowson's *Verses* (1896).

Text: *Verses* (1896).

They are not long, the weeping and the laughter,
Love and desire and hate:
I think they have no portion in us after
We pass the gate.

2
They are not long, the days of wine and roses: 5
Out of a misty dream
Our path emerges for a while, then closes
Within a dream.

Lionel (Pigot) Johnson (1867–1902)

Lionel Johnson was born at Broadstairs in Kent into a wealthy military family with literary connections (a cousin was one of Yeats's lovers). He was educated at Winchester and New College Oxford, from where he graduated with a first-class degree in Classics in 1890. Heavily influenced by Walter Pater at Oxford, he none the less eventually converted to Roman Catholicism. After graduation, he moved to London where he wrote for journals, worked on his poetry, and produced, in 1894, an important critical study, *The Art of Thomas Hardy*. Johnson, never fully at home in Decadent culture, became a member of the Rhymers' Club, contributing to the two volumes of the *Book of the Rhymers' Club* (1892, 1894). Taking up the Irish nationalist cause, his friendship with W. B. Yeats – who would commemorate him in 'In Memory of Major Robert Gregory' and in *Autobiographies* – deepened. So unfortunately did Johnson's dependence on alcohol (partly perhaps a consequence of a repressed homosexuality). His volumes of poetry – austere, pained, haunted by distant beauties – were *Poems* (1895) and *Ireland: With Other Poems* (1897). This learned, troubled man died after falling drunkenly from a bar stool in the Green Dragon pub in Fleet Street.

Oxford

Lionel Johnson was aloof from Decadence, and the knowledgeable, nostalgic idealism of this vision of Oxford makes peculiarly clear his distance from the fevered, absinthe-tinted world of Ernest Dowson (667–71) and Arthur Symons (657–66), or the Whistleresque charms of Oscar Wilde's (587–605). This is not the Baudelairean city of the *flâneur*, but an intellectual ideal. Crafted in the spare Classical language of 'By the Statue of King Charles at Charing Cross', 674–6, the poem constructs a Platonic notion of Oxford as a university and city set out of time, haunted by the shades of its great men, its values and learning immutable. The poet is wrapped up with a myth, from which he must none the less part. He is, like the poet of 'By the Statue of King Charles', soli-tary. There are ghosts and memories, a spectral homosociality. But the city is empty of the living.

'Oxford' (written 1890) invites comparison with Matthew Arnold's 'The Scholar-Gipsy', 298–305, which records the story of an Oxford student who leaves the university to seek the wisdom of the gipsies and preserve his intellectual integrity. In Johnson's poem, the university itself retains its integrity, a city apart from the world. Lionel Johnson was educated at Winchester and New College Oxford – both founded by the same Bishop of Winchester and Chancellor of England, William of Wykeham (1324–1404).

Text: *Poetical Works* (1915).

> Over, the four long years! And now there rings
> One voice of freedom and regret: Farewell!
> Now old remembrance sorrows, and now sings:
> But song from sorrow, now, I cannot tell.

> 2
> City of weathered cloister and worn court;   5
> Gray city of strong towers and clustering spires:
> Where art's fresh loveliness would first resort;
> Where lingering art kindled her latest fires.

> 3
> Where on all hands, wondrous with ancient grace,
> Grace touched with age, rise works of goodliest men: 10

Next Wykeham's[1] art obtain their splendid place
The zeal of Inigo,[2] the strength of Wren.[3]

4

Where at each coign[4] of every antique street,
A memory hath taken root in stone:
There, Raleigh[5] shone; there, toiled Franciscan[6] feet;   15
There, Johnson[7] flinched not, but endured, alone.

5

There, Shelley[8] dreamed his white Platonic dreams;
There, classic Landor[9] throve on Roman thought;
There, Addison[10] pursued his quiet themes;
There, smiled Erasmus,[11] and there, Colet[12] taught.   20

6

And there, O memory more sweet than all!
Lived he,[13] whose eyes keep yet our passing light;
Whose crystal lips Athenian speech[14] recall;
Who wears Rome's purple[15] with least pride, most right.

7

That is the Oxford, strong to charm us yet: 25
Eternal in her beauty and her past.
What, though her soul be vexed? She can forget
Cares of an hour: only the great things last.

8

Only the gracious air, only the charm,
And ancient might of true humanities: 30
These, nor assault of man, nor time, can harm;
Not these, nor Oxford with her memories.

9

Together have we walked with willing feet
Gardens of plenteous trees, bowering soft lawn:

[1] *Wykeham* William of Wykeham, Bishop of Winchester, founded New College Oxford in 1379. See headnote, 672.
[2] *Inigo* Inigo Jones (1573–1652), English architect: part of St John's College Oxford is attributed to him.
[3] *Wren* English architect Sir Christopher Wren (1632–1723) studied at Wadham College, and designed the Sheldonian Theatre, Oxford.
[4] *coign* corner.
[5] *Raleigh* Sir Walter Raleigh (1554?–1618), explorer, poet, educated at Oriel College.
[6] *Franciscan* Franciscan philosophy was prominent in medieval Oxford in the persons of such thinkers as Roger Bacon (1210/14–after 1292) and Roger Grosseteste (1175–1253).
[7] *Johnson* Dr Samuel Johnson (1709–84), English poet, critic and lexicographer, educated briefly at Pembroke College until forced to withdraw by poverty.
[8] *Shelley* Percy Bysshe Shelley (1792–1822), English poet, expelled from University College.

[9] *Landor* Walter Savage Landor (1775–1864), English poet and critic, educated at Trinity College.
[10] *Addison* Joseph Addison (1672–1719), English critic, educated at Queen's College and Magdalen.
[11] *Erasmus* (*c.* 1467–1536), Dutch humanist, who visited Oxford.
[12] *Colet* John Colet (1466–1519), Christian humanist who studied at Oxford and lectured on the New Testament there (heard by Erasmus).
[13] *he* probably Walter Pater (1839–94), fellow of Brasenose and author of *The Renaissance* (1873). Pater had resigned his college position in 1883.
[14] *Athenian speech* generally, as skilled as an orator of ancient Athens (but also, perhaps, a covert acknowledgement of Pater's homosexuality).
[15] *purple* imperial colour.

Hills, whither Arnold[16] wandered; and all sweet   35
June meadows, from the troubling world withdrawn:

10

Chapels of cedarn[17] fragrance, and rich gloom
Poured from empurpled panes on either hand:
Cool pavements, carved with legends of the tomb;   40
Grave haunts, where we might dream, and understand.

11

Over, the four long years! And unknown powers
Call to us, going forth upon our way:
Ah! turn we, and look back upon the towers,
That rose above our lives, and cheered the day.   45

12

Proud and serene, against the sky, they gleam:
Proud and secure, upon the earth, they stand:
Our city hath the air of a pure dream,
And hers indeed is an Hesperian[18] land.

13

Think of her so! the wonderful, the fair,   50
The immemorial, and the ever young:
The city, sweet with our forefathers' care;
The city, where the Muses[19] all have sung.

14

Ill times may be; she hath no thought of time:
She reigns beside the waters yet in pride.   55
Rude voices cry: but in her ears the chime
Of full, sad bells brings back her old springtide.

15

Like to a queen in pride of place, she wears
The splendour of a crown in Radcliffe's dome.[20]
Well fare she, well! As perfect beauty fares;   60
And those high places, that are beauty's home.

---

[16] *Arnold* Matthew Arnold (1822–88), poet and critic, educated at Balliol. Cf. Arnold's 'The Scholar-Gipsy', 298–305.

[17] *cedarn* of cedars.

[18] *Hesperian* of the Hesperides, singing nymphs who lived beyond the sunset in Greek myth and guarded the golden apples.

[19] *Muses* divinities on whom mortals relied for inspiration in Greek myth.

[20] *Radcliffe's dome* dome of the Radcliffe Camera, now part of the Bodleian Library.

By the Statue of King Charles at Charing Cross

Ezra Pound (1885–1972) said pertinently of Lionel Johnson's poetry that it continually gave the 'impression of . . . small slabs of ivory, firmly combined and contrived. There is a constant feeling of neatness, a sense of inherited order.' 'By the Statue of King Charles at Charing Cross' (written 1889, published in *The Book of the Rhymers' Club*, 1892) is a poem of ivory precision, its syntax and diction resonating conviction. Graver and more learned than the writing of Ernest Dowson, 667–71, or Arthur Symons, 657–66, the affective force of Johnson's text comes through its restraint. 'By the Statue of King Charles' is a brief, severe theodicy that affirms in contrast to Thomas Hardy's perception of the governing powers of the universe (cf. 'Hap', 510–11) the presence of impersonal order guiding all things.

Hubert Le Sueur's bronze statue of King Charles I (1633) faces down Whitehall in the centre of London. King Charles (1600–49) was the second Stuart monarch of England, a proud man with a strong sense of the divine right of kings. His conflicts with Parliament led to the English Civil War (1642–51). Charged with treason by Cromwell's side, the King was sentenced to death on 27 January 1649 and executed outside the Banqueting House at Whitehall Palace on a freezing 30 January. For some, Charles died a martyr, maintaining a defence of the Church against the secular power (the Society of King

Charles the Martyr was founded in England in 1894 shortly after this poem was written).

'By the Statue' pays tribute to the monarch as a model of heroic fortitude; its homoeroticism is self-evident. Johnson wrings affirmation from Charles's apparent failure. He meditates on masculine solitariness and dignity, writing himself as an isolated, insomniac contemplative. On different versions of the solitary poet of the 1890s, cf. Arthur Symons's 'The Absinthe Drinker', 658–9, and 'Prologue', 660–2. On the idealizing tendency of Johnson's verse and a similar self-construction, see 'Oxford', 672–4. 'By the Statue of King Charles', with its language of neo-Classical austerity, reflects a late Victorian revival of interest in the achievement of the previous century that included a renewed enthusiasm for Augustanism and the literature and thought of the high eighteenth century in general.

Text: *Poems* (1895).

Sombre and rich, the skies;
Great glooms, and starry plains.
Gently the night wind sighs;
Else a vast silence reigns.

2

The splendid silence clings   5
Around me: and around
The saddest of all kings
Crowned, and again discrowned.

3

Comely and calm, he rides
Hard by his own Whitehall:[1]   10
Only the night wind glides:
No crowds, nor rebels, brawl.[2]

4

Gone, too, his Court: and yet,
The stars his courtiers are:
Stars in their stations set;   15
And every wandering star.

5

Alone he rides, alone,
The fair and fatal king:
Dark night is all his own,
That strange and solemn thing.   20

---

[1] *his own Whitehall* Whitehall Palace in London was the English monarch's principal residence 1530–1698.

[2] *No crowds . . . brawl* Charles I's execution attracted a large crowd.

676   *Lionel (Pigot) Johnson (1867–1902)*

Which are more full of fate:
The stars; or those sad eyes?
Which are more still and great:
Those brows; or the dark skies?

7
Although his whole heart yearn   25
In passionate tragedy:
Never was face so stern
With sweet austerity.

8
Vanquished in life, his death
By beauty made amends:[3]   30
The passing of his breath
Won his defeated ends.

9
Brief life, and hapless?[4] Nay:
Through death, life grew sublime.
Speak after sentence? Yea: 35
And to the end of time.

10
Armoured he rides, his head
Bare to the stars of doom:
He triumphs now, the dead,
Beholding London's gloom.   40

11
Our wearier spirit faints,
Vexed in the world's employ:
His soul was of the saints;
And art to him was joy.[5]

12
King, tried in fires of woe!   45
Men hunger for thy grace:
And through the night I go,
Loving thy mournful face.

13
Yet, when the city sleeps;
When all the cries are still: 50
The stars and heavenly deeps
Work out a perfect will.

---

[3] *his death . . . amends* Charles remained composed
throughout the events leading to his death; his last words
were reported as 'I go from a corruptible to an
incorruptible Crown, where no disturbance can be'.

[4] *hapless* unfortunate.
[5] *art to him was joy* Charles invited the painters Van Dyck
and Rubens to work in England, and bought pictures by
Raphael and Titian.

The Dark Angel

Lionel Johnson's 'The Dark Angel' (written 1893, published in *The Second Book of the Rhymers' Club*, 1894) is a spare account of a tortured sensibility, its lean, controlled diction, syntax and verse form straining against the violence it describes. The description of the Dark Angel – a concise psychological account of mental torment dramatized through personal demonology – is saturated with the language of desecration. The Angel destroys all thoughts, content, music, inspiration and natural beauty as it infests the mind. The solitary contemplative poet of 'By the Statue of King Charles at Charing Cross', 674–6, and 'Oxford', 672–4, is replaced here by the lonely man's psychological battle. The language of 'aching lust',

'evil ecstasy' and 'ardour of red flame' implies the Dark Angel's sexual nature, and the poem may be influenced by Johnson's awareness of his repressed homosexuality. More plainly, its origin is Johnson's wrestle with alcoholism. For other late period contemplations of fractured or divided identities, cf. Gerard M. Hopkins, 'My own heart let me more have pity on', 544, Michael Field, 'Sometimes I do despatch my heart', 563–4, and Charlotte Mew, 'Madeleine in Church', 682–7, and 'The Forest Road', 680–2.

Text: *Poems* (1895).

Dark Angel, with thine aching lust
To rid the world of penitence:
Malicious Angel, who still dost
My soul such subtile[1] violence!

2
Because of thee, no thought, no thing,   5
Abides for me undesecrate:
Dark Angel, ever on the wing,
Who never reachest me too late!

3
When music sounds, then changest thou
Its silvery to a sultry[2] fire: 10
Nor will thine envious heart allow
Delight untortured by desire.

4
Through thee, the gracious Muses[3] turn
To Furies,[4] O mine Enemy!
And all the things of beauty burn   15
With flames of evil ecstasy.

5
Because of thee, the land of dreams
Becomes a gathering place of fears:
Until tormented slumber seems
One vehemence of useless tears.   20

6
When sunlight glows upon the flowers,
Or ripples down the dancing sea:

[1] *subtile* of fine or delicate texture (subtle).

[2] *sultry* oppressively hot (and also hot with anger or lust).

[3] *Muses* divinities on whom, in Classical myth, writers and artists depended for creativity.

[4] *Furies* Greek goddesses of retribution who brought punishment for murder and other crimes.

Thou, with thy troop of passionate powers,
Beleaguerest, bewilderest, me.

7

Within the breath of autumn woods,   25
Within the winter silences:
Thy venomous spirit stirs and broods,
O Master of impieties!

8

The ardour of red flame is thine,
And thine the steely soul of ice: 30
Thou poisonest the fair design
Of nature, with unfair⁵ device.

9

Apples of ashes, golden bright;⁶
Waters of bitterness, how sweet!
O banquet of a foul delight,   35
Prepared by thee, dark Paraclete!⁷

10

Thou art the whisper in the gloom,
The hinting tone, the haunting laugh:
Thou art the adorner of my tomb,
The minstrel of mine epitaph.   40

11

I fight thee, in the Holy Name!
Yet, what thou dost, is what God saith:
Tempter! should I escape thy flame,
Thou wilt have helped my soul from Death:

12

The second Death,⁸ that never dies,   45
That cannot die, when time is dead:
Live⁹ Death, wherein the lost soul cries,
Eternally uncomforted.

13

Dark Angel, with thine aching lust!
Of two defeats, of two despairs: 50
Less dread, a change to drifting dust,
Than thine eternity of cares.

14

Do what thou wilt, thou shalt not so,¹⁰
Dark Angel! triumph over me:

⁵ *unfair* with the sense of 'fair' as 'good-looking' or 'appealing'.
⁶ *Apples . . . bright* cf. the Golden Apples of Greek myth, a wedding present from the Earth to Zeus and Hera, which were guarded by the Hesperides (nymphs).
⁷ *Paraclete* Holy Spirit.

⁸ *second Death* hell.
⁹ *Live* an adjective.
¹⁰ *thou shalt not so* ironically recalls l. 2 of John Donne's 'Death be not proud': 'Death be not proud, though some have called thee / Mighty and dreadful, for, thou art not so'.

Lonely, unto the Lone[11] I go;
    Divine, to the Divinity.[12]   55

---

[11] *Lone* the wilderness of his temptation, but also God, sole creator of the universe.

[12] *Divine . . . divinity* despite the persistence of the Dark

Angel, the poet expresses confidence that he is made and defended by God.

Charlotte Mew (1869–1928)

Charlotte Mew was the third of seven children born to Frederick Mew (a successful and prosperous architect) and his often sick wife Anna Maria. Three of Mew's four brothers died in childhood, events that deeply affected her. She was educated at Gower Street School by the suffragist and enthusiast for women's poetry Lucy Harrison, editor of Spenser and author of *The Place of History in the School Curriculum* (1880). Mew's remaining brother became mentally ill by the late 1880s and was confined to hospital; Freda, the youngest daughter, also developed signs of insanity and was locked away in an asylum on the Isle of Wight. Mew was to be haunted by the horror of congenital mental illness. In 1898 there was more suffering: Mew's father died, leaving only Charlotte and her younger sister Anne to take care of their invalid mother. No compensation was to be found in love, either, as Charlotte's affections for Ella D'Arcy and later May Sinclair were unrequited. She was always to be alone. Although Mew published a story in the *Yellow Book* (1894), her first volume of poems, *The Farmer's Bride*, was issued only in 1916. It attracted notice, and an invitation to visit Thomas Hardy at Max Gate (she nervously talked too much, but managed somehow to continue a friendship with Hardy's wife Florence afterwards). In 1927, Anne died of cancer and Charlotte, who by now was the recipient of a Civil List pension, was left entirely by herself. Her solitariness became intolerable and her sanity was affected. Convinced that Anne had died as a result of poor hygiene, Mew killed herself by drinking the contents of a bottle of Lysol, a household disinfectant. Her second volume of poetry, *The Rambling Sailor*, appeared posthumously in 1929 but it seems she may have destroyed a significant amount of her work.

The Forest Road

Like the other Mew texts in this anthology, 'The Forest Road' (first published 1916) became public in the twentieth century. But in spirit, it is neatly placed at the crossing point of the late Victorian and the modern, poised between the *fin de siècle* and the psychological explorations of Virginia Woolf and Dorothy Richardson. Stretching away in long lines like free-flowing prose, Mew's poem takes the reader, painfully and without resolution, into the core of a conflictual female personality, caught in an emotional stalemate. (The speaker is formally ungendered but the silent invitation is to associate her with the poet's own voice.) Poetry here documents the interior life: it claims no other *raison d'être*. And isolation dominates it. The speaker is not addressing anyone and she is contemplating separation from her lover: Mew's poem is poignantly expressive of a woman's loneliness.

The monologist seeks to end her sexual relationship. Like Michael Field's work (see 557–65), 'The Forest Road' implicitly brings lesbian sexuality into the public domain of writing. Needing to distance herself from her partner, the speaker aspires to take the 'forest road', the route of the soul, rather than continue with the demanding emotional life her fragile companion requires, poignantly figured in Mew's image of hands searching for the speaker in sleep. But if this unspecific, mystical solitude is preferable, the speaker, who articulates a Swinburnean fantasy of the lover's dead body, neither concentrates on its joys nor acts at the end of the poem to obtain it. The poem closes with that peculiarly *fin de siècle* posture of dissatisfied passivity that also ends 'Madeleine in Church', 682–7.

Text: *The Farmer's Bride*, new edition with 11 new poems (1921).

The forest road,
The infinite straight road stretching away
World without end:[1] the breathless road between the walls
Of the black listening trees: the hushed, grey road

---

[1] *World without end* from the Christian doxology: 'Glory be to the Father, and to the Son, and to the Holy Spirit. As it was in the beginning, is now, and ever shall be, world without end. Amen.'

Beyond the window that you shut to-night   5
Crying that you would look at it by day –
There is a shadow there that sings and calls
But not for you. Oh! hidden eyes that plead in sleep
Against the lonely dark, if I could touch the fear
        And leave it kissed away on quiet lids –   10
If I could hush these hands that are half-awake,
        Groping for me in sleep I could go free.
I wish that God would take them out of mine
And fold them like the wings of frightened birds
Shot cruelly down, but fluttering into quietness so soon.   15
Broken, forgotten things; there is no grief for them in the green Spring
        When the new birds fly back to the old trees.
But it shall not be so with you. I will look back. I wish I knew that God would stand
        Smiling and looking down on you when morning comes,
                To hold you, when you wake, closer than I,   20
So gently though: and not with famished lips or hungry arms:
        He does not hurt the frailest, dearest things
        As we do in the dark. See, dear, your hair –
        I must unloose this hair that sleeps and dreams
        About my face, and clings like the brown weed   25
To drowned, delivered things, tossed by the tired sea
Back to the beaches. Oh! your hair! If you had lain
        A long time dead on the rough, glistening ledge
        Of some black cliff, forgotten by the tide,
The raving winds would tear, the dripping brine would rust away   30
        Fold after fold of all the loveliness
        That wraps you round, and makes you, lying here,
        The passionate fragrance that the roses are.
        But death would spare the glory of your head
        In the long sweetness of the hair that does not die: 35
        The spray would leap to it in every storm,
        The scent of the unsilenced sea would linger on
In these dark waves, and round the silence that was you –
Only the nesting gulls would hear – but there would still be whispers in your hair;
Keep them for me; keep them for me. What *is* this singing on the road   40
        That makes all other music like the music in a dream –
Dumb to the dancing and the marching feet; you know, in dreams, you see
        Old pipers playing that you cannot hear,
And ghostly drums that only seem to beat. This seems to climb:
Is it the music of a larger place? It makes our room too small: it is like a stair,   45
        A calling stair that climbs up to a smile you scarcely see,
Dim, but so waited for; and *you* know what a smile is, how it calls,
        How if I smiled you always ran to me.
        Now you must sleep forgetfully, as children do.
        There is a Spirit sits by us in sleep   50
Nearer than those who walk with us in the bright day.
I think he has a tranquil, saving face: I think he came
Straight from the hills: he may have suffered there in time gone by,
        And once, from those forsaken heights, looked down,
        Lonely himself, on all the lonely sorrows of the earth.   55
It is his kingdom – Sleep. If I could leave you there –
If, without waking you, I could get up and reach the door – !
        We used to go together. – Shut, scared eyes,
        Poor, desolate, desperate hands, it is not I

Who thrust you off. No, take your hands away –   60
I cannot strike your lonely hands. Yes, I have struck your heart,
It did not come so near. Then lie you there
Dear and wild heart behind this quivering snow
With two red stains on it: and I will strike and tear
Mine out, and scatter it to yours. Oh! throbbing dust,   65
You that were life, our little wind-blown hearts!
The road! the road!
There is a shadow there: I see my soul,
I hear my soul, singing among the trees!

Madeleine in Church

Mew was preoccupied by poetry's potential to dramatize conditions of female psychological conflict. 'The Forest Road', 680–2, provides a window onto an emotionally demanding relationship and the solitariness of its speaker. 'Madeleine in Church' (1916), pushing the syntax of poetry as close to prose as possible, similarly concerns a woman's sexual relationships and the fundamentally isolated self. Entirely gone is any confidence that sexual relationships could provide authentic connections between human beings and respite from the tumult of life (cf. Arnold's The Buried Life', 296–8).

With its roots in the poetics of the end of the nineteenth century, 'Madeleine in Church' involves a *fin de siècle* entanglement of sexuality and Catholicism. Its title suggests the Biblical figure of Mary Magdalene, traditionally identified as the sinner who bathed Jesus's feet with expensive ointment, wiping them with her hair (Luke 7). Tradition also has it that her offences were sexual. But unlike Augusta Webster's 'Circe', 450–5, or Amy Levy's 'Xantippe', 630–6, Mew's poem does not give a voice to a female figure marginalized by history. Her monologue offers a modern, sexually experienced woman, a 'new' and very different Magdalene/Madeleine. The 'sinner' of the New Testament experienced Jesus's forgiveness

directly. Mew's speaker wrestles continually with her faith, neither able to free herself from doctrines of sin and live without them, nor fully able to embrace the Church.

Dominating the poem is the representation of an uncomfortable, guilty, sexual self. The speaker recalls her lovers – Monty, Redge, Jim – yet only one moment of real affection. Sexual content has eluded Madeleine as much as spiritual. Beyond the messiness of ordinary life and seemingly at an impossible distance is the ideal of Jesus. The speaker sees herself remote from God but closer to human figures like the malefactors crucified with Jesus at Golgotha. And yet she cannot cast Christianity off altogether: 'If there were no one else, could it be You?' Like the speaker of 'The Forest Road', Madeleine takes no decisive action: she is fundamentally divided. The struggling with passivity, religious faith and sexual guilt in 'Madeleine in Church' locates it in the very last moments of Victorian writing, while the nature of Mew's exploration of complex and conflictual female psychology suggests a terrain later Modernist writers would claim their own.

Text: *The Farmer's Bride*, new edition with 11 new poems (1921).

Here, in the darkness, where this plaster saint[1]
Stands nearer than God stands to our distress,
And one small candle shines, but not so faint
As the far lights of everlastingness
I'd rather kneel than over there, in open day   5
Where Christ is hanging,[2] rather pray
To something more like my own clay,
Not too divine;

---

[1] *plaster saint* statue of saint present for devotional purposes in a Catholic church.   [2] *hanging* on a Crucifix.

For, once, perhaps my little saint
Before he got his niche and crown,   10
Had one short stroll about the town;
It brings him closer, just that taint
And anyone can wash the paint
Off our poor faces, his and mine!

Is that why I see Monty[3] now? equal to any saint, poor boy, as good as gold,   15
But still, with just the proper trace
Of earthliness on his shining wedding face;
And then gone suddenly blank and old
The hateful day of the divorce:
Stuart got his, hands down, of course   20
Crowing like twenty cocks and grinning like a horse:
But Monty took it hard. All said and done I liked him best, –
He was the first, he stands out clearer than the rest.
It seems too funny all we other rips[4]
Should have immortal souls; Monty and Redge quite damnably   25
Keep theirs afloat while we go down like scuttled ships. –
It's funny too, how easily we sink,
One might put up a monument, I think
To half the world and cut across it 'Lost at Sea!'
I should drown Jim, poor little sparrow, if I netted him to-night –   30
No, it's no use this penny light[5] –
Or my poor saint with his tin-pot crown –
The trees of Calvary[6] are where they were,
When we are sure that we can spare
The tallest,[7] let us go and strike it down   35
And leave the other two still standing there.[8]
I, too, would ask him to remember me
If there were any Paradise beyond this earth that I could see.[9]

Oh! quiet Christ who never knew
The poisonous fangs that bite us through   40
And make us do the things we do,
See how we suffer and fight and die,
How helpless and how low we lie,
God holds You, and You hang so high,
Though no one looking long at You,   45
Can think you do not suffer too,
But, up there, from your still, star-lighted tree
What can You know, what can You really see
Of this dark ditch, the soul of me!

We are what we are:[10] when I was half a child I could not sit   50
Watching black shadows on green lawns and red carnations burning in the sun,

[3] *Monty* her first lover.
[4] *rips* colloq., worthless, dissolute women.
[5] *penny light* the speaker or someone else has paid one penny for a devotional candle.
[6] *the trees of Calvary* the three crosses at Jesus's crucifixion (see Luke 23.33): his own, and those of the two malefactors.
[7] *tallest* Jesus's cross.
[8] *two . . . there* crosses of the malefactors.

[9] *I, too . . . see* one of the crucified malefactors acknowledged Jesus's innocence, saying, ' "Lord, remember me when thou commest into thy kingdome" '. Jesus replied, ' "Uerily, I say vnto thee, to day shalt thou be with me in Paradise" ' (Luke 23.42–3).
[10] *We are what we are* cf. Tennyson's 'Ulysses', 'that which we are, we are; / One equal temper of heroic hearts' (ll. 67–8).

Without paying so heavily for it
That joy and pain, like any mother and her unborn child were almost one.
I could hardly bear
The dreams upon the eyes of white geraniums in the dusk,   55
The thick, close voice of musk,
The jessamine[11] music on the thin night air,
Or, sometimes, my own hands about me anywhere –
The sight of my own face (for it was lovely then) even the scent of my own hair,
Oh! there was nothing, nothing that did not sweep to the high seat   60
Of laughing gods, and then blow down and beat
My soul into the highway dust, as hoofs do the dropped roses of the street.
I think my body was my soul,
And when we are made thus
Who shall control   65
Our hands, our eyes, the wandering passion of our feet,
Who shall teach us
To thrust the world out of our heart; to say, till perhaps in death,
When the race is run,
And it is forced from us with our last breath   70
'Thy will be done'?[12]
If it is Your will that we should be content with the tame, bloodless things[,][13]
As pale as angels smirking by, with folded wings.
Oh! I know Virtue, and the peace it brings!
The temperate, well-worn smile   75
The one man gives you, when you are evermore his own:
And afterwards the child's, for a little while,
With its unknowing and all-seeing eyes
So soon to change, and make you feel how quick
The clock goes round. If one had learned the trick –   80
(How does one though?) quite early on,
Of long green pastures under placid skies,[14]
One might be walking now with patient truth.
What did we ever care for it, who have asked for youth,
When, oh! my God! this is going or has gone?   85

There is a portrait of my mother, at nineteen,
With the black spaniel, standing by the garden seat,
The dainty head held high against the painted green
And throwing out the youngest smile, shy, but half haughty and half sweet.
Her picture then: but simply Youth, or simply Spring   90
To me to-day: a radiance on the wall,
So exquisite, so heart-breaking a thing
Beside the mask that I remember, shrunk and small,
Sapless and lined like a dead leaf,
All that was left of oh! the loveliest face, by time and grief!   95

And in the glass, last night, I saw a ghost behind my chair –
Yet why remember it, when one can still go moderately gay – ?
Or could – with any one of the old crew,[15]

---

[11] *jessamine* (jasmine) climbing shrub with white flowers.
[12] *'Thy will be done'* from the Lord's Prayer: 'Thy kingdome come. Thy will be done, in earth, as it is in heauen', Matthew 6.10.
[13] *[,]* this is a full stop in the original.
[14] *Of long green pastures under placid skies* cf. Psalm 23.1–2: 'The Lord is my shepheard, I shall not want. He maketh me to lie downe in greene pastures.'
[15] *old crew* previous lovers.

But oh! these boys! the solemn way
They take you, and the things they say –   100
This 'I have only as long as you'
When you remind them you are not precisely twenty-two –
Although at heart perhaps – God! if it were
Only the face, only the hair!
If Jim had written to me as he did to-day   105
A year ago – and now it leaves me cold –
I know what this means, old, old, *old!*
Et avec ça – mais on a vécu, tout se paie.[16]
That is not always true: there was my Mother – (well at least the dead are free!)
Yoked to the man that Father was; yoked to the woman I am, Monty too;   110
The little portress at the Convent School, stewing in hell so patiently;
The poor, fair boy who shot himself at Aix.[17] And what of me – and what of me?
But I, I paid for what I had, and they for nothing. No, one cannot see
How it shall be made up to them in some serene eternity.
If there were fifty heavens God could not give us back the child who went or never came; 115
Here, on our little patch of this great earth, the sun of any darkened day,
Not one of all the starry buds hung on the hawthorn trees of last year's May,
No shadow from the sloping fields of yesterday;
For every hour they slant across the hedge a different way,
The shadows are never the same.   120

'Find rest in Him' One knows the parsons' tags –
Back to the fold, across the evening fields, like any flock of baa-ing sheep:
Yes, it may be, when He has shorn, led us to slaughter, torn the bleating soul in us to rags,
For so He giveth His belovèd sleep.[18]
Oh! He will take us stripped and done,   125
Driven into His heart. So we are won:
Then safe, safe are we? in the shelter of His everlasting wings –
I do not envy Him his victories. His arms are full of broken things.

But I shall not be in them. Let Him take
The finer ones, the easier to break.   130
And they are not gone, yet, for me, the lights, the colours, the perfumes,
Though now they speak rather in sumptuous rooms,
In silks and in gem-like wines;
Here, even, in this corner where my little candle shines
And overhead the lancet-window[19] glows   135
With golds and crimsons you could almost drink
To know how jewels taste, just as I used to think
There was the scent in every red and yellow rose
Of all the sunsets. But this place is grey,
And much too quiet. No one here,   140
Why, this is awful, this is fear!
Nothing to see, no face,
Nothing to hear except your heart beating in space
As if the world was ended. Dead at last!

---

[16] *Et avec ça – mais on a vécu, tout se paie* obscure and
inaccurate French. Perhaps 'Is there anything else[?] – but
I/we have lived [and] everything must be paid for'.

[17] *Aix* Aix-en-Provence, city in Provence, south of
France.

[18] *belovèd sleep* cf. Psalm 127.2, 'It is vaine for you to rise vp
early, to sit vp late, to eate the bread of sorrowes: for so hee
giueth his beloued sleepe'.

[19] *lancet-window* narrow window with acutely pointed head,
a feature of ecclesiastical Gothic.

Dead soul, dead body, tied together fast.　　　145
These to go on with and alone, to the slow end:
No one to sit with, really, or to speak to, friend to friend:
Out of the long procession, black or white or red
Not one left now to say 'Still I am here, then see you, dear, lay here your head.'[20]
Only the doll's house looking on the Park　　　150
To-night, all nights, I know, when the man puts the lights out, very dark.
With, upstairs, in the blue and gold box of a room, just the maids' footsteps overhead,
Then utter silence and the empty world – the room – the bed –
The corpse! No, not quite dead, while this cries out in me,
But nearly: very soon to be　　　155
A handful of forgotten dust –
There must be someone. Christ! there must,
Tell me there *will* be some one. Who?
If there were no one else, could it be You?

How old was Mary out of whom you cast　　　160
So many devils?[21] Was she young or perhaps for years
She had sat staring, with dry eyes, at this and that man going past
Till suddenly she saw You on the steps of Simon's house[22]
And stood and looked at you through tears.
I think she must have known by those　　　165
The thing, for what it was that had come to her.
For some of us there is a passion, I suppose
So far from earthly cares and earthly fears
That in its stillness you can hardly stir
Or in its nearness, lift your hand,　　　170
So great that you have simply got to stand
Looking at it through tears, through tears.
Then straight from these there broke the kiss,
I think You must have known by this
The thing for what it was, that had come to You:　　　175
She did not love You like the rest,
It was in her own way, but at the worst, the best,
She gave you something altogether new.
And through it all, from her, no word,
She scarcely saw You, scarcely heard:　　　180
Surely You knew when she so touched You with her hair,
Or by the wet cheek lying there,
And while her perfume clung to You from head to feet all through the day
That You can change the things for which we care,
But even You, unless You kill us, not the way.　　　185

This, then was peace for her, but passion too.
I wonder was it like a kiss that once I knew,

[20] '*Still I am . . . head*' cf. Matthew 11.28, 'Come vnto me all yee that labour, and are heauy laden, and I will giue you rest'.

[21] *So many devils* Luke 8.2 notes that Jesus cast 'seuen deuils' out of 'Mary called Magdalene'.

[22] *Simon's house* it was at the house of Simon the Leper, according to Matthew 6.26, that the woman traditionally identified as Mary Magdalene anointed Jesus; Luke has a Pharisee's house. Lines 160–201 are based on various Biblical narratives of the supposed Mary Magdalene. The main story is in Luke 7: 'And behold, a woman in the citie which was a sinner, when shee knew that Iesus sate at meat in the Pharisees house brought an Alabaster boxe of ointment, And stood at his feet behind him, weeping, and began to wash his feete with teares, and did wipe them with the haires of her head, and kissed his feet, and anointed them with the ointment' (37–8).

The only one that I would care to take
Into the grave with me, to which if there were afterwards, to wake.
Almost as happy as the carven dead   190
In some dim chancel lying head by head
We slept with it, but face to face, the whole night through –
One breath, one throbbing quietness, as if the thing behind our lips was endless life,
Lost, as I woke, to hear in the strange earthly dawn, his 'Are you there?'
And lie still, listening to the wind outside, among the firs.   195
So Mary chose the dream of Him for what was left to her of night and day,
It is the only truth: it is the dream in us that neither life nor death
                              nor any other thing can take away:
But if she had not touched Him in the doorway of the dream could she have cared so much?
She was a sinner, we are what we are: the spirit afterwards, but first, the touch.
And He has never shared with me my haunted house beneath the trees   200
Of Eden[23] and Calvary, with its ghosts that have not any eyes for tears,

And the happier guests who would not see, or if they did, remember these,
Though they lived there a thousand years.
Outside, too gravely looking at me, He seems to stand,
And looking at Him, if my forgotten spirit came   205
Unwillingly back, what could it claim
Of those calm eyes, that quiet speech,
Breaking like a slow tide upon the beach,
The scarred,[24] not quite human hand? –
Unwillingly back to the burden of old imaginings   210
When it has learned so long not to think, not to be,
Again, again it would speak as it has spoken to me of things
That I shall not see!

I cannot bear to look at this divinely bent and gracious head:
When I was small I never quite believed that He was dead: 215
And at the Convent school I used to lie awake in bed
Thinking about His hands. It did not matter what they said,
He was alive to me, so hurt, so hurt! And most of all in Holy Week[25]
When there was no one else to see
I used to think it would not hurt me too, so terribly,   220
If He had ever seemed to notice me
Or, if, for once, He would only speak.[26]

[23] *Eden* Adam and Eve's Paradise, before the Fall: Genesis 2–3.
[24] *scarred* by the nails of the Crucifixion.
[25] *Holy Week* the week in the Christian calendar from Palm Sunday leading up to Easter Day, commemorating the events of Jesus's entry into Jerusalem, trial and crucifixion, before the Easter celebration of his resurrection.
[26] *He would only speak* a rather different perspective on Christianity is suggested by the poem 'Exspecto Resurrectionem' ('in expectation of the resurrection'), which directly follows 'Madeleine in Church' in the second edition of *The Farmer's Bride*: 'Oh! King who hast the key / Of that dark room, / The last which prisons us but held not Thee / Thou know'st its gloom. / Does Thou a little love this one / Shut in to-night, / Young and so piteously alone, / Cold – out of sight? / Thou know'st how hard and bare / The pillow of that new-made narrow bed, / Then leave not there / So dear a head! . . .'

The Trees are Down

Another of Mew's poems focused on the interior life, but this time with a more public voice. In recounting the chopping down of 'great plane-trees' at the end of gardens – in fact the work of speculators clearing the south side of Euston Square Gardens to replace it with houses and pavements in 1922 – Mew elegiacally figures the pattern of time's movement as loss. The loved, English, personalized landscape of the past is destroyed in favour of the advancing modern city, and with it, something of the poet herself is unmade. One of the very last of the Victorian poets, Mew sees some of her own precious history wiped away by the inevitable changes of a new world (the poem before this in the volume from which it is taken, *The Rambling Sailor* [1929], is 'On Youth Struck Down'; the one after, 'Smile, Death').

Where the speakers of 'The Forest Road', 680–2, and 'Madeleine in Church', 682–7, confess their isolation, revealing failed connections between themselves and others, the speaker of 'The Trees are Down' acknowledges a bond. But it is with trees, not human beings. The men here are bringers of severance and destroyers of community, radically different from the complex female identity that is in affective communion with the natural world. The dead rat was actually seen as a child and it stayed in Mew's mind, appearing again in her last, unfinished story. Its outcast nature – it is 'a god-forsaken thing' – figures an extreme of Mew's own poetic persona, haunted by isolation; it is a motif of the insistently dead.

Text: *The Rambling Sailor* (1929).

> – and he cried with a loud voice:
> Hurt not the earth, neither the sea, nor the trees –
> (Revelation)[1]

They are cutting down the great plane-trees at the end of the gardens.
For days there has been the grate of the saw, the swish of the branches as they fall,
The crash of the trunks, the rustle of trodden leaves,
With the 'Whoops' and the 'Whoas,'[2] the loud common talk, the loud common laughs of the men, above it all.   5

I remember one evening of a long past Spring
Turning in at a gate, getting out of a cart, and finding a large dead rat in the mud of the drive.
I remember thinking: alive or dead, a rat was a god-forsaken thing,
But at least, in May, that even a rat should be alive.

The week's work here is as good as done. There is just one bough   10
On the roped bole,[3] in the fine grey rain,
Green and high
And lonely against the sky.
(Down now! –)
And but for that,   15
If an old dead rat
Did once, for a moment, unmake the Spring, I might never have thought of him again.

It is not for a moment the Spring is unmade to-day;
These were great trees, it was in them from root to stem:
When the men with the 'Whoops' and the 'Whoas' have carted the whole of the whispering 20
loveliness away
Half the Spring, for me, will have gone with them.

It is going now, and my heart has been struck with the hearts of the planes;
Half my life it has beat with these, in the sun, in the rains,
In the March wind, the May breeze,   25

[1] *and he . . . the trees* adapted from Revelation 7.2–3: 'And I saw another Angel ascending from the East, hauing the seale of the liuing God: and he cried with a loud voice to the foure Angels to whom it was giuen to hurt the earth and the Sea, Saying, Hurt not the earth, neither the sea, nor the trees, till wee haue sealed the seruants of our God in their foreheads'.
[2] *'Whoas'* pron. 'woes'.
[3] *bole* tree trunk.

In the great gales that came over to them across the roofs from the great seas.
There was only a quiet rain when they were dying;
They must have heard the sparrows flying,
And the small creeping creatures in the earth where they were lying –
But I, all day, I heard an angel crying: 30
'Hurt not the trees.'

Select Bibliography

This is an indicative, not a comprehensive, bibliography of criticism on poetry included in this volume. Its suggestions are largely confined to selections of some recent texts that refer *directly* to individual poems anthologized. Where a critic's name has been cited in headnotes – e.g., Carol Christ, Catherine Maxwell – the reference is to the appropriate volume of his/her work listed here.

1 Victorian Poetry

Isobel Armstrong, *Language as Living Form in Nineteenth-century Poetry* (1982).
——, *Victorian Poetry: Poetry, Poetics and Politics* (1993).
Joseph Bristow, ed., *The Cambridge Companion to Victorian Poetry* (2000).
Matthew Campbell, *Rhythm and Will in Victorian Poetry* (1999).
Alison Chapman, Richard Cronin and Antony H. Harrison, eds, *A Companion to Victorian Poetry* (2002).
Carol Christ, *The Finer Optic: The Aesthetic of Particularity in Victorian Poetry* (1975).
Richard Cronin, *Romantic Victorians: English Literature, 1824–1840* (2002).
Eric Griffiths, *The Printed Voice of Victorian Poetry* (1988).
Margaret Homans, *Women Writers and Poetic Identity* (1980).
Robert Langbaum, *The Poetry of Experience* (1963).
Angela Leighton, *Victorian Women Poets: Writing Against the Heart* (1992).
——, ed., *Victorian Women Poets: A Critical Reader* (1996).
Catherine Maxwell, *The Female Sublime from Milton to Swinburne: Bearing Blindness* (2001).
Matthew Reynolds, *The Realms of Verse, 1830–1870: English Poetry in a Time of Nation-building* (2001).
Cynthia Scheinberg, *Women's Poetry and Religion in Victorian England: Jewish Identity and Christian Culture* (2002).
E. Warwick Slinn, *The Discourse of Self in Victorian Poetry* (1990).

Journals including work on Victorian poetry

Journal of Victorian Culture
Victorian Newsletter
Victorian Poetry
Victorian Review
Victorian Studies

There are also many specialist journals concentrating on a single poet or small group, e.g., *Browning Society Notes*; *Studies in Browning and His Circle*; *Brontë Society Transactions*; *The Kipling Journal*; *Tennyson Research Bulletin*, etc.

2 Selected Individual Authors

Elizabeth Barrett Browning

Joseph Bristow, ed., *Victorian Women Poets: Emily Brontë, Elizabeth Barrett Browning, Christina Rossetti* (1995).
Angela Leighton, *Elizabeth Barrett Browning* (1986).
Dorothy Mermin, *Elizabeth Barrett Browning: The Origins of a New Poetry* (1989).
Margaret Morlier, 'Elizabeth Barrett Browning and Felicia Hemans: The "Poetess" Problem', *Studies in Browning and His Circle*, 20 (1993): 70–9.
Marjorie Stone, *Elizabeth Barrett Browning* (1995).

Alfred Tennyson

James Chandler, 'Hallam, Tennyson, and the Poetry of Sensation: Aestheticist Allegories of a Counter-public Sphere', *Studies in Romanticism*, 33 (1994): 527–37.
Anthony H. Harrison, *Victorian Poets and the Politics of Culture: Discourse and Ideology* (1998).
Gerhard Joseph, *Tennyson and the Text: The Weaver's Shuttle* (1992).
Francis O'Gorman, 'Tennyson's "The Lotos-Eaters" and the Politics of the 1830s', *Victorian Review*, 29 (2003).
Christopher Ricks, *Tennyson* (1989).
Marion Shaw, *Alfred Lord Tennyson* (1988).
Herbert F. Tucker, *Tennyson and the Doom of Romanticism* (1988).
Jane Wright, 'A Reflection on Fiction and Art in "The Lady of Shalott"', *Victorian Poetry*, 41 (2003): 287–90.

Robert Browning

David J. DeLaura, 'The Context of Browning's Painter Poems: Aesthetics, Polemics, Histories', *PMLA*, 95 (1980): 367–88.

Daniel Karlin, ed., *Robert Browning and Elizabeth Barrett Browning: The Courtship Correspondence, 1845–1846* (1989).

Loy D. Martin, *Browning's Dramatic Monologues and the Post-Romantic Subject* (1985).

Catherine Maxwell, 'Robert Browning and Frederic Leighton: "Che farò senza Euridice?"', *Review of English Studies*, 44 (1993): 362–72.

Francis O'Gorman, 'Robert Browning's *Men and Women* and the Idea of Posterity', *Studies in Browning and His Circle* (forthcoming).

W. David Shaw, *The Dialectical Temper: The Rhetorical Art of Robert Browning* (1968).

Herbert F. Tucker, *Browning's Beginnings: The Art of Disclosure* (1980).

John Woolford, *Browning the Revisionary* (1988).

Emily Brontë

Margaret Homans, *Women Writers and Poetic Identity: Dorothy Wordsworth, Emily Brontë, and Emily Dickinson* (1980).

Lyn Pykett, *Emily Brontë* (1989).

Anne Smith, ed., *The Art of Emily Brontë* (1976).

Arthur Hugh Clough

Suzanne Bailey, '"A Garland of Fragments": Modes of Reflexivity in Clough's *Amours de Voyage*', *Victorian Poetry*, 31 (1993): 157–70.

Katharine Chorley, *Arthur Hugh Clough: The Uncommitted Mind: A Study of his Life and Poetry* (1962).

Christopher M. Kierstead, 'Where "Byron used to ride": Locating the Victorian Travel Poet in Clough's *Amours de Voyage* and *Dipsychus*', *Philological Quarterly*, 77 (1998): 377–95.

Matthew Reynolds, *The Realms of Verse, 1830–1870: English Poetry in a Time of Nation-building* (2001).

Matthew Arnold

Miriam Allott, ed., *Essays and Studies: Matthew Arnold, A Centennial Review* (1988).

William E. Buckler, *On the Poetry of Matthew Arnold: Essays in Critical Reconstruction* (1982).

John Coates, 'Two Versions of the Problem of the Modern Intellectual: "Empedocles on Etna" and "Cleon"', *Modern Language Review*, 79 (1984): 769–82.

Manfred Dietrich, 'Arnold's "Empedocles on Etna" and the 1853 Preface', *Victorian Poetry*, 14 (1976): 311–24.

Park Honan, 'Matthew Arnold, Mary Claude, and "Switzerland"', *Victorian Newsletter*, 16 (1978): 369–75.

Nicholas Shrimpton, 'Introduction' to *Matthew Arnold* (Everyman's Poetry, 1998).

John Woolford, 'Arnold on Empedocles', *Review of English Studies*, 50 (1999): 32–52.

Adelaide Anne Procter

Gill Gregory, *The Life and Work of Adelaide Procter: Poetry, Feminism, and Fathers* (1998).

George Meredith

LuAnne Holladay, 'Movement as Metaphor in George Meredith's *Modern Love*', *Journal of Pre-Raphaelite Studies*, 5:2 (1985): 33–40.

Dorothy Mermin, 'Poetry as Fiction: Meredith's *Modern Love*', *ELH: Journal of English Literary History*, 43 (1976): 100–19.

Dante Gabriel Rossetti

J. B. Bullen, *The Pre-Raphaelite Body: Fear and Desire in Painting, Poetry and Criticism* (1998).

Andrew Leng, 'Three Cups in One: A Reading of "The Woodspurge"', *Victorian Newsletter*, 78 (1990): 19–22.

Jerome J. McGann, *Dante Gabriel Rossetti and the Game that Must be Lost* (2000).

David H. Riede, *Dante Gabriel Rossetti and the Limits of Victorian Vision* (1983).

Christina G. Rossetti

D. M. R. Bentley, 'The Meretricious and the Meritorious in "Goblin Market": A Conjecture and Analysis', in *The Achievement of Christina Rossetti*, ed. David Kent (1987).

Alison Chapman, *The Afterlife of Christina Rossetti* (2000).

Eric Griffiths, 'The Disappointment of Christina G. Rossetti', *Essays in Criticism*, 47 (1997): 107–42.

Antony H. Harrison, *Christina Rossetti in Context* (1998).

William Morris

Constance W. Hassett, 'The Style of Evasion: William Morris' *The Defence of Guenevere, and Other Poems*', *Victorian Poetry*, 29 (1991): 99–114.

Fiona MacCarthy, *William Morris: A Life for Our Time* (1994).

John M. Patrick, 'Morris and Froissart: "Geffray Teste Noire" and "The Haystack in the Floods"', *Notes and Queries*, 203 (1958): 425–7.

W. David Shaw, 'Arthurian Ghosts: The Phantom
Art of "The Defence of Guenevere"', *Victorian
Poetry*, 34 (1996): 299–312.

Augusta Webster

Susan Brown, 'Economical Representations: Dante
Gabriel Rossetti's "Jenny", Augusta Webster's "A
Castaway", and the Campaign Against the
Contagious Diseases Acts,' *Victorian Review*, 17
(1991): 78–95.
Christine Sutphin, 'The Representation of
Heterosexual Desire in Augusta Webster's "Circe"
and "Medea in Athens"', *Women's Writing*, 5
(1998): 373–93.

Algernon Charles Swinburne

Michael A. Joyner, 'Of Time and the Garden:
Swinburne's "A Forsaken Garden"', *Victorian
Poetry*, 35 (1997): 99–105.
Francis O'Gorman, '"Death lies dead": The
Allusive Texture of Swinburne's "A Forsaken
Garden"', *Victorian Poetry*, 41 (2003): 348–52.
Rikky Rooksby and Nicholas Shrimpton, eds, *The
Whole Music of Passion: New Essays on Swinburne*
(1993).
Francis Jacques Sypher, 'Swinburne's Debt to
Campbell in "A Forsaken Garden"', *Victorian
Poetry*, 12 (1974): 74–8.
Melissa F. Zieger, *Beyond Consolation: Death,
Sexuality, and the Changing Shapes of Elegy*
(1997).

Thomas Hardy

Tom Paulin, *Thomas Hardy: The Poetry of Perception*
(1975).
F. B. Pinion, *A Commentary on the Poems of Thomas
Hardy* (1976).
Paul Zietlow, *Moments of Vision: The Poetry of
Thomas Hardy* (1974).

Gerard M. Hopkins

Gillian Beer, *Open Fields: Science in Cultural
Encounter* (1996).
Margaret Johnson, *Gerard Manley Hopkins and
Tractarian Poetry* (1997).
Robert Bernard Martin, *Gerard Manley Hopkins: A
Very Private Life* (1991).
Margaret Morlier, '"Barbarous in beauty": The
Violence of Time in the Poetry of Gerard Manley
Hopkins', *Victorian Poetry*, 35 (1997): 215–32.

Tom Paulin, *Minotaur: Poetry and the Nation State*
(1992).

Michael Field

Francis O'Gorman, 'Browning's Manuscript
Revisions to Michael Field's *Long Ago* (1889)',
Browning Society Notes, 25 (1998): 38–44.
Yopie Prins, 'A Metaphorical Field: Katherine
Bradley and Edith Cooper', *Victorian Poetry*, 33
(1995): 129–48.
——, *Victorian Sappho* (1999).
Chris White, '"Poets and lovers evermore":
Interpreting Female Love in the Poetry and
Journals of Michael Field', *Textual Practice*, 4
(1990): 197–212.

Four Victorian Hymns

Percy Dearmer, *Songs of Praise Discussed* (1933).
J. R. Watson, *The English Hymn: A Critical and
Historical Study* (1997).

W[illiam] E[rnest] Henley

Sabine Coelsch-Foisner and Holger Klein, eds,
Private and Public Voices in Victorian Poetry
(2000).

Oscar Wilde

Karen Alkalay-Gut, 'The Thing he Loves: Murder
as Aesthetic Experience in *The Ballad of Reading
Gaol*', *Victorian Poetry*, 35 (1997): 349–66.
Richard Ellmann, *Oscar Wilde* (1988).

John Davidson

Gioia Angeletti, 'The Poetry of John Davidson:
Tradition and Innovation between Victorianism
and Modernism', *Rivista di studi vittoriani*
(Pescara), 10 (2000): 71–92.
John Sloan, *John Davidson, First of the Moderns: A
Literary Biography* (1995).
James Townsend, *John Davidson: Poet of
Armageddon* (1961).

Amy Levy

Linda Hunt Beckman, *Amy Levy: Her Life and
Letters* (2000).
Cynthia Scheinberg, 'Recasting "Sympathy and
Judgement": Amy Levy, Women Poets, and the
Victorian Dramatic Monologue', *Victorian Poetry*,
35 (1997): 173–92.

Arthur Symons

Karl Beckson, *Arthur Symons: A Life* (1987).

Ernest Dowson

Karen Alkalay-Gut, 'Ernest Dowson and the Strategies of Decadent Desire', *Criticism*, 36 (1994): 243–63.
Christopher S. Nassaar, 'Dowson's Cynara', *Explicator*, 54 (1996): 168–70.

Charlotte Mew

Gary Day and Gina Wisker, 'Recuperating and Revaluing: Edith Sitwell and Charlotte Mew', in Gary Day and Brian Docherty, eds, *British Poetry, 1900–50: Aspects of Tradition* (1995), 65–80.
Penelope Fitzgerald, *Charlotte Mew and her Friends* (1984).
Linda Mizejewski, 'Charlotte Mew and the Unrepentant Magdalene: A Myth in Transition', *Texas Studies in Literature and Language*, 26 (1984): 282–302.

3 Other Anthologies

Isobel Armstrong and Joseph Bristow with Cath Sharrock, eds, *Nineteenth-century Women Poets: An Oxford Anthology* (1996).
Virginia Blain, ed., *Victorian Women Poets: A New Annotated Anthology* (2001).
Thomas J. Collins and Vivienne J. Rundle, eds, *Victorian Poetry and Poetic Theory* (1999).
Valentine Cunningham, ed., *The Victorians: An Anthology of Poetry and Poetics* (2000).
Angela Leighton and Margaret Reynolds, eds, *Victorian Women Poets: An Anthology* (1995).
Brian Maidment, ed., *The Poorhouse Fugitives: Self-taught Poets and Poetry in Victorian Britain* (1987).
Christopher Ricks, ed., *The New Oxford Book of Victorian Verse* (1987).
J. R. Watson, ed., *Everyman's Book of Victorian Verse* (1982).

Index of Titles

'Absinthe Drinker, The'   658
Amours de Voyage   228
'Amy's Cruelty'   59
'Anactoria'   480
'Andrea del Sarto'   189
'Apple-Gathering, An'   371
'As kingfishers catch fire'   535
'*Ave Atque Vale*: In Memory of Charles
    Baudelaire'   500

'Babylon the Great'   393
Ballad of Reading Gaol, The   588
'Ballad of Religion and Marriage, A'   642
'Bertha in the Lane'   18
'Binsey Poplars'   542
'Birthday, A'   372
'Bishop Orders his Tomb at St Praxed's
    Church, The'   175
'Burden of Nineveh, The'   350
'Buried Life, The'   296
'By the Statue of King Charles at Charing
    Cross'   674

'Caliban upon Setebos'   207
'Carmagnola to the Republic of Venice'   554
'Castaway, A'   456
'Charge of the Light Brigade, The'   165
'Charles Edward to his Last Friend'   556
'"Childe Roland to the Dark Tower
    Came"'   195
'Christmas Carol, A'   390
'Circe'   450
City of Dreadful Night, The   394
'Concerning Geffray Teste Noire'   438
'Crossing the Bar'   169
'Cry of the Children, The'   25
'Crystal Palace, The'   618
'Cyclamens'   563

'Dark Angel, The'   677
'Darkling Thrush, The'   512
'Day thou gavest, The'   566
'Defence of Guenevere, The'   428
'Dover Beach'   312
'Drummer Hodge'   511
'Dying Swan, The'   62

'Empedocles on Etna'   268
'Epic, The/Morte d'Arthur'   76
'Eurydice to Orpheus: A Picture by
    Leighton'   214
'Extreme Unction'   668

'Faded'   471
'Fallopius to his Dissecting Knife'   555
'Fantaisies Décoratives: II. Les Ballons'   587
'Forest Road, The'   680
'Forsaken Garden, A'   506
'Fra Lippo Lippi'   179
'From Théophile Gautier: Posthumous
    Coquetry'   657
'Fuzzy-Wuzzy'   644

'Girl, A'   562
'Goblin Market'   373
'God's Grandeur'   536
'Gunga Din'   646

'Hands'   663
'Hap'   510
'Harry Ploughman'   541
'Haystack in the Floods, The'   423
'Henry Edward Bartle Frere'   448
'High waving heather'   217
'Hiram Powers' *Greek Slave*'   51
'Horatius: A Lay made about the Year of
    the City CCCLX'   1
'Hymn to Proserpine'   476

'Iceland First Seen'   445
'If –'   654
Imaginary Sonnets   553
'In an Artist's Studio'   370
In Hospital   571
'In life our absent friend'   391
In Memoriam A.H.H.   88
'In Tenebris I'   516
'In the Old Theatre, Fiesole'   513
'Inapprehensiveness'   215
'Inversnaid'   539
'It was deep April'   564

'Javanese Dancers'   659
'Jenny'   358

'La Gioconda'   558
'Lady of Shalott, The'   71
'Lambs of Grasmere, The'   387
'Latest Decalogue, The'   262
'Laura to Petrarch'   553
'Laus Veneris'   487
'Lausanne: In Gibbon's Old Garden'   519
'Lay of the Trilobite'   627
'Legend of Provence, A'   320
'Lord Walter's Wife'   55

'Lotos-Eaters, The' 60

'Madeleine in Church' 682
'Maids, not to you my mind doth change' 557
'Mariana' 64
'Minor Poet, A' 636
Modern Love 328
'Morte d'Arthur' 76
'Musical Instrument, A' 57
'My God, how wonderful Thou art' 569
'My Last Duchess' 173
'My own heart let me more have pity on' 544

'Nests in Elms' 565
'New Medusa, The' 545
'Night-Wind, The' 218
'No coward soul is mine' 225
'No worst, there is none' 543
'*Non sum qualis eram bonae sub regno Cynarae*' 670
'Now sleeps the crimson petal' 87
'Nuns of the Perpetual Adoration' 667
'Nuptial Sleep' 358

'Onward Christian Soldiers' 567
'Oxford' 672

'Paris' 662
'Philip and Mildred' 314
'Pied Beauty' 537
'Porphyria's Lover' 171
'Portrait, A: Bartolommeo Veneto' 560
'Prisoner, The: A Fragment' 223
'Prologue' 660

'Recessional, A Victorian Ode' 650
'Remembrance' 222
'Resurgam' 392
'Revisitation, The' 520
'Rime of the Duchess May' 29
'Ruined Maid, The' 514

'Say not the struggle naught availeth' 227
'Scholar-Gipsy, The' 298

'Self Unseeing, The' 516
'Sestina. Of the Lady Pietra degli Scrovegni' 356
'Shall earth no more inspire thee[?]' 219
'Shelley's Skylark' 517
'Shut Out' 388
'Snow' 616
'Sometimes I do despatch my heart' 563
'Song: When I am dead, my dearest' 385
'Song 8: The Woodspurge' 368
Sonnets from the Portuguese 52
'Spring and Fall' 534
'Stanzas from the Grande Chartreuse' 305
'Stella Maris' 664
'Summer Night, A' 264
'Symphony in Yellow' 588

'Take my life, and let it be' 567
'That Nature is a Heraclitean Fire' 540
'Thirty Bob a Week' 606
'To Imagination' 220
'To Marguerite – Continued' 267
'To the Marquis of Dufferin and Ava' 167
'Toccata of Galuppi's, A' 202
'Tommy' 649
'Trees are Down, The' 687
'Two in the Campagna' 204

'Ulysses' 85

'*Vitae summa brevis spem nos vetat incohare longam*' 671

'Way through the Woods, The' 655
'White Heliotrope' 663
'White Man's Burden, The' 652
'Windhover, The' 538
'Winter: My Secret' 386
'Woman and Her Son, A' 609
'World, The' 389
'Wreck of the *Deutschland*, The' 525

'Xantippe: A Fragment' 630

Index of First Lines

'A crystal, flawless beauty on the brows'   561
'A girl'   562
'A mountain's giddy height I sought'   627
'A spirit seems to pass'   519
'Against these turbid turquoise skies'   587
'Ah face, young face, sweet with
    unpassionate joy'   471
'An omnibus across the bridge'   588
'And if you meet the Canon of Chimay'   439
'As I lay awake at night-time'   520
'As kingfishers catch fire'   536
'Asleep or waking is it?'   487
'At Francis Allen's on the Christmas-eve'   77
'At length their long kiss severed'   368
'At times our Britain cannot rest'   168

'Belovèd, thou hast brought me many
    flowers'   54
'Bend down and read – the birth, the
    death, the name'   449
'But do not let us quarrel any more'   189
'But give them me, the mouth, the eyes,
    the brow!'   215
'But, knowing now that they would have
    her speak'   428
'"But why do you go?" said the lady'   55
'By day she wooes me, soft, exceeding fair'   390
'By this he knew she wept with waking eyes'   329

'Calm, sad, secure; behind high convent
    walls'   667
'Cloud-puffball, torn tufts, tossed pillows
    flaunt forth'   540
'Cold in the earth and the deep snow piled
    above thee!'   222
'Contraption, – that's the bizarre, proper
    slang'   619
'"Courage!" he said, and pointed toward
    the land'   67

'Dark Angel, with thine aching lust'   677
'Do you hear the children weeping'   25

'Fair Amy of the terraced house'   60
'From depth to height, from height to
    loftier height'   392
'Foul is she and ill-favoured, set askew'   393

'Gently I wave the visible world away'   659
'Glory be to God for dappled things'   537
'Go, for they call you, shepherd, from
    the hill'   299
'God of our fathers, known of old'   651

'Grown strangely pale?'   546

'Had she come all the way for this'   424
'Half a league, half a league'   166
'Hard as hurdle arms, with a broth of
    goldish flue'   541
'"Has he come yet?" the dying woman asked'   610
'He did not wear his scarlet coat'   589
'Here, in the darkness, where this plaster
    saint'   682
'Here is the ancient floor'   516
'Here is the phial'   637
'High waving heather 'neath stormy blasts
    bending'   217
'Historic, side-long, implicating eyes'   559
'How do I love thee? Let me count the ways'   54

'I am poor brother Lippo, by your leave!'   179
'I caught this morning morning's minion'   538
'I couldn't touch a stop and turn a screw'   607
'I have lived long enough'   477
'I hear my death-bell tolling in the square'   554
'I leant upon a coppice gate'   512
'I never gave a lock of hair away'   53
'I plucked pink blossoms from mine
    apple tree'   371
'I stand on the mark beside the shore'   45
'I tell my secret? No indeed, not I'   386
'I thought once how Theocritus had sung'   53
'I traced the Circus whose gray stones
    incline'   514
'I went into a public-'ouse to get a pint o'
    beer'   649
'I wonder do you feel to-day'   205
'If but some vengeful god would call to me'   510
'If I leave all for thee, wilt thou exchange'   54
'If you can keep your head when all about
    you'   654
'In a coign of the cliff between lowland and
    highland'   507
'In life our absent friend is far away'   392
'In our Museum galleries'   351
'In summer's mellow midnight'   218
'In the bleak mid-winter'   390
'In the deserted, moon-blanched street'   265
'In the dungeon-crypts, idly did I stray'   223
'It little profits that an idle king'   85
'It was deep April'   564

'Last night, ah, yesternight, betwixt her
    lips and mine'   670
'Lazy laughing languid Jenny'   358
'Let there be laid, when I am dead'   657

'Light flows our war of mocking words' 296
'Lingering fade the rays of sunlight' 315
'Lo from our loitering ship a new land at last to be seen' 445
'Lo, thus, as prostrate' 395
'Lors Porsena of Clusium' 1

'Maids, not to you my mind doth change' 558
'Márgarét, áre you gríeving' 535
'Morning and evening' 374
'My aspens dear, whose airy cages quelled' 542
'My first thought was, he lied in every word' 196
'My God, how wonderful Thou art' 569
'My heart is like a singing bird' 372
'My life is bitter with thy love' 480
'My life is like a music-hall' 661
'My own heart let me more have pity on' 544
'My Paris is a land where twilight days' 662

'No coward soul is mine' 225
'No worst, there is none' 543
'Now shalt thou have thy way' 555
'Now sleeps the crimson petal' 88

'O 'Melia, my dear, this does everything crown!' 515
'Oh Galuppi, Baldassaro, this is very sad to find!' 203
'On either side the river lie' 72
'One face looks out from all his canvasses' 371
'Onward Christian soldiers' 568
'Over, the four long years!' 672
'Over the great windy waters, and over the clear-crested summits' 229

'Poor little diary, with its simple thoughts' 456
'Put the broidery-frame away' 19

'Say not the struggle nought availeth' 228
'Shall Earth no more inspire thee' 219
'Shall I strew on thee rose or rue or laurel' 501
'So all day long the noise of battle roll'd' 78
'Sombre and rich, the skies' 675
'Sometimes I do despatch my heart' 563
'Somewhere afield here something lies' 518
'Strong Son of God, Immortal Love' 89
'Sunset and evening star' 170
'Sweet Florentine that sitteth by the hearth' 554
'Swept into limbo is the host' 642

'Take my life, and let it be consecrated, Lord, to Thee' 567
'Take up the White Man's burden' 652
'That's my last Duchess painted on the wall' 174
'The day thou gavest, Lord, is ended' 566
'The door was shut' 389
'The feverish room and that white bed' 664

'The forest road' 680
'The light's extinguished, by the hearth I leant' 321
'The little hands too soft and white' 663
'The morning mists still haunt the stony street' 572
'The mules, I think, will not be here this hour' 269
'The plain was grassy, wild and bare' 63
'The rain set early in to-night' 172
'The rooks are cawing up and down the trees!' 565
'The sea is calm to-night' 312
'The sun drops luridly into the west' 451
'The upland flocks grew starved and thinned' 387
'The world is charged with the grandeur of God' 537
'They are cutting down the great plane-trees at the end of the gardens' 688
'They are not long, the weeping and the laughter' 671
'They are terribly white' 563
'They say Ideal beauty cannot enter' 51
'They shut the road through the woods' 655
'They throw in Drummer Hodge to rest' 511
'This darksome burn' 539
'Thou bottle, thou last comrade that is worth' 556
'Thou mastering me' 526
'Thou shalt have one God only' 263
'Through Alpine meadows soft-suffused' 306
'To the belfry, one by one' 31
'To the dim light and the large circle of shade' 356
'Twitched strings, the clang of metal, beaten drums' 660

'Upon the eyes, the lips, the feet' 669

'Vanity, saith the preacher, vanity!' 176

'We two stood simply friend-like side by side' 215
'We've fought with many men acrost the seas' 645
'What, have I waked again?' 631
'What was he doing, the great god Pan' 58
'When I am dead, my dearest' 385
'When weary with the long day's care' 221
'"Who affirms that crystals are alive?"' 616
'Will sprawl, now that the heat of day is best' 207
'Wintertime nighs' 517
'With blackest moss the flower-pots' 64

'Yes! in the sea of life enisled' 267
'You may talk o' gin and beer' 647